KT-229-592

CURRENT TRENDS IN LINGUISTICS

VOLUME 13

☆

CURRENT TRENDS IN LINGUISTICS

Edited by

THOMAS A. SEBEOK
Research Center for the Language Sciences
Indiana University

VOLUME 13

Historiography of Linguistics

☆

Associate Editors:

HANS AARSLEFF, ROBERT AUSTERLITZ, DELL HYMES, EDWARD STANKIEWICZ

Assistant to the Editor:

DONNA JEAN UMIKER-SEBEOK

1975
MOUTON
THE HAGUE · PARIS

UNIVERSITY LIBRARY NOTTINGHAM

© Copyright 1975 in The Netherlands
Mouton & Co. B.V., Publishers, The Hague

LIBRARY OF CONGRESS CATALOG CARD NUMBER: 74-78499
ISBN 90 279 3224 7

Printed in The Netherlands by Mouton & Co., The Hague

CONTENTS

VI PART THREE: BIBLIOGRAPHY

MASTER LIST OF ABBREVIATIONS

AA	*American Anthropologist.* Menasha, Wisconsin.
AAntH	*Acta Antiqua Academiae Scientiarum Hungaricae.* Budapest.
AAWL	*Abhandlungen der Akademie der Wissenschaften und der Literatur in Mainz, Geistes- und Sozialwissenschaftliche Klasse.* Wiesbaden.
ABORI	*Annals of the Bhandarkar Oriental Research Institute.* Poona.
AC	*L'Antiquité Classique.* Louvain.
AcAs	*Acta Asiatica.* Bulletin of the Institute of Eastern Culture Tō hō Gakkai. Tokyo.
ACIL	*Actes du congrès international des linguistes.*
A[2]CIL	*Actes du deuxième congrès international des linguistes.*
AClass	*Acta Classica.* Verhandelinge van die Klassieke Vereniging van Suid-Afrika / Proceedings of the Classical Association of South Africa. Cape Town.
ACLS	*American Council of Learned Societies Newsletter.* New York.
ACom	*Acta Comeniana.* Archiv pro bádání o *životě* a díle Jana Amose Komenského. Prague.
AcOr	*Acta Orientalia.* Ediderunt Societates Orientales Danica Norvegica Scecica (Le Monde Oriental). Copenhagen.
AEHU-HPh	*Annuaire de l'Ecole pratique des Hautes Etudes. IVe Section: Sciences historiques et philologiques.* Paris.
AES	*American Ethnological Society.* New York.
Aevum	*Aevum.* Rassegna di scienze filologiche, linguistiche e storiche. Milan.
AFLT	*Annales publiées par la Faculté des Lettres de Toulouse.* Toulouse.
AfVPhon	*Archiv für vergleichende Phonetik.* Berlin. (Superseded by ZPhon.)
AGI	*Archivio Glottologico Italiano.* Florence.
AGR	*American-German Review.* Philadelphia.
AION-L	*Annali, Istituto Universitario Orientale, Sezione Linguistica.* Naples.
AIV	*Atti dell'Istituto Veneto di Scienze, Lettere ed Arti, Classe di scienze morali e lettere.* Venice.
AJPh	*American Journal of Philology.* Baltimore.
AKM	*Abhandlungen für die Kunde des Morgenlandes.* Leipzig.
AL	*Acta Linguistica Hafniensia.* International journal of structural linguistics. Copenhagen.
Al-Andalus	*Al-Andalus.* Revista de las Escuelas de estudios árabes de Madrid y Granada. Madrid and Granada.
ALB	*The Adyar Library Bulletin.* Adyar, Madras, India.
ALH	*Acta Linguistica Academiae Scientiarum Hungaricae.* Budapest.
ALMA	*Archivum Latinitatis Medii Aevi.* Bulletin du Cange. Brussels.
Altertum	*Das Altertum.* Herausgegeben von der Sektion für die Wissenschaften zu Berlin. Berlin.

AM	*Asia Major.* New Series. London.
AmA	*American Anthropologist.* Menasha, Wisconsin.
AMAT	*Atti e Memorie dell'Accademia Toscana di Scienze e Lettere 'La Colombiana'.* Florence.
Amp	*Ampurias.* Barcelona.
Anglia	*Anglia.* Zeitschrift für englische Philologie. Tübingen.
AnL	*Anthropological Linguistics.* Bloomington, Indiana.
AnnIPhO	*Annuaire de l'Institut de Philologie et d'Histoire orientales et slaves.* Brussels.
Antichthon	*Antichthon.* Journal of the Australian Society for Classical Studies. Sydney.
AO	*Archiv Orientální.* Prague.
AOH	*Acta Orientalia Academiae Scientiarum Hungaricae.* Budapest.
AOR	*Annuari de l'Oficina Romànica de Lingüística i Literatura.* Barcelona.
APhS	*Acta Philologica Scandinavica.* Tidsskrift for nordisk sprogforskning. Copenhagen.
APS	*American Philosophical Society.* Philadelphia.
APS-P	*American Philosophical Society. Proceedings.* Philadelphia.
A&R	*Atene e Roma.* Rassegna trimestrale dell'Associazione Italiana di Cultura Classica. Messina and Florence.
Arabica	*Arabica.* Revue d'études arabes. Leiden.
Arbor	*Arbor.* Revista general de investigacion y cultura. Madrid.
Arch	*Archivum.* Revista de la Facultad de Filosofia y Letras, Universidad de Oviedo. Oviedo.
ArchL	*Archivum Linguisticum.* A Review of Comparative Philology and General Linguistics. Glascow.
ArchSlav	*Archiv für slavische Philologie.* Berlin.
Arkiv	*Arkiv för nordisk Filologi.* Lund.
AS	*American Scientist.* Published in the interest of scientific research. Society of Sigma XI, Scientific Research Society of America. New Haven, Conn.
ASAW	*Abhandlungen der Sächsischen Akademie der Wissenschaften zu Leipzig, Philologisch-Historische Klasse.* Berlin.
ASLU	*Acta Societatis Linguisticae Upsaliensis.* Uppsala.
ASNP	*Annali della Scuola Normale Superiore di Pisa.* Lettere, storia e filosofia. Florence.
ASNS	*Archiv für das Studium der neueren Sprachen.* Braunschweig.
ASPS	*Atti della Società Italiana per il Progresso delle Scienze.* Rome.
ASt	*Anatolian Studies.* Manchester.
AUI	*Analele Ştiinţifice ale Universităţii 'Al. I. Cuza'. Sectiunea III.* Jassy.
ÅVsLund	*Vetenskaps-societeten i Lund, Årsbok / Yearbook of the New Society of Letters at Lund.* Lund.
BAB	*Académie royale de Belgique, Bulletin de la Classe des Lettres et des Sciences morales et politiques / Koninklijke Belgische Academie, Mededelingen van de Klasse der Letteren en der Morele en Staatkundige Wetenschappen.* Brussels.
BAE-B	*Bureau of American Ethnology, Bulletin.* Washington, D.C.
BAE-R	*Bureau of American Ethnology, Annual Report.* Washington, D.C.
BAGB	*Bulletin de l'Association Guillaume Budé.* Paris.
BB	*Beiträge zur Kunde der indogermanischen Sprachen ("Bezzenbergers Beiträge).*
BBF	*Bulletin des bibliothèques de France.* Paris.
BCO	*Bibliotheca Classica Orientalis.* Dokumentation der altertumswissenschaftlichen Literatur der Sowjetunion und der Länder der Volksdemokratie. Berlin.
BDC	*Bulletin of the Deccan College Research Institute.* Poona.
BECh	*Bibliothèque de l'Ecole des Chartes.* Paris.
BEFEO	*Bulletin de l'Ecole Française d'Extrême-Orient.* Saigon.
Belfagor	*Belfagor.* Rassegna di varia umanità. Florence.
BF	*Boletim de Filologia.* Lisbon.
BFon	*Biuletyn fonograficzny / Bulletin phonographique.* Poznan.
BFS	*Bulletin de la Faculté des Lettres de Strasbourg.* Strasbourg.

BGPMA	*Beiträge zur Geschichte der Philosophie und Theologie des Mittelalters.* Münster.
BHPh	*Bulletin historique et philologique du Comité des travaux historiques et scientifiques.* Paris.
BhV	*Bhā ratīya Vidyā*. Bombay.
Biblica	*Biblica.* Commentarii editi Pontificii Instituti Biblici. Rome.
BIBR	*Bulletin de l'Institut Historique Belge de Rome.*
BICC	*Boletín del Instituto Caro y Cuervo.* Bogotá. Starting with vol. VII, 1951, title changed to *Thesaurus.*
BICS	*Bulletin of the Institute of Classical Studies of the University of London.* London.
BIHP	*Zhō ngyā ng yánjiuyuàn lìshi yuyán yánjiusuo jìkā n / Bulletin of the Institute of History and Philology, Academia Sinica.* Taipei (Taiwan).
BiHR	*Bibliothèque d'Humanisme et Renaissance.* Geneva.
BL	*Bibliographie linguistique publiée par le Comité International Permanent des Linguistes / Linguistic Bibliography.* Utrecht and Antwerp.
BNF	*Beiträge zur Namenforschung, Neue Folge.* Heidelberg.
BPhSC	*Bulletin of the Philological Society of Calcutta.* Calcutta.
BPTJ	*Biuletyn polskiego towarzystwa jezykoznawczego / Bulletin de la Société polonaise de Linguistique.* Wroclaw and Cracow.
BRPh	*Beiträge zur romanischen Philologie.* Berlin.
BS	*Behavioral Science.* Ann Arbor, Mich.
BSGW	*Berichte über die Verhandlungen der Sächsischen Gesellschaft der Wissenschaften.* Leipzig.
BSL	*Bulletin de la Société de Linguistique de Paris.* Paris.
BSLP	*Bulletin de la Société de Linguistiqye de Paris.* Paris.
BSOAS	*Bulletin of the School of Oriental and African Studies, University of London.* London.
BVSAW	*Berichte über die Verhandlungen der Sächsischen Akademie der Wissenschaften zu Leipzig, Philologisch-historische Klasse.* Berlin.
BVSpr	*Beiträge zur vergleichenden Sprachforschung auf dem Gebiete der arischen, celtischen und slavischen Sprachen.* Berlin, F. Dümmler, 1858-76.
BZAW	*Beihefte zur "Zeitschrift für die alttestamentl. Wissenschaft".*
CB	*Classical Bulletin.* Chicago, Ill.
CF	*Classical Folia.* Studies in the Christian perpetuation of the Classics.
CFS	*Cahiers Ferdinand de Saussure.* Geneva.
CHM	*Cahiers d'Histoire Mondiale.* Paris.
CHum	*Computers and the Humanities.* New York.
CILP	*Conférences de l'Institut de Linguistique de l'Université de Paris.* Paris.
CJ	*The Classical Journal.* Menasha, Wisconsin.
CJL	*Canadian Journal of Linguistics / Revue Canadienne de Linguistique.* Toronto.
CLex	*Cahiers de Lexicologie.* Besançon.
CLG	*Cours de Linguistique générale.* 3rd. ed., prepared by Charles Bally and Albert Sechehaye. Paris, Payot, 1931. Later editions are merely reprints of this one, including the numerous misprints it contains.
CLG(E)	*CLG.* Critical edition, prepared by Rudolf Engler, vol. I. Wiesbaden, O. Harrassowitz, 1968.
CLing	*Cercetări de Lingvistică.* Cluj.
CLTA	*Cahiers de linguistique théorique et appliquée.* Bucharest.
C&M	*Classica et Mediaevalia.* Revue danoise de philologie et d'histoire. Copenhagen.
ČMF	*Časopis pro moderní Fiolologii.* Prague.
CollE	*College English.* Chicago, Ill.
Convivium	*Convivium.* Rivista di lettere, filosofia e storia. Turin.
CPh	*Classical Philology.* Chicago, Ill.
CQ	*The Classical Quarterly.* New Series. London.
CR	*The Classical Review.* New Series. London.

CRAI	*Comptes Rendus de l'Académie des Inscriptions et Belles-Lettres.* Paris.
CSCA	*California Studies in Classical Antiquity.* Berkeley and Los Angeles.
CTL	*Current Trends in Linguistics,* vols. 1-13. The Hague, Mouton.
CW	*The Classical World.* New York. Formerly - until 1958 - *The Classical Weekly.*
DAb	*Dissertation Abstracts.* Ann Arbor, Mich.
De Homine	*De Homine.* Centro di Ricerca per le Scienze Morali e Sociali. Florence.
DJbVk	*Deutsches Jahrbuch für Volkskunde.* Berlin.
DS	*Danske Studier.* Copenhagen.
DSIJa	*Doklady i soobščenija Instituta jazykoznanija Akademii Nauk SSSR.* Moscow.
DU	*Der Deutschunterricht.* Beiträge zur Praxis und wissenschaftlichen Grundlegung. Stuttgart.
DVLG	*Deutsche Vierteljahrschrift für Literaturwissenschaft und Geistesgeschichte.* Stuttgart.
EClás	*Estudios Clásicos.* Madrid.
EETS	*Early English Text Society.* London.
EGerm	*Etudes Germaniques.* Revue trimestrielle de la Société des Etudes Germaniques. Paris.
EI	*Encyclopedia of Islam.* Leiden and London.
EJ	*Encyclopedia Judaica.* Jerusalem, 1971.
ELH	*Enciclopedia Lingüística Hispanica.*
Em	*Emérita.* Boletín de lingüística filología clásica. Madrid.
EM	*Enşiqlopediyya Migrāvit.* Jerusalem, 1958 -.
EMC	*Echos du Monde Classique.* Classical News and Views.
Eos	*Eos.* Commentarii Societatis Philologicae Polonorum. Wroclaw.
EPhK	*Egyetemes Philologiai Közlöny.* Archivum Philologicum. Budapest.
Eranos	*Eranos.* Acta philologica Seucana. Uppsala.
ES	*English Studies.* A Journal of English Letters and Philology. Amsterdam.
Esprit	*Esprit.* Paris.
EStn	*Englische Studien.* Marburg.
Ethnology	*Ethnology.* International Journal of Cultural and Social Anthropology. Pittsburgh, Penn.
Euphorion	*Euphorion.* Zeitschrift für Literaturgeschichte. Heidelberg.
E&W	*East and West.* Quarterly published by the Istituto Italiano per il Medio ed Estremo Oriente. Rome.
FdS	*Ferdinand de Saussure.*
FF	*Forschungen und Fortschritte.* Berlin.
Filologija	*Filologija.* Zagreb.
Filosofia	*Filosofia.* Turin.
FL	*Foundations of Language.* International Journal of language and philosophy. Dordrecht, The Netherlands.
FM	*Le Français Moderne.* Revue de linguistique française. Paris.
FoL	*Folia Linguistica.* Acta Societatis Linguisticae Europaeae. The Hague.
FPhon	*Folia Phoniatrica.* Journal international de phoniatrie. Basel and New York, Karger.
FR	*French Review.* American Association of Teachers of French. Eastern Michigan University. Ypsilanti, Mich.
FS	*French Studies.* Oxford.
FUF	*Finnisch-ugrische Forschungen.* Zeitschrift für Finnisch-ugrische Sprach- und Volkskunde. Helsinki.
FWCJS	*Fourth World Congress of Jewish Studies.* Jerusalem, 1968. World Union of Jewish Studies.
GGA	*Göttingische Gelehrte Anzeigen.* Göttingen.
GIF	*Giornale Italiano di Filologia.* Naples.
GL	*General Linguistics.* Lexington, Kentucky.
GLECS	*Comptes rendus du Groupe Linguistique d'Etudes Chamito-Sémitiques.* Paris.

GLL	*German Life and Letters.* Oxford.
Glossa	*Glossa.* A Journal of Linguistics. Burnaby, B.C.
Glotta	*Glotta.* Zeitschrift für griechische und lateinische Sprache. Göttingen.
Gnomon	*Gnomon.* Kritische Zeitschrift für die gesamte klassische Altertumwissenschaft. Munich.
GQ	*German Quarterly.* Appleton, Wisconsin.
GR	*The Germanic Review.* New York.
GRM	*Germanisch-Romanische Monatsschrift.* Heidelberg.
GSAI	*Giornale della Società Asiatica Italiana.* Florence.
Gymnasium	*Gymnasium.* Vierteljahreszeitschrift für humanistische Bildung. Heidelberg.
GZH	*Gdanskie Zeszyty Humanistyczne.* Gdansk.
HandNFC	*Handelingen van het Nederlands Filologencongres.* Groningen.
HBVk	*Hessische Blätter für Volkskunde.* Giessen.
HCL	*Hebrew Computational Linguistics.* Ramat-Gan, Israel.
Helmantica	*Helmantica.* Revista de humanidades clásicas. Salamanca.
Hermes	*Hermes.* Zeitschrift für klassische Philologie. Wiesbaden.
Hesperia	*Hesperia.* Journal of the American School of Classical Studies at Athens. Athens.
HJAS	*Harvard Journal of Asiatic Studies.* Cambridge, Mass.
HUCA	*Hebrew Union College Annual.* Cincinnati, Ohio.
Humanitas	*Humanitas.* Revista do Instituto de Estudos Clássicos da Faculdade de Letras da Universidade de Coimbra. Coimbra.
HW	*Hebräische Wortforschung.* Festschrift zum 80. Geburtstag von Walter Baumgartner. Supplements to Vetus Testamentum, 16. Leiden, 1967.
HZnMTL	*Handelingen van de Koninklijke Zuidnederlandse Maatschappij voor Taal- en Letterkunde en Geschiedenis.* Brussels.
IBK	*Innsbrucker Beiträge zur Kulturwissenschaft.* Innsbruck.
IBLA	*Revue de l'Institut des Belles Lettres Arabes.* Tunis.
IEJ	*Israel Exploration Journal.* Jerusalem.
IF	*Indogermanische Forschungen.* Zeitschrift für Indogermanistik und allgemeine Sprachwissenschaft. Berlin.
IHQ	*Indian Historical Quarterly.* Calcutta.
IIJ	*Indo-Iranian Journal.* The Hague.
IJ	*Indogermanisches Jahrbuch.* Berlin.
IJAL	*International Journal of American Linguistics.* Baltimore, Maryland.
IL	*Indian Linguistics.* Journal of the Linguistic Society of India. Poona.
IRAL	*International Review of Applied Linguistics in Language Teaching /Internationale Zeitschrift für angewandte Linguistik in der Spracherziehung.* Heidelberg.
Isis	*Isis.* An International Review devoted to the History of Science and Civilization. Cambridge, Mass.
Italica	*Italica.* American Association of Teachers of Italian. Chicago and New York.
It Beaken.	*It Beaken.* Meidielingen fan de Fryske Akademy. Assen.
ITL	*Review of the Institute of Applied Linguistics.* Louvain (Belgium).
IUPAL	*Indiana University Publications in Anthropology, Folklore and Linguistics.* Bloomington, Ind.
Iura	*Iura.* Rivista internazionale di diritto romano e antico. Naples.
IZAS	*Internationale Zeitschrift für Allgemeine Sprachwissenschaft.* Leipzig, J.A. Barth, 1884-90.
IzvAN	*Izvestija Akademii Nauk SSSR.* Otdelenie literatury i jazyka. Moscow and Leningrad.
JA	*Journal Asiatique.* Paris.
JAOS	*Journal of the American Oriental Society.* New Haven, Conn.
JASA	*Journal of the Acoustical Society of America.* Chicago.
JASB	*Journal of the Asiatic Society of Bengal.* Calcutta.
JASBo	*Journal of the Asiatic Society of Bombay.* Bombay.
JbBAW	*Jahrbuch der Bayerischen Akademie der Wissenschaften.* Munich.

JBRAS	*Journal of the Bombay Branch of the Royal Asiatic Society.* Bombay.
JBL	*Journal of Biblical Literature.* Philadelphia.
JCLA	*The Journal of the Canadian Linguistic Association / Revue de l'Association canadienne de linguistique.* Edmonton, Alberta.
JCS	*Journal of Cuneiform Studies.* New Haven, Conn.
JEGPh	*The Journal of English and Germanic Philology.* Urbana, Ill.
JHI	*Journal of the History of Ideas.* Lancaster and New York.
JJewS	*The Journal of Jewish Studies.* London.
JL	*Journal of Linguistics.* Journal of the Linguistic Association of Great Britain. London.
JOIB	*Journal of the Oriental Institute, M.S. University of Baroda.* Baroda, India.
JOR	*Journal of Oriental Research.* Madras.
JOS	*Języki obce w szkole.* Warsaw.
JPsych	*Journal de Psychologie normale et pathologique.* Paris.
JQR	*Jewish Quarterly Review.* Philadelphia.
JRAS	*Journal of the Royal Asiatic Society of Great Britain and Ireland.* London.
JSD	*Journal of Speech Disorders.*
JSHD	*Journal of Speech and Hearing Disorders.* Washington, D. C.
JSHR	*Journal of Speech and Hearing Research.* Washington, D. C.
JSS	*Journal of Semitic Studies.* Manchester.
JVLVB	*Journal of Verbal Learning and Verbal Behavior.* New York.
JWI	*Journal of the Warburg Institute.*
Kenyon Review	*Kenyon Review.* Kenyon College, Gambier, Ohio.
KLL	*Kuntr^esīm L<u>^e</u> 'Iny^enē Lāšōn.* Bulletin of Hebrew Language Studies, ed. by H. Yalon. 1937-43. Reprinted Jerusalem, 1963.
KNf	*Kwartalnik Neofilologiczny.* Warsaw.
Kratylos	*Kratylos.* Kritisches Berichts- und Rezensionsorgan für indogermanische und allgemeine Sprachwissenschaft. Wiesbaden.
KrS	*Kirjath Sepher.* Bibliographical Quarterly of the Jewish National and University Library. Jerusalem, The Hebrew University.
KZ	*Zeitschrift für vergleichende Sprachforschung auf dem Gebiete der indogermanischen Sprachen.* Begründet von A. Kuhn. Göttingen.
Langages	*Langages.* Paris.
Laryngoscope	*Laryngoscope.* A monthly journal on diseases of the ear, nose, and throat. American Laryngological, Rhinological and Otological Society. Collinsville, Ill., Laryngoscope Co.
Latomus	*Latomus.* Revue d'études latines. Brussels.
LB	*Leuvense Bijdragen.* Tijdschrift voor Germaanse Filologie. Louvain.
LBer	*Linguistische Berichte.* Braunschweig.
LbR	*Limba Română.* Bucharest.
LEC	*Les Etudes Classiques.* Namur.
Lesonénu	*Lesonénu.* Quarterly of Hebrew (In Hebrew). Jerusalem.
LeSt	*Lingua e Stile.* Quaderni dell'Istituto di Glottologia dell'Università degli Studi di Bologna. Bologne.
Lexis	*Lexis.* Studien zur Sprachphilosophie, Sprachgeschichte und Begriffsforschung.
LF	*Listy Filologickí.* Prague.
Lg	*Language.* Journal of the Linguistic Society of America. Baltimore.
LGRP	*Literaturblatt für germanische und romanische Philologie.* Heilbronn.
Lingua	*Lingua.* International Review of General Linguistics / Revue Internationale de linguistique générale. Amsterdam.
Linguistic Inquiry	*Linguistic Inquiry.* Toronto.
Linguistics	*Linguistics.* An International Review. The Hague.
Linguistique	*La Linguistique.* Revue internationale de linguistique générale. Paris.
LKK	*Lietuviu kalbotyros klausimai / Voprosy litovskogo jazykoznanija.* Vilnius.

LLA	*Lesonenu La'Am.* Jerusalem, The Academy of the Hebrew Language.
LM	*Les Langues Modernes.* Paris.
Logos	*Logos.* Naples, Libreria Scientifica Editrice.
LS	*Language Sciences.* Bloomington, Ind.
L&S	*Language and Speech.* Teddington, Middlesex.
LSA	*Linguistic Society of America.* Washington, D. C.
LTS	*Lexique de la terminologie saussurienne.* Comp. by Rudolf Engler. Utrecht and Antwerp, Spectrum, 1968.
Lustrum	*Lustrum.* Internationale Forschungsberichte aus dem Bereich des Klassischen Altertums. Göttingen.
MA	*Le Moyen Age.* Revue d'histoire et de philologie. Brussels.
MAGL	*Mittelalterliches Geistesleben.* Vols. I-III. Munich.
Maia	*Maia.* Rivista di letterature classiche. Bologna.
MAP	*Memorie dell'Academia Patavina di Scienze, Lettere e Arti.* Padova.
MAPS	*Memoirs of the American Philosophical Society.* Philadelphia.
MASB	*Memorie dell'Accademia delle Scienze (dell'Istituto) di Bologna.*
MC	*Il Mondo Classico.* Turin.
Mea	*Meander.* Miesięcznik Poswięcony Kulturze Swiata Starożytnego. Warsaw.
MH	*Museum Helveticum.* Schweizerische Zeitschrift für klassische Altertumswissenschaft / Revue Suisse pour l'étude de l'antiquité classique. Basel.
Mind	*Mind.* A quarterly review of psychology and philosophy. London.
MLF	*Modern Language Forum.* Los Angeles.
MLJ	*Modern Language Journal.* Ann Arbor, Mich.
MLN	*Modern Language News.* Baltimore.
MLR	*The Modern Language Review.* Cambridge.
Mn	*Mnemosyne.* Bibliotheca Philologica Batava. Leiden.
MPh	*Modern Philology.* Chicago.
MPhon	*Le Maître Phonétique.* Organe de l'Association Phonétique Internationale. London.
MS	*Mediaeval Studies.* Toronto.
MSFOu	*Mémoires de la Société Finno-ougrienne.* Helsinki.
MSLL	*Monograph Series on Language and Linguistics, Georgetown University.* Washington, D.C.
Mu	*Muttersprache.* Zeitschrift zur Pflege und Erforschung der deutschen Sprache. Mannheim.
Muséon	*Le Muséon.* Revue d'études orientales. Louvain.
MUSJ	*Mélanges de l'Université Saint-Joseph.* Beirut, Libanon.
MW	*The Muslim World.* Hartford Seminary Foundation. Hartford, Conn.
NAWG	*Nachrichten von der Akademie der Wissenschaften in Göttingen, Philologisch-historische Klasse.* Göttingen.
N&C	*Nigeria and the Classics.* Ibadan.
NDVŠ-F	*Naučnye doklady Vysšej školy, Filologičeskie nauki.* Moscow.
NF	*Neue Forschung.* Arbeiten zur Geistesgeschichte der germanischen und romanischen Völker. Berlin.
NGGW	*Nachrichten von der Gesellschaft der Wissenschaften zu Göttingen.* Berlin.
NJAB	*Neue Jahrbücher für antike und deutsche Bildung.* Leipzig. Replaced in 1943 by *Die Antike.*
NoVidSF	*Det Kongelige Norske Videnskabers Selskabs Fordhandlinger.* Trondheim.
Nph	*Neophilologus.* Groningen.
NphM	*Neuphilologische Mitteilungen.* Bulletin de la Société neophilologique de Helsinki. Helsinki.
NS	*Die Neueren Sprachen.* Frankfurt am Main.
NT	*Novum Testamentum.* An International Quarterly for New Testament and Related Studies. Leiden.
NTF	*Nordisk Tidsskrift for Filologi.* Copenhagen.

NTg	*De Nieuwe Taalgids.* Groningen.
NTS	*Norsk Tidsskrift for Sprogvidenskap.* Oslo
NTTS	*Nordisk Tidsskrift for Tale og Stemme.* Copenhagen.
NyK	*Nyelvudományi Közlemények.* A Magyar Tudományos Akadémia nyelvtudományi bizottságának megbizásából. Budapest.
OE	*Oriens Extremus.* Wiesbaden.
OLZ	*Orientalistische Literaturzeitung.* Berlin.
Onoma	*Onoma.* Bulletin d'information et de bibliographie / Bibliographical and Information Bulletin. Louvain.
Orbis	*Orbis.* Bulletin international de documentation linguistique. Louvain.
Oriens	*Oriens.* Milletlerarasi Sark Tetkikleri Cemujeti Mecmuasi / Journal of the International Society for Oriental Research. Leiden.
Orpheus	*Orpheus.* Rivista di umanità classica e cristiana. Catania.
OS	*Orientalia Suecana.* Uppsala.
Paideia	*Paideia.* Rivista letteraria di informazione bibliografica. Brescia.
PAPhilos	*Proceedings of the American Philosophical Society.* Philadelphia.
PBA	*Proceedings of the British Academy.* London.
PBB(H)	*Beiträge zur Geschichte der deutschen Sprache und Literatur.* Begründet von H. Paul und W. Braune. Halle.
PBB(T)	*Beiträge zur Geschichte der deutschen Sprache und Literatur.* Tübingen.
PCA	*Proceedings of the Classical Association.* London.
PCLS	*Papers from the Regional Meeting of the Chicago Linguistic Society.*
PE&W	*Philosophy East and West.* Journal of oriental and comparative thought, University of Hawaii (Honolulu).
PF	*Prace Filologiczne.* Warsaw.
Philologica	*Philologica Academia Republicii Socialiste România,* Centrul de Istorie, Filologie si Etnografie din Craiova, Philologica. Bucuresti.
Philologus	*Philologus.* Zeitschrift für das klassische Altertum. Berlin and Wiesbaden.
Philosophy.	*Philosophy.* Journal of the Royal Institute of Philosophy. Macmillan Ltd., Basingstoke, Hampshire.
Phoenix	*The Phoenix.* The Journal of the Classical Association of Canada. Toronto.
Phonetica	*Phonetica.* Internationale Zeitschrift für Phonetik / International Journal of Phonetics. Basel and New York.
PhP	*Philologica Pragensia.* Prague.
PhQ	*Philological Quarterly.* Iowa City.
PhR	*Philologische Rundschau.* Bremen.
PICL	*Proceedings of the ... International Congress of Linguists.*
P4ICPS/H	*Proceedings of the Fourth International Congress of Phonetic Sciences, held at the University of Helsinki, 4-9 September, 1961.* Edited by Antti Sovijärvi and Pento Aalto. The Hague, Mouton, 1962.
P5ICPS/M	*Proceedings of the Fifth International Congress of Phonetic Sciences, held at the University of Münster, 16-22 August, 1964.* Edited by Eberhard Zwirner and Wolfgang Bethge. Basel and New York, Karger, 1965.
PiL	*Papers in Linguistics, 1934-51,* by John Rupert Firth. London, Oxford University Press, 1957.
PLG	*Probleme de lingvistică generală.* Bucharest.
PMLA	*Publications of the Modern Language Association of America.* New York.
PMS	*Publications in Mediaeval Studies.* University of Notre Dame.
PoL	*Portraits of Linguists: A biographical sourcebook.* Edited by Thomas A. Sebeok, 2 Vols. Bloomington and London, Indiana University Press, 1966.
PP	*La Parola del Passato.* Rivista di Studi Classici. Naples.
PUF	*Presses Universitaires de France.* Paris.
QIGB	*Quaderni dell'Istituto di Glottologia dell'Università di Bologna.* Bologna.
QPR	*Quarterly Progress Report.* Research Laboratory of Electronica, MIT, Cambridge,

	Mass.
QUCC	*Quaderni Urbinati di Cultura Classica.* Urbino.
RAAD	*Revue de l'Académie Arabe de Damas.* Damascus.
RACF	*Revue archéologique du Centre de la France.* Vichy.
RAI	*Rendiconti della Classe di Scienze Morali e Storiche dell'Accademia d'Italia.* Rome
RAL	*Rendiconti della Classe di Scienze Morali, Storiche e Filologiche dell'Accademia dei Lincei.* Rome.
RALinc	*Atti della Accademia Nazionale dei Lincei.* Rendiconti della Classe di Scienze Morali, Storiche e Filologiche. Serie VIII. Rome.
RBPh	*Revue Belge de Philologie et d'Histoire / Belgisch Tijdschrift voor Filologie en Geschiedenis.* Brussels.
RCCM	*Rivista di cultura classica e medioevale.* Rome.
RCL	*Revista Clasică.* Bucharest.
REA	*Revue des Etudes Anciennes.* Bordeaux and Paris.
REC	*Revista de Estudios Clásicos.* Mendoza (Argentina).
REG	*Revue des Etudes Grecques.* Paris.
REL	*Revue des Etudes Latines.* Paris.
RELO	*Revue de l'Organisation international pour l'étude des langues anciennes par ordinateur.* Liège.
RES	*The Review of English Studies.* London.
RESI	*Revue des Etudes Slaves.* Paris.
RF	*Romanische Forschungen.* Vierteljahrschrift für romanische Sprachen und Literaturen. Frankfurt am Main.
RFE	*Revista de Filología Española.* Madrid.
RFHC	*Revista de la Faculdad de Humanidades y Ciencias.* Univ. de la Republica. Montevideo.
RFIC	*Revista di Filologia e d'Istruzione Classica.* Turin.
RFV	*Russkij filologiceskij vestnik.* Warsaw, later on Moscow, and eventually Kazan, 1879-1918. Reprinted in Düsseldorf, Brücken Verlag, 1972.
RHLF	*Revue d'Histoire Littéraire de la France.* Paris.
RhM	*Rheinisches Museum für Philologie.* Neue Folge. Frankfurt am Main.
RIL	*Rendiconti dell'Istituto Lombardo di Scienze e Lettere, Classe di lettere e scienze morali e storiche.* Milan.
RJaŠ	*Russkij Jazyk v Škole.* Moscow.
RJb	*Romanistisches Jahrbuch.* Hamburg.
RKJW	*Wrocławskie Towarzystwo Naukowe, Rozprawy Komisji Językowej.* Wroclaw.
RLaR	*Revue des Langues Romanes.* Montpellier.
RO	*Rocznik Orientalistyczny.* Warsaw.
Romanoslavica	*Romanoslavica.* Bucharest.
RomPh	*Romance Philology.* Berkeley and Los Angeles.
RPh	*Revue de Philologie, de littérature et d'histoire anciennes.* Paris.
RRLing	*Revue Roumaine de Linguistique.* Bucharest.
RSlav	*Ricerche Slavistiche.* Rome.
RUB	*Revue de l'Université de Bruxelles.* Brussels.
SAO	*Studia et Acta Orientalia.* Bucharest.
SbBAW	*Sitzungsberichte der Bayerischen Akademie der Wissenschaften, Philosophisch-historische Klasse.* Munich.
SbDAW	*Sitzungsberichte der Deutschen Akademie der Wissenschaften zu Berlin, Klasse für Sprachen, Literatur und Kunst.* Berlin.
SbOAW	*Sitzungsberichte der Osterreichischen Akademie der Wissenschaften, Philosophisch-historische Klasse.* Vienna.
SbSAW	*Sitzungsberichte der Sächsischen Akademie der Wissenschaften zu Leipzig, Philosophisch-historische Klasse.* Berlin.
Science	*Science.* American Association for the Advancement of Science. Washington, D.C.
SCL	*Studii şi Cercetări Lingvistice.* Bucharest.

SClas	*Studii Clasice.* Bucharest.
ScS	*Scandinavian Studies.* Publication of the Society for the Advancement of Scandinavian Study. Menasha, Wisconsin.
SDHI	*Studia et Documenta Historiae et Iuris.*
Semiotica	*Semiotica.* Journal of the International Association for Semiotic Studies. The Hague, Mouton.
SFFUK	*Sborník Filozofickej Fakulty Univerzity Komenského, Philologica.* Bratislava.
SG	*Studium Generale.* Berlin, Göttingen and Heidelberg.
SH	*Scripta Hierosolymitana.* Jerusalem, The Hebrew University.
SicGym	*Sicularum Gymnasium.* Rassegna semestrale della Facoltà di Lettere e Filosofia dell'Università di Catania. Catania.
SIFC	*Studi Italiani di Filologia Classica.* Florence.
SIL	*Studies in Linguistics.* Buffalo, New York.
SJA	*Southwestern Journal of Anthropology.* Albuquerque, New Mexico.
SL	*Studia Linguistica.* Revue de linguistique générale et comparée. Lund.
SLFriul	*Studi Linguistici Friulani.* Udine.
SM	*Les Sources manuscrites du CLG de FdS.* By Robert Godel. Paris, Minard and Geneva, Droz, 1957.
SNPh	*Studia Neophilologica.* A Journal of Germanic and Romance Philology. Uppsala.
SovFU	*Sovetskoe finno-ugrovedenie / Soviet Finno-Ugric Studies.* Tallinn.
Speculum	*Speculum.* A Journal of Mediaeval Studies. Cambridge, Mass.
SPFB	*Sborník Pedagogické Fakulty Brněnskó University.* Řada jazyková a literáarní. Brno.
SPh	*Studies in Philology.* Chapel Hill, North Carolina.
Sprache	*Die Sprache.* Zeitschrift für Sprachwissenschaft. Vienna.
SprB	*Språkliga bidrag.* Meddelanden från Seminarierna för slaviska språk, jämförande språkforskning, finsk-ugriska språk och östasiatiska språk vid Lunds Universitet. Lund.
SprPAN	*Polska Akademia Nauk.* Sprawozdania z prac naukonych wydziału nauk społecznych. Warsaw.
SS	*Slovo a Slovesnost.* Prague.
SSL	*Studi e saggi linguistici.* Supplemento alla rivista 'L'Italia dialettale'. Pisa.
SSlav	*Studia Slavica Academiae Scientiarum Hungaricae.* Budapest.
StRo	*Studi Romani.* Rivista Bimestrale dell'Istituto di Studi Romani. Rome.
Strumenti Critici	*Strumenti Critici.* Turin.
STZ	*Sprache im Technischen Zeitalter.* Stuttgart.
SUL	*Per lo Studio e l'Uso del Latino.* Bollettino Internazionale di Studi, Ricerche, Informazioni.
SvTs	*Svensk Tidsskrift.* Stockholm.
Symposium	*Symposium.* A Journal devoted to Modern Foreign Languages and Literatures. Syracuse, New York.
TAPA	*Transactions and Proceedings of the American Philological Association.* Lancaster, Pennsylvania.
Tarbiz	*Tarbiz.* A Quarterly Review of the Humanities. (In Hebrew), Jerusalem.
TBL	*Tübinger Beiträge zur Linguistik.* Tübingen.
TCLC	*Travaux du Cercle Linguistique du Prague.* Prague.
Textus	*Textus.* Annual of the Hebrew University Bible Project. Jerusalem.
Theoria	*Theoria.* A Swedish Journal of Philosophy. Lund.
TIL	*Travaux de l'Institut de Linguistique, Faculté des Lettres de l'Université de Paris.* Paris.
TLL	*Travaux de Linguistique et de Littérature.* Publiés par le Centre de Philologie et de Littératures romanes de l'Université de Strasbourg. Strasbourg.
TLP	*Traveaux Linguistiques de Prague.* Prague.
TP	*T'oung Pao.* Archives concernant l'histoire, les langues, la géographie et les arts de l'Asie Orientale. Leiden.

TPhS	*Transactions of the Philological Society*. Oxford.
Traditio	*Traditio*. Studies in Ancient and Medieval History, Thought and Religion, New York.
TsNTL	*Tijdschrift voor Nederlandse Taal- en Letterkunde*. Uitgegeven vanwege de Maatschappij der Nederlandse Letterkunde te Leiden. Leiden.
UAJb	*Ural-Altaische Jahrbücher*. Wiesbaden.
UCPEAP	*University of California Publications in East Asiatic Philology*. Berkeley and Los Angeles.
UCPL	*University of California Publications in Linguistics*. Berkeley and Los Angeles.
Universitas	*Universitas*. Zeitschrift für Wissenschaft, Kunst und Literatur. Stuttgart.
USDHEW	*United States Department of Health, Education and Welfare*. Washington, D.C.
Us Wurk	*Us Wurk*. Meidielingen fan it Frysk Institüt oan de Rijksuniversiteit yn Grims. Groningen.
UUÅ	*Uppsala Universitets Årsskrift / Recueil de Travaux publié par l'Université d'Uppsala*. Uppsala.
UZDušPI	*Učenye zapiski Dušanbinskogo gosudarstvennogo pedagogič-eskogo instituta in T.G. Ševčonko*. Filologičeskaja serija. Dušanbe.
UZLU	*Učenye zapiski Leningradskogo ordena Lenina gosudarstvennoge Universiteta in A.A. Ždanova*. Leningrad.
UZMU	*Učenye zapisko Moskovskogo gosudarstvennogo universiteta*. Moscow.
UZTarU	*Tartu rükliku ülikooli toimetised / Ucenye zapiski Tartuskogo gosudarstvennogo Universiteta*. Tartu.
VDI	*Vestnik Drevnej Istorii*. Moscow.
Vir	*Virittäjä*. Kotikielen seuran aikakauslehti. Helsinki.
Vox	*Vox Romanica*. Annales Helvetici explorandis linguis Romanicis destinati. Bern.
VT	*Vetus Testamentum*. A Quarterly published by The International Organization of Old Testament Scholars. Leiden.
WHJP	*World History of the Jewish People*. Rutgers University Press.
Wissenschaft und Weltbild	*Wissenschaft und Weltbild*. Zeitschrift für die Grundfragen der Forschung. Vienna.
WJA	*Würzburger Jahrbücher für die Altertumswissenschaft*. Würzburg.
Word	*Word*. Journal of the Linguistic Circle of New York. New York.
WSlav	*Die Welt der Slaven*. Vierteljahrsschrift für Slavistik. Wiesbaden.
WSlJb	*Wiener Slavistisches Jahrbuch*. Vienna.
WW	*Wirkendes Wort*. Deutsches Sprachschaffen in Lehre und Leben. Düsseldorf.
WZKM	*Wiener Zeitschrift für die Kunde des Morgenlandes*. Vienna.
WZKSO	*Wiener Zeitschrift für die Kunde Süd- und Ostasiens und Archiv für indische Philosophie*. Vienna.
WZUB	*Wissenschaftliche Zeitschrift der Humboldt-Universität, Berlin*. Gesellschafts- und sprachwissenschaftliche Reihe.
WZUG	*Wissenschaftliche Zeitschrift der Universität Greifswald*. Gesellschafts- und sprachwissenschaftliche Reihe.
WZUH	*Wissenschaftliche Zeitschrift der Martin Luther-Universität*. Gesellschafts- und sprachwissenschaftliche Reihe. Halle - Wittenberg.
WZUJ	*Wissenschaftliche Zeitschrift der Universität Jena*. Gesellschafts- und sprachwissenschaftliche Reihe. Jena.
WZUL	*Wissenschaftliche Zeitschrift der Karl Marx-Universität*. Gesellschafts- und sprachwissenschaftliche Reihe. Leipzig.
WZUR	*Wissenschaftliche Zeitschrift der Universität Rostock*. Gesellschafts- und sprachwissenschaftliche Reihe. Rostock.
YCS	*Yale Classical Studies*. New Haven, Connecticut.
YFS	*Yale French Studies*. New Haven, Connecticut.
ZAA	*Zeitschrift für Anglistik und Amerikanistik*. Berlin.
ZAnt	*Ziva Antika / Antiquité vivante*. Skopje.

ZAW	*Zeitschrift für die alttestamentliche Wissenschaft.* Berlin.
ZDA	*Zeitschrift für deutsches Altertum und deutsche Literatur.* Wiesbaden.
ZDAlt	*Zeitschrift für deutsches Altertum.* Leipzig.
ZDL	*Zeitschrift für Dialektologie und Linguistik.* Wiesbaden. Formerly ZMaF.
ZDMG	*Zeitschrift der Mörgenländischen Gesellschaft.* Wiesbaden.
ZDPh	*Zeitschrift für deutsche Philologie.* Berlin.
ZEthn	*Zeitschrift für Ethnologie.* Organ der deutschen Gesellschaft für Volkerkunde. Brunswick.
ZfdU	*Zeitschrift für den deutschen Unterricht.* Leipzig.
ZFSL	*Zeitschrift für französische Sprache und Literatur.* Wiesbaden.
ZII	*Zeitschrift für Indologie und Iranistik.* Leipzig.
ZJKF	*Zprávy Jednoty klasických filologie Cpri SA V.* Prague.
ZMaF	*Zeitschrift für Mundartforschung.* Wiesbaden. See also ZDL.
ZPhon	*Zeitschrift für Phonetik, Sprachwissenschaft und Kommunikationsforschung.* Berlin.
ZRPh	*Zeitschrift für romanische Philologie.* Tübingen.
ZSl	*Zeitschrift für Slawistik.* Berlin.
ZSlPh	*Zeitschrift für slavische Philologie.* Heidelberg.
ZVPs	*Zeitschrift für Völkerpsychologie und Sprachwissenschaft.* Berlin, F. Dümmler, 1860-90.

PART ONE

THE WESTERN TRADITION

INDIA

ROSANE ROCHER

> Hindus of reflective tendencies have always been much given to linguistic analysis and speculation. All Indian systems deal more or less with problems of the nature of language, the relation of sound to sense, etc. When the time comes for a general History of Linguistic Theories, the Indian section will bulk large. (Edgerton 1928:171)

0. INTRODUCTION

0.1 The reader who first consults the table of contents of this volume might be struck by the fact that India is considered part of the Western tradition, whereas the Far East, the Near East, and the American Indian tradition are viewed as 'areal'. It is the purpose of this paper to show how Indian linguistics indeed became a part of the Western tradition, and how the study of the Indian grammarians relates to general linguistics today. This is not a study of features of linguistic analysis which the West may have learned from India (on this, see Emeneau 1955; Kunjunni Raja 1958).

0.2 Attention is focused on trends, rather than exhaustive bibliographical data. Recent developments are emphasized. Earlier researches have been treated in depth — although from a different angle — by Renou in three successive reports (1940, 1957a, 1969), which contain extensive bibliographical references. It will be found that certain approaches which Renou (1969, article written in 1966) still considered marginal, have developed into new trends and attitudes.

0.3 Perforce the Pāṇinian tradition is the focus of the following pages. This is partly due to the orientation of the writer, but it is also true that Pāṇini and his followers have been the core of the Indian tradition as it has been integrated in the history of general linguistics. Pali, Prakrit, and Dravidian linguistics have been less influential, and are treated more summarily. Indian philosophy of language is not taken into account: it has been described recently in this series (Staal 1969); an updated version of that article is to appear shortly (Staal Ms.1).

1. COMPARATIVE LINGUISTICS

1.1 It is common knowledge that comparative linguistics began in earnest after the discovery of Sanskrit by Western scholars (Burrow v; Pedersen 21). It has been argued that what made the impact of Sanskrit greater than that of other Indo-European languages known at the time was 'the peculiar structural clarity of the language' (Pedersen 21–2), the fact that Sanskrit 'is above all an analyzable language' (Whitney 1884:279). Whitney contended that it admits 'of the easy and distinct separation of ending from stem, and of derivative suffix from primitive word, back to the ultimate attainable elements, the so-called roots' (1884:279). In fact, what made Sanskrit more analyzable on that score was less its own perspicuity, than the fact that Westerners learned it through an Indian tradition of grammar that provided them with such an analysis (Brough 1951:27; Lassen 112; Windisch 1917–20: 54–5). In one of the most fundamental features of Indo-European, the ablaut, Sanskrit is unquestionably less clear than Greek. Still, and in spite of the fact that Sanskrit had lost the qualitative ablaut, the Indian grammatical analysis of *guṇa* and *vṛddhi* served as a basis for the description of Indo-European ablaut (Emeneau 1955:147).

1.2 The first Europeans to learn Sanskrit did so with the help of native pandits, according to indigenous methods, and using traditional Sanskrit grammars. This was true of the pioneers Halhed and Wilkins, and of the founders Jones and Colebrooke. Their private oriental collections contained manuscripts of Sanskrit grammatical treatises (Rocher Ms.; Master 187). Emeneau (1955:148–9) has shown how the Pāṇinian system influenced Jones; Master's critique of his article has only reinforced the conviction that, even if Jones did not study Pāṇini's grammar itself, he definitely used a grammar in the Pāṇinian tradition (Emeneau 1971:960–2). The early Sanskritists not only provided the West with information on a distant and ancient Indo-European language; they also brought an analysis of these data that was to serve as a basis for the analysis of other Indo-European languages, and of reconstructed Indo-European itself (Schulze 1921, 1923, repr. 1934:5–6, 93–4).

1.3 The influence of the Indian grammatical tradition on comparative linguistics was essentially unconscious. No effort was made to study the Pāṇinian method systematically, and use it as a model. The distinction between root and suffix, primary and secondary suffixes, stem and endings, the analysis of compounds, the system of ablaut, were taken over as general guiding principles; there was no attempt to pattern the description of Indo-European languages after the detailed treatment of Sanskrit by the Pāṇinian tradition.

1.4 This influence was also short-lived. It was the initial spark that set comparative linguistics on its course. The historical character of comparative Indo-European linguistics precluded a lasting link. The Pāṇinian system, which is essentially descriptive, synchronic, and focused on one language to the exclusion of all other, had little in common with the drawing of historical trees, and the comparison of distant languages or of different stages of the same linguistic group. Once the Pāṇinian morphological analysis had been made an integral part of Western linguistic methods, the Indian linguistic tradition was of no further use or interest to comparatists. Comparatists developed their own historical methods; Pāṇini's grammar became the province of indologists.

2. INDOLOGY

2.0 Although comparative and historical Indo-European linguistics owes much to the Indian grammarians, comparatists never attempted to study Pāṇini's work directly. It was for the indologists to engage in the study of Indian grammar, and to introduce the original texts to the Western scholarly world. Most of the solid groundwork on Indian grammar is due to indologists.

Not that Pāṇini and other Indian grammarians ever imposed themselves as one of the main topics of study for Western indologists. Most indologists are primarily interested in the culture of India, as revealed in its literature. Technical branches of learning are not part of the central picture. Indologists are not more likely to be interested in Indian grammatology, mathematics, or astronomy, than students of German literature are expected to devote themselves to German dialectology, physics, or chemistry. For most indologists, as for most students of a foreign culture, language is only a tool, a necessary key to the cultural scene, an indispensable part of one's apprenticeship. Only a minority of indologists are interested in language and linguistics per se. When the term indologists is used from this point, it refers to those scholars who devoted at least part of their researches to Indian languages and Indian grammatology.

2.1 Not only were not all indologists interested in linguistics, not all linguistically oriented indologists have been appreciative of the Indian grammatical tradition.

The first grammars of Sanskrit published by Westerners, such as those by Colebrooke (1805), Carey (1806), Wilkins (1808), and Forster (1810), relied explicitly on the native tradition. Their authors had learned Sanskrit in India, with pandits, and it was natural for them to describe the language along the lines of their own experience. But, right from the beginning, a certain degree of dissatisfaction with the Indian method appears in European grammars of Sanskrit. Although Colebrooke claims to have followed the Indian system (iii–iv), he adds that its 'arrangement, indeed, is ill adapted to facilitate study' (iv). This point was to be made time and again in later years, even by scholars who otherwise valued the Indian grammatical tradition. When writing his Sanskrit grammar, Bopp deliberately turned his back to the native tradition, an attitude for which he incurred Lassen's criticisms. Bopp felt that the Indian system did not allow to distinguish between the general and the particular (Lassen 22); moreover, he wanted to write a historical grammar that would explain the origin of Sanskrit forms (Lassen 26). In spite of criticisms by Lassen, Schlegel (31–7), and Böhtlingk (1845), Bopp's attitude represented the trend of the times. The traditional Indian system ran against several desiderata. It was not historical. It was not comparative, a basic disadvantage at a time when no scholar approached Sanskrit without a firm knowledge of Greek and Latin. It was not based on the familiar Aristotelian categories. And, above all, it was exceedingly complex. The general sentiment was that, whatever its scientific merits, the Indian method had no didactic use for Westerners. Max Müller judged it 'not suited to the wants of English students, least of all to the wants of beginners' (vi); Macdonell considered that it 'rendered Sanskrit unnecessarily hard to learn' (vii). To this day, even admirers of Pāṇini rarely use his grammar to introduce their students to Sanskrit.

2.2.1 What prompted indologists to study the Indian grammarians was not their methods of description and techniques, but their testimonial value. Indian grammatical texts were viewed as one of the sources of evidence on the Sanskrit language. The obvious course of action was to match the teachings of Sanskrit grammarians with the language used in literary texts. A correlative preoccupation was to ascertain which stage in the evolution of the Sanskrit language Pāṇini described. Two prominent studies of that type appeared about the turn of the century; both were devoted to case-syntax, and compared the grammarians' teachings with the language of the Aitareyabrāhmaṇa (Liebich 1886) and the older Upaniṣads (Wecker 1905–6). Such comparative studies of Pāṇini's Sanskrit and the Sanskrit of literary texts did not flourish as might have been expected. From a chronological point of view they demonstrated that, generally speaking, Pāṇini's Sanskrit is later than the Brāhmaṇas, and older than the Upaniṣads; but they also confirmed what had already been repeatedly affirmed: that the Sanskrit of the grammarians does not tally exactly with the language of any text. This conclusion made the testimony of the grammarians suspect in the eyes of many, and worthless in the opinion of some.

In the controversy that developed, the main protagonist, and relentless critic of the grammarians was Whitney, who was convinced that Pāṇini and his followers had created an artificial language out of their own imagination. His attitude was one of total condemnation: the Indian grammarians' mode of presentation was 'perverse' and 'a failure' (1884:280); their categories were 'crude' and 'unphilosophical' (1893a:171–2); but their ultimate flaw was that they taught forms that were 'false and never-used' (1884:280); as a result, they could not be considered 'as the foundation of our knowledge of the Sanskrit language' (1893a:171). For his own Sanskrit grammar, Whitney made it very clear that he was not about to follow the example of the earliest grammars, which had relied on the native grammarians 'at the expense of clearness and proportion, as well as of scientific truth' (1879: v–vi). His tone was markedly different from that of other Sanskrit grammars (Max Müller: x–xi; Benfey 1852: I.v.) What set Whitney apart was the extreme character of his statements; he was convinced that 'it is characteristic of Hindu science generally not to be able to stop when it has done enough' (1884:290). Yet, the suspicion that Indian grammarians had invented forms which never existed in the language was wide-spread. Even Benfey acknowledged that he omitted rules which were not countenanced by literature, 'and which, for all we know, may be the result of grammatical speculation rather than the productions of the language as once spoken by the classical writers of ancient India' (1863: xiv). Overstatement aside, Whitney's attitude was more representative of his times than that of Böhtlingk (1885, 1893), who not only attempted to refute Whitney's criticisms, but even entertained thoughts of composing a Sanskrit grammar based on his extensive researches on the Indian grammatical tradition (Windisch 1917–20: 241–2). It is significant that the work was never completed.

2.2.2 Whitney's ire focused especially on the Dhātupāṭha, the list of roots annexed to Pāṇini's grammar (1884: 280–4; 1893a: 183). He dismissed it in the supplement to his Sanskrit grammar (1885b: vii; reaction by Kielhorn 1886) in the same way that he had written the grammar itself without relying on Pāṇini. For him, and for his student Edgren (1882), most of the roots listed in the Dhātupāṭha were figments of the grammarians' imagination: 'more than half — actually more than half — of them never have been met with, and never will be met with, in the Sanskrit literature of any age' (Whitney 1884:282). Böhtlingk (1885, 1893) and Liebich (1891:51–61) reacted against Whitney's contentions. In an attempt to answer Whitney's and Edgren's attacks, Bühler (1894) outlined a general program which has been only partly realized since. There were several reasons why this controversy developed. First, the textual tradition was extremely poor. Pāṇini's Dhātupāṭha has not been preserved; the tradition only records late, swollen recensions. Whitney knew the Dhātupāṭha from Westergaard's work, and, later, from the list annexed to Böhtlingk's second edition of Pāṇini's grammar (1887). Since then, Liebich (1919b, 1920a, 1921, 1930; important remarks by Thieme 1932) and Palsule (1955, 1958b, 1961) have done much to collate the different lists, and present a less inflated original list. But the difficulty did not lie in the source materials only; the critics of the Dhātupāṭha were also guilty of ethnocentrism. Whitney followed his teacher Bopp (1867) in condemning the Indian grammarians for calling *dhātu* 'root' elements which were not considered roots in Western grammar, such as the stems of denominative verbs. He also wanted to exclude elements which were at the basis of nominal forms; for him, root meant only verbal root. Even if we set aside these two basic causes of misunderstanding, there remains in the Dhātupāṭha a residue of roots which indeed are not countenanced by Sanskrit literature. Franke (1894) produced evidence from Pali for some of these unattested roots (for the Pali Dhātupāṭhas, see Katre 1940), while Kittel (1893) drew similar arguments from Dravidian sources. The program outlined by Bühler included a recourse to dialectal variations; Rocher (1965b) has recently argued for caution in that respect. The fact remains that a number of roots listed in the Dhātupāṭha are still unexplained. A comprehensive examination of that intriguing problem might throw valuable light on the structure of Sanskrit, and allow a glimpse in the workshop of Indian grammarians; but Rocher's announced vast scale project (1965b:707) has lain dormant. Little attention has been devoted to these matters of late, for the approach to Indian grammar has shifted away from the indological viewpoint. Matching the Sanskrit of literature with the grammarians' Sanskrit is no longer a focal point in research.

2.2.3 Attempts to answer Whitney's criticisms on other aspects of grammar have been equally rare (Chatterji 1952–3). In fact, the controversy all but died with its initial protagonists. Agreement was reached that, although the language described by Pāṇini is close to that of the older Brāhmaṇas and Sūtras, it does not match any extant text; Pāṇini codified a spoken, Northwestern variety of Sanskrit. Although few scholars would care to revive the issue, for lack of a better alternative, this characterization of Pāṇini's Sanskrit remains uneasy. The term 'spoken' in this case carries not only its normal positive semantic load, but also covers the failure to discover certain features of Pāṇini's Sanskrit in any written text. Moreover, it raises intricate questions: spoken by whom? in what circumstances? The Prakrits were also spoken in Pāṇini's days. Even if we assume the learned brahmins of the time to have used Sanskrit as their normal medium, the situation may not be dissimilar to that of the Sanskrit spoken by pandits today. It does not necessarily mean that the spoken Sanskrit described by Pāṇini was anyone's native tongue, nor that it was used in all aspects of life. Pāṇini's Sanskrit may not be more than a variety of language that was never written, but was spoken in one region of India by certain people in certain circumstances. As a result, Pāṇini's Sanskrit has lost much of its importance in the eyes of indologists. A wedge appears to have been driven between studies of the Sanskrit language and of the Sanskrit grammarians. Studies of the Sanskrit language by Western scholars focus on the language attested in texts; the grammarians' data are treated as marginal. There are exceptions, to be sure, such as Wackernagel's (1914) historical study of the seventh aorist, which takes into account the testimony of Pāṇini's sūtra 7.3.73 together with the Kāśikā's commentary (refutation by Cardona 1964); but such studies are the exception rather than the rule. On the other hand, studies of the grammarians have by and large become introverted; they concentrate on the internal problems of interpretation of the grammatical treatises, rather than on the language described. Comparative studies such as those by Liebich (1886) and Wecker (1905–6) are no longer in style. A few Indian scholars have taken pains to note un-Pāṇinian forms in various texts, such as the Matsyapurāṇa (Kantawala), the Yogavāsiṣṭha (Satya Vrat), the Rāmāyaṇa (N. Sen), and the Mahābhārata (Kulkarni 1943-51; Gokhale; Sil 1960–1, 1966). These are bare listings, which, as Renou (1969:493 n.30) noted, are of little relevance to the fundamental problem. Of greater interest is a recent study by Palsule (1968a), which goes beyond listing forms, and attempts to find out why some types of nominal derivations have not been described by Pāṇini, although they are well attested in the literature. An answer is sought in terms of Pāṇinian technique. Although the article concludes on a question mark, this appears to be a more profitable line than emphasizing the contrast between Pāṇini and literary evidence.

It is probable that a more thorough and wide ranging examination of the literature would corroborate some of the Pāṇinian data for which literary evidence is lacking so far; witness van Nooten's (1970b) recent note on the rare — and Pāṇinian — future form *gaṃsyate*. Editions of texts, which often normalize the readings of manuscripts, are likely to conceal part of the evidence. But whether exhaustive use of the literature, including variant readings in manuscripts, will ever vindicate all the teachings of the Indian grammatical treatises, is very doubtful at the present time. Certainly it no longer retains the attention of many scholars. An indologist who encounters an unusual form in his readings, or in editing a text, is more likely to check Whitney's, Renou's, or Wackernagel's grammar, than open his edition of the Aṣṭādhyāyī; unless, like van Nooten, he happens to be interested in Pāṇinian grammar per se. Western indologists have accepted, for the time being, that there is some degree of difference between the testimony of the Sanskrit grammarians, and that of the texts. Reconciling them is not a current trend of indological research.

The testimonial value of ancient grammars of Dravidian languages does not appear to be contested, if one is to judge by the works of Ramaswami Aiyar, Radhakrishnan, and Rama Subbiah. But this writer is not qualified to speak on that topic.

2.2.4 The fact that there are occasional differences between literary Sanskrit and the grammarians' Sanskrit represents a Western standpoint, which is at variance with the traditional Indian view. According to tradition, Indian grammarians, and particularly the munitraya, the trio of sages Pāṇini–Kātyāyana–Patañjali, do not represent a local, isolated, and otherwise unattested type of Sanskrit. They are the final authority on Sanskrit usage, so much so that V. L. Joshi (1965) can insist that today's Sanskrit should conform to the sandhi taught by grammarians. One difficulty is that the teachings of the three munis are in occasional disagreement. The traditional explanation, in grammar as in law, or in any other branch of Hindu learning, tends to prove that none of the great sages of antiquity was wrong. In the case of grammar, Indian traditional scholarship has marshalled an interpretation learned from the West: a historical view of language. Whenever Pāṇini, Kātyāyana, and Patañjali disagree, they are supposed to reflect different stages of the language. Needless to say, Patañjali, who is also our only source for Kātyāyana's work, never hints at a historical perspective. The arguments of the traditional scholars rest on the opinion voiced by Bhandarkar in the Wilson Philological Lectures (repr. 1927–33: IV.267–74,583ff.). They are articulated in the following fashion. (1) Sanskrit was a living, spoken language, at least until Patañjali's time; it must have undergone changes. (2) Pāṇini has been generally acclaimed as a great grammarian; it is inconceivable that he should have committed as many mistakes as the additions and corrections by his successors seem to indicate. (3) The only way to vindicate both Pāṇini and Kātyāyana–Patañjali, is to assume that they describe different stages in the evolution of the language. These assertions have been reiterated most recently by Devasthali (1960–1) in a spirited refutation of Rocher 1962, which itself attempted to oppose the views of Sarma (1944–55). Although Rocher (1962) may have overstated her case, her point was neither to rule out the possibility of linguistic changes in Sanskrit, nor to denigrate the Indian grammarians, as Devasthali was led to believe. She represented the long standing Western conviction that differences between commentators can be accepted as evidence of linguistic change, only if they are corroborated by a similar evolution in the language used in literature. Such correlations do exist, e.g. in the case of the periphrastic perfect (Rocher 1968:272–81). One of Devasthali's collaborators, Laddu, has devoted a 1966 Ph.D. thesis to the 'evolution of the Sanskrit language from Pāṇini to Patañjali'; unfortunately, the work is unpublished, and the validity of its methods cannot be ascertained. The controversy led a third and most distinguished member of the University of Poona, S. D. Joshi, to insert a section on 'reinterpretation versus historical development' in the introduction to the second volume of his translation of Patañjali's Mahābhāṣya (1968–73), in which he soberly argues that 'the question, whether we can infer an evolution of Sanskrit from the examples, must be answered in the negative' (x).

Whereas the question appears to have been hotly debated in India, it passed unnoticed in the West. Indeed, for some years, Western students of Indian grammar have treated the question of linguistic change, and the bearing of grammatical treatises on the history of the Sanskrit language generally, as matters of peripheral interest. In India, the relevance of the grammarians' evidence for the development of Sanskrit and Indo-Aryan, remains a point of central interest; so much so that scholars whose main field is in more modern stages of language occasionally devote attention to Pāṇini's testimony. The general theme of the loosely connected remarks that Sumukar Sen (1970) made in a series of three lectures at Calcutta Sanskrit College, is Pāṇini's evidence for the history of Indo-Aryan languages.

2.2.5 The relevance of Indian grammar for Vedic studies is an even more difficult question, and one which is still very much debated today. The problem is complicated by the fact that Pāṇini's aim was to describe the *bhāṣā*, the spoken Sanskrit with which he was familiar; his treatment of archaic forms is occasional, presented as footnotes as it were to the main body of his grammar. Later grammarians either referred 'Vedic' rules to a separate section, or dropped them altogether.

Whitney (1893b; refutation by Lévi 1906–8) dismissed Pāṇini on this as on other scores, and concentrated on the study of the Vedic texts themselves (e.g. 1956). The basic work devoted to the relation between Pāṇini and the Veda is Thieme's Habilitationsschrift (1935a). Written partly against Whitney, the work proves that

Pāṇini's teachings on archaic usages are consistent; it does not claim that they are to be treated as an important source for Vedic exegesis. This is a point on which Western and Indian scholars seem to part ways, inasmuch as most of the voices that urge the use of Pāṇinian grammar in Vedic interpretation come from India, whereas most of the doubts are expressed by Western scholars.

Renou, whose entire career oscillated between the study of the Veda and that of the grammarians — as evidenced by his series *Etudes védiques et pāṇinéennes* — and who analyzed the treatment of the Vedic language by Pāṇini (1955:115–7), Patañjali (1953b), and other grammarians (1956c), was of the definite opinion that the grammarians do not provide many useful data for the interpretation of the Veda (1960a: §§ 33–4; 1969:492). Kuiper expresses similar misgivings in a review of Bhawe's work on the Soma hymns of the Ṛgveda (1957–62). Bhawe attempted to interpret the Veda systematically in the light of Pāṇini's 'Vedic' rules, thereby putting into practice a theory which he had outlined earlier (1955), and of which he had already given a minor illustration (1954). As opposed to Kuiper's, Varma's review (1966) approved of the endeavor, as could be expected from a scholar who had presented 'a plan for the evaluation of Pāṇini on the Vedic language' (1953b). Another unmitigated attempt to interpret the Veda through Pāṇini's rules is represented by Patañjali's book. Other works reflect the same line of inquiry, but show an awareness of the dangers and pitfalls that may lie in such a path (Devasthali 1963, 1966, 1968b). Varma (1950) has also expressed concern about the phonetic limitations of Pāṇini's system, and urged that more attention be given to other sources, such as the Śikṣās. He has shown the lead in this direction with his book (1929, repr. 1961) on the phonetic observations of Indian grammarians, which pays special attention to the Śikṣās and Prātiśākhyas. These texts have since been superbly studied by Allen (1953, 1962; see also, from a different point of view, Renou 1960b). These studies, excellent as they are, have not drawn Vedic exegesis away from Pāṇini. They have demonstrated the high level which the study of phonetics had reached in ancient India, particularly in the Prātiśākhyas and Śikṣās, but they have not shaken the pre-eminence of Pāṇini's grammar in all matters of language. Although the Prātiśākhyas and Śikṣās are essentially Vedic, whereas Pāṇini's Vedic rules are marginal, research remains dominated by Pāṇini's towering figure.

The question of the value of Pāṇini's rules vis-à-vis the Veda is particularly crucial in the matter of the accent. Balasubrahmanyam has put out a series of articles (1962–3, revised 1965, 1966a, 1969) in which he attempts to bring together Vedic and Pāṇinian data with regard to the accentuation of single words. Laddu (1969b) has devoted a more ambitious, but somewhat confused article to accentuation as treated by the trio of sages Pāṇini–Kātyāyana–Patañjali.

The reliance to be placed on the teachings of the grammarians for Vedic interpretation can be debated; the nature of the Vedic texts they knew and attempted to account for is unquestionably a matter of great interest. This was the main contribution of Thieme's book (1935a; see also, on a minor scale, Thieme 1937c).

Since then, Vedic quotations in a variety of grammatical texts have been studied. Wackernagel–Debrunner examined Vedic quotations in Patañjali's work. A recent article by Palsule (1969) is more restricted in scope. Gopal devoted a few pages to Vedic quotations in the Kāśikā and the Siddhāntakaumudī (on the latter, see also Varma 1953c). Perhaps the most interesting recent contribution to this field is a short note by van Nooten (1968), pointing out a quotation from the White Yajurveda in the Mahābhāṣya. The attribution of this quote to Kātyāyana rather than Patañjali may be debatable; the lesson that is drawn from it remains valid in any case. Since Pāṇini, a Northerner, did not know the White Yajurveda, an eastern school (Thieme 1935:75–81), differences between Pāṇini and his commentators need not be explained as evidence of historical change, but can be interpreted as evidence of geographic distribution. This is said in part against Sarma (1968, which reprints 1944–59).

In another approach to the relationship between grammar and Veda, G. T. Deshpande has devoted several articles to the unprofitable stand that much of Pāṇini's method stems from the Padapāṭha.

2.3 Indian grammatical literature, like any other branch of literature, has been culled for realia. Arguments and discussions are not of a linguistic nature; they revolve around historical facts. This is particularly evident in religious matters, as exemplified by the heated controversy that opposed, among others, Bhattacharjee and Subrahmanyam in the 20's on the antiquity of Vāsudeva worship. Pāṇini's mention of the word Vāsudeva, and its meaning for the origins of Vaiṣṇavism, have been taken up again recently from a different, and most unlikely angle by Buddha Prakash.

Religion is only one of the aspects to which scholars have turned their attention. Mookerji has drawn data for literature (1923), history (1935), and education (1947) from the works of Sanskrit grammarians. More recently, Choudhary has extracted historical data on Mithilā from a Prakrit metrical treatise. There are also articles on such minor items as parts of chariots (S. K. Limaye). This line of research reached its apex in the numerous articles published by Agrawala from the late 30's to the early 50's, which culminated in his book *India as known to Pāṇini* (1953, 2nd ed. 1963; see also the critique by Venkatacharya). Puri has produced a similar work for Patañjali.

All this is of little relevance for the study of the grammarians themselves, except that such works throw light on the dates and regional origins of the grammarians, or on the corpus of literature they knew and used for linguistic description. Still, one reads with pleasure Sukumar Sen's (1952–3) delightful story of Devadatta, the hero of the grammatical examples in the Mahābhāṣya.

Western scholars have contributed less than their Indian colleagues to this kind of research, although they have occasionally produced articles for Festschriften in this vein. Thieme's article (1962) on chess and backgammon in the W. N. Brown volume is based principally on grammatical texts, particularly Patañjali's Mahābhāṣya. His contribution (1964b) to the Morgenstierne volume, devoted to Patañjali's interpretation of a Vedic verse in praise of the god Varuṇa, is of greater importance from a linguistic vantage point, since it deals with a religious justification of the study of grammar, and thereby echoes one of his early articles (1921), which analyzed the justifications which Sanskrit grammarians gave for the study of grammar.

2.4.1 One of the primary tasks that indologists took upon themselves was to date the several grammatical treatises. This was only a part of the general drive to ascertain the absolute and relative chronology of the whole body of Indian literature. The grammatical texts proved no easier to date than other branches of the Indian tradition. It was necessary to analyze occasional mentions of historical events, quotations from literary and other sources in the grammatical literature, quotations of grammatical treatises by other grammatical texts as well as by other bodies of literature, testimonies by foreign — mainly Greek and Chinese — sources, etc. This used to engage much of the indologists' attention. Most books and papers on Indian grammar were prefaced by remarks on the date of the textual materials. No lesser an indologist than Weber (1862) devoted a full length disquisition to the date of Pāṇini. Great names, such as those of Liebich (1899, 1903) and Lévi (1903), are recorded in an argument on the date of Candragomin. Controversies were often fierce, as those that opposed Bhandarkar (1872, 1873a, b, c, d) to Weber (1873a, b, c, d, 1875), and the same Bhandarkar (1883–5, 1885) to Peterson (1883–5, 1885), on the date of Patañjali.

There is little point in recalling these debates; they have long ceased to retain the interest of scholars, at least in the West. Some general agreement has been reached on probable dates; most scholars rest content with cautious statements of the type: Pāṇini (? 4th century B.C.), Patañjali (? 2nd century B.C.), Candragomin (? 5th century A.D.). Most of these dates, with the relevant bibliography, have been recorded by Renou (1940, 1957a, 1969).

Even the relative chronology of texts receives much less attention than it used to. The relative chronology of Pāṇini and the Prātiśākhyas, which was the center of a lively debate in the 30's (on the Ṛkprātiśākhya: Ghosh 1934, 1938, 1939, Thieme 1935a, 1937a, 1939, Chattopadhyaya 1937, 1938, Chaturvedi 1938, 1940; on the Vājasaneyiprātiśākhya: Thieme 1935a, 1937b, Keith 1936 following Weber 1862, 1873a), is no longer a burning issue. The same has been true for the relative chronology of Pāṇini and Yāska since 1935, when Thieme (1935c), proposed as a likely working hypothesis the posteriority of Yāska vis-à-vis Pāṇini. This theory has received additional support from Mehendale (1968c:1–14) and Laddu (1967a), but the evidence is adduced in much more cautious terms than with previous generations of scholars. Cardona (1972:172) probably reflects the general opinion when he holds to the conclusion: 'non liquet'.

Most of the texts can be placed in a reasonably certain succession; they quote their predecessors, and are quoted in turn. However, such evidence is not always available; it happens that no clear pattern of influence emerges, and that the data can be interpreted either way. The problem is particularly acute when one tries to establish a relative chronology between texts from different schools, which ignore one another, and reflect divergent views on language and linguistic analysis. Reference has already been made to Pāṇini and the Prātiśākhyas, and to Pāṇini and Yāska (see a recent grammatical analysis by Bhate of some derivations of Yāska's, without any attempt at conclusions on chronology). An equally vexed problem is the chronological order of the Phiṭsūtras, the Uṇādisūtras, and Pāṇini's Aṣṭādhyāyī, which has recently been the subject of a note by Abhyankar (1970).

Generally speaking, controversies on dates receive less attention in the field of grammar, as in other branches of Indian literature. Few scholars, in India and in the West, feel now inclined to emulate Gode, who, throughout his long career, made it his task to assign dates to a variety of Sanskrit texts, some of which are of a grammatical nature (e.g. 1939, 1940; for a full bibliography up to 1959, consisting of several hundred titles, see Hariyappa–Patkar xix–xlvi). Not that the issue is completely skirted; it is now dealt with where it can be profitably discussed: in the introductions to editions of texts, or in other places in which the argument is intimately linked with textual interpretation. A good example of this attitude is Birwé 1964. Chronology, whether absolute or relative, is no longer a central issue; scholars approach the subject only when they feel that the materials at hand allow conclusions that have not been put forth before.

2.4.2 The authorship of works has sometimes been debated with as much heat as their dates. Grammatical literature is not in any better position than other branches of Sanskrit literature on that score. Manuscript evidence is often lacking, or contradictory. Authors are known to have composed treatises under the names of their masters, or brothers, to whom they intended to pay homage. It is not rare to find an author write commentaries on his own works. The same names recur again and again in the literary history of India, and it is often difficult to sort out the productions of these homonyms. A single treatise may go by several titles. Moreover, the prestige of Pāṇini's name has brought about in the tradition a coalescence of works of different origins. The authorship of the Pāṇinīyaśikṣā, and particularly that of the Uṇādisūtras, have been hotly debated. Current thinking on these questions has been reported by Renou (1940, 1957a, 1969).

Controversies on matters of authorship arise even today, particularly when new editions of texts appear. One such debate opposed two scholars from Poona on the late work Laghuśabdaratna. Abhyankar, who attributes the work to Haridīkṣita (1951), reacted (1964) to the advance publication of appendices to the edition of the text by V. L. Joshi (1966), which attributed the work to Haridīkṣita's disciple Nāgeśa.

The current renewed interest in Bhartṛhari has led to discussions regarding the authorship of works attributed to him. Aklujkar (1972) has recently defended the traditional attribution of the commentary on Bhartṛhari's Vākyapadīya to Bhartṛhari himself, against Biardeau's challenge and attribution to Harivṛṣabha. Swaminathan's article 'Bhartṛhari's authorship of the commentary on the Mahābhāṣya' (1963) is, in spite of its title, less concerned with problems of authorship than with the description of a manuscript of this important and long lost text, which he later published (1965). Aklujkar has also devoted two articles to an assessment of the authenticity of the titles Vākyapadīya (1969) and Mahābhāṣyadīpikā (1971a), by which two of Bhartṛhari's works are known.

The old problem whether Candragomin can be credited with the commentary on his own grammar, has been taken up again by Birwé (1968b). This was motivated by Chatterji's (1953–61) challenge of the generally accepted attribution of both works to Candra proposed by Liebich (1895, 1899, 1902, 1903, 1918), in notes to his new edition of the texts. Unfortunately, Birwé's article is an example of criticism carried too far — a trait also present in his book of 1966. He suggests that the commentary be attributed to two distinct authors: Candra himself, and one of his disciples. This is based on flimsy arguments, and is subject to a number of difficulties which are not convincingly solved. Birwé himself admits that there are no internal contradictions in the commentary. This is quite different from the situation in the Kāśikā, which is known to have been written by two authors, and which does contain internal contradictions, most recently and thoroughly analyzed by Ojihara (1961a, 1962).

2.5 Indologists have discovered, deciphered, and reported on many grammatical texts. They have introduced and generally described to the scholarly world the vast number of grammatical treatises which are still extant. A great example of consistent work to reveal or better characterize a vast number of grammatical treatises is to be found in the section on Indian grammarians in Kielhorn's *Kleine Schriften* (1969). Closer to us, the scholar who has been engaged in this task on the most extensive scale is Renou, who covered an uncommon range of texts in his series of articles 'Etudes pāṇinéennes' in the *Journal asiatique* (1953a, b, 1956a, b, c), and his collection of essays *Etudes védiques et pāṇinéennes* (Pāṇinian studies appear in vol. 1, 1955; 2, 1956a; 3, 1957b; 8, 1961a), as well as in a number of separate articles, mostly in the *Journal asiatique* (for a bibliography of Renou's works, see Filliozat 1967b). Renou's reports (1940, 1957a, 1969), already quoted on several occasions, describe extensively the progress of research on the most important treatises.

Even though most major texts are known and published in a more or less critical form, it is fair to assume that much of the grammatical tradition remains to be discovered. Some texts, although published, remain little known. The pioneering task of introducing texts, with identification of author, date, and general description of contents, is still with us. Recently, Banerjee has given a brief description of a Prakrit grammar (1963), and identified another (1965). Miller (1963, 1965) has done superb work on Tibetan grammar, in the tradition of Bacot. Shanmugam and Vijayavenugopal have analyzed the phonological theories of two ancient Tamil grammars; these are hardly newly discovered works, but they have still not received the attention they deserve. On the Sanskrit side, a major work has recently been devoted to the Prakriyāsarvasva by Venkitasubramonia Iyer (1972). Kunjunni Raja (1964) has described the Niruktavārttika, the discovery of which had been announced by Kunhan Raja (1943), and which had occupied Kunhan Raja (1940–1, 1944) and Bishnupad Bhattacharya (who still described it as a lost treatise in 1950).

The grammatical literature mentions names of grammarians who are still otherwise unknown. V. P. Limaye (1966b) has mentioned, and Laddu (1967b) has attempted to identify two such grammarians. More work is needed on manuscript resources. This may be the most important contribution that indologists can make in the present stage of research. Needless to say, Indian scholars are best placed to examine the holdings of their public and private manuscript collections, and publish either the full texts, or analyses of contents, depending on the merits of each case. Grammatical literature needs the same type of relentless exhumation that Kulkarni (1953, 1955, 1968, 1968–71; Kulkarni–Dixit; Kulkarni–Gokhale) and other scholars are devoting to lexicographical works (see also, in the West, the excellent contributions by Birwé 1965, 1967, 1968a).

2.6.1 We thus come to the editing of texts, and textual criticism. This has been the main contribution of indologists, and the foundation on which all other research is necessarily built. In this area, however, a noticeable change has taken place over the years. The first critical editions of grammatical texts, as of other Sanskrit texts, were the work of Western scholars, particularly German. Although the founder of Pāṇinian studies, Böhtlingk, who edited Pāṇini's grammar (1839–40), gave the first full-fledged edition-translation of the Aṣṭādhyāyī (1887, repr. 1964), and edited and interpreted the Uṇādisūtras (1844) and Vopadeva's Mugdhabodha (1847), relied primarily on texts first published in India, other scholars soon followed with their own critical editions: Aufrecht, the editor of Ujjvaladatta's commentary on the Uṇādisūtras; Roth, the editor and interpreter of Yāska's Nirukta; Kielhorn, the editor and translator of the Phiṭsūtras (1866, repr. 1967), and of Nāgeśa's Paribhāṣenduśekhara (1868, 1871–4), whose most important contribution was an edition of Patañjali's invaluable Mahābhāṣya (1880–5, 3rd ed. by Abhyankar 1962–2); Eggeling, the editor of the Kātantra (1874–8) and the Gaṇaratnamahodadhi (1879–81); Kirste, the editor of Hemacandra's Uṇādisūtra (1895) and Dhātupāṭha (1899); Liebich, the editor of the Kṣīrataraṅgiṇī (1930), who also provided most of the work on Candra's grammar: an edition of the text (1902) and of its commentary (1918), as well as an analysis of the text (1895) and of its commentary (1920b).

Scholars from other Western nations have also contributed, although to a lesser extent. An early edition-translation of the Laghusiddhāntakaumudī was published by Ballantyne. Much more recently, Renou (1940–56) has given an edition-translation of the Durghaṭavṛtti. Grammars of later stages of Indo-Aryan owe much to the French school: Senart edited and translated Kaccāyana's Pali grammar;

Nitti-Dolci provided editions and translations of Prakrit grammars (1938a, 1939); an untimely death cut short her career. Interest in Vedic studies has been wide-spread around the world, and has fostered editions-translations of several Prātiśākhyas: of the Ṛgveda by Regnier (1856–8) and Max Müller (1869); of the Vājasaneyins by Weber (1858); of the Atharvaveda and of the Taittirīyas by Whitney (1862, 1871); of the Sāmaveda by Burnell (1879).

The situation has changed considerably in the past few decades. Western scholars are contributing far less to the task of editing grammatical texts. Rau has published a new fragment of the Candravṛtti (1964b), and described manuscripts of the Vākyapadīya (1962, 1964a, 1971), hopefully to lead to a critical edition of the text. Van Nooten has in manuscript a new edition of the Āpiśaliśikṣā. On the whole, Indian scholars are more prominent in this area of activities. Texts have long been edited in India, but Indian editions have not always met the requirements of textual criticism. Now, Indian editors not only publish more texts; their labors also show an increasing critical quality. The notion of a critical edition is expanding beyond the circle of scholars who were educated in Western style universities. An effort is being made to reach the traditionally educated scholars, the pandits. These tremendously learned men, who are usually attached to institutions of learning and libraries, and have an unmatched familiarity with and devotion to the texts, have often been used in the past as minor and anonymous participants in the task of editing. They have spent selfless hours copying and collating manuscripts for other scholars, Western and Indian. But they are now becoming full-fledged editors. One of the most interesting and potentially important books that have appeared in recent years, is the first volume of an edition of the Prauḍhamanoramā and its commentary the Śabdaratna, by V. L. Joshi (1966). The editor, who is a traditionally trained pandit, and has spent some time in England and the U.S., has included a long introduction (110 pages) in Sanskrit, in which he explains the methods of textual criticism. His own edition contains that still too rare feature, a stemma codicum. We may hope that he will reach his fellow pandits, who have long been separated by a language barrier. Introductions to textual criticism written in English, like that of Katre (1954), remained inaccessible to most of them. The matter is all the more urgent, since panditic scholarship is extinguishing rapidly. This underrated and underpaid profession is ceasing to be a family tradition; the pandits' sons are now directed toward more profitable careers, like engineering or chemistry.

Different types of grammatical texts in a number of languages and traditions are being published, often in critical editions, in all parts of India. Passing over former works, already recorded by Renou (1940, 1957a, 1969), let us consider the major productions of recent years. The most important text to be published for the first time, is probably Bhartṛhari's long lost commentary on the Mahābhāṣya. It was worked on independently in Poona (Abhyankar–Limaye 1963–9), and in Banaras (Swaminathan 1965). Unfortunately, the editions had to be based on a single Berlin manuscript, which does not always offer an understandable text. The French indological institute in Pondicherry is about to publish the first instalment of an ambitious project: a critical edition of all extant commentaries on Patañjali's Mahābhāṣya (Narasimhacharya); no project could be more welcome. Parts of the Vākyapadīya, Bhartṛhari's great work, and of its commentary, have been edited from several sources, but none of them amounts to a complete edition (see Aklujkar 1969; complete bibliography, with critical comments, in Rau 1971:45–9). Abhyankar has published a critical edition of a collection of eighteen works on Paribhāṣās 'meta-rules', belonging both to the Pāṇinian and other schools of grammar (1967), and has reedited the Paribhāṣenduśekhara (ed. by Kielhorn 1868), with a commentary by his father (1962). Another scholar from Poona, Devasthali (1967b), has reedited the Phiṭsūtras, also originally edited by Kielhorn (1866); he has edited for the first time the Sārasiddhāntakaumudī (1968a). To Tripathi, who had published earlier, jointly with Caturvedi, Jainendra's grammar and its commentary, we owe a recent edition of Śākaṭāyana's grammar and its commentary. Among lesser works, Krishnamacharya has published the short treatise Laghūpasargavṛtti at Adyar, using only one of several available manuscripts. Mimamsak pursues a steady program of editions at Ajmer (1943, 1957, 1962, 1965). The continuing publishing efforts of the Jain community have included grammars: Doshi published in Ahmedabad a Sanskrit grammar by Malayagiri; earlier, Vaidya had published in Sholapur a Prakrit grammar by Trivikrama, with its commentary (1954; he has since also published in Poona in 1958 the Prakrit grammar of Hemacandra, the latter not in a Jain series). The Prakrit metrical treatise Prākṛtapaiṅgala was published and analyzed by Vyas in Banaras. In Banaras also, Sitaram Sastri (1960, 1964) has published again well-known works of Nāgeśabhaṭṭa and Bhaṭṭojidīkṣita. The old Tamil grammar Tolkāppiyam has been published in parts and in toto in several editions.

Not all these editions can be considered critical. Much good work is being done; yet, much more is needed. In this important aspect of research, Indian indologists are taking a definite lead.

2.6.2 Most questions of textual criticism are encompassed in editions of texts. However, a number of specific problems have been treated separately. This is the supreme application of philological skills, and it may not be surprising that contributions tend toward extremes, good and bad.

Collections of passages from lost treatises, such as Mimamsak's work on the Bhāgavṛtti (1964), are precious, and above controversy. In the same vein, Birwé (1964) has attempted to reconstruct Nārāyaṇa Daṇḍanātha's commentary on a section of Bhoja's grammar. V. P. Limaye (1964–5) has proposed a number of corrections and additions to Sarup's edition of the commentaries on Yāska's Nirukta. Kunjunni Raja (1962) has studied a ghost word in the Siddhāntakaumudī. Jani has recently returned to a sūtra which had already puzzled Chaturvedi (1942). Variant readings in the Prākṛtaprakāśa have been studied by Ghosal (1966). The discussion by V. P. Limaye (1967) of the text of Pāṇini's sūtra 6.1.121 is not valid textual criticism; it is not based on textual evidence, but represents an attempt to improve on the text that was preserved. In the same way, there is no textual justification for Laddu's proposed emendations of a word in the Kāśikā (1964) and of one of Kātyāyana's vārttikas (1966).

Some of the best contributions to textual criticism in recent years come from Aklujkar (1969, 1971b). A year of collaboration with Rau, which he is about to begin, promises rich returns for the study of Bhartṛhari. Sadhu Ram's contribution (1956) is not to be trusted.

One of the most difficult and debated areas of Indian grammar, the Dhātupāṭhas, or lists of roots, has received superb treatment at the hands of Palsule. Extensive preparatory work, such as an edition of Vopadeva's Kavikalpadruma (1954), a painstaking concordance of Dhātupāṭhas (1955), and ample articles devoted to the analysis of various problems or techniques (1957, 1958a, b), has been crowned by the publication of a critical study of the Sanskrit Dhātupāṭhas (1961). This is excellent work, in the tradition of Liebich's ground breaking studies (1919b, 1920a, 1921, 1930). Next to this, Sengupta's contribution (1966, apparently unaware of Palsule's work) looks very pale indeed.

The Gaṇapāṭha, another appendix to Pāṇini's grammar, has received critical attention from Ayachit and Sengupta (1961), and, most of all, from Birwé (1958, 1961). Birwé's works are particularly difficult to assess. It was said earlier that contributions to textual criticism tend toward extremes, good and bad. In the case of Birwé, they are present in the very same works: it is textual criticism carried to its outmost limits. In the case of the Gaṇapāṭha, the balance was definitely positive, and the reviews favorable (see particularly Renou 1961b; Gonda 1963; Ojihara 1965b; Palsule 1965). Through a careful consideration of all lists of gaṇas, the groups of words to which specific rules of Pāṇini's grammar apply, Birwé attempted to reconstruct a list as original as the available sources would allow, and to answer questions regarding the relationship between the Gaṇapāṭha and the main body of the grammar (on this, see also Ojihara 1959). There were already, however, some signs of hypercriticism, which were noted by Palsule (1965): Birwé rejected words that were well represented in the various lists, when their inclusion appeared unnecessary from the point of view of the grammar.

This tendency to require the texts to be rigorously logical and absolutely consistent, regardless of the state of the textual tradition, was carried to its extreme in Birwé's book of 1966. This time, the topic was no longer the poorly preserved Gaṇapāṭha, but the well established text of the Aṣṭādhyāyī. Birwé expurgated from the text of the grammar all rules that do not conform to the most exacting standards of rigor and consistency. As a result, he distributed Pāṇini's grammar, that masterpiece of cohesion, between a minimum of six independent authors. This was to go far beyond the critical stand that he had always taken with regard to interpolations in Pāṇini's grammar (1955). Renou, who saw the work prior to publication, prophesied that its 'unexpected conclusions are likely to provoke strong reactions among scholars'

(1969:484). The reactions have come. Reviewers have been less than convinced (Rocher 1967; Palsule 1970). Moreover, Scharfe's recent book on Pāṇini's metalanguage (1971) has been prompted in part by Birwé's stand. This hypercritical attitude situates Birwé in the tradition of Sköld (1926a), who viewed as suspect any rule that was not commented on in the Mahābhāṣya. Not that the possibility of interpolations can be negated offhand; Palsule (1952b), hardly a critic of Pāṇini's grammar, has also pointed out such an occurrence. What seems to be needed is a blend of criticism and respect for the text. The modern scholar's task is to study the text critically and to point out eventual difficulties, not to rewrite or rearrange the text according to his own wishes.

2.7 Considering the interest and all the work done in Indian grammar, it might look surprising at first glance, that more progress has not been made in the task of translating texts into Western languages (we shall not consider here translations into modern Indian languages). Edition-translations of several texts have been mentioned above. Of the major texts, only Pāṇini's Aṣṭādhyāyī has been translated completely: first into German (Böhtlingk 1887, repr. 1964), then into English (Vasu 1891, repr. 1962; the same scholar also translated the Siddhāntakaumudī 1906, repr. 1962), and finally into French (Renou 1947–54, revised ed. 1966). A comparison between these translations reveals the nature of the task and the difficulties at hand. Vasu's English translation is unreliable, and generally follows blindly the interpretation of the Kāśikā. Böhtlingk attempted to translate the Aṣṭādhyāyī as purely as possible. His translation is generally not dependent on the interpretation of the text by later commentators, although their help has been sought on occasion. The main problem in translating Pāṇini's text is the technique of anuvṛtti, whereby a word, a group of words, or even a whole sūtra, remains valid in the following rules, without being repeated. The difficulty is that no indication is given that an anuvṛtti begins, nor when it ends; this has to be discovered by an examination of the domain of application of each rule, or by relying on the views of commentators, who are not always in agreement. Böhtlingk opted for a straight translation, which does not repeat the words carried over by anuvṛtti; some indication is given in the margin. As a result, his translation gives a true rendering of the Sanskrit text; it maintains most of its characteristic terse style. On the other hand, it is as cryptic as the Sanskrit original, in spite of the addition of a few examples in notes. Renou, on the contrary, tried to make his translation more readable. He spells out anuvṛttis, repeated, rule after rule, in parentheses. As a result, his translation is over-explicit, and totally unlike the original text; perforce, it also relies more on later commentaries, especially the Bhāṣāvṛtti, which may or may not give a slant to Pāṇini's text (see Thieme's 1956 criticisms on that score).

Commentaries are equally difficult to translate, although for somewhat different reasons. Patañjali's Mahābhāṣya, the secondmost important text in the Indian grammatical tradition, would appear, at first sight, to be an easier proposition than

Pāṇini's grammar; at least, the text proceeds in full sentences and in topical arguments. However, so much is left unsaid, formulated in bare allusions, hidden in the convolutions of a supposed dialogue, that one scholar (Cardona, oral communication) once branded 'useless' a literal translation of the text. The fact is that, for specialists of Sanskrit grammar, no plain translation is as clear as the Sanskrit original. Yet, for other scholars, translations, particularly annotated translations, appear desirable, perhaps even necessary. The only attempt at a comprehensive translation (Subrahmanya Sastri 1944–62) ended far short of its goal — 28 āhnikas out of 85 — and can be described as a failure. It effectively translates straightforward passages only, it takes over Sanskrit terminology when comment and interpretation are needed, and provides no answer when the reader faces a serious difficulty. Other translations are more explicit, and add explanatory comments, but are partial. The first āhnika was translated into German by Danielsson, and into English by Chatterji (2nd ed. 1957, 3rd ed. 1964); there is a German translation by Trapp of the first five āhnikas; recently, Abhyankar — whose father translated the complete text into Marathi, in seven volumes — and Shukla have published the first part (āhnikas 1–2) of a proposed translation into English of the first nine āhnikas; Ojihara has offered a French translation of sūtra 1.1.56 (1961b, 1963a), as a first instalment of a translation of the eighth āhnika.

The most hopeful development in the direction of a full and truly useful translation of the Mahābhāṣya is the project initiated by S. D. Joshi. Four volumes of an English translation have appeared (1968–73, the last three in collaboration with Roodbergen), covering āhnikas 19–22; they will hopefully culminate in a complete translation of the work. Joshi's work on the Mahābhāṣya is being published in a series which looks particularly promising for this type of research. Class C of the Publications of the Centre of Advanced Study in Sanskrit, located in the University of Poona, is devoted to texts 'edited with introduction, translation, and critical and exegetical notes' (to quote the subtitles of the volumes published in this series). Besides the aforementioned books on the Mahābhāṣya, it includes a similar work on the Sphoṭanirṇaya (chapter 14 of the Vaiyākaraṇabhūṣaṇasāra), also by Joshi (1967a), and editions by Devasthali of the Phiṭsūtras (1967b) and the Sārasiddhāntakaumudī (1968a). The works published so far in this series are of importance and of a consistently high quality, although their emphasis varies. The main interest of Joshi's work lies in the translation and in the extensive explanatory notes; the text itself generally follows existing editions. Devasthali's contributions are true editions, but do not provide as deep an analysis of the contents.

Ojihara and Renou (1960–7, vol. 3 by Ojihara alone) have translated into French the first pāda of the first adhyāya of the Kāśikā. This painstaking, detailed treatment should make obvious what has been stated elsewhere (Rocher 1968a:346–7), namely that this commentary is less simple than it appears, and that, if one is truly to understand why the Kāśikā says what it says, and why it quotes the examples it quotes, an analysis of the earlier tradition is indispensable. Another partial translation of this text was published by Liebich (1892).

For the Paribhāṣenduśekhara, the only translation remains that of Kielhorn in English (1871–4, 2nd ed. by Abhyankar 1960; critical remarks by Scharfe 1954). Liebich (1919a) has translated the Kātantra into German. Sukthankar has translated into German the first pāda of Śākaṭāyana. Ghosal (1962–3) has given the text and an English translation with notes of the Vājasaneyiprātiśākhya. Of the Vākyapadīya and its commentary, we have a few partial translations (listed in Rau 1971:50).

All these translations are individual endeavors, and do not amount to a coordinated program. Few such efforts sustain the enthusiasm of their authors throughout their career; none survives after their death. Although this is one of the most important aspects of the study of Indian grammar, it is also one in which it appears impossible to discover trends, or foresee developments.

2.8.1 One reason which has prevented much effort to be devoted to translations of grammatical texts, is the feeling that translations are not always as helpful as they should be; that, on many occasions, they are less clear than the original texts. Besides translations, detailed presentations and elucidations of the texts are needed. In such cases, the focus tends to be on selected passages from the texts.

In this type of studies, Ojihara stands out as the most scrupulous and painstaking. In between a first article on vocalic *ḷ* in the Aṣṭādhyāyī (1956), and a recent comparative study of the Pali grammar Saddanīti and Pāṇini's work (1971), his production has centered around the Mahābhāṣya and the Kāśikā. His series of articles entitled *Causerie vyākaraṇique* includes studies of Patañjali's involved discussions on the text of the Aṣṭādhyāyī (1958-60, followed up in a separate article 1965a and in a translation of the relevant section of the Mahābhāṣya 1961b, 1963a; 1959; 1963b; 1967), and of internal discrepancies in the Kāśikā (1961a, 1962). Since his review (1965b) of Birwé's (1961) work on the Gaṇapāṭha, he has published a string of articles on textual evidence for successive adaptations of the Gaṇapāṭha (1968b, 1967–8, 1970, quoted in order of composition, disturbed by publication delays). His article 1969a, in response to Abhyankar 1966, is a model of integration of textual criticism and textual interpretation. His works are not easy to read, but they are consistently trustworthy.

Studies of Pāṇini's grammar and of the direct Pāṇinian commentatorial literature have moved on to other concerns, which will be better studied in chapters 3 and 4; lesser texts, and lesser known texts, continue to be presented mainly according to this philological approach. Contributions by Dave (1963), Banerjee (1966), and Ghosal (1968–9) to the study of Prakrit grammarians, continue the tradition of Grierson (1925, 1929). An article by Meisezahl on Tibetan grammar is not without relevance for Sanskrit grammar.

Studies of Indian etymology, and of semantics and linguistic philosophy, have occupied a number of scholars. These are quite distinct from studies on the grammarians, and the scholars who have contributed to these fields have formed a separate circle from those concerned with Pāṇinian studies. Staal (1969) has reported on Sanskrit philosophy of language, and an updated version of this report is about to appear (Staal Ms. 1). Since no such survey exists for etymology, a rudimentary bibliography of recent studies of the Nighaṇṭu and Nirukta is included here (besides the classical works of Sköld 1926b, 1928, see Bhate; Bishnupad Bhattacharya 1958; Viman Ch. Bhattacharya; Chapekar; Kunjunni Raja 1957a; Simonsson; Varma 1953a — unreasonably attacked by Gupta —; and the works of Mehendale, the most persistent student of the Nirukta).

2.8.2 In the Indian linguistic tradition more than in any other, texts are more profitably studied in relationship with each other. This is all the more important, since most texts assume the form of commentaries on other texts. An important type of contribution by indologists has been to follow the grammatical tradition, the evolution of concepts in the long history of Indian linguistic thought.

One of the first problems was to determine the relationship between the three authoritative sages Pāṇini-Kātyāyana-Patañjali. This topic received much attention in the late 19th century, and was highlighted by contributions of Bhandarkar (1876), Böhtlingk (1876a, b), and Kielhorn (1876, repr. 1963, 1965). Since then, Kielhorn's views have not been seriously challenged. The only recent work that has been ostensibly devoted to that subject (Sarma 1968), prints a Master's thesis of the late 30's, some chapters of which had already been printed over the years (beginning with 1940a, b, 1940–1). How much out of touch the author has since been with the field is evidenced by his claim that 'although a long time has elapsed since this was written, so far as I know, no further work of any importance has been done on the textual or subject side of Pāṇini in recent years' (1968:vii). Already when it was written, the work was obsolete, still fighting the views of Goldstücker (1861, repr. 1940, 1965, 1966), which Kielhorn had long since antiquated.

The 40's and the 50's witnessed a proliferation of articles devoted to the study of pre-Pāṇinian grammar (e.g. Ghosh 1940, 1945; Chaturvedi 1941; Agrawala 1940–1, 1950; R. S. Bhattacharya 1951, 1952, 1952-6; Palsule 1957; Krishnamurthy). Articles in that vein are now relatively uncommon (see, however, Balasubrahmanyam 1967).

Current studies tend to focus on the contribution by Pāṇinīyas to the development of linguistic thought. They follow the arguments of commentators, and attempt to distinguish when they give a straightforward commentary and when they amplify on their own. Thieme has given exemplary models of this kind of endeavor as early as 1935b (not reprinted in his *Kleine Schriften* 1971), and again in 1957b, but it is his article (1956) occasioned by Renou's (1947-54) translation of Pāṇini inspired by commentators, which has had the most programmatic impact. Thieme has described in a masterly way the precarious balance between respect for the Pāṇinīyas as witnesses of a long standing tradition, and critical appreciation of each one as an individual author. One of his latest contributions to the field (1964a) describes vividly the Pāṇinīyas groping for an explanation for a compound word quoted as an example in Pāṇini's grammar, which they no longer understood, and provides the author's own explanation.

It is in this line of inquiry that a very promising maiden article by Madhav Deshpande is to be placed: it evaluates the interpretations which the Pāṇinīyas gave of Pāṇini's use of the anubandha *t*. Other contributors, such as Laddu (1964, 1967c, 1969a, b), restrict their studies to the trio of sages Pāṇini-Kātyāyana-Patañjali. At the other end of the Pāṇinian school, Venkitasubramonia Iyer (1970) has recently pointed out differences between Bhaṭṭojidīkṣita and Nārāyaṇabhaṭṭa.

On the whole, the direct Pāṇinian school remains the center of attention, in spite of efforts (such as Renou 1936) to bring to the fore other important grammarians like Candragomin. We still lack the necessary tools for consistent contrastive study, both within and without the Pāṇinian school. More concordances such as that of Pāṇini and Patañjali (Lahiri) and that of Pāṇini and Candra (Liebich 1928), are needed. The trend even appears to run against the exegesis of other schools of grammar, now that the study of Indian linguistics is shifting away from the philological indological approach toward a linguistic appreciation of techniques of description, and the comparison between Western and Indian methods. Pāṇini and his school are often treated as practically synonymous with Indian linguistics.

Even within the Pāṇinian school, later commentators are often treated in a stepmotherly fashion. Among the younger generation of Western Pāṇinian scholars, Cardona stands out as the one who tries most consistently to examine the views of later Pāṇinīyas. Whether he is right in often accepting their interpretation of Pāṇini (1964, 1967a, b, 1967-8, 1968a, 1971) is a matter for debate, and an issue which cannot be settled in general terms, but has to be decided according to the merits of each case (for a case in which Cardona is more critical of the views of the Pāṇinīyas, see 1970b). New articles in print (Cardona Ms. 1, Ms. 2) should provide new test cases.

2.8.3 What is sorely needed is a history — or histories — of Indian linguistics, covering not only the treatises on Sanskrit, but also the grammars of Prakrit, Pali, and Dravidian languages. The attempts that have been made are pioneer works, which stand in need of revision. The history of Pali grammar and lexicography by Franke dates back to 1902. For Prakrit, the 1938b doctoral dissertation of Nitti-Dolci remains the latest word, so much so that a recent English translation was judged warranted. The work of Subrahmanya Sastri (1934; critical remarks by Filliozat 1937), which presents itself as a history of grammatical theories in Tamil and of their relation to the grammatical literature in Sanskrit, is organized in such a way that the succession of grammarians does not appear clearly. Sarkar's sketch of the migration of Sanskrit grammar to Indonesia has whetted the appetite for a full investigation of grammatical literature in Greater India.

Meanwhile, the Sanskrit grammatical literature itself, which has been better investigated than any other, has still not been the subject of a full description in a Western language. Belvalkar's work, great as it was in his time (1935) and circumstances, is hardly satisfactory. It would be highly desirable to translate into English the history of Sanskrit grammatical literature which Mimamsak (1950–62, revised ed. of vol. 1, 1963) has published in Hindi. Although it lacks critical acumen, it is a mine of information. It is not altogether surprising that the only recent history of Sanskrit grammatical literature is available in an Indian language. Only Indian scholars educated in the panditic tradition have a sufficiently broad familiarity with the whole extent of the literature; these scholars rarely know English well enough to write a book of such proportions. Western scholars, and Indian scholars educated in Western style universities, shrink before the awe inspiring task of familiarizing themselves with a multitude of minor treatises. Some recent contributions whose titles might advertise as histories of Sanskrit grammatical literature, do not answer that objective. Staal's (Ms. 2) sketch of the origin and development of linguistics in India is highly selective, and drawn in the broadest terms. Orara's account of the tradition down to Patañjali's Mahābhāṣya rests on antiquated data.

2.9 For indologists, Indian grammar is only a part of Indian literature. The style in which Pāṇini has couched his rules, that of the sūtra, has been studied by Dave (1962–3) and Renou (1963). Renou (1961c) has included the Nirukta in an analysis of the form of Sanskrit texts. He has also taken pains to describe the relationship between grammar and other branches of Indian literature (1956b, 1957c, 1961a), as well as between grammar and ritual (1941–2). Except for the relationship between grammar and ritual (on which see below 3.5), this line of approach may have died — for a while at least — with Renou. These are delicate questions, which may retain an indologist's attention, but which prove less fascinating to linguists. The trend appears to run toward an increasing linguistic view of Indian grammar.

With Renou, one of the two towering figures in Pāṇinian studies has disappeared, and in this case it means even more than the end of a brilliant series of contributions to the study of Indian grammar. Renou was the best informed man on every aspect of Pāṇinian studies. Not only did he keep abreast of publications, he often received advance copies of manuscripts prior to publication, and he dispensed information freely. Whoever visited him came back with a harvest of helpful notes. Renou was a great source of encouragement for young scholars. Upon receipt of offprints, he used to send by return mail handwritten notes which proved that he had read the articles, for which he always seemed to find complimentary words. Now that he has disappeared, and that Thieme appears to be more interested in other types of studies, the field has been taken over by a relatively young generation of students of Pāṇini, who often have a different approach, and different concerns. They will provide most of the materials for the following two chapters. To be sure, they were already at work before Renou's death, and Renou (1969) reports, sometimes in puzzled tones, on these new developments. But Renou's disappearance has left them without the referee from whom some controversies might greatly benefit.

3. INDIAN LINGUISTICS

3.0 For indologists, Indian grammar is essentially a part of the cultural heritage of India, a branch of Indian learning. It is interesting as one — brilliant — aspect of the Indian intellectual production. In Renou's contributions, for example, the element that comes to the fore is that Indian grammar is one facet of the Indian genius; the fact that it happens to be linguistic science is secondary. In recent years, however, the emphasis has been reversed: what interests most Western scholars in Indian grammar is that it is grammar; the fact that it developed in India is of lesser importance. Indian grammarians, Pāṇini particularly, are studied for their linguistic descriptive techniques; the fact that they describe Sanskrit is incidental. Obviously, most scholars are India based, inasmuch as they control the language and have some understanding of associated Indian sciences. Still, the emphasis has unmistakably shifted away from a general indological standpoint to a linguistic appreciation. The pivot of research on Indian grammar at the present time is an interest in descriptive methods, in linguistic technique. The avowed goal of many publications is to make available to general linguists ready information on the linguistic methodology that was developed from early times in India.

The origin of this shift is to be traced back to the dramatic pronouncement by Bloomfield in the first chapter of his most influential work: 'The grammar of Pāṇini ... is one of the greatest monuments of human intelligence. It describes, with the minutest detail, every inflection, derivation, and composition, and every syntactic usage of its author's speech. No other language, to this day, has been so perfectly described' (1933:11). This was a repetition of words used in a much more detailed but less known analysis of Pāṇini's grammar, published four years earlier, in which Bloomfield stated: 'The descriptive grammar of Sanskrit, which Pāṇini brought to its highest perfection, is one of the greatest monuments of human intelligence and (what concerns us more) an indispensable model for the description of language. The only achievement in our field which can take rank with it is the historical linguistics of the nineteenth century, and this, indeed, owed its origin largely to Europe's acquaintance with the Indian grammar' (1929:268).

Bloomfield's appreciation was based on a deep knowledge of Pāṇinian grammar, evident in his articles of 1927 and 1929. It has even been suggested (Bloch 90; Hall 121; Kukenheim 113 n.2) that Pāṇini's example was largely responsible for Bloomfield's interest in synchronic and descriptive linguistics. Be that as it may, it is certain that renewed interest in Pāṇini coincided with the surge of synchronic and descriptive grammar. Although the discovery of Sanskrit and Indian grammar was at the basis of Indo-European comparative linguistics, interest in Pāṇinian methods could not then be sustained, because Pāṇini's grammar was neither comparative nor historical. The newer school of linguistics, on the contrary, found in the ancient Indian grammar so highly recommended by Bloomfield, a model of linguistic description. The spotlight turned increasingly on Pāṇini's methods, on Indian descriptive techniques.

Even in India, where Sanskrit is now mostly taught in Western style universities according to Western linguistic principles, whereas traditional panditic training is on the wane, Pāṇinian grammar has to a certain extent become a foreign linguistic method, which needs to be translated in more familiar terms. Even in its original home, Pāṇinian grammar is more and more studied on account of its techniques, less and less as the regular introduction to Sanskrit.

3.1 Pāṇini's metalanguage has always retained the attention of scholars, if for no other reason than its difficult and intricate character, and because understanding it is a prerequisite for approaching the text. The emphasis on Pāṇinian linguistic techniques has, however, led to a proliferation of studies of this kind. These range from simple lists and helpful notes to full-fledged critical inquiries into Pāṇini's use of metalinguistic devices, and analyses of the categories to which the technical terms refer.

The anubandhas, the conventional diacritic metalinguistic markers, had been included by Böhtlingk (1887) in his list of grammatical elements, together with other metalinguistic elements that were not borrowed from the object language. The use of anubandhas is particularly important with regard to the Dhātupāṭha; those used in that text were studied by Liebich (1920a), and more recently by Palsule (1958a). The most extensive study devoted to anubandhas is that of Devasthali (1967a). Useful as it is, as a list of anubandhas used in Pāṇinian grammar, as a survey of the specific purposes for which they have been used, and as a study of the paribhāṣās 'metarules' that apply to them, much more is needed. Devasthali's work is a description and enumeration of the anubandhas, not a critical study of Pāṇini's technique on that score. It is a useful reference work, still waiting for an in depth analysis.

3.2 Technical terminology has been repeatedly studied over the years. Approaches have varied, and have not always emphasized metalinguistic methods. As early as 1814, Hamilton published a list of terms of Sanskrit grammar (Rocher 1968b: 79–80). In Böhtlingk's work (1887), Pāṇini's technical terms were distributed in two separate indices: 'grammatical elements' when the terms were purely metalinguistic, without counterpart in the object language; 'Pāṇini's vocabulary' when they were borrowed from the object language. The second category also included non-technical terms, words of the object language quoted in the grammar. In these first, and most often used appendices, the criterion for the listing of technical terms thus rested on their standing in the object language, not on their role in the metalanguage.

Indices to grammatical treatises are helpful reference works, although they lump together the whole vocabulary, whether metalinguistic or not. Such are Pathak and Chitrao's indices to Pāṇini's grammar (1935) and Patañjali's commentary (1927).

Recently, Katre (1968–9) has published a dictionary of Pāṇini, which also includes the entire vocabulary — technical and non-technical — used by Pāṇini, together with English translations or definitions. The fact that this study is conceived as a dictionary, not an analysis, is evident from the fact that it painstakingly notes the several declensional forms in which each term appears — an irrelevant consideration from the point of view of metalinguistic usage —. This is a mechanical listing, akin to a previous work by the same author (1967), which provides an alphabetical index of Pāṇini's rules, a text of the Dhātupāṭha (without critical apparatus), and an alphabetical list of the roots mentioned in the Dhātupāṭha.

Of greater interest are studies specifically devoted to Indian grammatical terminology, such as Chaturvedi 1937, and several articles by Chatterji, leading to a comprehensive treatise (1948, 2nd ed. 1964), unfortunately left incomplete, in spite of additional chapters in the second edition, building on subsequent articles. Most precious of all are Renou's monumental *Terminologie grammaticale du Sanskrit* (1942, repr. 1967; see also the extensive review by Thieme 1958), and Abhyankar's invaluable *Dictionary of Sanskrit grammar* (1961). These works have the advantage of offering a survey of grammatical terminology that reaches far beyond Pāṇini's work. They also attempt to define and interpret each term, and add appropriate references and quotations. Although by no means final, Renou's and Abhyankar's works are the most informative sources on the metalanguage of Sanskrit grammarians. However, their format, with alphabetical listing, prevents a comprehensive and coherent analysis of metalinguistic usage. Also, such works are bound to rely primarily on the interpretation of commentators, and present in the same articles usages belonging to various strata of the development of linguistic theories. Although they constitute indispensable reference works, they often fail to give complete and satisfying answers to specific problems. Renou himself, in his characteristically modest and unassuming manner, acknowledged that his was only a step; he deliberately encouraged challenge, and looked forward to a new generation improving on his work. No one as yet has felt equal to the task. Specific items have been examined; the general scope of the project has not been touched.

In his review of the second edition of Renou's *Terminologie*, Thieme (1958) endeavored to correct and amplify a number of entries. Since then, several contributions have been added to the literature on the subject. Sukumar Sen (1962) has listed the names given to compounds by Pāṇini. Kapil Deo has devoted a few articles to the definitions given by Bhartṛhari of a number of terms. Palsule (1967) has exhaustively studied the contexts in which Pāṇini uses the word *saṃjñāyām*, in order to determine what is meant by this term which is not defined in the Aṣṭādhyāyī. Another recent contribution by the same author (1968b) lists and defines the numerous technical terms built on the root *kṛ*. Although more descriptive than interpretative, this article constitutes an excellent basis for further research. All this is done from a point of view which is quite different from that revealed in the attempt to explain the term *karmadhāraya*, which Palsule (1952a), Abhyankar, and Edgerton debated in 1952. The intention then was not to study metalinguistic usage, but to determine the original meaning of a term the technical use of which was perfectly clear.

Scharfe (1965) has argued against the interpretation of *vacana* as 'number' in Pāṇini, as opposed to the well established use of the term with that meaning by later commentators. This rigorous adherence to each author's own use of metalinguistic terms, and the willingness to break the general grammatical tradition in discrete entities to be studied primarily by internal critique, is particularly apparent in Rocher's articles (1964, 1966). This is very much in the Thieme (1956) tradition, as is the deliberate attempt to give one single interpretation for one metalinguistic term, and distinct interpretations for different metalinguistic terms. This attitude has been challenged by Cardona — curiously enough, a direct student of Thieme's — who is of the opinion that the meaning of a term, whether metalinguistic or not, should be decided according to its immediate context, and who is much more willing to accept the tradition of the commentators. Neither position is unbending, but the results of researches carried out along these opposite methodological lines have led to different conclusions (apropos *hetu*: Rocher 1964b, Cardona 1971; apropos *bhāva* and *kriyā*: Rocher 1966, Cardona 1970c).

3.3 There is more to the study of Pāṇini's metalanguage than the quest for exact definitions of technical terms. Recent contributions emphasize how the metalanguage operates. A good example of this type of study is Cardona's (1968a) analysis of Pāṇini's definition, description, and use of *svarita*. The article goes as far as to argue that the reason why Pāṇini cared to define *svarita* does not lie in the object language, but in its importance as a metalinguistic marker.

The first attempt at a comprehensive examination of Pāṇini's metalanguage is a recent monograph by Scharfe (1971). Although likely to be controversial, this study has the merit to bring together aspects of the metalanguage that had been studied in a haphazard manner so far. It is in part meant as a rebuttal of Birwé's (1966) view of the Aṣṭādhyāyī as a hodge-podge of incompatible metalinguistic usages. It may be daring to offer at this time a comprehensive grammar of Pāṇini's metalanguage, and the work stands to be corrected in more than one way. Some misgivings have already been expressed by Rocher (1973). Cardona (Ms. 4, Ms. 5) and Aklujkar (Ms.) intend to criticize it on several points. Still, it appears to represent an important step in this field of research, an occasion for discussion, and an instrument of further progress.

3.4 A problem of great importance is the relationship between grammar and logic. They often share terminology, but concepts are not always in agreement. The problem has been approached repeatedly, both from the philosophical and the grammatical standpoints. Without going into philosophy of language (on which see Staal 1969, Ms. 1), it might be proper to record a few contributions to the comparative study of logic and linguistics. On the philosophers' side, Frauwallner has studied the influence of linguistic theories on Indian philosophy (1959) and, conversely, philosophical principles in the Mahābhāṣya (1960); Matilal (1960, 1966, 1972) has attempted to determine the treatment given certain concepts in both grammar and logic. On the linguistic side, and particularly about the Mahābhāṣya, we have, besides an early article by Strauss (1927a), a doctoral dissertation by Scharfe (1961), devoted to a comprehensive study of logic in the Mahābhāṣya. This is a delicate and ambitious task, and it is no wonder that it has met with criticisms on specific points (Staal 1963a; Oberhammer). Moreover, Scharfe's interpretation of the terms *anvaya* and *vyatireka* in the light of logical usage has been criticized by Cardona (1967–8), who has sought to establish the metalinguistic meaning of the terms in the Mahābhāsya, and has drawn arguments from later commentators. Cardona (1967b) has also come back to negations in Pāṇini, and opposed Scharfe's interpretation of Mahābhāṣya 1.4.57, along with Renou's (1942) and Staal's (1962b, 1963a) statements about types of negations in grammar. Negations in logic have been the topic of Matilal's (1968) doctoral dissertation.

Whereas Cardona aims at establishing the usage of grammarians by a rigorous examination of the linguistic tradition, Staal's interest runs to studies which bring together linguistic, logical, and philosophical usage. A mathematician and philosopher by training, Staal has turned later to indology, and finally to linguistics. Many of his articles indicate a determination to compare and blend linguistic, logical, and philosophical usage (e.g. 1960a, b, 1961, 1962b, c, d, 1966c). An article most representative of Staal's approach is his contribution to the Bocheński volume (1965c). In a collection of papers dedicated to a logician, Staal's concerns lie in linguistics as well as in logic. The paper also represents its author's desire to arrive at general statements, on the basis of the Indian evidence. It is natural that Staal should show a strong attraction for Chomskian theories, since both scholars appear to work on the frontier of linguistics and logic, and are both intent on generalizations. A curious feature of Staal's article in the Bocheński volume is, however, that it is accompanied by an annex by Hartmann, destined to provide the views of a 'linguist' on the subject. Another clear indication of Staal's central concern is his inaugural address (1963c) at the university of Amsterdam — which he has left since — which he later revised and published in English (1965a). What may appear at first glance to be a preposterous juxtaposition of such different authors as Euclid and Pāṇini, ends up as a justification of systematization, formalization, and conceptualization to be obtained by logic and mathematical linguistics.

3.5 Besides the relation of grammatical terminology and categories with those found in logic, there is also the vexed question of their relation with the ritual. Some scholars have followed the lead of Renou (1941–2), and have postulated a ritual basis for much of the linguistic terminology, whereas others have rejected that view absolutely, as an instance of a Western tendency to find magico-religious elements in everything Indian. Staal's (1963a) objections to the ritualistic views of Scharfe (1961) have been challenged in turn by Wezler (Ms.). Another article by Wezler (1972) also traces the grammatical term *sthānin* back to ritualistic origins. The issue involves more than the question whether or not Indian grammarians were imbued with ritual. The fact is that, if a scholar attempts to trace the history of terms throughout different branches of Indian literature, he is bound to find a ritualistic origin: the preserved texts which are older than or contemporaneous with Pāṇini's work are essentially concerned with ritual. The very nature of the texts runs against the discovery of a lay origin. To present the history of Indian terminology as one coherent and linear development that runs across very different types of literature presents grave dangers, but so does the view that Indian grammar came about in a vacuum, without ties with other branches of Hindu thought.

Even more acute is the debate which opposes Al-George and Cardona. The issue here is part of a more general controversy, in which many scholars have taken part, and which will be considered later (3.8). The specific point of contention between Cardona (1967, 1970a) and Al-George (1957, 1968, 1970) is that the former views the kārakas as linguistic, syntactic categories, whereas the latter considers them to be extra-linguistic categories, issued from Vedic ritual categories. Like every other aspect of the kāraka controversy, the debate has picked up momentum, as is proved by the rapid succession in which three articles (Cardona 1967; Al-George 1969; Cardona 1970a) have appeared in issues of the same journal.

3.6 Recent years have been marked by a renewed interest in paribhāṣās, the meta-rules of Indian grammar. A major difficulty here is that most paribhāṣās have not been formulated by Pāṇini, but stem from the interpretation of his text by later commentators. Other schools of grammar have also developed their own paribhāṣās. Collections and commentaries on paribhāṣās are late works. Boudon's early article, and, more recently, Renou's (1956a) and the Rochers' contributions dealt mainly with the position of the later grammarians vis-à-vis paribhāṣās. Recent work has increasingly focused on the degree to which paribhāṣās formulated at a later time can be considered valid and understood in Pāṇini's work, and on the ways in which they affect or could affect the operation of grammatical rules. Most of the work on the subject has been incidental to the study of the grammar itself (e.g. Nath) or of general principles of logical argumentation (e.g. Staal 1962b).

Two works have recently appeared, and one is in progress, which are entirely devoted to the study of paribhāṣās. Abhyankar's book (1967, already announced in 1955) is essentially an edition of collections of and commentaries on paribhāṣās, with general comments in its introduction. Wezler's doctoral dissertation (1969) is a historical inquiry in the German tradition, an attempt to pinpoint the author of a number of paribhāṣās, in the continuous stream of grammatical literature. Of Devasthali's proposed work only an introduction and general survey (1969) have been published; judging by that limited evidence, and considering the author's other publications, it is likely to present a comprehensive picture of traditional thinking on the subject.

Much of the excellent work that has been done recently stems from the importance of paribhāṣās for questions of rule-ordering. Since the emphasis in this case lies with a matter of concern for general linguistics, it will be examined in the following chapter (4.2).

3.7 The best study of the relation of paribhāṣās with the text of the Aṣṭādhyāyī remains Buiskool's doctoral dissertation (1934 in Dutch, shorter version in English 1939). It also has the merit of being a systematic study of the last three pādas of the grammar. Such in depth analyses of chapters in Pāṇini's grammar have been exceedingly rare, and, like Buiskool's work, happen to have been mostly Ph.D. dissertations. Shefts has presented a study of the treatment of present stems in the Aṣṭādhyāyī, together with the views of the Mahābhāṣya and the Kāśikā. Although sūtras 3.1.68–85 do not constitute an āhnika, they represent a sequence of rules, the study of which helps establish Pāṇini's train of thoughts. Unfortunately, Shefts has left this field for Tibetan studies; as was the case with Buiskool, her dissertation was not followed by further publications. More recently, Rocher (1968a) has analyzed Pāṇini's treatment of the voices of the verb in a comprehensive study of the14th āhnika of the Aṣṭādhyāyī and of a number of commentaries in the Pāṇinian school. Curiously, Pāṇini's description of the verbal system appears to have received more attention than other points of the grammar. Besides Shefts' and Rocher's dissertations, we have had a survey of the theory of the tenses of the verb, which goes into less detail, but was drawn by Renou's masterly hand (1960c).

Wezler's (1973) Habilitationsschrift, which analyzes part of the secondary suffixes, and is based on section 5.1.119–136 of the Aṣṭādhyāyī, is about to be published. The publisher's announcement describes the study as a presentation of Pāṇini's replacement technique.

On the whole, scholars have been more tempted to study Pāṇini's treatment of what they themselves — or Western linguistics — view as topics than to accept Pāṇini's own outline. The only noteworthy exception to that tendency has been the great amount of interest given the Śivasūtras, which are not really a section of the Aṣṭādhyāyī, but a preface to the grammar. Besides a paper by Sköld (1926a II), and articles by Faddegon (1929), Breloer (1929, 1935–6), Chatterji (1934), Kunhan Raja (1957), and Staal (1962a), we now have in Cardona 1969 an excellent study of the Śivasūtras and of their relationship to the Aṣṭādhyāyī, together with relevant facts from the commentatorial literature, and comparison with the Prātiśākhyas.

Sections of the Aṣṭādhyāyī should receive the same degree of analysis. Scholars have put too much stress on the elements which show that the place where a rule is formulated in the grammar is indifferent for its application. Rules are not formulated in a random succession — excepting the necessities of anuvṛtti; there are sections of the Aṣṭādhyāyī which deal with a common topic, even though they may also refer to rules formulated in some other part of the grammar. It is regrettable that more scholars have not been led to examine systematically what Pāṇini himself conceived and presented as chapters. Studies of that type bring to the fore Pāṇini's approach in a way that studies of isolated or scattered rules cannot.

3.8 Studies of Pāṇini's anubandhas, technical terminology, and general metalinguistic usage, of his possible indebtedness to logic and ritual, of the application of metarules, and of chapters of the Aṣṭādhyāyī, all aim at an understanding of Pāṇini's method of linguistic description. Rocher (1965–6) has made some general remarks on the subject; it may also be the topic of a recent article by J.D. Singh, which could not be consulted. Other studies have attempted to analyze Pāṇini's principles and technique by observing his treatment of a problem, and drawing from whatever relevant material is to be found in his grammar. The precursor of this type of study, and the initiator of many modern trends in the study of Pāṇini, was Faddegon (1936). Renou (1937, 1940:10 n.1) found Faddegon's work odd at times, but also compelling. Strikingly, most members of the young generation of Pāṇini scholars, who have not been under Faddegon's direct influence, discover much that is congenial in his work, such as his description of Pāṇini's principles as 'mnemotechnical economy, logical division, and associative digression' (1936:49).

This approach to Indian grammar is essentially Western, although Chaturvedi read at meetings of the All-India Oriental Conference papers on the techniques of anuvṛtti (1946), anticipation (1949), and preference (1953) in the Aṣṭādhyāyī. Some recent Indian contributions, such as Balasubrahmanyam's (1966b) study of three anomalous suffixes, are inspired by Western themes, as is evident from the terminology, and the references to Trager, Bloomfield, and Faddegon. Along more traditional lines, there are contributions such as V.L. Joshi's (1971) study of the treatment of loanwords in Sanskrit grammar.

The title "A method of linguistic description" given to Staal's (1962a) study of the order of consonants in the Śivasūtras, and the subtitle "Un exemple de description linguistique" given to Rocher's (1965a) analysis of Pāṇini's treatment of the periphrastic future, are representative of many scholars' approach to Pāṇinian technique: a deliberate attempt to describe Pāṇini's techniques in terms not of Sanskrit, but of linguistic method, for the benefit of linguists, rather than indologists. Beyond that stated goal, however, the contents of contributions can vary greatly. Witness two papers bearing similar titles, which happened to be read at the 27th International Congress of Orientalists, and which were published in the same volume of *Foundations of language*. Rocher's paper "The concept of verbal root in Indian grammar" (1969) analyzes the semantic value assigned to the verbal root by Pāṇini and his early commentators. Van Nooten's study "Pāṇini's theory of verbal meaning" (1969) attempts to go beyond the morphological operation of the grammar, and to raise the semantic part to a new dimension, that of a link between the grammar and its user. This paper was meant in part to refute a statement by Cardona, that characterized Pāṇini's work as an attempt 'to formulate concise and consistent rules for the derivation of Sanskrit forms and sentences' (1965b:306). Cardona's line of thought was then akin to views expressed by his teacher Thieme (1957a) in a contribution to the Whatmough volume, which has often been debated since.

The point of Thieme's (1957a) article was that the reason why Pāṇini cared to define *anunāsika* and *svarita,* whereas he does not normally deal with phonetics, is that these are complex, not simple, features. This issue has since been taken up by Cardona (1968a), who sees the reason for such definitions in the fact that these elements are part of Pāṇini's metalanguage, and not only of the object language. The main impact of Thieme's article, however, does not stem from the specific issue he discussed, but from general statements he made by way of introduction. He declared that it is inaccurate to speak of Pāṇini's work as a grammar, since it is not a full description of speech usage: 'Pāṇini's work is exclusively concerned with defining ... the procedures of regular word-formation ... anything else does not fall within its scope' (Thieme 1957a:263). Among missing items, Thieme listed word order, gender, and phonetics, while he noticed that unanalyzable nominal stems are summarily dismissed. This followed another article of his (1956), in which he noted that Pāṇini's work is not concerned with sentences (1956:4). The absence of rules on gender, phonetics, and unanalyzable stems does not constitute a problem, since they are dealt with in specialized treatises; and there is general agreement that word order in Sanskrit is a matter of style, which is not grammatically significant (Staal 1967). The case of the sentence is different; scholars have reacted strongly to Thieme's pronouncement, and have attempted to describe how, within his methodological framework, Pāṇini can account for syntactic features. Thieme's (1957a:263) statement quoted above was accepted by Cardona (1965a:225), in an analysis of Pāṇini's morphophonemic principles that goes beyond the Śivasūtras, and offers an excellent contrastive view of Pāṇini's and other grammarians' use of the principle of *sāvarṇya* 'homogeneity'. When dealing with syntax, however, Cardona (1967a:213 n. 19, 1967b:35 n. 3) voiced disagreement with Thieme's (1956:4) views. Among other scholars who have opposed Thieme's views on the sentence are S.D. Joshi (1969b), van Nooten (1969), and Kiparsky–Staal. This issue was considered all the more important, since syntax is presently the most eagerly studied chapter in general linguistics.

Recent years have witnessed a controversy in which participants have managed to grow steadily apart, instead of realizing a consensus of opinion. The by now famous kāraka controversy has its roots in Faddegon's (1936) views. Faddegon defined the kārakas as 'the logical or ideational relations between a noun and a verb, or more precisely between an object or anything conceived after the analogy of an object and an action or anything conceived after the analogy of an action' (1936:19). This definition was very different from that of Whitney, who viewed the kārakas as 'ideal case-relations' (1893a:171). The controversy was sparked by recent contributions of Al–George (1957) and Rocher (1964a), which, on the surface, appeared to be in general agreement. They contrasted Pāṇini's definition of the agent — and object in Rocher 1964a — with the concept of subject — and object in Rocher 1964a — in Western grammar. They emphasized that Western grammar has a constant correspondence between the linguistic expression (nominative ending) and the grammatical category (subject), whereas in Indian grammar, the agent — and the same would be true of the other kārakas — finds different linguistic expressions, such as the verbal active and middle endings, the instrumental ending, suffixes, etc. Both contributions therefore defined the kārakas as non-linguistic, or extra-linguistic, categories; both were attacked by Cardona (1967a), who insisted that the kārakas are linguistic, semantic categories. It has already been mentioned above that Al-George (1968, also 1970) has since developed his ideas into a theory that links the kāraka categories to Vedic ritual. The prima facie agreement of his views with those of Rocher (1964a, b) has thereby disappeared. Although Rocher (1964a, b) has been interpreted by Kiparsky–Staal (109) as having 'come close to suggesting' that the kārakas have an ontological significance, a point which is emphatically made by Al-George (1970), she does not trace the origin of Pāṇini's categories back to Vedic ritual. She has rested her case after her initial articles (1964a, b), but the controversy has not lacked participants. Staal (1967) and Kiparsky–Staal have interpreted the kārakas in terms of deep structure. They speak of kārakas as relations, a position which echoes that of Faddegon, but is in disagreement with both Rocher's and Cardona's (1967a: 202 n. 2, 1970e: 236) views. Cardona 1971, although mainly directed against Rocher's (1964b) interpretation of *hetu*, one of the kārakas, also expresses disagreement with Kiparsky–Staal. In short, there may be occasional agreement between some scholars on some specific aspects of the problem, but no two participants in the kāraka controversy have reached a common view on the total issue. Recently, van Nooten (1970a: 15 n. 4) has attempted to review and synthetize this side of the controversy — excluding Al-George's views — but the issue may not be dead yet: Cardona (Ms. 3) is planning to return to it. Meanwhile, the discussion has had echoes in India, with Ananthanarayana's (1970) article inspired by Kiparsky–Staal, and a rebuttal of Kiparsky–Staal and Ananthanarayana by D. M. Joshi, a student of Cardona's.

The kāraka controversy is revealing of the trend in current researches on Sanskrit grammar. It made such a stir mainly because it touches the core of syntax, as treated by Indian grammarians, at a time when syntax is the most assiduously studied part of general linguistics. Whereas the difference of opinion between Cardona and Rocher appears determined only by different interpretations of Pāṇini's text, other contributors have brought to the problem extraneous elements, which depend on their respective positions with regard to general linguistics. The setting is European structuralism with Al-George, Chomskian deep structure with Kiparsky–Staal, and Fillmore's case grammar with Ananthanarayana.

3.9 All this reveals attitudes which are very different from those of yesteryears, as will be eloquently illustrated with the publication of Cardona Ms. 6. Entitled *Pāṇini*, this voluminous work will have very little to do with the concerns of similarly titled works by Goldstücker and Liebich (1891). It will not be 'an investigation of some literary and chronological questions', as the subtitle of Goldstücker's *Pāṇini* announced. Nor will it provide 'a contribution to Indian literature and grammar', like Liebich's *Pāṇini*. This will be a thorough study of Pāṇini's technique in all aspects of the grammar; it will reflect the fact that present day research is essentially concerned with methodology.

4. GENERAL LINGUISTICS

4.0 In the latest survey of Pāṇinian studies, Renou noted: 'Research has recently taken on extreme forms, namely toward a "formalization" of the Aṣṭādhyāyī (and of the language seen through the Aṣṭādhyāyī). Ten years ago one would hardly have imagined such a development' (1969:496–7). What was only incipient then has now established itself as one of the main trends in current research. The issue goes beyond attempts at formalization; it is essentially a new way of looking at Indian grammar. We have seen in the preceding chapters, that research shifted increasingly from a study of Pāṇini as part of the Indian tradition (2), to interest in his linguistic methods (3). In this final chapter, we shall examine studies which have their origin in problems of general linguistics.

As is to be expected for a new trend in research, opinions are still divided on the validity of this essentially external approach to Pāṇini. Rocher (1968a), who clearly stated that her goal was to present Pāṇinian technique in terms understandable to linguists (1968a:9), voiced some scepticism with regard to comparative studies of Western and Indian methodology: 'On s'est trop souvent hâté d'établir des rapports, alors que l'ensemble du système indien n'était pas suffisamment connu' (1968a:339). Cardona has been most explicit along these lines: 'I do not think we have yet arrived at a sufficiently detailed understanding of Indian grammatical methods to make a comparison with Western methods truly useful. After such an understanding has been attained, it will be both welcome and valuable to make comparisons' (1969:3). Cardona referred specifically to works by Misra (1966) and Staal (1967); he elaborated on his objections in his review (1970e) of Staal 1967. This provoked a spirited response by Staal (1970) in his review of Cardona 1969. Staal offered 'a general comment on outlook and methodology ... Doubtless overgeneralizing, it could be argued that Cardona approaches his subject in the first place historically and as a philologist. Others prefer to approach it in the first place systematically and as linguists' (1970:505), and went on to deny 'any methodological priority of philology over linguistics' (1970:506). On the contrary, he declared that 'Pāṇini was not a philologist but above all a linguist, and he deserves to be treated as such' (1970:506). Discussions expressed in general statements, with personal undertones, usually obfuscate the issue. Studies that compare Western and Indian methods, and incorporate them into general linguistic theory are the ultimate goal. Unfortunately, quite a few studies written along these lines have been unfaithful to Pāṇini. When one technique is more familiar than another, it is natural that consciously or unconsciously the foreign one be interpreted in terms of that which is better known. In that sense we witness here the highest point of a process that has integrated Indian linguistics into the Western tradition. It is futile to discuss whether such attempts are premature. The fact is that they are being made, and in increasing numbers. There can be no question of stopping the trend. The only issue that remains is to examine whether these contributions act like a bed of Procrastes, or are true to Pāṇini's genius.

4.1 Formalizing Pāṇinian rules means nothing more than translating them into another language. The point of the endeavor is, however, to present them in a form which allows immediate and automatic comparisons with rules formulated by other systems of grammar. The first attempt made in that direction was Staal's article 'Context-sensitive rules in Pāṇini' (1965b, repr.1968), which explicitly borrows Chomskian terminology and techniques, and applies them to Pāṇini's rules on vowel sandhi. Like any other translation, formalization requires a certain degree of interpretation, on which disagreement can arise. It led Cardona (1965b) to object to a number of formalizations proposed by Staal. Cardona did not question the usefulness of the formalizing process, but insisted on a strict formalization of Pāṇini's rules, without a 'translation' into Western terms. The formalization should also be such as not to obliterate the difference between the Pāṇinian method and that of other Indian grammarians; it should also make clear why Pāṇinian commentators could give varying interpretations to the same rules. Cardona even argues that, like Patañjali, modern interpreters should recognize their inability always to arrive at a unique solution. In short, he warns against conscious or unconscious tampering with Pāṇini's rules, even if the result retains obscurities. In spite of disagreements on the correct interpretation of specific rules, Staal's lead toward formalization has been followed, notably by Cardona (1969). Staal (1970) has in turn objected to the fact that Cardona's formalizations observe the traditional interpretation of commentators: 'on Kātyāyana's interpretation context-sensitive rules are reinterpreted as context-free rules, of course at a considerable cost' (1970:505). In other words, the criterion of Cardona's objection to Staal's treatment is fidelity to the text and the tradition; that of Staal's objection to Cardona's treatment desirability for general linguistic theory.

Further remarks on the difficulty of the translating and formalizing process were made by van Nooten (1967). Van Nooten argues that the formalized statements adopted by Staal (1965b, repr.1968) and Cardona (1965b) are not adequate to render the replacement operations by which Pāṇini describes the active finite verb, and proposes a different formalization. He insists that Pāṇini's categories and operations make sense only within the framework of his grammar. He also resists the temptation to interpret as allomorphic the various conjugational suffixes of the finite verb, in spite of the obvious advantages of such a formulation. For him it is a matter of principle: 'Pāṇini's linguistic outlook was not oriented to the allo-eme concept; his whole grammar is stated in terms of replacement formulations' (1967:889). Van Nooten (1970a) has developed that approach in an article devoted to vocalic declension. In this article he defends the use of plus-rules to reflect Pāṇini's ekādeśa substitutions, although such rules have found little favor with modern linguists. He opposes Staal's (1965b) use of dummy constituents to avoid such rules, since Pāṇini, who knows dummy constituents, does not use them in this particular case (1970a:26 n.9). It is not enough that formalization give a true rendering of isolated Pāṇinian rules; it must also be in keeping with Pāṇini's general theory of language and methodological approach.

4.2 The problem of rule-ordering has been prominent in recent contributions; it is a natural echo of the importance given that question in general linguistics. Curiously enough, the first contribution to the topic is the work of a scholar who has not participated in Pāṇinian studies in any other way. Fowler's article "How ordered are Pāṇini's rules?" is a singularly unsympathetic article; its main point appears to be that Pāṇini's grammar does not deserve the high praise which it usually receives. Fowler expresses preference for the order of the Siddhāntakaumudī, although he admits that it necessitates the rewording of many Pāṇinian rules, and so would the improvements he suggests before subjecting the grammar to an automaton. Fowler's criticisms were convincingly refuted by Staal (1966b), who pointed out, among other things, that, for Pāṇini, the order in which sūtras appear in the grammar does not coincide with the order in which operations take place. The order of sūtras depends on matters of economy, of anuvṛtti 'dittoing', etc.; this is a feature which Faddegon (1936) had sought to highlight. The order of operations is different; it depends on metarules, which create ordered pairs. Reordering rules along Fowler's suggestions would require not only considerable rewriting, but create great difficulties with regard to the metarules. Since Staal's article, studies of rule-ordering in Pāṇinian grammar have concentrated on the ordering of operations, not on the succession of sūtras in the grammar.

A good example of the attraction that rule-ordering in Pāṇinian grammar has exercised on linguists who do not make it their field of specialty, is Ghatage's article in the Katre volume. Noting that in Pāṇini's grammar the place in which rules occur relative to others does not affect their operation or scope of operation, Ghatage proceeds to study a vārttika on sūtra 1.4.32, which he takes to be 'probably the first place in Sanskrit grammatical literature where a strict ordering of rules is envisaged, in the sense of their sequential application and not in a purely mnemonic or abbreviatory sense' (150).

The most explicit attempt to analyze Pāṇini's position vis-à-vis rule-ordering as a model for general grammar, is van Nooten 1970a. Already in previous articles (1967, 1969), van Nooten had emphasized the mechanical, automatic character of Pāṇini's grammar. Continuing on that track, and using the example of vocalic declensions, his 1970a article extrapolated 'about the operation of a hypothetical grammar in which rules are ordered at random and in which the only significant principle of ordering is the context of the constituents in the base form' (13). Van Nooten contrasts Pāṇini's technique with Chafe's, and goes as far as to rewrite rules of French grammar in the framework of Pāṇini's system.

Perhaps the most lucid contribution to the study of Pāṇini's stand on rule-ordering is Cardona's (1970b) article in the first issue of the *Journal of Indian philosophy*. Cardona surveys principles according to which Pāṇinian rules operate, and which are recognized by Pāṇinian commentators. He shows, however, that commentators replaced Pāṇini's principle of limited blocking with a spatial ordering of rules (*paratva*, requiring that a rule formulated later in the grammar take precedence over a rule formulated earlier), with regrettable results.

Tiwary, a student of Cardona's, devoted his maiden publication to an analysis of another metarule on rule-ordering, and attempted to describe the various aspects that were subsumed under the general principle providing that an *antaraṅga* 'internal' rule take precedence over a *bahiraṅga* 'external' rule. This is a particularly intricate problem, which appears prominently in the commentatorial literature, and is of importance for the general question of rule-ordering.

4.3 Linguists have been understandably struck by the convergence of Indian grammar with modern linguistic trends. It has been tempting for them to emphasize those points that echo features of the particular school of linguistics to which each of them belongs.

Al–George (1966) has studied the name given the consonant by Indian phoneticians (followed by the Tibetan grammatical tradition). He argues that the consonant is called *vyañjana* 'sign', because it implies the vowel, because it is a subordinate element which cannot, by itself, constitute a syllable. He likens this view to that of European structuralism, particularly that of Hjelmslev's glossematics. His paper (1970), read at the 10th International Congress of Linguists, addresses the issue in a more general fashion. After having reviewed a number of aspects which militate in favor of a structural label for Indian linguistics, Al–George proceeds to investigate the reasons for such a convergence. He rejects Collinder's view of a direct filiation between Indian linguistics and modern structuralism, even though he is ready to accept an indirect filiation, and possible occasional borrowings. His argument may be lost on people who have not been nourished on Lévi–Strauss and Eliade, but his point appears to be that the origin of structural linguistics — whether Indian or European — lies in the ontological abstractions of archaic thought. In India, the link is direct, since Vedic ritual, which has fashioned linguistic categories, embodies the symbolic thought of the archaic world. In Europe, the link is indirect, and is to be found in

Plato's and the Neo-Platonists' doctrine of forms, which is a philosophical transposition of archaic thought. Several of these points are also made in another of his articles, more specifically devoted to the semiosis of zero according to Pāṇini (1967), which attempts to compare and contrast the views of Pāṇini and Western structuralism. In this case, Al–George's conclusion is that Pāṇini's zero is closer to the mathematical zero than to the zero of European structuralism.

4.4 The major current trend is to liken Pāṇini's method to generative and transformational grammar. In this, as in many other cases, the impulse has come from Staal. His first article in this vein (1966a) reveals the perception he has of his role in the field of Sanskrit linguistics: 'narrowing the gap between Sanskrit and linguistics' (165). At that point, Staal still envisaged two paths: 'either it can be attempted to present the methods and techniques of Indian grammarians in such a way that a linguist can derive benefit from it; or it can be attempted to describe Sanskrit with the help of modern linguistic tools' (167). He then proceeded to study nominal composition according to Pāṇini's system — in a rudimentary fashion — and according to a system of generative syntax — his own — with a scathing attack on Harweg in between. He observed that a generative approach constituted in some respects 'a return to Pāṇini' (189), 'small extensions' of his system (198), and that 'the most recent methods of linguistic description known as "generative grammar" are in some respects reminiscent of Pāṇini's method and system' (198). However, he cautioned that 'this parallelism should not be overstated since there are indubitable innovations, in particular in the realm of formalization as well as linguistic theory, which go beyond what would be easily dealt with within a purely Pāṇinian framework' (189).

His quest was carried a step further in his monograph bearing the programmatic title *Word order in Sanskrit and universal grammar* (1967). Indian grammarians were now presented as having 'paid attention ... to what is nowadays referred to as deep structure. ... In this connection transformational relations were discovered, and much attention was given to the semantic relations between transformationally derived sentences' (50). The contributions by Western Sanskritists were — politely — dismissed as 'based upon a specifically selected corpus of Sanskrit texts' (59); they treated Staal's study with similar polite indifference (Gonda 1969; Burrow 1969). According to Staal, the essential difference between the two approaches is that Western Sanskritists were mainly interested in performance, while the Indian grammarians were primarily concerned with competence. After analyzing these two views of Sanskrit, Staal proceeded to work out a theory of Sanskrit syntax in terms of deep and surface structures. Staal's work is much more concerned with universal grammar than with Sanskrit. He acknowledges that word order has no grammatical significance in Sanskrit. In fact, what he deals with in this book is what in Sanskrit serves the same purpose as word order in English. These are the kārakas, which elicited the controversy examined above (3.8). Not surprisingly, Staal's monograph has been better received by linguists than by Sanskritists. Zgusta accepts that Pāṇini's doctrine 'is very close to the transformational approach of our days' (412), although he goes on to caution against the temptation 'to simplify things and to interpret Pāṇini simply in transformational terms' (413), and to point out some differences between the two methods. Kiefer, although objecting to Staal's making word order a matter of deep structure, generally approves of the work, and probably summarizes the opinion of many linguists when he says: 'Staal has convinced me that Pāṇini's ideas could be very well exploited for modern linguistic theory' (420). Students of Pāṇini have been less impressed. Although Cardona (1970e) voiced his objections in stronger terms than most, he probably represents the position of many Pāṇinīyas on the accuracy of Staal's presentation of Pāṇini's technique.

A further article by Kiparsky and Staal represents an even higher stage in the assimilation of Pāṇini's techniques with generative methods. It concludes that 'Pāṇini's syntactic rules, with respect to certain of their formal properties, are closer to *realization rules* of the kind encountered in the "neo-Firthian" syntax of Halliday and the stratificational grammar of Lamb than they are to transformations', but insists that 'in other ways, however, Pāṇini's rules show some transformational properties' (107). The disturbing aspect of this article is that it dismisses as unimportant features of Pāṇini's analysis which appear cumbersome from a Western point of view. On the matter of the agent, for example, it states 'that the subject is expressed by the Nominative along with the verbal ending, as in *pacati devadattaḥ*$_1$ "Devadatta cooks", is not explicitly stated by Pāṇini, but must be inferred from the rule which defines the nominative as the unmarked case, i.e., as that which designates nothing but the gender and the number of the nominal stem notion' (96–7). This sweeping remark conceals two facts: that Pāṇini does not know the category of subject, and that, for Pāṇini, in the sentence quoted as example, the verbal ending alone expresses the agent. In fact, the tyranny of Latin grammar, which Staal (1966a:165) rejoices to have seen overthrown, has been replaced by a tyranny of English grammar. D.M. Joshi has objected to Kiparsky–Staal's article on these grounds. The dichotomies subject/predicate, and noun phrase/verb phrase, are not easily reconciled with Pāṇini's method, as the chart in S.D. Joshi 1969b clearly shows.

The tyranny of English grammar appears even in the works of Indian scholars. Pandit has credited the inflectional character of Sanskrit as the reason why 'it does not offer a possibility, due its very nature, to lay down a general rule or formula regarding the structure of a sentence as do some other languages like English in which the order or position of a word is of utmost importance' (1963:60–1); he went on to say that it is due to this fact that Pāṇini had to concentrate on word-structure, not on sentence-structure. He thereby offered an unexpected rationale for Thieme's opinion that Pāṇini was not concerned with syntax (see above 3.8). This article, of course, antedates Staal 1967, which raised the kārakas to a level equivalent to word order in English.

Ananthanarayana (1969) described the feminine formations in Pāṇini's grammar, and added introductory and concluding remarks inspired by Halle, Chafe, and Lakoff. These remarks were merely a setting for the description, and did not influence the analysis itself. His article of 1970, on the contrary, imposes Western concepts on his analysis of the kārakas. His avowed goal is to compare Pāṇini's description of Sanskrit with Fillmore's case grammar. Although he concludes that the two approaches cannot be equated, Western theory distorts his analysis. It leads him summarily to dismiss *hetu* from the number of kārakas, and to ascribe a syntactic value to the nominative ending, against Pāṇini's express statement. He claims that Pāṇini was aware of the distinction between deep structure and surface structure, and that he 'may be said to have given us the first case grammar which excels in many respects even the most modern grammars of Generative grammarians' (1970:25).

S.D. Joshi has also been drawn recently toward a generative interpretation of Pāṇini. A knowledgeable and skillful interpreter of the Pāṇinian tradition — his translation of the Mahābhāṣya (1968-73) embodies many observations by later grammarians — he has attempted over the years to describe the discussions of Pāṇinīyas in terms inspired by modern linguistics (1962, 1966a, b, 1967b, 1968). His choice of topics also appears to have been influenced by their relevance to modern linguistics. Recently, under direct influence of Kiparsky, he has given a description of sentence-structure according to Pāṇini which is squarely placed in a generative framework (1969). There is, however, a world of difference between his treatment and that of Ananthanarayana. Joshi remains careful, and warns repeatedly that the terms 'deep structure', 'generative grammar', etc., are used in a somewhat different way when applied to Pāṇini. He insists that 'in P's generative grammar, the idea of generating one equivalent sentence from the items of another sentence is not there' (25). This statement is unfortunately watered down in a note, accompanied by an acknowledgment to Kiparsky.

On the whole, once drawn to a comparison between Pāṇini's method and generative grammar, scholars have tended to become more assertive, not more circumspect. A similar evolution can be found between van Nooten's articles of 1967 and 1970a. The first was 'not intended as a demonstration of the parallelism of Pāṇini's thinking with any one of the present-day linguistic theories (although many such parallels exist)' (1967:883), whereas the latter compares Pāṇini's procedures with Chafe's. Even in this latter article, van Nooten remains mindful of differences between the two approaches; yet, more and more comparison is unmistakably the trend.

4.5 Some scholars have pushed the comparative spirit even further, and emphasized those features of Indian grammar which are akin to various forms of Western descriptivism. This posture, which had legitimate beginnings in Allen's (1955) article on 'Zero in Pāṇini', has generally led to unsatisfactory results. The prominent contributors in this area have been Misra and Pandit. Their aim is essentially to point out features of modern Western linguistics which were anticipated in India a long time ago.

Misra's book *The descriptive technique of Pāṇini* (1966; chapter 4 published separately 1964b; previewed 1964a) has drawn much criticism. Zgusta, Cardona (1968b, 1970d), and Rocher (1970) have pointed out a number of obscurities and misrepresentations in his analysis of Pāṇini's technique. Cardona (1968b) and Zgusta have also voiced doubts about Misra's correct understanding of the modern linguistic principles with which he compares Pāṇini's technique. All have objected to the uncritical way in which he imposes modern terminology and outlook on Pāṇini's work. Misra excerpts isolated points from various modern linguistic schools each time that he perceives a faint echo of them in Pāṇinian grammar. Pāṇini's work emerges from his treatment as a hodge-podge of unrelated principles and techniques. Although the author appears to have intended to extol Pāṇini's greatness by pointing out all the modern 'discoveries' which he anticipated, the picture that is presented to general linguists is a highly unsatisfactory mix of irreconcilable standpoints.

The contributions of M.D. Pandit, although of a different order, also attempt to praise Pāṇini's anticipation of modern techniques. His views, formulated in 1963a, have been developed in a series of articles. His contention that Pāṇini was aware that 'it is the phonemes alone, and not the phones, which are of use in constructing the grammar of a language' (1963a:53) served as a basis for an article (1969) in which he attempts to find out the number of phones from which the phonemes of the Sanskrit language — which he equates with the elements listed in the Śivasūtras — are derived. A study of non-compounded word-structures (1963b), followed by one of compound word-structures (1963c), is more traditional than what the use of foreign terminology such as nucleus and satellite leads to believe. The same is true for a study of the Pāṇinian *it-saṃjñā* (1966a), in spite of some curious remarks on the reasons for introducing sounds of the language as symbols. Pandit views the introduction of 'an artificial formal i.e. meta-formal plane or level' (86) as a matter of consistency in the grammar, but also appeals to the oral tradition. According to him, Pāṇini had to create symbols at a time when 'writing was either unknown or was not used for the purpose of handing down any text' (87). He had therefore no other choice than to use symbols which could be handed down orally, namely sounds. Which symbols Pāṇini would have used if writing had been adopted, Pandit does not say, but, judging from his other contributions, he certainly thinks of mathematical symbols. There is indeed a mathematical trend in his publications. His articles 1962 and 1963a had indicated that Pāṇini used the mathematical principle of division and factorization, and had raised the question whether Pāṇinian technique was influenced by mathematics, or vice versa. This led to a study entitled "Mathematical representation of some Pāṇinian sūtras" (1966b). Although the author judges the evidence he provides too limited for a final decision, he is of the opinion that an extensive study of Pāṇini's grammar along mathematical lines might settle the issue. He has also attempted to make a case for statistical studies

(1964, 1969, 1971). His latest contribution (1971, expanding 1964) is the boldest so far. It states that Pāṇini's linguistic observations and generalizations are unthinkable without comprehensive recording of linguistic forms and statistical activity, and goes on to retrace the steps of these proceedings. His study of 1969 attempted to ascertain statistically the number of sounds, starting from the Śivasūtras. His article of 1971 computes that each single root gives out 1498 finished forms according to Pāṇini's rules, and concludes that the Sanskrit language is of a generative nature. Moreover, 'the simplicity and straightforwardness with which the above forms are calculated will convince one of the highest type of generative character of Pāṇini's grammar' (1971: 207). This inference is similar to that drawn in 1963a, according to which the definition of prātipadika by factorization or division reveals Pāṇini as 'a thorough structuralist' (60). Evidently, the goal is to present Pāṇini in the setting of reputable modern Western schools of linguistics. The same desire animated Ananthanarayana (1969, 1970; see above 4.4).

What is happening in such cases is a remarkable convergence of Western influence and traditional interpretation. It is traditionally accepted in India that authoritative texts be reinterpreted periodically to account for later developments. The view that a text is to be interpreted in the confines of its own place and time is a Western historical standpoint. Indian traditional learning holds the view that authoritative texts — such as Pāṇini's — are ageless and perfect; it is the role of commentators to extract from the text the lessons which it contains, in a process of continuous revelation. (See, at the other end of the traditional spectrum, V.P. Limaye 1967, which proposes the addition of a few vārttikas to Pāṇini's grammar, to account for Avestan.) Misra's and Pandit's contributions represent this trend carried to its extreme. Other authors, such as Paranjpe, content themselves with describing Pāṇini's technique in terms inspired by modern Western linguistics, without attempting to draw further conclusions.

A similar situation appears to prevail for ancient grammars of Dravidian languages. On the face of it, contributions by Sankaran and Sankaran–Menon are hyperbolic when it comes to appreciating the modern discoveries which were anticipated by the ancient authors. George, also laudatory, speaks in more measured terms. Shanmugam Pillai is matter of fact. Whether he is right in assimilating *cāriyai* in the Tamil grammar Tolkāppiyam with the empty morph in modern linguistics, this writer does not venture to ascertain, any more than voice an opinion on Dravidian subjects generally.

4.6 Excesses in comparing Pāṇini's technique with that of modern linguistics have led to confusion, the best example of which is Zgusta's puzzled "Pāṇini — descriptivist or transformationalist?". This review of Misra 1966 and Staal 1967 concludes with a warning against incautious use of loaded terms.

In spite of obvious flaws in many comparative ventures, there is little doubt that they have helped bring Pāṇinian grammar into the main stream of linguistic studies.

As is the case with public relations, the impact of these studies does not depend on the degree to which they are true to Pāṇini's word. The fact is that comparing is a difficult task. It requires scholars to be equally versed in Pāṇinian and modern linguistics, a combination which is still rare. But the trend is unmistakable, and affects even scholars whose training and preferences lie elsewhere. Witness Aklujkar's (1970) attempt 'to look at the Indian semantic tradition from the point of view of the western semantic tradition, though my first and better acquaintance has been with the Indian semantic tradition and though the other point of view proves to be more profitable and convenient in some other comparative studies of Indian semantics' (13). He gives a perfect description of the task eventually to be achieved: 'a clear, well-ordered and comprehensive treatment of this subject in rigorously chosen English by a mind that has full grasp of the Sanskrit śāstric "theoretical" texts and profound awareness of the relevance of this subject to problems in modern linguistics and philosophy' (12 n.).

Meanwhile, we have to be satisfied with a slow, and sometimes erratic, progress. At least it appears that the Indian grammatical tradition has found a permanent place in general linguistics. The signs are clear, when it is deemed desirable — and commercially feasible — to publish *A reader on the Sanskrit grammarians* (Staal 1972), when a bibliography in the history of linguistics assumes the title *Pāṇini to Postal* (Salus), and when this very volume opens on an Indian chapter.

REFERENCES

Abhyankar, Kashinath Vasudev. 1951. Date and authorship of the Śabdaratna and the Bṛhad-śabdaratna. ABORI 32.258–60.

——. 1952. The term karmadhāraya. ABORI 33.238–44.

——. 1955. A short note on paribhāṣā works in Sanskrit grammar. ABORI 36.157–62.

——. 1961. A dictionary of Sanskrit grammar. GOS, 134. Baroda, Oriental Institute.

—— (ed.). 1962. The paribhāṣenduśekhara of Nāgojībhaṭṭa with the commentary Tattvādarśa of MM. Vasudev Shastri Abhyankar. Poona, BORI.

——. 1964. Authorship of Laghuśabdaratna. ABORI 45.152–8.

——. 1966. A dissertation on a doubtful passage in the Kāśikāvṛtti on P.I.1.4 and two passages in the Taittirīya Āraṇyaka Prapāṭhaka 4. ABORI 47.101–4.

——. 1967. Paribhāṣā-saṃgraha. Poona, BORI.

——. 1970. A brief note on the chronological order of the Phiṭ-sūtras, the Uṇādisūtras and the Aṣṭādhyāyī. JOIB 19.331–2.

Abhyankar, Kashinath Vasudev, and V. P. Limaye (eds.). 1963–9. Mahābhāṣyadīpikā. Supplements to ABORI 43, 44, 45, 46, 47, 50.

Abhyankar, Kashinath Vasudev, and J. M. Shukla. 1968. Patañjali's Vyākaraṇa-mahābhāṣya-(Navāhnikī), fasc. 1 (Āhnikas 1 and 2), with English translation and notes. Poona, Sanskrit Vidya Parisamstha.

AGRAWALA, VASUDEV S. 1940–1. Pūrvācārya saṃjñās for lakāras. NIAnt 3.39–40.

——. 1950. Pre-Pāṇinian technical terms. Siddheshwar Varma vol. 2.135–7.

——. 1953. India as known to Pāṇini. Lucknow, University. 2nd ed. 1963, Banaras, Prithvi Prakashan.

——. 1963. Gotras in Pāṇini. Banaras, Prithvi Prakashan.

AKLUJKAR, ASHOK. 1969. Two textual studies on Bhartṛhari. JAOS 89.547–63.

——. 1970. Ancient Indian semantics. ABORI 51.11–29.

——. 1971a. Mahābhāṣya-dīpikā or Tripādī? ALB 35.159–71.

——. 1971b. The number of kārikās in Trikāṇḍī, book 1. JAOS 91.510–3.

——. 1972. The authorship of the Vākyapadīya-vṛtti. WZKS 16.181–98.

——. Ms. Review of Scharfe 1971. OLZ.

AL-GEORGE, SERGIU. 1957. Le sujet grammatical chez Pāṇini. SAO 1.39–47.

——. 1966. La fonction révélatrice des consonnes chez les phonéticiens de l'Inde antique. CLTA 3.11–5.

——. 1967. The semiosis of zero according to Pāṇini. E&W 17.115–24.

——. 1968. The extra-linguistic origin of Pāṇini's syntactic categories and their linguistic accuracy. JOIB 18.1–7.

——. 1970. L'Inde antique et les origines du structuralisme. ACIL X 2.235–40.

ALLEN, W. SIDNEY. 1953. Phonetics in ancient India. London, Oxford University Press.

——. 1955. Zero and Pāṇini. IL 16.106–13.

——. 1962. Sandhi: the theoretical, phonetic, and historical bases of word-junction in Sanskrit. Janua linguarum, 17. The Hague, Mouton.

ANANTHANARAYANA, H.S. 1969. The feminine formations in Pāṇini's grammar. IL 30.1–12.

——. 1970. The kāraka theory and case grammar. IL 31.14–27.

AUFRECHT, THEODOR (ed.). 1859. Ujjvaladatta's commentary on the Uṇādisūtras. Bonn.

AYACHIT, S.M. 1961. Gaṇa-pāṭha: a critical study. IL 22.1–63.

BACOT, JACQUES. 1928. Les ślokas grammaticaux de Thonmi Sambhoṭa. Paris, Geuthner.

BALASUBRAHMANYAM, M.D. 1962–3. The accentuation of *arya-* in Pāṇini and the Veda. BDC 23.94–100.

——. 1965. An accentual note on *vikaṭa-* in Pāṇini and the Veda. IL 26.18–26.

——. 1966a. An accentual problem in Pāṇini and the Veda. A propos of the word *hāyana-*. BDC 25.43–58.

——. 1966b. The three Pāṇinian suffixes *ṆaC*, *inUṆ* and *Ktri*. JUP 23.123–38. Repr. 1966 PCASS A6.

——. 1967. Patañjali on the pre-Pāṇinian anubandhas *Ṅ* and *C*. JUP 25.77–82. Repr. 1966 PCASS A11.

——. 1969. *Arya-*: an accentual study. IAnt III 3.112–27.

BALLANTYNE, J.R. 1849. The Laghu-kaumudī, a Sanskrit grammar by Varadarāja: with an English version, commentary, and references. Mirzapur.

BANERJEE, SATYA RANJAN. 1963. A skeleton grammar of Prakrit attributed to Jīva Gosvāmī. BPhSC 4.10–31.

——. 1965. Caṇḍīdeva's Prākṛta-dīpikā, a commentary on Kramadīśvara's Prakrit grammar — identical with the Vṛtti of Jūmaranandi. BPhSC 5.33–40.

——. 1966. Some phonological distinctions of the eastern Prakrit grammarians. BPhSC 6.116–29.

BELVALKAR, SHRIPAD KRISHNA. 1915. An account of the different existing systems of Sanskrit grammar. Poona.

BENFEY, THEODOR. 1852. Vollständige Grammatik der Sanskrit-Sprache. Leipzig.

——. 1863. A practical grammar of the Sanskrit language. London.

BHANDARKAR, RAMKRISHNA GOPAL. 1872. On the date of Patañjali and the king in whose reign he lived. IAnt 1.299–302.

——. 1873a. Note on the above [Weber 1873b]. IAnt 2.59–60.

——. 1873b. Patañjali's Mahābhāṣya. IAnt 2.69–71.

——. 1873c. On the interpretation of Patañjali. IAnt 2.94–6.

——. 1873d. Reply to Professor Weber. IAnt 2.238–40.

——. 1876. Āchārya, the friend of the student, and the relations between the three āchāryas. IAnt 5.345–50.

——. 1883–5. The date of Patañjali: a reply to Professor Peterson. JBBRAS 16.199–222.

——. 1885. Date of Patañjali no. II: being a second reply to Professor Peterson. Bombay.

——. 1927–33. Collected Works, ed. N.B. Utgikar. 4 vols. Poona, BORI.

BHAT, M.S. 1966–7. The Vedic stem *rātrī* and Pāṇini. JASBo 41–2.8–11.

BHATE, SAROJA. 1968. Some primary and secondary suffixes known to Yāska. JUP 27.121–32. Repr. 1968 PCASS A15.

BHATTACHARJEE, UMESH CHANDRA. 1925. The evidence of Pāṇini on Vāsudeva-worship. IHQ 1.483–9.

——. 1926a. The evidence of Pāṇini on Vāsudeva-worship. IHQ 2.409–10.

——. 1926b. Evidence of Pāṇini on Vāsudeva-worship. IHQ 2.865.

BHATTACHARYA, BISHNUPAD. 1950. Niruktavārttika: a lost treatise. IHQ 26.159–65.

——. 1958. Yāska's Nirukta and the science of etymology: an historical and critical survey. Calcutta, Mukhopadhyay.

BHATTACHARYA, RAM SHANKAR. 1951. Some principles of tracing pre-Pāṇinian portions in Pāṇini's works. JGJRI 8.407–18.

——. 1952. Pāṇini's notion of the authoritativeness of the views of his predecessors. JGJRI 9.163–81.

——. 1952–6. Some chief characteristics of Pāṇini in comparison to his predecessors. JOIB 2.165–73; 5.10–8.

——. 1955. Some characteristics of the ancient vṛttis on the Aṣṭādhyāyī. IHQ 31.168–74.

Bhattacharya, Viman Ch. 1959. The Nirukta and the Aitareya Brāhmaṇa. IHQ 35.109–19.

Bhawe, Shrikrishna Sakharam. 1954. Interpretation of some Rigvedic compounds. JOIB 4.315–29.

——. 1955. Pāṇini's rules and Vedic interpretation. IL 16.237–49.

——. 1957–62. The Soma hymns of the Ṛgveda: a fresh interpretation. 3 vols. Baroda, Oriental Institute.

Biardeau, Madeleine. 1964. Bhartṛhari, Vākyapadīya Brahmakāṇḍa avec la Vṛtti de Harivṛṣabha. Paris, de Boccard.

Birwé, Robert. 1955. Interpolationen in Pāṇinis Aṣṭādhyāyī. Kirfel vol. 27–52.

——. 1958. Variae Lectiones in Adhyāya IV und V der Aṣṭādhyāyī. ZDMG 108.133–54.

——. 1961. Der Gaṇapāṭha zu den Adhyāyas IV und V der Grammatik Pāṇinis. Wiesbaden, Harrassowitz.

——. 1964. Nārāyaṇa Daṇḍanātha's commentary on rules III.2,106–121 of Bhoja's Sarasvatīkaṇṭhābharaṇa. JAOS 84.150–62.

——. 1965. Fragments from three lost kośas. I. Vācaspati's Śabdārṇava. JAOS 85.524–43.

——. 1966. Studien zu Adhyāya III der Aṣṭādhyāyī Pāṇinis. Wiesbaden, Harrassowitz.

——. 1967. Fragments from three lost kośas. Vyāḍi's Utpalinī. II. JAOS 87.39–52.

——. 1968a. Some more fragments from Vācaspati's Śabdārṇava. JAOS 88.345–7.

——. 1968b. Ist Candragomin der Verfasser der Candra-Vṛtti? Renou vol. 127–42.

Bloch, Bernard. 1949. Leonard Bloomfield. Lg 25.87–94.

Bloomfield, Leonard. 1927. On some rules of Pāṇini. JAOS 47.61–70.

——. 1929. Review of Liebich 1928. Lg 5.267–76.

——. 1933. Language. New York, H. Holt. Several reprints.

Böhtlingk, Otto. 1839–40. Pāṇinis Acht Bücher grammatischer Regeln. 2 vols. Bonn.

——. (ed.). 1844. Die Uṇādi-Affixe. St. Petersburg.

——. 1845. Bemerkungen zur zweiten Ausgabe von Franz Bopps Kritischer Grammatik der Sanskrita-Sprache in kürzerer Fassung. BHPh 3.113–37.

——. (ed.). 1847. Vopadevas Mugdhabodha. St. Petersburg.

——. 1876a. Kātyāyana oder Patañjali im Mahābhāṣya. ZDMG 29.183–90.

——. 1876b. Das Verhalten der drei kanonischen Grammatiker in Indien zu den im Wurzelverzeichnis mit ṣ und ṇ anlautenden Wurzeln. ZDMG 29.483–90.

——. 1885. Zur indischen Lexicographie. ZDMG 39.532–8.

——. 1887. Pāṇinis Grammatik. Leipzig. Repr. 1964, Hildesheim, Olms.

——. 1890. Versuch, eine jüngst angefochtene Lehre Pāṇinis in Schutz zu nehmen. BVSAW 42.79–82.

——. 1893. Whitney's letzte Angriffe auf Pāṇini. BVSAW 45.247–57.

Bopp, Franz. 1824–7. Ausführliches Lehrgebäude der Sanskrita Sprache. 3 vols. Berlin.

——. 1830. Glossarium comparativum linguae Sanscritae. Berlin. 2nd ed. 1867. 3rd ed. 1867.

Boudon, Pierre. 1938. Une application du raisonnement par l'absurde dans l'interprétation de Pāṇini: les jñāpakasiddhaparibhāṣā. JA 230.65–121.

Breloer, B. 1929. Studie zu Pāṇini. ZII 7.114–35.

——. 1935–6. Die 14 pratyāhārasūtras des Pāṇini. ZII 10.133–91.

Brough, John. 1951. Theories of general linguistics in the Sanskrit grammarians. TPhS 27–46.

Buddha Prakash. 1967. On Pāṇini's sūtra IV.3.98, *vāsudevārjunābhyāṃ vun*. KURJ 1.1–9.

Bühler, Georg. 1894. The roots of the Dhātupāṭha not found in literature. WZKM 8.17–42, 122–36; also IAnt 23.141–54, 250–5.

Buiskool, H.E. 1934. Pūrvatrāsiddham: analytisch onderzoek aangaande het systeem der Tripādī van Pāṇini's Aṣṭādhyāyī. Amsterdam, H.J. Paris.

——. 1939. The Tripādī: being an abridged English recast of Pūrvatrāsiddham. Leiden, Brill.

Burnell, A.C. 1879. Ṛiktantravyākaraṇa: a prātiśākhya of the Sāmaveda. Part I. Bangalore.

Burrow, T. 1955. The Sanskrit Language. London, Faber & Faber.

——. 1969. Review of Staal 1967. JRAS 87–8.

Cardona, George. 1964. The formulation of Pāṇini 7.3.73. JOIB 14.38–41.

——. 1965a. On Pāṇini's morphophonemic principles. Lg 41.225–37.

——. 1965b. On translating and formalizing Pāṇinian rules. JOIB 14.306–14.

——. 1967a. Pāṇini's syntactic categories. JOIB 16.201–15.

——. 1967b. Negations in Pāṇinian rules. Lg 43.34–56.

——. 1967–8. *Anvaya* and *vyatireka* in Indian grammar. ALB 31–2.313–52.

——. 1968a. Pāṇini's definition, description, and use of *svarita*. Kuiper vol. 448–61.

——. 1968b. Review of Misra 1966. Lg 44.643–9.

——. 1969. Studies in Indian grammarians. I. The method of description reflected in the Śivasūtras. TAPS n.s. 59,1. Philadelphia.

——. 1970a. A note on Pāṇini's technical vocabulary. JOIB 19.196–212.

——. 1970b. Some principles of Pāṇini's grammar. JIP 1.40–74.

——. 1970c. Review of Rocher 1968a. Lingua 25.210–22.

——. 1970d. Review of Misra 1966. IIJ 12.226–32.

——. 1970e. Review of Staal 1967. IIJ 12.232–9.

——. 1971. Cause and causal agent: the Pāṇinian view. JOIB 21.22–40.

——. 1972. Review of Mehendale 1968c. Lg 48.171–9.

——. Ms. 1. Indian grammarians on adverbs. H. Kahane vol.

——. Ms. 2. Pāṇini's use of the term *upadeśa* and the *ekānta* and *an-ekānta* views regarding *anubandhas*. PISC I.
——. Ms. 3. Pāṇini's kārakas: agency, animation, and identity.
——. Ms. 4. On Pāṇini's metalinguistic use of cases; an analysis of Pāṇini 1.1.49, 66, 67 and 3.1.2. Charudeva Shastri vol.
——. Ms. 5. Review of Scharfe 1971. IIJ.
——. Ms. 6. Pāṇini.
CAREY, WILLIAM. 1806. Grammar of the Sanskrit language. Serampore.
CHAPEKAR, N.G. 1956–8. Nighaṇṭu words for man. BhV 16.84–96; 18.56–69.
CHATTERJI, KSHITISH CHANDRA. 1934. The Śiva Sūtras. JDL 24,2. 10p.
——. 1948. Technical terms and technique of Sanskrit grammar. Part I. Calcutta, Visvanath Chatterji. 2nd supplemented ed. 1964, Calcutta, University Press.
——. 1952–3. Pāṇini and Whitney. CcR 125.55–8; 126.49–52.
——. (ed.). 1953–61. Cāndravyākaraṇa of Candragomin. SIAL, 13. 2 vols. Poona, Deccan College.
——. 1957. Patañjali's Mahābhāṣya. Paspaśāhnika (introductory chapter). 2nd ed. Calcutta, A. Mukherjee. 3rd ed. 1964.
CHATTOPADHYAYA, KSHETRESH CHANDRA. 1937. Pāṇini and the Ṛkprātiśākhya. IHQ 13.343–9.
——. 1938. Thieme and Pāṇini. ICult 5.95–8.
CHATURVEDI, S.P. 1937. Technical terms of the Aṣṭādhyāyī. PAIOC IX.1191–208.
——. 1938. Pāṇini and the Ṛk-Prātiśākhya. NIAnt 1.450–9.
——. 1940. Dr. Ghosh on Pāṇini and the Ṛk-Prātiśākhya. NIAnt 2.723–7.
——. 1941. On references to earlier grammarians in the Aṣṭādhyāyī and the forms sanctioned by them. JNU fasc. 7.46–54.
——. 1942. On Pāṇini's sūtra VII.I.90: wrong wording or corrupt reading? ABORI 23.77–9.
——. 1946. Some aspects of the anuvṛtti procedure in the Aṣṭādhyāyī. PAIOC XIII 2.109–12.
——. 1949. On the technique of anticipation in the application of the Pāṇinian sūtras. SPAIOC XV.189.
——. 1953. A study into the principles of preference in the application of Pāṇinian sūtras and their working. SPAIOC XVII.91–2.
CHOUDHARY, RADHAKRISHNA. 1963. The Prākṛtapaiṅgalam: an important source of Mithilā's political history. VIJ 1.322–8.
COLEBROOKE, HENRY THOMAS. 1805. A grammar of the Sanskrit language. Part 1. Calcutta.
COLLINDER, B. 1962. Les origines du structuralisme. ASLU n.s. 1,1.15p.
DANIELSSON, O.A. 1883. Die Einleitung des Mahābhāṣya. ZDMG 37.20–53.
DAVE, T.N. 1962–3. Technique of the sūtra-writing. JIRID 1.21–28; 2.1–10; 3.1–7, 55–68.
——. 1963. Geographical lay-out of the Prakrit dialects indicated from Vararuci. SPP 3.81–4.

Deshpande, G. T. 1965. Pāṇinian concept of pada. JNU 16.62–9.
——. 1967a. Import of the term *devavāṇī*. JNU 17.193–208.
——. 1967b. On the accent of the vocative (āmantrita). JNU 18.113–20.
——. 1967c. Pāṇini: sūtras VII.1.9 and 10. JNU 18.199–200.
Deshpande, Madhav. 1972. Pāṇinian procedure of taparakaraṇa: a historical investigation. KZ 86.207–54.
Devasthali, G. V. 1960–1. The aim of the vārtikas of Kātyāyana. BhV 20–1.52–63.
——. 1963. Sāyaṇa utilising Pāṇini in his Ṛg-veda-bhāṣya: a study of Sāyaṇa's commentary on RV 1.1–19. JASBo n.s. 38.165–73.
——. 1966. Pāṇini as an aid to Ṛgvedic interpretation. Velankar vol. 20–6.
——. 1967a. Anubandhas of Pāṇini. PCASS B2. Poona, University.
——. 1967b. Śāntanava: Phiṭsūtras. PCASS C1. Poona, University.
——. 1968a. Sārasiddhāntakaumudī of Varadarāja. PCASS C4. Poona, University.
——. 1968b. Pāṇini and Ṛgvedic exegesis. ABORI 48–9.75–81. Repr. 1967 IAnt III 2,3.1–8; 1968 PCASS A22.
——. 1969. Paribhāṣā: introduction and general survey. IAnt III 3.1–13.
Doshi, Bechardas J. (ed.). 1967. Ācārya Malayagiri's Śabdānuśāsana with autocommentary. L.D.series, 30. Ahmedabad, L.D.Institute of Indology.
Edgerton, Franklin. 1928. Some linguistic notes on the Mīmāṅsā system. Lg 4.171–7.
——. 1952. Karmadhāraya. JAOS 72.80–1.
Edgren, A. Hjalmar. 1882. On the verbal roots of the Sanskrit language and of the Sanskrit grammarians. JAOS 11.1–55.
Eggeling, Julius. (ed.). 1874–8. The Kātantra, with the commentary of Durgasiṃha. BI, 81. Calcutta.
—— (ed.). 1879–81. Vardhamāna's Gaṇaratnamahodadhi, with the author's commentary. 2 vols. London, Trübner.
Emeneau, Murray B. 1955. India and linguistics. JAOS 75.145–53.
——. 1971. Review of The letters of Sir William Jones, ed. by Garland Cannon. Lg 47.959–64.
Faddegon, Barend. 1929. The mnemotechnics of Pāṇini's grammar. I. The Śivasūtra. AcOr 7.48–65.
——. 1936. Studies on Pāṇini's grammar. VKNA n.s. 38,1. Amsterdam.
Filliozat, Jean. 1937. Review of Subrahmanya Sastri 1934. JA 229.512–7.
——. 1967a. Louis Renou et son oeuvre scientifique. JA 255.1–11.
——. 1967b. Bibliographie des travaux de Louis Renou. JA 255.13–30. Repr. 1968. Renou vol. XIII–XXIX.
Forster, H. P. 1810. An essay on the principles of Sanskrit grammar. Part I. Calcutta.
Fowler, Murray. 1965. How ordered are Pāṇini's rules? JAOS 85.44–7.
Franke, R. Otto. 1894. Einige Belege aus dem Pāli für unbelegte Wurzeln und Wurzelbedeutungen des Dhātupāṭha. WZKM 8.321–31.

——. 1902. Geschichte und Kritik der einheimischen Pāli-Grammatik und -Lexicographie. Strassburg.

Frauwallner, Erich. 1959. Das Eindringen der Sprachtheorie in die indischen philosophischen Systeme. ITag 239–43.

——. 1960. Sprachtheorie und Philosophie im Mahābhāṣya des Patañjali. WZKSO 4.92–118.

George, K. M. 1968. Līlātilakam and the Tamil-Malayalam relationship. Emeneau vol. 95–8.

Ghatage, A. M. 1968. Pāṇini 1.4.32. IL 29.150–4.

Ghosal, S. N. 1962–3. Vājasaneyi Prātiśākhya. ISPP 4.113–39, 369–74; 5.93–6.

——. 1966. On the text of a sūtra in Vararuci's Prākṛta Prakāśa. VIJ 4.173–7.

——. 1968–9. The Ārṣa Prākrit as Hemacandra viewed it. JOIB 18.304–14.

Ghosh, Batakrishna. 1934. Pāṇini and the Ṛkprātiśākhya. IHQ 10.665–70.

——. 1938. Thieme and Pāṇini. ICult 4.387–99.

——. 1939. Mr. Chaturvedi on Pāṇini and the Ṛkprātiśākhya. NIAnt 2.59–61.

——. 1940. Pūrvācāryas in Pāṇini. D. R. Bhandarkar vol. 21–4.

——. 1945. Aspects of pre-Pāṇinian Sanskrit grammar. B. C. Law vol. 1.334–45.

Gode, P. K. 1939. Date of the grammarian Bhīmasena: before A.D.600. NIAnt 2.108–10.

——. 1940. A new approach to the date of Bhaṭṭoji Dīkṣita. ASVOI 1.117–27.

Gokhale, V. D. 1955–6. Unpāṇinian forms and usages in the critical edition of the Mahābhārata. IL 17.121–8.

Goldstücker, Theodor. 1861. Pāṇini: his place in Sanskrit literature. London. Repr. 1914, Allahabad, Pāṇini Office; 1965, ChSSt, 48, Varanasi; 1966, Osnabrück, Zeller.

Gonda, Jan. 1963. Review of Birwé 1961. ZDMG 113.362–3.

——. 1969. Review of Staal 1967. Lingua 22.248–53.

Gopal, Ram. 1968. Vedic quotations in the Kāśikā and Siddhānta-kaumudī. ABORI 48–9.227–30.

Grierson, George A. 1925. The eastern school of Prakrit grammarians and Paiśācī Prakrit. Asutosh Mukerji vol. 3, 2.119–41.

——. 1929. The Prakrit dhātvādeśas according to the western and the eastern schools of Prakrit grammarians. MASB 8, 2.77–170.

Gupta, S. K. 1965–6. Appreciation of Yāska as an etymologist. JGJRI 22.55–96.

Hall, R. A. 1951. American linguistics, 1925–50. ArchL 3.101–25.

Hamilton, Alexander. 1814. Terms of Sanskrit grammar. London.

Hariyappa, H. L., and M. M. Patkar (eds.). 1960. Professor P. K. Gode commemoration volume. Poona, Oriental Book Agency.

Hartmann, Peter. 1965. Einige linguistische Bemerkungen zum vorstehenden Thema [Staal 1965c]. Bocheński vol. 188–92.

Harweg, Roland. 1964. Kompositum und Katalysationstext vornehmlich im späten Sanskrit. Janua linguarum, series practica 5. The Hague, Mouton.

JANI, A.N. 1963. An emendation of a sūtra of Pāṇini. JUB 12.71–3.
JOSHI, D.M. 1971. On expressing kārakas apropos of Pāṇini 2.3.1. IL 32.107–12.
JOSHI, S.D. 1962. Verbs and nouns in Sanskrit. IL 23.60–3.
——. 1966a. Two methods of interpreting Pāṇini. JUP 23.53–61. Repr. 1965 PCASS A5.
——. 1966b. Patañjali's definition of a word: an interpretation. BDC 25.65–70.
——. 1967a. The Sphoṭanirṇaya (ch. XIV of the Vaiyākaraṇabhūṣaṇasāra) of Kauṇḍa Bhaṭṭa. PCASS C2. Poona, University.
——. 1967b. Adjectives and substantives as a single class in the 'parts of speech'. JUP 25.19–30. Repr. 1966 PCASS A9.
——. 1968. Word-integrity and syntactic analysis. JUP 27.165–73. Repr. 1968 PCASS A28.
——. 1968–73. Patañjali's Vyākaraṇa-Mahābhāṣya. PCASS C3, 5, 6, 7. 4 vols. (vols. 2 to 4 in collaboration with J.A.F. Roodbergen). Poona, University.
——. 1969. Sentence-structure according to Pāṇini. IAnt III 3.14–26.
JOSHI, V.L. 1965. Pāṇini and the Pāṇinīyas on saṃhitā. IL 26.66–71.
—— (ed.). 1966. Prauḍha Manoramā with commentary Śabdaratna. Vol. 1. Poona, Deccan College.
——. 1971. Treatment of loan words in Sanskrit grammar. IL 32.113–22.
KANTAWALA, S.G. 1962. Some linguistic peculiarities of the Matsya-purāṇa. IL 23.66–71.
KAPIL DEO SHASTRI. 1963. Significance of the word *prakāra* in the sūtras of the Aṣṭādhyāyī. VIJ 1.239–46.
——. 1964a. Bhartṛhari on the relation between upamāna and upameya. VIJ 2.87–92. = Bhartṛhari's discussion on the relation between the upamāna and upameya in his Vākyapadīya. IL 25.229–33.
——. 1964b. Bhartṛhari's discussion on sāmānādhikaraṇya. ALB 28.41–54.
——. 1965. Upamāna, upameya and sāmānyavacana according to the Vākyapadīya of Bhartṛhari. VIJ 3.19–28.
KATRE, S.M. 1940. The roots of the Pāli Dhātupāṭhas. BDC 1.228–317.
——. 1941. Introduction to Indian textual criticism. Poona, Deccan College. 2nd ed. 1954.
——. 1967. Pāṇinian studies I. Poona, Deccan College.
——. 1968–9. Dictionary of Pāṇini. 3 vols. Poona, Deccan College.
KEITH, A. BERRIEDALE. 1936. Pāṇini and the Veda. ICult 2.735–48.
KIEFER, FERENC. 1969. Review of Staal 1967. ALH 19.419–22.
KIELHORN, FRANZ. 1866. Śāntanava's Phiṭsūtra. AKM 4,2. Leipzig. Repr. 1967, New York.
—— (ed.). 1868. The Paribhāṣenduśekhara of Nāgojibhaṭṭa. Part 1. Bombay.
——. 1871–4. The Paribhāṣenduśekhara of Nāgojibhaṭṭa. Part 2. Translation and notes. Bombay. 2nd ed. by K.V. Abhyankar, 1960, Poona, BORI.
——. 1876. Kātyāyana and Patañjali: their relation to each other and to Pāṇini.

Bombay. Repr. 1963, Varanasi, Indological Book House; 1965, Osnabrück, Zeller.

—— (ed.). 1880–5. The Vyākaraṇa-mahābhāṣya of Patañjali. 3 vols. Bombay. 2nd ed. 1892–1909. 3rd ed. by K.V. Abhyankar, 1962–72, Poona, BORI.

——. 1886. Review of Whitney 1885b. IAnt 15.86–7.

——. 1969. Kleine Schriften mit einer Auswahl der epigraphischen Aufsätze, ed. Wilhelm Rau. 2 vols. Wiesbaden, Steiner.

KIPARSKY, PAUL, and J.F. STAAL. 1969. Syntactic and semantic relations in Pāṇini. FL 5.83–117.

KIRSTE, J. (ed.). 1895. Das Uṇādi Gaṇasūtra des Hemacandra mit dem selbstverfassten Commentare des Autors. Vienna.

—— (ed.). 1899. The Dhātupāṭha of Hemacandra, with the author's own commentary. Vienna–Bombay.

KITTEL, FERDINAND. 1893. Dravidische Elemente in den Sanskrit-Dhātupāṭhas. Roth vol. 21–4.

KRISHNAMACHARYA, V. (ed.). 1962. Laghūpasargavṛtti. ALB 26.81–90.

KRISHNAMURTHY, P. GOPALA. 1959. Pāṇini and the earlier grammarians. SPAIOC XX.71.

KUIPER, F.B.J. 1965. Review of Bhawe 1957–62. IIJ 8.245–7.

KUKENHEIM, L. 1962. Esquisse historique de la langue française et de ses rapports avec la linguistique générale. Leiden, Universitaire Pers.

KULKARNI, E.D. 1943–51. Unpāṇinian forms and usages in the critical edition of the Mahābhārata. ABORI 24.83–97; BDC 4.227–45; NIAnt 6.130–9; BDC 5.13–33; BDC 11.361–78.

—— (ed.). 1953. Śālihotra of Bhoja. SIAL, 33. Poona, Deccan College.

—— (ed.). 1955. Ekārthanāmamālā and Dvyakṣaranāmamālā of Saubhari. SIAL, 34. Poona, Deccan College.

—— (ed.). 1968. Dharaṇikośa of Dharaṇidāsa. Part I. Poona, Deccan College.

—— (ed.). 1968–71. Paramānandīyanāmamālā of Makarandadāsa. 2 vols. Poona, Deccan College.

KULKARNI, E.D. and M.C. DIXIT (eds.). 1971. Paryāyaśabdaratna of Dhanaṃjayabhaṭṭa. Part I. Poona, Deccan College.

KULKARNI, E.D. and V.D. GOKHALE (eds.). 1955. Nāmamālikā of Bhoja. SIAL, 50. Poona, Deccan College.

KUNHAN RAJA, C. 1940–1. Niruktavārttika. AOR 5, 2.5–16.

——. 1943. Discovery of a manuscript of the Niruktavārttika. ALB 7.268.

——. 1944. The author of the Niruktavārttika. ALB 8.191.

——. 1957. The Śiva sūtras of Pāṇini: an analysis. AOR 13. Sanskrit section 65–81.

KUNJUNNI RAJA, K. 1957a. Yāska's definition of the 'verb' and the 'noun' in the light of Bhartṛhari's explanations. AOR 13. Sanskrit section 86–8.

——. 1957b. Diachronistic linguistics in ancient India. JUM 29.127–30.

——. 1958. The Indian influence on linguistics. JUM 30.93–111.

——. 1962. *Prārthayanti*: a ghost word discussed by the grammarians. ALB 26.26–7.

——. 1964. The Niruktavārttika of Nīlakaṇṭha: a metrical commentary on Yāska's Nirukta. ALB 28.250–62.

——. 1965. Pāṇini's attitude towards lakṣaṇā. ALB 29.177–87.

LADDU, S. D. 1964. Pāṇini and the *akālakaṃ vyākaraṇam*. IL 25.187–9.

——. 1966. Kātyāyana's vārttika on Pāṇini 3.1.33 and its bearing on the text of the Mahābhāṣya. VIJ 4.14–8.

——. 1967a. A possible light on the relative age of Yāska and Patañjali. VIJ 5.58–62.

——. 1967b. Who is the grammarian Vardhamāna? IAnt III 2, 3.18–25.

——. 1967c. A pre-Patañjalian grammatical observation. IAnt III 2, 4.40–1.

——. 1969a. The sphere of reference of the technical term *tṛjādi* according to Kātyāyana and Patañjali. JUP 29.1–10. Repr. 1968 PCASS A23.

——. 1969b. The laukika, vaidika and yājñika accentuation with the munitraya of Sanskrit grammar. IAnt III 3.93–111.

LAHIRI, PRABODH CHANDRA. 1935. Concordance Pāṇini–Patañjali (Mahābhāṣya). Indische Forschungen, 10. Breslau, Marcus.

LASSEN, CHRISTIAN. 1823–30. Ueber Herrn Prof. Bopps Grammatisches System. Indische Bibliothek 3, 1.1–113.

LÉVI, SYLVAIN. 1903. La date de Candragomin. BEFEO 3.38–53.

——. 1906–8. Des préverbes chez Pāṇini. MSL 14.276–9.

LIEBICH, BRUNO. 1886. Die Casuslehre der indischen Grammatiker verglichen mit dem Gebrauch der Casus im Aitareya-Brāhmaṇa: ein Beitrag zur Syntax der Sanskrit-Sprache. BB 10.205–34; 11.273–315.

——. 1891. Pāṇini: Ein Beitrag zur Kenntnis der indischen Literatur und Grammatik. Leipzig.

——. 1892. Zwei Kapittel der Kāśikā. Breslau.

——. 1895. Das Cāndra-vyākaraṇa. NGGW 272–321.

——. 1899. Das Datum des Candragomin. WZKM 13.308–15.

——. 1902. Cāndra-vyākaraṇa: Die Grammatik des Candragomin. AKM 11, 4. Leipzig.

—— (ed.). 1903. Das Datum des Candragomin und Kālidāsas. JSG 81.24–34.

—— (ed.). 1918. Candra-vṛtti: Der Original-Kommentar Candragomins zu seinem grammatischen Sūtra. AKM 14. Leipzig.

——. 1919a. Zur Einführung in die indische einheimische Sprachwissenschaft. I. Das Kātantra. SbHAW fasc. 4. Heidelberg.

——. 1919b. Zur Einführung ... II. Historische Einführung und Dhātupāṭha. SbHAW fasc. 15. Heidelberg.

——. 1920a. Zur Einführung ... III. Der Dhātupāṭha. SbHAW fasc. 10. Heidelberg.

——. 1920b. Zur Einführung ... IV. Analyse der Candra-vṛtti. SbHAW fasc. 13. Heidelberg.

——. 1921. Materialien zum Dhātupāṭha. SbHAW fasc. 7. Heidelberg.

——. 1928. Konkordanz Pāṇini-Candra. Indische Forschungen, 6. Breslau, Marcus.

—— (ed.). 1930. Kṣīrataraṅgiṇī: Kṣīrasvāmin's Kommentar zu Pāṇinis Dhātupāṭha. Breslau, Marcus.

LIMAYE, S.K. 1966. On the meaning of *sukeśī rathyā.* JNU 17.18–20.

LIMAYE, V.P. 1964–5. Additions and corrections to Sarup's edition of the commentaries on Yāska's Nirukta. VIJ 2.221–38; 3.29–56, 205–38.

——. 1966a. Necessity for new vārttikas to Pāṇini 1.1.27 and 5.2.39. VIJ 4.5–13.

——. 1966b. Dhyānagraha-kāra or Dhyāna-kāra: a pre-Bhartṛhari grammarian. VIJ 4.228–9.

——. 1967. Pāṇini 6.1.121: *avapathāsi ca* or *apavathāsi ca*? VIJ 5.193–5.

MACDONELL, A.A. 1927. A Sanskrit grammar for students. 3rd ed., Oxford, University Press.

MASTER, ALFRED. 1956. Jones and Pāṇini. JAOS 76.186–7.

MATILAL, BIMAL KRISHNA. 1960. The doctrine of *karaṇa* in grammar-logic. JGJRI 17.63–9.

——. 1966. Indian theorists on the nature of the sentence (*vākya*). FL 2.377–93.

——. 1968. The navya-nyāya doctrine of negation. HOS, 46. Cambridge, Mass.

——. 1971. Epistemology, logic, and grammar in Indian philosophical analysis. The Hague, Mouton.

MEHENDALE, MADHUKAR ANANT. 1965a. Nirukta notes, series 1 [1–9]. Poona, Deccan College.

——. 1965b. Nirukta notes, X: on *anūpa.* V.V. Mirashi vol. 104–7.

——. 1965c. Nirukta notes, XI: *ardhanāma.* IL 26.203–6.

——. 1967. Nirukta notes, XII: *vibhakti.* Gopinath Kaviraj vol. 17–9.

——. 1967–8. Nirukta notes, XIV: *jāmi* and *ajāmi* in the Nirukta 4.20. BDC 28.197–201.

——. 1968a. Nirukta notes, XIII: on *brahman.* Renou vol. 519–21.

——. 1968b. Nirukta notes, XV: *aikapadika* in the Nirukta 1.14. IL 29.90–6.

——. 1968c. Some aspects of Indo-Aryan linguistics. Bombay, University.

MEISEZAHL, R.O. 1966. Über *jñīṃ* in der tibetischen Version der Regel *ṃ̊ chandasi* der Sārasvata-Grammatik. IIJ 9.139–46.

MILLER, ROY ANDREW. 1963. Thon-mi Sambhoṭa and his grammatical treatises. JAOS 83.485–502.

——. 1965. Some minor Tibetan grammatical fragments. ZDMG 115.327–40.

MIMAMSAK, YUDHISTHIR (ed.). 1943. Daśapādyuṇādivṛtti. Banaras, Government Sanskrit College.

——. 1950–62. Saṃskṛta vyākaraṇa-śāstra kā itihāsa. Vol. 1. Dehradun, Vaidika Sadhana Asrama. Revised ed., Ajmer, Bharatiya Pracyavidya Pratisthanam.

Vol. 2, Ajmer, Bharatiya Pracyavidya Pratisthanam.

—— (ed.). 1957. Kṣīrataraṅgiṇī. Amritsar, Ramlal Kapur Trust.

—— (ed.). 1962. Daivam. Ajmer, Bharatiya Pracyavidya Pratisthanam.

—— (ed.). 1964. Bhāgavṛtti-saṃkalanam. Ajmer, Bharatiya Pracyavidya Pratisthanam.

—— (ed.). 1965. Nirukta-samuccayaḥ. Ajmer, Bharatiya Pracyavidya Pratisthanam.

——. 1965–6. Kāśakṛtsna-dhātuvyākhyānam. Ajmer, Bharatiya Pracyavidya Pratisthanam.

MISRA, VIDYA NIWAS. 1964a. The structural framework of Pāṇini's linguistic analysis of Sanskrit. PICL IX.743–7.

——. 1964b. Pāṇini's grammar as a mathematical model. IL 25.157–78. [= ch. 4 of 1966.]

——. 1966. The descriptive technique of Pāṇini: an introduction. Janua linguarum, series practica 18. The Hague, Mouton.

MOOKERJI, RADHA KUMUD. 1923. History of Sanskrit literature from the works of Pāṇini, Kātyāyana and Patañjali. IAnt 52.22–4.

——. 1935. Further historical data from Patañjali's Mahābhāṣya. ICult 2.362–3.

——. 1947. Ancient Indian education. London, Macmillan. 2nd ed. 1951. 3rd ed. 1960, Delhi, Motilal Banarsidass. 4th ed. 1969.

MÜLLER, FRIEDRICH MAX. 1866. A Sanskrit grammar for beginners. London.

——. 1869. Rig-veda-prātiśākhya: das älteste Lehrbuch der vedischen Phonetik. Leipzig.

NARASIMHACHARYA, M. S. (ed.). 1973. Mahābhāṣya Pradīpa vyakhyānāni. Vol. 1: adhyāya 1, pāda 1, āhnika 1–4. PIFI, 51,1. Pondicherry.

NATH, N. C. 1970. Are feminine bases prātipadikas according to Pāṇini? VIJ 8.82–5.

NITTI-DOLCI, LUIGIA. (ed.). 1938a. Le Prākṛtānuśāsana de Puruṣottama. Paris, Société asiatique.

——. 1938b. Les grammairiens prakrits. Paris, Adrien–Maisonneuve. Engl. transl. by Prabhakara Jha, 1972, Delhi, Motilal Banarsidass.

——. 1939. La première śākhā du Prākṛta-kalpataru de Rāmaśarman. BEHE 273. Paris.

OBERHAMMER, GERHARD. 1964. Gedanken zur historischen Darstellung indischer Logik. OLZ 59.6–19.

OJIHARA, YUTAKA. 1956. Quelques remarques sur *ḷ* voyelle dans l'Aṣṭādhyāyī. JIBS 4.597–1 [reverse pagination].

——. 1958–60. Causerie vyākaraṇique. I. 1.1.62 vis-à-vis de 1.1.56. JIBS 6.305–2; 8.370–69.

——. 1959. Causerie vyākaraṇique. II. Antériorité du Gaṇapāṭha par rapport au Sūtrapāṭha. JIBS 7.797–85.

——. 1961a. Causerie vyākaraṇique. III,1. Incohérence interne chez la Kāśikā. JIBS 9.753–49.

——. 1961b. Le Mahābhāṣya, adhyāya I, āhnika 8: un essai de traduction. MIK 2.9–22.

——. 1962. Causerie vyākaraṇique. III,2. Incohérence interne chez la Kāśikā. JIBS 10.776–66.

——. 1963a. Mahābhāṣya ad Pāṇini 1.1.56: un essai de traduction. AcAs 4.43–69.

——. 1963b. Causerie vyākaraṇique. II Addenda et corrigenda: la nécessité ultime des sū. 1.1.34–36. JIBS 11.852–46.

——. 1964. Causerie vyākaraṇique. III,3. Incohérence interne chez la Kāśikā. JIBS 12.847–5.

——. 1965a. A la recherche de la motivation ultime du Pāṇini-sūtra 1.1.62. MIK 6–7.69–85.

——. 1965b. Review of Birwé 1961. IIJ 8.285–93.

——. 1967. Causerie vyākaraṇique. IV. *Jāti* 'genus' et deux définitions pré-patañjaliennes. JIBS 16.459–1.

——. 1967–8. Sur l'énoncé pāṇinéen *astrīviṣaya* (IV.1.63): deux interprétations et leur rapport avec le Gaṇapāṭha. ALB 31–2.125–43.

——. 1968a. Read *parṇáṃ ná véḥ*: Kāśikā ad P.1.1.4: a notice. ABORI 48–9.403–9.

——. 1968b. Les discussions patañjaliennes afférentes au remaniement du Gaṇapāṭha. Renou vol. 565–76.

——. 1970. Les discussions patañjaliennes afférentes au remaniement du Gaṇapāṭha. IIJ 12.81–115.

——. 1971. Un chapitre de la Saddanīti comparé aux données pāṇinéennes. JA 259.83–97.

OJIHARA, YUTAKA, and LOUIS RENOU. 1960–7. La Kāśikā-vṛtti (adhyāya I, pāda 1), traduite et commentée. PEFEO, 48. 3 vols. (vol. 3 by Ojihara alone). Paris.

ORARA, EMMANUEL DE GUZMAN. 1967. An account of ancient Indian grammatical studies down to Patañjali's Mahābhāṣya: two traditions. ASt 5.369–76.

PALSULE, GAJANAN BALKRISHNA. 1952a. An interpolated passage in the Aṣṭādhyāyī. ABORI 33.135–44.

——. 1952b. A new explanation of the term karmadhāraya. ABORI 33.245–50.

—— (ed.). 1954. Kavikalpadruma of Vopadeva. SIAL, 15. Poona, Deccan College.

——. 1955. A concordance of Sanskrit Dhātupāṭhas (with index of meanings). Poona, Deccan College.

——. 1957. A survey of the pre-Pāṇinian grammatical thought in the matter of the verbal root. IL 18.116–39.

——. 1958a. Groupings, anubandhas and other technical devices used in the Dhātupāṭhas. BDC 19.1–30.

——. 1958b. A brief account of the different Dhātupāṭhas. IL 19.103–33.

——. 1961. The Sanskrit Dhātupāṭhas: a critical study. Poona, Deccan College.

——. 1965. Review of Birwé 1961. ABORI 46.183–5.

——. 1967. *Saṃjñāyām* in Pāṇini. JUP 25.31–75. Repr. 1966 PCASS A10.
——. 1968a. Some primary nominal formations missing in Pāṇini. JUP 27.145–51. Repr. 1968 PCASS A18.
——. 1968b. The role of √*kṛ*- in the Sanskrit grammatical terms. JUP 29.11–29. Repr. 1968 PCASS A24.
——. 1969. Patañjali's interpretation of RV 10.71.2. IAnt III 3.27–9.
——. 1970. Review of Birwé 1966. ABORI 51.274–9.
PANDIT, M.D. 1962. Zero in Pāṇini. JUB 11.53–66.
——. 1963a. Some linguistic principles in Pāṇini's grammar. IL 24.50–69.
——. 1963b. Pāṇini: a study in non-compounded word-structures. VIJ 1.224–38.
——. 1963c. Pāṇini: a study in compound word-structures. JUB 12.81–98.
——. 1964. Statistical picture of Pāṇinian word-formations. Pade Shastree vol.
——. 1966a. Pāṇinian *it-saṃjñā*: a symbolic zero. BDC 25.77–94.
——. 1966b. Mathematical representation of some Pāṇinian sūtras. JUP 23.139–52. Repr. 1966 PCASS A7.
——. 1969. Pāṇini: a statistical picture of Sanskrit sounds. I. IAnt III 3.128–38.
——. 1971. Pāṇini: statistical study of Sanskrit formations. ABORI 52.175–209.
PARANJPE, V.W. 1959. Analysis of case terminations in Sanskrit with special reference to the sūtras of Pāṇini. PICO XXIV.574–7.
PATANJAL, DEO PRAKASH. 1963. A critical study of Rigveda (1.137–163), particularly from the point of view of Pāṇinian grammar. Delhi, Patañjali Publications
PATHAK, SHRIDHAR, and SIDDHESHVAR CHITRAO. 1927. Word-index to Patañjali's Vyākaraṇa-mahābhāṣya. Poona, BORI.
——. 1935. Word-index to Pāṇini-sūtra-pāṭha and Pariśiṣṭas. Poona, BORI.
PEDERSEN, HOLGER. 1931. Linguistic science in the 19th century. Cambridge, Mass., Harvard University Press. Repr. 1959. The discovery of language. Bloomington, Indiana University Press.
PETERSON, PETER. 1883–5. Note on the date of Patañjali. JBBRAS 16.181–9.
——. 1885. The Aucityālaṃkāra of Kṣemendra, with a note on the date of Patañjali. Bombay.
PURI, BAIJ NATH. 1957. India in the times of Patañjali. Bombay, Bharatiya Vidya Bhavan. 2nd ed. 1968.
RADHAKRISHNAN, R. 1966. Tolkāppiyam on intervocalic stops. IIJ 9.209–10.
RAMA SUBBIAH. 1968. Tolkāppiyam and phonetics. IIJ 10.251–60.
RAMASWAMI AIYAR, L.V. 1964. Līlātilakam on unique Tamil-Malayalam sounds. IL 25.270–4.
RAU, WILHELM. 1962. Über sechs Handschriften des Vākyapadīya. Oriens 15.374–98.
——. 1964a. Handschriften des Vākyapadīya. Zweiter Teil. Oriens 17.182–98.
——. 1964b. Ein neues Fragment der Candra-vṛtti. ZDMG 113.521–9.
——. 1971. Die handschriftliche Überlieferung des Vākyapadīya und seiner Kommentare. Munich, Fink.

Regnier, Adolphe. 1856–8. Etudes sur la grammaire védique: Prātiśākhya du Rig-Véda. JA V 7.163–239, 344–407, 445–74; 8.255–315, 482–526; 9.210–47; 10.57–111, 374–450, 461–74; 11.289–379; 12.137–220, 329–94, 535–93.

Renou, Louis. 1936. Les 'innovations' de la grammaire de Candragomin. Etudes de grammaire sanskrite 1.86–143.

——. 1937. Review of Faddegon 1936. OLZ 40.318–9.

——. 1940. Aperçu de la littérature grammaticale en sanskrit [= 1940–56, fasc. 1:5–44].

——. 1940–56. La Durghaṭavṛtti de Śaraṇadeva. 2 vols. in 6 fasc. Paris, Belles Lettres.

——. 1941–2. Les connexions entre le rituel et la grammaire en sanskrit. JA 233.105–65.

——. 1942. Terminologie grammaticale du sanskrit. BEHE 280–2. 3 vols. Paris, Champion. Repr. 1 vol., 1957.

——. 1947–54. La grammaire de Pāṇini. 3 vols. Paris, Klincksieck. 2nd revised ed. 1966, 2 vols. Paris, Ecole française d'Extrême-Orient.

——. 1953a. Les transitions dans la grammaire de Pāṇini. Etudes pāṇinéennes, 1. JA 241.417–27.

——. 1953b. Le Veda chez Patañjali. Etudes pāṇinéennes, 2. JA 241.427–64.

——. 1955. Les nipātana-sūtra de Pāṇini et questions diverses. EVP 1.103–30.

——. 1956a. Etudes pāṇinéennes. EVP 2.

——. 1956b. Amarasiṃha et Pāṇini. Etudes pāṇinéennes, 4. JA 244.369–77.

——. 1956c. Le Veda chez les grammairiens non-pāṇinéens. Etudes pāṇinéennes, 5. JA 244.377–89.

——. 1957a. Introduction to J. Wackernagel's Altindische Grammatik, 1957 ed. of vol. 1. Göttingen, Vandenhoeck & Ruprecht.

——. 1957b. Etudes pāṇinéennes. EVP 3.

——. 1957c. Grammaire et Vedānta. JA 245.121–33.

——. 1960a. Le destin du Veda dans l'Inde. EVP 6. Engl. transl. 1965, Delhi, Motilal Banarsidass.

——. 1960b. La forme et l'arrangement interne des Prātiśākhya. JA 248.1–40.

——. 1960c. La théorie des temps du verbe d'après les grammairiens sanskrits. JA 248.305–37.

——. 1961a. Grammaire et poétique en sanskrit. EVP 8.105–31.

——. 1961b. Review of Birwé 1961. Kratylos 6.150–3.

——. 1961c. Sur la forme de quelques textes sanskrits. JA 249.163–211.

——. 1963. Sur le genre du sūtra dans la littérature sanskrite. JA 251.165–216.

——. 1969. Pāṇini. CTL 5.481–98.

Rocher, Ludo, and Rosane Debels [later Rocher]. 1960. La valeur des termes et formules techniques dans la grammaire indienne, d'après Nāgeśabhaṭṭa. AnnIPhO 15.129–51.

Rocher, Rosane. 1962. The Hindu grammarians and linguistic changes. JOIB

11.260–8.

——. 1964a. 'Agent' et 'objet' chez Pāṇini. JAOS 84.44–54.

——. 1964b. The technical term *hetu* in Pāṇini's Aṣṭādhyāyī. VIJ 2.31–40.

——. 1965a. La formation du futur périphrastique sanskrit selon Pāṇini: un exemple de description linguistique. AION-L 6.15–22.

——. 1965b. Dhātupāṭha et dialectologie indienne. ZMaF Beihefte n.s. 4, 2.699–707.

——. 1965–6. Les grammairiens indiens: leurs buts et leurs méthodes. RUB 18.78–88.

——. 1966. *Bhāva* 'état' et *kriyā* 'action' chez Pāṇini. Linguistic research in Belgium, ed. by Yvan Lebrun, 113–20. Wetteren, Universa.

——. 1967. Review of Birwé 1966. JAOS 87.582–8.

——. 1968a. La théorie des voix du verbe dans l'école pāṇinéenne: le 14e āhnika. Brussels, Presses Universitaires de Bruxelles.

——. 1968b. Alexander Hamilton (1762–1824): a chapter in the early history of Sanskrit philology. American Oriental Series, 51. New Haven, Conn.

——. 1969. The concept of verbal root in Indian grammar: a propos of Pāṇini 1.3.1. FL 5.73–82.

——. 1970. Review of Misra 1966. JAOS 90.357–9.

——. 1973. Review of Scharfe 1971. JAOS 93.112–4.

——. Ms. Nathaniel Brassey Halhed's collection of Oriental manuscripts. AOR.

ROTH, RUDOLF. 1852. Yāska's Nirukta, sammt den Nighaṇṭavas. Göttingen.

SADHU RAM. 1956. Authorship of some kārikās and fragments ascribed to Bhartṛhari. JGJRI 13.51–79.

——. 1966. Lakshman Sarup's translation of the Nirukta: some corrections and emendations. ALB 30.122–9.

SALUS, PETER H. 1971. Pāṇini to Postal: a bibliography in the history of linguistics. Linguistic bibliography series, 2. Edmonton-Champaign, Linguistic Research, Inc.

SANKARAN, C. R. 1951. Phonemics of Old Tamil. Poona, Deccan College.

——. 1961. Tolkāppiyam and the science of phonemics. TCult 9.117–30.

SANKARAN, C. R., and K. M. N. MENON. 1960–1. Līlātilakam and modern phonemics. BhV 20–1.392–4.

SARKAR, HIMANSU BHUSAN. 1966. The migration of Sanskrit grammar, lexicography, prosody and rhetoric to Indonesia. JASB n.s. 8.81–99.

SARMA, K. MADHAVA KRISHNA. 1940a. Patañjali, lakṣyaikacakṣus: his lofty realism. JOR 14.204–9.

——. 1940b. Technical terms in the Aṣṭādhyāyī. JOR 14.259–67.

——. 1940–1. Kātyāyana. PO 5.126–32; 6.74–92.

——. 1944–59. Patañjali and linguistic changes. QJMS 35.134–42; 49.263–70.

——. 1968. Pāṇini, Kātyāyana and Patañjali. Delhi, Lal Bahadur Shastri Samskrita Vidyapeetha.

SASTRI, SITARAM (ed.). 1960. Bṛhacchabdenduśekhara by Nāgeśabhaṭṭa. 3 vols. Varanasi, Sarasvati Bhavan.

—— (ed.). 1964. Prauḍhamanoramā of Śrī Bhaṭṭoji Dīkṣita and Laghuśabdaratna of Śrī Nāgeśa Bhaṭṭa. Vol. 1. HVNRSS, 8. Varanasi.

SATYA VRAT. 1963. Un-Pāṇinian forms in the Yogavāsiṣṭha. VIJ 1.247–66.

SCHARFE, HARTMUT. 1954. Kleine Nachlese zu Kielhorns Übersetzung von Nāgojibhaṭṭas Paribhāṣenduśekhara. Friedrich Weller vol. 570–4.

——. 1961. Die Logik im Mahābhāṣya. Berlin, Akademie-Verlag.

——. 1965. *Vacana* 'numerus' bei Pāṇini? KZ 79.239–46.

——. 1971. Pāṇini's metalanguage. MAPS 89. Philadelphia.

SCHLEGEL, AUGUST WILHELM. 1832. Réflexions sur l'étude des langues asiatiques. Bonn–Paris.

SCHULZE, WILHELM. 1921. Vom Altertum zur Gegenwart. 2nd ed., Leipzig.

——. 1923. Zur Bildung des Vokativs im Griechischen und im Lateinischen. Wackernagel vol. 240–54.

——. 1934. Kleine Schriften. Göttingen, Vandenhoeck & Ruprecht.

SEN, NILMADHAV. 1955. Un-Pāṇinian nominal declension in the Rāmāyaṇa. JOIB 5.169–86.

——. 1956. Un-Pāṇinian pronouns and numerals in the Rāmāyaṇa. JOIB 5.266–71.

SEN, SUKUMAR. 1952–3. The story of Devadatta in the Mahābhāṣya. IL 12.9–16.

——. 1962. The names of the samāsas in Pāṇini's grammar. BPhSC 3.90–2.

——. 1970. Paninica. Calcutta, Sanskrit College.

SENART, EMILE. 1871. Kaccāyanappakaraṇam: grammaire pālie de Kaccāyana. JA VI 17.103–351, 361–540.

SENGUPTA, SAILENDRANATH. 1961. Contribution towards a critical edition of the Gaṇapāṭha. JASB n.s. 3.89–96.

——. 1964. Uṇādi suffixes and words derived with such suffixes. JASB n.s. 6.123–206.

——. 1966. Contribution towards a critical edition of the Dhātupāṭha. JASB n.s. 8.191–217.

SHANMUGAM, S.V. 1967. Nacciṇārkkiṇiyar's conception of phonology. Annamalai, University.

SHANMUGAM PILLAI, M. 1964. Ca:riyai vaṟṟu in Tolka:ppiyam. IL 25.105–7.

SHEFTS, BETTY. 1961. Grammatical method in Pāṇini: his treatment of Sanskrit present stems. American Oriental Series, Essay 1. New Haven, Conn.

SIL, HARENDRA CHANDRA. 1960–1. A study of the un-Pāṇinian verb-forms in the critical edition of the Ādiparvan of the Mahābhārata. IHQ 36.35–57; 37.38–47.

——. 1966. The un-Pāṇinian causative verb-forms in the Ādiparvan of the Mahābhārata. BPhSC 6.28–39.

SIMONSSON, NILS. 1961. Audumbarāyaṇa's theory of sound. OS 10.22–30.

SINGH, J.D. 1971. Pāṇini's theory of language. KURJ 5.73–86.

SKÖLD, HANNES. 1926a. Papers on Pāṇini and Indian grammar in general. Lund–

Leipzig, Gleerup–Harrassowitz.
——. 1926b. The Nirukta: its place in Old Indian literature: its etymologies. Lund–Leipzig, Gleerup–Harrassowitz.
——. 1928. Untersuchungen zur Genesis der altindischen etymologischen Literatur. Lund–Leipzig, Gleerup–Harrassowitz.
STAAL, J.F. 1960a. Correlations between language and logic in Indian thought. BSOAS 23.109–22.
——. 1960b. The construction of formal definitions of subject and predicate. TPhS 89–103.
——. 1961. The theory of definition in Indian logic. JAOS 81.122–6.
——. 1962a. A method of linguistic description: the order of consonants according to Pāṇini. Lg 38.1–10.
——. 1962b. Negation and the law of contradiction in Indian thought. BSOAS 25.52–71.
——. 1962c. Contraposition in Indian logic. Proc. 1960 Internat. Congress for Logic, Methodology, and the Philosophy of Science 943–9.
——. 1962d. Philosophy and language. T.M.P. Mahadevan vol. 10–52.
——. 1963a. Review of Scharfe 1961. JAOS 83.252–6.
——. 1963b. Review of Shefts. Lg 39.483–8.
——. 1963c. Euclides en Pāṇini: twee methodische richtlijnen voor de filosofie. Amsterdam, Polak & Van Gennep.
——. 1965a. Euclid and Pāṇini. PE&W 15.99–116.
——. 1965b. Context-sensitive rules in Pāṇini. FL 1.63–72. Repr. 1968 Emeneau vol. 332–9.
——. 1965c. Reification, quotation and nominalization. Bocheński vol. 151–87.
——. 1966a. Room at the top in Sanskrit: ancient and modern descriptions of nominal composition. IIJ 9.165–98.
——. 1966b. Pāṇini tested by Fowler's automaton. JAOS 86.206–9.
——. 1966c. Analyticity. FL 2.67–93.
——. 1967. Word order in Sanskrit and universal grammar. FL suppl. ser., 5. Dordrecht, Reidel.
——. 1969. Sanskrit philosophy of language. CTL 5.499–531.
——. 1970. Review of Cardona 1969. Lg 46.502–7.
——. 1972. A reader on the Sanskrit grammarians. Cambridge, Mass., MIT Press.
——. Ms. 1. Sanskrit philosophy of language. History of linguistic thought and contemporary linguistics, ed. by H. Parret.
——. Ms. 2. Origin and development of linguistics in India. Traditions and paradigms, ed. by Dell Hymes.
STRAUSS, OTTO. 1927. Mahābhāṣya ad Pāṇini 4.1.3 und seine Bedeutung für die Geschichte der indischen Logik. Richard Garbe vol. 84–94.
SUBRAHMANYA SASTRI, P.S. 1934. History of grammatical theories in Tamil and their relation to the grammatical literature in Sanskrit. Madras, University.

——. 1944–62. Lectures on the Mahābhāṣya. 6 vols. Annamalainagar, Annamalai University and the author. Vol. 1, 2nd ed., 1960.

SUBRAHMANYAM, K.G. 1926a. A note on the evidence of Pāṇini on Vāsudeva-worship. IHQ 2.186–8.

——. 1926b. A short note on Mr. Jayaswal's interpretation of a Mahābhāṣya passage in his 'Hindu Polity'. IHQ 2.416–8.

——. 1926c. Evidence of Pāṇini on Vāsudeva-worship. IHQ 2.864–5.

SUKTHANKAR, V.S. 1921. Die Grammatik Śākaṭāyanas (Adhyāya 1, Pāda 1). Berlin. Repr. 1945 Sukthankar Memorial volume II.1.

SWAMINATHAN, V. 1963. Bhartṛhari's authorship of the commentary on the Mahābhāṣya. ALB 27.59–70.

—— (ed.). 1965. Mahābhāṣya ṭīkā by Bhartṛhari. Vol. 1. HVNRSS, 11. Varanasi.

THIEME, PAUL. 1931. Grammatik und Sprache: ein Problem der altindischen Sprachwissenschaft. ZII 8.23–32.

——. 1932. Zur Geschichte der einheimischen indischen Grammatik. OLZ 4.236–42.

——. 1935a. Pāṇini and the Veda: studies in the early history of linguistic science in India. Allahabad, Globe Press.

——. 1935b. Bhāṣya zu Vārttika 5 zu Pāṇini 1.1.9 und seine einheimischen Erklärer: ein Beitrag zur Geschichte und Würdigung der indischen grammatischen Scholastik. NGGW n.s. 1, 5.171–216.

——. 1935c. Zur Datierung des Pāṇini. ZDMG 89.*21–4.

——. 1937a. Pāṇini and the Ṛkprātiśākhya. IHQ 13.329–43.

——. 1937b. On the identity of the Vārttikakāra. ICult 4.189–209.

——. 1937c. *Hemantaśiśirau* und *ahorātre* (Pāṇ. II.4.28). G.N. Jha vol. 415–9.

——. 1939. A few remarks on Indian Culture IV [Ghosh 1938]. ICult 5.363–6.

——. 1956. Pāṇini and the Pāṇinīyas. JAOS 76.1–23.

——. 1957a. Pāṇini and the pronunciation of Sanskrit. Whatmough vol. 263–70.

——. 1957b. The interpretation of the learned. S.K. Belvalkar vol. 47–62.

——. 1958. Review of Renou 1942. GGA 212.19–49.

——. 1962. Chess and backgammon (tric-trac) in Sanskrit literature. W. Norman Brown vol. 204–16.

——. 1964a. Die Kobra bei Pāṇini. KZ 79.55–68.

——. 1964b. Patañjali über Varuṇa und die sieben Ströme. Morgenstierne vol. 168–73.

——. 1971. Kleine Schriften, ed. by G. Buddruss. 2 vols. Wiesbaden, Steiner.

TIWARY, K.M. 1971. Asiddham bahiraṅgamantaraṅgam: a meta-rule of rule-ordering in Pāṇini's grammar. IL 32.241–57.

TRAPP, VALENTIN. 1933. Die ersten fünf Āhnikas des Mahābhāṣyam. Leipzig, Harrassowitz.

TRIPATHI, SAMBHUNATHA (ed.). 1971. Śākaṭāyanavyākaraṇa. Delhi, Bharatiya Jnanapitha Prakasana.

TRIPATHI, SAMBHUNATHA, and MAHADEVA CATURVEDI (eds.). 1956. Jainendra-vyākaraṇam by Pujyapāda Devānandi, with Jainendra Mahāvṛtti of Śrī Abhayānandi. Varanasi, Bharatiya Jnanapitha.

VAIDYA, P. L. (ed.). 1954. Prakrit grammar of Trivikrama with his own commentary. Sholapur, Jaina Samskrti Samraksaka Samgha.

—— (ed.). 1958. Prakrit grammar of Hemacandra. Poona, BORI.

VAN NOOTEN, BAREND A. 1967. Pāṇini's replacement technique and the active finite verb. Lg 43.883–902.

——. 1968. The grammarian Kātyāyana and the White Yajurveda school. IL 29.43–6.

——. 1969. Pāṇini's theory of verbal meaning. FL 5.242–55.

——. 1970a. The vocalic declensions in Pāṇini's grammar. Lg 46.13–32.

——. 1970b. Sanskrit *gaṃsyate*: an *aniṭ* future. JAOS 90.159.

—— (ed.). Ms. Āpiśaliśikṣā.

VARMA, SIDDHESHWAR. 1929. Critical studies in the phonetic observations of Indian grammarians. London, Royal Asiatic Society. Repr. 1961, Delhi, Munshiram Manohar Lal.

——. 1950. The Vedic accent and the interpreters of Pāṇini. JBBRAS 26.1–9.

——. 1953a. The etymologies of Yāska. Hoshiarpur, Vishveshvaranand Indological Institute.

——. 1953b. A plan for the evaluation of Pāṇini on the Vedic language. SPAIOC XVII 104–5.

——. 1953c. The Vedic limitations of the Siddhānta-kaumudī. SPAIOC XVII 105–6.

——. 1963. Scientific and technical presentation of Patañjali as reflected in the Mahābhāṣya. VIJ 1.1–36.

——. 1966. Review of Bhawe 1957–62. VIJ 4.94–105.

VASU, SRISA CHANDRA. 1891. The Aṣṭādhyāyī of Pāṇini. 2 vols. Allahabad. Repr. 1962, Delhi, Motilal Banarsidass.

——. 1906. The Siddhānta Kaumudī of Bhaṭṭoji Dīkṣita. 2 vols. Allahabad. Repr. 1962, Delhi, Motilal Banarsidass.

VENKATACHARYA, T. 1959. A critique on Dr. Agrawala's 'India as known to Pāṇini'. JUG 10.85–112.

VENKITASUBRAMONIA IYER, S. 1970. The difference between Bhaṭṭoji Dīkṣita and Nārāyaṇa Bhaṭṭa with regard to certain phonetic observations. VIJ 8.87–102.

——. 1972. Nārāyaṇabhaṭṭa's Prakriyāsarvasva: a critical study. Trivandrum, University of Kerala.

VIJAYAVENUGOPAL, G. 1968. A modern evaluation of Nannul (Eḻuttatikāram). Annamalainagar, Annamalai University.

VYAS, BHOLA SHANKER. 1959–62. Prākṛtapaiṅgalam. Prakrit Text Society Series, 2 and 4. 2 vols. Varanasi.

WACKERNAGEL, JACOB. 1914. Zur Bildung des 7. Aorists im Altindischen. KZ

46.273–5.

WACKERNAGEL, JACOB, and ALBERT DEBRUNNER. 1942. Vedische Zitate bei Patañjali. KZ 67.178–82.

WEBER, ALBRECHT. 1858. Das Vājasaneyi-Prātiśākhyam. IndSt 4.65–171, 177–331.

——. 1862. Zur Frage über das Zeitalter Pāṇinis. IndSt 5.1–176.

——. 1873a. Das Mahābhāṣya des Patañjali. IndSt 13.293–496.

——. 1873b. Remarks on parts X and XI [of IAnt 1]. IAnt 2.57–9.

——. 1873c. On the date of Patañjali. IAnt 2.60–4.

——. 1873d. On Patañjali, &c. IAnt 2.206–10.

——. 1875. On the Yavanas, Mahābhāṣya, Rāmāyaṇa and Kṛṣṇajanmāṣṭamī. IAnt 4.244–51.

WECKER, OTTO. 1905–6. Der Gebrauch der Kasus in der älteren Upaniṣad-Literatur verglichen mit der Kasuslehre der indischen Grammatiker. BB 30.1–61, 177–207.

WESTERGAARD, N. L. 1841. Radices linguae sanscritae. Bonn.

WEZLER, ALBRECHT. 1969. Paribhāṣā IV, V und XV: Untersuchungen zur Geschichte der einheimischen indischen grammatischen Scholastik. Bad Homburg, Gehlen.

——. 1972. Marginalien zu Pāṇini's Aṣṭādhyāyī, I. *Sthānin.* KZ 86.7–20.

——. 1973. Bestimmung und Angabe der Funktion von Sekundär-Suffixen durch Pāṇini. Wiesbaden, Steiner.

——. Ms. Some observations on the grammatical terminology of Pāṇini. Marginalien zu Pāṇini's Aṣṭādhyāyī, II. German scholars on India, 2. Delhi.

WHITNEY, WILLIAM D. 1856. Contributions from the Atharva-veda to the theory of Sanskrit verbal accent. JAOS 5.387–419.

——. 1862. The Atharvaveda Prātiśākhya or Śaunakīya Caturādhyāyikā. JAOS 7. Repr. 1962, Varanasi, Chowkhamba Sanskrit Series Office.

——. 1871. The Taittirīya-prātiśākhya with its commentary, the Tribhāṣyaratna. JAOS 9.1–469.

——. 1879. Sanskrit Grammar. Leipzig. 2nd revised ed. 1889; often reprinted.

——. 1884. The study of Hindu grammar and the study of Sanskrit. AJPh 5.279–97. Repr. IAnt 14.33–43.

——. 1885a. The roots of the Sanskrit language. TAPA 16.5–29.

——. 1885b. The roots, verb-forms, and primary derivatives of the Sanskrit language. Leipzig.

——. 1893a. On recent studies in Hindu grammar. AJPh 14.171–97.

——. 1893b. The Veda in Pāṇini. GSAI 7.243–54.

WILKINS, CHARLES. 1808. A grammar of the Sanskrita language. London.

WINDISCH, ERNST. 1917–20. Geschichte der Sanskrit-Philologie und indischen Altertumskunde. 2 vols. Strassburg; Berlin–Leipzig.

——. 1921. Philologie und Altertumskunde in Indien. [1917–20, vol. 3.] AKM 15, 3.1–38.

ZGUSTA, L. 1969. Pāṇini: descriptivist or transformationalist? In margins of two recent publications. AO 37.404–15.

CLASSICAL ANTIQUITY: GREECE*

JAN PINBORG

1. THE BEGINNINGS OF GRAMMAR

1.1 *Presocratic Speculations on Language*

Speculations on the nature of language arose early within Greek philosophy. The ability of language to depict reality adequately was soon questioned, most vigorously by Parmenides (5th century B.C.). This in turn provoked the famous controversy among the sophists who asked whether language — like other cultural phenomena — was given by nature (φύσει, *phýsei*) or by convention (νόμῳ, *nómō*).[1] The problem involved is the semantic question whether language corresponds to reality or imposes an arbitrary structure upon it. The sophists saw this problem exclusively in terms of the correctness of names. A one-sided acceptance of one view to the exclusion of the other, if ever held by anybody, was soon abandoned. Already Protagoras (cf. Plato, Protagoras 322a) seems to advocate a compromise which accepts that both factors play a role in the description of the relationship between names and reality, and an exact and balanced exposition of this solution was given in Plato's dialogue *Kratylos*. This attitude was preserved by all subsequent thinkers, even if their interpretations of what 'natural' correspondence might mean differed considerably (cf. Fehling 1965: 218f.; Pinborg 1961:124f.).

* For several reasons I have not been able to discuss exclusively the historiography of Greek grammarians within the last 25 years or so. Studies in this field have been few and sporadic. They have mostly been discussions on rather special subjects and have always presupposed a knowledge of the general accounts given in the 19th and the early 20th centuries. Moreover, the mines of information hidden in the excellent edition of the *Grammatici graeci* have so far not been exhausted. I have therefore found it more convenient to give an account of our present knowledge on the subject, thereby indicating where studies would be most welcome. The problems of demarcation have been great. I have decided not only to discuss what would today exclusively be considered topics of linguistics, but I have also included related disciplines which the Greeks found could not be separated from grammar. I regard this as a necessity, considering the fact that most of the grammatical concepts originated in some other or broader context, in logic, or in philosophy of language. The Stoics have received a rather more exhaustive treatment than the few fragments we possess seem to justify. Most of the literature on Greek grammar written in this century has in fact centered on the Stoics. And this with good reason. The science of grammar originated with the Stoics, and their approach to linguistic problems was to be characteristic for a large part of what in antiquity was termed Greek grammar.

[1] The general background of this theory is given by F. Heinimann (1945). Cf. also W. K. C. Guthrie 1969 (204–23), which gives a well-balanced report of the state of question.

Most of our sources for this controversy are of Neoplatonic origin. In their usual way the Neoplatonic commentators tried to systematize the transmitted doctrines, and in the case of philosophy of language they took as their frame of reference the dichotomy of *physis* versus *thesis*. This model however must be used with care. The Neoplatonists themselves were often more interested in the exposition of systematically possible doctrinal positions rather than in a correct evaluation of historical sources. Furthermore, the opposition between *physis* and *thesis* tends to effect a confusion of two different problems, the semantic problem outlined above and the problem of the origin of language. As a matter of fact the Neoplatonists were often confused in this regard and many modern scholars have followed them in this.

This confusion was perhaps latent in Greek thought which always tended to confuse explaining a phenomenon with giving an account of its origin. In Greek linguistic thought etymology was continuously used as a device for semantic explanation. Nevertheless the two problems were never so entangled as to make the acceptance of a natural correspondence between words and things dependent on a natural origin of language. Two fundamentally different theories of the origin of language existed (cf. especially Fehling 1965). The most widespread of the two saw the origin of language in the efforts of one or more givers of names, who tried to make names as effective tools as possible. This theory is found with minor differences from Plato via Aristotle and the Stoa to the Neoplatonists, often combined with a theory of etymology which uses onomatopoetic explanations and distinguishes between original and derivate words (cf. Fehling 1965:222–3; Pinborg 1961:125f.; below, 2.6.2).[2] It was ridiculed by the advocates of an empiricist solution who dispensed with the impossible giver of names and instead saw the creation of language as the collective action of an evolving society. The best representative of this theory is Epicurus.[3]

Common to both theories was the so-called stoicheion theory of language according to which language is seen as an atomic system where elements are added together into more and more complex systems: syllables, words, and sentences, but where a tendency to explain everything from the nature of the elements prevails, thus effacing the boundaries between the different levels of language (cf. especially Gentinetta 1961:61f., 98f.). This tendency was first opposed by Plato and Aristotle.

More detailed investigations into language and its structure were caused by the sophists' principal aim of teaching how to speak well. This called for an interpretation of the authoritative texts of the poets. Even if their interpretation cannot be called interpretation by any modern standards (cf. Pfeiffer 1968:32f.) it resulted in some valuable grammatical observations.

As has been rightly stressed (Robins 1967:12–13), the invention of the Greek

[2] The general background of this conception is the theory of the first inventor of sciences; cf. W. Spoerri 1959. For the importance of the distinction between primitive and derivate words (πρώτη vs. δεύτερα θέσις), cf. J. Pinborg 1972:24f.

[3] The most important literature on Epicurus' philosophy of language is the Lucretius editions of C. Giussani (1896–98:I, 267f.) and of C. Bailey (1947:III, 1486–96). Further Ph. de Lacy 1939:85f. and P. H. Schrijvers 1970, especially 91–127; C. W. Chilton 1962:159–67; A. A. Long 1971a.

alphabet was a first specimen of acute linguistic observation. Further observations in phonetics followed: in Plato's *Kratylos* a distinction between vocals, semivocals and consonants is presupposed, and Xenokrates (Plutarch, *Quaestiones Convivales* VIII, 9,733 A), and later Ariston of Chios (cf. Gentinetta 1961:112–13) play with the idea of combinatorics in constructing and calculating the syllables which can be formed from the elements. This approach which has some affinity to phonemic analysis remained preponderant in Greek phonological analysis (cf. Pagliaro 1956:140–5), whereas phonetics in the strict sense was less satisfactorily developed (cf. Robins 1967:24f.).

Protagoras was aware of some grammatical distinctions such as that between different types of sentences (answer, question, command, prayer; cf. Koller 1958) and that between the genders of the noun, and Prodikos gave analyses of synonyms, but we have no reason to suspect any developed grammatical systematization.

1.2 *Plato*

Plato's most comprehensive account of language is to be found in the dialogues *Kratylos* and *The Sophistes*. But the chief importance of these dialogues lies in their contribution to logic and philosophy, less in their contribution to grammar.

In the *Kratylos* Plato shows the impossibility of using language as a direct evidence of the nature of things. Language is a tool, a tool which may be improved, but it can never take the place of philosophy or dialectics. In the preceding pages mention was made of the place of this conception within the development of the philosophy of language, and some elements of linguistic importance were likewise mentioned.

The literature on the *Kratylos* is legion. A survey covering the years 1950–57 was offered by Cherniss (1959:75–9). From recent literature I should like to refer to the following papers: Demos 1964; Ackrill 1963; Lorenz and Mittelstrass 1967; Weingartner 1970; Kretzmann 1971; Derbolav 1972, with extended bibliography.

In the *Sophistes* some improvements are made, the most important of which affects the theory of predication. Here (262 A) we find for the first time a definition of subject (*ónoma*) and predicate (*rhễma*)[4] respectively as that which applies to 'what performs actions' and that which applies to 'actions', even if the subsequent development shows that some confusion between the concept of word class and that of syntactic constituent is at work. Plato's theory of the intermingling of ideas made possible a theory of predication which does not conceive of a sentence as a mere juxtaposition of words, but also envisages different semantic roles to be played in order that a sentence may be generated. For literature on the *Sophistes* I again refer to Cherniss and should like to add Wiggins 1970.

[4] The distinction is mentioned in the *Kratylos* at 425a with no explanation, and may thus have been known before Plato.

1.3 *Aristotle on the Parts of Speech*

1.3.1 *General remarks*

Aristotle nowhere left a coherent exposition of his thoughts about language. His doctrine must be collected from scattered remarks in his voluminous writings. Nevertheless his importance to the development of grammar was immense. The best all-round description has been given by McKeon (1946–47).

Most relevant to the history of grammar are the introductory chapters of *Peri hermeneias* and the enigmatic Chapter 20 of the *Poetics*. In both places Aristotle offers an enumeration of the 'parts of speech'. The two expositions are not identical, but differ according to the different aim of the texts. In *Peri hermeneias* Aristotle is concerned with the logical analysis of statements and therefore only mentions the meaningful parts of speech (*mérē tou lógou*): noun (*ónoma*), verb (*rhḗma*), and sentence (*lógos*); whereas the *Poetics*, which aims at an analysis of the vocal level of speech, gives a more comprehensive and exhaustive list of the *mérē tḗs léxeōs*: letter (*stoicheîa*), syllable (*syllabḗ*), conjunction (*sýndesmos*), article (*árthron*), case (*ptṓsis*), *onoma, rhema, logos*. This list shows that Aristotle is not describing word classes, but rather segments of speech. As every significant part of speech according to Aristotle corresponds to some segment of speech I shall treat the different parts of speech according to the order in the *Poetics*.

1.3.2 *The non-significative segments*

The non-significative (*ásēmoi*) segments according to Aristotle include the level of phonetics (letters and syllables) and the 'level' of particles (grammatical vs. lexical words).

Aristotle developed the phonetical distinctions of his predecessors and added some elementary observations on the articulatory basis of sounds. He seems to have considered letters 'passions of the voice' which were defined as being distinctive and combinable. Human speech alone can be articulated in this way which accounts for the fact that we know of various human languages, whereas all other animals can only utter sounds in accordance with their specific nature (cf. Pagliaro 1955:140–5; Engels 1962:90).

The syllable is defined as the combination of consonant(s) and one vocal; there is, however, a textual difficulty in this definition.

The definitions of the two following segments of speech are hopelessly corrupt. The generally printed text is the following (the segmentation is that of Gallavotti 1954):

a) the *syndesmos* is a non-significative expression

b) which neither prevents nor effects (the formation of) one significative expression out of several expressions

c) apt to be placed along with other signs at the ends or in the middle (of a sentence?)

d) which cannot stand absolutely first in the sentence

e) as *men, étoi, de*

f) or a non-significative expression

g) which is apt to effect one significative expression out of at least two significative expressions

h) the *arthron* is a non-significative expression

i) which shows the beginning, end, or division (*diorismós*) of a sentence

l) as e.g., *to phēmí* (or *to amphí*) and *to perí* etc.

m) or a non-significative expression

n) which neither prevents nor effects (the formation of) one significative expression out of several expressions

o) apt to be placed at the ends or in the middle

As rightly emphasized by Gallavotti (1954) the main difficulties are: 1. Aristotle here gives alternative and even contradictory definitions of the same segments of speech or gives the same definition to different segments; and 2. that later rhetorical and grammatical traditions (cf. notes 12–13 below) tell us that Aristotle only knew three parts of speech, not including the *arthron*, and that Aristotle nowhere else uses *arthron* as a technical term. (1) is by far the stronger argument for corruption, as (2) is counterbalanced by the fact that Aristotle's contemporary, Anaximenes of Lampsakos (*Rhet. ad Alex.* 1435 a 35) and later the Stoics knew *arthron* as a technical term for a separate part of speech, exemplified by the deictic word *houtos*.

This state of affairs has produced various attempts at a solution, none of which is wholly convincing. One reaction is to declare the whole chapter spurious (latest Lohmann 1953).[5] There are, however, so many points of contact between the 20th chapter of the *Poetics* and the *Peri hermeneias* that I find it difficult to believe that the chapter as a whole is written by some later grammarian. Steinthal's argument in this connection (1890–91: I, 265) that any later grammarian would have made a better job of it than the pioneer Aristotle also seems plausible. Another type of solution argues that any mentioning of *arthron* is a later interpolation which leaves us with several definitions of the *syndesmos*. Rostagni, in his commentary on the *Poetics* (1945:117), and Pohlenz (1939:162) suggest that Aristotle had different sub-classes of conjunctions in mind, though it is very difficult to achieve any precise results. So far the most ingenious solution along these lines is that of Gallavotti (1954), who takes *arthron* in a non-technical sense, changes the 'or' (ἢ) of (f) to 'the' (ἡ) before which he with some support within the textual tradition inserts 'for not' (οὐ γὰρ), and deletes (m)-(o) which is redundant. With some minor adjustments he arrives at the following text:

a) the conjunction is a non-significative expression

[5] Koller's hypothesis (1958:29) to the effect that Aristotle's *syndesmos* means copula is only possible under this supposition. But even so it is in conflict with Aristotle's use of the term *syndesmos*, which always means conjunction or connected words.

b) which neither prevents nor effects (the formation of) one significative expression out of several expressions

c) apt to be placed along with other signs at the ends or in the middle

d) which cannot stand absolutely first in speech

e) as e.g. *men* or *de*

f-g) for the expression which is apt to effect one significative expression out of at least two, already significative expressions, is not non-significative

h) but the non-significative expression is a mere connecting link (*arthron*)

i) which is used to mark the beginning or the end of a sentence or an interval (*diorismos*) between two significative expressions

l) as examples, I can mention *kai* and *hóper*.

This solution, however, has some awkward points. Gallavotti explains (b) so that a *syndesmos* (= conjunction) can be omitted or added without any effect upon the construction of the sentence. This limits the meaning of 'syndesmos' to the particles, which is possible of course, but it leaves the Aristotelian enumeration of segments far from exhaustive. The worst problem, however, is that it is difficult to see which significant segement of speech Aristotle envisages in (f-g).[6]

Finally, a third type of solution tries to save both *arthron* and *syndesmos*. The best and most courageous attempt was made by Pagliaro (1955:88–103). At least some of his interpretations cast a genuine light on the text though the interpretation as a whole can hardly be accepted. He explains the double definitions as a result of Aristotle's wish to define the segments both from a lexical-morphological point of view and from a logical-syntactic. This interpretation has its drawbacks though. It is difficult to see how the element (c-d) of the first *syndesmos*-definition can be morphological or lexical. Even if (b) and (g) are not overtly contradictory they look more like an attempt at a division than like two complementary definitions of the same. Furthermore, the morphological definition of *syndesmos* and *arthron* are substantially identical. Finally, Aristotle's definitions of the other segments of speech are not formally divided according to these two approaches.

Most impressing are Pagliaro's interpretations of (b) and (i-l). According to him (b) is a rather clumsy attempt at describing the concept of 'consignificance', e.g., that the connectives are non-significative in themselves but can be part of a significative complex and are as such able to signify along with and according to the significative segments with which they are combined. This at least agrees with the interpretation of Neoplatonists and the grammarians (cf., for example, *Commentaria in Aristotelem*

[6] In this unobtrusive place I shall venture a suggestion. If we in (c) read πεφυκυῖαν with manuscript tradition, it is not the *syndesmos* which is thus determined but the prevented or effected unit of meaning. This unit of meaning can enter into a syllogism as a major, minor (ἐπὶ τοῦ μέσου) or middle (ἐπὶ τῶν ἄκρων) term. A unit of meaning of this kind must come into existence through nominalization. Nominalization is not prevented nor effected by a *syndesmos*. The article on the other hand always effects nominalization. This would account for the function of the opposition between (c) and (g), but it still leaves a lot of the text to be explained, and I do not see how except by using some very vehement philology.

Graeca IV, 5, 11 and Priscian, *Grammatici Latini* II, 54,7). In (i-l) Aristotle describes the function of the article and the demonstrative pronoun which is to determine the source (subject), the goal (object), and the modality of the action; the latter is exemplified by *amphí* and *peri* which are not instances of *arthra* but indicate the anaphorical and the deictic function of the demonstrative pronouns respectively. Aristotle uses a similar linguistic device in the *Rhetorics* (1457 a 19), where he indicates the different cases by mentioning the different caseforms of the demonstrative pronoun. If (i-l) is really a definition of *arthron* and not of the *syndesmos* this proves an ingenious solution.

It might seem preposterous to use so much space to report the failure of scholars to understand these definitions from the twentieth chapter of the *Poetics*. But perhaps we can here gain an insight into the difficulties which Aristotle encountered when trying to define the segments of speech, and to achieve an understanding of the criteria he envisaged when setting about this task: his analysis is not an analysis of formal linguistic features on the level of expressions, but an analysis conducted in terms of meaning and logic.

1.3.3 *The significative segments*

The definitions of noun and verb in the *Poetics* are identical with those given in the *Peri hermeneias* except for one point. Where the *Poetics* speak of them as composed *synthetḗ*, the *Peri hermeneias* uses the term *kata synthḗkēn*, which is generally translated as 'according to convention' or 'arbitrarily'. J. Engels (1962) has shown that a translation of *kata synthḗkēn* as a synonym of *synthetḗ* gives by far a better sense in the context of *Peri hermeneias.*[7] This, of course, does not imply that Aristotle did not accept the conventional theory of language, but only that he was not thinking about it when he defined a noun, a verb, and a sentence in the *Peri hermeneias*. The opposition here is not between nature and convention, but between natural inarticulate sounds and articulate sounds achieved through combination.

Common to noun and verb is that they are both minimal significative units. They are to be distinguished in so far as the verb additionally signifies the present time. This concept of 'additionally signifying' (*prossēmaínein*) was to play a prominent role in Medieval speculative grammar.

According to Aristotle verbs can be resolved into the corresponding participle and the copula. This makes a verb a kind of name for accidents which are inherent in the subject, which however also signifies the inherence by means of the implicit copula.

[7] Engels does not know of any previous explanation along these lines. However Nikephoros Blemmydes, the Byzantine philosopher of the 13th century, in his logical epitome (*Patrologia graeca* 142, 888 A) offers the same explanation. Even if this is a late testimony it shows that the explanation was felt to be linguistically possible by someone speaking Greek. Coseriu's interpretation (1969:68) — that Aristotle intends to say 'der Name ist Laut der als eingerichtet bedeutet' thus emphasizing the historical facticity (*Gegebensein*) of meaning — is interesting, but appears to me to strain the Greek wording.

The copula thus is what constitutes a sentence and accordingly plays a pivotal role in Aristotle's philosophy.

The semantic conception involved in these definitions and their context is rather primitive.[8] The written symbols are arbitrary signs of the spoken symbols which are arbitrary signs of the mental concepts which in turn are natural 'likenesses' of the things themselves. This conception presupposes a theory of natural 'forms' according to which the forms embodied in the things and giving them their nature is grasped directly by the intellect. The semantics of the *Peri hermeneias* thus depend rather heavily on Plato, which can be observed also from the fact that Plato uses the same term (*páthēma en tē psychē*, 'passion in the mind') for the concepts which are imitated by words (*The Republic* 382 B). The semantics of the mature Aristotle as expressed especially in the *Metaphysics* are much more sophisticated. They were, however, not to play any important role in the development of grammar, at least not until the Middle Ages.

Both in the *Peri hermeneias* and in the *Poetics* Aristotle distinguishes sharply between noun and verb on the one side and *ptosis* on the other. He reserves the terms noun and verb for the basic function of these word classes, viz. to be subject and predicate in a simple sentence in the present indicative. *Ptosis* signifies any deviation from this basic form. Barwick (1957:46) enumerates all the various examples of *ptosis*: case, number, mood (or rather linguistic tasks of the sentence, cf. 2.4.3), tense, derivations (adverbs, adjectives, etc.).[9] This is the generally accepted range for the term *ptosis* in Aristotle. Pagliaro (1955:108f.), however, thinks that Aristotle also included the basic forms under *ptosis* and interpreted them all as deviations from the indefinite noun (*aóriston*) or verb which is to be identified with the lexical item which has as yet not received any grammatical modification. It is difficult to see how this interpretation can be connected with the explicit formulations of Aristotle as to the descriptions of *ptosis* and the indefinite noun and verb in the *Peri hermeneias*.

The meaning of the metaphor *ptosis* (= 'fall') has given rise to many fanciful explanations in the grammatical literature of ancient and modern times. The most famous explanation is that of Sittig (1931), which takes it as a metaphor from the play of astragalus or from the play of dice. Barwick (1933) has strong reservations concerning this hypothesis, especially because Sittig presupposes a developed grammatical theory in the 6th century B.C., and because originally the term *ptosis* was not limited to the cases. Another (late) explanation was from the stilus which may fall perpendicularly or obliquely. A good summary of these discussions has been given by Hiersche et al.

[8] For a very interesting and relevant discussion of the doctrine of the *Peri hermeneias* I refer to Ackrill's commentary (Oxford, 1963).

[9] In Chapter 21 of the *Poetics* Aristotle mentions some species (εἴδη) of the noun for which he does not use the term *ptosis*. He distinguishes simple and compound words and nouns of different genders. The latter are divided according to their different terminations. Aristotle probably here develops theories of the Sophists. It is interesting to note that the grammarians were later to use this principle of division as a starting point for their flexional canons.

(1955), who finally accept the rather vague use of the term to signify a change of word form, normally expressed by the composite verb *metapiptein*.

Aristotle's definition of the sentence is not very satisfactory, as it also includes the phrase: 'A sentence is a significant expression, part of which is significant in separation.' Aristotle, however, clearly has the simple sentence in mind.[10] In the *Peri hermeneias* he is especially interested in statements which can be defined by their admitting of truth or falsity, something which nouns and verbs in isolation can never do. He does not attempt to extend this description to the other types of sentences. For a further discussion of these problems I refer to Ackrill's commentary on the passages in question.

Even if Aristotle's conceptualization within the field of language may be severely criticized, his importance cannot be overestimated. He created the frame within which the problems of language were to be discussed for the following centuries. It may be said that his contribution to grammar is small, but grammar as it was then developed in Greece is unexplainable without Aristotle.

2. THE STOICS

2.1 *The sources*

A decisive role in the development of grammatical theory was played by Stoic philosophers from Zenon (335–263) onwards, especially by Chrysippos (280–207) and his pupil Diogenes of Babylon (240-150). Unfortunately no authentic Stoic text on grammar has come down to us; we have to rely on doxographical reports incorporated into later grammatical and logical manuals, and on a few direct quotations. This material includes:

1. A short, but systematical exposition by Diogenes Laertius (4th century A.D.).[11]

2. A historical survey discussing how and why and by whom the different parts of speech were distinguished. This exposition has come down to us in the version of Tryphon (later half of 1st century B.C.), probably through Apollonios Dyskolos (see *Grammatici Graeci* II, 3, 30f.).[12] Most of the fragments on Stoic parts of speech in the *Grammatici Graeci* and *Grammatici Latini*[13] are dependent on this doxographical report (according to Fehling 1957: 52–3).

3. Some reports on the Stoic doctrine of case, tense and predicate types, transmitted

[10] His remarks on what makes a sentence one, and on compound sentences are very obscure (cf. Ackrill's commentary on chapter 5. Cf. also Brekle 1970).

[11] Main chapters of grammatical interest: *Vitae philosophorum* VII 55–9; 63–8; 71–3. This exposition probably goes back to Diokles Magnes (1st century BC) and seems, at least for 55–9, to draw heavily, but not exclusively, on the τέχνη περὶ φωνῆς of Diogenes of Babylon.

[12] A slightly different version is to be found in rhetorical tradition: Dionysios of Halikarnassos (contemporary of Tryphon), *De compositione verborum* c.2 (p. 6) and Quintilian (end of 1st century AD), *Institutio oratoria* I, 4, 18–21.

[13] *Grammatici Graeci* I, 3,214, 18f.; 356, 7f.; 517, 33f. *Grammatici Graeci* II, 1,5, 13f. *Grammatici Graeci* II, 2,43, 14f.; 94, 12f.; 436, 24f. *Grammatici Latini* II (Priscian), 54, 5f.; 548, 1f. I do not include other instances from *Grammatici Latini*, as they offer nothing new.

both in grammatical and logical tradition;[14] the most extensive ones reflect the combined teaching of grammar and logic in the Neoplatonic school of Alexandria.[15]

4. Finally, some direct quotations from later Stoic writers, namely from Poseidonios (1st century B.C.)[16] and from Chairemon (time of Nero),[17] transmitted through Apollonios Dyskolos, all concerning the divisions of conjunctions.[18]

The character of this tradition indicates that some caution is necessary. Though it may be taken for granted that most of the material in the doxographical reports refers to the elder Stoics, it often happens that the reports themselves use a terminology alien to the Stoa. This often leads to misinterpretations, especially when it is not clear whether a given term is used in its Stoic or, say, Aristotelian or Platonic meaning. The danger is immanent with the Neoplatonic commentators and with the grammarians as well. Moreover, the reconstruction of Stoic thought must necessarily make use of other sources where Stoic influence is suspected, in order to make a coherent interpretation of the scattered fragments possible. This method has been masterly, but often too optimistically used by Barwick (1922, 1957). It must not be forgotten that the discussion of linguistic topics did not take place within or between hermetically closed 'schools', so that a Stoic answer and an opposing Alexandrian one exist for any grammatical question. I find, like Fehling (1958:173), that it is more useful to look upon hellenistic grammar as a unity, to the development of which each school contributed research, but not totally different versions. J. Mau (1957:147f.) has shown that the same interpretation can be applied to the development of hellenistic logic. Actually, in every hellenistic techne, including philosophy, we meet an eclectic tendency to incorporate the findings of every school into a common picture. So we cannot from the Stoic flavor or Stoic elements of a text conclude that we possess a genuine Stoic fragment which can be used directly as a testimony of the Stoic contribution to grammar. Despite these difficulties the reconstruction of Stoic grammar remains of very great importance for the history of linguistics.

[14] *Case*: *Commentaria in Aristotelem Graeca* IV, 5 (Ammonios, 5th century A.D.), 42, 30f. *Commentaria in Aristotelem Graeca* XVIII, 3 (Stephanos, 7th century A.D.), 10, 22. Cf. also *Stoicorum veterum fragmenta* I, 65. *Tense*: *Grammatici Graeci* I, 3 (Stephanos), 250, 26f. *Grammatici Latini* II, 414, 26f. *Mood*: *Diogenes Laertius* VII, 66f. Sextus Empiricus *Adversus mathematicos* VIII, 70f.; *Commentaria in Aristotelem Graeca* IV, 5 (Ammonios), 2, 26f. Martianus Capella IV, 391. *Grammatici Latini* II, 421f. *Grammatici Latini* V (Macrobius, 4th century A.D.), 611, 36f. *Voice*: *Grammatici Graeci* I, 3:230, 27f. *Grammatici Graeci* II, 1,115, 9f. *Grammatici Graeci* II, 2,403, 1f.; 430, 1f. *Grammatici Latini* III (Priscian): 211, 19f. *Commentaria in Aristotelem Graeca* VIII (Simplikios, 7th century A.D.), 310, 13f. *Commentaria in Aristotelem Graeca* XVIII, 3, 11, 8f. *Commentaria in Aristotelem Graeca* IV, 5, 44, 11f. *Diogenes Laertius* VII, 65.

[15] For this double aspect of Alexandrinian teaching see di Benedetto (1958:171f.).

[16] Though Schneider and others (*Grammatici Graeci* II, 1, fasc. 2:217) identify this Poseidonios with a pupil of Aristarch's, I have no doubt that the famous Stoic of the 1st century B.C. is meant, as implicitly acknowledged by Pohlenz (1939:165). Camerer (1965:202), too, argues for this solution. The doctrine of the passages is specifically Stoic, and according to *Diogenes Laertius* VII, 60 Poseidonios wrote περὶ λέξεως εἰσαγωγή. He is also known to have worked on logic.

[17] *Grammatici Graeci* II, 1, fasc. 2,248 gathers all evidence on Chairemon.

[18] *Grammatici Graeci* II, 1,214, 4f. (Poseidonios, cf. *Grammatici Graeci* II, 2:488, 1f.). *Grammatici Graeci* II, 1,248, 1f. (Chairemon, cf. also *Grammatici Graeci* I, 3.212, 24f.). *Grammatici Graeci* II, 1,213, 9f.; 218, 20f.; 250, 15f.; 251, 19f. (all unspecified).

The 'fragments' were first collected by R. Schmidt (1839), but not all of them are included in von Arnim's *Stoicorum veterum fragmenta* (*SVF*). The most thorough interpretations of the fragments are those given by Pohlenz (1939), Müller (1943), and Barwick (1957).

2.2 *Grammar and Logic*

Before discussing the fragments in detail, it is worth discussing their place in the Stoic system of philosophy. It must first be stated that the Stoics did not conceive of any science corresponding exactly in scope and methods to grammar in our sense. Thus it is not surprising that we have no Stoic definition of grammar.[19] What we call grammatical problems were treated by the Stoics within the field of logic. This is a consequence of the Stoic conception of logic which again is dependent on their theory of meaning. They distinguish three components in the analysis of meaning:[20] 1. the sign or the expression signifying (*sēmaínōn* or *phōnḗ*); 2. what is signified (*sēmainómenon* or *lektón*); and 3. the object referred to (*tynchánon*). The expression and the object are corporeal entities (*sōmata*), while what is signified is incorporeal (*asṓmatos*) and thus cannot act upon anything. The *sēmainómena*, accordingly, must not be identified with the concepts. 'In Stoic theory acts of thought are private physical modifications of the *hēgemonikón* ('soul') but the sense of words in which they (i.e., the concepts) are expressed is immaterial, objective and something which others can grasp' (Long 1971:83–4).

Stoic logic is concerned with two of these components, expressions and what is signified, and consequently falls into two sections, the *tópos peri phōnḗs* and the *tópos peri sēmainoménou*, of which the former was considered dependent on the latter. The *topos* of linguistic expressions (*peri phonḗs*) also included the study of rhetorics and poetics as well as certain parts of logic (predicables, divisions, amphibology; see *Diogenes Laertius* VII, 44 and 45). The *topos* of linguistic contents or meanings also included the study of propositions and logical forms (*Diogenes Laertius* VII, 43 and 69). This means that what later grammarians and we bring together under one title, 'grammar', were two different approaches to language for the Stoics. To the doctrine of expression belonged the studies of phonology and morphology, whereas the study of case, tense, mood, and predicates belonged to the theory of meaning.[21] This was clearly understood by Schmidt (1834), but was forgotten by later interpreters, except

[19] The definition of grammar which Marius Victorinus (*Grammatici Latini* VI, 4, 7) quotes from Ariston cannot be ascribed to the Stoic Ariston of Chios of the 3rd century B.C., but seems to reflect a later stage of grammatical discussions (see Barwick 1922:220).

[20] Sextus Empiricus *Adversus mathematicos* VIII, 11–12 (= *Stoicorum veterum fragmenta* II, 166). My interpretation here and in the following is dependent on Müller (1943), Mates (1953), Christensen (1962), Kneale and Kneale (1962) and Long (1971).

[21] Cf. also the list of Chrysippean writings (*Diogenes Laertius* VII, 190f.) which is ordered according to the two topoi, thus dividing the 'grammatical' writings of Chrysippos according to the indications above.

Müller (1943). It is apparent, however, that these different approaches may account for several of the difficulties of interpreting Stoic 'grammar'.

2.3 *Ptosis*

2.3.1 *Ptosis as meaning*

It seems relevant to start with a discussion of meanings before considering the reflection of meaning-categories in the language expressed. Now, meanings or *lekta* are either complete or deficient. Unfortunately we find no exact definition of completeness; *Diogenes Laertius* VII, 63, gives the most explicit account: complete meanings are those which have a completed expression, as, for example, 'Socrates writes'.[22] A deficient *lekton* leaves a question in the mind of the hearer ('Writes' — 'Who writes?') or as Augustine says (*Dialectica* c.2) '*expectat aliquid ad completionem sententiae*'. Complete *lekta* are either atomar or molecular propositions. An atomar proposition consists of subject (*ptṓsis*) and predicate (*katēgórēma*), molecular propositions are characterized by containing a conjunction (*sýndesmos*). Because of the crucial place thus conceded to *ptosis* and *kategorema* an extended discussion of these two concepts seems appropriate. Though they primarily belong to logic it will appear that they were to play an important role in the development of Greek grammatical theory.

The *lekta* seem to function in the same way as the concepts and propositions of Aristotle. They are common, objective entities, and the universals with which scientific thinking is concerned are identified as *lekta*. But in contrast to what Aristotle thought, they are not likenesses of the objects referred to. There exists nothing which corresponds to a *lekton*, only individual somata exist. This is explicitly stated for some kinds of meanings, viz. predicates and propositions in an important letter from Seneca (ep. 117, 13). As regards the subjects (*ptoseis*) of propositions there seems to be some doubt. As the proposition which is a complete *lekton* is said to consist of *ptosis* and *kategorema* (Plutarch, *Quaestiones platonicae* 1009 C), most interpreters take *ptosis* to be one kind of deficient *lekta*, predicates another. A. A. Long, however (1971:105), takes *ptoseis* simply to be the 'means of referring' to something, not deficient *lekta* at all. As a proof of this, he mentions: a. that *ptoseis* are never mentioned as instances of deficient *lekta*; and b. that nouns are said to signify qualities which according to Stoic ontology are corporeal. Thus Long emphasizes the difference between subjects and predicates: they have different semantic roles corresponding to their different grammatical functions. But I doubt whether this observation allows the conclusion that *ptoseis* are not (deficient) *lekta*. Actually, Sextus Empiricus (*Adversus Mathematicos* VIII, 11 and 75) mentions *Dion* as an instance of a *lekton*, though he might at least at VIII, 11, as Long thinks, mean to say '... is Dion'. Augustine, however, does give subjects as examples of deficient *lekta* (*Dialectica* 2). Furthermore it must not

[22] Τὰ ἀπηρτισμένην ἔχοντα τὴν ἐκφοράν, οἷον Γράφει Σωκράτης.

be forgotten that the *ptosis* itself is conceived of as something incorporeal,[23] i.e., it is not identical with the thing referred to nor with the noun as a sign; but then it has to be a meaning. Haller (1962) and Mates (1953:36) give an instructive example: Chrysippos stated (*Stoicorum veterum fragmenta* II, 220a) that the proposition *this man is dead* is impossible, since *this man* always refers to something existing in virtue of the deictic pronoun *this*; but the proposition *Dion is dead* is possible. I take that only deictic pronouns refer in the strict sense, whereas nouns always signify something along with their reference, in this aspect partaking in the properties of a predicate;[24] this *significatum* or *ptosis* can be used as a subject, regardless of the actual existence or non-existence of the object referred to.

Therefore, when nouns are said to signify qualities I think it imperative to interpret these qualities as meanings, as is done by Mates (1953:17) and Christensen (1962:50). This interpretation is confirmed by a passage in Simplikios (*Commentaria in Aristotelem Graeca* VIII, 105,7f.; *Stoicorum veterum fragmenta* II, 278; cf. also *Stoicorum veterum fragmenta* I, 65) where the Stoic understanding of common qualities is discussed. We must consider, says Simplikios, how the *ptoseis* are expressed in language according to the Stoics, how they call common qualities 'nothings' (i.e., meanings), and how we are led into the sophism *Nobody* when we do not realize that not every entity in the category of substance signifies an individual. *Ptosis* and quality thus seem to be two words for the same, with quality implying the physical reality behind language, *ptosis* the logical structure as seen in itself.

The same distinction between meanings that refer to existing individuals and those that do not stand for anything outside of language is used by Klemens in the passage mentioned above.[25] Klemens here solves the sophism 'What you say passes through your mouth. You say *house*. Therefore, a house passes through your mouth' by distinguishing the *soma* and the *ptosis* of the house, i.e., the house as existing and the house as meaning. The same distinction is used by Galen when solving the sophism *Nobody* mentioned above (*Stoicorum veterum fragmenta* II, 153), though he uses the

[23] This is stressed by Müller (1943:46f.), who mentions Plutarch, *Quaestiones platonicae* 1009 C and *Diogenes Laertius* VII, 192 as (indirect) evidence. Add to this Klemens Alexandrinus (*Stromata* VIII, 9, 96, 23f., Stählin), where it is explicitly stated that *ptṓsis* is an *asṓmaton*, and Sextus Empiricus *Adversus Mathematicos* XI, 28f., where *ptṓsis* is called a *sēmainómenon*. Both passages will be discussed below.

[24] Cf. Cicero, *Lucullus* 21f., where propositions with deictic pronouns as subjects and adjectives as predicates are considered basic, whereas propositions containing nouns are derivate, i.e., imply an activity of the intellect (for this activity cf. below, 2.6.1).

[25] I translate the section in full as it is not printed in any of the collections of fragments: 'According to this the causes are causes of predicates (κατηγορημάτων) or as it is said by some 'of lekta' — Kleanthes and Archedemos call the predicates *lekta* — or to put it better: some causes are causes of predicates, as, e.g., τέμνεται, the *ptosis* of which is τέμνεσθαι, others are causes of propositions as, e.g., that *a ship is built* (ναῦς γίνεται), the *ptosis* of which is ναῦν γίγνεσθαι. Aristotle, however, says that they are causes of nouns (προσηγοριῶν) as, e.g., of a house, a ship, a fire (καύσεως), a cutting (τομῆς) (cf. Sextus Empiricus *Pyrrhōneioi Hypotypōseis* III, 14). The *ptosis* is incorporeal, as everybody will concede. Thus the following sophism is solved: 'What you say passes through your mouth' which is true; 'you say a house, thus a house passes through your mouth', which is false. We do not speak of the house which is corporeal but of the incorporeal *ptṓsis*, which refers to the house (ἧς οἰκία τυγχάνει).'

term *ousía* instead of *sôma* (cf. also Augustine, *De magistro*, c.8). What is spoken about in the minor premisses of this sophism is not the extramental thing, but the meaning (*ptosis*) itself.

In the same passage of Klemens we find two incidental remarks according to which the *ptosis* of a finite verb is its infinitive, and the *ptosis* of a proposition its corresponding accusative with infinitive. The traditional interpretation that *ptosis* here has its wide meaning flectional form, in case mood, has no point as Klemens explicitly defines *ptosis* as a meaning, not a form. *Ptosis* must accordingly be interpreted as any meaning which functions as object of reference, including meanings that substitute for other meanings and have no exact counterpart in reality, as is the case with the infinitive which is used when the verbal meaning shall function as subject-term. On the level of expressions this corresponds to the description of the infinitive-form as the name of the verb or as the most 'general' verb (*Grammatici Graeci* II, 1,129,16f. Cf. also *Grammatici Graeci* II, 2,43, 5–16; 45,13–46,2).

Here we find *in nuce* a theory of types which is part of a theory of ambiguity (see below, 2.6.4). Analogous passages can be found in many later Neoplatonic texts (cf. Pinborg 1972:21. Further: Augustine, *De dialectica*, c.9f. *De magistro*. Marius Victorinus, *De def.* c.2). As it is very difficult to assess which parts of the doctrine can be attributed to the Stoa, and as the doctrine is of more logical than grammatical mportance, I shall refrain from further discussion.

2.3.2 *The notion of case*

What has been said on *ptosis* so far does not throw much light on the grammatical notion of *ptosis* 'case'. Nevertheless I think that the preceding observations are necessary as preliminaries to the question: what did the Stoics mean when they used *ptosis* in connection with the case forms of the nominals? This question has caused a good deal of discussion. It is generally conceded that the Stoics must have meant something different from Aristotle, because they included the nominative among the cases but on the other hand excluded all non-nominal inflections.

Some of the proposed interpretations of the metaphor 'case' have been discussed above in connection with Aristotle (1.3.3). I shall here discuss the interpretations of Barwick (1933), Pohlenz (1939), and Müller (1943), together with some etymological explanations offered by Neoplatonic commentators. I should like to say in advance that we cannot be sure that the Stoics had one and only one etymology and explanation. They took over a current term and gave it a special meaning within their system, probably giving different etymological *ad hoc* explanations to justify their use. This at least conforms with Chrysippos' procedure in other cases (e.g., *Stoicorum veterum fragmenta* II, 1084).

Barwick begins by refuting the theories of Sittig (see above). For the Stoic use of the metaphor *ptosis* he accepts the interpretation of Ammonios (*Commentaria in Aristotelem Graeca* IV, 5, 42,30f., *Stoicorum veterum fragmenta* II, 164). Ammonios' text reflects discussions between later Peripatetics and Stoics, where the Peripatetics could only accept the use of *ptosis* for the oblique cases, because they 'fall from' the nominative, whereas it would be a *contradictio in adiecto* to call the nominative a fall, because it has nothing from which it can fall. To this the Stoics are reported to have answered that all case forms fall from concepts in the mind; when we want to express this concept the word forms fall from the soul, then first to the nominative, the archetype of the other cases.

Pohlenz (1939:169–71) criticizes this interpretation for the following reasons: 1. 'Dieses Bild ist für das Verhältnis von Gedanken und Wort der Stoa sonst durchaus fremd.' It is an instance of the general theory which distinguishes an 'internal' *logos* from an 'external', the former corresponds to the concepts, the latter to the spoken or written word. Pohlenz (1939:191f.) has proven that this theory does not belong to the Stoa but rather to the Peripatetics or Platonists, though others (Mühl 1962), but without sufficient evidence, have tried to attribute it to the Stoa; 2. This metaphor is not consistent with the Stoic use of *ptosis* for the nominals only. As was already shown by the Neoperipatetics this explanation can be used to show that every 'extern' word is a *ptosis*, also verbs, conjunctions, etc. Therefore, Pohlenz regards this explanation as a 'nachträgliche, gekünstelte Rechtfertigung'. I think this must be the case, especially because *ptosis* in this explanation is interpreted as a flectional form, and not as a meaning.

As a starting point for his own interpretation Pohlenz takes the distinction between *orthē* and *plagiai ptoseis*. We have no evidence that the Stoa ever thought of the metaphor from the play of astragalus (see above, 1.3.3). For Pohlenz *orthos* means *Normalfall*, while *plagios* is used when the noun is governed by the verb and thereby pressed away from its normal disposition (*Haltung*). Thus Pohlenz has to admit that the use of *ptosis* for the nominative is abusive, and he explains this by the assumption that the meaning of the term *ptosis* already was so *abgeschliffen* that the original image no longer prevented the use of the term for the nominative. Pohlenz here agrees with the common interpretation of the grammarians (except Apollonios; cf. *Grammatici Graeci* II, 3, 65–6). As we saw above this comes also very close to the general interpretation of the term given by Hiersche et al. (1955).

Perhaps Pohlenz' observation on the *Abgeschliffenheit* of the term *case* is confirmed by some further mutually exclusive explanations of *ptosis* given by Sextus Empiricus and Simplikios. Though both explanations are ascribed to the Academy, their contexts show a strong Stoic flavour, though it is impossible to say whether they reflect explanations of the old Stoa. Sextus (*Adversus Mathematicos* XI, 28; cf. Long 1971:105) uses *ptosis* as a meaning under which the denotata of the term 'fall'. Simplikios (*Commentaria in Aristotelem Graeca* VIII, 209, 10f.) brings *ptosis* into etymological connection with the verb *tyncháno*. Here the meaning 'fall' seems altogether discarded and replaced by the meaning 'being grasped by' (the external object) which places *ptosis* in the semantic triangle described by the Stoics.[26]

[26] ἐκάλουν ... τὰς πτώσεις τευκτὰς ἀπὸ τοῦ τυγχάνεσθαι καὶ ⟨τὰ⟩ κατηγορήματα [καὶ] συμβάματα ἀπὸ τοῦ συμβεβηκέναι. Does the *tynchanon* of Stoic semantic theory after all not mean 'what we happen to be talking about' (Long 1971:107, note 9) or 'whatever happens to exist' (Pohlenz 1955:

Traglia (1956:65) agrees in general with Pohlenz. He, too, regards the interpretation offered by Ammonios as a rational afterthought. Nevertheless, he attaches some importance to an alternate explanation given by Ammonios in the same place (but in a passage excluded by the editor Busse) and by Apollonios Dyskolos (*Grammatici Graeci* II, 3:65–6) that the case-form falls from some general noun which is undetermined as to grammatical determinations. There is no direct evidence that this is a Stoic answer; it might, however, reflect the sensible conception that the *ptosis* of a noun is one general meaning which may be realized differently in different propositions. This is probably what Schmidt (1839:59) had in mind when he gave the definition *significatio quatenus variis modis in ipsis enunciatis comparere possit.* This explanation also explains the fact that the nominative is a 'fall'. Pagliaro (1955:125), however, thinks that this *aóriston ónoma* is part of the Aristotelian doctrine, but I do not find his argumentation conclusive (see above, 1.3.3).

A fresh and original approach to the matter along these lines was given by Müller (1943:94f.). He interprets the relation between *ptosis* and predicate (*kategorema*) as that between cause and effect. His main evidence is Sextus Empiricus (*Adversus Mathematicos* IX, 211; *Stoicorum veterum fragmenta* I, 89): The noun is cause, for some object, of a predicate. The relevance of this approach is confirmed by the context of the Klemens fragment discussed above, where the causes are precisely the topics discussed. Now, according to the Stoa, every cause is a physical object (*soma*), while the effect is probably a state of the *soma* or *somata* involved (see below, 2.4.1). The *ptoseis* are reflections of these *somata* on the level of meanings. They correspond as *aitiai* (causal explanations) to the corporeal *aitia* (cf. *Stoicorum veterum fragmenta* II, 336). The nominative corresponds to the most important cause (the *synektikón*), which is the efficient cause which cannot be absent if the effect is to take place. The oblique cases correspond to other 'falls' of causes. Müller's interpretation has the advantage that it gives a reason why only nominals have *ptoseis* and supplements a general concept (cause) which justifies the use of *ptosis* for the *orthos* and *plagiai* cases. I think his interpretation is fundamentally right in its description of the semantic role ascribed to *ptoseis.* But I doubt whether the interpretation of *ptosis* as 'fall of the cause' can be upheld. There is no evidence for this concept and the exact correspondences of the oblique cases in the realm of causes may very well be questioned (see below, 2.3.3).

I would suggest the following tentative conclusion: The cases are various 'cases' of one nominal (i.e., referential) meaning being used in different contexts reflecting different relations between the objects in question, the most important (*orthos*) being

II, 22)? Has it a transitive meaning 'Whatever gets (a meaning in order to be expressed)'? Cf. the Klemens text in the preceding note: πτῶσιν ... ἧς οἰκία τυγχάνει. A close parallel is Aristotle, *Eudemian Ethics* 1241a16: τυγχάνοντες ταύτης τῆς προσηγορίας (I owe this reference to Johnny Christensen). Ammonios (*Stoicorum veterum fragmenta* II 166 and 236) also takes *tynchanon* in an active sense, but here it is the objects referred to which are grasped by us. This does not seem to be consistent with the active form *tynchanon.* The explanations of *tynchanon* seem to be as many as those of *ptosis* and as hard to disentangle.

that of referring to the agent cause of an effect. To illustrate this conception of case various metaphors have been used, of which probably none was as old as the term itself — the Stoics have taken over an already established term.

2.3.3 *The number of cases*

The Stoics enumerated five cases. Four of them are certain and well-documented: the nominative, the accusative, the genitive, and the dative. But what was the fifth? Two candidates appear: the adverb and the vocative. We have no direct evidence for either.

It seems natural to vote for the vocative, as this was the case which was later accepted as the fifth by the grammarians. Steinthal (1890–91: I, 302 *Amn.*), however, detected a difficulty. A vocative is equivalent to a proposition; it is a complete meaning according to the examples given by *Diogenes Laertius* VII, 67. Hjelmslev (1935) also argues convincingly that it is very difficult to give a consistent description of case which also includes the vocative. This is a serious difficulty which is not solved by Pohlenz (1939:169) when he says that the syntactical relations within meanings do not prevent the formal inclusion of the vocative among the cases of the noun. We saw, however, that the *ptoseis* cannot be distinguished formally (i.e., according to their vocal form) because they are meanings.[27] The same goes for Barwick's solution (1933:592) that Chrysippos accepted the vocative as a case-form without case-meaning. Steinthal's suggestion of listing the adverb as the fifth case also has the advantage of accounting for the adverb which is difficult to place within the Stoic system of parts of speech (see below, 2.9.2).

Nevertheless, the Stoic approach was not always consistent, as we shall see in several cases. They separated categories of meaning, but they were often inclined to depart from factual formal-linguistic distinctions which were thought to embody distinctions and connections of meanings. So they might after all have accepted the vocative as a case, because it had 'kinship' (*syngéneia*) with the nominative and the accusative, and because it was included in the paradigms of nominal inflections being used in schools (for an example of this see Pohlenz 1939:175). Müller (1943:117f.) accordingly explains the vocative as a meaning which corresponds to a situation in which the person calling (the nominative) and the person being called (the accusative) are involved. Thus it should have a certain internal kinship with these two cases.

The meaning and concept of the nominative and the vocative was referred to above. The nominative is the upright (or normal?) case, where the noun is used in its primary function of referring to the agent or to give him a name. Hence it is often called *onomastikḗ*. The vocative is used in the calling situation, hence *klētikḗ* (from *kaleín* 'to call').

The meanings of the terms for the oblique cases have been discussed intensely ever

[27] Cf. *Grammatici Graeci* (I, 3:551, 11f.) where *ptosis* is conferred to the level of meaning because one case of one word may have several phonetic representations. Consistently employed, this must imply that every morpheme (or *accident*) is a unit of meaning. This conception is part of the Stoic heritage to Greek grammar.

since antiquity. Generally speaking, there seem to exist two kinds of explanations for these case-names, one explaining them from some common use of the case (what Hjelmslev [1935:6] calls the principle of *metonymi*), and one trying to give a more general semantic description of the nature of the case. De Mauro (1965:171) very relevantly asks if we possess any evidence that suggests whether this latter explanation is historically possible, i.e., if it can be shown that the theory of cases is older than the grammarians and if it originated in a philosophical context where the semantic explanation alone seems possible. He answers in the affirmative: We have evidence that the philosophers of the 4th and 3rd centuries had a knowledge of the five cases, and we have evidence that the names were not uncommon and disputed in this same period. Moreover, it must be emphasized with de Mauro (187) that Aristotle and the Stoics did not impose arbitrary names upon their technical terms but rather *nomi parlanti*. So the road is free to attempt a semantic explanation of the case-names. We possess some starting points in the grammatical tradition of antiquity. An enumeration of all the sources from antiquity which discuss the meaning of the case-names can be found in de Mauro 1965 (189–92).

The accusative or *aitiatikḗ*. The metonymic explanation derives this case from the verb *aitiásthai* 'to accuse'. This is probably also the explanation for the Latin form *accusativus*. Most Greek scholiasts, however, agree that it has something to do with *aitía*, or cause. Trendelenburg (1836), Pohlenz (1939), and de Mauro (1965) think of the Aristotelian term *aitiatón* 'effect', so that the accusative signifies the effect of the cause signified by the nominative. If the term is of Stoic origin this explanation is imprecise and Müller must be right in opposing it. The effect in the strict sense of the word is not a corporeal object but has to be a predicate according to the Stoa. So the accusative cannot be identified with the effect but must, in agreement with the indications of the scholiasts, be interpreted as a cause. According to Müller it corresponds to the accessory, material cause (*synaitía*) which is indispensable in any act of causation (as the object acted upon). This *synaitía* is in some cases identical with the agent and might then be left unexpressed (cf. 2.4.2). De Mauro, however, interprets his effect in exactly the same way, so the explanations are perhaps not so different after all.

For the genitive, *genikḗ*, several etymologies are mentioned. Most scholiasts accept the metonymic derivation from the general Greek usage of name-giving where the genitive expresses the father's name. Another theory put forward by the grammarians (e.g., *Grammatici Graeci* I, 3, 384,5f.) takes the genitive as the (formal) source of the other oblique cases; this is hardly Stoic as it only reflects formal considerations. Pohlenz (1939:172–4) will derive it from *génos*, not in its metonymic sense as proposed by Steinthal (1890–91: I, 302) who thinks of the fact that the genus to which something belongs is expressed with the genitive, but in the sense that the genitive is the most general of the oblique cases, because it can be constructed with every part of speech. Müller derives it from *gignesthai* and interprets the genitive as the case denoting the ultimate source of the effect (the *aitía prokatarchtikḗ*); there is no antique evidence of this, nor can the explanation account for the general use of the genitive.

De Mauro finally accepts Steinthal's interpretation, but emphasizes the semantic generic relation, not the accidental fact that some such constructions are used.

As regards the dative, *dotikḗ*, de Mauro was the first to posit the problem why this case has so far only been given a metonymic explanation from constructions with the verb *didōnai* 'to give'. He justly remarks that this is an asymmetry which ought if possible to be removed, especially as the term *dotikós* 'what is given', does not express the receiver adequately, and as it is the receiver who is in the dative in the construction with *didomi.* The dative accordingly must be interpreted as the case of what is given, i.e., of what is not the end of the action, but the 'given' conditions under which the action is realized. There is one late text which offers some support to this interpretation (*Ars anon. Bernensis, Grammatici Latini*, VIII, 87: *Dativus aliquid extrinsecus addi demonstrat vel accedere*). It is possible that Müller with his identification of the dative with the synergon-cause, has the same in mind though he chooses the translation *Gebeursache.*

The most general opposition within this system of case is the opposition *orthós*: *plagíos.* Apollonios (*Grammatici Graeci* II, 2, 236,7f.) interprets this as an opposition *enérgeia*:*páthos.* This seems to correspond, moreover, to the Stoic division of the *kategorema* (2.4.2), and it seems natural to take the accusative as the most direct expression of the pathos (witness the de Mauro/Müller interpretation of the accusative given above). However, the genitive is also a serious candidate for the position of being the most important oblique case; it is placed immediately after the nominative in the paradigms, it expresses the agent of the passive clause, and it is called 'general'. The conclusion from this must be, in agreement with Hjelmslev (1935:8–9), that the Greek grammarians did not possess any definite conception of the oppositional relations of the cases. According to Hjelmslev (11f.) the localist interpretation of the cases given by Planudes is systematically the most satisfactory case-theory of Greek grammar. According to this, the dative is the unmarked case, whereas the accusative and the genitive are marked for approach and withdrawal, respectively. This theory, however, is certainly older than Planudes. It goes back at least to Heliodoros (*Grammatici Graeci* I, 3, 549,23f. 8th century) and possibly goes as far back as Apollonios Dyskolos (cf. *Grammatici Graeci* II, 3, 68). But there is no reason to connect it with the Stoics.

2.4 *Kategorema*

2.4.1 *Kategorema as meaning*

The other part of the proposition, the predicate (*kategorema*), is distinguished from the *ptosis* by having an indefinite reference. It does not denote anything if it is not connected with a *ptosis*; then *ptosis* and *kategorema* together denote an individual *soma.* The *kategorema* is that which is said of the *ptosis* or what is effected in it. It is said to be the case (*hypárchein*) when the effect signified really lies in the object denoted. In this case the Stoics seem to speak of accidents or occurrences (*symbebē-kóta*; cf. *Stoicorum veterum fragmenta* II, 509).

The Stoics distinguished a compound and a simple predicate (*sýntheton* and *ásyntheton*). A simple predicate is that which is signified by a verb (*Diogenes Laertius* VII 58). A compound predicate, accordingly, must be either a noun with copula (*A is B*), as Pohlenz thinks (1939:166 with reference to *Stoicorum veterum fragmenta* II, 199, which however does not apply),[28] or the combination of a verb and an oblique case, as Müller thinks. I am inclined to follow Müller, especially as we nowhere find a Stoic discussion of a proposition of the copula type. This, however, leads to two difficulties: 1. How did the Stoics explain a copula proposition? and 2. How can a *ptosis* (even an oblique one) be part of a predicate?

We have some evidence that universal copula propositions were interpreted as compound propositions (man is an animal → if something is a man, it is an animal, cf. Christensen 1962:90). This still leaves the propositions of the type: pronoun + copula + predicate to be explained. A theoretically possible explanation is that copula + predicate is to be interpreted as a hidden verb — this would be the exact opposite of the Aristotelian analysis of the predicate which reduces the verb to copula + participle. To the Stoics, in fact, participles and verbal substantives were equivalent nominalizations of verbs (cf. *Grammatici Latini* II, 548,148, together with *Grammatica Graeci* I, 3:518,17). Moreover, every noun expresses a quality and is thus in a sense always a predicate, and as predicates according to Stoic ontology always express something which happens, the prototype of a predicate must be a verb: *Dion walks → This is Dion* (→ *this has all the movements which we characterize by* '*Dion*') and *this walks*. Here, however, we are on very uncertain ground.

Neither do I know an answer to how a *ptosis* may be part of a predicate. There seems to be an inconsistency in the fact that the *ptosis* denotes and the predicate does not, except through a *ptosis*. This inconsistency, however, was probably blurred by the fact that a predicate containing an oblique case though denoting the affected object was still predicated of the agent. I should like to add that Vincent Ferrer, a Medieval logician, whose semantics show definite similarities with the Stoic doctrine, is subject to the same difficulties (cf. Trentman 1969:955).

What seems to me important and certain in these speculations is the fact that the Stoics offer a highly abstract theory of linguistic description, which involves several levels, that by means of a sort of transformation must in principle be reduced to a basic level containing semantic primitives, the most important of which seem on the subject side to be *this* (*hoútos*) and *some* (*tís*) (cf. below, 2.7.2) and on the predicate side *moves* or analogous expressions (cf. Christensen 1962:49).

[28] Barwick (1957:19) agrees with Pohlenz and refers to SVF II, 153, but this is unwarranted, too. Ἄνθρωπός ἐστιν is not a predicate but a proposition with dubious reference (cf. 2.3.1 p. 81).

2.4.2 *Types of predicate* (*voice*)

The Stoics distinguished several types of predicate.[29] (I am here following the exposition of Müller which is by far the most explicit and coherent.)

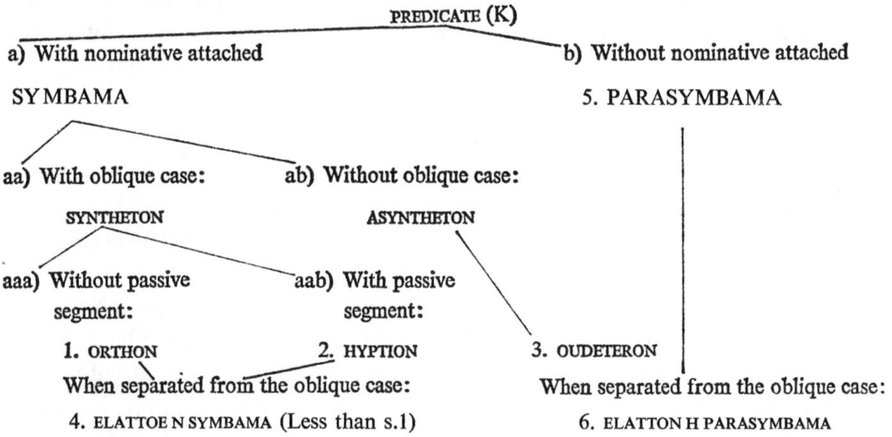

Ad 1. A *kategorema* or *symbama orthon* is a transitive predicate in the wide sense, i.e., a predicate which requires one of the oblique cases attached in order to effect a complete statement. Lest we should forget that we are speaking of meanings, not of word-forms, Diogenes exemplifies transitive predicates by referring to both active and passive forms: *akoúei, dialégetai.* This type of proposition reflects the typical causal scheme: A (*casus rectus*) causes something (predicate) in respect of (*pros*) B (*casus obliquus*). For this parallel, cf. Simplikios (*Commentaria in Aristotelem Graeca* VIII, 310,13f.). Both the agent and predicate verb have the same character (*diáthesis*), namely the active (*energētikḗ*).

Ad 2. A *hyption* predicate is the predicate of a passive proposition, characterized by the passive segment, by *hypó* (cf. Steinthal 1890–91 I, 299 and Müller). We note that meaning distinctions are judged by the presence or absence of certain linguistic forms (cf. 2.5). Again here we find the same diathesis in subject and verb, this time the passive (*pathetikḗ*):

Ad 3. *Oudeteron* is a predicate which expresses the pure *poíēsis*, i.e., does not include another cause except the agent who in a sense can be said to act on himself (cf. *Stoicorum veterum fragmenta* II, 979).

It is manifest that these distinctions have something to do with the later distinctions of voice: active, passive and neuter. The term *diathesis*, which should later become the technical term for voice, seems, however, not to be used in this technical sense yet. As we shall see, the term was originally also used to describe modal relations perhaps even relations of tense.

Naturally we find no trace of the voice *deponens* with the Stoics as it is not a category of meaning but an anomaly in the sense that expression and meaning do not corre-

[29] For the sources cf. note 14 above.

spond (Pohlenz 1939:179). Our sources, however, mention one further type of predicate, the 'reflexive' (*antipeponthós*) which Diogenes Laertius refers to as to a special form of 2. His example is *keíretai* (he cuts or has his hair cut off), and his definition a type 2 predicate which nevertheless is an action (*enérgēma*) because the agent includes itself in the sense that it is acted upon by itself or in respect of itself. Thus this type of predicate seems to be the passive counterpart of 3. It is obvious that some such description is the starting point for the concept of medium, 'which is in a sense both active and passive' (cf. *Grammatici Graeci* I, 3, 245,28f.).

Ad 4. The examples show that 'less than a *kategorema*' are transitive verbs without their complement.

Ad 5. *Parasymbama* or *parakategorema*. We have here a type of predicate without a subject in the nominative case. Nevertheless we seem to have a complete statement. It might be asked if the distinction between *kategoremata* and *parakategoremata* is a relevant distinction of meaning. It might be another case of the Stoics being seduced by a distinction in the linguistic expression to establish different categories of meaning. The term *parasymbama* perhaps indicates that no feature is common to subject and predicate.

Ad 6. There is some doubt in the sources, whether this type is exemplified by the impersonal verb alone or by a transitive *parakategorema* without complement. We cannot see how the Stoics accounted for constructions as the accusative with infinitive or the *genetivus absolutus*. Perhaps they were called *asymbamata*, a term which is only transmitted in the garbled version of Priscian.

There is some confusion between types of predicates and types of propositions in these distinctions. Perhaps the doubly transmitted names, viz. *symbama* and *kategorema*, indicate that the Stoics originally distinguished predicates from constructions. Whichever is the case, there can be no doubt that although these distinctions were to result in the distinctions between the different voices of the verb, they were also relevant to syntax. Through the mediation of Priscian the Middle Ages took up the Stoic distinction and used the opposition transitivity/intransitivity to divide all possible constructions.

2.4.3 *Mood*

We have no evidence that the Stoics established the category of mood. But again we find in the Stoa distinctions of types of meaning which were later to play a role in the distinctions within this linguistic category. The Stoics elaborated the Protagorean and Aristotelian distinction of various speech functions.[30] According to the Stoa the central function of speech was embodied in the statement (*axíōma*) which was either true or false i.e. comparable to reality. This does not apply to the other types of complete meanings such as questions, commands, etc. We do not know how they treated these other functions of speech. There is some indication that they elaborated

[30] The most extended discussion of this subject is Aristotle, *Poetics* 1456b 9f.; cf. Koller 195 (819f.).

a system of questions which were to be asked in connection with every subject and were perhaps organized according to the categories. A reflection of this system can possibly be seen in the rhetorical doctrine of status (cf. especially Quintilian III, 6).

With these divisions categories of meanings rather than of sentences were envisaged which cannot thus be identified with strictly grammatical categories. Plutarch (*De repugnatia stoicorum* 1037D) gives an example of one sentence being associated with three different complete *lekta*, an *axioma*, a command and a prohibition. 'The Stoic doctrine seems to be that a number of distinct linguistic jobs can be performed by means of a single sentence, depending on which of the complete *lekta* associated with that sentence is actually communicated on a given occasion of its use' (Kretzmann 1967:364–5).

Nevertheless, it is clear that the *axioma* is most often associated with the indicative, the command with the imperative, the wish with the optative, etc. This association is clearly emphasized by later grammarians (e.g., Varro X, 31, where mood however still holds a special place as against the other accidents of the verb, and Martianus Capella IV, 391f.). In this connection it is suggestive that Apollonios Dyskolos distinguishes the mood of the question from the indicative (*Grammatici Graeci* II, 2, 349).

There is some further but slight evidence that the doctrine of mood as such originated with the Stoics. In a late fragment (*Grammatici Latini* V, 611,36f.) we are told that the Stoics called the indicative *orthos* and the other moods *plagiai* ('oblique'), employing the terminology we know from their doctrine of case. Furthermore the term *diathesis* which we have just discussed in connection with voice seems also to have some relation to mood. Apollonios Dyskolos uses *diathesis* of the moods (e.g., *Grammatici Graeci* II, 2:351,8f.), and *diathesis* here seems to express a state of the predicate corresponding to the linguistic job performed as opposed to the mere signification of the action involved. I do not understand how Hahn (1951:31) can translate it simply as 'distinction'. Choeroboskos (*Grammatici Graeci* IV, 2:5,4–7) states that the older grammarians did use *diathesis* both for voice and mood, the distinction between psychical (mood) and physical (voice) *diathesis* being of a later date. This corresponds to the Stoic doctrine where at least some of the latter verbal accidents are interpreted as expressions of states of the predicate in relation to the subject or the speaker. Apollonios (*Grammatici Graeci* II, 2:354,11) also speaks of *diathesis* in connection with tense. Camerer (1965:193) shows that *diathesis* was the technical term for specifically verbal meanings. It is no argument against this that Dionysios Thrax uses *diathesis* only in the restricted sense of voice, since it is disputed whether the treatise transmitted under the name of Dionysios Thrax is genuine (cf. 3.1). Apollonios in fact uses *diathesis* rather vaguely (cf. Hahn: 34) in a sense corresponding to the above suggestion. The infinitive was not a 'mood' in this sense, but was probably considered the name of the verbal act (cf. 2.3.1 and *Grammatici Graeci* II, 2:43, 14); the participle was probably considered a noun (cf. 2.4.1).

2.4.4 *Tense*

Perhaps the most effusively discussed section of Stoic linguistic thought is the distinction between the tenses of the Greek verb. Why did the Stoics take an interest in the analysis of tenses? Steinthal (I, 308) suggests that it grew out of their consideration of inference (*sēmeîa*; cf. *Adversus Mathematicos* VIII, 254f.) where they had to distinguish the tense of the propositions involved from the time of the inference itself. The latter is always present, because it is either true or false now, whereas the consequent may be future and the antecedent past and therefore do not exist now except as meanings. Past and future may be factual, but they are not real now (they do not *hyparchein*). Though the present time is fleeting and strictly speaking consists of both past and future, we choose to speak of a certain amount of time as present. (For an opposite but to my estimation false interpretation of time, see Hadot 1969; for a rejoinder to Hadot see V. Goldschmidt 1972).

From our rather scanty sources (cf. note 14 above) we learn that the Stoics called the present *enestṓs paratatikós* because it also stretches into the future (*parateínetai*). The imperfect they called *paróchēmenos paratatikós*, because he who uses the imperfect states that he has performed most of the action, but not completed it. Present and imperfect thus have a 'kinship' (*syngeneia*) because both are incomplete (*atelés*) or durative (*paratatikós*). The perfect was called *enestṓs syntelikós*, the pluperfect *téleios parōchēménos*. There seems to be no doubt that the distinction between *paratatikos* and *syntelikos/teleios* is to be interpreted as a distinction between action in progress and result (cf. Lohmann 1953:189, who aptly refers to Sextus Empiricus *Adversus Mathematicos* X, 91f.). We have no sure indication as to how the Stoics viewed the aorist and the future, but some of Stephanos' further remarks in the passage mentioned above (cf. note 14) may have Stoic sources. Pohlenz (1939:177f.) and Lohmann (1953:185) think that *aoristos* means 'undetermined with respect to the opposition complete/incomplete'). This is plausible, though the use of *aoristos* in the sense of 'undifferentiated' seems unprecedented within the Stoa. Barwick's interpretation (1957:53f.) that we do not know exactly when an action (as expressed by an aorist or a future) begins is derived from Stephanos, who says that it is uncertain whether the aorist should be determined by *palai* ('long ago') as to effect a pluperfect, or with *arti* ('recently') as to effect a perfect. It is a difficulty that Stephanos takes the aorist in opposition to perfect/pluperfect, as this does not agree very well with the Stoic system of distinctions. But Stephanos' words here are not explicitly ascribed to the Stoa and might reflect the later system of the grammarians, who distinguished 1 future, 1 present and 4 past tenses (more or less receding from the present time). This reinterpretation of the grammarians was followed up by a new system of nomenclature which effaced the Stoic pairs of opposition (cf. Barwick 1957:54f.).

The data of the sources have been brought into three different systems by modern interpreters, which can be schematized as follows:

1. Pohlenz (1939:177)

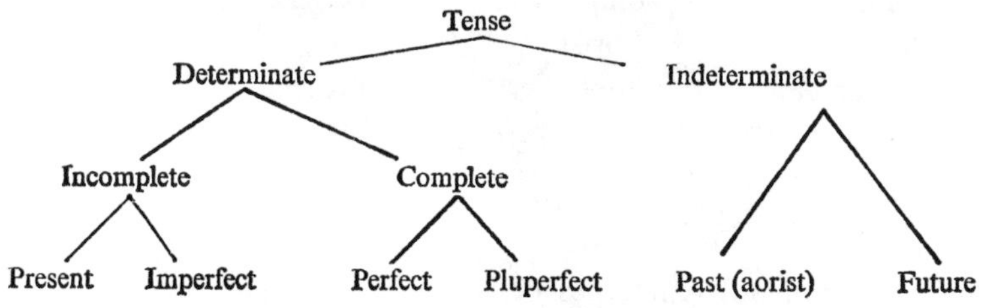

2. Lohmann (1953:185)

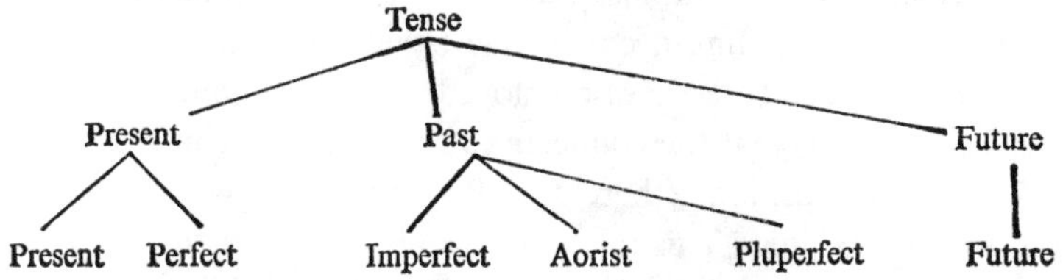

3. Barwick (1957:53)

	Tense		
	Present	Past	Future
Aspect regarding beginning of action:			
Undetermined:	0	Aorist	Future
Determined			
Aspect regarding end of action:			
a) Incomplete:	Present	Imperfect	Future
b) Complete:	Perfect	Pluperfect	Attic Future

Barwick's paradigm is perhaps unnecessarily complicated, and we have no evidence which helps to fill out or even establish the existence of the empty place in the system. The distinction between the two futures is supported only by slight evidence, though we find it in Varro and rather implicitly in Stephanos; but it was never common grammatical tradition. The double placing of the future is not satisfactory.

Lohmann's paradigm fails to account for the formal 'kinship' between the future and the aorist noticed by our sources. This is dismissed by Lohmann as a secondary theorization, but it corresponds rather well with the Stoic conception that kinship of forms expresses kinship of meaning.

Pohlenz' paradigm takes aspect as the fundamental division. This is against all evidence of the Stoic doctrine of time which departs from the temporal division of past, present and future. Also the terminology itself with the temporal terms as heads of construction speaks against Pohlenz' theory, as does the fact that the term *determinate* (*horismenos*) tense is not documented. A paradigm like the following thus seems indicated:

	Past	Present	Future
Complete	Pluperfect	Perfect	
Neutral	Aorist		Future
Incomplete	Imperfect	Present	

2.5 *Propositions and Connectors*

The Stoic divisions of different types of sentences also have grammatical interest, because they were based on a categorization of the different particles involved and were thus important for the grammar of particles and connectors.

The main division of propositions is into simple and compound propositions. The latter are defined by including a connective (*syndesmos*) and are accordingly categorized by the types of connectives employed. These of course reflect logical considerations, and it seems that the connectives were mostly defined by the truth tables of the compound propositions; there are also traces of interdefinability of the connectors (cf. Mates 1953:55). This raises the problem whether the connectives had any meaning of their own, for a discussion of which see below, 2.7.2.

The simple propositions were of several types, too. At least three different negative types were distinguished according to the kind of negative involved: (sentential) negation, negative pronoun or privativum; and three different affirmative types, according to the subject of proposition: indetermined (*aoriston*) with the subject *tis* 'somebody', determinate (*kategoreutikon* or *horismenon*) with the subject *houtos* 'this', and intermediate (*meson* or *kategorikon*) where the subject is a noun and therefore not necessarily deictic (cf. 2.3.1), but neither wholly indeterminate.

2.6 *Meanings and Expressions*

2.6.1 *Meanings and concepts*

It was stated above that meanings must not be identified with concepts *qua* psychical entities. This, however, does not imply that concepts and meanings have nothing to do with each other. On the contrary, meanings exist together with concepts, just as they exist together with expressions. Meanings are also conceptual contents of the concepts. Now, concepts are formed from impressions according to certain laws which partly describe mechanical processes in the impressions, e.g., they are combined, augmented, minimized or (wholly or partly) exchanged, partly describe some conditions under which these mechanical processes are to be effected (some sort of relation between the impressions involved must exist, as the changes are effected when the intellect compares impressions). Meanings, being correlative to concepts, can be described in an analogous way. Thus some meanings are derivative in relation to others and this derivation can be described in the same terms as were used for the derivation of concepts (cf. Barwick 1957:32–3).

2.6.2 *The natural correlation between words and things*

These considerations are important for linguistics, because the Stoics thought that linguistic change was analogous to derivation of concepts and meanings. The theoretical background for this was that the Stoics accepted the existence of isomorphism between the level of meaning and the level of expression. As Lloyd (1971:65) has remarked, this is really a semantic relation, but it was — rather infatuously, according to Lloyd — interpreted as an etymological relation. Actually, ancient etymology was more of a device for semantic description than a means of exploring the history of language.

It is Barwick (1957) who has treated this natural relation or isomorphism in greatest detail. In a previous paper I have followed him rather closely (Pinborg 1962). Now I should like to be more cautious. The main problem is that for his main sources Barwick uses Augustine and Varro. It is generally admitted that Augustine depends heavily on Varro, so we are left with Varro, who, as we shall see (3.2), is a source to be handled with extreme caution.

Now Barwick has without any doubt proved that in Varro and Augustine there existed a consistent theory of isomorphism which contained the following theorems:

1. It is necessary to distinguish primitive words from derivative words. The basis for this distinction is not phonetic nor is it in the strict sense semantic (as was the case in Aristotle's theory of *paronymi*, and in the corresponding Stoic theory of meanings), but it was rather constructed *ad hoc*, i.e., primitive words are such as fulfill the conditions denoted by theorem 2.

2. All primitive words are given by the giver of names as imitations of the things signified. This imitation may be onomatopoetic, synaesthetic (*mel*, 'honey', is equally soft to the ear and to the tongue) or gestural (when I say *nos*, 'we', the gesture of the lips points inwards, when I say *vos*, 'you', outwards).

3. From these primitive words derivate words are made, which are used to denote things which have some semantical relation to the things designated by primitive words. Augustine mentions three main semantic relations: similarity, proximity and contrariety.

4. Along with this 'translation' (*metábasis*) of words from signifying one thing to signifying another similar thing mechanical processes in the expression take place, according to the four principles mentioned above (2.6.1). Some of these correspond to our derivation, some to flexion, some have no linguistic relationship at all except a vague vocal similarity.

5. The so-called rhetorical 'tropes' are formed in the same way as derivate expressions but without any change in the expression.

6. Through these processes words are removed more and more from their origin or 'nature'. This is what makes anomaly possible, i.e., the state of affairs which we can observe that some words do not correspond to their meanings. In this way we use privatives for positive facts and conversely; we use sentences including but one word though complex in meaning, the subject being implicit in the verb, etc. (cf.

Stoicorum veterum fragmenta II, 151 and 177f.). The derivate words are only isomorphic with meanings as to the formal principles of change; they are no longer images of their corresponding meaning. The doctrine of anomaly apparently is a systematic development of Protagorean observations (cf. 1.1).

7. Nevertheless a semantic isomorphism remains, in the sense that an expression and its meaning are coordinate. Both expression and meaning are united in the sign taken as *logos* (cf. 2.6.3 and Pinborg 1962:164).

How many of these theorems can be attributed to the Stoa? Barwick (1952) thought that all of them were of Stoic origin but others have expressed some doubt. Theorems 1 and 2 are well-documented for the Stoa. 3 corresponds to the processes which are used to describe the formation of concepts (cf. 2.6.1). This Stoic description, however, includes more semantic relations than the three mentioned by Augustine. In this connection Schmidt (1960:249) has noted that the three concepts mentioned have an exact counterpart in Aristotle (*De memoria et reminiscentia* 451b, 19–20). So the Augustinian form of Theorem 3 might reflect a non-Stoic systematization. Other non-Stoic systematizations occur in Augustine's text (cf. Barwick 1957: 14 and 22 and Pinborg 1962:175). Probably the most general division of the text into *origo, vis, declinatio, ordinatio* is non-Stoic, too; cf. Lloyd (1971:58) and 2.7.3 below. Fehling (1958:167–8) has objected that these principles cannot be seen to function in any of the etymologies we know from Stoic sources. Minimally, this implies that they do not function within the Stoic doctrine in the same strict way as in Augustine. Nevertheless some sort of semantic relation between explicandum and explicatum must have existed also for the Stoics; cf. Theorem 3.

Ad 5. It is not possible to show that the theory of tropes was of Stoic origin. In fact, Fehling (1958) is able to show that it was of a different origin, and that the systematization which brought the tropes together with the doctrine of the origin of language is secondary. This, however, does not exclude the possibility that the Stoics themselves made this combination. The system of metaplasms, tropes and figures of speech and thought reconstructed by Barwick certainly has a Stoic flavor and reflects a courageous attempt to make order in the chaos of rhetorical devices as described by the textbooks. But Fehling is right to interpret it as a secondary systematization, not as the original theory.

Ad 6 and 7. It is a fact that the Stoics accepted a natural relation between expression and meaning, that they interpreted this etymologically, and that they had a theory of anomaly according to which words were not always images of their meanings.

Not every detail of the reconstructed system is necessarily Stoic, but there can be no doubt that the system owed a great deal to the Stoics. It is perhaps possible to say that it represents an 'idealized' Stoic system, developing implicit features of Stoic theory (cf. Pinborg 1962:151–2).

I shall refrain from further description of Stoic etymology which I do not find very interesting in itself. One modern critique of the theory exposed above deserves to be mentioned, as it sheds light on some central concepts of the Stoa with regard to language and grammar. Lloyd (1971:63f.) shows convincingly that there is 'a latent and unacknowledged conflict between the Stoic theory of meaning and the Stoic theory of etymology'. It is difficult to compare things and words, so in most cases you will have to compare meanings and words, thereby committing a fallacy as meanings cannot be grasped except as connected with thought or impressions or words. This would account for the fact that the etymological theory describes the derivation of words as a parallel to the formation of concepts.

A similar discrepancy is noted by Gentinetta (1961:77f.). The Stoic etymology tends to find meaningful relations between language and reality already on the level of minimal vocal elements and from there on through the more complex levels of language, thus following the stoicheia-theory of the *Kratylos* (cf. Barwick 1957:70f.), whereas the Stoic theory of meaning distinguishes sharply between the levels of language and does not ascribe any meaning to the lower levels (cf. 2.6.3). A word *qua* expression is not necessarily associated with any meaning (cf. 2.6.4). This suggests that the Stoics failed to separate their valid insight into the coordination of expression and meaning from a doubtful etymological theory of similarity between expression and meaning. Nevertheless this rather unhappy confusion had positive aspects, as it motivated Stoic logicians to search for categories of expressions corresponding to the categories of meanings. And this was to have important consequences for the grammatical theory of Greece (cf. 3.3).

2.6.3 *Levels of language*

As all Greek theoreticians of language the Stoics saw language as a hierarchy of levels (cf. *Stoicorum veterum fragmenta* II, 148; *Diogenes Laertius* VII, 55f.). On the lowest level we find pure sound. When articulated into phonemes, these may be combined, first into syllables, later into words and sentences. Only words and sentences can be associated with a meaning (thereby not, however, excluding the possibility of one phoneme being a word or even an [elliptical] sentence). The articulated sound, considered without its meaning, is called *lexis*; when the meaning is included the Stoics speak of *logos*. This is the interpretation of Traglia and Müller, whereas Steinthal (1890–91: I, 194) only accepts the use of *logos* for sentence + meaning. He seems, however, to be refuted by the fact that *lexis*, as shown by Müller from *Diogenes Laertius* VII, 59, stands for sentences (considered as phonetic strings) and by the explicit expression of Ammonios (*Commentaria in Aristotelem Graeca* IV, 5,13,7–9). Thus *lexis* becomes the formal object of the *techne peri phones*, in other words, of grammar. But as a consequence of the idea that distinctions of grammar had to be associated with distinctions of meaning, an interplay of these two levels can be observed in any part of grammar treated by the Stoics: meaning cannot be excluded from grammar. As we shall see, the so-called parts of speech were to play a pivotal role in this connection. In one sense they are the phonic material of *logos* that we find before us when we want to express ourselves. On the other hand they are always endowed with a meaning. This is probably the background of the Augustinian distinction between *verbum* and *dictio* (cf. *De dialectica* c.2f.) which has no exact counterpart in Stoic terminology.

Literary prose and poetry were considered to be a further level of language. The natural, 'straightforward' form of expression was thought to undergo certain transformations described by the four mechanical criteria mentioned above (2.6.1) with the intention of making a stronger impression on the hearer (cf. Pinborg 1962:167, 172).

2.6.4 *Ambiguity and disambiguation*

We have concluded that meanings and expressions are isomorphic in the sense that they coexist and have denotation together. We also concluded that an anomaly might nevertheless exist between the two aspects of the meaningful sign. How are we to assess the exact relation between word and meaning? Has every expression one and only one meaning? The existence of anomaly suggests that this is not necessarily the case, which is confirmed by the fact that Chrysippos states that every word (= expression) is ambiguous (Gellius 1913: XI, 12). We do not know much about the Stoic doctrine of ambiguity. It is a fact that they considered it part of the science of expressions, which is perfectly sensible since only expressions can be ambiguous. Thus, if we define 'word' as an expression associated with one and only one meaning we can have no ambiguous words. This was the standpoint of Diodoros Chronos (Gellius 1913: XI, 12), who says that we cannot utter an ambiguous word, because this would mean that we intended to say two things at the same time, which is impossible (this same point is made by Aristotle in his discussion of the principle of contradiction, *Metaphysics* III). When Chrysippos states that every word is ambiguous, he probably means that even if the speaker intends only one thing, the recipient cannot decide which meaning is associated with the word uttered and which linguistic job it is going to perform. Consequently the ambiguity can only be disambiguated from the context of the utterance. Augustine's *Dialectica* (c.8) gives some highly interesting examples of such disambiguating which seem to presuppose Stoic doctrine. The predicate may show us if the subject is intended to be used or mentioned (cf. the discussions in 2.3.1 and 2.4.3), or whether we use a word in its proper meaning or according to some translation (cf. 2.6.2).

2.7 *Formal Grammar*

2.7.1 *Phonetics*

Apparently the Stoics did not add anything significant to the Aristotelian distinctions of sounds. So it is no use to dwell upon their phonetics here. Perhaps it ought to be said that the Stoics in accordance with Aristotle but contrary to the Alexandrinian grammarians tended to regard sounds prior to the letters, as witnessed by their terminology, where the sound or phoneme is called *stoicheion*, whereas the letter is the 'figure' (*kharaktḗr*) of the *stoicheion* (cf. *Diogenes Laertius* VII, 57).

2.7.2 *The parts of speech*

According to general consensus the Stoics originally (or at least from Chrysippos onwards) acknowledged the existence of five parts of speech: *onoma, prosēgoría, rhēma, arthron, syndesmos.* They took over four of these from their predecessors and divided the noun into two parts, individual and common name. This division was imposed upon them by the importance which they attributed to the ontological distinction between common and individual qualities. Later Stoics — Antipater from Tarsos is expressly mentioned — added a sixth part of speech, *mesótēs,* the adverb or rather the adverbs derivated from nouns.

The *onoma* was defined by Diogenes from Babylon (*Diogenes Laertius* VII, 58) as a part of speech signifying an individual quality, e.g., *Dion.* The prosegoria was analogously defined as a part of speech signifying a common quality. For further discussion of these definitions cf. 2.3.1.

The *rhema* (verb) is defined as a part of speech which signifies a simple predicate (cf. 2.4.1). Diogenes Laertius adds another definition which is more formal, as it defines the verb by virtue of its having no case. The definition is probably of a later date though Steinthal (1890: I, 297) takes it to be the definition of Chrysippos (cf. also Pohlenz 1939:182).

The definition of *arthron* given by Diogenes Laertius is not expressly ascribed to Diogenes from Babylon, and I find it extremely improbable that the definition should derive from him. It defines *arthron* as if it only meant 'article' in the narrow sense, as a part of speech which shows the gender of the noun. This is quite out of character with the previous, purely semantic definitions. So it is probably a late definition influenced by the Alexandrinian grammarians. The original Stoic definition of *arthron* must be the one reflected in Apollonios Dyskolos (*Grammatici Graeci* II, 1, 9,9), according to which the *arthron* signifies existence (*ousia*) without quality, i.e. the mere existence of a denotatum. This agrees perfectly with the Stoic theory of the deictic and infinite pronoun (cf. 2.3.1) and with the fact that *arthron* was originally used of the deictic *houtos* (cf. 1.3.2). According to the Stoics there were two principal classes of *arthra*: definite and indefinite. This corresponds with their division of simple propositions according to their subject (2.5). The prototype of definite *arthra* was *houtos* ('that!'); the personal pronouns were probably associated with the demonstratives. The prototype of the indefinite *arthra* was *tis* ('some'). To this category belonged also the anaphoric *arthra* which were not strictly deictic but referred to an already mentioned object, e.g., the article and *ekeinos* (cf. *Diogenes Laertius* VII, 70). The interrogative and relative pronouns were probably also classified here (for sources cf. note 13 and Varro, *De lingua latina* VIII, 51, which Fehling [1958:165] does not understand perfectly). The distinction between pronouns and articles was not known to the Stoics, but was an accomplishment of later grammarians. If we trust Apollonios Dyskolos (*Grammatici Graeci* II, 1,5,18–19) even Dionysios Thrax did not distinguish pronouns and articles as two parts of speech (cf. 3.1).

As regards the conjunction (*syndesmos*) Diogenes Laertius again gives only a formal definition as a 'caseless part of speech which connects (other) parts of speech'. Again Apollonios brings us back to a discussion which involves a more semantic approach (cf. note 18). Some later Stoics insisted that the *syndesmoi*, which according to them included prepositions and preverbs, have a meaning. This appears from the fact that the *syndesmoi* are not interchangeable. It is not certain whether this reflects an old Stoic tradition since, as we have seen, some of the most important *syndesmoi*, the connectors of the compound proposition, were considered interdefinable and thus perhaps did not have any meaning of their own. On the other hand this 'extensional approach' to the connectors can refer to the fact that they have no denotation except in connection with noun and predicate; but this does not exclude that they have meaning. The Stoics seem to have established a comprehensive number of categories of *syndesmoi* in accordance with the claims of logic. Most of these categories are enumerated in *Diogenes Laertius* VII (71f.) and in Apollonios' treatise on the conjunctions (*Grammatici Graeci* II, 1, 213f.).

Whether the adverb, before being established as a separate part of speech, belonged to the noun or to the verb is difficult to decide. It has formal kinship with the nouns and was considered by Aristotle as a *ptosis* of the noun (*Topica* 106b29). Whether the Stoics followed him in this is debatable (cf. 2.3.1). They might also have considered it part of the predicate as it most frequently functions as a determination of the verb (hence the later name *epirrhēma*). An indication of this interpretation is given in *Grammatici Graeci* I, 3,95,20, where it is said that the philosophers called the adverb a *kategorema*, and perhaps in the description of the adverb as an adjective of the verb (*Grammatici Latini* II, 54,10). But already Apollonios was in doubt as to how the Stoics described the adverb. The Stoic Antipater's establishing it as a separate part of speech was probably influenced by the grammarians, but this was not to have any significance for Stoic semantics and logic. The examples offered by Antipater show that he only had in mind the adverbs which were derived from nouns. We find no mention of local and temporal adverbs.

We have noted above (2.6.3) that words could be considered at two levels, as formal entities (*lexeis*) and as significant elements of *logos*. This means that they may be categorized according to two principles. But there is no doubt that the definition according to semantic values was considered primary, owing to the fact that the expressions were isomorphic with and dependent on meanings (2.6.2). So the Stoic system of parts of speech is in principle an attempt to constitute the main semantic categories of human *logos*. As we have seen, they were often tempted to universalize the ascertainable expression categories of Greek.

There can be no doubt that the Stoic parts of speech correspond to fundamental Stoic categories of meaning, except perhaps the *syndesmoi* and the later established adverb. Moreover, there are obvious connections with the so-called Stoic categories, so that it is virtually certain that the categories must reflect the meaning categories as related to reality (Christensen 1962; Lloyd 1971). The categories are classes of denotata of meanings. In this sense they are all included in the first category of being; this reflects the fact that the other meaning categories only denote in connection with a pronoun. They are different types of names referring to the same *somata*, indicating different 'aspects' of the entity whose existence is acknowledged by the pronoun, approximately according to this paradigm:

arthron	*onoma*	*prosegoria*	*rhema*	
ousia	individual	common	simple predicate	
	quality (*ptosis*)			
			intransitive	transitive[31]
hypokeimenon	*poion*		*pōs echon*	*pros ti pōs echon*

2.7.3 *Accidents, inflection*

As we have seen, the Stoics established categories of meaning which somehow corresponded to several of the later grammatical parts of speech and their accidents. From this fact and from the exposition of Varro in *Lingua latina*, Barwick (1952) concluded that the Stoic *Techne peri phones* also included a discussion of virtually all accidents mentioned by later grammarians, except perhaps the accident of *figura*. This presupposes a notion of inflection which Barwick reconstructs from the Varronian discussions. According to him inflection (*klisis*) comprised both derivation and inflection in the latter sense; these two forms were later distinguished as extrinsic and intrinsic inflection, of which the former was irregular and the latter regular. Fehling (1958) has opposed this interpretation, mainly because he can find no other evidence than Varro for this comprehensive use of *klisis*. Aristotle's use of *ptosis* (cf. above, 1.3.3) for both derivation and inflection as well as the early grammarians use of the term *enklisis* in the same sense seem to support Barwick. Perhaps the two forms of systematic change on the level of expression are not as different as suggested by Fehling, especially not when the basis of the distinctions is an approach to language, the primary aim of which is to establish categories and dependencies of meanings. From this point of view both derivations and inflections modify the primitive meaning of the word. As Robins (1957:58) noted, even the Alexandrinian grammarians did not distinguish between inflectional and derivational categories in their listing of the accidents of the parts of speech.

Nevertheless I find Barwick's reconstruction of the Stoic theory of inflection too optimistic. I do not think that the Stoics made lists of inflections or even discussed them systematically. Lloyd (1971:58) has observed that inflection is not mentioned in the otherwise very comprehensive list of subjects covered in Chrysippos' grammatico-logical writings. Diogenes from Babylon may have included something on inflection, influenced by the Alexandrinian grammarians, but on the whole the *Techne peri*

[31] I here follow Christensen's suggestion (1962:50). Other scholars think that this category corresponds to the *syndesmos* which I find rather improbable as the *syndesmos* cannot be predicated of anything, and to be predicated was probably the function of the categories (cf. Lloyd 1971).

phones was probably a rather meagre compendium of the kind found in early grammatical papyri (cf. di Benedetto 1958:185f.) which only included definitions of the main categories with a few examples.

I also think that Barwick goes too far in vindicating the category of accidents for the Stoa. He thinks (1922:97f.) that the term accident (*symbebekos*) is the Stoic equivalent of the *parepómena* of the grammarians, in the sense of a secondary morphological category. But his evidence is very feeble indeed. He quotes a passage from Dionysios of Halikarnassos (*De Demosthene* c.52) which according to Barwick must be a piece of Stoic doctrine because the description of the letters uses Stoic terminology. If the Stoics invented and used the term accidents of grammatical categories, they cannot have had the thought in mind which Barwick (1952:48) imposes on them, viz. that the accidents signified accidental as against essential features of the parts of speech. This purely Aristotelian concept of accident is inconsistent with Stoic epistemology.

This problem is more important than it seems, because Barwick's whole reconstruction of the development of Roman grammar, as depending directly on the Stoics, not through Dionysios Thrax, demands that the Stoics had a concept of accidence and that they called it *symbebekos*. But if we, like di Benedetto, consider Dionysios Thrax' *Techne* spurious and Roman grammarians dependent on Alexandrinian grammarians of the first century B.C., the problem may be of less importance (cf. 3.1).

On the other hand, it is clear that the Stoics had established a series of meaning categories, which were to be the starting point of grammatical classifications. For the nouns we have considered case; gender was no doubt known to the Stoics as it was already known to Protagoras, and we find the Stoic Chaeremon distinguishing the expression category of gender from the meaning category of sex (*Grammatici Graeci* II, 1,248,1f.) but this is admittedly a late testimony. Roman grammarians, contrary to their Greek colleagues, maintained that diminution and comparation were accidents of the noun (Barwick 1957:48); this corresponds with the Stoic meaning categories of *auxēsis* and *meiōsis* (cf. *Diogenes Laertius* VII, 53; cf. also 2.6.1). For the verb we have considered categories corresponding to mood, voice and tense, while we have found no direct evidence of person and number.

In conclusion I should like to say that we do not know who first took the decisive step of commuting the Stoic meaning categories into strictly formal categories of expressions, which were structured according to a hierarchical system of primary and secondary categories. It might have happened in some Stoic *techne peri phones*, but it is much more probable that this step, which involves an approach to linguistic science other than the preponderant semantic approach of the Stoa, was taken by some grammarian outside the narrow philosophical circles of the Stoics (cf. 3.3).

2.7.4 *Syntax*

Our knowledge of Stoic syntax is slight. Chrysippos' treatise on the *syntaxis* of the parts of speech according to Dionysios of Halikarnassos (*De compositione verborum* c.4, p. 19) mostly treated the logical aspects of the sentence. The Stoic distinctions of *symbamata* (cf. 2.4.2) and their definition of *soloikismos* as a sentence which is constructed incongruently (*akatallēlōs*) show, however, some awareness of syntactic relations. The definition of *soloikismos* implies a concept of congruence, possibly developed in connection with the investigation into the common *diathesis* of subject and predicate in the *symbama*. Thus they probably inaugurated the Greek type of syntax which was based on analysis of the possible constructions of the parts of speech. This is for the main part the conclusion of Barwick (1957:25f.; cf. also *Grammatici Graeci* II, 2:271f.).

3. HELLENISTIC GRAMMAR

3.1 *The Techne of Dionysios Thrax and Its Authenticity*

In the authoritative expositions of the history of grammatical doctrines, the *Techne grammatike* attributed to Dionysios Thrax plays a pivotal role. Not only was this treatise to be the model of all important grammatical work for the next two millennia, but it also appears to be the oldest extant grammatical text in the western tradition. In this treatise grammar is understood in approximately the same way as it is today, and we find a grammatical system which at several points is radically different from the earlier philosophical approach to grammar. To be emphasized is the establishment of the eight canonical parts of speech which are defined formally, i.e., in terms of morphology, formal paradigms of inflections, or of syntax, position and function in relation to other words in the sentence (cf. Robins, 1951:41), and it only eventually takes the meaning of the word forms into consideration. This new approach to grammar 'jumps out' with the *Techne* 'like Athena from the head of Zeus' (di Benedetto 1958–59:204), but it is thought to have its roots in the grammatical and literary studies of the Alexandrinian grammarians. Nevertheless it is difficult to account for the many deviations from the Stoic systematization on this assumption, not to speak of the obvious misinterpretations of Stoic doctrine which, to put it mildly, are very surprising as early as in the 2nd century B.C.

The *Techne* begins with an introduction, which contains a definition of grammar and a division of it into six parts: 'first, accurate reading (aloud) with due regard to the prosodies; second, explanation of the literary expressions in the works; third, the provision of notes on phraseology and subject matter; fourth, the discovery of etymology; fifth, the working out of analogical regularities; sixth, the appreciation of literary composition which is the noblest part of grammar' (translation by Robins 1967:31). Under none of these six headings is grammar envisaged in our technical sense, except perhaps as part of the fifth. Nevertheless, the remaining parts of the *Techne* discuss this aspect of grammar exclusively. Obviously a discrepancy exists between the declared intentions of the introduction and their realization.

Under these circumstances it is hardly surprising that the authenticity of the *Techne* has been doubted ever since antiquity. But since M. Schmidt's investigations (1852–

53), the authenticity of the *Techne* has been considered established. Not until 1957 was the question reopened by di Benedetto. His paper, however, has not been seriously discussed so far. At best it is mentioned in footnotes, characterized by attributes such as 'interesting (if true)', 'exaggerated', etc. Since the question of the authenticity and the date of the *Techne* is of vital importance to the understanding of the development of grammatical theory in hellenistic times, a discussion of di Benedetto's arguments appears to be a necessary first step for anyone wanting to describe the history of Greek grammar.

Di Benedetto's arguments are many but not equally conclusive. I shall only try to give the main line of his argument:

Some of the ancient scholia already express their doubt as to the authorship of Dionysios Thrax. Through an analysis of the sources of these scholia, di Benedetto (171–8) establishes that 'the refutation of authenticity does not seem to be the hypothesis of an anonymous scholiast, but the conviction of a whole school of erudites', viz. the Alexandrinian school of Ammonios. Moreover, at least one of the scholiasts had, according to di Benedetto, access — if perhaps indirectly — to an early grammatical treatise, probably from the first century B.C. This, of course, does not prove that the scholiast is right, but his sources need not be completely contemnable.

The case for the authenticity is no better supported. The first direct quotations from the *Techne* under the name of Dionysios are from the fifth century, not much earlier than the oldest manuscript tradition. The only exception to this is Sextus Empiricus' quotation from the introduction. This part of the *Techne*, however, might go back to Dionysios Thrax himself; but it is obvious that the connection between the introduction and the rest of the *Techne* is so loose that the authenticity must be proved for each separately. None of the quotations collected by M. Schmidt (1852–53) and Uhlig (*Grammatici Graeci* I, 1) to show the dependence of hellenistic grammarians on the *Techne* are conclusive. They are far too general to prove dependence specifically on the *Techne* rather than on some work similar to the papyri known from the first centuries A.D.

A closer comparison with the 10 papyri dealing with technical grammatical questions (185–96)[32] offers the following observations:

1. The earliest papyri do not resemble the *Techne* very much: they are mere

[32] The following papyri are discussed:

a) *Papyrus Yale* 446. Ed. by Hubbell 1933. Classical Philology 28. 188–98. 1st century A.D.

b) *Papyrus Heidelbergensis* 197. Ed. by Siegmann 1956. Literarische griechische Texte der Heidelberger Papyrussammlung. 1st century A.D.

c) *Papyrus Heidelbergensis* 198. Ed. by Siegmann 1956.

d) *Papyrus Rendel-Harris* 59. The Rendel Harris Papyri of Woodbroke College, Birmingham, ed. by Y. E. Pavell. 1936, Cambridge. 2nd century A.D.

e) *Papyrus Osloensis* II, 13. Papyri Osloenses, ed. by S. Eitrem and L. Amundsen I-III. 1925–36. Oslo. II:1931. 2nd century A.D.

f) *Papyri fiorentini*, ed. by di Benedetto 1957. Annali della scuola normale superiore di Pisa, serie 2, lettere, storis e filosofia 26. 180–5.

g) *Papyrus Oxyrhynchus* III, 469. The Oxyrhynchus Papyri, ed. by B. P. Grenfell and A. S. Hunt. 1898f. London. 3rd century A.D.

enumerations with short definitions of their categories and their subcategories, but they contain no inflectional paradigms. Even if they were perhaps introductions to collections of inflectional paradigms (cf. Fehling 1958:247, note 1), such examples are not incorporated into the text as is the case with the *Techne*.

2. The papyri of the 2nd century A.D. seem to show a richer and more profound treatment of the single grammatical questions. 'Of course this evaluation must be regarded cautiously, because of the accidents involved in the discovery of papyri. Nevertheless it agrees perfectly with what we know of the development of grammar in the first and second centuries A.D., culminating with the work of the two *technikoi par excellence*, Apollonios Dyskolos and Herodian' (di Benedetto 1958:187). So much is certain that we cannot establish, for this period, the existence of a canonical grammatical textbook; in the schools we find a great variety of opinions and tendencies (189).

3. First with the papyri of the 3rd and 4th century we find close parallels to the *Techne*.

A most serious argument against the authenticity of the *Techne* is the fact that the one comprehensive account of Hellenistic Greek grammar, the treatise of Apollonios Dyskolos, nowhere alludes to the *Techne*. Neither can it be shown that Apollonios even indirectly takes the *Techne* into account. Whenever he quotes Dionysios Thrax, the quotations cannot be verified in the *Techne*. And these quotations do not regard minor points, as claimed by Pfeiffer (1968:271). According to Apollonios, Dionysios Thrax 1. distinguished *onoma* and *prosegoria* as two separate parts of speech; 2. defined the verb as signifying a simple *kategorema*; and 3. called the pronouns deictic *arthra*. Thus di Benedetto can conclude (210): 'Dionysios is to Apollonios a grammarian of the second order, who as regards the technical part of grammar is only mentioned because he adhered to Stoic doctrine with some slight modifications. From this testimony on the most famous grammarian of Antiquity can we learn what, incidentally, was to be expected from an Alexandrinian grammarian of the 2nd century B.C., namely that he made no original contribution to technical grammatical questions: whenever he happened to examine some of the logico-grammatical categories

---

h) *Papyrus Amhertensis* II, 21. Amherst papyri, ed. by B. P. Grenfell and A. S. Hunt I-II. 1900–01. London. 3–4th century A.D.

i) *Papyrus Londonensis* 126 verso. Greek Papyri in the British Museum, ed. by F. G. Kenyon. 1893 ff. 'Pseudo-Tryphon'. 4th century A.D. (according to Pfeiffer 1968:327, note 112).

j) Papiri greci e latini I, 18, ed. by Teresa Lodi. 1912f. Publicazioni della Società italiana per la ricerca dei papiri greci e latini in Egitto. Firenze. 5th century A.D. Contains the *Techne*.

The *Papyri Würzburg*, 19 (1934. Mitteilungen aus der Würzburger Papyrussammlung von Ulrich Wilschen. Berlin, Akademie), mentioned by Pfeiffer (1968:270) as a possible second century testimony to the *Techne* of Dionysios Thrax, is a treatise on the tropes. Even if della Corte's rather audacious reconstruction (*RFIC* 14, 1936:406–9) is accepted, we learn no more than that one Dionysios in his *Techne grammatike* treated of the tropes. This is, however, exactly one of the points, in which the *Techne* differs from most ancient grammatical tradition: nowhere does it mention the tropes or the *virtutes* and *vitia orationis*, a point which has been stressed, perhaps unduly, by Barwick (e.g., 1922 *passim*).

which he used for his critical and philological activity, he could do no better than to accept the definitions and theories of the Stoics.'

The first authors of technical grammatical writings mentioned in our sources, and the first authors who defined grammar with special regard to the technical parts, are, according to di Benedetto, Tyrannion and Asklepiades of Myrleia, both of the 1st century B.C. Perhaps Tauriskos, a pupil of Krates of Pergamon, who lived in the 2nd century B.C., should be added. He is said to have written on the 'logical' part of grammar which included *lexeis* and *tropoi* (*Adversus Mathematicos* I, 248; cf. Barwick 1922:218). It is not certain, however, that these categories have any grammatical significance. Mette (1952:56–7) interprets them as rhetorical terms.

These remarks lead us to the most important point: di Benedetto claims that his hypothesis of the non-authenticity of the *Techne* accounts for the known facts in a way far superior to any account based on the acceptance of the *Techne* as a genuine work of the 2nd century B.C. According to him the semantic grammar of the Stoics in the first century B.C. was replaced by a new grammatical science of Alexandrinian and rhetorical inspiration. The main names are Tyrannion, Asklepiades and Tryphon. The first centuries of this new science are characterized by a great variety of opinions, definitions, and approaches. Through the work of Apollonios Dyskolos and Herodian uniformity is achieved; this uniformity is codified in later writings, among which the *Techne* attributed to Dionysios Thrax was to have exceptional success.[33]

There can be no doubt that this exposition of the development of grammatical doctrine mirrors a more organic evolution than the traditional account. Before further discussing its correctness (cf. 3.3) it will be convenient to consider what we know about grammar in the Alexandrinian school, Dionysios excepted.

3.2 *Analogy and Alexandrinian Grammar*

Di Benedetto has emphasized the fact that we have no indications that the early Alexandrinian grammarians (including Dionysios Thrax) ever wrote treatises on technical grammar. As far as we can see they only wrote philological commentaries on classical authors, above all on Homer. We also find lexicographical discussions of words and their meanings, arranged in accordance with some systematic point of view; this latter was perhaps characteristic of Krates and his school at Pergamon. These activities made acute linguistical observations in the usages of Greek literary language imperative. A masterly account of the Hellenistic contribution to philology

[33] The latter part of di Benedetto's paper intends to show that the *Techne* can only be understood as a work of post-Apollonian scholarship. Its definitions are often abbreviations of Apollonian ones, perhaps through an intermediary source. That abbreviation is the right description emerges from the fact that many definitions of the *Techne* contain ambiguities and can only be understood when compared to the more complete versions to be found in Apollonios or in Roman grammarians. Some of the analysis of details in this section ought doubtlessly to be revised, but I do not think that this will endanger the general interpretation.

is to be found in Pfeiffer 1968. In the course of their exegesis the grammarians must, at least occasionally, have employed and perhaps described grammatical categories. (For some examples of this see the doctrines of Dionysios Thrax mentioned above or the description of the pronouns attributed to Aristarch by Apollonios, *Grammatici Graeci* II, 1,3,12.) From the sources we cannot with any degree of certainty decide just how many categories were in fact employed, neither can we tell anything about which relations were thought to exist between these categories. A systematic examination of the grammatical doctrine of e.g. Aristarch as presupposed by his philological work has so far not been carried out. That Aristarch acknowledged eight parts of speech, as mentioned by Quintilian (I, 4,18), is thus probably a later construction, made by a grammarian who sought to secure the authoritative support of Aristarch for his own theories. Perhaps he based this on a collection of categories which Aristarch mentioned unsystematically. But whichever the case the testimony remains isolated.

More exact information is available in connection with the famous controversy of analogy versus anomaly. A recent and provocative examination of these two concepts by Fehling (1956–57) remains almost as undiscussed as the paper of di Benedetto.

The starting point of Fehling is the 'obvious discrepancy between the rigid, completed doctrine of traditional grammar before and after Varro on the one side, and on the other side Varro whose unsystematic exposition leaves the impression of a doctrine still in the making' (218). Fehling sets out to explain this discrepancy from the rather unprecedented methods and procedures of Varro.

Even if this discrepancy is weakened if we accept the late date for the *Techne* given by di Benedetto, the fact nevertheless remains that Varro, even where his sources can be shown to agree with later grammatical theories, introduces arbitrary systematizations of his own. This evaluation of the character and scope of Varro's innovations and procedures is confirmed through the studies of Fuhrmann (1960:69f., 163) into other scientific works of Varro (cf. also the similar results in J.E. Skydsgaard 1968).

It is not my task here to discuss the position of Varro in the history of Roman linguistics. So I shall refrain from discussing the second part of Fehling's paper, which shows in detail how the Varronian systematizations originated. It should be said though that some of Fehling's observations on Varro probably ought to be revised if the theory of di Benedetto is accepted, to see if this might account for some of the peculiarities and uncertainties presented. But I think that even in this case Fehling's general conclusions as to Varro's employment of his sources will not be affected. This is of special importance in our connection, as Varro's *De lingua latina* has been used as the main source for Greek grammatical theory of the 3rd to 1st centuries B.C. Fehling's studies have shown that Varro is to be used with extreme caution, if at all, as he apparently did not add anything substantial from his sources to what we can learn from other and more reliable sources. Thus the later grammatical texts constitute far better materials for the reconstruction of Greek grammar (Fehling 1957:100).

The main part of Fehling's first paper consists of a thorough examination of the meaning and functions of analogy according to all extant sources. The main results of this examination are in Fehling's own words (1956:258):

Wir finden bei Griechen und Lateinen einen in allen wesentlichen Punkten übereinstimmenden Typ einer Flexionslehre vor, die auf den Begriff der Analogie aufbaut. Sein Prinzip ist, die Wörter gleicher Grundformen zusammenzustellen und mit Hilfe von bestimmten Unterscheidungen Regeln zu finden, nach denen sich die Flexion der Wörter bestimmt. Die grammatischen Faktoren, die zur Unterscheidung gebraucht wurden, wurden beim Nomen zum Kanon der Bedingungen der Analogie zusammengefasst,[34] während man beim Verb einen solchen nicht bedurfte. Die Flexionslehre steht unter dem Gesichtspunkt der Sprachrichtigkeit, für die vier Kriterien[35] angenommen werden, unter denen die Analogie[36] einen hervorragenden Platz einnimmt. Dieser Typ der Flexionslehre ist der einzige, den unsere Überlieferung kennt, sehr wahrscheinlich der einzige, der jemals existierte. Die Schriften, die die Flexionslehre behandelten, trugen in erster Linie den Titel 'Techne peri hellenismou' ... (259) ... Alle Stellen, die uns über sie Analogie unterrichten stammen aus der Einleitung der Techne peri Hellenismou.

The specific *Techne peri hellenismou* upon which all our extant sources depend seems to be a work from about 50 B.C., perhaps to be attributed to Tyrannion (Fehling 1956:259). The doctrine of inflection, however, cannot be an innovation of the first century B.C. It must be older, since the canon of conditions upon which it is constituted (cf. note 34) already is in the work of Aristophanes of Byzantium and Aristarch. Fehling concludes that these two scholars established the theory of inflection as we know it only from later sources. With Aristarch's pupils (e.g., Dionysios Thrax)[37] we already find 'das Stadium der Erstarrung' (1956:260). Since then the doctrine of inflection has never changed in principle. Aristophanes and Aristarch continue the

[34] This 'canon of conditions' according to Aristarch (*Grammatici Latini* I:117; cf. Barwick 1922: 180f.) comprised the following items: Nouns compared should have the same gender, case, termination, number of syllables, sounds and figura (primitive or derivate). Fehling (1956:241f.) observes that the awareness of these conditions in fact corresponds to the establishment of grammatical 'accidents'.

[35] *Etymologia*, *analogia*, *synētheia* (usage) and *historia* (*auctoritas*). For these four criteria cf. Barwick 1922:258f., though I do not agree with his attributing the first two to the Alexandrinians and the two remaining to the Stoics (cf. Pinborg 1961:36–8).

[36] Cf. Fehling's definition (1956:237): 'Analogie heisst das, was wir als "regelmässige Flexion" bezeichnen würden. Die Aufgabe des Grammatikers der sich mit der Analogie befasst ist es, die sich in der Flexion gleich verhaltenden Wörter zusammenzustellen und die Regel aufzustellen, nach der sie verändert werden.' This is how the word 'analogy' is in fact used in all sources except one, where it is used in its original meaning of proportion (cf. Fehling 1956:239).

[37] Fehling's comments on the place of Dionysios Thrax in grammatical tradition agree very well with di Benedetto's evaluation, even if the absolute dates are different: 'Die fertige Flexionslehre muss auch dem Dionysios Thrax bei der Auffassung seiner Grammatik vorgelegen haben. Man hat zwar gemeint, seine Schrift sei gewissermassen das Gerippe, das erst die nachfolgende Forschung mit Fleisch und Blut ausgefüllt hätte, und stehe mithin fast noch am Anfang der grammatischen Forschung, doch scheint mir diese Vorstellung geradezu absurd zu sein. Wie sollte es möglich sein, dass in einer Wissenschaft ein knapper, aber das System erschöpfend und endgültig darstellender Abriss sozusagen den Auftakt der Forschung darstellt? ... Vielmehr setzt im Gegenteil Dionysios Thrax in jedem Paragraphen die fertige Flexionslehre voraus, ja die vielen an ihm bemerkten Unebenheiten zeigen, dass er schon der Epoche der Kompilatoren und Abschreiber angehört' (Fehling 1956:260).

observations of Aristotle (*Poetics* 1458a; cf. 1.3.3) completing them from their extended experience of literary usage. The principle of proportion or analogy is not the starting point of this development, but a descriptional device which was introduced at a later stage, perhaps influenced by the science of medicine (1956:261–4).

It must be added, though, that Fehling has not proved the existence of systematic treatises on inflection composed e.g. by Aristarch and his immediate pupils. Their observations on such matters are determinant factors for the later *Techne peri hellenismou,* but this does not necessarily imply the existence of any systematic textbook. Rather the goal of the first Alexandrinian grammarians was interpretation of the poets, not establishment of inflectional paradigms (cf. Barwick 1922:180 and di Benedetto 1958–9:180).

What then becomes of the famous controversy between analogy and anomaly? In short: almost nothing of importance to grammatical theory. It did not play any important role for the doctrine of inflection as maintained e.g. by Steinthal on the basis of Varro.[38] At best it was a controversy on the significance of linguistic regularities in choosing the 'right' linguistic form. (The connection between the controversy and problems of rhetoric has been emphasized in an important paper by Dihle [1957].) Fehling's arguments against the significance of the controversy for the formation of the doctrine of inflection are the following: 1. The preceding reconstruction of the development of the doctrine of inflection shows that there is no room for the controversy as described by Varro. Aristophanes and Aristarch had already formulated the canon of the conditions for analogy which are supposed to have been introduced as modifications of an original theory according to which analogy dominated the whole of language without exceptions. I agree with Fehling that it is hard to understand how any grammarian of the Alexandrinian type could ever have maintained a theory so obviously refutable (cf. also Pinborg 1961:138). Krates of Pergamon opposed Aristarch's analogies on some points, but there is no reason to suppose that he wanted to give up the whole doctrine of inflection nor to introduce a wholly different grammatical system of his own. 2. The only source of the controversy understood in this way is Varro. Sextus Empiricus, who uses many of the same arguments as the 'anomalist' in Varro's *De lingua latina* to refute the possibility of any grammatical science and uses the word *anomaly* in the same sense, i.e., deviation from inflectional

[38] The traditional view has been aptly described by Fehling (1956:265): 'Der Streit über Analogie und Anomalie soll, durch einen Angriff des Krates auf Aristarch eröffnet, von da an bis auf Varro, also rund 100–150 Jahre lang, alle Grammatiker in zwei Schulen gespalten haben, eine reiche Literatur an Streitschriften an beiden Seiten hervorgebracht und auf die gleichzeitige Entwicklung der Grammatik, insbesondere der Flexionslehre, einen bedeutenden Einfluss gehabt, ja sogar ihre Ausgestaltung erst veranlasst haben. Dabei sollen die "Analogisten" die Herrschaft der grammatischen Regeln über die Sprache, die "Anomalisten" die alleinige Geltung des Sprachgebrauchs verfochten haben. Die "Analogisten" werden mit den Alexandrinern, die "Anomalisten" mit den Pergamenern (und oft dann ohne weiteres auch mit den Stoikern) identifiziert. Varro soll bei der Niederschrift seiner Analogiebücher aus dieser Streitschriftenliteratur geschöpft und für das achte Buch "anomalistische", für das neunte Buch "analogistische" Quellen benutzt haben.'

regularity,[39] never mentions the controversy as such nor the name of Krates. Varro only names Krates twice, quotations which hardly justify the customary conviction that all the 'anomalistic parts' of Varro's *De lingua latina* as well as of Sextus Empiricus are 'fragments' of Krates (cf. Mette 1952. Dahlmann [1932] more cautiously speaks of pupils of Krates).

Varro's possible source for the controversy according to Fehling (1956:269) was the same Introduction to the *Techne peri hellenismou* used elsewhere by Varro. This Introduction seems to have given an account of Krates' various points of critique against Aristarch, a fact which seems to be corroborated by other sources. The form of *in utramque partem disserere* imposed by Varro on the subject matter is more of a literary device than of an historically exact exposition. Even if Fehling's thesis may be somewhat too harsh, as Varro may have included other sources which discussed anomaly in terms of preferable usage, I feel convinced that he has successfully proved that the viewpoint of anomaly had no part in the formation of inflectional theory, though it may still have contributed to a better description of some points of detail.

3.3 *The Development of Grammatical Theory in Hellenistic Times*

At first sight the hypotheses of di Benedetto and Fehling seem to be incompatible. Their main point of controversy is over the determination of the creative period of Greek grammar. Where Fehling thinks of Aristarch, di Benedetto thinks of the first century B.C. Pfeiffer (1968:272) remarks against di Benedetto that we have no evidence that the grammarians of the first century were so important. But this argument is not conclusive, since we have even less certain evidence of technical grammar before that time. I think two developments have to be distinguished: The accumulation of linguistic observations which were abundant from Aristotle through the Stoa to the Alexandrinian grammarians, and the incorporation of all these observations into a single grammatical system. I agree with di Benedetto that this last did not take place till the first century B.C.

This point of difference between di Benedetto and Fehling must not make us overlook the very definite similarity in the approach of the two authors. To both, the grammatical theory of Greece as we know it from the extant technical literature is a product of grammarians who use the observations of their predecessors and incorporate them into *one* grammatical system. We do not find different versions of Greek grammar: e.g., a Stoic-Pergamenic one which is at the base of Roman grammar, and an Alexandrinian one, most perfectly embodied in the *Techne* of Dionysios, or an analogistic versus an anomalistic grammar, but we find one single grammatical science with uniform methods and a uniform approach to language, which is basically different from philosophical grammar. Of course, this does not mean that there existed no disagreement among grammarians at all, but these differences did not constitute totally different versions of grammar (cf. 2.1).

[39] This is the only place in Greek literature where the term *anomaly* is used in this sense. Elsewhere it is always used in the Stoic sense (cf. 2.6).

If I am right in accepting the theories of di Benedetto and Fehling to the extent indicated above, the whole history of grammatical theory in Hellenistic times will have to be rewritten. This can of course not be done here, but I should like to outline the main phases of its development as seen in the light of these new interpretations.

The pioneer work of Aristotle was continued by the Stoics and the Alexandrinian grammarians. The Stoics concentrated on establishing categories of meaning, and their theory of isomorphism between categories of meaning and of expression made their work valuable for a linguistic description of the Greek language. We concluded that some of their meaning categories seemed to be founded on observations of expressional categories. The Stoics thus distinguished five or six parts of speech and treated most secondary categories of language. However, we have no information as to how they conceived of the relationship between the primary categories or parts of speech and the secondary categories. On the whole the balance of the question seems to show that they thought of the meaning categories as diverse lexical items which could or could not be brought together (*sympiptein?*) in the same linguistic form. The later systematization in terms of propriety (*idion*) and accidence seems to be of Aristotelian inspiration and inconsistent with Stoic epistemology. According to Fuhrmann (1960:144) no other hellenistic science used the term 'accident' for its systematizations. This could point to a direct peripatetic influence on grammar which otherwise is difficult to prove. But it is probably not accidental that Dionysios of Halikarnassos who used peripatetic sources is our first witness to the use of the term *accident* as a technical term of grammar.[40]

The Alexandrinian grammarians, Aristophanes of Byzantium, Aristarch and Dionysios Thrax observed inflectional regularities of language and described the conditions under which such regularities existed. It is perhaps relevant to repeat that the same approach to language is foreshadowed in the *Poetics* of Aristotle (1458a; cf. 1.3.3). According to Fehling, these conditions are the origin of the later accidents. (Perhaps the formulation of Scaurus [*Grammatici Latini* I, 320,27]: 'nomini accidunt *observationes* hae, genus, numerus etc.' might be taken as a slight confirmation of this theory.) These conditions, however, did not correspond exactly to the latter secondary categories as they included e.g. the number of syllables and the terminations which were later to be discarded. Still, in the enumeration of the accidents in Dionysios of Halikarnassos (cf. note 40) some unusual accidents of this type seem to linger on. The goal of the Alexandrinian grammarians was the interpretation of texts. They did not try to write systematic expositions of grammar or of inflections. To them grammar was an *empeiria* (as stated e.g. in the probably genuine part of Dionysios Thrax' *Techne*). Couched in modern terms they only aimed at observational adequacy (cf. Langendoen 1966 though I do not agree with the actual use he makes of these labels in characterizing the different grammatical schools). We are not able to

[40] Dionysios of Halikarnassos, *De admirabili vi dicendi in Demosthene*, c.52 mentions among the accidents: contraction, extension, accentuation, gender, case, number, mood. Cf. also *De compositione verborum* c.25 (p. 135).

describe the interplay between Stoic and Alexandrinian grammar in details, but we have seen that the Alexandrinians took over some Stoic definitions and categorizations. It is not impossible that Alexandrinian grammar in turn inspired the Stoa, e.g., by describing 'kinships' (*syngeneiai*) of expressions which the Stoics could then use for their own ends.

The school of Pergamon seems to have advocated the study of common (literary) usage and to have denied the significance of analogy for determining the right norms of usage. But they did not formulate a rival grammar. The Pergamenic *Techne grammatike* in which Barwick has so much trust seems to be a construction without sufficient support in the sources.

'Classical' ancient grammar, as we know it, has been masterly characterized by Robins (1957) who took the *Techne* of 'Dionysios Thrax' as his paradigm. It is different from the earlier phases of Greek grammar because it considers grammar an autonomous[41] *techne* or science. This means that it aims at descriptive adequacy[42] and tries to build up grammar as a coherent system of categorizations and rules. This was done in systematic expositions or *technai* dating from the 1st century B.C. onwards. (There can be no doubt that they drew inspiration from the Stoic *technai peri phones* and *peri semainomenou* when they chose this form.) Two types of *technai* existed: the *Techne peri hellenismou* which discussed the criteria of correct usage, faults and virtues of speech, and gave canons of inflections — and the *Techne grammatike* which discussed parts of speech and their accidents. Fehling (1956:247, note 1) has suggested that the *Techne grammatike* originated in the elaboration of the introduction to the *Techne peri hellenismou* as it is often called 'prolegomena to the canones'. This is an attractive suggestion since it may account for the fact that virtues and vices of speech were often discussed in the *technai grammatikai*. (This is a matter of fact in all Roman treatises but only in a few Greek ones. I do not, however, think that this in itself constitutes an important difference between Greek and Roman grammar which must make us posit different origins for the grammars of the two languages, as Barwick wants to do. Cf., in the same sense, Calboli 1962:144f.) Besides

[41] Cf. Wendel's (1939:744) concluding characterization of Tryphon: 'Tryphon ist also grundsätzlich gewillt, die Sprache aus sich selbst zu erklären, hat sich aber doch von den philosophischen Konstruktionen der älteren Grammatik noch nicht völlig freigemacht.' With these words the pioneer work of the grammarians of the 1st century is aptly characterized. Nevertheless Wendel believes in the authenticity of the *Techne*.

[42] As noted by Langendoen (1966) we have very slight evidence of a desire for explanatory adequacy. To the example from Varro other passages could be added (e.g., *Grammatici Graeci* II, 2, 142, 1f., which gives the causes for the invention of the noun and its accidents). Medieval grammarians were later to object to ancient grammar especially on this point. But the Greek grammarians probably thought that their description in so far as it employed notional categories reflected universal structures of the world and of the human mind. This at least is what is implied by the Hellenistic and Neoplatonic theoreticians of semantics who gave ancient grammar its semantic foundations (cf. 3.7). Their explanation was based on the Aristotelian theory that the concepts were common to all human minds (cf. above, 1.3.3). We find no systematic account of how spoken and written language differed from the language of concepts (the deep structure), but the fact of 'difference' is often mentioned and the 'anomaly' explained by the conventional character of language.

these *technai* we find monographs on special grammatical subjects on a much larger scale. Among these monographs we find the first discussions of syntax (cf. 3.6).

In the *Technai grammatikai* we find a discussion of phonetics (cf. 3.4) and of morphology according to the parts of speech and their accidents (cf. 3.5). As previously stated, we have no evidence of the existence of *technai* till the first century B.C.: di Benedetto justly speaks of a new science of grammar (1958:200) and tries to outline the main factors which made the emergence of this new science possible (202f.). He first mentions the need for the preservation of classical (as against contemporary) usage which was already the main motive behind the efforts of the early Alexandrinian grammarians. Secondly, he mentions the growing exchange between the Greek and Roman cultural world which made it imperative for Greek students of language to aim at descriptive adequacy in order to achieve a common basis of understanding. Thirdly, he mentions the center of Rhodes where both grammatical and rhetorical studies flourished. As a fourth factor I should like to add a general trend of the time which was to collect the observations of their predecessors into systematic manuals, a trend which was strongly influenced by the practice of the Stoa (cf. Fuhrmann 1960:154f.).

It is difficult to assess the contribution of the individual grammarians of the first century B.C. Though we possess collections of fragments for some of them,[43] these fragments only inform us of minor points in their doctrine as most of them are transmitted by Apollonios Dyskolos who refers explicitly to his predecessors only when criticizing details of the grammatical system. We have, however, indications that Apollonios was far more dependent e.g. on Tryphon than it appears directly (cf. Wendel 1939:744). The wish for a *Quellenanalyse* of the Greek scholia (cf. Fehling 1957:99)— and I would like to add also of Apollonios — on this background becomes even more urgent. So far we possess a corpus of texts which do not allow us to describe the development of grammatical theory between the first century B.C. and the third century A.D. The main results of this development, however, were summarized in the *Compendium* attributed to Dionysios Thrax which had an astonishingly great success. Most grammatical work in Greece after the 4th century took on the form of commentaries on 'Dionysios Thrax'.

The reconciliation of the data of Roman grammatical tradition with the sketch given above is mostly of concern to the historian of Latin grammatical doctrine. It has however some repercussions on our understanding of developments in Greece, so I am bound to mention some of the problems involved. To Barwick (1932) the starting point of Latin grammar was the Pergamenic *Techne peri phones* which was transmitted to Rome, probably in the first century B.C. A grammatical *techne* is first mentioned in the *Auctor ad Herennium*, and a similar treatise is presupposed by Varro. Latin grammar, as we know it from manuals of the 3rd to the 6th century, reflects the tradition of Roman schools, and its doctrine is to be explained as successive modifica-

[43] Tryphon: *Tryphonis grammatici Alexandrini fragmenta*, 1853. Habron: Berliner philologische Wochenschrift 35, 1915. Didymos: *Didymi Chalcenteri grammatici Alexandrini fragmenta*, 1854. Cf. also the surveys by Wendel (1939 and 1948).

tions of the original Pergamenic (and Varronian) type. The most important modifications were introduced by Palaemon (time of Nero), who adhered closely to Dionysios Thrax (without mentioning him) and introduced the canonical system of eight parts of speech with their traditional accidents into Rome. The main lines of this exposition can be reconciled with the picture of Greek grammar given above. We only have to reject the Pergamenic *techne* and substitute the work of Tyrannion and his contemporaries. This is successfully accomplished by Calboli (1962:144f.) who shows that Roman grammar is perfectly explainable when derived from a *techne* of the Alexandrinian type (as embodied in the works of Tyrannion and Asklepiades). Similarly Palaemon cannot be dependent on 'Dionysios Thrax', but rather on a more extended Greek work on grammar, perhaps by Tryphon. But it seems very doubtful that he was the first to introduce the eight parts of speech into Roman grammar (cf. Calboli 1962:173f. and Fehling 1956–57 who prove that Varro's systematizations presuppose the division into eight parts). Di Benedetto, however, thinks that he can prove an influence from Apollonios Dyskolos, even in passages which according to Barwick are fragments of Palaemon. On the evidence available it is not possible to decide whether Barwick has been too optimistic in his reconstruction of Palaemon, or di Benedetto ascribes too much originality to Apollonios Dyskolos (what he takes to be Apollonian influence might be influence from Apollonios' sources). The evidence of the sources will have to be sifted once more. In this connection I should like to point to Scaurus, a Roman grammarian of the 2nd century A.D., as a figure of importance. His fragments are collected by Barwick (1922:238). His definitions prove to be remarkably oldfashioned when compared to the definitions attributed to Palaemon by Barwick.

3.4 *Phonetics*

For this section the best survey is that by Robins (1957:84–90). I have little to add to his observations, from which I should like to quote the following more general remarks:

(84): 'Although Greek linguistic analysis was able to distinguish orthography from the phonic material of the language, one cannot feel that an adequate separation was made between the statement of the alphabet and the spelling of Greek words on the one hand, and the phonetic and phonological analysis on the other; nor can one find an explicit acknowledgement of the difference between phonetic analysis and phonological analysis.' (Bearing in mind that both the sound (*dynamis*) and the letter were taken as accidents of the same *stoicheion*, a confusion between alphabet and phonetic elements is predictable.)

(85): 'Bearing in mind their lack of a clear distinction between phonetics and phonology and of interest in language other than Greek, one may not inappropriately compare this (their definition of the basic element [*stoicheion*] as the minimal part of language) with the (modern) definition of the phoneme...' [44] (cf. also 1.3.2).

[44] Some awareness of this distinction is evidenced by the fact that allophonic differences are mentioned (*Grammatici Graeci* I, 3, 32, 3–5. Cf. Robins 1967:32).

Chronological table of the grammarians mentioned

	Philosophers		
4th cent. B.C.	Aristotle (384–322)		
	Theophrastos (270–285)		
3rd cent. B.C.	(Stoics)	*Alexandrinian grammarians*	
	Zenon (335–263)	Zenodotos (a. 325–270)	
	Chrysippos (280–207)	Aristophanes of Byzantium (257–180)	
	Diogenes of Babylon (240–150)	Aristarch (217–145)	
2nd cent. B.C.			*Other grammarians*
	Antipater of Tarsos	Dionysios Thrax	Krates of Pergamon
			Tauriskos
1st cent. B.C., first half	Poseidonios (135–50)		
		Technikoi	
		Tyrannion	
		Asklepiades	
1st cent. B.C., 2nd half		Tryphon	Dionysios of Halikarnassos
			Varro (116–27)
1st cent. A.D.	Chairemon	Habron	Palaemon
2nd cent. A.D.		Apollonios Dyskolos	Scaurus
		Herodian	
3rd cent. A.D.			
and following		Techne of ‘Dion. Thrax’	Extant Artes.
		Scholia	

(86): 'It would be reasonable to credit Dionysios Thrax and his commentators with the awareness that linguistic elements operate in a language not only by their paradigmatic differences, but also by their possibilities of syntagmatic sequence and combination one with another in structures.' (Note that the consonants are generally defined as letters which can combine with vocals to form a syllable, even if the more 'phonetic' definition that they cannot be expressed alone sometimes can be found.)

(86): 'On the descriptions of the articulations employed in Greek one cannot credit Dionysios Thrax and his commentators with any very striking phonetic insight.'

(86): 'Thrax shifts his classification of the consonants onto morphological, or even morphophonemic, grounds. He tells us which consonants can be final in nouns of the three genders, though without referring to the rather striking restriction in the number of Greek consonants that can be final in any words in the language.'

The statements of the grammarians on phonology have been employed extensively for the reconstruction of the pronunciation of Ancient Greek. But we urgently need a comprehensive account of the Greek grammarians' theory of phonology, including the combinatoric aspect emphasized by Robins. Also their study of the syllable which includes the doctrine of phonetic change, accentuation, quantity and prosody, in close connection with the study of metrics, merits fresh consideration.

3.5 *Morphology*

In all extant texts we find the canonical number of eight parts of speech: noun, pronoun, verb, participle, article, adverb, preposition and conjunction. We find some evidence that this system had to overcome several rival systems which acknowledged from five to eleven parts of speech. This of course is partly due to the origin of the doctrine of the parts of speech, but individual grammarians also tended to combine the traditional data in different ways, sometimes introducing new parts of speech which, however, seldom succeeded in becoming generally acknowledged. Thus we have indications that the infinitive, the interjection (cf. Pinborg 1961:133–4, with note 27) and the appellative (in accordance with Stoic doctrine) were often given separate status.

The concept of 'part of speech' is somewhat heterogeneous as a consequence of its historical origin. It is used of a segment of a string (identified with a word) and of classes of such segments. Aristotle seems to have used the term exclusively in this way. It is then used of classes established as semantic classes (especially by the Stoics) and of classes of words undergoing similar inflections. The traditional exposition of the eight parts of speech reflects a conglomeration of these different approaches.

The traditionally accepted system was probably the work of Tryphon, who at least was the first to make the participle a separate part of speech, according to the direct testimony of our sources (*Grammatici Latini* II, 548,6; cf. *Grammatici Graeci* I, 3,518,17f., the argument of which probably goes back to Tryphon; cf. Fehling 1957: 52–3). This testimony has not been accepted at its face value, because Dionysios

Thrax was already thought to have separated the participle when he wrote the *Techne*. Tyrannion comprised the participle within the noun (cf. Wendel 1948:1817).

The accidents also received canonical status and number though some discrepancies are still to be detected, especially as regards arrangement. They are clearly described as secondary categories (*parepomena* or *accidentia*) through which something is indicated along with (*paremphainetai*) the main signification of the word *qua* part of speech.[45]

The definitions given are mostly formal (cf. above, 3.1), but notional criteria are not excluded. They appear overtly in the most extended corpus of grammatical texts transmitted to us, the grammatical writings of Apollonios Dyskolos. Here it is stated that the parts of speech can only be distinguished according to their meanings, and notional criteria are used in the definitions of the main parts of speech along with the strictly formal ones.

The existence of both notional and formal criteria is hardly surprising when the origins of Greek grammar are taken into account. It corresponds well to the Stoic theory that categories of language had to be based both on distinctions of meaning and on distinctions of forms of expressions. But it is only fair to mention that in the *technai* the formal criteria are preponderant. The parts of speech are mainly defined in terms of inflection and syntax (cf. Robins 1957:96f.). Notional criteria are mostly used to describe already established inflectional categories. When Apollonios speaks of meaning as the definiens of the parts of speech, he has not so much logical categories of meaning in mind as the fact that the mere observation of the phonological components of a word does not account for its linguistic role: homonyms (*synemptoseis*) may belong to different parts of speech; the same morpheme may have different phonological realizations (cf. note 27 above). In other words: Apollonios is not so much thinking of the lexical meaning of single words as of the more abstract meaning relations (difference, identity, etc.) though he does not express this explicitly.

There are some examples of a syntactical reinterpretation of the secondary categories of the main parts of speech: Gender is thought of in terms of syntactic concord, not as a reflection of natural sex (cf. *Grammatici Graeci* I, 3:218, 19–20). Person and number of the verb are not semantic categories of the verb, but reflections of its concord with the subject (cf. *Grammatici Graeci* II, 2:324,11–325,8). Mood is explained as the correspondent of an (abstract) verb + infinitive, the optative, e.g. as a combination of *thélo* [I will] or similar verbs and the infinitive. This has something to do with the concept of substitution (cf. 3.7). The two strings are, however, not strictly equivalent; whereas the combination of abstract verb + infinitive signifies a diathesis in the mind of the speaker, the use of the optative performs this diathesis as it embeds

[45] This use of *paremphainein* is typical of Apollonios. It is also found in Dionysios of Halikarnassos, *De compositione verborum* c. 6 (p. 29), perhaps the oldest extant discussion of some of the accidents of the parts of speech as such. For the noun number, case, gender and figure are discussed, for the verb voice (where *ortha* are distinguished from *hyptia*, note that the Stoic terms are used, not the terms which were to be used later in grammatical tradition), mood (*enklisis*, also called *ptosis rhematike* — Aristotelian influence?) and tense (note the formulation of the question: ποίας παρεμφαίνοντα διαφορὰς χρόνων).

it into the lower sentence where it appears along with (*paremphainetai*; cf. note 45) the statement.

Apollonios' approach to language is grammatical in the narrow sense of the word. 'Morphology or word structure was not given a distinct status within grammar, and the inflectional systems of the inflected words were handled by what Hockett has called the 'word and paradigm' method, wherein one form is selected as basic (e.g., the first person singular indicative active, in verbs), and the other forms associated with it are listed after it.[46] Their failure to analyze inflected words into root and inflectional elements is no doubt largely to blame for the comparative inability of Greek scholars to make any very useful contribution to etymological studies'[47] (Robins 1957:92–3).

A general description of Apollonios' grammar is sorely missed. The last monograph on the most important grammarian of Greece is the one by Egger from 1854. Some initial steps have recently been taken by Hahn (1952) and Camerer (1965), who however accomplish both too little and too much. They very sensibly confine themselves to fairly manageable parts of the Apollonian doctrine, the concept of mood and the conjunction *an* respectively. But feeling the need for a more comprehensive basis of understanding they tend to generalize their observations though their material is far too restricted. Hahn has too little knowledge of the philosophical background of Apollonios, and though Camerer sees the necessity for the cooperation of philosophers and linguists in interpreting Apollonios, her own essay is not convincing in its evaluation of the more general aspects. But both the papers mentioned are valuable contributions to the problems studied. However we need more such studies of the terminology of Apollonios, not only of the categories established, but also of the terms used to describe grammatical facts and relations, perhaps in the form of a terminological dictionary as advocated by Cousin. A starting point of this work can be found in the commentaries of Schneider on Apollonios (*Grammatici Graeci* II) and in the paper of Thierfelder (1935). On the basis of such studies we can then hope for a comprehensive account of Apollonios and of the type of grammar he envisaged.

The *Compendia*, especially the *Techne* attributed to Dionysios Thrax, offer a seemingly more consistent formal approach. However, I suspect that one of the main reasons for this lies in its very shortness; the secondary categories, for example, are generally not defined. Whenever these short or missing definitions are to be explained, e.g., in the scholia, we find the same mixture of formal and notional criteria as in Apollonios.

[46] This was often expressed so that the basic form was considered a word of the first thesis, whereas the derived forms were attributed to the second thesis. The inflections were described by giving inflectional paradigms according to classes. It is an interesting fact that these classes were established according to the final consonant of the nouns, the procedure already inaugurated by Aristotle. The Roman grammarian Palaemon seems to be the first who thought of classifying according to the different ways of forming the genitive (cf. Barwick 1922:236–7). This is even more peculiar as the Greek grammarians had already thought of classifying the verbs according to more effective criteria which led to the establishment of only three *syzygiai*.

[47] For a recent, thorough discussion of ancient etymology I refer to the article by I. Opelt (1941: 797–844).

3.6 *Syntax*

It was mentioned above that syntax was generally discussed in separate monographs. The oldest extant Greek monograph on syntax is written by Apollonios Dyskolos (*Grammatici Graeci* II, 2). We have some evidence that similar monographs were written before, by Chrysippos (cf. 2.7.4), Tryphon and Habron. (For a suggestive discussion of Greek theories of syntax see now Householder 1972.)

Isolated statements on syntax can be found in the *Techne* and in the scholia as well (cf. Robins 1957:103f.). This bears witness to the fact that syntax was not an autonomous part of grammar. Donnet (1967) has convincingly shown that syntax was only conceived of in terms of words and of the morphological categories already established. This in turn led to the failure of the Greek grammarians to describe syntax on the base of the grammatical relations between constituents. Instead grammarians turned to logic for their concepts, which is of course in keeping with the origin of syntax in Stoic discussions. Donnet mentions the definition of the complete sentence (cf. 2.3.1), the classification of propositions and conjunctions (cf. 2.5) — where especially the failing distinction between coordination and subordination is to be mentioned — and the priority ascribed to the noun over the verb because the noun signifies a substance and the verb an accident. It is easy to see that this deficient conceptual frame of reference not only affects the theoretical status of syntax, but also the power of syntactic descriptions (for examples, cf. Donnet 1967a: 40f.).

Questions of word order were also treated within a philosophical frame. Donnet has shown that the terms *syntaxis* and *synthesis* are used in questions of word order as well as in questions of construction. Sometimes only the place of a word in the sentence is mentioned in the section on its syntax, whereas its different constructions are not mentioned at all. At the very least it must be said that the two different aspects were not sufficiently distinguished. Apollonios begins his exposition of syntax with an examination of the 'structure' of language. Its minimal element are phonemes and letters which according to certain rules form syllables, these again words and sentences. Apollonios describes the relation word: sentence in analogy with the relation letter: syllable. Just as we find a 'rational' order of the letters in the alphabet, we find a 'rational' order of the parts of speech. The order of the *technai*: noun, verb, participle, pronoun, article, preposition, adverb, conjunction is not arbitrary but is a reflection of the complete sentence (*Grammatici Graeci* II, 2, 16,12). This order primarily expresses the relative importance of the parts of speech in the sentence, only secondarily the actual word order. The noun is the first part of speech, that about which something is stated; the verb is second because it expresses the statement of the sentence. These two parts of speech are analogous to the vocals, as they alone can form a sentence (just as the vocals alone can form a syllable), while no sentence can exist without them. The other parts of speech (like consonants) can only contribute to the formation of a whole along with the principal parts. This has some consequences for the word order: ideally the noun has to precede the verb, the verb the adverb and so on. This can, however, be deviated from for stylistic reasons (cf. 2.6.2). Though some vague notion of dependency is probably at work here, the confusion introduced through the failing distinction of constituent relations and questions of word order make any consistent syntactic theory impossible.

Apollonios then goes on to discuss the constructions of the single parts of speech, thus giving further proof of the basically morphological approach to syntax. A good deal of his discussion is directed to attempts at explaining particular features of Greek constructions, where semantic and formal explanations are mingled in a very unsystematic way (cf. Robins 1967:38).

The framework of description used in this connection is not without theoretical interest. We find some terms used which may foreshadow genuine syntactic concepts. Robins (1967:37–8) mentions the concordial relations (*katallēlótēs, akolouthía*) 'which hold, for example between a finite verb form and a nominative case noun or pronoun in respect of number and person, but not between a finite verb and an oblique case form'. Camerer (1965) has shown that the term *katallelotes* also covers collocation or propriety, which leaves the term somewhat vague. Robins further mentions 'the relationship of constituent structuring (*paralambánesthai* 'to be taken together') to refer to the construction of participle and main verb in a sentence, or of noun or pronoun and verb' and 'the use of *symparalambánesthai* 'to be taken along in addition' where something analogous with the modern concepts of immediate constituency and hierarchical ranking seems to be envisaged.' It remains to be seen how far these terms are used with any consistency and precision. Once more we are made aware of the fact that much work on Apollonios still needs to be done.

3.7 *Semantics*

Semantics were not a part of Greek technical grammar. Lexicography, however, was one of the main activities of ancient grammarians as evidenced by the early collections of glosses on difficult Homeric or dialect words and forms and by the comprehensive lexica of the Hellenistic age. The words discussed were generally explained through synonyms or through etymologies (cf. note 47). An example of this can be seen in the grammarians' use of the method of substitution (*anthypágesthai*). One or more words are substituted for the term or the phrase to be explained; from the nature and different possibilities of these substitutions conclusions as to categories of language may be drawn. Such arguments played a certain role in the discussions about the number of the parts of speech and the inclusion of single words into this frame. The same method was also used to distinguish between homonyms (*synemptṓseis*); cf. Thierfelder (1935:42f. and 55f.). Apart from this we do not find any systematic expositions of semantic concepts or problems. In a grammar of the Greek type, however, which defines many categories by what is signified by them, the presence of an implicit semantic theory is strongly felt. The observation of di Benedetto (1958:171f.), according to whom some of the grammatical scholia show a close relationship with the Neoplatonic tradition of commentaries on Aristotle, offers a clue as to where we can find the semantic theory of Greek grammar expressed. Actually we find penetrating semantic observations in the text of the *Commentaria in Aristotelem Graeca* which seem to be consistent with the approach of the grammarians. An obvious example of this is the handling of the parts of speech (cf., e.g., *Commentaria in Aristotelem Graeca* IV, 5, 11). It is interesting to see that the reinterpretation and modification of Stoic semantics and logic in Aristotelian terms which can be observed in the Neoplatonic commentaries, can be ascertained also in the grammatical sources where, for example, a tendency to identify meanings and concepts prevails. Identical discussions on the not overtly expressed subject of the verbs of 1st and 2nd person can also be exemplified in both types of sources. Unfortunately this aspect of the commentators' doctrine is strongly neglected. In a recent book (Pinborg 1972:34–41) I have made some tentative steps in order to reopen this field of study, but it is only a very modest beginning. A closer scrutiny of the semantic doctrines of the commentators and of the doctrinal similarities between them and the grammarians would doubtlessly be rewarding.

3.8 *A Note on Byzantine Grammar*

The study of Byzantine grammar is in its beginnings. We strongly need critical and commentated editions along the lines of Donnet's (1967b) edition of the 12th century grammarian Gregorios of Korinth. This edition incidentally also offers a good starting point for the discussion of some grammatical concepts of the general Greek tradition. For the study of Byzantine grammar the edition of the scholia in Dionysios Thrax (*Grammatici Graeci* I, 3) and the edition of Choiroboskos (10th century?, *Grammatici Graeci* IV) are indispensable. Other Byzantine grammarians are still unedited or to be found in old editions and collections of Anecdota. Only when critical editions and investigations into the sources of the Byzantine grammars are present will it be possible to give any precise account of the contribution of Byzantium to grammatical theory. So far we have no evidence that it went beyond the classical sources. The theories of case, for which Hjelmslev praised Byzantine grammarians, in the main have classical models (cf. 2.3.3).

REFERENCES

A. *Ancient Authors*

ANAXIMENES OF LAMPSAKOS. Rhetorica ad Alexandrum (*Rhet. ad Alex.*), edited among the works of Aristotle.

ARISTOTELE POETICA. Testo e commento di A. Rostagni. 1945. Torino.

ARISTOTELES. 1831. Ed. by I. Bekker. Berlin, Akademie.
AUGUSTINUS. 1857. Dialectica, ed. by W. Crecelius. Programm Elberfeld.
BLEMMYDES, NIKEPHOROS. 1857–66. Patrologiae cursus completus omnium ss. patrum, doctorum scriptorumque ecclesiasticorum. Series graeca. Accurante J.-P. Migne. Paris.
CLEMENS ALEXANDRINUS. 1905–09. Ed. by Otto Stählin. Die griechischen christlichen Schriftsteller der ersten drei Jahrhunderte. Leipzig, J.C. Heinrichs.
COMMENTARIA IN ARISTOTELEM GRAECA, I-XXII. 1882f. Berlin, Akademie. [Reprinted Berlin, de Gruyter.]
DIDYMOS. 1854. Didymi Chalcenteri Alexandrini fragmenta, ed. by M. Schmidt.
DIOGENES LAERTIUS. 1964. Vita philosophorum, ed. by H.S. Long. Oxford, Oxford University Press.
DIONYSIOS OF HALIKARNASSOS. 1899–1929. Opera, ed. by Usener and Rademacher. Leipzig, Teubner. [Mentioned above: De compositione verborum. De Demosthene.]
GELLIUS, AULUS. 1913. Noctes Atticae, ed. by Hosius. Leipzig, Teubner.
GRAMMATICI GRAECI, I-IV. 1878f. Ed. by G. Uhlig and R. Schneider. Leipzig, Teubner.
GRAMMATICI LATINI, I-VIII. 1857ff. Ed. by H. Keil. [Reprinted Hildesheim, 1961. Olms.]
HABRON. 1915. Ed. by R. Berndt. Berliner philologische Wochenschrift 35.
M. TULLII CICERONIS Academicorum reliquiae cum Lucullo. 1922. Recognovit O. Plasberg. Leipzig, Teubner.
PLUTARCH. Opera. 1925ff. Leipzig, Teubner. [Mentioned above: Platonicae quaestiones. De repugnantia stoicorum.]
QUINTILIAN. 1907–35. Institutio oratoria, ed. by L. Radermacher. Leipzig, Teubner.
SENECA. 1965. Epistulae morales, ed. by L. Reynolds. Oxford, Oxford University Press.
SEXTUS EMPIRICUS. 1914–61. Adversus mathematicos, I-XI. Leipzig, Teubner. [Mentioned above: Pyrrhōneioi Hypotypōseis.]
STOICORUM VETERUM FRAGMENTA. 1921–24. Ed. by J. von Arnim. Leipzig, Teubner.
T. LUCRETI CARI De rerum natura libri sex. Revisione del testo, Commento e studi introduttivi di. C. Giussani, I-IV. 1896–98. Torino.
T. LUCRETI CARI De rerum natura libri sex. Ed. with prolegomena, critical apparatus, trans. and commentary by Cyril Bailey, I-III. 1947. Oxford.
TRYPHON. 1853. Tryphonis grammatici Alexandrini fragmenta, ed. by A. de Velsen. Berlin. [Reprinted 1965. Amsterdam, Hakkert.]
VARRO. 1910. De lingua latina, ed. by Goetz and Schoell. Leipzig, Teubner.

B. *Modern Authors*[48]

ACKRILL, J. 1963. Retort to Demos. Journal of Philosophy 61.610–13.

BARWICK, KARL. 1922. Remmius Palaemon und die römische 'ars grammatica'. Philologus, suppl. 15. Leipzig.

——. 1933. Review of SITTIG 1931. Gnomon 9.587f.

——. 1957. Probleme der stoischen Sprachlehre und Rhetorik. ASAW 49(3). Berlin, Akademie.

BREKLE, H.E. 1970. A note on Aristotle's De interpretatione. Folia linguistica 4. 167–73.

CALBOLI, GUALTIERO. 1962. La tendenza grammaticale dell'auctor ad Herennium. Studi grammaticali, 141–242. Bologna, Zanichelli.

——. 1966. I modi del verbo greco e latino. Lustrum 11.175–84.

CAMERER, RUTH. 1965. Die Behandlung der Partikel ἄν in den Schriften des Apollonios Dyskolos. Hermes 93.168–204.

CHERNISS, H. 1959. Plato (1950–1957). Lustrum 4.5–308.

CHILTON, C.W. 1962. The Epicurean theory of the origin of language. American Journal of Philology 83.159–67.

CHRISTENSEN, JOHNNY. 1962. An essay on the unity of Stoic philosophy. København, Munksgaard.

COSERIU, E. 1969. Die Geschichte der Sprachphilosophie. Tübingen, Romanisches Seminar.

DAHLMANN, HELLFRIED. 1932. Varro und die hellenistische Sprachtheorie. Problemata, 5. Berlin, Weidmannsche.

DELACY, PH. 1939. The epicurean analysis of language. American Journal of Philology 60.85ff.

DE MAURO, TULLIO. 1965. Il nome del dativo e la teoria dei casi greci. Atti della accademia nazionale dei lincei, serie ottava, rendiconti, classe di scienti morali, storiche e filologiche 20.151–211.

DEMOS, R. 1964. Plato's philosophy of language. Journal of Philosophy 61.595–610.

DERBOLAV, JOSEF. 1972. Platons Sprachphilosophie im Kratylos und in den späteren Schriften. Darmstadt, Wiss. Buchgesellschaft.

DI BENEDETTO, V. 1958–59. Dionysio Trace e la Techne a lui attribuita. ASNP 27.169–210 and 28.87–118.

DIHLE, A. 1957. Analogie und Attizismus. Hermes 85.170–205.

DONNET, D. 1967a. La place de la syntaxe dans les traités de grammaires grecques des origines au XIIe siècle. AC 36.22–48.

——. 1967b. Le traité περὶ συντάξεως λόγου de Grégoire de Corinthe. Études de philologie, d'archéologie et d'histoire anciennes publiés par l'institut historique belge de Rome, 10. Bruxelles.

EGGER, E. 1854. Apollonius Dyscole. Paris, Durand.

[48] Mrs. K. M. Fredborg has helped me in compiling the list of recent contributions to the historiography of Greek grammar.

ENGELS, J. 1962. Origine, sens et survie du terme boécien *secundum placitum*. Vivarium 1.87–114.

FEHLING, DETLEV. 1956–57. Varro und die Grammatische Lehre von der Analogie und der Flexion. Glotta 35.214–70 and 36.48–100.

——. 1958. Review of BARWICK 1957. GGA 212.161–73.

——. 1965. Zwei Untersuchungen zur griechischen Sprachphilosophie. RhM 108. 212–29.

FUHRMANN, M. 1960. Das systematische Lehrbuch. Göttingen, Vandenhoeck & Ruprecht.

GALLAVOTTI, C. 1954. Il syndesmos in Aristotele. PP 9.241–55.

GENTINETTA, P.M. 1961. Zur Sprachbetrachtung bei den Sophisten und in der Stoisch-Hellenistischen Zeit. Wintherthur, Keller.

GOLDSCHMIDT, V. 1972. Ὑπάρχειν et ὑφιστάναι dans la philosophie stoicienne. REG 85.332-44. Paris

GUTHRIE, W.K.C. 1969. A history of Greek philosophy, III. Cambridge.

HADOT, P. 1969. Zur Vorgeschichte des Begriffs 'Existenz' YΠAPXEIN bei den Stoikern. Archiv für Begriffsgeschichte 13.115–27. Bonn, Bouvier.

HAHN, E.A. 1951. Apollonius Dyscolus on mood. TAPA 82.29–48.

HALLER, R. 1962. Untersuchungen zum Bedeutungsproblem in der antiken und mittelalterlichen Philosophie. Archiv für Begriffsgeschichte 7.57–119. Bonn, Bouvier.

HEINIMANN, F. 1945. Nomos und Physis. Schweizerische Beiträge zur Altertumswissenschaft 1. Basel.

HIERSCHE, R., E. ISING, and G. GINSCHEL. 1955. Entstehung und Entwicklung des Terminus πτῶσις. Aus der Arbeit an einem Historischen Wörterbuch der sprachwissenschaftlichen Terminologie. SbDAW 3. Berlin, Akademie.

HJELMSLEV, L. 1935. La catégorie de cas. Acta Jutlandica 9. Aarhus.

HOUSEHOLDER, FRED W. Introduction in: Syntactic theory I, Structuralist. Selected readings. London, Penguin.

KNEALE, W. and M. 1962. The development of logic. Oxford, Oxford University Press.

KOLLER, H. 1958. Die Anfänge der griechischen Grammatik. Glotta 37.5–40.

KRAUSE, W. 1962. Problemkreise der antiken Grammatik. Serta Philologica Aenipontana, Innsbrucker Beiträge zur Kulturwissenschaften 7–8.215–37.

KRETZMANN, N. 1967. Semantics, History of. The encyclopedia of philosophy, ed. by P. Edwards.

——. 1971. Plato on the correctness of names. American Philosophical Quarterly 8.126–38.

LAMACCHIA, R. 1961. Per una storia del termine deponente. SIFC 33.185–221.

LANGENDOEN, D.T. 1966. A note on the linguistic theory of M.T. Varro. FL 2.33–6.

LLOYD, A.C. 1971. Grammar and metaphysics in the Stoa. Problems in Stoicism, ed. by A.A. Long, 58–74. London, Athlone.

LOHMANN, J. 1953. Gemeinitalisch und Uritalisch. Lexis 3.169–217.
——. 1968. Über die stoische Sprachphilosophie. SG 21(3).250–7.
LONG, A. A. 1971a. Language and thought in Stoicism. Problems in Stoicism, ed. by A. A. Long, 75–113. London, Athlone.
——. 1971b. Aisthesis, Prolepsis and linguistic theory in Epicurus. BICS 18.114-33. London.
LORENZ, K., and J. MITTELSTRASS. 1967. On rational philosophy of language: The programme in Plato's Cratylus reconsidered. Mind 76.1–20.
MATES, B. 1953. Stoic logic. Los Angeles, University of California Press.
MAU, JÜRGEN. 1957. Stoische Logik. Hermes 85.147–58.
MCKEON, RICHARD. 1946–47. Aristotle's conception of language and the arts of language. Classical Philology 41.193–206 and 42.21–50.
METTE, H. J. 1952. Parateresis, Untersuchungen zur Sprachtheorie des Krates von Pergamon. Halle, Niemeyer.
MORPURGO-TAGLIABUE, G. Linguistica e stilistica di Aristotele. Filosofia e critica, 4. Roma, Ateneo.
MÜHL, MAX. 1962. Der λόγος ἐνδιάθετος und προφορικός von der älteren Stoa bis zur Synode von Sirmium 351. Archiv für Begriffsgeschichte 7.7–56.
MÜLLER, H. E. 1943. "Prinzipien der stoischen Grammatik". Unpublished dissertation. Rostock. [I have used the copy of the Universitätsbibliothek, Rostock.]
MURRAY, G. 1946. The beginnings of grammar. Greek Studies. Oxford.
NUCHELMANS, GABRIEL. 1973. Theories of the proposition. Ancient and Medieval conceptions of the bearers of truth and falsity. Amsterdam, North-Holland. [This important book has been of special relevance for the section on the Stoa.]
OPELT, I. 1941. Etymologie. In Rellexikon für Antike und Christentum, ed. by Th. Klauser, VI, 797–844. Stuttgart.
PAGLIARO, A. 1955. Il capitolo linguistico della Poetica di Aristotele. Nuovi saggi di critica semantica, 77–131. Firenze, d'Anna.
——. 1958. La dottrina dell'analogia e i suoi precedenti. Richerche linguistiche 4.1–18.
PECORELLA, G. B. 1962. Dionisio Trace. Bologna.
PFEIFFER, R. 1968. History of classical scholarship from the beginning to the end of the hellenistic age. Oxford, Oxford University Press.
PINBORG, JAN. 1961. Interjektionen und Naturlaute. C&M 22.117–38.
——. 1962. Das Sprachdenken der Stoa und Augustins Dialektik. C&M 23.148–77.
——. 1972. Logik und Semantik im Mittelalter. Problemata, Stuttgart, Frommann.
POHLENZ, MAX. 1939. Die Begründung der abendländischen Sprachlehre durch die Stoa. NAWG, Neue Folge 3(6).151–98.
——. 1955. Die Stoa, I-II. Göttingen, Vandenhoeck & Ruprecht.
ROBINS, R. H. 1951. Ancient and mediaeval grammatical theory in Europe. London, Bell & Sons.

——. 1957. Dionysios Thrax and the western grammatical tradition. TPhS 1957. 67–106.

——. 1966. The development of the word class system of the European grammatical tradition. FL 2.3–19.

——. 1967. A short history of linguistics. London, Longmans.

SCHMIDT, K. 1960. Review of Barwick 1957. Gymnasium 67.249–51.

SCHMIDT, M. 1852–53. Dionys der Thraker. Philologus 7.360–82 and 8.231–53; 510–20.

SCHMIDT, R. 1839. Stoicorum grammatica. Halle. [Reprinted, 1967. Amsterdam, Hakkert.]

SCHRIJVERS, P.H. 1970. Horror ac divina voluptas. Amsterdam, Hakkert.

SITTIG, E. 1931. Das Alter der Anordnung der Kasus und der Ursprung ihrer Bezeichnung als Fälle. Tübinger Beiträge zur Altertumswissenschaft 13. Tübingen.

SKYDSGAARD, J.E. 1968. Varro the scholar. Analecta Romana Instituti Danici IV, Supplementum. København.

SPOERRI, W. 1959. Späthellenistische Berichte über Welt, Kultur und Götter. Basel.

STEINTHAL, H. 1890–91. Geschichte der Sprachwissenschaft bei den Griechen und Römern, I–II. Zweite Ausgabe. Berlin. [Reprinted 1961. Hildesheim, Olms.]

THIERFELDER, ANDREAS. 1935. Beiträge zur Kritik und Erklärung des Apollonios Dyskolos. ASAW 43(2).

TRAGLIA, A. 1956. La sistemazione grammaticale di Dionisio Trace. Studie classice e orientale 5.38–78.

TRENDELENBURG, FR. A. 1836. Accusativi nomen quid tandem sibi velit. Acta Societatis Graecae 1.117–24.

TRENTMAN, JOHN A. 1969. Vincent Ferrer and his fourteenth-century predecessors on a problem of intentionality. Actes du quatrième congres international de philosophie médiévale, 949–56. Paris, Vrin.

WEINGARTNER, R.H. 1970. Making sense of *Cratylus*. Phronesis 15.5–25.

WENDEL, CARL. 1939. Tryphon. Realencyclopädie der classischen Altertumswissenschaft (Pauly-Wissowa) 2, Reihe VII A 1 (dreizehnter Halbband), 726–44.

——. 1948. Tyrannion. Realencyclopädie der classischen Altertumswissenschaft (Pauly-Wissowa) 2, Reihe VII A 2 (vierzehnter Halbband), 1811–19.

WIGGINS, D. 1970. Sentence meaning, negation and Plato's problem of non-being. Plato I: Metaphysics and epistemology, ed. by G. Vlastos, 268–303. Modern Studies in Philosophy. New York, Doubleday.

CLASSICAL ANTIQUITY: ROME

LUIGI ROMEO

INTRODUCTION*

Anyone daring to delve into general historiography with regard to definitions, theoretical tenets, current problems, past schools and so forth, would be an audacious soul; the subject matter requires constant battle against an infinite number of obstacles and variables. But, worse, anyone planning to treat historiography in particular (in our case that of linguistics) must be either a masochist or a fool. And if historiography of linguistics is restricted to Rome, then the researcher is both a masochist and a fool.

Since each author participating in this volume probably has his own conception of historiography in general and in particular, I am forced to display my understanding and application of some concepts involved in this term. It is proper thus that terminology be traced briefly in order to reveal a few trends in the development of meaning and its interpretations. Perhaps it would not hurt to review both 'historiography' and 'historiographer' along an etymological path since in English (the medium of communication for this chapter) it has a lengthy semantic history. By assuming ἱστοριογράφος and ἱστοριογραφία (not attested in ancient Greek), it is not difficult to accept *historiographus* and *historiographia* of which the former is attested as a post-classical word (Julius Capitolinus, *Gordiani tres*, II, 21) in the third century after Christ. The latter term appears in the Renaissance through Cornelius Heinrich Agrippa (1486–1535) (1531:II, 5, pp. 2, 27). In English scholarship the first evidence is in *Wits Trenchmour* (p. 13) by Nicholas Breton (1545?–1626) where *historiographie* ('Haue you not beene a little red in historiographie?' [1597:D3]) means the art of employment of writing history or just history. A similar acceptation is found the first time it appears, with "modern" spelling, in *Contemporary Review* (50[1886].291): "The Modern school of Historiography." The meaning of *historiography* begins to assume a specific connotation in Campanella 1613 (243) as 'the art of writing history correctly (*read* truth-

* This introduction constitutes a drastically abridged version of a much longer text, which had to be reduced at the request of the publisher. The full text will hopefully appear, completed and updated, at a later date.

fully)'. According to Abbagnano (1971:843), this meaning stabilized as such in French and English but in Italian it acquired, under the influence of Croce (1911),[1] the connotation of historical knowledge in general or the complex of historical sciences. In view of the ambiguity and differences involving 'history' and 'historiography' of linguistics, it is thus useful to accept a proper term that would distinguish historical knowledge from historical reality. Distinctions were necessary as early as the first third of the nineteenth century, as typified by the *Dictionnaire des Dictionnaires* (2 [1837].127): 'L'historiographe rassemble les matériaux, l'historien les met en ordre.' This somewhat prosaic distinction was to linger in most Western cultures for almost a century.

The most illuminating essay designed to clarify the distinction between history and historiography is, in my judgment, the entry "storiografia" in Abbagnano 1971 (843–6). Abbagnano, of course, needs no introduction from me, since he is internationally known — at least among philosophers. His *Dizionario della filosofia*, moreover, is not a mere dictionary of terms *à la* Philosophical Library but a collection of essays properly documented by bibliography.

Abbagnano says there are two possible interpretations for such historical knowledge (as 'awareness'), namely (a) universal historiography and (b) pluralistic historiography. The interpretation of historical knowledge as universal history corresponds to the interpretation of historical reality as world, i.e. cosmic (*Weltgeschichte*) as the knowledge of the providential level of the historical world (Hegel 1905:52). Interpretation of historiography as pluralistic history, however, corresponds to the interpretation of historical reality as an object capable of definition or acceptance only through the tools of research at our disposal (cf. Romeo and Tiberio 1971:23). It seems to me that historiography of linguistics falls into (and can be interpreted within) (b), i.e. pluralistic historiography which is primarily characterized by the rejection of concepts such as 'historical world' or 'universal history', and by the acceptance of plurality of forms of both historical knowledge and its dependence at our disposal and on principles which guide our historical selection. Paraphrasing Abbagnano more closely, from this viewpoint the authentic historical knowledge always converges on defined and definable objects, and never on the totality of history. Although Greek antiquity has endowed us with excellent examples of historiography in this sense (e.g. the contributions of Thucidides and of Polybius), the cornerstones of what is now historiography begin to appear clearly starting only with the Renaissance and have found their definitions by historians and philosophers only in recent years (cf. Fueter 1911, Soranzo 1950, and Bulferetti 1965, as well as the four volumes of the collection *Questioni di storia contemporanea* [Milano, Marzorati 1952–56], especially volume 3 con-

[1] Other works influencing both the terminology and the concepts it represented were his first writings on theory and history of historiography that appeared in 1912 and later published in Croce 1917.

taining a gold mine of essays on history of historiography and a rich bibliography).

Abbagnano's views on historiography, although seen within philosophy, history and literature, are readily applicable to linguistics. No one, so far, has tried to specifically relate historiography to linguistics or any theory of how history could be viewed at the comparative level except for some concerns expressed at a few Linguistic Society of America Institutes through an attempt to inject Kuhn's paradigms (see Romeo & Tiberio 1971:24) into courses of history of linguistics. In correspondence with E.F.K. Koerner I have discussed some topics on this matter and, as I understand it, he has in mind to treat at least part of it. Judging from an advance copy of an abstract dated April 26, 1971, Koerner plans to read a paper, at the XI International Congress of Linguists, entitled "Paradigms for the epistemology of the 19th and 20th century history of linguistics: Schleicher-Saussure-Chomsky". In it he says: 'Histories available at the present time content themselves with presenting linguistic ideas in an almost exclusively chronological manner disregarding the advances in the (other) sciences and tend to judge the validity and adequacy of ideas proposed in the past from the strictly modern point of view. There is no doubt that this treatment of the history of linguistics thought is quite inadequate and misleading since it ignores the impact of social, political, and economic conditions under which these ideas were developed and, in particular, the advancement of science which has had an impact on the intellectual atmosphere of the time; the mistreatment has been compounded by viewing science in the light of the understanding today.' I hope that Koerner's concern for the last two centuries will be spread back to the Graeco-Roman era concerning which most misunderstanding occurs. In a letter dated November 18, 1971, he wrote to me: 'I do not believe that we have something we could rightly call a historiography of linguistic science but, as you may gather from the enclosed mimeographic summary above, I hope to propose a few principles on which something like a linguistic historiography may be based on the occasion of the 11th Congress of Linguists.' What will happen in the next few years remains to be seen. Meanwhile it is tentatively possible to assume a couple of definitions for historiography related to linguistics. Already, even in popular United States dictionaries, definitions generally have been changed. For example, the 1st edition of *Webster's New International Dictionary* (1920) says: "Historiography ... The art or employment, or a work, of a historiographer.' And 'Historiographer ... A historian; a writer of history; esp., one appointed or designated to write a history; also a title bestowed by some governments upon historians of distinction.' Just half a century later, we find at least four definitions in *The Random House Dictionary* (1966) where only the fourth reflects a 19th-century legacy stemming from the *Dictionnaire des Dictionnaires,* while definition 2 and 3 show quite a concern and an awareness as to what historiography could be. In our case, thus, we assume and combine both definitions 2 and 3 in order to analyze how scholars have expressed and written their views on histories of Roman linguistics (in actuality, segments of this never-written history). What are the trends? Are these based on facts? Are these reflections a monogenetic trend? Is this "correct"? What are the methods of analysis? How were they devised?

Is there enough material for an objective dissection, account, and evaluation? In essence can we really speak of historiography of linguistics as a genre? (Cf. *Dizionario Enciclopedico della Letteratura Italiana* (1966–70) 5.200–1.)

Perhaps some answers to these and many other questions can be obtained by "historiographicizing" the tradition. Is there an 'antitradition'? There should be, otherwise we cannot have any 'historiography' proper.

It is hardly appropriate to speak of conclusions at the end of a phase of historiography, and I can offer two reasons for that. In my own judgment, the primary one could be expressed by either Horatius' 'Parturiunt montes, nascetur ridiculus mus,' or Seneca's 'Magna promisisti, exigua video.' That would be seconded by the conviction that in historiography conclusions can only be characterized by trends. What are these trends? For me, they exist at two separate levels. At the first level we can consider the 'art' as incorporating the actual processes of learning, teaching and working with the language, i.e. Latin. Even there I sense two other different facets. On one hand there is the true, irreversible and inescapable reality that the total demise of 'Latin' is imminent. The causes for that are several, but perhaps the most obvious fact is that the humanities themselves are moribund in this world of technology, of material aims, and immediate concern for biological survival. This psychosis is further aggravated by the fact that even at institutions of higher learning emphasis is now aimed toward 'everything in translation,' an analgesic but hardly a cure for the disease. On the other hand I sense that, because of the stimulus given by transformational generative grammar to studies on Latin, there is an upsurge of interest with attendant hopes for a revival. I fear this is an illusion, however, because the human reservoir required for such an endeavor has been fed mostly by a now-old generation of tradition-ingrained young scholars (including R. Lakoff). Most assuredly there are manifestations of interest, even in Italy, the land that gave Latin its birth.[2] For instance, the pioneering work by Calboli 1968a and 1970 is certainly an exceptional case, if not a miracle in itself. Morelli 1970 is another, followed by Zirin 1971. I firmly believe that others will be added to this line but, sadly, they are all within the realm of a dying art. What can be expected to come out of the next one or two generations of translation-trained scholars? It is at the first level, then, that continuity

[2] Just a few hours before sending my original typescript to the editor-in-chief, I received an airmailed copy of Calboli 1972 [= Gualtiero Calboli, *La linguistica moderna e il latino; I casi*. Bologna, Pàtron]. Too late to include it in the bibliography and to digest it properly, I can only say that Calboli's work is an exceptional, unique, original presentation of a topic that had never been treated systematically in a transformational key. To the historiographer of linguistics for the Seventies, Calboli will be remembered gratefully not only for his excursus of the cases in Greek and Latin grammar (Chapter 2), but also for Chapters 3 and 4 in which he covers the cases respectively during the structural period and with regard to transformational grammar. (Cf. Traina 1963–64). Attention should be paid to pp. 94–97 in which Calboli *seems* to accept the 'tradition'. This is reinforced by the fact that in the bibliography the suspiciously intuitive Della Corte 1937 and the massively documented Funaioli 1946–48 are conspicuously absent.

of the "species" must be determined. As for the other, the historiographic level, I hold slightly more optimism. But that halcyonic emotion is dampened somewhat by a premonition that any activity there must perforce be finite. Once exhausted by the regard to the history of Latin linguistics, will such activity rally enough strength to save the language and the symbols it embodies from oblivion? I see Latin, and all it implies, as an enchanted swan singing her *Totenlieder*. Some visionaries among us may hope to someday know every historical fact on this elusive subject but by that time it could be found only in zoological museums. If my views appear obsessive they remain nevertheless strong and persistent, not confined to matters of Latin alone but extending to other components comprising the very essense of western civilization which is based upon Greek and Latin culture from which *homo sapiens* developed into *homo oeconomicus* in the Aristotelian sense. If I should wager upon the outcome of this state of affairs, nothing could please me more than to lose. Then, every blow from whipping criticism would be a pang of joy in the proof that, once more, 'Errare humanum est!'

BIBLIOGRAPHY

AALTO, PENTTI. 1949. Untersuchungen über das lateinische Gerundium und Gerundivum. Suomalaisen Tiedeakatemian Toimituksia. Sarja B, Nid. 63, No. 3. Helsinki.

——. 1953. Die statistische Methode in der Sprachforschung unter besonderer Berücksichtigung des Lateinischen. Eranos 51.232–6.

ABBAGNANO, NICOLA. 1971². Dizionario di filosofia. Torino, Unione Tipografica Editrice Torinese.

ABBOTT, K.M. 1943. The grammarians and the Latin accent. In Classical studies in honor of W.A. Oldfather, 1–19. Urbana, University of Illinois Press.

——. 1944. Ictus, accent and statistics in Latin dramatic verse. TAPA 75.127–40.

ABEL, W., and G. REINCKE, eds. 1941. Bibliotheca philologica classica. Leipzig, Reisland.

ACCADEMIA TOSCANA DI SCIENZE E LETTERE. 1970. Mille: I dibattiti del Circolo Linguistico Fiorentino, 1945–1970. Firenze, Olschki.

ACTA ANTIQUA PHILIPPOLITANA. Studia historica et philologica. VIe Conférence Internationale d'Études Classiques des Pays Socialistes, Plovdiv, 24–28 avril 1962. 1963. Sofia, Academie des Sciences.

ACTA CONGRESSUS MADVIGIANI. Proceedings of the Second International Congress of Classical Studies. 1954. Köbenhavn, Munksgaard.

ACTA OMNIUM GENTIUM AC NATIONUM CONVENTUS LATINIS LINGUAEQUE FOVENDIS A

DIE XIV AD DIEM XVIII MENSIS APRILIS A. MDCCCCLXVI Romae habiti. 1968. Roma, Colombo.

ACTAS DEL PRIMER CONGRESO ESPAÑOL DE ESTUDIOS CLÁSICOS. 1958. Madrid, Sociedad Española de Estudios Clásicos.

ACTAS DEL II CONGRESO ESPAÑOL DE ESTUDIOS CLÁSICOS. 3 vols. 1964. Madrid, Consejo Superior de Investigación Científica.

ACTAS DEL III CONGRESO ESPAÑOL DE ESTUDIOS CLÁSICOS. (Madrid, 28 de marzo-1 de abril de 1966). 1968. Madrid, Sociedad Española de Estudios Clásicos.

ACTES DU PREMIER CONGRÈS DE LA FÉDÉRATION INTERNATIONALE DES ASSOCIATIONS D'ÉTUDES CLASSIQUES. 1951. Paris, Klincksieck.

ACTES DU VIII° CONGRÈS, ASSOCIATION GUILLAUME BUDÉ, Paris 5–10 1968. Paris, Les Belles Lettres.

AGRIPPA VON NETTESHEIM, HENRY CORNELIUS. 1531. De incertitudine et vanitate scientiarum et artium atque excellentia verbi Dei declamatio. Antwerp.

AHLBERG, A. W. et al. 1945. Latinsk-svensk ordbok. Stockholm, Svenska.

AKABOGU, G. 1958. The teaching of Latin in Nigerian schools. In FERGUSON 1958: 56–64.

——. 1962. The traditional versus the modern method of teaching. In FERGUSON 1962:54–64.

ALESSIO, G. 1939. Imprestiti, calchi e rifacimenti latini dal greco. RFC 17.145–63.

——. 1953. Calchi linguistici greco-latini nell'antico territorio della Magna Grecia. Atti dell'VIII° Congresso internazionale di Studi Bizantini I, 237–99.

ALLARDICE, J. T. 1929. Syntax of Terence. Oxford, University Press.

ALLEN, W. SIDNEY. 1953. Phonetics in Ancient India. London, Oxford University Press.

——. 1965. Vox Latina: A guide to the pronuniciation of Classical Latin. London, Cambridge University Press.

——. 1968. Vox Graeca: A guide to the pronunciation of Classical Greek. London, Cambridge University Press.

——. 1969. The Latin accent: A restatement. JL 5.193–203.

ALTHEIM, FRANZ. 1951. Geschichte der lateinischen Sprache von den Anfängen bis zum Beginn der Literatur. Frankfurt, Klostermann.

AMATUCCI, A. G. 1954. Appunti di bibliografia classica. Paideia 9.283–7.

ANDRÉ, JACQUES. 1948. Étude sur les termes de couleur dans la langue latine. Unpublished dissertation. Paris.

——. 1958. Accent, timbre et quantité dans les emprunts du latin au grec postérieurs au IIIe s. après J.-C. BSL 53.138–58.

——. 1968a. Philologie latine. AEHE-HPh 1967–68.225–7.

——. 1968b. Les changements de genre dans les emprunts du latin au grec. Word 24.1–7.

——. 1969. Philologie latine. AEHE-HPh 1968–69.203–4.

——. 1970. Philologie latine. AEHE-HPh 1969–70.281–4.

ANDREWS, E. A. 1860. A copious and critical Latin-English lexicon founded on the larger Latin-German lexicon of Dr. William Freund with additions and corrections from the lexicons of Gesner, Facciolati, Scheller, Georges, etc. New York, Harper and Brothers.

ANONYMOUS. 1940. Il contributo dell'Istituto di Studi Romani agli studi sul latino attraverso i suoi congressi. SUL 2.119–22.

ANONYMOUS. 1949. O reaparecimento do Thesaurus linguae Latinae. Humanitas 2.432–5.

ANONYMOUS. 1956. El Primer Congreso Español de Estudios Clásicos, realidad y promesa. Helmantica 7.177–81 and 289–311.

ANONYMOUS. 1959 (1961). A situação dos estudos clássicos no Brasil. BECh 3.93–6.

ANONYMOUS. 1961. Philologia classica in Republica Populari Dacoromana. ZJKF 3.168–70.

ANONYMOUS. 1962. Il latino nel mondo (Stati Uniti, Inghilterra, Finlandia, Repubblica Democratica Tedesca). Orpheus. Supplement IX(1).22–8.

ANONYMOUS. 1969. Cinquième Congrès de la Fédération Internationale des Associa tions d'Études Classiques. RACF 8.366–7.

ANTIKE UND MITTELALTER IN BULGARIEN. 1960. See BEŠEVLIEV et al. 1960.

ARAMON I SERRA, R. 1952. El Primer Congrés d'Etudis Clàssics. Butlletí de la Soc. Catalana d'Estudis Historics, 80–2.

ARENS, HANS. 1955. Sprachwissenschaft. Der Gang ihrer Entwicklung von der Antike bis zur Gegenwart. Freiburg, Alber. [2nd edition 1969.]

ARON, RAYMOND. 1959. Introduction à la philosophie de l'histoire. Paris, Gallimard.

ARROWSMITH, R. 1943. Tendances et lacunes des études de métrique latine. In Mémorial des études latines, 117–22. Paris, Les Belles Lettres.

BACCI, ANTONIO. 1963. Lexicon vocabulorum quae difficilius latine redduntur. Romae, Studium.

BADER, FRANÇOISE. 1964. La formation des composés nominaux du latin. Paris, Les Belles Lettres.

——. 1968 (1969). Vocalisme et redoublement au parfait radical en latin. BSL 63. 160–96.

BARBU, N. I. 1969. De consecutione temporum Latina. Latinitas 17.25–34.

BARDON, H. 1956. Le Premier Congrès Espagnol d'Études Classiques. REA 58. 437–8.

BARTOLI, M. 1941. Tradizione e rivoluzione nella storia del latino e dell'italiano. Romana V.621–31.

BARTONĚK, A. 1956. [The Latin grammarians' conception of the seventh and eighth cases.] Sborník Prací Filosofické Fakulty Brněnské University, Řada Archeologicko-Klasická E(1).173–82.

——. 1960. [IIIe Congrès International d'Études Classiques, Londres, août-sept. 1959.] SPFB, 9(E5).157–60.

——. 1962. Der Latein- und Griechischunterricht in der Tschechoslovakischen Sozialistischen Republik. Romanitas 4.369–84.

——. 1963. [On the application of new methods to the study of Latin and Greek.] LF 11.197–206.

BARWICK, KARL. 1922. Remmius Palaemon und die römische ars grammatica. Leipzig, Dietrich. [Reprinted 1967. Hildesheim, Olms.]

BASSETT, E. L. 1945. The genitive absolute in Latin. CPh 40.108–14.

——. 1949. Classical studies in Holland. CJ 44.328–32.

BASSETT, S. E., and J. W. SPAETH, JR. 1947–48. Classical articles in non-classical periodicals. CJ 43.57–61.

BASSOLS DE CLIMENT, M. 1945. Sintaxis histórica de la lengua latina. I, Introducción, género, número, casos. Barcelona, Consejo Superior de Investigación Científica.

——. 1948. Sintaxis histórica de la lengua latina. II, Las formas personales del verbo. Barcelona, Instituto Nebrija.

——. 1956. Sintaxis latina. Enciclopedia clásica, 3–4. Madrid, Consejo Superior de Investigación Científica.

——. 1962. Fonética latina. Madrid, Consejo Superior de Investigación Científica.

BATILLE HUGUET, P. 1943. Inscripciones Romanas inéditas de Tarragona. Amp 5.79–94.

BATTISTI, CARLO. 1961. Orientamenti generali della linguistica in Italia, 1930–1960. In MOHRMANN et al. 1961:240–82.

BEACH, G. B. 1957. The Congress for Living Latin: Another view. CJ 53.119–22.

——. 1962. De statu hodierno rei classicae in Civitatibus Foederatis Americae Septentrionalis. Romanitas 4.353–9.

BEAUJEU, J. 1956. Premier Congrès International pour le Latin Vivant. L'Information littéraire 8.156.

BELOVA, N. N., et al. 1968. [Classical studies at the University of the State of Urals]. VDI 104.206–12.

BELTRÁN, A. 1955. El II Congreso Internacional de Estudios Clásicos en Copenhague. Caesaraugusta 6.284–7.

BENDZ, G. 1945. Some critical Latin word studies. Eranos 43.36–57.

BENFEY, THEODOR. 1869. Geschichte der Sprachwissenschaft und orientalischen Philologie in Deutschland. Munich, Cotta.

BENVENISTE, ÉMILE. 1962. Pour l'analyse des fonctions casuelles: le génitif latin. Lingua 11.10–18.

——. 1969. Diffusion d'un terme de culture: latin *orarium*. Studia Pagliaro I.213–18.

BERGSLAND, K. 1942. Remarques sur la valeur des temps latins. Serta Eitremiana, 25–31.

BERNARDI PERINI, GIORGIO. 1964. L'accento latino. Cenni teorici e norme pratiche. Bologna, Pàtron.

BERTOLDI, V. 1940. Storia di un dialettismo nel latino dell'Urbe. RFC 18.22–33.

BEŠELÍEV, V., et al. 1960. Antike und Mittelalter in Bulgarien. Berlin, Akademie-Verlag.

BIBLIOGRAFÍA DE LOS ESTUDIOS CLÁSICOS EN ESPAÑA, 1939–1955. Madrid, Sociedad Española de Estudios Clásicos.

BIBLIOGRAFÍA DE LOS ESTUDIOS CLÁSICOS EN ESPAÑA, 1956–1965. 1968. Madrid, Sociedad Española de Estudios Clásicos.

BIGNONE, ETTORE, ed. 1951. Introduzione alla filologia classica. Milano, Marzorati.

BJÖRCK, GUDMUND, et al. 1952. Bibliografisk översikt. Eranos 50.164–245.

BLAKE, FRANK R. 1942. Review of GRAY 1939. AJPh, 63.337–42.

BLATT, F. 1946. Latinsk Syntaks i Hovedtraek. Paa Grundlag af den klassiske Sprogtilstand. København, Gyldendal.

——. 1952. Précis de syntaxe latine. Lyon, I.A.C.

——. 1964. Gli studi di filologia classica e medievale in Danimarca. Aevum 30. 30.286–300.

BLOCH, B., and G. L. TRAGER. 1942. Outline of linguistic analysis. Baltimore, Md., The Linguistic Society of America.

BLOIS, J., et al. 1968. Problèmes de la traduction automatique. Paris, Klincksieck.

BLOMGREN, S. 1939. De hodierno linguae latinae in Suecia usu atque statu. SUL 2.34–41.

BLOOMFIELD, LEONARD. 1933. Language. New York, Holt.

——. 1939. Review of GRAY 1939. MLF 24.198–9.

BODSON, A. 1968a. Le programme d'analyse automatique du latin. Les machines dans la linguistique. Colloque international sur la mécanisation et l'automation des recherches linguistiques, 117–30. Prague, Academia.

——. 1968b. Le laboratoire d'analyse statistique des langues anciennes. REL 46.19–21.

——, and E. ÉVRARD. 1966. Le programme d'analyse automatomatique du latin. RELO 2.17–46.

BOECKH, AUGUST. 1886. Formale Theorie der philologischen Wissenschaft. In E. Bratuscheck, ed., Enzyklopädie und Methodenlehre der philologischen Wissenschaften, 1. Leipzig, Klussmann.

BOLELLI, T. 1943. Osservazioni sul suono intermedio fra *i* e *u* in latino. RAI (Serie VII) IV.193–204.

BOLLING, G. M. 1944. Acceleration of language teaching and the classics. CPh 39. 101–6.

BOLOGNESI, GIANCARLO. 1951. Profilo storico-critico degli studi linguistici greci e latini. In BIGNONE 1951:369–452. [Part III, Lingua Latina, 421–52.]

BONFANTE, GIULIANO. 1946. Semantics, language. In HARRIMAN 1946:838–70.

BONIOLO, MARIA. 1962. La pronuncia del latino nelle scuole dell'antichità al Rinascimento, Parte I. Torino, Università degli Studi.

BONNELL, EDUARD. 1962. Lexicon Quintilianeum. Hildesheim, Olms.

BOROVSKIJ, J. M., et al. 1968. [Classical philology at the University of Leningrad.] VDI 104.145–9.

BORZSÁK, ISTVÁN. 1952. A magyar klasszika-filológiai irodalom bibliográfiája, 1925–1950. Budapest, Akadémiai Kiadó.

BOS, GYSBERTHA F. 1967. L'adverbe en latin. Tentative de classification structurale. BSL 62.106–22.

BOSCHERINI, SILVANO. 1964. Filologia e linguistica. A&R 9.108–11.

BOTTAI, G. 1939. Roma nella scuola italiana. Roma, Istituto di Studi Romani.

——. 1942. Vitalità e funzione del latino nella nuova scuola. Quaderni del Centro Nazionale per il Latino 4.53–6.

BOWER, E. W. 1961. Some technical terms in Roman education. Hermes 89.462–77.

BOYANCÉ, P. 1951. Le Premier Congrès de la Fédération Internationale des Associations d'Études Classiques. Paris, 28 août-3 septembre 1950. REA 53.89–91.

——. 1961. Les études latines à Rome. In MAROUZEAU 1961: 81–2.

BRAJER, F. 1965–66. Kongres klasičnih filologa. Madarska Akademia Nauka (Magyar Tudom. Akad.), Budapest, 1–7 nov. 1965. ŽAnt 40.503–4.

BRANDENSTEIN, W. 1950. Einführung in die Phonetik und Phonologie. Wien, Gerold.

——. 1951. Kurze Phonologie des Lateinischen. In ALTHEIM 1951:481–98.

BRASH, I. F., and F. W. WALBANK. 1946. Les études classiques en Grande-Bretagne pendant la guerre. BAGB (n.s.) 1.73–105.

BRAVO LOZANO, MILLÁN. 1965. Un aspecto de la latinización de la terminología filosófica en Roma: κατηγορία/praedicamentum. Em 33.351–80.

BRITANNICA REVIEW OF FOREIGN LANGUAGE EDUCATION. 1ff. 1968 ff. Chicago, Encyclopaedia Britannica, Inc.

BRÉGUET, ESTHER. 1969. *Urbi et orbi.* Un cliché et un thème. Hommages Renard 1.140–52.

BRETON, NICH[OLAS]. 1597. Wits trenchmour in a conference had [sic] betwixt a scholler and an angler. London, N. Ling.

BROCCIA, S. 1946. Breve nota di grammatica latina. Annali della Facoltà di Lettere, Filosofia e Magistero della U. di Cagliari 14.13–22.

BRØNDAL, VIGGO. 1958. Théorie des prépositions. Copenhague, Munksgaard.

BROUGHTON, T. R. S. 1946. Les études classiques en Amérique, 1940–1945. BAGB (n.s.) 1(2).44–65.

BRUNO, MARIA GRAZIA. 1969. Il lessico agricolo latino. 2nd ed. Amsterdam, Hakkert.

BÜCHNER, KARL, and J. B. HOFMAN. 1951. Lateinische Literatur und Sprache in der Forschung seit 1937. Bern, Francke.

BUCK, C. D. 1933. Comparative grammar of Greek and Latin. Chicago, University Press.

BUDAGOV, R. A. 1961. K teorii otnošenij meždu slovom, slovosočetaniem i predloženiem v latinskom jazyke. In Issledovanija v oblasti latinskogo i romanskogo jazykoznanija, 5–36.

BUESCU, V. 1947. Os estudos clássicos na Roménia. Humanitas 1.186–202.

BULFERETTI, L. 1965. Introduzione alla storiografia. Milano, Marzorati.

BURCK, E. 1955. Pronunciation du latin. In Premier Congrès International pour le latin vivant, 58–65.

BURIAN, J., and VIDMAN, L., eds. 1967. Pro antiquitate viva. Colloque sur la part revenant à la culture antique dans l'enseignement tenu à l'occasion du Congrès International "L'antiquité classique et nos jours" à Brno les 12 et 13 avril 1966. Praha, Státní Pedag. Naklad.

——. 1968. Acta Congressus internationalis habiti Brunae diebus 12–16 mensis Aprilis MCMLXVI. Praha, ČSAV.

BURNET, I.G. 1969. Linguistic 'normality' in Tacitus: *promitto* and *polliceor*. BICS 16.63–6.

BURSILL-HALL, G.L. 1959a. "The doctrine of Partes Orationis in the speculative grammars of the Modistae". London, University of London. Unpublished Ph.D. Dissertation.

——. 1959b. French Quadri-phonematic Clusters. JCLA 5.35–45.

——. 1971. Speculative grammars of the Middle Ages. The Hague, Mouton.

BUSA, R. 1951. Rapida e meccanica composizione e pubblicazione di indici e concordanze di parole mediante macchine elettrocontabili. Aevum 25.479–93.

——. 1968. Un lexique latin électronique. In MATER & STINDLOVÁ 1968:251–69.

——. 1969. Actes du Seminaire International sur le Dictionnaire Latin de Machine. Pisa, Centro Nazionale Universitario di Calcolo Elettronico, 27–29 marzo 1968. In RELO, 2–3.

CALBOLI, GUALTIERO. 1965. Questioni di linguistica latina. QIGB 7.67–86.

——. 1966. I modi del verbo greco e latino, 1903–1966. Lustrum 11.173–349.

——. 1968a. Sintassi latina e linguistica moderna. LeSt 3.307–17.

——. 1968b (1969). I modi del verbo greco e latino, 1903–1966. Lustrum 13.405–511.

——. 1969. Il congresso di Bonn sull'antichità classica. Maia 21.370–8.

——. 1970. Il latino della grammatica. LeSt 5.107–36.

CALCATERRA, ANTONIO. 1968. Struttura del linguaggio giuridico-precettivo romano. Contributi. Bari, Cacucci.

CALDER, W.M. 1968. Die klassische Philologie in den Vereinigten Staaten. Altertum 14.45–55.

CALLMER, C., et al. 1963. Bibliografia översikt. Eranos 61.183–275.

CAMILLI, A. 1949. Trattato di prosodia e metrica latina. Firenze, Sansoni.

——. 1950. La pronuncia normale del latino nel primo secolo dell'impero. MPhon 94.26–7.

CAMPANELLA, TOMMASO. 1613. Philosophia Rationalis partes quinque, videlicet Grammatica, Dialectica, Rhetorica, Poetica, Historiographia, iuxta propria principia. Paris.

CAMPANILE, ENRICO. 1961. Elementi dialettali nella fonetica e nella morfologia del latino. SSL 1.1–21.
——. 1965. Rapporti linguistici fra il mondo celtico e il mondo latino e neo-latino. Napoli, Corvino.
——. 1968. Studi sulla posizione dialettale del latino. SSL 8.16–130.
——. 1969. Valutazione del latino di Britannia. SSL 9.87–110.
CAMPOS, J. 1966a. Omnium gentium ac nationum conventus latinitas litteris linguaeque fovendis. Helmantica 17.121–33.
——. 1966b. III Congreso Español de Estudios Clásicos. Helmantica 17.135–42.
CAPPELLI, A. 1949. Dizionario di abbreviature latine ed italiane. Milano, Hoepli.
CARO, M.A. 1950. Del ritmo acentual en la versificación latina. BICC 6.369–83.
CARRIÈRE, G. 1949. Les études classiques à Ottawa. Phoenix 3.40–1.
CARROLL, JOHN B. 1953. The study of language. A survey of linguistics and related disciplines in America. Cambridge, Harvard University Press.
CATAUDELLA, Q. 1952. Rassegna di libri di filologia classica. SicGymn 5.243–63.
——. 1956. Rassegna di studi di filologia classica. SicGymn 9.118–31.
——. 1962. Rassegna di libri di filologia classica. SicGymn 15.254–99.
——. 1963. Rassegna di libri di filologia classica. Sic Gymn 16.200–47.
CATONE, NICOLA. 1964. Grammatica enniana. Firenze, Vallecchi.
CEVOLANI, GIUSEPPE. 1960. Studi critici di sintassi latina. Bologna, Cappelli.
CHANTRAINE, P. 1964. [Le IVe Congrès International des Études Classiques de Philadelphie.] CRAI, 305–6.
CHAPOUTHIER, F., et al. 1950. Chronique des études anciennes. REA 187–98 and 372–8.
CHARPIN, F. 1965 (1966). Coniunctiones causales et rationales. REL 43.396–405.
CHAUSSERIE-LAPRÉE, J.P. 1963 (1964). Les structures et les techniques de l'expression narrative chez les historiens latins. REL 41.281–96.
——. 1969. L'expression narrative chez les historiens latins. Histoire d'un style. Paris, de Boccard.
CHEVALLIER, R. 1960. Les études supérieures de latin: Initiation à la recherche. Paris, Société d'Education et d'Enseignement.
CHOMSKY, NOAM. 1957. Syntactic structures. The Hague, Mouton.
——. 1966. Cartesian linguistics. New York, Harper and Row.
——. 1968. Language and mind. New York, Harcourt, Brace, and World.
——. 1972. Language and mind. Enlarged edition. New York, Harcourt, Brace, Jovanovich.
CIARDI, JOHN. 1969. Manner of speaking. The Saturday Review 24 May. 34–9.
CICCHITTI, V.V. 1960. Tercer Congreso Internacional de Estudios Clásicos. REC 7.165–9.
CIRESOLA, TEODORO. 1960. Sintassi latina. Milano, Garzanti.
CLASSICAL STUDIES IN HONOR OF W.A. OLDFATHER. 1943. Urbana, University of Illinois Press.

COHEN, J. G. 1939. A few words on words. CW 32.280.
COLE, T. 1969. The saturnian verse. YCS 21.3–73.
COLEMAN, R. T. 1936a. Two linguistic topics in Quintilian. CQ 13.1–18.
——. (1963b) 1962. Some allophones of Latin /i/ TPhS 80–104.
COLLART, JEAN. 1954a. Pour une anthologie des textes grammaticaux latins. REL 32.88–92.
——. 1954b. Varron grammairien latin. Paris, Les Belles Lettres.
——. 1954c. Varron, De lingva latina, livre V. Paris, Les Belles Lettres.
——. 1959. Quelques observations statistiques sur les parties du discours. REL 37.215–29 (1 dépliant).
——. 1960. À propos des études syntaxiques chez les grammairiens latins. BFS 38.267–77.
——. 1963. Analogie et anomalie. In VARRON 1963:117–40.
——. 1965. Quelques observations sur Aulu-Gelle, grammairien. REL 43.384–95.
——. 1966. Grammaire du latin. Paris, Presses Universitaires de France.
——. 1967. Histoire de la langue latine. Paris, Presses Universitaires de France.
CONWAY, R. S. 1933. The Pre-Italic dialects. 3 vols. Cambridge, Harvard University Press.
COPPA, J. 1966. Linguae Latinae per orbem terrarum fortuna. Latinitas 14.141–6 and 226–30.
——. 1969. Linguae Latinae per orbem terrarum fortuna. Latinitas 17.58–65.
CORDIER, A. 1939. L'allitération latine. Le procédé dans l'Enéide de Virgile. Paris, Vrin.
——. 1947. Les débuts de l'hexamètre latin: Ennius. Paris, Vrin.
CORREA RODRÍGUEZ, J. A. 1966. *s* sonora en latín, ¿variante o fonema? Estudio Diacrónico. ACEEC 3.85–91.
COSTELLOE, M. J. 1950. A First International Classics Meeting (Le ler Congrès de la Fédération Internationale des Associations d'Études Classiques). CB 27.8–10.
COUSIN, JEAN. 1939. Review of MAROUZEAU 1939 in REA 41.290–1.
——. 1944. Evolution et structure de la langue latine. Paris, Les Belles Lettres.
——. 1951. Bibliographie de la langue latine (1880–1948). Paris, Les Belles Lettres.
CROCE, BENEDETTO. 1911. La filosofia di G. B. Vico. Bari, Laterza.
——. 1917. Teoria e storia della storiografia. Bari, Laterza.
CRUSIUS, FRIEDRICH. 1955². Römische Metrik. München, Huber.
CUNNINGHAM, M. P. 1941. The singular and plural of substantives in Latin poetic diction. Doctoral dissertation, University of California.
——. 1957. Some phonetic aspects of word order patterns in Latin. PAPhilosS 101.481–505.
——. 1965. A theory of the Latin sentence. CPh 60.24–8.
CUPAIUOLO, FABIO. 1960. Appunti di grammatica storica latina. Napoli, Libreria Scientifica Editrice.
——. 1961. Appunti di storia della lingua latina e di grammatica storica. Napoli,

Libreria Scientifica Editrice.
D'AGOSTINO, V. 1949. Contributi allo studio del lessico latino. Torino, Ruata.
DAHLÉN, ERIC, 1964. Études syntaxiques sur les pronoms réfléchis pléonastiques en latin. Stockholm, Almqvist & Wiksell.
DAHLMANN, HELLFRIED, ed. 1940. Varro, De Lingua Latina, 7. Hermes, 8. Berlin Weidmann. [Reprinted 1960.]
——. 1964². Varro und die hellenistische Sprachtheorie. Berlin, Weidmann.
DAIN, A. 1954. Congrès et commémorations. REL 32.72–3.
DALL'OGLIO, GAETANO. 1959. Punti controversi di sintassi latina. Bologna, Zanichelli.
DALTON, R. H. F. 1963. Latin in Africa. The cultural point of view. G&R 10.183–8.
DA NÓBREGA, V. L. 1962. A cultura clássica no Brasil. Romanitas 4.457–65.
DAUBE, DAVID. 1969. Roman law: Linguistic, social and philosophical aspects. Edinburgh, University Press.
DAVIS, GEORGE TOBEY. 1959. "A study in Latin prosody". Ph.D. dissertation, University of Pennsylvania. Dab 20.1773.
DE DIEGO LÓPEZ, V. G. 1947. Orientaciones sobre el género en latín, con especial estudio de la sinonimia genérica. Sevilla, Suárez.
De FELICE, E. 1948. La pronuncia del latino classico. Arona, Paideia.
DE GROOT, A. W. 1948. The history of Latin grammar. In Studia varia Carolo Guilielmo Vollgraff a discipulis ablata, 62–70. Amsterdam, North Holland.
——. 1956. Classification of the uses of a case illustrated on the genitive in Latin. Lingua 6.8-66.
DELATTE, L., and É. ÉVRARD. 1961. Un laboratoire d'analyse statistique des langages anciennes à l'Université de Liège. AC 30.429–44.
——. 1968. Listes de fréquence en ordre décroissant des mots des quatre livres des *Odes* d'Horace à l'exclusion du 'Carmen saecular', repartis selon leur catégorie grammaticale. RELO 6.11–89.
DELBRÜCK, B. 1884². Einleitung in das Sprachstudium. Leipzig, Härtel.
DELFINO, MARIA GIOVANNA. 1958. Il problema dei rapporti linguistici tra l'osco e il latino. In Serta Eusebiana, 27–86. Publicazione dell'Istituto di Filologia Classica, No. 11. Università di Genova.
DELLA CASA, ADRIANA. 1969. Il libro X del De lingua latina di Varrone. Genova, Bozzi.
DELLA CORTE, FRANCESCO. 1937. La filologia latina dalle origini a Varrone. Torino, Bona.
DELL'ERA, ANTONIO. 1968. Appunti sulla paraipotassi latina. RCCM 10.193–218.
DE MAURO, TULLIO. 1959. Accusativo, transitivo, intransitivo. RAL 14.233–58.
DE MATOS, L. 1947. Dos estudos clássicos em França. Humanitas 1.172–6.
DE OLIVEIRA. See LOURENÇO DE OLIVEIRA.
DERATANI, N. F. 1958. [Classical philology at the University of Moscow during the last 40 years.] Vestnik Moskovskogo Universiteta (istor. sekcija) 1.123–9.

De Ruyt, F. 1947–48. Les études anciennes en Italie (1937–1947). BIBR 24.193–272.
——. 1949. Les études anciennes en Italie. BIBR 25.343–408.
——. 1958. Les études anciennes en Italie. BIBR 31.301–410.
De Saint-Denis, E. 1947a. Syntaxe du latin parlé dans les 'Res Rusticae' de Varron. RPh, 141–62.
——. 1947b. Vocabulaire des animaux marins en latin classique. Paris, Klincksieck.
De Sousa Pereira, T. 1959. Varia noscenda [chronicle of classical studies in the world]. Euphrosyne 2.285–320.
Deutsch, R.E. 1939. "The pattern of sound in Latin". Dissertation, Bryn Mawr.
Deuxième Congrès International pour le Latin Vivant. 1960. Avignon, Aubanel.
De Villapadierna, T. 1959. Tercer Congreso Internacional de Estudios Clásicos. Londres, 31 agosto-5 Septiembre. Helmantica 10.443–4.
Devoto, G. 1939a. Un aspetto della storia della lingua latina. Romana 4.225–33.
——. 1939b. Gli Studi italiani di storia della lingua latina nell'ultimo quinquennio. ASPS (Riunione XXVII, Dec. 1). 81–82.
——. 1940a. Bibliographie der Jahre 1938–40, Italico. IJ 24.287–301.
——. 1940b. Storia della lingua di Roma. Bologna, Chiappelli.
——. 1951. I giorni [comments on the 1st Congress of Classical Studies, Paris, 1950]. A&R (n.s.) Mai Juin (2 and 17).
——. 1968. Geschichte der Sprache Roms, trans. by Ilona Opelt. Heidelberg, Winter.
——. 1970. Un esempio di modestia. In Accademia Toscana di Scienze e Lettere, 1–6.
De Witt, Norman W. 1941–42. Review of Gray 1939. CJ 37.174–5.
DeWitt, N.J. 1954. Grammar and linguistics. CW 47.193–6.
Díaz y Díaz, Manuel C. El latín de la península ibérica. In Enciclopedia lingüística hispánica 1.153–7 ('Rasgos lingüísticos') and 237–50 ('Dialectalismos').
Di Benedetto, Vincenzo. 1958. Dioniso Trace e la Techne a lui attribuita. Annali della Scuola Normale di Pisa 27.169–210.
——. 1959. Dioniso Trace e la Techne a lui attribuita. Annali della Scuola Normale di Pisa 28.87–118.
Dictionnaire des Dictionnaires ... donnant, de plus: tous les termes de littérature ... de grammaire ... de philologie, de linguistique ... 1837. 2 vols. Bruxelles, Hauman, Cattoir et Co.
Dihle, A. 1957. Analogie und Attizismus. Hermes 85.170–205.
Dik, Simon C. 1968. Coordination. Its implications for the theory of general linguistics. Amsterdam, North-Holland.
Di Marco, E. 1941. Il verbo latino. Nuova teoria dei tempi. Roma, Perrella.
Dinneen, Francis P. 1963. Linguistics and classical philosophy. Report of the fourteenth round table meeting on linguistics and language studies. 16. Washington, D.C., Georgetown University Press.
——, ed. 1966. Report of the seventeeth annual round table meeting on linguistics

and language studies. Washington, D.C., Georgetown University Press.
——. 1967. An introduction to general linguistics. New York, Holt, Rinehart and Winston.
DIVER, WILLIAM. 1964. The system of agency of the Latin noun. Word 20.178–96.
DIXON, ROBERT M.W. 1965. What is language? London, Longmans Green.
DIZIONARIO ENCICLOPEDICO DELLA LETTERATURA ITALIANA. 1966–70. 6 vols. Bari, Laterza-Unedi.
DOBROIU, E. 1968. Artifices phoniques employés par les écrivains romains pour suggérer certaines particularités de prononciation. Analele Universite Bucureşti 18.443–8.
DOLC, M. 1951. El Congreso Clásico de Grenoble. EClás 1.100–3.
DONALDSON, JOHN WILLIAM. 1844. Varronianus: A critical and historical introduction to the ethnography of Ancient Italy and to the philological study of the Latin language. London, Parker.
DORFMAN, EUGENE. 1960. University selected for linguistics program. After Hours 3(1).2(March).
DOWNEY, CHARLOTTE MARIE. 1969–70. Latin, a person oriented language. SIL 21.43–8.
DRĂGANU, NICOLAE. 1970. Storia della sintassi generale. Bologna, Pàtron.
DREXLER, HANS. 1969. Zur Syntax und Prosodie von *ille* und *iste* bei Plautus und Terenz. GIF 21.147–55.
DUCKWORTH, G.E. 1940. Recent trends in classical training in the United States. SUL 2.83–8.
——. 1962. Structural patterns and proportions in Vergil's Aeneid: A study in mathematical composition. Ann Arbor, University of Michigan Press.
——. 1967 (1968). Five centuries of Latin hexameter poetry. TAPA 98.77–150.
——. 1969. Vergil and classical Hexameter poetry. A study in metrical variety. Ann Arbor, University of Michigan Press.
DUGAS, C., et al. 1946. Chronique des études anciennes. REA, 148–50 and 301–6.
——, et al. 1947. Chronique des études anciennes. REA, 369–86.
DURRY, M. 1950. Le Premier Congrès International des Études Classiques. BAGB (n.s.) 12.5–9.
——. 1962. Les études latines en France. Romanitas 4.194–199.
DYER, R.R. 1969. The new philology. An old discipline or a new science? CHum 4.53–64.
EGGER, E. 1854. Apollonius Dyscole. Essai sur l'histoire des théories grammaticales dans l'antiquité. Paris, Durand.
EGITTO ANTICO E MODERNO. 1941. Milano, I.S.P.I.
EGLI, URS. 1967. Zur stoischen Dialektik. Inauguraldissertation Universität Bern.
——. 1970. Zwei Aufsätze zum Vergleich der stoischen Sprachtheorie mit modernen Theorien. Universität Bern, Institut für Sprachwissenschaft, Arbeitpapier 2, 1–40.

EHLERS, W. 1968. Der Thesaurus Linguae Latinae: Prinzipien und Erfahrungen. Antik und Abendland 14.172–84.

EMENEAU, M. B. 1940. Review of GRAY 1939. CPh 35.311-15.

ENCICLOPEDIA CLASSICA. 1968. Sezione II, Lingue e lett. Vol. VI, La lingua latina nei mezzi della sua espressione, ed. by Giovanni Battista Pighi. Tomo I, G. B. Pighi: Storia della lingua latina. Tomo II, G. B. Pighi: La metrica latina. Torino, Società Editrice Internazionale.

ENCICLOPEDIA ITALIANA DI SCIENZE, LETTERE ED ARTI. 1929–39. 36 vols. Roma, Istituto Giovanni Treccani.

ENCICLOPEDIA LINGÜÍSTICA HISPÁNICA. 1960ff. Madrid, Consejo Superior de Investigación Científica.

ENGELMANN, W. 1880–82^{8}. Bibliotheca scriptorum classicorum. Leipzig.

ENK, P. J. 1951. Étude des langues et littératures classiques dans les pays germaniques. In Actes du Premier Congrès de la Fédération Internationale des Associations d'Études Classiques, 333. Paris, Klincksieck.

——. 1953. The Latin accent. Mnemosyne 6.93–109.

——. 1955. De Latijnse philologie in onze tijd. In Ut pictura poesis, 7–21.

——. 1962. L'état actuel de la philologie latine en Hollande. Romanitas 4.318–22.

ENTWISTLE, WILLIAM JAMES, and WILLIAM SIDNEY ALLEN. 1967. Language. Chambers' Encyclopaedia 8.347–57.

ERNOUT, ALFRED. 1940. Review of GRAY 1939. RPh (ser. 3) 14.270–1.

——. 1953^{3}. Morphologie historique du latin. Paris, Klincksieck.

——. 1954. Aspects du vocabulaire latin. Paris, Klincksieck.

——. 1969a. Du latin aux langues romanes. RPh 43.7–14.

——. 1969b. Angerona. Hommages Renard 1.335–8.

——, and A. MEILLET. 1939. Dictionnaire étymologique de la langue latine. Histoire des mots. Nouvelle édition revue, corrigée et augmentée d'un index. Paris, Klincksieck.

——. 1951^{3}. Dictionnaire étymologique de la langue li) e. Histoire des mots. Paris, Klincksieck.

ERNST, J. 1939. L'enseignement du latin en Suisse. SUL 1.59–62.

——. 1949. Les études classiques après la guerre. Bulletin du Conseil de la Philolophie et des Sciences Humaines, 33–42. Paris, UNESCO.

——. 1953. À travers les revues d'études classiques. IL 5.33–4 and 111–13.

——. 1957. Actualités philologiques. Réflexions d'une bibliographe. BAGB 3.28–38.

——. 1958a. À travers les revues d'études classiques. IL 10.34–5; 124–6.

——. 1958b. Bibliographies critiques des études latines. REL 36.97–9.

——. 1960. Lo stato attuale degli studi classici nel mondo. SicGym 13(1).117–26.

——. 1961. À travers les revues d'études classiques. IL 13.33–5 and 128–30.

——. 1962. À travers les revues d'études classiques. IL 14.32–4 and 131–3.

——. 1963. À travers les revues d'études classiques. IL 15.37–9 and 131–3.

——. 1964a. À travers les revues d'études classiques. IL 16.37–8 and 128–9.

——. 1964b. El estado actual de los estudios clásicos en el mundo y el papel de la bibliografía y de la documentación. EClás 8.107–19.

——. 1964c. La Fédération Internationale des Associations d'Études Classiques. Son origine, son but, son activité. REL 43.89–98.

——. 1965. À travers les revues d'études classiques. IL 17.38–9 and 130–2.

ESAN, O. 1966. The Classics in Africa. Didaskalos 2(1).119–26.

FABBRI, P. 1939. Quam utile sit latinam linguam latine docere. SUL 1.167–9.

FABRICIUS, J. A. 1728. Bibliotheca latina. Venezia. [The 'first' edition was published in Hamburg, 1697; the 'last' was updated by J. A. Ernesti, Leipzig, in 1773–1774.]

FAIDER, P. 1939. Belgium latinum. Essai sur l'usage et l'étude de la langue latine en Belgique des origines à nos jours. SUL 1.12–30.

FARAGO, LADISLAS. 1967. The broken seal: The story of operation magic and the Pearl Harbor disaster. New York, Random House.

FARIA, E. 1945. A renovação atual dos estudos latinos. Rio de Janeiro, Faculdade de Letras da Universidade.

——. 1955. Fonética histórica do latim. Rio de Janeiro, Libraria Acadêmica.

——. 1958. Gramática superior da língua latina. Rio de Janeiro, Livraria Acadêmica.

——. 1959 (1961). II Congresso Internacional de Estudos Clássicos. BEC 3.101–4.

FEHLING, DETLEV. 1956a. Varro und die grammatische Lehre von der Analogie und der Flexion. Dissertation Kiel.

——. 1956b. Varro und die grammatische Lehre von der Analogie und der Flexion. Glotta 35.214–70.

——. 1957. Varro und die grammatische Lehre von der Analogie und der Flexion. Glotta 36.48–100.

——. 1969. Noch einmal der *passer solitarius* und der *passer* Catullus. Philologus 113.217–24.

FERGUSON, J., ed. 1958. Nigeria and the Classics [I]. Papers read at a conference on the Classics organised by the Department of Extra-Mural Studies and the Classics Department and held at the University College, Ibadan, Dec. 16–20, 1957. Ibadan, University Press.

——. 1962. Nigeria and the Classics, V. Ibadan, University Press.

——. 1963. Nigeria and the Classics, VI. Ibadan, University Press.

——. 1964. Nigeria and the Classics, VII. Ibadan, University Press.

——. 1966. Some Aspects of the Classics at Ibadan. Didaskalos 2.(1).111–18.

FERNALD, JAMES C. 1943. Grammar. Encyclopedia Americana 13.112–15.

FERRANTE, D. 1962. Curiosità etimologiche nel Cratilo di Platone e nel De lingua latina di Varrone. GIF 15.163–71.

FERRARINO, P. 1939. L'allitterazione. Bologna, Azzoguidi.

FILIN, F.P., et al. 1967. Sovetskoe Jazykoznanie za 50 let. Moskva, Izdatel'stvo Nauka.

FINK, ROBERT O. 1969. A long vowel before *m* in Latin? AJPh 90.444–52.

FISCHER, I. 1960a. Note de lingvistică latină. SClas 2.317–19.

——. 1960b. Bibliographie classique roumaine, 1958–1959. SClas 2.413–30.

——. 1962. Bibliographie classique roumaine. SClas 4.367–79.

——. 1963. Bibliografia clasică romînească. SClas 5.375–86.

——. 1965. Bibliografia clasică românească. SClas 7.407–17.

FLETCHER, G.B.A., ed. 1948. The year's work in Classical studies. (Vol. 33, 1939–1945.) Bristol, Arrowsmith.

FLOR DE OLIVEIRA, M. DE L.N. 1962. Os estudos clássicos em Portugal, I. Romanitas 4.456.

FOERSTER, A. 1939. De variis lingua latinae casibus in scholis Hungariae. SUL 1.224–5.

FOLEY, J. 1965. Prothesis in the Latin verb *sum*. Lg 41.59–64.

FONTÁN, ANTONIO. 1965. Historia y sistemas de los demostrativos latinos. Em 33.71–107.

——. 1966. El Congreso para el Estudio del Latín organizado por el Istituto di Studi Romani. EClás 10.211–13.

FONTENROSE, J. 1944. The meaning and use of 'sed enim.'. TAPA 75.168–95.

FORMIGARI, F. 1961. Rinnovamento degli studi classici. Roma, Armando.

FRAENKEL, GERD. 1964. The decline of Latin as a model for linguistic analysis. PICL 9.730–7.

FRIEDLÄNDER, P. 1943–44. Greek behind Latin. CJ 39.270–7.

FRIEDRICH, W.H. 1939. Der gegenwärtige Stand des Lateinstudium in Deutschland. SUL 2.18–21.

FRIES, C.C. 1957. Structural linguistics and language teaching. CJ 52.265–8.

FUCHS, HAROLD, 1947. Rückschau und Ausblick im Arbeitsbereich der lateinischen Philologie. MH 4.147–98.

FUETER, E. 1911. Geschichte der neueren Historiographie. München/Berlin, Oldenbourg.

FUGIER, H. 1969. Pour une systématique des termes de coordination en latin. REL 47.45–8. [Abstract.]

FUGLSANG, P. 1940. On the Latin future infinitive passive and related expressions in Archaic and Classical Latin. C&M 3.236–52.

FUNAIOLI, HYGINUS, ed. 1907. Grammaticae romanae fragmenta. Leipzig, Teubner.

——. (GINO). 1932. Filologia classica. Enciclopedia Italiana 15.339–42.

——. 1933. Grammatica. Enciclopedia Italiana 17.648.

——. 1946. Studi di letteratura antica. Spiriti e forme, figure e problemi delle letterature classiche, I. Bologna, Zanichelli.

GAENG, PAUL A. 1971. Introduction to the principles of language. New York, Harper and Row.

GAGKAEV, K.E. 1957. Kurs lekciĭ po istorii jazykoznanija. Odessa, Odesskii Gosudarstvenni Universitet.

GALERKINA, B.L., et al. 1962. [Deuxième Conférence sur la Philologie Classique, Léningrad.] VDI 1.194–200.

GALIANO, M.F. 1951. La reunión de Sociedades Clásicas de Cambridge. EClás 218–20.

GARCÍA GUAL, C. 1966. Análisis sintáctico y categorías semánticas. Emerita 34. 289.94.

GAREY, H.B. 1954. Review of Tesnière 1953. Lg 30.512–13.

GEBAUER, G.J. 1941. Prolegomena to the Ars Grammatica Bonifacii. Doctoral Dissertation, University of Chicago.

GEESTESWETENSCHAPPELIJK ONDERZOEK IN NEDERLAND. 1948. Amsterdam, North-Holland.

GERCKE, A., and E. NORDEN. 1927⁴. Einleitung in die Altertumswissenschaft. Leipzig, Teubner.

GEROV, B. 1960. Die klassische Philologie in Bulgarien. In Antike und Mittelalter in Bulgarien, 104–8.

GERSCHEL, L. 1958. Varron logicien, I: Étude sur une séquence du De lingua latina. Latomus 17.65–73.

GETTY, ROBERT J. 1963 (1964). Classical Latin metre and prosody 1935–1962. Lustrum 8.103–60.

GHEDINI, GIUSEPPE. 1951. Bibliografia generale. In BIGNONE 1951:343–67.

GHISELLI, ALFREDO, 1951. Commento alla sintassi latina, I, Introduzione e particolarità sintattiche. Firenze, Valmartina.

——. 1954. Commento alla sintassi latina. Firenze, Valmartina.

——. 1961. Grammatica e filologia. Studi e ricerche di grammatica latina. Firenze, Sansoni.

GIARRATANO, CESARE. 1951. La storia della filologia classica, in BIGNONE 1951:1–72.

GIGLI, A. 1941. Repertorio della sintassi latina. Firenze, Barbera.

GIGON, O. 1946. Les études classiques en Suisse de 1939 à 1945. BAGB (n.s.) 1(2). 66–76.

GLEASON, H.A., JR. 1965. Linguistics and English grammar. New York, Holt, Rinehart and Winston.

GODEL, ROBERT. 1961. Sur l'évolution des voyelles brèves latines en syllabe intérieure. CFS 18.53–69.

GOIDANICH, P.G. 1943. Rapporti culturali e linguistici tra Roma e gli Italici. Origine antica della cultura in Roma. L'iscrizione arcaica del foro romano e il suo ambiente archeologico. Suo valore giuridico. Atti Reale Accademia d'Italia, Memorie Classe di Scienze morali e storiche. Serie VII, vol. III, fasc. VII, 1–501.

GOLDSMITH, ULRICH K. 1959. Stefan George: A study of his early work. Boulder, University of Colorado Press.

——. 1970. Stefan George. New York, Columbia University Press.

GONDA, J. 1969. Latin obsc(a)enus. Studia Pagliaro 2.259–72.

GORDON, ARTHUR E. 1969. On the origins of the Latin alphabet: Modern views CSCA 2.157–70.

GOUGENHEIM, G. 1968a. L'évolution des oppositions linguistiques. BSL 63(1).13–17.

——. 1968b. Le latin, banc d'essai de la traduction automatique. In BLOIS 1968: 71–81.

GRAHAM, H. F. 1961. The Classics in the Soviet Union. CW 54.205–13.

GRASSI, CESARE. 1966. Problemi di sintassi latina. Consecutio temporum e aspetto nel verbo latino. Firenze, La Nuova Italia.

GRASSI, CORRADO. 1968. Note linguistiche sulle 'Compositiones' di Scribonio Largo. AGI 53.104–10.

GRAUR, AL., and L. WALD. 1965^2. Scurtă istorie a lingvisticii. Bucureşti, Editura Ştiinţifica.

GRAUR, A. 1969. *quidam* chez Apulée. In Hommages Renard 1.378–82.

GRAY, LOUIS H. 1939. Foundations of language. New York, Macmillan.

GREENBERG, JOSEPH H. 1965. Linguistics. In LYSTAD 1965:416–41.

GRÉGOIRE, A. 1939. La linguistique. Paris, Delagrave.

GRÉGOIRE, H. 1961. Rapport sur le Seconde Congrès Espangol d'Études Classiques tenu à Madrid et à Barcelone du 4 au 10 avril 1961. BAB 47.126–9.

GRILLI, A. 1965. La situazione delle lingue classiche nella scuola italiana. Didaskalos 1(3).47–52.

GROGNET, ALLENE, and WILLIAM NEMSER. 1971. Interview with LSA President Eric Hamp. LSA Bulletin 48.36–42.

GROUNDSTROEM, A. 1941. Über die Stellung des Lateins in Finnland. SUL 3.49–52.

GUARINO, A. 1955. Il II Congresso Internazionale di Studi Classici. (Copenhagen, 23–28 Agosto 1954). Iura 6.544–5.

GUDEMAN, ALFRED. 1907. Grundriss zur Geschichte der klassische Philologie. Leipzig, Teubner.

GUENTHER, R. 1962. Altertumswissenschaft im sozialistischen Deutschland. Altertum 8.251-6.

GUILLÉN, J. 1950. Humanidades, filología y lingüística. Helmantica 1.9–29.

——. 1954^2. Estilística latina. Salamanca, Sígueme.

——. 1969. El latín de las XII tablas. [4.] Ambientación histórica. Helmantica 20. 67–103.

GUIRAUD, PIERRE. 1970. Gustave Guillaume and generative grammar. LS 10.1–60.

——. 1971. Lucien Tesnière and transformational grammar. LS 15.1–7.

GUZZO, A. 1939. Scuole del duemila. ASPS Riunione 27(Sept. 6).371–3.

HAFTER, H. 1949. Bericht über den Thesaurus linguae Latinas. JbBAW, 43–8.

HAHN, E. ADELAIDE. 1941. Quintilian on Greek Letters lacking in Latin and Latin Letters lacking in Greek. (XII, 10, 27–29). Lg 17.24–32.

——. 1952. The moods in indirect discourse in Latin. TAPA 83.242–66

——. 1953. Subjunctive and optative, their origin as futures. New York, Hunter College.

——. 1960 (1961). The origin of the Greek accusative in Latin. TAPA 91.221–38.

——. 1969. Naming-constructions in some Indo-European languages. Cleveland, American Philological Association.

HAKAMIES, R. 1952. Aperçu sur les études latines en Finlande. A&R, 2.147–50.

HALL, ROBERT A., JR. 1946. Classical Latin noun inflection. CPh 41.84–90.

——. 1969. Coerenza e realismo nella ricostruzione del protoromanzo. LeSt 4. 399–404.

HALPORN, JAMES WERNER, et al. 1963. The meters of Greek and Latin poetry. London, Methuen.

HAMMER, S. 1948. Historia filologii klasycznej w Polsee. Kraków, Polska Akad.

HAMP, ERIC P. 1969. 1. Latin *insula.* 2. *hedera* is not ivy. AJPh 90.463–4.

——. 1971. See GROGNET and NEMSER 1971.

HANDFORD, S.A. 1947. The Latin subjunctive: Its usage and development from Plautus to Tacitus. London, Methuen.

HARMATTA, J. 1948. Les études grecques et latines en Hongrie de 1939 à 1946. BAGB (n.s.) 5.126–50.

HARRIMAN, P.L. 1946. Encyclopedia of psychology. New York, Philosophical Library.

HARRIS, Z.S. 1940. Review of GRAY 1939. Lg 14.216–31.

HARSH, PHILIP WHALEY. 1958 (1959). Early Latin meter and prosody 1935–1955. Lustrum 3.315–50.

HAUGEN, EINAR. 1950. First grammatical treatise. Baltimore, LSA.

HAURY, A. 1956. Écho du Congrès International pour le Latin Vivant. REA 58.438–40.

HEGEL, G.W.F. 1905. Philosophie der Geschichte. Leipzig, Dürr.

HEILMANN, LUIGI. 1958. Origini, prospettive e limiti dello strutturalismo. Convivium (n.s.) 5.513–26.

——. 1959. Linguistica e filosofia. Quaderni del Collegio Borromeo, 1–21.

HEINIMANN, F. 1948. Gli studi di filologia classica in Svizzera. Belfagor 3.474–6.

HENRIKSSON, K.E. 1962. A note on Classical studies in Finland. Romanitas 4.347–50.

HERESCU, N.I., et al. 1939–40. Bibliografia clasica in România. RCl 11–12.304–36.

——. 1946. Poètes linguistes. REL 24.71–4.

——. 1960. La poésie latine. Étude des structures phoniques. Paris, Les Belles Lettres.

HERMAN, J. 1961. Posit (= posuit) et questions connexes dans les incriptions pannoniennes. Essai de géographie linguistique. AAntH 9.321–31, 1 carte.

——. 1965. Aspects de la différenciation territoriale du latin sous l'Empire. BSL 60.53–70.

Hermann, E. 1942. Grammatik und Sprachwissenschaft. NJAB 4.114–23.

Hernández Vista, V. Eugenio. 1969. Redundancia y concisión: su naturaleza lingüística. Funcionamiento estilistico en Tácito (Historias 1.2–3). Em 37.149–58.

Herrero, Víctor José. 1965. Introducción al estudio de la filología latina. Madrid, Gredos.

Highet, G. 1942. Review of Rostagni 1939. AJPh 63.92–104.

Hill, Archibald A. 1954. Juncture and syllable division in Latin. Lg 30.439–47.

——, ed. 1969. Linguistics today. New York, Basic Books.

Hjelmslev, Louis. 1941. Review of Gray 1939. AL 2.122–6.

Höeg, C. 1948. Research in Classical philology. In The humanities and the sciences in Denmark during the Second World War, 118–24. København, Munksgaard.

——. 1949. Les études classiques et l'Unesco. BAGB (n.s.) 8.32–4.

Hoenigswald, H.M. 1947. On Varro, De lingua latina, V, 15. AJPh 68.198–9.

Holborn, H. 1953. History and the study of the Classics. JHI 14.33–50.

Hombert, M., and C. Préaux. 1946. Les études d'antiquité classique en Belgique. BAGB (n.s.) 1.123–35.

Hommages à L. Herrmann. 1960. Berchem-Bruxelles, Coll. Latomus, 44.

Hommages à Marcel Renard. 3 vols. 1969. Bruxelles, Latomus.

Hommel, H. 1951. Internationaler Kongress der Altertumwissenschaft, Paris 1950. Gymnasium 58.92–3.

Hook, Sidney, ed. 1969. Language and philosophy. New York, New York University Press.

Horecký, J. 1949. Fonologia latinčiny. Bratislava, Acad. Scientiarum et Artium Slovaca.

Hornsby, R.A. 1959. From other [non-classical] journals. CJ 54.372–4.

Hosek, R. 1949. La philologie classique en Tchécoslovaquie (1938–1948). BAGB (n.s.) 7.108–15.

Høst, Gerd. 1962. A linguistic-historical contribution to the history of Rome. NoVidSF 35.28*-40* (*sic*).

Houghton, H.P. 1948–49. The study of the Classics in the United States in the seventeenth, eighteenth, nineteenth and twentieth centuries. Humanitas 2.345–59.

Householder, F.W., Jr. 1947. A descriptive analysis of Latin declension. Word 3.48–58.

——. 1969. Review of Lakoff 1968. LS 6.11–18.

——. 1970. Review's reply [to Lakoff 1970]. LS 10.35–6.

Howald, E. 1940. Das Lateinische und die Schweiz. SUL 2.89–93.

Hughes, John P. 1962. The science of language. New York, Random House.

The Humanities and the Sciences in Denmark during the Second World War. 1948. København, Munksgaard.

Hunt, R.W. 1943. Studies on Priscian in the eleventh and twelfth centuries. Medieval and Renaissance Studies 1.194–232.

——. 1950. Studies on Priscian in the eleventh and twelfth centuries. Medieval and Renaissance Studies 2.1–56.

HUS, ALAIN. 1969. *intelligentia* et *intellectus* en latin impérial. In Hommages Renard 1.449–62.

HUZAR, E. 1957. Structural linguistics and language teaching. CJ 52.268–74.

IMBS, PAUL. 1959. De la grammaire normative à la linguistique descriptive. NS 5.5–17.

IORDACHE, R. 1964. Verbe cu prefix şi fără inchiderea vocalei din radical în limba latină. Analele Univ. din Bucureşti (Filol.) 13.305–18.

IRMSCHER, J. 1962. Die lateinischen Studien in der Deutschen Demokratischen Republik. Romanitas 4.228–52.

ISSLEDOVANIJA V OBLASTI LATINSKOGO I ROMANSKOGO JAZYKOZNANIJA. 1961. Kišinev.

IVENS, P.E. 1951. Grammaticale begrippen in verband met het Latijn. HZnMTL 5.58–77.

IVIĆ, MILKA. 1963. Pravci u lingvistici. Ljubljana, Državna založba Slovenije.

——. 1965. Trends in linguistics. The Hague, Mouton.

JAKOVIDI, F.V. 1941. Vinitel'nyj s neopredelennym v latinskom jazike. Učenyje Zapiski Leningrad 7.37–40.

JANÁČEK, K. Hundert Jahre klassischer Philologie im Verband der tschechischen Philologen und im Verband der klassischen Philologen. LF 91.360–70.

JANKO, J. 1941. Latinskij ablativ zkoumán zvukovou analysou. LF 68.117–22.

JANSSEN, H. 1941. De kenmerken der Romeinsche dichtertaal. Nijmegen, Dekker.

——. 1947. De positie der geminatae in het Latijnsche consonantsysteem. Neophilologus 31.125–7.

——. 1952. Historische grammatica van het Latijn. I, De klanken. Den Haag, Servire.

——. 1957. Historische grammatica van het Latijn. II, De vormen. Den Haag, Servire.

JENNINGS, A.C. 1940. A linguistic study of the Cartulario de San Vicente de Oviedo. New York, Vanni.

JENSEN, P.J. 1941. Det latinske Perfektsystem. Studier i kategorierne modus og tempus i Ciceros sprog. København, Munksgaard.

JESPERSEN, OTTO. 1922. Language; its nature, development and origin. London, Allen and Unwin.

JIMÉNEZ DELGADO, J. 1958. De orthographia latina. Barcelona, Lauria.

——. 1959. El II Congreso Internacional en pro del Latín Vivo. EClás 5.206–9.

——. 1961. II Congreso Español de Estudios Clásicos. Helmantica 12. 369–78.

——. 1962. Panorama de los estudios clásicos en España. Romanitas 4.253–67.

——. El latín y su pronunciación. Datos recientes a favor de la pronunciación clásica. Helmantica 14.325–31.

JONES, T.B. 1939. The Classics in Colonial Hispanic America. TAPA 88.37–45.

JOSEPHSON, A. 1952. Un decennio di filologia latina in Svezia. A&R 2.98–108.
JOURNOUD, SYLVAIN. 1967. Aulu-Gelle philologue. Actas Classica Universitatis Scientiarum Debreceniensis 3.63–6.
JOVÉ, M. 1953. Pronunciación clásica del latín. Helmantica 4.53–79.
JURET, C. 1921. Manuel de phonétique latine. Paris, Hachette.
——. 1942. Dictionnaire étymologique grec et latin. Mâcon, Protat.
JUREWICZ, O. 1960. De studiis classicis in Hungaria cultis. Meander 15.189–95.
KAHN, DAVID. 1967. The codebreakers; the story of secret writing. New York, Macmillan.
KAISER, L. (ed.) 1957. Manual of phonetics. Amsterdam, North-Holland.
KARAKULAKOV, VI. V. 1964. K voprosu o sootnesennosti častej reči stoikov s ich logičeskimi kategorijami. SClas 6.83–6.
——. 1965a. Pergamskaja i morphologičskaja klassifikacija častej reči u Varrona. UZDušPI 33(vyp. 18).113–34.
——. 1965b. Rol' Varrona v razvitii učenija ob uslovijach pravil'nosti analogii v sisteme sloviozmenenija. *Ibid.*, 135–59.
——. 1965c. K istorii razrabotki učenija o slove kak edinstve zvučanija i značenija (Varro, *De lingua latina*, 37–38; i. X, 83–4; VIII, 39–41 i IX, 40–42, X, 63–72). *Ibid.*, 161–71.
——. 1965d. K voprosu o 'troičnosti' v sisteme akcidencij imeni u Varrona. *Ibid.*, 173–80.
——. 1965e. Ob odnom opyte sintaksičeskoj klassificacii častej reči v antičnom jazykoznanii (Varro, *De lingua latina*, VIII, 12). In Omagiu Rosetti, 437–9.
——. 1966. K istorii razrabotki učenija o kategorii zaloga v antičnom jazykoznanii (Varro, *De lingua latina*, VIII, 59–58, IX, 106–107, X, 33.) RRLing 11.147–54.
KARDOS, T. 1941. L'insegnamento del latino in Ungheria. SUL 63–67.
KAZIK-ZAWADZKA, IRENA. 1952–53 (1955). Nowsze badania nad językiem łacinskim (na podstawie czasopim *Revue des Études Latines i Glotta*, 1948–1952). Eos 46(2).93–111.
KELLY, DAVID H. 1967. Distinctive features analysis in Latin phonology. AJPh 88.67–77.
——. 1968. Transformations in the Latin nominal phrase. CPh 63.46–52.
KENT, R. G. 1932. The sounds of Latin. Baltimore, LSA.
——. 1940[2]. The sounds of Latin. Philadelphia, LSA. [3rd ed. 1945. Baltimore, LSA.]
——. 1940–41. Review of GRAY 1939. CW 34.249–51.
——. 1946. The forms of Latin. A descriptive and historical morphology. Baltimore, LSA.
——. 1948. A problem of Latin prosody. Mélanges Marouzeau, 303–8.
KIECKERS, ERNST. 1931. Historische lateinische Grammatik, mit Berücksichtigung des Vulgärlateins und der romanischen Sprachen. München, Hueber.
——. 1960. Historische lateinische Grammatik, mit Berücksichtigung des Vulgär-

lateins und der romanischen Sprachen. I, Lautlehre; II, Formenlehre. München, Hueber.

Kindermann, K. 1960a. Die klassische Philologie in Rumänien. Gymnasium 47. 446–50.

——. 1960b. Klassische Philologie in Sowjetrussland. Gymnasium 67.450–1.

Kirchconnell, W., and Woodhouse, A.S.P. 1947. The humanities in Canada. Ottawa, Humanities Research Council of Canada.

Kirk, W.H. 1942. The syntax of the gerund and the gerundive. TAPA 166–76 and 293–307.

Kleve, K. 1962. La situation des études classiques en Norvège. Romanitas 4.367–8.

Klussmann, R., ed. 1809–13. Bibliotheca scriptorum classicorum. Leipzig, Reisland.

Knös, B., and G. Rudberg. 1946. Les études classiques en Suède pendant la guerre. BAGB 1.119–22.

Kobov, I.U. 1955. [La doctrine des cas chez les grammairiens anciens.] Lvov, University dissertation.

——. 1961. Pochodžennja hramatyčnych terminiv supinum, gerundium, gerundivum. Pytannja klasyčnoji filolohiji 2.36–42.

Koepstein, H. 1965. Altertumskundliche Publikationen erschienen in der Deutschen Demokratischen Republik, 1956–1964. BCO 10.322–451.

Koerner, E.F.K. 1970. Review of Salus 1969. Lingua 25.419–31.

——. 1971. Bibliographie linguistique: An assessment of the sad 'state of the art'. LBer 16.62–3.

Koller, Hermann. 1951. Praesens historicum und erzählendes Imperfekt. Beitrag zur Aktionsart der Praesensstammzeiten in Lateinischen und Griechischen. MH 8.63–9.

Kollmann, E.D. 1968. Remarks on the structure of the Latin hexameter. Glotta 46.293–316.

Korževa, K.P. 1968. [Classical studies at the University of Kazakh.] VDI 104. 212–15.

Kraft, Peter. 1969. Varro, *De lingua latina*, 5, 1. RhM 112.306–11.

Krahe, H. [1948]. Bibliographie des Jahre 1941. IX. Italisch. IJ 27.186–95.

Krause, Wilhelm. 1962. Problemkreise der antiken Grammatik. In Serta philologica Aenipontana, 215–37.

Kravar, M. 1960. [Le Troisième Congrès International d'Études Classiques, Londres, 31.VII-5.IX, 1959.] ZAnt 10.398–400.

——. 1962. L'enseignement classique en Yougoslavie. Romanitas 4.305–12.

——. 1968. Zur Frage des lateinischen Verbalaspekts. ZAnt 18.49–66.

——. 1969a. Nochmals zum historischen Präsens im Lateinischen. ZAnt 19.25–9.

——. 1969b. Vidsko-vremenska značenja latinskoga futura II. ZAnt 19.217–25.

Kretschmer, Paul. 1927. Sprache [= Vol. 1 of A. Gercke and E. Norden, Einleitung in die Altertumswissenschaft]. Leipzig, Teubner.

——. 1946. Introducción a la lingüística griega y latina, trans. by S. Fernández

Ramírez and M. Fernández-Galiano. Madrid, Instituto Nebrija.

KROLL, W. 1928. Historia de la filología Clásica. Barcelona, Labor.

KUJORE, O. 1969. Notes on the Latin aspirates. N&C 11.1–5.

KUKENHEIM, LOUIS. 1962. Esquisse historique de la linguistique française et de ses rapports avec la linguistique générale. Leiden, Universitaire Pers.

KUMANIECKI, K. 1962. La philologie classique en Pologne. Romanitas 4.288–96.

——. 1967. Twenty years of classical philology in Poland, 1945–1965. G&R 14. 61–75.

KURE, S. 1955. Les études latines au Japon. REL 33.100–3.

LABHARDT, A. 1945. La philologie classique. AM 2.431–42.

LAKOFF, R.T. 1967. "Studies in the transformational grammar of Latin. The complement system". Dissertation Harvard University.

——. 1968. Abstract syntax and Latin complementation. Cambridge, Mass., M.I.T. Press.

——. 1969. Transformational grammar and language teaching. Language Learning 19.117–40.

——. 1970. More on abstract syntax. LS 10.30–5. [Reply to HOUSEHOLDER 1969.]

LAMB, POSE. 1967. Linguistics in proper perspective. Columbus, Ohio, Merrill.

LAMBRINO, S. 1951. Bibliographie de l'antiquité classique, 1896–1914. Paris, Les Belles Lettres.

LANGENDOEN, D. TERENCE. 1966. A note on the linguistic theory of M. Terentius Varro. Foundations of Language 2.33–6.

LANGLOIS, P. 1967–68. Philologie classique. Bibliographie. AEHE-HPh 229.

——. 1968–69. Philologie classique. Bibliographie. AEHE-HPh 205–6.

LANOWSKI, J. 1966. Antyk w USA. Eos 56.367–72.

LASCU, N. 1961. Ovidio linguista. SClas 3.305–11.

LAST, H. 1939. The Position of Latin in the universities of Great Britain. SUL 1.111–16.

LATIMER, J.F. 1969. The Fifth International Congress of Classical Studies. CW 63.116–18.

LAURAND, L., and A. LAURAS. 1955. Manuel des études grecques et latines, II, Rome. Géographie ... grammaire historique latine. New ed. Paris, Picard. ['Grammaire historique latine' (fasc. vi), 401–611.]

LAVENCY, M. 1969. A propos de la syntaxe des cas en latin classique. LEC 37. 325–37.

LEBEL, M. 1947. Les études classiques au Canada de 1939 à 1945. BAGB (n.s.) 4.130–6.

LEE, M. OWEN. 1969. Word, sound, and image in the Odes of Horace. Ann Arbor, The University of Michigan Press.

LEEMAN, A.D. 1959. [Third International Congress of Classical Studies.] Hermeneus 31.64–5.

LEES, R.B. 1957. Review of CHOMSKY 1957. Lg 33.375–408.

LEJEUNE, MICHEL. 1949a (1940–48). La curiosité linguistique dans l'antiquité classique. CILP 8.45–61.

——. 1949b. La posición del latín en el dominio indoeuropéo, trans. by C.A. Ronchi March. Buenos Aires, Coni.

LENZ, F.W. 1959. Der dritte internationale Kongress für Altertumwissenschaft. Orpheus 6.153–6.

LEO, ULRICH. 1963. Il Passero solitario: ein Motivstudie. In Wort und Text: Festschrift für Fritz Schalk, 400–21.

LEONE, A. 1949. L'uso del congiuntivo in latino. Principi di sintassi ragionata. Catania, Coniglione e Giuffrida.

LEONE, EUGENIO. 1969. *Dominus*: la storia della parola e le origini dei titoli onorifici *don e donna*. AMAT 34.329–411.

LEPSCHY, G.C. 1962. Il problema dell'accento latino. Rassegna critica di studi sull'accento latino e sullo studio dell'accento. ASNP 31.199–246.

——. 1969. Riscoperta di Sapir. Libri Nuovi [Einaudi], April, p. 5.

LEROY, LUCIEN. 1962. Notes de grammaire latine. IV, Le style indirect. Montréal, Éd. Fides.

LEROY, MAURICE. 1963. Les grands courants de la linguistique moderne. Brussels, Presses Universitaires.

——. 1967. The main trends in modern linguistics. Oxford, Oxford University Press.

——. 1969. Le Congrès des Études Classiques de Bonn. BAB 55.310–11.

LEUMANN, M. 1947. Die lateinische Dichtersprache. Musem Helveticum 4.116–39.

——. 1957. Lateinische Laut- und Formenlehre, 1940–1955. Glotta 36(i/2).123–51.

——, J.B. HOFMANN, and A. SZANTYR. 1963^5. Lateinische Grammatik auf der Grundlage des Werkes von Friedrich Stolz und Joseph Hermann Schmalz. I Band, Manu Leumann, Lateinische Laut- und Formenlehre. München, Beck. II Band, J.B. Hofmann, Lateinische Syntax und Stilistik. München, Beck. (First ed., 1926–28.]

——. 1964. Lateinische Laut- und Formenlehre 1955–1962. Glotta 42.69–120.

LIEBERG, GODO. 1967. Structura. Di nuovo sulla storia di un termine. LeSt 2.199–211.

LIÉNARD, EDMUND. 1969. Réflexions sur l'accent latin. In Hommages Renard 1. 551–60.

LINDSAY, WALLACE MARTIN. 1894. The Latin language. An historical account of Latin sounds, stems, and flexions. Oxford, Clarendon.

——. 1963. The Latin language. New York, Hafner. [Reproduction of the original edition, Oxford 1894.]

LIVE, ANNA HARRIS. 1959 (1960). Pre-history of Latin phonemic structure. University of Pennsylvania dissertation 1959. DAb 20(1959–60).2280.

——. 1963 (1964). The nature of changes in the prehistory of the Latin phonemic system. SIL 17.99–106.

LÖFSTEDT, EINAR. 1928. Syntactica, Studien und Beiträge zur historischen Syntax des Lateins. I, Über einige Grundfragen der lateinischen Nominalsyntax. Lund, Gleerup.

——. 1933. Syntactica, Studien und Beiträge zur historischen Syntax des Lateins. II, Syntaktisch-stilistische Gesichtspunkte und Probleme. Lund, Gleerup.

——. 1942². Syntactica. I, Ueber einige Grundfragen der lateinischen Nominalsyntax. Lund, Gleerup.

Loi, V. 1969. Note sulla terminologia battesimale. In Studia Pagliaro 3.67–84.

Loicq, J. 1962a. Minutiae latinae. I, A propos de la nasale dorsale: le problème de sa date et de sa notation. II, Le traîtement des groupes *-ngn-et*-nkn-. AC 31(1–2).130–47.

——. 1962b. La quantité de la voyelle devant *-gn-* et la nature de la quantité vocalique. Latomus 21(2).257–78.

López Kindler, A. 1967. El subjuntivo independiente latino y la funciones elementales de la lengua. Emerita 35.109–36.

Lord, H.G. 1960. A structural Latin course. London, University Press.

Lo Torto, Gino. 1972. Per una storia della linguistica latina. Roma, Calende Greche.

Lounsbury, Floyd G. Language and culture. In Hook 1969:3–29.

Lourenço de Oliveira, J. 1956. Ars grammatica. Kriterion 9.423–76.

Lucot, J. 1969. Sur l'accent de mot dans l'hexamètre latin. Pallas 16.79–106.

Ludvíkovský, J. 1949. Filologia klasyczna w Czechosłowacji. Meander 4.202–8.

Lugli, G. 1951. [Les grandes entreprises internationales et les instruments de travails, encyclopédies, répertoires, catalogues, indices, lexiques.] In Actes du Premier Congrès de la Fédération Internationale des Associations d'Études Classiques, 133–8.

Luria, S. 1962. Die klassischen Studien in der UdSSR. Romanitas 4.297.

Lyne, R.O.A.M. 1969. The constraints of metre and the 'Ciris': A brief note. Latomus 28.1065–7.

Lyons, John. 1968. Introduction to theoretical linguistics. Cambridge, University Press.

——. Chomsky. 1970. London, Collins.

Lystad, Robert A., ed. 1965. The African world. A survey of social research. New York, Praeger.

MacKay, L.A. 1941. A syntactical experiment of Sallust. CPh 36.280.

McDonough, J.T. 1959. Computers and Classics. CW 53.44–50.

——. 1968. Computers and the Classics. CHum 2.37–42.

McElwain, M.B. 1939. Further reflections of the forgotten student. CJ 34.198–212.

McGuire, Martin R.P. 1961. Introduction to Classical scholarship. A syllabus and bibliographical guide. New and revised ed. Washington, D.C., The Catholic University of America Press.

McKay, A.G. 1962. Latin Studies in Canada. Romanitas 4.323–31.

MACHADO, JOSÉ PEDRO. 1942. Breve história da lingüística. Lisboa, Inquérito.
MACHADO, R. 1940. Questões de gramática latina. I, Pronúncia do latim e elementos de fonética histórica latina. Lisboa, Teixeira.
——. 1941. Questões de gramática latina. II, Morfologia geral e elementos de morfologia histórica. Lisboa, Teixeira.
MACREA, D. 1957. Necesitatea unei istorii a lingvisticii. LbR 6.5–10.
MAGNIEN, VICTOR. 1942. Grammaire comparée du grec et du latin. I, Phonétique. Lyon et Grenoble, Les Éditions de la France Nouvelle.
——. 1949. Grammaire comparée du grec et du latin. III, Morphologie, le verbe, les mots invariables. Tables. Paris, Bordas.
MAGUINNESS, W. S. 1962a. The Classics in England. Romanitas 4.187–93.
——. 1962b. Les études classiques en Grande-Bretagne. Revue de la Franco-Ancienne (Paris). No. 140 (Nov.).196–203.
——. 1962–63. Los estudios clásicos en Gran Bretaña. EClás 7.333–42.
MAJNARIČ, N. 1961. La filologia classica a Zagabria dal 1945. Helikon 1.537–42.
——. 1966. Klassische Philologie in Kroatien von 1953 bis heute. Altertum 12.51–64.
MALCLÈS, L. N. 1958. Review of Ernst 1957. BBF 3.248–50.
MALCOVATI, E. 1954. Il Congresso di Studi Classici di Copenhagen (Agosto 1954) e la commemorazione di J. N. Madvig. RIL (Parte Generale e Atti Ufficiali) 87.
——. 1956a. Il Primo Congresso Spagnolo di Studi Classici. A&R (n.s.) 1.203–8.
——. 1956b. Il Congresso Internazionale di Avignone 'Pour le latin vivant'. RIL (Parte generale e Atti ufficiali) 89–90.1–8.
——. 1959. Il secondo Congresso Internazionale 'Pour le latin vivant'. RIL (Parte Generale) 93.1–10.
——. 1964. Il Terzo Congresso Internazionale 'Pour le Latin Vivant'. StRo 12.73–6.
MALKIEL, YAKOV. 1969. Morphological analogy as a stimulus for sound change. BeSt 4.305–27.
MALMBERG, BERTIL. 1962. Nya Vägar inom Språkforskningen: En orientering i modern lingvistik. Stockholm, Svenska Bokförlaget.
——. 1964. New trends in linguistics: An orientation, trans. by E. Carney. Stockholm, Naturmetodens Sprakinstitut.
——. 1966. Les nouvelles tendances de la linguistique. Paris, Presses Universitaires de France.
——. 1968². Les nouvelles tendances de la linguistique. Paris, Presses Universitaires de France.
MALUNOWICZ, L. 1960. [Introduction to Classical Philology, with a methodology of intellectual and scientific work.] Lublin, Towarzystwo Naukowe Katolickiego Uniwersytetu Lubelskiego.
MANDELBAUM, DAVID D. 1968. Sapir, Edward. International Encyclopedia of the Social Sciences 14.9–15.
MANIET, A. 1950a. Bibliographie choisie de la langue latine. Les Études Classiques 18.55–92.

——. 1950b. L'evolution phonétique et les sons du latin ancien. Louvain, Arta.
——. 1969. Plaute. Lexique inverse, listes grammaticales, relevés divers. Hildesheim, Olms.

Manzo, G. 1953. Dizionario della sintassi latina. Roma, Signorelli.

Marache, R. 1954. À propos de l'analogie et de l'anomalie. AFLT (Pallas) 2.31–8.

Marcillet-Jaubert, Jean. 1960. Philologie et inscriptions. REA 62.362–82.

Marcovich, M. 1965–66. IV Internacionalni Kongres Klasičnih Studija, University of Pennsylvania, Philadelphia, 24–29 augusta 1964. ŽAnt 15.253–4.

Marg, W. 1950. Der erste Kongress der Fédération Internationale des Associations d'Études Classiques, Paris, 1950. Gnomon 22.198–9.

——. 1954. Der zweite internationale Kongress für klassische Studien. Gnomon 26.494–5.

Mariner Bigorra, Sebastián. 1957a. Valor fonemático de los diptongos del latín clásico. Helmantica 8.17–30.

——. 1957b. Estructura de la categoría verbal 'modo' en latín clásico. Emerita 25. 449–86.

——. 1958. Caracterización funcional de los fonemas del latín clásico. Em 26.227–33.

——. 1962. Fonemática latina. In Bassols de Climent 1962, Appendix.

——. 1965. Noción básica de los modos en el estilo indirecto latino. Em 33.47–59.

Mariotti, Giuseppe. 1970. Ricerche sulla grammatica latina. I, 1. Roma, Ateneo.

Mariotti, Italo. 1958. Stilistica latina (Rassegna bibliografica). A&R (n.s.) 3. 65–76.

Mariotti, Scevola, and Gerardo Sani. 1960. Sintassi latina. Firenze, La Nuova Italia.

Marouzeau, Jules. 1927–28. Dix années de bibliographie classique [1914–1924]. Paris, Les Belles Lettres.

——. 1938. L'ordre des mots dans la phrase latine. II, Le verbe. Paris, Les Belles Lettres.

——. 1939a. Les études latines dans le monde. REL 14.52–4.

——. 1939b. L'emploi du latin comme langue de communication scientifique. REL 14.56–7.

——. 1939c. L'enseignement du Latin en France. SUL 1.31–6.

——. 1939d. Chronique des études latines. REL 17.39–47.

——. 1940a. Chronique des études latines. REL 18.43–7.

——. 1940b. Review of Gray 1939. REL 18.188–9.

——. 1940c. Virgile linguiste. In Mélanges Ernout, 259–65.

——. 1941a. Chronique des études latines. REL 19.46–54.

——. 1941b. Introduction au latin. Paris, Klincksieck.

——. 1942. Chronique des études latines. REL 20.29–34.

——. 1943. Lexique de la terminologie linguistique. Français, allemand, anglais, italien. Éd. augmentée et mise à jour. Paris, Geuthner.

——. 1944a. La linguistique ou science du language. Paris, Geuthner. [2nd ed. 1944.]

——. 1944b (1943–44). Chronique des études latines. REL 21–2, 67–74.

——. 1945. L'adverbe dans la phrase latine. REL 23.182–202.

——. 1946a. Chronique des études latines. REL 24.57–66.

——. 1946b. La construction des subordonnants. REL 24.247–60.

——. 1946c. Traité de stylistique latine. Paris, Les Belles Lettres. [3rd ed. 1954.]

——. 1947. Place de la préposition. REL 25.298–327.

——. 1948a. Les études latines dans le monde. REL 26.89–90.

——. 1948b. La construction des particules de liaison. REL 26.235–67.

——. 1948c. Quelques vues sur l'ordre des mots en latin. Lingua 1.155–61.

——. 1949a. Les études latines dans le monde. REL 27.100–5.

——. 1949b. L'ordre des mots dans la phrase latine. III, Les articulations de l'énoncé. Paris, Les Belles Lettres.

——. 1949c. Quelques aspects de la formation du latin littéraire. Paris, Klincksieck.

——. 1950a. Les études latines dans le monde. REL 28.76.

——. 1950b. Chronique des études latines. REL 28.66–8.

——. 1955[4]. La prononciation du latin. Histoire, théorie, pratique. Paris, Les Belles Lettres.

——. 1956. Chronique des études latines. REL 34.76–84.

——. 1958. Les études latines dans le monde. REL 36.100–4.

——. 1959. Quelques observations statistiques sur les parties du discours. REL 37.215–29.

——. 1960a (1961). Chronique des études latines. REL 38.79–86.

——. 1960b (1961). Sur un aspect de la corrélation en latin: les cas de l'énoncé-fonction. REL 38.172–81.

——. 1961. Chronique des études latines. REL 39.81–6.

——. 1962. Chronique des études latines. REL 40.103–8.

——. 1964. Pour prendre congé. REL 42.84–6.

Marques de Oliveira Filho, A. 1955. Vocalismo, sonantismo e consonantismo do latim. Reexame dos mesmos, na expectativa de uma nova síntese do indo-europeu. Rio de Janeiro, Livraria Principal.

Martins, F. 1947. O Instituto de Estudos Romanos. Humanitas 1.162–71.

Masaracchia, A., and B. Boettger. 1962. Notiziario bibliografico. Helikon 2. 309–27.

Mater, Erich, and J. Stindlová. 1968. Les machines dans la linguistique. Prague. Academia.

Matsudaira, C. 1962. Classical Studies in Japan. Romanitas 4.313–17.

Matthews, P.H. 1967. Word classes in Latin. Lingua 17.153–81.

Mattoso Câmara, J. 1962. "History of linguistics". Unpublished mimeographed notes used at the University of Washington.

——. 1968. Dicionário de filologia e gramática. Rio de Janeiro, Livraria Acadêmica.

MAURER, TH. H., JR. 1948. A morfologia e a sintaxe do genitivo latino (estudio histórico). São Paulo, Universidade de São Paulo.

MAYER, ANTON. 1953. Die Entstehung des lateinischen Perfektsystems. Glotta 32. 261–82.

MAYOR, D. 1950. Sobre la pronunciación del latín. Humanidades 2.103–7.

MAZZUOLI-PORRU, GIULIA. 1955. Italico. [Bibliography for 1947–48.] IJ 30.214–53.

MEILLET, ANTOINE. 1933³. Esquisse d'une histoire de la language latine. Paris, Hachette.

——, and J. VENDRYES. 1948². Traité de grammaire comparée des langues classiques. Ed. revised and augmented. Paris, Champion.

MÉLANGES DE LINGUISTIQUE OFFERTS À CHARLES BALLY. 1939. Genève, Georg.

MÉLANGES DE PHILOLOGIE DE LITTÉRATURE ET D'HISTOIRE ANCIENNES OFFERTS À A. ERNOUT. 1940. Paris, Klincksieck.

MÉLANGES DE PHILOLOGIE, DE LITTÉRATURE ET D'HISTOIRE ANCIENNES OFFERTS À J. MAROUZEAU PAR SES COLLÈGUES ET ÉLÈVES ÉTRANGERS. 1948. Paris, Les Belles Lettres.

MÉLANGES NIEDERMANN. 1944. Neuchâtel, Faculté des Lettres de l'Université.

MÉMORIAL DES ÉTUDES LATINES. 1943. Paris, Les Belles Lettres.

MENÉNDEZ PELAYO, M. 1950–53. Bibliografía hispano-latina clásica. I, Accio-Catón; II, Catulo-Cicerón; III, Cicerón-Historia augusta; IV, V and VI, Horacio; VII, Hostio-Plauto; VIII, Quintiliano-Virgilio: IX, Virgilio-Vitruvio; X, Miscelánea y notas para una bibliografía greco-hispana. Santander, C.S.I.C.

MERLO, C. 1939. Il latino nelle province dell'impero e il problema delle lingue romanze. Romana 4.1–14.

MERONE, E. 1967. Innovazioni linguistiche in Calpurnio Siculo. Napoli, Intercontinentalia.

METTE, H. J., and A. THIERFELDER, eds. 1956 (1957). Lustrum. Internationale Forschungsberichte aus dem Bereich des klassischen Altertums. 1956ff., Iff. Göttingen, Vandenhoeck & Ruprecht.

MICHAEL, IAN. 1970. English grammatical categories and the tradition to 1800. Cambridge, University Press.

MICHEL, A. 1964. Le Quatrième Congrès de la Fédération Internationale des Associations d'Études Classiques. REL 42.87–9.

MIĘTUS, A. 1962. [Symposion des philologues classiques polonais à Cracovie.] JOS 6(1).51–2.

MIGNOT, XAVIER. 1969. Les verbes dénominatifs latins. Paris, Klincksieck.

MIHĂESCU, H. 1939. Gramaticii latini şi barbarismul. Iaşi.

——. 1943. Puncte de vedere asupra lingvisticii latine. Buletinul Institutului de Filologie Romîne 10.91–152.

——. 1950. O barbarismo segundo os gramáticos latinos. Trans. by M. de Paiva Boléo and V. Buescu. Coimbra, Casa do Castelo.

——. 1960a. Cercetările asupra limbii latineşti în ultimii cincisprezece ani. SCL 11.131–4.

——. 1960b. Limba latină în provinciile dunărene ale imperiului roman. Bucureşti, Editura Academiei Republicii Populare Romîne.

MIKKOLA, EINO. 1964. Die Abstraktion im Lateinischen. Eine semantisch-morphologische Untersuchung auf begriffsanalytischer und literaturgeschichtlicher Grundlage. I, Die hypostative Abstraktivität im vorklassischen Gebrauchslatein. Suomalaisen Tiedeakatemian Toimituksia, Sarja B, 133. Helsinki.

MIOC, V. 1939. Studium linguae latinae in realibus gymnasiis Iugoslaviae. SUL 2.53–6.

MIR, J. 1956. Primer Congreso Internacional en pro del latín vivo. EClás 3.478–80.

——. 1969. Historia y enseñanza en un Congreso. IV Congreso internacional de Vita Latina. Helmantica 20.347–64.

MISSIR, L. A. M. 1957. Los estudios clásicos en Turquía. Humanidades 9.123–32.

MOGNI, V. 1951. Il pronome latino negli scrittori classici. Genova, Lupa.

MOHRMANN, CHRISTINE. 1947. Transformations linguistiques et évolution sociale et spirituelle. Vigiliae Christianae 1.186–90.

——. 1950. Les emprunts grecs dans la latinité chrétienne. CVhr 4(4).193–211.

MOLINA YÉVENES, J. 1966. Los pronombres latinos de ausencia de flexión. Emerita 34.87–93.

MOMIGLIANO, ARNALDO. 1958. L'eredità della filologia antica e il metodo storico. Rivista Storica Italiana 70.442–58.

——. 1960. Secondo contributo alla storia degli studi classici. Roma, Edizioni di Storia e Letteratura.

MONTFORD, J. F., and J. T. SCHULTZ. 1962. Index rerum et nominum in scholiis Servii et Aelii Donati tractatorum. Hildesheim, Olms.

MORALEJO, JOSÉ L. 1968. Notación de la aspiración en el latín de la República (Testimonios epigráficos datados). Bologna, Compositori.

MOREAU, B. 1968. Le rôle des cas dans les tours prepositionnels en attique et en latin classique. CJL 14.31–9.

MORELLI, GIUSEPPE. 1970. Ricerche sulla tradizione grammaticale latina I(1). Roma, Edizioni dell'Ateneo.

MORPURGO-TABLIABUE, ANNA. 1967. Linguistica e stilistica di Aristotele. Roma, Ateneo.

MOSES, ELBERT R., JR. 1964. Phonetics: History and interpretation. Englewood Cliffs, Prentice-Hall.

MOSSÉ, F. 1942–45. Review of GRAY 1939. BSL 125.3–4.

MOST, W. G. 1960. Latin by the natural method. Revised ed. 3 vols. Chicago, Regnery.

——. 1962a. Latin as language. CF 16.71–86.

——. 1962b. Teacher's manual for Latin by the natural method. Revised ed. Chicago, Regnery.

MOULTON, WILLIAM G. 1961. Linguistics and language teaching in the United States, 1940–1960. Trends in European and American Linguistics, ed. by Christine Mohrmann, Alf Sommerfeldt and Joshua Whatmough, 82–109. Utrecht, Spectrum.

——. 1969. The nature and history of linguistics. In HILL 1969:3–17.

MOUNIN, GEORGES. 1967. Histoire de la linguistique des origins au XXe siècle. Paris, Presses Universitaires de France.

MOUNTFORD, J. 1963. Investment in the Classics. PCA 60.9–23.

MULJAČIĆ, ŽARKO. 1964. Fonološki status latinskoga [w]. Radovi Razdio Lingvističko-Filološki (3) 5(5).62–9.

——. 1966a. Per un'analisi binaristica dei fonemi latini. Omagiu Rosetti, 599–605.

——. 1966b. Due analisi binarie del sistema fonematico italiano. LeSt 1.265–79.

——. 1967. Distinktivna obilježja latinskih fonema. Filologija 5.83–105.

MÜLLER, HANS-ERICH. 1943. Die Prinzipien der stoischen Grammatik. Rostock, Dissertation Universität Rostock.

MUSCA, DORA ALBA. 1966. Apuliae et Calabriae Latinarum lexicon. Bari, Istituto di Diritto Romano dell'Università.

MYNORS, R. 1966. Classics, pure and applied. PCA 63.13–17.

NAGY, F. 1939. [Grammaticus and grammatica.] EPhK 57–65.

NAIRN, J.A. 1939. Classical handlist. Oxford, Blackwell.

NARO, ANTHONY J. 1971. Directionality and assimilation. Linguistic Inquiry 2. 57–67.

NASCENTES, A. 1962. A filologia românica no Brasil. Romanitas 4.402–9.

NATUNEWICZ, C.F. 1967. The Classics in post-War Poland. CW 60.271–2; 275–80; 282.

NAVIA, A.M. 1939. La pronunciación clásica del latín. Estudios de crítica fonética sobre la pronunciación que estuvo en uso durante la edad de oro, y su aplicación al latín moderno como lengua hablada. Bogotá, Escuelas Gráficas Salesianas.

NELSON, H.L.W. 1963. Klassieke Studie conferentie 1963. Hermeneus 34.219–20.

NENCIONI, G. 1939. Innovazioni africane nel lessico latino. SIFC 16.1–50.

——. 1940. Lessico giuridico e tradizione mediterranea. ASNP 9.21–33.

——. 1941. La lingua latina nell'antico Egitto. In Egitto antico e moderno, 305–29.

NEPPI MODONA, A. 1964. Il IV Congresso Internazionale di Studi Classici. Maia 16.373–87.

——. 1968. L'Associazione Classica dell'Africa Centrale. A&R 13.49–50.

NETTLESHIP, H. 1886. Latin grammar in the first century. Journal of Philology 15.189–214.

NIČEV, A. 1968. Les études classiques en Bulgarie. Euphrosyne (n.s.) 2.199–208.

NIDA, EUGENE A. 1971. [Report of the] Committee to examine the Society's relationship with CIPL. LSA Bulletin 48 (February).19.

NIEDERMANN, MAX. 1907. Historische Lautlehre des Lateinischen. Heidelberg, Winter.

——. 1939. Tendances euphoniques en latin. In Mélanges Bally, 423–8.
——. 1948a. Elementi di fonetica storica del latino. Trans. by C. Passerini. Bergamo, Istituto Italiano Arti Grafiche.
——. 1948b. Iotacismus, labdacismus [sic], mytacismus. RPh 22.5–15.
——. 1953³. Historische Lautlehre des Lateinischen. Revised ed. Heidelberg, Winter.
——. 1953³. Phonétique historique du latin. Paris, Klincksieck.
NILSSON, M. P. 1948. Die klassiche Altertumwissenschaft in Schweden seit dem Jahre 1940. WJA 3.321–4.
NORBERG, D. 1943. Syntaktische Forschungen auf dem Gebiete des Spätlateins und des frühen Mittellateins. Uppsala, Lundeqvist.
——. 1944. Beiträge zur spätlateinischen Syntax. Uppsala, Almqvist & Wiksell.
——. 1952. L'origine de la versification latine rythmique. Eranos 50.83–90.
NORTON, MARY E. 1971a. A selective bibliography on the teaching of Latin and Greek: 1920–1969. New York, MLA/ERIC.
——. 1971b. A bibliography on the value of the Classics. ERIC Report FL 001957. Washington, D.C., Office of Education, USDHEW.
——. 1971c. Pedagogogical literature on the teaching of Latin and Greek: 1920–1970. CW 64.191–3.
NOVOTNÝ, FRANTIŠEK. 1955. Historická mluvnice latinského jazyka. II, Skladba, nauka o slohu, přehled dějin latinského jazyka. Praha, Československá Akad. Věd.
NUMMINEN, P. 1967. Les études classiques en Finlande. Euphrosyne (n.s.) 1.193–205.
NURMELA, R. 1947. Latinan kielen c: n ääntäminen suomalaisena kulttuurikysymyksenä. Vir, 92–5.
NUSSBAUM, J. 1942. La linguistique, élément de culture dans l'enseignement secondaire moderne. In Mélanges Niedermann, 185–8.
NYE, I. 1939. Some facts concerning the study of Latin in the United States of America. SUL 1.126–32.
OLIVA, P. 1965. [IVe Congrès International d'Études Classiques.] ZJKF 7.63–5'
OLIVER, REVILO P. 1966. Apex and Sicilicus. AJPh 87(2). 129–70.
OLMSTED, DAVID L. 1967. History of linguistics. Encyclopedia Americana 16:721.
OMAGIU LUI ALEXANDRU ROSETTI. 1965 (1966). Bucureşti, Ed. Acad. Republicii Socialiste România.
OPELT, ILONA. 1969. La coscienza linguistica dei Romani. A&R 14.21–37.
OPPERMANN, H. 1962. Geisteswissenschaft und Elektronenrechnen. Das Johanneum, Mitteilung des Verehemaliger Schüler des Johanneums Hamburg.49.175–9.
ORBERG, H. 1962. Les études classiques au Danemark. Romanitas 4.351–2.
ORMANNI, A. 1954. Il Congresso Internazionale di Studi Classici (Copenhagen, 23–28 ag. 1954). SDHI 20.538–41.
OUDOT, J. 1964. Syntaxe latine. Paris, Les Belles Lettres.
OWEN, S. G., ed. 1939. The year's work in Classical Studies. Bristol, Arrowsmith.

PACITTI, G. 1960. Il latino lingua viva. Il Secondo Congresso Internazionale per il Latino Vivente. StRo 8.62–8.

PACKARD, D.W. 1969. Publishing Scholarly Compilations by Computer. CHum 4.75–80.

PAGLIARO, ANTONINO. 1930. Sommario di storia linguistica arioeuropea. Roma, L'Universale.

——. 1947. La dottrina linguistica di Dante. Quaderni di Roma 1.485–501.

——. 1956. Filosofia del linguaggio. Roma, Edizioni dell'Ateneo.

PALMER, L.R. 1954. The Latin language. London, Faber & Faber.

PALUZZI, G.C. 1939. L'attività dell'Istituto di Studi Romani durante l'anno 1938–1939. Roma, Istituto di Studi Romani.

PANCONCELLI-CALZIA, G. 1957. Earlier history of phonetics. In KAISER 1957:3–17.

PARATORE, ETTORE. 1948. Letteratura latina. Doxa 1.5–39.

PARIENTE, A. 1946. Notas al vocabulario jurídico latino. Madrid, CSIC.

——. 1949. Estudios de fonética y morfología latina. Salamanca, Universidad de Salamanca.

PARIGGER, F.H. 1941. Aanschouwelijkheidsgraad als factor bij de betekenisontwikkeling der Latijnsche praepositie. Utrecht, Oosthoek.

PARKER, WILLIAM RILEY. 1964. The case for Latin. PMLA 79.4 (Part 2).3–10.

PASCUCCI, G. 1962^2. I fondamenti della filologia classica. Firenze, Sansoni.

——. 1966. A proposito di 'muta cum liquida'. SIFC 38(2).63–9.

PASOLI, ELIO. 1961. Saggi di grammatica latina. Bologna, Università degli Studi.

PASQUALI, G. 1940. I risultati raggiunti dalla filologia classica italiana nell'ultimo sessennio. Roma, A.S.P.S. [Riunione XXVIII].

PAULI, A.F., and J.W. SPAETH. 1939. Classical articles in non-Classical periodicals. CJ 34.381–4, and 509–12.

PAVLOVSKAJA, A.I. 1962. [VIe Conférence Internationale des Études Classiques à Plovdiv.] VDI 79.173–7.

PEDERSEN, HOLGER. 1924. Sprogvidenskaben i det nittende aarhundrede; metoder og resultater. Copenhagen, Nordisk.

——. 1931. Linguistic science in the nineteenth century. Trans. by J.W. Spargo. Cambridge, Harvard University Press. [Reprinted 1962, Indiana University Press.]

PEI, MARIO A. 1945. Language for war and peace. New York, Vanni.

——. 1965. Invitation to linguistics. A basic introduction to the science of language. Garden City, Doubleday.

PELLICER, ANDRÉ. 1966. Natura. Étude sémantique et historique du mot latin. Paris. Presses Universitaires de France.

PEPE, L. 1946. Accio, Lucilio e la *geminatio*. SIFC 20.105–20.

PEREIRA DE FIGUEIREDO, ANTONIO. 1752. Novo método de gramática latina. Lisboa.

PÉREZ RIOJA, J.A. 1958. Las lenguas clásicas como instrumentos de agilidad mental. Actas del Primer Congreso Español de Estudios Clásicos, 223–4.

PERRENOUD, A. 1942. Linguistique et pédagogie. In Mélanges Niedermann, 179–84.

——. 1956. Rapport sur le Congrès pour le Latin Vivant. REL 34.62.

——. 1962. Les études latines en Suisse. Romanitas 4.268–77.

PERRET, J. 1964. Présent et imparfait dans le subjonctif latin. Latomus 23.197–212.

PERROT, J. 1966. Le fonctionnement du système des cas en latin. RPh 40.217–27.

PETRUŠEVSKI, M.D. 1951. Elementa. ŽAnt 1.137–44.

PFEIFFER, RUDOLF. 1968. History of Classical scholarship from the beginnings to the end of the Hellenistic Age. Oxford, Clarendon.

PFISTER, RAIMUND. 1969. Strukturalismus und Lateinunterricht. Gymnasium 76. 457–72.

PHILOLOGISCHE STUDIEN FÜR JOSEPH M. PIEL. 1969. Heidelberg, Winter.

PIANKO, G. 1952. Filologia klasyczna w Polsce. Bibliografia zu lata 1945–1949. Warszawa, Min. Szkol. Wyzsz. i Nauki.

PIGHI, GIOVANNI BATTISTA. 1939a. L'insegnamento del latino. Aevum 12.222–36.

——. 1939b. Pronunzie del latino. SUL, 105–10.

——. 1968. See ENCICLOPEDIA CLASSICA 1968.

PINBORG, JAN. 1962. Das Sprachdenken der Stoa und Augustins Dialektik. C&M 23.148–77.

PINKSTER, H. 1969a. Latijnse taal. Recente publicatie op het gebied van de Latijnse taalkunde. I, Tempus, aspect en Aktionsart in het Latijnse verbum. Lampas 2.167–93.

——. 1969b. A B & C-Coordination in Latin. Mn 22.258–67.

PIPPIDI, D.M. 1946. Les études classiques en Roumanie de 1939 à 1945. BAGB (n.s.) 1.77–81.

——. 1958. Les études classiques en Roumanie 1946–1957. Dacia (n.s.) 2.499–511.

——. 1965. Al IV-lea Congres International de Studii Clasice (Philadelphia, August 1964). SClas 7.365–6.

PIRIE, J.W. 1941. Review of GRAY 1939. CR 55.38–40.

PISANI, VITTORE. 1948²a. Introduzione alla linguistica indoeuropea. Arona, Paideia.

——. 1948b. Grammatica latina storica e comparativa. Torino, Rosenberg & Sellier.

——. 1960. Casus interrogandi. In Hommages Herrmann, 624–38.

——. 1962. Manuale storico della lingua latina. I, Storia della lingua latina. Part I, Le origini e la lingua letteraria fino a Virgilio e Orazio. Torino, Rosenberg & Sellier.

PLATNAUER, M., ed. 1950. The Year's work in Classical Studies. Bristol, Arrowsmith.

——, et al. 1954. Fifty years of Classical scholarship. Oxford, Blackwell.

PLEZIA, M. 1946. tacina, której nie znamy. Mea 1.350–68.

POMAR, J.M.F. 1957. Entidades de estudios clásicos en Inglaterra. EClás 4.115–25.

PONCELET, R. 1948. Précision et intensité dans la prose latine. REL 26.134–56.

——. 1964 (1965). Statisme et évolution dans l'histoire du latin écrit. REL 42. 400–28.

PORRU, GIULIA. 1949. Bibliographie der Jahre 1942 und 1943. IX, Italico. IJ 28. 172–200.

POTTER, S. 1941. Review of GRAY 1939. MLR 26.117–19.

POUSA, R.F. 1941. La enseñanza del latín en la nueva España. SUL 1–8.

PREMIER CONGRÈS INTERNATIONAL POUR LE LATIN VIVANT. Avignon, 3–6 septembre 1956. 1956. Avignon, Aubanel.

PRIESEMANN, G. 1962. Grundfragen und Grundlagen des altsprachlichen Unterrichts. Göttingen, Vandenhoeck & Ruprecht.

PULGRAM, ERNST. 1950. Spoken and written Latin. Lg 26.458–66.

——. 1954. Accent and ictus in spoken and written Latin. KZ 71.218–37.

——. 1957a. A report on the International Congress for Living Latin. CJ 52.301–8.

——. 1957b. A reply [to BEACH 1957]. CJ 53.123.

——. 1958. The tongues of Italy. Cambridge, Harvard University Press.

——. 1965. The accentuation of Greek loans in spoken and written Latin. AJPh 86.138–58.

PYLES, TH. 1939. A history of the pronunciation of learned Latin loanwords and foreign words in English. Dissertation Johns Hopkins University.

QUINN, K. 1955. Les études latines en Nouvelle-Zélande. 33.103–4.

RADCIG, S.I. 1965 (1966). Vvedenie v klassicheskuiu filologuiu. Moscow, I. Moscow Univ.

RADET, F., et al. 1939. Chronique des études anciennes. REA 41.101–9; 207–12; 305–8; 388–91.

RAMBAUD, M. 1959. Le IIe Congrès International pour le Latin Vivant. IL 11.214–16.

RANDALL, J.H. 1958. Nature and historical experience. New York, Columbia University Press.

RAPALLO, UMBERTO. 1969. Per una definizione diacronica e tipologica dei calchi ebraici nelle antiche versioni del Levitico. (Studio sui LXX, la Vulgata e la Vetus). RIL 103.369–437.

RAPISARDA, EMANUELE. 1951. Avviamento allo studio della lingua e letteratura latina. Parte III, Vol. I, Rassegna espositiva di studi di lingua latina. Catania, Reina.

——. 1964. Il movimento europeo per la difesa del latino: programma per il 1964. 1964. Orpheus 11.33–6.

RAVEN, D.S. 1965. Latin metre. An introduction. London, Faber & Faber.

REGULA, M. 1948. Streifzüge auf dem Gebiet der lateinischen Syntax und Stilistik. Glotta 31.72–92.

REHM, A. 1944. Bericht über den Thesaurus linguae Latinae in den Geschäftjahren 1940/41 bis 1943/44. JbBAW, 63–9.

——. 1948. Bericht über den Thesaurus linguae Latinae in den Geschäftjahren

1944–45 bis 1947–48. JbBAW, 82–6.

REINERT, HARRY. 1972. Truth in packaging ... for foreign languages. MLJ 56. 205–9.

RICHER, ERNEST. 1962. Lieux linguistiques et latin classique. Montréal, Centre Pédagogique des Jésuites Canadiens.

RICHTER, W. and G. PACITTI. 1966. A proposito del Congresso Internazionale per il Latino. StRo 14.445–52.

RIGHI, GAETANO. 1962. Breve storia della filologia classica. Firenze, Sansoni.

——. 1967. Historia de la filología clásica. Trans. by J. M. García de la Mora. Barcelona, Labor.

——. 1969². Breve historia de la filología clásica. Trans. by J. M. García de la Mora. Barcelona, Labor.

RISICATO, ANTONINO. 1948. L'evoluzione fonetica del latino. Lineamenti storici con cenni di fonetica italiana e di prosodia. Messina, D'Anna.

——. 1950. Grammaticalia, profili storici sull'aspetto nel verbo latino e sul deponente. Messina: Editrice Universitaria.

——. 1961. Fattori linguistici generali e vicende fonetiche principali del latino. Messina, D'Anna.

ROBINETT, BETTY WALLACE, et al. 1953. Classics and linguistics. CW 46.97–100.

ROBINS, R. H. 1951. Ancient and Medieval grammatical theory in Europe, with particular reference to modern linguistic doctrine. London, Bell.

——. 1957 [1958]. Dionysius Thrax and the Western grammatical tradition. TPhS 67–106.

——. 1964a. Ancient grammarians and modern linguistics. Didaskalos 1(1).81–9. [Reprinted, with an introduction, in ROBINS 1970:101–11.]

——. 1964b. General linguistics: An introductory survey. Bloomington, Indiana University Press.

——. 1966. The development of the word class system of the European grammatical tradition. FL 2.3–19.

——. 1968. A short history of linguistics. Bloomington, Indiana University Press.

——. 1970. Diversions of Bloomsbury. Amsterdam, North-Holland.

ROBINSON, T. W. 1967. The computer and classical languages. EMC 11.39–46.

ROCHA PEREIRA, M. H. 1953–54. Os estudos clássicos em Espanha. Humanitas 5/6.192–200.

ROCHER, L. 1957–58. Les philologues classiques et les débuts de la grammaire comparée. Revue de l'Université de Bruxelles 10.251–86.

RODRÍGUEZ ADRADOS, F. 1951. El Congreso de la Federación de Estudios Clásicos. EClás 1.103–5.

——. 1952. La lingüística y la ensenanza de las lenguas clásicas. EClás 1.322–35.

——. 1964. Sobre los congresos internacionales de estudios clásicos. EClás 8.235–7.

ROMANELLI, PIETRO. 1955. Il Secondo Congresso Internazionale di Studi Classici. StRo 3.195–7.

——. 1960. Il Terzo Congresso Internazionale di Studi Classici. StRo 8.56–8.

——. 1964. L'unité des études classiques. REL 42.99–112.

——. 1966. Il Congresso Internazionale per il Latino. StRo 14.262–8.

ROMANELLI, R. C. 1963. Do morfema indo-europeu n em latim. Contribuiçao ao estudo da lexicologia latina. Belo Horizonte, Imprensa Universitária de Minas Gerais.

ROMEO, LUIGI. 1966. Review of WATERMANN 1963. Annali dell'Istituto Orientale di Napoli. Sezione Linguistica 7.218–26.

——. 1967. On the phonemic status of the so-called 'geminates' in Italian. Linguistics 29.105–16.

——, and G. E. TIBERIO. 1971. Historiography of linguistics and Rome's scholarship. LS 17.23–44.

ROMERO, N. 1948. L'argument historique et la pronunciation du latin. Rio de Janeiro, Olympio.

RONCONI, ALESSANDRO. 1946. Il verbo latino. Principi di sintassi storica. Bologna, Zanichelli.

——. 1958. Interpretazioni grammaticali. Padova, Liviana. [Revised ed. 1971. Roma, Ateneo.]

——. 1959a. La sintassi latina. Firenze, Sansoni.

——. 1959b. Il verbo latino. Problemi di sintassi storica. Le Monnier.

——. 1962a. Gli studi di latino in Italia. Romanitas 4.466–77.

——. 1962b. I nomi dei casi e le ire di un linguista. A&R 7.91–5.

——. 1964. Appunti per un parallelo tra filologia e linguistica. RCCM 6.1–14.

ROSÉN, HAIIM B. 1961. Arrius' speech again (Catullus 84). Mn Ser. 4, 14(3).224–32.

——. 1968. Die Grammatik des Unbelegten. Dargestellt an den Nominal-Komposita bei Ennius. Lingua 21.359–81.

ROSS, DAVID O. 1969. Style and tradition in Catullus. Cambridge, Harvard University Press.

ROSSBRUCKER, I. 1944. "Zur Wegvorstellung im Lateinischen". Dissertation Wien. [Typewritten.]

ROSSI, L. E. 1960. Storia e storicismo nella filosofia contemporanea. Milano, Lerici.

——. 1969. La pronuntiatio plena, sinalefe in luogo d'elisione. RFIC 97.433–47.

ROSTAGNI, A. 1939. La letteratura di Roma repubblicana ed augustea. Bologna, Capelli.

RÖTTGER, GERHARD. 1969. Lateinische Grammatik. Römisches Sprachdenken zur Zeit Ciceros und Cäsars. Frankfurt, Fischer.

RUBENHAUER, H. 1944 (1945). Aus der Arbeit am Thesaurus linguae Latinae. JbBAW, 6–15.

RUBIO, LISARDO. 1966. Introducción a la sintaxis estructural del latín. I, Casos y preposiciones. Barcelona, Ariel.

RUCH, M. 1969a. Objectivité et subjectivité dans la période hypothétique latine. RRLing 14.101–9.

——. 1969b. Le participe futur en *-turus* dans la conditionelle. LEC 37.152–61.

Sacconi, J. M. Rivas. 1941. Il latino nella letteratura e nella scuola columbiana. SUL 3.12–22.

Saddington, D. B. 1968. The Classics in South Africa. Euphrosyne (n.s.) 2.215–20.

Sadler, J. D. 1969. Idiosyncrasies of suffixes. CB 46.8–11 and 16.

Safarewicz, J. 1948. Fonologiczna wartość lacińskich dwugłosek. SprPAUm 49. 264–6.

——. 1949. Lacińskie imperfectum w ujęciu składniowym. SprPAUm 50.227–8.

——. 1950. Grammatyka historyczna języka lacińskiego. II Składnia. Warszawa, Państwowe Zakłady Wynawnictw Szkolnych.

——. 1953. Zarys gramatyki historycznej języka łacińskiego. Fonetyka historyczna i fleksja. Warszawa, Państwowe Wydawnictwo Naukowe.

——. 1961 (1962). Oznaczanie iloczasu w inskrypcjach rzymskich I wieku n.e. SprPAN 4.12–26.

——. 1962. Oznaczanie aspiracji w inskrypcjach rzymskich I wieku n.e. Eos 52. 337–49.

——. 1963. Chronologia rozwoju łacińskich grup spółgłoskowych. PF 17(1).179–94.

——. 1964a. Rozwój łacińskiego systemu spółgłokowego. SprPAN 7, No. 2 (33). 11–31.

——. 1964b. O spółgłoskach geminowanych w języku łacińskim. SprPAN 7, No. 4 (35).1–19.

——. 1965. Stanowisko Enniusza w historii języka łacińskiego. SprPAN 8, No. 1 (36).1–19.

——. 1966 (1968). Charakterystyka fonologiczna łaciny klasycznej. Eos 56.100–7.

——. 1969. Notes sur le vocabulaire de Cicéron. Studia Pagliaro 3.193–215.

——. 1969a. Nanik iloczasu w języku łacińskim. SprPAN 12, No. 2 (53).1–13.

——. 1969b. Historische lateinische Grammatik. Halle (Saale), Niemeyer.

——. 1969c. À quelle époque commence le latin dit vulgaire. In Studia Pisani 2.863–72.

Salus, Peter H. 1969. On language. Plato to Humboldt. New York, Holt, Rinehart, and Winston.

Sánchez Ruipérez, M. 1954a. El II Congreso Internacional de Estudios Clásicos celebrado en Copenhague (23–28 de agosto de 1954). Arbor 29.511–16.

——. 1954b. El II Congreso Internacional de Estudios Clásicos. EClás 2.396–8.

——. 1954c. II Congreso Internacional de Estudios Clásicos (Copenhague, 23–28 de agosto de 1954). Zephyrus 5.230–1.

——. 1956. I Congreso Español de Estudios Clásicos. Arbor 34.260–2.

——. 1964. Panorama actual de la gramática griega y latina. In Actas del II Congreso Español de Estudios Clásicos, 63–95.

Sánchez Vallejo, F. 1956. Congreso Internacional para el Latín Vivo. Humanidades 8.267–74.

——. 1959. El movimento por el latín vivo. 2a etapa. Lyon, 1959. Humanidades 11.333–41.

SANDYS, JOHN EDWIN. 1903–08. A history of Classical scholarship. 3 vols. Cambridge, University Press.

SAYCE, A.H. 1911[11]. Grammar. Encyclopaedia Britannica 12.326–32.

SBORDONE, FRANCESCO. 1955. Ai margini della sintassi latina. I, Sintassi nominale. Napoli, Loffredo.

——. 1957. Ai margini della sintassi latina. II, Sintassi del verbo e del periodo. Napoli, Loffredo.

SCAGLIONE, ALDO S. 1970. Ars grammatica. The Hague, Mouton.

SCHILLING, R. 1963. La situation des langues classiques dans l'enseignement français. Didaskalos 1.37–44.

SCHMIDT, J.H. HEINRICH. 1968. Handbuch der lateinischen und griechischen Synonymik. Amsterdam, Hakkert.

SCHODER, R.V. 1949. John Bull on Helicon. The state of the Classics in England. CJ 44.332–4.

SCHOENHEIM, U. 1969a. Inexpensive books for teaching the Classics. 9th Annual list. CW 62.173–86.

——. 1969b. Textbooks in Greek and Latin. CW 62.311–23.

SCHOFIELD, HARRY. 1968. The application of linguistics to the problem of teaching pupils to translate complex Latin sentences into English. IRAL 6.187–94.

SCHROETER, R. 1959a. Le riviste tedesche di filologia classica. AGR 4.140–4.

——. 1959b. Studien zur Varronischen Etymologie. Wiesbaden, Steiner.

——. 1963. Die Varronische Etymologie. In VARRON, 79–116.

SCHWEIGER, F.L.A. 1830–32. Handbuch der klassischen Philologie. Leipzig, Fleischer.

——. 1834. Handbuch der classischen Bibliographie, II, Lateinische Schriftsteller. Leipzig, Fleischer. [Reprinted 1962. Amsterdam, Hakkert,]

SCIUTO, SALVATORE. 1967. Grammatica della lingua latina. Manuale di consultazione per studenti ed insegnanti. Torino, Società Editrice Internazionale.

SEEL, OTTO. 1964. Römertum und Latinität. Stuttgart, Klett.

SEMAAN, KHALIL I. 1968. Linguistics in the Middle Ages: Phonetic studies in Early Islam. Leiden, Brill.

SEMERANO, GIOVANNI. 1951. Bibliografia degli autori greci e latini. In BIGNONE 1951:453–655.

SEMI, FRANCESCO. 1969. Manuale di filologia classica. Padova, Liviana.

SERRA I RAFOLS, J. DE C. 1951. Participation de l'Espagne dans les entreprise internationales. In Actes du Premier Congrès de la Fédération Internationale des Associations d'Études Classiques, 183–4.

SERTA EITREMIANA. Opuscula philologica S. Eitrem septuagenario 28 dec. 1942 oblata. 1942. Oslo, Brögger.

SERTA PHILOLOGICA AENIPONTANA. 1962. IBK, 7–8. Innsbruck, Sprachwissenschaftliches Institut der Universität.

SEVERYNS, A. 1964. Note sur le Quatrième Congrès Internationale des Études Classiques à Philadelphie. AC 33.444–7.

SHIPP, G.P. 1969. Supertitio and ἐπίσταμαι. Antichthon 3.29–31.

SIBILLA, GAETANO. 1967. Sintassi della lingua latina, positiva, filosofica. Roma, A.BE.T.E.

SIEGART, H.K. 1939. Die Syntax der Tempora und Modi der ältesten lateinischen Inschriften (bis zum Tode Caesars). Würzburg, Triltsch.

SIMEON, RIKARD. 1969. Enciklopedijski riečnik lingvističkih naziva. 2 vols. Zagreb, Matica Hrvatska.

SIMONS, PH.J. 1950. Moderne en antieke taalwetenschap. Vergelijkingen en synthesen. NT 43.75–83.

SINANOĞLU, S. 1959. [Congrès du Latin Vivant.] Ankara Univ. Dil. Tar.-Coğr. Fak. Derg. 17(1–2).99–104.

SMUTS, F. 1960. Classical scholarship and the teaching of Classics at Cape Town and Stellenbosch. AClass 3.7–31.

——. 1962. Classical studies in South Africa. Romanitas 4.360–6.

SOLIN, HEIKKI. 1969. Zur Datierung ältester lateinischer Inschriften. Glotta 47. 248–53.

SOMMER, FERDINAND. 1914. Handbuch der lateinischen Laut- und Formenlehre. Heidelberg, Winter.

SORANZO, G. 1950². Avviamento agli studi storici. Milano, Marzorati.

SOUBIRAN, JEAN. 1969. Les hexamètres spondaïques à quadrisyllabe final. Problèmes de liaisons syllabiques. GIF 21.329–49.

SOUTER, A., et al., eds. 1968. Oxford Latin Dictionary. Fasc. 1, A-Calcitro. Oxford, Clarendon.

——. 1969. Oxford Latin Dictionary Fasc. II, Calcitro-Demitto. Oxford, Clarendon.

SOUTHAN, J.E. 1962. A survey of Classical periodicals. Union Catalogue of Periodicals Relevant to Classical Studies in Certain British Libraries. BICS, Suppl. XIII. London, Institute of Classical Studies.

SPECHT, FR. 1952. Die Herkunft der Griechen und Römer und ihre Sprachen. Lexis 3.69–74.

SPITZER, LEO. 1930. Die Umschreibungen des Begriffes 'hunger' im Italienischen; stilistisch-onomasiologische Studie auf Grund von unveröffentlichtem Zensurmaterial. Halle, Karras.

SPRINGER, L.A. 1958. Aulus Gellius on historical and descriptive linguistics. CJ 54.121–8.

SPRINGHETTI, AEMILIUS. 1962. Lexicon linguisticae et philologiae. Romae, apud Pontificiam Universitatem Gregorianam.

STATI, SORIN. 1961. Limba latină în inscripţiile din Dacia şi Scythia minor. Bucureşti, Editura Academiei Republicii Populare Romîne.

STECJUK, V. 1951. Istoryčna hramatyka latynsk'koji movy. I, Fonetyka. München, Ukrajins'kyj Vil'nyj Univ.

STEINTHAL, H. 1863. Geschichte der Sprachwissenschaft bei den Griechen und Römern mit besonderen Rücksicht auf die Logik. 2 vols. Berlin, Dümmler.

——. 1890. Geschichte der Sprachwissenschaft bei den Griechen und Römern mit besonderer Rücksicht auf die Logik. Berlin. [2nd ed. 1891; reprinted 1961. Hildesheim, G. Olms.]

STOCK, BRIAN. 1969. The poverty of philology: The need for new directions in Classics and Medieval Studies. American Council of Learned Societies Newsletter 20(3).1–7.

STOLZ, FRIEDRICH. 1911. Geschichte der lateinischen Sprache. Sammlung Göschen, 492. Berlin.

——. 1953[3]. Geschichte der lateinischen Sprache. Berlin, de Gruyter.

STRUNK, KLAUS. 1969. 'Besprochene und erzählte Welt' im Lateinischen? Eine Auseinandersetzung mit H. Weinrich. Gymnasium 76.269–310.

STRZELECKI, L. 1949. Studia prosodiaca et metrica. Kraków, Polska Akad. Umiejętnosci.

STUDI LINGUISTICI IN ONORE DI VITTORE PISANI. 1969. 2 vols. Brescia, Paideia.

STUDIA CLASSICA ET ORIENTALIA ANTONINO PAGLIARO OBLATA. 3 vols. 1969. Roma, Herder.

STUDIA VARIA CAROLO GUILIELMO VOLLGRAFF A DISCIPULIS ABLATA. 1948. Amsterdam, North-Holland.

STURTEVANT, E. H. 1939. The pronunciation of Latin *qu* and *gu*. Lg 15.221–3.

——. 1940. The pronunciation of Greek and Latin. Philadelphia, LSA.

——. 1947. An introduction to linguistic science. New Haven, Yale University Press.

——. 1968[2]. The pronunciation of Greek and Latin. Groningen, Bouma's Boekhuis.

SUETONIUS TRANQUILLUS, GAIUS. 1830. De illustribus grammaticis, ed. by M. de Goldberg. Paris, Panckoucke.

SUNDWALL, J. 1939. Das Studium des Lateinischen in Finland [sic]. SUL 1.208–10.

SVENNUNG, J. 1948. En språkets skattammare. Dess förhistoria, skapande och ovissa framtidsöde. SvTs 35.547–51.

SVOBODA, K. 1939a. [New trends in Classical Philology.] LF 66.1–8.

——. 1939b. [The Czech Classic Philologists as professors in Russia.] LF 66.349–64.

——. 1955. [La disposition de la linguistique.] LF (n.s.) 3.153–61.

SVOBODOVÁ, E. 1964. [Conférences d'Études Classiques à Liblice, 9–11 mars 1964.] LF 12.391–2.

SWANSON, DONALD C. 1940. Review of GRAY 1939. Lg 16.231–5.

SWEET, WALDO. 1957. Latin. A structural approach. Ann Arbor, University of Michigan Press.

——. 1967. The continued development of the structural approach. Didaskalos 2(2).141–59.

SZEMERÉNYI, O. 1941. Die idg. Liquidae sonantes im Lateinischen. Budapest.

——. 1942. A latin névmási ragozás történetéhez. EPhK 66.337–43.

SZIDAVROSZKY, J. 1939. [Zur Frage der lateinischen Sprachwissenschaft.] EPhK 64.129–143.

TACCONE, A. 1947. Cenni bibliografici e notizie varie. MC 14.9–21.

TAGLIAVINI, CARLO. 1934. Linguistica. Enciclopedia Italiana di Scienze, Lettere ed Arti 21.207–14.

——. 1936. Cenni storici. In Introduzione alla glottologia generale comparata, 5–105. Padova, Gruppo Universitario Fascista [= Bologna, La Grafolito].

——. 1942². Introduzione alla glottologia. Bologna, Pàtron. [First ed. 1936.]

——. 1949. Cenni di fonetica e morfologia storica del latino. Bologna, Pàtron.

——. 1968². Panorama di storia della linguistica. Revised ed. Bologna, Pàtron.

——. 1969⁷. Introduzione alla glottologia. 2 vols. Bologna, Pàtron.

TANNER, R. G. 1962. Latin in Australia. Romanitas 4.385–98.

TAYLOR, DANIEL JENNINGS. 1970. "A study of the linguistic theory of Marcus Terentius Varro". Ph.D. Dissertation, University of Washington, Seattle.

TEETER, KARL V. 1964. Descriptive linguistics in America: Triviality vs. irrelevance. Word 20.197–206.

——. 1966. The history of Linguistics: New lamp for old. In DINNEEN 1966:83–95.

TESCARI, ONORATO. 1957. Sintassi latina. Torino, S.E.I.

TESNIÈRE, LUCIEN. 1953. Esquisse d'une syntaxe structurale. Paris, Klincksieck.

——. 1959. Éléments de syntaxe structurale. Paris, Klincksieck.

——. 1968. Pour prononcer le grec et le latin. Paris, Didier.

THEANDER, C. 1941. In Suecia quis et fuerit et hodiernis maxime temporibus set linguae latinae usus. SUL 3.9–11.

THÉODORE-AUBANEL, ÉDOUARD. 1958. Latein — die internationale Sprache. Altertum 4.186–92.

THEORY AND PRACTICE IN HISTORICAL STUDY: A REPORT OF THE COMMITTEE ON HISTORIOGRAPHY. 1942 [1946]. New York, Social Science Research Council.

THESAURUS LINGUAE LATINAE, editus auctioritade et consilio quinque Germanicarum Berolinensis Gottingensis Lipsiensis Monacensis Vindobonensis. 1942. Vol. 5, No. 2, fasc. 11, Expavesco-Expono. Lipsiae, Teubner. Vol. 8, fasc. 5, Membrum-Mercor. *Ibid.*

THIERFELDER, A., ed. 1956. Jahresbericht über die Fortschritte der klassischen Altertumswissenschaft. 285 (1944–55). Göttingen, Vandenhoeck & Ruprecht.

THOMPSON, L. A. 1966. The Classics in Nigeria, 1956–1966. N&C, 46–61.

THOMSEN, VILHELM. 1902. Sprogvidenskabens historie: en kortfattet fremstilling. Copenhagen, Gad.

——. 1945. Historia de la lingüística. Trans. by J. de Echave-Sustaeta. Barcelona, Labor.

THORNTON, HARRY and AGATHE. 1962. Time and style: A psycho-linguistic essay in Classical literature. London, Methuen.

THUROT, CHARLES. 1869. Extraits de divers manuscrits latins pour servir à l'histoire des doctrines grammaticales au Moyen Age. Paris, Imprimerie Impériale.

THYLANDER, H. 1962. L'étude des langues classiques en Suède. Romanitas 4.282–97.

TIBILETTI, G. 1959. II Congress of Classical Studies. Labeo 5.411–13.

TOGEBY, K. 1969. Prépositions latines et prépositions romanes. LeSt 4.413–21.

TOSATTI, Q. 1956. II Congresso di Avignone per il Latino Vivente. StRo 4.584–9.

TOVAR, ANTONIO. 1944. Lingüística y filología clásica. Su situación actual. Madrid, Revista de Occidente.

——. 1946. Gramática histórica latina. Sintaxis. Madrid, Aguado.

——. 1969a. Lucilio y el latín de España. In Studi Pisani 2.1019–1031.

——. 1969b. Catón y el latín de Hispania. In Studien Piel, 201–8.

TOWNEND, G.B. 1969. Some problems of punctuation in the Latin hexameter. CQ 19.330–44.

TOYNBEE, A.J. 1943. A study of history. London, Oxford University Press.

TRAGER, G.L. 1962. History of linguistics. Encyclopaedia Britannica 14.163–4.

TRAGLIA, A. 1950. La flessione verbale latina. Trattato di morfologia storica. Torino, SEI.

——. 1963. Dottrine etimologiche ed etimologie varroniane con particolare riguardo al linguaggio poetico. In VARRON, 33–77.

——, ed. 1967. La lingua latina [di] M. Terenzio Varrone, Libro X. Roma, Ateneo.

TRAINA, ALFONSO. 1955. Esegesi e sintassi. Studi di sintassi latina. Padova, Liviana.

——. 1957. L'alfabeto e la pronunzia del latino. Bologna, Pàtron.

——. 1959. Tra filologia e linguistica. Maia 11.67–81.

——. 1961. Attrazione e no. A&R (n.s.) 6.25–30.

——. 1963–64. La sintassi latina e la linguistica moderna. Scuola e didattica 9. 132–4; 245–7; 361–3.

——, and T. BERTOTTI. 1966. Sintassi normativa della lingua latina. 3 vols. Bologna, Cappelli.

TROISIÈME CONGRÈS INTERNATIONAL POUR LE LATIN VIVANT, Strasbourg, 2–4 sept. 1963. 1963. Avignon, Aubanel.

TRONSKIJ, I.M. 1953. Očerki iz istoriji latinskogo jazyka. Moskva, Izdatel'stvo Akademiia Nauk SSSR.

——. 1960a. Istoričeskaja grammatika latinskogo jazyka. Moskva, Izdatel'stvo Literatury na Inostrannych Jazykach.

——. 1960b. Zametki o vido-vremennój sisteme latinskogo glagola. In Voprosy grammatiki (Mélanges Meščaninov), 434–45.

——. 1967. Klassičeskie jazyki. In FILIN et al. 1967:143–57.

TROST, P. 1939. Zum lateinischen Kondizionalsatz. Glotta 27.206–11.

TRUBETZKOY, N.S. 1939. Grundzüge der Phonologie. TLP, 7. Prague.

——. 1949. Principes de phonologie. Trans. by J. Cantineau. Paris, Klincksieck.

UHLFELDER, M.L. 1963. The Romans on linguistic change. CJ 59.23–30.

UITTI, KARL K. 1969. Linguistics and literary theory. Englewood Cliffs, N.J., Prentice-Hall.

ULLMAN, B. L., et al. 1946. German and Italian publications in Classics, 1940–1945. CW 40.15–16; 40; 56; 63–4.

USSANI, V. 1939. La missione unificatrice dell latino nella storia della civiltà. SUL 1.197–207.

UT PICTURA POESIS. Studia latina Petro Iohanni Enk septuagenario oblata. 1955. Leiden, Brill.

VÄÄNÄNEN, V. 1947. Latinaisperäisten sanojen etuvokaalia edeltävän c: n ääntämisestä. Vir 51.95–9.

VALENTINI, G. 1939. Albania Latina. SUL 2.6–12.

VAN BERCHEM, D. 1952. Poètes et grammairiens. Recherche sur la tradition scolaire d'explication des auteurs. MH 9.79–87.

VAN BUREN, A. W. 1947. War-time productivity in Italy. AJPh 68.1–20.

VAN DER HARST, L. L. A. 1944. Beschouwingen omtrent de beteekenis van het Latijn als algemeene omgangstaal in den naklassieken tijd. Hermeneus 16.3ff. and 23ff.

VANDVIK, E. 1942. Genetivus und ablativus qualitatis. Oslo, Dybwad.

VAN HAMEL, A. G. 1946. Geschiedenis van de taalwetenschap. The Hague, Servire's Encyclopaedie in Monographieën.

VAN OMME, A. N. 1946. 'Virtus', een semantiese studie. Utrecht, Kemink.

VAN OOTEGHEN, J. 1961. La prononciation de 'mihi' et 'nihil'. Les Études Classiques 29(3).310–12.

VARCL, L. 1964. [Conférence d'Études Classiques à Léningrad, 9–14 avril 1964.] LF 12.392–3.

VARRON, 1963. Vandoeuvres-Genève, Fondation Hardt. Entretiens sur l'Antiquité Classique, IX.

VELKOV, V. 1966. [Conférence sur les Études Classiques réunie en Hongrie.] Arch (Sophia) 8(1).68–9.

VENDRYES, J. 1939². Le language. Introduction linguistique à l'histoire. Paris, La Renaissance du Livre.

——. 1951. Language. A linguistic introduction to history. Trans. by P. Radin. New York, Barnes and Noble.

VENEDIKOV, I. 1942. [Phonetics of the Latin Inscriptions in Bulgaria.] Acta Seminatiorum Facultatis Historico-philologicae Universitatis Sancti Clementis Achridensis Serdicae 1.227–46.

VEREMANS, J. 1969. Évolution historique de la structure verbale du deuxième hémistiche du pentamètre latin. Hommages Renard 1.758–67.

VIDMAN, L. 1961. Philologia classica a. 1960. Bibliografia librorum Bohemicorum et Slovacorum. ZJKF 3.114–17.

——. 1966a. [Colloque sur les études classiques dans l'enseignement, Londres 1965.] ZJKF 8.44–7.

——. 1966b. Bibliographia studiorum Graecorum et Latinorum in Bohemoslovenia,

MCMLI-MCMLX. Praha, Státni, Knihovna CSSR.
VITA LATINA. 1954ff. 1ff. Avignon, Aubanel.
VOLLGRAFF, C.W. 1946. Les études classiques en Hollande pendant la guerre. BAGB (n.s.) 1.106–18.
——. 1949. Elementum. Mn 4e Ser., 2.89–115.
VON FRITZ, KURT. 1949. Ancient instruction in 'grammar' according to Quintilian. AJPh 70.337–66.
——. 1959. Quomodo duabus demum vocalibus in se ipsas coeundi natura sit. Hermes 87.118–26.
VON HENTIG, H. 1962. Die klassische Bildung in Deutschland. Versuch einer Standortbestimmung. Romanitas 4.200–27.
——. 1966. Linguistik, Schulgrammatik, Bildungswert. Eine neue Chance für den Lateinunterricht. Gymnasium 73.125–46.
VOPROSY GRAMMATIKI. Sbornik statej k 75-letiju akademika I.I. Meščaninova. 1960. Moskva, Izdatelstvo Akademiia Nauk SSSR.
VORONKOV, A.I. 1961. [Ancient Greece and Ancient Rome. Bibliographic index of the publications made in USSR between 1895 and 1959.] Moscow, Akad. Nauk.
WAERN, I. 1962. Classical studies in Sweden. Romanitas 4.278–81.
WAGENVOORT, H. 1941. Imperium. Studiën over het 'mana'-begrip in zede en taal der Romeinen. Amsterdam, H.J. Paris.
——. 1947. Roman Dynamism. Studies in Ancient Roman thought, language and custom. Oxford, Blackwell.
——. 1948. Klassieke philologie. In Geesteswetenschappelijk onderzoek in Nederland, 139–58.
WAGNER, J. 1939a. De usu linguae latinae in Hungaria post bellum gentium. SUL 1.63–8.
——. 1939b. Iuventus budapestinensis. SUL 1.73–4.
WAITE, S.V.F. 1969. Computers and the Classics. CHum 3.25–9.
WARMINGTON, E.H. 1940. Remains of Old Latin. IV, Archaic Inscriptions. London, Heinemann.
WARSLEY, A.E. 1939. Latin in U.S.A. SUL 1.71–3.
WASSERMANN, F.M. 1959. Third International Congress of Classical Studies. CW 53.51–3.
WATERMAN, JOHN T. 1963. Perspectives in linguistics. Chicago, University Press.
WATKINS, CALVERT. 1969. A Latin-Hittite etymology. Lg 45.235–42.
WEBER, MAX. 1967. Il metodo delle scienze storico-sociali. Trans. by P. Rossi. Torino, Einaudi.
WEIJERMANS, L.H. 1949. De genitivus inhaerentiae in het Latijn. Nijmegen, Centrale Drukkerij.
WEINRICH, HARALD. 1966. Die lateinische Sprache zwischen Logik und Linguistik. Gymnasium 73.147–63.
WELCH, JOHN JOSEPH. 1962. Latin initial syllables: An historical phonological study.

Dissertation, University of Pennsylvania. DAb 23(Nov. 1962).1961.

WESTERMANN, J. F. 1939. Archaïsche en archaïstische woordkunst. Nijmegen, Dekker.

WESTMAN, R. 1968. Bibliographie abrégée des études classiques en Finlande, 1947–1966. Euphrosyne (n.s.) 2.209–14.

WHATMOUGH, J. 1943. Review of BLOCH and TRAGER 1942. CPh 38.210–11.

WHITE, D. S. 1953. Classics and linguistics. CW 47.43–4.

WHITNEY, WILLIAM DWIGHT. 1875. The life and growth of language. New York, Appleton.

——. 1911[11]. Philology. Encyclopaedia Britannica 21.415–30.

WHITTAKER, C. R., et al. 1962. Ex Africa. Latin in Rhodesia. [Salisbury], University College of Rhodesia and Nyasaland.

WHITTKOWER, R. 1939. Grammatica, from Martianus Capella to Hogarth. JWI 2.82–4.

WILKINS, J. 1966. In translation? Didaskalos 2.91–100.

WINGO, ELVIS OTHA. 1963. Latin punctuation in the Classical age. Dissertation University of Illinois. DAb 24(June 1964).5395.

WINKLER, H. 1962. Die klassischen Studien in Oesterreich. Romanitas 4.332–46.

WINNICZUK, L., and J. DOMAŃSKI. 1949. L'antiquité en Pologne. Mea 4(10).518–33.

WINNICZUK, L., and Z. PISZCZEK. 1968. Antyk w Polsce. Bibliografia za rok 1966. Mea 23.215–79.

WISTRAND, E. 1941a. Über das Passivum. Göteborg, Wettergren & Kerber.

——. 1941b. Der Instrumentalis als Kasus der Anschauung im Lateinischen. Göteborg, Wettergren & Kerber.

——. 1946. Nach innen oder nach aussen? Zum geographischen Sprachgebrauch der Römer. Göteborg, Elanders Boktryckeri Aktiebolag.

WOODCOCK, E. C. 1959. A new Latin syntax. London, Methuen.

WORT UND TEXT: FESTSCHRIFT FÜR FRITZ SCHALK. 1963. Frankfurt am Main, Klostermann.

YAMADA, A. 1960. [Classical education in Italy.] JCS 8.93–6.

ZAMBALDI, F. 1968. Elementi di prosodia e metrica latina. Torino, Loescher.

ZAMBONI, ALBERTO. 1966. Contributo allo studio del latino epigrafico della X Regio Augustea (Venetia et Histria). Introduzione. Fonetica (Vocalismo.) AIV 124. 462–517.

——. 1968. Contributo allo studio del latino epigrafico della X Regio Augustea (Venetia et Histria). Morfologia. MAP 80.139–70.

——. 1969. Contributo allo studio del latino epigrafico della X Regio Augustea (Venetia et Histria). Il lessico. SLFriul 1.110–82.

ZEBIAN, G. 1965. The relative use of ablatives of quality and respect in Latin literature. AJPh 86.240–57.

ZEWEN, F. 1962. La situation actuelle du latin dans les écoles du Grand-Duché de Luxembourg. Romanitas 4.298–304.

ZICÀRI, MARCELLO. 1968. Due note al capitolo di Quintiliano sulla pronuntiatio. QUCC 5.109–11.

ZIEGLER, KONRAT. 1969. *Mater magna* oder *Magna mater*? Hommages Renard 2.845–55.

ZIELINSKI, T. 1939a. De societate linguae latinae usui internationali adaptandae Varsoviae consistente. SUL 1.160–1.

——, et al. 1939b. Corrispondenze, rassegne, informazioni sullo studio e l'uso del latino. SUL 1.97–104 and 186–95.

ZIRIN, R.A. 1967. "The phonological basis of Latin prosody". Dissertation Princeton University. DAb 28, 661A.

——. 1971. The phonological basis of Latin prosody. The Hague, Mouton.

ZUCCARELLI, U. 1967. Psicologia e semantica di Tacito. Brescia, Paideia.

ZUCCHELLI, BRUNO. 1969. Studi sulle formazioni latine in -lo non diminutive e sui loro rapporti con i diminutivi. Brescia, Paideia.

ZWIRNER, E., and K. ZWIRNER. 1970. Principles of phonometrics. Trans. by H. Bluhme. University, Alabama, The University Press.

THE MIDDLE AGES

G. L. BURSILL-HALL

0.0 INTRODUCTION

In his *The Structure of scientific revolutions*, T.S. Kuhn has suggested[1] that one result of a scientific revolution is that even the subject matter of a science must change. The study of grammar in the Middle Ages affords us an almost classical example of this dictum, though the historian of Medieval philosophy has rarely succeeded in recognising the full implication of the change in the nature and status of grammar that occurred as a result of the modifications in the intellectual paradigm of the 11–12th century.

The study of grammar held a privileged position in the Medieval programme of studies and this statement can be said to apply to the period prior to the rise of the Medieval university just as well as to the golden period of scholasticism when the university replaced the monastery as the centre of learning *par excellence*; it also applied to northern and southern Europe equally, and this is part of the Medieval inheritance from the world of Greek and Roman antiquity.

The history of linguistics in the Middle Ages provides us, furthermore, with an excellent example of the progression of change that occurs with the change of paradigm, and it shows quite clearly that development-by-accumulation cannot provide a valid explanation for the change, but that, as Robins points out (1967:5), changes can and do arise from outside as well as inside a science, since a science, in addition to its own intrinsic properties, is also the product and part of its intellectual context. A change may be the result of some intervention from outside which has the effect of completely reversing the direction of intellectual and scholarly progress generally, or more usually it is the result of a piecemeal process and it is in many instances impossible to discern the original impetus. No science operates in a vacuum; it is the obvious inheritor of its own past and also the creature of its environment, and obviously will see itself in a light quite different from the view that succeeding generations will have of it. This must have a debilitating effect on any attempt to see the changes that have occurred as a simple process of accretion; it means also that in order to give a more adequate account of the state of linguistic theory at any point in time, an account of the intellectual tenor of the time is a necessary prerequisite, so it is

[1] Kuhn, Thomas S., *The structure of scientific revolutions*. Chicago, University Press, 1962.

imperative that in our account of a theory we try at least to see how the creators of such a theory saw themselves and were seen by their contemporaries. The implications of this for general linguistics and in particular for the history of linguistics are profound and far-reaching; Ferdinand de Saussure saw language in two-dimensional terms, i.e. synchronic and diachronic. Neither can supersede the other; indeed both are necessary. The same is true of general linguistics, and the history of linguistics represents the diachronic dimension of general linguistic theory.

The study of grammar in the Middle Ages can be said, then, to have followed the lines of development as characterised by Kuhn, i.e. traditional practice, revolution, "mop-up"; the new will itself become traditional practice until the next revolution exercises its characteristic influence and the new cycle is worked out. The line of progress can be thought of as lines which converge and then separate only to merge and separate once more; this means that work on the currently accepted lines will continue to be carried on all the while that the new line is being inaugurated. This is so because it is a normal fact of life, and in this sense linguists are no different from other scientists, i.e. there are leaders and followers; the leader is the innovator who creates a new school of thought while the followers are responsible for the "mop-up" operation, and they will themselves be replaced by the leaders and followers who will wreak the changes in established theory and practice.

0.1 Until the 11th century, grammar was taught as the key to textual interpretation; based on the models provided by Donatus and Priscian, it became the propaedeutic for a literary culture. By the 11th century, it is possible to discern certain rumblings of change within grammar, but, as one might expect, additional research has made it harder to answer questions such as: who first conceived of grammar in the new light, or who first questioned the authority of Priscian? The external factor, which was to have a Copernican-like effect on Medieval grammatical theory, was the rediscovery of the complete corpus of Aristotle's logical work. Together they had the effect of making grammar a highly speculative, theoretical subject, no longer the hand-maid of literary learning but the associate of logic and metaphysics. It is not that grammar disappeared or rather was absorbed into logic, which many commentators of the medieval scene have suggested[2] (this of course reveals an excessively one-sided view of grammar), but that grammar changed, which is fully in keeping with the idea of a scientific revolution in grammar, and this is fully confirmed by the nature of the textbooks that we have from the 12th and 13th centuries, viz. the commentaries by William of Conches, Peter Helias, and Robert Kilwardby on Priscian, and the speculative grammars of the Modistae. The achievement of Peter Helias is most significant; it may well be that his originality as a grammarian does not equal that of his teacher, William of Conches, but his work represents the pennant of the revolution by virtue of its systematic

[2] Paetow (1910:45) is a typical example, i.e. 'very little more can be said about grammar at the great university of France [after the death of John of Garland — G.L.B-H.]. Logic and philosophy now held full sway in the arts course'.

incorporation of the ideas of the new spirit into grammatical theory and paved the way for developments in grammar culminating in the theories of the Modistae which represent the first successful attempt in the history of Western Europe at a fully integrated theory of language.

The Modistae were in turn succeeded by the Nominalist grammarians of the 14th century, and grammatical activity of the 14th century appears to have consisted of a rivalry between these two schools of thought, until they were in turn superseded by the humanist grammarians of the Renaissance. The intellectual climate had by then become completely incompatible with the type of theoretical speculation so characteristic of the Middle Ages; this is the inevitability of scholarly progress. Nevertheless, developments in grammatical theory between the 11th and 14th centuries do possess all the hall-marks of a Kuhnian scientific revolution; it is the purpose of this chapter to provide the details of these developments. The account will unfortunately be redolent with lacunae, since one of the most immediate problems facing the historian of this period is the dearth of a satisfactory critical apparatus; despite yeoman efforts by one or two modern scholars, we possess no usable texts of the grammatical writing from the period 1100–1260.

0.2 The Middle Ages, no matter how one attempts to define it, is an enormous period in time, and the period often referred to as the High Middle Ages, was a period of intense intellectual and scholarly ferment. It is inevitable, therefore, that in an account such as this, much will perforce be omitted; indeed it has been the author's specific intent to restrict himself to the period between the 11th and the middle of the 14th centuries, which can be regarded as his termini. It is a period which coincides with the introduction of dialectic into logical argument, the so-called Renaissance of the 12th century, the discovery of the complete logical works of Aristotle, the founding of the universities, the age of universals, the Realist-Nominalist controversy, the achievements of the Speculative grammarians of the 13th and early 14th centuries and ending with the period of Ockham and the Nominalist grammarians of the 14th century. The account therefore will not include an account of grammatical work prior to the 11th century, largely because little work of any originality has emerged (if indeed it ever existed), and, although the study of grammar was continued during this period, it would seem that grammarians of the time were content to repeat the arguments of the great Roman grammarians Donatus and Priscian. The account will not include a discussion of the work of the Arab and Jewish grammarians of the 11th and 12th centuries; this is in part an admission of the author's inability to handle the material but, in addition, there is no evidence to suggest that their work was known to the grammarians of the Middle Ages which is, to say the least, strange, since knowledge of Aristotle whose influence in the Middle Ages was all-pervasive was to a great extent transmitted to the West through the translations and commentaries of the Arab and Jewish philosophers. It should also be pointed out that even if the work of Arab and Jewish grammarians had been available, it is doubtful whether the schoolmen would have been able to make use of their work, since, with the notable exception of Roger Bacon, none of the leading grammarians had a working knowledge of these languages.

A further omission will be all reference to the work of Irish and Scandinavian grammarians (cf. Robins 1967:69–74); in their case too, their work, though relatively well known to modern scholarship, appears to have had no impact whatsoever on Medieval scholarship. The most serious omission will be that of Byzantine linguistic scholarship; modern scholars, e.g. Hjelmslev, Jakobson, and Robins, have all referred to the significance of grammatical work carried on in the Eastern Empire after the collapse of Rome. One of the greatest problems facing the student of linguistic work in the Middle Ages is the almost complete dearth of workable editions of the works of these grammarians, and, as far as the Byzantine grammarians are concerned, their work, though extensively preserved in manuscript form in the libraries of Europe, is not to be found in usable form. Finally, the *terminus ad quem* is quite arbitrary and yet it represents a logical cut-off point; the great rivals, i.e. Modistic and Nominalist grammarians, were by then no longer of interest to the philosopher of language, and together they may be said to have left the field to the humanist grammarian, and this can be safely said despite the fact that grammars in a Modistic or Nominalist frame continued to be written until well into the 16th century.

0.3 The Middle Ages inherited from the world of Ancient Greece and Rome a grammatical tradition and a fully developed philosophical tradition; this is not to suggest that this occurred in one fell swoop, and the aim of this chapter is to portray the progressive incorporation into Medieval thought of these ancient traditions. This was to become an original and sophisticated language theory and represents one of the signal achievements of Medieval scholasticism, but one which has often been overlooked or unappreciated by students of the Middle Ages. The chapter will also include a section which seeks to give an account of the different contributions to our knowledge of Medieval linguistic activities which have been made in the 20th century, because, despite the remark at the end of the previous sentence, Medieval language theory has not escaped the scrutiny of the scholar, although the majority of linguists have, until recently, tended to accept without examination the assertion that the grammatical theories of the Middle Ages contained nothing of interest to the modern linguist. The chapter will also contain a list of the grammarians of the Middle Ages and their works as well as a detailed bibliography of discussions of the various aspects of Medieval linguistic work which, although it cannot claim to be exhaustive, does contain the significant contributions of linguists, philosophers, logicians, and historians writing in the 20th century.

1.0 HISTORIOGRAPHY

The technical literature, i.e. logical, philosophical, and grammatical literature of the

Middle Ages, has often been considered a closed book to historians of philosophy and grammar alike; written in Latin, it often presents an obscurity which is due to a lack of a familiarity with a tradition in logic and grammar which was of course an integral part of the scholarly world to which the authors of these obscurities belonged. Modern scholarship has often been too preoccupied with the great theological and metaphysical syntheses of the great masters of the Middle Ages and have ignored the logico-grammatical tradition of the period which provided the basic training for the schoolmen and without which the sophistication of so much Medieval theology and philosophy would not have been possible.

In recent decades, the exegesis of Medieval logic has been relatively rich; we possess workable versions of many of the leading logicians of the Middle Ages, and there are a number of scholarly works which relate to the development of logic, in particular terminist logic, supposition and signification (de Rijk 1962–67), and the theory of consequences. The history of Medieval grammatical theory has not fared nearly so well; one consults in vain many of the compendious histories of Medieval philosophy to find only a passing reference to the Medieval grammarian and then usually to the normative grammarian, ignoring completely the highly sophisticated grammatical work of the 12th and 13th century, so surprisingly "modern" in their interests, and which destroys the myth that speculative or universal grammar originated in the 17th or 18th century. One can sympathise with the lament of one modern scholar (Hunt 1941–43:194) that so little work had been done on the development of grammatical doctrines in the Middle Ages since the appearance of Thurot's monumental work (Thurot 1869). Indeed, for our knowledge of these developments we have to rely on the work of a handful of scholars in addition to Thurot, e.g. Grabmann, Lehmann, Hunt, Roos, Robins, Paetow, de Rijk, and Pinborg.

The achievements of our predecessors demonstrate the significance of Medieval language study and the value of this work is not restricted to the historian of linguistics but is of considerable interest to the historian of ideas inasmuch as Medieval grammatical theory is a vital source for understanding Medieval thought, and this for two reasons: 1. it was a compulsory study, and 2. the basis for grammar lay in reality and that language mirrored the reality underlying the phenomena of the physical world.

It is the duty of the historian to indicate those studies that he considers to be particularly significant; with one important exception, the scholars whose work will be discussed in this section are of the 20th century. It is often argued that general linguistics is a relatively young science; if this is indeed so, though the existence of this chapter would seem to belie this, the history of linguistics, even though it has received rapid acceptance as a *bone fide* subject and an integral part of general linguistic study, is an even younger discipline.

It is inevitable, therefore, that linguists, with a few notable exceptions, have so far contributed little to our understanding of Medieval language theory; this is not hard to explain. We have had reason to complain on more than one occasion of the paucity of usable research material; the manuscript tradition is very rich[3] but unless the linguist-historian is *pari passu* sufficiently skilled in the delicate art of palaeography to be able to work with the original manuscript, he is regrettably excluded from a mine of information. The work of Danish scholars such as Father Roos and Jan Pinborg is particularly worthy of mention in this context; in addition, the present author has undertaken to edit the works of some of the more important Medieval grammarians.[4] Series of texts have been launched or proposed, e.g. the *Corpus philosophorum Danicorum Medii Aevi*, edited by Fathers A. Otto and H. Roos and published in Copenhagen, *The Classics of Linguistics*, edited by D. Abercrombie and R. H. Robins and published by Longmans in England, and the *Grammatica Speculativa*, edited by Pinborg (Copenhagen) and Kohlenberger (Tübingen) and published by the Frommann-Holzboog Verlag (Stuttgart) will do a great deal to alleviate the situation, but there will still remain several life-times of work before all the grammatical treatises on grammar are available in a modern edition. Section 1.1 is striking proof of the dearth of a critical apparatus; Pinborg lists many anonymous Modistic grammars (Pinborg 1967: 309–23), and there are many more treatises which have found no mention whatsoever in the accounts we possess of Medieval language study. There is an additional problem which may account for the difficulties that are encountered in research in Medieval language theory; unlike the 20th century, when it has become possible to label a student as a 'linguist', the Middle Ages knew no such degree of autonomy and it is necessary for an understanding of Medieval grammatical theory to be conversant with Medieval logic, philosophy, and metaphysics. Grammar was taught in an intellectual climate very different from that of today; today linguists trained in one school of thought often find it difficult to make the shift to another school of thought, and the problem becomes much more acute when it is a matter of coping with a metalanguage and system of thought so unlike those of our own day. Interpretation becomes to all intents and purposes impossible, the net result being that we possess few commentaries by the modern linguist of those few grammatical works to be found in modern editions. Unless one has a firm control of the *res gestae*, one has no choice but to refer to secondary material prepared by non-linguists. On the other hand, studies on the philosophy and historical background are much less sparse though they have tended to overlook the contributions of the Medieval grammarian and have concentrated on the theological and philosophical achievements of the period.

The work of certain scholars, both linguists and historians, stand out as being of signal importance in the history of the Middle Ages. Linguists have not in the past

[3] We would all do well to remember the warning of P. O. Kristeller that unless something is done to protect and preserve the valuable manuscript material housed in so many collections, 'Medieval and Renaissance civilization may suffer the same fate as ancient civilization did through the destruction of the library in Alexandria'; cf. Paul O. Kristeller. 1965. Latin Manuscript books before 1600. Rev. ed. New York, Fordham University Press.

[4] In particular the Priscian commentaries of Peter Helias and Robert Kilwardby.

paid a great deal of attention to the history of linguistics and the Middle Ages are to many modern linguists still in the "Dark Ages" (cf. Romeo and Tiberio 1971:23); however, the work of two scholars are particularly worthy of our attention. R.H. Robins was probably the first modern linguist to see that our more distant predecessors in language study were not the unsophisticates that tradition would have us believe, and he has shown that there is a continuous line of activity from the Ancient Greeks to the end of the Middle Ages in which language study was the very core of the programme. Pinborg has contributed a very significant series of studies in which he traces the development of grammatical theory from the 11th to the end of the 15th century and, although there are areas which he has not described in depth, he had given clear indication of the many points which warrant further investigation; in one major study (Pinborg 1967), he has discussed the developments in grammatical theory, in medieval descriptive metalanguage, word-class theory, and syntax. In the same study, he has traced the developments within the group known as the Modistae who cover a period of some 70–80 years of intense activity at a time when interest in language was very high. His work also includes a study of the Nominalist grammarians of the 14th century; this appears to be the only examination by a modern linguist of this group of grammarians, and the controversy between Modistae and Nominalists is of the greatest significance in the history of linguistics of this period. Father F.P. Dinneen has included a section on the grammatical theories of the Ancient and Medieval world in his *Introduction to general linguistics* (1967:Chapter 12); the value of his contribution is that once more it draws attention to the all-pervasive influence of Aristotle on all Medieval language theory. The present author has contributed two studies on the Modistae. One (Bursill-Hall 1972) is an examination of the grammatical work of Thomas of Erfurt, whose speculative grammar (*Grammatica speculativa*) is in many respects the most complete and at the same time a very typical example of Modistic theory. The other (Bursill-Hall 1971) is a detailed examination of the metalanguage, word-class theory, and syntactic theories of the Modistae seen from the standpoint of the modern linguist.

As one might expect, we know far more about the intellectual background and history of philosophy in the Middle Ages than we do about their grammatical theories. There are a number of histories of Medieval philosophy, but the most significant is surely that of E. Gilson (1955) who has always demonstrated an awareness of language study and its importance for an understanding of the Medieval paradigm;[5] other

[5] His "Discours de réception à l'Académie française" is worth repeating once more in this context: 'Avec une audace qui les honore, les maîtres du XIIIe siècle ont porté jusque dans l'étude du langage leur intellectualisme impénitent et leur goût passionné de l'universel. Par delà toutes les grammaires particulières qui s'embarrassent dans la diversité des idiomes, des constructions et des formes, ils imaginèrent une grammaire générale ou, comme ils disaient: théorique, qui ne devait retenir de faits particuliers que les lois du langage humain en général. Que les mots ne fussent pas les mêmes dans les diverses langues, ou que savoir la grammaire d'une langue ne permit pas de comprendre ceux qui en parlent une autre, c'était là, pour nos vieux maîtres, des accidents sans importance. Qui sait une

histories of significance are those of Father Copleston (1951ff.) and van Steenberghen (1955b, 1966) and, in addition, there are studies by Leff, Knowles, and Vignaux which are essential to an understanding of the thought of the period. It would, however, be quite fruitless to attempt a survey of the vast literature, and it must suffice that we should refer to the most important contributions of 20th century scholarship, and in particular to the relatively narrow field of language theory.

In the historiography of Medieval linguistics, one name stands out in the 20th century above all the rest; Martin Grabmann's contribution must be regarded as monumental and it is safe to say that he has done more than any other single scholar to make us aware of the details of Medieval linguistic scholarship. His researches in the manuscript book collections of many European libraries have provided details of the extant works of both logicians and grammarians of the period and the bibliography of his scholarship in the third volume of his *Mittelalterliches Geistesleben* (1956) is testimony to his work; supplemented by Lehmann 1944, Hunt 1941–43, Pinborg 1967, de Rijk 1967, and Thurot 1869 — the only scholarly work prior to the 20th century to be referred to in the context of this chapter — Grabmann has provided us with the necessary details of the primary sources for the principal works of the main figures in the development of grammatical theory in the 12th and 13th centuries. In particular, he has described (1916, 1928, 1936, 1937b, 1938, 1939, 1941, 1950) the impact of Aristotelian logic on the Medieval scholarly world and a necessary understanding of this is a prerequisite to our understanding of the whole Medieval achievement;[6] he has also described (1923, 1937a, 1937b, 1940) the work of 12th and 13th century logicians whose work was very much influenced by contemporary grammatical theory (cf. Mullally 1945:XXXIXff.). For our purposes, his most significant contributions (1922, 1940, 1943, 1951) are those in which he traces the development of Medieval grammatical theory — he uses the term *Sprachlogik* — from the 12th century to the Modistae; Grabmann established that the grammar, which had been for many years ascribed to Duns Scotus, was in fact the work of Thomas of Erfurt, and his monograph (1943) on Thomas of Erfurt provides us with a very thorough survey of the grammatical literature of the period. Grabmann's studies, along with Thurot's massive work, are indispensable for our knowledge of Medieval grammatical theory; it is inevitable that they will be superseded by modern scholarship, e.g. it has been shown (Pinborg 1967:202) that the list of the Modistae (Grabmann 1943:95) is inaccurate, that Johannes Aurifaber and Erhardus Knaab de Zwiefalten were in fact Nominalist grammarians and thus anti-Modistic, and Thurot's study was restricted to manuscripts in French libraries whereas the Modistic tradition, for example, was far more widespread as can be seen from the lists of Modistic texts given by Lehmann (1944) and Pinborg (1967).

grammaire, disaient-ils, ne sait pas toutes les langues, mais il sait toutes les grammaires, car il n'y en a qu'une: celle de cette intelligence dont les opérations sont identiques chez tous les hommes, bref, la grammaire universelle de l'esprit humain.'

[6] Van Steenberghen's account (1955a) is a most useful and important supplement, since it provides a picture of the Aristotelian invasion of the University of Paris in the 13th century.

This is no animadversion of their work, for without them modern scholarship would be faced with the necessity of building the pioneer spade-work which we fortunately now possess.

For some time, it was thought that Peter Helias was responsible for the infiltration of dialectic into grammar in the middle of the 12th century; this has been shown (Hunt 1941–43) to be incorrect, and thanks to Hunt's incomparable knowledge of the manuscript tradition, we know that from about the middle of the 11th century the commentators on Priscian introduced the methods and doctrines of dialectics into the exposition of grammar. We do not know the full details of this important change in direction when grammar was no longer the handmaid of literature but the companion of logic, but as a result of Hunt's work, we can point to two very significant facts, i.e. William of Conches emerges as a figure of prime importance and his criticism of Priscian (cf. Robins 1967: 76) must be construed as a demand for greater adequacy of theory, and Peter Helias, under the influence of William, established grammar as an autonomous art by his systematic statement of the grammatical theories of his day, as a result of which grammar was able to develop along its own lines without being swamped by dialectic. The relation between logic and grammar in the 11th and 12th centuries is one theme that emerges from L.M. de Rijk's very important study (1967; Vol. II, Part I), in which he confirms the results of Hunt's researches and expands our knowledge of the interpenetration of logic and grammar during this period. As a result we can see the extent to which logic was influenced by grammar, whereas it is often imagined that the contrary was the case, and this cooperation was fruitful in that it produced, not only terminist logic, but also the speculative grammar (*Summa modorum significandi*) of the later 13th and early 14th centuries. Furthermore, de Rijk shows that grammatical theory made important contributions to the theory of properties of terms and to the theories of signification and supposition which must be regarded among the more significant contributions of Medieval scholars to language theory and which are of much more than antiquarian interest. The work of other scholars (Boehner 1952; Kneale 1962; Moody 1953; Henry 1960, 1964; Colish 1969; Michaud-Quantin 1969; Chojnacki 1969) is also useful for an understanding of these earlier developments.

The Modistae represent the apogee of Medieval grammatical theory; in addition to the work of Grabmann and Thurot already mentioned there are other studies available (Roos 1946, 1948, 1952, 1959, 1969; Pinborg 1964, 1967, 1968, 1969a; Robins 1951, 1967; Dinneen 1967; O'Mahoney 1964; Bursill-Hall 1963, 1966a, 1966b, 1970, 1971; Wallerand 1913), on the Modistae. Roos (1952) and Pinborg (1967) have given us details of the development of this group of grammarians, while Robins (1951, 1967) and Bursill-Hall (1971, 1972) have examined their theory but more particularly from the standpoint of the modern linguist. In addition, we possess critical editions of the Danish Modistae, Martin of Dacia (Roos 1952), Boethius of Cacia (Pinborg and Roos 1969), John of Dacia (Otto 1955), and Simon of Dacia (Otto 1963), which must be regarded as masterpieces of the art.

We have so far been concerned with the discussion of scholarly contributions to our understanding of the more theoretical aspects of language study in the Middle Ages; we tend to lose sight of the fact that grammar was taught as a necessary part of the undergraduate curriculum and there is a vast amount of pedagogical material available from the Middle Ages — we are not concerned here with actual teaching methods which, if Thurot's account is true (1869:121), would fill both the teacher and student of today with horror. There were a number of teaching texts, i.e. Alexander de Villa-Dei *Doctrinale*, Eberhardus Bethuniensis *Graecismus*, Hugutio Pisanus *Lexicon* (or *Derivationes magnae*), Papias *Elementarium*, Jean de Janua *Catholicon*, all of which enjoyed a wide currency in their day, and there is in addition a vast amount of unedited material. Unfortunately, this is an aspect of Medieval language study which has not, so far as we have been able to determine, received much attention from modern scholarship, and furthermore there tends to be an uneven attitude towards this particular activity, i.e. that after the 12th century grammar disappeared to all intents and purposes, or else normative grammar was completely divorced from the more speculative views of grammar. The vast amount of material is clear proof of the continued activity of the grammar teacher but grammatical instruction by the 14th century (at least in England, cf. Hunt 1964) seems to have shifted down to the grammar school, and there appear to have been two types of instruction, i.e. the normative type based on Priscian and Donatus, who in the later Middle Ages were superseded by the *Doctrinale* and *Graecismus*, and the speculative type in which grammar is treated as part of word science (*sermocinalis scientia*). Two studies (Brother Bonaventure 1961 and Hunt 1964) tell us something about grammar instruction in Oxford and England in the Middle Ages, and apart from anything else Hunt recounts that the Oxford grammar masters used the doctrines of speculative grammar which is evidence of the widespread success of 'logical' grammar. A third study (Murphy 1961) draws attention to the fact that one neglected area of contemporary Medieval scholarship is the teaching of *all* forms of discourse. Even in the Middle Ages, successful language instruction implied familiarity with current theory, and we should know more about the extent of the fertilisation of normative grammar by speculative grammar after an examination of the commentaries on the *Doctrinale* and *Graecismus.* The popularity of these teaching texts is clearly revealed by the richness of the manuscript tradition and there are in addition a large number of unedited commentaries which could throw a great deal of light on Medieval discussions of language pedagogy.

The picture that emerges is one of broad detail and, apart from the contributions of a relatively small number of scholars who have thrown some light into a few dark corners, there remains a great deal to do before we claim a full understanding of Medieval language theory. There are huge gaps in our knowledge of theoretical developments, for example in syntactic theory, meaning, descriptive procedures, word-class theory and description; historians of logic know far more about developments in the logic of the 14th century and yet this is intimately connected with grammatical theory of the same period. We need to know far more about the inter-connections between theory and pedagogical practice as well as between the linguistic grammarians and the early burgeonings of humanistic grammar in the 14th century. These are merely some of the preliminaries to an appreciation of the extent and sophistication of Medieval language theory.

1.1 *Textual Material*

The extent of our knowledge of Medieval linguistic activity must depend on the availability of edited texts, and in this respect the picture, as we have already implied, is not a happy one. Mention has already been made of such texts as are available, and Thurot (1869), Hunt (1941–43, 1950), Pinborg (1967), and de Rijk (1962–67), especially the two last named, have provided us with versions of many anonymous texts; Scaglione 1970 also contains bibliographical details of textual material. Even so, the problem is acute, indeed one of urgency, as the following list of grammarians and their works, which concludes this section, will show.

There are a large number of unpublished and unedited manuscript books from the Middle Ages which contain grammatical writings; a census of these manuscripts at present in progress lists more than 3000 manuscript books which contain such material, and in many instances these books contain more than one grammatical treatise; for example, Codex 849 of the monastery library at Melk (Austria) contains a *Doctrinale* commentary (ff. 2–277a), a Donatus commentary (ff. 279a–340a), questions on the *Doctrinale* (ff. 340a–66b), grammatical rules, and a treatise on syntax (ff. 401–10). Many of these works are anonymous and it is at present impossible to state with absolute certainty just how many of these are significant, but a rough estimate is that at least 1000 of these treatises are of importance to the historian of linguistics. Many are clearly important (cf. Pinborg 1967); the others, that is those that cannot be ascribed to a particular author, consist of treatises on grammar and syntax, rules, commentaries on Priscian or Donatus or on one or other of the great teaching grammars of the Middle Ages, for example Alexander de Villa-Dei's *Doctrinale.*

The following list contains only those works that can be ascribed to a known author; it does not include the many anonymous treatises on grammar and logic to be found in various European manuscript book collections. There were in the Middle Ages no 'pure' grammarians in the sense that their sole concern was grammar (as opposed to the modern linguist who may, for example, be a specialist in phonology); the works of some of the schoolmen who contributed to language theory without writing a treatise which can be specifically labelled 'grammatica' have also been included. It is becoming increasingly clear that we must think of Medieval 'language theory', since grammar and logic were often inseparably intertwined; it is perhaps significant in this context that Robert Kilwardby in his *De ortu scientiarum* created a division '*sermocinalis scientia*' which consists of grammar, logic and rhetoric.

The list is laid out in alphabetical order since it is difficult to construct a reliable chronological list in view of the paucity of reliable dates, and in many instances all that can be provided is an approximate date (for the work in question). The list will include the incipit (*Inc.*) of the work and in the case of a published work the necessary bibliographical details (*Ed.*). It is, however, not possible to include all the details of the manuscripts but further information about them and about the works themselves, both attributed and anonymous, can be found in the works of Thurot (1869), Grabmann (1943), Lehmann (1944), Pinborg (1967), de Rijk (1967), and the author's forthcoming "Census of Medieval Latin Grammatical Manuscripts"; even so, the information available will not be exhaustive:

1. Albertus. (ca. 1285). Questiones de modis significandi.
   Inc: Queritur utrum de gramatica sit scientia ...
   Ed: Wynham de Worde, London (ca. 1500).
2. Albert of Saxony. Summa logicae.
   Ed: Petrus Aurelius Sanutus. 1522. Venice.
3. Albertus Swebelinus. (ca. 1300). *Martin of Dacia commentary*. (Cf. No. 35).
   Inc: In libro ethicorum scribit philosophus: Bonum est ...
   Ed: Nil.
4. Alexander de Villa-Dei. (ca. 1200). Doctrinale.
   Inc: Scribere clericulis paro doctrinale novellis ...
   Ed: D. Reichling. 1893. Monumenta Germaniae Paedagogica, Bd. 12. Berlin, A. Hofmann.
5. Anselm. (ca. 1070). De grammatico.
   Inc: De grammatico peto ut me certum facias utrum sit substantia an qualitas ...
   Eds: i) J.P. Migne. 1863. Patrologia Latina 158. cols. 561–2.
   ii) Desmond P. Henry. 1964. PMS, 18. Notre Dame, University Press.
6. Boethius Dacus. (ca. 1270). Questiones super Priscianum maiorem.
   Inc: Secundum quod vult Aristoteles in primo celi et mundi ...
   Ed: Jan Pinborg and Heinrich Roos. 1969. Corpus Philosophorum Danicorum Medii Aevi 4, Part 1. Copenhagen, Gad.
7. Bonus de Lucca. (ca. 1200). Summa grammatice.
   Inc: Gerundia dicitur quasi duo gerentia ...
   Ed: Nil.
8. Eberhardus Bethuniensis. (ca. 1200). Graecismus.
   Inc: Quoniam ignorantie nubilio turpiter ...
   Ed: J. Wrobel. 1887. Corpus Grammaticorum Medii Aevi, 1. Breslau, G. Koebner.
9. Erhardus Knaab de Zwiefalten. (1452). Determinatio de modis significandi.
   Inc: Ut gramatici et modistae veteres pluresque ...
   Ed: Nil.
10. Gentilis de Cingulo. (ca. 1290). Questiones super Priscianum minorem.
    Inc: Queritur utrum gramatica sit scientia ...
    Ed: Nil.
11. Gentilis de Cingulo. (ca. 1290). *Martin of Dacia commentary*. (Cf. No. 35).

Inc: Quaelibet ars habet sua organa quibus exercet ...
Ed: Nil.

12. Gosvin de Marbais. (ca. 1250). Questiones super Priscianum minorem.
Inc: Sicut testatur Plato in Tymeo ...
Ed: Nil.

13. Henricus de Crissay. (ca. 1400). *Iohannes Josse de Marvilla commentary*. (Cf. No. 25).
Inc: Horti florem vernalis odoris vallis ...
Ed: Nil.

14. Hoygensis. (ca. 1250). Summa super Priscianum.
Inc: Sicut dicit Aristoteles cognitio superioris valet ...
Ed: Nil.

15. Hugo de Abbatisvilla. (ca. 1260). Questiones super Priscianum minorem.
Inc: Queritur utrum de sermone possit esse scientia ...
Ed: Nil.

16. Hugo de St Victor. (early 12th century). De grammatica.
Inc: Quid est grammatica? ...
Eds: i) J. Leclerq. 1943–45. Archives d'histoire doctrinale et litteraire du moyen âge, 14, 263–322. Paris.
ii) Roger Baron. 1966. Hugonis de Sancto Victore opera propaedeutica. PMS, 20. Notre Dame, University Press.

17. Hugo Spechtsart de Reutlingen. (ca. 1340). Speculum grammaticae.
Inc: Ut speculum varias rerum formas manifestat ...
Ed: Nil.

18. Hugutio Pisanus. (ca. 1200). Lexicon.
Inc. Cum nostri protoplasti suggestiva ...
Ed: Nil.

19. Hugutio Pisanus. (ca. 1200). Summa grammatice.
Inc: Ad communem disceptare volentium ...
Ed: Nil.

20. Ion Suessionensis. (ca. 1300). Super Doctrinale Alexandri.
Inc: Antequam ulterius in dictis procedam, quaeso Dei filius ...
Ed: Nil.

21. Iohannes Aurifaber. (ca. 1330). Determinatio de modis significandi.
Inc: Nominativo hic magister ...
Ed: Jan Pinborg 1967:215–32.

22. Iohannes Avicula de Lotharingia. (ca. 1300). Questiones super modos significandi.
Inc: Sicut dicit Plato in Timaeo ...
Ed: Nil.

23. Iohannes Balbis de Janua. (ca. 1280). Catholicon.[7]

[7] There were several editions of this work published between 1460–1520.

Inc: Prosodia quedam pars gramatice nuncupatur ...
Ed: Nil.

24. Iohannes Dacus. (1280). Summa Grammatica.
Inc: Cum grammatica quam antiqua auctoritas latina ...
Ed: Alfred Otto. 1955. Corpus Philosophorum Danicorum Medii Aevi, 1. Copenhagen, Gad.

25. Iohannes Josse de Marvilla. (1322). Tractatus metricus de modis significandi.
Inc: Ut flos grammaticae pingatur corde minorum ...
Ed: Nil.

26. Iohannes de Rus. (ca. 1250). Tractatus de constructione.
Inc: Eorum quae accidunt litterae et syllaba ...
Ed: Nil.

27. Iohannes de Soncino. (ca. 1400). Questiones super summam 'Artes liberales sunt septem'.
Inc: Quaero utrum artes (liberales sint septem ...) vero quod non ...
Ed: Nil.

28. Iohannes de Soncino. (ca. 1400). Notabilia grammaticae.
Inc: Grammatica est scientia principaliter inventa ad exprimendum conceptum mentis ...
Ed: Nil.

29. John Buridan. Summula de dialectica.
Eds: Paris 1504, Oxford 1637, London 1740.

30. John of Garland. (ca. 1230). Compendium grammaticae.
Inc: Gramaticum trivialis apex subicit sibi firmo pro pede ...
Ed: Nil.

31. John Gerson. De modis significandi et de concordia metaphysicae cum logica.
Ed: Louis Ellies du Pin. 1706. Opera omnia (5 vols.). Paris/Antwerp.

32. John of Salisbury. (1159). Metalogicon.
Ed: Clement C. J. Webb. 1929. Oxford, Clarendon Press.

33. Jordanus de Saxonia. (ca. 1210). *Priscian minor commentary.*
Inc: Sermocinalis scientia sit de sermone...
Ed: Nil.

34. Lambert d'Auxerre. Summulae logicales. (ca. 1255).
Inc: Ut novi artium auditores plenius intelligant...
Ed: Nil.

35. Ludolfus de Luckowe. (13th century). Flores grammaticae.
Inc: Flores grammaticae propono scribere...
Ed: Nil.

36. Martinus Dacus. (ca. 1270). De modis significandi.
Inc: Cum cuiuslibet artificis. .
Ed: Heinrich Roos. 1961. Corpus Philosophorum Danicorum Medii Aevi, 2) Copenhagen, Gad.

37. Mattheus de Bononia. (ca. 1260–70). Questiones super grammaticam et modos significandi.
Inc: Quoniam de principiis in qualibet constructione ...
Ed: Nil.
38. Michel de Marbais. (ca. 1285). Summa modorum significandi.
Inc: Secundum quod vult philosophus in principio secundi veteris metaphysicae id quod solus homo ...
Ed: Nil.
39. Nicholas de Bohemia. (ca. 1300). Questiones de modis significandi.
Inc: Quoniam ignoratis communibus necesse est artem ignorare ...
Ed: Nil.
40. Nicholas de Paris. (ca. 1250). In Barbarismum Donati.
Inc: Grammatica aliter dividitur a Donato, aliter a Prisciano ...
Ed: Nil.
41. Nicholas de Paris. (ca. 1250). In de accentu Prisciani.
Inc: Sermocinales scientiae sunt viae ad alias scientias ...
Ed: Nil.
42. Nicholas de Paris. (ca. 1250). Rationes super libro peryermenias.
Inc: Omne iudicium precedit apprehensio et hoc apparet in cognitione sensitiva ...
Ed: Nil.
43. Papias. (ca. 1050). Elementarium.
Inc: Filii utique karissime debui si potuissem ...
Ed: Nil.
44. Papias. (ca. 1050). Ars grammatica.
Inc: Petistis a me, karissimi ex arte grammatice ...
Ed: Nil.
45. Petrus Abailard. Dialectica.
Ed: Lambertus M. de Rijk. 1956. Wijsgerige Teksten en Studies van het Filosofisch Instituut der Rijksuniversiteit te Utrecht, deel I. Assen, Van Gorcum.
46. Petrus Abailard. Introductiones parvulorum.
Ed: Mario Dal Pra. 1954. Pietro Abelardo, Scritti Filosofici. Rome/Milan, Nuova Biblioteca Filosofica.
47. Petrus Abailard. Logica ingredientibus.
Ed: Bernard Geyer. 1919–27. Peter Abaelards Philosophische Schriften. BGPMA 21(4). Münster.
48. Petrus de Alliaco. (ca. 1390). Destructiones modorum significandi.
Inc: Naturae vinculo astrictus non modicum in scientiis ...
Ed: Hain 833.
49. Petrus de Croccus. (ca. 1275). Glosa in Doctrinale.
Inc: Sicut dicit sapiens Timor domini fit negotiatio tua ...
Ed: Nil.
50. Petrus Helias. (ca. 1150). Summa super Priscianum.

Inc: Ad maiorem artis grammaticae evidentiam ...
Ed: Nil.

51. Petrus Helias. (ca. 1150). De constructione.[8]
Inc: Absoluta cuiuslibet disciplinae perfectio ...
Ed: Nil.

52. Petrus Hispanus. (ca. 1230–35). Summulae logicales.[9]
Eds: i) Innocentius M. Bocheński. 1947. Turin, Marietti.
ii) Joseph P. Mullally. 1945. University of Notre Dame Publications in Medieval Studies, 8. Notre Dame, University Press.

53. Petrus de Insolellis. (beg. 13th century). Summa grammaticae.
Inc: Ut ad sapientiam per grammaticam venire possumus ...
Ed: Charles Fierville. 1886. Une grammaire inédite du XIIIe siècle. Paris, Imprimerie Nationale.

54. Ralph de Beauvais. (ca. 1170). Liber Titan.
Inc: Quandoque nomini quod per appellationem uni soli convenit ...
Ed: Nil.

55. Ralph de Beauvais. (ca. 1170). Summa super Donatum.
Inc: Quia grammatica prima est artium, in eius principium ...
Ed: Nil.

56. Radulphus Brito. (ca. 1290). Questiones super Priscianum minorem.
Inc: Circa Priscianum minorem queritur utrum gramatica ...
Ed: Nil.

57. Robert Blund. (ca. 1180). Summa in arte grammatica.
Inc: Iustas parit petentium preces necessitas ...
Ed: Nil.

58. Robert Blund. (ca. 1180). Glosa super Priscianum.[10]
Inc: Promisimus nos succincta brevitate festinare ad litteram ...
Ed: Nil.

59. Robert Grosseteste. (ca. 1210). De generatione sonorum.[11]
Inc: Cum sonativum percutitur violenter partes ipsius...
Ed: Nil.

60. Robert Kilwardby. (ca. 1250). Super Priscianum maiorem.
Inc: Sicut scribitur in primo posteriorum, quod non est, non contingit scire ...
Ed: Nil.

[8] This has been ascribed to Peter Helias by de Rijk (1967:24). Hunt informs me (personal communication) that it is *not* the work of Peter Helias but of a Petrus Hispanus (not Pope John); Hunt is preparing an edition of this important treatise.

[9] A critical edition is being prepared by L. M. de Rijk; cf. also his series of articles in *Vivarium* (de Rijk 1968–70).

[10] Cf. de Rijk 1967:255–7.

[11] There is one treatise *De lingua* with the incipit 'Lingua congruit in duo nature opera'; many copies of this are to be found, especially in British libraries, where it is usually ascribed to Robert Grosseteste. This ascription has been strongly denied by Thomson (1940). It is not, however, a grammatical treatise.

61. Robert Kilwardby. (ca. 1250). Super Priscianum minorem.
Inc: Sicut dicit Aristoteles in 2° de anima, lingua congruit ...
Ed: Nil.
62. Robert Kilwardby. (ca. 1250). In de accentu Prisciani.
Inc: Accidentia ut dicit Aristoteles in libro de anima ...
Ed: Nil.
63. Robert Kilwardby. (ca. 1250). In Barbarismum Donati.
Inc: Cum omnes homines natura scire desiderant ...
Ed: Nil.
64. Robert Kilwardby. (ca. 1250). Sophismata grammaticalia.
Inc: Quoniam circa orationes grammaticas ...
Ed: Nil.
65. Robert Kilwardby. (ca. 1240). De ortu scientiarum.
Inc: Scientiarum alia est divina, alia humana ...
Ed: Nil.
66. Roger Bacon. (ca. 1260). Summa grammaticae.
Inc: Oratio grammaticae aut sit mediante verbo ...
Ed: R. Steele. 1940. Opera hactenus inedita Rogeri Baconi, 15. Oxford, Clarendon Press.
67. Siger de Courtrai. (ca. 1300–10). Summa modorum significandi.
Inc: Quoniam grammatica est sermocinalis scientia ...
Ed: Gaston Wallerand. 1913. Les Philosophes Belges, 8, 93–125. Louvain, Institut Supérieur de philosophie de l'université.
68. Siger de Courtrai. (ca. 1300–10). Sophisma "Amo est Verbum".
Inc: Amo est verbum, hoc est sophisma propositum ...
Ed: Gaston Wallerand. 1913. Les Philosophes Belges, 8, 129–37.
69. Siger de Courtrai. (ca. 1300–10). Sophisma "Magistro legente pueri proficiunt".
Inc: Magistro legente pueri proficiunt, hoc est sophisma circa quod quaeritur unum, scilicet, utrum ablativus ...
Ed: Gaston Wallerand. 1913. Les Philosophes Belges, 8, 137–43.
70. Siger de Courtrai. (ca. 1300–10). Sophisma "O Magister".
Inc: O Magister, haec oratio grammaticalis proposita de qua potest quaeri utrum congrua vel incongrua ...
Ed: Gaston Wallerand. 1913. Les Philosophes Belges, 8, 143–54.
71. Simon Dacus. (ca. 1290). *Martin of Dacia commentary.* (Cf. no. 35).
Inc: Rhetorice primo scribitur a philosopho "Turpe est ignorare quod omnibus scire contingit ...
Ed: Nil.
72. Simon Dacus. (ca. 1290). Questiones super secundum minoris Prisciani.
Inc: Quaeritur utrum grammatica sit scientia ...
Ed: Alfred Otto. 1963. Corpus Philosophorum Danicorum Medii Aevi, 3, 91–178. Copenhagen, Gad.

73. Simon Dacus. (ca. 1260). Domus grammaticae.
Inc: Sicut domus tribus partibus integratur ...
Ed: Alfred Otto. 1963. Corpus Philosophorum Danicorum Medii Aevi, 3, 3–88. Copenhagen, Gad.
74. Thomas of Erfurt. (ca. 1310). De modis significandi sive Grammatica Speculativa.
Inc: Quoniam quidem intelligere et scire ...
Eds: i) M. Fernández García. 1902. Florence.
ii) Geoffrey L. Bursill-Hall. 1972. The classics of linguistics. London, Longmans.
75. Vincentius Heremita. (ca. 1260). Compendium modorum significandi.
Inc: Quoniam ut dicit Boethius docilem reddit scriptura ...
Ed: Nil.
76. Walter Burleigh. De puritate artis logicae.
Ed: Philotheus Boehner. 1955. Franciscan Institute Publications. Text series 9. St. Bonaventure, N.Y.-Louvain.
77. William of Conches. (ca. 1120). Glosa in Priscianum.
Inc: Quoniam in humanis inventionibus nihil ex omni parte posse esse perfectum ...
Ed: Nil.
78. William of Ockham, Summa totius logicae. Pars I-III.
Ed: Philotheus Boehner. 1951–57. Franciscan Institute Publications. St. Bonaventure, N.Y.-Louvain.
79. William of Sherwood, Introductiones in logicam.
Eds: i) Martin Grabmann. 1937. Sitzungsbericht der Bayerischen Akademie der Wissenschaften. Phil. Hist. Klasse, Heft 10. München.
ii) Norman Kretzmann. 1966. Minneapolis, University Press.
80. William of Sherwood, Syncategoremata.
Eds: i) J. Reginald O'Donnell. 1941. MS 3.46–93.
ii) Norman Kretzmann. 1968. Minneapolis, University Press.

2.0 GRAMMAR IN THE MIDDLE AGES

Language events occur in contexts of situation which have to be stated as part of their meaning; a similar statement can be made with reference to theories of language. An understanding of their intellectual environment is a necessary premise to an account of the theory, and this is no less true (indeed one might argue that it is all the more so) for a theory from the more remote past than it is for a theory of today. This makes very real demands on the historian, as he cannot become a participant in the context of situation and yet he must try to do so as closely as he can, and for the reason that this will prevent his account from degenerating into apologia or mere chronicle.

There is no shortage of histories of Medieval philosophy; there are histories of Medieval logic but there is at present no completely adequate history of Medieval language theory. In any such endeavour there are at least four factors which would have to be taken into account, namely the influence of Aristotle, the Liberal Arts, the division of sciences, and the developing and changing status of grammar in relation to these. It is a common-place to say that the seven liberal arts formed the basis of the Medieval curriculum, and to emphasise the fact that grammar was the first member of the liberal arts is also not very informative about the nature and status of grammar, though one might be inclined to think that, by virtue of the privileged position that it held, grammar would have attracted a great deal of attention.

This appears indeed to be the case but what has not generally been recognised is the fact that grammatical theory in the Middle Ages, as a result of the changing intellectual atmosphere, changed out of all recognition, and this can be attributed to the different climates of opinion which characterise the 11th, 12th, 13th and 14th centuries.

2.1 *The Medieval Paradigm*

The Medieval curriculum was based on the seven liberal arts, an inheritance from Boethius (died ca. 524) who has been described (Dinneen 1967:27) as the greatest single influence on education in the Middle Ages; the Liberal Arts were divided into the Trivium and Quadrivium, but it is with the Trivium that we are concerned. It consisted of grammar, logic, and rhetoric and dealt with man's expression of knowledge — indeed it is sometimes referred to as *sermocinalis scientia*.[12] In the earlier Middle Ages only grammar and rhetoric survived and were the key to the preservation of classical learning, and the grammars of the period based on Priscian and Donatus provided a model for subsequent grammars in the more creative period of Medieval grammatical scholarship. From the middle of the 11th century (approximately) a radical change in grammatical theory took place, and we must concern ourselves more with the causes of this, which cannot be attributed to the Liberal Arts, and with the status of grammar in such a scheme of things. The teaching of the liberal arts formed, as Father Weisheipl has shown in a very important series of papers (1964, 1965, 1966, 1969), a continuous tradition as a preparation for the higher faculties at both Oxford and Paris, and the Faculty of Arts was, as he points out (Weisheipl 1969:209), regarded throughout the 14th century as the 'fundamentum et radix aliarum [scientiarum]'. This does not mean, however, that the subject matter of each discipline remained the same throughout this period, and this is particularly true of grammar. One has only to compare, for example, the differences in the definitions of linguistic science in the 12th and 13th centuries, for example Peter Helias: 'Grammatica est scientia gnara recte scribendi et recte loquendi', and Siger de Courtrai: 'Grammatica est sermocinalis scientia, sermonem et passiones eius in communi ad exprimendum principaliter mentis conceptus per sermonem coniugatam considerans.'

[12] Robert Kilwardby in his *De ortu scientiarum* divided the sciences into the speculative sciences, and the practical sciences, which he divided into the moral sciences, the mechanical arts, and word-science; this latter he divided into grammar, logic, and rhetoric; cf. Sharp (1934) and Weisheipl (1965).

The earlier Middle Ages had used the legacy of Rome as the model for their institutions, for example the Church, the law and Education, and Roman culture as their model for literature, especially poetry and rhetoric. Though the influence of the Greek world was not entirely unknown in this period, i.e. Platonic and neo-Platonic ideas had been transmitted to the Middle Ages and part of Aristotle's logic had been translated into Latin by Boethius, it was the fuller appreciation of the Greek tradition and incorporation of the complete Aristotelian *Organon* which was to produce what is often referred to as the 'Renaissance of the 12th Century' (Bursill-Hall 1971:23).[13] The 12th century was more a period of assimilation (van Steenberghen 1955a:24) but by 1200 (according to van Steenberghen 1955a:62) the greater part of Aristotle was available in Latin translation. The 13th century saw the complete absorption of Aristotelian philosophy and logic as well as the works of his Arab commentators into the teaching of the Trivium; more than any other single factor, this will explain the differences in grammatical thought which characterise this period. The details of the "invasion" of the Northern schools of Europe by Aristotle are set out in a number of studies, in particular van Steenberghen (1955a), which also contains references to many other studies; in addition, one should refer to the work of Grabmann, Gilson, de Wulf, and de Rijk. The result of the new spirit, as far as grammar was concerned, was that by 1215 classical authors were absent from the University of Paris (Paetow 1909 and Bursill-Hall 1971), and grammar was no longer associated with literary studies but became instead a philosophical, theoretical and speculative discipline.

The influence of Aristotle was all-pervasive; historians have treated aspects of the influence of his thought, but so far there has been no adequate discussion of the impact of his thought on grammatical theory; it does not after all tell as a great deal to learn that the distinction between the *modus significandi essentialis* and the *modus significandi accidentalis* was created by analogy with Aristotle's distinction of substance and accident, or that Modistic syntactic theory was based on Aristotle's four causes, i.e. the material referring to the individual constructibles, the formal to the actual combination of constructibles, the efficient to the realization of the construction by virtue of the selection of the relevant modes of signifying, with the final, since the object of syntax is the complete expression of a compound concept, representing the sum of the other causes. It is equally unrevealing to point to the frequent reference to Aristotle in the various grammatical treatises of the time; a searching examination of the influence of Aristotle on Medieval grammatical theory is a real necessity because this way we shall perhaps begin to understand the causes of the intimacy between grammar and logic in the creative period of Medieval linguistic scholarship and the links between language theory and philosophical speculation.

Historians of logic, for example Bocheński, Kneale and de Rijk, have pointed to the three stages of Medieval logic, that is *logica vetus*, *logica nova*, and *logica moderna*, which coincide with: a. the period when Aristotle was known through the translations

[13] It might, however, be more appropriate to accept de Rijk's suggestion (1967:126) and speak of the '11th century Renaissance'.

of Boethius; b. the period when the whole Aristotelian corpus and the wealth of philosophical and scientific commentary from Byzantine, Arab and Jewish sources were being assimilated and incorporated into the intellectual system; and c. the period when western scholars began to develop their own particular and original brand of logic which resulted from their complete mastery of Greek logical work. The progress of grammar follows on very similar lines (a more detailed account will follow in the next section) and the fortunes of both disciplines are closely interwoven. During the period of the *logica vetus*, grammar like logic was not remarkable for any novelties; in the period of the *logica nova*, grammar was in danger of being swamped by logic but this was a time when there was a real revival in the teaching of both disciplines. This was followed by a period when logic was investigating new problems, especially the properties of terms (*proprietates terminorum*), while grammar was establishing its autonomy and refining its own technical terms; during the 12th century logic was, in a sense, in the ascendant whereas in the 13th century the position is somewhat reversed, so that Petrus Hispanus worked out his logic in terms of the formal relationships between words in syntactic structures (McCanles 1965–66:136–7). The period of the later 13th century completes the synthesis between terminist logic and grammar; the modes of thought are dictated by the formal structure of language which serves to express them. We encounter for the first time an attempt at a fully fledged, one might even be tempted to call it an 'over-all', theory of language which is also a theory of semiotics, since grammar was clearly the basis on which the main semiotic problems were developed (Bocheński 1961:150). It is quite misleading to claim (viz. Colish 1969:785) that the Middle Ages can be divided into an age of rhetoric, an age of grammar, and an age of dialectic; it would seem much more appropriate, certainly from the point of view of language theory, to talk about a period of rhetoric which lasted up to the middle of the 11th century, a period of linguistics which lasted up to the middle of the 14th century, and then a period of logic which saw a shift in interest from the *scientiae sermocinales* to the *scientiae reales* (Weisheipl 1966:52), a period when the Nominalists were more interested in epistemological problems (Pinborg 1967:202).[14] What is perhaps significant is that Medieval grammatical theory, and to all intents and purposes all language work in the Middle Ages was theory oriented, expanded and refined itself as a result of its association with logic (the *scientiae sermocinales* consisted really only of logic and grammar with rhetoric playing no real part at all). It seems reasonable to claim, therefore, that linguistic theory (in the strict sense of the term) does thrive when the association between logic and grammar are as close as they were, for instance, in the 12th and 13th centuries.

One of the most important results of the full incorporation of the Aristotelian

[14] The grammatical texts in use at the time also suggest this; the first period used Priscian and Donatus without commentary, the second period used Priscian and Donatus critically and with original commentary, and in the third period, i.e. by 1366 Alexander de Villa-Dei's *Doctrinale* and Eberhardus Bethuniensis' *Graecismus* replaced Donatus and Priscian in the University of Paris (Weisheipl 1969:211). At Oxford, though Priscian continued to be read, grammar lost much of its former prominence (Weisheipl 1969:211).

corpus into Medieval teaching was that the classification of the sciences — it should be remembered that learning in the Middle Ages tended to be encyclopedic — which was an inheritance from antiquity and in particular Boethius, at last became fully intelligible to the schoolmen of the 13th century (Weisheipl 1965:54). It is not so much the classification itself, however, which is our immediate concern but rather the idea of science since it implied a new and universally applicable method (Gilson 1955:312). The Medieval notion of science was, as may be well imagined, very different from that of today. The term was used to designate a profound intellectual grasp of a situation or object, and was used of knowledge which explained a situation thoroughly through its true causes (Weisheipl 1965:54), i.e. it referred to any field in which causal explanations could be discovered. This was to have the most profound implications for grammar, since William of Conches demanded that one function of the grammarian was to examine and explain the discovery procedures (*causae inventionis*) for the word-classes and their accidents (Hunt 1941:211–14). The significance of this is that grammar was thereafter required to provide a more adequate explanation.[15] The idea of science, that is necessary knowledge justified by strict demonstration, along with the notion of art, that is a systematic body of principles and consequences, became a part of all Medieval education, which affected grammar just as much as any other field of study.

2.2 *The Status of Grammar*

One can discern two lines of grammatical thought in the Middle Ages, one which followed the literary tradition inherited from the classical world and one which in the 13th century became the dominant trend at least as far as the schools of Northern Europe were concerned, and which was in a sense a renewal of the logical tradition also inherited from the classical world. The details of the 'struggle for supremacy' between the study of literature and the "new" grammar of the 12th and 13th centuries and of the eclipse of belletristic studies have been well reported (Paetow 1909 and 1914; Robins 1951; Sandys 1903), and a very useful bibliographical survey of the whole tradition is to be found in Scaglione 1970. His account, which carries through to the period of the humanist grammarians, demonstrates, despite the presence of certain factual errors concerning Medieval work, the richness of Ancient, Medieval, and Renaissance grammatical work. It is to be regretted that his concern with literary grammar should have led him to say so little about speculative grammatical theory, but his study is, nevertheless, one that the student of the period must not overlook. The result was a new imbalance in the Trivium; rhetoric took very much a back seat, and grammar was justified, no longer by reference to Classical literature, but by systems of logic and metaphysical theories of reality.

The result of this change and the introduction of the notion of science into the

[15] Cf. R. H. Robins (1967:76) and Bursill-Hall (1972:25).

whole field of intellectual activity meant, as far as grammar was concerned, that it could be considered a science only if it was the same for all men, which was one of the requirements made by Robert Kilwardby,[16] that grammar should be the same for all languages, and that rules peculiar to any one language are only accidentally a concern of grammar. Roger Bacon, who was himself convinced of the value of learning languages,[17] observed that in every language there are two kinds of problem, some which concern the language in question and others which are common to all languages;[18] the first sort could not be the object of scientific study but the second kind, on account of their generality, could be. In this way grammar could become a science because its object was universal and its conclusions deducible from principles. Bacon conceived of the possibility of a general grammar of human language, its object being to teach the rules followed by the human intellect in expressing itself (Gilson 1955:313).[19]

As a result of the change in emphasis, grammar came to be associated with the formulation of concepts of reality and their expression by language. This led to the belief that the universality of reality, as conceived and understood by the universality of human reason, could be expressed in the universal language, Latin. The study of such a language became the true object of grammatical science. For the 13th century grammarian, then, linguistics was concerned with the study of the expression of the concept; the concept, however, is the prime concern, whereas its expression is secondary and accidental. Superficially, grammar remained what it had been since the beginning, that is to say a commentary on Priscian; but Priscian was normative and so too were the earliest commentaries, and something more was required in order to satisfy the requirements of science, which is to say that mere grammatico-philological commentaries (Roos 1959:98) were quite inadequate since they do not embody the philosophical element necessary for the explanation of the universal properties of language.

The treatises of the Modistae represent the culmination of Medieval linguistic speculation; the logicisation of grammar was complete and grammar was justified by systems of logic and metaphysical theories of reality. Grammar remained a statement of Latin, but in the hands of the Modistae it also became the study of the word-classes and syntax of the idealised perfect language, and the methods used were speculative in the sense that language mirrors the reality underlying the phenomena of the physical world (Bursill-Hall 1971:26–31). Grammatical systems were for the Modistae to be explained in terms of semantic theories, the concern of their authors being much more with "deep" rather than with "surface" grammar, and in this way grammar could be

[16] Robert Kilwardby: 'Cum scientia maneat eadem apud omnes, et subiectum eius idem manet, quare subiectum grammaticae debet manere idem in omnibus. Sed oratio constructa vel vox literata ordinabilis propter congruum non idem manet apud omnes; quare non erit subiectum grammaticae'.

[17] Cf. Chapter III: 'De utilitate grammaticae' in his *Opus maius*.

[18] Roger Bacon, *Grammatica Graeca* (ed. by Nolan and Hirsch), p. 27: 'Grammatica una et eadem est secundum substantiam in omnibus linguis, licet accidentaliter varietur'.

[19] The implication is, of course, that one could know the language without knowing the literature; such an attitude aroused the hostility of the humanists, and one may add wryly that this is not unlike the hostility that modern linguists have encountered from students of literature and the humanities.

the object of scientific study and be taught as true learning because its object, grammar, was universal. Grammatical theory now rested on the study of words and their properties as the signs of things (*signa rerum*) which are capable of signification (Bursill-Hall 1971:41, 1972:29). The mind seizes upon the property of these things but, not satisfied with mere understanding, it seeks to give linguistic formulation to what it has understood and does so by means of the modes of signifying. The meaning is not the possession of the thing since it is the mind that bestows meaning, and the process continues until the word can not only denote but also signify, i.e. function syntactically. Grammar thus became the study of the formulation of these concepts of the mind; there was no confusion in this for the Modistae, who were insistent on the discreteness of logic whose function was to distinguish right from wrong.[20] The word-classes serve, by means of their modes of signifying, to substantiate things and the properties of things perceived by the mind which now seeks to express them. Details of Modistic semantics are to be found in Robins 1967 (78–88), Pinborg 1967 (30–45, 109–23), Roos 1946 (104–9) and 1948 (205–14), and Bursill-Hall 1971 (37–46) and 1972 (28–36). The next section will describe in more detail the development of Medieval grammatical thought from the repetition of normative grammar as laid down by Donatus and Priscian to the very original theory of speculative grammar, a trend which lasted until well into the 14th century, which became the scene of the controversy between the Modistic and Nominalist grammarians, and which will close our account of Medieval grammatical theory.

3.0 MEDIEVAL GRAMMATICAL THEORY

The study of grammar in the Middle Ages can be divided into two distinct parts, but it is only the second part which is of any real interest to the historian of linguistics, since it is a period which coincides with the introduction of the full Aristotelian logic into the northern schools, the revival of dialectic, and the revival of learning. The earlier period is much more one of preservation and the characteristic feature of the grammatical activity of this earlier period seems to have been a faithful adherence to Priscian and Donatus, with few, if any, attempts at innovation. Other disciplines fared no better, but this was a period when civilisation survived 'by the skin of its teeth'.[21] It would, however, be quite wrong to dismiss this earlier period as being of no importance whatsoever in the history of linguistics. The Greeks and Romans possessed their own grammatical traditions, which the Middle Ages inherited as well as the Greek philosophical tradition, which was transmitted (in part at least) to the Middle Ages by the translations of Boethius; in other words, the earlier Middle Ages inherited

[20] Siger de Courtrai: 'Sicut logica defendit animam nostram a falso in speculativis et a malo in practicis, sic grammatica defendit virtutem nostram interpretativam ab expressione conceptus mentis incongrua in omnibus scientiis'.

[21] Cf. Clark, Kenneth, *Civilisation*, Chapter 1. London, B.B.C. & John Murray, 1969.

a successful model and preserved it throughout a period in history when human intellectual fortunes were at their lowest. This enabled grammarians throughout the 12th, 13th and 14th centuries, a period of great creativity in scholarship, to construct their own model of grammar which they did largely in the form of commentaries on Priscian.

The development of grammatical theory in the second part of the Middle Ages has been variously characterised, but it would seem that, given the present state of knowledge, the best picture is to be obtained from the scheme suggested by Pinborg (1967: 55–6), to which can be added the names of scholars who were significantly active:

a) *Grammatical theories of antiquity*. This in effect means Donatus and particularly Priscian, whose work enjoyed a position of particular privilege in the curriculum of the Medieval university. Priscian, by his own admission, had based his work on the model of the Alexandrian grammarians Dionysius Thrax and Apollonius Dyscolus. Few of the scholars of the Middle Ages knew Greek, but the achievements and originality of Greek linguistic scholarship was made known to Medieval scholarship through Priscian, which thus ensured the continuity of the tradition. Varro was unquestionably a linguist of real originality, but he cannot be included in this account since he does not appear to have exercised any influence on Medieval grammatical theory. Varro occurs between Thrax and Apollonius and it would seem that he exercised no influence on Priscian, which would perhaps account for his lack of influence in the Middle Ages. It has been suggested elsewhere (Bursill-Hall 1971:20) that there appear to be certain similarities between suggestions made by Varro and the Modistae, but there is no evidence at present to suggest that these similarities were anything more than fortuitous.

b) *Interpenetration of logic and grammar*. The history of grammar in the Middle Ages is divided by the period of Abelard, i.e. during the 11th century, when dialectic began to infiltrate grammar as well as theology (de Rijk 1967:99), and this influence was both doctrinal as well as methodological in nature. This period coincides with the teaching of Anselm and Abelard, and there is overwhelming evidence (Hunt 1941–43: 1944ff.) to support the claim that there was a great revival in grammatical teaching,[22] but what is even more significant is that it was at this time that we have the first indications of a change of direction which was to lead to a complete revolution in grammatical thought. The details of this important change in direction are not yet fully known, and it may well prove impossible to point exactly to the originator of the change, but one figure emerges, William of Conches,[23] as a grammarian of considerable significance in the history of grammar of the 11th and 12th centuries. If for nothing else, he is worth remembering for his criticisms of Priscian and the latter's lack of explanatory power, which have a modern ring to them, and for his criticisms of the ignoring by the traditional grammarian of discovery procedures (*causae inventionis*)[24]

[22] Pinborg (1967:23) points out that the nature of Medieval pedagogy was another factor that prevented grammar from being swallowed up by the new and vigorous logic.

[23] Cf. Jeauneau (1960), Hunt (1941–43), and de Rijk (1967) for details of the extant manuscripts of William's Priscian commentary.

[24] I am grateful to my colleague, E. W. Roberts, who suggested this rendering of *causa inventionis*.

for the word-classes and their accidents, the argument being that these discovery procedures (rather than blind reiteration of authority) would explain the word-classes and thus determine their proper grammatical function. It is not yet possible to make a completely valid assessment of William's work, but it is clear that he laid the groundwork for Petrus Helias, who must be regarded as the first grammarian of real originality in the Middle Ages. Furthermore, William exemplifies a spirit of interplay and interconnection which was to prove successful and creative for both grammar and logic in the 12th and 13th centuries. As a result of the stimulus given to dialectic by Abelard and the change in direction given to grammar by William of Conches, there was a marked change in the Trivium; the earlier intimacy between grammar and rhetoric in the study of literature is now replaced by a greater accent on the logical aspects of language, so that grammar is now much more concerned with the language of logic and verbal context in relation to meaning.

c) *The autonomy of grammar*. Recent research (Hunt 1941–43; de Rijk 1967) has shown that the claim that Petrus Helias was the first to embody in grammar the new dialectic inspired by the discovery of Aristotelian logic is unfounded. This does not, however, minimise the importance of Peter. His achievement as far as grammatical theory is concerned is very significant and this serves to justify the position of pre-eminence that he has been traditionally allocated in Medieval grammatical studies. Hunt (1941–43:241ff.) and de Rijk (1967:99–108) have shown that 11th century commentators on Priscian consciously constructed their commentaries in such a way as to fit the requirements of dialectic which was fully in keeping with the new approach to learning that was evolving. Pinborg points out (Pinborg 1967:22) that by the 12th century the liberal arts had receded in importance and the position of grammar was in real jeopardy. Logic took a leap forward and became the first discipline par excellence, and grammar was, so to speak, saved only by its association with logic. Indeed, there would appear to have been the real danger that, as a result, grammar, having abandoned its traditional function of providing the key to a literary text, might be absorbed into logic and dialectic.

It was Peter Helias,[25] inspired by his teacher, William of Conches, who seems to have found the answer; his commentary on Priscian is not a continuous commentary but rather a systematic discussion of contemporary opinions on Priscian. It is not that he was anxious to abandon dialectic, especially as a method of analysis, but rather that he discerned clearly the difference and at the same time the intimacy between them, and his purpose was thus a two-fold one, to free grammar from questions that are unrelated to its purpose (Hunt 1950:32) and to embody in his account of grammar those aspects of dialectic and its methodology which are valuable to its purpose. This

[25] There are many manuscript versions of Peter's Priscian commentary and of the treatise, *De constructione*, ascribed to him by de Rijk (1967:24). There is another treatise, of which there are many manuscript versions, which has been wrongly attributed to Peter (cf. Thurot 1869:22), and indeed, in many manuscript catalogues it is listed as pseudo-Peter Helias. It is a metrical commentary on Priscian with a further commentary by Magister Johannes Sommerfelt with the incipit 'Sicut ab esse rei soliti rem promere dicunt'.

is not the first nor the last time in the history of linguistics that grammar has been held in thrall by sister disciplines, but the achievement of Peter lies in the fact that he allowed grammar to achieve a marked degree of autonomy by reason of his thorough systematisation of the theories of his predecessors, and, coupled with the impetus given to speculative scholarship in logic and philosophy by the full incorporation of the Aristotelian logical corpus into the programme of studies, he encouraged speculation in a new direction on the nature of grammar and language. His status is clearly indicated by the respect shown to his work by later commentators and grammarians.

The work of a third master, Ralph of Beauvais,[26] must be mentioned in this context, since the grammarians of the generation immediately following Peter Helias achieved a synthesis between grammar and the study of classical authors, especially in the study of syntax (Hunt 1950:39), though, as Hunt also points out, grammatical theory did not develop along the lines that Ralph had laid down. As we have already pointed out, the study of literature was superseded by the study of logic. It is from this period that we find the first independent treatises on syntax, and it is generally recognised that the study of syntax is one of the important achievements of Medieval grammatical theory (de Rijk 1967:112–13). What is even more important is that this expansion of grammatical theory into syntax continued the close association between logic and grammar which culminated in the speculative grammars of the Modistae, but this was, as Hunt and de Rijk have also shown, the result of the full assimilation of Aristotle and his commentators and not from a renewed association between grammar and literature.[27]

d) *Universal grammar*. There is a gap in our knowledge of the details of the progress and changes in grammatical theory in the 100 years that separate Ralph of Beauvais and the Modistae, but it is clear that this was a period of consolidation. Once more, the historian is handicapped by the absence of usable texts, and it is certain that modern editions of William of Conches, Peter Helias and Ralph of Beauvais will allow us to fill in many details of the developments in grammatical doctrine in the very interesting formative period of the 12th century. The problem of universals, for instance, was one of the great controversies of the Middle Ages, and grammar did not escape from some of the implications of the problem. It is, however, not so much the matter of universals, which for the schoolmen was not a question of language universals as we think of them today, although the problem was for them unquestionably a linguistic one, which is of immediate concern, but rather the idea that, although there are superficial, i.e. phonetic, differences between languages, the meanings remain the same. The full impact of Aristotle had taught Medieval scholars that a science, in order

[26] Cf. Hunt (1950:11–16) for details of Ralph and his work.

[27] De Rijk (1967:113) stresses the importance of syntactic studies in the context of the second half of the 12th century in that it created the foundation for a very fruitful relationship between grammar and logic. He also points out (de Rijk 1967:263) that the grammatical theory of the late 12th century is a vital source for understanding developments in logic which was very much influenced by developments in grammar.

to be recognised as a science, must be universal, that is, it must be the same for all men and describable in the form of universal rules; furthermore, it was not sufficient to describe the data, but they must be explained and necessarily so. In the 12th century one encounters, according to Pinborg (1967:24–5), occasional recognition of this, but it was not incorporated into their understanding of grammar, and it is not until, again according to Pinborg, the early 13th century, specifically in Jordan of Saxony's Priscian minor commentary (ca. 1220), that this requirement is built into grammatical theory. This involves a tremendous shift in interest, with vital implications for subsequent developments. Peter Helias had earlier been concerned with concrete facts relating to what we might call surface features of language, in that he saw grammar as closely related to practical problems connected with natural languages, whereas Jordan required of grammar that it should be concerned with speech in terms of meaning or the content which was common to all men. At much the same time, we find the requirement, expressed in an unpublished manuscript,[28] that grammar should not be concerned with individual languages but with general rules of language as such, that grammar is not, according to Pinborg (1967:26), concerned with concrete facts but with "sermo ut quoddam abstrahens a quolibet sermone secundum generales virtutes'. On these terms, then, grammar becomes a science.

e) *Pre-Modistic grammar*. The first half of the 13th century is the last stage prior to the creation of Modistic grammar, which represents the ultimate refinement in the concept of universal grammar and of the modes of signifying (*modi significandi*), and which provides us with the first attempt in the western world with a fully worked out general theory of grammar. In this period, two grammarians stand out as being of particular significance, Robert Kilwardby (died 1279) and Roger Bacon (ca. 1220–92). Kilwardby was a scholar of real distinction, philosopher, theologian, logician, and grammarian; he wrote numerous commentaries on Aristotle and an extensive commentary on both the Priscian *Maior* and *Minor*, as well as a number of grammatical sophismata. He was often referred to by later grammarians as an authority, but once again we are hampered in our interpretation of his work through the absence of any edition of his grammatical writings. Kilwardby and Bacon (who was very much influenced by Kilwardby) are significant by virtue of their insistence on the universal nature of grammar. For Kilwardby, the object of grammar is 'sermo significativus prout abstrahitur ab omni lingua speciali', and it is only in this sense that language can be considered a science. This proposal of the unity of grammar, which Kilwardby likened to geometry, i.e. irrespective of the superficial differences between languages or the shapes and sizes of different diagrams (Thurot 1869:127), was developed further by Bacon, who argued that grammar was one and the same in all languages in its substance, and that there were only accidental variations in their surface differences. The status of Roger Bacon is one which requires more careful definition. Grabmann described him as one of the first speculative grammarians, but he was not one of the Modistae — indeed they referred to him somewhat disparagingly (Pinborg 1967:57).

[28] Paris, Bibliothèque Nationale, Cod. Lat. 16617.

He was, by Medieval standards, a skilled practical linguist, but his position will not be established until his grammatical theories have been examined. His *Summa gramatice* is to be found in a modern edition; this is, rather than a systematic treatise, a collection of grammatical sophismata which discuss various syntactic problems.

Another important aspect of grammatical work of the immediate pre-Modistic period was the refinement of technical terms such as *modus significandi*, its concomitant term *consignificare*, and word-class (*pars orationis*); this is discussed in some detail by Pinborg (1967:30–45), and this whole matter of their very specialised terminology is basic to an understanding of the theory of grammar taught by the Modistae. Their technical language may seem strange to us today, but they did use it to talk about language, and, with certain obvious restrictions and provisions, it could (Robins 1967: 87–8) be used to talk about language today.

Boethius (Thurot 1869:150) introduced the terms *modus significandi* and *consignificare*, but not as technical terms. He used *modus significandi* in two senses, as the various means of designating something, and as a specific way of designating, e.g. the verb differs from the noun in that it has a different *modus significandi* since it designates by means of time. *Consignificare* was derived from the translation of two Greek terms, one of which implied a constitutive element in the definition of a term and the other that a word has meaning only in context. *Modus significandi* as used by Boethius was coextensive with *consignificare*, and throughout the period under discussion they were closely associated and together developed analogously into related technical terms.

Consignificare was at first used as an equivalent term for syncategorematic in that terms such as *omnis, nullus* must be combined with significant terms if they are to express anything. In later grammatical use, it came to be applied to all accidents of the word-classes. Peter Helias used *consignificare* in the form of *modus consignificandi* to refer to the indeclinables and syncategorematic expressions; he introduced the terms *secundariae significationes* to refer to accidents with specific meanings, such as number and tense, and *communes proprietates* to refer to different word forms. It was not until the 13th century that any systematic use emerges and during this period *consignificare* and *accidentia* came closer together, so that *consignificare* and *modus significandi* almost completely converge, and with the Modistae *consignificare* becomes the instrument by means of which the *modus significandi* is established, which is to say that the word acquires its meaning from the intellect but the mind also confers consignification, which assigns the word to a word-class; it is by virtue of its consignification, i.e. its syntactic or grammatical function, that a meaningful word is assigned to a particular word-class.

Boethius had used *modus significandi* in two ways and both are to be found in Abelard. As a result the idea was used for all accidents of the word-class insofar as they have any meaning. Grammarians began to use the concept not only to show that word-classes were constituted of *modi significandi*, but that the word-classes can by this means be further distinguished. Peter Helias failed in his attempt to restrict the term to the definition of the word-classes, and it is not until the 13th century that we find once more system being brought to bear on scattered suggestions; the idea of the *significatio generalis* in contrast to the *significatio specialis* of separate words was introduced with reference to those distinctions of meaning which constitute word-classes. These terms did not supersede *modus significandi*, but, as a result of the distinction, the *modi significandi* were divided into essential modes, which constitute word-classes, and accidental modes, which constitute accidents, the essential modes being further subdivided into general and special modes. From that point, it is only a short step to the Modistic view that a mode of signifying is a property of a thing consignified by a word. The refinement of these terms, which, with the Modistae, achieve the status of *termini technici*, throughout the 12th and 13th centuries is an excellent example of the interplay between grammar and logic, but to understand the change fully one must refer to early Scholastic semantic theory.

f) *Modistic grammar*. In the second half of the 13th century, a completely new type of grammatical literature appeared which represents a very systematic account of the philosophy and logic of language which had been developing through the previous one hundred years; it also represents the blend into a single theory of the various trends and developments which were recounted in the previous parts of this section. The authors of these grammars stated their theory in the form of treatises on the modes of signifying (*Tractatus de modis significandi*), and have come to be known as the Modistae.

They were the heirs of a grammatical tradition created by Peter Helias and fostered by Robert Kilwardby. They achieved a remarkable synthesis of i. the Aristotelian and Platonic philosophical traditions, which, by the middle of the 13th century, had been fully incorporated into the schools of Northern France, ii. the Aristotelian tradition transmitted to the Middle Ages through the translations of Boethius, iii. the literary grammatical tradition exemplified by Dionysius Thrax and Apollonius Dyscolus in Greece and Donatus and Priscian of Rome, and iv. the innovations and refinements introduced into grammatical theory by William of Conches, Peter Helias, Robert Kilwardby, Jordan of Saxony, etc.

Our knowledge of them is relatively slight and the scholarly literature relating to them is not extensive. The best account so far is Pinborg's (1967), in which he also relates in summary fashion the development in grammatical theory prior to the Modistae as well as an account of post-Modistic grammar; he does not attempt a detailed analysis of the grammatical doctrine of the Modistae, but instead provides us with details of the Modistae themselves. Therefore it is now possible to see them as a group consisting of a first generation made up of the Danish Modistae (cf. Roos 1969:195), a second generation who were mostly commentators on the work of the previous generation, and a third group who were generally later and who do not, so far as we can tell, appear to have had close contact with the Danish Modistae and their commentators, though they all studied in Paris, but whose contribution to Modistic theory was vital. We are referring to Michel de Marbais, Siger de Courtrai, Thomas of Erfurt, the latter's *Grammatica speculativa* often being regarded as the most complete statement of Modistic grammatical doctrine. Pinborg points out, however (1968:177–8), that Thomas did not produce any new thesis in grammar which his predecessors had not already put forward; his work is much more a summary and review of all previous work which corrected the mistakes of the earlier Modistae and which could be used as a suitable introduction to and presentation of the Modistic tradition. That this was so is shown by the number of extant commentaries on the text and by the fact that it enjoyed widespread use in central Europe (cf. the manuscript tradition (Pinborg 1967:318)) as a starting-point for lectures and discussion. Details of their grammatical theory can also be found in two studies (Bursill-Hall 1971 and 1972) and in this sense they complement Pinborg's very important treatise. These accounts were written from the standpoint of a modern linguist and concentrate on the works of the last-named Modistae. The first one is in fact a detailed description of Modistic grammatical method and is based for the most part on Siger de Courtrai and Thomas of Erfurt. The second contains the text (with translation) of Thomas's treatise, and is a more detailed account of Thomas's descriptive procedure. Pinborg (1969) has also provided us with a summary account of Modistic theory, and this too has been stated in the terms of the modern linguist. We do not at present possess an account of the Modistae which is sufficiently detailed to account for the changes and developments which undoubtedly took place; the work of the later Modistae give clear evidence of the refinements of time, and a full study of the Modistae, taking into account the differences in the details of presentation, and which would permit a fuller appreciation of this important period in the history of linguistics, is very much to be desired.

In addition to Pinborg's valuable study, we possess an account of Martin of Dacia (Roos 1952) which should be supplemented by further studies (Roos 1946 and 1948) in which Father Roos has provided more detail of the nature of Martin's grammatical thought. There is another summary account of Modistic thought (O'Mahoney 1964) written more from the standpoint of the philosopher of language than the linguist.[29] Fr. O'Mahoney's account is valuable in that it explains the leading technical terms, such as *consignification* and *mode of signifying*, used by the Modistae, and he emphasises the fact that this technical language which is admittedly complicated and at times obscure is a necessity for an understanding of all medieval linguistic thought. Modistic metalanguage was a natural outcome of its context of situation and an understanding of it will lead to a fuller appreciation of the strength and validity of the dialectical doctrine of the Trivium, which was the instrument of all scholastic intellectual activity. Two studies by Robins (1951 and 1967) are also worthy of mention. The first must be

[29] Fr. O'Mahony makes the very important point that interest in the great achievements of Medieval theology and metaphysics has led scholars to overlook (we might even add misunderstand) the linguistic culture which constituted the very foundation of all Medieval education and thought.

He also points out (pp. 484–6) that although the Modistae undoubtedly exaggerated the parallels between linguistic categories and the structure of thought and reality, they were working entirely within a framework which was the result of the Aristotelian-scholastic vision of reality; within such narrow confines their speculation had a valid foundation. Their limitation was the limitation of their epistemology.

regarded as a pioneer effort since it represents probably the first attempt by a modern linguist to view without disparagement the linguistic views of another period in its own terms and to relate them to their historical ancestors. The second study is part of a remarkable work of synthesis in which Robins captures in the space of one relatively small volume and in eminently readable form the salient features of the development of linguistic theory from the Ancient Greeks to the present. The picture that emerges of the Modistae is that of a coherent theory of language which achieved a marked degree of success and one which was very much a product of their time; their failure, if one must talk in such terms, was not the result of the lack of internal validity, but of the intellectual context in terms of which modistic theory was constructed. Intellectual climates change and linguistic theory changes with them.

The Modistae covered a period of approximately eighty years; we know the names of some twenty four authors of modistic treatises and commentators, though in some cases our knowledge is very slim, e.g. Pinborg refers (1967:93) to an incunabula edition of a collection of questions on the modes of signifying written by a certain Magister Albertus, but denies any attribution to Albertus Magnus. Pinborg also refers to some 260 manuscripts (most unpublished) containing Modistic material; his list is to all intents and purposes exhaustive and reveals a rich tradition since it refers to some eighty different treatises and commentaries. If we accept the dates suggested by Pinborg (and we recognise that they can, for the most part, be only approximate), we can begin to see something more of the progression:

1260–70:	Vincentius Heremita, Matthew of Bononia.[30]
1270–80:	Martinus Dacus, Boethius Dacus, Petrus de Alvernia, Petrus de Croccus.
1280–90:	Johannes Dacus, Simon Dacus, Magister Albertus, Michel de Marbais.[31]
1290–1300:	Albertus Swebelinus, Gentilis de Cingulo, Radulphus Brito.
1300–1310:	Ion Suessionensis, Johannes Avicula de Lotharingia, Nicholas de Bohemia, Thomas Chirmister, Siger de Courtrai, Thomas of Erfurt.
1320+	Johannes Josse de Marvilla, Johannes de Soncino, Magister Fredericus, John Seward, Henricus de Crissay.[32]

The creative period was between 1270–1310; thereafter, although grammars in a Modistic strain were written up to the 16th century,[33] the tradition by the mid-14th century had become sterile.

30 Pinborg (1967) describes these as precursors whose work is somewhat more elementary than the treatises of the Danish Modistae, in particular Martin and Boethius.

31 The unedited manuscripts of Michel's treatise have been reported in Pinborg 1967 (316); unfortunately, the section on syntax to which Michel himself referred has not been found.

32 By this time Modistic grammar had lost much of its originality; treatises from this period were either repetitions of earlier work or else polemical, since they were presumably engaged in answering the criticisms of the nominalists. The controversy between the later Modistae and the Nominalist grammarians is in a curious way not unlike the controversy in the 20th century between the structural linguists and the transformationalists.

33 There is, for instance, a 16th century manuscript in the University Library in Bologna (Cod. 153, f. 46^{v}–129^{r}); its title is 'Tractatus de modis significandi qui dicitur grammatica speculativa et artificalia' with the incipit 'Ut dicit philosophus...' which is not very revealing but which we have not encountered elsewhere among Modistic work.

The Modistae must be thought of as the second generation of speculative grammarians who systematised and codified the work of grammarians from Peter Helias onwards. They believed that the basis of grammar lay outside language itself and was dependent upon the structure of reality and the laws of thought; this means that, in their view, there was one universal grammar dependent on the structure of reality, and, as a result, grammatical rules are independent of any natural language which might be used to express them. There was one grammatical system universally valid for all languages and it was the task of the philosopher of language to discover them. They retained the grammatical system of Priscian but restated the categories and definitions in terms suitable to the new spirit; in other words, their purpose was to state the functional nature of the formal categories which Priscian had described but stated the criteria in terms of the correlates of reality to which they corresponded.

The broad line of their procedure was a statement in three parts which can be labelled metalanguage, word-class theory and syntax.[34] The metalanguage serves as an account of their technical language, in particular the processes and categories required in the descriptive process beginning with expression and culminating in the word as a grammatical unit. The word-classes (*partes orationis*) are then described by means of the technical language which consists of two inter-related procedures, namely *vox* ('expression'), *signum* ('sign'), *dictio* ('word'), *pars orationis* ('word-class'), and *modus essendi* ('mode of being'), *modus intelligendi* ('mode of understanding'), and *modus significandi* ('mode of signifying').

The word-classes are in effect described by means of the modes of signifying, which are divided into essential and accidental. The essential mode is used to set up the class in terms of its essence, and therefore the class, or perhaps more appropriately the archipars,[35] will share its essence with another class, so that the division of general and special is introduced in order to explain the substantial similarities of the classes and their formal differences. The classes are then described in terms of their accidental modes, which to a large extent coincide with the traditional accident but which represent in the Modistic scheme variations of the essence without effecting any change in it. The metaphysician recognised in the world of things two primary elements, permanence and becoming; their expression is the province of the grammarian who used the noun and pronoun to express permanence and the verb and participle to express becoming. The device of matter and form was introduced to distinguish the noun and pronoun, and the verb and participle; this device was borrowed from the language of the metaphysician but is used as a terminological distinction without further implica-ions, e.g. the verb and participle share the same matter but differ in form.

If one were guided by the manuscript tradition, one would be led to imagine that the Medieval grammarian and particularly the Modistae looked upon word-class descrip-

[34] The terms used were *Prooemium*, *Etymologia*, and *Diasynthetica* (cf. Bursill-Hall 1971:42–3).
[35] One Modista, Siger de Courtrai, proposed an analysis of the word-classes (cf. Bursill–Hall 1971: 109–11) into three meta-classes in terms of their essence, and these were subdivided into specific aspects of their essence in order to achieve the eight traditional word-classes.

tion as their most important function. However, it is generally recognised that the Medieval grammarian made significant contributions to syntactic theory[36] and Modistic syntax must be looked upon as the most original aspect of their work. Once the word-classes had been described, they proceeded to the third stage, which is the syntax of these word-classes, and which is done by means of three stages, construction, congruity, and completion.[37] The construction represents the combinations of words into constructions; there are two types of construction, each of which can be further divided into two sub-types, which closely resemble the endocentric and exocentric constructions of modern structural linguistics; in other words, we are dealing with a rudimentary form of phrase-structure syntax.[38] The second stage of congruity states the requirements for correctness which include concord, government and collocational appropriateness.[39] The final stage of completion states any further criteria, for example all dependences of the constructibles must be completed, which are necessary for the expression and understanding of a compound concept of the mind.[40]

It is obvious that the modern linguist could not operate with a procedure structured on the Modistic scheme, but Modistic theory contains much to interest the modern linguist. It represents a fully articulated theory expressed in terms of its intellectual environment; it reveals not only a pattern of change and development not unlike the movements of the 20th century but also the fluctuating fortunes and the fickleness of varying attitudes towards the problem of language description. There are many problems of intense interest to the modern linguist which did not originate with him, and if these problems receive more attention today than they did from the Modistae, it does not mean that the Modistae were not aware of them or that they did not discuss them. This greater awareness simply reveals the progress which is a portion of the historical progression within a science. It is not so much the method *per se*, but its relationship to its intellectual world, which counts, and a less adequate intellectual paradigm will of necessity imply a less adequate theory of language.

g) *Nominalist grammar*. The last stage of Medieval grammar is represented by the Nominalist grammarians of the 14th century and for our knowledge of them we have to rely entirely on Pinborg's accounts (Pinborg 1967:172–85, 202–10 and 1968:178–85). This reveals once more the value and importance of Pinborg's study. It is not only that he has filled in some of the gaps in our knowledge, but a careful examination of his book will show precisely the need for further research in specific areas and, if supplemented by our own study (Bursill-Hall forthcoming), it should

36 Cf. Bursill-Hall 1971:288–90; de Rijk 1967:112–16.

37 The terms used were *constructio, congruitas, perfectio* (cf. Bursill-Hall 1971:301–9).

38 Pinborg (forthcoming) states: 'Die syntaktische Analyse der Modistae ähnelt der antiken grammatischen Analyse darin, dass sie keine Analyse von 'oben', vom Satze her ist, sondern bei den constructibilia (den Wörtern) anfängt und zeigt, wie sich diese zu grösseren Einheiten zusammenfügen'.

39 The terms used were *similitudo, proportio,* and *proprietas* (cf. Bursill-Hall 1971:64–5, 303–7).

40 Thomas of Erfurt: 'conceptum mentis compositum exprimere, et perfectum sensum in animo auditoris generare' (Bursill-Hall 1972:314).

provide the appropriate basis of a paradigm of investigation on which the history and an appreciation of the details of the history of linguistics in the Middle Ages can be constructed.

The first clash between Realists and Nominalists in terms of grammar seems to have taken place at Erfurt (Pinborg 1967:139 and Roos 1969:195), which appears to have been a very active centre in the 13th and 14th centuries. Pinborg refers, however, to four authors in particular who can be described as Nominalist grammarians, though in this instance epithets such as 'Nominalist' must be regarded (as indeed they themselves described language) as a system of labels, since 'each Medieval master is a distinct historical case' (Gilson 1955:402). Johannes Aurifaber must be considered one of the most important and radical members of this group, since he appears to have begun the attack on the Modistic tradition. His *Determinatio contra modos significandi* was written in 1332 and, according to Pinborg's account, this seems to have aroused considerable controversy among the other grammarians of Erfurt. Petrus Alliacus (Pierre d'Ailly) wrote his *Destructiones modorum significandi* about 1372–90, John Gerson his *De modis significandi* in 1426, and Erhardus Knaab de Zwiefalten his *Determinatio de modis significandi* in 1452; of these, a modern, edited version of Aurifaber's treatise, along with a number of other anonymous texts, constitute the fourth part of Pinborg's study (1967:215–32), but there are no modern versions of the others. Pinborg (1967:152–66) refers to other anonymous manuscripts which also include the work of Aurifaber's opponents.

Aurifaber framed his attack on Modistic grammar in a sophisma "Nominativo hic magister" which marks the entry of nominalist language theory into the field of grammar, and the influence of William of Ockham is apparent throughout his whole argument. The main thrust of his criticism was directed against the Modistic theses that the *modus significandi* and the *ratio significandi* of the word are something attributed to the expression by the intellect; his claim was that such an attribution was completely superfluous for language theory, i.e. one can explain the function of language without having recourse to such devices. The gist of Aurifaber's argument was that, since the meaning of a word is nothing more than the use which the intellect makes of it, the modes of signifying are unnecessary, and furthermore they are ontologically impossible since they are merely relations set up by the intellect and hence have no reality. The result, as far as grammatical theory is concerned, was revolutionary because grammatical science in these terms lost its philosophical relevance; the result was that the grammarian had nothing more to contribute to the philosopher.

It is not easy, because of the dearth of usable texts, to assess Nominalist grammatical theory, and one must remain content with Pinborg's summary accounts (1964, 1967, 1968); Nominalist grammar does clearly represent a most important development in Medieval language theory. The Modistae were concerned with purely grammatical problems, whereas the Nominalists were much more concerned with the logical and epistemological aspects of language. Despite the fact that we are unable to point to a detailed account of Nominalist grammatical theory which would allow us to make a reasonable assessment of their achievement, they are important not only because of their opposition to the Modistae and other Realist grammarians, but because of the link they provide with the universalist grammarians of the 17th and 18th centuries. The Nominalists were the most effective opponents of the Modistae, and the 14th century seems to have been a linguistic battlefield from which the Modistae do not appear to have emerged as victors. Grammars in a Modistic form continued to be written, but the whole tradition had grown sterile, because the concept of '*modus significandi*' was no longer of interest to the philosopher of language. 'In this area of 14th century scholasticism (i.e. meaning and grammar) almost everything remains to be investigated and understood' (Moody 1964:74).

This has not been, intentionally so, an exhaustive account of grammatical theory in the Middle Ages; rather we have sought to indicate the main lines of development, the sources of our knowledge and the principal figures who contributed much to a discipline which did enjoy a great prestige and a considerable degree of autonomy and which attracted some of the best minds among the Schoolmen. The account has also tried to indicate the main gaps in our knowledge and it will be the purpose of the next section to describe the research still required, and it is extensive, in a rich scholarly field and of a period when the study of language rather than the learning of languages was one of the principal activities of the Medieval student. We leave the discussion of Medieval theories of grammar, which for some, at least, was a categorical semasiology, at a point when, weakened by the requirements of their rigour and the controversies between the Modistae (who were moderate Realists) and the Nominalist grammarians, it had become an easy target for the attacks of the humanist grammarians.

The study of linguistic theory in the Middle Ages is important because it gives us the opportunity of seeing a fully developed theory in terms of an intellectual environment very different from that of today. Medieval grammatical theory is also important because its practitioners raised certain problems which periodically have emerged to plague students of grammar and which are also of great contemporary concern. Above all, though the problem was itself never clearly and specifically articulated in the Middle Ages, it raised the question of theory versus data orientation which is one that must be resolved if linguistics is ever to achieve the status of a mature science.

4.0 RESEARCH

So far the discussion has centered around what we already know; the purpose of this section is, however, to indicate what still needs to be done. We are far from knowing the details of developments in grammatical doctrine in the period from mid-11th to the 15th century. In order to fill in this enormous gap in our knowledge we can establish certain clear-cut research priorities and without these, the account of grammar in the Middle Ages must remain very much a second-hand chronicle. The history of linguistics in the Middle Ages, or for that matter of any period, deals with the *res gestae*, which Collingwood has defined[41] as the actions of human beings in the past. In this instance, the actions in question are the way or ways that the medieval schoolmen saw language and these are preserved in a large number of extant manuscripts. Collingwood further points out that history proceeds by the interpretation of the evidence; this can be done only in terms of a clearly stated theory which for the history of linguistics at present is lacking. Such a theory, which should be sufficiently general for application to any period, is a matter of urgent necessity; it may well be that history, i.e. historiography or the history of science, has much to provide, but our justification for the practice of the history of linguistics will ultimately lie in the possession of an adequate theory of history.

In terms then of priorities, the first requirement for the history of linguistics in the Middle Ages is the provision of an adequate primary apparatus; the manuscript tradition is a rich one. There are excellent editions of the Danish Modistae, of whom Boethius of Dacia and Martin of Dacia are the most important; there are also editions available of Siger de Courtrai (Wallerand 1913) and Thomas of Erfurt (Garcia 1902; Bursill-Hall 1972), though a critical edition of the latter's *Grammatica speculativa* would be useful. Of the other known Modistae, in particular Michel de Marbais, we have no editions at all and, in addition, there are at least forty anonymous treatises (cf. Pinborg 1967:309–27), none of which are available in modern form.

One method of writing a grammatical treatise which was commonly practised in the Middle Ages was to write a commentary on Priscian or Donatus; there are over 500 manuscripts of Priscian's *Institutiones grammaticae* still extant and the majority of these, especially if they were written in the 11th and 12th centuries, contain marginal annotations and commentaries which are in some instances very extensive. They are almost always anonymous and difficult to read, having been written in a very small hand (Hunt 1941–43:195); from the 13th century onwards, the practice of marginal annotation was for the most part abandoned and full length commentaries took their place. The Priscian commentaries and glosses of the 11th and 12th centuries are a vital source of information about changes in grammatical theory at a very important stage in its development. They are at present being investigated by M. Gibson of Liverpool University, and it is hoped that this will throw a great deal of light on developments in grammatical theory at a time when grammar and dialectic were very closely associated. There are also many commentaries on Priscian and Donatus dating from the 13th century; most of these are anonymous and none have been published, but they will be of the greatest use in filling in some of the gaps in our knowledge of developments in the period between Peter Helias and the Modistae. The most serious gap is that there are no editions of the works of the most important grammarians prior to the Modistae, i.e. William of Conches, Peter Helias and Robert Kilwardby, nor of the 13th century commentaries on Priscian by Jordan of Saxony and Nicholas de Paris. All this represents an enormous fund of important matter but which will require many years of solid and painstaking work before it becomes really accessible. In addition there

[41] Robin G. Collingwood, *The idea of history*, p. 9. Oxford, University Press, 1946.

are many anonymous treatises on syntax, *quaestiones*, *regulae*, and commentaries on various teaching texts, e.g. Alexander de Villa-Dei's *Doctrinale*, all of which represent a veritable mine of fascinating research material.

Of equal importance to the publication of texts will be the commentaries on the works of the major grammarians: in a sense, it is appropriate that the historian should write his account in the form of commentaries on these medieval grammars, inasmuch as they themselves used this format in order to state their views. In addition to the scholars already mentioned, there are other grammarians who deserve commentary; Roger Bacon is clearly a figure of importance and an examination of his grammatical writings will do much to place him in relation to both his predecessors and successors. There is a need for a new edition of Siger de Courtrai,[42] who occupies an important position among the Modistae and modern scholarship, since the edition of this work was published some sixty years ago, and in this particular instance has much to contribute. There is need for a more detailed examination of the Modistae; we know a lot about the structure of this group and the basic principles of their grammatical doctrine. There are ten we know by name and there are, as has already been pointed out, many more anonymous *Summa modorum significandi*. These commentaries must also take into account contemporary philosophical problems, since the Medieval approach to learning was much more encyclopedic than it is today.

With the establishment of the textual material and the commentaries on the key figures of the period, we should then be in a position to tackle problems of a more purely historical and chronological nature. There is much we need to know of activities in the 11th and the first half of the 12th centuries; without this, we shall not be in a position to place William of Conches, and particularly Peter Helias, in their proper perspective, since it was due to their work that grammar was able to enjoy a position of considerable autonomy in the studies of the Trivium of the late 12th and 13th centuries. We need to know a great deal more about developments in the fifty to sixty years after Peter Helias. If we regard the work of William and Peter as tantamount to a scientific revolution in grammatical theory, then the work of Ralph of Beauvais and lesser figures such as Bonus de Lucca, Gosvin de Marbais, Hugutio Pisanus, not to mention anonymous treatises, must be treated as the exploitation of the innovatory ideas of William and Peter. We need to know more of the development of certain ideas introduced into grammatical theory in the first half of the 13th century; mention has already been made of the introduction of the idea of universal grammar and the refinement of the concept of mode of signifying (*modus significandi*) and consignification (*consignificatio*). Admirable though Pinborg's (1967) study is, it is not sufficiently detailed to allow us to describe *in extenso* the details of these developments.[43] By the same token,

[42] An edition is in preparation for the *Grammatica speculativa* series, edited by Jan Pinborg and Helmut Kohlenberger.

[43] Apart from its intrinsic value as the most significant account of the development of Medieval grammatical theory, Pinborg's book is valuable for its indication of further research necessary for a fuller understanding of the details of these developments.

we need to establish the status as grammarians of scholars such as Jordan of Saxony, Nicholas de Paris, Robert Kilwardby, and Roger Bacon, since this will help to fill in the gaps in our knowledge of grammatical work between Peter Helias and the Modistae. It is especially important to establish, in so far as it is possible for this period, the exact chronology of events as a necessary prolegomena to a fuller appreciation of the achievements of the Modistae.

Even so, we would not yet be in a position to write the history of linguistics in the Middle Ages, since any such study must take into account i. Medieval theories of meaning, ii. theories of syntax, iii. theories of the sign, iv. the relationship between grammar and logic, and v. Medieval metalanguage. It would also have to take into consideration the intellectual relationship between the scientific and scholarly world of the Middle Ages, since the Medieval schoolmen sought for a unified system of knowledge, so that any account of Medieval grammatical theory must be fitted into a framework which embraces all intellectual activity. Meaning was all-pervasive in the grammatical work of the period and it simply will not do, as was so often the case in the past, to dismiss Medieval theory as mentalistic, since the schoolmen were concerned, and this has of course an interesting modern twist, much more with problems of adequacy, universals, deep structure than with the descriptive approaches to linguistic statement, and they did this from the standpoint that the semantic and psychological components of language are the true base for all linguistic investigation. A recent study (Pinborg forthcoming) may well throw considerable light on the problem of the interpenetration of logic, grammar, and meaning in the Middle Ages. Pinborg writes with penetrating insight and understanding about Medieval theories of language, and combines a real appreciation of Medieval and modern linguistic theory with a first-hand knowledge of the manuscript tradition. This most recent book of his traces the development of logical and semantic theories from the Greek logicians to the Middle Ages and includes a chapter on medieval linguistic theory, in which he compares medieval logical and grammatical sentence analysis. Though it is not possible at this stage to discuss in detail the content of his thesis, he is concerned to show that both disciplines sprang from the same source, the *logica vetus*, and that both saw their purpose as the setting up of rules for the creation and confirmation of correct sentence construction; and yet despite their mutual fertilisation, both disciplines were fully convinced of their autonomy, viz. Simon of Dacia's commentary on Martin of Dacia's treatise *De modis significandi*: 'Non debet sumi bonitas orationis ex principiis vel bonitate intellectus, sed debet sumi ex propriis principiis intrinsecis constructionis vel orationis'.[44] We have in effect two quasi- parallel types of analysis, namely the logical, which was concerned with the meaning of terms within a particular context, and the grammatical, which was concerned with linguistic structure, so that together they could provide a reference system which would describe both the logical 'deep structure' as well as the grammatical 'surface structure', not of a language but of language, and in this way satisfy the requirements of a science.

[44] Quoted by Pinborg, *op. cit.*

Meaning was made to include formal syntactic relations, at least by implication, so that the study of syntax — generally regarded as one of the major achievements of Medieval grammarians — must be closely related to meaning. In this respect, technical terminology, which was often subtle and complex, will throw a great deal of light on the inter-relationships between various disciplines since their descriptive processes and concomitant technical terms are replete with concepts borrowed from contemporary metaphysics, such as matter and form, act and potentiality, which were incorporated into their statements, not in their philosophical acceptance, but with descriptive function (Bursill-Hall 1971:48–55). As a result of the intimacy between reality, the conceptualisation of reality, and the expression of the concept by means of grammar, meaning becomes in effect the formulation of these concepts in the oneness of language and the task of the grammarian was to discover the universal validity of the rules which govern language. The resultant statement is often complicated and obscure, but the unravelling produces a picture of a close inter-penetration of logic, metaphysics, psychology, epistemology, and grammar, all of which must be subsumed under language in this instance.

We can therefore set out in tabular form[45] the research still necessary (in conjunction with what we know as set out in 2.0 and 3.0) for a complete picture of Medieval grammatical activity:

1. The publication of texts; there are at least three series of scholarly publications, which are already in existence, i.e. i. Corpus Philosophorum Danicorum Medii Aevi, ii. The Classics of Linguistics, and iii. Grammatica Speculativa. The extent of the problem has already been discussed.
2. Commentaries on the works of the key figures and themes of the period.
3. The activity of the period of Abelard and the school of Chartres; the status of William of Conches and Peter Helias.
4. The chronology of events between Peter Helias, i.e. mid-12th century, and the Modistae, i.e. mid-13th century.
5. A detailed comparison of the Modistae who, though they shared the same theoretical point of view, showed, and this may be a simple matter of time, marked differences of presentation.
6. The Nominalist grammarians of the 14th century, of whom, apart from Pinborg's short account, we know very little.
7. The study of meaning which is closely connected to syntax and logic; Medieval grammarians concentrated on grammar and, because of their concern for matters relating to deep structure, little or no attention appears to have been given to the study of phonology. Under this topic, we may subsume problems such as:
   a. technical terminology
   b. sign theory
   c. universal properties

[45] The paradigm of investigation has also been discussed in our forthcoming paper to appear in the collection 'Traditions and paradigms' edited by Dell H. Hymes.

d. the idea of modus significandi

8. Studies on Donatus and Priscian.

9. Pedagogical grammars of the Middle Ages: The manuscript tradition contains a large number of items which were directed towards practical instruction in Latin. This pedagogical literature assumed a variety of forms, e.g. commentaries on Donatus or on the *Doctrinale*, which was itself a teaching grammar in verse. Much of it will be of little value, i.e. those items that are in effect lists of paradigms, mnemonic rules, etc., but, on the other hand, there are many items, in particular the various commentaries (which are not always easy to identify from the entries in manuscript catalogues), which do contain a lot of valuable information about Medieval grammatical theory. Language pedagogy was influenced by Modistic grammatical doctrine (viz. Hunt 1964:177–8), and we should remember that this '*grammatica positiva*' formed the basis for so much subsequent language instruction. Indeed, much of what we might call secondary grammatical literature, i.e. *quaestiones*, *regulae*, and *notabiliae*, will probably prove to be a rich source of information about Medieval views on language; for instance, one unedited manuscript (discovered by Grabmann 1934 — Barcelona, Archivo de la Corona de Aragón, Cod. Ripoll 109, f. 134r-158v) contains what amounts to a student's *vademecum* written to cope with the problems of a diverse curriculum and the consequent variety of examination questions. The book contains a description of the books used in the course of study in the Faculty of Arts in the University of Paris in the early 13th century, a set of typical questions, and a series of answers. The book is a useful guide for an examination of the growth of Aristotelianism in the University of Paris in the first half of the 13th century, but what is of particular and immediate interest is that it provides a very unequal treatment of the subjects despite its clearly stated practical aim, in that of the 100 columns, some 23 are devoted to a discussion of speculative grammatical theory, some 60 columns to logic, and the remainder, i.e. 17 columns, are reserved for all the other subjects, e.g. ethics, physics, metaphysics, and rhetoric.

10. The interpenetration of grammar and the general intellectual and philosophical trends of the Middle Ages; the history of science in the Middle Ages has much to contribute here.

There are, in addition, a number of related but not directly dependent problems, e.g. Byzantine grammarians, Arab and Jewish language study, the Humanist grammarians, compilers of dictionaries, e.g. Hugutio of Pisa, Papias. These may not add a great deal to our knowledge of grammatical theory of the Middle Ages, but would nevertheless serve to fill out the picture of a period of intense and extensive language activity in an intellectual atmosphere very different from that of today but which had nonetheless a purpose very much akin to the motive that has prompted so much recent linguistic activity.

5.0 BIBLIOGRAPHY

This does not aim at exhaustiveness — that would be quite impossible. Furthermore, standard works of reference and standard histories of philosophy in the Middle Ages have not been included. Insofar as it has been possible, all the writings by modern linguists on Medieval grammatical theory have been included. It contains the works consulted in writing this chapter as well as the studies which are useful for ideas about Medieval theories of language; it has been divided into two parts: (5.2) linguistic, and (5.3) Medieval, the latter being used to include all the studies which do not refer specifically to Medieval grammarians and Medieval language theory.

5.1 *Texts*

ALEXANDER DE VILLA-DEI. Doctrinale. Ed. by D. Reichling. Monumenta Germaniae Paedagogica, Bd. 12. Berlin, A. Hofmann.

ANSELM. 1964. De grammatico. Ed. by Desmond P. Henry. PMS, 18. Notre Dame, University Press.

BOETHUNIUS DACUS. 1969. Questiones super Priscianum maiorem. Ed. by Jan Pinborg and Heinrich Roos. Corpus Philosophorum Danicorum Medii Aevi 4. Copenhagen, Gad.

EBERHARDUS BETHIENSIS. 1887. Graecismus. Ed. by J. Wrobel. Corpus Grammaticorum Medii Aevi, 1. Breslau, G. Koebner.

HUGO, DE ST. VICTOR. 1966. Hugonis de Sancto Victore opera propaedeutica. Ed. by Roger Baron. PMS 20. Notre Dame, University Press.

IOHANNES DACUS. 1955. Summa Grammatica. Ed. by Alfred Otto. Corpus Philosophorum Danicorum Medii Aevi, 1. Copenhagen, Gad.

MARTINUS DACUS. 1961. De modis significandi. Ed. by Heinrich Roos. Corpus Philosophorum Danicorum Medii Aevi, 2. Copenhagen, Gad.

ROGER BACON. 1902. Grammatica Graeca. Ed. by E. Nolan and S.A. Hirsch. Cambridge, University Press.

——. 1940. Summa grammaticae. Ed. by R. Steele. Opera hactenus inedita Rogeri Baconi, 15. Oxford, Clarendon Press.

SIGER DE COURTRAI. 1913. Summa modorum significandi. Ed. by Gaston Wallerand. Les Philosophes Belges, 8. Louvain, Institut supérieur de philosophie de L'université.

SIMON DACUS. 1963. Questiones super secundum minoris Prisciani. Ed. by Alfred Otto. Corpus Philosophorum Danicorum Medii Aevi, 3. Copenhagen, Gad.

——. 1963. Domus grammaticae. Ed. by Alfred Otto. Corpus Philosophorum Danicorum Medii Aevi, 3. Copenhagen, Gad.

THOMAS OF ERFURT. 1902. De modis significandi sive Grammatica speculativa. Ed. by M. Fernández García. Florence.

——. 1972. De modis significandi sive Grammatica speculativa. Ed. by Geoffrey L. Bursill-Hall. The Classics of Linguistics. London, Longmans.

5.2 *Linguistic*

ARENS, HANS. 1969². Sprachwissenschaft. Rev. ed. Freiburg-München, K. Alber.

BARON, ROGER. 1966. La grammaire de Hugues de St. Victor. Studi Medievali. 3e série, 835–55.

BISCHOFF, BERNARD. 1961. The study of foreign languages in the Middle Ages. Speculum 36.209–24.

BROTHER BONAVENTURE, F.S.C. 1961. The teaching of Latin in later Medieval England. MS 23.1–20.

BURSILL-HALL, GEOFFREY L. 1963. Medieval grammatical theories. CJL 9.39–54.

——. 1966a. Notes on the semantics of linguistic description. In In Memory of J.R. Firth, ed. by C.E. Bazell, J.C. Catford, M.A.K. Halliday, R.H. Robins, 40–51. London, Longmans.

——. 1966b. Aspects of Modistic grammar. MSLL 17.133–48.

——. 1971. Speculative grammars of the Middle Ages. Approaches to Semiotics, 11. The Hague, Mouton.

——. 1972. Thomas of Erfurt. Grammatica speculativa. The Classics of Linguistics. London, Longmans.

——. Forthcoming. Toward a history of linguistics in the Middle Ages. (1100–1450). In Traditions and paradigms, ed. by Dell H. Hymes. Bloomington, Indiana University Press.

CASSIRER, ERNST. 1923. Die Philosophie der symbolischen Formen. Vol. I, Die Sprache. Berlin, Bruno Cassirer.

CHENU, MARIE-DOMINIQUE. 1935. Grammaire et théologie aux XIIe et XIIIe siècles. Archives d'histoire doctrinale et littéraire du moyen âge 10.5–28.

——. 1967. Un cas de platonisme grammatical au XIIe siècle. Revue des sciences philosophiques et théologiques 51.666–8.

CHEVALIER, JEAN C. 1968. Histoire de la syntaxe. Naissance de la notion de complément dans la grammaire française (1530–1750). Publications romanes et françaises, 100. Geneva, Droz.

CUNNINGHAM, FRANK A. 1961. Speculative grammar in St Thomas Aquinas. Laval théologique et philosophique 17.76–86.

CURTIUS, ERNST R. 1947. Das mittelalterliche Bildungswesen und die Grammatik. RF 60.1–26.

DELHAYE, PHILIPPE. 1958. 'Grammatica' et 'Ethica' au XIIe siècle. Recherches de théologie ancienne et médiévale 25.59–110.

DIEHL, ADOLF. 1910. Speculum grammaticae und forma discendi des Hugo Spechtsart von Reutlingen. Mitteilungen der Gesellschaft für deutsche Erziehungs- und Schul-geschichte 20.1–26.

DINNEEN, FRANCIS P. 1967. An introduction to general linguistics. New York, Holt.

DIXON, ROBERT M.W. 1965. What is language? A new approach to linguistic description. London, Longmans.

FIERVILLE, CHARLES. 1886. Grammaire latine inédite du XIIIe siècle. Paris, Imprimerie nationale.

GILSON, ETIENNE. 1969. Linguistique et philosophie. Paris, J. Vrin.

GODFREY, ROBERT G. 1960. The language theory of Thomas of Erfurt. SPh 57.22–9.

——. 1965. Late Medieval linguistic meta-theory and Chomsky's Syntactic structures. Word 21.251–6.

——. 1967. A Medieval controversy concerning the nature of a general grammar. GL 7.79–104.

GRABMANN, MARTIN. 1922. Die Entwicklung der mittelalterlichen Sprachlogik (Tractatus de modis significandi). Philosophisches Jahrbuch der Görres-Gesellschaft 35.121–35, 199–214. [MFGL I, 104–46.]

——. 1940. Der Kommentar des sel. Jordanus von Sachsen zum Priscianus minor. Archivum Fratrum Praedicatorum. 10.1–19. [MAGL III, 232–42.]

——. 1943. Thomas von Erfurt und die Sprachlogik des mittelalterlichen Aristotelismus. SbBAW, Heft 2. München.

——. 1951. Die geschichtliche Entwicklung der mittelalterlichen Sprachphilosophie und Sprachlogik. Ein Überblick. Mélanges Joseph de Ghellinck, S.J., 421–33. Gembloux. [MAGL III, 243–53.]

HEIDEGGER, MARTIN. 1916. Die Kategorien- und Bedeutungslehre des Duns Scotus. Tübingen, Mohr.

HEINIMANN, SIEGFRIED. 1963. Zur Geschichte der grammatischen Terminologie im Mittelalter. ZRPh 79.23–37.

HUNT, RICHARD W. 1941–43, 1950. Studies on Priscian in the eleventh and twelfth centuries. Mediaeval and Renaissance Studies 1.194–231; 2.1–55.

——. 1950. Hugutio and Petrus Helias. Mediaeval and Renaissance Studies 2.174–8.

——. 1964. Oxford grammar masters in the Middle Ages. Oxford Studies Presented to Daniel Callus. Oxford Historical Society, N.S. 14.163–93.

IVIĆ, MILKA. 1965. Trends in linguistics. Janua Linguarum, 42. The Hague, Mouton.

JENSEN, SØREN S. 1964. Some remarks on the Medieval etymology of *congruitas* and its background. Fides quaerens intellectum. Festskrift tilegnet Heinrich Roos, S.J., 60–5. Copenhagen, Forst-Hansen.

JOLIVET, JEAN. 1966. Quelques cas de "platonisme" grammatical du VIIe au XIIe siècle. Mélanges R. Crozet 1.93–9. Poitiers, Sociéte d'Etudes Médiévales.

——. 1969. Arts du langage et théologie chez Abélard. Paris, J. Vrin.

——. 1970. Grammaire et language chez Boèce de Dacie. MA 76.307–22.

KUKENHEIM, LOUIS. 1951. Contributions à l'histoire de la grammaire grecque, latine, et hébraïque. Leiden, E.J. Brill.

——. 1962. Esquisse historique de la linguistique française et de ses rapports avec la linguistique générale. Leiden, Universitaire Pers Leiden.

LANGENDOEN, D. TERENCE. 1966. A note on the linguistic theory of M. Terentius Varro. FL 2.33–6.

LEUNINGER, HELEN. 1969. "Scholastische und transformationelle Sprachtheorie. Ein Beitrag zur Theorie der allgemeinen Grammatik." Frankfurt am Main. Dissertation.

LYONS, JOHN. 1968. Introduction to theoretical linguistics. Cambridge, University Press.

MARTINELLI, LUCIEN. 1963. Thomas d'Aquin et l'analyse linguistique. (Conférence Albert-le-Grand). Institut d'Etudes Médiévales, Université de Montréal. Montréal, Institut d'Etudes Médievales.

MCCANLES, MICHAEL. 1965–66. Peter of Spain and William of Ockham: From metaphysics to grammar. The Modern Schoolman 43.133–41.

MICHAEL, IAN. 1970. English grammatical categories. Cambridge, University Press.

MOUNIN, GEORGES. 1967. Histoire de la linguistique des origines au XXe siècle. Paris, Presses Universitaires de France.

NEHRING, ANTON. 1953. A note on functional linguistics in the Middle Ages. Traditio 9.430–4.

O'MAHONEY, BRENDAN E. 1964. A Medieval semantic: The Scholastic 'Tractatus de modis significandi'. Laurentianum 5.448–86.

PAETOW, LOUIS J. 1909. The Arts course at Medieval universities with special reference to grammar and rhetoric. The University of Illinois Studies, vol. 3, no. 7. Urbana.

PINBORG, JAN. 1961. Interjektion und Naturlaute. C&M 22.117–38.

——. 1964. Mittelalterliche Sprachtheorien. Fides quaerens intellectum. Festskrift tilegnet Heinrich Roos, S.J., 66–84 Copenhagen, Forst-Hansen.

——. 1967. Die Entwicklung der Sprachtheorie im Mittelalter. BGPMA, 42, Heft 2. Münster/Copenhagen.

——. 1968. Die Erfurter Tradition im Sprachdenken des Mittelalters. Miscellanea Mediaevalia 5.173–85.

——. 1969a. Pour une interprétation moderne de la théorie linguistique du moyen âge. Bulletin du Cercle Linguistique de Copenhague 1967–68. AL 12.239–44.

——. 1969b. Miszellen zur mittelalterlichen lateinischen Grammatik. Cahiers de l'Institut du Moyen Age grec et latin 1.13–20.

——. 1971. Bezeichnung in der Logik des XIIIten Jahrhunderts. Miscellanea Mediaevalia 8.238–81.

——. Forthcoming. Logik und Semantik im Mittelalter. Stuttgart, Frommann-Holzboog.

REICHLING, ANTON. 1948. What is general linguistics. Lingua 1.8–24.

ROBINS, ROBERT H. 1951. Ancient and medieval grammatical theory in Europe. London, Bell.

——. 1966. The development of the word class system of the European grammatical tradition. FL 2.3–19.

——. 1967. A short history of linguistics. London, Longmans.
ROMEO, LUIGI, and GAIO E. TIBERIO. 1971. Historiography of linguistics and Rome's scholarship. Language Sciences 17.23–44.
ROOS, HEINRICH. 1946. Martius de Dacia und seine Schrift 'De modis significandi'. C&M 8.87–115.
——. 1948. Sprachdenken im Mittelalter. C&M 9.200–15.
——. 1952. Die Modi Significandi des Martinus de Dacia. Forschungen zur Geschichte der Sprachlogik im Mittelalter. BGPMA, 37. Münster/Copenhagen.
——. 1959. Die Stellung der Grammatik im Lehrbetrieb des XIIIten Jahrhunderts. Artes Liberales, ed. by Josef Koch, 94–106. Leiden/Köln, Brill.
SAARNIO, UUNO. 1959. Betrachtungen über die scholastische Lehre der Wörter als Zeichen. Acta Academiae Paedagogicae Jyvräskyldensis 17.215–49.
SALMON, PAUL. 1962. Über den Beitrag des grammatischen Unterrichts zur Poetik des Mittelalters. ASNS 199.65–84.
SALUS, PETER H. ed. 1969. On language: Plato to von Humboldt. New York, Holt.
SCAGLIONE, ALDO D. 1970. Ars grammatica. Janua Linguarum, series minor 77. The Hague, Mouton.
TEETER, KARL V. 1966. New lamps for old. MSLL 19.83–95.
THUROT, CHARLES. 1869. Notices et extraits de divers manuscrits latins pour servir à l'histoire des doctrines grammaticales au moyen âge. Notices et Extraits des manuscrits de la Bibliothèque Impériale, 22. Reprinted 1964. Frankfurt am Main, Minerva.
VANDERWALLE, CHARLES B. 1929. Roger Bacon dans l'histoire de la philologie. Extrait de la France franciscaine 11.315–410; 12.45–90, 161–210.
WATERMAN, JOHN T. 1963. Perspectives in linguistics. Chicago, University Press.
WERNER, KARL. 1877. Die Sprachlogik des Johannes Duns Scotus. SbÖAW, 85. Vienna.

5.3 *Medieval*

ABELSON, PAUL. 1906. The seven liberal arts. New York, Teachers' College, Columbia University.
ARNOLD, ERWIN. 1952. Zur Geschichte der Suppositionstheorie. Jahrbuch für Philosophie 3.1–134.
ARTZ, FREDERICK B. 1953. The mind of the Middle Ages. New York, Knopf.
BARRETT, HELEN M. 1940. Boethius. Some aspects of his time and work. Cambridge, University Press.
BEONIO-BROCCHIERI FUMAGALLI, MARIA T. 1970. The logic of Abelard. Dordrecht, D. Reidel.
BOCHEŃSKI, INNOCENTIUS M. 1947. Summulae logicales Petri Hispani. Turin, Marietti.
——. 1961. A history of formal logic. Trans. by Ivo Thomas. Notre Dame, University Press.

BOEHNER, PHILOTHEUS. 1935. Der Aristotelismus im Mittelalter. Franziskanische Studien 22.338–47.

——. 1952. Mediaeval logic. Manchester, University Press.

——. 1958. A Mediaeval theory of supposition. Franciscan Studies 18.240–89.

BOLGAR, ROBERT R. 1954. The classical heritage and its beneficiaries. Cambridge, University Press.

CALLUS, DANIEL A.P., O.P. 1944. The introduction of Aristotelian learning to Oxford. London, H. Milford.

——. 1964. The function of the philosopher in thirteenth century Oxford. Miscellanea Mediaevalia 3.153–62.

CARLO, WILLIAM E. The Medieval battle of the liberal arts: A key to contemporary philosophy. Actes 4.745–50.

CARRÉ, MAYRICK H. 1945. Realists and Nominalists. Oxford, Clarendon Press.

CHOJNACKI, PIOTR. 1969. L'essor de la logique au XIIIe siècle. Actes 4.887–94.

COLISH, MARCIA L. 1968. The mirror of language: A study in the Medieval theory of knowledge. New Haven, Yale.

——. 1969. Eleventh-century grammar in the thought of St Anselm. Actes 4.785–95.

COPLESTON, FREDERICK C. 1951ff². A history of philosophy. Vols. 2–3. London, Burns, Oates & Washbourne.

——. 1955. Aquinas. London, Penguin.

CROMBIE, ALISTAIR C. 1953. Robert Grosseteste and the origins of experimental science. Oxford, Clarendon Press.

CURTIUS, ERNST R. 1953. European literature and the Latin Middle Ages. London, Routledge & Kegan Paul.

——. 1960. The Medieval basis of Western thought. Gesammelte Aufsätze zur romanischen Philologie, 28–39.

D'ALVERNY, MARIE-THÉRÈSE. 1968. Les traductions d'Aristote et de ses commentateurs. Revue de synthèse 89.49–52, 125–44.

DELHAYE, PHILIPPE. 1947. L'organisation scolaire au XIIe siècle. Traditio 5.211–68.

——. 1969. La place des arts libéraux dans les programmes scolaires du XIIIe siècle. Actes 4.161–73.

DÜRING, INGEMAR. 1968. The impact of Aristotle's scientific ideas in the Middle Ages. Archiv für Geschichte der Philosophie 50.115–33.

FOREST, ANDRÉ, FERNAND VAN STEENBERGHEN, and MAURICE DE GANDILLAC. 1951. Le mouvement doctrinal de XIe au XIVe siècle. Paris, Bloud & Gay.

GHELLINCK, JOSEPH DE. 1946. L'essor de la littérature latine au XIIe siècle. Bruxelles. L'Edition universelle.

——. 1946-49. Patristique et moyen âge; études d'histoire littéraire et doctrine. 3 vols. Gembloux, J. Duculot.

GIBSON, MARGARET T. 1969. The 'Artes' in the eleventh century. Actes 4.121–6.

GILSON, ETIENNE. 1932. L'esprit de la philosophie médiévale. 2 vols. Paris, J. Vrin.

——. 1952². La philosophie au moyen âge des origines patristiques à la fin du XIVe

siècle. Augmented edition. Bibliothèque historique. Paris, Payot.
——. 1955. A history of Christian philosophy in the Middle Ages. New York, Random House.
GRABMANN, MARTIN. 1916. Forschungen über die lateinischen Aristotelesübersetzungen des XIIIten Jahrhunderts. BGPMA 17, Heft 5–6. Münster.
——. 1923. Die logischen Schriften des Nikolaus von Paris und ihre Stellung in der aristotelischen Bewegung des 13ten Jahrhunderts. BGPMA Supplementband II, 119–46. [MAGL I, 222–48.]
——. 1926–56. Mittelalterliches Geistesleben. 3 vols. München, Max Hueber Verlag.
——. 1928. Mittelalterliche lateinische Aristotelesübersetzungen und Aristoteleskommentare in Handschriften spanischer Bibliotheken. SbBAW, Heft 5. München.
——. 1934. Eine für Examinazwecke abgefasste Quaestionensammlung der Pariser Artistenfakultät aus der ersten Hälfte des 13ten Jahrhunderts. Revue Néoscolastique de Philosophie 13.211–29. [MAGL II, 183–99.]
——. 1936. Aristoteles im Werturteil des Mittelalters. [MAGL II, 63–102.]
——. 1937a. Die Introductiones in logicam des Wilhelm von Shyreswood. SbBAW, Heft 10. München.
——. 1937b. Bearbeitungen und Auslegungen der aristotelischen Logik aus der Zeit von Peter Abaelard bis Petrus Hispanus. Abhandlungen der Preussischen Akademie der Wissenschaften, Phil. Hist. Klasse 5, Berlin.
——. 1938. Ungedruckte lateinische Kommentare zur aristotelischen Topik aus dem 13ten Jahrhundert. Archiv für Kulturgeschichte 28.210–32. [MAGL III, 142–57.]
——. 1939. Methoden und Hilfsmittel des Aristotelesstudium im Mittelalter. SbBAW, Heft 5. München.
——. 1940. Die Sophismataliteratur des 12ten und 13ten Jahrhunderts mit Textausgabe eines Sophisma des Boethius von Dacien. BGPMA 36, I. Münster.
——. 1941. Gentile de Cingoli, ein italienischer Aristoteleserklärer aus der Zeit Dantes. SbBAW, Heft 9. München.
——. 1950. Aristoteles im zwölften Jahrhundert. MS 12.123–62. [MAGL III, 64–127.]
HALLER, RUDOLF. 1962. Untersuchungen zur Bedeutungsproblem in der antiken und mittelalterlichen Philosophie. Archiv für Begriffsgeschichte 7.1–57.
HASKINS, CHARLES H. 1923. The rise of universities. New York, Holt.
——. 1927. The Renaissance of the twelfth century. Cambridge, Mass., Harvard University Press.
HEER, FRIEDRICH. 1961. The Medieval world. New York, Mentor.
HENRY, DESMOND P. 1958. Why *grammaticus*? ALMA 28.165–80.
——. 1960. St Anselm's De grammatico. Philosophical Quarterly 10.115–26.
——. 1963. The early history of *suppositio*. Franciscan Studies 23.205–12.

——. 1964. The De grammatico of St Anselm. PMS, 18. Notre Dame, University Press.

——. 1967. The logic of St Anselm. Oxford, Clarendon.

HUNT, RICHARD W. 1948. The Introductiones to the 'Artes' in the twelfth century. Studia mediaevalia in honorem R.J. Martin, 85–112. Bruges.

JEAUNEAU, EDOUARD. 1960. Deux rédactions des gloses de Guillaume de Conches sur Priscien. Recherches de théologie ancienne et médiévale 27.213–47.

JOURDAIN, AMABLE L.M.M.B. 1960. Recherches critiques sur l'âge et l'origine des traductions latines d'Aristote et sur des commentaires grecs au arabes employés par les docteurs scholastiques. Rev. ed. et aug. par Charles Jourdain. New York, B. Franklin.

KNEALE, WILLIAM and MARTHA. 1962. The development of logic. Oxford, Clarendon Press.

KNOWLES, DAVID. 1962. The evolution of Medieval thought. London, Longmans.

KOCH, JOSEF ed. 1959. Artes liberales. Von der antiken Bildung zur Wissenschaften des Mittelalters. Leiden, Brill.

KOYRÉ, ALEXANDRE. 1944. Aristotélisme et platonisme dans la philosophie du moyen âge. Gants du ciel 4.75–107.

KRETZMANN, NORMAN. 1966. William of Sherwood's Introduction to logic. Minneapolis, University of Minnesota Press.

——. 1968. William of Sherwood's Treatise on syncategorematic words. Minneapolis, University of Minnesota Press.

——. 1970. Medieval logicians on the meaning of the *propositio*. Journal of Philosophy 67.767–87.

LACOMBE, GEORGES. 1939. Aristoteles Latinus. Pars Prior. Corpus Philosophorum Medii Aevi. Bruges, Desclee de Brouwer. [Rev. et aug. 1957.]

LEFF, GORDON. 1958. Medieval thought from Saint Augustin to Ockham. London, Penguin.

——. 1968. Paris and Oxford universities in the thirteenth and fourteenth centuries. New York, Wiley.

LEHMANN, PAUL. 1909. Einleitung in die lateinische Philologie des Mittelalters. Traube, Ludwig. 1906–20. Vorlesungen und Abhandlungen, Band 2. München, Beck.

——. 1914. Vom Mittelalter und von der lateinischen Philologie des Mittelalters. Traube, Ludwig. Quellen und Untersuchungen zur lateinischen Philologie des Mittelalters. Band 5. Heft 1. München, Beck.

——. 1944. Mitteilungen aus Handschriften VIII. SbBAW. München.

——. 1959ff. Erforschungen des Mittelalters. 5 vols. Stuttgart, Hiersemann.

LOHR, CHARLES H. 1969. Aristotle in the West. Traditio 25.417–31.

LUQUET, GEORGES H. 1904. Aristote et l'Université de Paris pendant le XIIIe siècle. Paris, E. Leroux.

LUSCOMBE, DAVID E. 1969. The school of Peter Abelard. Cambridge, Univ. Press.

MANITIUS, MAX. 1911–31. Geschichte der lateinischen Literatur des Mittelalters. 3 vols. München, Beck.

MANTHEY, FRANZ. 1937. Die Sprachphilosophie des hl. Thomas von Aquin und ihre Anwendung auf Probleme der Theologie. Paderborn, F. Schöningh.

MARKUS, R.A. 1961. The impact of Aristotle on Medieval thought. Blackfriars 42.96–102.

MCKEON, RICHARD P. 1942. Rhetoric in the Middle Ages. Speculum 17.1–32.

MCMULLIN, ERNAN. 1965. The concept of matter in Greek and Medieval Philosophy. Notre Dame, University Press.

MICHAUD-QUANTIN, PIERRE. 1969. L'emploi des termes *logica* et *dialecta* au Moyen Âge. Actes 4.855–62.

MINIO-PALUELLO, LORENZO. 1957. Les traductions et les commentaires aristotéciens de Boèce. Studia Patristica 2.358–65.

——., ed. 1961ff. Aristoteles Latinus. Corpus Philosophorum Medii Aevi. Leiden, E.J. Brill. (International Union of Academics.)

MOODY, ERNEST A. 1953. Truth and consequence in Medieval logic. Amsterdam, North-Holland.

——. 1964. A Quodlibetal question of Robert Holcot O.P. on the problems of the objects of knowledge and of belief. Speculum 39.53–74.

——. 1966. The medieval contribution to logic. SG 19.444–52.

MORAUX, PAUL. 1968. Aristoteles in der neueren Forschung. Darmstadt, Wissenschaftliche Buchgesellschaft.

MULLALLY, JOSEPH P. 1945. The Summulae logicales of Peter of Spain. PMS, 8. Notre Dame, University Press.

——. Trans. 1964. Peter of Spain, Tractatus syncategorematum. Introduction by Joseph P. Mullally and Roland Houde. Milwaukee, Marquette University Press.

MURPHY, JAMES J. 1961. The arts of discourse, 1050–1500. MS 23.194–205.

NEMETZ, ANTHONY A. 1956. Logic and the division of the sciences in Aristotle and St. Thomas Aquinas. The Modern Schoolman 33.91–109.

O'DONNELL, J. REGINALD, C.S.B. 1941. The Syncategoremata of William of Sherwood. MS 3.46–93.

OTTO, ALFRED. 1955. Magister Johannes Dacus und seine Schriften C&M 13.73–86.

PAETOW, LOUIS J. 1914. The Battle of the Seven Arts. Memoirs of the University of California, Vol. 4, No. 1. Berkeley.

PARÉ, GÉRARD M., ADRIEN M. BRUNET, and PIERRE TREMBLAY. 1933. La renaissance du XIIe siècle. Les écoles et l'enseignement. Publications de l'Institut d'Etudes. Médievales d'Ottawa, 3. Paris/Ottawa.

PATCH, HOWARD R. 1935. The tradition of Boethius: A study of his importance in Medieval culture. New York, Oxford University Press.

PELZER, AUGUSTE. 1964. Etudes d'histoire littéraire sur la scolastique médiévale. Philosophes médiévaux, 8. Louvain, Publications universitaires.

Perreiah, Alan R. 1971. Approaches to supposition theory. New Scholasticism 45.381–408.

Rashdall, Hastings. 1936. The universities of Europe in the Middle Ages. 3 vols. Rev. F.M. Powicke and A.B. Emden. Oxford, Clarendon Press.

Régis, Louis-M. 1969. L'être du langage et l'humanisme médiéval et contemporain. Actes 4.281–94.

Rijk, Lambertus M. de. 1956. Abelard Dialectica. Assen, Van Gorcum.

——. 1962–67. Logica modernorum. A contribution to the history of early Terminist logic. 3 vols. Assen, Van Gorcum.

——. 1968–70. On the genuine text of Peter of Spain's Summule logicales. Vivarium 6.1–34, 69–101; 7.8–61, 120–62; 8.10–55.

Roos, Heinrich. 1968. Der Unterschied zwischen Metaphysik und Einzelwissenschaft nach Boethius von Dacien. Miscellanea Mediaevalia 5.105–120.

——. 1969. Le 'Trivium' à l'université au XIIIe siècle. Actes 4.193–7.

Sajó, Géza. 1963. Boetius de Dacia und seine philosophische Bedeutung. Miscellanea Mediaevalia 2.454–63.

Sandys, John E. 1903–08. A history of classical scholarship. Cambridge, University Press.

Sharp, Dorothea E. 1934. The De ortu scientiarum of Robert Kilwardby. The New Scholasticism 8.1–30.

Sikes, Jeffrey G. 1932. Peter Abailard. Cambridge, University Press.

Sommer-Seckendorff, Ellen M.F. 1935. Robert Kilwarby und seine philosophische Einleitung De ortu scientiarum. Historisches Jahrbuch 55.312–24.

Southern, Richard W. 1953. The making of the Middle Ages. London, Hutchinson's University Library.

——. 1970. Medieval humanism and other studies. Oxford, Blackwell.

Steenberghen, Fernand van. 1955a. Aristotle in the West. Louvain, E. Nauwelaerts.

——. 1955b. The philosophical movement in the 13th century. Edinburgh, Nelson.

——. 1966. La philosophie au XIIIe siècle. Philosophes médiévaux, 9. Louvain, Publications Universitaires.

Taylor, Henry O. 1903. The classical heritage of the Middle Ages. New York, Macmillan.

——. 1938[4]. The mediaeval mind. 2 vols. London, Macmillan.

Thomson, S. Harrison. 1938. Robert Kilwardby's commentaries In Priscianum and In Barbarisnum Donati. New Scholasticism 12.52–65.

——. 1940. The writings of Robert Grosseteste, Bishop of Lincoln 1235–1253. Cambridge, University Press.

Trentman, John. 1968. Extraordinary language and Medieval logic. Dialogue 7.286–91.

Vignaux, Paul. 1938. La philosophie au Moyen Âge. Paris, Armand Colin.

VYVER, A. VAN DE. 1929. Les étapes du développement philosophique du haut moyen-âge. RBPh 8.425–52.

WEISHEIPL, JAMES A., O.P. 1964. Curriculum of the Faculty of Arts at Oxford in the early fourteenth century. MS 26.143–85.

——. 1965. Classification of the sciences in Medieval thought. MS 27.55–90.

——. 1966. Developments in the arts curriculum at Oxford in the early fourteenth century. MS 28.151–75.

——. 1969. The place of the liberal arts in the university curriculum during the 14th and 15th centuries. Actes 4.209–13.

WULF, MAURICE DE. 1922. Philosophy and civilisation in the Middle Ages. Princeton, University Press.

——. 1932. Courants doctrinaux dans la philosophie européenne du XIIIe siècle. Revue néoscolastique de philosophie 34.5–20.

——. 1934–47[6]. Histoire de la philosophie médiévale. 3 vols. Louvain, Institut supérieur de philosophie.

THE GRAMMATICAL TRADITION AND THE RISE OF THE VERNACULARS

W. KEITH PERCIVAL

1.0 The term *Renaissance*, as used by general historians, is ambiguous, sometimes referring to an intellectual movement and at other times to a period of history. The intellectual movement in question is customarily described by such expressions as 'the revival of classical learning' or 'the imitation of Greek and Roman design in the fine arts', while the period designated by the term is usually thought to extend from the mid-fourteenth century to the middle or end of the sixteenth. However, historians have held widely divergent opinions both as to the character of the intellectual movement and the precise boundaries of the period.

Though historians of linguistics may not have discovered this fact yet, a similar uncertainty affects the history of linguistics. Whether there ever was a characteristically Renaissance approach to language and grammatical theory is very much a debatable issue, as also is the question of the chronological boundaries of such a linguistic subtradition, if indeed such a thing can be demonstrated to have existed.

For the purpose of this essay I choose to consider as relevant to Renaissance grammatical theory certain trends in the grammatical tradition of southern Europe (in this instance Provence and Northern Italy) which coexisted in part with the development of modistic grammar in Northern France and Germany. It was in fact this southern version of the western grammatical tradition, flourishing in the thirteenth and fourteenth centuries, which provided a theoretical foundation for the grammatical productions of the fifteenth century humanists. One may therefore consider Renaissance linguistics to be nothing more than a further step in the development of medieval grammatical theory, a mere offshoot of one local variety of the medieval grammatical tradition.

From about the end of the fifteenth century, however, what looks like two genuinely novel features make their appearance: radical criticism of traditional grammatical concepts and the advent of vernacular grammatical writing. One might accordingly argue that the real break with the medieval past was signalled by such works as the Elder Scaliger's *De causis linguae Latinae* (1540) and Nebrija's Spanish grammar (1492). However, it can also be plausibly argued that Scaliger's book really points ahead to the philosophical and rational grammars of the seventeenth century, and that the beginnings of an interest in vernacular grammar go back to the Middle Ages (notably in the area of Provençal).

If we add a geographical dimension to the picture the problem of defining Renaissance linguistics becomes even more intractable. While humanistic grammars were being written in Italy, say in the mid-fifteenth century, the rest of Europe was still content with the medieval linguistic literature. (See Thurot's interesting remarks [1869:485–90].) Similarly, the vernacular grammatical writing of the fifteenth and sixteenth centuries was confined almost exclusively to Italy, France, and the Iberian peninsula. In England only two grammars appeared in the sixteenth century and each of them exists in no more than a single copy at the present time. In Eastern Europe, the Russian or Church Slavonic grammatical tradition continued to follow the Byzantine model, unaffected by developments in the West.

One must conclude, therefore, that the problem of periodization is not likely to receive a neat, esthetically satisfying solution, here as in other areas of historical research. But a much more serious problem affects the study of Renaissance linguistics, namely our relative ignorance of the primary source material. An enormous amount of grammatical literature is known to have been produced between 1350 and 1600, but so far very little of this literature has been examined by historians of linguistics, and very few grammatical works have been critically edited.

The historian must therefore be prepared to grapple with the primary sources in their pristine form. Much material from the fourteenth and early fifteenth centuries exists only in manuscript form. When printing arrived in Italy in the 1460s, many popular grammars were immediately issued in widely disseminated printed editions. But many other basic texts of the preceding period for one reason or another never appeared in print. Ideally, therefore, the historian of linguistics should be well versed in both paleography and bibliography. In practice, however, most historians of this period of linguistics confine their attention to printed sources, and in many instances make no attempt either to use the earliest known printed editions or to ascertain when and where the earliest known edition appeared. Needless to say, this practice has at times led them to formulate some rather bizarre hypotheses. For instance, Otto Funke (1941:14) hazards the supposition that in matters of linguistic theory Guarino Veronese (1374–1460) followed the example of Lorenzo Valla (1407–57), no doubt misled by the relative chronology of the *printed* editions to which he had access. As a matter of fact the direction of influence, if any existed, must have been the reverse: Guarino was already seventy years old when Valla's *Elegantiarum linguae Latinae opus* appeared around 1444.

A further obstacle in the way of an understanding of Renaissance grammatical theory is constituted by the existing secondary literature, which is scattered in innumerable journals, monographs and bibliographies, and has never been adequately surveyed. Furthermore, scholars working on the Latin grammatical tradition have been largely unaware of or at least uninterested in the work of scholars working on the vernacular traditions, and vice versa. A general picture of the development of linguistics in this period has therefore not emerged.

The aim of the present essay is to review some of the significant secondary literature about Renaissance linguistics. To make this review more understandable I shall first briefly survey the grammatical tradition itself, Latin, Greek, and vernacular, from the mid-fourteenth to the end of the sixteenth century. The essay will therefore fall into two halves, the first devoted to primary sources, the second to secondary literature. In each half there will be four main topics discussed: the late medieval grammars of Latin produced in Italy and Provence, the Latin grammars of the Renaissance humanists, Greek grammars of the late Middle Ages and Renaissance, and finally the vernacular grammatical traditions. The bibliography at the end of the chapter will be in two parts: the first a list of primary sources referred to in the essay, and the second a list of the secondary literature reviewed.

1.1 Renaissance linguistic theory had its origins in a tradition of lexicographic and grammatical writing which emerged in northern Italy and Provence in about the eleventh century and developed to some degree independently of the familiar northern tradition represented by the modistic treatises and the verse grammars (the *Doctrinale* of Alexandre de Villedieu and the *Graecismus* of Evrard de Béthune). The peculiarity of this southern tradition was that it was oriented towards rhetoric rather than dialectic, rhetoric in this instance being not the art of forensic eloquence but the techniques of written composition, or the *ars dictandi*, as it was called in those days.

The best known lexica produced in this tradition are the *Vocabularium* of Papias (1053), the *Derivationes magnae* of Uguccione (Hugutio) of Pisa (late twelfth century), and the *Catholicon* of John of Genoa (Ioannes Ianuensis de Balbis) (1286). In the area of grammar a number of influential works appeared: a grammatical compendium by Pietro da Isolella, based in part on an earlier work by the Provençal Sponcius, both from the thirteenth century; and from the early part of the same century a *Summa in grammaticam* by a Master Bene, who taught grammar in the University of Bologna. Both Uguccione and John of Genoa wrote grammars; that of the latter was extremely influential since it formed the introductory portion of the *Catholicon*. In the fourteenth century a number of grammars appeared, of which the following are especially noteworthy: the *Regule* of the Pisan Francesco da Buti, a compendium by the Cremonese Master Folchino dei Borfoni, and a treatise on syntax by a Master Philippus of Florence. Since these latter works appeared shortly before the advent of Renaissance humanism and quite clearly influenced the content and style of Renaissance grammars, it may be of interest to examine them in some detail.

Typically a grammar in this tradition consisted of a rather loose assemblage of short treatises on topics ranging from orthography to lexical semantics. Such grammars were intended to supplement the information found in elementary pedagogical grammars rather than to replace them. Generally a considerable amount of space was devoted to syntax, and especially to the phenomenon of verbal government. In some grammars we find general discussions of fundamental syntactic concepts (this is true, for instance, of the grammar of Folchino dei Borfoni). As a general rule, however, some of the most basic theoretical terms are left undefined and unexplained, their use being simply taken for granted. The terminology varies somewhat from grammar to grammar, but the bulk of the concepts involved are common to them all.

The main sentence constituents are described somewhat differently from the way they are treated in more familiar medieval sources. In a sentence such as *Antonius amat Martinum* 'Anthony loves Martin', *Antonius* is referred to as the agent (*persona agens*) and *Martinum* as the patient (*persona patiens*[1]). In the corresponding passive sentence *Martinus amatur ab Antonio* 'Martin is loved by Anthony', *Martinus* is the patient and *Antonio* the agent. The terms *subiectum* 'subject' and *praedicatum* 'predicate' are not used.[2] In their place we find the terms *suppositum* and *appositum*, the former designating the nominal expression to the left of the verb in the natural order, and the latter any nominal expression right of the verb.[3]

Thus in the first sentence the agent *Antonius* is the suppositum, and the patient *Martinum* the appositum, while in the second sentence the suppositum is *Martinus* and the appositum *Antonio.* The terms 'agent' and 'patient' are assigned on purely semantic grounds, so that, for example, in a sentence such as *ego gaudeo tuo bono* 'I rejoice in your good' the suppositum *ego* is the patient and the appositum *tuo bono* the agent. The terms *suppositum* and *appositum*, on the other hand, are applied on a formal basis.

Verbs are classified as personal or impersonal on morphological grounds (only personal verbs are conjugated in both numbers and all three persons), and also in terms of their associated *supposita:* personal verbs are preceded by a nominative, impersonals by an oblique case (e.g., *me taedet vitae* 'I am tired of life' with the accusative *me* left of the impersonal verb *taedet*). Verbs are then further subclassified on the basis of their associated *apposita.* For example, active verbs (i.e., those which have corresponding passive forms) govern a nominative on the left and on the right either a single appositum in the accusative, as in *Antonius amat Martinum*, or a pair of apposita, one of which is in the accusative and the other in one of the oblique cases. An active verb which governs an accusative and a genitive (e.g., *ego accuso Petrum furti*

[1] These examples and those which follow are from the *Regule* of Francesco da Buti. I am quoting from Bodleian MS. Canon. Misc. 196.

[2] John of Genoa, for instance, makes it clear that the terms *subiectum* and *praedicatum* are logical, not grammatical terms. See *Catholicon*, sig. f6vb.

[3] John of Genoa's definitions of these two terms are at variance with the usage of later grammarians, in that for him the *appositum* includes the main verb and hence is referentially equivalent to the logicians' term *praedicatum*: 'Scias quod partes constructionis sunt duae, scilicet suppositum et appositum. Suppositum est illud de quo loquimur, et dicitur in dialectica *subiectum.* Appositum est illud quod de altero dicitur, et appellatur in dialectica *praedicatum.* Et scias quod quicquid praecedit verbum principale vel intellegitur praecedere est suppositum. Verbum vero principale cum toto illo quod sequitur est appositum' (*Catholicon*, sig. f6vb.). The notion that the natural order of constituents is subject — verb — object appears to be shared by all medieval grammarians. Compare the following verses from the *Graecismus* (XXVII, verses 14–18; Wrobel 1887:247):

Vult, si *praeveniat* verbum, rectus tibi fiat
Regula, nam verbo personam reddere dico.
Si *sequitur* verbum, datur haec tibi regula: verbum
Omne vocativum substantivumque vel altrum
Istis consimile casus similes habet in se...

'I accuse Peter of theft') is called a *possessive* active verb; one which governs an accusative and a dative (e.g., *do tibi filium meum* 'I give you my son') is termed an *acquisitive* active; one which takes two accusatives (e.g., *ego doceo Petrum grammaticam* 'I teach Peter grammar') a *transitive* active; one which governs an accusative and an ablative (e.g., *ego impleo Petrum virtutibus* 'I fill Peter with virtues') an *effective* active; and finally one which governs an accusative and an ablative preceded by the preposition *a/ab* (e.g., *averte faciem tuam a peccatis meis* 'turn thy face away from my sins') a *separative* active.

Neuter verbs (i.e., verbs which have only an active voice) and deponent verbs (i.e., verbs which conjugate only in the passive voice) are similarly classified. Thus neuter possessives govern a genitive (e.g., *ego egeo denariorum* 'I need money'), neuter acquisitives a dative (e.g., *tu oboedis magistris* 'you obey the masters'), neuter transitives an accusative (e.g., *ego laboro terram* 'I cultivate the soil'), and so forth.

It was customary in these grammars to describe each verbal subclass in formulaic terms and to append a list of its members. The enumerated items were quoted in their principal parts (e.g., *emo is emi emptum*) and followed by a vernacular gloss (*per comprare*). Semantic or syntactic peculiarities of some of the verbs listed (verbs governing different cases with a change of meaning and so forth) were discussed at the end of each section, sometimes in the form of a mnemonic verse, and a sentential example was occasionally added together with a vernacular translation.

The verb was said to govern the various nominal expressions in the sentence by virtue of certain specified "influences" which caused the governed noun to be in such and such a case rather than some other. Thus the nominative *suppositum* to the left of the verb was said to be governed by virtue of *intransitio* (*nominativus regitur a parte ante ex natura intransitionis*), and the accusative *appositum* to the right by virtue of *transitio* (*accusativus regitur a parte post ex natura transitionis*).[4] The rationale behind the terms *intransitio* and *transitio* lay in the notion that the action denoted by a verb in a sentence containing both a subject and an object passes (*transit*) from the person denoted by the subject to that denoted by the object, whereas no such transition of action takes place in a sentence which lacks an object. The two types of construction involved were termed *transitive* and *intransitive* respectively, and the relation between a verb and its object (in those cases where an object occurs) was called 'transition' and the relation between a verb and its subject 'intransition'.[5] Hence in a transitive construction both transition and intransition were present, the one account-

[4] I am quoting here from the grammar of Francesco da Buti, Bodleian MS. Canon. Misc. 196, fol. 2r.

[5] The division of constructions into transitive and intransitive goes back (in the Latin grammatical tradition) to Priscian (XIV, 14; XIII, 23) and seems to have been adhered to by all medieval grammarians. Compare the following statement in the *Doctrinale* (Verses 1370–73; Reichling 1893:87):

In geminas species constructio scinditur: illi
Transitio debet intransitioque subesse.
Cum partes, per quas constat constructio plena,
Signant diversa, constructio transeat illa...

ing for the case of the object and the other for the case of the subject. In this way the concept of transition functioned both to classify constructions and to explain the workings of verbal government.

Other verb-noun relations could of course not be explained in this way, and a whole battery of explanatory notions had to be elaborated to handle them all.[6] Use was made, for example, of the four Aristotelian causes. Thus the ablative case in a sentence such as *ego impleo Martinum virtutibus* 'I fill Martin with virtues' was said to be governed by virtue of the material cause (*ex natura causae materialis*), and the ablative in passive sentences (e.g., *ego amor a Petro* 'I am loved by Peter') by virtue of the efficient cause (*ex natura causae efficientis*). In other cases the explanatory term chosen was purely *ad hoc*; for example, the genitive in sentences such as *extimo istam domum centum librarum* 'I estimate the value of that house at a hundred pounds' was said to be governed by virtue of *pretium* 'price'. The same case could be governed by virtue of many different 'natures' in different constructions. Indeed in the grammar of Francesco da Buti a list of the different ways in which each case can be governed is provided. The genitive and dative, it seems, can be governed in four ways, the accusative and ablative in eight. The nominative can be governed by a verb in two ways: on the left by virtue of intransition, as we have seen, and on the right by virtue of *similis copulatio* as in sentences such as *ego sum bonus* 'I am good'.

Grammarians did not, however, agree in all instances as to what explanatory term was appropriate for a given verb-noun relation. For example, the second accusative in sentences such as *ego doceo te grammaticam* 'I teach you grammar' seems to have caused a great deal of trouble, some grammarians claiming that it was governed *ex vi causae materialis* 'by virtue of the material cause', others that it was governed *ex natura transitionis accidentalis* 'by virtue of accidental transition' (Folchino dei Borfoni), or *ex natura secundi actus* 'by virtue of the second action' (Francesco da Buti).[7]

Another feature of some grammars in this tradition is the use of several different terms to designate the phenomenon of government. Thus Francesco da Buti uses the terms *regere* and *velle* to refer to the influence of a verb on the case of its associated nominal expressions, and the term *determinare* to refer to the converse relation holding between a nominal expression and the verb or other word which governs it. Thus nouns occurring to the right of passive, neuter, and deponent verbs are said to determine the verbs which govern them, or more precisely such verbs are said to be deter-

[6] Compare the passages from Petrus Helias (12th century) cited by Thurot (1869:244–5). In the *Doctrinale* the formula is *ex vi* or *per vim* rather than *ex natura* (see Verses 1081, 1248, 1250, 1254, 1270; Reichling 1893:71, 81, 82).

[7] See the article on *doceo* in the *Catholicon*, sig. r7rb: 'Quidam tamen dicunt, quod primus [accusativus] regitur ex natura transitionis, et alius ex vi causae materialis... Ex qua autem natura praedicta verba regant duos accusativos duplex est opinio posita, et potest addi tertia: quod videlicet praedicta verba regant duos diversos accusativos ex natura transitionis hac ratione, quia pertinent ad duos actus. Nam quicumque docet agit due: agit enim in discipulum quem docet, et agit in artem quam ostendit, et ideo duos accusativos regunt. Sed quia illae duae transitiones sunt diversarum naturarum, non debent copulari, quia una transitio est dependens, altera perficiens, et haec opinio magis mihi placet.'

mined by them. Thus Francesco da Buti describes the passive verb as follows: 'The passive verb requires to be preceded by a nominative patient and to be determined by an ablative agent' (*vult suppositum per nominativum rei patientis et determinari per ablativum rei agentis a vel ab mediante*).[8] However, this converse relation does not hold between the object of an active verb and the verb it governs: such a constituent was not said to be determined by the nouns which occur to its right.

In some grammars in this tradition the modistic terms *terminare* and *dependere* also make their appearance. Thus in the grammar of Master Philippus of Florence the syntax of the passive verb is described thus: 'The passive verb establishes a dependency to its right by virtue of the (semantic) mode "action exerted by the other (i.e., by the referrent of the other nominal expression)" whereby it governs an ablative agent which is the terminating constituent of the grammatical dependency (of the verb)' (*Verbum passivum dependet a parte post per modum actus illati ab altero, per quem modum regit ablativum mediante a vel ab personae agentis qui terminat suam propriam dependentiam, ut doceor a te*).[9]

To sum up, the main features of the syntactic theory of grammars in this tradition were the following: Sentences are described as if the constituents occur in the natural order, i.e., subject, verb, object. The verb governs all the nominal expressions in the sentence, including the subject. The noun denoting the performer of the action is called the agent (*persona agens*), and the undergoer of the action the patient (*persona patiens*). The nominal constituents to the left and right of the verb are called the *suppositum* and *appositum*, respectively. Verbs are allotted to subclasses depending on what case or set of cases they govern to the right. Government is assumed to involve a semantic influence exerted by the verb on the various nominal expressions in the sentence. These influences are categorized in such a way that the choice of a particular case after the verb can be attributed to one of them. The list of these influences varies somewhat from grammar to grammar.

In general, however, many quite basic grammatical concepts are left undefined, and their meanings can only be inferred from the way in which they were used. In the grammars I have so far examined it is not clear, for example, what the precise extension of the term *appositum* was. Did it apply to a substantive governed by a preposition to the right of a verb (as for instance the *ecclesiam* 'church' in a sentence such as *vado ad ecclesiam* 'I go to church')? It seems reasonably clear that the terms *suppositum, appositum, persona agens*, etc., referred to single nouns and not to whole noun phrases. Clauses were called 'sentences' and were sometimes referred to in rules. In the grammar of Folchino dei Borfoni, for instance, a subject clause is called *oratio posita loco nominativi* 'a sentence replacing a nominative'.

Finally a salient feature of the grammars in this tradition is the emphasis placed on correct translation of vernacular constructions into Latin and the regular use of vernacular glosses and translations throughout. Such grammars were designed to pre-

[8] Bodleian MS. Canon. Misc. 196, fol. 2v.

[9] Florence, Biblioteca Medicea-Laurenziana, Ashburnham 243, fol. 2r.

pare the student to compose correctly in Latin. It was necessary therefore to catalogue the various ways in which Latin and the vernacular differed.

1.2 The fourteenth century humanists were satisfied with the existing grammatical literature and did nothing to add to it. It was not until the fifteenth century that something new was produced. The first area to receive attention was orthography. The discovery of earlier (Carolingian) manuscripts of the Roman authors and the study of inscriptions led to the general realization that the system of Latin orthography then in vogue was in many instances (e.g., in the matter of diphthongs) at variance with the usage of the ancients. Several humanists such as Coluccio Salutati and Niccolò Niccoli, tried their hand at the problem, but it was Gasparino Barzizza who made the first major contribution (c. 1418), to be followed some years later by Giovanni Tortelli who produced an encyclopedic dictionary entitled *De orthographia* (c. 1450).

As regards elementary texts, the humanists continued to use the ones which had been popular in the thirteenth century, i.e., the *Doctrinale* of Alexandre de Villedieu and the *Graecismus* of Evrard de Béthune (both c. 1200), the *Ars Minor* of Donatus, and a widely disseminated anonymous compilation with the incipit *Ianua sum rudibus primam cupientibus artem*,[10] which was Priscianic in inspiration. (The latter was still appearing in printed editions in the late sixteenth century).[11]

In the area of syntax, however, a reform of the medieval system was undertaken by Guarino Veronese (1374–1460), who wrote the first humanistic grammatical treatise, the *Regulae grammaticales* some time before 1418. Guarino's grammar was the prototype on which all subsequent humanistic grammars of Latin were based. It was an extremely popular work and appeared in a large number of manuscript and printed editions, generally together with his lexicographical work, the *Carmina differentialia*, or *Versus differentiales*, which was concerned with the differentiation of synonyms, homonyms, and related phenomena. Frequently Guarino's orthographical treatise *De diphthongis* was also included in such editions.

A number of grammars by Italian humanists show unmistakable signs of Guarinian influence, such as for example the grammar of Gasparo Veronese who taught in Rome during the pontificate of Nicolas V (1447–55). The first complete Latin grammar in the new humanistic style was the *Rudimenta grammatices* of Niccolò Perotti (1468). This work (catechetical in style) consists of three parts: an elementary morphology, a syntax in the style of Guarino's *Regulae*, and a treatise on epistolary composition. Perotti's grammar like Guarino's, was reprinted many times, in Italy as well as in Germany and France. The German version was edited by Bernard Perger (Passau, 1482, or possibly earlier), and was entitled significantly *Grammatica nova* 'New grammar'. The middle section of Perotti's grammar is rather more elaborated than Guarino's *Regulae.*

[10] Thurot describes a manuscript of the *Ianua* in the Bibliothèque Nationale (1869:47).

[11] I am familiar with the following edition: Aelius Donatus, *Erudimenta grammatice* (Venice, Ioannes Gryphius), 1572. For a list of incunabular editions see the *Gesamtkatalog der Wiegendrucke* (VII:662–75, Nos. 8987–9028).

Other Latin grammars written in Italy closely resemble those of Guarino and Perotti. Thus the *Erudimenta grammatices latinae linguae* (1510) attributed to Benedictus Philologus (Benedetto Riccardini) consists of a Guarinian syntax followed by a manual of epistolary style similar to the one provided by Perotti. The famous Venetian printer Aldo Manuzio also wrote a grammar, the *Institutionum grammaticarum libri quattuor* (1493), which contains an elementary morphology (like Perotti's grammar), a syntax and a treatise on metrics.

The influential Guarinian syntactic system has the following salient features: The concepts *suppositum* and *appositum* are avoided, but the notions 'agent' and 'patient' occupy the same crucial position as they did in the fourteenth century grammars; the terms *transitio* and *intransitio* are dispensed with altogether. The notion of government remains at the heart of the system, and the terms *ante se* 'left of the verb' and *post se* 'right of the verb' are regularly used in definitions of the verbal subclasses. Thus the acquisitive active verbs are described as follows: 'There are certain active verbs which require to the left of them a nominative agent and to the right of them an accusative patient and in addition to the accusative they govern a dative, as in *do tibi panem* 'I give you bread'. (*Nota quod sunt quaedam verba activa quae volunt ante se nominativum personae agentis et post se accusativum personae patientis, et ultra accusativum volunt dativum, ut* do tibi panem).[12]

Guarino's syntax is then in fact a medieval syntax with certain crucial concepts excised. In other words grammatical theory may be said to have undergone a purge at the hands of Guarino, and though some medieval concepts (e.g., the notions *appositum* and *suppositum*) survived into the sixteenth century in some grammars,[13] Guarino's intervention seems to have been decisive.

It should, however, be emphasized that throughout the fifteenth and well into the sixteenth century, medieval grammatical works continued to be transcribed and printed, and hence, we must assume, widely used. Modistic grammars, for example, were still being reprinted in the sixteenth century and modistic concepts are clearly discernible in some philosophical discussions of language, as for example in the

[12] I am quoting from an early incunabular edition of which there is a copy in the Biblioteca Marciana in Venice (Guarnaschelli 3.58, No. 4528; Hain lists it as No. 8108 and claims that it was printed by Jensen, which cannot have been the case; see Brown 1891:12). The passage on acquisitive active verbs is on fol. 6v. It should be pointed out that like Francesco da Buti Guarino does not use the terms *acquisitive*, *possessive*, etc., in referring to active verbs, but only for the neuter and deponent classes. This is a practice which is also followed by Perotti, who numbers the active subclasses and uses the epithets to refer to the neuter and deponent subclasses. Folchino dei Borfoni, on the other hand, uses the epithets for all subclasses. Note that I have simplified my exposition by following Folchino's practice in this regard. It is, of course, small details such as this one which allow one to establish historical relations between grammars.

[13] The term *suppositum* puts in an occasional appearance in Perotti's *Rudimenta*, but only in the treatise on epistolary style, not in the main body of the grammar. The following statement is a sample: 'Nam cum in oratione plura sunt supposita, verbum sequi debet ultimum suppositum, ut *ego te de grammatica, tu me de epistolis percontaris*.' (Note the allusion here to Cicero, *De re publica*, 6.9). In the sixteenth century the term still crops up; see, for example, the *Minerva* of Francisco Sánchez, Book I, Chapter 12, fol. 28v).

important *De veris principiis et vera ratione philosophandi contra pseudophilosophos by* Mario Nizzoli (Parma, 1553, sig. C2r). Traces of modistic terminology can be seen in many of the more heavily interpolated editions of Guarino's *Regulae grammaticales* in definitions of the parts of speech. In Spain and Portugal the pre-humanistic grammar of Juan Pastrana (the *Compendium grammatice*) was still popular in the sixteenth century in spite of the impact of the works of the humanist Antonio de Nebrija.[14] In Italy and Germany the *Catholicon* of John of Genoa was printed a number of times in the incunabular period. We also know from statements by Francisco Sánchez de las Brozas that medieval grammar and logic persisted at the University of Salamanca until well into the sixteenth century (see *Minerva*, sigs. A3r-A4v).

The humanists, however, kept up a constant campaign against medieval Latinity and medieval grammatical and lexicographical literature, at least from the mid-fifteenth century onwards. The work which epitomized this attitude was the *Elegantiarum linguae Latinae libri sex* of Lorenzo Valla (c. 1444), a massive, rather disorganized stylistic manual which was immensely popular for the next two centuries. However, explicit criticisms of particular medieval grammatical concepts do not occur in the *Elegantiae* and the book does not contain, as far as I am aware, any references to modistic theory or any attack on the basic theoretical notions I have discussed above in connection with the Italian medieval tradition.

The real assault on medieval grammatical theory began in the closing years of the fifteenth century. Alexander Hegius, a north German humanist, for instance, attacked modistic grammar in his *Invectiva in modos significandi* (c. 1486). The verse grammars had frequently been referred to in disparaging terms by the Italian humanists (Valla poured scorn on the *Graecismus* in his *Elegantiae* (Preface to book II)[15] and even wrote a short treatise pointing out certain mistakes in the *Doctrinale*), but it was not until the turn of the century that the actual banning of these medieval textbooks from the school curriculum was undertaken, chiefly by northern humanists. The grammars of the Flemish humanist Jan Despauter (early sixteenth century) may be said to be an attempt to provide a complete corpus of grammatical texts to replace the medieval ones.[16]

[14] Nebrija was the author of an extremely popular primer entitled *Introductiones in latinam grammaticen* (first edition Salamanca, 1481). See Palau X:459.

[15] 'Post hunc [sc. Isidorum] Papias aliique indoctiores, Eberhardus, Hugutio, Catholicon, Aymo, et ceteri indigni qui nominentur, magna mercede docentes nihil scire, aut stultiorem reddentes discipulum quam acceperunt' ('After him [viz. Isidore of Seville] came Papias and others more ignorant: Evrard [de Béthune], Uguccione, [the author of] the *Catholicon*, Aymo, and others not worthy of mention, who in exchange for a large fee taught students to know nothing, turning out pupils who were more stupid than they had been when admitted'), *Opera* (Basel, Henricus Petrus), 1543, p. 41.

[16] Despauter's grammars were extremely popular in France and the Low Countries throughout the next century and a half. A convenient collection of them was published by the Parisian printer Robert Estienne (Robertus Stephanus) in 1537, entitled *Commentarii grammatici*. They were originally written between about 1500 and 1520 and include a *Rudimenta* (1514), a morphology entitled *Prima pars grammaticae* (1512), the *Syntaxis* (1511, reprinted as late as 1744), treatises on metrics, figures, orthography, and epistolary style. In general Despauter relied on the old device of mnemonic verses, interspersed with commentary.

Erasmus, the greatest northern humanist of them all, indulged in acrimonious criticism of the modistic system. However, his own contribution to grammatical literature was modest: he published a treatise on syntax (*Libellus de octo orationis partium constructione*), a dialogue on the correct pronunciation of Latin and Greek (*De recta latini graecique sermonis pronunciatione dialogus*), and an alphabetically arranged summary of the *Elegantiae* of Lorenzo Valla (*Epitome in elegantiarum libros Laurentii Vallae*). His most substantial linguistic work was a manual of style, which may be said to epitomize the humanistic approach to the problem of literary composition (*De copia verborum ac rerum libri duo*).[17]

Philipp Melanchthon, the foremost Protestant humanist, wrote an elementary manual (*Elementa Latinae grammatices*, 1526), and a syntax (*Syntaxis*, 1526).

In England the popular text-book was the so-called *Short introduction of grammar*, a grammatical compilation written by a number of different hands and subsequently most often attributed to William Lily.

In the sixteenth century the grammarians began to criticize the grammatical tradition itself. Signs of this were already apparent in some of the writers of the preceding century. Lorenzo Valla, for example, while declaring an admiration for the triumvirate Donatus, Servius, and Priscian (Preface to book II of the *Elegantiae*), did not scruple to criticize them harshly on occasion.

The supreme example of the destructive critic of the grammatical tradition was, however, Julius Caesar Scaliger, whose *De causis linguae Latinae libri tredecim* (1540) influenced subsequent grammatical theorizing in both the Latin and the vernacular traditions. Scaliger's book is, as he saw it himself, a philosophical rather than a grammatical treatise,[18] and was written from an Aristotelian viewpoint, the prevailing purpose being to exhibit the wrongheadedness of the terminology and definitions of the grammarians. Significantly the book is not provided with a table of contents, but with a list of the errors corrected in each chapter! In the course of these criticisms, however, Scaliger makes a multitude of interesting observations and constructive suggestions some of which entered the grammatical tradition and became part and parcel of subsequent theories. Above all the underlying rationalist attitude to tradition (witness such remarks as the following: 'Verum interest philosophi placitis

[17] The text of the works mentioned can be found in the *Opera omnia* (ed. Le Clerc), volume 1.

[18] In a later publication, the *Poetics*, Scaliger makes the following significant remark (Book I, Chapter 5): 'Quare stultissime nobis grammatici nomen imponunt ex libro nostro *De causis linguae latinae*. Omnia enim illa ad libellam philosophiae appensa sunt. Nam quemadmodum probare potest artifex principia sua? Atqui probamus ibi nos, quaecunque a grammaticis pro notis accipiuntur.' At the same time, however, Scaliger claimed that grammar was part of philosophy, invoking the authority of Aristotle: 'Cuius [sc. Aristotelis] profecto iudicio Grammaticam non solum esse philosophiae partem, id quod nemo sanus negat, sed ne ab eius quidem cognitione dissolvi posse intellegeremus' (*De Causis*, Preface). Needless to say, this view of the relation between grammar and philosophy was highly unorthodox. The traditional view assigned grammar to the propaedeutical disciplines, which furnished the student with a preparation to enable him later to attack the study of philosophy and theology.

humanis anteponere rationem; nihil enim pretiosius veritate: ea enim hominis solius sola meta est' — Book II Chapter 63, p. 108) was immensely influential.

As a sample of Scaliger's method we may consider his discussion of verb classes (Book V, Chapter 110, pp. 221–2). He repudiates the traditional division of verbs into active, passive, neuter, common, and deponent, and replaces it by a simple dichotomy, viz. active versus passive. Actives he then subdivides into transitive (those which take an object) and absolute (those which do not), and passive verbs into those which occur with a subject, and those which do not. He abolishes entirely the class of impersonal verbs by demonstrating that such verbs have covert personal subjects.

Earlier works in a similar vein to Scaliger's *De causis* were the brilliant *De emendata structura latini sermonis libri sex* (1523) by the English humanist Thomas Linacre, and two works by Italian humanists, the *De rebus non vulgaribus* (1504) by Curio Lancellotto Pasi da Ferrara, and the *Mercurius maior* (1531) by Agostino Saturnio. Linacre's work is notable in that it emphasized the distinction between normal and figurative construction (*constructio iusta* and *constructio figurata*), i.e., syntax strictly in accordance with the rules of grammar as against syntax involving a (permissible) breach of normal grammatical rules due to some syntactic figure. Linacre is responsible for the famous theory of ellipsis which was to be so popular in subsequent centuries (book VI). He also rejected the system of describing verbal syntax which had been customary hitherto, i.e., the system of verbal subclasses as expounded in such grammars as Perotti's *Rudimenta*.

An equally uncompromising stance against tradition was adopted by Pierre de la Ramée (Petrus Ramus) in his *Scholae grammaticae* (1559). Ramus applied his logical method of dichotomies to grammatical theory — with dubious success, it must be admitted.

The final outcome of the revolution set in motion by these critics of the grammatical tradition was a new orthodoxy, a synthesis of the old and new, represented above all by two works by humanists from the Iberian peninsula, Francisco Sánchez de las Brozas (Franciscus Sanctius Brocensis) and Manoel Alvares (Immanuel Alvarus). Of these two Alvares was the more traditional in his approach. His *De institutione grammatica*, the first edition of which was printed by João de Barreira in Lisbon in 1572, became the official Latin grammar of the Jesuit order and was reprinted scores of times in the next two centuries, even appearing in a number of vernacular translations. (A Japanese translation appeared in 1594!). It covers the entire field of grammar as understood at that time: rudimenta, morphology, syntax and metrics. The overall arrangement is methodical and unusually perspicuous. The author makes use of mnemonic verses and vernacular glosses (in this he continues the southern grammatical tradition). There are long theoretical discussions interspersed in the text in which the opinions of both the ancient and modern grammarians are carefully weighed and balanced.

Francisco Sánchez wrote a number of grammatical works, the most famous of which is the *Minerva seu de causis linguae latinae* (Salamanca, 1587). Unlike Alvares' grammar the *Minerva* is an extremely complex work,[19] badly organized, and written in a polemical and at times almost vituperative style.[20] Sánchez appears to disagree with all his predecessors in the grammatical tradition. In fact, however, the *Minerva* shows unmistakable evidence of the influence of Thomas Linacre (in the theory of ellipsis), Julius Caesar Scaliger (in the basic classifications and definitions), and Petrus Ramus (in the underlying pedagogical theory). Indeed at times Sánchez did not scruple to plagiarize from authors whose ideas he elsewhere attacked most virulently.[21]

In the area of grammatical theory the two salient features of the *Minerva* are the attack on the customary theory of government and the claim that each of the nominal cases has the same basic meaning in all constructions in which it appears. Sánchez denied that the verb governs all the nominal constituents in the sentence: 'The nominative is never governed (by the verb), for in the sentence *Cato writes, Cato* is not governed by the verb, nor is *writes* governed by *Cato.* Rather there is agreement between noun and verb, and Cato is the *suppositum,* not the agent or patient, as grammarians have vainly argued' (Book II, Chapter 2, fol. 45v).[22]

The following is an example of the way in which he argues for his case theory: 'The genitive always denotes the possessor, either in the active or the passive sense, e.g., *father's love, Achilles' wound.* Hence the genitive cannot be governed by the verb. For the possessor and the thing possessed are relative terms, as the logicians call them,

[19] The book consists of two separately foliated parts (272+16+7 unnumbered leaves), the second of which is a reprint of Sánchez' earlier *Verae brevesque grammatices latinae institutiones* (first edition Lyons, Sebastian Gryphius, 1562). The first part, however, is by no means a simple bibliographical entity, being composed of an expanded version of an earlier treatise entitled *Minerva,* which Sánchez had appended to some editions of the *Institutiones,* together with several sections from another earlier book of his entitled *Paradoxa,* which had appeared in Antwerp in 1582. The *Minerva* proper is in four books, only the first three of which consist of numbered chapters. In seventeenth and eighteenth century editions the chapters of Book IV were numbered. I have made references to the *Minerva* by book and chapter number, to facilitate reference to later editions, and have added the leaf numbers (followed by *r* or *v* for *recto* and *verso* respectively) of the first edition.

[20] An extreme example of Sánchez' contumely is his tirade against Agostino Saturnio, the author of the *Mercurius maior,* of which the following remark is a sample: 'O mentis inops, quae te vexat dementia? hic tecum fustibus agendum erat, non rationibus' (Book III, Chapter 1, fol. 88v).

[21] The most interesting example of this is Sánchez' reproof of Quintilian in Book I, Chapter 2. He attacks Quintilian for including in grammar the interpretation of the poets (*enarratio poetarum,* see Quintilian I, 4.2): 'Vulgi errorem secutus est Quintilianus. Dicebantur enim quondam grammatici vulgo, qui primis rudimentis pueros instituebant, et eis poetas enarrabant, quo in munere subeundo adhibebant praeter grammaticam variarum artium cognitionem. Neque tamen vulgus intellegebat doctorem illum musicae, astrologiae, philosophiae esse peritum.' (fols. 8r–8v). Compare this passage with the following from Ramus's *Distinctiones in Quintilianum* (Paris, A. Wechel, 1559): 'Qui error ex imperitae plebeculae ... errore profectus est. Dicebantur enim quondam grammatici vulgo, qui in litteris pueros instituebant, et eis poetas enarrabant, quo in munere adhibenda esset artium praeter grammaticam variarum cognitio. Nec tamen vulgus intellegebat doctorem illum, qui in poetis explicandis varias artes doceret, esse quoque et historicum, et musicum, et astrologum, et philosophum, et rhetoricae peritum, non autem grammaticum tantum' (pp. 30–1).

[22] 'Rectus praeterea nunquam regitur, nam in hac oratione *Cato scribit, Cato* non regitur a verbo, nec *scribit* a *Cato.* Sed concordia est nominis et verbi, et *Cato* suppositum est, non persona agens aut patiens, ut somniant grammatici.'

since the one cannot be understood without the other. Verbs can denote 'possess', but never 'possessor'. Since the grammarians were unaware of this fact they set up various subclasses of verbs which govern the genitive. Such errors must be dispelled one by one. In verbs denoting price and estimate the genitive which sometimes accompanies them is governed by a noun, not by the verb. For example, in *magni emi* 'I bought it at a large price', the word *pretio* 'price' is understood, for the whole sentence is essentially *emi hoc magni aeris pretio.* (Book II, Chapter 3, fol. 46r).[23]

Sánchez adopts Scaliger's division of verbs into active and passive, but does not further subdivide the active class into transitive and absolute, on the grounds that in a sentence containing an intransitive verb a cognate object is understood. Thus in the case of the so-called neuter verbs, *vivo* 'to live', *ambulo* 'to walk', and *sedeo* 'to sit', the cognate accusatives *vitam* 'life', *ambulationem* 'walk', and *sessionem* 'sitting position' are understood (Book III, Chapter 3, fols. 93r-v, 116v). With regard to passive verbs Sánchez defends the position that the accompanying ablative with *a* or *ab* cannot possibly denote the agent since in many cases it is not present at all and cannot be supplied from the context. Hence his rule: 'Passivum verbum nihil praeter suppositum desiderat' (Book III, Chapter 4, fol. 122v).

In spite of the paradoxical character of some of Sánchez' discussions the *Minerva* was a very influential work. This is due to the fact that it was discovered by Caspar Schoppe and reprinted with notes by him in 1663 (Padua, Paulo Frambotti), and a year later in a widely disseminated Amsterdam edition (published by Judocus Pluymer). Schoppe also adopted many of Sánchez' ideas in his influential *Grammatica philosophica* (Milan, 1628). Sánchez' influence can also be detected in the *De arte grammatica libri septem* of Gerardus Vossius (Amsterdam 1635), and the Port-Royal *Nouvelle Méthode pour apprendre facilement ... la langue latine* (1644, 1650, 1653, etc.), from the second edition of that work onwards.

Editions of the *Minerva* continued to appear well into the nineteenth century. From 1687 editions were provided with copious footnotes by Jacob Perizonius, in which a great many of Sánchez' less defensible notions were corrected. By a strange quirk of fortune, therefore, the *Minerva* became one of the most influential grammatical works in the western grammatical tradition, outlasting much more original productions such as the *De Causis* of the Elder Scaliger to which it owed so much.

Summing up the whole development, one may say that there were roughly three periods in the development of Renaissance grammar. In the first period only medieval grammatical handbooks were used. In the second period, which was inaugurated by Guarino's *Regulae* (early fifteenth century), medieval theories of syntax were aban-

[23] 'Genitivus perpetuo significat possessorem, sive active sive passive capiatur, ut *amor patris, vulnus Achillis*, unde fit ut a verbo regi non possit. Nam possessor et res possessa nomina relata sunt, ut vocant dialectici, cum alterum sine altero nequeat intellegi. Possidere verba significabunt, at possessionem nunquam. Haec cum ignorarent grammatici, varias species statuerunt verborum quae genitivum regerent, quae peccata singillatim discutienda sunt. In verbis pretii et aestimationis si sit genitivus, a nomine non a verbo regitur, ut *magni emi*, deest *pretio*; integrum enim erat *emi hoc magni aeris pretio*.'

doned and replaced by new ones, the operation being in the nature of an anatomical excision of undesirable parts of the medieval tradition. However, little in the way of original or novel concepts was introduced at this time. The abandonment of medieval syntax was, it seems, motivated chiefly by considerations of pedagogical effectiveness rather than by any deep-seated theoretical misgivings, and indeed much of the medieval system remained intact.

In the third period, the hostility to medieval grammar intensified, medieval textbooks were finally driven out of the schools, and at the same time a genuine attempt was made to rethink whole portions of traditional grammatical lore. The result of this was an uneasy period of rebellion, epitomized by the Elder Scaliger's *De causis linguae Latinae* (1540), and the Ramist movement. By the end of the sixteenth century, however, the revolution had been contained and new authorities arose (the textbooks of Sánchez and Alvares) which were to hold sway until the nineteenth century.

1.3 Until the sixteenth century almost all Greek grammars were written by Greeks.[24] A vigorous tradition of grammatical writing — continuing the familiar Alexandrian tradition which so profoundly influenced Roman grammarians such as Remmius Palaemon and Priscian — existed throughout the Middle Ages in the Byzantine Empire. The culminating work in this tradition was the *Erotemata* of Manuel Moschopulos (c. 1265–1316), an elementary grammar written in the catechetical style.

The main characteristics of the inflectional model used by the Byzantine grammarians were the following: Verbal conjugations were described according to the system we see exemplified in the grammar of Dionysius Thrax (2nd century B.C.) while nominal declensions were treated in the manner of Theodosius of Alexandria (4th century A.D.). Nouns were classified into patterns according to the ending of the nominative singular, not as in the West according to the genitive singular ending. This principle of classification yielded a total of 56 patterns — clearly a very cumbersome system. The only Greek grammar which classified nouns on the basis of their genitive singular endings was the one by Roger Bacon, i.e., a westerner, and he obviously arrived at this result by applying the familiar Palaemonian system to Greek.

Some simplifications were introduced by two fourteenth century grammarians: Nilus Diassorinus and Manuel Calecas. The former organized the nouns into parisyllabic and imparisyllabic (depending on whether all members of the paradigm had the same number of syllables or not). The first real revolution in the system was due to Manuel Chrysoloras, the Greek scholar who was invited to teach Greek in Florence in 1396 and inaugurated the study of Greek in the Latin West. His *Erotemata* was composed in the final decade of the fourteenth century for use in teaching the language to westerners. Building on the reform of Diassorinus Chrysoloras reduced the usual 56

[24] The only Greek grammar written by a westerner in the Middle Ages, as far as I am aware, was the remarkable one by the Franciscan Roger Bacon, see the edition by Nolan and Hirsch (1902). The first Renaissance Greek grammar written by a non-Greek was by another Franciscan, Urbano Bolzanio (the *Institutiones graecae grammaticae*, printed in Venice in 1497).

nominal patterns to 10, and in this all subsequent Greek grammars which appeared in the West followed suit, conforming to Chrysoloras' system with occasional minor modifications.

The early Italian humanists, prior to the arrival of Chrysoloras in Florence, knew little Greek. Francesco Petrarca, the father of Italian humanism, studied the rudiments of the language from a Calabrian monk in 1342 and later received from another Greek friend a copy of the Homeric poems, but he was never able to read them with any understanding. The first westerner to attain a profound knowledge of the language was Guarino Veronese, who spent the years 1403 to 1408 in the Chrysoloras household in Constantinople.

Guarino in fact was responsible for the version of Chrysoloras's *Erotemata* which first became widely known in Italy. A little before 1418 he made a summary of the work for the use of his pupils, and the summary was translated into Latin. The first Greek grammar to appear in print later in the fifteenth century was this Guarinian version of the *Erotemata* in both languages (c. 1475). Chrysoloras's original text did not appear in print for another twenty years (c. 1496).

By this time other grammars had been written by exile Greeks in Italy: the *Erotemata* of Constantin Lascaris (first printed edition in Milan by Dionigi Paravicino in 1476), which was soon to be translated into Latin by Giovanni Crastone da Piacenza and published thereafter in bilingual fashion as the *Compendium octo orationis partium*; the *Eisagoge* of Theodore Gaza (first printed edition by Aldo Manuzio in 1495); and others. Erasmus translated part of Gaza's grammar into Latin. In 1497 there appeared the *Institutiones graecae grammaticae* of Urbano Bolzanio (Venice, Aldo Manuzio). The *Erotemata* of Manuel Moschopulos was also made available in a printed edition, together with the grammar of Demetrius Chalcondylas (Milan, 1493).

Once the study of Greek had become established in the West the number of grammars produced increased. These grammars were written in Latin, both because they were intended to be used by students who already knew Latin, and because they were destined for an international public. Two very popular grammars were the *Institutiones linguae graecae* by Nicolas Cleynaerts (Clenardus), which first appeared in Louvain in 1530, and the *De omnibus graecae linguae grammaticae partibus* by Francisco Vergara, published first at Alcalá in 1537. The grammatical theory of these sixteenth century grammars of Greek was thoroughly westernized. The Italian method of dealing with verbal government (in the style of Perotti's *Rudimenta*) had already been adopted, for example, by Lascaris.

From the point of view of the history of the western grammatical tradition, therefore, the Greek grammars of the Renaissance present few surprises. The influence of the eastern tradition, attenuated already in Chrysoloras's *Erotemata*, was effectively eliminated in the course of the sixteenth century. It should, however, be pointed out that one of the grammars printed by Aldo Manuzio in the final years of the fifteenth century was the Syntax of Apollonius Dyscolus, which came to be quite widely read.

The grammar of Dionysius Thrax, on the other hand, was not printed in the west until the eighteenth century.[25]

1.4 The rise of the vernaculars and the development of vernacular grammatical traditions were extremely slow and gradual processes. At the height of medieval civilization, say in the twelfth century, Latin was the written language used almost exclusively in both lay and ecclesiastical circles. Moreover the people who used Latin acquired the language so early in life and used it with such frequency that they were capable of turning it to almost any use:[26] one might say, therefore, that Latin functioned for them as a second native language. The common people, of course, spoke the vernaculars and so did the ruling classes for ordinary conversational purposes. Vernacular literature in the Middle Ages, therefore, tended to be either of the oral variety (for the lower classes), or to consist of courtly poetry for the delectation of the aristocracy. It should be recalled that in countries where the feudal system was entrenched (i.e., in France, Germany, and England) an urban middle class existed only in embryo.

In southern Europe, and in particular in the flourishing cities of northern Italy, the situation was rather different. Here a vigorous mercantile middle class arose quite early (from about the tenth century on), and was able to assert its claims against the great feudal powers. This class of people were relatively uninterested in the type of literature being written for the feudal aristocracies of western Europe, and were furthermore so busily engaged in money making that they had little time to acquire a scholarly, i.e., Latinate, education. It was this kind of environment that produced the literary flowering of the Tuscan dialect associated with the names of Dante Alighieri, Giovanni Boccaccio, and Francesco Petrarca.

It may seem strange, however, that although a vigorous vernacular literature existed in Italy by the early fourteenth century, no attempt at writing an Italian grammar was made until the middle of the fifteenth century. It must be borne in mind that a Latin grammatical tradition has long been a necessity precisely because Latin was a second language which had to be acquired by study in school and university. No such need existed in the case of the vernacular dialects of Italy. Other vernaculars, such as French and Provençal, had acquired some measure of international status — French as a result of the Crusades, and Provençal on account of the courtly literature written in it — and hence pedagogical grammars of these two languages had been written in the Middle Ages (see for instance Marshall 1969).

In any case the term *grammatica* was practically synonymous with Latin,[27] and many people expressed the view that grammatical regulation of a vernacular dialect

[25] In volume 7 of the *Bibliotheca graeca*, edited by Johann Albert Fabricius (Hamburg, 1715).

[26] See, for instance, the interesting passages of medieval Latin quoted by Migliorini (1960:123–4). I do not need to expatiate on the remarkable development of popular Latin verse in the Middle Ages, as exemplified by the Cambridge Songs, the *Carmina Burana*, the poems attributed to Walter Map, and so forth.

[27] Compare the following remark by Dante in his *De vulgari eloquentia* (I, 1, 3): 'Est et inde alia locutio secundaria nobis, quam Romani gramaticam vocaverunt' with the opening sentence of the

was a difficult if not impossible venture.[28] As late as the fifteenth century there was a famous dispute among scholars as to whether Latin had ever been the language of the common people of Rome in ancient times. It seemed more likely to these humanists that Latin had always been a learned language, and that the dichotomy between Latin and the vernacular had always existed.[29] It was largely to refute such notions that Leon Battista Alberti wrote his *Regole della lingua fiorentina* (c. 1450) in which he attempted to describe the grammatical structure of the Tuscan of his day ('l'uso della lingua nostra', as he put it). The first Italian grammar was therefore in the nature of a theoretical demonstration that it was possible to write a grammar for the vernacular.[30] Naturally enough, Alberti's grammar is unexciting from the point of view of grammatical theory, for if it had needed to depart radically from the Latin mold the experiment would have been accounted a failure by its author! Thus slavish imitation of the Latin grammatical tradition had a definite place in the development of a vernacular grammatical tradition.

By the early sixteenth century in Italy the vernacular had already begun to threaten the traditional status of Latin as the exclusive language of scholarship and serious literature. Counterattacks were then launched against the encroachments of the vernacular: the partisans of Latin assembled arguments to champion the continued use of Latin in its traditional functions.[31] Acrimonious conflicts also broke out in the vernacular camp over the precise choice of a standard dialect, the alternatives being 1. an archaizing form of Tuscan close to the usage of the great fourteenth century writers, 2. the contemporary speech of Tuscany, or 3. some kind of 'common Italian' more acceptable to non-Tuscans. The issue was eventually resolved in favor of the first alternative with some concessions being made to appease the non-Tuscans.

---

thirteenth century Provençal grammar by Uc Faidit: 'Las oit partz que om troba en gramatica troba om en vulgar provençhal...' (The eight parts of speech which one finds in Grammar one finds in Provençal...) (Marshall 1969:88).

[28] Witness the following remarks by the German monk Otfried (died c. 870): 'Huius enim linguae barbaries, ut est inculta et indisciplinabilis, atque in sueta capi regulari freno grammaticae artis, sic etiam in multis dictis scriptum est, propter literarum aut congeriem aut incognitam sonoritatem difficilis' (Braune and Helm 1949:111). As late as the mid-sixteenth century Giovan Battista Gelli presented a paper to the Florentine Academy with the suggestive title *Ragionamento sopra la difficoltà di mettere in regole la nostra lingua*.

[29] The view that Latin was only used by the learned in ancient times was expressed by Leonardo Bruni in a letter to Flavio Biondo; see Leonardus Aretinus, *Epistolarum libri octo* (Basle, 1535), sigs. S2r–S8r. The opposite view was defended by Poggio Bracciolini; see *Poggii Florentini ... Operum* etc. (Strassburg, 1513, fols. 24v–20v.).

[30] Thus the *Regole* begins as follows: 'Que che affermano la lingua latina non essere stata comune a tutti e populi latini, ma solo propria di certi docti scolastici, come hoggi la vediamo in pochi; credo deporrano quello errore: vedendo questo nostro opuscholo in quale io racolsi l'uso della lingua nostra in brevissime annotationi: qual cosa simile fecero gl'ingegni grandi e studiosi presso a Graeci prima, e po presso de e latinij: et chiamorno queste simili ammonitioni apte a scrivere e favellare, senza corruptela, suo nome Grammatica. Questa arte quale ella sia in la lingua nostra leggietemi e intenderetela.' (Trabalza 1908:535).

[31] The most famous attempt to defend the retention of Latin was the oration entitled *De linguae latinae usu retinendo*, delivered at Bologna in 1529 by Romolo Amaseo (see his collected *Orationum volumen*, Bologna 1563–64).

Outside Italy the issue of the status of the vernacular *vis-à-vis* Latin was resolved in the same way, with the vernacular encroaching more and more as time went on. The problem of choosing a standard dialect, on the other hand, was less acute in countries like Spain, France, and England which had a strong central government.

The first full-scale grammar of a vernacular (apart from Alberti's brilliant but uninfluential sketch of Tuscan) was the Castilian grammar of the Spanish humanist Antonio de Nebrija, which appeared in 1492. It covers the entire domain of grammar (including syntax). Nebrija's grammatical theory is, as one might expect, completely traditional. The description of verbal government, for instance, follows the procedure familiar from contemporary Latin grammars: 'Los verbos personales o passan en otra cosa o no passan. Los que passan en otra cosa llamánse 'transitivos', como diziendo *io amo a dios, amo* es verbo transitivo por que su significación passa en *dios*. Los que no passan en otra cosa llamánse 'absolutos', como diziendo *io bivo, bivo* es verbo absoluto, por que su significación no passa en otra cosa. Los que passan en otra cosa, o passan en el segundo caso, cuales son estos ... Otros passan en dativo cuales son estos ... Otros passan en accusativo, cuales son estos ... Otros verbos allende del accusativo demandan genitivo cuales son estos', etc. (IV, 3). Quite clearly this is the Guarinian system of verbal government, in some instances with the very same examples used.

Italian grammatical discussions of the sixteenth century can be classified into three types, according to the position their authors adopted toward the 'questione della lingua': those which advocated an archaizing form of Tuscan, such as Cardinal Bembo's celebrated *Prose della volgar lingua* (Venice, 1525); those which defended the prerogatives of the contemporary dialect of Tuscany, such as Pier Francesco Giambullari's *Della lingua che si parla e scrive in Firenze* (Florence, 1551); and finally those which proposed the creation of a pan-Italian standard based on the contemporary dialects, such as Gian Giorgio Trìssino's *Castellano* (1528). The earliest Italian grammar of the sixteenth century was the *Regole grammaticali della volgar lingua* by Francesco Fortunio (Ancona, 1516), which falls into the first category. The final codification of the archaizing Tuscan, which emerged as the victor in the linguistic controversies of the sixteenth century, was undertaken by Leonardo Salviati in his influential *Degli avvertimenti della lingua sopra 'l Decamerone* (1584).

The earliest grammars of French were written in English: the sketchy *Introductions in Frensshe* by Pierre Valence (printed in London in 1528 by Wynkyn de Worde), and the earliest full-scale grammar, entitled *Lesclaircissement de la langue françoyse* by the Englishman John Palsgrave (London, 1530). The first French grammar to appear in France was by the humanist Jacques Dubois (Iacobus Sylvius) and was entitled *In linguam Gallicam Eisagoge* (Paris, 1531). The first grammarian of real stature to write about French in French was Louis Meigret. He was also the first in a series of orthographic reformers who tried, without much success, to introduce a more rational spelling system for the French language. His grammar of French was entitled *Le tretté de la grammère francoèze*, and appeared in Paris in 1550. Pierre de la Ramée

(Petrus Ramus) published a French grammar (the *Gramere*) in 1562, printed in part in an orthography of his own invention (though in fact modelled in many respects on that of Meigret). The grammatical system underlying the *Gramere* was an application to French of ideas which Ramus had already experimented with in his *Scholae grammaticae* three years earlier. The famous humanist printer Robert Estienne and his son Henri distinguished themselves in the area of French grammar. Robert wrote the *Traicte de la Grammaire françoise* (Paris, 1557), to which his son wrote a sequel, entitled *Hypomneses de Gallica lingua* (1582). A popular French grammar explicitly directed to non-native speakers was the *Gallicae linguae Institutio* written by Jean Pillot (first edition Paris, 1550, and many subsequent reissues). A work in a similar vein was written by Jean Garnier, entitled *Institutio Gallicae linguae in usum iuventutis germanicae* (Marburg, 1558).

In both Germany and England the output of vernacular grammars in the sixteenth century was rather meagre. William Bullokar's *Bref Grammar for English* appeared in 1586 and is, as its title suggests, a mere sketch. An English grammar written in the Ramist framework was published in 1594 by Paul Greaves and was entitled *Grammatica Anglicana.* In Germany it has already been the practice in the fifteenth century to translate the *Ars Minor* of Donatus into the vernacular. The first real German grammar was written by Valentin Ickelsamer and was published some time before 1537, presumably in Augsburg. It was composed in German and was entitled *Teutsche Grammatica.* In 1573 two grammars of very similar style and content appeared: one by Laurentius Albertus entitled *Teutsch Grammatick oder Sprach-Kunst*, and the other by Albert Ölinger (*Underricht der Hoch Teutschen Spraach: Grammatica seu institutio verae Germanicae linguae*, Strassburg). The most popular grammar to appear in the sixteenth century was the *Grammatica Germanicae linguae* by Johann Clajus (1578). All these grammars were modelled closely on the prevailing canons of Latin grammatical writing. In both Germany and England the first really substantial vernacular grammars did not appear until the seventeenth century, namely the *Teutsche Sprachkunst* by Justus Georg Schottelius (1641) and the *Grammatica linguae Anglicanae* by John Wallis (1653).

2.0 I shall not comment on the views which general historians have held about the nature of the Renaissance. The interested reader should consult the valuable study by Wallace K. Ferguson entitled *The Renaissance in historical thought* (1948). For more recent discussions of the same topic he may turn to Garin's article 'Interpretazioni del rinascimento' (1954), and E. F. Jacob's 'Introduction' in the volume *Italian Renaissance studies* (1960). On the nature of Italian humanism opinion is still divided. Kristeller (1956) equates humanism with the grammatical and rhetorical disciplines, the so-called *studia humanitatis*, while Garin (1947) emphasizes the wider social significance of Renaissance humanism.

The now classic treatment of Renaissance culture is Jacob Burckhardt's essay *Die*

Kultur der Renaissance in Italien, which first appeared in 1860. A recent general history of the period is Ferguson's *Europe in transition, 1300–1520* (1962). The classic works on humanism are Georg Voigt's *Die Wiederbelebung des klassischen Altertums*, which first appeared in 1859, and Ludwig Geiger's *Renaissance und Humanismus in Italien und Deutschland* (1882), strongly Burckhardtian in flavor.

There is no general guide to the study of the relevant primary sources. McKerrow (1927) has written a useful introduction to the study of early printed books. A concise introductory manual of paleography is Battelli's *Lezioni di paleografia* (1949). The basic catalogue of incunabula is still Hain's two volume *Repertorium bibliographicum* (reprinted in 1925) with its various supplements. Of the *Gesamtkatalog der Wiegendrucke* (1925–38) only seven volumes have so far appeared, reprinted in 1968. Kristeller's *Iter Italicum* (1963, 1967) is a catalogue of manuscripts in Italian libraries not hitherto catalogued, and must be used in conjunction with the series founded by Mazzatinti entitled *Inventari dei manoscritti delle biblioteche d'Italia*, which is itself far from complete. A catalogue of incunabular holdings in Italian libraries is Guarnaschelli's *Indice generale degli incunaboli delle biblioteche d'Italia* (1943–65), also incomplete. The *Manual del librero hispano-americano* (1948 ff.), edited by Palau y Dulcet is not confined to the incunabular period. Among library catalogues those of the British Museum and the Bibliothèque Nationale are perhaps the most generally useful. Edmund Stengel published in 1890 a catalogue of French grammars from the end of the fourteenth to the end of the eighteenth century, and R.C. Alston is at present compiling a multi-volume bibliography of English linguistic literature from the invention of printing until 1800. For Spanish and Portuguese imprints one may consult volume 3 of *La ciencia española* by Menéndez y Pelayo (1888).

2.1 The Italian and Provençal grammatical tradition of the Middle Ages has been little studied. Charles Fierville published in 1886 the text of the grammar of Pietro da Isolella,[32] to which he added a lengthy extract from the grammar of Sponcius (Poncius). In his introduction to the edition he emphasizes the unsystematic arrangement of the various chapters of the grammar of Pietro da Isolella, and claims that it was based on Priscian rather than on the *Doctrinale:* 'le *Doctrinal* est à peu près complètement laissé de côté, au profit de Priscien' (1886:IX). He describes the style of presentation as lucid and relatively free of logical subtleties. He shows that the section on syntax in the grammar of Pietro da Isolella was borrowed from the grammar of Sponcius. But beyond this Fierville has little to say about the place of these two grammars in the history of the southern grammatical tradition.

Manacorda (1914:213–45) presents a valuable survey of grammatical studies in Italy. He divides the development into four periods: the first including the famous grammars of late antiquity from Donatus to Cassiodorus; the second, the grammars of the Carolingian era; the third, the grammars produced in the episcopal schools

[32] It should be noted that Fierville did not attribute the work to Pietro da Isolella, but rather to a Master Cesar, whose name appears in one of the manuscripts. On the question of authorship see Hunt 1950:177.

(including the *Doctrinale* and the *Graecismus*); and the fourth, the era of humanistic reform beginning with Valla, Guarino, and Perotti. He places the grammars of Francesco da Buti and Folchino dei Borfoni in his third period but has little to say about the content of these grammars. His account is, however, useful in that it contains a great deal of bibliographical information and also provides manuscript locations.

Of fourteenth century grammarians only Francesco da Buti and Folchino dei Borfoni have been discussed in the secondary literature. Sabbadini (1902:310–11, 1906:115) transcribed a passage from the grammar of Folchino dei Borfoni, and in an earlier publication (1896:40–1) presented an account of the structure of the grammar of Francesco da Buti. These discussions were, however, in the context of Sabbadini's investigations into the historical sources of the *Regulae grammaticales* of Guarino Veronese. In 1896 he was content to demonstrate the parallels between the *Regulae* and the grammar of Francesco da Buti, drawing from this comparison the conclusion that 'Guarino's book is merely a summary of a work similar to that of Buti's' (1896:41). In the two later publications (1902, 1906) he no longer mentioned Francesco da Buti, but rather concentrated his whole attention on the parallels between Guarino's grammar and that by Folchino dei Borfoni, which he claimed was the *earliest* grammar in which the method and terminology of Guarino's *Regulae* existed in fully developed form (1902:310). In other words Sabbadini was interested in these two fourteenth century grammars only in so far as they threw light on the origins of Renaissance grammar.

The question of the relation between the two grammars and their place in the development of the southern tradition of grammatical writing was not touched on by Sabbadini. He was, however, able to trace back this style of grammar composition to Priscian and Apollonius (1902:311; 1906:118).

Our knowledge of the grammar of Master Bene is extremely meagre. Pinborg (1967:38fn.) transcribes a short but interesting passage from it in which the author discusses the distinction between object-language and metalanguage.[33] Hunt (1950:177) maintains that Bene's grammar is the source of the grammatical section of the *Catholicon* of John of Genoa. About the contents of the latter work, however, little is known at present, beyond a few observations by Manacorda (1914:237).

2.2 The earliest survey of humanistic grammar can be found in Georg Voigt's *Wiederbelebung des klassischen Altertums* (1893 II:373–81). His account is, in general, still serviceable. He pays a great deal of attention to works on Latin orthography (373–6). In discussing Guarino's reform of grammar (376) he claims that Guarino

[33] I should like to suggest a couple of small but I think justifiable emendations to the text transcribed by Pinborg, as follows: 'Nominum aliud prime impositionis, aliud secunde. Prime impositionis sunt nomina rerum, ut *homo*, *animal*, *albus*, et *niger*; secunde impositionis sunt nomina vocum, ut *nomen*, *verbum*, *participium*, *categorica*, *hypotetica*. Videndum ergo, quod si adiectivum secunde impositionis determinet substantivum prime [proprie *cod.*], locutio est incongrua, ut [et *cod.*] *tu habes nasum adverbialem*, quia tale adiectivum non depingit tale substantivum, unde talis sensus penitus evanescit.' (MS. Pisa, Biblioteca Cateriniana del Seminario 66, fol. 3rb.).

was motivated by a desire to reduce the amount of material the student needed to master, so that he could be initiated into the study of the ancient writers as soon as possible. Too much time spent on grammar would dampen the enthusiasm of the beginner, it was felt.

Voigt also raises the interesting question as to who was the first humanist to have the idea of composing a 'short' grammar and throws out the following suggestion (II:376): "Perhaps it was Zomino da Pistoia, who taught grammar after the conclusion of the Council of Constance, but his *Regulae grammaticales* was not popular (*fanden keine Verbreitung*)." However, since Zomino was younger than Guarino it is more likely that he got his ideas from the older man than the other way round, but the problem of priority still awaits investigation.[34]

The fundamental work on Guarino's life and pedagogical activity is Sabbadini's *La scuola e gli studi di Guarino Guarini Veronese* (1896). A more recent summary can be found in Garin (1965:122–32). Guarino's grammar has been discussed briefly by Golling (1900:647–9) and in greater detail in various publications of Remigio Sabbadini. In his 1896 monograph (38–47) Sabbadini claims that the *Regulae* has four historical sources: 1. the Italian grammatical tradition, as represented by the grammar of Francesco da Buti; 2. the *Doctrinale*; 3. the *Ianua*, and 4. Priscian's *Institutiones.* In each case of the third and fourth putative sources, however, objections can be raised to his conclusions.

The definitions which Guarino shares with the *Ianua* can also be found in other grammars in the Italian tradition, hence Sabbadini's contention that Guarino copied them from the *Ianua* must be regarded as unproven. Sabbadini would also have us believe that in some passages in the *Regulae* Guarino was directly influenced by Priscian. Here again quoting documentary evidence is not sufficient. The passage which he cites in full from the *Regulae* (Sabbadini 1896:44) was quite probably not part of the original version of the work. Guarino's *Regulae* suffered the fate of many popular medieval and post-medieval grammatical texts — scribes did not hesitate to interpolate material into the text whenever it suited their purpose. Furthermore, the Italian grammatical tradition was already heavily Prisçianic in content. It is difficult, therefore, to distinguish the direct influence of Priscian from the indirect influence which he exerted through the tradition.

The Guarinian system of verbal government has been described by Sabbadini (1902, 1906), and also by Golling (1900:647–9). For a discussion of other grammars by Italian humanists we must again turn to Golling, who has short accounts of the grammars of Perotti (650), Sulpizio (650), Mancinelli (651), Pasi (651), and Saturnio (652–4). Baebler (1885:135–9) carefully describes Perotti's *Rudimenta.* The position of grammar in the educational system of Italian humanism was studied by William H. Woodward in a number of publications (1904, 1906, 1921). Especially valuable is Woodward's free translation of the treatise *De ordine docendi ac studendi* by Guarino's

[34] Zomino's dates are 1387–1458. An autograph manuscript of his grammar exists in the Bodleian Library (MS. Lat. Misc. e.110).

son, Battista Guarini (1921:161–78). Battista's account throws light on the pedagogical motivations underlying Guarino's *Regulae* and his attitude (lenient, it would seem) toward the *Doctrinale* (165).

The secondary literature on Lorenzo Valla is vast. Still invaluable are the biographies by Mancini (1891) and Wolff (1893). Useful summaries can be found in histories of literature such as Rossi 1945 (80–90), and Garin 1965 (198–226). Valla's general approach to philological matters is discussed in a recent book by Gaeta (1955). The *Elegantiae* is discussed in some detail by Barozzi and Sabbadini (1891:161–73), Wolff (1893:93–7), and Mancini (1891:115–16, 263–75). The Latin text of the preface to each of the six books of the *Elegantiae*, together with Italian translations, was published by Garin (1952:594–631). Garin has also given a survey of Valla scholarship in two publications (1952:522, 1965:345–6). Valla's works have recently been reprinted in two volumes under the editorship of Garin by the Bottega d'Erasmo in Turin (1962). The first volume is a photographic reproduction of the *Opera* published by Henricus Petrus at Basel in 1540 and 1543. A critical edition of the *Elegantiae* does not exist.

On the content of the *Elegantiae* the best sources of information are still Barozzi's and Mancini's discussions, quoted above. It is generally agreed that the main novelty of the work lay in that it set forth the rules of correct Latinity with reference to concrete examples from the great writers of antiquity (Barozzi and Sabbadini 1891:161, 166; Golling 1900:646; Apel 1963:183). It has also been asserted that Valla's aim in writing the *Elegantiae* was to replace the medieval handbooks of grammar (Manacorda 1914:240; Ising 1970:53), and that the book was therefore indirectly responsible for the eventual demise of the *Doctrinale-Graecismus* tradition (Thurot 1869:492).

The notion that Valla established his prescriptions strictly on the basis of classical usage is generally supported by the following quotation from the *Elegantiae* (Book III, Chapter 17): 'As regards elegant usage I accept as authoritative whatever was agreeable to the great writers.'[35] Verburg (1952:109, fn. 1) has pointed out, however, that this statement has been quoted out of context. What Valla was in fact arguing at this point was almost the very opposite, namely that although one should as a general rule follow the usage of the ancients, one ought not to imitate every turn of phrase which can be found attested in some author or other. Verburg's point is well taken. In fact Valla makes a similar remark later in the same book (Chapter 64), where he advises against a certain locution although he is aware that it was used on one occasion by Horace. In other words, he recommends that the usage of the ancients should be followed, but with discrimination.

At the same time Valla was prepared to admit that in certain rare instances usage seems to violate the rules of grammar, as happens, for instance, in the following passage from the *Rhetorica ad Herennium* (IV, 29.40), which he quotes in Book III, Chapter 22 of the *Elegantiae*: 'The state was at that time greatly endangered by —

[35] 'Quamquam, quod ad elegantiam pertinet, ego pro lege accipio quicquid magnis auctoribus placuit.'

should I call it the stupidity of the consuls, or their deliberate criminal intent, or both?'[36] where there appears to be no agent noun (in this case a *suppositum*) to which the main verb (*obfuit*) could be in construction. Valla observes: 'In the straits between Boeotia and Euboea or in those between Sicily and the mainland the violent surge of the waters will compel a boat to sail in the opposite direction to the way the wind is blowing, and similarly a sentence which might have followed the normal grammatical pattern is inhibited by the very force of well established usage.'[37] He then proceeds to show that the sentence from the *Rhetorica ad Herennium* could be rewritten grammatically in either of two ways.

It should also be pointed out in this connection that although Valla commonly backs up his prescriptions by quotations from the classical writers, he does not always do so. For instance, in describing the meaning of the verb *peto* 'to strive after' (Book V, Chapter 58), he points out that the goal of the action may be either good or evil, and invents a set of examples: 'A doctor strives after the health of his patient, a father after the glory of his son, you strive after wealth, I after pleasure. Likewise many sons strive after the death of their fathers, slaves after the death of their masters, and doctors strive to lengthen disease.'[38]

Valla was also not averse to coining new words not found in the classical writers (such as *bombarda*) and vociferously defended this practice against puristic critics. In his first invective against Bartolomeo Fazio (*Opera* 504), for example, he asserts roundly that new objects require new words to designate them.[39]

As regards his attitude to medieval grammarians, it was quite clearly a negative one. However, if one examines the detailed criticisms which he levels at various writers for their misinterpretations of specific words (*Elegantiae*, Book VI) it is significant that the medieval grammarians and lexicographers are not mentioned. Valla was chiefly interested in that section in attacking the late classical grammarians, such as Nonius Marcellus, Servius, Macrobius, and Aulus Gellius, and the jurists (Justinian and the authors of the *Pandects*). In other publications he criticized the Latinity of his contemporaries Poggio Bracciolini, Antonio da Rho, and Bartolomeo Fazio, and he wrote a very short verse treatise on the first declension for King Alfonso of Aragon, the *Emendationes quorundam locorum ex Alexandro* (see Mancini 1891:200), in which he corrected certain mistakes in the *Doctrinale*. But he never launched a full-scale attack on the verse grammars or the lexica, nor did he ever, as far as I know, refer to the modistic treatises, of whose existence he must have been aware.

This forebearance toward his immediate predecessors may be due, I should like to suggest, to the fact that he was aware of the extent to which he stood on their shoul-

[36] 'Obfuit eo tempore plurimum rei publicae consulum — sive stultitiam sive malitiam dicere oportet, sive utrumque.'
[37] 'Sed sicut in Euripo aut Siciliae freto inflata vento vela, aquarum impetus retroire cogit, ita orationem lege grammatica euntem auctoritas ipsa consuetudoque inhibet ac repellit.'
[38] 'Medicus sanitatem aegri petit, pater laudem filii, tu divitias, ego voluptatem peto. Item multi filii petunt mortem patris, servi mortem dominorum, medici longitudinem morbi.'
[39] 'At nova res novum vocabulum flagitat.'

ders. No detailed study of the relation between the *Elegantiae* and the medieval lexica has yet been made, but instances in which Valla repeats information to be found in the earlier dictionaries are not difficult to find. For example, he insists (Book V, Chapter 56) that *devenio* and *pervenio* (both with the meaning 'to reach') differ in that the former has the connotation 'downward movement'. According to Valla, therefore, it is not so good (*minoris rationis*) to say *devenimus in montem* 'we reached the mountain' as to say *pervenimus in montem*. Similarly one should say *pervenimus ad divitias* 'we attained to wealth', but *devenimus in paupertatem* 'we sank into poverty'. It is, however, difficult to square these assertions with the way the two verbs are actually used by classical writers, and it is significant that Valla makes no effort to quote real examples, but invents his own. The question therefore arises as to where he got the idea that *devenio* has the connotation 'downward movement'. Part of the answer is provided by Valla himself: he cites two other verbs containing the prefix *de-* which definitely have this connotation (*devolvo* 'to roll down', *despicio* 'to look down upon'). But this is not the complete answer, since after all many verbal derivates in *de-* quite clearly do not have this shade of meaning (e.g., *despolio* 'to plunder', *deservio* 'to serve zealously', *deligo* 'to select'). Perhaps Valla was aware that John of Genoa had defined *devenio* in the *Catholicon* (article on *venio*) as '*deorsum venire*' ('to come down'), and the ultimate explanation for this assertion and perhaps many others may be that he did not in fact arrive at his prescriptions by an inductive process, but rather by correcting the assertions of his predecessors whenever he thought he had reason to do so on the basis of his wide acquaintance with the Roman authors. But in cases in which the interpretations offered in the older lexica did not seem to him to be erroneous he clearly has no cause to reject them. Thus Valla's real attitude to the medieval lexica may have been somewhat different from the opinion he expressed in writing about them. But clearly this matter requires a detailed study.

Summing up, I should like to suggest that the novelty of Valla's approach to language lay in his attempt to make grammar accountable to the facts of usage, or in his refusal to allow grammar to continue its separate, hermetically sealed existence. From a technical point of view Valla certainly does not rank with the great grammarians of the western tradition. The *Elegantiae* is singularly lacking in organization and fails to cover many topics which were considered integral parts of grammar at that time. But Valla represents a new hard-headed attitude to the validity of grammatical statements: what a Latin grammarian prescribes should be in harmony with the usage of the Roman writers.

Moving now to humanistic grammars written by non-Italians, one notes an almost complete absence of secondary literature. Casual references to the German grammarians Johannes Heinrichmann and Johannes Brassikan, both Tübingen professors, were made by Geiger (1882:400). A recent study by Terrence Heath (1971) discusses commentaries on the *Doctrinale* by Gerhard von Zütphen and by later humanists (Alexander Hegius and Johannes Synthen) and proceeds to give an interesting account of the adoption of humanistic grammar north of the Alps. It is clear, however, that this historical process was an extremely complex one. Italian humanistic grammars continued a local tradition of grammatical writing. In Germany, however, the confrontation between medieval and humanistic grammar was more extreme. Unfortunately, we are poorly informed about the history of the grammatical tradition in Germany immediately prior to the advent of Renaissance humanism. Heath draws an interesting contrast between the grammar of Johannes Turmair (Aventinus), which is humanistic in approach, and the grammatical section of the *Margarita philosophica* by Gregor Reisch, which has an unmistakable medieval flavor. It would be interesting to know more about the historical sources of Reisch's grammatical theory.

Two grammars of the sixteenth century have received a great deal of attention in the secondary literature: the *Scholae grammaticae* of Petrus Ramus, and Francisco Sánchez' *Minerva*. Scaliger's *De Causis linguae latinae*, on the other hand, still awaits detailed analysis. Benfey (1869:212) praises Scaliger's comparison of Greek and Latin phonetics, accuses him of apriorism, but compares him favorably with Sánchez. Arens (1969:69), however, places the *Minerva* higher than Scaliger's work in terms of scientific significance. Verburg (1952:165), on the other hand, asserts that Scaliger and Sánchez did not differ on essentials. Robins (1967:110) finds the *Minerva* a less theoretical work than Scaliger's *De Causis*. On the sources of Scaliger's ideas nothing certain is known. Hjelmslev (1928:11) hazards the claim that Scaliger's grammatical theory rested exclusively on scholasticism, which he equates with Aristotelianism. It would seem, however, that Scaliger's Aristotelianism was not of the scholastic variety. A general statement of the main theoretical positions which Scaliger advances in the *De Causis* has never been attempted. Scaliger's relations to earlier grammarians (especially Linacre, Pasi, and Saturnio) also await investigation.

Ramus' three Latin grammars (the *Scholae grammaticae*, *Rudimenta*, and *Grammatica*, all first published in 1559) have been described by Walter Ong (1958b:310–12, 323–4, 331–2), who is of the opinion that Ramus had little genuine originality as a grammarian. Ong describes the *Grammatica* as follows (1958b:311): 'Thus ... the whole of grammar is divided into etymology (words taken singly) and syntax (words taken conjointly) — an initial division based on a quantitative norm. By taking a further quantitative norm, etymology is divided into words with number ('nouns' or *nomina*, substantive and adjective, and verbs) and words without number (all other parts of speech). These words without number are thereupon divided into those which are themselves coupled to another word (thus constituting a two-piece quantitative unit) and those which join other words to each other (a three-piece quantitative unit). The latter are conjunctions, the former adverbs.' Ong concludes (1958b:312): 'The division of grammar into etymology and syntax is based directly on Ramus' preference for two-part divisions, not on any particular insight at all. ... He attributes the two-part division to no one but himself.'

Regarding Ramus' initial two-part division of grammar into etymology and syntax (rather than the traditional four part division into orthography, prosody, etymology, and syntax) it should be borne in mind that in practice Ramus adheres to the traditional division by simply treating orthography and prosody in the first section of the grammar together with noun morphology. He then handles the morphology of the verb and other parts of speech in the second section, and syntax in the two concluding sections. Ramus' definition of etymology and syntax is in essence also traditional — etymology is concerned with single words, syntax with sentences, i.e., word combinations. The 'quantitative norm' which Ong refers to here is a legacy of the tradition as well as part of Ramus' logical methodology.

Kukenheim (1962:18) maintains that Ramus was the first to describe sounds articulatorily in the *Grammatica*. It is clear, however, that many grammarians had discussed the articulatory nature of the sounds of Latin and Greek in some detail (see, for instance, Nebrija's treatise *De vi ac potestate litterarum*, published at Salamanca in 1503, and Erasmus' later *De recta latini graecique sermonis pronunciatione*, both discussed by Bywater (1908)).

The so-called Ramist consonants *j* and *v* (see Robins 1967:110) were already being consistently employed for consonantal *i* and *u* in the first edition of Nebrija's Castilian grammar of 1492, and some years later were advocated (independently?) by Trìssino (Trabalza 1908:98). However, in the absence of a comprehensive study of Ramus' grammatical writings and those of his immediate predecessors one can come to no firm conclusions concerning his originality. In any event it is clear that even if Ramus fell short of being entirely original he was immensely influential.

The most illustrious Ramist grammarian was the Spanish humanist Francisco Sánchez de las Brozas (1523–1601), who was however careful not to mention Ramus' name in print, since to do so in Philipp II's Spain would have been extremely dangerous. In this way the details of Sánchez' indebtedness to Ramus have been obscured: Aubrey Bell (1925:75), for instance, considered Sánchez 'not so much a "ramista" as has sometimes been supposed'.

Sánchez' life and scholarly activity were described by Mayans y Siscar (1766) in the preface to the first of a four-volume set of all Sánchez' works except the *Minerva*. In addition to Mayans' account the interested reader should consult the highly readable monograph by Aubrey Bell (1925), which, however, relies heavily on Mayans.

The *Minerva* has been much discussed by historians of linguistics. Extracts from it in translation are provided by Arens (1969:69) and Lakoff (1969:357–63). The popularity of the *Minerva* was commented on by Benfey (1869:213) and its influence on Claude Lancelot, the author of the Port-Royal *Nouvelle Méthode*, by Sainte-Beuve (1952 II:462–3). Lázaro Carreter (1949:27) attempts to situate the *Minerva* in the age-old nature versus convention debate.

A generally favorable, at times even laudatory, account of Sánchez' linguistic and grammatical theories is provided by Constantino García (1960). His theory of ellipsis is analyzed by Sánchez Barrado in two publications (1919a, 1919b), to which I have not had access. Most modern linguists have expressed disapproval of the concept of ellipsis (see, for instance, Verburg 1952:165), a notable exception being Lakoff (1969), who regards it as a prefiguration of the notion of deletion in transformational grammar.

As for Sánchez' relations to his predecessors García (1960) maintains throughout that his ideas were both original and superior to those of all other grammarians of that period. In a similar vein Lakoff (1969) portrays Sánchez as reacting against the excessive preoccupation with surface structure characteristic, so she believes, of both Valla and Scaliger. However, both Valla and Scaliger made use of such devices as ellipsis and subaudition. They cannot therefore be characterized as proponents of surface grammar, nor were they so characterized by Sánchez. In any event the issue on which Lakoff imagines Sánchez taking a position did not exist in the fifteenth and sixteenth centuries.

García and Lakoff both pay a great deal of attention to the question of the relevance of Sánchez' ideas to modern linguistics. García goes through the *Minerva* section by section comparing Sánchez' position with what he calls *las concepciones modernas*, by which he means the theories of Hjelmslev, Jespersen, Marouzeau, Meillet, Vendryes, and others. Lakoff, on the other hand, finds parallels between Sánchez' theories and transformational grammar.

Alvares' Latin grammar has received very little attention in the secondary literature. A laudatory remark by Morhof (1732 I:831): 'Deliria veterum grammaticorum primus ostendit, et saniora substituit Emanuel Alvarez' was picked up and translated by Sandys (1908:163). It is likely that Morhof got his high opinion of Alvares' work from Caspar Schoppe's essay *De veteris av novae grammaticae Latinae origine, dignitate et usu* which formed the preface to his *Grammatica philosophica* (Milan, 1628).

On possible relations between Sánchez and Alvares little is known. It is at least reasonably clear that they differed radically in their pedagogical approach. For example, Alvares advises Latin masters to teach their pupils to speak Latin and not worry them too much about the underlying rationale behind grammatical phenomena: 'neque sit magister solicitus de nominativi et verbi consensu; priusque si fieri poterit, discipulos doceat bene latine loqui, quam causas bene loquendi' (quoted from the Venice edition of 1581, p. 38). Sánchez, on the other hand, was convinced that pupils would never learn to write Latin elegantly if they were constantly exposed to incorrect conversational Latin ('Qui latine garriunt corrumpunt ipsam latinitatem' *Minerva*, Book IV, f. 267^{v}). Moreover, Sánchez accepted Scaliger's rationalistic approach to grammar and hence rejected the notion that there was nothing to be gained from inquiring into the rationale behind grammatical rules (*Minerva*, Book I, Chapter 1). However, whether Sánchez had Alvares' position specifically in mind in this connection is not clear.

2.3 Fifteenth century grammars of Greek are competently discussed by Pertusi (1962). The earlier account by Kukenheim (1951) is full of factual errors (see Pertusi's remarks 1962:322, fn. 1). Pertusi concentrates on the development of the system for describing nominal inflection up to and including Chrysoloras' *Erotemata*.

The study of Greek in the Latin Middle Ages is discussed by Sandys (1903:583–5) and Tiraboschi (1823:676–98). Voigt (1893 I:47–50) describes Petrarca's attempts to learn Greek.

Sabbadini (1922:17–27) gives an interesting account of the methods used by the Italian humanists in learning and teaching Greek. Guarino's contribution to Greek studies has also been documented by Sabbadini (1896:38–9).

On Greek studies outside Italy we are less well informed. Aubrey Bell in his useful monograph on the Spanish Renaissance (1944:44–56) has provided a certain amount of information on the work of Spanish humanists in this area.

2.4 The study of vernacular languages in the medieval and early modern periods has been discussed at great length by Arno Borst in his monumental work *Der Turmbau von Babel* (1957–63). Migliorini (1960) describes the position of Latin vis-à-vis the vernacular in Italy in the thirteenth (123–5), fourteenth (198–202), fifteenth (253–64), and sixteenth centuries (311–28). The early use of the vernacular in the elementary stages of Latin instruction has been recently discussed by Erika Ising (1970:21–31). The paleographer Bernard Bischoff (1961) has made a number of perceptive observations about the extent to which the various vernacular languages were studied in the Middle Ages.

As is well known Dante discussed the use of the vernacular for certain genres of literature, e.g., the *canzone*, in two treatises, one written in Italian and entitled the *Convivio*, the other, *De vulgari eloquentia* composed in Latin. The latter work is of great interest to linguists in that it contains a general discussion of language, a classification of the Romance languages, and a comparative survey of the Italian dialects. The most authoritative edition of the *De vulgari eloquentia* is by Aristide Marigo, and was first published in 1938; the third edition, revised by Pier Giorgio Ricci, appeared in 1968. This latest Marigo-Ricci edition contains the Latin text and an Italian translation on facing pages, and a survey of recent secondary literature on the work.

Dante's notions about language have been discussed by a number of scholars (see Ewert 1940; Pagliaro 1947; Migliorini 1949; 1960:180–6). It is often not realized that the *De vulgari eloquentia* was unfinished and never published in Dante's lifetime, and that it had no influence on subsequent developments until it was discovered in the early sixteenth century (see Hall 1942:16–17; Migliorini 1960:345–8; Grayson 1960b: 14–15).

An excellent edition of the Provençal grammar by Uc Faidit (13th century) has been recently published by Marshall (1969). It contains the Provençal and Latin versions on facing pages and a full critical apparatus. The text of another Provençal grammar, *Las Rasos de trobar* by Raimon Vidal, was published by Edmund Stengel in 1878. Kathleen Lambley (1920) has written about the study of French in England from the fifteenth century on.

There is a great deal of literature about the Italian *questione della lingua.* The basic accounts are Migliorini's 1949 article, summarized in his later *Storia della lingua italiana* (1960:339–60), and Robert Hall's lucid essay (1942). Cecil Grayson's inaugural lecture (1960b) presents a useful summary of the main issues. Grayson (1960a) has also written about the linguistic views of Niccolò Machiavelli and Lorenzo de' Medici, showing clearly that Machiavelli's arguments in his *Dialogo intorno alla lingua* (c. 1514) reveal unmistakable signs of being influenced by Dante's *De vulgari eloquentia.* Kristeller (1956:473–93) has attacked the widely held view that fifteenth century humanism set the literary development of the vernacular back a century. The grammatical and lexicographical notes of Leonardo da Vinci have been collected and published by Augusto Marinoni (1944).

The Italian vernacular grammatical tradition received monographic treatment at the hands of Ciro Trabalza in 1908. In spite of Scalgione's recent condemnation of Trabalza's book (1970:38), his treatment will undoubtedly remain an indispensable guide for future research.

On Leon Battista Alberti's grammatical sketch a great deal has been written. The question of the authorship of the work has been, it seems to me, definitively resolved by Cecil Grayson (1963). The text of the grammar was published by Trabalza (1908: 535–45) and more recently by Grayson (1964) with a full critical apparatus (general introduction, facsimile of the manuscript, transcription, and notes). Grayson attempts to demonstrate Alberti's especial indebtedness to Priscian's *Institutiones*, an interesting hypothesis but one which will need to be scrutinized by future investigators.

The French grammatical tradition has been ably described by Charles-Louis Livet (1859) and Ferdinand Brunot (1906). An edition of Palsgrave's grammar was published in 1852 by Génin. A detailed analysis of Palsgrave's ideas has recently been offered by Neumann (1959). In general both Livet and Brunot have a low opinion of all the grammarians of the sixteenth century, including Petrus Ramus. Graves, on the other hand, wrote an extremely laudatory account of Ramus' grammatical writings (1912:121–32), and it is this account, rather than those of Livet and Brunot, which has influenced the opinion of historians of linguistics concerning Ramus (Verburg 1952: 172–80; Robins 1967:102–3). Walter Ong (1958b:346–8) accepts Brunot's evaluation of the *Gramere* and is on the whole skeptical concerning the value of Ramus' contribution to grammatical theory (1958b:311–12). For bibliographical information on Ramus' various grammatical works see Ong 1958b (310–48, 431, 433). Ong's general approach to Ramus and Ramism is expounded in a monograph entitled *Ramus: method and the decay of rhetoric* (1958a). Ramus' influence on Sánchez has been pointed out by Bement (1928:320) and Graves (1912:211). Both Verburg (1952:177) and Kukenheim (1962:18) regard Ramus as a forerunner of twentieth-century structuralism. Verburg reasons, not very convincingly it seems to me, that Ramus' method of dichotomies is tantamount to the structuralist notion of binary oppositions, while Kukenheim asserts that Ramus described each language in its own terms. The only evidence for Kukenheim's claim is the title of Ramus' Greek grammar, which reads 'Greek grammar in so far as it differs from Latin'. This, however, is a consequence of Ramus' pedagogical principle according to which disciplines should not overlap.

The German grammatical tradition received detailed treatment from Max Jellinek

(1913–14), who treats all the grammarians up to and including Adelung (late eighteenth century), in his first volume chronologically by author and in the second by topic. Erika Ising (1970) concentrates on the role of Donatus' *Ars minor* in the development of the vernacular grammatical tradition in German-speaking countries and in eastern Europe.

Otto Funke published a useful edition of Paul Greaves' *Grammatica Anglicana* and a short study of Bullokar's *Bref Grammar* in 1938. Bullokar and Greaves are also discussed *passim* in Funke's monograph *Die Frühzeit der englischen Grammatik* (1941). Vorlat (1964) traces the development of English grammatical writing into the eighteenth century, concentrating on the treatment of morphology. Her discussion of the intellectual background of the periods she covers is chiefly based on secondary sources, especially on Funke's earlier studies. She handles grammatical theory chronologically by part of speech, ignoring syntax almost entirely. Ian Michael (1970) has produced the most comprehensive and richly documented study of the English grammatical tradition to appear so far.

The text of various Spanish grammars of the late fifteenth and sixteenth centuries is reprinted in Viñaza's *Biblioteca histórica de la filología castellana* (1893:189–264), including Nebrija's *Gramática sobre la lengua castellana* (189–228). Other editions of Nebrija's grammar are Walberg 1909, González-Llubera 1926, Rogerio Sánchez 1931, and Galindo and Oritz 1946. The last named contains a facsimile of the first edition, a transcription and notes. Valuable discussions of Nebrija's significance as a grammarian can be also found in the earlier editions mentioned. Walberg (1909:V–XV) also provides useful bibliographical information about the original editions. The early Portuguese grammar of Fernão d'Oliveira (1536) was reprinted in 1871 by the Visconde d'Azevedo e Tito de Noronha in an indifferent edition. Useful bibliographical information on early Portuguese imprints can be found in King Manuel's *Livros antigos portuguezes* (1929–35).

The indebtedness of the early vernacular grammarians to the Latin grammatical model has been emphasized by all investigators. Corti (1955) has documented the influence of the various ancient and medieval grammarians on the Renaissance grammarians, both vernacular and Latin, and in particular on Ateneo Carlino, who published a vernacular grammar in 1533. Vorlat (1964:192) claims that Bullokar based his sketch on the *Short introduction of grammar*, a popular Latin grammar regarding the authorship of which C.G. Allen has written an interesting article (1954). Since historians of the vernacular traditions have paid relatively little attention to syntax, possible influence of the Guarinian system of verbal government on writers of vernacular grammars has never been investigated. Trabalza (1908:161–3) has asserted that Giambullari modelled his syntactic theory on that of Linacre's *De emendata structura latini sermonis*. It is clear also that Sánchez' syntactic notions influenced the authors of the *Grammaire générale et raisonnée* (see Lakoff 1969).

BIBLIOGRAPHY

1. *Primary Sources*

ALBERTI, LEON BATTISTA. 1908. Regole della lingua fiorentina, 535–45. Editions Trabalza. Grayson, 1964.

ALBERTUS, LAURENTIUS. 1573. Teutsch Grammatick oder Sprach-Kunst. Vienna, Michael Manger.

ALEXANDRE DE VILLEDIEU. Doctrinale. Critical edition by Reichling (1893).

ALVARES, MANOEL. 1572. De institutione grammatica libri tres. Lisbon, Joao de Barreira. Many subsequent editions. Here quoted from the edition published by Alexander Gryffius, Venice, 1581.

AMASEO, ROMOLO. 1563–64. Orationum Volumen. Bologna.

ARETINUS, LEONARDUS. 1535. Epistolarum libri octo. Basle, Henricus Petrus.

ATENEO CARLINO, MARCO ANTONIO. 1533. La grammatica volgar dell' Atheneo. Naples, Giannes Sultzbach.

AVENTINUS. See TURMAIR.

BEMBO, PIETRO. 1525. Prose della volgar lingua. Venice, Giovanni Tacuino. Many subsequent editions.

BENE. Summa in grammaticam. MS. in Biblioteca Cateriniana del Seminario, Pisa. Shelfmark 66. Widely disseminated.

BENEDICTUS PHILOLOGUS. See RICCARDINI.

BRASSIKAN, JOHANN. 1508. Institutiones grammaticae. Strassburg, Johannes Prusser.

BULLOKAR, WILLIAM. 1586. Bref grammar for English. London, Edmund Bollifant. Copy in Bodleian Library, Oxford: shelfmark Tanner 67. Edition by Max Plessow. 1906. Palaestra 52.331–85.

CHALCONDYLAS, DEMETRIUS. 1493. Erotemata. First printed edition Milan, Ulderico Schinzenzeler. Gesamtkatalog No. 8250.

CHRYSOLORAS, MANUEL. Erotemata. According to Pertusi (1962:324–5) written before 1397. First printed edition 1471 (abbreviated bilingual version). Venice, Adam von Ambergau. Copy in Milan, Biblioteca Braidense (AP. XVII. 21). Original Greek text appeared c. 1496, probably printed by Lorenzo de Alopa (Gesamtkatalog No. 6694, Guarnaschelli No. 2778).

CLAJUS, JOHANN. 1578. Grammatica germanicae linguae ... ex bibliis Lutheri Germanicis et aliis eius libris collecta.

CLEYNAERTS, NICOLAES. 1530. Institutiones linguae graecae. Louvain.

DESPAUTER, JAN. 1537. Commentarii grammatici. Paris, Robertus Stephanus.

DONATUS, AELIUS. 1572. (Supposititious) Erudimenta grammatice. Venice, Ioannes Gryphius. See IANUA.

——. De partibus orationis ars minor. Critical edition by Keil (1864: XXI–XLI, 353–66).

DUBOIS, JACQUES. 1531. In linguam gallicam Isagoge, una cum eiusdem grammatica latino-gallica, ex Hebraeis, Graecis et Latinis authoribus. Paris, R. Stephanus.

ERASMUS, DESIDERIUS OF ROTTERDAM. 1703. Opera omnia ... studio et opera Ioannis Clerici. Vol. 1. Leiden, Petrus Vander Aa.

ESTIENNE, HENRI. 1582. Hymomneses de Gallica lingua peregrinis eam discentibus necessariae. Geneva.

ESTIENNE, ROBERT. 1557. Traicté de la grammaire françoise. Paris, Robert Estienne.

EVRARD DE BÉTHUNE. Graecismus. Critical edition by Wrobel (1887).

FAIDIT, UC. 1878. Lo donats proensals. Stengel. Marshall edition, 1969.

FOLCHINO DEI BORFONI. No printed editions. Quoted here from manuscript copy in the Biblioteca Ambrosiana, Milan. Shelfmark H 66 Inf. No other known copies.

FORTUNIO, GIOVANNI FRANCESCO. 1516. Regole grammaticali della volgar lingua. Ancona, Bernardino Vercellese. Many subsequent editions.

FRANCESCO DA BUTI. Regule gramatice. No printed editions. On the author see Silva 1918. Here quoted from manuscript copy in the Bodleian Library, Oxford. Shelfmark MS. Canon. misc. 196. Widely disseminated.

GARNIER, JEAN. 1558. Institutio gallicae linguae in usum iuventutis germanicae. Geneva, J. Crispin.

GASPARO VERONESE. Latin grammar without title. I have consulted the following manuscript copies: Rome, Biblioteca Casanatense, DV 27 (285), fols. 2r–61r; Florence, Biblioteca Laurenziana, Plut. 52, Cod. 19; Venice, Biblioteca Marciana, MS. Latin. XIII, 53 (=4417). The latter was erroneously attributed to Francesco Petrarca by an eighteenth century manuscript cataloguer (see Kristeller 1967:244).

GAZA, THEODORE. 1495. Eisagoge. Venice, Aldo Manuzio. Hain No. 7500, Guarnaschelli No. 4181.

GELLI, GIOVAN BATTISTA. See GIAMBULLARI, PIERFRANCESCO.

GERHARD VON ZÜTPHEN. 1491. Glosa notabilis seconde parte Alexandri. Deventer. Quoted by Heath (1971:15).

GIAMBULLARI, PIERFRANCESCO. 1551. Della lingua che si parla e scrive in Firenze, e un Dialogo di Giambattista Gelli, Sopra la difficoltà dell'ordinare detta lingua. Florence, Lorenzo Torrentino.

Grammaire générale et raisonée. By le Sieur D.T., i.e. De Trigny, pseudonym. Assumed to have been written by Antoine Arnauld and Claude Lancelot. Paris, Le Petit, 1660.

GREAVES, PAUL. 1594. Grammatica anglicana, praecipue quatenus a Latina differt ad unicam P. Rami methodum concinnata. Cambridge, J. Legatt. Only known copy in British Museum: shelfmark G. 7479.

GUARINI, BATTISTA. 1489. De modo et ordine docendi ac studendi. Heidelberg, Heinrich Knoblochtzer. Guarnaschelli No. 4521.

GUARINO VERONESE. Regulae grammaticales. MS. in the Biblioteca Marciana, Venice. Shelfmark MS. Lat. XIII, 143 (= 4042). Incunabular edition quoted from here is Guarnaschelli No. 4528 = Hain No. 8108. For incunabular editions see Hain Nos. 8105–23, Guarnaschelli Nos. 4528–41.

HEGIUS, ALEXANDER. Contra modos significandi invectiva. Written in 1486. Included in Dialogi, Deventer, Rich. Pafraet, 1503.

HEINRICHMANN, JACOB. 1506. Grammaticae institutiones. Pforzheim, Thomas Anselm.

HUGUTIO, See UGUCCIONE.

IANUA. Elementary medieval grammatical manual. Manuscript in the Bibliothèque Nationale described by Thurot (1869:47). Wrongly attributed to Donatus in the fifteenth and sixteenth centuries. See Gesamtkatalog Nos. 8987–9029.

ICKELSAMER, VALENTIN. Ein teutsche Grammatica. No place, no date.

JOHN OF GENOA. (Iohannes de Ianua, Iohannes Ianuensis de Balbis). Summa que vocatur Catholicon. Here quoted from an incunabular edition (Venice, Hermann Liechtenstein, 1483. Hain No. 2257). For location of manuscript copies see Marigo 1936. For incunabular editions see Gesamtkatalog Nos. 3182–3205.

LA RAMÉE, PIERRE DE. See RAMUS, PETRUS.

LASCARIS, CONSTANTINE. 1476. Erotemata. Milan, Dionigi Paravicino. Guarnaschelli No. 5690.

——. 1480. Compendium octo orationis partium. Latin translation of Lascaris' Erotemata by Giovanni Crastone da Piacenza. Milan, Buono Accorsi. Guarnaschelli No. 5691.

LINACRE, THOMAS. 1524. De emendata structura Latini sermonis libri sex. London, R. Pynson. Many subsequent editions.

MANCINELLI, ANTONIO. 1490. Epitoma seu regulae constructionis. Rome. Guarnaschelli No. 6059.

MANUZIO, ALDO. 1493. Institutiones grammaticae. Venice. Guarnaschelli No. 6139.

MEIGRET, LOUIS. 1550. Le tretté de la grammère françoèze. Paris, C. Wechel.

MELANCHTHON, PHILIPPUS. 1526. Syntaxis. Hagenau, J. Secerius, and Paris, Robertus Stephanus.

——. 1526a. Elementa latinae grammatices. Cologne.

MOSCHOPULOS, MANUEL. 1493. Erotemata. First printed edition Milan, Ulderico Schinzenzeler. Gesamtkatalog No. 8250.

NEBRIJA, ANTONIO DE. 1481. Introductiones in latinam grammaticam. Salamanca.

——. 1492. Gramática sobre la lengua castellana. Salamanca. Modern editions Walberg 1909, Gonzáles-Llubera 1926, Rogerio Sánchez 1931, Galindo and Ortiz 1946.

——. 1503. De vi ac potestate litterarum. Salamanca, Gysser.

NIZZOLI, MARIO. 1553. De veris principiis et vera ratione philosophandi contra pseudophilosophos libri quattuor. Parma, Viotti.

NOUVELLE MÉTHODE pour apprendre facilement et en peu de temps la langue latine. 1644. Paris, A. Vitré. Written by Claude Lancelot. Many subsequent editions.

ÖLINGER, ALBERT. 1573. Underricht der Hoch Teutschen Spraach: Grammatica seu institutio verae Germanicae linguae. Strassburg, Nicolaus Wyriot.

Oliveira, Fernão d'. 1536. Grammatica da lingua Portugueza. Lisbon, German Galhard.

Palsgrave, Jehan. 1530. Lesclarcissement de la langue françoyse. London, Pynson, Haukyns.

Papias. Vocabularium. For incunabular editions see Hain Nos. 12378–81. Manuscript copies I have consulted are the following: Florence, Biblioteca Laurenziana, Ashburnham 63, and Lucca, Biblioteca Feliniana del Capitolo della Cattedrale, Cod. 614, fols. 1ra–179ra. Both these copies contain the grammar. There is also a copy of the grammar in the British Museum, Harley 2514.

Pasi, Curio Lancellotto da Ferrara. (Curius Lancillotus Pasius Ferrariensis). 1504. De arte grammatica libri octo seu de rebus non vulgaribus. Reggio, Mazalis.

Pastrana, Juan de. c. 1485. Compendium gramatice brevissimum ac utilissimum: thesaurus pauperum sive speculum puerorum. Salamanca. Palau y Dulcet 12. 360. Facsimiles of pages from the 1512 Lisbon edition in Manuel II, 1.228–36.

Perger, Bernard. c. 1482. Grammatica nova. Passau. See Hain Nos. 12602–19.

Perotti, Niccolò. 1468. Rudimenta grammatices. Autograph manuscript in the Vatican Library (Vatic. Lat. 6737), discussed by Mercati 1925:59–61, 131–2, facsimile of one page 170. Many printed editions. Hain Nos. 12635–95. Guarnaschelli Nos. 7431–90.

Philippus of Florence. Regulae grammaticales. No printed editions. Manuscript copy in the Biblioteca Marciana, Venice. Shelfmark MS. Lat. XIII, 29 (=4473). Widely disseminated.

Pietro da Isolella. 1886. Compendium grammaticae. Edition by Fierville. For location of manuscript copies see Hunt 1950:177.

Pillot, Jean. 1550. Gallicae linguae institutio, latino sermone conscripta. Paris, S. Grouleau.

Poggio, Bracciolini. 1513. Poggi' Florentini Operum. Strassburg, Johann Knoblauch.

Priscian. Prisciani Caesariensis institutionum grammaticarum libri XVIII. Critical edition by Keil 1855–58.

Ramus, Petrus. 1559. Grammaticae libri quattuor. Paris, A. Wechel.

——. 1559. Rhetoricae distinctiones in Quintilianum. Paris, A. Wechel. First edition Paris, M. David, 1549.

——. 1559. Scholae grammaticae. Paris, A. Wechel.

——. 1560. Grammatica graeca, quatenus a latina differt. Paris, A. Wechel.

——. 1562. Gramere. Paris, A. Wechel.

——. 1569. Scholae in liberales artes. Basel, Eusebius Episcopius.

Reisch, Gregor. 1496. Margarita philosophica. Heidelberg. Hain No. 13852. Many subsequent editions.

RICCARDINI, BENEDETTO. (Benedictus Philologus). 1510. Erudimenta grammatices latinae linguae. Florence, Filippo Giunta.

SALVIATI, LIONARDO. 1584–86. Avvertimenti della lingua sopra 'l Decamerone. Vol. I, Venice, Guerra. Vol. II, Florence, Giunti.

SÁNCHEZ, FRANCISCO DE LAS BROZAS. 1562. Verae brevesque grammatices Latinae institutiones. Lyons, Sebastian Gryphius.

——. 1582. Paradoxa Antwerp, Christophorus Plantinus.

——. 1587. Minerva: seu de causis linguae Latinae. Salamanca, Ioannes & Andreas Renaut, fratres. Many subsequent editions.

SATURNIO, AGOSTINO (Augustinus Saturnius Lazaroneus). 1546. Mercurii maioris, sive grammaticarum institutionum libri decem. Basel, J. Oporini.

SCALIGER, JULIUS CAESAR. 1540. De causis linguae Latinae libri tredecim. Lyons, Seb. Gryphius. Many subsequent editions.

——. 1561. Poetices libri septem. Geneva, J. Crispin. Here quoted from the fourth edition, Heidelberg, in Bibliopolio Commeliniano, 1607.

SCHOPPE, CASPAR. 1628. Grammatica philosophica, non modo tironibus linguae latinae ... sed et latine doctissimis ... necessaria. Accessit praefatio de veteris ac novae grammaticae latinae origine, dignitate, et usu. Milan, J.B. Bidelli.

SCHOTTELIUS, JUSTUS GEORG. 1641. Teutsche Sprachkunst. Braunschweig, Balthasar Grubern.

Short Introduction of Grammar. First published with the title An introduction of the eyght partes of speche (London, Thomas Berthelet, 1542). Often reprinted together with the Brevissima institutio grammatices cognoscendae, which was first published separately with the title Institutio compendiaria totius grammaticae (London, Thomas Berthelet, 1540.)

SPONCIUS. Summa de constructione. Manuscript described by Thurot (1869:38). Extract in Fierville 1886:177–92.

STEPHANUS. See ESTIENNE.

SULPIZIO, GIOVANNI. (Sulpitius Verulanus). 1475. De arte grammatica opusculum compendiosum. Perugia.

SYLVIUS, IACOBUS. See DUBOIS, JACQUES.

SYNTHEN. 1491. Glosa Joannis Sinthen super secunda parte Alexandri. Deventer. Quoted by Heath (1971:19).

TORTELLI, GIOVANNI. 1471. Commentariorum grammaticorum de orthographia dictionum e Graecis tractarum opus. Rome, Ulricus Gallus Teutonicus. Hain Nos. 15563–78.

TRÌSSINO, GIAN GIORGIO. 1528. Dialogo intitulato: Il Castellano, nel quale si tratta della lingua italiana. Vicenza, Tolomeo Ianiculo da Bressa.

TURMAIR, JOHANNES. (Johannes Aventinus). 1512. Grammatica. Munich, Schobsser.

UGUCCIONE. Derivationes magnae. No printed editions. For location of manuscript editions see Marigo 1936.

——. Summa grammatice. Manuscript in Munich, Staatsbibliothek. Shelfmark Clm. 18908.

URBANO BOLZANIO. 1497. Institutiones graecae grammatices. Venice, Aldo Manuzio. Hain No. 16098. Copy in Milan, Biblioteca di Brera, AO. XI. 1.

VALENCE, PIERRE. 1528. Introductions in Frensshe. London, Wynkyn de Worde.

VALLA, LORENZO. (Laurentius Vallensis). 1543. Opera, Basle, Henricus Petrus. Incunabular editions of the Elegantiarum linguae Latinae Opus Hain Nos. 15799–823.

VERGARA, FRANCISCO. 1537. De omnibus graecae linguae grammaticae partibus. Alcalá.

VIDAL, RAIMON. 1878. Las rasos de trobar. Edition by Stengel.

VOSSIUS, GERARDUS. 1635. De arte grammatica libri septem. Amsterdam.

WALLIS, JOHN. 1653. Grammatica linguae Anglicanae, cui praefigitur De loquela sive sonorum formatione tractatus grammaticophysicus. Oxford, Leon. Lichfield.

ZOMINO DA PISTOIA. Grammatical notes without title. Autograph manuscript in the Bodleian Library, Oxford. Shelfmark MS. Lat. misc. e. 110.

2. *Secondary Sources*

ALLEN, C.G. 1954. The sources of 'Lily's Latin Grammar': A review of the facts and some further suggestions. The Library, 5th Series, Vol. 9, No. 2, 85–100.

ALSTON, R.C. 1965. A bibliography of the English language from the invention of printing to the year 1800. 8 vols. Leeds, E.J. Arnold.

APEL, KARL OTTO. 1963. Die Idee der Sprache in der Tradition des Humanismus von Dante bis Vico. Archiv für Begriffsgeschichte, 8. Bonn, H. Bouvier.

ARENS, HANS. 1969². Sprachwissenschaft: der Gang ihrer Entwicklung von der Antike bis zur Gegenwart. Freiburg/Munich, Karl Alber.

AZEVEDO E TITO DE NORONHA, VISCONDE DE. 1871. Grammatica de Linguagem Portugueza por Fernão d'Oliveira. Segunda edição, conforme a de 1536. Porto, Impensa Portugueza.

BAEBLER, J.J. 1885. Beiträge zu einer Geschichte der lateinischen Grammatik im Mittelalter. Halle a.S., Verlag der Buchhandlung des Waisenhauses.

BAROZZI, L., and SABBADINI, REMIGIO. 1891. Studi sul Panormita e sul Valla. R. Sabbadini: cronologia della vita del Panormita e del Valla. L. Barozzi: Lorenzo Valla. Florence, Le Monnier.

BATTELLI, GIULIO. 1949³. Lezioni di paleografia. Città del Vaticano, Pont. Scuola Vaticana di Paleografia e Diplomatica.

BELL, AUBREY FITZ GERALD. 1925. Francisco Sánchez el Brocense. Hispanic Notes and Monographs 8. Oxford, University Press.

——. 1944. El renacimiento español. Traducción y prólogo de Eduardo Julia Mártinez. Zaragoza, Ebro, S.L.

BEMENT, NEWTON S. 1928. Petrus Ramus and the beginnings of formal French grammar. Romanic Review 19.309–23.

BENFEY, THEODOR. 1869. Geschichte der Sprachwissenschaft und orientalischen Philologie in Deutschland seit dem Anfange des 19. Jahrhunderts mit einem Rückblick auf die früheren Zeiten. Munich, Cotta'sche Buchhandlung.[Reprinted New York and London, Johnson Reprint Corporation, 1965.]

BISCHOFF, BERNARD. 1961. The study of foreign languages in the Middle Ages. Speculum 36.209–24.

BORST, ARNO. 1957–63. Der Turmbau von Babel: Geschichte der Meinungen über Ursprung und Vielfalt der Sprachen und Völker. 4 vols. bound in 6. Stuttgart, Hiersemann.

BRAUNE, W., and HELM, K. 1949. Althochdeutsches Lesebuch. Halle, Niemeyer.

BROWN, HORATIO F. 1891. The Venetian Printing Press. London, John C. Nimmo.

BRUNOT, FERDINAND. 1906. Histoire de la langue française des origines à 1900. Tome II: le seizième siècle. Paris, Armand Colin. [Reprinted Armand Colin, 1967.]

BURCKHARDT, JACOB. 1860. Die Kultur der Renaissance in Italien: ein Versuch. Basel, Schweighausers Verlagsbuchhandlung.

BYWATER, INGRAM. 1908. The Erasmian pronunciation of Greek, and its precursors. London and Oxford, Henry Frowde.

CORTI, MARIA. 1955. Marco Antonio Ateneo Carlino e l'influsso dei grammatici latini sui primi grammatici volgari. Cultura Neolatina 15.195–222.

COSENZA, MARIO EMILIO. 1962. Biographical and bibliographical dictionary of the Italian Humanists and of the World of Classical scholarship in Italy, 1300–1800. 6 vols. Boston, G.K. Hall.

EWERT, A. 1940. Dante's theory of language. Modern Language Review 35.355–66.

FABRICIUS, JOHANN ALBERT. 1715. Bibliotheca graeca. Volume 7. Accedunt nunc primum edita Grammatica Dionysii Thracis etc. Hamburg, Christian Liebezeit.

FERGUSON, WALLACE K. 1948. The Renaissance in historical thought; five centuries of interpretation. Boston, Houghton Mifflin.

——. 1962. Europe in Transition, 1300–1520. Boston, Houghton Mifflin.

FIERVILLE, CHARLES. 1886. Une grammaire latine inédite du XIIIe siècle, extraite des manuscrits No. 465 de Laon et No. 15462 (Fonds latin) de la Bibliothèque Nationale. Paris, Imprimerie Nationale.

FUNKE OTTO. 1938a. Grammatica Anglicana von P.Gr. (1594) nach dem Exemplar des britischen Museums herausgegeben und mit einer Einleitung versehen von Otto Funke. Wiener Beiträge zur englischen Philologie, 60. Vienne and Leipzig, Wilhelm Braumüller.

——. 1938b. William Bullokars Bref Grammar (1586), ein Beitrag zur Geschichte der frühneuenglischen Grammatik. Anglia, neue Folge. 50.116–37.

——. 1941. Die Frühzeit der englischen Grammatik. Schriften der literarischen Gesellschaft Bern, Neue Folge der Neujahrsblätter 4. Bern, Herbert Lang & Cie.

GAETA, FRANCO. 1955. Lorenzo Valla: filologia e storia nell'umanesimo italiano. Napoli, Istituto italiano per gli studi storici.

GALINDO ROMEO, PASCUAL, and ORTIZ MUÑOZ, LUIS. 1946. Antonio de Nebrija, Gramatica castellana, texto establecido sobre la ed. 'princeps' de 1492. 2 vols. Madrid, Edición de la Junta del Centenario.

GARCÍA, CONSTANTINO. 1960. Contribución a la historia de los conceptos gramaticales: la aportación del Brocense. Revista de Filología Española, Anejo 71. Madrid.

GARIN, EUGENIO. 1947. Der italienische Humanismus. Bern, Francke.

——. 1952. Prosatori latini del quattrocento. La Letteratura Italiana: Storia e Testi, vol. 13. Milan and Naples, Riccardo Ricciardi.

——. 1954. Interpretazioni del rinascimento. In Medioevo e Rinascimento: Studi e Ricerche, 90–107. Bari, Laterza.

——. 1965. La letteratura degli umanisti. In Storia della litteratura italiana, ed. by Emilio Cecchi and Natalino Sapegno, volume 3, Il Quattrocento e l'Ariosto, 7-353. Milan, Garzanti.

GEIGER, LUDWIG. 1882. Renaissance und Humanismus in Italien und Deutschland. Berlin, G. Grote.

GÉNIN, F. 1852. L'éclaircissement de la langue française [de Jehan Palsgrave], suivi de la Grammaire de Giles du Guez. Paris, Imprimerie nationale.

GESAMTKATALOG DER WIEGENDRUCKE. 1968. Herausgegeben von der Kommission für den Gesamtkatalog der Wiegendrucke. 7 vols. Stuttgart/New York, Hiersemann & Kraus.

GOLLING, JOSEPH. 1900. Zur Behandlung der lateinischen Syntax im 15. und 16. Jahrhundert. In Festschrift Johannes Vahlen zum siebzigsten Geburtstag gewidmet von seinen Schülern, 645–63. Berlin.

GONZÁLEZ-LLUBERA, IG. 1926. Nebrija: Gramática de la lengua Castellana, Muestra de la historia de las antigüedades de España, Reglas de orthografía en la lengua castellana. London, Humphrey Milford.

GRAVES, FRANK PIERREPONT. 1912. Peter Ramus and the educational reform of the sixteenth century. New York, Macmillan.

GRAYSON, CECIL. 1960a. Lorenzo, Macchiavelli and the Italian language. In Jacob 1960:410–32.

——. 1960b. A Renaissance controversy: Latin or Italian? An inaugural lecture delivered before the University of Oxford on 6 November 1959. Oxford, Clarendon Press.

——. 1963. Leon Battista Alberti and the beginnings of Italian grammar. Proceedings of the British Academy 49.291–311.

——. 1964. [Leon Battista Alberti.] La prima grammatica della lingua volgare. Bologna, Commissione per i testi di lingua.

GUARNASCHELLI, TERESA MARIA. 1943–65. Indice generale degli incunaboli delle biblioteche d'Italia ... compilato da T.M. Guarnaschelli e E. Valenziani. 4 vols. Rome, La libreria dello stato.

HAIN, LUDWIG. 1925. Repertorium bibliographicum, in quo libri omnes ab arte typographica inventa usque ad an. MD typis expressi ordine alphabetico vel simpliciter enumerantur vel accuratius recensentur. 2 vols. Berlin, Josef Altmann.

HALL, ROBERT A. 1942. The Italian Questione della Lingua: an interpretative essay. University of North Carolina Studies in the Romance Languages and Literature, No. 4. Chapel Hill, University of North Carolina.

HEATH, TERRENCE. 1971. Logical grammar, grammatical logic, and humanism in three German universities. Studies in the Renaissance 18.9–64.

HJELMSLEV, LOUIS. 1928. Principes de grammaire générale. Det kongelige danske videnskabernes selskab, historiskfilologiske meddelelser, XVI, 1. Copenhagen, Bianco Lunos Bogtrykkeri.

HUNT, R.W. 1950. Hugutio and Petrus Helias. Mediaeval and Renaissance Studies 2.174–8.

ISING, ERIKA. 1970. Die Herausbildung der Grammatik der Volkssprachen in Mittel- und Osteuropa. Berlin, Akademie-Verlag.

JACOB, E.F. 1960. Italian Renaissance studies: A tribute to the late Cecilia M. Ady. London, Faber & Faber.

JELLINEK, MAX HERMANN. 1913–14. Geschichte der neuhochdeutschen Grammatik von den Anfängen bis auf Adelung. 2 vols. Germanische Bibliothek herausgegeben von Wilhelm Streitberg. 2. Abt.: Untersuchungen und Texte. 7. Bd. Heidelberg, Carl Winter.

KEIL, HEINRICH. 1855–58. Grammatici Latini ex recensione Henrici Keilii. Vols. 2–3: Prisciani institutionum grammaticarum libri XVIII ex recensione Martini Hertzii. Leipzig, Teubner.

——. 1864. Grammatici Latini ex recensione Henrici Keilii. Vol. 4: Probi Donati Servii qui feruntur de arte grammatica libri ex recensione Henrici Keilii. Leipzig, Teubner.

KRISTELLER, PAUL OSKAR. 1956. Studies in Renaissance thought and letters. Storia e Letteratura: Raccolta di studi e teste, 54. Rome, Edizioni di Storia e Letteratura.

——. 1963. Iter italicum: A finding list of uncatalogued or incompletely catalogued humanistic manuscripts of the Renaissance in Italian and other libraries. Volume 1: Agrigento to Novara. London, the Warburg Institute and Leiden, E.J. Brill.

——. 1967. Iter italicum: A finding list of uncatalogued or incompletely catalogued humanistic manuscripts of the Renaissance in Italian and other libraries. Volume 2: Orvieto to Volterra, Vatican City. London, the Warburg Institute and Leiden, E.J. Brill.

KUKENHEIM, LOUIS. 1951. Contributions à l'histoire de la grammaire grecque, latine et hébraïque à l'époque de la Renaissance. Leiden, E.J. Brill.

——. 1962. Esquisse historique de la linguistique française et de ses rapports avec la linguistique générale. Leiden, Universitaire Pers.

LAKOFF, ROBIN. 1969. Review of Grammaire générale et raisonnée, ed. by Herbert H. Brekle. Language 45.343–64.

LAMBLEY, KATHLEEN. 1920. The teaching and cultivation of the French language in England during Tudor and Stuart times, with an introductory chapter on the preceding period. Manchester, the University Press.

LÁZARO CARRETER, FERNANDO. 1949. Las ideas lingüísticas en España durante el siglo XVIII. Revista de filología española. Anejo 48. Madrid.

LIVET, CHARLES-LOUIS. 1859. La grammaire française et les grammairiens du XVIe siècle. Paris, Didier & Durand.

MCKERROW, RONALD BRUNLEES. 1927. An introduction to bibliography for literary students. Oxford, Clarendon Press.

MANACORDA, GUISEPPE. 1914. Storia della scuola in Italia. Vol. 1. 2 parts. Milan, R. Sandron.

MANCINI, GIROLAMO. 1891. Vita di Lorenzo Valla. Florence, G.S. Sansoni.

MANUEL II. 1929–35. Livros antigos portuguezes, 1489–1600, da bibliotheca de sua Majestade fidelissima. Descriptos por S. M. El-Rei D. Manuel. Vol. 1, 1929; Vol. 2, 1932; Vol. 3, 1935. London, Maggs Bros.

MARIGO, ARISTIDE. 1936. I codici manoscritti delle 'Derivationes' di Uguccione Pisano: saggio d'inventario bibliografico con appendice sui codici del 'Catholicon' di Giovanni da Genova. Istituto di Studi Romani. Rome.

——. 1968. De vulgari eloquentia, ridotto a miglior lezione, commentato e tradotto da Aristide Marigo, con introduzione, analisi metrica della canzone, studio della lingua e glossario. Terza edizione con appendice di aggiornamento a cura di Pier Giorgio Ricci. Firenze, Felice le Monnier. [First edition 1938.]

MARINONI, AUGUSTO. 1944. Gli appunti grammaticali e lessicali di Leonardo da Vinci. Edited by Augusto Marinoni. 2 vols. Milan.

MARSHALL, J.H. 1969. The Donatz Proensals of Uc Faidit. London, Oxford University Press.

MAYANS Y SISCAR, GREGORIO. 1766. Francisci Sanctii Brocensis opera omnia, una cum ejusdem scriptoris vita, auctore Gregorio Maiansio. 4 vols. Geneva, Frères de Tournes.

MAZZATINTI, GIUSEPPE. 1890ff. Inventari dei manoscritti delle biblioteche d'Italia. 76 vols. Florence, L.S. Olschki.

MENÉNDEZ Y PELAYO, D. MARCELINO. 1888³. La ciencia española. 3 vols. Colección de escritores castellanos. Madrid, Pérez Dubruli.

MERCATI, GIOVANNI. 1925. Per la cronologia della vita e degli scritti di Niccolò Perotti, arcivescovo di Siponto. Studi e testi 44. Rome, Biblioteca apostolica vaticana.

MICHAEL, IAN. 1970. English grammatical categories and the tradition to 1800. Cambridge, Cambridge University Press.

MIGLIORINI, BRUNO. 1949. La questione della lingua. In Questioni e correnti di storia letteraria, ed. by U. Bosco et al., 1–75. Problemi ed Orientamenti

Critici di Lingua e di Letteratura Italiana 3, ed. by Attilio Momigliano. Milan, Carlo Marzorati.

——. 1960². Storia della lingua italiana. Florence, Sansoni.

MORHOF, DANIEL GEORG. 1732³. Polyhistor literarius, philosophicus et practicus. 2 vols. Lübeck, Peter Böckmann.

NEUMANN, SVEN-GÖSTA. 1959. Recherches sur le français des XVe et XVIe siècles et sur sa codification par les théoriciens de l'époque. Etudes romanes de Lund, 13. Lund, C.W.K. Gleerup and Copenhagen, Ejnar Munksgaard.

NOLAN, EDMOND, and S.A. HIRSCH. 1902. The Greek Grammar of Roger Bacon and a fragment of his Hebrew grammar. Cambridge, The University Press.

ONG, WALTER J., S.J. 1958a. Ramus: Method, and the decay of dialogue. Cambridge, Mass., Harvard University Press.

——. 1958b. Ramus and Talon Inventory. Cambridge, Mass., Harvard University Press.

PAGLIARO, A. 1947. La dottrina linguistica di Dante. Quaderni di Roma 1.485–501.

PALAU Y DULCET, ANTONIO. 1948ff. Manual del librero hispano-americano. 22 vols. Barcelona, Libreria Palau.

PERTUSI, A. 1962. 'Ερωτήματα. Per la storia e le fonti delle prime grammatiche greche a stampa. Italia medioevale e umanistica 5.321–51.

PINBORG, JAN. 1967. Die Entwicklung der Sprachtheorie im Mittelalter. Beiträge zur Geschichte der Philosophie und Theologie des Mittelalters, Band XLII, Heft 2. Münster, Achendorffsche Verlagsbuchhandlung and Copenhagen, Arne Frost-Hansen.

POGGIO, BRACCIOLINI. 1513. Poggi' Florentini Operum. Strassburg, Johann Knoblauch.

REICHLING, DIETRICH. 1893. Das Doctrinale des Alexander de Villa-Dei: kritisch-exegetische Ausgabe mit Einleitung, Verzeichniss der Handschriften und Drucke nebst Registern. Berlin, A. Hofmann.

ROBINS, R.H. 1967. A short history of linguistics. Indiana University Studies in the History and Theory of Linguistics. Bloomington, Indiana/London, Indiana University Press.

ROGERIO SÁNCHEZ, JOSÉ. 1931. Gramática Castellana por D. Antonio de Nebrija. Madrid, Hernando.

ROSSI, VITTORIO. 1945³. Il Quattrocento. Storia Letteraria d'Italia, 5. Milan, Francesco Vallardi.

SABBADINI, REMIGIO. 1896. La scuola e gli studi di Guarino Guarini Veronese (con 44 documenti). Catania, F. Galati.

——. 1902. Dei metodi nell'insegnamento della sintassi latina: considerazioni didattiche e storiche. Rivista di filologia 30.304–14.

——. 1906. Elementi nazionali nella teoria grammaticale dei Romani. Studi italiani di filologia classica 14.113–25.

——. 1922. Il metodo degli umanisti. In appendice l'elenco di tutti i lavori umanistici dell'autore. Florence, F. Le Monier.

SAINTE-BEUVE, C.A. 1952–55. Port-Royal. Texte présenté et annoté par Maxime Leroy. Paris, Gallimard.

SÁNCHEZ BARRADO, MOISÉS. 1919a. Estudios sobre el Brocense. Revista crítica Hispano-Americana 5.1–26.

——. 1919b. La elipsis según el Brocense en relación con su sistema gramatical. Segovia.

SANDYS, JOHN EDWIN. 1903. A history of classical scholarship from the sixth century B.C. to the end of the Middle Ages. Cambridge, University Press.

——. 1908. A history of classical scholarship. Vol. 2. Cambridge, University Press.

SCAGLIONE, ALDO D. 1970. Ars grammatica. Janua Linguarum, Series minor 77. The Hague, Mouton.

SILVA, PIETRO. 1918. Lo studio Pisano e l'insegnamento della grammatica nella seconda metà del sec. XIV. In Raccolta di studi di storia e critica letteraria dedicata a Francesco Flamini da' suoi discepoli, 475–93. Pisa.

STENGEL, EDMUND. 1878. Die beiden ältesten provenzalischen Grammatiken: lo donatz proensals und las rasos de trobar, nebst einem provenzalisch-italienischen Glossar, von neuem getreu nach den Hss. herausgegeben von Edmund Stengel. Marburg, N.G. Elwert.

——. 1890. Chronologisches Verzeichniss französischer Grammatiken vom Ende des 14. bis zum Ausgange des 18. Jahrhunderts, nebst Angabe der bisher ermittelten Fundorte derselben. Oppeln, G. Maske. Berlin, Wilhelm Gronau.

THUROT, CHARLES. 1869. Extraits de divers manuscrits latins pour servir à l'histoire des doctrines grammaticales au moyen âge. Paris, Imprimerie Impériale. [Reprinted, 1964. Frankfurt, Minerva.]

TIRABOSCHI, GIROLAMO. 1823. Storia della letteratura italiana. Tomo V. Dall'anno MCCC fino all'anno MCCCC. Parte seconda. Milan, Società tipografica de'-classici italiani.

TRABALZA, CIRO. 1908. Storia della grammatica italiana. Milano, Ulrico Hoepli. [Reprinted, 1963. Bologna, Arnaldo Forni.]

VERBURG, P. A. 1952. Taal en functionaliteit: Een historisch-critische studie over de opvattingen aangaande de functies der taal vanaf de prae-humanistische philologie van Orléans tot de rationalistische linguistiek van Bopp. Wageningen, H. Veenman & Zonen.

VIÑAZA, CIPRIANO MUÑOZ Y MANZANO, CONDE DE LA. 1893. Biblioteca histórica de la filología castellana. Madrid, Manuel Tello.

VOIGT, GEORG. 1893[3]. Die Wiederbelebung des classischen Alterthums oder das erste Jahrhundert des Humanismus. 2 vols. Berlin, Georg Reiner.

VORLAT, EMMA. 1964. Progress in English grammar, 1585–1735: A study of the development of English grammar and of the interdependence among the early

English grammarians. 4 vols. Luxembourg, A. Pfeiffer.

WALBERG, E. 1909. Antonio de Nebrija, Gramática Castellana. Halle, Niemeyer. [Reproduction phototypique de l'édition princeps (1492).]

WOLFF, MAX VON. 1893. Lorenzo Valla, sein Leben und seine Werke: eine Studie zur Litteratur-Geschichte Italiens im XV. Jahrhundert. Leipzig, Seemann.

WOODWARD, WILLIAM HARRISON. 1904. Desiderius Erasmus concerning the aim and method of education. Cambridge, University Press.

——. 1906. Studies in education during the age of the Renaissance, 1400–1600. Cambridge, University Press. [Reprinted, 1965. New York, Russell & Russell.]

——. 1921. Vittorino da Feltre and other humanist educators: Essays and versions. An introduction to the history of classical education. Cambridge, University Press. [Reprinted, 1964. New York, Bureau of Publications, Teachers College, Columbia University.]

WROBEL, IOH. 1887. Eberhardi Bethuniensis Graecismus. Corpus grammaticorum medii aeui, 1. Bratislav, Koebner.

THE SEVENTEENTH CENTURY

HERBERT E. BREKLE

INTRODUCTION

In accordance with the intentions of the Editorial Board this chapter is not meant to be a full-scale history of the linguistic achievements of the seventeenth century; it is rather a critical report on some aspects of research that has been carried out in this field during the last few decades pertaining to grammar and the theory of language. At some places the available material is supplemented by readings and interpretations that occurred to the present writer as he looked through various sources. Moreover, it should be borne in mind that this article is — at least in principle — restricted to an evaluation of works and contributions dealing with questions of general linguistics and some adjacent areas, like, e.g., language philosophy and semiotics. Consequently, no attempt is made to discuss the endless number of grammars and grammatical treatises dealing with some particular language or special aspects of one or another language.[1]

Furthermore, it is not the intention of this article to determine with reasonable accuracy the various influences of earlier writers on grammatical doctrines developed during the seventeenth century; at certain points, however, where reliable work on special influences on certain grammarians is available, such results will be included in our survey. Another problem consists in describing possible cross-relationships between authors belonging to the period under consideration. Due to the lack of a relatively complete history of linguistics in the seventeenth century only fragmentary informations can be given on this point.

In most of the recently published full-scale works on the history of linguistics, e.g. Verburg 1951, Borst 1957–63, Tagliavini 1964, Ivič 1965, Kukenheim 1966, Robins 1967, Mounin 1967, Arens 1969, and Leroy 1971, the seventeenth century is not treated as fully as one would wish in view of the many important philosophical and linguistic contributions stemming from this century.[2] More specialized works, as for example Rossi 1960, Kretzmann 1967 and Formigari 1970 will be discussed in the proper places.

[1] References for this chapter of the history of linguistics are, e.g. Benfey 1869, Stengel 1890, Trabalza 1908, Jellinek 1913, Brunot 1922–24, Vorlat 1963, Kukenheim 1966, Alston 1965–67, Michael 1970.

[2] In the same vein P. Rossi (1968:2) utters his complaints: 'A chi ... nutre invece un qualque interesse per la storia dei problemi filosofici e delle idee nel Seicento, questi testi fanno una

Among the works dealing with the history of linguistics Verburg's somewhat neglected book, *Taal en functionaliteit* (1951), occupies a special place. Its subtitle says that it is meant to be 'a historical-critical study of the conceptions of the functions of language extending from the pre-humanistic philology of the Orléans-school to Bopp's rationalist linguistics'. As far as the seventeenth century is concerned Verburg presents a philosophically and linguistically well-founded discussion of the main lines of language philosophy and linguistics. Verburg places Bacon among such Renaissance philosophers as Giordano Bruno, Tommaso Campanella, and Montaigne. Further subdivisions are 'Het scientale rationalisme' and 'Het practicale rationalisme'. Verburg considers Descartes, Hobbes, Locke, Leibniz and the inventors of philosophical languages (e.g. Wilkins) as falling under what he calls 'scientific rationalism', whereas the Port-Royal Grammar and its various successors in the eighteenth century (Harris, Dumarsais, Beauzée, Condillac *et al.*) are placed under the heading of 'practical rationalism'. This distinction between these two tendencies, may — at first sight — seem to be somewhat strange, but if one reads carefully Verburg's argumentation (1951:321ff.) it becomes acceptable insofar as the linguistic philosophy of Descartes, Locke, and Leibniz (Locke in this connection is a bit problematic) does not take into consideration the psychological or pragmatic functions of language to the same extent as the more practically minded rationalists. For the present writer there is no doubt that Verburg's work is indeed a rich source for the more philosophically oriented linguist (Chomsky would have done well to study Verburg's book before entering the stage of linguistic history).

Borst (1957–63) is an impressive work in six volumes. Its title, *Der Turmbau von Babel: Geschichte der Meinungen über Ursprung und Vielfalt der Sprachen und Völker*, gives a rough idea as to its aims and scope. The method of Borst's book is exclusively historical and is rooted deeply in the German tradition. Borst's aim is to delineate the cultural and religious history of the idea of the seventy-two languages extant after Babylonian linguistic confusion. He produces masses of sources relating not so much to the history of linguistics — even if taken in its broad sense — but rather to the history of religious beliefs concerning the number, pre-eminence and age of various languages. This he does also for the seventeenth century where he depicts in his typical erudite manner a broad prospect of practically all European countries with their respective peculiarities and cross-relationships centering around the main theme of the book.[3]

---

curiosa impressione. Leggendoli, nella vana ricerca di una illuminazione, da parte dei "competenti", sulle discussioni relative al linguaggio, ci si trova di fronte, nel piú dei casi, a conclusioni molto deludenti, a formule passivamente riprese e ripetute, travasate da un libro all'altro ...'. See also the various reviews in Malkiel and Langdon 1968.

[3] Tagliavini (1964:384) gives the following evaluation of Borst's monumental work: 'Una diffussissime (ed anzi troppo prolissa) storia delle teorie sull'origine del linguaggio e sulla differenziazione linguistica ...'.

Tagliavini (1964:35-50) in his chapter "Dal Rinascimento al secolo XVIII" deals briefly with etymological and other achievements in diachronic linguistics. He mentions Ménage 1650 and several early grammars of non-Indoeuropean languages, e.g. De Rhodes 1651, Rivola 1624, Petraeus 1649, Maggio 1670, Dias 1697.

Ivič (1965:26–9) presents only a few remarks on 17th century linguistics. She mentions the Port-Royal Grammar as a representative of linguistic theory in the period under discussion and Franciscus Junius (1589–1677) and George Hickes (1642–1715) as the founders of comparative philology.

Kukenheim (1966) dedicates eight pages to the 17th century. He states briefly the dominance of Bacon, Descartes, Hobbes, Spinoza, Locke, and Leibniz not only in philosophical but also in linguistic matters. A few disparaging remarks on the chapter "De Ellipsi" in Scioppius 1628 betray clearly Kukenheim's positivistic position. Finally he mentions two Dutch scholars Franciscus Junius (the Younger) and Petrus Montanus (Pieter Berch). The latter is noteworthy for his phonetic treatise *Spreeckonst* (1635).[4] Kukenheim's main topic, however, is the development of French grammar. On six pages (32–8) he glosses over the main linguistic events in 17th century France: Malherbe's normative influence, the foundation of the 'Académie française' in 1635, Vaugelas' doctrine of the 'bon usage' as sketched in his *Remarques sur la langue françoise* (1647), and, among some lexicographical matters,[5] a short description of the main ideas of the Port-Royal *Grammar* (1660).

Robins (1967) deals with the 17th century within his chapter "The Renaissance and after" (94–132). After sketching the philosophical background of the century (Bacon, Locke, Berkeley, Descartes, Leibniz) he gives a short description of Bishop Wilkins's *Essay* (1668). He goes on to discuss briefly several works on phonetics (e.g. Wallis 1653, Holder 1669) followed by a few remarks on grammars by Wallis (1653), Jonson (1640), Gill (1619), and Cooper (1685). Finally, he gives a clear description of the linguistic theory embedded in the Port-Royal Grammar together with a cautious attempt to link this position with linguistic doctrines in the line of Hjelmslev (1928) and Chomsky (1964).

Mounin (1967:124–41) displays a sense of systematicity insofar as he first mentions some works dealing especially with 'la deuxième articulation' (i.e. phonology), e.g. Cordemoy 1668a, Petrus Montanus 1635, A. Hume 1617, Holder 1669, Dalgarno 1680, Lodwick 1647, Beck 1657, Wilkins 1668. In the second section, dealing with 'la première articulation', he comments on the grammatical system of the Port-Royal *Grammar*. The next two sections contain lists of various descriptive grammars (including treatises on exotic languages) and several attempts related to historical studies of languages (e.g. Guichard 1606, Ménage 1650). Mounin is noteworthy for his special section on Giambattista Vico (1668–1744). He presents

[4] See Verschuur 1924 for an evaluation of this early treatise on Dutch phonetics.

[5] See also Brunot 1924 (43, 262–70).

Vico's *Principi di una scienza nuova* (1744³) as a theory on the origin and development of languages.

Arens (1969)[6] can be characterized — at least as far as his chapter on 17th century linguistics is concerned — as an anthology of necessarily fragmentary texts translated into German and derived from works by Bacon (1623), Wallis (1653), Locke (1690), Port-Royal (1660), Leibniz. The commentaries connecting the various excerpts contain mainly factual information on other well-known 17th century grammarians. At certain points, however, Arens sets out to pronounce judgments on the validity and fruitfulness of certain theoretical trends; his main target is the Port-Royal *Grammar*. In this connection Arens speaks of the Port-Royal method as a 'Tyrannei der Räson'. For him comparative philology as developed during the 19th century seems to be the only gauge with which linguistic theories can be judged as to their usefulness.[7]

Leroy (1971) has nothing relevant to say on seventeenth century linguistics. His few remarks on the Port-Royal *Grammar* and on Cordemoy's position in the history of phonetics (see below, 5.3.) are prejudiced, contradictory or factually wrong. He speaks (1971:12f.) of the *Grammaire générale* (1660) as 'balayant les observations de bon sens que Vaugelas avait émises quelques années plus tôt dans ses célèbres *Remarques sur la langue française* dont l'ambition était de constater et de décrire — il faudra attendre deux siècles pour revenir à cette méthode saine — la grammaire de Port-Royal veut expliquer les faits, démontrer que le langage, image de la pensée, est fondé sur la Raison, bref construire selon la logique une espèce de schéma du langage auquel, bon gré mal gré, doivent se plier les multiples apparences de la langue réelle.' If it is the aim of the Port-Royal *Grammar*, as Leroy himself admits, to explain linguistic facts within some linguistic theory, then universal grammarians cannot be accused of disregarding empirical data as given by language usage, etc. It is rather the so-called 'pure descriptivists' that must cope with questions as to the scientific status of their descriptive results.[8]

Whitehead's dictum in his *Science and the modern world* adequately expresses the relevance of seventeenth century ideas, this is especially true for language philosophy and linguistics:

> A brief, and sufficiently accurate, description of the intellectual life of the European races during the succeeding two centuries and a quarter up to our own times is that they have been living upon the accumulated capital of ideas provided for them by the genius of the seventeenth century. (Whitehead 1925)

[6] Compared with the first edition (1955) the chapter under discussion did not undergo substantial modifications. On p. 93 (1969), however, we find the sweeping remark that 'man schließlich doch finden wird, daß ihr [sc. grammatical treatises for the 17th–19th centuries] Nutzen und Erkenntniswert für die heutige Forschung mager sind.'

[7] See also p. 93: 'All das — die allgemeine Grammatik ... — geriet mit dem Anbruch der modernen vergleichenden Sprachwissenschaft langsam in Mißkredit, zumal diese kaum irgendwelchen Nutzen daraus ziehen konnte.'

[8] See *Grammaire* (1676:II, ch. IX) on the famous controversy with Vaugelas (1647) about the nature of relative clauses. Cf. Chomsky's discussion of this point (1966:56f.).

In agreement with Professor Aarsleff — the author of the chapter on eighteenth century linguistics — this chapter will contain nothing on Leibniz's linguistic conceptions, nor shall the special case of relationships between Locke and Leibniz be dealt with here.

The bibliography appended to this chapter has two parts; the first part lists the primary sources that are mentioned in the text, the second part gives secondary sources, i.e. works dealing in one way or another with the primary sources.[9]

1. LINGUISTICS IN SEVENTEENTH CENTURY ENGLAND

1.1 *The Philosophical Ascent*

1.1.1 *Bacon*

It is not only for chronological reasons that a presentation of topics relating to 17th century linguistic doctrines should open with a discussion of relatively recent interpretations of Baconian linguistic philosophy. Most of the themes dealt with by the 'learned Verulam', especially in his works *The advancement of learning* (1605) and in the revised and enlarged Latin version of this work (*De augmentis scientiarum*, 1622–3), are taken up again in the writings of other linguists and philosophers of the seventeenth century.[10]

In the last four decades or so we find a number of treatises trying to interpret the numerous passages in Bacon's works that can be said to be of some relevance for the philosophy and theory of language or languages (Funke 1926; Wallace 1943; Verburg 1951:185–219; Rossi 1957 (English translation 1968); De Mas 1963; Apel 1963:286–96; Rosiello 1967:19–29; Kretzmann 1967:375–376; Formigari Cubeddu 1968 and Formigari 1970). The last work mentioned has come to my attention only very recently; it is noteworthy for its competent discussion of linguistic philosophy in connection with the epistemological tendencies prevalent in 17th century England. There is relatively little disagreement between these authors as to their interpretation of Bacon's semiotic and grammatical conceptions.

In the following we shall not try to sum up for the ninth time Bacon's doctrine of the four idols, nor shall we try to delineate again the well-known Baconian system of sciences and the exact place of semiotics, grammar, or linguistics therein (for a survey of the latter see Funke 1926, reprinted in Funke 1965 (51–77) and Rossi 1968 [Ital. 1957]:152–66). What we shall do instead is to discuss certain theoretical positions contained in Bacon's work that seem to be of special interest for an understanding of Bacon's linguistic and metalinguistic conceptions and which, at

[9] At this point the present writer feels obliged to express his gratitude towards several of his co-workers: to Mrs. Asbach-Schnitker, M.A., who helped in preparing the sub-chapter on Comenius, to Mrs. Krefft, who did a fine job in typing the difficult text, and to Mr. Köllner for his help in bibliographical matters.

[10] See e.g. Rossi (1960:201–8), where Bacon's influence on a group of scholars such as Wilkins and Webster is demonstrated.

the same time, appear to be relevant for present-day discussions on various problems of general linguistics.

It is in the sixth book of Bacon's *De dignitate et augmentis scientiarum* that our author deals with the properties and subdivisions of what he calls 'the art of transmission'. Nowadays we would classify the topics mentioned here as belonging to various branches of semiotics or theory of communication.[11]

Bacon places his 'art of transmission' *(ars traditiva)* alongside other 'intellectual arts', whose total number is assumed to be four. These four arts, Bacon declares, are 'divided according to the ends whereunto they are referred; for man's labour is to *invent* that which is *sought* or *propounded;* or to *judge* that which is *invented*; or to *retain* that which is *judged*; or to *deliver over* that which is *retained*. So as the arts must be four: Art of Inquiry or Invention; Art of Examination of Judgment; Art of Custody or Memory; and Art of Elocution or Tradition.' (*De augmentis*, V, 1; Works 3.384f.)

Bacon wants the art of tradition (or 'transmission') to include all the arts which relate to words and discourse.

The art of transmission is divided into three parts:

a) the doctrine concerning the Organ of Discourse
b) the doctrine concerning the Method of Discourse, and
c) the doctrine concerning the Illustration or adornment of Discourse.

In the following we shall concentrate on Bacon's 'doctrine concerning the Organ of Discourse'. It is discussed in the first chapter of the sixth Book of *De augmentis*. The other two parts of Bacon's art of transmission are not taken into consideration here. By 'Method of Discourse' Bacon means the composition of a text or various sorts of texts following certain didactic and pragmatic criteria; this leads to the third part 'Illustration or adornment of Discourse' — commonly called rhetoric — where various types of figures and literary forms are considered as to their effect on the hearer or reader.[12]

When Bacon refers to the parts of his 'doctrine concerning the Organ of Dis-

[11] Cf. Apel (1963:286–96) who refers to Bacon's semiotics and linguistics as having great importance for the historical movement called 'Sprachhumanismus'. Apel discovers in Bacon's program 'die technisch-szientifische Umdeutung des genuin humanistischen Sprachdenkens von einer im Kern nominalistischen Position aus' (286). That Apel's judgment is essentially correct can be seen from Bacon's numerous hints and remarks on the usefulness of his 'art of transmission' for further research in such fields as psychology, anthropology, rhetoric etc. See, for example, Bacon's lengthy discussion on the merits of 'common' and 'private alphabets' (*Works* 4). By 'common alphabets' he understands our normal orthographical systems, any reform of these 'in which the spelling should agree with the pronunciation' he regards as belonging to the 'class of unprofitable subtleties' (444). By 'private alphabets' he understands ciphers or codes 'agreed upon by particular persons'. Bacon himself proposes a binary code made up of combinations of the two letters *a* and *b*.

[12] See on the latter subject the extensive treatment of Baconian rhetoric in K. R. Wallace 1943. For an overall discussion of problems concerning logic and rhetoric in England from 1500–1700 see Howell's well-documented work 1956. Bacon receives special attention in the sixth chapter in connection with Lamy 1675 (Engl. 1676), Hobbes 1637 and Glanvill 1678.

course' he expressly does not restrict himself to the elements and structure of ordinary spoken or written languages but wants to include any system of symbolic representation, be it pictorial or gestural. For him 'it seems that the art of transmission has some other children besides Words and Letters.' (*De augmentis* VI, 1; *Works* 4.439). A general criterion valid for any semiotic system to be used for human communication is laid down in the following lines:

> . . . whatever can be divided into differences sufficiently numerous to explain the variety of notions (provided those differences be perceptible to the sense) may be made a vehicle to convey the thoughts of one man to another.

From Bacon's own words it is clear that this criterion should cover any semiotic system; natural languages being 'doubly articulated' (Martinet 1960) and hieroglyphic systems or systems of 'real characters' where there is not necessarily a level of second articulation. That Bacon recognizes the principle of 'double articulation' is shown by his division of Grammar into the two parts: 'Speech' (*locutio*) and 'Writing' (*scriptio*). He justifies this division by quoting Aristotle who 'says rightly that "words are the images of thoughts and letters are the images of words".' (Bacon, *Works* 4.439; Aristotle *De Interpretatione* I, 1).[13]

In modern terms we might try to interpret this in such a way that Bacon's grammar would consist of a component dealing with matters of 'speech' (syntax, semantics, lexicon, and prosody) and of a component where graphematic and phonological matters are described. That Bacon also wants phonology to be included as a part of grammar is shown by a later passage where he declares that 'To grammar

[13] The English translation of Aristotle's statement (Bacon, *Works* 4.439) concerning the relation between 'words' and 'letters' is liable to be misunderstood (at least by present-day readers). We may paraphrase Aristotle's statement as: 'words, written or spoken, are the images of thought, and letters, written or spoken, are the images of words'. This interpretation would seem a possible one for Bacon's own ideas on the relation between words and letters. Even if we consider Bacon's original Latin version, where the quotation from Aristotle reads as follows: 'Cogitationum tesserae verba, verborum literae', we cannot be completely certain that Bacon would have agreed with the essence of Aristotle's statement, namely that 'Words spoken are symbols or signs of affections or impressions of the soul; written words are the signs of words spoken' (this is H. P. Cook's close translation of the Greek text, Cook 1962:115). It is evident that the Aristotelian judgment on the indirect relation between written words and their content is identical with de Saussure's (cf. 1916:45). A thin thread of evidence for a possible difference between Bacon's and Aristotle's position can be found a few lines further on in *De augmentis* (*Works* 1.652) where Bacon is not content to say 'verba volant, scripta manent' but expressly specifies this by saying: '. . . verba prolata volant, scripta manent'. So, *verbum* alone could really mean, with Bacon, 'spoken or written word'. This, together with his general semiotic principle (see *Works* 4.439), would then mean that Bacon would not be strictly against the glossematic principle postulating the systematic independence of graphematic representations of linguistic content-structures form respective acoustic sequences. (See Hjelmslev 1963:103f.) This whole problem, if it is one, was not seen by other authors dealing with Baconian linguistics. Wallace (1943:9) distorts Bacon's division of grammar into 'locutio' and 'scriptio' by interpreting it as a division between 'Speech' and 'Words'. Funke (1926:28), too, is not very clear when paraphrasing Bacon like this: '. . . die Worte sind Zeichen für die Gedanken, die Buchstaben für die Worte. B[acon] stimmt darin überein, daß die Grammatik von beidem, von der Sprache und der Schrift, zu handeln hätte.'

[Editor's note: Cf. Bacon's own version in Bacon 1605 (*Works* 3.399): 'Words are the images of cogitations, and letters are the images of words.']

also I refer all accidents of words, of what kind soever; such as Sound, Measure, Accent' (*Works* 4.442). Moreover, there exists a tradition in writing grammars, which goes right back to antiquity, of presenting jointly (under such headings as 'de literis') the elements of the alphabet and the respective sounds of a language. The term *litera* is used to mean both graphemic and phonemic/phonetic elements; if necessary a distinction is made between *figura* and *potestas* (phonetic value) of a letter.

Within the more general scope of semiotics Bacon distinguishes between two kinds of signs that without the help or intervention of spoken or written words may carry significations:

one *ex congruo,* where the note has some congruity with the notion, the other *ad placitum,* where it is adopted and agreed upon at pleasure. Of the former kind are Hieroglyphics and Gestures; of the latter the Real characters above mentioned. The use of Hieroglyphics is very old, and held in a kind of reverence, especially among the Egyptians, a very ancient nation. So that they seem to have been a kind of earlier born writing, and older than the very elements of letters . . .[14] it is plain that Hieroglyphics and Gestures have always some similitude to the thing signified, and are a kind of emblems. Whence I have called them 'notes of things by congruity'. Real characters on the other hand have nothing emblematic in them, but are merely surds, no less than the elements of letters themselves,[15] and are only framed *ad placitum,* and

[14] Rosiello (1967:21f.) compares Bacon's thesis of the symbolic origin of our alphabets with views brought forth a hundred years later by G. Vico, who in his *Principi di Scienza Nuova* (1725) not only assumes a symbolic origin of the alphabets of languages but even considers this symbolic origin as being closely related to the natural origin of language. Apel (1963:368) comments on Vico's ideas along the following lines: Vico's assumption that man's first medium of language was not sounds but symbols can be taken seriously if the term symbol is interpreted as including all sorts of gestures, symbolic actions (e.g. dance). Such a 'symbolic language' may either have antedated the development of a sound language, or, more probably, may have co-existed with certain primitive sound-patterns. This hypothesis would mean that the generally accepted view of the priority of spoken language over symbolic language would have to be modified. See also Rossi 1968 (168) where Bacon's idea of the symbolic origin of natural languages is brought together with Vico's claim concerning a sensory origin of languages in gestures.

[15] As I see it, there is again a problem of interpretation. What is meant by 'Real characters . . . are merely surds, no less than the elements of letters themselves'? In the Latin original we read: '. . . Characteres Reales . . . plane surdi sunt; non minus quam ipsa elementa literarum . . .'. A 'real character', e.g. an element of some nautical flag code, may be said to be surd (or a surd) if by *surd* we mean 'exhibiting no analogical connection with the thing or idea it stands for'. This clearly distinguishes a real character from some hieroglyph or some other iconic sign. As for the meaning of *surd* or Neo-latin *surdus* a little bit of etymology can help to clarify this peculiar expression in our context: according to the OED *surd* (n.) can mean 'irrational number'. *Surd* acquired this mathematical sense by way of a mistranslation of Greek *alogos* — meaning also 'speechless' — into Latin *surdus.* Thus *surd* in our context can be interpreted as 'speechless, speaking not of its own', as compared with those signs that carry significations *ex congruo.* Another problem lies in the comparison of 'real characters' to 'elements of letters'. There seems to be a difficulty with the equation 'elements of letters' = *elementa literarum.* Apel (1963:289) gives a meaningful translation of *elementa literarum* as 'Buchstaben der Schrift'. In my opinion *literae* here means 'inventory of sounds or letters'. We may now paraphrase the passage as: 'Real characters are not self-explaining, they do not exhibit an analogical connection with the thing or idea they stand for, no less than the sounds or letters of the alphabet with regard to some set of notions, both are only framed *ad placitum,* and silently agreed upon by custom.'

silently agreed on by custom. It is evident however that a vast multitude of them is wanted for writing; for there ought to be as many of them as there are radical words. (*Works* 4.440)

From this passage we may infer that Bacon was well acquainted with the distinction between signs signifying *ex congruo* and those signifying *ad placitum*; this distinction goes back at least to Aristotle.[16] From the earlier English version of our text (*The advancement of learning* 1605) we learn that Bacon did not restrict the *ad placitum* criterion to 'real characters' but wants also the words of natural languages to be determined by this principle.[17] This is also confirmed by what he has to say on the use of etymology for the solution of semantic questions. Bacon by no means approves 'of that curious inquiry, which nevertheless so great a man as Plato did not despise; namely concerning the imposition and original etymology of names; on the supposition that they were not arbitrarily fixed at first (supponendo ac si illa [nomina] jam a principio ad placitum indita minime fuissent), but derived and deduced by reason and according to significance; a subject elegant indeed, and pliant as wax to be shaped and turned... but yet sparingly true and bearing no fruit.'

As to the usefulness of semantic or etymological analyses of ordinary language expressions for discovering scientific truths Bacon's position is that of a cautious sceptic.[18] Compare the following two passages, the first taken from the *Novum organum* (1620), the second from *De augmentis* (1623).

But the Idols of the Market-place are the most troublesome of all: idols which have crept into the understanding through the alliances of words and names. For men believe that their reason governs words; but it is also true that words react on the understanding; and this it is that has rendered philosophy and the sciences sophistical and inactive. Now words, being commonly framed and applied according to the capacity of the vulgar, follow those lines of division which are most obvious to the vulgar understanding. And whenever an understanding of greater acuteness or a more diligent observation would alter those lines to suit the true divisions of nature, words stand in the way and resist the change. (*Works* 4, 60f.)

16 See Coseriu 1967:87ff. In his otherwise extensive survey on the history of 'l'arbitraire du signe' Coseriu does not mention Bacon's position.

17 *Works* 3.400: '*Ad placitum* are the Characters Real before mentioned, and Words: although some have been willing by curious inquiry, or rather by apt feigning, to have derived imposition of names from reason and intendment.'

18 In Formigari Cubeddu 1968 (161f.) we find an interesting parallel relating to this question between Bacon and one of his contemporary philosophers, namely Francesco Sánchez (this is not the famous grammarian but a namesake, who lived from 1551-1623. See *Enciclopedia de la cultura española*, vol. 5. Madrid, 1963). Both authors are sceptical as to the possibility of describing or defining in a precise way the semantic side of words (synchronically and diachronically). Sánchez, known as 'el Escéptico', agrees in the main with Bacon, although stressing the fact that it is within the context of vulgar, ordinary languages that we learn to speak: 'Verborum significationes magis aut omnio a vulgo pendere videntur, ab eoque proinde petendas esse: quis enim nos loqui docuit nisi vulgus ... In vulgo autem an aliqua certitudo et stabilitas? Necquiquam ... Dices forsan quaerendum esse qua significatione qui primum imposuit usus fuerit. Quaere igitur: non invenies.' (*Quod nihil scitur in Opera philosophica*, ed. J. de Carvalho, Coimbra 1955:5).

Certainly words are the footsteps of reason, and the footsteps tell something about the body (*Works* 4.441)

This latter passage should be seen in its context. After his general semiotic discussion Bacon goes on to divide grammar into two types: 'the one being Literary,[19] the other Philosophical. The one is used simply for languages, that they may be learned more quickly or spoken more correctly and purely; the other ministers in a certain degree to philosophy' (*ibid.*). This philosophical grammar 'should diligently inquire, not the analogy of words with one another, but the analogy between words and things, or reason; not going so far however as that interpretation which belongs to Logic' (*ibid.*).

Bacon places his 'philosophical grammar' on the boundaries between linguistics and logic; his 'philosophical grammar' would correspond to something like general or universal linguistic semantics where relevant categories and propositional structures should be set up, whereas it would fall within the province of Logic to deal in the truth-functions and deductions.

In addition, Bacon wants his 'philosophical grammar' to fulfil tasks both of comparative linguistics and of ethnolinguistics. To Bacon the results of such studies are profound. First, all languages would not only be 'enriched by mutual exchanges, but the several beauties of each may be combined (as in the Venus of Apelles) into a most beautiful image and excellent model of speech itself, for the sight expressing of the meanings of the mind' (*Works* 4.442).[20]

Second, such inquiries will produce valuable information 'concerning the disposition and manners of peoples and nations, drawn from their languages' (*ibid.*).

To conclude, we must mention briefly Bacon's treatment of phonetic and prosodic phenomena. According to him 'The primary formation of simple letters [sounds] indeed (that is by what percussion of the tongue, by what opening of the mouth ... the sound of each letter is produced) does not belong to Grammar, but is part of the doctrine concerning Sounds, and to be handled under Sense and the Sensible' (*Works* 4.442f.). Thus articulatory phonetics would be considered as belonging to the physical sciences. But, he continues, 'the sound which I speak of as belonging to Grammar relates only to sweetnesses and harshnesses' (443), meaning that Bacon wants certain phonotactic regularities to be described by Grammar. Furthermore he considers 'measure' and 'accent' as accidents of words: 'measure' as exhibited in 'the style and form of words: that is to say, metre or verse; wherein the art we have is a very small thing, but the examples are large and innumerable' (443), and 'accent' as exhibited in the rule-governed accentuation of words. In

[19] In the second book of *The advancement of learning* (1605) we read: 'the one popular ... the other philosophical, examining the power and nature of words as they are the footsteps and prints of reason ...' (*Works* 3.401).

[20] We find a very similar idea put into practice in Wolfius 1578. He demands that a common German language should take over the best from all German dialects: 'una tamen quaedam communis lingua est Germanorum, que ex omnibus optima quaeque et minime aspera deligit ...' (see Jellinek 1913:1, § 30).

contradistinction to the well-known stressing rules of words, Bacon sets down as wanting the doctrine concerning the accentuation of sentences. Bacon obviously alludes here to patterns of accent and pitch variations related to different sentence types (assertive, interrogative etc.):

> . . . it is common to all mankind almost to drop the voice at the end of a period, to raise it in asking a question, and other things of the kind not a few. (*Works* 4.444)

It was the aim of the foregoing remarks to give a rough idea of the scope of Bacon's linguistic conceptions which — with the exception of Kretzmann's lengthy article on the history of semantics (1967) — did not stand in the center of most of the monographs and articles mentioned at the beginning of this section. These contributions lay more stress on wider philosophical aspects of Bacon's work, or, in the case of Wallace 1943, on literary and rhetorical ideas.

1.1.2 *The case Webbe vs. Brookes (ca. 1630): Language learning by way of pattern drills or by application of rules of grammar*

In her very informative review of Chomsky 1966, Vivian Salmon (1969) presents a very interesting piece of evidence against Chomsky's over-simplified discussion of the history of the innateness hypothesis. In a way it is unfortunate that Salmon has buried this information in a review-article; in order to remedy this, Salmon's discussion of the case Webbe vs. Brookes shall be reproduced here in some detail. The material evidence of the case is preserved in the British Museum in the Sloane MS. 1466. According to Salmon (1969:184) the controversy between Webbe and Brookes must have taken place early in the 1630's. According to Salmon (1969: 183f.) Chomsky (1966:29) 'appears to regard Bloomfield, Saussure, Hockett and others who exemplify for him "modern linguists" as deviating from an earlier tradition in which it was normal to regard language acquisition as dependent on innate ideas and not on pattern-learning. This is also an over-simplification, since the Bloomfield school was reviving, although unwillingly, a view current in the seventeenth century, and very much the subject of debate in the decade before Descartes's first publication appeared. This debate, in terms of "patterns" as opposed to "judgment" had begun early in the sixteenth century as a result of the growing necessity for the teaching both of the vernaculars and of Latin, as a means of international communication; and towards the end of the century scholars were engaged in a "grammar war" between those who thought that Latin could be taught by the repetition of patterns and those who concentrated on the teaching of grammar, so that the learner could produce sentences in accordance with deliberately acquired rules.'

Biographical details on the two English schoolmasters, Joseph Webbe and William Brookes, can be gained from Salmon 1964.[21] The following quotations

[21] See also Salmon 1961 (287–96), where she argues for a probable cooperation between Joseph Webbe and the dramatist and grammarian James Shirley. Shirley's Latin grammar (1649) was

show that they conducted a rather heated discussion on the respective usefulness of the pattern learning method and the method of learning language by means of expressly stated and deliberately acquired grammatical rules.

Joseph Webbe held the pattern-drill position, he had invented and patented a method of language teaching by patterns, and had published textbooks in which the method was used. William Brookes, the defender of the rule-governed method of language teaching, was employed by some interested lay patron in order to evaluate Webbe's work.

Webbe's argument, slightly reminiscent of modern behaviorism, runs as follows:

> Looke uppon Children in their learninge languages, nature teaceth them to use the sense before the judgment: they are asked wilt thau have some drinke? they heare, but are not able yet to form any word, nor understand the meaning there they see a pott or glasse ... by some few repetitions of the wordes and reiterations of the same actions of shewing potts and puttinge it to theyre mouths and often tasting thereof, they ... will at lenght [sic] never see a pott, but it will put out the hand, and beginne to crye drinke: Wherin I rather [see] an action of memory taken from the outward sense than of judgement or understandinge. As in doggs, that once hearinge the bell and presently feeling the lash, will never after heare the bell, but will runne away barking or crying. ... God forbidd we should call this judgement or understandinge. (MS. f.267, as quoted in Salmon 1969:184).

Brookes' more rationalist counterposition can be clearly derived from the following:

> Now where the memory is first furnished, the judgment must receive from it what soever it hath: and this, because it is contrary to the course of nature will be long a doeing. But where the understanding is first informed, the memory will soone be qualified by it sufficiently for the habitt: because this is accordinge to natures order. (MS. Sloane 1466,f.278, as quoted in Salmon 1969)

Interestingly enough it is the 'rationalist' Brookes who refers to psychology applied to language-learning; he notes, for example, that there are certain pragmatical factors determining the meaning of sentences. According to Brookes certain words 'expresse not the matter of the clause but the affection of the speaker makinge praeparation to the matter as interjections, vocative cases and some Adverbs' (MS. f.278, as quoted in Salmon 1969).

published by Thomas Philipps in 1726 under the somewhat exaggerating title: *An essay towards an universal and rational grammar*. Salmon 1961 is also very instructive as to the treatment 'of at least two major seventeenth-century grammatical problems and of contemporary attempts at solutions — the problem of the classification of the parts of speech, and that of a terminology to describe the structure of the sentence.' (287). As to the first problem, Salmon shows convincingly how three methods of classifying the parts of speech were evaluated by grammarians such as Shirley, Lilly, Hewes, and others. The three methods are: the formal (i.e. morphological), the structural (by the position of parts of speech in a sentence) and the semasiological or semantic (by their relationship to the categories of reality). See in this connection especially Michael 1970 where a very full discussion of the various systems of grammatical categories used in 17th century English grammars can be found. As to the second problem Salmon (1961:293ff.) sketches the historical development of the scholastic categories 'suppositum' and 'appositum' to the modern pair 'subject' and 'predicate'.

More generally Brookes views syntax as dependent on Reason. His conceptions of a sort of 'innate ideas' which he called 'praecognita'[22] seem to be influenced by Scaliger (1540). The term 'praecognita' occurs frequently in the Webbe/Brookes discussion, where, perhaps for the first time, it was applied to linguistic matters.

Salmon (1969:185) concludes her exposition of the controversy with a surprising quotation from Webbe, who, commenting on the generative power of language from small resources seems to overcome the narrow bonds of his pattern-drill method:

> Doe wee not first out of twenty Letters make an hundred syllables, and out of these hundred syllables make a thousand words, and of these 1000 wordes make a million of Clauses and propositions, and to goe forward allwayes from a Contraction of all things in a Center of the diffusion of them. (MS. f.263, as quoted in Salmon 1969)

The case of Brookes vs. Webbe is one more example that demonstrates clearly that the so-called Cartesian originality in the Port-Royal *Grammar* and *Logic* need not be of Cartesian origin, but that Arnauld and Lancelot wrote in the middle of a stream of linguistic theories current throughout Western Europe between, roughly, 1570 and 1650, e.g. Ramus.

1.1.3 *Locke, Berkeley, Hobbes*

This is certainly not the place where a thorough discussion of the linguistic and metalinguistic conceptions of these three great English philosophers may reasonably be expected. Nevertheless, in a more or less rounded picture of the history of seventeenth century linguistics some information on the main linguistic ideas embedded in this part of English philosophy should not be lacking.

Cassirer (1953, 1:73ff.) sees the fundamental tendency of these philosophers in the fact that they seek not to relate language to some 'logic ideal' but to understand language according to its empirical foundations and its social or pragmatic functions. Both Hobbes and Locke justify to a great extent Cassirer's judgment that one of the main theses of empiricism — as far as language is concerned — is that language serves as an instrument for gaining and securing knowledge; language is not only conceived as a means to the analysis of the ideas of a thinking individual; language must be seen to be *the* instrument for interhuman communication and cooperation.

For Hobbes it is therefore self-evident that questions of language philosophy are no longer situated in the realm of metaphysics:

> Names are signs not of things, but of our cogitations. But seeing names ordered in speech (as is defined) are signs of our conceptions, it is manifest they are not signs of the things themselves; for that the sound of this word stone should be the sign of a

[22] Salmon (1969:184) mentions the diarist Hartlib who 'notes in his *Ephemerides* for 1635 that, while working on his [Brookes'] method for teaching Latin, Brookes was to reade Scaliger de causis linguarum. That will give him divers occasions to perfect his praecognita philologica'. (On Hartlib see Turnbull 1947 and Webster 1970.)

stone, cannot be understood in any sense but this, that he that hears it collects that he that pronounces it thinks of a stone. And, therefore, that disputation, whether names signify the matter or form, or something compounded of both, and other like subleties of the metaphysics, is kept up by erring men, and such as understand not the words they dispute about. (*De corpore,* ch. 2, § 5)

For Locke, too, it became clear that any speculation on epistemological problems could profitably take into account the semantic structure of various sorts of linguistic expressions:

I must confess, then, that, when I first began this Discourse of the Understanding, and a good while after, I had not the least thought that any consideration of words was at all necessary to it. But when, having passed over the original and composition of our ideas, I began to examine the extent and certainty of our knowledge, I found it had so near a connexion with words, that, unless their force and manner of signification were first well observed, there could be very little said clearly and pertinently concerning knowledge: which being conversant about truth, had constantly to do with propositions. And though it terminated in things, yet it was for the most part so much by the intervention of word, that they seemed scarce separable from our general knowledge. At least they interpose themselves so much between our understandings, and the truth which it would contemplate and apprehend, that, like the medium through which visible objects pass, the obscurity and disorder do not seldom cast a mist before our eyes, and impose upon our understandings.

(*Essay,* Book III, ch. IX, § 21)

Cassirer (1953–7, 1:73ff.) interprets the development of the above-mentioned main thesis of empiricism — i.e. the instrumental function of language — along the line Bacon–Hobbes–Locke–Berkeley as a dialectic movement: if language is not the instrument to represent things but ideas, then it is exactly the generality of ideas that endangers the foundation of knowledge in sense-data. From this Berkeley draws the conclusion that it is the main task of the philosopher to criticize language thus freeing the human mind from all sorts of errors hidden in the use of words and sentences.

Berkeley's recommendation 'to draw the curtain of words' (1710:§24) runs straight against empiristic fundamentals held by Bacon, Hobbes, and Locke. Hobbes wanted language philosophy to be free from metaphysics in order to serve as a useful philosophical instrument; Berkeley denied the utility of language for cognitive purposes altogether. This is a point of extreme disagreement between the early Berkeley and Hobbes because for the latter truth resided not in things or ideas but in the use of words: 'veritas in dicto, non in re consistit' (*De corpore*, *Computatio sive Logica*, cap. III, §7).

According to Cassirer, however, Berkeley's development turns full circle in his last work *Siris* (1744) where he frees the 'idea' from its empirical and psychological bonds by reinterpreting it as a Platonic entity. The consequence of this 'conversion' is, finally, the reintroduction of language as a means of representing ideas and cognitive acts.

After having outlined Cassirer's evaluation of some of the main ideas of Hobbes, Locke, and Berkeley as far as language philosophy is concerned an attempt will be made to discuss the central notions in the works of Thomas Hobbes (1588–1679) and John Locke (1632–1704) as far as linguistic theory is concerned. The following discussion draws on the one hand on considerations stemming from the present writer, on the other hand attention is paid to relevant results to be found in such works as e.g. Verburg (1951:234ff.), Kretzmann (1967:376–8), and Formigari (1970:141–55).

Hobbes has laid down his views on language mainly in his works *De corpore, De homine*, and in his *Leviathan*.[23]

At the beginning of his treatise *De corpore*, Hobbes defines philosophy as 'such knowledge of effects or appearances, as we acquire by true ratiocination from the knowledge we have first of their causes or generation: And again, of such causes or generations as may be from knowing first their effects' (Molesworth I:3). By ratiocination Hobbes means computation in analogy to arithmetics. In order to carry out computational operations successfully man has to rely on sensible marks or 'moniments' because men's thoughts are inconstant and fading. 'For no man is able to remember quantities without sensible and present measures.... So that whatsoever a man has put together in his mind by ratiocination without such helps, will presently slip from him, and not be revocable but by beginning his ratiocination anew.' (*De corpore* II,1). From this it follows for Hobbes 'that for the acquiring of philosophy, some sensible moniments are necessary, by which our past thoughts may not only be reduced, but also registered every one in its own order'. (*De corpore* II,1).

For Hobbes the words or names of natural languages supply both necessities, namely, to serve as marks of men's thoughts and as signs by which man may make his thoughts known to others. Names standing alone are only marks for someone's conceptions; for names to become real signs with which thoughts may be communicated to others they must be connected to form well-ordered utterances. Moreover, Hobbes believes it to be unquestionable that, originally, words or names were imposed arbitrarily by our 'first parents' on their conceptions. But, in order to serve as efficient means for communicating thoughts to others, people will have to agree upon such primary decisions.[24]

For Hobbes it is manifest that names ordered in speech are signs of our conceptions; they are not signs of the things themselves, for, he argues, 'that the sound of

[23] Quotations are from Hobbes 1839–1845b, vols 1 and 3.

[24] Verburg (1951:236f.) develops further Hobbes's distinction between *notae* and *signa*: '*Notae* ut recordari, *signa* ut demonstrare cogitationes nostras valeamus.' (*De Corpore* I, 2. § 3). Verburg recognizes a genetic dependency of the socially determined sign-function on the prior existence of 'notae': 'De notae vormen de oertaal, de "*lingua Adamica*"; of liever: *de oer-functie der taal*.' (1951:240). On the whole Verburg gives a rather close reading of Hobbes's main texts concerning semiotics and linguistics. Verburg's criticism of Hobbes will be taken into consideration after the presentation of our exposition.

this word *stone* should be the sign of a stone, cannot be understood in any sense but this, that he that hears it collects that he that pronounces it thinks of a stone' (*De corpore* I, 2, § 5). We note that Hobbes does not speak of general ideas as the meaning of some sign occurring in speech, but rather of some individualized conception such as e.g. 'a stone'. Thus, for Hobbes, it is not necessary that every name should be the name of some really existing thing.[25] It is therefore quite natural for Hobbes to distinguish between 'positive' and 'negative' names: '*Positive* are such as we impose for the likeness, equality, or identity of the things we consider; *negative*, for the diversity, unlikeness, or inequality of the same' (*De corpore* I, 2, §7).

Hobbes's second distinction between different kinds of names is made between common names and proper names. Hobbes considers as proper names not only simple names such as *Homer*, etc.; but also individual descriptions like *he that writ the Iliad* or indexical expressions like *this man, that man*. In defining his concept of a common name Hobbes distinguishes implicitly between names of divided and undivided reference (class nouns as opposed to mass nouns): 'a common name, being the name of many things severally taken, but not collectively of all together (as man is not the name of all mankind, but of every one, as of Peter, John, and the rest severally) is therefore called an *universal name*; and therefore this word *universal* is never the name of any thing existent in nature, nor of any idea or phantasm formed in the mind, but always the name of some word or name ...' (*De corpore* I, 2, §9).

From this explanation of the term *universal* Hobbes proceeds to his third distinction of names. The distinction between names of the first and those of the second intention enables Hobbes to avoid category mistakes of the sort made by several 'writers of metaphysics'.

> Of the *first intention* are the names of things, a *man, stone* etc.; of the second are the names of names and speeches, as *universal, particular, genus, species, syllogism,* and the like. (*De corpore* I, 2, § 10)

Hobbes's fourth distinction relates not so much to isolated names, but rather to different sorts of quantifications occurring in noun phrases, insofar as he allows some names to be of 'certain and determined, others of uncertain and undetermined signification' (*ibid.*). By 'certain and determined signification' Hobbes understands individual and definite plural descriptions, e.g. *this tree, that living creature* and *all, every, both tree(s)*, respectively. 'Uncertain and undetermined significations' are those where descriptions or noun phrases contain such quantifiers as *some*; these he calls 'particular names'.[26] What Hobbes considers as 'indefinite names' would

[25] In the same vein see Kretzmann 1967 (377): 'At any event, Hobbes nowhere suggested that "stone" occurring in speech was a *name* of some mental entity'.

[26] Kretzmann (1967:377) criticizes Hobbes's ideas on quantification. Kretzmann regards Hobbes's discussion of names of "certain and determined" and of "uncertain and undetermined" signification as being 'a badly distorted remnant of supposition theory'.

today be looked at as cases of universal quantification. Hobbes's definition runs as follows:

> . . . a common name set by itself without any note of universality or particularity, as *man, stone,* . . . is called an *indefinite name* . . . (*De corpore* I, 2, § 11)

Formigari (1970:149) amplifies these considerations of pragmatic conditions determining the use equivocal names by paraphrasing ideas expressed in *Leviathan* (Hobbes 1839–1845b, 3.28):

> Benché la natura di ciò di cui abbiamo nozioni sia sempre la stessa, pure la diversa constituzione dei corpi e i pregiudizi derivanti dalle diverse opinioni danno ad ogni cosa una coloritura determinata dalle nostre diverse passioni. Di qui la necessità di cautelarsi contro le parole, le quali, oltre ad un significato primario, hanno anche un significato derivante della natura, disposizioni ed interesse di colui che parla.

Speaking of quantifiers, Hobbes expressly states that 'these words, *all*, *every*, *some*, etc. are not names, but parts only of names . . .' (*De corpore* I, 2, §11). Moreover, for Hobbes it is evident 'that the use of signs of this kind [quantifiers], is not for a man's own sake, or for his getting of knowledge by his own private meditation (for every man has his own thoughts sufficiently determined without such helps as these) but for the sake of others; that is, for the teaching and signifying of our conceptions to others . . .' (*De corpore* I, 2, §11). It seems that in this point Hobbes's predilection for differentiating between the private and social functions of signs has carried him too far.

In his fifth distinction Hobbes separates univocal from equivocal names. His example is: '. . . the name *triangle* is said to be *univocal,* because it is always taken in the same sense; and *parabola* to be *equivocal,* for the signification it has sometimes of allegory or similitude, and sometimes of a certain geometrical figure'. (*De corpore,* I, 2, §12). Kretzmann (1967:377) points out — correctly — that Hobbes's univocal-equivocal distinction does not primarily concern words as such but must be understood pragmatically: there is always someone who uses words univocally or equivocally.

Sixthly, for Hobbes some names are *absolute*, others *relative*. Relative names are such as imply some relation (Hobbes speaks of 'comparison') as *father*, *cause*, *like*, *equal*, etc.

Hobbes's seventh and last distinction is between simple and compounded names. With Hobbes this is not a grammatical distinction, his motives for this dichotomy derive from philosophical grounds: '. . . among philosophers *sentient animated body* passes but for one name, being the name of every living creature . . .' (§14). Hobbes's criteria for distinguishing between simple and compounded names are, more precisely, logical or semantic ones. To put it briefly, for Hobbes simple names are conceptual or semantic primitives, such as 'body'; the name *man* would be compounded (*animated rational body*).

Having dealt with different properties and sorts of names in the second chapter of *De corpore*, Hobbes goes on in the third chapter to deal with propositions or judgments. This is the classical scheme of constructing logical or epistemological treatises; it was to be resumed a couple of years later in the Port-Royal *Logic*.[27]

The linguistic relevance of the chapter "Of Proposition" seems to be rather slight. It presents essentially the classical subject-predicate logic plus the usual propositional operations and relations.[28] Nevertheless, some points in this chapter deserve to be mentioned explicitly.

Hobbes has 'divers kinds of speech' depending on the 'connexion or contexture of names' in utterances; in more modern terms we would speak of different pragmatically founded sentence modalities, such as interrogation, declaration etc. Hobbes mentions 'interrogations' and 'prayers' as examples of the significations of desires and affectations of men. In philosophy, however, 'there is but one kind of speech useful . . . most men call it *proposition*, and is the speech of those that affirm or deny, and expresseth truth or falsity.' (*De corpore* I, 3, §1).

Hobbes defines a proposition to be 'a speech consisting of two names copulated, by which he that speaketh signifies he conceives the latter name to be the name of the same thing whereof the former is the name; or (which is all one) that the former name is comprehended by the latter' (§2).

Hobbes's anti-metaphysical attitude clearly breaks through when he assigns the categories true or false to propositions only. More precisely, for him 'truth consists in speech, and not in the things spoken of . . . truth and falsity have no place but amongst such living creatures as use speech.' (*De corpore* I, 3, §7f.). This makes it clear that 'truth' and 'falsity' are conditioned by pragmatic principles. The following quotation shows that Hobbes did recognize the ambivalent function of language for arriving at 'true ratiocinations':

> . . . as men owe all their true ratiocination to the right understanding of speech; so also they owe their errors to the misunderstanding of the same; and as all the ornaments of philosophy proceed only from man, so from man also is derived the ugly absurdity of false opinions. For speech has something in it like to a spider's web . . . for by contexture of words tender and delicate wits are ensnared and stopped; but strong wits break easily through them. (*De corpore* I, 3, § 8)

[27] Arnauld 1965:23: 'Cet art [la logique] consiste dans les reflexions que les hommes ont faites sur les quatre principales operations de leur esprit, *concevoir, juger, raisonner,* et *ordonner*.' Formigari (1970:153) also mentions the connection between Hobbes's conception of the processes of reasoning and the ideas of Arnauld and Nicole on the principal operations of the mind. Formigari discusses briefly the critical attitude of Arnauld and Nicole towards Hobbes's ideas on the processes of reasoning. Formigari sees a misunderstanding on the Port-Royalist side of Hobbes's ideas (see Arnauld 1965:31f.) insofar as Hobbes's idea that reasoning is nothing else than assembling names by means of the word *est* can only be understood within some theory of calculus. Formigari (1970:153) concludes correctly that 'Per Hobbes, come per i portorealisti, il "concepire" è la prima operazione dello spirito; il dissidio reale verte sugli strumenti di tale concepire (solo fantasia corporea, o anche la "force et . . . application interieure" dello spirito).'

[28] See Kretzmann 1967 (377f.) for some discussions of Hobbes's ideas on propositional logic. See in this connection also Formigari's interpretation of the third chapter of Hobbes's *Logica* (Formigari 1970:150ff.).

Hobbes's ideas on the various functions of language (argumentative, emotional, esthetic, social) receive a succinct interpretation in Formigari (1970:141–55) under the heading "La semiotica di Hobbes". In her discussion of Hobbes's more general semiotic conceptions Formigari takes her starting-point in *Leviathan* and in *De Homine*. In these texts Hobbes distinguishes between two main functions of language: general and special ones. According to Formigari (1970:142) the general function or use of language is the one,

> grazie al quala gli uomini registrano i loro pensieri, li richiamo alla memoria, e instaurano quei rapporti intersoggettivi senza i quali non vi sarebbe ni stato né società civile; traducono insomma il discorso mentale in discorso verbale, la serie dei pensieri in serie di parole.

On the basis of this general function of language several pragmatically or socially determined functions can be distinguished: a) the transmission of acquired knowledge, and, dependent on this b) the acquisition of the arts; c) the manifestation of an individual will in order to pursue practical aims, and, finally, d) the various esthetic functions of language. Formigari clearly differentiates the heuristic-demonstrative function (a and b) from the others (c and d). These latter functions serve to express or arouse passions or feelings. Hobbes as an empirically-minded philosopher goes as far as correlating these various functions with grammatical phenomena: the indicative corresponds with functions a and b, whereas the other functions are reflected by sentence modalitaties other than assertion (indicative): verbs of command, advice etc. It seems not to be far-fetched if one recalls in this context quite recent deliberations of Wittgenstein, J. L. Austin and other scholars, who have rediscovered the linguistic importance of other sentence modalities than assertion.

It is also in *Leviathan* (1839–45b. 3.20ff.) that Hobbes draws the necessary logical consequences concerning the applicability of the notion of truth-value to various types of sentences or discourses. It can be inferred from Hobbes's considerations that the meta-linguistic predicates 'true' and 'false' cannot be applied to sentences evoking emotions, passions and the like. This would again mean that such ideas can be understood as foreshadowing J. L. Austin's 'felicity conditions' applicable to all sorts of modal sentences.[29] In this connection Hobbes's ideas as to when actions are justified seem to be particularly pertinent; at this point Hobbes's principle of the arbitrariness of linguistic signs converges with his principle of the arbitrariness of moral judgments.[30]

In order to conclude our discussion of interpretations and judgments on Hobbes's language philosophy two objections put forward by Verburg (1951:246ff.) shall be

[29] See e.g. Austin 1962. Formigari (1970:144) has the following interpretation: 'Nel caso del discorso inteso a suscitare passioni, il problema della verità, invece, non si pone affatto: non ha alcuna importanza che l'opinione espressa sia vera o falsa . . .'

[30] See *De corpore* I, 6, § 7 and *Leviathan* (3.130ff.). Formigari's concise paraphrase of this principle is this: 'Giudicare la giustizia di un'azione significa constatare se essa sia conforme a meno ad una norma positiva, istituzionale' (1970:145).

mentioned. According to Verburg Hobbes overstresses the instrumental function of language and linguistic signs. Formigari (1970:148f.), without mentioning Verburg, argues convincingly against this objection:

Hobbes insiste sulla funzione fondamentale della generalizzazione linguistica ai fini conoscitivi, prima ancora che communicativi.

Her examples proving this are drawn from *Leviathan* (3.21).

Verburg's other objection that for Hobbes language predetermines the structure of thought processes seems to be more convincing. He lends some precision to it by saying

. . . de taal als 'taal' niet zo zeer het denken structureert, als wel dat ze de hele werkelijkheid — of liever, de de taal als ordeningsmiddel gebruikende mens doet dit — gestructureerd tegemoet treedt op een categoriaal-eigenwettige wijze. (1951:247)

It is commonly agreed that Hobbes, but also lesser known writers such as Digby (1664) and Burthogge (1678), exerted considerable influence on John Locke's linguistic and philosophical ideas.[31] Kretzmann (1967:380) elaborates his overall critical attitude towards Locke's conceptions on semantics by saying that 'Locke's account of words as the signs of ideas shows little of the sensitivity to the complexities of language that had characterized the work of many of his predecessors, including Hobbes. Except for one very short, cryptic chapter on "particles" (by which he evidently meant syncategorematic words but perhaps also verbs), the semantics of words in Book III [of Locke's *Essay concerning human understanding* (1690)] is exclusively a semantics of "names" — names of "simple ideas", of "mixed modes", and of "natural substances" — with no suggestion that anything has been left out of consideration.' One important difference between Locke and Hobbes is stated in Formigari (1970:155):

. . . in Locke le idee generali sono a loro volta segni, e segni non isomorfi rispetto ai dati prelinguistici; mentre per Hobbes ciò per cui sta l'universale è una nozione o immagine, intesa ancora come segno naturale della cosa.

Among the recent contributions[32] dealing with Locke's ideas on language philosophy and linguistics there seems to be a broad agreement as to the aims and content of the linguistic side of Locke's *Essay* as well as to points of criticism.

Verburg (1951:253–265) gives a critical account of Locke's linguistic philosophy; he classifies Locke as a 'a-historisch-synchronisch denker' (254) in contradistinction to Hobbes, who considered also genetic-historical factors within his linguistic

[31] See e.g. Kretzmann 1967 (379) and Formigari 1970 (155–73) where Formigari dedicates a whole chapter ('Problematicà del rapporto semantico. Da Kenelm Digby a John Locke') to the problem.

[32] See e.g. Zobel 1928; Verburg 1956:253–65, Aarsleff 1964; Kretzmann 1967:379–81; Rossi 1968; Danto 1969; Hook 1969 (and other contributions in the same volume); Formigari 1970: 173–209; Aarsleff 1971.

theory. Verburg's further criticisms refer to Locke's failing to consider the semantic structure of propositions and sentences:

Terwijl Hobbes het inzicht heeft, dat in de *verbinding* der woorden tot proposities en van deze weer tot syllogismi het *veritas in dicto* begrepen ligt, komt Locke niet verder dan een steriel vergelijken van losse woorden met de, even losse, door hen betekende ideas. . . . (Verburg 1951:258)

However, Verburg qualifies this summarizing statement when he comes to discuss Locke's chapter on the 'particles' (*Essay* III, c. 7).[33] It is well known that Leibniz in his *Nouveaux essais* (ed. Gerhard, 5.311ff.) made a special point of this weakness of Locke's semantics. Inspite of Verburg's sometimes a bit idiosyncratic line of argumentation his criticism of Locke seems to be well-balanced and not without justification.

Aarsleff's well-documented article from 1964 is mainly historically oriented. Besides shedding more light on the historical circumstances under which Locke conceived his *Essay* Aarsleff centers his interest on the many details of the famous Leibniz-Locke controversy.[34] It is the aim of this article to deal with one stage of the interrelations between the philosophy of language and Natural Philosophy in the seventeenth century. His aim is to 'help to clarify and fix some fundamental aspects of Locke's doctrines and method in the *Essay*, which have been either poorly understood or have received interpretations that are too diverse for comfort and conviction' (Aarsleff 1964:166). Although Aarsleff succeeds to a large extent in clarifying possible misunderstandings within the Leibniz-Locke controversy, it is not very easy — and this seems to be due largely to Aarsleff's immanent-historical method — to detect the real substance of Locke's linguistic theory.

Kretzmann's position (1967) is highly critical towards Locke's semantics. The final passage of the article clearly shows that Kretzmann's evaluation criteria are of a rather panchronic nature:

Locke's strictly subjectivist, nominalist theory of signification in the opening chapters of Book III, which gave him so much trouble in its application, may represent nothing more than his overzealous attempt to state precisely such characteristically commonsensical observations as can be found in his *Conduct of the understanding*, Section 29, where he advised 'those who would conduct their understanding right, not to take any term . . . to stand for anything, till they have an *idea* of it. . . .'

Another important point in Locke's philosophical conceptions relating more indirectly to language is his rejection of the innate ideas-hypothesis as put forward

[33] Verburg 1956:259: 'Dit is de enige plaats, waar Locke verder gaat dan een lexicaal voorbeeld.' Formigari 1970:175 stresses the same point: 'Il nodo problematico delle dottrine linguistiche di Locke non è la semantica della proposizione, ma il rapporto fra nomi e cose . . .'
[34] Because of the agreement made between Aarsleff and the present writer (see our introductory chapter), these problems are not dealt with here.

by Descartes and his followers. The somewhat heated recent discussion of this problem is reflected in Aarsleff 1971, Danto 1969, and Hook 1969. (As far as Chomsky's standpoint in this debate is concerned, the reader is referred to our fifth chapter, "Linguistics in 17th century France").

In his course of lectures[35] dealing with the "Geschichte der Sprachphilosophie von der Antike bis zur Gegenwart (Teil I: Von der Antike bis Leibniz)", Eugenio Coseriu gave a fairly concise but illuminating interpretation of Locke's semantic conceptions.

After criticizing Locke's views on the nature of individual ideas, on the process of abstraction leading to general idea and on the nature of linguistic meanings Coseriu nevertheless regards Locke's ideas on semantics as useful for establishing certain foundations of modern structural semantics. Following de Saussure, Coseriu takes it for granted that meanings of words should be established by means of well-structured meaning differences.

Locke posits — apart from particles — three kinds of names. Although he uses only substantives and adjectives as examples, his distinctions are very probably valid for verbs and adverbs as well.

1. Names for 'simple ideas'. These ideas are directly given by experience; they cannot be analyzed, and, consequently they cannot be defined by means of other ideas. Examples are: 'motion', 'light', 'warm', etc.

2. Names for the so-called 'mixed modes'. These ideas arise through combinations of ideas; they are constructions of the human mind. It is not necessary for them to have counterparts in empirical reality; their creation is due to specific interests pursued by members of some social group in order to cope with all sorts of phenomena, be they real or fictitious. Because of their mixed nature these ideas are relatively easy to analyze. It is evident that a large portion of lexical elements in one or another language belong to this second class. Examples: 'justice', 'triangle', 'incest', etc.

3. Names for 'substances'. These refer to spatio-temporal continua of extralinguistic reality. The names for substances share the composite nature of the 'mixed modes', but in contradistinction to these the names for substances represent such combinations of ideas that also co-occur in reality. In this case things are necessarily prior to the respective names. Examples: 'man', 'gold', 'horse', etc.

As to the existence of 'species' and 'genera' it is Locke's aim to show that this difference is due to a distinction made by human minds on the ground of their experience and their interests. This is clear in the case of 'mixed modes'. According to Locke it is precisely in the domain of 'mixed modes' that the lexical structure of various languages may differ considerably. In the case of the names for substances Locke admits a lesser degree of arbitrariness with regard to the combinatorial possibilities of ideas or features forming a substance name. Yet, according to the needs

[35] Winter term 1968/69, University of Tübingen. See Coseriu 1968–69, especially 139–48.

and interests of individuals or social groups the conceptual and lexical boundaries between various 'substances' can be drawn differently. Locke uses here the example of 'water' and 'ice'; a similar distinction does not occur with other liquids. Some kinds of things may be divided into different species, if we have different non-synonymous names for these species.

Coseriu criticizes some of Locke's conceptions; in particular he questions Locke's aim to draw a neat line between an empirical classification of reality and a classification dependent on linguistic criteria.

Inspite of these and other criticisms Coseriu recognizes the following positive points in Locke's ideas on semantics:

1. Locke's conception of three basic semantic categories or lexematic classes: names for 'simple ideas'; names for 'mixed modes', and names for 'substances'. In the case of 'simple ideas' the lexematic expression stands for just one 'lexeme' or semantic feature.

2. Locke's identification of a class of meanings as 'mixed modes': here the intended phenomena are necessarily given in the meaning of words like *uncle* insofar as speakers construe such entities as 'uncle' or 'brother'.[36]

3. Locke's conception of a class of meanings as 'substances'. As mentioned above, the semantic structure of substance names may depend on various choices made by language-users from the overall set of objective features characterizing some substance (e.g. 'gold', 'mountain', 'hill', etc.).

Coseriu is certainly correct in stating that these problems must be dealt with in any serious theory on semantics and that is was John Locke who did a good deal towards paving the way for a workable theory of linguistic semantics.

Formigari's chapter on 'John Locke. Logica semiotica e teoria del significato' (1970: 173–95) besides giving an overall view of Locke's semiotic and linguistic ideas, pays special attention to Locke's postulate that abstraction processes are a necessary condition for language to function as an instrument of knowledge as well as an instrument for communication. From this postulate various consequences for the nature of different semantic wordclasses are drawn. That Locke — like many of his predecessors — adheres to the principle that linguistic signs are arbitrary as to the relation expression-content is quite evident from Locke's text (see, for example, *Essay* III, 2, 1). More important, however, is Locke's explanation of the so-called 'mixed modes'. The determining factor constituting these 'non è l'esistenza di un modello in natura, d'una connessione reale fra le idee tra loro congiunte, ma una finalità in senso lato pratica, in cui intervengono fattori di costume, abitudine e simili' (Formigari 1970: 183). This explains for Locke that in one language there are words not encountered in another language. What we have here is, clearly, an important extension of the principle of arbitrariness applied to the

[36] For a recent discussion on the non-objectivity of kinship terms see Lounsbury 1969 (especially 16ff.).

relatively arbitrary assembling of semantic elements within the content of some given word.[37]

Appended to Formigari's convincing discussion of the main elements of Locke's semiotics and semantics we find a brief presentation of various objections stemming from Locke's first critics. Among these the most noteworthy seems to be Stillingfleet[38] with whom Locke exchanged several letters concerning such ontological matters as the possible reduction of 'substance' to 'nominal essence'. (See Formigari 1970:196–209). Formigari concludes this section with a discussion of Lee's objections[39] together with a brief outlook on Leibniz's *Nouveaux essais.*

1.2 *Projects for Universal and/or Philosophical Languages*

In the course of the last two or three decades there has been a continuous flow of publications dealing with various aspects of projects on 'universal' or 'philosophical' languages stemming from the seventeenth century.[40] Although the primary motivation for these contributions is to eludicate the historical setting and the reasons for the various activities concerning the construction of universal and/or philosophical languages around the middle of the seventeenth century, there are also hints as to the possible usefulness of these early attempts for the clarification of present-day problems in theoretical linguistics, especially in the domain of universal phonetics and universal semantics.[41]

[37] See Formigari 1970:185: '... il nome non è arbitrio soltanto in quanto suono non avente alcun legame necessario col suo significato, ma in quanto l'idea stessa che connota è un'arbitraria classificazione (*sorting*) della realtà.'

[38] See Stillingfleet 1696.

[39] Lee 1702. According to Formigari (1970:203f.) Lee's main criticism amounts to this: '... ci sono proposizioni, sia pratiche sia speculative, che non sono ricavabili dall'esperienza e senza le quali l'esperienza non è possibile; negando tali princìpi la "way of ideas" conduce inevitabilmente allo scetticismo.'

[40] Couturat and Leau 1903 deals very briefly (11–22) with the essential features of projects proposed or discussed by Descartes, Dalgarno, and Wilkins. More recent and more detailed contributions to this special field in the history of linguistics are: Funke 1929, Jones 1932, Emery 1947/48, McCracken 1948, Cohen 1954, Elliott 1957, de Mott 1958, Funke 1959, Rossi 1960, Knowlson 1965, Linsky 1966, Robins 1967 (114–117), Salmon 1972. [Editor's note: the best treatment is still to be found in Couturat 1901.]

[41] See e.g. Linsky 1966:60: 'His [Wilkins's] views reflect not only the state of the 17th-century linguistics but that of the centuries to come. And it would not be overestimation to say that Wilkins was the man to foresee those burning problems which are even haunting scientists and scholars today. A careful examination may prove that a lot of problems treated in his book are highly up to date and urgently calling for further investigations.' In this connection see also Chomsky 1967 (402): 'The importance of developing a universal semantics and universal phonetics ... was clearly recognized long before the development of modern linguistics. For example, Bishop Wilkins in his *Essay towards a real character and a philosophical language* (1668) attempted to develop a universal phonetic alphabet and a universal catalogue of concepts in terms of which, respectively, the signals and semantic interpretations for any language can be represented.' In fact, Chomsky is mistaken in this at least as far as the phonetic side is concerned; Wilkins did not devise a universally applicable phonetic or phonological scheme.

The relevance of some 'projects of a universal character' (mainly those devised by Dalgarno, Wilkins, and Leibniz) for the development of modern systems of symbolic logic is critically assessed in Cohen (1954:49–63).

Before entering upon a more detailed discussion of recent work done in this field a — be it brief — explanation of the disjunctive term 'universal and/or philosophical language' seems to be called for.

The latest monograph on universal language schemes, Vivian Salmon's excellent study of the writings of Francis Lodwick in the intellectual context of the 17th century (Salmon 1972), distinguishes clearly between 'two separate currents in this particular stream of linguistic research, one leading towards the creation of a colloquial medium of intercourse, and the other towards a medium which would reflect accurately in its notation the facts of nature as discovered by "true philosophy", and would serve as an instrument of scientific discovery as well as a means of communication' (Salmon 1972:12). The fact that many projects of an artificial language that were proposed in the 17th century deal in varying degrees with these two main functions — universal and philosophical — may justify the use of the coverterm 'universal and/or philosophical language'.

Among the recent publications on projects on universal and/or philosophical languages (Rossi 1960:201–38, Formigari 1970:81–139, Salmon 1972) Salmon's monograph deserves special mention. Although her primary aim is to comment on Lodwick's works on universal language[42] she presents a wealth of well-organized information on the more general topic: problems of communication and views on language in the seventeenth century.

The second chapter ("The development of universal language schemes", 12–42) consists on the one hand of a survey of the many projects on 'universal characters' (i.e. symbolically represented 'philosophical languages'), on the other hand various schemes of 'universal languages' (i.e. relatively developed philosophical languages that may serve also as a means for oral communication) are presented. From Salmon's discussion it again becomes clear that — especially with 'universal languages' — the distinction between the practical and philosophical functions cannot always be drawn easily.

Salmon (1972:13f.) sees in Bacon 'the first English scholar to discuss in any detail — and probably at all — the topic of universal character . . .'. The next Englishman to publish his ideas in this topic was John Wilkins. His *Mercury, or the secret and swift messenger* (1641) is considered by Salmon (1972:15) as 'a critique of various modes of communication by such methods as bells, birds, bullets and arrows and included a chapter on universal character'. Salmon continues to outline the various relations between such scholars as John Webster,[43] Hartlib,[44] Mer-

[42] Salmon's book contains the text of Lodwick's printed works (1647, 1652, and 1686) together with texts drawn from various manuscripts collections (see Salmon's list of the writings of Francis Lodwick, 1972:159–62).

[43] See Webster 1654.

[44] See Turnbull 1947 and Webster 1970.

senne,[45] Comenius, Lodwick and others, all of which in one way or another were connected actively as authors or as critics with projects on universal characters or philosophical languages. In considerable detail Salmon (1972:18ff.) discusses the influences of Lodwick's *A common writing* (1647) on Dalgarno's *Ars signorum* (1661) and Wilkins' *Essay* (1668). Lodwick's aim was to produce simply a written character and not a philosophical language; nevertheless 'his work does involve some theoretical consideration of linguistic categories' (Salmon 1972:18). Dalgarno first started on the level of 'written characters' but it soon became evident to him that with such characters — partly based on earlier plans for shorthand-systems[46] — the need for a philosophically workable instrument could not be satisfied. According to Salmon (1972:21) 'it is strange that they [the defects of universal characters] were not equally obvious to continental scholars, some of whom continued to work on the same unsatisfactory lines during the following decade.'[47] Beck 1657 and Kircher 1663 were the last works that can be considered as projects of some importance with the aim of constructing universal characters that were not based on a conceptual classification.

The second part of Salmon's chapter 'the development of universal language schemes' is dedicated to a thorough comparison of various works on universal or philosophical languages. Salmon (1972:22) stresses the fact that it was again Lodwick who 'was the earliest language-planner to publish an attempt at a more scientific medium of communication, which proclaimed the necessity for a "truer description" of things as an "easie and quick entrance to the things themselves".' What is meant here is Lodwick's *Ground-work* (1652) where he touches on two different aspects of a philosophical language: on the one hand such a language should avoid the many ambiguities of the words of natural languages and procure the means for conceptual classification and notation of things and ideas, on the other hand a truly philosophical language should serve as an instrument for logical deductions in order 'to enable men to think more precisely and clearly without being misled by the varying connotations of words in a natural language' (Salmon 1972:23). Of these two aspects only the first was elaborated to some extent in the works of the language-planners around the mid-century. The second aspect was to receive detailed attention later in Dalgarno 1680 and more notably in Leibniz 1666.

Also within her chapter "The development of universal language schemes" Salmon elaborates the somewhat intricate relationships between language-planners around the middle of the 17th century. Salmon describes the pivotal role played by Hartlib who was closely connected with practically everybody working on projects of universal and/or philosophical languages. The following list of names shows at once the widespread activity in this field: the Oxford mathematician and astron-

45 See Mersenne's *Harmonie universelle* (1636; repr. 1963) and Mersenne 1932, 2:323–29.
46 See on this aspect Salmon 1972:114f., 144f.
47 See e.g. Becher 1661 (on Becher, see Waffenschmidt 1962), Kircher 1663.

omer Seth Ward,[48] a founder-member of the Royal Society, displayed considerable interest in linguistics and language-planning; Descartes's thoughts and criticism were known in England mostly via Mersenne and Hartlib; Comenius and other continental scholars were friends of Hartlib who brought them into contact with English scholars such as Lodwick, Dalgarno, and Wilkins. Salmon (1972:29f.) also makes clear that the last-mentioned two authors worked on their projects within a circle of scholars who were members of the Royal Society.[49]

In her third chapter ("The works of Lodwick in their intellectual context: problems of communication in the seventeenth century") Salmon (1972:43–71) delivers an impressive report on such topics as 'religion, commerce, science and language; education and language, communication at speed, in secret, at a distance; communication with the deaf and dumb'.

The fourth chapter ("Views on language in the 17th century", 72–104) deals — in Salmon's view — with the three most important problems: 'the relationship of "words and things" (the common contemporary phrase used in dealing with problems of meaning); the origin of language; and the standardization of the vernacular' (Salmon 1972:72). Again Salmon displays her wide range of knowledge and insight not only in strictly linguistic matters but also in adjacent areas, e.g. theology and philosophy.

Salmon's fifth chapter is expressly dedicated to the works of Lodwick and their sources (1972:105–56). Salmon does not rely on more or less superficial similarities between Lodwick's works and those of his predecessors; instead she analyzes in considerable detail three lines of enquiry for a philosophical language that were relevant for Lodwick: 'first, the discovery and classification of the basic concepts of the human mind, and their arrangement in some kind of logical order; secondly, an analysis of the relationships which are possible between such concepts; thirdly, the provision of appropriate symbols, written and spoken, for both the concepts and their relationships' (Salmon 1972:105).

Salmon states clearly that Lodwick did 'never create a genuinely philosophical language based on conceptual classification' (*ibid.*); nevertheless she demonstrates successfully that Lodwick was now and then aware of and interested in the vast problems of such a language. It seems to be a fair judgment that Lodwick's attempts went more into the direction of a universal language with special attention towards the written representation of linguistic elements.[50] This is made clear from

[48] Ward (1654) was written in reaction to Webster (1654), who believed that the language which God spoke to Adam could serve as a possible model for an universal language. See Salmon 1972 (95f.) for a discussion of mystic movements which influenced 17th century linguistic thought, e.g. Jacob Boehme's *Signatura rerum* (1635; English trans. 1651).

[49] See Formigari 1970:81ff. for a discussion of the role of the Royal Society within the language-planning process going on in the middle of the 17th century.

[50] See however Lodwick 1686 (Salmon 1972:235–46) where phonetic problems receive due attention. See also the earlier treatment on Lodwick as a phonetician by Abercrombie (1948: 2–11).

Lodwick's preface to his *Common writing*[51] where he describes his work as '... an Essay of a *Common writing*, invented, that may be common to all Languages, that is, that one skilled in the same, shall have no need, for what is written with this writing, to learne any other language then his mother Tongue, which he already hath, although the writing were written by one, who understood not the readers Language, and writ the said writing according to his owne Language. So that what is once written with this writing, will be legible and intelligible, in all Languages whatoever ... The reason hereof is, for that this writing hath no reference to letters, ... but, being rather a kind of hieroglyphical representation of words ...' (Salmon 1972:167).

In this connection it seems useful to recall De Mott's distinction between two periods in the development of projects on universal/philosophical languages: 'the first (ca. 1635–47) marked by efforts to devise a *universal* language that would function as an easily learned substitute for existing language; the second (ca. 1650–68) marked by efforts to devise a universal *and* philosophical language that would be adapted to the exact and perfect representation of things' (De Mott 1958:10).

De Mott (1958:4) maintains that the decisive step in the development of a philosophical language from mere lists and alphabets of 'radical characters' was partly due to the influence of Comenius, whose visit to England occurred in 1641, and of Kinner, who came to England in 1648.[52] As evidence for the influence of these scholars De Mott mentions certain documents written by Kinner found among Hartlib's papers. 'In the late 1630's Comenius was the best known European proponent of a new language; his writings — especially *Via Lucis*[53] — seem to have been largely responsible for the interest in the idea that first appeared in England around this time; his visit to England in 1641 brought him into contact with several of the linguistic projectors' (De Mott 1958:4).

It was Comenius's idea that the framers of a new language should 'follow the guidance of things themselves, since everything in our new language must be adapted to the exact and perfect representation of things' (Comenius 1938:191). He suggested furthermore that the projectors instead of compiling lists of radical words of an existing language[54] should begin by attempting to make a 'correct definition of the Kinds, the ideas, and the qualities of things'. He argued that the new language

[51] See the reprint of this and other works by Lodwick in Salmon 1972 (166ff.).

[52] For details see De Mott 1958 (1–11) and De Mott 1955 (1069ff.). Another East European initiative connected with the development of Dalgarno (1661) is described in Salmon 1966a (354ff.). It was one Faustus Morstyn, a Pole, who brought Dalgarno to Hartlib's notice (see also Turnbull 1947). According to Salmon, Morstyn took an active part in the process of developing elementary brachigraphy toward a real universal language. Further information about Comenius's influence on projects of that sort can be found in Formigari 1970 (131ff.) and in Rossi 1960 (211ff.)

[53] See the translation of this work in Comenius 1938.

[54] This was the policy followed by Wilkins (1641). Similar tendencies can be seen in other attempts: Francis Lodwick 1647, Urquhart 1653, Kircher 1663, Becher 1661, Edmundson 1655, Beck 1657.

'cannot be real and true unless it has been made apt to things, nor can it be made apt in this sense until the foundations, the relative order, the mutual connections of all things have been exactly revealed' (Comenius 1938: 219).

De Mott (1958:6ff.) produces sound evidence for his thesis that it was in great part the joint influence of Kinner and Comenius that caused Wilkins to reject the idea of using a vocabulary of 'conventional' primitive words and to decide in favour of terms and symbols that would express a series of philosophical classifications. Moreover, De Mott convincingly shows that Wilkins' basic plan for his *Essay* (1668) originated with writers like Comenius and Kinner and scientists like Ward and Boyle,[55] whose interest in philosophical languages antedated his own — and Dalgarno's — by several years.[56]

It is readily acknowledged by all writers on philosophical languages dating from the seventeenth century that Wilkins' *Essay towards a real character and a philosophical language* (1668) represents the most highly developed work of its kind. This justifies the fact that the following descriptive outline of a universal and philosophical language is restricted to Wilkins' *Essay*. Wilkins' general idea of his language is that 'all things and notions are reduced into such a frame, as may express their natural order, dependence, and relations' (1668, 2).

The monumental work is divided into five parts:

I. The "Prolegomena" (1–21) deal with the general philological ideas of the mid-seventeenth century. Wilkins presents a survey of the world's languages, he discusses briefly problems relating to the origin of language and to the rise and decline of languages. Furthermore he mentions various aspects of the orthographical and phonetic side of languages, and in doing so he supplies valuable information on orthographical and phonetic matters concerning certain 17th century standards of the English language.

II. The second part — "Universal Philosophy" (22–296) — is dedicated to the representation of Wilkins' system of categories. He posits six genera superimposed on the predicaments (substances and accidents); these genera he calls 'transcen-

[55] As to Boyle's role in the discussion of various linguistic projects see Formigari 1970 (85f.) *et passim*.

[56] For a thorough discussion of the evolution of Dalgarno 1661 and its relationship both to Wilkins 1668 and to Lodwick's works, see Salmon 1972 (30f.) and Funke 1929 (37ff.). In the light of more recent results Funke's claims as to the originality of Dalgarno 1661 compared with Wilkins 1668 stand in need of some modification; see especially De Mott (1958). In connection with Dalgarno 1661 it seems interesting to note that at about the time when Dalgarno 1661 was published Isaac Newton occupied himself with a project 'of an universall language'. The manuscript (35 pages), which belongs to the period just before or after Newton's entry into Trinity College, Cambridge, in 1661, was not published until Elliott 1957. He suggests that 'the most likely work to have influenced Newton was Dalgarno's *Ars signorum* which he probably knew before beginning his first draft ...' (Elliott 1957:2). Although Newton's scheme for a universal language is not as complete as Dalgarno's — let alone Wilkins's — it emphasizes especially quantificational and relational problems that must needs occur if somebody sets out to write a grammar, be it of a universal or a natural language.

dental relations': 1. general: kind, cause, diversity, end, means, modes; 2. mixed: quantity, quality; 3. of action: simple, comparate, business, commerce, events, ition; 4. discourse: elements of speech, words, grammar, logic, common to both, modes of it; 5. creator; 6. world: spiritual, celestial, land, water, animate, circles by which it is divided.

Wilkins has thus 14 genera 'substance' and 20 genera 'accident'.

Seen as a whole, the second part contains the hierarchically ordered lexicon of Wilkins' lingua universalis.

III. The third part — "Concerning Natural Grammar" (297–383) — deals with the structure of speech and with systems of graphemic and phonetic substances as representations of written or spoken language.

In presenting his scheme of a universal grammar, Wilkins quotes freely from Scotus, Scaliger, Vossius, Caramuel, and Campanella. One interesting point should be noted: Wilkins set up two main word classes: 'Integrals' (substantives and adjectives; the latter seem to comprise verbs as well) and 'Particles' (copula, pronouns, prepositions, conjunctions, interjections, and derivational suffixes).[57] The third part concludes with an extensive discussion of articulatory phonetics. It is on pages 376 and 378 that Wilkins set out to make speech visible by using two kinds of symbols. The first kind is meant to represent the various positions of articulation of vowels in combination with preceding and following consonants; the second kind of symbol tries to depict the relevant positions and movements of the organs of speech (1668:378). Wilkins assesses the relative merits of his two kinds of 'Visible Speech' in the following way: 'The former being more facil and *simple*, the other more *complicate*; but with this advantage, that it hath in the shape of it some resemblance to that configuration which there is in the Organs of speech upon the framing of several letters. Upon which account it may deserve the Name of a *Natural character* of the Letters.' (1668:375).[58]

IV./V. The last part of Wilkins' *Essay* — "Concerning a Real Character and a Philosophical Language" (385–454) — contains the practical application of the theoretical foundations set out in the previous chapters. Wilkins presents two representational systems, one graphemic and one phonetic, whose function is to express the various semantic structures of sentences in his philosophical language. Both systems supply the same semantic information, between graphemic and phonetic symbols, be they simple or complex, there is a one to one mapping relation so that the more or less complex semantic structure of a single word of Wilkins's philosophical language can be directly inferred from the combination of various strokes and diacritic elements — these are the primitive elements of the graphemic

[57] Funke (1929:28) notes that Wilkins's ideas on different functions of prepositions are taken up again by John Horne-Tooke in his *Diversions of Purley* (1798/1805).

[58] See also the short discussion of other enterprises of this sort in Brekle and Wildgen 1970 (XII–XVIII) in connection with Wolfgang von Kempelen's (1791) attempt to construct a 'speaking machine'.

system, each element represents a certain category, differences or species; the 'internal syntax' of a combination of such elements representing the semantic structure of a word is regulated by simple topological criteria (left, right; above, below). These are the main ideas of Wilkins' graphemic system, or as he designates it, of his 'Real Character' (1668:376, 385ff.).

The corresponding phonetic system is based on various combinations of vowels and consonants; each combination of a consonant and a vowel — this process may be iterated — represents some category, difference, or species. In addition there are several rules for the derivation of adjectives, plural-formation etc.[59] As was pointed out before the elements of some word in a phonetic representation stand in a one-to-one mapping relation to their respective graphemic elements.

Without entering on a discussion of the relative merits or faulty assumptions and premises of Wilkins' entire scheme, it should nevertheless be stated that Wilkins' succeeded to a certain degree in devising both graphemic and phonetic systems for representing the internal semantic or conceptual structure of the meaningful elements ('words') of his 'philosophical language'.

On the other hand, his treatment of the syntactic organization of words within a sentence is clearly less adequate. From one example — The Lord's Prayer (reprinted in Funke 1929 (29, 32)) — one can infer that the arrangement of words in Wilkins' philosophical language follows closely the surface structure ordering of the respective English text. Wilkins does, however, provide for various sets of 'isolated particles' whose function would be to establish some degree of semantic organization in a sentence. Among these 'isolated particles' we find: symbols for the copula, 18 pronouns, 36 prepositions, 27 adverbs, 24 conjunctions, and symbols for modal and temporal categories.

Wilkins sees a definite advantage of his language over 'natural languages':

> But then for the Philosophy of this Language, it hath many great advantages above any other. Every word being a description of the thing signified by it; Every letter being significant, either as to the Nature of the Thing, or the Grammatical variations of the Word, which cannot be said of any of the rest; besides the constant Analogy observed in all kind of Derivations and Inflexions. (1668:440)

It seems certain that Wilkins' *magnum opus* must be considered as a major contribution to the theory of linguistics and to the development of 'Real Characters' or 'Begriffsschriften', of which in our times we have witnessed such admirable results in the series of works by Frege–Peano–Russell–Whitehead.[60]

[59] See Linsky 1966 (58ff.) for a set of examples of Wilkins's way of handling various metaphorical relationships between words. This aspect of his work would correspond to a sort of paradigmatic semantics.

[60] See Funke 1929 (36f.) for a short outline of the influences of Wilkins's *Essay* on linguistics and logic in the eighteenth and nineteenth centuries.

1.3 *Grammatical Studies in Seventeenth Century England*

In the course of the last twenty-five years appeared two monographs dealing with grammatical works stemming from seventeenth century English authors. Poldauf 1948 is arranged chronologically and gives a list of 100 English grammars which appeared in the seventeenth and eighteenth centuries (1948:21–39) together with useful biobibliographical and linguistic commentaries. Covering a total of 273 texts, Michael (1970) has a systematical arrangement of topics: the first part deals with the medieval tradition of divisions of grammar, parts of discourse and speech, and classification within the parts of speech; the second part of Michael's impressive work covers systematically the development of English grammatical categories as they are used in 17th and 18th century grammatical treatises. Michael's *magnum opus* will certainly prove to be indispensable for any sort of future research work done in the field of the history of English linguistics.

According to Poldauf (1948:70ff.) the first thorough grammatical work dealing with English is Gill 1619. His concern is above all the relation between the way English is written and the way it is pronounced, but, unlike his predecessors,[61] he treats of syntax at great length. Gill compares English with Latin, Greek, Hebrew and even some modern languages. In the preface to his work the idea of comparative philology emerges for the first time in a grammar of English. Gill, however, is not so much attracted by similarities of sound between languages as by differences in various structural layers. He thinks it necessary to define the features he considers to be most characteristic of English, for 'uti omnis alia lingua, sic etiam Anglica suos habet idiotismos, qui latine vix aut omnino reddi non possunt' (Gill 1621:75). This can be seen as one of the first attempts to liberate English grammar from the bonds of Latin grammar; in Wallis's work (1653) we find this revolutionary idea most clearly expressed. On the other hand Gill was rather conservative; in contrast to his contemporary, the dramatist Ben Jonson, he chooses as the linguistic material for his investigations the language of the 'docti aut culte eruditi viri'. Gill likewise recognized the sovereign to be the highest authority in grammatical questions, or, rather, in questions of usage. Gill's intention is to distinguish strictly between the literary and the spoken language.

Unlike Gill, Jonson's main concern in his *English grammar*[62] was the 'common speech'. Appealing to Quintilian, Jonson declares custom to be decisive in forming the rules of grammar. In his opinion it is the grammarian's task to present the system of a language in the best way possible. The grammatical rules and the exceptions should be derived from experience and observation only. In Poldauf's opinion, Jonson's grammar 'is sketchy and from the philological point of view most unsatisfactory, for the most part owing to Raméesque systematism' (1948:74).

[61] A. Hume (1617), Bullokar (1586); see also Funke (1938).
[62] Written around 1620, printed posthumously in 1640. See Jonson 1620.

After Gill and Jonson it was John Wallis (1616–1700), a mathematician and divine, who with his *Grammatica linguae anglicanae* (1653)[63] set up a land-mark for further grammatical descriptions of the English language. In a way Wallis tried to meet the demands expressed by Bacon, who had called for a physiological study of sounds and a grammatical characterization of every single language (*Works* IV, 442f.). Wallis's treatise "De loquela sive sonorum formatione. Tractatus grammatico-physicus", which is prefixed to his *Grammatica* (1653), is classified by Poldauf (1948:79) as 'the first description of the sounds of a language that can claim to be scientific'. Wallis here describes with an astonishing degree of precision the place and the manner of articulation of English sounds.[64] In the description of the grammatical structure of English Wallis tries to detach himself from the Latin tradition; he is thereby led by the observable data of his mother-tongue. He refuses to introduce a new terminology for his subject unless he is sure that it will simplify his description. He gives great attention to problems of word-formation; whereas syntax is somewhat neglected because English is 'a language most simple in itself' ('Lingua in se facillima'). Poldauf's appraisal of Wallis's work is certainly correct: '. . . there is a scientific foundation in Wallis's work, austerely simple, empirical and rational, which leaves Wallis without a match among the English grammarians of more than a hundred years after him . . . undoubtedly Wallis is in more than one respect a symbol of his age, the age of classicism and enlightenment, the age of Dryden and Newton' (1948:82).

During the second half of the seventeenth century we have a number of English grammars pursuing mainly practical aims (see Poldauf 1948:86ff.). Two grammars, however, can be said to be on the same lines as Wallis': Miège 1688, based on the theoretical parts of Miège 1685 and Cooper 1685.

According to Poldauf (1948:88) 'Miège brings into English grammar the spirit of the French Academy. The nimble style and keen observation of a Frenchman who had become naturalized in England, with the ambitions of a scholar, and the universal interest of that time in problems of education'. His keen interest in problems of lexicography caused him to write two dictionaries, a French-English dictionary, published in 1677, and Miège 1679. After having written a French Grammar (1678) he published an English Grammar for the French, his *Nouvelle méthode*, which is really a contrastive grammar of the two languages. The success of this work seems to have made him write the *English grammar* (1688). Miège stressed the importance of language-learning, native and foreign, for the general

[63] See Lehnert 1936 for a description of the life and personality of Dr. John Wallis together with an evaluation of his *Grammatica*. In the series *The classics of linguistics* a new edition with translation and commentary of Wallis 1653 has appeared in Wallis 1972. Unfortunately the date of publication made it impossible to use this edition.

[64] There are many phoneticians who follow Wallis's scheme of description: Holder (1669) who questioned Wallis's method and results to a certain extent; Sibscota (1670), La Fin (1692) and Amman (1700) applied Wallis's articulatory phonetics for the cure of the deaf and dumb. See for a detailed discussion Kökeritz 1935, Firth 1946, and Abercrombie 1948.

education of young people: 'Could I have my option, all young people that are designed for any thing of good education should begin with the grounds of their language. And, as it is fit for travellers to be capacitated first to give an account of their native country before they launch into foreign parts, I think it very proper, before a young man be turned over to the Latin tongue, to know the nature and principles of his own. Twould be in a manner a prelude and introduction, which would facilitate unto him the learning of other languages. (Quoted after Poldauf 1948:89)

Miège is a systematic and witty observer of the language of the common people. He distinguishes four kinds of pronunciation of English:[65] National, Provincial, Grave and Familiar. The national pronunciation is the most universal, it is in a way a standard for the nation.[66] Starting from graphematic elements, Miège develops pretty clear-cut correlations with the respective sounds; moreover he continually contrasts English sounds with French ones.

In the second part Miège 1749 treats of Words and Sentences within the traditional framework of the eight parts of speech. However, he ridicules the Latin inflexional paradigm with its six cases,[67] instead he recognizes only the two prepositional phrases with *of* and *to* as equivalents for the Genitive and Dative in English.

Miège has an extensive chapter on English word-formation; he distinguishes between compounds and derivatives; for Miège compounds also include prefixal combinations such as *inhabit*, *undergo*, etc.

Remarkably enough, Miège makes a clear difference between combinations fully analysable on a native basis and those where this is not the case:

> . . . une grande partie des Composés qui tirent leur Origine du Latin n'ont pas leurs Simples en Usage. Ainsi on dit bien *to permit, promise, intercept* . . . etc. Otez-en la préposition, le reste n'est qu'un Corps sans Ame. (Miège 1749:58)

[65] The following quotations are taken from a later edition of Miège's *Nouvelle méthode* (1749). This edition of Miège's grammar contains also a vocabulary, familiar phrases and dialogues drawn from Boyer's *French grammar* (1698). According to Poldauf (1948:90) 'Miège's grammar became one of the most frequently reprinted English grammars on the continent in the 18th century.' In 1718 the first edition of the combined Miège-Boyer grammar appeared in Holland.

[66] Miège (1749:19): '... les Anglois ont, comme nous, plusieurs Sortes de Prononciation. Ils ont la Prononciation Universelle et la Particulière, la Familière et la Grave, Par l'Universelle j'entends la véritable Prononciation du Pais, et par la Particulière, celle des Provinces. La Prononciation Familière est celle dont on se sert ordinairement dans les Discours Familiers, et la Grave est celle dont l'Usage consiste dans les Discours graves et serieux. ... Les Règles que j'avance sur la Prononciation de l'Anglois sont néanmoins formées sur ce Modèle [la Prononciation Familière]; puis que c'est la Prononciation familière qui a le plus d'étendue, et dont l'Usage est le plus nécessaire.'

[67] 'Les Grammairiens à la vieille Mode, qui prennent toutes Leurs Mesures de la Langue Latine, et qui se croiroient perdus s'il s'en écartoient tant soit peu, déclinent nos Noms (à la manière des Latins) avec six cas en chaque Nombre. Ils y font venir à toute force le Nominatif, le Genitif, le Datif, l'Accusatif, le Vocatif et l'Ablatif; qui sont autant de Fantômes dans nos Langues Vulgaires ... il n'y a rien de tel dans l'Anglois ni dans le François, à quoi bon multiplier les choses sans nécessité, et remplir les Grammaires d'un Fatras inutile.' (Miège 1749:78).

One further quotation shall suffice in order to show that Miège's judgment on peculiarities of the English language reaches a certain degree of empirical as well as theoretical adequacy. He recognizes clearly that in French there are two genders, whereas in English there is no such difference; in other words Miège here states the difference between the syntactical-morphological function of gender in French and the semantic category of sex in English:

Les Genres des Noms Anglois ne se distinguent pas, comme les nôtres, par la Terminaison des Noms, mais par la différence des Sexes. (Miège 1749:76)

Cooper 1685, the last English grammar written in Latin, is clearly influenced by Wallis 1653. Cooper, too, deals mainly with problems of pronunciation, spelling, and word-formation. Nevertheless he has some new points to contribute to the general theory of English grammar. Cooper is probably the first to discuss the problem of Expanded vs. Simple Form of English verbs. He divides the 'vox activa' of English verbs into two modes 'vel per adjectivum et copulam; id est, si adjectivum activum in loco passivi ponuntur: vel per unum verbum, quod continet adjectivum et copulam ... *I am preparing* ... *I was* ... *I have been* ... *I had been* ... *I shall* vel *will be preparing* ...' (Cooper 1685:147). As a first approximation to an explanation of the semantic function of this peculiar English construction Cooper is not too far from the truth:

Sed hujus modi adjectiva actum significant tantum praesentem in actu, non praeteritum nec finitum; quamvis enim persona agens dicitur esse vel in praesenti vel praeterito, vel futuro tempore, quod denotant copulae *am, was;* vel signa copulis praeposita *have been, had been, shall* vel *will be:* attamen adjectivum *preparing* et hujusmodi semper loquuntur de praesenti; ideoque hoc modo ... actum absolutum enunciare non possumus. Quandocumque igitur exprimendus occurrit actus absolute finitus, fit per unam dictionem, quam emphatice verbum nuncupamus, quod copulam et actum comprehendit ... [*I prepare* ...] (Cooper: 1685:147)

Finally, mention shall be made of the English grammarian A. Lane. As a schoolmaster at Leominster, Herefordshire, then at Mile End Green, Stepney, Lane might have been expected to concentrate his attention upon the didactic side of English grammar. Instead, his main interest lies in universal grammar. Lane intermingled two conceptions of universal grammar current in his days: the one took for universal everything that seemed indispensable in a language,[68] the other regarded as universal what was common to inflected languages, such as Latin and Greek. In his two works, 1695 and 1700, Lane clung fairly closely to the system of traditional Latin grammar. As an English grammarian, however, Lane deserves some attention because, according to Poldauf (1948:93) he 'is the first ... to proceed from a philosophical basis in order to find grammatical rules of general validity'. For Lane there are four sorts of words, for 'whatever is in the whole universe, is either a thing, or the manner of a thing, the action of a thing, or the manner of an

[68] Cf. e.g. Lewis 1674.

action' (quoted after Poldauf 1948:93).

Poldauf (1948:93) assumes that Lane did not know the Grammar of Port-Royal. Lane's work is certainly inferior to the *Grammaire générale*, yet he seems to foreshadow the approaching age of English rationalism.[69]

2. SEVENTEENTH CENTURY LINGUISTICS AND PHILOLOGY IN GERMANY

The still valuable two-volume work by Max Hermann Jellinek (1913) provides detailed information on the lives and works of grammarians dealing with the German language. Jellinek's standpoint is mainly an historical and comparative one; the value of his work resides more in the diligent and painstaking accumulation of primary data on the external structure of a multitude of grammatical treatises of the High-German language and various German dialects than in the not so satisfactory treatment of the philosophical and theoretical background of the works discussed.

Jellinek's statement (1913:I,30) that 'Eine Geschichte der Sprachphilosophie des 16. bis 18. Jahrhunderts fehlt, ebenso eine Geschichte der allgemeinen Grammatik' still holds true, especially for German works written during the seventeenth century.[70]

Verburg (1951) does not deal with the development of German linguistics and philology in the first three quarters of the seventeenth century, probably because in Verburg's judgment the theoretical aspect is not the dominating one in the works of such grammarians as Ratichius (Ratke), Helvicus (Helwig), Alsted, and Schottelius.

Although this may be true to some extent for Ratke and Helwig, it is certainly not valid for Alsted and Schottelius. From the philosophical and logical side the vast corpus of works by Heinrich Alsted, who was Comenius's teacher at Herborn, has already received some attention,[71] his studies on the theory of grammar, however, have been so far neglected by the historiographers of linguistics. As is well known Alsted did much to propagate Ramus's ideas in logic and linguistics in the Protestant countries; the methodological background of Ratke's and Helwig's works derives also from Ramistic sources.

[69] Cf. the so-called *Brightland grammar* (1711). (See Flasdieck 1928.) It consists of an English grammar at the top of every page and a 'universal' grammar in footnotes. These notes are more or less a translation of the Port-Royal *Grammar*. See Poldauf 1948 (104f.) for further information.

[70] Cf. the older works Reichard 1747, Reichenbach 1842 and Loewe 1829. It was impossible for me to see Reichenbach 1842; Jellinek describes this Halle dissertation as a short summary of the views of some philosophers on the relation between language and thought. Loewe's dissertation is nothing more than an annotated bibliography of several general grammars going back only to the eighteenth century.

[71] See especially Rossi 1960 (179–184) and Yates 1966 (375f.).

There are at least two models that can be said to have influenced the work of German grammarians in the seventeenth centuries: the Melanchthon type of grammar going back to medieval and classical models, the other — often mixed with the first — is derived from Ramus's linguistic and logical conceptions.

The structure of Melanchthon's Latin grammar (1525/26) served as a prototype for many grammatical works written during the seventeenth century; it aimed at a classificatory treatment of linguistic data within four components of a grammar: 1. Orthographia, 2. Prosodia, 3. Etymologia, 4. Syntaxis.

By 'orthographia' is meant the presentation of the phonological and alphabetical inventory of a language. 'Prosodia' deals with syllabic elements, especially as to quantity and stress. 'Etymologia' comprises the morphological and functional properties of words: an enumeration of the traditional eight 'partes orationis' (Nomen, Pronomen, Verbum, Participium, Adverbium, Praepositio, Coniunctio, Interiectio) together with a list of their respective 'accidentia' (if any) as e.g. 'Genus', 'Numerus', 'Casus', 'Declinatio' for the 'Nomen', and 'Genus', 'Tempus', 'Modus', 'Persona', 'Coniugatio', etc. for the 'Verbum'. 'Syntaxis' is the component where grammatical relations are discussed such as congruence, case relationships (both morphological and semantic) between verbs and nouns and nouns and nouns, and conjunctions combining sentences.

The logical and grammatical conceptions of Petrus Ramus (1515–1572) can be viewed as another model for several German grammarians during the first half of the seventeenth century, especially as regards his dichotomizing method, his didactic orientation, and his respect for questions of linguistic usage.[72]

At the beginning of the seventeenth century Wolfgang Ratke (1571–1635) tried to disseminate his plans for an educational reform which were developed under the influence of Ramus. One of his guiding principles was: 'omnia docenda per notiora'. Its implication for the teaching of languages — mainly Latin — was that the pupils should first become acquainted with grammatical notions applied to their mother tongue, i.e. one or another dialect variant of German. Thus the teaching of German grammar had a twofold purpose: on the one hand to teach a somewhat normalized version of High German, on the other hand to make available a generally valid grammatical system that might profitably be applied to the study of Latin, Greek, and Hebrew. Moreover, Ratke held the belief that teaching German grammar could serve as an instrument 'die teutsch Sprach vnd Nation mercklich zu beßern vnd zu erheben'.[73]

Similar ideas on language planning can be found in the works of most German grammarians during the seventeenth century. Later on this striving for a linguistic

[72] See e.g. Ramus's *Gramere* (1562). On Ramistic theories and their influences in Europe in the 16th and 17th centuries see Rossi 1960 (133–142) and Risse's Introduction in Ramus 1964. A detailed discussion of Ramus' linguistic theory is found in Verburg (1951:172–84). See also Ong 1958a.

[73] See Stötzner 1892 (vol. 1, 26). More bibliographical details on Ratichius and other grammarians of this period are found in Jellinek 1913 (vol. 1, 85ff.).

norm is combined with investigations into the history of the German or Germanic languages in order to demonstrate the venerable age and purity of German.

From Ratke and his collaborators we have a Latin and a German version of a didactically orientated general grammar (Ratke 1619a and 1619b).[74]

The theoretical substance of this work is rather traditional; by way of questions — supplemented by examples to be given by the teacher — the pupils are expected to become acquainted with the traditional grammatical distinctions and categories.

Christoph Helwig (Helvicus) (1581–1617) was one of Ratke's collaborators. In 1619 his widow published Helwig 1619a and 1619b. Helwig's grammar is a definite improvement over Ratke's work. Helwig is less traditional, he reduces the number of eight 'partes orationis' to three main categories, namely, 'Nännwort' (Nomen), 'Sagwort' (Verbum), and 'Beiwort' (Advocabulum); furthermore he admits only four cases for German, whereas Ratke adhered in both cases to the grammatical tradition dating back to classical antiquity.

In 1630 Heinrich Alsted adopted Helwig's 'grammatica universalis' for his *Encyclopaedia* under the title *Delineatio grammaticae germanicae*. Alsted has his own chapter on general or universal grammar where modistic and Ramistic influences can be discovered. He describes the method and task of a general grammar in the following way: 'Praecipuum Grammaticae generalis officio in eo est, ut Grammatices notiones (seu entia Grammaticae) componat cum notionibus seu entibus Logicis' (Alsted 1630:C.VII, 271b). Due to the lack of penetrating studies Alsted's influence on later grammarians cannot be established with reasonable certainty.

Between 1620 and 1663 — the date when Schottelius' masterpiece *Ausführliche Arbeit Von der Teutschen HaubtSprache* left the press for the first time — a number of other German grammarians were at work.[75] Their grammars brought certain improvements over earlier treatises, especially as regards didactic questions and the system of German morphology.

There is no doubt that Justus Georg Schottelius (1612–1676) was the dominating German grammarian in the seventeenth century. He was of Low-German origin (born at Eimbeck); he earned his living as a jurist in the service of the House of Brunswick. The influence of his works is acknowledged by Leibniz; it lasted throughout the first half of the eighteenth century.

Schottelius' first grammatical treatise was published in 1641. Together with his next work, from 1643 — written in verse — his 1641 treatise can be viewed as being preparatory for Schottelius' *magnum opus*, Schottelius 1663.[76] Hankamer (1927:124) qualifies this work justly as a 'barocke summa philologica'.

[74] Reprinted in Vogt 1894. Cf. also the recent edition of the works in Ratichius 1959. See also Ising 1960 (367–74) where something is said of the development of linguistic conceptions in early German grammars. On the pedagogical and didactic side of Ratke's work see Rioux 1963.

[75] E.g. Olearius 1630. See Jellinek 1913 (vol. 1, 95ff.) for further references.

[76] Second the 1737 edition, Hildesheim. The work comprises five books (ca. 1500 pages in quarto). There is a recent Zürich dissertation (1967) by Josef Plattner which aims at elucidating Schottelius's notion of language. Plattner's contribution is quite useful as to biographical and other

In the same vein as e.g. the Dutch scholar Simon Stevin, whom Schottelius quotes several times, one of Schottelius's aims in his main work is to prove that German can also be used as a medium for scientific discourse. For this Schottelius adduces historical as well as functional criteria. Before Leibniz it was Schottelius who insisted on the relevance of the historical aspect for the description and evaluation of a language.[77] For Schottelius the permanent element in language was the structure of the word. In contradistinction to later grammarians Schottelius's grammar is based on the word and its variations and not on the sentence. That this is so can be seen from the fact that Schottelius took over the notion 'root' or 'stem' from earlier Hebrew grammars; this notion is one of his central theoretical concepts. Schottelius's axiom of the primacy of the word is common with most of his German and Dutch contemporaries, it is also one of the cornerstones of the linguistic-didactic doctrines of the great Czech language philosopher Johannes Amos Comenius (see below our chapter on Comenius' linguistic doctrines).

Schottelius's fame as the German 'praeceptor grammaticae' during the second half of the seventeenth century rests on his extensively elaborated theory of the German word-structure. His theory displays both aspects of language description: diachrony and synchrony. This qualifies him as a forerunner of nineteenth century historical and comparative linguists. He did, however, not share the wide-spread conviction of nineteenth-century linguists and philologists that older stages of a language — or some hypothetical 'Urgermanisch' or 'Indogermanisch' — are per se more venerable or more perfect than more modern languages. For Schottelius a language does not just fall into decay; at least for the German language he postulates a certain structural stability throughout its historical development; he calls this the 'Grundrichtigkeit' of the German language.[78] Schottelius explicitly charac-

---

historical data, however, he restricts his discussion of Schottelius's notion of language to such notions as 'analogy' and 'language as a codified system'. Plattner does not try to apply more modern linguistic categories to a differentiated interpretation of Schottelius's linguistic ideas.

[77] Cf. Metcalf 1953 for a recent discussion of diachronic aspects in Schottelius 1663. Metcalf stresses the close connection of Schottelius's general linguistic doctrine with the role of German in linguistic history which prevents a sharp division between the synchronic-functional and diachronic aspects of Schottelius 1663.

[78] See in this connection Fricke 1933. The title of Fricke's contribution is rather misleading insofar as he deals only with German grammarians and — in the seventeenth century — only with Schottelius. Nevertheless, Fricke's judgment on Schottelius's fundamental category — the 'Grundrichtigkeit' of the German Language — still seems quite acceptable; it shows that Schottelius' conceptions on the philosophy of language can be said to foreshadow somehow the romantic and idealistic ideas of Hamann, Herder and other German philosophers like Fichte: 'Das zentrale Prinzip der GRUNDRICHTIGKEIT faßt den objektivistischen Sprachbegriff der ganzen Epoche klar and folgerecht zusammen. Es bestimmt die ganze grammatische Konzeption Schottels. Hier ist die Sprache wirklich zu einer ewigen und unveränderlichen Wesenheit geworden, sie ist absolut geworden, den Gesetzen von Zeit und Raum ebenso entrückt wie der Relativität der Dinge und der Willkür der Menschen. ÜBER der bewegten, von Unwissenheit und roher Willkür verzerrten und mißhandelten GESPROCHENEN Sprache in der Mannigfaltigkeit ihrer Dialekte liegt die unveränderliche richtig und eigentliche deutsche Sprache, der Schottel einen viel höheren Wirklichkeitsgehalt beimißt. Sie ist Idee — wenn man ihr jenen absoluten ding-

terizes among the four developmental stages of German that of Luther as the stage where refinement, as well as vigor, replaced many old crudities.[79] In Schottelius' view every language has a definite structural system; it is the task of the grammarian describing some given language to uncover its particular structure that may vary from language to language. The grammarian should expose the fundamental and unchanging pattern of the word-structure of a language so that usage can conform with it. Usage, or empirical evidence, is not to be regarded as the overriding criterion for the work of a grammarian; for the determination of the basic structure — essentially unchangeable — the grammarian has to rely upon his intuitive etymological analysis of the language.

He distinguishes three elements that enter into the formation of a complete word, i.e. a word as used in syntactic constructions: 1. the stem ('Stamm- oder Wurzelwort', 'literae radicales'); 2. derivational ending ('Hauptendung', 'terminatio derivandi'); 3. inflectional ending ('zufällige Endung', 'literae accidentales'). These three classes of elements are definite as to their number; once these classes and the regularities governing their combination are found out, the fundamental system ('Grundrichtigkeit') of a language is described and explained.[80] Schottelius postulates that these elements should be monosyllabic which leads him into difficulties with a number of stem-forming vowels or suffixes.[81]

One of the most lasting merits of Schottelius' main work lies in the fact that he was the first to develop a relatively consistent theory of word-formation, supplemented by ample lists of examples. Even if the relationship between derivation and composition is not seen clearly in all its consequences, the guiding principles are nevertheless sound ones:

> Die Ableitung [derivation] wird von der Verdoppelung [composition] hierin unterschieden, dieweil die Verdoppelung oder die verdoppelten Wörter aus zweyen, dreyen oder vieren, an sich etwas bedeutenden Wörteren gemacht werden: Die Ableitung aber besteht darin, wenn etzliche gewisse Endungen [derivational suffixes], die an sich selbst nichts bedeuten, dem Nennworte beygefüget worden, und zwar nur zu ende, da in den gedoppelten solches bald vorn, bald in der Mitte, und bald an zweyen, bald an dreyen örtern zugleich, bald zu ende, geschiehet. (Schottelius 1663:318)

Obviously, Schottelius considers words with inseparable prefixes as belonging to the compositional system. In the sixth 'Lobrede' he gives the following classifica-

lichen Realitätsgrad zuerkennt, den das Mittelalter mit seinen Ideen verband. Sprache ist also bei Schottel nicht mehr bloßes Material in der gesetzgebenden Hand des Grammatikers. Sie ist aller Willkür auch des Grammatikers entrückt; der gelehrte Forscher denkt sie nicht NEU — er denkt sie nur NACH, er liest ihre Regeln ab.' (Fricke 1933:120f.).

[79] See Schottelius 1663 (I, 49) *et passim* together with Metcalf's discussion of Schottelius' somewhat ambiguous position (Metcalf 1953:117f.).

[80] Cf. Schottelius (1676:6): '... solche grundmäßige Abmerkung, und ordentlich untriegliche Eintheilung dieser Letteren [i.e. stems, derivational and inflexional endings] verursachen die in Teutscher Sprache verhandene gewißmäßige Grundrichtigkeit, die man schon bey Caroli M. Zeiten beginnen abzumerken.'

[81] See Jellinek 1913 (vol. 1, 137f.) for a detailed discussion.

tion of German nominal compounds: 1. Combination of several substantives; 2. Combination of a substantive and a deverbal substantive; 3. Combination of one or several prepositions with a substantive; 4. Combination of stem-words with one or two derivational suffixes.

The leading theoretical concepts in Schottelius' doctrine on German word-formation are still in use today; as far as nominal compounds are concerned he divides them into two elements: the 'Grundwort' and the 'Beygefügte'. It is easy to discover in this dichotomy such notions as 'head'/'modifier' or 'determinatum'/ 'determinans'. For Schottelius this distinction is also valid for compounds consisting of more than two elements:

Ist demnach zuwissen, daß ein jedes verdoppeltes Wort abgeteihlet werde in zwey Glieder oder Stükke: Das eine heisset *Grund,* das andere Beyfügig; also daß aus einem Grundworte, und aus einem oder mehr Beygefügten die Verdoppelung in Teutscher Sprache geschehen muß. (Schottelius 1663:75)

Moreover, Schottelius clearly recognized the overall communicative function of derived and compounded words; starting from his already mentioned assumption — which we would regard as true today — that we have in every language only a finite list of stem-words and 'endings', he goes on to state a sort of generative principle (valid only in the domain of word-formation; Schottelius's conceptions about syntax being rather traditional, i.e. restricted to statements about 'congruence' and 'rection'):

. . . daß eine jede Sprache eine gewisse und nur wenige Anzahl Stammwörter habe, gegen der großen Menge derer Dinge, so da unterschiedlich zu benahmen seyn . . . Zu dem, weil die Stammwörter durch und in sich allein fast keine, oder gar eine geringe Rede machen können, als muß ihnen die hüfliche [sic] Hand stets gebohten werden von jhren *abgeleiteten* und *verdoppelten* Wörtern. (Schottelius 1663:74)

In diesen dreyen / den Stammwörtern / abgeleiteten und verdoppleten / besteht die volle Gerechtschaft [justification] der Teutschen Sprache / mächtig und gnugsam / fast alles was in der Welt ihr auszudeuten nötig / auch auszudeuten.

(Schottelius 1663:1247)

The encyclopedic nature of the 'Ausführliche Arbeit' makes it impossible to give even a summarizing description of its content; besides a lexicon of German stem-words it contains a "poetica germanica" (fourth book), a list of proverbs, a historical sketch of German writers, etc.[82]

Between Schottelius and Leibniz, who acknowledged Schottelius's merits for the historical description of German,[83] we find a number of 'grammatici minores'[84] whose dependency on and partial progress beyond Schottelius are sketched in Jellinek 1913 (vol. 1, ch. 6.).

[82] For a critical evaluation of Schottelius's phonological, morphological and relatively meagre syntactical doctrines see Jellinek 1913 (vol. 2).

[83] On the connections between Schottelius and Leibniz's see also Aarsleff 1964 (169f.).

[84] E.g. Bödiker 1690; Prasch 1687; Pudor 1672.

3. JOHANN AMOS COMENIUS ON LANGUAGE

Johann Amos Comenius (1592–1670) was a member of the Bohemian-Moravian Brethren, a religious sect founded in 1457. While studying at different places, he came into contact with numerous famous scholars. At the Calvinist Academy of Herborn in Nassau, where he pursued his studies under Alsted, he became acquainted with some ideas of the Spaniard Ludovico Vives.[85] Vives, although a precursor of Jesuit educational ideas, had a strong influence on the protestant Comenius, who adopted from him certain suggestions regarding training in language which he was to develop later on.

On one of his many journeys through Europe, it was in 1642 that Comenius had a conversation with René Descartes in Leiden. According to Geissler, Comenius discussed with Descartes the question whether language was merely a means to internalize traditional doctrines — a view propounded by the Jesuits (cf. Geissler 1959:25). After their first meeting Comenius remained in contact with Descartes. But Comenius — like Bacon and Spinoza no mathematician — was incapable of following Descartes' mathematical and rationalistic way of thinking. He attacked the dualism Descartes had set up between the soul (= *res cogitans*) and the body (= *res extensa*). Besides the existence of the *res cogitans* and the *res extensa* Descartes also attempted to prove the existence of God who was conceived of as being separated from the world of reality. Therefore — he believed — language cannot be inspired by God and 'les mots que nous avons n'ont quasi que des significations confuses, auxquelles l'esprit des hommes s'étant accoutumé de longue main, cela est cause qu'il n'entend presque rien parfaitement' (Descartes 1963:231–232, letter to Mersenne of 20 November 1629).

The ideal, then, would be to establish 'un ordre entre toutes les pensées qui peuvent entrer en l'esprit humain, de même qu'il y en a un naturellement établi entre les nombres; . . .' (Descartes 1963:230).

According to Descartes, the invention of a philosophical language

> dépend de la vraie Philosophie, car il est impossible autrement de dénombrer toutes les pensées des hommes, et de les mettre par ordre, ni seulement de les distinguer en sorte qu'elles soient claires et simples, qui est à mon avis le plus grand secret qu'on puisse avoir pour acquérir la bonne Science. Et si quelqu'un avait bien expliqué quelles sont les idées simples qui sont en l'imagination des hommes, desquelles se compose tout ce qu'ils pensent, et que cela fût reçu par tout le monde, j'oserais espérer ensuite une langue universelle, fort aisée à apprendre, à prononcer et à écrire, et ce qui est le principal, qui aiderait au judgement, lui représentant si distinctement toutes choses, qu'il lui serait presque impossible de se tromper . . .
>
> (Descartes 1963:231)

Following Ernst Cassirer, Geissler points out that 'because of these remarks in his [= Descartes'] letter to Mersenne, the problem of language, having been a methodo-

[85] For a recent discussion of Vives's theory of language see Coseriu 1971a and 1971b.

logical one in antiquity, has become a mere technical problem, consisting basically in the difficulty of establishing a natural order of basic concepts' (Geissler 1959:26).

The rise of a new scientific conception of the world provided the background for the discussion between Comenius and Descartes. The conflict with the old christian-aristotelian conception of the world made Comenius hesitate about the Copernican hypothesis and he may fairly be judged to have hardly taken part in the change in western thought (cf. Geissler 1959:26).

In opposition to Descartes, Comenius believed in the traditional theory concerning the inspiration of the Bible; he developed a mystical theory of *Pansophia* that was supposed to sketch a new conception of the world. Descartes admitted that the views propounded by Comenius, were justified to a certain extent and he waited for the further elaboration of Comenius's work. Descartes remained in contact with Comenius through his [Descartes'] correspondent Mersenne.

Comenius was familiar with the work of the German mystic Jacob Boehme,[86] who was the most prominent representative of the German type of mysticism; his works were widely circulated in Europe. As a student at the University of Herborn, Comenius met his teacher Heinrich Alsted and also became interested in the work of Wolfgang Ratke. Ratke's ideas on the philosophy of language — according to Geissler — were so impressive that he was sponsored by several German princes and towns; moreover the Professors Helwig and Jungius for a while left their University posts and followed him.[87] After Ratke had abandoned the idea of teaching Hebrew in every school as a second language he turned to the teaching of the native language (i.e. German). The essence of the Ratke method as concerns the teaching of foreign languages, was to use the vernacular as the medium for instruction and the formulation of the rules of grammar.[88] From Ratke Comenius adopted the idea of giving a proper instruction in the mother tongue before teaching Latin to children. In contradistinction to Alsted's method of teaching, Comenius enunciated a new principle according to which the teaching of the native language had absolute priority.[89]

The international fame of Comenius began to develop in 1633 with the publication of his famous text-book *The gateway of languages unlocked* (*Janua linguarum reserata*).[90] According to his own statement this work was based on the *Janua linguarum* written by Spanish Jesuits and its various multi-lingual compilations. In 1629 it was worked out in eight different languages. Patočka points out that Co-

[86] See, for instance, Klaus Schaller's "Einleitung" in Comenius 1964 (8–11).

[87] See Brekle 1965 (82ff.) for some discussion of Jungius's ideas.

[88] Ratke elaborated his views on universal language-learning in Ratichius [Ratke] 1619a and 1619b.

[89] According to Geissler (1959:48), Comenius's first pedagogical work (of which no copy has come down to us) *Grammaticae facilioris praecepta* (1616, Prague), was especially influenced by Ratke's suggestions.

[90] For some details on the *Janua linguarum reserata* see Schaller 1967 (318–31), Salmon 1972 (60 *et passim*) and Formigari 1970 (129ff.).

menius's *Janua* was — according to Bayle — the most widely circulated book in Europe during the second half of the 17th century — with the exception only of the Bible (cf. Patočka 1971:31).

In his *Janua* Comenius gives an outline of his well-known principle that things have priority in relation to words and that the lexicon of a language is more important than its grammar. This view is, of course, a result of Comenius's conviction that the formation of concepts is the result of perceptional processes.[91] Sadler criticizes this point made by Comenius in remarking that he 'greatly over-estimated the accuracy of observation through the senses but especially visual observation' (Sadler 1966:156).

In the work in question Comenius is primarily concerned with the 'nomenclatura', the correct denotation for the things in the universe. For Comenius words are the images of things if they are used in a correct relation to the world of God; this is Comenius's standpoint as regards the age-old controversy on the relation between words and things.

In regard to length, the second longest of Comenius's writings is the *Linguarum methodus novissima* (1648), which is concerned mainly with theoretical and methodological questions; it shows an attempt to systematize his theory and — according to Geissler — it can with some justification be called 'scientific' (cf. Geissler 1959:119). It was hardly known during Comenius's lifetime and never received much attention. There has been no German translation of this work and — as far as we know — the only scholarly investigation of the work is Liese 1904.

The *Methodus* is chiefly concerned with Latin, but Comenius claimed that it could be adapted to all other languages including vernaculars.

In this work Comenius emphasizes again that language is an image of things; the structure of language reflects the structure of the world and of the human mind; language is a means of communicating ideas to other people. Language is an artistic fabric, its harmonious structure corresponds to the harmonious structure of the world of things which is founded in the human mind.[92]

According to Geissler (1959:139), Demokrit in a similar way drew a comparison between the structure of sentences and nature; the sounds, then, corresponded to the atoms.

Comenius believes that there are the same differences between things as there are between words; if the relations between words are understood, then the differences between things can easily be recognized. This, he goes on to explain, is the reason why 'a good grammarian can easily be a good logician, a good logician, a

[91] See in this connection Rossi 1960 (184ff.) on Comenius's relation to earlier projects related to Lullist ideas on the 'ars memoriae'. Similar interpretations are given by Formigari 1970 (128f.).

[92] 'Hoc linguae apparatum, in sua perfectione spectetur, praegrande quid esse, ut mundus ipse, quem repraesentatum it, et amplum capaxque, ut mens ipsa, cuius conceptibus exhauriendis, et in alterius mentem transfundendis sufficere debet et denique concinnum quid, omnia sua tam harmonice contexens et connectens, ut harmoniam rerum, cuius mensuras in se animus humanus continet, recte exprimat.' (*Methodus* II:15).

good philosopher, politician, theologian and even a good christian...' (*Methodus* 1649:V,40; cf. Geissler 1959:139).

Because language as a whole takes part in the harmony of all being, only few devices are necessary to constitute a perfect language: the *Nomenclatura*, an unequivocal list of the names of things, that is: a list of words resembling the *Janua*; the *Lexicon* of the phonetic alphabet which gives the names of the sounds; and the *Grammatica*, the system of rules for the correct use of language.

It is fairly obvious that the *Methodus* was influenced by the views of Vives. Comenius puts forward the idea that Latin is the ideal universal language. It is known throughout the world and is exact and easy to write and to pronounce. Therefore it is necessary for everybody to learn Latin. He abandons the idea of the restoration of the *natural* Adamitic language and believes in finding new possibilities for the future in the Latin language.

The true method, Comenius emphasizes again and again, has to teach man to perceive words and things together, to understand and to pronounce them simultaneously in one single step.[93] This is a difficult task for the student because there are a good many rules and exceptions to confuse him. In order to help the student the teacher has to anticipate this knowledge of all things. A sound knowledge of Latin is of great value to man although it is impossible to learn Latin perfectly. Therefore it is necessary to rediscover the fundamentals of language. These are: a) the radical words with their regular inflections; b) the structure of language, i.e. the possibility to reproduce by the use of language the relation to things; c) stylistic subtleties.[94]

Another one of Comenius's writings, the *Triertium catholicum* — published after his death in 1681 — is also of great importance for Comenius's philosophy of language. It is an attempt to deal with the relation between thought, language and action. These three human faculties are based on 'mens', 'lingua' and 'manus'. The problem discussed in this work is still a central problem of modern philosophy of language. Comenius assumes that the traditional theory about language being merely an image of thought does not suffice to account for action. His idea of a 'Pansophical parallelism' can in his view lead to a harmonious union of the three faculties as well as the three sciences associated with thought, language and action which are logic, grammar and pragmatics. These in turn are linked with pansophical metaphysics, the 'sapientia prima'.

In the *Triertium catholicum* Comenius recapitulates certain ideas already put forward in the *Methodus*.

> The things create the thoughts; thoughts create speech; thought and speech lead to action; actions are things, so that the circle is closed again. The purpose of language is to achieve knowledge of things which is immediately put into action.
>
> (Geissler 1959:138; cf. *Triertium catholicum* II)

[93] 'Vera igitur methodus res et verba simul accurate intueri, concipere, exprimere doceat labore uno, simplici, non distracto' (*Methodus* IX:4).

[94] See *Methodus* IX:19.

Language, as well as thought and action consists of seven parts. Because we are mainly interested in language, we will only enumerate the elements of language: sounds, syllables, words, phrases, sentences, groups of sentences (periods), and complete speeches (or written books).[95]

Words are considered by Comenius to be the most important parts of language, they are perceptible signs of our thoughts. In this Comenius is consonant with Schottelius (1663). According to Sadler (1966:156), Comenius is overestimated the importance of 'word' as opposed to 'sentence'. However, he points out, that as a translator Comenius did not make this mistake, and that he was well aware of the effect context had on meaning. To admit this 'would seem to invalidate the argument that each word should correspond with a thing "in such a way that it is impossible to attribute it to another thing"' (Sadler 1966: *ibid.* and *Panglottia, Tentamen*; 3). In so far Comenius is opposed to the principle of arbitrariness insisted on by most modern linguists.

Another work by Comenius, the *Clavis grammatica*,[96] can be said to be connected with the *Triertium catholicum*. It contains the complete arrangement of language which is the fundament of his *Janua*. He divides grammar into three parts:

1. *Etymology*. Etymology deals with the sounds of human languages (which Comenius lumps together with letters), as well as with syllables and words. The parts of speech are enumerated as follows: Noun, Ad-noun, Pro-noun, Verb, Participle, Adverb, Preposition, Conjunction, Interjection, Ad-jection. Furthermore there are meaningful combinations of words (= phrases), sentences, sentence-periods and complete speeches.

2. *Syntax* (syntaxis) constitutes the second part of grammar. It deals with the combinations of sounds, words, etc. and their inflections and includes German and Latin examples.

3. The third part is called *Orthoepeia*, the correct expression of language. It includes the *Orthotonia*, *Orthographia* and *Prosodia*. It is governed by the principle of a close correspondence between the written and the spoken form of language. Various dictionaries are necessary to supplement this grammar.

Comenius also emphasizes the social function of language; language is necessary to man to communicate his ideas to others. In his *Lexicon reale pansophicum*[97] Comenius points out that language considered as a tool for communication is a result of the processes of ideation and imagination. According to Geissler, the term *imago* is intended by Comenius to characterize his understanding of the relation between words and things. *Sermo*, (speech), then, is a *picta imago rerum*. The identification of words and things is understood as the mental process of combining certain conceptions. The word is 'nihil nisi imago mentis'.

[95] See Comenius, *Triertium catholicum*, pp. 24–25 and the German translation of the relevant passage in Hofmann 1970b (88–90).

[96] See Comenius 1657, Part 2: 303–40.

[97] See the recent edition Comenius 1966 and Hofmann 1970a.

On the whole it may be said that Comenius's view on the purpose of language is rather undetermined; he emphasizes its rational and pragmatic character, as well as its social and ethical functions, he recognizes its relation to truth and wisdom.

The *Pampaedia* is his work on education which includes, explains and completes the others. Comenius elaborated it until his death.

In the *Panglottia* Comenius gives an outline of what he conceives as a new universal and perfect language. He emphasises again that language is an image of the things in the universe, even of those things which are non-existent. There are barbarian and cultured languages but he agrees that only among the angels could speech really be perfect. Comenius defines his idea of a perfect language as follows:

> It is firstly an extension of the world in its totality, secondly, an equal richness of the mind whose concepts it communicates to others, and thirdly, a regularity, like musical harmony, by which it establishes between things and concepts and between concepts and words a context in which it is possible to conceive things as they are and to express them as they are conceived. (Sadler 1966:150–51; quoted from *Panglottia* III:6)

Sadler's contention that Comenius was 'working under the influence of the English language reformers, though he did not attempt, like Dalgarno and Wilkins, to devise a complete system but rather to give a new orientation to the whole problem' (1966:151) cannot be upheld in view of recent research.[98] The relationships between Comenius and English scholars like Hartlib, Lodwick, Dalgarno, and Wilkins must have been mutual ones.

Comenius was well aware that a comparative study of languages was necessary as a basis for a universal language in order to combine the best features to be found in each language.[99] To avoid the irregularities and difficulties of natural languages Comenius devises a system which consists of a number of monosyllabic roots; nouns and verbs should be formed from the same root.

The constant harmony between words and things is guaranteed in so far as every root can be modified by simple suffixes; e.g. *hom* = 'man', *home* = 'little child', *homi* = 'boy', *homei* = 'young man' etc. (cf. Geissler 1959:155). Each thing, Comenius insists, must have a different name; there will be no adjectives, no signs devoid of meaning and no synonyms. From each noun three types of verbs can be derived, actives, passives and essentials. Gender and plural are marked as well. Comenius is convinced that his new language would be easy to learn and that it could be understood by everybody. There are no exceptions from the rules, similar things have similar sounds; every word is at the same time a complete definition of the thing or the concept of the thing; because its foundations lie in Metaphysics; misunderstanding will be impossible. Different denotations correspond to different meanings. 'Quidquid aliter significat, aliter determinetur.' (*Panglottia* VIII).

> Summi termini rerum notandi sunt certis notis sonorum et facile nunc voces componere, quemadmodum res componuntur. (*Panglottia:*97)

[98] See Formigari 1970 (129ff.) and Salmon 1972 (17, 124 *et passim*).

[99] This is, basically, Bacon's idea; see our section 1.1 on Bacon.

The *Panglottia* represents an attempt to construct a universal language which can be used for perfect communication and transmission of ideas and which at the same time was to be in accordance with the principles of logic. For Comenius it seemed inconceivable that speech should be irrational and that the rules of grammar were not basically determined by logic. But the *Panglottia* remained fragmentary, due mainly to the fact — according to Geissler — that Comenius tried to invent a language which could be used for both tasks. From a modern point of view, we know, that Comenius's aims can be reached in principle, but only if the tasks are dealt with separately. Thus an artificial language like *Esperanto* can be said to be quite useful for certain types of communication and numerous successful attempts have been made to construct 'logical languages' (cf. Geissler 1959:158).[100]

4. LINGUISTIC THEORY IN SEVENTEENTH CENTURY ITALY AND SPAIN

This chapter will deal only with some of the main theoretical conceptions of three grammarians or philosophers: Benedetto Buonmattei (1581–1647), Tommaso Campanella (1568–1639), and J. Caramuel y Lobkowitz (1606–1682). This restriction may seem justified if one looks e.g. into Trabalza 1908, where Buonmattei is considered as being 'il principe de' grammatici' (300) of the 17th century. Astonishingly enough, neither Vitale (1967) nor Trabalza (1908) even mention the name of Tommaso Campanella. Perhaps he was not considered to be a grammarian; indeed, he did not take part in the more politically oriented discussions of his compatriots on the question which Italian dialect should be taken as the linguistic norm (see e.g. Vitale 1967:84ff., "Posizioni toscane e liberalismo linguistico").

Trabalza (1908) deals with linguistic and grammatical ideas discussed during the 'Seicento' in three chapters: X: "Il trattato grammaticale con fondamento speculativo. Nuove elaborazioni integrative (Il Buonmattei e il Cinonio)"; XI: "Con e contro la Crusca. Verso la grammatica filosofica"; XII: "Gli albori della scienza (G. D. Vico)".

Vitale (1967:303–15) presents an anthology of Italian grammarians of the 17th century comprising short passages from Palo Beni 1612, Allessandro Tassoni 1612, Carlo Dati 1657, Benedetto Buonmattei 1643, Benedetto Fioretti 1620–1639, Daniello Bartoli 1670, and Lorenzo Magalotti 1667. These passages are mainly concerned with problems of usage, the rise of the Italian language, lexical problems and similar questions. Vitale in his chapter "La questioni della lingua nel secolo XVII" does not discuss explicitly the status of theoretical linguistics or

[100] Editor's note: The handiest bibliography of Comenius's works is Brambora 1971. There is an immense bibliography in Čeněk Zirbt, *Bibliografie České Historie*, 5 (Prague 1912), 325–930. The secondary literature in German is listed in Bethke 1971. There is a very full bibliography of primary and secondary works in Schaller 1967 (482–523) and in Blekastad 1969 (728–98). For a short introduction with basic bibliography to 1969, see Aarsleff 1971b, where the reader will also find a critical remark regarding Sadler 1966.

general grammar. Buonmattei is mentioned as 'il fondatore della grammatica metodica e in qualque modo precorritore del logicismo grammaticale nella sistemazione e divisione della parti del discorso e nella disposizione delle norme linguistiche . . .' (Vitale 1967:79.)

The title of Buonmattei's first book, *Delle cagioni della lingua toscana* (1623), indicates some relationship to Scaliger 1540 and to Sanctius 1587. This relationship is not a superficial one, in fact, Buonmattei was the first Italian grammarian to apply logico-philosophical principles to his mother tongue without, however, leaving out of account the empirical foundations, namely, the literary norm and speech usage. As may be seen from Buonmattei's main work (1643)[101] which includes his first treatise, it was its principal purpose to serve as a descriptive grammar in exposing 'i veri elementi delle regole della nostra Lingua' (Buonmattei: Dedication).

Trabalza (1908:303f.) is certainly right in pronouncing Buonmattei a forerunner of French rationalist grammar of the later seventeenth century: 'Di *ragione*, di *logica*, d'*intelletto* è piena, specie nel primo libro, la sua grammatica.'.

The preface to the second book displays neatly Buonmattei's methodological distinctions between theory and practice on the one hand, and between linguistic philosophy and language on the other hand:

> Gia s'è veduto nel primo Libro, e quel che sia parola, e come se ne faccia Orazione; per palesare: concetti della nostra mente, e insieme delle sue cagioni; clioè de quelle cose, che a formarla concorrono. . . . Era necessario . . . trattar prima di quelle cose che prima sono: e discendere a quelle poi, che da esse procedono. (99)

If, however, there should be a more fact-oriented reader, Buonmattei recommends him to start with the second book 'e quando si conoscerà impossessato di ciò che s'insegna in esso; allora potrà con suo comodo farsi dal primo, che gli riuscirà men difficile, a più fruttuoso . . .' (99).

The first of the overall nineteen 'treatises' of the book tries to answer the question 'Che cosa sia Lingua, e quel que per Lingua s'intenda.'. Besides problems of usage, language typology and similar matters Buonmattei presents four 'causes' of language in the sixth chapter ("Delle cagioni della Lingua").

These four 'causes' are to be considered as formal universals; they are not restricted to the domain of language because,

> tutte le cose composte, o naturali, o artificiali, che sieno; son composte di quelle quattro cagioni: materiale; formale; efficiente, e finale. (37)

Buonmattei's application of these essentially scholastic distinctions to language shows that they constitute a sort of semiotic framework including syntactic, semantic and pragmatic dimensions. The essence of Buonmattei's theory of communication can be derived from the following quotation:

[101] In the following, quotations are taken from the 'ultima impressione Veneta più accurata, e con particolar diligenza ricorretta' (Venezia 1735). This edition also contains a most complete account of Buonmattei's life written by Giovanni Battista Casotti.

Tutte queste cagioni si trovano in tutte le cose, e perciò anche nelle lingue, e in spezie nella nostra.

La materiale son le parole, delle qualisi compon l'orazione; perchê senza le parole l'orazion non si potrebbe mai fare.

La formale è il significato di esse parole, onde l'orazion è composta: perchè s'elle non significassero, elle non sarebbon parole.

L'efficiente sono i popoli che le parlano, e in proposito nostro, cagione efficiente della nostra lingua si può dir che sieno i popoli della Toscana, perchè essi, oltre all averla da principio trovata, la nobilitarono poi; e ora familiarmente la parlano.

La finale è esplicare i concerti dell' animo: perchè mentre uno parlo, o scrive, non parla, o scrive per altro che per palesare altrui i concetti dell' animo. (37f.)

In the second treatise ("Dell' orazione") Buonmattei defines 'speech' (spoken and written) as the suitable arrangement of words, suitable in so far as it is able to represent human thoughts ('i concetti dell' animo', 38). In order to show how this representational relationship between words and thoughts may be conceived, Buonmattei, in the second chapter of the second treatise, treats of the question: "Intelletto umano come discorra" (38f.).

In the opening passage our author draws a parallel between the cognitive and communicate power of angelical and human beings, a theme that was to be dealt with again twenty-five years later by the Cartesian Cordemoy.[102] According to Buonmattei

L'intelletto umano è simile in parte allo angelico; ... E' simile nello 'intendere: ma è diverso nel modo di esso 'intendere. Perche siccome l'Angelico intende in uno istante, e in uno istante fa intendersi; l'umano non intende, nè si fa intendere, se non per via di discorso. (38)

In order to make himself understood in the course of a communicative process man has to rely upon his senses, they serve as the instruments that transmit the 'message' from the speaker to the hearer and vice versa. Buonmattei speaks of the senses as the 'ministri, nunzi, famigliari, o segretari dello 'ntelletto' (38). In discussing the relative value of the senses for the human mind Buonmattei takes the Baconian position that in principle any medium can serve as the 'material cause' of language or of sign-systems, but he concludes that for human beings it is the eye and the ear that are most apt to serve as transmitting instruments. He declares — using the term *colore* in a somewhat peculiar way to mean 'visible distinction' — that

L'udito ha per instrumento l'orecchio, e per oggetto il suono; la vista ha per instrumento l'occhio, e per oggetto il colore. E per colore intendiamo tutto quel che per mezzo della luce si può discerner dall' occhio. (30)[103]

The sounds are divided into two kinds: 'simple sounds' and 'special sounds'. Simple sounds are not produced by the human vocal tract, they have other natural or

[102] See especially the seventh chapter of Cordemoy 1970 [1677]. There are now two available critical editions of this work: Cordemoy 1968 and Cordemoy 1970.

[103] The last word is misprinted in Trabalza 1908 (309) as *orecchio*.

artificial origins; special sounds are again of two kinds: inarticulate, like cries, laughing, etc. and articulate ('voce formata'):

Voce formata è quella, che si manda fuori dagli nomini nel pronunziar l'orazione: con la quale può ragguagliarsi chi si trova presente d'ogni nostro occulto pensiero. Per questa l'uomo è dagli altri animali distinto ... Il parlare ha gran virtù d'esplicare i concetti; e non solo di fargli 'ntendere a chi ascolta; ma di persuadere ogni gran cosa a chi attentamente lo sta a sentire ... (40)

In the field of visual perception Buonmattei sets up similar distinctions between 'perfect' or 'imperfect' signs. Among the latter sort are counted natural and artificial signs or marks. Natural marks occur independently of our will (blushing etc.), artificial marks depend on conventions (smoke, fire as material for such signs).

The class of 'perfect signs' (*color perfetto*) is divided into pictures and scriptures. The obvious advantage of the latter symbolic sort of signs over pictorial or iconic signs can be seen from Buonmattei's following argument:

... e non solo si può con essa [i.e. la scrittura] manifestare i fatti; ma palesar le cagioni, e scoprire i pensieri, e i fini, e l'occasioni, che anno indotto a fare, o a tralasciar quella impresa. (41)

A closer comparison between Buonmattei's semiotic outline and the semiotic distinctions drawn in the Port-Royal *Logic*[104] forty years later reveals that our Italian grammarian had already a considerable insight into the diverse problems connected with human sign usage. A remarkable degree of empirical adequacy can also be detected in Buonmattei's treatment of the relationship between spoken and written linguistic representations. It is in the fifth chapter of the second treatise ("Che differenza sia tra la scrittura, e la voce") that we find the following explications:

La scrittura (come s'è visto) e la voce (la voce que dicemmo forma) sono i particolari sensibili, onde i concetti dell' animo si possono altrui palesare. Ma la voce è più della scrittura espressiva.

Perchè se la scrittura manifesta il fatto, il pensato, o le cagioni; ella le rappresenta con tutto ciò senz altra vivezza di quella, che le seppe dar lo scrittore con la convenevol' union delle parole, e con la ornata espression de' concetti: ma la voce vi aggiunge lo spirito, e l' affetto; alzando, e abbassando; ingrossando, e assottigliando; sostenendosi, e velocemente correndo, secondo che richiede il bisogno.

Ma la scrittura è per un'altro rispetto più ragguardevole. Perchè la voce s'alltontana per poco spazio: non si potendo parlar, se non a chi si truova presente: dove la scrittura s'allarga ancora alle persone lontanissime, e di luogo, e di tempo potendosi avvisar con essa ciò che ne occorra fin di là dall' America; e sino dentro al Giappone.

A tal che senza derogare alla preminenza dell' una, o dell' altra; diciamo che cias-

[104] See the critical edition of Arnauld and Nicole's collective work (first edition 1662) in Arnauld 1965–67. The fourth chapter of the first part ("Des idées des choses et des idées des signes") was added to the *Logic* only in 1683. The two Jansenist authors follow — in this respect — rather closely the patristic tradition, especially St. Augustine's *De doctrina christiana* (Migne 34, 35–49).

cuna è bastante ad esplicare i concetti: l'una coll'ajuto dell'occhio; l'altra per via dell' orecchio. Perchè sempre ch' e' si forma orazione, o ella si sente dalla voce; o ella si vede nella scrittura: che in questo son tanto unite, che l' una potrebbe dirsi il ritratto dell' altra: avvenga che niuno per ordinario che regolatamente scriva; scrive diversamente da quel ch' e' parla. (41)

It is impossible to cover completely the substance of Buonmattei's nineteen 'trattati'. We shall, however, try to sketch at least the contents of the first book, which treats of general linguistics.

The third to the sixth treatises contain matters belonging to the level of the second articulation: "Delle lettere" (42–60). There we find—quite surprisingly—a succinct and basically correct theoretical framework of graphemics and phonology. Buonmattei seeks to describe both systems of linguistic expression in terms of minimal distinctive features. This is not so much astonishing for the phonological system, where he works with articulatory features; Buonmattei's merit in this part of his grammar — as I see it — lies in his painstaking efforts to analyze the graphemic inventory, the alphabet, into its minimal constituents. After considering various etymologies for the latin term *litera* he goes on to say

. . . che lettera nel suo proprio, e stretto significato, si pigli per una parte della scrittura. Poiche la lettera si fa di linee: la linea può cancellarsi: ma cancellar non si può, se prima non è formata: ed essendo formata in modo ch' ella possa leggersi; avrà sembiante di scrittura, e non di pura favella.

Ch'ella riceva l'esser dalle linee si vede. Perchè le linee (come le arti matematiche insegnano) sono o rette, o curve.

Di linee rette appariscono formate A. E. F. H. I. L. M. N. T. V. Z.

Di curve. C. O. Q. S.

Di rette, e di curve: B. D. G. P. R.

Ma qui ci potrebb' essere opposto: che se la lettera è formata di linee; adunque non la lettera ma la linea, anzi il punto, onde la linea ha principio, dovrà dirsi parte indivisibile del parlare.

A che brevemente rispondo, che la linea non è parte della favella, in quanto ell' è pura linea: perche mentr'ella si stane' suoi termini, ogni buon gramatico la stimerà cosa informe, come gramatico; perche ella non concorre alla formazion del parlare; facciasi per esempio una quantità di linee rette, e curve quanto si vuole I – I I 3) chi le stimerà mai parte del parlare? Ma quando quelle linee sono unite in maniera ch' elle formino una lettera A.B. ecco subito creata una parte della favella la quale per esser la più piccola, si puo, e dee chiamar'indivisibile. (42)

The fourth to the sixth treatises treat of the properties of syllables (where several phonotactic regularities are described in great detail), of diphthongs, and of various sorts of accents or suprasegmentals.

The seventh and last treatise of the first book is entitled "Delle parole" (75–98). It is in this part of Buonmattei's grammar that we find an analysis of the various aspects of the level of first articulation; e.g. cap. I: "Parola, che sia"; cap. II: "Se il parlare sia naturale, o per arte"; cap. III: "Se i nomi sien posti con ragione, o a caso"; cap. IV: "Come s'intenda ad arbitrio del primo"; cap. V: "Parola di che sia formata"; cap. VI: "Parole di quante sorte sieno"; cap. IX: "Dell' alterazion naturale delle parole"; cap. X: "Dell' accidentale alterazion delle parole"; cap. XIX: 'Delle parole composte"; cap. XX: "Della significazion delle parole". This incomplete enumeration of the content already demonstrates the theoretical relevance of Buonmattei's masterpiece. To conclude, a few quotations shall be added in order to demonstrate Buonmattei's well-reasoned judgment on some fundamental linguistic questions. Words as arbitrary representations of concepts:

Parola è un segno d'una spezie dell' animo secondo la voce, posto a quella cosa di che ella è spezie, ad arbitrio del primo imponente. (75)

Relationship between spoken and written words:

Ma perchè l'Uomo non si può sempre servir di tal segno [spoken word]: perch'e non può far sempre sentir la sua voce all' orecchio; ella si ripone spesso nella scrittura, che la conserva per appresentarla poi a suo tempo alla vista. Di maniera, che se la voce, è un segno della spezie; la scrittura è un segno della voce. E quindi si scorgerà, che se il cavallo è nella natura, la forma del cavallo è nello 'ntelletto, il segno di quella forma è nella voce, e 'l segno di quella voce è nella scrittura. E in questa maniera la parola, è segno d' una specie del' animo. (76)

Relationship between words (signs), things, and concepts:

Non una spezie dell' animo, ma il SEGNO: perchè la spezie del cavallo è segnata con questa parola CAVALLO.

Non segno della cosa, ma DELLA SPEZIE: perchè quella parola cavallo non è segno del cavallo, ma di quella immagine intenzionale, che si considera in astratto per rammemorarci il cavallo.

Non di più spezie, ma D'UNA; perchè s'ella fosse di più ella non sarebbe parola, ma orazione. (76)

The foregoing remarks and quotations should suffice to show that Buonmattei's grammar well deserves a more thorough interpretation, both from the purely theoretical side and as to its merits as one of the earlier Italian grammars exhibiting a relatively high degree of empirical adequacy.

Unlike Buonmattei the two other linguists or linguistic philosophers dealt with here briefly, Tommaso Campanella and Juan Caramuel de Lobkowitz, have so far not received an adequate treatment in handbooks on the history of linguistics. In both cases thorough studies on the respective linguistic theories must be classed as desiderata.

Both Campanella and Caramuel were monks adhering to the scholastic tradition, who, however, were destined to lead vastly different lives. Because of certain philosophical opinions held by the Dominican Campanella, he had to face several accusations and proceedings before the Holy Office which resulted in his imprisonment. Five years before his death in Paris (1639), Pope Urban urged him to flee to France. One year before his death Campanella published his *Philosophia rationalis* (1638) which contains a universal grammar, and treatises on rhetoric, poetry, and historiography.

In her review of Chomsky 1966, Salmon (1969) refutes conclusively Chomsky's claim as to the overwhelming Cartesian influence on the Port-Royal *Grammar* and *Logic*. Within her very detailed discussion of sixteenth and seventeenth century works on linguistic theory she also sketches several pertinent grammatical conceptions set forth by Campanella and Caramuel.

When first mentioning Campanella in connection with possible Cartesian influences on 17th century grammatical works, Salmon explains that Campanella's *Grammatica philosophica* (the first part of Campanella 1638), 'although it came from a Parisian press, could hardly have been affected by Cartesian ideas' (172), because — as was already mentioned above — Campanella did not arrive in France until 1634 when Descartes had already moved to Holland. After giving more detailed arguments as to the impossibility of Campanella's having been influenced by Descartes' philosophy, Salmon goes on to outline some of Campanella's more important grammatical ideas. For Campanella grammar should have the status of a science. His statement that 'Grammatica est ars instrumentalis' can perhaps be best interpreted as meaning 'Grammar is an auxiliary science', together with logic, rhetoric and poetic it forms a group of 'artes non mechanicae, sed speculativae' (Salmon 1969:172). It may be a little problematic to equate 'ars' with 'science' because at least in the seventeenth and eighteenth centuries and already in the Middle Ages philosophers and grammarians usually distinguish between 'scientia' and 'ars'.[105] Campanella himself clarifies this point when positing two kinds of grammar, 'Civil' and 'Philosophical':[106] 'Civil [grammar] is a technique, not a Science. It depends on the authority and usage of eminent authors. . . . Philosophical [grammar], however, depends on reason, and this indicates a science' (Salmon 1969:172–73).

Salmon (1969:173) then quotes a hint as to Campanella's evaluation of the scientific climate in the 1630's:

> Grammarians of the Vernacular [*Grammatici vulgares*] condemn this [philosophical grammar] . . . they condemn Scotus, St. Thomas, and others, who speak rather from the nature of the thing.

This quotation shows clearly Campanella's leaning towards scholastic positions; this again implies that he felt himself to be a theoretician, rather than a 'grammaticus vulgaris'. Nevertheless, his investigation of general grammar relies on a large number of data and examples drawn from classical, modern and oriental languages. Moreover his work is interesting 'for its attempt to suggest rules for an invented philosophical language'[107] (Salmon 1969:173).

[105] Cf. for a short discussion of this point Brekle in the third chapter of the introduction to Meiner 1781.

[106] All quotations and translations from Campanella and Caramuel are taken from Salmon 1969.

[107] For technical reasons I was unable to get hold of a copy of Campanella 1638 in time; it is for this reason that neither Campanella's scheme of a philosophical language nor his overall linguistic conceptions can be discussed in this paper.

In questioning Chomsky's claim 'that grammar prior to Port-Royal had been concerned with classification rather than with explanation', Salmon (1969:177) comes much nearer to the historical truth by saying that Chomsky's predilection for Port-Royal in this case, too, 'is something of a simplification; Port-Royal's "explanations" were better and fuller than those of their predecessors, but they were by no means a Cartesian novelty'. With both, Campanella and Caramuel it was well-known that case-relationships may be expressed by way of declension or by way of structural words.[108]

In other languages, however, one has structural words [*artículos*] as signs of their cases instead of declension ... Therefore it is not essential to words to be declinable, but either to be declined, as with the Romans, or to be linked by structural words, as among speakers of the vernaculars and the Hebrews, or both, as with the Greeks ... (Salmon 1969:177)

Again, Port-Royal's treatment of the linking function of relative pronouns (1676: 66–87) is foreshadowed in Campanella:

Every relative makes a sentence [*orationem*] double, and is like a nominal conjunction of sentences, nor can a simple sentence be discovered into which a relative enters. (Salmon 1969:178)

In Campanella we find interesting statements as to the function of adverb/conjunctions as modals (Salmon 1969:182). They relate to the disposition of the mind — 'pertinentia ad animae circunstantiam'. 'For the mind either affirms or denies ... or doubts, or questions or addresses ... from all these relationships of the mind to objects [*ex omnibus hisce animae extensionibus ad objecta*] adverbs arise.' Campanella gives as examples such 'adverbs' as *non, cur, ne, cave*. In his *Dialectic* Campanella elaborates further on the problem of modalities. He suggests three principles from which there arise imperative, indicative and optative clauses: the principles of volition, cognition and possibility. In this connection Campanella describes the semantic properties of various infinitive clauses.

Juan Caramuel y Lobkowitz (1606–1682) was a Spanish Cistercian monk who excelled in the most diverse fields: speculative and practical grammar, logic, mathematics, theology, jurisprudence, poetry, music. In his bibliography 262 titles are listed (cf. *Enciclopedia universal ilustrada* ..., t. 11, Madrid 1958). However, apart from his grammatical and logical treatises — his *Grammatica audax* (Frankfurt 1651 (?)/1654), his *Grammatica critica* (1654) and his *Herculis logici labores tres* (Frankfurt 1651) — no high degree of originality can be claimed for his other publications. In contradistinction to Campanella, Caramuel lived and worked peacefully within the pale of the church. He saw most of Europe as ambassador, as abbot and bishop. Caramuel is remarkable for his knowledge of Asiatic languages, especially Chinese. Because of technical difficulties — lack of suitable characters — his Chinese grammar was never printed.

108 Cf. chapter VI (second part) of the Arnauld 1966 where Campanella's explanation of the equivalence of cases and prepositions is — in its essence — repeated.

For Caramuel, Campanella's works together with those of Duns Scotus and Scaliger were acknowledged sources. The fact that John Wilkins (1668) mentions not only Campanella and Caramuel, but also Duns Scotus, shows that the medieval traditions of speculative grammar run uninterruptedly straight into the second half of the seventeenth century.[109]

In the same vein as Campanella and plainly reminiscent of Bacon, Caramuel distinguishes two kinds of grammar:

Speculative grammar is, so to speak, a more remote (kind of grammar), nobler and more excellent than the more immediate kind of grammar. It does not refer to any region or nation in particular, but contains the most abstract ideas which prescribe laws of discourse for every nation and language. It is also, as it were, a Designer, who forms sounds on which he imposes various meanings, so that he may make clear to others what he thinks. (Salmon 1969:173)

Following the doctrine of the medieval 'modistae' Caramuel equates *verbum mentis* with the logical concept of *intellectio* — which is the first operation of the understanding in traditional logic — and *verbum oris* with *dictio*, i.e. the meaningful linguistic sign.[110] Like other of his contemporaries, e.g. Alsted (1630), Caramuel considers logic and grammar as being closely related. For Caramuel, logic is the 'life and soul' [*vita et anima*] of reason and speech as well as the 'scientific faculty' [*facultas scientifica*] which, as mental dialectic, directs the 'operations of the mind' [operationes mentis] and, as verbal dialectic 'utterances of the tongue' [linguae prolationes]. Logic was not only the 'art of thinking well' but the total art of mental or verbal discourse. (Salmon 1969:176)[111]

From Salmon's discussion of the historical development of theories concerning restrictive and explanatory modification in relative clauses and Adj + N constructions we learn that Caramuel continued the medieval discussion of this topic. He distinguished between 'restrictio' and 'ampliatio'. 'Restrictio' involves the 'narrowing of the term from its wider to its narrower meaning'; in contrast, 'ampliatio' is the extension of the term from its narrower to its wider meaning. To quote Salmon (1969:180) more fully:

Caramuel also discusses the topic under 'description' and 'definition' . . . After discussing further . . . examples where the adjectives 'restrict' or 'determine', he describes modification by terms which are *explanantes,* that is, which 'explain and declare, by showing some property of the thing signified' . . . In the proverb *Optat ephippia bos*

[109] The works of Duns Scotus — his *grammatica speculativa* is ascribed to Thomas von Erfurt — were reprinted in Paris in 1605 and were edited by Lucas Wadding in 1639, being published at Leiden. See Bursill-Hall 1971 for a thorough presentation of Modistic grammatical theories.

[110] Cf. H. Roos (1952:143), who interprets the relationship between the expression and content side of words as expressed in the *modi significandi* by Martinus de Dacia in the following way: 'Die Verknüpfung einer bestimmten "vox" mit einem bestimmten "significatum speciale" geschieht durch den Intellekt. Dieser Prozeß, den die Grammatik voraussetzt, heißt "prima articulatio vocis" . . . Das Resultat dieses intellektuellen Prozesses ist die "dictio"; d.h. die Verknüpfung eines bestimmten Lautphänomens mit einem bestimmten Inhalt.'

[111] Cf. Nicole's discussion in the "Second discours" of the *Logique de Port-Royal* on the suitability of such expressions as 'l'art de penser' or 'l'art de bien raisonner'. See Arnauld 1965–67, vol. 2, 42f.

piger ('The lazy ox prefers the saddle'), *piger* denotes a characteristic of all oxen — to be lazy. If, however, there existed any ox which was not lazy, then 'that epithet does not explain, but restricts' (1654:13).

One last point should suffice to show that for Caramuel the distinction between surface and deep or logical structure of sentences was a well-established one.[112] In analyzing a sentence like 'Petrus demolitur domum' Caramuel can be said to foreshadow Bach's and McCawley's conceptions on the treatment of predicates and noun phrases in a semantically or logically based generative grammar.[113] Caramuel (Salmon 183) relates the sentence 'Petrus demolitur domum' to an 'underlying' logical structure like 'Petrus demolitur, id quod est domus'. From this it is no far cry to a predicate logical formula as used by McCawley (1971:223):

$$\text{demoliri}_y\ (x_1, x_2) \wedge \text{Present}\ (y) \wedge \text{Petrus}\ (x_1) \wedge \text{domus}\ (x_2).$$

These few remarks on Caramuel's *Grammatica audax* should be enough to arouse a more thorough interest in theoretically oriented grammars of the early seventeenth century.

5. LINGUISTICS IN SEVENTEENTH CENTURY FRANCE

This chapter will be restricted to a discussion of three topics, each of which has received considerable attention during the last six or eight years, namely, 1. "Cartesian linguistics?"; 2. "Port-Royal linguistics"; 3. "Cordemoy's *Discours physique de la parole* (1677)". There is, of course, much more to be said about linguistics in seventeenth century France. Because of lack of space the reader is referred to some critical notes below.[114]

5.1 *Cartesian Linguistics?*

It is well known that it was Chomsky's 1966 book with the subtitle "A Chapter in

[112] Cf. Salmon 1969 (183) and the extended discussion of Sanctius 1587 in connection with Lancelot 1644 in R. Lakoff 1969 (355ff.).
[113] See especially Bach 1968 and McCawley 1968 and 1971.
[114] General information about the period in question may be gleaned from Livet 1859, Minckwitz 1897, Leser 1912, Brunot 1922–24, Nyrop 1925 (vol. 5), Harnois 1929, Kukenheim 1966 (31–8), Mounin 1967 (124–33), Robins 1967 (144–62), Arens 1969 (88–93), Hall 1969. The older contributions are to be used with some reservation as far as judgments on linguistic matters are concerned. Sahlin (1928:1–21) accentuates especially tendencies connected with the development of universal grammars; for some criticism of Sahlin see R. Lakoff 1969 (359, fn. 5). Works dealing with special problems are Manz 1909 and Winkler 1912. Vaugelas is discussed in Wüllenweber 1877, Mok 1968, Weinrich 1960 and Hall 1969. As for bibliographical matters Stengel 1890 is still indispensable. Stengel gives detailed bibliographical information on French grammars that were written from the end of the 14th till the end of the 18th century. For the 17th century he lists 183 French grammars. It is evident that many indications as to libraries are no longer relevant. Stengel has indices relating to authors, titles, and places of publication.

the History of Rationalist Thought" that provoked quite a stir among philosophers, historians, and linguists. It is the aim of this sub-chapter to evaluate to a certain degree the various criticisms as well as such large-scale critiques as Aarsleff 1970 and 1971 and Percival 1972 that were directed against Chomsky's idea of 'Cartesian linguistics'.

First of all some of the more relevant reviews will be taken into consideration.[115] Practically all reviewers agree on the catalytic function of Chomsky 1966. This 'preliminary and fragmentary sketch of some of the leading ideas of Cartesian linguistics' (Chomsky 1966:2) has certainly had the most salutary effect in that both historically oriented philosophers and linguists started to reconsider historical problems of their respective fields. Especially in the field of theoretical linguistics Chomsky's much-critized contribution may eventually result in a long needed turn to its historical dimension, not so much in the more traditional 'immanent' style but exactly in the way Chomsky tried — even if not very successfully — to interpret older theories and results in the light of present-day linguistic conceptions (*pace* Hall 1969:223–9).

As to the term 'Cartesian linguistics' Chomsky himself freely admits that 'the aptness of the term... may well be questioned on several grounds' (Chomsky 1966:2). A majority of the reviewers and other critics are, however, not satisfied by this apologetic remark.[116] Salmon's 1969 review of Chomsky 1966 adduces abundant evidence for the fact that above all the linguistic doctrines of Port-Royal together with their fundamental methodological conceptions are not derivable in any straightforward way from the scant references to linguistic theory to be found in Descartes' works, nor can the Port-Royal position be considered as highly original in its application of its theory to the description and explanation of language. According to Salmon (1969:167) 'Such an assumption would be a distortion of the facts, or at the very least an oversimplification.' In order to prove her claim Salmon produces a host of well-organized and consistently interpreted quotations

[115] The present writer is of the opinion that another summary of Chomsky 1966 here — as far as the seventeenth century is concerned — would be of no great help. Four reviews of Chomsky 1966 will not be discussed explicitly: Kampf 1967, Szépe 1967, Prideaux 1967, and Harman 1968. The reason for this is that these rather short papers do not contribute much to the historical problems that are relevant to this chapter.

[116] Bracken (1970) does not call into question this much-debated label. For him Chomsky is 'the true inheritor of the tradition of seventeenth-century Cartesian linguistics' (1970:191). Brekle (1969) does not deal with the historical and philosophical implications of the term in question; his — perhaps too pragmatic standpoint — is: 'If, however, we consider the term "Cartesian linguistics" as "une définition de nom" for a general rationalist attitude towards certain fundamental linguistic problems more or less inherent in all of the works discussed here, it may well be accepted as a practical cover term' (Brekle 1969:75). If we follow Aarsleff (1971) this would mean that Chomsky was wrong in excluding Locke, Condillac and others from his list of rationalist philosophers and linguists. Aarsleff's point that a wholesale use of such labels as 'rationalist' and 'empiricist' does not further the understanding of these authors is certainly a valid one.

from a number of pre-Port-Royalist and pre-Cartesian linguistic treatises.[117] If one is willing to use the dichotomy of 'deep' and 'surface structure' at all in connection with grammatical works dating from the seventeenth century — in a non-technical way this seems to be quite feasible — then, according to the well-substantiated claims advanced by Salmon (1969:174f.), the idea 'that deep and surface structures need not be identical is not necessarily... a specifically Cartesian feature, as Chomsky (33) apparently claims.' Salmon regards it justly — in view of her weighty evidence — as a major distortion of Chomsky's to claim a dominant Cartesian influence on the Port-Royal *Grammar*. Moreover, Salmon's thesis that the Port-Royalists were mainly interested in Descartes' philosophy 'because they saw it as "a revival of Augustinian thought and therefore an ally of their own kind of theology" (Kneale 1962:316)' (Salmon 1969:185) is corroborated by independent research done by Rodis-Lewis.[118]

Zimmer (1968:290) sees in Chomsky 1966 'the major effort to date in Chomsky's campaign to rehabilitate an important pre-descriptivist and pre-comparativist tradition in the study of human language . . .'. However, he duly warns Chomsky that his 'determined efforts to make the pendulum swing away from the extreme position of wholesale debunking of Cartesian linguistics do not perhaps result in his pushing it too far in the opposite direction, thereby producing a flock of *ex post facto* generative grammarians' (290f.). Another critical point — a very pertinent one — is raised by Zimmer (1968:295ff.) when he demonstrates clearly that between Chomsky's conception of 'deep-surface structure' as put forward in *Aspects* (1965:9) and the sort of 'deep-surface structure' that Chomsky seeks to locate in Port-Royal and later developments there are considerable differences. Chomsky (1968:16f.) declares that:

> The clear intent of philosophical grammar was to develop a psychological theory... The theory holds that the underlying deep structure, with its abstract organization of linguistic forms, is 'present to the mind', as the signal, with its surface structure, is produced or perceived by the bodily organs. And the transformational operations

[117] A number of quotations go back to such medieval grammarians as Robert Kilwardby and Duns Scotus (or, rather, Thomas of Erfurt). Other possible sources for Port-Royal theories are Sanctius 1587, Bacon 1623, Alsted 1630, Vossius 1635, Campanella 1638, Caramuel 1642. See in this connection also R. Lakoff 1969 where she adduces interesting material from Lancelot 1644, and from Sanctius 1587 in order to prove that Lancelot, Arnauld's collaborator in writing the Port-Royal *Grammar* (1660), did work along fairly precise transformational lines, but that he did so under considerable influence from Sanctius' *Minerva* (1587). (See below 5.2.)

[118] Rodis-Lewis (1950:133) arrives at the following conclusion: '... c'est ... à leur commune résonance augustinienne que l'on attribue le rapprochement entre le cartésianisme et la doctrine de Port-Royal. Dès 1642, faisant état de la satisfaction avec laquelle Arnauld avait accueilli les réponses de Descartes à ses objections, Mersenne annonçait à Voetius: "plus un homme sera savant dans la doctrine de Saint Augustin, et plus sera-t-il disposé à embrasser la philosophie de Descartes" (Lettre de Mersenne à Voetius, 13 décembre 1642, A.T. 3; 603).' Another hint as to the predominance of Augustinian doctrines in Arnauld's philosophical standpoint is found in du Pac de Bellegarde and Hautefage's introduction to volume 38 (XI) of their edition of Arnauld's complete works (1775–81): 'ce docteur avait auparavant trouvé dans Saint Augustin ce que Descartes établissait pour fondement et pour principe premier de sa philosophie.'

relating deep and surface structure are actual mental operations, performed by the mind when a sentence is produced or understood.

If we knew more about our mental operations, such a psychological theory of the 'deep-surface structure' dichotomy could undergo a serious discussion and might, eventually, be validated. But in view of our present knowledge it must be doubted whether the syntax-based Chomskyan type of generative transformational grammar could ever be a useful model for the attainment of this goal. In fact, it seems for Zimmer (1968:297) 'much more appropriate to say that in the Port-Royal view semantic content determines deep structure than that deep structure determines semantic content . . .'[119] Brekle (1969:86ff.) after refuting Chomsky's claim that the Port-Royal *Logic* (1662) succeeded in developing 'a partial theory of relations' (Chomsky 1966:44, whatever 'partial' may mean in this connection), maintains similarly that 'There is no question . . . that for the linguistic side of the whole problem [an analysis of a rather complex sentence] this last analysis made in terms of a hierarchy of semantic relations gives more insight into the semantic structure of such a complex sentence than a traditional subject-predicate analysis [or a syntactic analysis à la Chomsky] could ever do.'

Percival 1972 regards it also as a mistake in Chomsky 1966 to equate 'his notion of deep structure with the set of basic propositions which, the Port-Royal grammarians claimed, underlie complex sentences'. It is now well known that for Chomsky deep structures merely *determine* the semantic interpretations of sentences. Contrariwise, the Port-Royal grammarians believed that the set of underlying propositions was equivalent to the semantic interpretation of the sentence. On the whole, Percival does succeed in proving his thesis implied in the title of his contribution: "On the Non-Existence of Cartesian Linguistics" if one agrees to take the term in question literally. Percival accuses Chomsky of not having demonstrated 'that an intellectual movement such as he has in mind really ever existed, call it whatever you will.' In the course of his arguments Percival disproves two crucial historical assumptions advanced by Chomsky: 'The first of these historical assumptions is that Descartes' statements about language represent a novel departure from the traditional position. The second is that Descartes' ideas about language influenced the writers of universal grammars in fundamental respects.'

Percival denies the admissibility of these assumptions by examining a number of

[119] Three other reviewers of Chomsky 1966 are much more lenient towards Chomsky's treatment of the 'deep-surface structure' problem in the Port-Royal *Grammar*. Harman (1968:234) is content to state that Chomsky's chapter "Deep and Surface Structure" (1966:31–51) 'is clear, interesting, and persuasive'. See Uitti 1969–70 (78) which merely reports Chomsky's position, although quoting Zimmer's skepticism on this point. Although Bracken (1970) is quite critical as to the 'Cartesian' quality of eighteenth and nineteenth century philosophers and linguists mentioned by Chomsky, he agrees with Chomsky that 'the theory of deep and surface structure as developed in the Port-Royal linguistic studies implicitly contains recursive devices and thus provides for infinite use of the finite means that it disposes, as any adequate theory of language must' (Chomsky 1966:41). The problem, however, is exactly the assumed 'implicit' existence of such devices in Port-Royal writings.

relevant passages in various works by Descartes and by taking up arguments from Sahlin 1928, Salmon 1969, and R. Lakoff 1969.

Another contribution, Miel 1969, criticizes Chomsky's predilection for assuming Cartesian ancestry for Port-Royal's linguistic doctrines on other grounds. Miel (1969:262) agrees with Rodis-Lewis (1950) that

> Cartesianism was accepted at Port-Royal precisely insofar as it was found to be compatible with Augustinianism; Descartes' philosophy actually served the useful purpose of arousing interest in Augustine as a philosopher among men who were already Augustinians in theology ... Arnauld and Nicole can be called 'Cartesians', then, only in a limited sense: as important critics and continuators (and even popularizers, as indeed in many parts of the *Logic*) of some features of Descartes' philosophy ... they were basically Augustinians who saw in some of Descartes' ideas a useful adjunct to their Augustinianism. (Miel 1969:267)

However, in the view of the present writer, Miel fails to make the theory plausible that it was Pascal to whom some of his 'co-solitaires' — especially Arnauld and Lancelot — were indebted in linguistic matters.

Miel (1969:269) overrates considerably the importance of Pascal's contribution to the Port-Royal *Grammar*: the sixth chapter of the first part ("D'vne nouvelle maniere pour apprendre à lire facilement en toutes sortes de langues") comprises two pages and amounts just to the recommendation to teach the phonetic value of letters directly to children without the intermediate stage of names for letters (like *ef, er, y grec* for [f], [r], [i]). Miel is certainly right — mentioning A. Church as his witness — in stating the considerably greater influence of Pascal on the Port-Royal *Logic*. But again it was most certainly not Pascal who contributed to the linguistic and semiotic parts of the *Logique* (see especially the first and second part); these parts (especially the first) rely heavily on the Augustinian doctrine of signs.[120]

In the final paragraphs of his article Miel takes great pains in producing evidence for his claim that it would surely not be 'unreasonable to suppose that his [Pascal's] theory of language might be more relevant to their [Arnauld and Lancelot] exposition than that of Descartes.' However, it is difficult to see how such few remarks like 'les propositions qui sont contradictoires dans les paroles, ne le sont pas toujours dans le sens' (Pascal 1954:977) and 'les langues sont des chiffres' (Pascal 1954:1096), even if Pascal's undoubtedly correct distinction between real and nominal definitions would be included, could possibly be regarded as something like a 'theory of language'. Even if Pascal did discuss linguistic matters with Arnauld and Lancelot, the evidence available (see R. Lakoff 1969 and Salmon 1969) does speak plainly in favour of Lancelot being influenced by Sanctius, Campanella, Caramuel and other sources.

[120] See Arnauld 1965–67 for factual evidence, especially in the second volume of this edition of the *Logique* where several passages from Augustine's *De doctrina christiana* are paralleled with Arnauld's own text: ch. IV. "Des idées des choses, et des idées des signes" (62–5). For a short discussion of some semiotic and semantic aspects in the *Logique* and in the *Grammaire* see Brekle 1964.

In concluding this sub-chapter on recently raised questions about 'Cartesian linguistics' a discussion of the arguments brought forth by Aarsleff (1970, 1971), surely the most fervent opponent of Chomsky on this point, seems unavoidable. It is to be understood that the following discussion only refers to such points raised by Aarsleff that fall within the span of time dealt with here, namely the seventeenth century.

Aarsleff's aim in both of his papers (1970, 1971) is to show that Chomsky's version of the history of linguistics 'is fundamentally false from beginning to end' (1970:583). In his 1971 paper — a reply to Verhaar 1971 — Aarsleff is eager to demonstrate that he had not changed his mind at all about 'Professor Chomsky's idiosyncratic historical chaos' (1971:2). Undoubtedly, Aarsleff's knowledge in matters of historical scholarship and in the domain of philosophy — especially in the seventeenth and eighteenth centuries — obviously surpasses that of Chomsky. Moreover, it is readily agreed that in order to make contributions to 'a true and significant history of linguistics' (Aarsleff 1971:2) scholars should have 'a reasonably comprehensive knowledge of the texts that are used and of the total work of each major figure' (Aarsleff 1970:571). One would also be *d'accord* that in order to avoid 'the worst errors ... an adequate acquaintance with the best secondary literature and the best editions' (*ibid.*) is most necessary. Aarsleff is fully justified in stating that — sometimes — Chomsky does rely 'on outright inferior sources!' (Aarsleff 1970:571).[121] Aarsleff is again correct — this time together with Zimmer (1968:302) — in criticizing Chomsky's interpretation of the innateness hypothesis both in connection with Cordemoy (1677) and Locke's *Essay*. In the case of Cordemoy, Zimmer is quite explicit:

> Cordemoy's conclusion that language learning presupposes the possession of reason is of course not what we are looking for in terms of specific assertions as to the nature of the innate knowledge that *must necessarily* be involved in language learning. Such assertions are, as far as I know, non-existent in Cartesian linguistics.
>
> (Zimmer 1968:302)

The present writer's objection to Aarsleff's critique of Chomsky 1966 and 1968 coincides partly with Verhaar's point (1971:1), who recognizes the necessity for a historiographer of linguistics to make explicit his 'frame of reference'. Aarsleff's argumentation is peculiar in that he never even tries to enter a discussion on the linguistic — not philosophical — substance of the works discussed in Chomsky 1966 on his own. Criticizing historical misconceptions is one thing, another — certainly not less important — is to judge the adequacy and consistency of

[121] See Brekle 1969 (86ff.) for a rather elaborate discussion of a case in point: 'It is probably for the sake of convenience that Chomsky has chosen the most recent English translation of the work [i.e. Dickoff/James's 1964 translation of the Port-Royal *Logic*] as the basis for his quotations. If, as in our case, we have to do with such a delicate subject matter that is extremely difficult to interpret fully and correctly, it would seem that using any translation is very liable to cause unnecessary difficulties'. One crucial example was Dickoff/James's translation of *proposition incidente* by 'incidental remark'.

Chomsky's linguistic interpretations of older texts. Aarsleff's main argument in this connection that 'the entire doctrine of "Cartesian linguistics" loses coherence and falls apart as a result of these errors' (Aarsleff 1971:4) sounds somewhat rash in view of certain parts of Chomsky (1966) — e.g. the chapter on "Description and Explanation in Linguistics" (52–59) — that seem to offer well-balanced and significant interpretations of texts related to the topics indicated in the heading of the chapter. [Editor's note: See also Joly 1972, listed below p. 381.]

To conclude, Chomsky 1966 exhibits quite a number of inadequacies and errors as far as historical scholarship and philosophical positions are concerned and this may at times even weaken or distort his strictly linguistic investigations in the field under discussion. Aarsleff has certainly produced a fine and intricately woven fabric of historical criticism, but, unfortunately, he did not consider it worthwhile to weigh the plainer linguistic substance of Chomsky's interpretations.[122] Obviously, this remark implies a host of fundamental problems of an epistemological and hermeneutic nature; this is not the place to discuss them in an adequate manner.

5.2 *Port-Royal Linguistics*

It is taken for granted that this heading will not provoke a debate as to its appropriateness, unlike the one that was discussed to a certain extent in the previous sub-chapter. The aim of this part of our 'tour d'horizon' is to review most of the recently published works dealing in one way or another[123] with the linguistic ideas that were put forward by 'le grand Arnauld' and his collaborators Lancelot and Nicole.

Before discussing some commentaries on several Port-Royal texts it would not seem out of place to mention first the recent editions and translations of the *Logic* and *Grammar* together with some relevant points raised in reviews of some recent editions.

1. Over the last few years three editions of the Port-Royal *Logic* have left the press. The first was published in 1964 with a short introduction by R. Roubinet; it contains a facsimile reprint of the fifth Paris edition (1683). In 1965 P. Clair and

[122] That there are various ways of interpreting e.g. Port-Royal texts relating to logic and grammar can be seen from Brekle 1964 and 1967 and from Donzé's more immanent interpretation of the Port-Royal *Grammar*. (1967).

[123] It is an albeit non too serious case of M.I.T. self complacency to state that 'The reason for the resurgence of interest in the *Grammaire générale et raisonnée (GGR)* is, of course [sic], its discovery and discussion by Chomsky, particularly in his recent *Cartesian linguistics* (CL, 1966), and *Language and mind* (1968)' (R. Lakoff 1969:343). As for counterexamples, see e.g. Brekle 1964 and Donzé 1967. Borodina 1959 is an example of a traditional treatment of some relations between logical and grammatical aspects contained in the Port-Royal *Grammar*. Borodina's final judgment in her French 'résumé' (236) amounts to this: 'En dépit de sa complication apparente, la *Grammaire* de Port-Royal se révèle, dans l'ensemble, plutôt primitive. Sa valeur actuelle est uniquement historique.'

François Girbal published their critical edition of *La Logiqve ov l'art de penser*. The basis of their text is again the 1683 Paris edition supplemented with exhaustive notes as to the textual development and as to allusions and quotations. Clair and Girbal's edition does not contain a facsimile text; the text is re-set in a somewhat modernized orthography.

In the years 1965–1967 another critical edition of the Port-Royal *Logic* was published (Arnauld 1965–67) in two volumes containing three parts: Tome I: "Nouvelle impression en facsimilé de la première edition de 1662" (1965, vol. 1); Tome II: "Supplément: Présentation synoptique des variantes de texte des éditions 1662–1683. Avec des annotations."; Tome III: "Supplément: Présentation synoptique des variantes de texe du MBSN Fr. 19915 et de l'édition de 1662. Avec des annotations." (T.II/III appeared in 1967 as vol. 2). This edition differs in several respects from the edition in Arnauld 1965. Arnauld 1965–67 starts from the first printed edition of the *Logique* (1662). The second volume of the edition shows the gradual development of the text from 1662 to 1683. The 'apparatus criticus' of this edition contains some forty textual variants which are not found in Arnauld (1965). Moreover, the second volume of Arnauld 1965–67 shows for the first time the text of a manuscript of the *Logique* in synoptical presentation with the 1662 text.[124]

There are three recent translations of the Port-Royal Logic: a Polish one by S. Romahnowa in Arnauld 1958; an English one by J. Dickoff and P. James in Arnauld 1964,[125] and an Italian one by Simone in Arnauld 1969. Simone's work also contains an Italian translation of the Port-Royal Grammar, based upon the French text in Arnauld (1966); his translation of the *Logic* is based on Arnauld 1965. Worth reading is his historical and critical introduction to both the Grammar and the Logic.

2. Mathiesen (1970) reviewed five recent editions and/or translations of the *Grammaire générale et raisonnée.* In 1964–1967 the classic 43-volume edition of Antoine Arnauld's complete works 1775–1781 was reprinted in Brussels. It includes to it, as vol. 43 the most valuable biography of Arnauld by Larrière (1783). This edition includes both the Grammar (vol. 41:I–III, 1–84) and the Logic (vol. 41: IV–V, 99–416).

In 1967 a reprint of the original edition of the Port-Royal Grammar (1660) was published by The Scolar Press together with a short anonymous introduction.

One year later we find a Geneva reprint of Bailly's 1846 edition of the *Grammar.* This edition 'contains not only the *Grammaire* (according to the Paris text of 1676) and relevant extracts from the *Logique*, both orthographically modernized, but also two important and influential eighteenth-century French commentaries on it: the *Remarques* of Duclos (printed part by part after each chapter of the *Grammaire*) and the *Réflexions* of the Abbé Fromant (printed as a whole at the end of the

[124] The manuscript can be dated to 1659 or 1660. See Arnauld 1965–67: vol. 3, 3–5.

[125] Brekle's judgment (Arnauld 1965–67, vol. 3, 23) as to the quality of this translation has to be corrected. See Brekle 1969 (86f.); actually, the Dickoff/James translation is unreliable and faulty.

volume). It is the latter two texts (and the editor's introduction) which make this edition worth the attention of a historian of linguistics' (Mathiesen 1970:130).

Also, in 1968, the Scolar Press reprinted the only published English translation of the *Grammar* (London 1753) together with the same introduction that was prefaced to the reprint of the 1660 edition of the *Grammar*. One can agree with Mathiesen (1970:130) that this translation of the Paris text of 1676 is 'extremely clear and readable . . . and seems to be quite accurate.'

The following remarks aim at supplying a cursory description of some of the relevant contributions to 'Port-Royal linguistics'.

In more recent years it was Brekle (1964) who tried to assess some semiotic and semantic aspects of the Port-Royal *Logic* and *Grammar* in the light of modern semiotics and semantics. In view of the fact that this contribution is one of the very first attempts to draw the attention of linguists to some fundamental aspects of the works in question some misgivings as to his interpretation would seem excusable.[126] Among other topics Brekle (1964) discusses the various semiotic categories and processes that are put forward mainly in the Port-Royal *Logic*; he discovers a clear parallel in the *Grammar* (1676:26f.) with the principle of 'double articulation' that characterizes any natural language. Finally he discusses (Brekle 1964:118ff.) Port-Royal's semantic conception of two sorts of components in the meaning of words: 'idée principale' — this would nowadays correspond to the cognitive meaning of a word — and 'idée accessoire' — this would correspond to connotative, value-based meaning constituents.

Brekle (1967)[127] discusses some specifically linguistic aspects of the Port-Royal *Grammar*. It is argued — in accordance with Chomsky — that Arnauld and Lancelot did try to arrive at a distinction in their *Grammar* similar to the 'deep-surface structure' dichotomy (if taken in a non-technical, or Wittgensteinian sense). Furthermore Brekle (1967:7f.) gives an interpretation of a passage in the *Grammar* (1676: 30–34) dealing with the notions 'substance' and 'accident' and their application to grammatical analyses. It is shown that the authors of the Port-Royal *Grammar* succeeded in transforming the ontology-based scholastic notions of 'substantia' and 'accidentia' into categories that are defined by intra-grammatical criteria in a way similar to the principles governing 'immediate constituent' analysis. Brekle (1967:

[126] The present writer is now of the opinion that his 1964 interpretation of the term 'manière de signifier' (*Grammaire* 1676:5 *et passim*) along the lines of a 'meaning = use' theory is untenable. The term in question is best understood as an equivalent to the medieval term 'modus significandi'; this would mean that some given semantic substance can take on various 'modes of meaning', i.e. function as a noun, verb, adjective etc. See on this problem now Donzé 1967 (71, 118f. *et passim*) and Foucault 1967 (11): '. . . les mots ne diffèrent pas tellement par leur sens que par la manière dont ils fonctionnent par rapport à l'objet . . . les différences qui sont pertinentes pour le grammairien ne concernent pas les choses signifiées par les mots, mais le mode sur lequel ils signifient.' At this point it should be noted that Hall's sweeping judgment on Foucault 1967, namely, that this article 'is a rather naïve presentation of Port-Royal's main approach and doctrines, taken *au pied de la lettre*' (Hall 1969:221) is unsubstantiated.

[127] This article was written early in 1965.

8–10) also tries to elucidate the Port-Royal notions 'signification distincte' and 'signification confuse' by connecting them with the theoretical background of more modern terms like 'lexical' and 'structural or grammatical meaning'.[128]

Brekle concludes his 1967 contribution with a discussion of the interrelation of the terms 'signification' (= intension), 'l'étendue d'une signification' (= extension), and 'détermination'; these concepts are central for Arnauld and Lancelot's famous discussion of Vaugelas' rule concerning the use of relative pronouns (*Grammaire* 1676:ch.X.79–87), and with a critical evaluation of chapter XIII: "Des Verbes: et de ce qui leur est propre et essentiel" (*Grammaire* 1676:94–104).

In volume 7 of *Langages* (1967) two important articles were published, both dealing with the *Grammaire générale de Port-Royal*. In the first article Foucault (1967) gives a consistent account of the fundamental linguistic conceptions of the *Grammar*. To start with, he explains the Port-Royalist idea of an 'art de penser' or an 'art de parler' in contradistinction to the idea of an 'art de bien penser/parler'. He argues in the following way, thereby clearly showing the Port-Royalist's ideas on the notion of 'rule':

> *Art* de penser et non point *art de bien* penser, parce qu'un art a toujours pour tâche de donner des règles; que les règles définissent toujours une action correcte et qu'il n'y a pas plus d'art de mal penser qu'il n'y a de règles pour peindre mal. La pensée incorrecte est une pensée sans règle ... (Foucault 1967:7)

Foucault then goes on to apply this argument to grammar:

> ... parler hors des règles revient à ne pas parler du tout; ... De là une conséquence importante: la grammaire ne saurait valoir comme les prescriptions d'un législateur donnant enfin au désordre des paroles leur constitution et leurs lois; elle ne saurait être non plus comprise comme un récueil des conseils donnés par un correcteur vigilant. Elle est une discipline qui énonce les règles auxquelles il faut bien qu'une langue s'ordonne pour pouvoir exister. (1967:7)

From these considerations Foucault is lead to posit a double meaning of 'grammar': 'il y a une grammaire que est l'ordre immanent à toute parole prononcée, et une grammaire qui est la description, l'analyse et l'explication, — la théorie — de cet ordre' (Foucault 1967:8). Thus, according to Foucault's interpretation of the Port-Royal conception of grammar, grammar is the set of rules governing man's speech and it is also the discipline in which these rules are to be discovered. As a consequence of this Foucault sets up the following distinction between the tasks of logic and grammar:

> La formule de la logique serait: dès que je pense la vérité, je pense vraiment; et il suffit que je réfléchisse sur ce qui est nécessaire à une véritable pensée pour que je

[128] See in this connection also the pertinent remarks in Donzé 1967 (69–71, 78f.). Mounin (1967: 128) seems to have missed Port-Royal's linguistic reinterpretation of the scholastic categories. His simplistic comment amounts to this: 'On y [in the Port-Royal *Grammar*] démontre que le substantif dénomme la *substance*, et que l'adjectif ne peut dénommer que l'*accident*, au sens scolastique de ces deux termes'.

sache à quelle règle obéit nécessairement une pensée vraie. La formule de la grammaire serait plutôt: dès que je parle véritablement je parle selon les règles; mais si je veux savoir pourquoi ma langue obéit nécessairement à ces règles, il faut que je les reconduise aux principes qui les fondent. (1967:8)

Furthermore Foucault (1967) — which, as a whole, is an extract from Foucault's preface to another as yet unpublished edition of the *Grammar* — discusses some semiotic aspects of both the *Grammar* and the *Logic*; finally he sets up a semantic system with six different strata that is meant to explain the parts-of-speech system contained in the *Grammar*. This scheme refers as a whole to the first nine chapters of the second part of the *Grammar* where the properties and functions of the essential parts of speech are investigated. On the whole Foucault's scheme seems to be quite convincing; he explains the function of the various grammatical categories by the following correlations (see Foucault 1967:13):

l'étendue du signe	:	article défini — indéfini[129]
		[singulier — pluriel]
la nature de l'idée	:	noms — verbes
l'extension de l'idée	:	noms propres — noms communs
la nature de l'objet	:	substantifs — adjectifs
les rapports entre objets	:	prépositions

The second relevant article in volume 7 of *Langages* is by Chevalier. His critique and evaluation of the *Grammar* in relation to modern linguistics, from Brunot to Chomsky, is more extensive than Foucault (1967). Chevalier (1967:17–24) discusses in some detail Foucault 1966, Chomsky 1966, and Snyders (1965). In connection with the latter work he justly emphasizes the pedagogical side of Lancelot's grammars for various languages. To quote Hall (1969:222), Chevalier 'points out the way in which Port-Royal subordinates the study of actual linguistic manifestations to that of "la proposition, cadre unique auquel on ramène tous les autres, puisqu'il est tenu pour le schéma nécessaire du raisonnement" (Snyders 1965:32), and then observes "Un outil remarquable par son abstraction est donc offert à une élite pour la réduction à l'unité d'un monde désordonné" (Snyders 1965:33)'.

In the final paragraph of his interesting and valuable article Chevalier summarizes his general critical attitude towards universalist tendencies in linguistics.

It is somewhat difficult to discuss Donzé's 1967 monograph here.[130] One readily agrees with Hall (1969:219) that 'Donzé's treatment of Arnauld's and Lancelot's grammar is outstanding for its thoroughness and its objectivity'. Although Donzé is on the whole quite sympathetic to the work of Arnauld and Lancelot, he is nevertheless ready to disagree with them on a number of points (see the list given in Hall 1969:221). In this connection one critical remark seems to be called for; if Donzé in his commendable zeal expounds on each point 'their [Arnauld/Lancelot]

[129] There seems to be an inconsistency here because Foucault 1967 (13) does not include the 'singulier-pluriel' distinction in the proper place.

[130] See the reviews by Uitti (1969–70:81–5) and Hall (1969:218–21).

premisses, analytical procedures, and conclusions, with his own answers to possible objections and also his own evaluation of their findings' (Hall 1969:220), then one might wish that Donzé had paid more attention to recent developments in the fields of semiotics and linguistics. He might then have found it easier to cope with a number of theoretical problems — e.g. his discussion of the Port-Royal division of the parts of speech according to logico-semantic criteria (63–66).

A glance through Donzé's bibliography reveals that modern linguistics — especially the Sapir-Bloomfield branch — and modern logic and semiotics are clearly underrepresented. Nevertheless the three main parts of Donzé's work — "La méthode de Port-Royal" (23–44), "Les mots" (45–124), and "Les fonctions" (125–71) — prove that Donzé acts not only as a historian but at least to the same degree as a linguist who did a fine job in writing this large-scale commentary on a famous but often ill-understood grammatical landmark.

There are two recent contributions to the ongoing discussion on Port-Royal linguistics that testify to the fact that Italian scholars, too, take a renewed interest in both historical and linguistic aspects of the field under discussion.

Rosiello 1967 is a very competent work; it is a successful attempt to describe in some detail what he calls 'la linguistica illuminista'. Rosiello's aim is to delineate the main ideas that were set out by philosophers and grammarians of the seventeenth and eighteenth centuries; particularly in the last chapter of his book,[131] Rosiello tries to draw connecting lines from earlier rationalist and more empirical theoretical standpoints to linguistic theories advanced in the nineteenth and twentieth centuries. It is especially this aspect of Rosiello's work, which is also clearly visible in other chapters of his book, that stands out most favourably against other contributions to the same field that sometimes exhibit tendencies of a rather arid historicism. Rosiello 1967 contains a special chapter "La grammatica generale" (105–166) where he presents a set of detailed discussions of the work of philosopher-grammarians like Arnauld, Lancelot, Du Marsais, Beauzée, and several others. In one sub-chapter (108–132) he deals specifically with Port-Royal linguistics. In a similar vein to Simone (1969) — the other Italian scholar whose introduction to his Italian translation of the Port-Royal *Grammar* and *Logic* will be considered here — Rosiello sheds some light on the scholastic and Renaissance background of the *Grammar*. In evaluating the respective contributions of Arnauld and Lancelot to their joint enterprise, Rosiello (1967:111) comes to the following conclusion:

> Nella collaborazione dei due autori, il Lancelot rappresentante della tradizione grammaticale scolastica trasmessa dai filosofi del Rinascimento, e l'Arnauld diretto interprete del razionalismo cartesiano [and, one would like to add, 'agostiniano'[132]], si

[131] Rosiello (1967:167–210): "La linguistica come scienza empirica."

[132] See Simone in Arnauld 1969 and, more specifically, Simone 1969. The latter contribution deals with St. Augustine's sign theory and its considerable influences on the Port-Royal *Logic* and *Grammar*.

può vedere il duplice aspetto della *Grammaire générale* di Port-Royal: essa, da un lato, chiude un'epoca di normativismo speculativo et pratico in cui l'assunzione del modello latino aveva creato le regole da applicarsi al buon uso delle lingue moderne, e, dall'altro, ne apre un'altra il cui inizio è caratterizzato dall'esigenza, emergente dalla filosofia cartesiana, di fondare una tassonomia generale delle lingue che rifletta la struttura logica della ragione.

With regard to the much-debated analogy between Port-Royal's distinction between the phonetic and semantic side of language on the one hand, and Chomsky's 'deep-surface structure' dichotomy on the other, Rosiello (1967:114) is somewhat critical of Chomsky's position. Rosiello brings in Descartes' well-known categories 'res extensa' and 'res cogitans' which have — as substances of reality — their linguistic counterparts in 'sound' and 'meaning'. According to Rosiello (1967:114) these two Cartesian substances are defined by Chomsky as 'modelli che rappresentano, l'uno l'organizzazione superficiale della unità che determina l'interpretazione fonetica, l'altro la forma astratta che determina l'interpretazione semantica della proposizione'.

In connection with the last mentioned problem Rosiello (115) points out — correctly — that in the Port-Royal *Grammar* two definitions of the 'word' are to be found, one reading the word as a special phonetic or graphemic unit, the other takes into account the semantic function of a word.[133]

Rosiello (1967:117ff.) has an interesting discussion of Port-Royal's Aristotelian subject-predicate logic as applied to grammar. In using arguments derived from modern predicate logic he criticizes both Port-Royal's theory of propositions and Chomsky's syntactic principles (regarding his NP-VP dichotomy):[134]

> ... Chomsky tenda a recuperare la tradizione sostanzialista della logica grammaticale di Port-Royal, e ..., in particolare, creda di scoprire nell'operazione riduttiva di tutti i tipi di proposizione allo schema *S è P* della proposizione attributiva l'antecedente del metodo trasformazionale ... (1967:119)

Rosiello's other interpretations of several important topics of the *Grammar* follows roughly the same lines as Brekle (1964 and 1967).

As was already indicated above, Simone's edition of Arnauld (1969) is a valuable source for historical as well as linguistic insights in matters connected with the two main Port-Royal texts. However, his criticism of Brekle (1964 and 1967) as being an uncouth case of 'repêchage' is not too convincing.[135] Simone's position would

[133] See *Grammaire* (1676:16): 'On appelle Mot ce qui se prononce à part, et s'écrit à part' and on p. 27: 'Ainsi l'on peut définir les mots, des sons distincts et articulez dont les hommes ont fait des signes pour signifier leurs pensés.'

[134] See on this point also Brekle 1969 (81ff.) for a short discussion on the historical development of relational logic. In our opinion the 1638 *Logica Hamburgensis* by Joachim Jungius would well deserve further attention, especially from the side of linguistics. See also Reichenbach 1947 (251–55) from whom Rosiello borrows some arguments.

[135] See Simone in Arnauld 1969:XXXV: 'Il *repêchage* ... si presenta invece in forme grossolane nei due saggi segnalati di Brekle [1964 and 1967]. ... Siamo qui, dome si vede, alla più totale confusione interpretativa, che non serve a niente proprio perché non contribuisce a far meglio penetrare il testo in esame.'

become more convincing if he had entered into a substantial discussion on some of the 'unhistorical' interpretations put forward in Brekle (1964 and 1967). However, when discussing some aspects of the distinction between a nominal and a real definition (see *Logic* 1662:I,ch.11f.) Simone (in Arnauld 1969:XLI) seems to agree with Brekle (1964:116f.). The same holds true for Simone's interpretation of the Port-Royal notion of 'idées accessoires' in relation to the 'idée principale' of a word.[136]

Among the few remaining more recent contributions to an interpretation of Port-Royal linguistics[137] R. Lakoff's (1969) evaluation of the *Grammaire générale et raisonnée* deserves special mention. She gives several examples of 'pre-transformational treatments of philosophical grammars' (Bloomfield 1933:6–7, Jespersen 1924:47, and Hockett 1961:4–5) and concludes therefrom that 'it is probably true that none of the scholars who discussed the GGR [= *Grammaire générale et raisonnée*] as a Latinizing grammar had read it very carefully' (R. Lakoff 1969:343f.). Speaking generally R. Lakoff is sympathetic to Chomsky's 'transformational' interpretation of the Port-Royal texts; on certain points, however, she gives a more differentiated picture of the relevant problems. She recognizes that although 'Lancelot and Arnauld describe a number of rules, which can be considered transformational in nature ... they are not really the same as our transformational rules: they are never precisely or formally stated' (1969:345). On the whole R. Lakoff is even very critical towards the idea that the *Grammar* can be considered the work of a proto-transformationalist:

> One feels the potential is there, but not enough is said, apart from hints, for one to legitimately draw any strong conclusion. (1969:346)

R. Lakoff's main claim in her review article is that it is not so much the *Grammaire générale* that can be said to contain seeds of a generative-transformational grammar, but that — instead — it is Lancelot's NML [= Lancelot 1644[138]] that can be viewed as a convincing example of a grammar which is transformational in nature. R. Lakoff's second claim is that the proto-transformational properties detectable in NML cannot be derived from Cartesian origins but go back to Sanctius' *Minerva* (1587), at least.[139] For R. Lakoff 'it looks as though the GGR is not meant

[136] See the discussion in Brekle 1964. The question is discussed in the *Logic* (1662:I, ch. XII) under the heading "D'vne autre sorte de définitions de noms, par lesquels on marque ce qu'ils signifient dans l'vsage".

[137] See Verburg 1951 (323–32), Chomsky 1964, Marx 1967, Rosetti 1969.

[138] Second largely revised and augmented 1650 edition (it is in this edition that Lancelot included significant parts of Sanctius' syntactic conceptions). There is a fifth edition (1656). See also the somewhat inconclusive discussion of the textual development of Lancelot 1644 in R. Lakoff 1969 (356f.).

[139] On Sanctius see Verburg 1951 (165f. *et passim*); on Sanctius' two seventeenth century commentators, Scioppius and Perizonius, see also Verburg 1951 (418ff.). Besides being known as a commentator of Sanctius' *Minerva*, Scioppius is also remembered as the author of a *Grammatica philosophica* (1628); this work, however, is not held in high esteem by a number of critics (see

to be used by itself: rather, it seems to have been viewed by its authors as a kind of abstract or summary of all their previous works, without reference to which the GGR is unintelligible'. (1969:347)

In order to substantiate her claims R. Lakoff gives examples from Lancelot 1644. Her interpretations (see especially her discussion of 'ellipsis', 352ff.) show that Lancelot 'holds a fairly well-developed theory of deep/surface structure distinction. His use of abstract elements prove this, though there is no evidence of this in the GGR'. (355)

R. Lakoff concludes her valuable contribution in pointing out that it was most certainly Sanctius' influence that was seminal for Lancelot's (proto-)transformational syntactic theory.

5.3 *Cordemoy's "Discours physique de la parole"* (1677)

There are now two editions available of Cordemoy's *Discours physique de la parole*: one is contained in Clair and Girbal's edition of Cordemoy (1968:193–256), the other is a separate edition of the work by Brekle in Cordemoy 1970. Clair and Girbal give the *Discours physique de la parole* in the form of the posthumous 1704 edition together with textual variants derived from earlier editions (1668, 1671, 1677, 1690), Brekle (Cordemoy 1970) gives a reprint of the 1677 edition — the last one that appeared during the lifetime of Gérauld de Cordemoy — together with bio-bibliographical data and commentaries on each chapter.[140]

Cordemoy's *Discours physique de la parole*, which must be seen in connection with and as a continuation of his 'Six discours sur la distinction et l'union du corps et de l'Ame' (first published in 1666),[141] has for various reasons recently aroused the interest of philosophers and linguists.[142]

Cordemoy's central question in his *Discours* is whether it is necessary to admit the existence of minds or souls other than his own. In close analogy to the Cartesian doubt Cordemoy advances the following consideration:

Je pense avoir au moins sujet de douter que ces Corps soient unis à des Ames, jusques à ce que j'aye examiné toutes leurs actions. (1970:2)

Verburg 1951:418f.). In the domain of classical philology it was Vossius 1635 that proved to be influential throughout the seventeenth and eighteenth century (see Verburg's comments, 1951: 423ff.).

140 See Cordemoy 1970 (IX–XIII) for a detailed discussion of the relative merits of the 1677 and 1704 versions of the text. There is a recent reprint of the work — no date is given — which is a facsimile of the 1704 edition. It appeared as supplement to No. 9 of *Cahiers pour l'analyse* (Paris) and can be conveniently used as a checking-instrument for Clair and Girbal's 1968 edition.

141 See Cordemoy's own explanations on this in his dedication of the work to Louis XIV (1677: ã i j and in the Preface ẽ i).

142 See Chomsky 1966 (6ff.), Rodis-Lewis 1966, Cordemoy 1968 (15–84), Arnauld 1969, Cordemoy 1970 (xvii–xli), Leroy 1970, Simone 1971.

As a result of the first step in his investigations Cordemoy states that quite a number of the actions and reactions of the bodies that are similar to his own can be explained by the purely mechanist principle of 'stimulus and response'. Cordemoy, however, also recognizes different sorts of behavior in these 'bodies' which cannot simply be explained by dispositions to respond automatically and predictably in such and such a way:

> ... il me semble que ie leur vois souvent faire des choses, qui ne se rapportent nullement à eux-mesmes ny à leur conservation ... quand ie vois qu'ils s'approchent avec fermeté de ce qui les va détruire, et qu'ils abandonnent ce qui les pourroit conserver, ie ne puis attribuer ces effets à cette proportion méchanique qui se rencontre entr'eux et les obiets ... (1970:6f.)

From this Cordemoy concludes that some actions of his fellow-creatures are governed by a will like his own. But, Cordemoy is not content with this criterion for the existence of other minds or souls. He immediately proceeds to his main theme which is whether language or rather, a satisfactory explanation of the verbal behavior of the seemingly human beings surrounding him, can possibly serve as the decisive criterion for a positive answer to his initial question. In order to arrive at a solution of his problem Cordemoy sets out to make 'un discernement exact de tout ce qu'elle [la parole] tient de l'Ame, et de tout ce qu'elle emprunte du Corps' (1970: Préface, ẽ). This amounts to nothing less than an examination of the phonetic *and* semantic aspects of language.

Cordemoy discusses various factually existing or hypothetically assumed models for communication:

1. A speaking machine: Cordemoy imagines that 'une pure Machine pourroit proferer quelques paroles' (1970:8f.) but the sound sequences produced by such a machine would differ radically from those uttered by human beings because their utterances 'n'ont presque iamais la mesme suite' (1970:9).

2. The language of animals: Cordemoy admits that animals can produce meaningful sounds, but — as in the case of parrots — Cordemoy is not willing to accept this as a criterion for parrots possessing language because 'parler n'est pas repeter les mesmes paroles dont on a eu l'oreille frappée, mais que c'est en proferer d'autres à propos de celles-là' (1970:19). Other sounds uttered by animals, groaning and whining, are regarded as 'natural signs' whose production is solely due to various relatively fixed dispositions in one or another species of animal (see 1970: 110–16).

3. The language of human beings: in the case of human language Cordemoy recognizes clearly two essential aspects, namely that human beings use well-ordered strings of phonetic events in order to convey their ideas to each other. This latter semantic aspect Cordemoy concludes after having run through a number of intricately designed arguments, 'ne peut estre que de la part de l'Ame' (1970: 117).

4. The language of spiritual beings ('angels'): To the discussion of this hypo-

thetical model of communication Cordemoy dedicates the last chapter of his work (1970:173–200). Cordemoy holds the opinion that spiritual beings can communicate with each other without using signs; this must necessarily be so because these beings are — by their very nature — not invested with a body. This non-semiotic kind of communication[143] constitutes for Cordemoy the ideal model.

The following remarks are intended to throw light on some specifically linguistic positions of Cordemoy. He continually stresses the importance of pragmatic aspects of language; this becomes clear when he defines language, or, rather the process of speaking:

Parler ... n'est autre chose que se faire connoistre ce que l'on pense, à ce qui est capable de l'entendre ... (1970:21)

By way of a *Gedankenexperiment* Cordemoy seeks to prove that interhuman communication is founded on an inventory of institutionalized signs; this is not only true for the commonly accepted inventory of the words of a language but also in a special case where 'ie puis convenir avec quelques-uns d'eux [other people], que ce qui signifie ordinairement une chose en signifie une autre, et que cela réussit de sorte, qu'il n'y a plus que ceux avec qui i'en suis convenu, qui me paroissent entendre ce que ie pense' (1970:22f.).

Another essential criterion for linguistic signs is seen by Cordemoy in their arbitrariness; the following quotation shows that he tries to separate neatly the age-old criteria for linguistic signs *ex arbitrio* and *ex instituto*:[144]

Vne des principales choses que ie trouve digne de consideration touchant ces signes, est qu'ils n'ont aucune conformité avec les penséés que l'on y joint par institution. (1970:32)

Moreover, Cordemoy does not restrict this criterion of non-conformity to some special medium used as linguistic substance, but extends it to all possible substances (spoken, written, gestatory). This means that Cordemoy takes the side of Bacon (see above 1.1.) and Hjelmslev (1963) and not de Saussure's position on the priority of spoken signs over written signs.

Cordemoy develops his ideas on the phonetic side of language in the third chapter of his *Discours*: 'Ce que c'est que la parole, à ne considérer que le corps' (1970:66–110).[145]

[143] See Simone 1971, where the historical and theological aspects of this question are competently discussed. This theme recurs also in Locke's *Essay* II, 23, 36: '... we cannot yet have any idea of the manner wherein they [spirits] discover their thoughts one to another: though we must necessarily conclude that separate spirits, which are beings that have perfecter knowledge and greater happiness than we, must needs have also a perfecter way of communicating their thoughts than we have, who are fain to make use of corporeal signs, and particular sounds ...'.
[144] See Coseriu's amply documented contribution to the history of these notion, in Coseriu 1967.
[145] See on this point Leroy 1970 and 1971. However, Leroy (1971:13) holds the erroneous view that 'il faudra ... attendre deux siècles pour voir reprendre l'étude des organes de la parole et celle de la production des sons selon la voie expérimentale qu'avait indiquée en 1668 Gérauld de Cordemoy ...'. In fact, there exists a continuing tradition in the work of experimentally-minded

In fine, there are many more most interesting linguistic points in Cordemoy's treatise that are undoubtedly still worth a close reading even by less historically-minded linguists. Chomsky is certainly right in stating that Cordemoy has convincingly demonstrated 'that there can be no mechanistic explanation for the novelty, coherence, and relevance of normal speech' (Chomsky 1966:7).

BIBLIOGRAPHY

Primary Sources

ALSTED, J. H. 1630. Scientiarum omnium Encyclopaedia septem tomis distincta. Herborn.

AMMAN, J. C. 1692. Surdus loquens, seu methodus quâ qui surdus natus est loqui discere possit. Amstelaedami.

——. 1694. The talking deaf man: or a method proposed, whereby he who is born deaf, may learn to speak . . . Done out of Latin into English, by D. Foote. London.

——. 1700. [Dissertatio de loquela]. Amsterdam. [A dissertation on speech. In which not only the human voice and the art of speaking are traced from their origin, but the means are also described by which those who have been deaf and dumb from their birth may acquire speech, and those who speak imperfectly may learn how to correct their impediments. Amsterdam, 1966. Repr. of the London ed. 1873.]

ARNAULD, A. 1775–83. Oeuvres de Messire Antoine Arnauld, Docteur de la maison et société de Sorbonne. Edited by Gabriel Du Pac de Bellegarde and Jean Hautefage. 43 vols. Paris, Sigismond d'Arnay et Compagnie.

——. 1964–67. Repr. of the 1775–83 edition. 43 vols. Brussels, Culture et civilisation. [Vol. 43 = biography of Arnauld by Noël de Larrière (1783).]

ARNAULD, A. and C. LANCELOT. 1846. Grammaire générale et raisonnée de Port-Royal, suivie, 1. de la partie de la Logique de P.-R. qui traite des propositions; 2. des Remarques de Duclos, de l'Academie françoise; 3. du Supplément à la Grammaire générale de P.-R., par l'abbé Fromant, et publiée sur la meilleure éd. originale. Avec une introduction historique par M. A. Bailly. Paris, Hachette. Slatkine [Reprints, Genève 1968.]

——. 1966. Grammaire générale et raisonnée ou La Grammaire de Port-Royal. 1676 Edition critique . . . par Herbert E. Brekle. 1, 2. Stuttgart-Bad Cannstatt.

——. 1967. Grammaire générale et raisonnée 1660. Menston, England, Scolar Press. [Facsim. ed.]

——. 1968. A general and rational grammar. (1753). Translated by Thomas Nugent. Menston, England: The Scolar Press Limited. [English linguistics

phoneticians throughout the seventeenth and eighteenth centuries. See e.g. Wallis 1653, Cooper 1685, Amann 1700, and von Kempelen 1791.

1500–1800: a collection of Facsimile Reprints, selected and edited by R. C. Alston, 73.]

——. 1969. Simone, R. Grammatica e Logica di Port-Royal. Le Grandi Opere. Collana di opere classiche. Roma, Ubaldini Editore.

ARNAULD, A. and P. NICOLE. 1958. Logica czyli sztuka myślenia. Przelozyla i poprzedzila węştepem Seweryna Romahnowa. Państwowe Wydawnictwo Naukowe.

——. 1964. Logique de Port-Royal (1683). Introduction par R. Roubinet. Lille, Librairie René Giard.

——. 1964. The art of thinking. Transl. by J. Dickoff and P. James. Indianapolis, Bobbs & Merill Comp.

——. 1965. La logique ou l'art de penser (1683). Ed. critique par P. Clair et F. Girbal. Le mouvement des idées au XVIIe siècle. Paris, Presses Univ. de France.

——. 1965–67. La logique de Port-Royal. (1662). Ed. par B. v. Freytag-Löringhoff et H. E. Brekle. 1–3. Stuttgart-Bad Cannstatt.

AUGUSTINUS. 1844–1855. De doctrina christiana, 1. II, cap. I–XVI. [Migne 1844–55, 34.]

BACON, F. 1605. The advancement of learning. London.

——. 1620. Novum organum scientiarum. London.

——. 1623. Opera . . . tomus primus: qui continet De dignitate & augmentis scientiarum, libros IX . . . Londini, In officina Joannis Haviland. [Published also under the title De augmentis scientiarum].

——. 1857–1874. The works of Francis Bacon. Coll. and ed. by J. Spedding, R. L. Ellis and D. D. Heath. 1–14. London. [Faksimile-Neudr., Stuttgart-Bad Cannstatt, 1963.]

BARTOLI, D. 1670. Il torto e 'l diritto del Non si può. In Bartoli 1844. Opere complete, XXXIV. Torino.

BECHER, J. J. 1661. Clavis convenientiae linguarum: character pro notitia linguarum universali: inventum steganographicum hactenus in auditum, quo quilibet suam legendo vernaculam, diversas, imo omnes linguas, unius etiam diei informatione explicare et intellegere potest. Francoforti.

——. 1661. Allgemeine Verschlüsselung der Sprachen (Character pro notizia linguarum universali, lat. u. dt.) Stuttgart 1962:21–44.

BECK, C. 1657. The universal character, by which all the nations in the world may understand one anothers conceptions, reading out of one common writing their own mother tongue. An invention of general use, the practise whereof may be attained in two hours space, observing the grammatical directions. Which character is so contrived, that it may be spoken as well as written. London.

BENI, P. 1612. L' Anticrusca ovvero il paragone della lingua Italiana. Padova.

BERKELEY, G. 1710. A treatise concerning the principles of human knowledge. Dublin. [Ed. by G. J. Warnock, London, The Fontana Library, 1962.]

——. 1948–57. The works of George Berkeley, Bishop of Cloyne. Ed. by A. A. Luce and T. E. Jessop. 9 vols. Edinburgh, Nelson and Sons.

BÖDIKER, J. 1690. Grund-Sätze der Deutschen Sprachen im Reden und Schreiben, samt einem Bericht vom rechten Gebrauch der Vorwörter. Cölln an der Spree.

BOEHME, J. 1635. De Signatura Rerum: das ist Bezeichnung aller dingen, wie das Innere vom Eusseren bezeichnet wird. [Amsterdam?].

——. 1651. Signatura rerum, or the Signature of all things, shewing the Sign and Signification of the several Forms and Shapes in the Creation, and what the beginning, ruin, and cure of everything is, ... (The 177 Theosophick Questions). Transl. by J. Ellistone. London.

——. 1955–61. Sämtliche Schriften. Faksimile-Neudruck der Ausgabe von 1730. Hrsg. v. W.-E. Peuckert. 11 Bde. Stuttgart-Bad Cannstatt.

BRIGHT, T. 1588. Characterie. [J. H. Ford, ed., 1888.]

——. 1628. The school-master to the art of stenography. London.

BULLOKAR, W. 1586. Bref grammar for English. London. [Repr. by M. Plessow, Berlin, 1906.]

BUONMATTEI, B. 1623. Delle cagioni della lingua toscana. Venezia.

——. 1626. Introduzione alla lingua toscane del signor Benedetto Bvommattei al serenissimo grandvca Ferdinando secondo. Nella qvale si tratta dell' origine, cagioni, & accrescimento di quell ... Con l'agiunta in questa seconda impression di due trattati vtilissimi. E la tauola de capitoli in fine. In Venezia, Gio. Salis.

——. 1643. Della lingua toscana ... libri due, impressione terza. Firenze, Z. Pignoni.

——. 1643. Della lingua toscana. Libri I, II. Venezia, 1735.

BURTHOGGE, R. 1678. Organum vetus et novum. Or, a discourse of reason and thruth. Wherein the natural logick common to mankind is briefly and plainly described. London.

CAMPANELLA, T. 1638. Philosophia rationalis partes quinque. Paris.

——. 1638. Philosophiae rationalis pars prima continens Grammaticalium libros tres. Paris.

CARAMUEL Y LOBKOWITZ, J. 1642. Rationalis et realis philosophia. Louvain.

——. 1651a. Herculis logici labores tres ... Frankfurt.

——. 1651b. Grammatica audax. Frankfurt.

——. 1654a. Praecursor logicus complectens grammaticam audacem. (Herculis logici labores tres ... sive Praecursoris logici pars altera). Frankfurt, Schönwettern.

——. 1654b. Grammatica critica.

COMENIUS, J. A. 1633. The gate of tongues unlocked and opened. [A trans. of Janua linguarum reserata (Leszno 1631)]. 2nd enlarged ed. by John Anchoran. London.

——. 1649. Linguarum methodus novissima. Leszno. Also in Comenius 1657: Part 2. 1–292.

——. 1657. Opera didactica omnia. 4 parts. Amsterdam. [Reprint in 3 vols. Sumptibus Academiae Scientiarum Bohemoslovenicae Pragae in aedibus Academiae Scientiarum Bohemoslovenicae. Prague, 1957.]

——. 1681. Sapientiae primae Usus Triertirum Catholicum appelandus... Leiden, Heeneman.

——. 1914–1938. Věskeré Spisy Jana Amosa Komenského. Brno, [Only 9 of a projected 30 vols. were published, but still the most comprehensive modern edition].

——. 1938. The way of light of John Amos Comenius. Tr. by E. T. Campagnac. Liverpool, The University Press. [234 pp.]

——. 1959. Janua linguarum reserata. Editio synoptica et critica quinque authenticos textus latinos necnon Janualem Comenii textum Bohemicum continens. Curavit Janomir Červenka. Praha. [xliv, 344 pp.]

——. 1964. Centrum securitatis, nach der deutschen Ausgabe von A. Macher aus dem Jahre 1737, eingeleitet und herausgegeben von Klaus Schaller. Heidelberg, Quelle & Meyer. [156 pp.]

——. 1965. Pampaedia. Lateinischer Text und deutsche Übersetzung herausgegeben von Dmitrij Tschizewskij in Gemeinschaft mit Heinrich Geissler und Klaus Schaller, 2nd ed. Heidelberg, Quelle & Meyer. 518 pp.

——. 1966. De rerum humanarum emendatione consultatio catholica. Sumptibus Academiae Scientiarum Bohemoslovacae Pragae in aedibus Academiae Scientiarum Bohemoslovenicae. 2 vols. Prague. [Herein: Panegersia 1.41–95; Panaugia 1.97–162; Pansophia 1.163–776; Pampaedia 2.9–145; Panglottia 2.147–204; Panorthosia 2.205–378; Pannuthesia 2.379–447; Lexicon reale pansophicum 2.449–681.]

Cooper, C. 1685. Grammatica linguae Anglicanae. London. 1912 [Repr. by]: John D. Jones (Neudrucke frühneuenglischer Grammatiken, ed. by R. Brotanek, vol. 5).

——. 1687. The English Teacher, or the discovery of the art, of teaching and learning the English tongue. London. [Reprinted by Bertil Sundby as 'Christopher Cooper's English Teacher 1687', Lund Studies in English 22. Lund, 1953.]

Cordemoy, L. G. de. 1668a. Discours physique de la parole. Paris.

——. 1668b. A philosophical discourse concerning speech, conformable to the Cartesian Principles... Englished out of French. John Martin: In the Savoy.

——. 1704. Discours physique de la parole. Les cahiers pour l'analyse. [Supplément to no. 9, no date.]

——. 1968. Oeuvres philosophiques avec une étude biobibliographique. Ed. critique par Pierre Clair et François Girbal. Le mouvement des idées au XVIIe siècle. Paris, Presses Univ. de France.

——. 1970. Discours physique de la parole [1677], ed. by H. E. Brekle. Stuttgart-Bad Cannstatt.

DALGARNO, G. 1661. Ars signorum, vulgo character universalis et lingua philosophica. Qua [sic!] poterunt homines diversissimorum idiomatum, spatio duarum septimanarum, omnia animi sua sensa (in rebus familiaribus) nonminus intelligibiliter, sive scribendo sive loquendo mutuo communicare, quam linguis propriis vernaculis. London.

——. 1680. Didascalocophus or the deaf and dumb man's tutor. Oxford.

DATI, C. R. 1657. Discorso dell' obbligo di ben parlare la propria lingua. Firenze. In B. Buonmattei 1735. Della lingua toscana. Venezia.

DESCARTES, RENÉ. 1897–1913. Oeuvres, ed. by Charles Adam and Paul Tannery. 13 vols. Paris. [Abbreviated A. & T.]

——. 1963. Oeuvres philosophiques (1618–1637), ed. by Ferdinand Alquié. Paris, Garnier.

——. 1967. Oeuvrcs philosophiques (1638–1642), ed. by Ferdinand Alquié. Paris, Garnier.

DIAS. 1697. Arte da lingua de Angola. Lisboa.

DIGBY, K. 1644. Two treatises. In the one of which, the nature of bodies; in the other, the Nature of man's soule; is looked into: in way of discovery, of the immortality of reasonable soules. Paris.

EDMUNDSON, H. 1655. Lingua linguarum, the natural language of languages.

——. 1658. ΣΥΝ ΘΕΩ, Lingua linguarum. The natural language of languages, in a vocabulary; . . . contrived and built upon analogy. London.

FIORETTI, B. 1620–1639. Proginnasmi poetici. I–V. Firenze.

GILL, A. 1619. Logonomia Anglica que gentis sermo facilius addiscitur. London. [Repr. by Otto L. Jiriczek, Berlin 1903.]

——. 1621. Alexander Gill's Logonomia anglica, nach der Ausgabe von 1621 diplomatisch hrsg. von O. L. Jiriczek. Strasburg, Trübner.

GLANVILL, J. 1678. A seasonable defence of preaching: and the plain way of it. London.

——. 1678. An essay concerning preaching: Written for the direction of a young divine; and useful also for the people, in order to profitable hearing. London.

GUICHARD, E. 1606. L'harmonie étymologique des langues hébraique chaldaïque, syriaque, grecque, latine, françoise, italienne, espagnole, allemande, flamande, angloise, etc. . . . Paris.

HELWIG, C. 1619a. Libri didactici Grammaticae Vniversalis, Latinae, Graecae, Hebraicae, Chaldaicae. Giessae, Chemlin.

——. 1619b. Sprachkünste: I. Allgemeine . . ., II. Lateinische, III. Hebraische.

HICKES, G. 1689. Institutiones grammaticae anglo-saxonicae et moeso-gothicae; acc. grammaticae island. rudimenta Runolphi Jonae cum dictionario island. Oxford.

HOBBES, TH. 1637. A briefe of the art of rhetoriqve. London. In Hobbes. 1839–1845b. Vol. VI.

——. 1650. De corpore, in Hobbes 1839–1845b. Vol. I.

——. 1651. Leviathan or the matter, forme and power of a commonwealth, ecclesiasticall and civill. London. Ed. A. R. Waller, Cambridge 1904.

——. 1839–1845a. Opera philosophica quae latine scripsit omnia in unum corpus nunc primum collecta. Ed. by G. Molesworth. Vol. I–V. Londini. [Repr. 1961, Aalen.]

——. 1839–1845b. The English works of Thomas Hobbes. Ed. by W. Molesworth. Vol. I–XI. [Repr. 1962, Aalen.]

HOLDER, W. 1669. Elements of speech. An essay on inquiry into the natural production of letters with an appendix concerning persons deaf and dumb. London.

HUME, A. 1612a. Grammatica nova. Edinburgh.

——. 1616b. Prima Elementa grammaticae. Edinburgh.

——. 1617. Of the orthographie and congruitie of the Britan tongue . . . Ed. by H. B. Wheatley. EETS 5.1865.

JONSON, BEN. 1620 [printed 1640]. The English grammar, for the benefit of all strangers, out of his observation of the English language now spoken, and in use. In Ben Jonson's Dramen in Neudruck hrsg. nach der Folio 1616 von Willy Bang, London, 1905. Vol. 2, 31–84. [Editor's note: The best edition is in Ben Jonson, ed. by C. H. Herford, and Percy and Evelyn Simpson. Oxford, Clarendon, 1925–52 in 11 vols. Here the English grammar is in vol. 8 (1947), 453–553.]

JUNGIUS, J. 1638 [1957]. Logica Hamburgensis. Ed. and tr. by R. W. Meyer. Hamburg.

JUNIUS, F. 1743. Etymologicum Anglicanum; ex autographo descripsit et access. permultis auctum ed. Edw. Lye: praemittuntur vita auctoris et grammatica anglosaxonica. Oxford.

KEMPELEN, W. v. 1791. Mechanismus der menschlichen Sprache nebst Beschreibung einer sprechenden Maschine. Wien. Faksimile-Neudruck mit einer Einleitung von Herbert E. Brekle und Wolfgang Wildgen. Stuttgart-Bad Cannstatt, 1970.

KINNER, C. 1648? A continuation of Mr. John-Amos-Comenius school-endeavours [published by Hartlib].

KIRCHER, A. 1636. Prodromus coptus sive aegyptiacus. Romae.

——. 1663. Polygraphia nova et universalis ex combinatoria arte detecta. Romae, Varesius.

LA FIN. 1692. Sermo mirabilis: or, the silent language, whereby one may learn . . . how to impart his mind to his friend in any language, whithout . . . noise, word, or voice. London.

LAMY, B. 1675. La rhétorique ou l'art de parler. Paris.

——. 1676. The art of speaking: written in French by Messieurs du Port Royal ... Rendred into English. London.
——. 1966. Entretiens sur les sciences dans lesquels on apprend comment l'on doit étudier les Sciences, & s'en servir pour se faire l'esprit juste, & le coeur droit. Ed. critique par F. Girbal et P. Clair. Paris, Presses Univ. de France.
LANCELOT, C. 1644. Nouvelle méthode pour apprendre facilement & en peu de temps la langue Latine, contenant les rudiments et les règles des genres, des declinaisons, des prétérits, de la syntaxe & de la quantité. Mises en François... Dediée au Roy. [5th ed. 1656, Paris.]
——. 1660. Nouvelle méthode pour apprendre facilement et en peu de temps la langue espagnole. Paris. [Published in Grammaire générale et raisonnée avec les nouvelles méthodes pour apprendre facilement et en peu de temps les langues italienne et espagnole.]
——. 1676. Nouvelle méthode pour apprendre facilement et en peu temps la langue espagnole. Bruxelles.
LANE, A. 1695. The rational and speedy method of attaining to the Latin tongue. London.
——. 1700. A key to the art of letters: or, English a learned language, full of art, elegancy and variety. Being an essay to enable both foreigners, and the English youth of either sex, to speak and write the English tongue well and learnedly, according to the exactest rules of grammar. After which they may attain to Latin, French, or any other foreign language in a short time, with very little trouble to themselves or their teachers. With a preface shewing the necessity of a vernacular grammar. London.
LEE, HENRY. 1702. Anti-scepticism: Or, notes upon each chapter of Mr. Locke's Essay. London.
LEIBNIZ, GOTTFRIED WILHELM VON. 1666. De arte combinatoria, in Sämtliche Schriften und Briefe, Series 6 Philosophische Schriften, vol. 1, 163–230. [Berlin, Akademie-Ausgabe 1930.]
LEWIS, M. 1670. Institutio grammaticae puerilis: Or the rudiments of the Latin and Greek tongues. Fitted to children's capacities, as an introduction to the larger grammars. London.
——. 1671. An apologie for a grammar. Tottenham.
——. 1674. An essay to facilitate the education of youth by bringing down the rudiments of grammar to the sense of seeing. London.
——. 1675? Plain, and short rules for pointing periods, and reading sentences grammatically, with the great use of them. London.
——. 1675. Vestibulum technicum: or, an artificial vestibulum. Wherein the sense of Janua linguarum is contained, and most of the leading words chapter by chapter, are compiled into plain, and short sentences, fit for the initiation of children. Each part of speech is distinguished by the character it is printed in (a method never used before) and a sufficient grammar is

brought down to the sense of seeing, in regard of the thing signified, contained in two pages. London.

LOCKE, J. 1690. An essay concerning human understanding. Printed by Eliz. Holt, for Thomes Basset. London. [5th ed. London, 1706.]

——. 1961[5]. Essay ed. by John W. Yolton. 2 vols. London, Everyman's Library, nos. 332 and 984. [This is currently the best available edition of the Essay.]

LODWICK, F. 1647. A common writing: whereby two, although not understanding one the others language, yet by the helpe thereof, may communicate their minds one to another. Composed by a well-willer to learning. Oxford.

——. 1652. The ground-work, or foundations laid (or so intended) for the framing of a new perfect language: And an universal or common writing. And presented to the consideration of the Learned. By a Well-willer to learning. n.p.

——. 1686. An essay towards an universal alphabet. Philosophical Transactions 16/No. 182. 126–133. [Followed by 'A second essay concerning the universal primer', 134–137; reprinted almost in full in John Lowthorp's abridgement of The philosophical transactions and collections to the end of the year 1700, vol. 3. 1705: 373–379; 2nd ed. 1716.]

LODWYCK. See SALMON, 1972, which reprints Lodwyck 1647, 1652, 1686.

MAGALOTTI, L. 1667. Lettera ad Apollonio Basetti. In: Magalotti 1825. Lettere dilettevoli e curiose. (Notizie intorno alla vita ... del conte L. Magalotti), ed. by B. Gamba. Venezia.

MAGGIO, F. M. 1670. Sintagma linguarum quae in Georgiae regionibus audiuntur.

MEINER, JOHANN WERNER. 1781. Versuch einer an der menschlichen Sprache abgebildeten Vernunftlehre oder philosophische und allgemeine Sprachlehre. Faksimile-Neudruck der Ausgabe Leipzig 1781 mit einer Einleitung von Herbert E. Brekle. Stuttgart-Bad Cannstatt, 1971.

MELANCHTHON, PHILIPP. 1525–26. Grammatica latina. 1540 ed. Jacob Micyllus.

MÉNAGE, G. 1650. Les origines de la langue françoise. Paris.

MERSENNE, M. 1636–37. Harmonie universelle contenant la théorie et la pratique de la musique. Où il est traité de la nature des sons, et des mouvements, des consonnances, des dissonnances, des genres, des modes, de la composition, de la voix, des chants, et de toutes sortes d'instruments harmoniques. Paris. [Facsimile of the 1636 original edition, with introduction by F. Lesure Vol. 2. Paris, 1963.]

——. 1932 –. Correspondance de Marin Mersenne, ed. by Cornelis de Waard et al. Paris, PUF. [12 vols. published to date.]

MIÈGE, G. 1677. A new dictionary French and English, with another English and French; according to the present use and modern orthography of the French. London.

——. 1678. A new French grammar ... To which are added ... a ... vocabu-

lary and a store of . . . dialogues. Besides four . . . discourses of cosmography in French. London.
——. 1679. A dictionary of barbarous French . . . taken out of Cotgrave's dictionary . . .
——. 1685. Nouvelle méthode pour apprendre l'anglois. Avec une nomenclature, Françoise et Angloise; un recueil d'expressions familières; et des dialogues, etc. Londres.
——. 1688. The English grammar, setting for the grounds of the English tongue and particularly its genius in making compounds and derivatives, with many other useful and curious observations. London.
——. 1749. Nouvelle grammaire angloise-françoise contenant une instruction claire et aisée pour acquérir, en peu de temps, l'usage de l'anglois: et enrichie de règles fondamentales et succinctes, pour parler purement . . . Rotterdam, Jean Daniel Beman.
MIGNE, J. P. 1844–1855. Patrologia Latina cursus completus. 221 vols. Paris.
OLEARIUS, TILEMAN. 1630. Deutsche Sprachkunst. Halle.
PASCAL, BLAISE. 1954. Oeuvres complètes, ed. by J. Chevalier et al. Paris, Bibliothèque de la Pléiade.
PETRAEUS, A. 1649. [Grammatica finnica]. Turku, Åbo.
PETRUS MONTANUS [van Delft]. 1635. Bericht van een niewe konst, genaemt Spraeckkonst, ontdekt en beschreven door P. M.
PRASCH, J. L. 1687. Neue kurtz- und deutliche Sprachkunst. Regensburg.
PUDOR, C. 1672. Der Teutschen Sprache Grundrichtigkeit und Zierlichkeit. Köln.
RAMUS, PETRUS. 1964. 1. Dialecticae institutiones. 2. Aristotelicae animadversiones (Paris 1543), ed. by Wilhelm Risse. Stuttgart, Frommann-Holzboog.
RATICHIUS [RATKE], WOLFGANG. 1619a. Grammatica universalis: pro didactica Ratichii. Köthen. [Also in Vogt 1894.]
——. 1619b. Allgemeine Sprachlehr nach der Lehrart Ratichii. Köthen. [Also in Vogt 1894 and Ratichius 1959 (2.23–48).]
——. 1957. Die Neue Lehrart: Pädagogische Schriften Wolfgang Ratkes, ed. with introd. by Gerd Hohendorf. Berlin, Volk und Wissen Volkseigener Verlag. [270 pp.]
——. 1959. Wolfgang Ratkes Schriften zur Deutschen Grammatik (1612–1630), ed. by E. Ising. Part 1 Abhandlung (119 pp.); Part 2 Textausgabe (332 pp.). Berlin, Akademie-Verlag.
——. 1970–1971. Wolfgang Ratke: Allunterweisung, Schriften zur Bildungs-, Wissenschafts- und Gesellschaftsreform, ed. by Gerd Hohendorf and Franz Hofmann with the assistance of Christa Breschke. Vol. 1 (1970), 478 pp.; vol. 2 (1971), 479 pp. = Monumenta paedagogica, vols. 8 and 9. Berlin, Volk und Wissen Volkseigener Verlag.
RHODES, ALEXANDRE DE. 1651a. Dictionarium annamiticum, lusitanum et latinum. Roma.

——. 1651b. Linguae annamiticae seu tunchinensis brevis declaratio. Roma.

RIVOLA, F. 1621. Dictionarium armeno-latinum. Mediol. [Paris 1633.]

——. 1624. Grammaticae armenae LL. IV. Mediol. [Paris 1634.]

SANCTUS, F. 1587. Minerva: seu de causis linguae Latinae. Salmanticae.

——. 1598? Quod nihil scitur. Opera Philosophica. ed. by J. de Carvalho, Coimbra, 1955. [See on the question of Sánchez's authorship: Palau y Dulcet, 1967. Manual del Librero Hispanoamericano. Tom. XIX.286.]

——. 1664. Minerva, sive de causis Latinae linguae commentarius, cui accedunt animadversiones et notae G. Scioppii (Grammatica latina, . . .). Amstelodami.

SCALIGER, J. C. 1540. De causis Linguae Latinae. Lugduni.

SCHOTTELIUS, J. G. 1641. Teutsche Sprachkunst darinn die . . . Hauptsprache der Teutschen auss ihren Gründen erhoben, der Eigenschafften . . . entdeckt . . . worden. Braunschweig.

——. 1643. Der Teutschen Sprach Einleitung, zu richtiger gewisheit . . . der Teutschen Haubtsprache. Lübeck.

——. 1663. Ausführliche Arbeit Von der Teutschen HaubtSprache, worin enthalten gemelter dieser Haubt-sprache Uhrankunft, Uhralterthum . . . Braunschweig. [Repr. Tübingen, 1967. 2 vols., edited by Wolfgang Hecht.]

——. 1676. Brevis et fundamentalis manductio ad orthographiam et etymologiam in lingua germanica. Braunschweig.

SCIOPPIUS, C. 1623. Paedia politices, sive suppetiae logicae scriptoribus politicis latae, adversus 'απαιδευσίαγ et acerbitatem plebeiorum quorundam judiciorum. Rome.

——. 1628. Grammatica philosophica, sive institutiones grammaticae latinae. Mediolanum.

SHIRLEY, J. 1649. Via ad latinam linguam complanata. The way made plain to the Latine tongue. The rules composed in English and Latine verse. London. [In 1726 edited by J. Thomas Philipps under the title: An essay towards an universal and rational grammar; together with rules for learning Latin, in English verse . . . London.]

——. 1651. Grammatica Anglo-Latina. An English and Latin grammar. London.

——. 1656. The rudiments of grammar. London.

——. 1660². Manductio: Or, a leading of children by the hand through the principles of grammar. London.

SIBSCOTA, G. 1670. The deaf and dumb man's discourse, or a treatise concerning those that are born deaf and dumb, containing a discovery of their knowledge or understanding; as also the method they use to manifest the sentiments of their mind. Together with an additional tract of the reason and speech of inanimate creatures. London.

STILLINGFLEET, E. 1696. A discourse in vindication of the doctrine of trinity. In Works, London, 1710, vol. III, cap. X. 503–505.

TASSONI, A. 1612. Pensieri diversi, 1. IX, quesito XV. In Prose politiche e morali, a cura di G. Rossi, Bari, 1930.

URQUHART, T. 1653. Logopandecteision or an introduction to the universal language.

USSHER, M. 1644. Vindex anglicus; or the perfections of the English language. Defendet, and asserted. Oxford.

VAUGELAS, C. F. DE. 1647. Remarques sur la langue Françoise, nouvelle édition comprenant le texte de l'édition originale, des remarques inédits, une clef inédite de Conrart, tous les commentaires du XVIIe siècle, des notes nouvelles, une introduction et une table analytique des matières par A. Chassang, t. I et II. Versailles, Cerf-Paris, J. Baudry, 1880.

VICO, G. B. 1725. Principi di una Scienza Nuova intorno alla natura dell nazioni, per la quale si ritruovano i principi di altro sistema del Diritto Naturale delle genti. Napoli. [In Opere, ed. by F. Nicolini. Milano-Napoli, 1953.]

VOSSIUS, G. J. 1635. De arte grammatica libri septem. Amsterdami.

WALLIS, J. 1653. Grammatica linguae Anglicanae. Cui praefigitur, de loquela sive sonorum formatione tractatus grammatico-physicus. Oxoniae.

——. 1972. Grammar of the English language, with an introductory grammatico-physical treatise of speech (or on the formation of all speech sounds). A new edition with translation and commentary by J. A. Kemp. London, Longman. [400 pp.]

WARD, S. 1654. Vindicae academiarum, containing some briefe animadversions upon Mr. Websters book, stiled, The examination of academies. Together with an appendix concerning what M. Hobbs, and M. Dell have published on this argument. Oxford, L. Lichfield.

WEBBE, J. 1627. Pueriles confabulatiunculae.

WEBSTER, J. 1654. Academiarum examen, or the examination of academies.

WILKINS, J. 1641. Mercury, or the secret and swift messenger. London.

——. 1668. An essay towards a real character and a philosophical language. (An alphabetical dictionary, wherein all English words . . . are either referred to their places in the philosophical tables, or explained by such words as are in those Tables.) London. [Repr. Menston, Scholar Press, 1968.]

WOLFIUS, H. 1578. De orthographia Germanica, ac potius Suevice nostrate.

Secondary Sources *

AARSLEFF, H. 1964. Leibniz on Locke on language. American Philosophical Quarterly 1.165–188.

——. 1970a. Review of Shapiro, B. 1969. John Wilkins 1614–1672, an Intellectual Biography. American Scientist 58.707–708.

——. 1970b. The history of linguistics and Professor Chomsky. Lg 46.570–585.

* See the Editor's note at the end of the bibliography, p. 380.

——. 1970c. Jacob Boehme. Dictionary of Scientific Biography [DSB], editor-in-chief Charles Coulston Gillispie. New York, Scribners (1970-) 2.222–224.

——. 1971a. 'Cartesian linguistics': History or fantasy? Language Sciences 17.1–12.

——. 1971b. John Amos Comenius. DSB 3.359–363.

——. 1971c. Locke's reputation in 19th century England. The Monist 55.392–422.

ABERCOMBIE, D. 1948. Forgotten phoneticians. TPhS 1–34.

ALLEN, C. G. 1954. The sources of Lily's Latin grammar; a review of the facts and some further suggestions. The Library, 5th ser., 9.85–100.

ALLEN, D. C. 1949. Some theories of the growth and origin of language in Milton's age. PhQ 28.1–16.

——. 1960. The predecessors of Champollion. Proceedings of the American Philosophical Society 104.527–547.

ALSTON, R., and B. DANIELSSON 1964. The earliest dictionary of the known languages of the world. English Studies presented to R. W. Zandvoort on the occasion of his 70th birthday, 9–13. Amsterdam.

ALSTON, R. C. 1965–. A bibliography of the English language from the invention of printing to the year 1800: 1. English grammars written in English and English grammars written in Latin by native speakers. 1965. 119 pp.; 2. Polyglot dictionaries and grammars. Treatises on English written for speakers of French, German, Dutch . . . and Russian. 1967. 311 pp.; 3. Part I: Old English, Middle English, Early Modern English, miscellaneous works, vocabulary. 1970. 205 pp.; 3. Part II. Punctuation, concordances, works on language in general, origin of language, theory of grammar. 1971. 66 pp.; 4. Spelling books. 1967. 277 pp.; 5. The English dictionary. 1966. 195 pp.; 6. Rhetoric, style, elocution, prosody, rhyme, pronunciation, spelling reform. 1969. 202 pp.; 7. Logic, philosophy, epistemology, universal language. 1967. 115 pp.; 8. Treatises on short-hand. 1966. 152 pp.; 9. English dialects, Scottish dialects, cant and vulgar English. 1971. 68 pp.

ANDRADE, E. N. DA C. 1936. The real character of Bishop Wilkins. Annals of Science I, 1.4–12.

APEL, K. O. 1963. Die Idee der Sprache in der Tradition des Humanismus von Dante bis Vico. Archiv für Begriffsgeschichte, 8. Bonn.

APOSTEL, L. 1967. Epistémologie de la linguistique. Logique et Connaissance scientifique, Encyclopédie de la Pléiade, volume publié sous la direction de J. Piaget.

ARENS, H. 1969². Sprachwissenschaft: Der Gang ihrer Entwicklung von der Antike bis zur Gegenwart. Freiburg/München.

ARMSTRONG, R. I. 1965. John Locke's doctrine of signs: A new metaphysics. Journal of the History of Ideas 26.369–382.

AUSTIN, J. L. 1962. How to do things with words. The William James Lectures delivered at Harvard University in 1955, ed. by J. O. Urmson. Oxford, Clarendon Press. [167 pp.]

BACH, E. 1968. Nouns and noun phrases. Universals in linguistic theory, ed. by E. Bach and R. T. Harms, 91–122.

BAILEY, M. L. 1914. Milton and Jakob Boehme. New York.

BAILLOU, J. 1936. L'influence de la pensée philosophique de la Renaissance italienne sur la pensée française. Revue des études italiennes, 1.116–153.

BAKOS, J. 1958. Comenius és a nyelvi nevelés néhány kérdése. Az Egri Pedagógiai Föiskola füzetei 83.5–33.

——. 1961a. Comenius és Vesalius. Az Egri Pedagógiai Föiskola füzetei 207. 135–142.

——. 1961b. Comenius és az emberi beszédhang vizsgálata. Az Egri Pedagógiai Föiskola füzetei 216.247–286.

——. 1961c. Varia Comeniana Hungarica. I. Nyelvészeti és müvelödéstörténeti vonatkozású adatok Comenius magyarországi utóéletéhez. Az Egri Pedagógiai Föiskola füzetei 218.305–314.

BALZ. A. C. A. 1931. Gérauld de Cordemoy, 1620–1684. The Philosophical Review, mai pp. 40.221–245.

——. 1951. Cartesian studies. New York, Columbia University Press.

BANOVIĆ, A. 1965. Le travail de J. A. Comenius à la réforme de l'enseignement des langues vivantes. ACom. 23.205–207.

BARROUX, ROBERT. 1922. Pierre de la Ramée et son influence philosophique: essai sur l'histoire de l'idée de la méthode à l'époque de la Renaissance. Ecole nationale des Chartes, Positions des thèses, 13–20. Paris, Librairie Alphonse Picard.

BATESON, F. W., ed. 1940. The Cambridge bibliography of English literature. I, 600–1660; II, 1660–1800. Supplement 1957. Cambridge University Press. [See also Watson 1971.]

BATTEN, J. M. 1944. John Dury. Chicago.

BENFEY, T. 1869. Geschichte der Sprachwissenschaft und orientalischen Philologie in Deutschland seit dem Anfang des 19. Jh. mit einem Rückblick auf die früheren Zeiten. Geschichte der Wissenschaften in Deutschland. Neuere Zeit 8. New York. London, Johnson, 1965. [Repr. of orig. ed. München 1869.]

BENNETT, J. 1971. Locke, Berkeley, Hume. Central Themes. Oxford.

BENVENISTE, E. 1966. Problèmes de linguistique générale. Paris.

BETHKE, HILDBURG. 1971. Bibliographie der deutschsprachigen Comenius-Literatur 1870–1970. Heydorn 2.105–189.

BLEKASTAD, MILADA. 1969. Comenius, Versuch eines Umrisses von Leben, Werk und Schicksal des Jan Amos Komenský. Oslo, Universitetsforlaget and Praha, Academie. [874 pp.]

BLOOMFIELD, L. 1933. Language. New York, Holt.

Bolelli, T. 1965. Per una storia della ricerca linguistica. Testi e note introduttive. Napoli.

Bolgar, R. R. 1958. The Classical heritage & its beneficiaries. Cambridge.

Bollnow, O. F. 1950. Comenius und Basedow. Die Sammlung 5/3.141 ff.

Bonfante, G. 1953–54. Ideas on the kinship of the European languages from 1200 to 1800. Cahiers d'histoire mondiale 1.679–699.

——. 1955. Una descrizione linguistica d'Europa del 1614. Paideia 10.224–227.

Borodina, M. A. 1959. Zagadnienia logiki i gramatyki w Grammaire générale et raisonnée Port-Royalu. KNf 6.225–236.

Borst, A. 1960. Die Geschichte der Sprachen im abendländischen Denken. WW 10.129–143.

——. 1957–1963. Der Turmbau von Babel. Geschichte der Meinungen über Ursprung und Vielfalt der Sprachen und Völker. 4 vols. in 6. Stuttgart.

Boutroux, E. 1948. La philosophie allemande au XVIIe siècle. Les prédécesseurs de Leibniz: Bacon, Descartes, Hobbes, Spinoza, Malebranche, Locke et la Philosophie de Leibniz. Paris.

Bracken, H. M. 1970a. Chomsky's Languages and mind. Dialogue 9.236–247.

——. 1970b. Chomsky's variations on a theme by Descartes. Journal of the History of Philosophy 18.181–192.

Bradley, H. 1921–23. On the text of Abbo of Fleury's Questiones grammaticales. Proc. Brit. Acad. 10.173–180.

Brambora, J. 1961. Der Saal. Das Meisterwerk von Komenskýs Sprachlehrbüchern. ACom 20.155–178.

——. 1965. Zu Komenskýs Buchtiteln. Erklärungen und Unterscheidungen. ZSlPh 32.254–262.

——. 1971. [Complete bibliography of Comenius' works]. Heydorn. 2.7–104.

Brekle, H. E. 1964. Semiotik und linguistische Semantik in Port-Royal. IF 69. 103–121.

——. 1967. Die Bedeutung der Grammaire générale et raisonnée — bekannt als Grammatik von Port Royal — für die heutige Sprachwissenschaft. IF 72. 1–21.

——. 1969. Review of Chomsky 1966. Linguistics 49.74–91. [Also in Linguistische Berichte 1/1.52–66.]

——, and W. Wildgen, eds. 1970. See Kempelen 1791.

Briggs, W. D. 1913–1914. On certain incidents in Ben Jonson's life. Modern philology 11.279–288.

Brunot, F. 1922–24. Histoire de la langue française des origines à 1900. III–IV. Paris.

Bursill-Hall, G. L. 1971. Speculative grammars of the Middle Ages: The doctrine of the partes orationes of the Modistae. Approaches to Semiotics, 11. The Hague, Mouton. [424 pp.]

Butler, E. H. 1951. The story of British shorthand. London.

CADET, F. 1898. Port-Royal education, tr. by A. D. Jones. London.
CAJORI, F. 1928–29. A history of mathematical notations. 2 vols. Chicago.
CANTEL, R. 1959. Les idées linguistiques de Vieira. IX Congresso internacional de linguistica românica, Universidade de Lisboa, 31.3.–4.4.1959. Actas I–II, Lisboa 1961 (= BF 19.63–75).
CARLTON, W. J. 1911. Timothy Bright, Doctor of Phisicke. A memoir of 'the father of modern shorthand'. London.
CARRÉ, I. 1887. Les pédagogues de Port-Royal. Paris.
CARRERAS Y ARTAU, J. 1946. De Ramón Lull a los modernos ensayos de formación de una lengua universal. Barcelona.
CASSIRER, E. 1953–1957. The philosophy of symbolic forms. 3 vols. New Haven, London.
CAVENAILE, R. 1969. L'enseignement du grec à Port-Royal. Mélanges de linguistique, de philologie et de méthodologie de l'enseignement des langues anciennes offerts à M. Reué Fohalle à l'occasion de son soixante-dixième anniversaire, ed. par Charles Hyart, 289–300. Gembloux.
CH'EN CH'I-HSIANG. 1958. Yü-yen-hsüeh shi kai-yao. Peking.
CHENU, M. D. 1936. Grammaire et théologie aux XIIe et XIIIe siècles. Archives d'histoire doctrinale et littéraire du Moyen Age 10.5–28.
CHEVALIER, J. C. 1967. La Grammaire générale de Port-Royal et la critique moderne. Langages 7.16–33.
——. 1968. Histoire de la syntaxe. Naissance de la notion de complément dans la grammaire française (1530–1750). Genève, Droz. [776 pp.]
CHOMSKY, N. 1964. Current issues in linguistic theory. Janua linguarum, series minor, 38. The Hague, Mouton.
——. 1965. Aspects of the theory of syntax. Cambridge, Mass.
——. 1966. Cartesian linguistics: A chapter in the history of rationalist thought. New York.
——. 1967. The formal nature of language. Appendix in Eric H. Lenneberg, Biological foundations of language, 397–442. New York, Wiley.
——. 1968. Language and mind. New York.
CHRISTENSEN, F. 1946. John Wilkins and the Royal Society's reform of prose style. Modern language quarterly 7.179–187, 279–290.
CHRISTMANN, H. H. 1965. Un aspetto del concetto humboldtiano della lingua e i suoi precursori italiani. Problemi di Lingua e Letteratura Italiana del Settecento, 328–333. Wiesbaden.
COGNET, L. 1950. Cl. Lancelot, Solitaire de Port-Royal. Paris.
COHEN, J. 1954. On the project of a universal character. Mind 63.49–63.
COOK, H. P. 1962. Aristotle. The categories. On interpretation. Harvard University Press.
COOKE, G. K. 1938. English grammarians 1450–1650: A critical survey. Unpublished M. A. Diss., Univ. of London.

CORNELIUS, P. 1965. Languages in seventeenth and early eighteenth-century imaginary voyages. Geneva.

COSERIU, E. 1967. L'arbitraire du signe. Zur Spätgeschichte eines aristotelischen Begriffes. Archiv für das Studium der neueren Sprachen und Literaturen 204.81–112.

——. 1968–69. Geschichte der Sprachphilosophie von der Antike bis zur Gegenwart. I: Von der Antike bis Leibniz. Hrsg. v. G. Narr u. R. Windisch. Tübingen, Romanisches Seminar der Universität.

——. 1971a. Zur Sprachtheorie Juan Luis Vives. Festschrift zum 65. Geburtstag Walter Mönch, hrsg. von W. Dierlamm und W. Drost, 234–255. Heidelberg.

——. 1971b. Das Problem des Übersetzens bei Juan Luis Vives. Interlinguistica, Festschrift zum 60. Geburtstag von Mario Wandruszka, hrsg. von K. R. Bausch und H. M. Gauger, 571–582. Tübingen, Niemeyer.

COUTURAT, L. 1901. La logique de Leibniz. Paris.

——. 1911. Des rapports de la logique et de la linguistique dans le problème de la langue internationale. Revue de Métaphysique et de Morale, Juillet 1911.

COUTURAT, L., and L. LEAU. 1903. Histoire de la langue universelle. Paris.

CUBEDDU. See Formigari.

DAL PRA, M. 1962. Note sulla logica di Hobbes. Rivista critica di storia della filosofia, 429ff.

DAMIRON, J. P. 1903. Essai sur l'histoire de la philosophie en France au XVIIe siècle. Paris.

DANTO, A. 1969. Semantical vehicles, understanding, and innate ideas. Hook 1969: 122–137.

DASCAL, M. 1972. Aspects de la sémiologie de Leibniz. Unpublished Doctoral Diss. Jerusalem.

DAVID, M. V. 1965. Le débat sur les écritures et l'hiéroglyphe aux XVIIe et XVIIe siècles et l'application de la notion de déchiffrement aux écritures mortes. Paris.

DE MAS, E. 1963. La filosofia linguistica e poetica di Francesco Bacone. Filosofia 14.495–542.

DE MAURO, T. 1965. Introduzione alla semantica. Bari.

DE MOTT, B. 1955. Comenius and the real character in England. PMLA 70. 1068–1081.

——. 1957. Science versus mnemonics: 'Notes on John Ray and on John Wilkins' Essay towards a real character and a philosophical language. Isis 48.3–12.

——. 1958. The sources and development of John Wilkins' philosophical language (1668). JEGPh 57.1–13.

DOBSON, E. J. 1957. English pronounciation 1500–1700. 2 vols. Oxford.

DONZÉ, R. 1967 La grammaire générale et raisonnée de Port-Royal: Contribution à l'histoire des idées grammaticales en France. Berne.

ELLIOTT, R. W. V. 1954. Isaac Newton as phonetician. MLR 49.5–12.

——. 1957. Isaac Newton's 'Of an universall language'. MLR 52.1–18.

Ellissen, O. A. 1913. Justus Georg Schottelius, 'Der Jakob Grimm seiner Zeit', 1612–1676. Bericht des Vereins für Geschichte und Altertümer der Stadt Einbeck und Umgebung 9.39–43.

Emery, C. 1947/48. John Wilkins' unversal language. Isis 38.174–185.

Enkvist, N. 1958. Paul Greaves, author of Grammatica Anglicana. Neuphilologische Mitteilungen 59.277–279.

Faithfull, R. G. 1962. Teorie filologiche nell' Italia del primo Seicento con particolare riferimento alla filologia volgare. Studi di Filologia 20.147–313.

Firth, J. R. 1946. The English school of phonetics. TPhS 92–132.

Flasdieck, H. M. 1928. Zur Verfasserschaft der Grammatik von J. Brightland (1711). Anglia, Beiblatt 39. 324–327.

Formigari Cubeddu, L. 1968. Empirismo e critica del linguaggio in Francesco Bacone. Atti della Academia Nazionale dei Lincei, Rediconti della Classe di scienze morali, storiche e filologiche, Ser. VIII, 23.157–175.

——. 1970. Linguistica ed empirismo nel seicento inglese. Bari.

Foucault, M. 1966. Les mots et les choses. Paris, Gallimard.

——. 1967. La Grammaire générale de Port-Royal. Langages 7.7–15.

Frege, G. 1879. Begriffsschrift, eine der arithmetischen nachgebildete Formelsprache des reinen Denkens. Halle.

Fricke, G. 1933. Die Sprachauffassung in der grammatischen Theorie des 16. u. 17. Jh. Zeitschrift f. deutsche Bildung 9.113–123.

Funke, O. 1926. Sprachphilosophische Probleme bei Bacon. Englische Studien 61.43ff. [Repr. in Funke 1965: 51–77.]

——. 1929. Zum Weltsprachensystem in England im 17. Jahrhundert. Anglistische Forschungen 69.145–155.

——. 1938. William Bullokars Bref grammar for English (1586), ein Beitrag zur Geschichte der frühneuenglischen Grammatik. Anglia 62.116–137.

——. 1938a. Grammatica Anglicana von P.Gr. 1594. Wiener Beiträge zur englischen Philol. 60.11–51.

——. 1940. Ben Jonsons English grammar. Anglia 62.116–134.

——. 1941. Die Frühzeit der englischen Grammatik. Bern.

——. 1954. On the system of grammar. Archivum Linguisticum 6.1–19.

——. 1959. On the sources of John Wilkins's Philosophical language (1668). ES 40.208–214.

——. 1965. Gesammelte Aufsätze zur Anglistik und zur Sprachphilosophie. Bern.

Gabrielson, A. 1929. Professor Kennedy's Bibliography of writings on the English language: A review with a list of additions and corrections. Studia Neophilologica 2.117–168.

——. 1935. Elisha Cole's Synkrisis, 1675, as a source of information on seventeenth century English. Englische Studien 70.149–152.

——. 1941/42. A few notes on Gil's Logonomia Anglica 1619. Studia Neophilologica 14.331–339.

De Gandillac, M. 1966. Histoire des théories du langage. Le Langage, Vol. II. Actes du XIIIe Congrès des Soc. de philos. de langue française, 69–82. Genève.

García, C. 1960. Contribución a la historia de los conceptos gramáticales. La aportación del Brocense. RFE 71.

Gargani, A. G. 1966. Idea, mondo e linguaggio in T. Hobbes e J. Locke. Annali della Scuola Normale Superiore di Pisa, Lettere Storia e Filosofia, serie II, 35.251–292.

Gauger, H.-M. 1967. Bernardo Aldrete (1565–1645): Ein Beitrag zur Vorgeschichte der romanischen Sprachwissenschaft. RJb 18.207–248.

Geissler, H. 1959. Comenius und die Sprache. Heidelberg.

Gibson, J. 1917. Locke's theory of knowledge and its historical relations. Cambridge.

Gibson, R. 1950. Francis Bacon: A bibliography of his works and of Baconiana to the year 1750. Oxford.

Gilbert, N. W. 1960. Renaissance concepts of method. New York.

Givner, D. A. 1959. A study of George Berkeley's theory of linguistic meaning. With a discussion of Locke's account of language and a consideration of the relevance of their philosophies of science. Columbia Univ. diss. [Microfilm].

——. 1962. Scientific preconceptions in Locke's philosophy of language. JHI 23.340–54.

Gleason, H. A. 1965. Linguistics and English grammar. New York.

Goudschaal, P. R. 1903. Ein holländisches Kurzschriftsystem aus dem Jahre 1650. Archiv für Stenographie 55.110–115.

Grana, G. 1965. Lingua italiana e lingua francese nella polemica galeani Napione-Cesarotti. Problemi di Lingua e Letteratura Italiana del Settecento, 338–353. Wiesbaden.

Greenwood, O. 1949. The curious history of English grammar. The Listener 42.13–14.

Guilhon, E., ed. 1950. Descartes et le cartésianisme hollandais. Paris et Amsterdam.

Gunderson, K. 1964. Descartes, La Mettrie, language and machines. Philosophy 39. 193–222.

Gundolf, F. 1930. Justus Georg Schottel. Deutschkundliches. Friedrich Panzer-Festschrift, hrsg. von H. Teske, 70–86. Heidelberg.

Gunther, R. T. 1925. The philosophical society. Early science in Oxford, vol. 4. Oxford.

Haase, A. 1935. Syntaxe française du XVIIe siècle, Nouvelle édition par M. Obert. Paris.

HALL, R. A. 1969. Some recent studies on Port-Royal and Vaugelas. Acta Linguistica Hafniensia 12.207–233.

HANKAMER, P. 1927. Die Sprache, ihr Begriff und ihre Deutung im sechzehnten und siebzehnten Jahrhundert. [Repr. Hildesheim, Olms, 1965.]

HANZELI, VICTOR EGON. 1969. Missionary linguistics in New France: A study of seventeenth-and-eighteenth-century descriptions of American Indian languages. Janua linguarum, Series maior, 29. The Hague, Mouton. [141 pp.]

HARMAN, G. 1968. Review of Chomsky 1966. The Philosophical Review 77.229–235.

HARNOIS, G. 1929. Les théories du langage en France de 1660 à 1821. Paris.

HASSINGER, H. 1951. Johann Joachim Becher 1635–1682. Wien.

HEEROMA, K. 1961. De Nederlandse bewerkingen van Comenius' 'Janua linguarum'. TsNTL 78.247–274.

HEINIMANN, S. 1965. Die Lehre vom Artikel in den romanischen Sprachen von der mittelalterlichen Grammatik zur modernen Sprachwissenschaft. Ein Beitrag zur Geschichte der grammatischen Begriffsbildung. Vox Romanica 24.23–43.

HELBIG, G. 1970. Geschichte der neueren Sprachwissenschaft. Leipzig.

HELLER, L. G. 1960. English linguistic terminology, 995–1645. Dissertation, Columbia University.

HENDRICH, J. 1937. Komenského logica. Archiv pra bádáni o životě a spisech J. A. Komenského 14.131–138.

HERCZEG, G. G. 1965. La struttura del periodo nel Settecento. Problemi di lingua a letteratura Italiana del settecento, 353–373. Wiesbaden.

HEUSSLER, H. 1889. F. Bacon und seine geschichtliche Stellung. Breslau.

HEYDORN, HEINZ-JOACHIM, ed. 1971. Jan Amos Comenius: Geschichte und Aktualität 1670–1970. 2 vols. Glashütten im Taunus, Detlev Auvermann.

HILLER, R. 1883. Die Lateinmethode des Comenius. Zschopau.

HJELMSLEV, L. 1928. Principes de grammaire générale. Copenhagen.

——. 1935. La catégorie des cas, étude de grammaire générale, I. Aarhus.

——. 1963. Prolegomena to a theory of language. Madison. Wisc.

HOCKETT, C. 1963. The problem of universals in language. Universals of language, ed. by J. Greenberg, 1–29. Cambridge, MIT Press.

HOFMANN, F. 1970a. Über den pädagogischen Gehalt des 'Lexicon reale Pansophicum' J. A. Komenskýs. In Schaller 1970: 74–84.

——. 1970b. SAL — Bildung zu vollem Menschentum. Eine pädagogische Betrachtung zu J. A. Komenskýs Spätwerk 'Triertium catholicum'. In Schaller 1970: 88–90.

HOOK, S, ed. 1969. Language and philosophy. New York.

HORÁLEK, K. 1968. Tradice a novátorství v jazykovědě (Komenský jako filosof jazyka). SS 29.22–26.

HORN, J. 1910. Das englische Verb nach den Zeugnissen und Grammatiken des 17. und 18. Jahrhunderts. Giessen.

HOWELL, A. C. 1946. Res et verba: Words and things. English literary history 13.131–142.

HOWELL, W. S. 1956. Logic and rhetoric in England, 1500–1700. Princeton University Press.

HUTIN, S. 1960. Les disciples anglais de Jacob Boehme. Paris.

ISING, E. 1957/58. Wolfgang Ratkes Deutsche Grammatiken. I, Einleitung. WZUB 7.405–406.

——. 1959. See Ratichius 1959.

——. 1960. Zur Entwicklung der Sprachauffassung in der Frühzeit der deutschen Grammatik. FuF 34.367–374.

ISRAEL, A. 1892. Das Verhältnis der Didactica magna des Comenius zu der Didaktik Ratkes. Monatshefte d. Com. Ges. 1. 173–195, 242–274.

IVIĆ, M. 1956. Trends in linguistics, trans. by Muriel Heppell. The Hague. [Transl. into German München, 1971.]

JAGEMANN, H. C. G. v. 1893. Notes on the Language of J. G. Schottel. PMLA 8.408–431.

JELLINEK, M. H. 1906. Zur Geschichte einiger grammatischen Theorien und Begriffe. IF 19.272–316.

——. 1913. Geschichte der neuhochdeutschen Grammatik von den Anfängen bis auf Adelung. 2 vols. Heidelberg.

JESPERSEN, OTTO. 1924. The philosophy of grammar. London.

JIRICZEK, O. L. 1902. Alexander Gill. Studien zur vergleichenden Literaturgeschichte, ed. Max Koch, 2.129–145.

——. 1903. See Gill 1621.

JONES, R. F. 1930. Science and English prose style in the third quarter of the seventeenth century. PMLA 45.977–1009.

——. 1932. Science and language in England of the mid-seventeenth century. JEGPh 31.315–331.

——, ed. 1951. The seventeenth century. Studies in the History of English Thought and Literature from Bacon to Pope, by Richard Foster Jones and Others, Writing in His Honour. Stanford/London.

——. 1953. The triumph of the English language. London.

KAMPF, L. 1967. Review of Chomsky 1966. College English 28.403–408.

KAYSER, W. 1930. Böhmes Natursprachenlehre und ihre Grundlagen. Euphorion 31.521–562.

KENNEDY, A. G. 1927. A bibliography of writings on the English language. Cambridge/New Haven.

KING, R. D. 1969. Historical linguistics and generative grammar. Englewood Cliffs, N.J.

KNEALE, W., and M. KNEALE. 1962. The development of logic. Oxford, Clarendon Press.

KNORRECK, M. 1938. Der Einfluss des Rationalismus auf die englische Sprache. Sprache und Kultur, 30. Breslau.

KNOWLSON, J. R. 1963. The ideal languages of Vieiras, Foigny, and Tyssot de Patot. Journal of the History of Ideas 24.269–278.

——. 1965. The idea of gesture as a universal language in the XVIIth and XVIIIth centuries. Journal of the History of Ideas 26.495–508.

KOBYLANS'KYJ, B. V. 1964. Korotkyj ohljad istoriji movoznavstva. Kyjiv.

KÖKERITZ, H. 1935. English pronunciation as described in shorthand systems of the 17th and 18th centuries. Studia Neophilologica 7.

——. 1938–39. Alexander Gill, 1621, on the dialects of South and East England. Studia Neophilologica 11.277–288.

KOLDEWEY, F. E. 1899. Justus Georg Schottelius und seine Verdienste um die deutsche Sprache. ZfdU 13.

KORNINGER, S. 1957. Edward Brerewoods 'Enqviries': Ein Beitrag zur Sprachtheorie des frühen siebzehnten Jahrhunderts. Studies in English Language and Literature, presented to ... Karl Brunner ... 70th birthday, ed. by S. Korninger, 87–102. Wien.

KRETZMANN, N. 1967. History of semantics. The Encyclopedia of Philosophy, ed. by Paul Edwards, 7.358–406.

——. 1968. The main thesis of Locke's semantic theory. Philosophical Review 77/2.175–198.

KROOK, D. 1956. Thomas Hobbes's doctrine of meaning and truth. Philosophy 31.3–22.

KUKENHEIM, L. 1962. De periodisering in de Franse linguistiek. HandNFC, 27.131–133.

——. 1966². Esquisse historique de la linguistique française et de ses rapports avec la linguistique générale. Leiden.

KUNOW, I. VON. 1921. Sprach- und Literarkritik bei Antoine Arnauld. Erlangen. Romanische Forschungen 39.67–200.

KVAČALA, J. 1888. Comenius und Baco. Beiträge zur Comeniusforschung. Pädagogium.

——. 1903–04. Die pädagogische Reform des Comenius in Deutschland bis zum Ausgange des XVII. Jahrhunderts. Monumenta germaniae paedagogica, (26 and 32). Berlin.

——. 1909. Thomas Campanella. Berlin.

LAKOFF, G. 1971. On generative semantics. In Semantics: An interdisciplinary reader in philosophy, linguistics and psychology, ed. by D. Steinberg and L. A. Jakobovits, 232–296. Cambridge University Press.

LAKOFF, R. 1969. Review of Arnauld/Lancelot 1966. Lg 45.343–364.

LAMBLEY, K. 1920. The teaching and cultivation of the French language in

England during Tudor and Stuart times, with an introductory chapter on the preceding period. Manchester.

LANGDON, M. 1968. See Malkiel.

LANTOINE, H. 1874. Histoire de l'enseignement secondaire en France au XVIIe siècle. Thèse, Paris.

LATTMANN, J. 1898. Ratichius und die Ratichianer. Göttingen.

LEHNERT, M. 1936. Die Grammatik des englischen Sprachmeisters John Wallis (1615–1703). Breslau.

——. 1937. Die Abhängigkeit frühneuenglischer Grammatiker. Engl. Studien 72.192–206.

——. 1938. Die Anfänge der wissenschaftlichen und praktischen Phonetik in England. Archiv für das Studium der neueren Sprachen 173.163–180; 174. 28–35.

LENDERS, W. 1968. Die Verwendung des Terminus 'Kommunikation' bei G. W. Leibniz u. Chr. Wolff. Institut f. Phonetik u. Kommunikationsforschung, IPK-Forschungsbericht 68/2. Bonn.

LEROY, M. 1960. Du Cratyle de Platon à la linguistique moderne. AUI Sec. III 6/2.41–45.

——. 1971[2]. Les grands courants de la linguistique moderne, Bruxelles. [First ed., 1963.]

——. 1966. Cordemoy et 'le Bourgeois gentilhomme'. Acad. Roy. de Belgique, Bulletin de la Classe des Lettres et des Sciences morales et politiques, 52. 76–95.

——. 1970. Un précurseur de la phonétique: Cordemoy. Actes du Xe Congrès Intern. des Linguistes, Bucarest, 2.307–311. Bucarest.

LESER, E. 1912. Geschichte der grammatischen Terminologie im 17. Jahrhundert. Dissertation, Freiburg.

LEVY, R. 1963. A survey of the evolution of French linguistics. MLJ 47.14–16.

LEWIS, G. See RODIS-LEWIS.

LIAÑO PACHECO, J. M. 1971. Sanctius el Brocense. Madrid. 114 pp. + 2 pp. facsimiles. Tesis doctoral, Universidad de Salamanca [Contains a minute bibliography of Sanctius 1587.]

LIESE, E. 1904. Die neueste Sprachenmethode des J. A. Comenius. Neuwied.

LINSKY, S. S. 1966. John Wilkins' linguistic views. ZAA 14.56–60.

LIVET, C.-L. 1859. La grammaire française et les grammairiens du XVIe siècle. Paris.

LOEWE, M. L. 1829. Historiae criticae grammaticae universalis seu philosophicae lineamenta. Dresden.

LOUNSBURY, F. G. 1969. Language and culture. In Hook, 1969: 3–29.

LOWISCH, M. 1889. Zur englischen Aussprache von 1650–1760 nach frühenglischen Grammatiken. Kassel.

MAJEWSKA-GRZEGORCZYKOWA, R. 1961. Teoria czasownika w 'Gramatyce ogólnej' Port-Royal. KNf 8.411–420.

MALKIEL, Y., and M. LANGDON. 1968. History and histories of linguistics. Romance Philology 22.530–574.

MANZ, G. 1909. Das Verbum nach den französischen Grammatiken von 1500–1700. Halle.

MARTIN, R. M. 1953/54. On the semantics of Hobbes. Philosophy and Phenomenological Research 14.205–211.

MARTINET, A. 1960. Eléments de linguistique générale. Paris.

MARX, O. 1967. The history of the biological basis of language. Appendix B in Lenneberg, E. H., Biological foundations of language, 443–469.

MAS, E. DE. See DE MAS.

MATHIESEN, R. 1970. Review of Arnauld 1964–67 and of Arnauld and Lancelot 1846, 1966, 1967, and 1968. Lg 46.126–130.

MAURO, T. DE. See DE MAURO.

MAZZONI, G. 1880. Il saggio sulla filosofia delle lingue. Firenze.

MCCAWLEY, J. D. 1968. The role of semantics in a grammar. In Universals in linguistic theory, ed. by E. Bach and R. T. Harms, 125–169.

——. 1971. Where do noun phrases come from. In Semantics . . ., ed. by D. D. Steinberg and L. A. Jakobovits, 217–231.

MCCRACKEN, G. E. 1948 Athanasius Kircher's Universal Polygraphy. Isis 39.215–228.

MELIN, O. 1927–29. Stenografiens historia. Stockholm.

MENDELS, J. I. H. 1936. Een phoneticus uit de 17de eeuw. Neophilologus 21. 219–225.

MERRILL, J. 1962. The presentation of case and declension in early Spanish grammars. ZRPh 78.162–171.

METCALF, G. J. 1953. Schottel and historical linguistics. GR 28.113–125.

——. 1966. Andreas Jäger and his 'De lingua vetustissima Europae' (1686). MLN 81.489–493.

MICHAEL, I. 1970. English grammatical categories and the tradition to 1800. Cambridge, University Press.

MIEL, J. 1969. Pascal, Port-Royal, and Cartesian linguistics. JHI 30.261–271.

MIGLIORINI, B. 1960. Storia della lingua italiana. Firenze.

MILES, K. 1933. The strong verb in Schottel's Ausführliche Arbeit von der Teutschen Haubt Sprache. Dissertation, University of Pennsylvania.

MINCKWITZ, M. J. 1897. Der Purismus bei Übersetzern, Lexikographen, Grammatikern und Verfassern von Observations und Remarques. Berlin, Gronau. [= Part I of the Phil. Diss.: Beiträge zur Geschichte der französischen Grammatik im siebzehnten Jahrhundert. Zürich, 1897.]

MIŠKOVSKÁ, V. T. 1959. La 'Panglottie' de J. A. Komenský. PhP 2.97–105.

——. 1961a. Linguarum methodi novissimae capita duo, XIV et XV. ACom 20.53–75.

——. 1961b. Empirisme ou invention à la base lexicale de la Panglottie [de J. A. Komenský]? ACom 20.189–197.

——. 1962. Comenius (Komenský) on lexical symbolism in an artificial language. Philosophy 37.238–243.

MOK, Q. I. M. 1968. Vaugelas et la 'désambigüisation' de la parole. Lingua 21.303–321.

MOORE, J. L. 1910. Tudor-Stuart views on the growth, status and destiny of the English language. Studien zur englischen Philologie 41. Halle.

MOTT, B. DE. See DE MOTT.

MOUNIN, G. 1959. Une illusion d'optique en histoire de la linguistique. TIL 4.7–13.

——. 1967. Histoire de la linguistique des origines au XXe siècle. Paris.

MULCASTER, R. 1925. The first part of the Elementarie (1582), ed. by E. T. Campagnac. Oxford.

MURRAY, DAVID. 1905–1906. Some early grammars and other school books in use in Scotland more particularly those printed at or relating to Glasgow. Royal Philosophical Society of Glasgow, Proceedings, 36.266–97; 37.142–91.

NELSON, W. 1952. The teaching of English in Tudor grammar schools. Studies in Philol. 49.119–143.

NYROP, K. 1925. Grammaire historique de la langue française, vol. 5. Copenhague, Gyldendalske Boghandel.

OGDEN, C. K. 1934. The magic of words. I: Idola fori; II: From Bacon to Berkeley; III: Berkeley's theory of signs. Psyche 14.9–87.

ONG, W. J. 1958a. Ramus, method, and the decay of dialogue. Cambridge.

——. 1958b. Ramus and Talon inventory; a short-title inventory of the published works of Peter Ramus (1515–1572) and of Omer Talon (ca. 1510–1562) in their original and in their variously altered forms . . . Cambridge.

OSSELTON, O. E. 1958. Branded words in English dictionaries before Johnson. Groningen Studies in English, 7.

OTTO, K. F. 1972. Die Sprachgesellschaften des 17. Jahrhunderts. Sammlung Metzler, M 109. Stuttgart.

PAFORT, E. 1946. A group of early Tudor school-books. Library, 4th ser., 26. 227–261.

PALMER, D. J. 1965. The rise of English studies. An account of the study of English language and literature from its origins to the making of the Oxford English School, published for the Univ. of Hull by the Oxford University Press.

PANCONCELLI-CALZIA, G. 1961. 3000 Jahre Stimmforschung. Die Wiederkehr des Gleichen. Marburg.

PATOČKA, J. 1971. Die Philosophie der Erziehung des J. A. Comenius. Paderborn, Schöningh.

PEI, M. 1958. One language for the world. New York.

PERCIVAL, W. K. 1969. The notion of usage in Vaugelas and in the Port-Royal grammar. PCLS 6.165–176.

——. 1972. On the non-existence of Cartesian linguistics. Cartesian Studies, ed. by R. J. Butler, 137–145. Oxford, Blackwell's.

PETERS, R. S. 1956. Hobbes. London.

PISANI, V. 1966. Profilo storico della linguistica moderna. Paideia 21.297–308.

PLATTNER, J. 1967. Zum Sprachbegriff von J. G. Schottel, aufgrund der 'Ausführlichen Arbeit von der Teutschen Haupt Sprache 1663. Dissertation, Zürich.

PLEZIA, M. 1966. Dzieje filologii klasycznej w Polsce od początku XVII do początku XX w. Studia i materiały z driejów nauki polskiej, Ser. A: Hist. nauk społecznych 9.65–85.

POLDAUF, I. 1948. On the history of some problems of English grammar before 1800. Prague Studies in English, 55. Praha.

PRANTL, C. 1855–1870. Geschichte der Logik im Abendlande. 4 vols. Leipzig.

PRIDEAUX, G. D. 1967. Review of Chomsky 1966. CJL 13.50.

PUPPO, M. 1957. Appunti sul problema della costruzione della frase nel Settecento. Boll. Ist. Lingue Estere 5.76–78. Genova.

QUINTANA, R. 1930. Notes on English Educational Opinion during the Seventeenth Century. Studies in Philol. 27.265–292.

RAUMER, R. v. 1870. Geschichte der germanischen Philologie vorzugsweise in Deutschland. München.

REICHARD, E. C. 1747. Versuch einer Historie der deutschen Sprachkunst. Hamburg.

REICHENBACH, H. 1947. Elements of symbolic logic. London, Macmillan.

REICHENBACH, R. E. W. 1842. Commentationes de linguae doctrina universali. Halle, Dissertation.

RICKEN, U. 1963. La discussion linguistique en France au 18e siècle, reflet de la lutte philosophique du siècle des lumières. AUI 9.71–88.

——. 1965. Un phonéticien philosophe du 17-ème siècle. Omagiu lui Alexandru Rosetti la 70 de ani, 761–765. Bucureşţi.

RIEMENS, K.-J. 1919. Esquisse historique de l'enseignement du français en Hollande du XVIe au XIXe siècle. Leyde.

RIOUX, G. 1963. L'oeuvre pédagogique de Wolfgang Ratichius. Paris.

RIVAUD, A. 1951. Claude Lancelot, éducateur janséniste. Revue des deux mondes 305–312.

ROBBE, M. 1955. Philosophy and politics in Hobbes. Philosophical Quarterly 5.125–146. [Also in Hobbes studies, ed. by K. C. Brown, Oxford, 1965.]

ROBINS, R. H. 1951. Ancient and mediaeval grammatical theory in Europe, with particular reference to modern linguistic doctrine. London.

——. 1952. Noun and verb in universal grammar. Lg 28.289–298.

——. 1966. The development of the word class system of the European grammatical tradition. FL 2.3–19.

——. 1967. A short history of linguistics. London.

[RODIS-]LEWIS, G. 1950. Augustinisme et cartésianisme dans Port-Royal. In Descartes et le cartésianisme hollandais, ed. by E. Guilhon, 131–182. Paris/ Amsterdam.

——. 1964. Le domaine propre de l'homme chez les cartésiens. Journal of the History of Philosophy 2. 157–188.

——. 1966. Langage humain et signes naturels dans le cartésianisme. Le Langage (Actes du XIIIe congrès des sociétés de philosophie de langue française), 132–136. Neuchâtel.

——. 1968. Un théoricien du langage au XVIIe siècle: Bernard Lamy. Le Français Moderne 36.19–50.

RÖSLER, M. 1919. Veraltete Wörter in der Grammatica Anglicana von 1594. Engl. Studien 53.168–195.

ROOS, H. 1952. Die Modi significandi des Martinus von Dacia: Forschungen zur Geschichte der Sprachlogik im Mittelalter. Beiträge zur Geschichte der Philosophie u. Theologie des Mittelalters, 37. Münster.

ROSENFIELD, L. D. COHEN. 1941. From beast-machine to man-machine; animal soul in French letters from Descartes to la Mettrie. New York, Oxford University Press.

ROSETTI, A. 1969. Actualité de la 'Grammaire' de Port-Royal. Wissenschaftliche Zeitschrift der Humboldt-Universität zu Berlin, Ges.-Sprachw. R, 18.587–588.

ROSIELLO, L. 1965. Analisi semantica dell' espressione genio della lingua nelle discussioni linguistiche del Settecento Italiano. Problemi di Lingua e Letteratura Italiana del Settecento, 373–385. Wiesbaden.

——. 1967. Linguistica illuminista. Bologna.

ROSIER, J. L. 1961. The sources and methods of Minsheu's 'Guide into the tongues' (1617). PhQ 40.68–76.

ROSSI, P. 1957. Francesco Bacone. Dalla magia alla Scienze. Bari. [English translation by S. Rabinovitch, 1968.]

——. 1960. Clavis universalis. Milano/Napoli.

——. 1968. Linguisti d'oggi e filosofi del Seicento. Lingua e Stile 3.1–20.

ROY, E. 1891. La vie et les oeuvres de Charles Sorel. Paris.

RUSSEL, L. J. 1939. Note on the term *Semeiotike* in Locke. Mind 48.405–6.

SADLER, J. E. 1966. J. A. Comenius and the concept of universal education. London.

SAHLIN, G. 1928. César Chesneau du Marsais et son rôle dans l'evolution de la Grammaire générale. Paris.

SAINTE-BEUVE, C. A. DE. 1953–55. Port-Royal. Texte presentée et annotée par Maxime Leroy. 3 vols. Paris, Bibl. de la Pléiade.

SAISSET, E. 1862. Précurseurs et disciples de Descartes. Paris.

SALMON, V. 1961a. James Shirley and some problems of 17th century grammar. ASNS 197.287–296.

——. 1961b. Joseph Webbe: Some seventeenth-century views on language-teaching and the nature of meaning. Bibliothèque d'humanisme et renaissance 23.324–340.

——. 1964. Problems of language-teaching: A discussion among Hartlib's friends. MLR 59.13–24.

——. 1966a. The evolution of Dalgarno's 'Ars signorum' (1661). Studies in language and literature in honour of Margaret Schlauch, 353–371. Warszawa.

——. 1966b. Language-planning in seventeenth-century England, its context and aims. In memory J. R. Firth, ed. by C. E. Bazell et al., 370–397. London.

——. 1969. Review of Chomsky 1966. JL 5.165–187.

——. 1972. The works of Francis Lodwick: A study of his writings in the intellectual context of the seventeenth century. London, Longman.

SALUS, P. H., ed. 1969. On language: Plato to von Humboldt. New York.

——. 1969. Pre-pre-Cartesian linguistics. PCLS 5.429–434.

SANDYS, J. E. 1915. A short history of classical scholarship, from the sixth century B.C. to the present day. Cambridge.

SAUSSURE, F. DE. 1916. Cours de linguistique générale. Paris.

SCHALLER, K. 1958. Pan: Untersuchungen zur Comenius-Terminologie. The Hague, Mouton.

——. 1967. Die Pädagogik des Johann Amos Comenius und die Anfänge des pädagogischen Realismus im 17. Jahrhundert. 2., durchges. Aufl. Heidelberg, Quelle & Meyer.

——. et al. 1970. Jan Amos Komenský: Wirkung eines Werks nach drei Jahrhunderten. Heidelberg, Quelle & Meyer.

SCHEUERWEGHS, G. 1960. English grammars in Dutch and Dutch grammars in English in the Netherlands before 1800. English studies 41.129–167.

SCHEUERWEGHS, G., and E. VORLAT. 1959. Problems of the history of English grammar. Eng. Studien 40.135–143.

SCHIAFFINI, A. 1953²a. Momenti di storia della lingua italiana. Roma.

——. 1953b. Aspetti della crisi linguistica italiana del Settecento. In Schiaffini 1953a: 91–132.

SCHLEIFF, A. 1938. Sprachphilosophie und Interpretationstheorie im Denken des 17. Jahrhunderts. Zeitschrift für Kirchengeschichte, III. serie, VIII, 57.133–152.

SCHMARSOW, A. 1877. Leibniz und Schottelius. Quellen u. Forschungen zur Sprach- und Culturgeschichte der germanischen Völker, No. 23.

SCHMIDT, S. J. 1968. Sprache und Denken als sprachphilosophisches Problem von Locke bis Wittgenstein. Den Haag, Nijhoff.

SCHOLEM, G. G. 1955³. Major trends in Jewish mysticism.

——. 1965. On the Kabbalah and its symbolism, trans. by R. Manheim.

SEBBA, G. 1964. Bibliographia cartesiana. La Haye.

SEGERT, STANISLAV, and BERÁNEK, KAREL. 1967. Orientalistik an der Prager Universität, Erster Teil; 1348–1848. Praha, Universita Karlova. [226 pp.]

SERRUS, C. 1933. Le parallélisme logico-grammatical. Thèse, Paris.

SHAPIRO, B. 1969. John Wilkins 1614–1672: An intellectual biography. Berkeley/ Los Angeles.

SHAW, A. E. 1901. The earliest Latin grammars in English. trans. by Bibl. Soc., 5.39–65.

SIMONE, R. 1969. Semiologia agostiniana. La cultura 7.88–117.

——. 1971. Communicazione semiotica e communicazione non-semiotica in Cordemoy. La cultura 9.376–391.

SIMONS, P. J. 1950. Moderne en antieke taalwetenschap: Vergelijkingen en synthesen. NT 43.75–83.

SKEAT, W. W. 1888. English grammars. Notes and queries, ser. 7, 6.121–122, 243–244, 302–303. [Repr. in his Student's pastime 1896 with slight omissions.]

SMIT, A. 1934. Mededeelingen betreffende een aantal Oud-Hollandsche handschriften over stenografie. De Groote schrijver, August 1934, 2–16.

SNYDERS, G. 1965. La pédagogie en France aux XVIIe et XVIIIe siècles. Paris, PUF.

SÖDERLIND, J. 1964. The attitude to language expressed by or ascertainable from English writers of the sixteenth and seventeenth centuries. Studia neophilologica 36.111–126. London.

SONG, SO-RYONG. 1964. Onohagui paltal. Chosonohak 5.78–83.

SPINGARN, J. E., ed. 1908. Critical essays of the seventeenth century, vol. 2. Oxford.

STARNES, T. DE WITT, and G. E. NOYES. 1946. The English dictionary from Cawdrey to Johnson, 1604–1755. Chapel Hill, N. Carolina.

STENGEL, E. 1890. Chronologisches Verzeichnis französischer Grammatiken vom Ende des 14. bis zum Ausgang des 18. Jahrhunderts. Oppeln.

STERNISCHA, H. 1913. Deux grammairiens de la fin du XVIIe siècle: L. Aug. Alemand et Andry de Bois-Regard. Thèse, Colin.

STIMSON, D. 1931. Dr. Wilkins and the Royal Society. Journal of Modern History 3.539–563.

STÖTZNER, P. 1892/93. Ratichianische Schriften I, II. Neudrucke pädagogischer Schriften. IX, XII, ed. by A. Richter. Leipzig.

SVOBODA, C. 1925. La grammaire latine depuis le Moyen Âge jusqu' au commencement du XIXe siècle. Rev. des Etud. Lat. 3.69–77.

SZATHMÁRI, I. 1965. István Geleji Katona und die deutschen Sprachgesellschaften des 17. Jahrhunderts. Acta Linguistica Acad. Sc. Hungaricae 15.323–330.

SZÉPE, C. 1967. Review of Chomsky 1966. Filologiai Közlöny 13.248–251.

TAGLIAVINI, C. 1964. Panorama di storia della linguistica. Bologna.

——. 1968. Panorama di storia della filologia germanica. Bologna.

TEETER, K. V. 1966. The history of linguistics: New lamps for old. Report of the

17th Annual Round Table Meeting on Linguistics and Language Studies, 83–95. Washington, D.C., Georgetown.

TELLE, JULIEN AIMABLE. 1874². Les grammairiens français depuis l'origine de la grammaire en France jusqu' aux dernières oeuvres connues. Paris, Firmin Didot. [Reprint Genève, Slatkine, 1967.]

THOMSEN, G. 1945. Historia de la lingüística. Madrid.

THOMSEN, V. 1927. Geschichte der Sprachwissenschaft bis zum Ausgang des 19. Jahrhunderts, übersetzt von H. Pollack. Halle. [1ere éd. danoise, 1902.]

TÖRNEBOHM, H. 1960. A study in Hobbes' theory of denotation and truth. Theoria 26.53–70.

TOLMER, L. 1938. Un appendice au discours physique de la parole de Cordemoy (1668): La leçon phonétique de J.-B. Hamel (1673). FM 6.243–251.

TOȘA, A. 1967. John Locke si problemele limbajului. CLing 12.199–205.

TRABALZA, C. 1908. Storia della grammatica italiana. Milano.

TURNBULL, G. 1947. Hartlib, Dury and Comenius. London, Liverpool Univ. Pr. and Hodder & Stoughton.

——. 1953. Samuel Hartlib's influence on the early history of the Royal Society. Notes and records of the Royal Society 10.101–130.

UITTI, K. D. 1969–70. Descartes and Port-Royal in two diverse retrospects. Review of Chomsky 1966 and Donzé 1967. Romance Philology 23.75–85.

VERBURG, P. A. 1951. Taal en functionaliteit: Een historisch-critische studie over de opvattingen aangaande de functies der taal vanaf de prae-humanistische philologie van Orleans tot de rationalistische linguistik van Bopp. Wageningen.

——. 1968. Ennoësis of language in 17th century philosophy. Lingua 21.558–572.

——. 1969. Hobbes' calculus of words. ITL 5.62–69.

VERHAAR, J. W. M. 1971. Philosophy and linguistic theory. Language Sciences 14.1–11.

VERSCHUUR, A. 1924. Een Nederlandsche Uitspraakleere der 17e eeuw: De Spreeckonst van Petrus Montanus van Delft (1635). Amsterdam.

VIANO, C. A. 1960. John Locke: Dal razionalismo all' illuminismo. Torino.

VICKERY, B. C. 1953. The significance of John Wilkins in the history of bibliographical classification. Libri 2.326–343.

VINAZA, CONDE DE LA. 1893. Biblioteca historica de la filología española. Madrid. [Libro segundo: De la gramática Primera Parte: Analogía y sintaxis, 189–385.] [Bibliography!]

VISCARDI, A. 1947. Il problema della costruzione nelle polemiche linguistiche del Settecento. Paideia 2.193–214.

VITALE, M. 1967. La questione della lingua. Palermo.

VOGT, GIDEON. 1894. Wolfgang Ratichius, der Vorgänger des Amos Comenius. Die Klassiker der Pädagogik, 17. Langensalza. [298 pp.]

VORLAT, E. 1963. Progress in English grammar 1585–1735. A study of the development of English grammar and of the interdependence among the early English grammarians. Catholic University of Louvain. 4 vols.

VOTRUBOVA, D. 1955. Einheit des Denkens und der Sprache bei Comenius. Český jazyk 5.169–188. Praha.

WAFFENSCHMIDT, W. G., (ed.). 1962. Zur mechanischen Sprachüberzetzung: Ein Programmierungsversuch aus dem Jahre 1661. J. J. Becher: Allgemeine Verschlüsselung der Sprachen ... Mit einer interpretierenden Einleitung von W. G. Waffenschmidt. Veröff. der Wirtschaftshochschule Mannheim 1,10. Stuttgart.

WALLACE, K. R. 1943. Francis Bacon on communication and rhetoric. Chapel Hill.

——. 1956. Aspects of modern rhetoric in Francis Bacon. Quarterly Journal of Speech 42.4.

WATANABE, S. 1958. Studien zur Abhängigkeit der frühenglischen Grammatiken von den mittelalterlichen Lateingrammatiken. Münster, Dissertation.

WATERMAN, J. 1963. Perspectives in linguistics. Chicago.

WATSON, F. 1903. Curriculum and textbooks of the English schools in the first half of the seventeenth century. Trans. Bibliogr. Soc. 6.159–267.

——. 1908. The English grammar schools to 1660: Their curriculum and practice. Cambridge.

——. 1912. English grammar: Historical development. A Cyclopedia of Education, ed. by P. Monroe, 3.132–133. New York.

WATSON, GEORGE, ed. 1971. The new Cambridge bibliography of English literature, 2: 1660–1800. Cambridge, University Press.

WEBSTER, CHARLES, ed. 1970. Samuel Hartlib and the advancement of learning. Cambridge, University Press. [220 pp.]

WEIMANN, K.-H. 1965. Vorstufen der Sprachphilosophie Humboldts bei Bacon und Locke. ZDPh 84.498–508.

WEINRICH, H. 1960. Vaugelas und die Lehre vom guten Sprachgebrauch. ZRPh 76.1–33.

——. 1968. Review of Brekle 1966. IF 73.362–364.

WELLS, W. H. 1878. Chronological catalogue of English grammars issued prior to 1801. Chicago. [= pp. 3–9 of his Historical authorship of English grammar, Chicago, 1878.]

WHITEHEAD, A. N. 1925. Science and the modern world. Lowell lectures. [18th printing, New York, Macmillan, 1967.]

WILL, W. VAN DER. 1969. Name, semeion, energeia: Notes on the permutation of language theories. In Essays in German language, culture and society, ed. by S. S. Prawer, R. H. Thomas, and L. Forster, 211–230. London.

WINCKEL, E. 1921. La Grammaire générale et raisonnée de Port-Royal. Bonn, Dissertation.

WINKLER, E. 1912. La doctrine grammaticale française d'après Maupas et Oudin. Halle.

WÜLLENWEBER, F. 1877. Vaugelas und seine Kommentatoren. Berlin, Programm.

YATES, F. A. 1954. The art of Ramón Lull. Journal of the Warburg and Courtauld Institutes 17.115–173.
——. 1964. Giordano Bruno and the Hermetic tradition. London.
——. 1966. The art of memory. London, Routledge & Kegan Paul. [400 pp.]
YOUNG, R. F. 1929. Comenius and the Indians of New England.
——. 1932. Comenius in England.
ZACHRISSON, R. E. 1914. Notes on some early English and French Grammars. Anglia, Beiblatt, 25.245–253.
——. 1927. English pronunciation at Shakespeare's time, as taught by William Bullokar. Uppsala.
ZELLER, H. 1930. Die Grammatik in der grossen französischen Enzyklopädie. Weißwasser O.-Lausitz, E. Hampel.
ZGUSTA, L. 1968. Review of Brekle 1966. Archiv Orientální 36.331–332.
ZIMMER, K. E. 1968. Review of Chomsky 1966. IJAL 34.290–303.
ZOBEL, A. 1928. Darstellung und kritische Würdigung der Sprachphilosophie John Locke's. Anglia 52.289–324.
ZWIRNER, E. 1969. Zum Begriff der allgemeinen Sprachwissenschaft und der allgemeinen Grammatik. Mélanges pour J. Fourquet, ... Réunis par P. Valentin et G. Zink, 407–415. München.

[Editor's note] Professor Brekle's contribution, "The Seventeenth Century", deals with only one aspect of linguistic studies in the seventeenth century, an aspect which that century itself did not consider particularly important. The major work of that century is left virtually untouched both in the text and in the bibliography. An adequate remedy not now being possible, the nature of the missing material can merely be suggested by (1) referring to some items in the Bibliography to Aarsleff's section on "The Eighteenth century, including Leibniz" which also contains material that pertains to the seventeenth century; and (2) adding a few titles that pertain specifically to the seventeenth century.

From the Leibniz bibliography in Aarsleff: HORMIA 1964, KANGRO 1969, LAKÓ 1969, LOEMKER 1961.

From the eighteenth-century Bibliography in Aarsleff: ADAMS 1917, AGRELL 1955, BAUMANN 1958, BERNHAGEN 1958, BOLTON 1966, BURSIAN 1883, CYŽEVŚKYJ 1939, DOUGLAS 1951, DÜNNINGER 1957, ECKHART 1711, EICHLER 1958 and 1967, EVANS 1956, FÜCK 1955, IVERSEN 1961, JENSEN 1912, KÜHLWEIN 1971, LANGEN 1957, MONROE 1970, PARAIN 1952, POWITZ 1959, QUEMADA 1967, RUSCH 1972, SANDYS 1903–08, SEGERT 1967, TUCKER 1961.

In addition the following titles, which of course by no means exhaust the wealth of material that is missing:

BARNER, WILFRIED. 1970. Barockrhetorik, Untersuchungen zu ihren geschichtlichen Grundlagen. Tübingen, Niemeyer. [Quellenverzeichnis, 456–487; Literaturverzeichnis, 488–521.]

BLOCHWITZ, WERNER, 1968. Vaugelas' Leistung für die französische Sprache. BRPh 7.101–130.

CHATEAU, JEAN, ed. 1969[4]. Les grands pédagogues. Paris, PUF. [375 pp.] [Therein P. Mesnard, La pédagogie des Jésuites, 57–119; J.-B. Piobetta, Comenius, 121–138.]

GARIN, EUGENIO. 1957. L'educazione in Europa (1400–1600), problemi e programmi. Bari, Laterza. [310 pp.] [In spite of the title's limitation to 1600, this work also covers the 17. century.]

——. 1964–67. Geschichte und Dokumente der abendländischen Pädagogik. 3 vols. (Mittelalter, Humanismus, Von der Reformation bis John Locke). Hamburg, Rowohlt. [This is a German translation of Garin 1957, greatly expanded by an excellent selection of sources in the original and in German, making up well over half the contents of each volume. Vol. 3 contains the last three chapters of Garin 1957 plus the sources, making it the best brief introduction to paedagogy in the seventeenth century, a subject intimately connected with the study of language and especially of grammar, not least universal grammar.]

GIRBAL, FRANÇOIS. 1964. Bernard Lamy (1640–1715), étude biographique et bibliographique. Paris, PUF. [194 pp.]

HANNAFORD, R. L. 1970. Animadversions on some recent speculations concerning the contemporary significance of "Cartesian linguistics". Actes du Xe congrès international des linguistics Bucarest, 28 août — 2 septembre 1967. 2.248–254.

HODGEN, MARGARET, 1964. Early anthropology in the sixteenth and seventeenth centuries. Philadelphia, University of Pennsylvania Press. 523 pp.

JOLY, ANDRÉ. 1972 Cartésianisme et linguistique cartésienne: Mythe ou réalité. BRPh 11.86–94.

KAYSER, WOLFGANG. 1932. Die Klangmalerei bei Harsdörffer: Ein Beitrag zur Geschichte der Literatur, Poetik und Sprachtheorie der Barockzeit. Palaestra 179. Leipzig, Mayer and Müller. [288 pp. Therein, Die Sprachtheorie als Grundlage für die Verwendung der Klangmalerei, 137–186, with a rich body of references to the relevant literature.]

METCALF, GEORGE J. 1953. Abraham Mylius on historical linguistics. PMLA 68.535–54.

NORDSTRÖM, JOHAN. 1924. Inledning til Georg Stiernhielms Filosofiska Fragment. Stockholm, Bonniers. [ccclxi pp. The best introduction to the intellectual world in which much work on language was done in the seventeenth century, Stiernhielm being one of the most notable exponents of that mode of study.]

POPELAR, INGE. 1967a. Probleme der französischen Lexicographie des 17. Jahrhunderts. BRPh 6.177–183.

——. 1967b. Die Etymologien Ménages im Lichte der modernen Wortforschung. BRPh 6.347–357.

——. 1968. Das Akademie-Wörterbuch von 1694. Das Wörterbuch des "honnête homme". BRPh 7.303–310.

SETÄLA, EMIL. 1902. Über den Hamburger Sprachforscher Martin Fogel. Verhandlungen des XIII. Internationalen Orientalisten-Kongresses in Hamburg. Section III.

STÅHLE, CARL IVAR. 1951. Språkteori och ordval i Stiernhielms författarskap. Arkiv 55.52–94.

VIËTOR, KARL. 1928. Probleme der deutschen Barockliteratur. Leipzig, Weber. [94 pp.]

THE EIGHTEENTH CENTURY, INCLUDING LEIBNIZ*

HANS AARSLEFF

In accordance with the title and purpose of this volume, it is the aim of my contribution to present a survey of recent literature devoted to the history of the study of language in the eighteenth century, including Leibniz. Thus, following the intent expressed in the title 'Current Trends' of the series to which this volume belongs, I am concerned with the historiography of the subject, not directly with its history, an enterprise of an altogether different sort. Both the subject matter and the method of history are not the same as those of historiography, and it would at the present time be premature, indeed hazardous and misleading to write the history of the study of language in the eighteenth century or any other period. My contribution will have achieved its aim if it helps the reader gain orientation and knowledge that can form a basis for further work so that it can be accomplished more easily, quickly, and safely. This orientation is provided by the bibliography and by the essay that precedes it. I deliberately here list them in that order. The bibliography must be counted at least half my contribution. In the essay that precedes it I do not make an effort to mention every item given in the bibliography. My aim has been to indicate major trends and their variety by drawing attention to the items, or more often clusters of items, which in my opinion merit discussion either for their positive or negative value. The organization and coverage of my contribution must be clearly stated.

First, though Leibniz by his dates (1646–1716), by intellectual background, and it might be argued by his work belongs as much to the seventeenth as to the eighteenth century, it has been deemed desirable that I should include him here. Since he is not, however, easy to integrate with the eighteenth century at large and since he is in any event a subject of fair proportions, I have found it best first to devote a separate section, Section 1, to Leibniz with discussion of recent work and bibliography, followed in Section 2 by treatment of the eighteenth century. The advantages of this arrangement seem to me so evident that they outweigh the slight inconvenience of a divided bibliography. To meet this difficulty, the bibliography to Section 1 will make cross reference to items whose main listing is in the bibliography to Section 2.

Secondly, the reader is entitled to know what limits I have imposed on the coverage.

* This essay was written in January of 1972. Some bibliographical items were added in December 1972, with corresponding revision and expansion of the text where necessary.

Let me therefore try to indicate them as clearly as possible so that the reader will not seek what he cannot expect to find. Time and space are inescapable bounds. Chronologically, it has been my aim to include all publications that pertain to the history of the study of language in regard to Leibniz as well as to the eighteenth century in so far as they have appeared by and large within the last generation. Naturally, no sharp line can be drawn, and there will be cases in which somewhat earlier items demand inclusion owing to their significance and influence. The reader must, however, bear firmly in mind that all I am attempting is a taking stock of the present state of knowledge, interpretation, and research. He should not assume that the body of work I deal with has now superseded earlier work so that, for instance, nineteenth-century or even later literature can now be forgotten or ignored as being outdated. It would be useless to approach such figures as Leibniz, Rousseau, Hamann, Herder, and Wilhelm von Humboldt without knowledge of work that is older than anything I can deal with here. I am afraid this warning is needed, for the history of the study of language appears suddenly to have become a fashionable subject; the results are evident: much inferior work is not only being done but also published. In particular, much writing shows conspicuous ignorance of primary texts and the intellectual milieus in which they were written.

Geographically, the limitations are the following. Not having the requisite skills, I do not (except for a single item) include literature in the Slavic languages. I am aware that this exclusion must be a considerable loss, but can only hope that someone else will some day supply the remedy. Professor Stankiewicz's "Bibliography of the History of Western Linguistics since 1945", at the end of this volume, contains some Slavic items that pertain to my period. Further, the coverage of items in Italian, Spanish, and Portuguese is spotty, not entirely for lack of skill but in some measure also owing to somewhat limited library resources and time. This is also a loss, for instance, in regard to the intellectual history of Italy and Spain in the eighteenth century and the influence of the French philosophers in those two countries. Similarly, I have not sought complete coverage for such smaller areas as Holland, Sweden, and Denmark, though I do have some items for each of those. Much of this material is both relevant and interesting, but there must be limits, at least for a chapter among many even though the volume is large. Anyone familiar with Swedish life and intellectual history in the seventeenth and eighteenth centuries and with the recent scholarship, written chiefly in Swedish, will know their importance also in regard to those centuries at large. The same is true of Denmark. A minor omission is the literature relating to the history of classical philology, a subject that has all along received not much perhaps but still steady attention. I am thinking of such an item as Getty 1962, which I have included to make this point.

With the exception of Slavic, my geographical limitations are also largely those of the annual *Bibliographie Linguistique* (BL), published under the auspices of UNESCO. It has, since 1948, devoted a separate section to the history of linguistics. The latest volume that has been available to me is the one for the year 1969. This bibliography is indispensable, but it must be noted that only the section on General Linguistics near the beginning of each volume contains a separate section on our subject. Items that fall within particular language areas appear in those sections, which have no similar sub-division. Like all comprehensive bibliographies, it is not complete, and since inclusion is usually determined by title, it cannot effectively take account of relevant material in books by single authors. Since the last couple of years, the annual bibliography of the *Publications of the Modern Language Association* (PMLA) also has a separate listing under the heading "History of Linguistics". *Language and Language Behavior Abstracts* (LLBA) has an index entry for History of Linguistics, in which, however, I have not encountered items for my period, most of the references being to work on much more recent events. Within these stated limitations, though with the exceptions listed after the next sentence, I have not knowingly omitted any item listed in BL. In fact, even for the years it covers (a span somewhat narrower than my coverage), I believe my bibliography has more items though there are undoubtedly items I would have included had I known about them. The exceptions are these: I have not attempted to include unpublished dissertations; I have made no effort to include reviews (which can be found in BL under the items reviewed); and with rare exceptions I do not include reprints and reprint introductions. This category is a vast one, the same item often being reprinted — or announced for reprinting — by several publishers. The competition has led to the practice of including introductions by 'experts', introductions which more often than not are so desultory and convey so much misinformation and oversimplification that the reader is better off without them. Primary works mentioned in the text are not all included in the bibliography — a reminder that my immediate concern is historiography and not history. I have sought to make their description in the text sufficient for the needs of readers who may wish to seek them out. The sort of general observations that are the stock-in-trade of introductions I have postponed to the final pages of Section 2.

SECTION 1. LEIBNIZ

Like his study of other subjects, Leibniz' interest in language was wide and thorough. To him all problems relating to language were interrelated — as indeed in his view was everything he studied — but we may for practical purposes observe that he directed his interest toward three sorts of problems: logical, philosophical, and historical. The first category includes the symbolic logic, the *ars combinatoria*, the *characteristica universalis*, and the philosophical language (Patzig 1969). This is perhaps the aspect of Leibniz that has been most precisely and fruitfully studied under the guidance and influence of such important works as Russell 1900, Couturat 1901, and Cassirer 1902. This tradition became so powerful that it created a tendency to view the logic as the heart and foundation of Leibniz' philosophy, a view that has recently been countered by G. H. R. Parkinson (1965). Except for some items that also pertain to the study of language at large as understood here, the present essay will not deal with this aspect of Leibniz scholarship. The bibliography is immense, the treatment of necessity often highly technical, and in this form it properly belongs with the logicians.

It is the last two categories that concern us here, i.e. the philosophical and historical modes of study, or as we might even call the latter the philological or linguistic study. Of these two the philosophical mode has no doubt received the greater attention both recently and in the past. There are several reasons for this concentration. The first volume of Cassirer's *Philosophy of symbolic forms*, first published in 1923, contained a stimulating and influential chapter on "The problem of language in the history of philosophy" (1953:117–76). Here Cassirer saw the essence of Leibniz' philosophy of language to lie in the problems pertaining to the 'universal logic,' thus in a way carrying the philosophical view of language back to logic: 'It was only with Leibniz, who restored the problem of language to the context of *universal logic* (which he recognized to be the prerequisite for all philosophy and all theoretical cognition in general) that the problem of a universal language was seen in a new depth ... Leibniz' *rationalism* achieves its ultimate confirmation and completion in the contemplation of language, which is seen purely as a means of cognition, an instrument of logical analysis' (129–30). Thus Cassirer concluded that in Leibniz, 'the specific character of language as a language of sounds and words, seems not so much acknowledged and explained, as ultimately negated' (132). It is clear that this view of Leibniz' study of language gives little encouragement to concern with his linguistic and philological work or even with the philosophical aspects that cannot easily be made amenable to the demands of logical analysis. Yet, no understanding that aims to comprehend Leibniz' over-all view and study of language is likely to be successful when the problem is conceived in this fashion. Of course, Cassirer is not to be blamed, for within his context and under his title, this emphasis is natural. But his important chapter has rarely been read with adequate awareness of that limit on his interest. It has been read rather as a history that presents a well-rounded view of the history of linguistic philosophy at large.

Independently of Cassirer's influence, there would seem to be another reason why greater attention has been paid to the philosophical than to the historical aspects of Leibniz' study of language: the inviting nature of the subject, the seeming ease of dealing with it, and the ready availability of texts that are known to be relevant, though these texts also contain much material that is relevant to the third category. They include the Preface to the Nizolius edition of 1670 as well as *Die Ermahnung an die Teutsche ihren Verstand und Sprache besser zu üben* first published in 1846, *Die Unvorgreiflichen Gedanken betreffend die Ausübung und Verbesserung der Teutschen Sprache* published in 1717, the "Brevis designatio" of 1710, and the *Nouveaux essais* first published in 1765.

Typical of work devoted to one or another or several of these pieces are Sokol 1941, Korninger 1958, Leroy 1966, and Huberti 1966. They do not, if at all, go much beyond an exposition that the reader could easily improve on by doing his own reading, they contain several errors, and they make the common mistake of making their analyses fit the dogmas of the accepted — one could almost say official — history of philosophy, a matter to which I shall return at the end of Section 2. Korninger's title is too general, for he deals with the narrower subject of 'Bedeutung der Sprache für Leben und Wissenschaft, ihrer Verbesserung, Erfassung und Verbreitung' (4). He further makes the error of citing the well-known opening words of Book III of Locke's *Essay* on the social nature of language, which also stand at the head of Book III in the *Nouveaux essais*, as if they were also Leibniz' words. Perhaps one may decide that Locke and Leibniz agree on this point, but there is surely no good reason to take such agreement for granted. It is clearly necessary to distinguish between the interlocutors in the long dialogue that makes up the *Nouveaux essais*, between Philalethe and Theophile who speak for Locke and Leibniz, a distinction that has often not been observed. Leroy tells the reader that the *Nouveaux essais* were published in 1704, which is approximately the time when they were written. It may not be very useful to speculate on the could-have-beens of history, but it seems quite certain that the entire course of language study during the eighteenth century would have been very different if that work — in many respects the longest, most explicit and finished we have from Leibniz — had been published early in the century rather than in 1765, when it had been so overtaken by events that its impact was very limited in regard to our subject. Characteristic of much history of linguistics written by linguists, Leroy's attitude is one of overbearing surprise 'de découvrir un Leibniz à la fois prisonnier du passé et précurseur des conceptions modernes' (202). Thus his discussion lacks a sense of basic issues, shows little knowledge of intellectual history, and is ill-informed about the texts.

Huberti's article is a more serious case, being on the one hand better informed about the texts, yet more bound by preconceptions and misled by the kind of reading of the *Nouveaux essais* that pays attention to what Leibniz says without critical awareness of what Locke had said. Huberti labors first of all under the common dogma that Locke's *Essay* and its philosophy represents 'sensualism', that is the view that all knowledge and ideas are derived from sensation, a notion which a simple reading of Locke should suffice to dispel, though in the course of the nineteenth century this interpretation became a commonplace so confirmed that it is hard to get rid of even today (cf. Aarsleff 1971a). Thus Huberti is able to find contrasts between the two philosophers which in fact did not exist. We are told, for instance, that Locke's view of language, 'erschöpft sich in der Brauchbarkeit des Wortschatzes; sie ist die Fülle mehr oder weniger geordneter Einzelwörter', while to Leibniz it also serves three other purposes, namely 'dass der Mensch für sich denke, dass er sich erinnere und dass er die Sprache als Zeichen für Definitionen benutzen könne' (363). That to Locke words have a crucial role in thinking should hardly need to be pointed out, and that he took them to have an equally crucial role for memory he says often, e.g. in the *Essay*'s Book III, ch. ii, par. 2: 'The use men have of these marks [is] ... to record their own thoughts for the assistance of their own memory.' (It should be recalled that Leibniz was using Pierre Coste's French translation (1700) of the *Essay*, a version that was produced under Locke's supervision, had his approval, and which in fact contained passages that did not appear in English till the fifth edition of 1706, which Locke had personally prepared for the press before he died.) One final example; with reference to the significant chapter vii in Book III, 'Of Particles,' Huberti says that while Locke 'die Verwendung der Partikel mehr als eine Frage der Eleganz des Sprechers betrachtet, weist Leibniz mit Ernst darauf hin, dass die Partikeln nicht nur die Sätze miteinander oder Satzteile untereinander verbinden ... sondern auch die Teile der Idee selbst, sofern diese sich auf verschiedene Arten aus der Kombination anderer Ideen ergibt' (369). It is true that Locke makes the point about style, but he also immediately explains what he means: 'To think well, it is not enough that a man has *ideas* clear and distinct in his thoughts, nor that he observes the agreement or disagreement of some of them; but he must think in train and observe the dependence of his thoughts and reasonings one upon another; and to express well such methodical and rational thoughts, he must have words to *show* what *connexion*, *restriction*, *distinction*, *opposition*, *emphasis*, etc., he gives to each *respective part of his discourse*' (III, vii, 2). This passage is in fact cited by Leibniz at that very point in his discussion so that it is hard to see any good reason for Huberti's statement, which misrepresents both Locke and Leibniz. Leibniz gives a correct version of what Locke said, though it is hazardous to assume that one can proceed with an enterprise such as Huberti's without a good independent knowledge of Locke's *Essay*. It is at the end of this very chapter that Leibniz observes, 'que je croye veritablement, que les langues sont le meilleur miroir de l'esprit humain, et qu'une analyse exacte de la signification des mots feroit mieux connoitre que toute autre chose, les operations de l'entendement'. This famous remark is a succinct statement of Leibniz' view, which in regard to language hardly varies from Locke's.

Verburg 1952 devotes pages 265–96 to Leibniz with exclusive attention to the 'rationalistic' and 'logistic' aspects of his philosophy of language without touching the historical aspects. Coseriu (1969:149–55) gives a brief and very selective account based on a few passages in the *Nouveaux essais* which offer little scope for a good understanding of either Locke or Leibniz. I cannot share Coseriu's opinion that there is no need to deal with Leibniz' attention to the problems of historical linguistics, 'da dies in der Geschichte der Sprachwissenschaften schon oft geschehen ist'. Coseriu also observes that Leibniz, unlike Locke, knew 'verschiedene Sprachen aus denen er Beispiele zu sprachphilosophischen Problemen anführen kann'. It is true that Leibniz knew and cited a vast number of examples, for instance in the *Nouveaux essais*, a reminder both of the intimate relationship he saw between the philosophical and the historical study of language, and of the danger that lies in separating them to a full understanding of Leibniz' conception of the nature of language. The possible implication, however, that Locke did not know a variety of languages is wrong; as a practical linguist he was almost certainly better prepared than Leibniz. Locke was at one time Greek lecturer at Oxford, studied Arabic and Hebrew, probably learnt Dutch while he lived in exile in Holland, and like Leibniz he wrote Latin and French with ease. His correspondence shows that he shared some of Leibniz' eagerness to learn about words and terms in distant parts of the world from travellers who went there (Aarsleff 1964:168). Thus, if he rarely cited particular words in the *Essay*, it was not for lack of knowledge of languages he might draw on. Further Leibniz' citation of words from different languages does not imply that he spoke those languages or even knew them well. He often determined to learn a Slavic language, but in fact never did. In so far as Coseriu's remark suggests that Locke was not much of a linguist, it is incorrect.

I have dealt with these items in greater detail than I shall have time for in the following in order to show how easily simplified and erroneous analyses are produced and gain acceptance, a failure that becomes more serious when we consider that such expositions generally form many students' first introduction to the subject and in large measure are the sources of expositions in books that do not reach back to the primary material. Leibniz' work on historical and plain descriptive linguistics has been spared this fate only because it has received little attention, chiefly because the relevant texts are not easily available, not widely known, or still unpublished. Since the remedy, both in regard to the philosophical and historical work, lies in better acquaintance with the bibliographical works and the texts, let me now briefly give a survey of these aids. If this will mean going back in time beyond the stated limits of this essay, the procedure is justified by the evident difficulty of mastering the basic bibliography without which no serious work can be done.

To approach Leibniz' work, both published and unpublished, is like entering a veritable maze in which there is no hope of finding one's way without good guidance. Bodemann's two volumes, 1966a and b, are indispensable guides to the manuscripts and the letters in the Leibniz collection in the 'Niedersächsische Landesbibliothek' in Hanover in Germany, even though a good part of the material has been published since those volumes appeared in 1889 and 1895. By the inclusion of quite extensive citations, both volumes give more than a mere enumeration of items. The published work is so extensive and has appeared in such a variety of places from Leibniz' lifetime until the present day that it is often very difficult to locate a particular text without the aid of Ravier 1937, which up to the date of its appearance lists every item and letter, an immense and demanding task for which one is grateful in spite of the fact that references and page numbers, also in the indexes, contain a fair number of errors. Ravier is indispensable not least as a source of cross-reference to locate an item for which the text of a particular edition is not readily available, since even very large libraries are not likely to have all the editions. On pages 535–669 Ravier lists the contents of all the major editions. Ravier should be supplemented and corrected by Schrecker 1938, but for the years following, during which a very large amount of publication has occurred, there is no similar guide. Wells 1957 and Loemker 1965 are useful surveys, though both are chiefly devoted to secondary works.

To the secondary literature, from the beginning to the date of publication, Müller 1967 is a superb guide, with 'Sprachforschung, Literaturgeschichte' on pages 121–8. Naturally, this bibliography is not complete — how could it be? It is being continued with great precision and fulness in Utermöhlen 1969, 1970, and Koch-Klose and Hölzer 1971, a task that will presumably be an annual feature of *Studia Leibnitiana*. These bibliographies also include new text editions. Guhrauer's two-volume work from 1846 is still the most comprehensive biography, but excellent guidance in the biography as well as other general matters is found in Totok and Haase 1966 and not least in Müller and Krönert 1969, which presents a detailed record of Leibniz' whereabouts and activities from month to month and sometimes even from day to day.

It is beyond my scope to list the editions, but the most important must be noted. The six-volume Dutens edition of 1768 is still the most extensive in coverage, though the text is not reliable. The last two volumes are devoted to philological matters. On the whole, this edition reprints eighteenth-century collections that are usually yet more difficult to come by than Dutens. Gerhardt 1965, a reprint from the late nineteenth century, is the handiest and most complete for the philosophical works. Influential and important is Couturat's great collection in Leibniz 1903, which contains much that pertains directly to the philosophy and study of language. Schmidt's edition in German translation in Leibniz 1960 is also useful, drawing chiefly on the Gerhardt and Couturat editions; I think readers will find the translations in the next two items more reliable. More extensive in coverage, though briefer, with a good introduction is Leibniz 1966. Also reliable and the most extensive collection in English is Loemker's in Leibniz 1969, with a full introduction and a useful annotated bibliography on pages 63–9. It is unfortunate that Langley's very old translation of the *Nouveaux essais* should still be widely used in the English-speaking world. Its philosophical terminology is outdated, and it is based on Gerhardt's text in Leibniz 1965 (vol. 5, first published in 1882), which has now been entirely superseded by the much better text in the Akademie-Ausgabe (Leibniz 1923–, Series 6, vol. 6 [1962]).

By far the most authoritative edition is the great Akademie Ausgabe, of which 14 volumes have so far appeared since 1923 (Leibniz 1923–). Owing to the great care that is excercised with every aspect of the presentation of the text, this edition supersedes all previous editions, though since it is not its aim to offer full annotation of the texts, there may still be editions of individual works that are fuller in this respect. Its progress has been slow owing both to the intervention of two World Wars and other political events and to the sheer magnitude of the task. The collection of manuscripts in the Niedersächsische Landesbibliothek is so vast that even today it has barely been completely catalogued, and new pieces are still turning up. At the end of the Second World War the register of manuscripts and prints contained some 52,500 pieces. The first eight volumes of series one, *Allgemeiner politischer und historischer Briefwechsel*, contains 3,668 letters. Each of the large volumes now contains less than one year's correspondence, yet Leibniz' mania for letter-writing does not peak until the period between 1700 and 1710, so that before this series is brought up to Leibniz' death in

1716 it will contain at least an additional 13,000 letters. If the entire edition is ever completed according to the original plan, it will comprise some 70 volumes. Even at the present more rapid rate of publication, the edition is not likely to be completed within the lifetime of any reader of these lines. Since the quality and even the possibility of the preparation of one series depends on correlation with information made available by work on the other series, the edition should ideally, in so far as possible, proceed chronologically through Leibniz' writings, but owing to a variety of practical difficulties this has not so far been entirely possible. This in turn means that it would be false to assume that all the most important material has been published by now. The volumes are indispensable to all serious work not merely because of the quality of the text, but also by virtue of the information that is made accessible by means of the indexes. With the exception of the early volumes, each volume contains a subject index; an index of works cited with author, title, and date; and index of persons; and for the correspondence volumes an index of correspondents with brief identifications. The vast possibilities opened up by such careful indexing need hardly be pointed out to the reader. For an account of the aims, principles, problems, and state of the edition in 1966, see Hochstetter 1966b and 1969, Hofmann and Schröter both 1969, and especially Müller 1969.

Volume six (1962) in series six presents the *Nouveaux essais*, edited by André Robinet and Heinrich Schepers, but so far none of the other works that pertain to the philosophical and historical study of language have been published in this edition. A good part of the latter are scheduled to appear in future volumes of series five, *Historische Schriften*. But much of the material on this subject is contained in the letters to and from Leibniz which are appearing in series one. Relevant material will increase steeply over the next ten years of the correspondence and continue until 1716. There are at least two reasons for this increase. In 1685 Leibniz undertook the task of writing the history of the House of Braunschweig-Lüneburg, a task that not only brought him face to face with early documents in a variety of languages and dialects, but also engaged him in wide correspondence that further stimulated his already strong interest in the historical study of language (Eckert 1971; Aarsleff 1969). The other reason was Leibniz' reading of Locke's *Essay*, which clearly seems to have turned his interest toward a variety of linguistic problems, both philosophical and practical.

Before I proceed to discuss some of the recent work devoted to Leibniz' study of language, let me mention two older works of unusual importance and richness. Guerrier 1873 contains a wealth of letters and pieces that illustrate Leibniz' lively and detailed interest in the languages that were spoken within the Czarist empire, from its European borders to the farthest reaches of the East, as well as in general problems of historical and comparative linguistics. The other work is Davillé 1909, a very hefty volume that presents a detailed account of Leibniz as an historian with a vast number of references to the correspondence, including many that bear on linguistic matters.

Leibniz' interest in natural languages was guided by a few basic conceptions which he stated again and again in his writings and letters. First, the study of languages and etymology formed an auxiliary discipline to history, as he said for instance in a letter written in the spring of 1691: 'Muss auch in etwas Migrationes Gentium et Origines Lingvarum betrachten. ... Ich glaube gänzlich dass die Harmonie der Sprachen das beste Mittel von Ursprung der Völcker zu urtheilen, und fast das einige so uns übrig blieben, wo die Historien fehlen. Es scheinet, dass in der that alle Sprachen vom Strohm Indo an, bis an das Mare Germanicum von einem Ursprung seyn' (Aarsleff 1969:174). Secondly, he believed that all languages ultimately had a common root — in spite of the slight qualification in this passage: 'Il semble en effect que prèsque toutes les langues ne sont que des variations, souvent bien embrouillées, des mêmes racines, mais qu'il est difficile de reconnoitre, à moins que de comparer beaucoup de langues ensemble; sans négliger les jargons, dont it seroit bon que les Sçavans de chaque pays prissent la peine de recueillir les mots particuliers' (*ibid.* 180). (The qualification is designed to take account of deliberately created artificial languages, such as Leibniz believed Chinese might possibly be — and thus also a sort of philosophical language [cf. Aarsleff 1969:181–2]. Leibniz did not wish to suggest that there might be natural languages outside the common source of origin.) The respect for dialects, as at the end of this passage, was especially characteristic of Leibniz; it is an expression of the continuity principle to which he was committed. Thirdly, in spite of the great diversity of mankind in different parts of the globe, he firmly believed that this diversity, 'n'empêche pas qve tous les hommes qvi habitent ce globe ne soyent tous d'une même race, qvi a esté alterée par les differens climats, comme nous voyons qve les bestes et les plantes changent de naturel et deviennent meilleurs ou dégénèrent' (*ibid.* 182). In this respect he agreed with Locke, sharing his lively interest in what we now call comparative anthropology. Fourthly, unlike Locke he believed that there is 'quelque chose de naturel dans l'origine des mots qui marque un rapport entre les choses et les sons et mouvemens des organes de la voix' (*ibid.* 179). Thus, 'supposé que nos langues soyent derivatives quant au fonds, elles ont néantmoins quelque chose de primitif en elles mêmes, qui leur est survenu par rapport à des mots radicaux nouveaux, formés depuis chez elles par hazard mais sur des raisons physiques' (*ibid.* 180). These principles leave no doubt of the direction which his general philosophy of language and mind gave to the detailed study of languages and etymology.

Bittner's (1931–32) tripartite monograph gives a clear and detailed account of Leibniz' interest in Slavic matters, which included both politics and linguistics. The monograph is based both on published and unpublished material, though some of the latter has since appeared in the Akademie-Ausgabe. Bittner first shows the great impetus that Leibniz's linguistic studies received from the journey he undertook — from November 1687 to June 1690 — to European archives in order to collect material for the history of the ducal house he served. Thus in Frankfort he met the oriental, Ethiopic and Slavic scholar Hiob Ludolf with whom a correspondence of over 60 letters now began, ended only by Ludolf's death in 1704, chiefly on linguistic matters.

Back in Hanover, Leibniz turned his attention toward the last remnants of a Slavic language known in the area between Uelzen and Dannenberg in present-day Lower Saxony, the Polabian dialect (Bittner 1931–32:169–89). He sent a letter in the form of a questionnaire to a high administrative official in the area: Had sepulchral urns or ancient burial mounds been found, how did they look, and were there other archeological remains, or noteworthy features of physical geography, flora and fauna? Finally, have books been printed in the Polabian language (the answer was no), a request for the Lord's Prayer in that language, a question about the difference between the German spoken by Polabians and normal German ('our German'), and last what is their word for German. Leibniz received more or less adequate answers to all these questions, including a version of the Lord's Prayer on which he promptly made a number of linguistic comments. (The letter to Leibniz and his comments will also be found in Leibniz 1923–, Series I, Vol. vii, pp. 513–19.) Soon after he sent back some additional comments, at the same time suggesting that if a country pastor or a schoolmaster could be found who knew the language, it would be desirable if he could be induced to make a vocabulary list and a sketch of the grammar. At least in regard to the former, this effort may have borne fruit according to Leibniz' suggestion, even though it may not have reached him. Leibniz gave a characteristic reason for his request: 'Je trouve que de tous les moyens de juger de l'origine ou connexion des peuples, celui des langues est le plus seur. Et les jargons et dialectes et sur tout les paroles qui ne sont en usage que parmi les paysans et le petit peuple y servent particulièrement. Car ce sont des restes de l'ancienne langue' (182–3). The method, the carefully framed questions and specific requests, the comments, the encouragement to further work, and the reason he gives for his interest are all typical of innumerable other efforts of the same kind which he directed toward all parts of the world as soon as he saw a chance to get back information from a correspondent or acquaintance. Bittner cites examples from the rich storehouse of Guerrier's book on Slavic and Asian languages, but the list can easily be extended to the rest of the world, China, the Far East, Africa, America, all parts of Europe, and of course Germany.

On pages 197–210, Bittner gives a good account of Leibniz' correspondence with the Swedish diplomat, scholar, and linguist, especially in Slavic, J. G. Sparwenfeld. Their correspondence, from 1695 to 1702, is perhaps the most significant and revealing of all the many that Leibniz maintained on linguistic matters with his far-flung correspondents. The letters contain requests for specific information and in addition rather full philosophical observations on language and its study. Though Leibniz' letters have been published, Sparwenfeld's have appeared only in excerpts, in Jacobowsky 1932. Leibniz was interested in Sparwenfeld's knowledge and linguistic activities, not least the polyglot Slavic lexicon he was preparing — I think it would be correct to say that Leibniz was picking Sparwenfeld's brain. Their correspondence also gives insight into a particular matter of some interest. In 1699 Leibniz had employed a young Hungarian, Matthias Zabani, as his amanuensis in linguistic matters, but not being able to afford to keep him (and perhaps to have an informant in Stockholm), he recommended him to Sparwenfeld as a man who would be useful in his service. He had not been there long, however, before Sparwenfeld wrote back that the young man was quite ignorant of the languages Leibniz had claimed he knew. This incident may show that Leibniz had small practical knowledge of some of the languages he dealt with.

Richter 1946 is a brief survey that quite lacks the thoroughness, insight, and detailed citation of sources found in Bittner. Without giving the source, she cites two rather long and important passages from Guerrier, which may be useful to readers who lack access to that work. Olesch 1967 and 1968 include Leibniz' interest in Polabian and the texts, though not the surrounding correspondence.

Bittner's monograph appears to have received as little attention in the scholarly world as Sigrid von der Schulenburg's excellent short work of 1937, the only one she had published before her death in 1945. But she had written several other essays which, having fortunately been preserved though in more or less complete and finished form, will be published from her manuscript in Schulenburg 1973. There is good reason to look forward to this publication. Schulenburg 1937 indicates that she planned a treatment of Leibniz' discussion of the origin of language and the original nature of words (9), a description of the manuscripts of the *Unvorgreiflichen Gedanken* (20), and a history of Leibniz' *Collectanea etymologica* (1717), including his marginalia in the copy now in the library in Hanover. We shall later see that she was planning yet a fourth Leibniz publication. It is rather striking proof of the neglect of Leibniz' historical linguistic work that these projects still remain among the desiderata of Leibniz scholarship. This neglect is undoubtedly a consequence of the steady but quite superficial attention that has been given to his philosophy of language, though this subject is poorly served so long as the discussion remains confined to the few texts that are generally used.

Schulenburg makes no reference to Bittner, but her exposition shows that Leibniz in regard to German followed the same procedure as with Slavic: again the busy correspondence to all sides, questionnaires, requests for specific information, statement of basic principles, and encouragement to engage in particular long-term projects — even the same suggestion that country pastors should be under obligation to send in ten 'Landwörter (voces rusticas)' (25) while the bishops would be responsible for a hundred. Schulenburg's monograph has a wealth of references to a large number of original manuscripts, thus affording a good understanding both of the richness of the material and the great complexity of the task of dealing with it. She emphasizes Leibniz' respect for dialects (as already brought out in a passage cited from Bittner), which unlike some of his correspondents he did not consider corruptions of a better standard language: 'Leibniz hat keine Mundart die Rolle zuerkannt, allein die echte deutsche Sprache zu besitzen. Er will ohne Unterschied die deutschen Worte von ihnen allen erbitten. Erst in ihrer Gesamtheit stellen sie ihm die deutsche Sprache dar. Vor allen Dingen lehnt er es ab, aus dem Alter eines Dialekts auf seine Vernünftigkeit zu schliessen' (14). In his respect for the linguistic importance of dialects, Leibniz may well show both insight and originality, but it may be recalled that on this matter Leibniz himself referred to the English botanist John Ray's *Collection of English Words*, which Leibniz knew before he visited London in 1676. Later he sent a copy to Gerhard Meier in Bremen, whom he was especially eager to convince of the significance of dialect words (5).

Owing to its clear awareness of the interrelations between the philosophical and the historical aspects of the study of language in Leibniz, Schulenburg's monograph suggests certain problems which I have tried to deal with in two articles. Being in equal measure devoted to Locke and Leibniz, the scope of Aarsleff 1964 is perhaps somewhat wider than the title may at first glance suggest. My aim is first to identify the separate positions of each both systematically and in terms of seventeenth-century doctrines about the nature of language, a subject whose basic features Locke knew quite as well as Leibniz. My thesis is that their ultimate opposition, in spite of much agreement, turns on the question whether language is conventional — *ex instituto* — or in some sense natural, and I try to demonstrate that Locke had deliberately taken his stand against the doctrines which Leibniz later advanced in his critique. In both, their doctrines of the nature of language resulted from the basic principles of their philosophical positions, a fact that is succinctly suggested by Henry Ollion's remark in 1908: 'Quoi qu'il en soit, Locke a certainement consideré la doctrine de l'innéité comme fondée sur un abus de mots' (183). At the very end of the *Essay*'s Book II Locke had observed that a discussion of 'words and language in general' would be necessary because he had found 'that there is so close a connexion between *ideas* and words, and our abstract *ideas* and general words have so constant a relation one to another, that it is impossible to speak clearly and distinctly of our knowledge, which all consists in propositions, without considering first the nature, use, and signification of language'. He wished to examine in detail what he called 'the cheat of words' in order to determine how well language served the needs of moral and natural philosophy. He concluded that language did not serve the needs of truth and knowledge as well as was often carelessly assumed. Following a suggestion in Bacon, he arrived at the important principle that 'languages in all countries have been established long before sciences. So that they have not been philosophers, or logicians, or such who have troubled themselves about forms and essences, that have made the general names that are in use amongst the several nations of men; but those more or less comprehensive terms have for the most part, in all languages, received their birth and signification from ignorant and illiterate people, who sorted and denominated things by those sensible qualities they found in them' (178). A corollary of this principle is Locke's doctrine of intranslatability. Anyone with a 'moderate skill in different languages' can readily observe a 'great store of words in one language which have not any that answer them in another. Which plainly shows that those of one country, by their customs and manner of life, have found occasion to make several complex ideas and gives names to them, which others never collected into specific ideas. This could not have happened if these species were the steady workmanship of nature, and not collections made and abstracted by the mind, in order to naming, and for the convenience of communication' (175). In this analysis of language and words, Leibniz agrees with Locke (176), a fact that needs to be recognized since several commentators see disagreement already on these points, usually owing to inadequate familiarity both with the *Essay* and with the *Nouveaux essais* — and as I have already suggested it is necessary to have knowledge of Locke's work also apart from Leibniz' presentation of it. Leibniz disagreement has another source that transcends the question of language alone, 'cependant les idées ne dependent point des noms' (179), a remark that is linked to Leibniz' conceptions of contingency and necessity.

The disagreement is over another fundamental linguistic problem. In order to guard against the claim often made with authority during the seventeenth century that there is somehow a natural connection between a given word and its meaning, Locke made it a cardinal principle that, 'words ... came to be made use of by men, as the signs of their ideas; not by any natural connexion that there is between particular sounds and certain ideas, for then there would be but one language amongst all men; but by a voluntary imposition, whereby such a word is made arbitrarily the mark of such an idea' (183). Here Leibniz could not agree, for committed to his principle of sufficient reason and 'cette admirable harmonie préestablie de l'âme et du corps', he was bound to assert against Locke: 'Il y a quelque chose de naturel dans l'origine des mots' (179) thus on principle making allowance, though with significant qualifications, for the doctrine of the language of nature so popular in the seventeenth century.

Here is the crux of the matter: how could Leibniz agree with Locke on the former principle, then assert that ideas do not depend on words, and finally disagree with Locke on the question whether language is conventional or natural? Leibniz' answer turns to a diachronic or historical view of language to meet these problems: 'Pour ce qui est des langues qui se trouvent faites depuis longtemps, il n'y en a gueres qui ne soit extrèmement alterée aujourdhuy. Cela est manifeste en les comparant avec les anciens livres et monuments qui en restent.' He therefore reasserts his belief in the single origin of mankind and of all languages: 'De sort qu'il n'y a rien en cela qui combatte et qui ne favorise plustost le sentiment de l'origine commune de toutes les Nations, et d'une langue radicale et primitive' (184). Thus Locke and Leibniz both show a precise knowledge of seventeenth-century doctrines; and it is a tribute both to the significant implications of those doctrines and to the consistency Locke and Leibniz showed in their debate with that century and among themselves (though Locke participated only with the text of the *Essay*) that the two philosophers confront each other over the age-old question whether language is conventional or natural. In Aarsleff 1969 I have examined Leibniz' conception of etymology, which is clearly a crucial problem in his understanding of the nature of language and its study. In that article I have again made an effort to relate philosophy and history. I have used it above to present a brief review of Leibniz' basic linguistic doctrines.

Heintz 1969 suggests a number of observations. The first aim of this article is to show that 'die These vom Weltbild der Sprache' — sometimes called the Sapir-Whorf thesis or the principle of linguistic relativity — is anticipated by Leibniz. On this matter of 'anticipation', that is so very common in the history of linguistics, especially recently, it may be observed that the search for forerunners in history is not useful; it is in fact incompatible with any intelligent conception of history. It poses two sorts of danger: that the doctrines found are conceived in the form of their later presentation rather than in the terms in which they were first understood, a procedure that can easily lead to serious misunderstanding; and secondly that the forerunner in fact does not occupy the special position claimed for him. (I have made some observations on this matter in Aarsleff 1967 (7–10). It is healthy to recall Alexandre Koyré's words: 'La manie de la recherche des "précurseurs" a bien souvent irrémédiablement faussé l'histoire de la philosophie'.) Heintz admits that Locke and Leibniz, in the principle of intranslatability, agree that each language expresses the particular needs of its speakers — though for Locke Heintz's argument is weakened by the use of supporting passages which only incidentally deal with this problem rather than the passages which Locke devotes directly to this subject. Heintz claims, however, that Leibniz carried his view beyond Locke to the doctrine that even the language of each individual is relative: 'Dabei ist seine Vorstellung von der einzelnen Sprache der von der Monade analog' (228). But Locke also, with his analysis of the nominal essence of gold, postulates that this essence to each speaker will constitute no more than he takes to be characteristic of gold. The underlying philosophical principles may be different, but the linguistic consequence is the same. It is hard to agree that, 'Sprache ist für Leibniz nicht, wie noch für Locke, ein verfügbares und welt-anschaulich indifferentes Mittel der Kommunikation, sondern in jeder Sprache spiegelt sich eine unverwechselbare Weltansicht' (229), for Locke's reason for the discussion of language is his profound concern over its rule over thought in any effort to gain knowledge and truth; if Locke had believed that language was an indifferent means of communication there would have been no need for Book III. Heintz's error emerges with yet greater clarity when he inserts his own explication into a citation from Wilhelm von Humboldt: '"Denn das Wort entsteht ja aus dieser Wahrnehmung, und ist nicht ein Abdruck des Gegenstandes an sich" — wie die sensualistische Ausfassung Lockes meint — "sondern des von diesem in der Seele erzeugten Bildes"' (230); for Locke's conception is surely not that words and ideas are impressions or copies of objects. By virtue of his strong sense of the active role of words in thinking, Locke has much in common with von Humboldt. It is not useful to assume that an analysis of Leibniz will show us Leibniz 'mit seinem vertieften Verständnis für psychologische Fragen von Locke Abstand nehmen, dessen Position überwinden und eine wesentliche Erkenntnis zur Metalinguistik beisteuern' (226).

Though it is correct to find a systematic presentation of the principle of linguistic relativity in Locke and Leibniz, it is not correct to assume that it was not known to the seventeenth century. With regard to Bacon and Locke this has been pointed out with effective succinctness and the citation of forceful passages by Weimann 1965, who also suggests, rightly I think, that this point has been missed chiefly because Locke did not devote a separate chapter of Book III to this subject. More than that, it is often not understood that Locke's linguistic remarks and influence on the history of the study of language is by no means confined to the contents of his book on'words and language in general'. The principle of linguistic relativity also had other sources, for instance the effort to raise the German language to a position of respect and importance among the European languages, an effort that showed this tendency in Justus-Georg Schottel's wonderful *Ausführliche Arbeit von der Teutschen Haubt-Sprache* (1663), which is a veritable anthology of the history of linguistic thought and a work on which Leibniz drew extensively (see Aarsleff 1964 *passim*, esp. 169–70, 186). In theological form the principle was stated by Boehme, whose influence and representativeness during the seventeenth century, especially in England, is not to be underestimated. 'God did likewise form the languages according to the property of every land and country,' he said. 'For seeing that people were to be dispersed into every country and climate, he opened to each people a language, according as it should be in a land. ... For, as the manifestation of the formed word was in the spirit of the world in every place, even so the spirit of God did form, through the nature of the properties, the language and speech in every country. First the seventy-two languages out of nature, and afterward the collateral affinities [dialects], proceeding from the senses of every head language; as we plainly see, that a man doth scarce find, in any place of the world, among all the head languages [Haupt-Sprachen], one and the same sense in any head language, within the compass of fifteen or eighteen miles' (*Mysterium magnum*, ch. 35, §§73–5 in John Sparrow's translation). Thus the principle of linguistic relativity generally attributed to von Humboldt was not original with him, and its history extends back in time at least to the seventeenth century. In the eighteenth century it received classical formulation in Condillac, who is the focal point of its later career.

Heintz's argument leads him to assert that Leibniz found that, 'es gibt so viele Sprachen wie Formen der Weltansicht, also keine Ursprache. Die reizvolle Idee einer solchen Urform von Sprache hat Leibnizens Einsicht in die sprachliche Wirklichkeit in ihrer Fragwürdigkeit durchschaut' (237). But that assertion is surely false, as a number of quotations above will amply demonstrate. Since I wrote those lines I have seen Heinekamp 1972, which is emphatic on this point: 'Wie zahlreihe Sprachtheoretiker der damaligen Zeit hält Leibniz die These für erwägenswert, dass die natürlichen Sprachen aus einem gemeinsamen Ursprung entstanden seien: "neque ego valde illis repugnem, qui plerasque linguas cogniti veteribus orbis ab eodem fonte fluxisse judicant", ebenso wie die verschiedenen Völker nach seiner Meinung von derselben Rasse sind' (469–470). Heinekamp also makes reference to this well-known passage from the *Nouveaux Essais*: '... il n'y a rien en cela qui combatte et qui ne favorise plustost le sentiment de l'origine commune de toutes les Nations, et d'une langue radicale et primitive.' I believe that the argument of Aarsleff 1964 shows how Leibniz solved at least one important problem that arose in this context.

Finally, it is part of Heintz's argument that Leibniz in his later years became so committed to the view of language that included the relativity principle that he rejected his earlier interest in the perfect artificial language of knowledge, the philosophical language. It may be true — though in the as yet imperfect state of publication of Leibniz' writings it is hard to say — that in regard to language his later years were mostly preoccupied with the study of actual languages, dialects, and etymology. But there is no proof that he had become disaffected with the philosophical foundations of the *scientia generalis*, and it is hard to see why there should in fact be any conflict between the two. If, however, Heintz were right, it would immediately increase the likelihood that Locke had an overwhelming influence on Leibniz, much greater than even I would be prepared to maintain. With reference to Huberti 1966 (373), Heintz refers to a remark Leibniz made in the *Nouveaux essais* (IV, iii, 18) about an unlicensed republication of his early *Dissertatio de arte combinatoria* (1666). H[4] was unhappy about this reissue of a work of his first adolescence, for it had made some people believe, 'que j'étois capable de publier une telle pièce dans un age avancé: Car quoi qu'il y ait des pensées de quelque conséquence, que j'approuve encore, il y en avoit pourtant aussi, qui ne pouvoient convenir qu'à un jeune étudiant.' Leibniz' concern is understandable, and there is surely no basis at all for Heintz's interpretation that he saw that early work as one of his sins of youth in regard to the philosophy of language at large: 'Nicht umsonst bezeichnet er selbst späterhin die Entwürfe zur 'Characteristica' als Jugendsünde. ... Denn im Laufe seiner Entwicklung muss er erkennen, welcher Grad von Sinnlichkeit in der Sprache liegt und wie hoch der Anteil der individuellen Einbildungskraft für die einzelsprachliche Begriffsbildung zu veranschlagen ist' (240). In this connection Heintz sees Leibniz' use of the metaphor of words as counters or money freely exchanged with the value of their assigned worth as an expression of the early idea of a 'Characteristica generalis', but the very import of this metaphor is opposed to the principles of a perfect language, and the metaphor is in any case traditional (Quintilian) and had been used by Bacon, Hobbes, Locke, and Robert South without the implication Heintz ascribes to it (cf. Aarsleff 1967: 233–4).

Thus in spite of its often interesting discussion I find Heintz's interpretation fundamentally mistaken. Like the earlier piece by Huberti, it unfortunately also shows slight acquaintance with Locke's argument in the *Essay*, with the usual consequence that some points on which Leibniz and Locke did not disagree are made the exclusive property of Leibniz.

Six months after I had written the last two paragraphs arguing against Heintz's version of what may perhaps be called the Cassirer tradition (in this case in fact the reverse of Cassirer's view but still a version of it), I had the opportunity to see the final proofs of Heinekamp 1972, whose title announces its relevance in this context, 'Ars characteristica and natürliche Sprache bei Leibniz'. This long and excellent essay, closely argued and rich in references to published and unpublished material, must be judged the best treatment we have of the main features of Leibniz' philosophy of language. It is true, Heinekamp argues, that Leibniz in his later years was chiefly preoccupied with natural language, but 'Daraus darf man jedoch nicht schliessen, er sei in seinem Alter von den Plänen einer characteristica universalis abgerückt. Für die Annahme einer Entwicklung im Sinne von Heintz sehe ich keine Anhaltspunkte. Noch kurz vor seinem Tode schreibt Leibniz: "Je voy qu'il est possible d'inventer une caractéristique générale, qui pourroit faire dans toutes les recherches capables de certitude, ce que l'Algebra fait dans les Mathématiques"' (449; the cited passage is from a letter written in 1716, eight months before Leibniz' death). For Leibniz, all human thinking is symbolic, it depends on signs. The instrument of knowledge is language. 'Da die Ideen den Dingen entsprechen und die Sprache den Ideen entsprechen soll, kann Leibniz sagen, "dass die Worte nicht nur den Gedancken, sondern auch der Dinge Zeichen seyn." Deshalb is die Sprache nicht nur Mittel zur Erkenntnis der Gedanken, sondern auch zur Erkenntnis der Wirklichkeit' (465). It was the aim of the characteristica universalis to be a perfect language in the sense that error, both in regard to logic and knowledge, would become as apparent as error in arithmetic or algebra when the symbols are before the eye. But Leibniz never fully worked out this idea, 'er hat nur wenige und nicht sehr weit durchgeführte Versuche hinterlassen. Seine Studien zum Aufbau der Characteristica stehen im Missverhältnis zu seinen programmatischen Äusserungen' (453). The natural languages, however, are also systems of signs that can serve as the instrument of knowledge. 'In dieser Hinsicht besteht zwischen der lingua rationalis und den Muttersprachen kein wesentlicher, sondern nur ein gradueller Unterschied' (469). But the artificial signs of the characteristica have a different relation to what they express than the words or signs of natural languages. The latter take their origin according to 'dem principium rationis sufficientis. ... Dabei is zu beachten, dass nach Leibniz nicht Dinge selbst die unmittelbare Ursache für das Benennen sind, sondern die Eindrücke (die affectũs), die die Dinge im Subject hervorrufen' (475). Here Leibniz distinguishes between rootwords and deviations. The rootwords may indeed be considered simple signs, 'aber ihnen entspricht nicht ein einfacher Begriff, sondern eine elementare Empfindung, eine einfache Perzeption' (478), whereas the characteristica operates with signs for simple concepts and for complex concepts; they are designed to serve as the vehicle and expression of such perfect knowledge as we may imagine to be natural to higher intellectual beings and to Adam before the fall, but not to man. But the artificial signs of the characteristica lose in width of applicability and use what they gain in precision, 'die Zwecksetzung der künstlichen Zeichensysteme ist eng begränzt. Diese Zeichensysteme zielen nur auf das Auffinden und Vergegenwärtigen von Erkenntnissen ab. In den natürlichen Sprachen spiegelt sich hingegen die gesamte Fülle des menschlichen Geistes. Die Sprache "ist eine Dolmetscherin des Gemüths and eine Behalterin der Wissenschaft". Sie ist ein Weg zur Erkenntnis des menschlichen Geistes "et de la merveilleuse variété de ses opérations". Deshalb konnte es nicht Leibniz' Absicht sein, so wird man folgern dürfen, die natürlichen Sprachen durch die characteristica zu ersetzen. Was die natürliche Sprache von der lingua philosophica trennt, ist der Unterschied zwischen sinnlicher Wahrnehmung und Vernufterkenntnis. Diese beiden

Gebiete berühren und durchdringen sich zwar an vielen Punkten, aber es ist (wenigstens vom Standpunkt des Menschen) nicht möglich, einen der beiden Bereiche auf den anderen zurückzuführen. Diesen Unterschied verwischt wer behauptet, Leibniz habe eine Kunstsprache vorgeschwebt, in die "alle umgangssprachlichen Äusserungen übersetzt werden können". Die characteristica sollte und konnte nicht alle Funktionen der natüralichen Sprachen übernehmen, sie sollte vielmehr nur im Bereich der Wissenschaften an die Stelle der Muttersprachen treten. Dadurch wird der Wert und die Bedeutung der Muttersprachen nicht herabgesetzt, sondern ihre Besonderheit wird gerade durch die Gegenüberstellung mit der lingua philosophica sichtbar. ... Deshalb gibt es keinen Widerspruch zwischen Leibniz' Projekt einer characteristica universalis und seinen Ausführungen über die natürlichen Sprachen, seine Monadologie bietet die Möglichkeit, beide Standpunkte miteinander zu vereinigen' (487–8). I have given so much attention to Heinekamp's excellent essay because it seems to me to be successful and definitive in removing once for all one of the most serious obstacles to a better view of Leibniz' study and philosophy of language, what I have above called the Cassirer tradition.

Two recent articles, Brekle 1971 and Dascal's critique (1971), raise some interesting issues. Citing a number of texts from Leibniz' scattered fragments on logic and the theory of language along with Brekle's own interpretation of them, Brekle tries to demonstrate that the idea of a generative grammar can be found in Leibniz. To this attempt and the conclusion that duly follows, it seems to me it may first be remarked that the conclusion is hardly surprising. For if it is true, as I think is generally granted, that transformational and generative grammar has strong roots in the conceptions and terminology that pertain to logic and have long been known there (e.g. Carnap), then it is no wonder that the application in turn of present-day principles and procedures of that grammar to such texts as the ones here under discussion, will reveal close similarities and even agreement. Thus the argument is in fact circular. This, however, is not the line Dascal follows. He grants that 'on the whole, I think that there are enough similarities, both in methodological and in substantive issues, between Leibniz' and the generativists' conceptions to justify Brekle's claim that there is an "idea of a generative grammar" in Leibniz' writings. However, I would like to see this claim better justified' (272). Dascal is refreshingly unorthodox and critical, for, as he says, 'Although my comments support the view that there is an analogy between generativism and Leibniz, who is placed by Chomsky in the tradition of "Cartesian linguistics", I do not accept most of Chomsky's own arguments in support of this view' (272). Dascal then first tries to show, I think successfully, that on Brekle's showing Leibniz' theory 'can be shown to be compatible with both generative and structuralist theories of language. ... And, in that case,' he asks, 'would it not be more proper to say that they contain an "idea of linguistic theory" *tout court*' (273). The discussion of this point occupies the major part of the article, which then in the final pages suggests a better justification of Brekle's claim. Unfortunately the paper ends on a somewhat inconclusive note, as if it were not quite finished according to its initial plan, but it remains successful both in its critique of Brekle and of some rather basic Chomskyan conceptions. One point of criticism is, I think, especially forceful because it applies to many current attempts to find instances and anticipations of recent doctrine in older texts by means of interpretations that are so careless that success is assured. Assuming that the cited texts would largely speak for themselves in favor of his argument, Brekle supplies only rather general interpretation. Dascal's answer has general import: 'This would not be a flaw if Leibnizian terminology were really unequivocally understandable by the contemporary reader. Unfortunately, this is not the case. As a matter of fact, there are changes in the meaning of Leibniz' terms even from text to text, so that the same term may express quite different concepts for him. *A fortiori*, it is by no means certain that the same terms have the same meanings today as they had for Leibniz. ... Some interpretative work is ... needed in order to ensure that the similarity is not merely a superficial and terminological one (in which case it may, in fact, conceal more profound dissimilarities)' (273).

Since it has more than local implications, I may perhaps comment on a point Dascal makes with reference to something I have said. In Aarsleff 1969 (179) I had stressed that Leibniz' law of sufficient reason for him also operates in natural languages. 'In my opinion,' Dascal continues, 'this clearly shows that Leibniz' linguistic studies [i.e. of natural languages] and his search for a "philosophical language", though different subjects, are closely connected, since they are based on the same principles. A clear recognition of this fact would have led Aarsleff (1970:579ff.) to admit that the "fusion of universal grammar and the origin of language", attributed by him to the work of the 18th century (particularly Du Marsais and Condillac) had already been accomplished, though perhaps without historical consequences, in the work of Leibniz' (283). The point is well taken and I entirely agree. There was no need, however, to make this point in that context, where I was only concerned with the fusion I pointed out, a fusion that is not historically traceable to Leibniz. It is another matter that there is here a profound connection between seventeenth- and eighteenth-century theories of language that is altogether missed, both actually and potentially, by 'Cartesian linguistics' and its epigones in what they consider 'history'. Not only Leibniz but also the seventeenth century at large are seriously misunderstood so long as it is assumed that all that pertains to the history of linguistics falls in the category of grammar, with the addition perhaps of the philosophical language. It is with considerable eagerness that one looks forward to Dascal's forthcoming "Aspects de la sémiologie de Leibniz".

It is not hard to see what tasks scholarship on Leibniz' study of language may set itself for the future. First of all, a more precise handling of the texts and the arguments than have often been the case. Secondly, further study of the interrelationships among the various aspects of his study in order to gain a fuller understanding of his philosophy of language. Thirdly, an effort to study and integrate the material that is becoming available in future volumes of the Akademie-Ausgabe. Fourth, the publication of relevant texts. Sigrid von der Schulenburg had done much work toward an edition of the unpublished "Epistolaris de historia etymologica dissertatio", but her work was lost in the closing months of the Second War. This unpublished manuscript consists of some eighty-five closely written folio pages written in response to his former secretary, J. G. Eckhart's *Historia etymologici lingvae germanicae* (1711), itself a significant work in the history of linguistics (the name is also spelled Eccard). The unfinished manuscript presents a history of etymological doctrines, organized by the original language they postulated: Hebrew, Greek, Latin, or some fourth language. Written late in life, it demonstrates Leibniz' vast knowledge of the subject and its bibliography. With its citation of some 250 little-known works that were important in their day, in the sixteenth and seventeenth centuries, the "Epistolaris" is among other things a bibliography of unequalled importance for the history of the study of language. I am preparing an edition of this manuscript. (For a brief description see Schulenburg 1937:5 and Aarsleff 1969:177 with quotations there and *passim*. On Eckhart, see Leskien 1965.)

A further task, of great proportions and very considerable difficulty, must be the examination of the linguistic and etymological collections Leibniz brought together for his own use and study. The items that are not by Leibniz in the *Collectanea etymologica* give an impression of what to expect, as does the section 'Philologie' in Bodemann 1966a. 125–165. Sixth, it will be necessary to study more carefully Leibniz' relationship to linguistic work and doctrines of language in the sixteenth and seventeenth centuries. As has been suggested above, without such an examination it is not possible to assess Leibniz' originality.

There is finally a problem of great fascination, if it can be reduced to manageable proportions. Leibniz carried on an extensive correspondence with other linguistic scholars, many of whom were the first to study distant and hitherto unknown languages, write grammars, compile dictionaries, and collect materials. Several of them were Jesuits. A few names will indicate what I mean: Grimaldi, La Loubère, La Croze, Hiob Ludolf, Gerhard Meier, Sparwenfeld, Nicolaas Witsen, and Melchisédech Thévenot. Employed in a variety of positions, why did these men take such an avid interest in linguistic phenomena? What were their motivations? In other words, Leibniz' profound interest in the practical study of language is only the best-known example of the learning and scholarship that flourished in his time, directed chiefly toward the non-classical languages and often toward non-European languages. This is ultimately a problem in the sociology of knowledge and scholarship. Most of these people are now little known; what we need first of all are good monographs that study each figure in depth in order to identify his intellectual profile, so to speak, studies that have precise bibliographies, lists of unpublished materials, and analyses of the main lines of their work. Monographs of that sort are not easy to write, and they unfortunately tend to gain little attention in the circles that ought to welcome them the most. Not least in the history of linguistics there has been a tendency to admire facile and spectacular claims of vast scope but little or no substance. We shall never have firm foundations until the solid monograph is given the respect it deserves.

As an example of the difficulty of studying these figures as well as of the fascinating insights that may be gained from such study, I can refer to Kangro's (1969) excellent essay on the Hamburg physician, traveller, scholar and linguist Martin Fogel (1634–1675), who was a student of Joachim Jungius. Though they never met or corresponded, Fogel and Leibniz shared several correspondents. Leibniz was, however, familiar with Fogel's work, and in 1678 Leibniz bought his library and manuscripts for the Hanoverian library, now the Niedersächsische Landesbibliothek, where they are still preserved. For readers unfamiliar with the nature and quality of the learned world of the seventeenth century, with its scholars and their lives, Kangro's essay is a most instructive introduction. Fogel is representative of a host of other scholars with similar interests and careers, men who have left their mark in history — and at the same time they may serve as a reminder that the so-called 'Cartesian linguistics' was by no means the most prominent mode of linguistic study in that century. The belief that it was, so widely held today, is a serious obstacle to our knowledge and understanding of the history of the study of language. The insights that may be gained from Kangro 1969 are fruitfully supplemented by Lakó 1969, also on Fogel, and Hormia 1964 which is devoted to a closely related subject.

Leibniz' influence is hard to assess at the present time. On balance I think one must admit that it has not been great and almost certainly less than has often been claimed. Again, the question cannot be answered until we have more precise knowledge. In general, one must agree with Sigrid von der Schulenburg's observation: 'Unter allen Anstössen, die Leibniz der deutschen Sprachwissenschaft gegeben hat, am nachhaltigsten gewirkt hat vielleicht sein ruheloses Drängen auf Erforschung der Mundarten und auf Sammlung ihrer besonderen Wörter. Ähnlich fruchtbare, zukunftsreiche Gedanken entwickelt er auf diesem Gebiete nur noch bei seinen Vorschlägen zur Sammlung und Erklärung der volkstümlichen Kunstwörter' (4). But in the present state of knowledge, it is not easy to indicate precisely how this effect showed itself.

Bibliography to Section 1

AARSLEFF, HANS. 1964. Leibniz on Locke on language. American Philosophical Quarterly 1.165–88.

——. 1967. See Bibliography to Section 2.

——. 1969. The study and use of etymology in Leibniz. Studia Leibnitiana. Supplementa 3.173–89.

——. 1970. See Bibliography to Section 2.

——. 1971a. Locke's reputation in nineteenth-century England. The Monist 55.392–422.

——. 1971b. 'Cartesian linguistics': History or fantasy? Language Sciences 17 (October 1971). 1–12.

——. 1975a. Schulenburg's 'Leibniz als Sprachforscher' with some observations on Leibniz and the study of language. Studia Leibnitiana 7. Heft 1. Forthcoming.

ARNDT, HANS W. 1967. Die Entwicklungsstufen von Leibniz' Begriff einer Lingua universalis. Das Problem der Sprache, ed. by Hans-Georg Gadamer, 71–9. München, Fink.

BELAVAL, YVON. 1947. Leibniz et la langue allemande. EGerm 2.121–32.

BERNARDINI, ANTONIO and GAETANO RIGHI. 1947. Il concetto di filologia e di cultura classica nel pensiero moderno. Bari, Laterza. [xlv, 687 pp. Leibniz, pp. 119–28.]

BITTNER, KONRAD. 1931–2. Slavica bei G. W. von Leibniz. Germanoslavica 1.3–32, 161–234, 509–57.

BODEMANN, EDUARD. 1966a [1889]. Die Leibniz-Handschriften der Königlichen Öffentlichen Bibliothek zu Hannover. Mit Ergänzungen und Register von Gisela Krönert und Heinrich Lackmann, sowie mit einem Vorwort von Karl-Heinz Weimann. Hildesheim, Olms. [383 pp.]

——. 1966b [1895]. Der Briefwechsel des Gottfried Wilhelm Leibniz in der Königlichen Öffentlichen Bibliothek zu Hannover, mit Ergänzungen und Register von Gisela Krönert und Heinrich Lackmann, sowie einem Vorwort von Karl-Heinz Weimann. Hildesheim, Olms. [463 pp.]

BÖCKMANN, PAUL. 1949. Die aufklärerische Sprachauffassung bei Leibniz. Formgeschichte der deutschen Dichtung; Vol. 1: Von der Sinnbildsprache zur Ausdruckssprache. Der Wandel der literarischen Formensprache vom Mittelalter zur Neuzeit, 477–83. Hamburg.

BREKLE, H.E. 1971a. Die Idee einer generativen Grammatik in Leibnizens Fragmenten zur Logik. Studia Leibnitiana 3.141–9.

——. 1971b. See Bibliography to Section 2.

CALLE, D.U. GONZÁLEZ DE LA. 1946. Orientación filológica de Leibniz. BICC, 2.233–76.

CASSIRER, ERNST. 1902. Leibniz' System in seinen wissenschaftlichen Grundlagen. Marburg. [549 pp.]

——. 1953. See Bibliography to Section 2.

COSERIU, EUGENIO. 1969. G.G. Leibniz. Die Geschichte der Sprachphilosophie von der Antike bis zur Gegenwart. Eine Übersicht. Part I, Von der Antike bis Leibniz, ed. by G. Narr and R. Windisch, 149–55. Tübingen.

COUTURAT, LOUIS. 1901. La logique de Leibniz. Paris, F. Alcan. [608 pp.]

——. See LEIBNIZ 1903.

CURRÁS RÁBADE, ANGEL. 1969. Consideraciones sobre la lengua universal leibniziana. Anales del Seminario de Metafísica 1969.7–39. Madrid.

DASCAL, MARCELO. 1971. About the idea of generative grammar in Leibniz. Studia Leibnitiana 3.272–90.

——. 1972. "Aspects de la sémiologie de Leibniz." Doctoral dissertation, Jerusalem.

DAVILLÉ, LOUIS. 1909. Leibniz historien. Paris. [798 pp.]

DE MAURO. 1969. See Bibliography to Section 2.

DREIKE, BEATE MONIKA. 1973. Herders Naturauffassung in ihrer Beeinflussung durch Leibniz' Philosophie. Studia Leibnitiana. Supplementa 10. Wiesbaden, Franz Steiner Verlag. [137 pp.]

DUTENS. See LEIBNIZ 1768.

ECKERT, HORST. 1971. G.W. Leibniz' Scriptores Rerum Brunsvicensium. Entstehung und historiographischer Bedeutung. Veröffentlichungen des Leibniz-Archivs, hrsg. von der Niedersächsischen Landesbibliothek, 3. Frankfurt am Main, Klostermann. [155 pp.]

EKOWSKI, FELIX and ANKE HÖLZER. 1973. Leibniz-Bibliographie. Neue Titel 1970–72. Studia Leibnitiana 4.304–19.

ERHARD, FR. and W. PLATZECK. 1972. Gottfried Wilhelm Leibniz y Raimundo Llull. Estudios Lulianos 16.129–93.

GERHARDT, C.I. See LEIBNIZ 1965.

GETTY, ROBERT J. 1962. Bentley and classical scholarship in North America. TAPA 93.34–50.

GRIMM, TILEMANN. 1969. China und das Chinabild von Leibniz. Studia Leibnitiana, Sonderheft 1, Systemprinzip und Vielheit der Wissenschaft, ed. by Udo Wilhelm Bargenda and Jürgen Blühdorn, 38–77.

GUERRIER, WALDEMAR. 1873. Leibniz in seinen Beziehungen zu Russland und Peter dem Grossen. Eine geschichtliche Darstellung dieses Verhältnisses nebst den darauf bezüglichen Briefen und Denkschriften. St. Petersburg and Leipzig. [xviii, 372 pp.]

GUHRAUER, G.E. 1846. Gottfried Wilhelm Freiherr von Leibniz. Eine Biographie. 2 vols. Breslau. [Reprinted Hildesheim, Olms, 1966.]

HAASE, CARL. See TOTOK 1966.

HANKAMER, PAUL. 1927. Die Sprache. Ihr Begriff und ihre Bedeutung im 16. und 17. Jahrhundert. Bonn. Leibniz, pp. 139–50.

HEINEKAMP, ALBERT. 1972. Ars characteristica und natürliche Sprache bei Leibniz. Tijdschrift voor Philosophie 34.446–88.

HEINTZ, GÜNTER. 1969. Point de vue. Leibniz und die These vom Weltbild der Sprache. ZDA 98.216–40. [Also in Zeitschrift für philosophische Forschung 27 (1973). 86–107.]

HOCHSTETTER, ERICH. 1966a. Leibniz-interpretation. Revue Internationale de Philosophie 21. 174–92.

——. 1966b. Zur Geschichte der Leibniz-Ausgabe. Zeitschrift für Philosophische Forschung, zum Gedenken an den 250. Totestag von Gottfried Wilhelm Leibniz 20.651–8.

——. 1969. Bericht über die Arbeiten der Leibniz-Forschungsstelle der Universität Münster. Studia Leibnitiana. Supplementa. 3.215–16.

HÖLZER. See KOCH-KLOSE 1971.

HÖLZER, ANKE and FELIX EKOWSKI. 1972. Leibniz-Bibliographie. Neue Titel 1970–72. Studia Leibnitiana 4.304–19.

HOFMANN, J.E. 1969. Bericht über die Herausgabe der mathematisch-naturwissenschaftlich-technischen Reihen III und VII innerhalb der Leibniz-Ausgabe. Studia Leibnitiana. Supplementa. 3.230–32.

HORMIA, OSMO. 1964. Über die finnougristischen Interessen von Olaus Rudbeck d. Ä. FUF 35.1–43.

HUBERTI, F.H. 1966. Bemerkungen zu Leibniz' Sprachverständnis an Hand des 3. Bandes der Neuen Essays über den Verstand. WW 16.361–75.

ISHIGURO, HIDE. 1972. Leibniz's philosophy of logic and language. London, Duckworth.

JACOBOWSKY, C.V. 1932. J.G. Sparwenfeld. Bidrag till en Biografi. Stockholm. [413 pp.]

KANGRO, HANS. 1969. Martin Fogel aus Hamburg als Gelehrter des 17. Jahrhunderts. UAJb 41.14–32.

KNEALE, MARTHA. See KNEALE and KNEALE 1962.

KNEALE, WILLIAM. 1966. Leibniz and the picture theory of language. Revue Internationale de Philosophie 21.204–15.

——, and MARTHA. 1962. The development of logic. Oxford. [761 pp.]

KOCH-KLOSE, ABEL and ANKE HÖLZER. 1971. Leibniz-Bibliographie. Neue Titel 1969–1971. Studia Leibnitiana 3.309–20.

KORNINGER, SIEGFRIED. 1958. G.W. Leibnizens Sprachauffassung. Sprache 4.4–14.

KRÖNERT. See BODEMANN 1966a and b, MÜLLER 1969.

LACKMANN. See BODEMANN 1966a and b.

LAKÓ, GYÖRGY. 1969. Martin Fogelius' Verdienste bei der Entdeckung der finnougrischen Sprachverwandtschaft. UAJb 41.3–13.

LANGLEY. See LEIBNIZ 1884.

LEIBNIZ. 1768. Opera omnia, ed. by L. Dutens. 6 vols. Geneva.

——. 1884. New essays concerning human understanding, tr. by A.G. Langley. La Salle, Illinois; Open Court. [3rd ed. unchanged 1949.]

——. 1903 Opuscules et fragments inédits de Leibniz, ed. by Louis Couturat. [682 pp.]

——. 1923– Akademie-Ausgabe. So far published:

Series I Allgemeiner politischer und historischer Briefwechsel, 8 vols. (1923–1970), covering the years 1668–1692.

II Philosophischer Briefwechsel, 1 vol. (1926), 1663–1685.

III Mathematischer, naturwissenschaftlicher und technischer Briefwechsel. Nothing published so far.

IV Politische Schriften, 2 vols. (1931, 1963), covering the years 1667–1687.

V Historische Schriften. Nothing published so far.

VI Philosophische Schriften, 3 vols. (1930–1966), covering the years 1663–1672 and Nouveaux essais.

VII Mathematische, naturwissenschaftliche und technische Schriften. Nothing published so far.

——. 1951. Selections, ed. by Philip P. Wiener. New York, Scribner's. [606 pp.]

——. 1960. Fragmente zur Logik, ed. and tr. by Franz Schmidt. Berlin, Akademie-Verlag. [547 pp.]

——. 1965. [1875–1890]. Die philosophischen Schriften, ed. by C.I. Gerhardt. 7 vols. Hildesheim, Olms.

——. 1966. Logical papers. A selection, ed. and tr. by G.H.R. Parkinson. Oxford. [148 pp.]

——. 1969². Philosophical papers and letters. A selection, ed. and tr., with an Introduction by Leroy E. Loemker. Dordrecht, Reidel. [736 pp.]

LENDERS, WINFRID. 1974. Leibniz on language and communication. In PARRET 1974.

LEROY, MAURICE. 1966. Les curiosités linguistiques de Leibniz. Revue Internationale de Philosophie 21.193–203.

LESKIEN, HERMANN. 1965. Johann Georg von Eckhart (1674–1730). Das Werk eines Vorläufers der Germanistik. Inaugural-Dissertation zur Erlangung der Doktorwürde der Philosophischen Fakultät der Julius-Maximillians-Universität zu Würzburg. München, Hermann Leskien. [227 pp.]

LOEMKER, LEROY E. 1961. Leibniz and the Herbarn Encyclopedists. Journal of the History of Ideas 22.323–38.

——. 1965. Leibniz in our time. A survey of recent Leibniz literature. PhR 13.83–111.

——. See LEIBNIZ 1969.

MERKEL, F.R. 1920. G.W. Leibniz und die China-Mission. Leipzig.

MLADENOV, STEFAN. 1950. Voltaire im Unrecht gegen Leibniz als genialen Sprachforscher. Miscellanea Academica Berolinensia. Gesammelte Abhandlungen zur Feier des 250-jährigen Bestehens der Deutschen Akademie der Wissenschaften zu Berlin. Vol. 2, part 1. 15–29.

MUGNAI, MASSIMO. 1973. Leibniz e la logica simbolica. Firenze, Sansoni. [91 pp.]

MÜLLER, KURT. 1967. Leibniz-Bibliographie. Verzeichnis der Literatur über Leibniz. Veröffentlichungen des Leibniz-Archivs, hrsg. von der Niedersächsischen Landesbibliothek. Vol. 1. Frankfurt am Main, Klostermann. [478 pp.]

——. 1969. Bericht über die Arbeiten des Leibniz-Archivs der Niedersächsischen Landesbibliothek Hannover. Studia Leibnitiana. Supplementa. 3.217–29.

——, and GISELA KRÖNERT. 1969. Leben und Werk von G.W. Leibniz. Eine Chronik. Veröffentlichungen der Niedersächsischen Landesbibliothek. Vol. 2. Frankfurt am Main, Klostermann. [331 pp.]

OLESCH, REINHOLD. 1967. G.W. Leibniz und das Dravänopolabische. Fontes lingvae dravaenopolabicae minores et chronica venedica J.P. Schvltzii, ed. by Reinhold Olesch, 269–76. Slavistische Forschungen. vol. 7. Köln/Graz, Böhlau Verlag.

——. 1968. Bibliographie zum Dravänopolabischen. Slavistische Forschungen, vol. 8. Köln/Graz, Böhlau Verlag. [126 pp.]

PARAIN, BRICE. 1942. Leibniz. Recherches sur la nature et les fonctions du langage, 117–36. Paris.

PARKINSON, G.H.R. 1965. Logic and reality in Leibniz's metaphysics. Oxford. [196 pp.]

——. See LEIBNIZ 1966.

PARRET, HERMAN, ed. 1974. History of linguistic thought and contemporary linguistics. The Hague, Mouton.

PATZIG, GÜNTHER. 1969. Leibniz, Frege und die sogenannte 'lingua characteristica universalis'. Studia Leibnitiana. Supplementa 3.103–12.

RAMOS, G. GORDEIRO. 1948. Leibniz e a investigacão linguística, Memórias da Academia das Ciñcias de Lisboa. Classe de Letras. Vol. 5. 99–123.

RAVIER, ÉMILE. 1937. Bibliographie des œuvres de Leibniz. Paris. [704 pp.]

RICHTER, LISELOTTE. 1946. Scythien, die Völkerschiede. Leibniz als Slawist. Leibniz und sein Russlandbild, 73–90. Berlin.

RIGHI, GAETANO. 1947. See BERNARDINI and RIGHI 1947.

RISSE, WILHELM. 1964. Die Logik der Neuzeit. Vol. 1, 1500–1640. Stuttgart-Bad Cannstatt. [573 pp.]

——. 1965. Bibliographia logica. Verzeichnis der Druckschriften zur Logik mit Angabe ihrer Fundstelle. Vol. 1, 1572–1800. Hildesheim, Olms. [292 pp.]

——. 1970. Die Logik der Neuzeit. Vol. 2, 1640–1780 Stuttgart-Bad Cannstatt. [749 pp. Leibniz, pp. 170–252.]

ROSSI, PAOLO. 1960. Le fonti della caracteristica Leibniziana. Clavis universalis. Arti mnemoniche e logica combinatoria da Lullo a Leibniz, 237–58. Milan.

RUSSELL, BERTRAND. 1900. A critical exposition of the philosophy of Leibniz, with an appendix of leading passages. London. [311 pp.]

RUTT, THEODOR. 1966. G.W. Leibniz und die deutsche Sprache. Mu 76.321–5.

SCHMIDT, FRANZ. 1955. Leibnizens rationale Grammatik. Zeitschrift für philosophische Forschung 9.657–63.

——. 1969. Zeichen, Wort und Wahrheit bei Leibniz. Studia Leibnitiana. Supplementa 3.190–208.

——. See LEIBNIZ 1960.

SCHRECKER, PAUL. 1938. Une bibliographie de Leibniz [Ravier 1937]. Revue Philosophique de la France et de l'Etranger 126.324–46.

SCHRÖTER, KARL. 1969. Bericht über den Stand der Leibniz-Ausgabe der Deutschen Akademie der Wissenschaften zu Berlin. Studia Leibnitiana. Supplementa 3.209–14.

SCHULENBURG, SIGRID VON DER. 1937. Leibnizens Gedanken und Vorschläge zur Erforschung der deutschen Mundarten. Abhandlungen der Preussischen Akademie der Wissenschaften. Philologisch-historische Klasse. 1937, No. 2. [37 pp.]

——. 1973. Leibniz als Sprachforscher. Frankfurt am Main, Klostermann. [328 pp.]

SOKOL, E.A. 1941. Leibniz and the German language, 193–202. Stanford Studies in Language and Literature, ed. by Hardin Craig.

TOTOK, WILHELM and CARL HAASE, eds. 1966. Leibniz; Sein Leben — sein Wirken — seine Welt. Hannover, Verlag für Literatur und Zeitgeschehen. [552 pp.]

UTERMÖHLEN, GERDA. 1969. Leibniz-Bibliographia 1967–1968. Studia Leibnitiana 1.294–320.

——. 1970. Leibniz–Bibliographie. Neue Titel 1968–1970. Studia Leibnitiana 2.302–20.

V.-DAVID, MADELEINE. 1961a. Leibniz et la 'Tableau de Cébès' (Nouveaux Essais IV, iii, 20) ou le problème du langage par Images. Revue Philosophique de la France et de l'Etranger 86.39–50.

——. 1965. See Bibliography to Section Two.

VERBURG, P. A. 1949. See Bibliography to Section 2.

——. 1952. See Bibliography to Section 2. On Leibniz pp. 265–6.

——. 1974. The idea of linguistic system in Leibniz. In PARRET 1974.

WATERMAN, JOHN T. 1963a. The languages of the world. A classification by G. W. Leibniz, 27–33. Studies in Germanic Languages and Literatures in Memory of Fred. O. Nolte, ed. by Erich Hofacker and Liselotte Dieckmann. St. Louis.

——. 1963b. See Bibliography to Section 2.

WEIMANN, KARL-HEINZ. 1965. Vorstufen der Sprachphilosophie Humboldts bei Bacon und Locke. ZDPh 84.498–508.

——. 1966a. Leibniz als Sprachforscher. TOTOK 1966:535–52.

——. 1966b. See BODEMANN 1966a and 1966b.

WELLS, RULON. 1957. Leibniz today. Review of Metaphysics 10.333–49.

WIENER. See LEIBNIZ 1951.

SECTION 2. THE EIGHTEENTH CENTURY

As in Section 1, this bibliographical essay will make no effort to mention every item that is listed in the bibliography. Further, since our view of the history of the study of language during the eighteenth century is at best fragmentary, I shall not attempt to write a unified essay but turn my attention to particular problems, figures, and areas of research. Without pretending to make systematic divisions, Section 2 will fall in five sections. The items will not normally be mentioned more than once. I shall begin with a survey of the bibliographical aids and other sources of information and orientation. I shall then, secondly, discuss the general works that cover the eighteenth century at large or substantial parts of it. Thirdly, I shall deal with some special areas of research which to me appear suggestive. Fourthly, I shall consider recent publication on some of the major figures. Finally, in an epilogue already promised early in Section 1, I shall deal with some of the problems that are raised by the history of the study of language, particularly in relation to the eighteenth century.

2.1 *Bibliographical Aids*

There is, not surprisingly, no general bibliography of the primary sources, a work it would be pointless to attempt until there is an adequate foundation for it in special studies that cumulatively cover most of the period. Subject bibliographies and systematic catalogues are not common in the eighteenth century, but there are some works which, once known and used with a little ingenuity, can be very useful. One such work is the *Allgemeines Repertorium der Literatur für die Jahre* 1785 *bis* 1800, which in two sets of three volumes a piece (for 1785–1790 and 1791–1795) and one set of two volumes (for 1796–1800) suggests how plentiful the material is even for such a short, though in this case important span as fifteen years. I have seen only the first two sets. Near the front of Volume One of each of these, Section Two is devoted to "Philologie," containing no less than 1,527 and 1,676 items covering not only German but also English and French items. One might suspect that the overwhelming majority of entries would pertain to classical studies, but there is in fact a very large number of items for such categories as philosophy of language, Chinese, Arabic, etc., etc. Volume three of these sets contain an alphabetical index of authors. There may be other works of a similar kind for other periods (though this work was not continued beyond 1800), but I am not aware of them. (I owe this reference to Stéfanini 1969:387, which on pp. 369–404 presents a rich bibliography of sources, both primary and secondary, even on the limited subject to which that work is devoted.) A much later work, Sommervogel 1890, gives a wealth of information on Jesuit writings, including the influential linguistic work in the eighteenth century. Thus the bibliography in Volume Ten, in the general section "Linguistique", has such categories as "Langues asiatiques" (including, e.g., Sanskrit and Chinese) and "Langues américaines" (pp. 970–77 and 978–84 respectively). I have mentioned the *Allgemeines Repertorium* and Sommervogel merely as examples of what can be found in works that may not come to our attention in the normal course of events. Provided one seeks a particular name or can find a fruitful subject entry, there is also much bibliographical information to be found in eighteenth-century encyclopedias and biographical reference works. It is obvious that the linguistic historian, like any other historian, must be familiar with and use such works. There is no reason to take seriously the charge of antiquarianism, which cannot legitimately be used of bibliography but only to point to lack of insight and proportion in the work that results from careful attention to bibliography.

For individual countries, a number of works give bibliography for particular subjects, especially grammar and lexicography. For French grammars, Stengel 1890 is immensely rich with very full indices of authors, titles, and places of publication. The introduction (1–18) also has much suggestive observation and information. For the study of the English language at large, Kennedy 1927 is still indispensable, and to my knowledge no work of similar scope exists for any other language. But for the primary grammatical literature it is now being superseded by Alston's (1965–) impressive project for a bibliography 'of the English language from the invention of printing to the year 1800', which began as an attempt to supplement Kennedy 1927. This immense one-man effort has so far produced nine volumes (with vol. 3 in two parts) of a planned total of twenty, of which the last will be a master index to the series. For each item it gives bibliographical description, location of copies in a large number of selected libraries (the same is true of Stengel 1890, but his information would now be unreliable), a brief indication of contents, significant manuscript notes in particular copies, and some information about modern editions, reviews, and critical studies. Each volume has separate indices of authors, of anonymous titles, and of subjects, editors, revisers, and translations. In addition a great many pages, chiefly title pages, are reproduced in facsimile. Naturally, in a work of such vast proportions perfection in every detail is not to be expected — the listing of secondary material, for instance, is spotty. Wider scholarly cooperation might have been desirable, but would almost certainly have endangered the safe progression of the work. Unfortunately, its considerable cost will for all but a few readers mean that it must be consulted in the library. Its chief virtue lies in the completeness of coverage, and on that score it is triumphant — though unless I have missed something it would appear that Thomas Nugent's English translation (1756) of Condillac's *Essai* (1746) is not found in vol. 3, part 2. Alston's work, though unfinished, has already borne fruit in Michael 1970, whose census of English grammars is based on Alston. Alston also presides over the facsimile reprint series of English linguistics from 1500 to 1800, which will contain some 365 titles produced at relatively modest prices (and some of them issued in paper), a service of great benefit to the history of linguistics.

For French grammar the admirable work Chevalier 1968 has a bibliography for items prior to 1800 on pp. 733–49. German grammars until Adelung near the end of the eighteenth century are listed in Jellinek 1913–14, vol. 1.3–19. On lexicography, Starnes and Noyes 1946 gives a "Bibliography and census of dictionaries in American libraries" on pp. 228–41. The amazing work by Quemada (1968) gives a "Relevé chronologique de répertoires lexicographiques français (1539–1863)" on pp. 567–634. This work testifies to the great upsurge in lexicography that has taken place in France in recent years, both in the form of new dictionaries (some already complete, others in the process of publication) and in the form of historical and systematic studies. This interest is only one aspect of the well-known, general increase in linguistic study which has also found expression in the publication of a rapidly increasing number of items, both articles and books, devoted to the history of linguistics. Readers would therefore do well to follow recent issues of such publications as *Langages*, *Français moderne*, and *Langue française*. Several recent items are listed in my bibliography. Some of them contain short bibliographies, for instance Clerico 1971 (22–4). Régaldo 1970 is a bibliography of primary sources by the 'idéologues' who were active and influential in philosophy, linguistic theory and education during the final decade of the eighteenth century and the early years of the nineteenth; it has a section on the philosophy of language and grammar. Joly 1970 is a republication of François Thurot's remarkable history of universal grammar first published in 1795 as the *Discours préliminaire* to a French translation of James Harris' Hermes. It must be one of the first writings ever to be devoted to the history of grammar. Useful also as a bibliographical source, it is an excellent work and has the special virtue of seeing its subject free of the distortions which the nineteenth century has interposed between us and the eighteenth century. It is worth noting that Thurot's introduction offers no support for the so-called 'Cartesian linguistics'. Near the beginning of the century was published quite a different work also devoted to the history of the study of language, Eckhart (or Eccard) 1711 (see Leskien 1965:31–58). Though obviously concerned chiefly with the work of the sixteenth and seventeenth centuries, this work is an important bibliographical source for the impressive number of writings that had already then been devoted to the origin and history of the Germanic languages. It reminds us — or those who need to be reminded — that grammar and grammatical theory was by no means the chief linguistic interest of the seventeenth century, a fact the history of linguistics cannot afford to ignore. If we admire the intellectual genius of that century, we must respect its universality.

Dünninger 1957 and Langen 1957 cover aspects of German work, though chiefly seen in the perspective of literary history and the sense of 'philology' that is now rare. As surveys both are informative and suggestive. Dünninger's bibliography is sparse, Langen's more ample.

The bibliographical aids that have so far been listed are quite comprehensive and give access to a good part of the primary literature. They indicate the wealth of material that is available, but clearly by no means exhaust it. The uncertain state of the bibliography, which in some measure reflects the difficulty of fixing the limits of the subject, directs attention to other items that provide general orientation both in regard to the subject and the literature. Among these are anthologies and works that discuss the philosophy and study of language in the context of other subjects. The rapid growth in the history of the study of language is shown by the number of anthologies that have appeared during the last few years. Texts which until recently could be found only in old publications in major libraries are now within reach of students at reasonable cost. Juncker 1948 led the way, but seems to have received little attention before it was superseded in 1955 by the first edition of Arens 1969 (which will be discussed in the next section). Opening with Locke and ending with Wittgenstein and Bulgakow, it has only German texts for the eighteenth century — Leibniz, Hamann, Herder, and Fichte. Tucker 1961 and Bolton 1966 are both confined to English texts, which is also true of Kühlwein 1971, a useful little volume with a large number of texts in rather short excerpts. With some overlap, Porset 1970 and Grimsley 1971 include a small number of important French texts, either entire or in substantial excerpts. From a somewhat different point of view, as indicated by the title, and also confined to France, Roudaut 1971 has texts that are not in Porset or Grimsley. It has a useful bibliography on pages 357–67. By far the largest, both in size and scope, is Jacob 1969. Its numerous short excerpts are organized in five major sections under the headings "Langage et philosophie," "Langage et art", "Langage et culture", "Langage et science", and "Langage et linguistique". These sections are divided in turn into sub-sections to make up the total of one hundred points of view. Thus the orientation of Jacob 1969 is not historical, but within each major section the selections are placed in chronological order. There is a bibliography for each of the 100 sections. It is in the nature of anthologies to cause disagreement about their inclusions and exclusions; reliance on a single anthology is not prudent, but used to supplement one another they constitute a welcome addition to the literature, not least for beginning students. We can no doubt look forward to the publication of other single texts or collections, especially perhaps from the house of Ducros in Bordeaux.

A number of items will serve as examples of what can be found in writings on related subjects. They especially offer much needed general orientation, and the best of them are models of research and exposition. No student can afford to ignore Wilbur Samuel Howell's two masterly volumes (1956 and 1971) on the history of British logic and rhetoric from 1500 to the first decades of the nineteenth century. Their immediate relevance speaks for itself. Other books of similar relevance — and I emphasize that these are only examples — are Blackall 1959, which should be supplemented by Kimpel's (1966) survey of recent literature attached to the German translation; Gerth 1960, Sørensen 1963; and Rauter 1970. Reichel 1968 calls attention to the importance of Pietism in German thought in the eighteenth century and as a preparation for Romanticism.

Since the study of language has in large measure found expression in scholarship and teaching, works on the history of these subjects are rich though often ignored sources of knowledge. Works of this kind include histories of learned societies, universities, academies, and in some cases publication series. Examples are Adams 1917, Douglas 1951, Evans 1956, Proust 1967b, and Lough 1968. One work merits special mention: Harnack's (1900) magnificent history of the Berlin Academy from its foundation by Leibniz in 1700 to the year 1900. I think it is fair to say that it is the single most significant work for gaining a wide knowledge and understanding of scholarship and learning during the eighteenth century. Lomholt (1942–61) performs a similar task for the Danish Academy, with relevant material especially 3.205–318 on etymology and lexicography. Lindroth 1967.715–88 has a chapter on the study of Swedish, a subject of particular interest owing to the tradition of linguistic speculation and scholarship in that country. The French *Encyclopédie* is so rich in material on the study of language that indispensable orientation must be sought in Proust 1967b and Lough 1968, which among their many uses give help in the identification of contributors. Though its immediate subject is quite different, Schwab 1950 is an excellent example of a work that offers much insight and information that relate to our understanding of the study of language. It is also a well-written and delightful book to read.

2.2 *General Works*

Among these, the first was a little book that has hardly received any attention, even in Denmark, though it was not only a pioneering effort but also a very reliable and informative survey, Lollesgaard 1925 on the philosophy and study of language in Denmark during the eighteenth century. It has an amazingly wide European orientation that might well have proved stimulating. Funke's two books (1927, 1934) are still useful and reveal a sympathetic understanding of their subject that was not common at the time.

But the best-known item is of course Harnois' brief monograph (1928), which has only recently received the attention it deserves. The Preface itself is almost prophetic, even its title: "Science et histoire des sciences; Linguistique et histoire de la linguistique" (7–11). Perhaps Harnois' interest was first roused by a statement he cites, made by Maurice Grammont in 1920 in a review of a book which devoted one of its last chapters to a sketch of the history of linguistics. Grammont's reaction was severe: 'Au début de ce chapitre, l'auteur consacre trop de pages à ce qui est antérieur au XIXe siècle et qui, n'étant pas encore de la linguistique, pouvait être expédié en quelques lignes' (1918–20:439). Disagreeing with Grammont, Harnois observed:

> Il est clair que la valeur d'une théorie ne peut être appréciée justement que si l'on sait à quelle autre elle succède et comment elle prévalut. L'histoire des sciences ne doit pas être séparée de la science; et surtout l'époque des erreurs ne doit pas être négligée dans cette histoire. Saisir et expliquer comment la physique a corrigé petit à petit diverses erreurs, n'est pas inutile pour se rendre compte de ce que représente exactement le physique dans son état actuel. ... Rien n'est plus faux et dans tous les cas rien n'est plus propre à faire méconnaître l'intérêt de l'histoire antérieure de ces sciences [archéologie, etnographie, épigraphie, sociologie, linguistique]. Sans doute n'est-il pas absolument sans raison de dire que la linguistique n'existait pas avant le XIXe siècle mais c'est peut-être qu'on donne à linguistique un sens trop étroit et trop exclusivement défini par un genre de méthode qui de fait n'est apparu qu'au cours du XIXe siècle. Or dans ce cas et en dépit de certaines apparences on pourrait avec au moins autant de raison imaginer pour la physique moderne un autre nom que celui qu'elle avait au XVIIIe siècle. (8–9)

I have quoted these remarks at some length because they seem to me both still very apposite and also historically interesting. To make his point Harnois gave an account of French theories of language from 1660 to 1821; he gave serious historical attention to the Port-Royal grammar, to Condillac, Maupertuis, Beauzée, Turgot, Du Marsais, and a few others — the small scope did not offer opportunity for details.

Harnois' accomplishment cannot be doubted, but he did introduce a mode of treatment which staked out the lines of development in a manner that has proved less than adequate. In spite of its title, much more than half of the work is devoted to grammatical theory, so that Rousseau, Turgot, and Leibniz have to be introduced as 'independents' in the fifth of the six chapters. Condillac figured among the grammarians, who were divided in rationalists and empiricists, with Condillac in the latter category. Condillac's influential theory of the origin of language thus becomes a grammatical subject; further, with only brief mention of the *Essai sur l'origines des connaissances humaines* (1746), Condillac, even on the origin of language, is allowed to speak only from the *Grammaire* first published in 1775. Thus the historical significance of the *Essai* is obscured, in fact missed. If the *Essai* had not been lost in this fashion, there would have been no reason to introduce a category of 'independents', which of course blocks historical continuity and coherence. Though Harnois is hardly the source of this error about the *Essai*, there is no doubt that he confirmed it. Failure to see the full significance of the *Essai* has proved the single most significant obstacle to our understanding of the history of the philosophy of language in the eighteenth century. This error has its roots in Condillac's official nineteenth-century reputation, which was based on a false ideological interpretation of his philosophy. Similarly, also recently, his linguistic philosophy is more often than not derived from the posthumous *Langue des calculs* (1798), which is obviously not the work by which he gained his influence as soon as the *Essai* appeared in 1746. (I deal in detail with this problem in Aarsleff 1974; there is also relevant matter in Aarsleff 1971a.) Within Harnois' French context, this distortion was perhaps not serious, but applied to Germany it confirmed the long-held belief that there was a complete separation between Condillac and Herder. Harnois' brief bibliography was perhaps the first to bring together a number of little-known titles on the study of language in eighteenth-century France.

Kuehner (1944), even briefer than Harnois, tried to redress the balance by dealing with the origin of language. He is no doubt right that Harnois had been chiefly interested in predecessors of modern linguistics and consequently had avoided 'reference to the theories on the origin of language wherever possible' (vi). Kuehner brings together a great deal of material, and his exposition is quite sound, except on Condillac. He describes his basic theory as postulating that language originates 'in a spontaneous response to sensations without necessary intervention of reason' (viii). There is no scope for an explanation here, except to say that Condillac postulates reason as innate to man; it finds expression in reflection and the 'liaison des idées', which make the use of signs both possible and productive. Condillac makes a sharp division between natural signs, which animals also have and which do not constitute the language whose origin Condillac is talking about, and the deliberate use of artificial, conventional signs which alone create the language that is man's special possession. The notion that Condillac derived all knowledge from sensation is as false about his doctrines as it is about Locke's, an error that has often made chaos of the intellectual history of the eighteenth century. Thus Kuehner's statement is not correct that Condillac 'draws no clear line of distinction between a non-thinking and a thinking human being, between unconscious and conscious language' (26). For the same reason, Kuehner cannot produce a coherent account of Condillac's argument.

Recently a book has appeared under the promising title *Philosophies of language in eighteenth-century France* by Pierre Juliard (1970). In it one will consistently find the name de Brosses spelt de Brosse, and William Templeton (59) occurs for William

Temple. One will further learn that 'The *Grammaire de Port-Royal* enjoyed great popularity and laid the foundations for nearly all works on language during the eighteenth century. Its disciples can be divided into two groups. The first of these is composed of grammarians like Dumarsais who produced innumerable grammars theoretically based on reason' (14). In a work under this title one might expect awareness that Condillac, building on Locke, is the focus of 'philosophies of language', and if the implication is that Du Marsais also wrote many grammars, it is false, for he in fact wrote at most one, though he did write on grammatical and linguistic subjects. About Condillac we learn that he 'could not picture man formulating a language at will. To perform such a task the mind could not have remained in a passive state as the abbé claimed it had done' (30); on page 45 we are told that according to Condillac 'all knowledge comes from sensations and evolves in a completely passive mind'. But in between we have read that 'Condillac allotted to man the most important role in language formation' (and we then read on: 'De Brosse regarded nature as the ultimate source, while Court de Gébelin attempted to combine nature and man without divorcing them entirely from divine inspiration'). Finally, near the end we are told that, 'Condillac showed how ideas could be developed in a passive mind through the use of signs' (102) — one wonders then who or what is using the signs and whether whatever it is, is passive in doing so. These examples indicate the level of understanding of this book. Not a single text has been adequately understood or correctly placed in relation to any other text. There is no sense whatever that the chronological sequence of texts might be relevant to proper understanding, thus also no sense of primary and influential arguments in relation to secondary ones. The exposition is throughout painfully disorganized to such a degree that the difficulty is not merely expository but lies in failure to comprehend the subject matter. In a brief attempt to deal with inversion, we read that, 'the most ridiculous part of this argument was that the authors involved believed that their own particular way of thinking reflected the only natural order possible' (52). A matter so important as the philosophical language in Descartes and Leibniz (56) is drawn from Preserved Smith, *A history of modern culture*. The intellectual context is assumed to be all-important, yet the author reveals no sense of it. A single example will suffice: 'The eighteenth-century philosophers ... did not have the aid of modern science or anthropology. Their efforts were aimed at finding a new solution with which to repudiate the Church's answer' (89). This little book of 104 pages and a very skimpy bibliography was a Ph.D. dissertation, and comparison with the typescript shows that it has been printed absolutely raw — even the most obvious errors have not been corrected. It appears inconceivable that it passed referees for publication and unlikely that the Professor who oversees this series has read it. Yet, this piece is sent forth in a series to which a large number of libraries have standing orders. Its publication is an act of irresponsibility. It may also indicate something about the popularity of the history of linguistics. One can only agree with Professor Christmann's assessment (1971:174) of, 'der haarsträubenden Inkompetenz dieser Schrift. Wer das Siegel B.E.R.M. der *Encyclopédie* nicht aufzulösen versteht und die elementarste Sekundärliteratur nicht kennt, hat keine Anspruch darauf, ernst genommen zu werden.'

Let me now discuss two substantial works, both German and covering more than the eighteenth century. Arens 1955 with its second expanded edition (with the same type increased from 568 pages to 816) and Borst 1957–63. No student of the history of linguistics can fail to recognize the importance and influence of Arens' great anthology. It has no doubt done more than any single work to promote the subject and smooth the way for the beginner. Its popularity was proved by the recent issue of a second edition that contains much new material. For our period, however, only nine lines from ten Kate (1969:105) and a single-paragraph selection from G. C. Lichtenberg are new (1969:129). For the rest — Leibniz, Condillac, Herder, etc. — the selections of texts are exactly the same. All other changes occur in the expository matter that links the selections. Mention of Christoph Besold (1955:87) has unfortunately been omitted, but new matter on Junius, Hickes, and ten Kate added (1969.104–5). Other additions occur under Horne Tooke (134), Kraus (140), and with the mention of Gyarmathi (148). The categories follow the conventional divisions of the 'official' version of intellectual history. Condillac is introduced as a typical representative of the French 'rationalistisch-psychologische Betrachtung', which, true to the category, is characterized by 'einer Ungeduld und Unduldsamkeit des Geistes gegenüber dem Leben, das man mathematisch nur bewältigen kann, wenn man es als einen reinen Mechanismus auffasst'. Thus 'die Sprache wird also überhaupt nicht als Lebensform und -ausdruck gesehen, sondern immer noch und nur als ein — an sich logisches — System von Zeichen für Vorstellungen und zum Ausdruck von Urteilen. Typisch für diese Geisteshalttung und Geistesschärfe ist ... Condillac' (1955:89; 1969:106–7). This, of course, is a travesty of Condillac. Arens denies him the very qualities that were central to his conception of the nature of man and of his achievements and progress in all modes of expression from poetry and art to philosophy and mathematics. Condillac is represented by one passage from the posthumous *Langue des calculs* (1798) and another yet briefer from the *Essai* (1746), both of which fail to indicate the nature of Condillac's philosophy of language. There is no inkling that it was Condillac who for the eighteenth century formulated the problem of the origin of language.

Herder is introduced under "Deutsche Richtung: Anthropologische Betrachtung", and here we learn that the problem of the origin of language had long been a topic in Germany, while in France it was treated only peripherally (1955:102–103; 1969:120–1). One consequence of Arens' conventional opinion of Condillac is that prominent aspects of Herder's *Ursprung* will appear more original and new than they were. We shall later meet other examples of this strange disregard of Condillac's overwhelmingly influential *Essai.* In 1969 Du Marsais has gained a single brief mention in connection with the Port-Royal grammar in the section on the seventeenth century. Still, for all its shortcomings, Arens' great anthology is a useful source and an instructive work. No other work presents so many important texts.

Arno Borst's great six-volume work (with continuous pagination from beginning to end) is surely one of the great scholarly compilations in recent time. One wonders how it was done, then whether it was worth doing in that form, and soon one also ponders the problem as to exactly what it is trying to do, for its scope and limits are by no means clear. It often — but not for every figure — contains more than strictly belongs under the subject as stated in the subtitle: 'Geschichte der Meinungen über Ursprung und Vielfalt der Sprachen.' It is organized in long sections under very general headings borrowed from intellectual history of the most schematic sort. The sections that concern us are "Aufklärung und Apologetik" (1395–1520) and the earlier part of "Revolution und Romantik" (1521–1629), both in Vol. 3, Part 2.

Within each section the subject-matter is organized geographically, thus in the former section in the order: England; France; Holland, Scandinavia, Russia; Germany; and Switzerland, Italy, and Spain. But in the latter a different order is followed: Germany; Germany's neighbors, including now England; America and France; and finally the other Romance languages. This geographical organization makes it virtually impossible to take adequate account of crosscurrents and influences except when they happen to come in the same order as this somewhat arbitrary disposition. For instance, with no America in the former section, William Penn (1644–1718) suddenly appears long past the mid-point of "Revolution und Romantik" (1597). Thus in spite of the subtitle, it is not easy to make history out of all this. But there is a second more serious difficulty: the facile acceptance of quite meaningless categories that are meant to refer to intellectual history — with the consequence already mentioned that intellectual history itself is left unaffected by the presentation. In connection with François Raynal, we learn: 'Hier ist ernst gemacht mit den Sätzen Johnsons und Condillacs, dass eine Sprache Spiegelbild ihres Volkes und Gradmesser seiner geschichtlichen Reife ist; schon das ist ein Schritt über die Aufklärung hinaus.' But is it really? And what becomes of the category Enlightenment when Johnson and Condillac are not in it? It continues: 'Wer sonst unter den Franzosen hätte statt der Sprache an sich die historischen Sprachen betrachtet, nicht als natürliche oder vernünftige Prinzipien, sondern als geschichtliche Fakten?' (1449). The answer is quite a few. And in regard to the view attributed to Johnson and Condillac, it was as we have seen found in both Locke and Leibniz.

The section on "Revolution und Romantik" opens with this ominous rhetorical flourish: 'Zwischen 1770 und 1830 bestimmten Deutsche Bewegung und Französische Revolution das Verhältnis von Religion und Geschichte zu Sprache und Volk grundlegend neu, im schöpferischen Widerspruch gegen Absolutismus und Aufklärung. Anders als der internationale Adel sah das jetzt aufsteigende Bürgertum in der Muttersprache das Abzeichen seiner Gemeinschaft, in der Nation der Gleichgesinnten die Gesellschaft selbst' (1521). Moving close to Herder: 'In Deutschland brachte die Deutsche Bewegung die Selbstbefreiung des deutschen Geistes von der romanischen Rationalität und den Durchbruch von den erstarrten Traditionen zur deutschen Wirklichkeit. ... Der eine Man, der dies alles begann, ... Herder, fasste den

Widerspruch gegen die Aufklärung, von Leibniz and Lessing bis Hamann und Möser, genial zusammen' (1522). But alas, a few pages later we learn that, 'Herder wurde von seinen Zeitgenossen gern als Aufklärer missverstanden' (1527). One more serious problem must be mentioned: the difficulty of telling the trivial opinion from systematic argument. Only if a particular argument or text is devoted wholly to the multiplicity of languages is there any hope of adequate representation. Thus N. F. S. Grundtvig (1783–1872) enters with a few bizarre opinions, but no mention — since it does not fall within the chosen framework — that he was an original and influential philologist (1590–91; cf. Aarsleff 1967:185–9). Pope enters with a few lines from "The Rape of the Lock" and Coleridge with some from "Frost at Midnight". A final long section under the title "Geschichte und Sprache" (1885–2046) attempts to tie it all together, but reading it one senses the impossibility of success as a consequence of the order and conception of the entire work. I have in recent secondary literature observed dependence on Borst for reliable information about the general linguistic views of the vast number of individual figures who parade through its many pages. For the reasons I have given, such faith is misplaced. Its use must lie in the access it gives to a vast number of texts that deal with, touch on, or barely suggest something about the multiplicity of languages. For that purpose — which is surely its own justification — a single alphabetical bibliography would have served as well, perhaps combined with compact chronological and geographical listings. Rightly used, however, Borst's *Turmbau* records a vast mass of material that has never been brought together before; but the disposition of that material shares some of the confusion that is its subject. Borst 1960 explores its subject by concentrating on six figures: Isidor of Seville, Dante, Luther, Locke, Condorcet, and Stalin. Within that framework it has useful citations. Both Arens and Borst tend to see their subject from a German point of view. (Cf. the very interesting collection of essays in Lämmert 1969.)

There is no work that deals with the philosophy of language in England comparable to what Harnois and Kuehner do for France and Arens for Germany and, secondarily, for France. There are, however, some important works on the history of English grammar. Of these the latest and most important is Michael 1970, which as already pointed out, is based on Alston's bibliographical collections. Confined to native English grammars, it covers no less than 273 individual works: two prior to 1600, 32 for the next one hundred years, and the rest in the eighteenth century. There is something positively Malthusian about the rate of increase, a tendency also borne out by Stengel (1890), though in France the increase would appear to have set in much earlier. Further, a table shows (277) that beginning with the decade 1751–1760 a proliferation of new grammars occurs which on the whole is maintained for the rest of the century. It is easy to think of reasons for this increase, chiefly no doubt simply greater demand owing to increased travel and perhaps also because women now were expected to show knowledge of foreign literature. It is a question whether the increase can be explained by an observation made by Poldauf (114): 'In a certain respect, the new period, opening with James Harris [Hermes 1751], may be said to link up with Wallis [*Grammatica linguae Anglicanae* 1653]. With Harris, grammar is again taken up by great thinkers of a stature comparable to Wallis's.' During the Thirty Years War a good hundred years earlier, practical foreign language grammars seem to have increased greatly in number on the Continent, no doubt partly owing to the growth in foreign language contact that was caused by the war. It would be interesting to have precise information on the means by which members of diplomatic missions became prepared to face their need for a ready knowledge of foreign languages. The fullness and liveliness of Michael's work are admirable, but its chief virtue lies in its unsurpassed attention to evidence and illustration, most clearly seen in the detailed examination that Michael devotes to the variety of systems which were devised to cope with the parts of speech. Michael is surely right that, 'the very little which had so far been written about these questions relied too much on "influence" — the assumed influence of one writer on another — as an organising concept; that the evidence was thin and the generalisations robust but unproductive' (vii). One is left with the impression that English grammar was much less monolithic, much less given to a few descriptive and prescriptive doctrines than has often been claimed. One is struck rather by the variety, freedom, ingenuity and originality shown by the best grammars, alternating with secondary, unimaginative and derivative solutions to grammatica problems. One firm conclusion is that 'perhaps the most important anticipation of reform is one of the commonest features of the [best] grammars, quite unremarked at the time, and only now known to have been so frequent: the use of syntactic criteria in defining the parts of speech' (516), in spite of the general dominance of Latin grammar. Michael's work is a model of its kind, and it supersedes such older works as Leonard 1929, which is perhaps the most striking example of modern disparagement of eighteenth century grammar and its doctrines.

Poldauf's pioneer work (1948), however, still deserves to be read. It covers the still impressive number of one hundred texts. Michael considered it unfruitful to relate his grammars to the cultural and intellectual background, but Poldauf found he could not avoid doing so, even though he would have preferred it, 'considering that some problems of English grammar were occasionally solved with reference to the grammatical conclusions sometimes attempted by these thinkers' (121) — Monboddo, Adam Smith, James Beattie, Thomas Reid, Dugald Stewart, and even J. D. Michaëlis and De Brosses. Poldauf's treatment is biased toward modern linguistic views. Vorlat 1963 is an immensely detailed examination of fourteen English grammars. It contains a great deal of 'bio-biographical' material as well as extensive quotations from the primary texts. But one wonders whether the subject can survive under the weight of such treatment that greatly surpasses the combined length of the primary texts.

These works on English grammar invite comparison with Jellinek's (1913–14) beautiful and classic work on the history of German grammar. Though linguistic doctrines have changed greatly over the intervening years, Jellinek is still unsurpassed for analysis, precision, and insight. As history, the current mode of laudatory interpretation in terms of 'Cartesian' linguistics or transformational-generative grammar is no more enlightened or reliable than Leonard's dependence on the descriptivist doctrines of his time.

Chevalier 1968 is a work of historical synthesis on a grand scale, moving from the early sixteenth century over J.C. Scaliger to Ramus, Sanctius and Port-Royal, to Du Marsais, Girard, Condillac, and the Encyclopédie. Michael and Chevalier are very different books. While Michael fixed his eye on the grammatical categories and stayed clear of intellectual history, Chevalier seeks the wider social meaning and epistemological implications of his subject matter. Like Michael, he engages in what he calls 'microanalyse', 'on est entré ici dans des détails minutieux, inlassablement repris', and he cites a passage by Beauzée on 'la nécessité pour tout grammairien ... d'entrer dans les détails les plus ténus, dans les arbres les plus branchus'. But, unlike Michael 1970, Chevalier's investigation is balanced by macroanalysis, 'parce que le développement des théories grammaticales ne se conçoit que très confusement, si on ne le rapporte pas aux systèmes des idées alors en cours ainsi qu'aux ensembles pédagogiques dans lesquels il prend place. ... Le paradoxe est donc que cette thèse prétend apporter une contribution — terme qui appelle l'adjectif "modeste" — aux recherches d'épistémologie historique en ne mettant pourtant qu'un pied effarouché en ce domaine royal' (10–11). He never forgets that, 'la grammaire n'est pas seulement une réflexion sur l'art de penser et du penser; elle entre aussi dans un processus de communication active ou, plus précisément, dans une praxis, puisqu'elle est outil d'enseignement. Pendant les deux siècles que nous envisageons, aucune grammaire française ne fut conçue en dehors de cette visée pédagogique. C'est à la fois une servitude et une force.' He is thus led to conclude that, 'la pédagogie ouverte de la Renaissance, fondée sur le mimétisme de la vie. ... se change en un enseignement de classe fermé. ... La notion de complément est partie d'un ensemble de puissances raisonnantes que la bourgeoisie se forge pour instrument de pensée' (728). It seems to me that Chevalier's brilliant and suggestive book may well be the most significant publication in the history of linguistics during the last decades. Chevalier has dealt with similar themes in a number of articles, for instance Chevalier 1971a. A worthy companion to Chevalier 1968 is Quemada 1967 on the dictionaries of modern French from 1539 to 1863, again a work that hardly has its equal in any other language.

A number of recent histories of linguistics have sections on the eighteenth century, Leroy (1963:8–14), Kukenheim (1966:38–48), Robins (1967:133–63), and Mounin (1967:133–51 including Vico). They differ considerably in degree of sympathy for the eighteenth century and in the number of figures and texts they treat. They should all be used with considerable caution, best perhaps only for every preliminary orientation. They all offer some bibliographical aid. By far the largest, most detailed and comprehensive history of linguistics is still Verburg 1952, which unfortunately has not received the attention it deserves. I understand that an English translation may soon be published.

2.3 *Special Studies*

Samuel Johnson's lexicography and opinions about language and style have steadily attracted a good deal of attention. Some of this work is thorough and scholarly, such as W. K. Wimsatt's illuminating volume. But Johnson has also been the favorite target of writers who thought they best demonstrated the 'scientific' nature of their linguistics by denigrating both Johnson and the eighteenth century at large, chiefly for their failure to respect usage. Leonard 1929 is the epitome of this attitude. I think it is fair to say that works of this sort now have little value except as examples of the rather extreme aberrations of historical myths. According to Leonard, Johnson, the eighteenth century, and even the Port-Royal grammar showed no respect for usage, wishing instead to be prescriptive in the terms of Latin grammar, a claim so doubtful that one wonders how it was possible to make it. Elledge 1967 shows the emptiness of these claims, in the process citing several amusing examples, e.g. a widely used college anthology which says that 'the philosophy of the eighteenth century was "inimical to scientific research in language" and that "the prevailing conceptions of language were (1) that language is a divine institution, originally perfect, but debased by man; (2) that English is a corrupt and degenerate offspring of Latin and Greek"' (280). This passage calls to mind another, cited in Teeter (1966:95), which said — in 1948 — that 'the theory of divine origin ... calls for no intellectual speculation', a statement which must be pure guesswork. Johann Peter Süssmilch's famous and influential essay on the divine origin of language is surely one of the most brilliant eighteenth-century pieces on the theory of language. Elledge concludes with a good survey of James Harris, Joseph Priestley, Monboddo, George Campbell, and Hugh Blair.

Another altogether different area of study has proved very fruitful and suggestive: the history of early Slavic studies in Germany. The literature on this subject is both extensive and distinguished; it also suggests the benefit to be derived from similar studies directed toward other instances in which cultural contact has had significant effects on linguistic scholarship. Much of this early study had a religious aim and was especially associated with Halle (Winter 1953), the center of pietism, an association that brings to mind Ernst Benz's brilliant examination of the relations between Wittenberg and Byzantium in the century of the Reformation. The first of these studies appeared just before the Second War, Cyževśkyj 1939. He observed: 'H. W. Ludolf und A. H. Francke, die miteinander in regen Briefwechsel standen, verband u.a. das gemeinsame Interesse für die orientalischen Kirche. Aus diesem Interesse erwuchs nun die Aufmerksamkeit, die die beiden der slavischen Welt zuwandten. Man darf eines nicht vergessen: an der Wiege der meisten Kinder der Neuzeit stehen die religiösen Bewegungen und der religiöse Ethusiasmus. Zu diesen Kindern der Neuzeit gehört auch die slavische Philologie' (17). Other aspects of this relationship are examined in Balazs 1956 and Tetzner 1956. Some element of religious motivation also occurs, more or less intensely, in Frisch, Hiob Ludolf, and his nephew H. W. Ludolf.

Five items are devoted to the remarkable figure Johann Leonhard Frisch (1666–1743): Bernhagen 1958, Powitz 1959, and Eichler 1958, 1966, and 1967. Taught by Leibniz' teacher Erhard Weigel, he travelled widely before he settled in Berlin to become headmaster of a gymnasium at the recommendation of Philipp Jacob Spener after he had declined A. H. Francke's invitation to accept a similar post in Moscow. In 1706 he became a member of the Berlin Academy, having been nominated by Leibniz, whom he knew, was influenced by, and is reputed (though that would seem doubtful) to have given instruction in Russian. He is known for significant contributions to entomology, ornithology, he performed chemical experiments, worked for the reclamation of swampy land, and promoted silk manufacture — much of his correspondence with Leibniz turns on this subject. He gave assistance to J. G. Wachter, and is known as a linguist for his contributions to Slavic studies and to German lexicography, for which he earned Jacob Grimm's admiration. Eichler 1967 examines his Slavic studies and Powitz 1959 presents a close examination of his *Teutsch-Lateinisches Wörterbuch* (2 vols. 1741), including an interesting demonstration of its historical background in German linguistic studies of the seventeenth century, especially Schottel and Harsdörffer. Thus the historical context within which he worked is much the same as that of Leibniz, by whom he was in turn influenced. Powitz shows how Leibniz' plans for the Berlin Academy, in line with other European academies, included the making of a German dictionary. *Die Unvorgreiflichen Gedanken* had called for three kinds of dictionaries, of the common language, of technical terms, and of etymology. These were combined in Frisch's great dictionary, in which the etymology drew heavily on his knowledge of the Slavic languages. Between 1727 and 1736 he published six treatises under the general title *Historia linguae slavonicae* (Eichler 1967:25–45). Powitz' monograph contains valuable bibliography of Frisch's works (190–3), of secondary literature (194–7), and for the linguistic historian an especially rich list of Frisch's linguistic sources for the dictionary (121–36), followed by a long bibliography of sources on other subjects (136–79). The value of these studies can hardly be overestimated, both for the light they shed on their immediate subjects and upon the scholarly and intellectual tradition within which these scholars worked, as in the case, for instance, of Frisch's dependence on German seventeenth-century work. Frisch is a figure who draws our interest toward a better understanding of the intellectual milieu, already mentioned in Section 1, which produced Leibniz' learned and productive scholar-correspondents.

The same fascinating question is illuminated by Baumann 1958 on the learned Orientalist and Slavicist Hiob Ludolf (1624–1704) and Tetzner 1955 on his nephew, the better known Slavicist H. W. Ludolf (1655–1712). Both travelled widely, performed diplomatic duties, had religious motives for their linguistic work, and pietistic leanings. Tetzner's monograph offers excellent insight into his intellectual milieu and concludes with 33 pieces of correspondence (97–143), including some letters to Francke and one to Leibniz. Though receiving their initial impulse from Cyževśkyj, who has done so much for the study of relations between the German and the Slavic worlds, all these studies have been encouraged by Eduard Winter, as a glance at the bibliography will indicate. Winter 1962 (247–317) contains nine essays on Peter Simon Pallas.

Berkov and Mazon — both 1958 — explore the relations between the Russian poet V. K. Trediakovskij and Gabriel Girard, best known for his *Synonymes français* and *Les vrais principes de la langue française*. Here again is a little known or even suspected example of intercultural contact with significant linguistic consequences. Jensen 1912 and Stender-Petersen 1960 record the history of Slavic studies in Scandinavia, with emphasis that naturally falls on the work of J. G. Sparwenfeld. Owing to its Baltic empire, Sweden became the first Western-European center of Slavic studies, and it was during a sojourn in Stockholm in 1649 that Hiob Ludolf first began the study of Russian.

A number of studies that treat special subjects indicate areas of research that deserve further investigation. Jonsson 1969 deals with Swedenborg's view of language, a subject of wide historical and intellectual implications, which also call his contemporary Linnaeus to mind. Reychman's two articles (1959, 1960) are devoted to the linguistic studies of two Polish figures who also happened to be correspondents of Sir William Jones, A. K. Czartoryski and Charles Reviczky. Reychman 1950 deals with the knowledge and teaching of oriental languages in Poland during the eighteenth century. Seeber 1945, Knowlson 1963, and Cornelius 1965 explore the ideal languages of imaginary voyages, a subject that brings out the utopian character of artificial linguistic projects. Cornelius has a rather full bibliography of primary and secondary literature (159–71). The interesting subject of hieroglyphics — to the seventeenth and eighteenth centuries a matter of wider import than is readily suspected — is treated in Allen 1953, V.-David 1961b, 1965, Iversen 1961, and Dieckmann 1969. Both in 1965 and in 1961a (in the Bibliography to Section 1), V.-David deals with Leibniz' considerable interest in this subject.

In the history of linguistics, I think it has generally been true, at least until recently, that discontinuities have been set up between present doctrine and practice and those of the past. In this respect it seems to differ from the history of natural science, which has generally sought (also before the recent distinguished work in that subject) and found continuities rather than discontinuities. This difference may point to important differences between linguistics and natural science. Whereas the development of the latter tends to be linear rather than cumulative — successful science destroys its own past, as Kuhn has observed — linguistics seems to be primarily cumulative rather than linear. But this accumulation does not equally affect the entire spectrum of linguistics, and thus one tradition will dominate in one period and others in other periods. Said differently, linguistics seems to be more historically oriented than science in practice but less so in its view of its own history. Thus the astonishing success of comparative and historical linguistics in the early decades of the nineteenth century has most often been seen as discontinuous with the past, for instance in the establishment of proof of linguistic kinship. Taking up this problem, both Bonfante 1954 and

Agrell 1955 try to show that there is in fact no such discontinuity as has been believed. At the beginning of his article, Bonfante observes that in the matter of kinship 'the lack of information of our contemporary books and encyclopedias is appalling. The work of centuries has simply been entirely forgotten or neglected. Our predecessors are accused more or less openly of an ignorance which is not theirs but ours' (1679). He presents a large number of names and citations that bear out his point, at the same time offering a wealth of references and bibliography that should prove suggestive for further work. It is interesting that one of his secondary sources is Eckhart 1711. How often is it acknowledged that works now over 250 years old may still be our best secondary sources? Agrell's much longer and more detailed study of the history of comparative phonology makes the same point. Concentrating on nine different changes (such as p–f–b; b–p–f), he finds that twelve Swedish scholars have made 64 observations of which 48 can be considered fully correct. Fifteen non-Swedish scholars have made 76 observations of which 58 are certain. His list has two figures from the sixteenth century, nine from the seventeenth, eleven in the eighteenth, and five in the early nineteenth century (see table p. 201; I have used the figures that exclude Grimm and J. H. Bredsdorff). Agrell has a very full bibliography of primary (printed and unprinted) and secondary material as well as a resumé in German. Bonfante 1956 presents a systematic survey of the contents of J. G. Wachter's *Glossarium Germanicum* (Leipzig 1737), again with the intent of supporting his argument that respectable comparative linguistics has a longer history than commonly known. It would be helpful if we had more such short accounts of works that are not available except in large libraries. Bonfante's and Agrell's studies are fruitful for several reasons: their method might well be imitated with good results in other particular subjects; they offer much information; and they are suggestive. If the early observations they record did in fact not have the effect that very similar work so dramatically created during the early decades of the nineteenth century, then our attention is drawn to the intellectual context, which presumably makes the difference. The internal history of a discipline, which these studies illustrate so well, is not sufficient to produce the sort of history that not only records but also connects. In a curious way, it is, I think, true that Bonfante and Agrell disprove the official history at the same time as they, by accepting its limitations, reveal its inadequacy. A model of what can be achieved is Diderichsen's (1960) excellent monograph of Rask's linguistics and its intellectual background.

Hanzeli 1969 is an interesting study of a significant subject. To my knowledge we have nothing like it for China, Japan, and South-East Asia, where the Jesuits were also active teaching and learning languages and bringing back the material that made Paris the center of Sanskrit studies. Filliozat 1941 gives a brief account of the history of these collections in the eighteenth century. The 34-volume Jesuit publication *Lettres édifiantes* (1707–1776) contains much linguistic observation that was frequently cited in the eighteenth century, not least by the Encyclopédie. It would be useful if this material were collected and published. In his conclusion Hanzeli observes:

'One can but hope that subsequent studies will be made not only of seventeenth- and eighteenth-century descriptions of other American Indian languages, but also in the following fields: the description of Asian languages and lesser European languages, research in the history of contemporary practical "teaching" grammars of various languages. From these studies, a new dimension in the history of the science of language would emerge: a history of language description would come to complement the history of grammatical theory and the history of Classical grammarianship — the two pillars upon which all histories of linguistic science have hitherto rested' (102). There is a good bibliography on pages 129–36. Fück 1955 deals with Arabic scholarship in Europe, with sections on the eighteenth century on pages 97–139. It is a well-written, lively book that shows a good understanding of the intellectual context.

Even the history of the teaching of European languages is a subject on which there are few studies, though Chevalier 1968 is likely to call attention to that subject. Sørensen 1971 is a useful study of this sort (though not inspired by Chevalier), and Snyders' (1965) excellent history of French pedagogy includes the teaching of grammar.

2.4 *Major Figures*

Let me now turn to some of the literature that has been devoted to the major figures in the philosophy of language in the eighteenth century, the subject for which that period is especially known. Dealing with such names as Vico, Condillac, Diderot, Rousseau, Turgot, D'Alembert, De Brosses, Du Marsais, Herder, and Hamann, the literature is immense, steadily growing, and very uneven. I can only deal with some of the relevant items. In no area does the present variety of interest in language — often vaguely understood — show so busily; but it seems to me that our understanding both of theories and of historical relationships have not gained as much as one might have hoped. In fact, the general scene is one of confusion, much generalization, and often limited knowledge. This is perhaps to be expected at the present stage of research; the important point is that these problems are now at last receiving serious and sympathetic attention. Here lies perhaps the greatest single challenge of the history of linguistics as it bears on our period.

In the English-speaking world at least, Vico has been a favorite subject since the publication of Fisch's and Bergin's translation of the *Autobiography* in 1944, with a long introduction on pages 1–106. The introduction made vast and indiscriminate claims for Vico's inordinate originality and influence in nearly all learned and philosophical disciplines, including the philosophy and study of language. Though an early review by René Wellek pointed out the weakness of these claims, there has since grown up a veritable Vico industry which perpetuates the claims with yet greater confidence. This is unfortunate, for no useful and reliable knowledge of Vico will come out of these uncritical claims; they are so exaggerated that common sense calls their plausibility in question. And he would quite easily remain a significant figure without these exaggerations. He is said, for instance, to have been a significant influence on Herder because their linguistic thought has obvious similarities. Yet as Wells (1969:99–102) has demonstrated, Herder could not have known of Vico till 1777, does not mention him until late in life in 1797, and gives no semblance of proof that he knew Vico's work in any depth. The same would appear to be true of Hamann (101).

In a detailed and scholarly examination of Vico's supposed influence on a number of influential Englishmen and Scotsmen as well as Montesquieu, Condillac, Rousseau, and Diderot, Wellek answers that there is no proof at all, only presumption based on postulated similarity. His conclusion has greater range than the geographical limits suggest, for many of the English and Scottish figures were in turn influential in Germany, some of them at least as early as 1750. Seeing no plausibility in the claims made by Fisch and Bergin, Wellek offers the only sensible conclusion: 'The most reasonable [solution] is the assumption that the ideas Mr. Fisch considers as peculiarly Vichian were known before Vico and were developed by English writers from other sources than Vico' (1969:218).

A similar conclusion is reached by Pons 1968. Is it possible, he asks, that all the great figures of the French enlightenment have pillaged and plagiarized Vico without acknowledgement, as has been widely claimed since the beginning of the nineteenth century? He shows that in regard to Montesquieu and Condillac this cannot be the case, or for Turgot's and Condorcet's philosophy of history, and that in other cases such claims are ruled out by errors in the chronology that has been used to support them. He suggests that the very assumption of any such influence is paradoxical since it comes from writers who at the same time make Vico an enemy of the Enlightenment before the fact, an antirationalist and too historicist for a century devoid of historical sense. Pons arrives at nearly the same conclusion as Wellek: 'Il faut sans doute réviser l'image traditionnelle que l'on s'est longtemps faite du XVIIIe siècle. Ce siècle nous commençons à le savoir, n'a pas ignoré l'histoire autant que l'a prétendu le siècle suivant. Au contraire, et surtout dans sa seconde moitié, il a été obsédé par le problème de l'origine historique des sociétés, des institutions, des religions, du droit, des langues, qu'il a cherché à dévoiler en particulier grâce à l'interprétation des mythes' (365–66). This seems to me true, and it must be borne in mind in the following paragraphs.

De Mauro 1969b is a cogent discussion which is aware that Vichian ideas regarding language are also found in, for instance, Locke and Leibniz, though it is not the purpose of his essay to examine these in detail. (Much of the material in this essay is also in De Mauro 1969a.) Vico 'intuited that philosophical research cannot be separated from linguistic research', and by way of summary of Vico's 'original conception of language', De Mauro cites this statement: 'Language is not an artificial medium which men have deliberately constructed to give expression to pre-existent ideas, but has evolved naturally, the course of its development being inseparable from that of the human mind itself' (291). Vico is said to have originated the idea that each language gives anthropological evidence about its speakers, and that poetic language preceded other kinds. Since these ideas are widely shared by Herder, Apel thinks that, 'es is schwer glaublich, das zwischen Herders Fragment "Von den Lebensaltern der Sprache" von 1766 und Vicos "Neuer Wissenschaft" ... keine reale Abhängigkeit bestehen sollte' (1963:376). Berlin observes that Vico's 'boldest contribution, the concept of "philology", anthropological historicism, the notion that there can be a science of mind which is the history of its development, the realization that ideas evolve, that knowledge is not a static network of eternal, universal, clear truths, either Platonic or Cartesian, but a social process, ... this transforming vision, was still in the future', i.e., in the future of Vico's own later writings' (1969:372).

Though it is possible that Vico made a new and original synthesis, there are a number of reasons that make it hard to accept the claims for originality that are here being made. These ideas are found separately in other figures before Vico. The quotations from De Mauro, as he is aware, contain ideas that are in, for instance, Leibniz and Locke, in some measure already in Bacon. These are familiar notions in the seventeenth century. The 'anthropological historicism' is clear in Leibniz, and Leibniz in turn had learned much from his German contemporaries and predecessors (who wrote mostly in Latin). The idea that a language somehow expresses the world of the people who speak it is in Bacon's doctrine — hardly his own — that language was first made by illiterate people for their own convenience according to their needs, an idea that was expanded and deepened by Locke. The priority of poetic language is an idea that was common in the literature of the seventeenth century, commonly suggested and supported by reference to the prophetic books of the Old Testament.

Apart from motives of national partiality (which seem to have played some role), there are several factors that have made such claims possible. First, we know far too little about the scholarly tradition of the seventeenth century, especially about the work of scholars in biblical and oriental languages and the wider conclusions that were drawn from this scholarship. It is revealing that Leibniz was intimately familiar with this tradition. Secondly, from the nineteenth century we have inherited a view of the eighteenth century that excludes some of its most significant features, as Pons and others have pointed out (see Aarsleff 1971a in the Bibliography to Section 1). But we should not rest confident that this version is correct. The third point is related to the second. Berlin observes that 'no one before Michelet seems to have had an inkling that Vico had opened a window to a new realm of thought' (377). If I am right that the nineteenth century's reading of the eighteenth century, of Condillac and Locke for instance, was distorted in a conservative reaction against their reputed materialism, sensationism, and so forth, then the discovery of Vico — carrying much little-known baggage of the seventeenth century with him — would come as a welcome revelation; at last an eighteenth-century mind that was congenial to the nineteenth centur[3]. It is likely that some of Vico's linguistic views can be isolated into original doctrines, but so far no such demonstration has been advanced in the literature I have seen. The important fact is that we are here, I think, on to a problem that may force us to revise the common tradition of intellectual history. If what is attributed to Vico was not foreign to the eighteenth century at large, then substantial revision of that history must follow. It also makes one not a little suspicious that the discussions I have seen have little to say about Vico's sources, even when they seem committed to dealing with them. Apel, for instance, makes Vico the end-point of his investigation, yet all he says about his sources is confined to a few lines about Bacon and Cusa. Apel also measures Vico as a forerunner, though in precisely what sense is never clear, of 'die Deutsche Bewegung', i.e. of for instance Herder, Hamann, and Wilhelm von Humboldt. According to De Mauro, Pagliaro 1959 is the best discussion of Vico's study and philosophy of language.

With other major figures such as Condillac, Maupertuis, and Herder we encounter much the same difficulty as with Vico, and the source is again in the factors I have stated above, that is essentially the nineteenth-century's creation of a view of the eighteenth century which precluded the sort of historical interrelations and the kinds of linguistic doctrines which in fact existed. In this case the force of our incomprehension has been exacerbated by the old fable convenue that Herder, an 'idealist' German, could not have had anything to do with a reputed materialist Frenchman like Condillac, except in the role of strong opponent. Consider for a moment such statements as the following: 'The style of the early nations of Asia was prodigiously figurative.' 'Everything confirms that each language expresses the character of the people who speak it.' 'It is to the poets that we owe the first and perhaps also the greatest of obligations [in regard to language]. ... The philosophers have only perfected it much later.' 'Among all writers, it is the poets who express the genius of languages in the most lively fashion. ... To a man who is well versed in languages they become like a painting of the character and the genius of each people.' Few who know the secondary literature will doubt that these statements are from Herder's *Ursprung*, but they are in fact all taken from Condillac's *Essai*. In the literature that deals with the study of language in the second half of the eighteenth century, Condillac has been neglected or ignored in two areas where his influence is decisive: in France among the philosophers and on the *Encyclopédie*, and in Germany on Herder and some of his contemporaries. Having dealt with these problems in Aarsleff 1974 (except for minor revisions completed in January 1969), I shall merely give a few examples.

Salmony 1949 offers a very detailed examination of Herder's linguistic philosophy as found in the *Abhandlung über den Ursprung der Sprache*, sharply contrasting it with Condillac's Essai. About Condillac's *Langue des calculs* (1798), however, Salmony observes that it shows, 'wie aus einer ursprünglicher Gebärdensprache (langue d'action) allmählich die artikulierte Sprache hervorgeht, die ausdrücklich keineswegs allein der Mitteilung und äusseren Verständigung, sondern vor allem dem Verstehen dient. ... Vom tierischen Ursprung der Sprache, von den "Schällen" und "Schreien der Empfindung" is hier nicht mehr die Rede' (42). This Salmony considers a doctrine that is much more significant — that is like Herder's — than the one that is presented in the *Essai* (Salmony 1949:67). But the doctrine attributed to the *Langue des calculs* in the passage just cited is exactly the same as that of the *Essai*. Similarly, with regard to Condillac's influence among his French contemporaries, Hunt 1938 says that Diderot in 1751 (in the *Lettre sur les sourds-et-muets*) found one precondition for the origin of language in gestures and inarticulate cries, a theory, Hunt says, that was later taken up 'by Condillac himself'. Again, its source was the *Essai*, in which the language of action, gestures, plays a crucial role. Knight (1968) has written an entire book which without hesitation attributes to Condillac the doctrine that knowledge comes about by the association of ideas — her understanding, it seems, of his term 'liaison des idées', though Condillac specifically makes the distinction between the voluntary use of the connection of ideas as opposed to the involuntary association of ideas. (It may be necessary to add that Locke calls the association of ideas a kind of madness; he considers it an irrational feature of the mind and destructive of knowledge.) It seems that opinion of Condillac has become so fossilized as to obviate a reading of him — our inheritance from the nineteenth century. Cassirer is only one of many who with reference to Herder will make this sort of remark: 'Alors apparait ... cette orientation vers la "réflexion" que Herder, dans son essai sur l'origine du langage, regard comme le facteur intellectuel décisif de toute création verbale' (1933: 30). This doctrine, however, is from the *Essai* (1746), in which reflexion is the active expression of reason and solely responsible for the creation of language. Condillac leaves no room for doubt on this point; there is no basis for saying that he postulates, as Knight and others say, that 'reason is acquired', whatever that might mean. It is curious that Herder scholars, for some 70 years, have missed or ignored that Herder before he wrote the *Ursprung* had read at least Part Two of Condillac's *Essai*, that is the part that contains his argument about the origin of language, which Herder in a note said he greatly admired. These matters may change, however; several very recent French publications pay some attention to Condillac, as does Chevalier 1968. Schottländer (1969a) argues for a better understanding of Condillac and his originality along the lines I have just indicated. Ricken in his two items (1961 and 1964) is also contributing to the revision of our view of Condillac and the history of linguistic philosophy in the mid-eighteenth century. (I have not had access to Ricken 1963 which, judging by its title, would appear to be relevant in this context.)

In Section 1, it was mentioned that the principle of linguistic relativity — "die Hypothese vom Weltbild der Sprache" — was known in the seventeenth century, is found, for instance, in both Locke and Leibniz, and that Condillac was its eighteenth-century focal point. Though its argument is somewhat tortuous, the interesting and reference-packed article by Christmann (1966) deals with this problem, chiefly with the aim of finding Wilhelm von Humboldt's source for it. Christmann is aware that this doctrine is also in Bacon and Locke, but is not dealing with that aspect of the question. He arrives at the conclusion that the doctrine is characteristic of the Enlightenment, making the further observation, which is as rare as it is true in regard to linguistic philosophy: 'Auf verschiedenen Gebieten hat ja die Forschung der letzten Jahrzehnte gezeigt, dass man gerade für die Anfänge der Romantik nicht aus-kommt mit der Annahme einer blossen Antithese zu der vorhergehenden Epoche, einer scharfen Grenze zur Aufklärung, sondern dass man auch eine gewisse Kontinuität in Rechnung stellen muss' (452). Indeed on Wilhelm von Humboldt, he says: 'Die These vom Weltbild der Sprache wird dann endgültig von Wilhelm von Humboldt formuliert. Einen Bruch gegenüber der Auffassung des 18. Jahrhundert ... vermögen wir nicht zu erkennen' (467). He seems reluctant, however, to admit Condillac as the source in Germany, though he allows it in Italy, where in addition he demonstrates the influence of J. D. Michaëlis. But, 'die Resonanz auf Michaëlis' Abhandlung [Beantwortung der Frage von dem Einfluss der Meinungen in die Sprache und der Sprache in die Meinungen, first published Berlin 1760] war in Deutschland noch stärker als in Frankreich, England, und Italien' (465). Thus Michaëlis is made the German source of the doctrine in Herder, Hamann, and Wilhelm von Humboldt. Still, the topic is as typical a Condillacian problem as one can imagine, as Maupertuis who framed it was well aware. (In the English translation, the title reads 'the influence of opinions on language and of language on opinions'; opinion here does not mean something like ill-founded belief or prejudice, but rather concept-formation.)

Still, it is a good question whether it is necessary to go this round-about way to find Humboldt's source. In the entire corpus of Humboldt's writings, I have never found any reference to Herder or Michaëlis that would substantiate Christmann's thesis, though it might of course retain its plausibility in the absence of other evidence. We do have such evidence, however. It is striking that Humboldt's decisive turn toward language occurs during his stay in Paris from November 1797 to late August 1799, followed by the Spanish journey September 1799 to April 1800, another year's sojourn in Paris, and the journey to the Basque Provinces and Spain from April to June 1801. On 21 December 1797 he wrote from Paris to his friend C. G. Körner that 'für die Kultur einer Nation ist schlechterdings nichts so wichtig, als ihre Sprache'. Almost two years later, in September 1800 while still in Paris, he wrote the long letter to Schiller on 'Wallenstein', in which he suddenly lapsed into a passage on Schiller's language and then on language in general. Here we find such Condillacian statements as the following: 'Die Sprache stellt offenbar unsre ganze geistige Tätigkeit subjektiv (nach der Art unsres Verfahrens) dar, aber sie erzeugt auch zugleich die Gegenstände, insofern sie Objekte unsres Denkens sind. Denn ihre Elemente machen die Abschnitte in unserm Vorstellen, das ohne sie in einer verwirrenden Reihe fortgehen würde. ... So bringt uns die Sprache unaufhörlich die Arbeit unseres Geistes. ... Das nun ist es, was ich die eigentliche Kraft der Sprache nennen möchte, ihre Fähigkeit, den Trieb und die Kraft zu erhöhen, immerfort — wie Sie es nennen wollen — mehr Welt mit sich zu verknüpfen oder aus sich zu entwickeln.' During the 1790s Humboldt had written a number of pieces devoted to the problem that especially interested him, the study of mankind and nations, the unity and diversity of mankind, a subject he then called comparative anthropology. But in these early writings (e.g. *Plan einer vergleichenden Anthropologie* [1795], *Das achtzehnte Jahrhundert* [1796–7], and *Ueber den Geist der Menschheit* [c. 1797]), there is no indication at all that he found language especially important to that enterprise; on the contrary, it is mentioned only casually along with customs, manners, and dress. But looking at the writings that immediately followed the Paris period, we find that they are wholly dominated by the conviction that language is not only the key to this study, but in fact itself the primary cause of the great variety of manifestations of universal human nature. What caused this reorientation in Humboldt's outlook and method, a change that determined the writings on language for which he is best known and most admired? From his first stay in Paris, we have a notebook in which he entered material that related, as he said, 'zu meinen Arbeiten über die Kenntniss der Menschen und Nationen', reports on books, conversations, and events. His philosophical acquaintances were all idéologues: Garat (who was chiefly responsible for Condillac's standing with that group and for the collected edition of his works published during the first half of 1798), Destutt de Tracy, Laromiguière, Condorcet's widow, and others. From his Kantian point of view, Humboldt deplored their metaphysics as they deplored his. In the midst of multifarious activities, he also within a month read all of Condillac's main works and took extensive notes on them—more extensive than on any other reading recorded in his notes. A dozen years later, after his brother Alexander had brought him materials on American Indian languages, Humboldt wrote (and, though unfinished, for once in a clear and succinct style) his *Essai sur les langues du nouveau continent* (1812, first published 1904), an essay that is replete with the doctrines of Condillac and his tradition in France to which Humboldt had been exposed during the Paris period. It is hard to see any good reason to believe that this influence was mediated through Herder, especially on a confirmed Kantian like Wilhelm von Humboldt.

Recently a book with a curious thesis has appeared, Penn 1972. The thesis is this: 'That Herder, Humboldt, Sapir and Whorf all advocated the extreme view [of linguistic relativity] will be suggested as having been in a sense necessary to Western thought — necessary to free us of the notion of innate ideas, e.g. Kant's categories' (11). It is hard to think of a less promising thesis, considering that, for instance, Leibniz and Humboldt were committed to what the author calls innate ideas, yet were strong advocates of the doctrine of linguistic relativity. She further suggests that 'the notions like Kant's categories were alive until after Whorf's time. The extreme hypothesis may have been offered as an antidote to the assumption of innate ideas,' though she also suggests that Humboldt, Sapir, and Whorf were not 'necessarily aware of combatting Kant's categories' (55). It would be an understatement to say that the book does not succeed in supporting its thesis, and one must wonder at the judgment that found it publishable.

In addition to Sahlin's great monograph (1928) on Du Marsais, which among other things pointed out the influence of Locke on DuMarsais (17), there are two recent monographs that deal with this influential figure. Though neither deals with Du Marsais as linguist, both Dieckmann 1948 and Gross 1955–56 throw much light on Du Marsais' philosophical position. Dieckmann finds no definite answer to the question whether Du Marsais wrote *Le philosophe*, but seems to incline to the view that he did not. Gross discusses the same problem at length and comes to the opposite conclusion, though on circumstantial evidence. He also discusses the authorship of other pieces, thus suggesting that the canon of Du Marsais' works is not settled. The collected edition of 1797 contains some works that are not by him and omit others that are. It is Gross's main thesis that Du Marsais illustrates a combination of confirmed anti-Cartesianism and radical attitudes towards established authority, especially the church and the monarchy, a thesis that is supported also by other treatments of French intellectual history but hard to prove beyond debate owing to the then prevalent practice of also voicing sentiments that would please the censors sufficiently to gain permission for publication. To show that Du Marsais was a representative of 'monistic materialism', Gross cites this passage from *De la raison*: 'Rien, dans la nature, ne peut parvenir à notre connoissance que par l'un de ces quatre moyens: l'expérience de nos sens, l'expérience de notre entendement, l'autorité humaine et l'autorité divine' (139). Though Gross's disposition is somewhat lacking in effectiveness and clarity, this is still an important monograph. Gross did not have access to Dieckmann. Both have very full bibliographies.

Since the bicentenary of his birth in 1946, Sir William Jones has been the object of many studies, in particular by Garland Cannon whose work includes a biography of Jones (1964) (which presents much of the material published in his earlier studies and a good bibliography) and more recently the fascinating two-volume edition of the letters. It contains 596 letters of which no less than 304 were previously unpublished. The effect of these publications, and especially of the letters, has been a substantial revision of our earlier image of Jones. This image was largely created by the biography of John Shore written very shortly after Jones's death. It was as Arberry remarks, 'marred by the author's too patent anxiety to make of his hero a prophet of Clapham evangelicalism, and to mitigate the harshness of his uncompromising politics' (1946b: 673). We have long known that Jones already early in life was an indefatigable and brilliant scholar, that he had amibitions to enter active political life as a member of Parliament, that his liberal views delayed the Indian appointment he sought, and that once in India he devoted himself to Sanskrit and Indian studies. But the extent of his political radicalism has not been clearly known. Some details from the letters will give an impression of Jones's beliefs and temper. He was fond 'both of fame and hard work; so here I am, a barrister. ... Glory I shall pursue through fire and water by night and day' (Jones 1970:85–6, with continuous pagination through the two volumes). In 1773 he wrote the mother of the young man whose tutor he was: 'There are three authors, with whom I hope, one day or other, to bring him acquainted, Euclid, Locke and Blackstone: the first will open to him the principles of all natural knowledge, the second will show him the nature and extent of human reason, and the third will offer him a specimen of that reason reduced to practice in the admirable Laws of our country' (121). Jones often voiced his commitment to Locke who was the foundation of his philosophical and political outlook. In 1778 he defended Locke's political doctrines against Josiah Tucker (276). In 1779, having briefly stated his grounds of religious belief, Jones wrote the following Lockian passage: 'I know too well the nature of evidence and the different degrees of it, to insist that this mode of reasoning amounts to strict *demonstration*, which, on such topics, is not to be expected, or, if expected, is not to be had; but though demonstration alone afford *certainty*, yet my argument affords the *highest probability*, which is sufficient to influence our actions and consequently to procure happiness' (329). Early in 1780, he attended John Hunter's lectures on comparative anatomy with great excitement; before attending them he hoped that afterwards 'I shall tolerably well have completed my Encyclopedia' (340, 329). In 1780 he expressed his desire to write 'an impartial history of the American war', a matter in which he was much involved with sympathies that lay entirely on the American side; he looked forward to visiting America first, however, in order to know more than he did, for 'no man ever became an historian in his closet' (440). (Jones's remark invites comparison with one that was made by James Mill when he was planning his *History of British India*, a work marked by its great lack of sympathy both for the Hindus and for Jones. It was Mill's opinion that 'a man who is duly qualified may obtain more knowledge of India in one year in his closet in England, than he could obtain during the course of the longest life, by the use of his eyes and ears in India' [Aarsleff 1967:142].) On a visit to Paris in 1782 he mentioned the Abbé de l'Epée, 'whose lessons on his Universal Language of signs I have attended pretty constantly' (560). In February of 1785, he was 'almost tempted to learn Sanskrit, that I may be a check on the Pundits of the court' (664). In October 1786 he wrote that 'the difficult study of Hindu and Mohammedan Laws, in two copious languages, Sanskrit and Arabic, [are studies] which are inseparably connected with my public duty' (714). Almost a year later he was happy to have been provided with a Sanskrit vocabulary of ten thousand words, 'but *things* are my great object; since it is my ambition to know India better than any other European ever knew it' (751). 'Philosophers take nothing for granted,' he wrote in September of 1787, 'and will not be satisfied with general propositions: they expect a detail of experiments, not the result merely. If Newton had given only general theorems without proof, ages would have passed, before he could have blazed into fame' (773). A week later he said, 'For the last sixteen years of my life, I have been in the habit of requiring evidence of all assertions' (778). Expressions of interest in the work of Linnaeus occur often in Jones, who himself was no mean botanist. Jones who had earlier had friendly and close relations with Edmund Burke, came to despise him after the publications of his *Reflections on the revolution in France*. 'Very grave unprejudiced men here,' he wrote, 'assure me, that it has the honor of being the wickedest, the silliest, and the worst written book in our language: if you love that man, you will never mind your rival' (898). With the publication of the letters Jones unmistakably emerges as one of the major figures in English intellectual life in the eighteenth century, and his influence on the Continent was such that it is doubtful whether any other Englishman, except Shakespeare, Milton, and Byron, have had similar impact. Unfortunately Cannon's fine edition does not include the letters to Jones, of which many are known to exist and not a few of them from linguistic scholars; it is to be hoped that it will some day be possible to accord them equal treatment. Cannon also makes clear that there is much other relevant material, for instance Lady Jones's letters back to England. On this basis we may perhaps look forward to the full biography which Jones so richly deserves.

For the history of the study of language the most urgent problems are first a close examination of Jones's studies seen in relation to his general orientation, and secondly an effort to trace his impact among his near contemporaries in greater detail and with fewer assumptions than has been the case in the past. Jones research is still dogged by the tendency to cite his famous statement about linguistic affinities in isolation from the context of all the *Anniversary Discourses* in which it occurred. From the first to the last, the discourses are linked by a firm over-all plan, which in a man so methodical as Jones cannot be disregarded, though more often than not that context is ignored (Hoenigswald 1963:2–3; cf. Aarsleff 1967:123–36). But the deeper question is suggested by Kuhn's remark, that it 'is a symptom of something askew in the image of science that gives discovery so fundamental a role' (1970:54), a principle that may be brought against Bonfante 1954 and Agrell 1955. After all, if historical understanding has any meaning, it follows that particular events that are roughly similar do not have the same effect in different contexts, a consideration which again reaffirms the significance of understanding the full context. If Filippo Sassetti and others had also noted Indo-European affinities, they had not lived in times that took note of their observations, they were not already widely known for their scholarship in oriental languages, they did not like Jones establish an Asiatic Society of Calcutta, and did not, as Jones also did, create a journal, the *Asiatic Researches*, to make their findings known to a world that was hungry for them. Finally, they did not have an Alexander Hamilton to spread the word.

In Rocher's excellent study of that little-known — and not very knowable — figure Alexander Hamilton, her subject emerges as a more important scholar and potentially a greater influence than before. On his relations with Friedrich Schlegel, she cites a contemporary source which emphatically shows that Hamilton did not share, in fact rather disapproved of Schlegel's enthusiastic flights of fancy over his new study: 'An der Einwirkung dieses Studium auf Phantasie und Gemüth seines Jüngers hatte A. Hamilton keinen Antheil. Er war der tüchtigste Sprachforscher, der beharrlichste und unausbündigste Handschriftenzifferer, ein höchst verständiger Mann, eine wackre, schönbegabte, klare und ausgeruhte Natur. ... Schlegel begnügte sich nicht mit einer Einzelheit der Anschauung, er umfasste mit Inbrunst das Ganze, und wollte es durchdringen mit der vollsten und brennendsten Fülle seiner Kraft' (46). Rocher concludes: 'The fact is that many of Schlegel's more mature opinions about India as expressed in his book [*Über die Sprache und Weisheit der Indier*] are in absolute agreement with opinions expressed by Hamilton long before. It would no doubt be a work of high interest to make a thorough comparison between Schlegel's work and Hamilton's writings ... with regard to comparative philology' (52). In his later life

Hamilton despaired over the impossibility of creating genuine interest in Indian studies in England, and Rocher suggests that he died a disappointed man. Here again we may see one of the effects of James Mill's attitude toward India and Sir William Jones. Hamilton never ceased to admire Jones. It is a pity that Rocher's study does not contain a bibliography of Hamilton's writings, though they will be found in the footnotes.

Cloyd 1972 is the first book-length biography of Monboddo ever and the first to draw on all the unpublished sources (listed on pages 180–1). Where none existed before, one must be grateful to have it. Being fully aware that Monboddo's chief interest as well as the basis of his reputation is his great work *Of the origin and progress of language*, Cloyd pays much attention to this subject, both in passages scattered throughout her book and in chapter four, "The natural history of language" (pp. 64–89), but her treatment is unfortunately vastly disappointing and falls far short of what one might expect from the sources available to her, printed as well as unprinted. She examines in some (though not much) depth Monboddo's intellectual milieu in Edinburgh, but about the impulses he may have received directly from France there is only bare mention of a few facts but no attempt to explore. During the fall of 1763, again during part of 1764 and also part of 1765, he was in Paris, where he spent much of his leisure time reading in the Bibliothèque nationale, and 'studied reports of savage nations in an effort to learn something of man's first ages ... interviewed the wild girl Memmie le Blanc, and encouraged his clerk, William Robertson, to translate and publish an account of her, to which he [Monboddo] wrote an introduction describing the interview'. These are all themes that relate directly to the contemporary French discussions of the origin of language and the nature of man as this problem had been defined by Condillac; yet Cloyd seems unaware of the relevance. In the years 1765–66, shortly after the visits to Paris, he wrote several essays on language and also wrote to James Harris that he contemplated 'a work showing the origin and progress of this most wonderful of all the arts of man, the art of speech' (22–8). Nowhere is there any mention that we learn from Monboddo himself in the Preface to his great work (I, ix) that he knew Condillac's *Essai* only from the extracts he had seen in a review from which he gathered, rightly I think, that their views were in basic agreement — in fact the similarity between both arguments and details of the two works is so striking that it is hard to escape the thought that Monboddo may after all have known the entire *Essai.* From the first volume of the *Origin and progress*, to which she devotes so much space, Miss Cloyd could also have learned that Monboddo while in Paris visited the Abbé de l'Épée (1:185). Neither Condillac nor de l'Épée are mentioned in her book. She shows that Monboddo was a meticulous keeper of notebooks, including notes on his reading, and at various periods of his life wrote a large number of essays, many of them on language and later incorporated in the *Origin and progress.* These are all in the unpublished sources she has examined or had access to, yet there is no attempt to sift the evidence in order to arrive at an understanding of the background and genesis of his work on language.

It is hard to understand that a biographer can be so helpless when confronted with material that virtually announces its own importance and the clues to successful treatment. The failure is in part explained when one encounters the assertion that according to Locke, 'all of the knowledge man has comes through the senses, just as all the knowledge a computer has comes through the programme it is given' (117). How is it possible that such error and confusion can find their way into print? Clearly, with such premises it is pointless to expect illumination. A unique opportunity to make a major contribution to the intellectual history of the eighteenth century has been lost.

At the same time it must be admitted that this failure is in part a consequence of still widely held attitudes about language study and its history. In typical fashion, rather than searching out and examining the intellectual context, Miss Cloyd lapses into discussion of more recent scholarly opinion on the origin of language, citing, for instance, Jespersen's opinion that there must have been a time when 'speech and song were not differentiated (77)' (which of course forms part of the argument in Condillac's Essai, though Miss Cloyd seems unaware of it). She observes that Monboddo studied and sought information on a variety of languages 'with as clear and unprejudiced an eye as was possible at the time: this is something almost no other man writing on these subjects in the last quarter of the eighteenth century attempted, or, perhaps, even thought of attempting' (82), a repetition of the nineteenth-century myth, for such studies of language had been current at least since the 16th century. She further speculates that Rask may have or could have learnt something from Monboddo, a possibility that can be firmly rejected on the basis of Rask's published correspondence and the meticulous examination of Rask's intellectual milieu in Diderichsen 1960. Still, we must be grateful to have Miss Cloyd's biography with its ready references to the printed and unprinted sources. A golden opportunity still awaits some future student who will devote a monograph to the problems her book leaves untouched.

Seigel 1969 is a very useful article. Though somewhat weak on the precise historical and philosophical context, it calls attention to a set of problems — deaf-muteness and also in part blindness — that occupy a significant role in the philosophy of language after Condillac's *Essai* and Diderot's *Lettre sur les aveugles* (1749) and *Lettre sur les sourds-et-muets* (1751), both inspired by the *Essai*. Seigel is chiefly concerned with the Abbé de l'Epée, whose important work is no doubt the most significant and lasting practical consequence of that interest in the philosophy of language.

2.5 *Epilogue*

Though the present bibliography of the historiography of eighteenth-century linguistics contains nearly four hundred items, not a single one of them attempts to deal with the study and philosophy of language at large as one of the distinct intellectual interests of that century, not even for a single country. This remarkable fact deserves closer examination. One possibility can be dismissed at the outset: the reason is not that this century has either resisted or not invited the study of its thought. On the contrary, the eighteenth century has long been granted unusual intellectual unity, felt even before 1800 and summed up in the word enlightenment and its German and French counterparts. Its literature, philosophy, painting, architecture, and crafts have been the subjects of many book length studies; its science and technology have more recently been studied as aspects of intellectual and social history. The possibility that the study of language is too recalcitrant, too difficult, forbidding, trivial or irrelevant for successful historical treatment can also be dismissed. As long ago as 1923, Cassirer remarked that 'a comprehensive work on the history of the philosophy of language is still a desideratum' (1953:117). The answer is not that the subject has been adequately dealt with in larger histories of linguistics that include the eighteenth century, or that it has found a place in the numerous histories of philosophy that have appeared since the middle of the eighteenth century, for such histories have largely ignored the study and philosophy of language.

There is, I think, general agreement about the situation I have described and also about at least one explanation that helps to account for it. In the form of comparative and historical philology, the study of language became during the nineteenth century the archetypal humanistic discipline. The philologist became the academic sage par excellence, enjoying greater prestige than his colleagues in other subjects. Full of vitality and the sense of excitement that goes with the opening up of new knowledge, philology undoubtedly attracted some of the best minds; its home was Germany where the universities under the impact of Wilhelm von Humboldt's reforms were ready to give it the best opportunities. It also had the luck to grow into its own during an age that had a strong though naive faith in positivism, that is in the belief that each discipline suddenly finds the right method and becomes mature, from that point on putting all past error behind it. Like natural science, it was felt, philology was somehow genuinely true and the only correct way of studying language. It is a curious and perhaps not entirely unrelated fact that the rise of Sprachwissenschaft in the German universities occurred during the years when their science faculties were dominated by Naturphilosophie — in the words of Emil du Bois-Reymond: 'Fast auf allen Punkten hatte die naturphilosophische Spekulation Boden gewonnen, und in fast allen Universitäten wurden ihre Hirngespinste sowohl von Philosophen von Fach, wie von Naturforschern und Ärzten als bare Weisheit verkündet und von einer irregeleiteten Jugend begierig aufgenommen' (1883,2:68). The success and confidence — one could also say pride — of nineteenth-century linguistics became a nearly insuperable obstacle to the creation of a genuine history of the study of language.

In varying degrees but still without hesitation, this attitude is found in all the standard introductions to linguistics, if they touch on the matter at all, e.g. Jespersen 1922, Bloomfield 1933, Meillet 1937, and Gray 1939. Lockwood 1969 credits Leibniz with giving a great impetus to linguistic studies generally by overcoming 'the prejudice that Hebrew had been the primitive speech of mankind, arguing that language was not the product of a uniform plan, but had arisen and evolved as a consequence of man's natural needs' (21). Even if this could be taken as a correct statement, which is doubtful, there is no obvious indication that Leibniz in fact had any influence by virtue of this view. It is not true that Hebrew until his day, or earlier, ever generally held the exclusive position claimed for it, and the belief that it did is typical of the convenient myths that gave the nineteenth century a comfortable sense of superior achievement and self-justification. Further, many who believed that Hebrew was the original language also believed that it had been lost in the Babylonian confusion. The tenacity of the nineteenth-century tradition is indicated by this statement from 1963, which could just as well have been written a hundred years earlier: 'Ce n'est qu'au XIXe siècle que ces raisonnements de type abstrait vont perdre peu à peu la face devant l'élargissement des horizons que procurent la connaissance de langues de plus en plus nombreuses ... [et] surtout, d'une méthode historique qui, rejetant tout apriorisme, prend conscience des réalités et travaille sur les faits tels qu'ils se présentent à l'observation' (Leroy 1963:14). All work before 1800 becomes pre-scientific in light of this extraordinary mixture of confidence and methodological naiveté. With regard to the eighteenth century especially, the nineteenth century has worked on us like a clever and very successful propaganda machine.

In the history of linguistics, the big stick of the nineteenth century has been especially hard on the eighteenth. Neither Benfey (1869) nor von Raumer (1870) mention Condillac and other important names of that time, but they construct detailed chronicles of scholars, works, and achievements that fit the canons of linguistics that enjoyed prestige in the 1860s. Thus the seventeenth century easily appeared more congenial than its successor, for Rask and Grimm had used such works as Junius' edition of Caedmon, William Somner's Anglo-Saxon dictionary, and George Hickes' grammar. Turgot's article on etymology (1756) in the *Encyclopédie* has received a great deal of attention and been treated as if it was exceptional in its time, though it is in fact a very derivative work. Referring to Herder and Horne Tooke as typical examples of the eighteenth-century mode, Vilhelm Thomsen observed in 1902 that although he granted that they might have some relevance in the history of ideas, he also believed that they had little to do with philology and that they had not, either directly or indirectly, brought it one inch forward. Their speculations being subjective, they were bound to miscarry for lack of any concept of philological empiricism, of the principles of the history of language, and of the life of language in general (Thomsen 1927:42-3; Aarsleff 1967:7–8). This attitude is still common. Some recent reviewers of Aarsleff 1967 (which has two chapters on Horne Tooke and his influence) express embarrassment to find so much space devoted to a man who didn't have the right method, almost as if paying any attention to him at all is an act of indiscretion. Yet there can be no doubt that Horne Tooke was a man of considerable intelligence — indeed brilliance —, extensive knowledge, and great influence on men of no mean intellectual stature, in other words no doubt that he does have a place in the history of the study of language.

Here we encounter a general problem in the history of linguistics of which the big-stick treatment of the eighteenth century is merely an example. If natural science has tended to form schools which sought ideological justification in particular versions of history, the study of language has rather formed sects with sharply opposed creeds, apostles and even something like curiae in charge of the purity of the doctrine. Dispassionate history has been rare and gained little attention. We need only to think of Bloomfieldian and Chomskyan linguistics, their opposition, and the ex post facto versions of history that have been created for both. What Kuhn says about scientific revolutions and the history of science is with even greater force true of linguistics. It is, he observes, 'only during periods of normal science that progress seems both obvious and assured' (1970:163). The result has led to 'a persistent tendency to make the history of science look linear or cumulative, a tendency that even affects scientists looking back at their own research' (139). The result has been what he calls textbook-preface history. Textbooks, 'being pedagogic vehicles for the perpetuation of normal science, have to be rewritten in whole or in part whenever the language, problem-structure, or standards of normal science change' (137). Thus, 'for reasons that are both obvious and highly functional, science textbooks ... refer only to that part of the work of past scientists that can easily be viewed as contributions to the statement and solution of the texts's paradigm problems. Partly by selection and partly by distortion, the scientists of earlier ages are implicitly represented as having worked upon the same set of fixed problems and in accordance with the same set of fixed canons that the most recent revolution in scientific theory and method has made seem scientific. ... The depreciation of historical fact is deeply, and probably functionally, ingrained in the ideology of the scientific profession that places the highest of all values upon factual details of another sort' (138). It is obvious that the tendencies Kuhn here analyzes have been much stronger in linguistics; one need only think of the Bloomfieldian curia's denigration of prescriptivism and Latinism in seventeenth and eighteenth century grammar, quite contrary to what the texts warrant.

The significant fact is, however, that developments during the last generation, in large measure under the influence of the distinguished work of Alexandre Koyré, have created a history of science that has overcome its former textbook-preface qualities and functions, thus becoming an autonomous discipline within the larger context of intellectual history, to which it has in the process significantly contributed. In spite of the fondness for calling linguistics a science (often helped along by the difficulty of finding more suitable English terms for some of the meanings of the German 'Wissenschaft'), it is surprising that it has learnt so little from the powerful example of the history of science. In this respect, its latest version in 'Cartesian linguistics' has been a very long step in the opposite direction. The history of linguistics is again more than ever engaged in the search for forerunners, a procedure that is of course incompatible with any genuine conception of history. I may perhaps again cite Koyré's words of warning: 'La manie de la recherche des "précurseurs" a bien souvent irrémédiablement faussé l'histoire de la philosophie.' They neatly sum up the attitude that has made the history of science the distinguished discipline it is today.

The tendency of most larger syntheses in the history of linguistics corresponds to the state of the history of science earlier in this century. Kuhn identifies two traditions. One saw 'scientific advance as the triumph of reason over primitive superstition.... Though vast scholarship, some of it still useful [as we find it in, for instance, Benfey and von Raumer], was sometimes expended on them, the chronicles which this tradition produced were ultimately hortatory in intent, and they included remarkably little information about the content of science beyond who first made which positive discovery when.' The other tradition we owe to 'practicing scientists ... who have from time to time prepared histories of their specialties. Their work usually began as a by-product of science pedagogy and was directed predominantly to science students.' Seen from the perspective of the present, this tradition has two serious limitations. First, 'excepting occasional naive asides, it produced exclusively internal histories which considered neither context for, nor external effects of, the evolution of concepts and techniques being discussed.' And, second, 'scientist-historians and those who followed their lead characteristically imposed contemporary scientific categories, concepts, and standards on the past. ... Inevitably, histories written in this way reinforced the impression that the history of science is a not very interesting chronicle of the triumph of sound method over careless error and superstition' (1971:288–90). It takes little knowledge and insight to see that this description fits the dominant tendency in the history of linguistics today.

It is very rare indeed to find a linguist who consistently and from the very start — not merely retrospectively — has given equal status to works both old and very recent as relevant to his own work. Of this procedure I know only one example, which is perhaps also unique, Viggo Brøndal. His four major works (listed in the bibliography and spanning the years 1928 to 1940), are devoted to the theoretical problem of linguistic universals, first announced in this form in 1928: 'Y a-t-il, autrement dit — puisque la langue réflechit la mentalité — une même base logique pour toutes les langues, ou y en a-t-il plusieurs?' (1948:24), a question that already indicates the affinity between Brøndal's and Chomsky's interests. His answer is that there is a single logical base, as stated for example in this passage:

Si l'on envisage ce mouvement ou cheminement de la pensée dans sa généralité ..., il semble qu'on le retrouve dans (ou plutôt; sous, derrière) toutes les langues: en chinois aussi bien que dans nos langues occidentales, chez les anciens et les primitifs comme chez les modernes et les civilisés. Il s'agit là d'une constante logique ou, si l'on veut, psychologique [which is also the sense in which Chomsky uses the term psychology], d'une condition générale de la réalisation ou de l'articulation d'une langue — dont l'étude sera d'importance capitale aussi bien pour la logique générale ou pure que pour la théorie linguistique. Rappelons que Husserl, l'un des penseurs les plus pénétrants de notre époque, a très bien vu qu'il y a connexion intime entre le discours et sa logique pure, d'où ressort, selon lui, que la syntaxe n'est que de la logique extériosée dans le langage: la logique sans syntaxe manquerait d'expression et resterait donc inaccessible; la syntaxe sans logique serait vide, et par conséquent incomprehensible (1937:66–7; cf. *ibid.* 56).

Brøndal 1948 [1928] is preceded by an epigraph from Wilhelm von Humboldt, who is often cited elsewhere in Brøndal's writings because he 'savait encore, et d'une façon géniale, maintenir aussi bien le point de vue historique que le point de vue philosophique, et les combiner d'une manière fructueuse, mais bientôt les préoccupations phonétiques l'emportèrent à tel point sur le souci logique que toute philosophie du langage en fut, pendant la plus grande partie du XIXe siècle, réduite à une existence tout à fait misérable' (31). Both points are emphatically restated in 1937: 'La linguistique comparée et historique — florissante, surtout en Allemagne, au XIXe siècle — fut, par réaction, nettement positive. Ses efforts principaux et trop souvent exclusifs portent sur l'histoire et les variations dialectales des langues; elle réagit consciemment et parfois avec une violence extrême (Steinthal) contre les prétensions universalistes de la grammaire générale; la plupart des linguistes, d'ailleurs, s'intéressent surtout à la forme extérieure: phonéticiens purs, ils négligent très souvent l'analyse conceptuelle' (50). And again in 1937: 'C'est Humboldt, le grand linguiste philosophe, connaisseur intime des langues les plus divergentes, qui pose ce principe qu'on ne pourra assez se figurer que le langage et la pensée sont identiques' (52). Brøndal 1948 [1928] opens and closes with reference to the same passage in Descartes: 'A la première page du *Discours de la méthode*, on peut lire que la raison est partout et toujours identique à elle-même: "Toute entière à vn chascun"' (9). It closes with these words: 'Le fondement logique est partout le même. Là ou il y a langue, il y a nécessairement formation de phrases. ... Les combinaisons sont ici aussi nombreuses que la base est simple. A cette multiplicité de combinaisons correspond la grande plasticité de l'esprit, et, par suite, des langues. A la simplicité du fondement répond par contre le *logos*: l'esprit humain, ou la raison, partout identique à elle-meme ou, pour citer les mots de Descartes: "Toute entière à vn chascun"' (173). These passages recall a great deal that we later encounter in Chomskyan linguistics and in Cartesian linguistics.

In retrospect, Brøndal's bibliographies of works that are actively used in his analyses are equally astonishing. His 1948 [1928] devotes more than a fourth of its pages to "Histoire de la terminologie" (24–30) and "Histoire des définitions" (30–69). A selection of items from the bibliography (14–21) gives the following: Adelung, *Umständliche Lehrgebäude* (1782); Beauzée, *Grammaire générale* (1767); Du Marsais, *Logique et principes* (1769); Thomas of Erfurt, *De modis significandi*; James Harris, *Hermes* (1751); Girard, *Vrais principes* (1747); six works by von Humboldt; Leibniz, *De arte combinatoria* (1666) as well as *Nouveaux essais* and Leibniz 1903; Meiner, *Versuch* (1781; see Brekle 1971b); Port-Royal *Grammar and Logic*; de Sacy, *Principes de grammaire générale* (1799); Sanctius Minera (1587); J. C. Scaliger, *De causis linguae latinae* (1540); Ch. Thurot, *Histoire des doctrines grammaticales* (1868); G. J. Vossius, *De arte grammatica* (1635); Christian Wolff, *Vernünftige Gedanken* (1719). In addition, these modern works: Boas, *Handbook* (1911); Cassirer 1902 and 1953 [1923];

Couturat 1901; Ogden and Richards, *The Meaning of Meaning* (1923); several items by Bertrand Russell, and Sapir, *Language* (1921). Brøndal 1932 repeats these items, adding Joachim Jungius, *Logica Hamburgensis* (1638) and Jellinek 1913–14. Brøndal 1950 [1940] adds Bacon, *Novum organon* (1620); Locke, *Essay*; Melanchthon, *Grammatica latina* (1560); Pascal; as well as these modern works: Carnap, *Logische Aufbau der Welt* (1928), *Logische Syntax der Sprache* (1934); Husserl, *Logische Untersuchungen* (1913–21).

Several of these items recur in the shorter Brøndal 1937, which, written for an encyclopedia, contains the most succinct statement of Brøndal's theories up to this time. I have earlier mentioned the fact, also I hope brought out by the citations, that there are inescapable affinities between Brøndal and what we find in Cartesian linguistics. It is therefore perhaps not without interest that Chomsky on 20 February 1959 took out the Brøndal volume that contains Brøndal 1937, renewing it on 27 March in the Princeton Library (as indicated by the library card and the borrower's signature). I have already cited several passages from that item, but two more may be justified.

Les éléments ainsi supposés à la base d'une langue quelconque et de ses constructions seront nécessairement de caractère extrêmement général puisqu'ils devront servir à la définition des formations morphologiques (classes, mots, formes) et syntaxiques (propositions, membres) même les plus abstraits. La recherche des ces éléments derniers du langage — la tâche la plus ardue sans doute et la plus important de la linguistique générale — doit de toute évidence se fonder, d'une part sur la permanence et l'identité universelle du discours (ce sera peut-être là le point de départ le plus commode pour la plupart des chercheurs), d'autre part sur cette monotonie frappante des catégories morphologiques qu'a souvent souligné le grand linguiste et grammairien que fut Antoine Meillet. En persévérant assez dans de telles recherches on arrivera peut-être à établir l'invariant linguistique ou l'ensemble des éléments et procédés nécessaires et suffisante pour définir le langage. (57).

Considérons maintenant la logique en tant que théorie générale et impartiale de la pensée ou théorie de tout système symbolique possible (ajoutons: et de son fonctionnement) ... Une langue, dans cette hypothèse, devra etre considérée comme une cristallisation particulière de possibilités inhérentes à la logique universelle; cristallisation qui dépend d'une choix systématique d'intervalles ou *quanta* logiques. (61)

I hope these pages on Brøndal will not be considered an irrelevant excursus, even though he is not entirely forgotten in recent literature. I introduced them first because I think it has a certain interest to see a modern linguist who in the process of addressing himself to theoretical problems actively uses a large number of very old items on an equal footing with modern ones, at the same times entirely bypassing the dominant nineteenth-century linguistics, whose particular quality is defined by contrast. Secondly, because I hope it will be granted that not only the aim but also some of the theoretical positions show affinity with modern theory. And, thirdly, because I think that the historical view that emerges has a good deal in common with what has later become known as Cartesian linguistics. On this point, however, there are significant differences. Brøndal did not use history retrospectively. He found Descartes and the

Port Royal representative but did not accord them any decisive innovative stature; they merge into the tradition he traces from the previous century: 'La grammaire générale, développée surtout en France aux XVIIe et XVIIIe siècles (Port-Royal, Encyclopédie), reflétait ... la philosophie de l'époque, à savoir le rationalisme dogmatique et universaliste: elle réduit, en principe, toute phrase possible au schéma de la logique' (1937.49). And he did not introduce a confusing doctrine of innate ideas to support his argument. He makes a perceptive observation on the persistence of rationalism. Even in the nineteenth century, 'cette théorie, ou ce dogme, de l'unité absolue de l'esprit humain eut encore beaucoup de partisans; ni le positivisme (August Comte), ni l'école anthropologique anglaise ([Sir Edward Burnett] Taylor, [Andrew] Lang et [Sir James] Frazer) ne trouvèrent de raison de la reviser. ... Cependant l'orientation empirique et historique qui — justement et surtout sous l'influence de Hume et de Rousseau (en partie par l'intermédiaire de Kant) — devint dominante au XIXe siècle, détourna peu à peu les esprits de ce postulat comme de beaucoup d'autres postulats rationalistes' (1948 [1928 :9). Thus Brøndal does not fall into the errors that make a historical dead end of Cartesian linguistics.

Today the program and success of nineteenth-century comparative and historical linguistics no longer stand in the way of efforts to create a coherent and informed history of the study of language, and Bloomfieldianism with its small interest and poor work in the subject did not become a hindrance. But with the recent arrival of new and exciting linguistic doctrines, the now familiar pattern has unfortunately repeated itself in the construction of another retrospective history, which 'partly by selection and partly by distortion' is supplying the 'text-book preface' history of the moment. True, the interest has shifted to problems and subject-matter that were previously given little attention, but hopes that a better, more comprehensive and balanced history would come out of this interest do not appear likely to be fulfilled. First propounded at length in Chomsky 1966 under the title that is now its general name, it has since by its advocates been pursued in a very large number of items which have tended to make it not more but much less promising than it was at the outset. It is again especially the eighteenth century that is getting into trouble. It will therefore be necessary to restate the main objections to Cartesian linguistics.

In her widely informed and severely critical review of Chomsky 1966, Vivian Salmon has convincingly demonstrated that the three features that are used to establish the dependence of the Port-Royal grammar on Descartes existed independently of Descartes in the grammatical tradition that reaches back into the Middle Ages and that these features are especially prominent in discussions found in the literature of the early seventeenth century prior to Descartes. Thus no causal link can be established between Cartesian doctrines and the form that linguistic and grammatical theory took in Port Royal — indeed one exponent of one of these principles was 'the founder of modern empirical philosophy, Francis Bacon' (170). Thus, referring to Chomsky's own admission of 'a certain distortion' owing to his approach (a distortion, incidentally, which both Chomsky and his followers have since tended to ignore or play down), Vivian Salmon can conclude that the major distortion 'is the attribution of the form taken by the Port-Royal grammar to Cartesian inspiration with little or no attempt to take into account the whole intellectual context in which it appeared' (185). Mrs. Salmon's argument gains support from the material offered in Lakoff 1969 and from the argument of Percival 1972, which concludes: 'That universal grammar began with Port Royal and had Cartesian origins is a hypothesis which sounds less and less plausible the more we learn about the development of linguistic theory since the Renaissance' (144). The significance of these facts and arguments is far-reaching, for it means that there is no specifically Cartesian element or novelty in the features that Chomsky finds in the Port-Royal grammar. In fact, the relationship is rather the reverse of the one postulated, namely that Descartes on these points was the exponent of views that were conventional and generally accepted in the period; comparing him with other philosophers of that century, one must surely agree with Percival's words that 'Descartes was relatively uninterested in language' (144). From the significance I have just pointed out a yet more important conclusion follows: if universal grammar can get along without any doctrine of innate ideas of the sort Chomsky sets up and attributes to Descartes and some others, also in the eighteenth century, then it will be possible to create a coherent view, that is a satisfactory history of linguistics from the seventeenth century through the eighteenth into the early decades of the nineteenth.

The insuperable obstacle to such a history lies in Chomsky's own and his followers' insistence on the version of innate ideas they either attribute to or withhold from various philosophers in ways that are at variance both with the texts they use for support and with interpretations that have gained respect and acceptance. On this point, their position has hardened since the rather moderate version of Chomsky 1966, which is why I said earlier that Cartesian linguistics has become steadily less promising as a framework for the history of linguistics.

The texts by Descartes that form the foundation of Cartesian linguistics are cited in the opening pages, with notes, of Chomsky 1966. Descartes observes that the most evident proof of a distinct difference between automatos and beasts on the one hand and human beings on the other is that only the latter 'use speech or other signs as we do when placing our thoughts on record for the benefit of others' ('pourraient user de paroles [et] d'autres signes en les composant, comme nous faisons pour déclarer aux autres nos pensées'), or 'make use of a true language' ('ut vera loquela uteretur'). What this shows is that 'brutes are devoid of reason' ('bestias cogitatione destitutas esse'), that 'reason is a universal instrument' ('que la raison est un instrument universel'), that language 'is the sole sign and the only certain mark of the presence of thought wrapped up in the body' ('loquela unicum est cogitationis in corpore latentis signum certum'). There is in man a 'power by which we are properly said to know things' ('vim illam, per quam res propriè cognoscimus'), a 'cognitive power' ('vis cognoscens'), 'it is properly called mind when it either forms new ideas in the fancy, or attends to those already formed' ('propriè autem ingenium appellatur, cum modò jam factis incumbit'). Nowhere in these passages or anywhere else in Descartes is man's ability to use language connected with, made dependent on, or taken to give proof of what Descartes called innate ideas. Language gives proof of reason and thought.

Whether one reads the texts cited in Chomsky's writings or the same and other texts entire from the seventeenth and eighteenth centuries, even the Port-Royal grammar and logic and Cordemoy, one will look in vain for any argument for or even bare comment on the necessity of innate ideas. Again, it is reason that is invoked, as, for instance, in this passage from Cordemoy cited in Chomsky 1966 (63), 'he concludes that language learning presupposes possession of "la raison toute entière; car enfin cette manière d'apprendre à parler, est l'effet d'un si grand discernement, et d'une raison si parfaite, qu'il n'est pas possible d'en concevoir un plus merveilleux".'

The difficulties are very considerable, both internal and external so to speak. Chomsky (e.g. 1966:60–62; 1968:70) makes a great deal of Herbert of Cherbury, especially his 'common notions' and of universal consent as the criterion of 'natural instinct'. But in several letters to Mersenne, Descartes explained that he disagreed with Herbert on those points as well as others. On the former he observed that Herbert took many things for common notions, 'qui ne le sont point; et il est certain qu'on ne doibt recevoir pour notion, que ce qui ne peut estre nié de personne' (A. & T. 2:629; Descartes to Mersenne 25 December 1639). He rejected universal consent: 'L'auteur prend pour règle de ses verités le consentement universel; pour moi, je n'ai pour règle des miennes que la lumière naturelle, ce qui convient bien en quelque chose: car tous les hommes ayant une même lumière naturelle, ils semblent devoir tous avoir les mêmes notions', but they do not because so few make good use of the light of nature, which means that many may well agree on the same error, while a great many things can be known by that light which no one has yet thought of (A. & T. 2:597–8; Descartes to Mersenne 16 October 1639). On both points Gassendi and Locke held the same positions as Descartes, rejecting the argument that natural instinct be determined by or is somehow shown in universal consent. They rejected the very disquieting qualification that such consent must occur 'among "normal men". That is, we must put aside "persons who are out of their minds or mentally incapable" and those who are "headstrong, foolish, weak-minded and imprudent"' (Chomsky 1966:61). Locke wondered whether 'those men will think it reasonable that their private persuasions, or that of their party, should pass for universal consent: a thing not infrequently done when men, presuming themselves to be the only masters of right reason, cast by the votes and opinions of the rest of mankind as not worthy of reckoning' (*Essay* I, iii, 20; cf. Gassendi 1641, esp. 277–85, e.g. 278 '... sans doute il ne faut écouter que des hommes disposant d'un jugement sain et entier. Mais, o généreux adversaire, quand bien même je vous accorderais cela de plein gré, ne s'élève-t-il pas une nouvelle contestation pour savoir quels sont ceux qui ont un jugement sain et entier? Encore ai-je à dessein laissé de coté les choses dont nous sommes, par une autre voie, certains et assurés: l'existence d'un Dieu, d'une Providence, des âmes immortelles, du droit naturel, du devoir de faire pour autres ce que nous voudrions qu'on fit pour nous, etc., choses qui ne sont pourtant pas si universellement admises que certains peuples (comme l'attestent de récentes relations sur le Nouveau Monde) et même une foule de philosophes (comme il ressort de l'histoire ancienne), persuadés du contraire, ne soient prêts, si je ne les tenais pas pour sains et entiers d'esprit, à dire que c'est plutôt moi qui suis malade et privé de jugement.') Descartes also observed that Herbert followed a procedure that was very different from his own by examining what Truth is, a notion which to Descartes was 'transcendalement claire' so that we have no means 'pour apprendre ce que c'est que la vérité, si on ne la connaissait de nature', and Descartes rejected Herbert's contention 'qu'il y ait en nous autant de facultés qu'il y a de diversités à connaître' (A. & T. 2:597–9). Yet, for Chomsky 'Herbert expressed much of the psychological theory that underlies Cartesian linguistics, just as he emphasized those aspects of cognition that were developed by Descartes' (1966:62). What is it then? On Chomsky's reading of Herbert it cannot also be Cartesian.

There is a second internal difficulty. Cartesian linguistics would be nothing without the contention that the doctrine of innate ideas implies the activity of the mind, not passivity. But on this point Descartes rather asserts passivity, e.g. in a letter to Mesland of 2 May 1644: 'Je ne mets autre différence entre l'âme et ses idées, que comme entre un morceau de cire et les diverses figures qu'il peut recevoir. Et comme ce n'est pas proprement une action, mais une passion en la cire, de recevoir diverses figures, il me semble que c'est aussi une passion en l'âme de recevoir telle ou telle idée, et qu'il n'y a que ses volontés qui soient des actions; et puis ses idées sont mises en elle, partie par les objets qui touchent les sens, partie par les impressions qui sont dans le cerveau, et partie aussi par les dispositions qui ont précédé en l'âme même, et par les mouvements de sa volonté' (A. & T. 4:113–14; cf. Beck 1967:151). Quite apart from the many passages in Descartes that raise great uncertainty about Chomsky's interpretation, this is a matter that has often been treated in the literature in ways that do not agree with Chomsky's reading.

A third internal difficulty emerges from a single sentence in Descartes' "La recherche de la vérité par la lumière naturelle". Eudoxe, leading the dialogue and with the young Poliandre (whose mind is pure and uncorrupted by false learning and prejudice) speaking for Descartes, says: 'Je désire que vous remarquiez la différence qu'il y a entre les sciences et les simples connaissances qui s'acquièrent sans aucun discours de raison, comme les langues, l'histoire, la géographie, et généralement tout ce qui ne dépend que de l'expérience seule' (A. & T. 10:502). Since this is so far as I know the only passage in which Descartes speaks directly to the question of language acquisition, it should be taken seriously by the doctrine of Cartesian linguistics. Yet it says in plain words that the acquisition of languages has nothing to do with reason (let alone innate ideas), but depends entirely on experience. Various interpretations may of course be possible or one may not wish to accept this statement as speaking for all of Descartes, as if it were a lapse or some unfortunate and careless statement. Yet, it is recalcitrant and cannot be lightly dismissed by readers who build a large and confident structure on Descartes' few statements regarding language and mind and on interpretations of which it would be a mild remark to say that they are doubtful.

As it has been formulated, Cartesian linguistics also creates very considerable difficulty externally, so to speak, that is in its bearing on the study of language during the eighteenth and early nineteenth centuries. It would be conceivable that neither Descartes' name nor the doctrine of innateness that is given such a significant role in Cartesian linguistics would be mentioned in subsequent writings if both were tacitly admitted and taken for granted in the tradition of universal grammar. But Descartes and his innate ideas are in fact challenged by Du Marsais, who rejects both in favor of Locke and his philosophy, yet without making any corresponding adjustment in his linguistic doctrines such as we would be forced to expect according to Cartesian linguistics. Du Marsais' philosophical alignment is plentifully evident in his writings and was well known to his contemporaries, who like Du Marsais himself also failed to see any conflict between Lockianism and universal grammar. Indeed, François Thurot writing a history of universal grammar in the last decade of the eighteenth century specifically denied that Descartes had any role in that tradition (Aarsleff 1971b:5). Further, when the problem of the origin of language was formulated and discussed at length by Condillac with heavy and acknowledged indebtedness to Locke, also fully known by Condillac's contemporaries, this problem was readily and without any sense of conflict fused with universal grammar. These are bothersome facts that cannot fail to raise serious doubts about Chomsky's formulation of Cartesian linguistics since it hardly seems inviting to argue that these men — many of whom also play distinguished roles in Chomsky's presentation, for example, Du Marsais and Beauzée — were too insensitive to the issues to see any conflict.

It is not without importance to note that Wilhelm von Humboldt also, voicing agreement with Condillac, rejected innate ideas. While in Paris during the spring of 1798 and within a year of the first journey to Spain and the Basque Provinces, he read Condillac's main works with marked eagerness. When he had completed Condillac's *Essai* (1746), he summed up the results in this fashion: 'In Condillac liegt der Ursprung noch aller heutigen Metaphysik in Frankreich. Zwei Dinge sind darin Hauptsächlich characteristisch. 1. sie nehmen keine angebornen Ideen an, und das mit Recht. Daher verwerfen sie alles *a priori*, weil sie keine andere Manier, als durch solche Ideen kennen ... 2. da sie dies nicht annehmen ist ihre Metaphysik bloss rationelle Psychologie. 3. sie legen unendlich viel Gewicht in die Verbindung der Begriffe mit Zeichen und daher scheint ihnen die allgemeine Grammatik ein so wesentlicher Theil der Metaphysik' (1916:449). As I have suggested earlier, it is very hard indeed to escape the impression that Humboldt's philosophy of language was strongly influenced, in fact initially it seems determined by, what he met in Paris. Humboldt of course postulated a sort of language power or speaking power, a point he often made, as, for instance, in a passage cited in Chomsky 1966:71. This conception is fully in agreement with Condillac. Though it has often been asserted in the secondary literature that Humboldt was influenced by Herder, I have never seen this claim substantiated.

It is for this reason that Locke's position in Cartesian linguistics becomes an important issue in the historical context, and it is only natural that the insistence on innate ideas has triggered off an awareness of this problem. Both Professors Goodman and Danto have raised this point, and two recent survey articles on Chomskyan linguistics appear to take for granted that Locke's philosophy, called empiricism, is incompatible with the rationalism of Cartesian linguistics (Searle 1972; Yergin 1972). Thus John Searle (1972:20) observes that 'the most spectacular conclusion about the nature of the human mind' in Chomsky is the vindication of the claims of seventeenth-century rationalists that 'there are innate ideas in the mind'. Searle continues: 'The empiricist tradition by contrast, from Locke down to contemporary behaviorist learning theories, has tended to treat the mind as a *tabula rasa*, containing no knowledge, except that they must be derived from experience by such mechanisms as the association of ideas or the habitual connection of stimulus and response.' But this is surely, as has often been observed, not Locke's view. To him experience was not only sensation but also reflection, the all-important role he gave to reason and intuition does place constraints on possible knowledge, and it should hardly be necessary to point out that association of ideas in Locke subverts reason and destroys the very possibility of knowledge. Further, if behaviorism somehow implies the passivity or non-creativity of the mind, it has in that respect nothing in common with Locke's philosophy, which for instance in the *Essay* and in the *Second treatise of government* attributes great activity and creativity to the mind, not least in regard to language. This is among other things the reason why Condillac can argue for the human creation of language on a Lockian basis. It is characteristic of rationalist grammarians that they, in accordance with their rationalism, advocated the learning of language first by routine rather than rules, a method advocated both by Locke and Cordemoy and later by Du Marsais, who cited Locke, among others, as authority for that method. Chomsky holds it to be a feature of empiricism that 'language is essentially an adventitious construct, taught by "conditioning" ... or by drill and explicit explanation' (1965:51), all of them means that Locke discourages.

Locke's position with Chomsky is not very clear. As early as *Aspects*, he cited Cudworth on '"the innate vigour and activity of the mind itself ..."', commenting that 'even in Locke one finds the same conception, as was pointed out by Leibniz and many commentators since' (1965:49; this has been repeated more recently in Chomsky 1971[8]). Here would seem to lie a possibility to deal with Locke in a manner that would not create difficulty in the eighteenth century, but it has not been pursued. On the contrary, in Hook 1969(73) we read: 'But consider the actual doctrines developed in the speculative psychology of rationalism, rather than Locke's caricature. Descartes, for example, argued that the idea of a triangle is innate. ...' It is curious to see the consideration of the triangle cited against 'Locke's caricature', for in Locke the very example of the triangle is cited several times — more often than in Descartes it would seem — with the same purpose and interpretation (Aarsleff 1971:8). It is not clear whether Chomsky would find Locke a representative of empiricist philosophy when he says that, 'we have a traditional philosophical claim — of empiricist philosophy ... from the 18th century onwards — that language is learnt by association of ideas and by reinforcing responses' (Aarsleff 1971:6). Unfortunately he does not say which philosophers said so in the eighteenth century. Perhaps some can be found (possibly La Mettrie and perhaps, though that would seem doubtful, Horne Tooke), but the overwhelming tradition that followed Locke certainly did not hold that view, for to them reason was the 'species-specific' human quality that governed the creation of language. These include Condillac and his well-known followers around the *Encyclopédie* in France, many important figures in the debate in the Berlin Academy in Germany (including Herder), and in England Monboddo and others. More recently, Chomsky has observed on the same subject: 'Rousseau holds that "although the organ of speech is natural to man, speech itself is nonetheless not natural to him ...". Again, I see no inconsistency between that observation and the typical Cartesian view that innate abilities are "dispositional", faculties that lead us to produce ideas (specifically, innate ideas) in a particular manner under given conditions of external stimulation, but that also provide us with the ability to proceed in our thinking without such external factors. Language, too, then is natural to man only in a specific way. This is an important and quite fundamental insight of the rationalist linguists that was disregarded, very largely, under the impact of empiricist psychology in the eighteenth century' (1972:21). But this is an insight that Rousseau owes to Condillac (to whom Rousseau specifically acknowledges his debt on linguistic theory in the work that is cited) and which stands at the core of the Locke-derived theory of the origin of language among all its practitioners just mentioned. The insight was certainly not disregarded, and it is not easy to understand who the empiricist psychologists could be that might have blocked it if they had been successful. David Hartley may perhaps be said to represent such a psychology, but he also knew well that his associationism was incompatible with Locke, and he does not appear to have had any appreciable influence on linguistic doctrine. Thus, it is pleasant to agree with Harman (1973) that 'Locke is clearly Cartesian in all relevant respects,' a point on which he appears to agree with me, but this interpretation is hardly compatible with Chomsky's reading of Descartes and Locke, and it has not been understood to be so in writings that rely on Cartesian linguistics. Yet, only if Descartes and Locke are so understood in regard to philosophy and linguistic theory is it possible to make sense of the actual course of the study of language in the eighteenth century. In addition Cartesian linguistics has had an unfortunate consequence, for which it cannot, of course, be held directly responsible, namely the tendency to narrow the study of language in a manner that misrepresents the entire seventeenth century at large and in good part also the eighteenth by ignoring that seventeenth-century linguistics was primarily engaged in the study of a very large variety of languages of the entire world, producing an enormous number of grammars and dictionaries. If the seventeenth was the century of genius and created a vast fund of intellectual capital, its genius was, so to speak, widely spread.

I think that at least one basic weakness of Chomsky's Cartesian linguistics as a historical framework derives from the acceptance of an extremely conventional version of the history of philosophy that sets up a few simple dichotomies such as seventeenth-century rationalism versus eighteenth-century sensualism, Descartes versus Locke, innateness versus sensationalism. Perhaps owing to its pedagogical convenience, this version has been widely disseminated until it has become the nearly ineradicable commonplace we face. But neither the texts nor the secondary literature that has dealt seriously and critically with them lend any support to it, and in spite of its success it has a very narrow base in the nineteenth-century conservative reaction against the eighteenth, most clearly represented by Victor Cousin followed in England by William Whewell and Adam Sedgwick, Sir William Hamilton, and later the editor of Locke, A. C. Fraser. But in that century it was in England rejected by much better informed and more critical minds, e.g. Dugald Stewart, Henry Rogers, J. S. Mill, G. H. Lewes, Robert Vaughan, and Edward Tagart, and by all substantial treatments in this century (on the nineteenth century, see Aarsleff 1971a). It has long been observed that Hume, not Locke, represents the cast of philosophy that has been known as empiricism. It is a consequence of this weakness that though Cartesian linguistics can note the change in linguistic orientation that occurs in the early decades of the nineteenth century, it has no means of explaining it, for though this orientation abandons the insights of rationalist theory, it is surely not a product of the reputed empiricist psychology of the eighteenth century.

Chouillet 1972 is an interesting article that explores the problem of the origin of language in relation to Cartesianism. He clearly sees that Cartesianism as formulated by Chomsky would create a rupture between the seventeenth and eighteenth centuries, but finds that there is in fact no evidence for such a rupture, even though Chouillet accepts the idea of a sensualist philosophy. He concludes: 'Il s'agit de savoir, pour revenir à notre problématique initiale, où, quand et comment se manifeste la véritable coupure par rapport à Descartes. Nous pouvons affirmer maintenant que ce n'est pas en France, et que ce n'est pas non plus chez les représentants attirés de la philosophie sensualiste.' In regard to the influence of Descartes, he therefore finds himself 'un peu en retrait par rapport à l'Americain Chomsky' (59). Chouillet is also, like Ricken 1964, aware of Locke's influence on Du Marsais.

It is curious that the years 1965 and 1966 saw the publication of two works that both sought to bring about a reorientation in the history of linguistics as part of a larger effort to introduce new views in linguistics, Chomsky 1966 and the first Italian edition of De Mauro 1969a. The major historical problems they identify are the same: the intellectual value of the linguistic work of the seventeenth and eighteenth centuries, the eclipse it suffered since the early nineteenth century until recently, and the need to return to what can generally be called mentalism. But the solutions and related historical interpretations they offer are diametrically opposed, a consequence of Chomsky's exclusion (at least at that time) of the semantic component, which for De Mauro is the very heart of the matter.

In the first third of his book, De Mauro presents a very interesting and compelling historical analysis. His linguistic interest is focused on the creation of a theory of the signified ('le signifié'), a task, he says, that has generally been considered insoluble, mysterious or meaningless, not least during the nineteenth century which explicitly or implicitly considered it impossible, 'pour une raison ou pour une autre, de construire une théorie du signifié' (15). His remedy is to change the perspective so that 'les signifiés ne sont plus considerés comme une fonction des formes linguistiques, une sorte de *virtus significativa* qui leur est inhérente, mais sont considerés comme résultat et fonction de l'acte significateur, du comportement linguistique de l'homme dans le contexte des collectivités historiques dans les quelles, avant tout à travers la solidarité sémantique, il s'insère et il vit' (11–12). In accordance with this culture-oriented linguistic theory, the first, that is the systematic aim of De Mauro's book is 'de faire ressortir la nécessité absolue de l'intégration interdisciplinaire et de la composition et de l'utilisation des différents points de vue passés et présents'. The second aim is to account for the virtual neglect of this problem in the history of the study of language, 'de retrouver les motifs historiques et culturels complexes qui ont mené, au cours des siècles, au paradoxe de tant d'ignorance face à une réalité aussi accessible que les signifié' (11). De Mauro shows an uncommon awareness, not least by contrast to Cartesian linguistics, of the tension between the actual history and the suppressions of this evidence in the historiography.

With its vast scope, De Mauro's analysis is unavoidably schematic and questions may be raised over details, but it remains compelling and persuasive. Saussure and others have identified the popular but simple-minded common man's view that language is like a repertory in which there are given signs for given things, as if the world has so to speak structured itself independently of language. This conception of 'la proposition-peinture et de la langue-image du monde' (37) has been widespread not only in the twentieth century but throughout history. De Mauro traces it to Aristotle and especially to a sort of conventionalized Aristotelianism which, having been established in antiquity, has held sway almost ever since. It has had two consequences: an excessive verbalism which has, in spite of some questioning (e.g. by Ockham), reigned until the early Renaissance; and an excessive logicism in grammar. They have been questioned only when the force of events have created a condition of crisis: 'La crise de la conception aristotélicienne est commencée lorsqu'il devient clair que ces deux conséquences, le verbalisme dans la science et le logicisme en grammaire, pèsent de manière négative sur la culture et sur la connaissance' (45). No single figure or event caused this crisis. Verbalism was drawn in doubt by the new science and the discovery of things for which there were no words, while anti-logicism arose from increasing awareness of the particularity of each vernacular language, a realisation that was forced upon the early translators of the Bible, to mention only one example. Thus Luther wrote that 'toute langue, y compris le latin, a sa "eigen Art", sa manière historique de représenter les choses, si bien que chacune, avec la même légitimité, peut et doit etre adoptée, comme instrument de transmission de la parole divine' (47–48). Having begun in the sixteenth century, this crisis gathers force during the seventeenth, 'enlevant ainsi des esprits l'idée que la langue est un reflet simple, immédiat et passif d'un monde de concepts et des choses déjà donnés. ... Les fruits de cette nouvelle façon de considérer le langage et les langues sont pleinement mûrs dans les œuvres de Francis Bacon, de Hobbes, de Locke, de Vico, de Leibniz, de Condillac, de Hamann et de Hume' (49). Thus in Locke's anti-verbalist and anti-innatist analyses of the relations between ideas and words of ordinary languages, we find an awareness of the 'historicity of languages' (50), soon taken up by others. The so-called Humboldtianism is much older than Humboldt — as we have seen in, for instance, Weimann 1965. In Vico, though he remained without disciples, we find the archetype 'de toute histoire linguistique qui délimite les problèmes de la croissance de la culture et de la civilisation d'une société, en rapport avec les problèmes de la communication linguistique des locuteurs et de l'adaptation continue de l'instrument de cette communication, la langue, aux exigences toujours renouvelées' (53). In agreement with Locke and Vico, we find in Leibniz that, 'non seulement une langue reflète l'histoire d'un peuple, mais elle peut aussi en conditionner la mentalité et les coutumes' (55). It is one of the reassuring aspects of De Mauro's analysis that it agrees with a number of other analyses, for example with Heinekamp's (1972) fundamental interpretation of the relationship between natural language and the *ars characteristica* in Leibniz (see especially De Mauro 1969b.57). The final result of this anti-Aristotelian renewal is the triumph of linguistic philosophy, as De Mauro sees it, at the middle of the eighteenth century.

But one hundred years later this philosophy has been rejected and virtually forgotten. This is the paradox: 'La linguistique scientifique, depuis la moitié du XIXe siècle, avec son orientation antisyntaxique et antisémantique marquée, a complètement trahi les objetifs et les raisons de sa naissance.' At the end of the century, 'le pouvoir des idées aristotéliciennes sur le langage était complètement restauré dans la culture européenne' (79–81), although there were a few dissenting voices, eg. J. N. Madvig and Michel Bréal. The study of language had become confined to three areas, 'des faits précis (c'est-à-dire phonétiques et morphologiques), des faits nombreux (c'est-à-dire très particuliers), des faits anciens' (78). De Mauro gives an answer that must surely have struck many: the silence of Kant (who, De Mauro argues, was not unfamiliar with the eighteenth-century tradition) on the philosophy of language which has caused it to disappear not only in the histories of philosophy but also in the histories of the study of language. Here is again the conflict between the actual history and the official historiography which calls Kuhn's observations to mind. 'La pensée de Kant a donc contribué à faire disparaître toute trace et tout souvenir de la philosophie du langage du XVII et XVIII siècles. A la moitié du XIXe siècle survinrent, pour en compléter l'œuvre, la crise formaliste et l'appauvrissement des idées et de la culture dans la linguistique scientifique' (71). One can think of several reasons for Kant's indifference. His attitude is perhaps indicated by a piece of information which his pupil and correspondent J. G. C. C. Kiesewetter, writing from Berlin on 5 November 1795, must have thought Kant would relish. It is about Daniel Jenisch, also known to Kant, who had then completed the work published in 1796, *Philosophisch-kritische Vergleichung und Würdigung von vierzehn ältern und neuern Sprachen Europens*, which had gained the prize for an essay topic set by the Berlin Academy. Kiesewetter had met the pastor of the Russian embassy, with whom Jenisch had sought instruction in Russian. When the pastor said he was too busy, Jenisch had asked him to recommend another informant. He recommended his coachman, 'Jenisch habe auch 14 Tage bei diesem Unterricht genommen und ihn dann mit einem Dukaten belohnt entlassen. Auf diese Weise had Jenisch den Geist der russischen Sprachen kennen gelernt' (Kant 1902:48).

De Mauro's analysis is interesting because it covers such a wide span in the study of language and creates a framework for the history of linguistics that must on the whole be accepted as persuasive and fruitful. Thus it explains not only the background and rise but also the decline and neglect of the great tradition of the seventeenth and eighteenth centuries. In this respect it differs markedly from Cartesian linguistics, but agrees with Brøndal who also aimed at a better semantic theory, as indicated outwardly by the subtitle of Brøndal 1950, 'introduction à une sémantique rationelle'. Of course, De Mauro's semantic orientation means that his great figures, such as Locke and Leibniz, are not Chomsky's, a fact that underscores the distortion that results when Leibniz is seen only in the framework of Cartesian linguistics. To be able to take full account of Leibniz is perhaps the best test of a genuine history of the study of language. As the dates of publication make likely, De Mauro wrote without knowledge of Chomsky 1966, except for a footnote that was perhaps added later or in the French edition (56). Its judgment is predictable. De Mauro sees Descartes as being committed to a typical Aristotelian view, as one of the voices that sound 'les dernières affirmations de la fidélité à une conception désormais vacillante'. Referring to a number of texts in Descartes (including several not used by Chomsky), De Mauro observes that none of these 'se présente dans un traité à l'organisation semblable à celle des traités non seulement de Locke, Leibniz ou Vico, mais même de Hobbes. Cela est naturel car pour Descartes le phénomène language est secondaire dans l'organisation et dans le développement de la vie cognitive et mentale', an observation with which Cartesian linguists may perhaps agree (how would it be possible to do otherwise?), but still a significant fact. (Cf. Aarsleff 1964:3: 'To Locke, unlike Descartes, the obstacle to good sense and knowledge was not merely a verbose enemy, not just some men's words, but words,' that is not merely as Descartes several times suggests a problem encountered in difficulty of precise expression.) De Mauro continues: 'Et c'est pourquoi it est absurde de vouloir faire de Descartes un précurseur de l'organicisme linguistique de Humboldt et de la notion de créativité, comme tend à le faire Chomsky.'

De Mauro's semantic orientation has another significant consequence that also sets it apart from Cartesian linguistics: emphasis on the cultural context of language. Thus he observes with justice: 'Lorsque récemment ... les idées sur la mutualité des rapports entre systématisation sémantique et structure syntaxique d'une part, et culture et *ethnos* d'autre part, revinrent à l'honneur, on parla, pour les désigner, des "hypothèses Sapir-Whorf" ... ou comme nous l'avons déjà signalé, des "idées de Humboldt". ... C'est peut-être la preuve la plus éclatante de l'oubli dans lequel a sombré, chez les linguistes, l'histoire de la linguistique du XVIIIe siècle' (61). Chevalier has already in several places pointed out that Cartesian linguistics ignores that all the grammars it deals with were designed to serve immediate pedagogical needs, not just in general, but for a particular class. Thus Chevalier observes: 'Sous les explications sociologiques, sous l'affirmation de la croyance dans les idées innées perce l'affirmation satisfaite que la bourgeoisie s'est fait son outil de réflexion; la Ratio devient un élément d'unification de classe. L'inventaire de la Renaissance ouvert sur le monde universel, devient une méthode fermée, fermée sur cette classe qui s'en donne l'usage exclusifs de la Raison' (1967:30).

It seems to me that the confrontation of De Mauro and Cartesian linguistics is interesting because they share certain basic concerns at the same time as they differ greatly on the solutions they offer. In spite of many troublesome points in De Mauro's analysis, it seems to me to offer much greater promise as a framework for a comprehensive and workable history of the study of language.

It is often assumed that the first and perhaps only raison d'être for such a history is the degree to which it can serve as a hand-maiden to current linguistics. This is perhaps not entirely the way of Cartesian linguistics in its original formulation in Chomsky 1966, but there is little doubt that it has been so understood. Thus there is an expectation that the history of linguistics will uncover new and fruitful views, but I see no indication that this has in fact happened. And since its method is to examine older texts in the light of current theory, how could it be expected that one would find more than the reflection of one's own image? Thus we get textbook-preface history and linguist-historians who impose current linguistic categories, concerns and standards on the past, to recall Kuhn's words. But this procedure will obviously miss the possibility of gaining insight into the thoughts, insights, methods, and achievements of past linguistic work. Missing that, it will in advance preclude the very benefit that is sought. More seriously for history, it will fail to satisfy the first aim of history, to gain a sense of coherence and texture in a collection of past events and to create understanding of intellectual traditions and influence. For clearly, these interrelations come about in response to the internal pressures of the context and not according to foreign categories that are imposed from the outside. There is nothing new in this; the problem is rather why the history of linguistics should have taken so long to recognize it or be so unwilling to accept it. No one expects the history of science to be a hand-maiden to science, so why should the history of linguistics be expected to perform such a task. If the history of science has become perhaps the most lively and exciting branch of intellectual history, there seems to be no good reason why the history of the study of language should not also free itself from its past and present subservience to non-historical interests. The history of science is already before us as a model. This also means that the history of linguistics must seek wider relations in the social, historical, and intellectual context of the times of the sort suggested by, for example, Chevalier when he calls attention to Snyders 1965 on the history of pedagogy. There is a vast amount of unexplored material that can be made to yield important knowledge, as shown by the fascinating books by Gossman 1968 and Stéfanini 1969. It is steadily becoming more evident that the neglect of the study of language in history, in all its forms, leaves a large gap in our understanding of the past.

Bibliography to Section 2

AARSLEFF, HANS. 1967. The study of language in England 1780–1860. Princeton. [279 pp.]

——. 1970. The history of linguistics and Professor Chomsky. Lg 46.570–85.

——. 1971a. See Bibliography to Section 1.

——. 1971b. 'Cartesian linguistics': History or fantasy? Language sciences, No. 17 (October 1971), 1–12.

——. 1974. The tradition of Condillac: origin of language in the eighteenth century and the debate in the Berlin Academy before Herder. In Hymes 1974. [Except for minor revisions, this essay was completed in January 1969.]

——. 1975b. Condillac's speechless Statue. Studia Leibnitiana. Supplementa XV – Akten des II. Internationalen Leibniz-Kongresses Hannover, 17.–22. Juli 1972. Vol. 4. Forthcoming.

ABERCROMBIE, DAVID. 1951. Steele, Monboddo and Garrick. Studies in phonetics and linguistics, 35–44. London, Oxford University Press. [1965.]

ACTON, H.B. 1959. The philosophy of language in revolutionary France. PBA 45.199–219.

ADAMS, ELEANOR. 1917. Old English scholarship from 1566 to 1800. Yale Studies in English, No. 55. New Haven.

ADLER, EMIL. 1968. Abhandlung über den Ursprung der Sprache. Herder und die deutsche Aufklärung, tr. from Polish by Irena Fischer, 122–30. Wien Frankfurt Zürich, Europa Verlag.

AGRELL, JAN. 1955. Studier i den äldra Språkjämförelsens allmänna och Svenska Historia fram till 1827. UUÅ 1955, No. 13. [220 pp.]

ALIPRANDI, G. 1950. Il Vico e l'etimologia. Aevum 24.423–33.

ALLEN, DON CAMERON. 1960. The predecessors of Champollion. PAPhilos S 104 (5) 527–47.

ALLEN, W.S. 1953. Relationship in comparative linguistics. TPhS 1953. 52–108.

ALLGEMEINES REPERTORIUM DER LITERATUR FÜR DIE JAHRE 1785 BIS 1790. 3 vols. (Jena 1793–94).

ALLGEMEINES REPERTORIUM DER LITERATUR FÜR DIE JAHRE 1791 BIS 1795. 3 vols. (Jena 1799–1800).

ALLGEMEINES REPERTORIUM DER LITERATUR FÜR DIE JAHRE 1796 BIS 1800. 2 vols. (Weimar 1807).

ALSTON, R.C. 1965–. A bibliography of the English language from the invention of printing to the year 1800.

1. English grammars written in English & English grammars written in Latin by native speakers. 1965. [119 pp.]
2. Polyglot dictionaries and grammars, treatises on English written for speakers of French, German, Dutch, Danish, Swedish, Portuguese, Spanish, Italian, Hungarian, Persian, Bengali. 1967. [311 pp.]
3. Part I: Old English, Middle English, Early Modern English, Miscellaneous Works, Vocabulary. 1970. [205 pp.]
3. Part II: Punctuation, Concordances, Works on language in general, Origin of language, Theory of grammar. 1971. [66 pp.]
4. Spelling books. 1967. [277 pp.]
5. The English dictionary. 1966. [195 pp.]
6. Rhetoric, style, elocution, prosody, rhyme, pronunciation, spelling reform. 1969. [202 pp.]
7. Logic, philosophy, epistemology, universal language. 1967. [115 pp.]
8. Treatises on short-hand. 1966. [152 pp.]
9. English dialects, Scottish dialects, Cant and Vulgar English. 1971. [68 pp.]
10. Education and language teaching. 1972. [75 pp.]

——. Supplement 1973. Additions and corrections vols. 1–10. List of libraries. Cumulative indexes. [117 pp.]

ANTONI, CARLO. 1951. [1942] Der Kampf wider die Vernunft, zur Entstehungsgeschichte des deutschen Freiheitsgedankens. Stuttgart, K. F. Koehler Verlag. [352 pp. Hamann, pp. 200–39, Herder, pp. 240–83. Tr. from the Italian: La lotta contro la ragione.]

APEL, KARL OTTO. 1963. Die Idee der Sprache in der Tradition des Humanismus von Dante bis Vico. Archiv für Begriffsgeschichte, vol. 8. Bonn, Bouvier. [398 pp.]

APPLETON, WILLIAM W. 1951. A Cycle of Cathay. The Chinese Vogue in England during the 17th and 18th centuries. New York.

ARBERRY, A.J. 1946a. Asiatic Jones. The life and influence of Sir William Jones (1746–1794). Pioneer of Indian studies. London, British Council. [40 pp. Reprinted in Arberry 1960; 48–86.]

——. 1946b. New light on Sir William Jones. BSOAS 11. 673–85.

——. 1960. Oriental essays. Portraits of seven scholars. London. [261 pp.]

ARENS, HANS 1955. Sprachwissenschaft, der Gang ihrer Entwicklung von der Antike bis zur Gegenwart. Freiburg/München, Verlag Karl Alber. [568 pp.]

——. 1969². Sprachwissenschaft… zweite, durchgesehene und stark erweiterte Auflage. [816 pp.]

ARNAULD, A. 1969. Grammaire générale et raisonnée avec les remarques de Ch. Duclos. Introduction by M. Foucault. Paris, Republication Paulet, No. 7.

AUERBACH, ERICH. 1932. Vico und Herder. DVLG 10.671–86.

BAHNER, WERNER. 1957. Zur Romanität des Rumänischen in der Geschichte der romanischen Philologie von 15. bis zur Mitte des 18. Jahrhunderts. RJ*b* 8.75–94.

BALAZS, JANOS. 1956. Zur Frage des Erwachsens der osteuropäischen Nationalsprachen. Die Berührungen zwischen den Universitäten Krakau, Wittenberg und Ungarn im 16. Jahrhundert auf dem Gebiet der grammatischen und orthographischen Literatur. WINTER FESTSCHRIFT 1956:33–73.

BATTAGLIA, SALVATORE. 1963. Le teorie linguistiche del settecento. Napoli. [133 pp.]

BAUDLER, GEORGE. 1970. 'Im Worte Sehen.' Das Sprachdenken Johann Georg Hamanns. Müncherner philosophische Forschungen Vol. 2. Bonn, Bouvier. [338 pp.]

BAUMANN, H. 1958. Hiob Ludolfs Anteil an den deutsch-russischen Beziehungen im 17. Jahrhundert und seine Bedeutung für die Entwicklung der slawischen Philologie und der Russlandskunde in Deutschland. WINTER 1958b;86–93.

BAUSANI, ALESSANDRO. 1970. Geheim- und Universalsprachen, Tr. from the Italian by Gustav Glaeser. Stuttgart, Kohlhammer. [175 pp.]

BEAL, M. W. 1973. Condillac as precursor of Kant. Studies on Voltaire and the eighteenth century 102.193–229.

BECK, L. J. 1967. The metaphysics of Descartes. A study of the Meditations. Oxford, Clarendon. [307 pp.]

BECK, LEWIS WHITE. 1969. Early German philosophy. Kant and his predecessors. Cambridge, Mass. [556 pp.]

BÉDARIDA, HENRI. 1927. Parme et la France de 1748 à 1789. "Sur le séjour et l'influence de Condillac à Parme," 412–26. Paris.

BELAVAL, YVON. 1969. Vico and Anti-Cartesianism. In Tagliacozzo 1969:77–91.

BENFEY, THEODOR. 1869. Geschichte der Sprachwissenschaft und orientalischen Philologie in Deutschland seit dem Anfange des 19. Jahrhunderts, mit einem Rückblick auf die früheren Zeiten. München. [836 pp.]

BENZ, ERNST. 1949. Wittenberg und Byzanz; zur Begegnung und Auseinandersetzung der Reformation und der östlich-orthodoxen Kirche. Marburg. [288 pp. Reissued 1971 in Forum Slavicum 6.]

BERÁNEK. See SEGERT 1967.

BERKOV, P.N. 1958. Des relations littéraires franco-russes entre 1720 et 1730: Trediakovskij et l'Abbé Girard. RESl 35.7–14.

BERLIN, ISAIAH. 1969. Vico's concept of knowledge. In TAGLIACOZZO 1969:371–8.

BERNHAGEN, W. 1958. Johann Leonhard Frisch und seine Beziehungen zu Russland. In WINTER 1958b:112–24.

BERTELSEN, HENRIK. 1926. Jens Pedersen Höysgaard og hans Forfatterskab. Copenhagen. [270 pp.]

BESTHORN, RUDOLF. 1963. Du-Marsais-Forschung? Bemerkungen zu den Arbeiten von Georg Gross. BRPh 2.5–26.

BEZARD, YVONNE. 1939. Le Président de Brosses et ses amis de Genève. Paris. [255 pp.]

BLACKALL, ERIC A. 1959. The emergence of German as a literary language 1700–1775. Cambridge. [539 pp.]

——. See KIMPEL 1966.

BLANCHARD, J. M. 1973. Grammaire(s) d'ancien régime. Studies on Voltaire and the eighteenth century 106.7–20.

BLOOMFIELD, LEONARD. 1933. Language. New York, Holt. [564 pp.]

BOLÊLLÎ, TRISTANO. 1965. Per una storia della ricerca linguistica. Testi et note introduttive. Napoli. [598 pp.]

BOLTON, W. F., ed. 1966. The English language. Essays by English and American men of letters 1490–1839. Cambridge. [228 pp.]

BONFANTE, G. 1954. Ideas on the kinship of the European languages from 1200 to 1800. CHM 1.679–99.

——. 1956. Il Glossarium di J. G. Wachter [1663–1757]. RIL 89/90.146–62.

BORST, ARNO. 1957–63. Der Turmbau von Babel. Geschichte der Meinungen über Ursprung und Vielfalt der Sprachen und Völker. 4 vols. in 6. Stuttgart, Anton Hiersemann.

——. 1960. Die Geschichte der Sprachen im abendländischen Denken. WW 10. 129–43.

BREKLE, HERBERT E. 1971a. See Bibliography to Section 1.

——. 1971b. Einleitung. Johann Werner Meiner, Versuch einer an der menschlichen Sprache abgebildeten Vernunftlehre oder philosophische und allgemeine Sprachlehre, *9–*44. Faksimile-Neudruck der Ausgabe Leipzig 1781. Stuttgart-Bad Cannstatt, Fromann Verlag.

BRENGUES, JACQUES. 1970. Correspondance de Charles Duclos (1704–1772). Saint-Brieuc, Presses Universitaires de Bretagne. [355 pp.]

——. 1971. Charles Duclos (1704–1772) ou l'obsession de la vertu. Saint-Brieuc, Presses Universitaires de Bretagne. [638 pp.]

BRØNDAL, VIGGO. 1948 [1928]. Les parties du discours. Partes orationis. Études sur les catégories linguistiques, tr. by Pierre Naert. Copenhague, Munksgaard. [173 pp.]

——. 1932. Morfologi og Syntax. Festskrift udgivet af Københavns Universitet i Anledning af Universitetets Aarsfest November 1932, 1–108.

——. 1937. Langage et logique. Essais de linguistique générale, publiées avec une bibliographie des œuvres de l'auteur, 49–71. Copenhague, Munksgaard. [1943. Pp. 49–71 First published in La grande encyclopédie française, July 1937.]

——. 1950 [1940]. Théorie des prépositions. Introduction à une sémantique rationelle, tr. by Pierre Naert. Copenhague, Munksgaard. [145 pp.]

BROWN, HARCOURT. 1963. Maupertuis Philosophe: Enlightenment and the

Berlin Academy. Studies in Voltaire and the eighteenth century, Vol. 24, 255–69.

BRUNET, PIERRE. 1929. Maupertuis. Étude biographique. 2 vols. Paris.

BRYAN, W. F. 1923. Notes on the founders of prescriptive English Grammar, 383–93. Manly Anniversary Studies. Chicago.

BURSIAN, CONRAD. 1883. Geschichte der classischen Philologie in Deutschland von den Anfängen bis zur Gegenwart. 2 vols. München/Leipzig. [Therein 1.260–356 Die classischen Studien in Deutschland während des 17. Jahrhunderts, 1.357–664 Die classischen Studien in Deutschland im 18. Jahrhundert bis auf Fr. Aug. Wolf.]

BUYSSENS, ERIC. 1961. Origine de la linguistique synchronique de Saussure. CFS 18.17–33.

CALCATERRA, C. 1946. L'ideologia illuministica negle studi linguistici italiani della seconda metà del settecento. Ideologismo e italianità nella transformazione linguistica delle seconda meta del settencento. Bologna.

CANNON, GARLAND. 1952. Sir William Jones, Orientalist. An annotated bibliography of his works. Honolulu, University of Hawaii Press. [88 pp.]

——. 1957. Sir William Jones and Edmund Burke. MPh 54. 165–86.

——. 1958. Sir William Jones's Persian linguistics. JAOS 78.262–73. [Also in SEBEOK 1966:36–57.]

——. 1964. Oriental Jones. A biography of Sir William Jones (1746–1794). London, Asia Publishing House. [215 pp.]

——. 1965–66. Sir William Jones and Dr. Johnson's literary club. MPh 63.20–37.

——. See JONES 1970.

CARRETER, LÁZARO. 1949. Las ideas lingüísticas en España durante el siglo XVIII. RFE 48.

CASSIRER, E. 1933. Le langage et la construction du monde des objets. *JPsych.* 30. 18–44. [Also in PARIENTE 1969.]

——. 1953. [1923] The philosophy of symbolic forms. Vol. 1: Language, Tr. by Ralph Manheim. New Haven. [328 pp.]

CHAMBERS, W. W. 1946. Language and nationality in pre-romantic and romantic thought. MLR 41.382–93.

CHATTERJI, SUNITI KUMAR. 1948. Sir William Jones: 1746–1794. In SEBEOK 1966: 18–36.

CHEVALIER, JEAN-CLAUDE. 1967. La Grammaire de Port-Royal et la critique moderne. Langages 7 (September 1967). 16–33.

——. 1968. Historie de la syntaxe. Naissance de la notion de complément dans la grammaire française (1530–1750). Genève, Droz. [776 pp.]

——. 1971a. La grammaire générale et la pédagogie au XVIIIe siècle. FM 39.40–51.

——. 1971b. Note sur la notion de synonimie chez trois grammairiens des XVIIe et XVIIIe siècles [Vaugelas, Girard, Beauzée]. Langages 10 (Décembre 1971). 40–47.

——. 1974. Les idéologues. Linguistique et société. In PARRET 1974.

CHOMSKY, NOAM. 1965. Aspects of the theory of syntax. Cambridge, Mass., MIT Press. [251 pp.]

——. 1966. Cartesian linguistics. New York, Harper & Row. [119 pp.]
——. 1968. Language and mind. New York, Harcourt, Brace & World. [88 pp.]
——. 1971. Problems of knowledge and freedom. The Russell Lectures. New York, Vintage Books. [111 pp.]
——. 1972. Language and freedom. TriQuarterly 23/24.13–33.
CHOUILLET, JACQUES. 1972. Descartes et le problème de l'origine des langues au 18e siècle. Dix-huitième siècle 4.39–60.
CHRISTMANN, H.H. 1966. Beiträge zur Geschichte der These vom Weltbild der Sprache, 441–69. Akademie der Wissenschaften und der Literatur. Abhandlungen der Geistes- und Socialwissenschaftliche Klasse. No. 7. Mainz.
——. 1971. Die Begegnung von deskriptiver und historischer Sprachbetrachtung in der 'Grammaire des grammaires.' RF 83.173–81.
CLARAPÈDE, EDOUARD. 1935. Rousseau et l'Origine du Langage. Annales de la Société Jean-Jacques Rousseau 34.95–119.
CLARK, ROBERT T. 1955. Herder. His life and thought. Berkeley.
CLERICO, G. 1971. Actualité de la grammaire générale. FM 39.16–24.
CLOYD, E.L. 1969. Lord Monboddo, Sir William Jones and Sanskrit. Ama 71. 1134–5.
——. 1972. James Burnett. Lord Monboddo. Oxford, Clarendon. [196 pp.]
CONDILLAC. See ROY 1947, 1953.
CONRADY, K.O. 1969. See LÄMMERT 1969.
CORNELIUS, PAUL. 1965. Languages in seventeenth- and early eighteenth-century imaginary voyages. Genève, Droz. [177 pp. Bibliography, pp. 159–71]
COSERIU, EUGENIO. 1967a. L'arbitraire du signe: zur Spätgeschichte eines aristotelischen Begriffes. ASNS 119.81–112.
——. 1967b. François Thurot [1768–1832], ZFSL 77.30–4.
——. 1968. Adam Smith und die Anfänge der Sprachtypologie. Wortbildung, Syntax und Morphologie. Festschrift zum 60. Geburtstag von Hans Marchand am 1. Oktober 1967, ed. by Herbert E. Brekle and Leonhard Lipka, 46–54. Janua Linguarum. Series Major, 36. The Hague, Mouton. [Also in SMITH 1970: 15–25.]
COSTA, GUSTAVO. 1970. Vico e Locke. Giornale critico della filosofia Italiani. Ser. 4, vol. 1. 344–61.
CYŽEVŚKYJ, D. 1939. Der Kreis A. H. Franckes in Halle und seine slavistischen Studien. (Ein vergessenes Kapitel aus der Geschichte der slavisichen Philologie.) ZbSlPh 16.16–68.
DE MAURO, TULLIO. 1969a [1965]. Une introduction à la sémantique, tr. from the Italian by Louis-Jean Calvet. Paris, Payot. [222 pp.]
——. 1969b. Giambattista Vico: From rhetoric to linguistic historicism. In TAGLIACOZZO 1969:279–96.
DERRIDA, JACQUES. 1967a. De la grammatologie. Paris. [447 pp.]
——. 1967b. La linguistique de Rousseau. Revue Internationale de Philosophie 82. 443–62.

DESCARTES, RENÉ. Oeuvres, ed. by Charles Adam and Paul Tannery. 13 vols Paris. [1897–1913. Abbreviated A. & T.]

DIDERICHSEN, PAUL. 1960. Rasmus Rask og den grammatiske Tradition. Studier over Vendepunktet i Sprogvidenskabens Historie. Historisk-filologiske Meddelelser udgivet af Det Kongelige Danske Videnskabernes Selskab. Vol. 38, No. 2. Copenhagen. [251 pp.]

——. 1966. The foundation of comparative linguistics: Revolution or Continuation? 340–63. Helhed og Struktur. Udvalgte Sprogvidenskabelige Afhandlinger. Copenhagen, Gad.

——. 1968. Sprogsyn og sproglig Opdragelse. Copenhagen. [254 pp.]

DIECKMANN, HERBERT. 1948. Le philosophe: Texts and interpretation. St. Louis.

DIECKMANN, LISELOTTE. 1970. Hieroglyphics: The history of a literary symbol. St. Louis, Washington University Press. [246 pp.]

DINNEEN, F.P., ed. 1966. Report on the seventeenth Annual Round-Table Meeting on Linguistics and Language Studies. Washington, D.C., Georgetown University Press. Monograph Series on Languages and Linguistics, No. 19. [258 pp.]

DOUGLAS, DAVID. 1951². English scholars 1660–1730. London. [291 pp.]

DOWNES, RACKSTRAW. 1962. Johnson's theory of language. A Review of English Literature (London) 3, No. 4. 29–41.

DROIXHE, DANIEL. 1971. L'Orientation structurale de la linguistique au XVIIIe siècle. FM 39.18–32.

DU BOIS-REYMOND, EMIL. 1883² Die Humboldt-Denkmäler vor der Berliner Universität. Reden, 2.249–84. 2 vols. Leipzig. [1912]

DUCHET, MICHÈLE. 1971. Anthropologie et histoire au siècle des lumières. Paris, Maspero.

DUCHET, MICHÈLE and MICHEL LAYNAY. 1967. Synchronie et diachronie: Essai sur l'Origine des langues et le second Discours. Revue Internationale de Philosophie 82.421–42.

DUFRENOY, M.L. 1963. Maupertuis et le progrès scientifique. Studies on Voltaire and the eighteenth century 25.512–88.

DÜNNINGER, JOSEF. 1952. Geschichte der deutschen Philologie. Deutsche Philologie im Aufriss, ed. by Wolfgang Stammler 1. 79–214. Berlin.

——. 1957². Geschichte der deutschen Philologie. Deutsche Philologie im Aufriss, ed. by Wolfgang Stammler, 1.83–222. Revised ed. Berlin, E. Schmidt. [On the eighteenth century 1.102–48.]

ECKHART, JOHANN GEORG VON. 1711. Historia studii etymologici linguae germanicae hactenus impensi; ubi scriptores plerique recensentur et diludicantur, qui in origines et antiquitates linguae teutonicae, saxonicae, belgicae, danicae, suecicae, norwegicae et islandicae, veteris item celticae, gothicae, francicae atque anglo-saxonicae inquisiverunt ... Hanover. [332 pp. The author's name is also written Eccard.]

EDGERTON, FRANKLIN. 1946. Sir William Jones: 1746–1794. JAOS 66.230–9. [Also SEBEOK 1966:1–18.]

EDRÖDI, J. 1970. Sajnovics (1733–1785), der Mensch und der Gelehrte. ALH 20.291–322.

EICHLER, ERNST. 1956. Joachim Christoph Stahl und seine slawistischen Studien. WINTER FESTSCHRIFT 1956:233–8.

——. 1958. Johann Leonhard Frisch und die russische Sprache. Ein Kapitel deutscher Russlandkunde. WINTER 1958b:94–111.

——. 1966. Josef Dobrovský und Johann Leonhard Frisch. WINTER FESTSCHRIFT 1966:401–5.

——. 1967. Die Slawistischen Studien Johann Leonhard Frisch. Ein Beitrag zur Geschichte der deutschen Slawistik. Berlin, Akademie-Verlag. [165 pp.] VISl 40.

ELLEDGE, SCOTT. 1967. The naked science of language, 1747–1786. Studies in Criticism and Aesthetics 1660–1800. Essays in Honor of Samuel Holt Monk, ed. by Howard Anderson and John S. Shea, 266–95. Minneapolis.

ELUNGU, MONIQUE. 1970. Les réflexions théoriques de Turgot sur la langue: un moment de l'histoire de la linguistique au dix-huitième siècle. Cahiers de littérature et de linguistique appliquée 1.90–99.

EMENAU, M. B. 1955. Indian and linguistics. JAOS 75.145–53.

EVANS, JOAN. 1956. A history of the Society of Antiquaries. [487 pp.]

FANO, GIORGIO. 1962. Saggio sulle origini del linguaggio, con una storia critica delle dottrine glottogoniche. Torino, Einaudi. 298 pp. 'Il settecento,' pp. 217–47; L'ottocento,' pp. 248–74.

FARKAS, JULIUS VON. 1948. Samuel Gyarmathi und die finnischugrische Sprachvergleichung. NAWG 1948. 110–36.

FIESEL, EVA. 1927. Die Sprachphilosophie der deutschen Romantik. Tübingen. [259 pp.]

FILLIOZAT, JEAN. 1941. Catalogue du Fonds Sanscrit. Bibliothèque Nationale. Département des Manuscrits. Paris. [xviii, 103, v pp. On history of 18th century acquisitions, pp. i–viii.]

FORMIGARI, LIA, ed. 1971. Maupertuis, Turgot, Maine de Biran: Origine e funzione del linguaggio. Bari, Laterza. [172 pp.] [Editor's introduction, with bibliography, pp. 5–69.]

——. 1972. Linguistica e antropologia nel secondo settecento. Messina, La libra. Biblioteca de filosofia moderna, No. 3. [357 pp.]

FOUCAULT, MICHEL. 1966. Les mots et les choses. Paris. [400 pp.]

——. 1967. La Grammaire générale de Port-Royal. Langages 7 (September 1967). 7–15. ['Cet article est extrait d'une Préface préparée par M. Foucault pour une réédition de la Grammaire Générale de Port-Royal. (Note des éds.)']

——. See ARNAULD 1969.

FRIEDRICH, HUGO. 1935. Die Sprachtheorie der französischen Illuminaten des 18. Jahrhundert. DVLG 13.293–310.

FÜCK, JOHANN. 1955. Die arabischen Studien in Europa bis in den Anfang des 20. Jahrhunderts. Leipzig, Harrassowitz. [335 pp.]

FUNKE, OTTO. 1927. Studien zur Geschichte der Sprachphilosophie. Bern, Francke.

——. 1934. English Sprachphilosophie im späteren 18. Jahrhundert. Bern, Francke. [162 pp.]

GAJEK, BERNHARD. 1967. Sprache beim jungen Hamann. Bern, Herbert Lang. [113 pp.]

GANCILLAC, MAURICE DE. 1966. Histoire des théories du langage. Le Langage 2.69–82. Actes du XIIIe Congrès des Sociétés de Philosophie de Langue Française.

GASSENDI, PIERRE. 1641. Lettre à Cherbury, tr. by Bernard Rochot. Actes du Congrès du tricentenaire de Pierre Gassendi (4–7 août 1955), 249–90. Paris, PUF [1957].

GERRETZEN, J. G. 1940. Schola Hemsterhusiana. De Herleving der grieksche Studien aan de nederlandsche Universiteiten in de achttiende Eeuw van Perizonius tot en met Valckenaer. Nijmegen/Utrecht. [408 pp.]

GERTH, KLAUS. 1960. Studien zu Gerstenbergs Poetik. Ein Beitrag zur Umschichtung der ästhetischen und poetischen Grundbegriffe im 18. Jahrhundert. Palaestra. Untersuchungen aus der Deutschen und Englischen Philologie und Literaturgeschichte. Vol. 231. [233 pp.]

GODFREY, JOHN S. 1967. Sir William Jones and Père Coeurdoux: A Philological footnote. JAOS 87.57–9.

GOSSMAN, LIONEL. 1958. Old French scholarship in the eighteenth century. The Glossary of La Curne de Sainte-Palaye. FS 12.346–61.

——. 1960. Berkeley, Hume and Maupertuis. FS 14.304–24.

——. 1968. Medievalism and the ideologies of the Enlightenment. The world and work of La Curne de Sainte-Palaye. Baltimore. [377 pp.]

GRAMMONT, MAURICE. 1918–20. Review of A. Grégoire, Petit traité de linguistique (1915). RLaR 60.436–40.

GRANATA, LAURA. 1970. Melchiorre Cesarotti linguista. RIL 104.111–44.

GRANGE, J. 1967. L'Essai sur l'origine des langues dans ses rapports avec le Discours sur l'origine de l'inégalité. Annales historique de la Révolution française. 39.291–307.

GRAY, LOUIS H. 1939. Foundations of language. New York. [530 pp.]

GRIMSLEY, RONALD. 1967a. Jean-Jacques Rousseau and the problem of the 'original' language. The Age of Enlightenment. Studies presented to Theodore Bestermann, ed. by W. H. Barber, J. H. Brumfitt, R. A. Leigh, R. Shackleton and S. S. B. Taylor, 275–86. Edinburgh.

——. 1967b. Some aspects of 'nature' and 'language' in the French Enlightenment. Studies on Voltaire and the eighteenth century 56.659–77.

——. 1968. Maupertuis, Turgot and Maine de Biran on the origin of language. Studies on Voltaire and the eighteenth Century, ed. by Th. Bestermann, Vol. 62, 285–307. Genève, Droz.

——. 1971. Sur l'origine du langage, suivie de trois textes [Maupertuis, Turgot, Maine de Biran]. Genève, Droz. [Introduction pp. 1–25 is French version of Grimsley 1968.]

GROSS, GEORG. 1955–56. César Chesnau Du Marsais. Ein Beitrag zur Geschichte der französischen Aufklärungsliteratur. WZUR 5.125–82.

GUERCI, LUCIANO. 1966. La composizione e le vicende editoriali del 'Cours d'Etudes' di Condillac. Miscellanea Walter Maturi. Torino, G. Giappichelli. pp. 185–220. [= Università di Torino. Facoltà di Lettere e Filosofia. Storia. Vol. 1.]

GUETTI, BARBARA J. 1969. The double voice of nature: Rousseau's Essai sur l'origine des langues. MLN 84. 853–75.

GUIN, CHARLES A. LE. 1960. Roland de la Platière [1734–1793] and the universal language. MLR 55.244–9.

GULYA, JÄNOS. [1964]. The eighteenth-century antecedents of the nineteenth-century linguistic revolution. In HYMES 1974.

GUNDERSON, KEITH. 1964. Descartes, La Mettrie, language and machines. Philosophy 39.193–222.

GUSDORF, GEORGES. 1973. Les sciences humaines et la pensée occidentale, vol. 6: L'avènement des sciences humaines au siècle des lumières. Paris, Payot. pp. 197–372 "Linguistique et histoire".

HAGSTROM, J.H. 1950. Dr. Johnson's rationalism. ELH 17.191–205.

HALL, ROBERT A., JR. 1941. G.B. Vico and linguistic theory. Italica 16.145–54.

——. 1963. Benedetto Croce and the influence of G. B. Vico. Idealism in Romance linguistics, 21–36. Ithaca, New York, Cornell University Press.

HAMANN, JOHANN GEORG. 1963. Hauptschriften erklärt. Vol. 4: Über den Ursprung der Sprache, erklärt von Elfriede Büchsel. Gütersloh. [285 pp.]

HAMPSHIRE, STUART. 1969. Vico and the contemporary philosophy of language. TAGLIACOZZO 1969:475–82.

HANZELI, VICTOR EGON. 1969. Missionary linguistics in New France. A study of seventeenth- and eighteenth-century descriptions of American Indian languages. Janua linguarum, Series major, No. 29. The Hague, Mouton. [141 pp.]

HARMAN, GILBERT. 1973. Review of 2nd ed. of Chomsky 1968. Lg 49.453-64.

HARNACK, ADOLF. 1900. Geschichte der Königlich Preussischen Akademie der Wissenschaften zu Berlin. 3 vols. Berlin.

HARNOIS, GUY. 1928. Les théories du langage en France de 1660 à 1821. Paris. [95 pp.]

HECHT, HANS. 1933. T. Percy, R. Wood und J. D. Michaëlis. Stuttgart.

HEINTEL, ERICH. 1967. Herders Sprachphilosophie. Revue Internationale de Philosophie 82.463–74.

HERDER, J.G. 1959 [1772]. Über den Ursprung der Sprache, ed. by Claus Träger. Deutsche Akademie der Wissenschaften zu Berlin. Schriftenreihe der Arbeitsgruppe zur Geschichte der deutschen und französischen Aufklärung, ed. by by Werner Kraus, Vol. 9. Berlin, Akademie-Verlag. [118 pp.]

——. 1960. Sprachphilosophische Schriften. Aus dem Gesamtwerk ausgewählt, mit einer Einleitung, Anmerkungen und Registern versehen von Erich Heintel. Philosophische Bibliothek. No. 248. [242 pp. 2nd enlarged edition 1964. Hamburg, Felix Meiner Verlag. 248 pp.]

——. 1964. Immanuel Kant. Aus den Vorlesungen der Jahre 1762 bis 1764. Auf Grund der Nachschriften Johann Gottfried Herders. Kantstudien. Ergänzungsheft, No. 88. Köln.

——. 1965 [1772]. Über den Ursprung der Sprache. Karl König's "Nachwort", 125–250. Nos. 33–34 in Denken – Schauen – Sinnen. Stuttgart. Verlag Freies Geistesleben. [150 pp.]

——. 1966 [1772]. Abhandlung über den Ursprung der Sprache, ed. by Hans Dietrich Irmscher. Stuttgart, Reclam. [176 pp.] Editor's "Nachwort", 137–75.

HINE, ELLEN MCNIVEN. 1973. Condillac and the problem of language. Studies on Voltaire and the eighteenth century 106.21–62.

HJELMSLEV, LOUIS. 1928. Principes de grammaire générale. Det Kongelige Danske Videnskabernes Selskab. Historisk-filologiske Meddelelser, Copenhagen. [362 pp.] Vol. 16, No. 1.

HOENIGSWALD, H.M. 1963. On the history of the comparative method. AnL 5, No. 1.1–11.

HOFFMAN, VOLKER. 1972. Johann Georg Hamanns Philologie zwischen enzyklopädischer Mikrologie und Hermeneutik. Stuttgart, Kohlhammer. [256 pp.] [= Studien zur Poetik und Geschichte der Literatur, vol. 24.]

HOOK, SIDNEY, ed. 1969. Language and philosophy. New York University Press. [301 pp.]

HOWELL, WILBUR SAMUEL. 1966. Logic and rhetoric in England 1500–1700. Princeton. [411 pp.]

——. 1971. Eighteenth-century British logic and rhetoric. Princeton. [742 pp.]

HUBER, THOMAS. 1968. Studien zur Theorie des Übersetzens im Zeitalter der deutschen Aufklärung 1730–1770. Deutsche Studien. Vol. 7. Meisenheim am Glahn. [134 pp.]

HUMBOLDT, WILHELM VON. 1916. Tagebücher, vol. 1, 1788–1798, ed. by Albert Leitzmann. Berlin, Behr. [644 pp.]

HUNT, J.J. 1938. Logic and linguistics. Diderot as grammairien-philosophe. MLR 33.215–33.

HYMES, DELL. 1963. Notes towar a dhistory of linguistic anthropology. AnL 5, No. 1.59–103.

——, ed. 1974. Studies in the history of linguistics. Indiana University Press.

IORDAN, IORGU. 1962. Einführung in die Geschichte und Methoden der romanischen Sprachwissenschaft, ins deutsche übertragen, ergänzt und teilweise neubearbeitet von Werner Bahner. Berlin, Akademie-Verlag. [521 pp.] [Einleitung: Die Vorgeschichte der romanischen Sprachwissenschaft, pp. 1–18.]

IRMSCHER, HANS DIETRICH. See HERDER 1966.

IVERSEN, ERIK. 1961. The myth of Egypt and its hieroglyphics, a European tradition. Copenhagen. [178 pp.]

JACOB, ANDRÉ. 1969. 100 points de vue sur le langage. 270 textes choisis et présentés avec introduction et bibliographie. Publications de la Faculté des lettres et sciences humaines de Paris-Nanterre. Points de vue, No. 1. Paris, Klincksieck. [637 pp.]

JELLINEK, MAX HERMANN. 1913–14. Geschichte der Neuhochdeutschen Grammatik von den Anfängen bis auf Adelung. 2 vols. Heidelberg, Winter. [392 and 504 pp.]

JENSEN, ALFRED. 1912. Die Anfänge der schwedischen Slavistik. Arch Slav. 33. 136–65.

JESPERSEN, OTTO. 1922. Language, its nature, development and origin. London. [448 pp.]

——. 1928. L'étude de la langue maternelle en Danemark. APhS 3.63–76.

JOLY, ANDRÉ. 1970. Introduction to ed. of Françoit Thurot's Discours préliminaire à 'Hermès' [de James Harris]. Bordeaux. [138 pp.]

——, ed. 1972a. James Harris, Hermès ou recherches philosophiques sur la grammaire universelle. Traduction et remarques par François Thurot (1796). Edition, introduction et notes par André Joly. Genève, Droz. [144 plus 469 pp.]

——. 1972b. Cartésianisme et linguistique Cartésienne: Mythe ou réalité. BRPh 11.86–94.

JONES, SIR WILLIAM. 1948. Bicentenary of his birth. Commemoration Volume 1746–1946. Calcutta. [173 pp.]

——. 1970. The letters of Sir William Jones, ed. by Garland Cannon. 2 vols. Oxford. [977 pp.]

JONSSON, INGE. 1969. Swedenborgs Språkuppfattning. In Jonsson, Swedenborgs Korrespondenslära, 203–36. pp. Acta Universitatis Stockholmiensis. Stockholm Studies in History of Literature. No. 10. Stockholm.

——. 1971. Emanuel Swedenborg, tr. from the Swedish by Catherine Djurklou. New York, Twayne. [224 pp.]

JOSEPHS, HERBERT. 1969. Diderot's dialogue of language and gesture: Le Neveu de Rameau. Ohio State University Press. [228 pp.]

JOYAUX, JULIA. 1969. Le langage, cet inconnu. Paris. [319 pp.]

JULIARD, PIERRE. 1970. Philosophies of language in eighteenth-century France. Janua Linguarum. Series Minor, No. 18. The Hague, Mouton. [111 pp.]

JUNKER, HEINRICH. 1948. Sprachphilosophisches Lesebuch. Heidelberg, Carl Winter. [302 pp.]

KANT, IMMANUEL. 1902. Gesammelte Schriften. Zweite Abteilung: Briefwechsel, vol. 3 (1795–1803). Berlin.

KEHR, KURT. 1969. Johann Georg Estors (1699–1733) kulturhistorische und germanistische Beiträge. Orbis 18.46–61.

KENNEDY, ARTHUR G. 1927. A bibliography of writings on the English language from the beginnings of printing to the end of 1922. Cambridge/New Haven. [517 pp.]

KILLY, W. 1969. See LÄMMERT 1969.

KIMPEL, DIETER. 1966. Bericht über neue Forschungsergebnisse 1955–1964. In Eric A. Blackall, Die Entwicklung des Deutschen zur Literatursprache, tr. [from Blackall 1959] by Hans G. Schürmann, 477–519. Stuttgart, Metzler.

KNIGHT, ISABEL F. 1968. The geometric spirit: The Abbé de Condillac and the French Enlightenment. New Haven. [321. pp.]

KNOWLSON, J.R. 1963. The ideal languages of Veiras, Foigny, and Tyssot de Patot. Journal of the History of Ideas 24.269–78.

——. 1965. The idea of gesture as a universal language in the XVIIth and XVIIIth centuries. Journal of the History of Ideas 26.495–508.

KÖNIG, KARL 1965. See HERDER 1965.

KOLB, GWIN J. See SLEDD 1955.

KONRAD, GUSTAV. 1937. Herders Sprachproblem im Zusammenhang der Geistesgeschichte. Eine Studie zur Entwicklung des sprachlichen Denkens der Goethezeit. Germanische Studien, No. 194. Berlin. [102 pp.]

KRAUS, ANDREAS. 1963. Vernunft und Geschichte. Die Bedeutung der deutschen Akademien für die Entwicklung der Geschichtswissenschaft im späten 18. Jahrhundert. Freiburg, Herder. [575 pp.]

KRAUSS, WERNER. 1962. L'Énigme du Du Marsais. RHLF 62.514–22.

KRÜGER, MANFRED. 1967. Der menschlich-göttliche Ursprung der Sprache, Bemerkungen zu Herders Sprachtheorie. WW 17.1–11.

KÜHLWEIN, WOLFGANG, ed. 1971. Linguistics in Great Britain. Vol. I: History of linguistics. English Texts ed. by Theo Stemmler, No. 14. Tübingen, Niemeyer. [148 pp.]

KUEHNER, PAUL. 1944. Theories on the origin and formation of language in the eighteenth century in France. Philadelphia. [54 pp.]

KUHN, THOMAS. 1970. The structure of scientific revolutions. 2nd enlarged ed. Chicago. [210 pp. 1st ed. 1962.]

——. 1971. The relations between history and history of science. Dædalus, Spring. 1971. 271–304.

KUKENHEIM, LOUIS. 1962. Esquisse historique de la linguistique française et de ses rapports avec la linguistique générale. Leiden. [205 pp.]

——. 1966². 'revue, corrigée et augmentée' of KUKENHEIM 1962. [285. pp]

LAKÓ, GYÖRGY. 1970a. Sajnovics und seine Demonstratio. ALH 20.269–89.

——. 1970b. János Sajnovics und die finnisch-ugrische Sprachvergleichung. SovFU 6.239–47.

LAKOFF, ROBIN. 1969. Review of Grammaire générale et raisonnée. Lg 45.343–64.

LÄMMERT, E., W. KILLY, K.O. CONRADY, P. v. POLENZ. 1969. Germanistik — eine deutsche Wissenschaft. Frankfurt am Main, Suhrkamp. [163 pp.]

LANGEN, AUGUST. 1957². Deutsche Sprachgeschichte vom Barock bis zur Gegenwart. Deutsche Philologie im Aufriss, ed. by Wolfgang Stammler, vol. 1,931–1356. revised ed. Berlin, E. Schmidt. [Therein 'Aufklärung,' 'Irrationalismus,'

'Klassik,' and 'Romantik' 1,1018–1260, with bibliography 1387–91.]

LAUCH, ANNELIES. 1969. Wissenschaft und kulturelle Beziehungen in der russischen Aufklärung, zum Wirken H. L. Ch. Bacmeisters. VISl, vol 51. Berlin, Akademie-Verlag. [444 pp.] ["Russisch-deutsches Transkriptionssystem," 160–70; "Bacmeisters Sprachvergleichende Sammlungen," 170–216.]

LAUCHERT, FRIEDRICH. 1894. Die Anschauungen Herders über den Ursprung der Sprache, ihre Voraussetzungen in der Philosophie seiner Zeit un ihr Fortwirken. Euphorion 1.747–71.

LAUNAY, MICHEL. See DUCHET 1967.

——. 1968. Problèmes de lexicologie politique selon Rousseau. CLex 13.61–74.

LÁZARO CARRETER, F. 1949. Las ideas lingüísticas en España durante el siglo XVIII. RFE. 48. Madrid. [294 pp.]

LEFÊVRE, ROGER. Condillac ou la joie de vivre. Présentation, choix de textes, bibliographie. Paris, Editions Seghers, Philosophes de Tous les Temps. [192 pp.]

——. 1967. Condillac, maître du langage. Revue Internationale de Philosophie 82.393–406.

LEONARD, STERLING A. 1929. The doctrine of correctness in English usage, 1700–1800. University of Wisconsin Studies in Language and Literature. No. 25. [361 pp.]

LEROY, MAURICE. 1960. Les langues du monde et la typologie linguistique. Mémoires et Publications de la Société des Sciences, des Arts et des Lettres du Hainaut 74.169–204.

——. 1963. Les grands courants de la linguistique moderne. Université Libre de Bruxelles, Travaux de la Faculté de Philosophie et Lettres, Vol. 24. Bruxelles and Paris. [198 pp.] [Also as Main trends in modern linguistics, tr. by G. Price. Berkeley, 1967.]

LESKIEN 1965. See bibliography to Section 1.

LETTRES édifiantes et curieuses, écrites des missions étrangères par quelques missionaires de la Compagnie de Jésus. 34 vols. Paris, 1707–1776. [New ed., Paris 1780–1783 in 26 vols.]

LINDROTH, STEN. 1967. Kungl. Svenska Ventenskapsakademiens Historia 1739–1818. Stockholm. 2 vols. in 3 parts.

LOCKWOOD, W.B. 1969. Indo-European philology, historical and comparative. London. [193 pp.]

LÖWITH, KARL. 1968. Vicos Grundsatz: verum et factum convertuntur. Seine theologische Prämisse und deren säkulare Konsequenzen. Sitzungsberichte der Heidelberger Akademie der Wissenschaften. Philologisch-historische Klasse 1969, No. 1. [36 pp.]

LOHUIZEN-DE LEEUW, J.E. VAN. 1948. Sir William Jones 1746–94. Orientalia Neerlandica, a volume of oriental studies, 288–97. Leiden.

LOLLESGAARD, JOHS. 1925. Sprogfilosoferen og Sprogforsken i Danmark ved det 18. Aarhundredes Midte. Copenhagen, Haase. [127 pp.]

LOMHOLT, ASGER, ed. 1942–61. Det Kongelige Danske Videnskabernes Selskab 1742–1942. Samlinger til Selskabets Historie. Copenhagen. 4 vols.

LOUGH, JOHN. 1968. Essays on the Encyclopédie of Diderot and D'Alembert. London. [xiv, 552 pp.]

——. 1973. The contributors to the "Encyclopédie." London, Grant and Cutler. [120 pp.]

MALKIEL, YAKOV, and MARGARET LANGDON. 1969. History and histories of linguistics. RomPh 22.530–74.

MASTER, ALFRED. 1946. The influence of Sir William Jones upon Sanskrit Studies. BSOAS 11.798–806.

——. 1956. [Sir William] Jones and Panini. JAOS 76.186–7.

MATORÉ, GEORGES. 1968. Histoire des dictionnaires français. Paris, Larousse. [278 pp.] [Lexiques et encyclopédies du XVIIIe siècle, pp. 88–108.]

MAZON, ANDRÉ. 1958. L'Abbé Girard grammairien et russisant. RES*l* 35.15–56.

MEILLET, A. 1937^{8}. Introduction à l'étude comparative des langues indo-européennes. Paris. [514 pp.]

MEISTER, PAUL. 1956. Charles [Pinot] Duclos (1704–1772). Genève, Droz.

METZKE, E. 1934. J. G. Hamanns Stellung in der Philosophie des 18. Jahrhunderts. Schriften der Königsberger Gelehrten Gesellschaft, Geisteswissenschaftliche Klasse. vol. 10, Heft 3.

MICHAEL, IAN. 1970. English grammatical categories and the tradition to 1800. Cambridge. [622 pp.]

MONROE, JAMES T. 1970. The study of grammar and lexicography. Islam and the Arabs in Spanish scholarship (Sixteenth century to the present), 23–45. Leiden, Brill.

MONTEVERDI, A. 1948. L.A. Muratori e gli studî intorno alle origine della lingua italiana. Atti e memorie dell' Arcadia 3 (1).81–93.

MOSCONI, JEAN. 1966. Analyse et Genèse: Regards sur la théorie du devenir de l'entendement au XVIIIe siècle. Cahiers pour l'Analyse 4.45–82.

MOUNIN, GEORGES. 1967. Historie de la linguistique des origines au XXe siècle. Paris, PUF. [226 pp.]

MUKHERJEE, S.N. 1968. Sir William Jones: A study in eighteenth-century British attitudes to India. Cambridge. [199 pp.]

NADLER, JOSEF. 1949. Johann Georg Hamann 1730–1788. Der Zeuge des Corpus Mysticum. Salzburg. [518 pp.]

NARR, GUNTER, See SMITH 1970.

NEUMANN, FRIEDRICH. 1971. Deutsche Sprach- und Literaturkunde bis zum Ende des 18. Jahrhunderts. Studien zur Geschichte der deutschen Philologie, aus der Sicht eines alten Germanisten, 22–38. Berlin, E. Schmidt.

NIDA, EUGENE A. 1965. See WONDERLY 1965.

NIKLIBORC, ANNA. 1961. Les Manuels du français publiées en Pologne au XVIIIe Siècle. RKJW 3.151–78.

NOYES. See STARNES 1946.

O'FLAHERTY, JAMES C. 1952. Unity and language: A study in the philosophy of Johann Georg Hamann. University of North Carolina Studies in the Germanic Languages and Literatures, No. 6. Chapel Hill. [121 pp.]

PACI, ENZO. 1969. Vico, structuralism, and the phenomenological Encyclopedia of the Sciences. TAGLIACOZZO 1969.497–516.

PAGLIARO, ANTONIO. 1959. La dottrina linguistica di G. B. Vico. Atti delle Accademia nazionale dei Lincei. Memorie. Classe di scienze morali, storiche e filologiche. Ser. 8, Vol. 8.379–486.

——. 1961. Lingua e poesia secondo G. B. Vico. Altri saggi di critica semantica. 297–444. Biblioteca di cultura contemporanea, No. 72. Firenze. [The same as Pagliaro 1959.] Firenze.

PALLUS, H. 1964. Die Sprachphilosophie Johann Georg Hamanns als eine Quelle für Herders Anschauungen über das Verhältnis von Sprache und Denken. WZUG 13.363–74.

——. See TETENS 1966.

PARAIN, BRICE. 1952. Recherches sur la nature et les fonctions du langage. Paris, Gallimard. [Bibliothèque des Idées. 187 pp.]

PARIENTE, JEAN-CLAUDE, ed. 1969. Essais sur le langage. Paris; Editions de Minuit. See CASSIRER 1933.

PARRET. See Bibliography to Section 1.

PEDERSEN, HOLGER. 1931. The discovery of language. Linguistic science in the nineteenth century, tr. by J. W. Spargo. Cambridge, Mass. [360 pp. First Danish ed. 1924.]

PENN, JULIA M. 1972. Linguistic relativity versus innate ideas. The origins of the Sapir-Whorf hypothesis in German thought. Janua linguarum, Series Minor, No. 120. The Hague, Mouton. [62 pp.]

PERCIVAL, W. KEITH. 1972. On the non-existence of Cartesian linguistics. Cartesian studies, ed. by R.J. Butler, 137–45. Oxford, Blackwells.

PINTO, V. DE SOLA. 1946. Sir William Jones and English literature, BSOAS 11. 686–94.

POLDAUF, IVAN. 1948. On the history of some problems of English grammar before 1800. Prague Studies in English, No. 55. [322 pp.]

POLENZ, P. v. 1969. See LÄMMERT 1969.

POLITZER, ROBERT L. 1957. A detail in Rousseau's thought: Language and perfectibility. MLN 72.42–7.

——. 1963. On some eighteenth-century sources of American and German linguistic relativism. Weltoffene Romanistik. Festschrift Alwin Kuhn, ed. by Guntram Plangg and Eberhard Tiefenthaler, 25–33. IBK 10. Innsbruck.

——. 1964. On the linguistic philosophy of Maupertuis and its relation to the history of linguistic relativism. Symposium 18.5–16.

PONS, ALAIN. 1968. Vico et la pensée française. Les études philosophiques 1968.

361–83. [Also in Tagliacozzo 1969:165–85 'Vico and French thought.']

PORSET, CHARLES, ed. 1970. Varia linguistica. Bordeaux, Ducros. [353 pp. A collection of texts by Maupertuis, Turgot, Condillac, Dumarsais, and Adam Smith.]

——. See also ROUSSEAU 1968.

PORZIG, WALTER. 1950. Das Wunder der Sprache. Probleme, Methoden und Ergebnisse der modernen Sprachwissenschaft. Bern. [415 pp.]

POWITZ, GERHARD. 1959. Das deutsche Wörterbuch Johann Leonhard Frisch. VIDSL 19. [viii, 209 pp.]

PROUST, JACQUES. 1967a. Diderot et les problèmes du langage. RF 79.1–27.

——. 1967b. Diderot et l'Encyclopédie. Paris, A. Colin. [624 pp.]

PUPPO, M. 1957. Discussioni linguistiche del settecento. Classici Italiani 63.

QUEMADA, BERNARD. 1967. Les dictionnaires du français moderne 1539–1863. Vol. I: Étude sur leur histoire, leurs types et leurs méthodes. Paris; Didier. [683 pp. Forthcoming vol. II: Bibliographie de répertoires des dictionnaires français.]

RAUMER, RUDOLF VON. 1870. Geschichte der Germanischen Philologie vorzugsweise in Deutschland. München. [743 pp.]

RAUTER, HERBERT. 1970. Die Sprachauffassung der englischen Vorromantik in ihrer Bedeutung für die Literaturkritik und Dichtungstheorie der Zeit. Frankfurter Beiträge zur Anglistik and Amerikanistik Vol. 1. Bad Homburg, Verlag Gehlen. [237 pp.]

READ, ALLEN WALKER. 1934. The Philological Society of New York, 1788. AS 9.131–6.

——. 1935. The contemporary quotations in Johnson's Dictionary. English Literary History 2.246–51.

——. 1936. American projects for an academy to regulate speech. PMLA 51.1141–79.

——. 1937. Projected English dictionaries, 1755–1828. JEGP 36.188–205, 347–66.

——. 1938. Suggestions for an academy in England in the latter half of the eighteenth century. MPh 36.145–56.

——. [1973]. Dictionary. Encyclopaedia Britannica. Forthcoming.

RÉGALDO, MARC. 1970. Matériaux pour une bibliographie de l'idéologie et des idéologues. Répertoire analytique de littérature française. No. 1.33–49. Nos. 2/3.27–39 [therein 'Philosophie du langage, linguistique et grammaire,' 34–9].

REICHEL, JÖRN. 1968. Dichtungstheorie und Sprache bei Zinzendorf. Ars poetica. Texte und Studien zur Dichtungstheorie und Dichtkunst. No. 10. [114 pp. Therein "Sprachtheorie", 66–94.]

REYCHMAN, J. 1950. Znajomósc i nauizanie jezyków orientalnych w Polsce XVIII w. Prace Wroclawskiego Towarzystwa Naukowego [Travaux de la société des sciences et des lettres de Wroclaw]. Ser. A, No. 35. [161 pp.]

——. 1959. Zur Beschäftigung mit der ungarischen Sprache in Polen des 18. Jahrhunderts. UAJb 31.336–43.

——. 1960. Les notes du Prince A. K. Czartoryski [1734–1823] concernant ses études de la langue turque. RO 23(2).57–82.

RICKEN, ULRICH. 1961. Rationalismus und Sensualismus in der Diskussion über die Wortstellung. Literaturgeschichte als geschichtlicher Auftrag. Festgabe für Werner Krauss, 97–122. Berlin, Akademie-Verlag.

——. 1963. La discussion linguistique en France au 18e siècle, reflet de la lutte philosophique du siècle des lumières. AUI 9.71–88.

——. 1964. Condillacs Liaison des Idées und die Clarté des französischen. NS 1964.552–67.

——. 1973. La critique sensualiste à l'encontre du 'Discours sur l'universalité de la langue française' d'Antoine Rivarol. Historiographica Linguistica 1.67–80.

ROBINS, R.H. 1967. A short history of linguistics. Bloomington, Indiana University Press. [248 pp.]

ROCHER, ROSANE. 1968. Alexander Hamilton (1762–1824). A chapter in the early history of Sanskrit philology. New Haven, American Oriental Society. [128 pp.]

RODIS-LEWIS, GENEVIÈVE. 1967. L'Art de parler et l'essai sur l'Origine des langues. Revue Internationale de Philosophie 82.407–20.

——. 1968. Un théoricien de langage au XVIIe siècle: Bernard Lamy. FM 36. 19–50.

ROSIELLO, LUIGI. 1961. Analisi semantica dell' espressione 'genio della lingua' nelle discussioni del settecento italiano. Quaderni dell' Istituto di Glottologia dell' Università di Genova 6.89–102.

——. 1967. Linguistica illuminista. Bologna, Il Mulino. [217 pp.]

——. 1968. Le theorie linguistiche di Vico e Condillac. Forum Italicum. A Quarterly of Italian Studies 2.386–93.

ROUDAUT, JEAN, ed. 1971. Poètes et grammairiens au XVIIIe siècle. Anthologie. Paris, Gallimard. [369 pp.]

ROUSSEAU, J.-J. 1964. Discours sur l'Origine et les fondéments de l'inégalité parmi les hommes, ed. by Jean Starobinski, 109–223. Oeuvres Complètes, Vol. 3. Paris, Pléiade.

——. 1968. Essai sur l'origine des langues, ed. by Charles Porset. Bordeaux, Guy Ducros. [245 pp.]

ROWBOTHAM, ARNOLD. 1942. Missionary and mandarin; the Jesuits at the Court of China. Berkeley. [374 pp.]

ROY, GEORGES LE. 1937. La psychologie de Condillac. Paris. [236 pp.]

——. 1947–51. Introduction à l'œuvre philosophique de Condillac, 1.vii–xxxv. Oeuvres philosophiques de Condillac, ed. by Georges le Roy, Paris, PUF. 3 vols.

——, ed. 1953. Condillac. Lettres inédites à Gabriel Cramer. Paris, PUF. [116 pp.]

RUSCH, JÜRG. 1972. Die Vorstellung vom goldenen Zeitalter der englischen Sprache im 16., 17., und 18. Jahrhundert. Schweizer Anglistische Arbeiten, vol. 69. Bern, Francke Verlag. [265 pp.]

SAHLIN, GUNVOR. 1928. César Chesnau Du Marsais et son rôle dans l'évolution de la grammaire générale. Paris, PUF. [490 pp.]

SALMON, PAUL. 1968. Herder's Essay on the origin of language and the place of man in the animal kingdom. GLL 22.59–70.

——. 1974. The beginnings of morphology: Linguistic botanizing in the 18th century. Historiographia linguistica 1.313–39.

SALMON, VIVIAN. 1969. Review of Chomsky 1966. JL 5.165–87.

SALMONY, H.-J. 1949. Die Philosophie des jungen Herder. Zürich, Vineta Verlag. [250 pp.]

SALVUCCI, PASQUALE. 1957. Linguaggio e mondo umano in Condillac. Urbino, S.T.E.U. [132 pp.] [= Publicazioni dell' Università di Urbino. Serie di lettere e filosofia. No. 5.]

SANDYS, JOHN EDWIN. 1903–08. A history of classical scholarship. Cambridge University Press. 3 vols. (Vol. 2 [498 pp.] From the revival of learning to the end of the eighteenth century (in Italy, France, England, The Netherlands, [and Germany]); vol. 3 [523 pp.] The eighteenth century in Germany, and the nineteenth century in Europe and the United States.)

SAPIR, EDWARD. 1907. Herder's Ursprung der Sprache. MPh 5.109–42.

SCHEURWEGHS, G. 1960. English grammars in Dutch and Dutch grammars in English in The Netherlands before 1800. ES 41.129–67.

——. 1961. The influence of the Latin grammar of William Lily on the early English grammarians in the Netherlands, pt. 1. LB 50.140–51.

SCHMIDT, SIEGFRIED J. 1968. Sprache und Denken als Sprachphilosophisches Problem von Locke bis Wittgenstein. The Hague, Nijhoff. [202 pp.]

SCHNEBLI-SCHWEGLER, BRIGITTE. 1965. Johann Gottfried Herders Abhandlung über den Ursprung der Sprache und die Goethe-Zeit. Winterthur. [113 pp.]

SCHOTTLÄNDER, RUDOLF. 1969a. Die verkannte Lehre Condillacs vom Sprachursprung. BRPh 8.158–65.

——. 1969b. Ursprungsbegriff und Wortursprung. Zeitschrift für philosophische Forschung 23.161–76.

SCHWAB, RAYMOND. 1943. Anquetil-Duperron, sa vie. Paris.

——. 1950. La Renaissance orientale. Paris. [526 pp.]

SCHWAB, RICHARD N., W. E. REX and JOHN LOUGH. 1971–72. Inventory of Diderot's 'Encyclopédie', vols. 1–3. Studies on Voltaire and the eighteenth century 80 (1971).1–213; 83 (1971).1–352; 85 (1972).347–679. To be continued.

SEARLE, JOHN. 1972. Chomsky's revolution in linguistics. New York Review of Books 18(12) (29 June 1972).16–25.

SEBEOK, THOMAS A., ed. 1966. Portraits of linguists. A biographical source book for the history of western linguistics 1746–1963. Bloomington, Indiana University Press. 2 vols. Vol. 1: From Sir William Jones to Karl Brugmann.

SEEBER, EDWARD D. 1945. Ideal languages in the French and English imaginary voyage. PMLA 60.586–97.

SEGERT, STANISLAV and KAREL BERÁNEK. 1967. Orientalistik an der Prager Universität. Erster Teil 1348–1848. Praha, Universita Karlova. [226 pp.]

SEILS, M. 1961. Wirklichkeit und Wort bei J. G. Hamann. Arbeiten zur Theologie, signs in France and England. Journal of the history of ideas 30.96–115.

SEILS, M. 1961. Wirklichkeit und Wort be J. G. Hamann. Arbeiten zur Theologie, No. 6.

SEMERARI, GUISEPPE. 1968. Intorno all'anticartesianesimo di Vico. Omaggio a Vico, 193–232. Napoli, Morano.

SLEDD, JAMES H. and GWIN J. KOLB. 1955. Dr. Johnson's Dictionary. Essays in the biography of a book. Chicago. [256 pp.]

SMITH, ADAM. 1963. Lectures on rhetoric and Belles Lettres, ed. by John M. Lothian. Edinburgh.

——. 1970 [1761]. A Dissertation on the origin of languages, ed. by Gunter Narr. Tübinger Beiträge zur Linguistik, No. 3. Tübingen. [104 pp. Narr's "Einleitung", 3–14.]

SNYDERS, GEORGES. 1965. La pédagogie en France aux XVIIe et XVIIIe siècles. Paris, PUF. [459 pp.]

SØRENSEN, BENGT ALGOT. 1963. Symbol und Symbolismus in den ästhetischen Theorien des 18. Jahrhunderts und der deutschen Romantik. Copenhagen. [332 pp.]

SØRENSEN, KNUD. 1971. The teaching of English in Denmark: a historical survey. Paedagogica historica. 11.90–101.

SOMMERVOGEL, CARLOS, ed. 1890. Bibliothèque de la Compagnie de Jésus. 11 vols. 1890–1932. [Bruxelles, Gregg Associates, 1960.]

SOUBLIN, FRANÇOISE. 1974 La théorie grammaticale de Du Marsais. In PARRET 1974.

STANKIEWICZ, EDWARD. [1968]. The dithyramb to the verb in 18th and 19th-century linguistics. In HYMES 1974.

STARKE, MANFRED. 1968. Helvetius and la Mettrie. BRPh 7.74–90.

STARNES, DE WITT T. and GERTRUDE E. NOYES. 1946. The English dictionary from Cawdrey to Johnson 1604–1755. Chapel Hill. [299 pp.]

STAROBINSKI, JEAN. 1967a. Rousseau et l'origine des langues. Europäische Aufklärung. Herbert Dieckmann zum 60. Geburtstag, ed. by Hugo Friedrich and Fritz Schalk, 281–300. München-Allach.

——. 1967b. Langage, nature et société selon Rousseau. Le Langage, Actes du XIIIe Congrès des Sociétés de Philosophie de langue française [1966]. Neuchâtel 1.143–46 [résumé of Starobinski 1967a].

STÉFANINI, JEAN. 1969. Un provençaliste marseillais: L'Abbé Féraud (1725–1807). Annales de la faculté des lettres et sciences humaines d'Aix-en-Provence. No. 67. [406 pp.]

STEINER, ROGER J. 1970. Two centuries of Spanish and English bilingual lexicography (1590–1800). Janua Linguarum. Series Practica, No. 108. The Hague, Mouton.

STENDER-PETERSEN, A. 1960. Zur Geschichte der nordischen Slavistik. Eine Skizze. WSlJb 8.141–53.

STENGEL, E. 1890. Chronologisches Verzeichnis französischer Grammatiken vom Ende des 14. bis zum Ausgange des 18. Jahrhunderts, nebst Angabe der bisher ermittelten Fundorte derselben. Oppeln. [151 pp.]

STOLPE, HEINZ. 1964. Herder und die Ansätze einer naturgeschichtlichen Entwicklungslehre im 18. Jahrhundert. Neue Beiträge zur Literatur der Aufklärung, 289–316. Berlin, Rütten und Loening. Neue Beiträge zur Literaturwissenschaft. Vol. 21.

TAGLIACOZZO, GIORGIO and HAYDEN V. WHITE, eds. 1969. Giambattista Vico, an international symposium. Baltimore. [636 pp.]

TASKA, BETTY KEENE. 1973. Grammar and linguistics in the Encyclopédie. FR 46.1159–71.

TEETER, KARL V. 1966. The history of linguistics: New lamps for old. DINNEEN 1966:83–95.

TETENS, JOHANN NICOLAUS. 1966 [1772]. Über den Ursprung der Sprachen und der Schrift, ed. with Introduction by H. Pallus. Berlin, Akademie-Verlag. [xxx, 64 pp.]

——. 1971 [1772]. Sprachphilosophische Versuche. Mit einer Einleitung von Erich Heintel, ed. by Heinrich Pfannkuch. Philosophische Bibliothek, No. 258. Hamburg, Felix Meiner Verlag. [xlvi, 245 pp.]

TETZNER, JOACHIM. 1955. H. W. Ludolf und Russland. VISl 6. Berlin, Akademie-Verlag. [152 pp].

——. 1956. Russica in den Anlagen zum Tagebuch A. H. Franckes. Neue Funde im Archiv der Frankischen Stiftung. Winter Festschrift 1956:193–209.

THOMSEN, VILHELM. 1902. Sprogvidenskabens Historie. En kortfattet Fremstilling. [87 pp. Also in Samlede Afhandlinger 1 (1919). 1–106.]

——. 1927 [1902]. Geschichte der Sprachwissenschaft bis zum Ausgang des 19. Jahrhunderts, kurzgefasste Darstellung der Hauptpunkte, tr. by Hans Pollak. Halle, Niemeyer. [101 pp.]

TUCKER, SUSIE I. 1961. English examined: Two centuries of comment on the mother-tongue. Cambridge. [154 pp.]

ULMER, K. 1951. Die Wandlung des Sprachbildes von Herder zu Jakob Grimm. Lexis 2.263–86.

UNGER, RUDOLF. 1905. Hamanns Sprachtheorie im Zusammenhange seines Denkens. Grundlegung zu einer Würdigung der geistesgeschichtlichen Stellung des Magus im Norden. München. [272 pp.]

V.-DAVID, MADELEINE. 1961b. En marge du mémoire de l'Abbé [J.-J.] Barthélemy sur les inscriptions phéniciennes (1758). CRAI 1961.30–42.

——. 1965. Le débat sur les écritures et l'hiéroglyphe aux XVIIe et XVIIIe siècles et l'application de la notion de déchiffrement aux écritures mortes. Paris,SEVPEN. [159 pp.]

VENTURI, FRANCO. 1939. La jeunesse de Diderot (1713–1753), tr. by Juliette Bertrand. Paris. [Especially 237–82: "La Lettre sur les sourds-et-muets."]

VERBURG, P. A. 1949. The background of the linguistic conceptions of Bopp. Lingua 2.438–68.
——. 1952. Taal en Functionaliteit. Wageningen. [490 pp.]
VERRA, VALERIO. 1957. Herder e il linguaggio come organo della ragione. Filosofia 8.663–702.
——. 1968. Linguaggio, storia e umanità in Vico e in Herder. Omaggio a Vico, 333–62. Napoli, Morano.
VERRI, ANTONIO. 1970. Origine delle lingue e civilità in Rousseau. In Appendice: Essai sur l'origine des langues. Ravenna; A. Longo. [280 pp.]
VESEY-FITZGERALD, S. G. 1946. Sir William Jones, the Jurist. BSOAS 11.807–17.
VIERTEL, JOHN. 1966. Concepts of language underlying the 18th-century controversy about the origin of language. DINNEEN 1966:109–32.
VITALE, MAURIZIO. 1955. Sommario di una storia degli studî linguistici romanzi. Preistoria e storia degli studî romanzi, ed. by A. Viscardi et al. Milan, pp. 5–169.
——. 1967. La questione della lingua. 4th ed. Palumbo. [381 pp.]
VORLAT, E. 1959. The sources of Lindley Murray's [1745–1826] The English grammar [1795]. LB 48.108–25.
——. 1963. Progress in English grammar 1585–1735. A study of the development of English grammar and of the interdependence among the early English grammarians. 4 vols. Louvain. Mimeographed.
WALEY, ARTHUR D. 1952. Anquetil-Duperron and Sir William Jones. History Today (January 1952).23–33.
WATERMAN, JOHN T. 1963a. See Bibliography to Section 1.
——. 1963b. Perspectives in linguistics. Chicago. [105 pp.]
WEBER, HANNA. 1939. Herder Sprachphilosophie. Eine Interpretation in Hinblick auf die moderne Sprachphilosophie. Germanische Studien, Heft 214. Berlin. [98 pp.]
WEIMANN 1965. See Bibliography to Section 1.
WELLANDER, ERIK. 1959. Kungl. Vetenskapsakademiens Insats för svenska Språkets Uppodlande. Kungl. Svenska Vetenskapsakademiens Årsbok 1959.369–404.
WELLEK, RENÉ. 1969. The supposed influence of Vico on England and Scotland in the eighteenth century. TAGLIACOZZO 1969:215–24.
WELLS, GEORGE A. 1969. Vico and Herder. TAGLIACOZZO 1969:93–102.
WHITE, HAYDEN V. See TAGLIACOZZO 1969.
WILLSON, A. LESLIE. 1964. A mythical image: the ideal of India in German Romanticism. Durham, N.C. [261 pp.]
WIMSATT, W.K. 1948. Philosophic words. New Haven. [xvi, 167 pp.]
WINDISCH, ERNST. 1917–1920. Geschichte der Sanskrit-Philologie und Indischen Altertumskunde. Strassburg. [2 parts. 460 pp.]
WINTER, EDUARD. 1953. Halle als Ausgangspunkt der deutschen Russlandkunde im 18. Jahrhundert. VISl 2. Berlin, Akademie-Verlag. [502 pp.]

——. 1954. Die Pflege der west- und südslavischen Sprachen in Halle im 18. Jahrhundert. Beiträge zur Geschichte der bürgerlichen Nationwerdens der west- und südslavischen Völker. VISl No. 5. Berlin, Akademie-Verlag. [292 pp.]

——. 1957. Die Registres der Berliner Akademie der Wissenschaften 1746–1766. Berlin, Akademie-Verlag.

——. 1958a. Ein Bericht von Johann Werner Paus aus dem Jahre 1732 über seine Tätigkeit auf dem Gebiete der russischen Sprache, der Literatur und der Geschichte Russlands. ZSl 3.744–70.

——, ed. 1958b. Die deutsch-russische Begegnung und Leonhard Euler. Beiträge zu den Beziehungen zwischen der deutschen und der russischen Wissenschaft und Kultur im 18. Jarhundert. Quellen und Studien zur Geschichte Osteuropas, Vol 1. Berlin, Akademie-Verlag. [196 pp.]

——, ed. 1962. Lomonosov, Schlözer, Pallas. Deutsch-russische Wissenschaftsbeziehungen im 18. Jahrhundert. Quellen und Studien zur Geschichte Osteuropas, Vol. 12. Berlin. ["Peter Simon Pallas (1741–1811)," 245–317.]

WINTER FESTSCHRIFT. 1956. Deutsch-Slawische Wechselseitigkeit in sieben Jahrhunderten. Gesammelte Aufsätze. VISl 9. Berlin, Akademie-Verlag. [708 pp.]

WINTER FESTSCHRIFT. 1966. Ost und West in der Geschichte des Denkens und der kulturellen Beziehungen. Festschrift für Eduard Winter zum 70. Geburtstag, ed. by W. Steinitz, P. N. Berkov, B. Suchodolski and J. Dolanský. Quellen und Studien zur Geschichte Osteuropas, Vol. 15. Berlin, Akademie-Verlag. [816 pp.]

WOKLER, ROBERT. 1974. Rameau, Rousseau, and the 'Essai sur l'origine des langues'. Studies on Voltaire and the eighteenth century 117.179–234.

WOLFF, HANS M. 1942. Der junge Herder und die Entwicklungsidee Rousseaus. PMLA 57.753–819.

WONDERLY, WILLIAM L. and EUGENE A. NIDA. 1965. Linguistics and Christian missions. AnL 5(4).104–44.

YERGIN, DANIEL. 1972. The Chomskyan revolution. New York Times Magazine (3 December). 42ff.

ZAICZ, G. 1970. The etymologist Sajnovics. ALH 20. 323–27.

ZSIRAI, MIKLÓS. 1951. Samuel Gyarmathi, Hungarian Pioneer of comparative linguistics. In SEBEOK 1966:58–70.

ZWOLINSKI, P. 1969. J. D. Hoffmann als Polonist und Etymologe. Ein Beitrag zur vorwissenschaftlichen Slawistik. Slawisch-Deutsche Wechselbeziehungen in Sprache, Literatur und Kultur, ed. by W. Krauss, Z. Stieber, J. Belic, V. I. Borkovskij, 575–80. VIS*l*, No. 44. Berlin, Akademie-Verlag.

SPRACHWISSENSCHAFT UND SPRACHPHILOSOPHIE IM ZEITALTER DER ROMANTIK

HELMUT GIPPER UND PETER SCHMITTER

VORBEMERKUNGEN

Ein Bericht über die Geschichte und Entwicklung der Sprachphilosophie und der Sprachwissenschaft im sog. Zeitalter der Romantik, wie ihn die Herausgeber dieses Bandes vorgesehen haben, stellt die Verfasser vor die schwierige Aufgabe, den betreffenden Zeitraum abzugrenzen, den geographischen Rahmen festzulegen und zu entscheiden, welche Gestalten und welche Entwicklungen berücksichtigt werden müssen. Ein Blick auf die vorliegende Sekundärliteratur, die ja in dieser historiographischen Darstellung im Vordergrund stehen soll, erleichtert dieses Vorhaben nicht. Im Gegenteil: es zeigen sich derartig verschiedene Ansichten, derart widersprüchliche Beurteilungen der Epoche und des Epochenbegriffs selbst, daß die Auswahl dessen, was aufzunehmen ist und was aufgrund des begrenzten Raumes beiseite gelassen werden darf, noch problematischer wird. Diese Schwierigkeiten müssen aber noch etwas verdeutlicht werden.

1. *Zum Begriff "Romantik" und der zeitlichen Abgrenzung dieser Epoche:*

Daß der Begriff "Romantik" und das zugehörige Adjektiv "romantisch" seit ihrem Aufkommen umstritten sind, ist hinreichend bekannt (Mason 1959; Wellek 1963, 1965; Prang 1968; Riese 1968; Oppel 1968; Behler 1972), und daß den Ausdrücken ursprünglich pejorative Konnotationen anhafteten, die gelegentlich auch heute noch nicht ganz überwunden sind, bedarf ebenfalls keiner besonderen Bestätigung. Es erscheint uns aber notwendig, eigens darauf hinzuweisen, daß die Ausdrücke "Romantik" und "romantisch" in recht verschiedenem Sinn verwendet werden können. So können sie einmal zur Charakterisierung einer gefühlsbetonten, naturnahen, gegen Zwänge jeder Art gerichteten Geisteshaltung mit metaphysischem, irrationalem Einschlag dienen, die zu allen Zeiten möglich ist. Sie können ferner eine bestimmte geistesgeschichtliche Epoche bezeichnen, in der diese Geisteshaltung besonders in Europa bestimmend wurde. (Unter diesem Gesichtspunkt drängt sich zugleich die Frage auf, wodurch dieses Denken ausgelöst wurde, welche Ziele es verfolgte und wogegen es sich richtete.) Schließlich kann man "Romantik" auch als einen rein traditionellen, wertneutralen Namen für einen bestimmten historischen Zeitraum verwenden, in dem zwar romantisches Denken eine bedeutende Rolle spielte, zugleich aber auch andere Strömungen nachzuweisen sind, die Beachtung verdienen.

In diesem letzteren rein zeitlichen Sinne wird man "Romantik" begreifen müssen, wenn — wie es in diesem Kapitel geschieht — alles berücksichtigt werden soll, was sprachphilosophisch und sprachwissenschaftlich relevant ist. Zur zeitlichen Begrenzung sieht man sich aber wieder auf den an 2.Stelle genannten Epochenbegriff "Romantik" selbst zurückverwiesen. Und dieser kann auch deshalb kaum umgangen werden, weil manches in der Entwicklung der Sprachphilosophie und der Sprachwissenschaft nur von dorther zu verstehen ist. Daher scheinen einige Erläuterungen hierzu unerläßlich.

Man pflegt den Begriff "Romantik" für jene in allen Kulturbereichen spürbare geistige Erneuerungsbewegung zu verwenden, die in der Mitte des 18. Jahrhunderts in England einsetzte, von da auf das kontinentale Europa übergriff, besonders stark Deutschland erfaßte und von dort aus nach allen Seiten ausstrahlte und so auch auf England selbst wieder zurückwirkte. Romantischer Einfluß reichte aber auch weit über Europa hinaus bis in die südamerikanischen Kolonialstaaten, wo er die Ausbildung eigener nationaler Literaturen förderte. Wenn man bedenkt, daß die geistesgeschichtlichen und politischen Voraussetzungen für das sog. romantische Denken in den europäischen Nationen sehr verschieden waren und sich zudem zahlreiche Einflüsse und Wechselwirkungen von Land zu Land ergaben, dann wird begreiflich, daß die Romantik in den verfügbaren Darstellungen zeitlich verschieden beurteilt und terminiert wird.

In England, wo bereits Dichter wie Edward Young (1683–1765), Thomas Gray (1716–1771) und James Macpherson (Ossian) (1736–1796) als wichtige Vorläufer gelten dürfen, ist die Abgrenzung einer eigentlichen "Romantik" kaum möglich. Die englischen Darstellungen bevorzugen eine Kennzeichnung ihrer geistesgeschichtlichen Epochen nach hervorragenden Gestalten, und so findet man Vertreter romantischer Anschauungen im sog. Age of Johnson (Samuel Johnson, 1709–1784), vor allem aber im Age of Byron (George Gordon Noel Lord Byron, 1788–1824) und auch noch im Age of Tennyson (Alfred Lord Tennyson, 1809–1892). Zur Bildung einer ausgesprochen romantischen Schule kam es aber nicht zuletzt deshalb nicht, weil die klassizistischen und aufklärerischen Strömungen in England nicht zu so heftigen Reaktionen Anlaß gaben, wie dies etwa in Frankreich der Fall war. Die englische Bewegung hat ihren Schwerpunkt in der Dichtung, die nie die Tradition des 18. Jahrhunderts ganz verleugnet.

In Frankreich darf zwar bereits Jean-Jacques Rousseau (1712–1778) als wichtiger Vorläufer romantischer Denkansätze gelten, aber die eigentliche französische Romantik setzt erst wesentlich später ein und steht stark unter dem Einfluß der deutschen Entwicklung. Madame de Staëls (Anne Louise Germaine Baronne de St. Holstein, geb. Necker, 1766–1817) berühmtem Werk *De l'Allemagne*, das 1813 erschien, kommt hier eine vermittelnde Schlüsselposition zu. Insgesamt gesehen umspannt die französische Romantik etwa den weiten Zeitraum von François René Vicomte de Chateaubriand (1768–1848) bis zu Victor Hugo (1802–1885), Alfred de Musset (1810–1857) und dem frühverstorbenen Übersetzer von Goethes Faust, Gérard de Nerval (eigentlich: Gérard Labrunie, 1822–1855). Sie erstreckt sich also bis weit in die zweite Hälfte des 19. Jahrhunderts hinein und konnte auch zu ausgesprochen kämpferischen Schulbildungen führen, weil es Anlaß genug gab, gegen die Regelstrenge klassizistischer und akademischer Doktrinen und gegen die Herrschaft des Ancien Régime anzukämpfen. So zeigt die französische Romantik, mitbedingt durch die umwälzenden politischen Ereignisse der französischen Revolution, den Aufstieg und Sturz Napoleon Bonapartes, die anschließenden Auseinandersetzungen zwischen Restauration und revolutionären Kräften, recht verschiedene Seiten: sie hat christlich-restaurative Züge, jedoch auch stark liberalisierende und soziale Tendenzen. In allen Bereichen des Geisteslebens zeigt sich ihre Wirkung, aber ihr Schwerpunkt liegt eindeutig im Literarischen.

In keinem Lande gewann die Romantik jedoch eine so zentrale Bedeutung wie in Deutschland. Hier erfaßte sie alle Bereiche des Geisteslebens mit gleicher Intensität, die Philosophie ebenso wie die Literatur, die Geschichtsschreibung, die Sprachwissenschaft und die schönen Künste. Vor allem aber spielt die Idee der Sprache in ihr eine entscheidende Rolle. Ihre Blütezeit liegt etwa zwischen 1790 und 1830. Nicht zu Unrecht hat man gesagt, die Sonderstellung der Romantik in Deutschland hänge damit zusammen, daß die romantische Geisteshaltung diesem Volke besonders gemäß gewesen sei, während Frankreich im Grunde immer mehr klassizistischen Auffassungen zugeneigt habe.

In Deutschland dominiert der romantische Einschlag sogar derart, daß die gleichzeitige deutsche Klassik, repräsentiert durch zentrale Gestalten wie Johann Wolfgang v. Goethe (1749–1832) und Friedrich v. Schiller (1759–1805), besonders im Blick ausländischer Betrachter völlig dahinter zu verschwinden droht. In Frankreich gelten z.B. Schiller und Goethe durchaus als Romantiker, aber wenn man sie mit den französischen Klassikern des 17. Jahrhunderts, Corneille und Racine, vergleicht, wird dieses Urteil verständlich.

In den deutschen Darstellungen ist es nun üblich, eine frühe oder ältere Romantik, auch Berliner oder Jenaer Romantik genannt (etwa von 1796–1806), zu unterscheiden von der jüngeren Hochromantik, die auch als Heidelberger Romantik bezeichnet wird. Diese reicht bis etwa 1815, und auf sie folgt noch die Spätromantik, der die sog. schwäbische Schule zugerechnet wird. Schlüsselfiguren der frühen Romantik sind Gestalten wie die Brüder Schlegel (August Wilhelm v. Schlegel, 1767–1845, und Friedrich v. Schlegel, 1772–1829) und der Dichter Georg Philipp Friedrich Freiherr von Hardenberg, genannt Novalis (1772–1803). Stellvertretend für die Hochromantik seien hier lediglich die für die Sprachwissenschaft bedeutsamen Brüder Grimm (Jacob Grimm, 1785- 1863, und Wilhelm Grimm, 1786–1859) und die durch ihre Volksliedsammlungen berühmten Dichter Clemens von Brentano (1778–1842) und Achim von Arnim (1781–1831) aufgeführt, und als Vertreter der Spätromantik sei schließlich noch auf Joseph Freiherr von Eichendorff (1788–1857) hingewiesen.

Die romantische Bewegung blieb jedoch keineswegs auf die bisher erwähnten Länder England, Frankreich und Deutschland beschränkt. Vielmehr wären etwa noch zu nennen für Italien Ugo Foscolo (1778–1827) und Alessandro Manzoni (1785–1873), für Spanien Ángel de Saavedra Duque de Rivas (1791–1865), für Polen Adam Mickiewicz (1798–1855) und für Rußland Alexandr Sergevič Puškin (1799–1837) und Michail Jurevič Lermontov (1814–1841).

Infolgedessen könnte man sogar von einer gesamteuropäischen Bewegung sprechen, die allerdings — wie dieser kurze Überblick deutlich machen sollte — ein äußerst vielschichtiges Phänomen ist. Aus diesem Grunde ist es auch unmöglich, allgemein verbindliche zeitliche Grenzen für die Epoche der Romantik anzugeben, und angesichts dieser Datierungsschwierigkeiten haben wir uns entschlossen, eine Terminierung vorzunehmen, wie sie z.B. von Colliers *Encyclopedia*, dem jüngst erschienenen großen amerikanischen Orientierungswerk, vorgeschlagen wird. Dort heißt es kurz und bündig: 'The three generations of men who dominated the intellectual scene in the Western World between 1770 and 1850 are known as Romanticists' (vol. 20, 1971).

In Bezug auf einige bedeutsame Männer dieser Zeit wie etwa die deutschen 'Klassiker' Schiller und Goethe oder die französischen Ideologen enthält dieser Satz wohl zweifellos ein unhaltbares Pauschalurteil; ansonsten aber scheint es uns durchaus vertretbar, dieser Definition entsprechend das letzte Drittel des 18. Jahrhunderts und die erste Hälfte des 19. Jahrhunderts — mit dem Schwerpunkt auf den Jahren 1800–1830 — als den Zeitraum zu bezeichnen, der in diesem Kapitel berücksichtigt werden sollte.

2. *Zur Frage des geographischen Schwerpunktes der Romantik:*

In fast allen Darstellungen der Geschichte der Sprachwissenschaft in dieser Epoche nehmen einige deutsche Gelehrte einen hervorragenden Platz ein. Zuweilen mag es dabei auch zu einseitigen Werturteilen gekommen sein, und so erhebt Hans Aarsleff in seinem Buch *The study of language in England 1780–1860* gegenüber den historischen Darstellungen Theodor Benfeys und Rudolf von Raumers den Vorwurf, daß beide 'also show a heavy bias toward the belief that all good work and advances in philology have been the product of German ingenuity' (Aarsleff 1967: 7–8). Ein solcher Lobpreis 'deutschen Geistes' ist natürlich ganz indiskutabel, aber trotzdem bleibt es eine Tatsache, daß es zwar u.a. in England oder Frankreich wichtige Ansätze gegeben hat, diese jedoch in ihrem eigenen Ursprungsland nicht auf günstigen Boden fielen. So führt z.B. Aarsleff selbst aus, daß in England die Voraussetzungen für neue linguistische Erkenntnisse nicht sehr günstig waren, weil die dortige Fachwelt lange Zeit unter dem beherrschenden Einfluß eines eigenwilligen Gelehrten und Gegners der spekulativen allgemeinen Sprachphilosophie stand, nämlich unter dem

Einfluß John Horne Tookes (1736–1812). Aarsleff bemerkt dazu: 'The reputation of Tooke's *Diversions* is one of the most remarkable phenomena in the intellectual and scholarly life of England during the first third of the nineteenth century. For thirty years it kept England immune to the new philology until the results and methods finally had to be imported from the Continent in the 1830's, and even then they met strong opposition' (1967:73).

Was Frankreich anbetrifft, so erklärt Georges Mounin in seiner *Histoire de la linguistique des origines au XXe siècle* (1970) das auffällige *silence des français* in dieser Zeit des Umbruchs mit den Sätzen: 'Quelques autres points de l'histoire de la grammaire comparée méritent une attention particulière, par la réflexion proprement historique qu'ils suggèrent. Le premier, très instructif, est le silence paradoxal de la science française en matière de grammaire comparée, durant plus de cinquante ans. Le paradoxe est ici, que les fondateurs de la discipline soient venus tous à Paris recevoir l'initiation au sanskrit. Silvestre de Sacy, qui a lu Gyármathi, et Wilkins, qui fait créer la chaire de sanskrit de Chézy, qui appuie les travaux de Burnouf et de Champollion, représente à lui seul l'explication du phénomène: la France alors est littéralement bloquée vis-à-vis de la science nouvelle, à cause de sa tradition culturelle nourrie de Port-Royal.' (1970:186).

Was Mounin hier für die vergleichende Sprachwissenschaft bemerkt, dürfte jedoch für das Gebiet der Sprachphilosophie nicht zutreffen. Neuere Untersuchungen, die H. B. Acton in seinem Aufsatz *The philosophy of language in revolutionary France* (1959) vorlegt, machen darauf aufmerksam, daß die sog. Ideologen, eine Gruppe von Gelehrten am Institut National des Sciences et Arts, in der napoleonischen Ära bereits wichtige sprachphilosophische Probleme erörterten, die bislang als Errungenschaften der neueren Sprachphilosophie betrachtet zu werden pflegten. Wir werden diese zu Unrecht vergessene Strömung einbeziehen. Daß sie damals allerdings ohne besondere Wirkung blieb, muß mit der turbulenten Entwicklung der politischen Verhältnisse in Frankreich und mit der kurzen Wirkungszeit der Ideologen in Zusammenhang gebracht werden.

In Deutschland dagegen erwiesen sich gerade die bedrückenden politischen Verhältnisse als günstig für das beginnende Pionier- und Entdeckungszeitalter der Sprachwissenschaft und die Entwicklung neuer Sprachideen. Zwar zeigt das Beispiel Franz Bopps, der in den Stunden entscheidender Ereignisse der europäischen Geschichte im Jahre 1814 in der Nationalbibliothek vom Paris seinen indologischen Studien nachging, wie unbeeinflußt die Wissenschaft von Tagesgeschehen bleiben kann, aber die Unterwerfung der deutschen Staaten unter die Herrschaft Napoleons hatte doch die Besinnung auf die eigene Geschichte, auf das Volk bzw. die Nation und ihre Sprache wesentlich gefördert. Die historisch-vergleichende Grammatik wurde dadurch erheblich begünstigt. Es konnte freilich nicht ausbleiben daß in den Befreiungskriegen auch nationale, ja nationalistische Töne laut wurden und zu einer polemischen Überbewertung der deutschen Sprache führten, aber es wäre falsch, die deutsche Romantik deshalb als eine Epoche des Nationalismus abzustempeln.

W. W. Chambers hat in seinem wichtigen Aufsatz *Language and nationality in German preromantic and romantic thought* (MLR 1946:382–392) mit Recht darauf hingewiesen, daß die romantischen Sprachideen schon seit Herder eher einen kosmopolitischen Charakter trugen und daß erst während der napoleonischen Kriege der Nationalismus durchschlug. Und außerdem muß noch beachtet werden, daß die Rede vom Nationalcharakter der Sprachen, vom Volksgeist, der schon bei Hegel vorkommt, nicht nationalistisch gemeint war, wie heute manchmal fälschlicherweise angenommen wird, sondern der Ausdruck für die in einem Volke bzw. einer Nation wirksamen schöpferischen Kräfte sein sollte.

Die romantische Epoche darf mit Recht als das Entdeckungs-und Pionierzeitalter der Sprachwissenschaft gelten, und genauer betrachtet lassen sich innerhalb dieses Zeitraums zwei große Entwicklungslinien verfolgen. Die erste verläuft mehr in sprachphilosophischer und anthropologischer Richtung. Sie führt zu einer auf breiter erkenntnistheoretischer Grundlage aufruhenden allgemeinen Sprachwissenschaft. Die zweite geht mehr in die sprachhistorische, genetisch-sprachvergleichende Richtung. Sie führt zur indogermanischen bzw. indoeuropäischen Sprachwissenschaft und zur Ausbildung der historischen Grammatiken in den Einzeldisziplinen Germanistik, Romanistik, Slawistik, usw.

Die Zuordnung der einzelnen Sprachforscher zu den beiden Richtungen ist nicht immer eindeutig. Die Brüder Schlegel z.B. haben sich in beiden Bereichen Verdienste erworben. Anregungen zur ersten Richtung gingen — um nur wenige Namen zu nennen — aus von Denkern wie Anthony Ashley-Cooper Earl of Shaftesbury (1621–1683), John Locke (1632–1704), Jean-Jacques Rousseau (1712–1778), Etienne Bonnot de Condillac (1715–1780), Johann Georg Hamann (1730–1788) und Johann Gottfried von Herder (1744–1803). Die Zentralgestalt ist Wilhelm von Humboldt (1767–1835), in dessen Werk die Grenzen zwischen Sprachphilosophie und Sprachwissenschaft fließend sind. Seine Sprachauffassung hat in der ersten Hälfte des 20. Jahrhunderts eine Renaissance erlebt.

Anregungen für die zweite Strömung gehen von Forschern und Gelehrten aus wie etwa Job Ludolf (1624–1704), Gottfried Wilhelm Leibniz (1646–1716), Christian Jakob Kraus (1753–1807), Sir William Jones (1746–1784) oder Sámuel Gyármathi (1751–1830). Vor allem aber gehören zu ihr Männer wie August Wilhelm von Schlegel (1767–1845) und Friedrich von Schlegel (1772–1829), die jedoch beide auch sprachphilosophisch interessiert waren; dann Rasmus Kristian Rask (1787–1832), Franz Bopp (1791–1867) und Jacob Grimm (1785–1863). Von ihnen führt der Weg zu den sog. Junggrammatikern und zu einer neuen Epoche positivistischer Sprachbetrachtung mit naturwissenschaftlichem Einschlag.

Karl Otto Apel hat in seiner bedeutenden Untersuchung *Die Idee der Sprache in der Tradition des Humanismus von Dante bis Vico* (1963) die großen Strömungen des europäischen Sprachdenkens mit ihren Verzweigungen aufgezeigt und die Verbindungen bis zur Antike hergestellt. Die Humboldtsche Linie wird über Herder und Giambattisto Vico (1668–1744), Francesco Petrarca (1304–1374), Dante Alighieri

(1265–1321) bis auf die Rhetorik Ciceros (106–43 v. Chr.) zurückgeführt und von Apel als *Sprachhumanismus* gekennzeichnet. Apel weist auch die Verbindung Humboldts zu der Seitenlinie nach, die über Hamann zurückgeht auf den Mystiker Jakob Böhme (1575–1624), auf Nikolaus von Kues (Cusanus, 1401–1464), Meister Eckehart (1260–1328) und letztlich Augustinus (354–430). Hier handelt es sich um die im Christentum verankerte Logos-Mystik, in die auch neuplatonische Gedanken eingegangen sind und deren Vermittler u.a. der englische Neuplatoniker James Harris (1709–1780) war. Schließlich zeigt Apel die Beziehungen der Humboldtschen Linie zu den Ideen von Roger Bacon (1212–1294) und John Locke auf, die er dem NOMINALISTISCHEN ZWEIG des europäischen Sprachdenkens zuordnet, den er über Wilhelm von Ockham (ca. 1300–1349) bis Aristoteles verfolgt.

Diese Humboldtsche Art des Sprachdenkens sucht Apel als transzendental-hermeneutische Betrachtungsweise zu kennzeichnen. Für sie ist charakteristisch, daß die Sprache als konstitutives Merkmal des Menschen gilt und die Sprachen der Welt als verschiedene geistige Zugänge zur Erfahrungswelt der Sprachgemeinschaften betrachtet werden. Sie werden damit als Bedingungen der Möglichkeit des Verstehens von Welt gedeutet, stellen also, philosophisch ausgedrückt, ein transzendentales Moment, eine Apriori-Bedingung menschlicher Erkenntnis dar. Dieser Sprachphilosophie haften idealistische Sehweisen an, und sie gerät deshalb in Widerstreit mit den mehr technisch-szientifischen Strömungen der Sprachphilosophie, für die Sprache in erster Linie ein Verständigungsmittel ist, dass mit positivistischen und behavioristischen Methoden zu beschreiben ist.

Durch die Synthese von Logos-Mystik und Sprach-Humanismus wird auch die europäische Entdeckung der Nationalsprachen, der 'Muttersprachen' als Gegenstände sprachwissenschaftlicher Forschung begünstigt. Für die moderne Sprachwissenschaft ist dieser Schritt von nicht zu unterschätzender Bedeutung. Nach Humboldt werden die hier skizzierten sprachphilosophischen Ideen dann in verschiedene Richtungen weitergeführt. Während Heymann Steinthal (1823–1899) den Weg von der Philosophie zur Psychologie beschreitet und damit zur Völkerpsychologie (Moritz Lazarus, 1824–1903, Wilhelm Wundt, 1832–1920) führt, sind im Bereiche der Sprachphilosophie selbst Gelehrte wie Benedetto Croce (1866–1952), Ernst Cassirer (1874–1945), Erich Rothacker (1888–1965), Martin Heidegger (geb. 1897), Hans-Georg Gadamer (geb. 1900), Bruno Liebrucks (geb. 1911), Johannes Lohmann (geb. 1895), Leo Weisgerber (geb. 1899) und Karl Otto Apel (geb. 1922) zu erwähnen.

Auf dem speziell linguistischen Gebiet müssen schließlich außer Steinthal Franz Nikolaus Finck (1867–1910) und Ernst Lewy (1881–1966), dann aber auch die ganze Reihe der sogenannten Neuhumboldtianer genannt werden, die sich neben Leo Weisgerber an der Weiterführung dieser Gedanken beteiligt haben. Zu nennen sind hier vor allem Gunther Ipsen (geb. 1899), Walter Porzig (1895–1961) und Jost Trier (1894–1970), ferner Hennig Brinkmann (geb. 1901), Hans Glinz (geb. 1913), und Johannes Erben (geb. 1925).

Außerdem kann eine Verbindung hergestellt werden zu verwandten Ansätzen in der amerikanischen Linguistik, vor allem zu Edward Sapir (1884–1939), Benjamin Lee Whorf (1897–1941) und zu den Forschern, die sich um eine Weiterführung und Verifizierung der sog. Sapir-Whorf-Hypothese verdient gemacht haben, also Forschern wie John Bissel Carroll (geb. 1916), Harry Hoijer (geb. 1940) u.a.m.

Kann man nun insgesamt die Humboldtsche Linie trotz ihrer empirischen Grundlage als 'idealistisch' im positiven Sinne ansprechen, so ist die Boppsche Linie eher als 'positivistisch' zu kennzeichnen. Denn es geht hier um ein streng faktenbezogenes Wissen mit dem Endziel technisch-szientifischer Exaktheit, wie es auch die moderne Linguistik, insonderheit den klassischen Strukturalismus, bestimmt hat. Im engeren Sinne führt die Linie Rask-Bopp-Grimm dann weiter zu den 'Junggrammatikern', den Entdeckern und Verfechtern der sog. Lautgesetze. Hier soll Sprachwissenschaft den Exaktheitsgrad der Naturwissenschaften erreichen, ein Ziel, das legitim und erstrebenswert ist, aber an der Inkommensurabilität der menschlichen Freiheit seine Grenzen findet.

Zum Schluß sei nur noch darauf hingewiesen, daß wir uns trotz aller Mühe nicht alle thematisch relevanten Arbeiten beschaffen konnten und daß uns bei der Überfülle der einzubeziehenden Literatur vielleicht auch das eine oder andere Werk entgangen ist, das hier hätte erscheinen sollen.

A. DIE BEGRÜNDUNG DER HISTORISCH-VERGLEICHENDEN SPRACHWISSENSCHAFT

I. *Vorstufen und Anfänge der vergleichenden Grammatik*

Eines der bedeutsamsten Ereignisse für die sprachwissenschaftlich orientierte Forschung der Romantik war zweifellos das Bekanntwerden der alten indischen Gelehrtensprache, des Sanskrit. Infolgedessen nimmt es auch nicht wunder, daß man bisweilen hier den Wendepunkt in der Geschichte der Linguistik ansetzt. Doch wie schon Otto Jespersen (1925:14–5) zu Recht betont, war es keineswegs die Entdeckung des Sanskrit allein, die eine neue Epoche der Linguistik einzuleiten vermochte. Hauptvoraussetzung dazu war vielmehr, wie Vilhelm Thomsen (deutsche Übersetzung durch Hans Pollak, 1927:43–4) einmal formulierte, 'die Erkenntnis, dass das, was einen zuverlässigen Führer durch die Mannigfaltigkeit der Sprachen zur Auffindung ihrer Verwandtschaft und zur Verfolgung ihrer historischen Entwicklung abgeben kann, nicht die Gleichheit einzelner Wörter ist, ... sondern ... einzig und allein eine methodische Behandlung des ganzen Sprachbaues, all des Grammatischen.' Die Abkehr von der naiven Vorstellung, man könne schon allein aufgrund der Ähnlichkeit einzelner Wörter auf eine Verwandtschaft der betreffenden Sprachen schließen, und die Forderung nach einem systematischen Vergleich ihrer grammatischen Strukturen sind also als die eigentliche Leistung dieser Epoche anzusehen, und daher ist es zu begrüßen, wenn z.B. Holger

Pedersen (1962:240–310), Francis P. Dinneen (1967:176–91) und R. H. Robins (1967:164–97) im Gegensatz etwa zu Walter Porzig ([2]1957:320–73) ihre Kapitel über die historische und vergleichende Sprachwissenschaft nicht erst mit Franz Bopp (1791–1867) bzw. William Jones (1746–1794) beginnen, sondern auch die Anfänge dieser Entwicklung in der Zeit vor der Entdeckung des Sanskrit aufzuzeigen suchen. Als wichtige Beiträge über die sprachvergleichenden Untersuchungen dieser früheren Epochen sind vor allem auch die Abhandlung *Studier i den äldre språkjämförelsens allmänna och svenska historia fram till 1827* von Jan Agrell (1955) und die beiden Aufsätze *Ideas on the kinship of the European languages from 1200 to 1800* von Giuliano Bonfante (1954) und *The foundation of comparative linguistics: Revolution or continuation?* von Paul Diderichsen (1966) zu nennen sowie ebenfalls die Studie *Some 18th century antecedents of the 19th century linguistics* von J. Gulya (1965), die sich allerdings weitgehend auf den finno-ugristischen Bereich beschränkt.

Ob es nun erforderlich ist, mit Paul Diderichsen (1966:341) und Francis P. Dinneen (1967:176) bereits bei der stoischen Sprachauffassung einzusetzen oder mit R. H. Robins (1967:165) bei Dante Alighieri (1265–1321), mag dahingestellt sein; auf jeden Fall aber ist es sinnvoll, so wie es etwa auch bei Vilhelm Thomsen (1927:25), Jan Agrell (1955:7–12), und Holger Pedersen (1962:240) geschieht, mit einem kurzen Blick die Zeit zu streifen, in der man aufgrund von äußerst willkürlichen Wortgleichungen das Hebräische als Ursprache der Menschheit zu erweisen suchte. Wie man hier im 16., 17. und auch noch im 18. Jahrhundert im einzelnen verfuhr, ist sehr anschaulich von Otto Jespersen (1925:3–4), Vilhelm Thomsen (1927:36–7), Francis P. Dinneen (1967:177–8) und Hans Arens (1969:73–80) beschrieben worden, doch ist für die weitere wissenschaftsgeschichtliche Entwicklung in erster Linie von Interesse, daß Gottfried Wilhelm Leibniz (1646–1716) dieses Spiel mit Worten als unhaltbar erweist und zur Klärung des Problems der Sprachverwandtschaft eine wissenschaftlich korrekte und weltumfassende 'collatio linguarum' fordert.

Wie Tullio de Mauro (1969:54–62) nachdrücklich hervorhebt und auch Hans Arens (1969:103) nahelegt, erhoffte Leibniz sich von einer derartigen Untersuchung außerdem nähere Auskunft über eventuelle Unterschiede im Denken und in der Erkenntnismöglichkeit der jeweiligen Völker. Daher zählt de Mauro ihn sogar zusammen mit John Locke (1632–1704) und Giambattista Vico (1668–1744) zu den großen Wegbereitern derjenigen These, die man heute in der Regel als SAPIR-WHORF-HYPOTHESE, THESE VOM WELTBILD DER SPRACHE oder THESE VOM SPRACHLICHEN RELATIVITÄTSPRINZIP (LINGUISTIC RELATIVITY) zu bezeichnen pflegt (Schaff 1964b:61–93, Brown 1967, Christmann 1967, Gipper 1972). Weil wir uns jedoch im Zusammenhang mit Wilhelm von Humboldt noch einmal etwas eingehender mit dem Gedanken vom Weltbild der Sprache befassen werden (vgl. S. 278ff.), können wir uns an dieser Stelle sogleich wieder dem Problem der Sprachverwandtschaft zuwenden, und hier hat in neuerer Zeit J. Gulya in dem bereits erwähnten Aufsatz (1965:162) schön gezeigt, daß Leibniz in concreto bei dem Sprachvergleich einmal das Vaterunser, dann aber auch Zahlwörter, Verwandtschaftsbezeichnungen, Körperteile, Nahrungsmittelbezeichnungen und dergleichen mehr im Auge hatte. Was nun an Leibniz' eigenen Anschauungen im Bereich der Etymologie und Sprachverwandtschaft der heutigen Kritik noch standhält, ist vor allem bei Bonfante (1954:692–5), Aarsleff (1969) und Jankowsky (1972:19–24) ausführlich gewürdigt. Da wir in diesem Rahmen aber lediglich die großen Linien verfolgen können, müssen wir von näheren Einzelheiten absehen und uns im Augenblick damit begnügen festzuhalten, daß Leibniz mit der Forderung nach einer weltumfassenden 'collatio linguarum' direkt oder indirekt alle großen Polyglottensammlungen des 18. und 19. Jahrhunderts angeregt hat.

So ist es zwar aufgrund der unterschiedlichen Lebenszeiten von Gottfried Wilhelm Leibniz (1646–1716) und Peter Simon Pallas (1741[und nicht 1744, wie Dinneen, 1967:178, irrtümlich verzeichnet]–1811) ausgeschlossen, daß der letztere, wie Milka Ivić (1971:27 Anm. 5) schreibt, direkt 'auf Zureden (!) des Philosophen Leibniz' sein großes Wörterbuch herausgab, doch ist das Erscheinen dieses wichtigen Werkes trotzdem auf die Initiative von Leibniz zurückzuführen. Denn dieser hatte schon Peter den Großen (1672–1725) dazu angeregt, Wort- und Textsammlungen der verschiedenen Sprachen seines weiten russischen Reiches anlegen zu lassen; und dieser Plan war dann von der an sprachlichen Dingen sehr interessierten Zarin Katharina II. (1729–1796) sogar persönlich in Angriff genommen worden. Über die einzelnen Stufen der Ausführung dieses Unternehmens, seine Überleitung in die Hände des damals weltberühmten deutschen Naturforschers und Weltreisenden Peter Simon Pallas sowie über Titel, Inhalt und Erscheinungsweise des schließlich von diesem im Auftrage der Zarin herausgegebenen Werkes informieren zwar auch etwa Thomsen (1927:39), Arens (1969:135–6) und vor allem Gulya (1965:168–9) recht ausführlich, doch ist es immer noch von Nutzen, die alte *Geschichte der Sprachwissenschaft und orientalischen Philologie in Deutschland seit dem Anfange des 19. Jahrhunderts mit einem Rückblick auf die früheren Zeiten* (1869) von Theodor Benfey mitheranzuziehen. Dieses Buch zeichnet sich nämlich nicht nur durch eine Fülle von interessanten Einzelheiten aus, die es über die neueren Abhandlungen hinaus berichtet, sondern auch z.B. durch die präzise Wiedergabe solcher wichtiger Dinge wie des Titels des Pallasschen Werkes. Denn während sich die heutigen Autoren durchweg auf ein mehr oder weniger stark gekürztes—und bisweilen auch noch falsches (vgl. R. H. Robins, 1967:193, Anm. 17)—Titelzitat beschränken, referiert Theodor Benfey (1869:266) wenigstens die bekanntere lateinische Version des ursprünglich in lateinischer und russischer Sprache publizierten Titels in seinem vollen Wortlaut *Linguarum totius orbis vocabularia comparativa, Augustissimae cura collecta. Sectionis primae, linguas Asiae et Europae complexae, pars prior* bzw. *pars posterior*. (Zur russischen Version vgl. etwa Gulya, 1965:168, oder die großen Kataloge der Bibliothèque Nationale in Paris oder der Library of Congress, und zwar *Catalogue générale des livres imprimés de la Bibliothèque Nationale*, Tome 129, Paris: Imprimerie Nationale 1934:446–7, sowie *A catalogue of books represented by Library of Congress printed cards*, vol. 113, Ann Arbor, Michigan: Edwards Brothers 1959:368.) Nun deutet zwar der Titel noch das Erscheinen einer weiteren 'sectio' an, doch blieb es bei der Veröffentlichung dieser ersten beiden Teile, wie z.B. im Bibliothekskatalog der Library of Congress (a.a.O.) ausdrücklich vermerkt wird. Dort ist selbstverständlich auch die Erscheinungszeit der 1. Auflage mit St. Petersburg 1787–1789 richtig angegeben, die in der wissenschaftsgeschichtlichen Literatur oft unzutreffend referiert wird (vgl. beispielsweise Dinneen 1967:178: '1768–1787'; Arens 1969:135: '1786'; oder Jespersen 1925:4; Pedersen 1962:10 und Mounin 1967:144: '1786–1787').

Was nun den Inhalt dieses vergleichenden Vokabulars angeht, so werden dort über 280 Wörter (Substantive, Adjektive, Verben, Verbalformen, Pronomina, Adverbien und Zahlwörter) aus 149 asiatischen und 51 europäischen Sprachen und Dialekten wiedergegeben. Und zwar ist man im einzelnen so verfahren, daß jedes der zugrundegelegten russischen Ausgangswörter, soweit es das gesammelte Material erlaubte, nacheinander in den übrigen 199 Sprachen aufgeführt wurde, wodurch dann eine nackte Wörterliste ohne besondere erklärende Zusätze entstand. In der zweiten Auflage, die von dem in Ungarn geborenen Jankovics de Mirijevo besorgt wurde und 1790–1791 in vier Bänden erschien, waren zwar sieben asiatische Sprachen der ersten Bearbeitung fortgelassen worden, dafür aber 22 andere asiatische, 4 europäische, 30 afrikanische und 23 amerikanische Sprachen neu hinzugekommen.

So stellt dieses Werk auf der einen Seite eine beachtenswerte Pionierleistung dar, da hier, wie schon Theodor Benfey (1869:268) ganz zu Recht betont, zum ersten Mal in der Geschichte eine so große Anzahl von Sprachen in einem Buch zusammengefaßt wurde. Daher ist es auch kein Wunder, daß dieses Vokabular bei seinem Erscheinen bedeutendes Aufsehen erregte und — worin alle seine heutigen Kritiker (vgl. z.B. Thomsen 1927:39; Gulya 1965:169; Arens 1969:136) völlig übereinstimmen — viel dazu beitrug, das Interesse für vergleichende Sprachstudien zu steigern.

Auf der anderen Seite war dieses Wörterbuch jedoch so fehlerhaft, daß Wilhelm von Humboldt beispielsweise in seinem Beitrag zu Johann Christoph Adelungs *Mithridates* (Bd. IV, 334) — auf dieses Werk werden wir gleich noch näher eingehen — darauf hinweist, daß von den ersten zwanzig baskischen Wörtern lediglich acht völlig einwandfrei sind. Aber nicht nur diese fehlerhafte Wiedergabe der fremdsprachigen Wörter wurde kritisiert, vielmehr rief auch schon die Konzeption, die dem Vokabular zugrundelag, heftige Kritik hervor. Neben J. L. L. Rüdiger, auf den Theodor Benfey (1869:268) in diesem Zusammenhange hinweist, ist hier vor allen Dingen der Königsberger Professor für Geschichte und Nationalökonomie Christian Jakob Kraus (1753–1807) zu nennen, dessen *Rezension des Allgemeinen vergleichenden Wörterbuchs von Pallas* so bedeutende und teilweise auch heute noch nicht überholte Gedanken enthält, daß Hans Arens (1969:136) sogar das größte Verdienst des Pallasschen Werkes darin sieht, diese Kritik veranlaßt zu haben. Im einzelnen entwickelt Kraus in seiner Besprechung, die er im Jahre 1787 in der *Allgemeine(n) Literatur-Zeitung* (Nr. 235–237) veröffentlichte, zuerst seine Gedanken über den Zweck der Sprachvergleichung und führt dann näher aus, wie man dabei methodisch richtig vorzugehen habe. Da wir hier jedoch nicht alle seine Darlegungen referieren können, sei an dieser Stelle lediglich hervorgehoben, daß er zum einen auf die großen Schwierigkeiten hinweist, die allein schon der korrekten 'lautlichen', wir würden heute sagen: der phonetischen bzw. phonologischen Beschreibung fremder Sprachen entgegenstehen, und zudem auf einige Probleme eingeht, die mit dem Zeichencharakter der Sprache sowie mit der bei den einzelnen Völkern unterschiedlichen gedanklichen und sprachlichen Erfassung der Welt zusammenhängen. Zum anderen aber — und das ist für unsere Thematik ganz besonders wichtig — lehnt Christian Jakob Kraus das bloße 'Geschäft der Wortvergleichung' ab und fordert eine systematische 'Vergleichung der charakteristischen Züge des grammatischen Baues', und zwar insbesondere der Deklinationen, Konjugationen, Steigerungsarten usw. Die bedeutendsten Passagen dieser Rezension, die in der älteren Literatur (vgl. Benfey 1869:268 mit Anmerkung, Thomsen 1927:44, Anm. 1, oder Agrell 1955:21) nur am Rand erwähnt wird, jetzt aber zu Recht wesentlich mehr Beachtung findet (siehe etwa Dinneen 1967:179–80, Robins 1967:169 und Jankowsky 1972:29–33), sind heute wieder leicht zugänglich bei Hans Arens (1955:118–27; ²1969:136–46), der sie — soweit wir sehen — auch zum ersten Mal in jüngerer Zeit angemessen würdigt und daher vielleicht als ihr Entdecker gelten kann.

Die Erkenntnis der von Christian Jakob Kraus so stark betonten Notwendigkeit, daß man bei der Sprachvergleichung das Hauptaugenmerk auf die grammatische Struktur der Sprachen richten müsse, hat aber — wie Vilhelm Thomsen (1927:44) ganz richtig hervorhebt — zu jener Zeit sozusagen in der Luft gelegen. Die Ansätze dazu kommen von verschiedenen Seiten, die wohl völlig unabhängig voneinander sind; und zwar ist hier wahrscheinlich als der erste überhaupt, der von der Bedeutung des grammatischen Strukturvergleichs für die Beurteilung der Sprachverwandtschaft spricht, Job Ludolf (1624–1704) zu nennen. Dieser Orientalist, den etwa Jan Agrell (1955:19–20; 205), Holger Pedersen (1962:240), Paul Diderichsen (1966:345–6) und Kurt R. Jankowsky (1972:23–4) zu Recht unter die großen Vorläufer der komparativen Linguistik rechnen, hatte sich nämlich intensiv mit dem Studium semitischer Sprachen beschäftigt (vgl. dazu Benfey 1869:236–7) und war dabei zu der für seine Zeit revolutionären Einsicht gekommen: 'Si linguam alteri dicere affinem velimus, necesse est, non tantum ut ea contineat nonnulla alterius cuiusdam linguae vocabula, sed etiam ut Grammaticae ratio, maxima sui parte, eadem sit, qualis convenientia cernitur in Orientalibus, Ebraea, Syriaca, Arabica et Aethiopica.' (Eine englische Paraphrase dieses Textes findet sich etwa bei Lockwood 1969:21, und eine deutsche bei Arens 1969:105–6).

Desweiteren ist, wie es auch durchweg in der neueren Literatur geschieht, auf zwei Männer hinzuweisen, die in der Geschichte der finnisch-ugrischen Sprachwissenschaft eine große Rolle spielen und ebenfalls die Bedeutung des grammatischen Baues für die Sprachvergleichung erkannt haben. Der erste dieser beiden, der ungarische Gelehrte P. Sajnovics, hat in seinem im Jahre 1770 in Kopenhagen publizierten Werk *Demonstratio idioma Ungarorum et Lapponum idem esse* die Identität des Ungarischen und Lappischen zu erweisen versucht und dabei nicht nur Wortentsprechungen, sondern auch Ähnlichkeiten in der Grammatik als Beweis herangezogen. Der unerschütterliche Nachweis dieser Sprachverwandtschaft ist aber nach allgemeinem Urteil erst dem zweiten dieser Männer, dem Ungarn Sámuel Gyármathi (1751–1830) gelungen, dessen Untersuchung *Affinitas linguae Hungaricae cum linguis Fennicae originis grammatice demonstrata. Nec non vocabularia dialectorum Tataricarum et Slavicarum cum Hungarica comparata* (Göttingen, 1799) Theodor Benfey (1869:278) die 'erste wirklich wissenschaftliche Sprachvergleichung' nennt. Dieses Lob scheint in der Tat nicht zu hoch gegriffen, denn wie etwa auch H. Pedersen (1962:105–6, 240–1) und H. Arens (1969:148) betonen, liegt mit diesem Werke eine Arbeit vor, in der erstmals eine Sprachverwandtschaft — genau so wie der Titel zu erkennen gibt — wirklich systematisch aufgrund der Ähnlichkeit in der grammatischen Struktur bewiesen wurde. Wie Gyármathi dabei im einzelnen vorging, hat Miklós Zsirai in dem Aufsatz *Sámuel Gyármathi, Hungarian pioneer of comparative linguistics* (1951) detailliert beschrieben, und zu Recht hebt Zsirai dabei auch hervor, daß Gyármathi im Gegensatz zu Sajnovics nicht nur das Ungarische mit dem Lappischen vergleicht, sondern die gesamte finnisch-ugrische Sprachfamilie behandelt.

Beachtenswerte Ansätze zu einem grammatischen Strukturvergleich finden sich jedoch auch noch bei dem Spanier Lorenzo Hervás y Panduro (1735–1809). Dieser Mann, der schon als vierzehnjähriger Junge in den Jesuitenorden eintrat, war 16 Jahre lang — und zwar bis zur Vertreibung der Jesuiten aus Amerika im Jahre 1767 — in den südamerikanischen Missionen tätig und lebte dann bis zu seinem Tod am 24.8.1809 in Italien, wo er unter Papst Pius VII (1740–1823) zum Leiter der Bibliothek im Quirinal ernannt wurde. Seine besondere Bedeutung für die Linguistik liegt nun einmal darin, daß die Nachwelt ihm die Kenntnis zahlreicher Indianersprachen zu verdanken hat. Denn wie schon Wilhelm von Humboldt, der sein 'grammatisches' Werk sehr schätzte und auch für seine eigenen Studien benutzte (vgl. z.B. Akademie-Ausgabe VI:134 mit Anm. 1, sowie VII:225, Anm. 2), rühmend hervorgehoben hat, hatte Lorenzo Hervás 'den lobenswürdigen Gedanken', seine ebenfalls aus Amerika vertriebenen Mitbrüder zu bitten, ihre Erinnerungen an die Eingeborenensprachen aufzuzeichnen. Die auf diese Art entstandenen Skizzen hat er dann gesammelt, nach eigenem Wissen ergänzt und soweit umgearbeitet, daß daraus eine Reihe instruktiver Grammatiken und Wortsammlungen entstand. Zum zweiten aber hat er im Jahre 1784 im 17. Band seiner groß angelegten einundzwanzigbändigen Enzyklopädie *Idea dell' Universo che contiene la storia della vita dell' uomo, elementi cosmografici, viaggio estatico al mondo planetario, e storia della terra e delle lingue* (1878–1787) einen *Catalogo delle lingue conosciute e notizia della loro affinità e diversità* veröffentlicht, von dem er etwa zwei Jahrzehnte später sogar noch eine stark erweiterte sechsbändige Fassung herausgab. Dieses Werk, das im Gegensatz zu der ersten Ausgabe nicht in italienischer, sondern in spanischer Sprache verfaßt war und von 1800 bis 1805 in Madrid erschien, trägt den Titel *Catálogo de las lenguas de las naciones conocidas y numeración, división, y clases de estas según la diversidad de sus idiomas y dialectos.* Wie bereits mit dieser Formulierung angedeutet wird, läßt sich Hervás bei dieser Untersuchung jedoch in erster Linie von ethnologischem Interesse leiten; denn sein Ziel besteht ja darin, die Verwandtschaft oder auch Verschiedenheit der bisher bekannten Völker aufzuzeigen. Aber da er diesen Nachweis aufgrund der Sprachverwandtschaft führen will, bietet sein Werk auch manche Aufzeichnungen, die für den Linguisten wertvoll sind. Hierunter fallen selbstverständlich auf der einen Seite ganz generell die Wortlisten und Kurzgrammatiken von über 300 Sprachen aus dem amerikanischen Bereich (Bd. I), den Inseln im Indischen und Pazifischen Ozean (Bd. II) sowie aus Asien (Bd. III) und Europa (Bd. IV–VI), die Lorenzo Hervás hier zusammenstellte. Auf der anderen Seite aber werden heute allgemein zwei Dinge als seine besondere Leistung auf sprachwissenschaftlichem Gebiet hervorgehoben: Und zwar ist hier erstens seine Klassifikation der amerikanischen Sprachen zu erwähnen, die Theodor Benfey (1869:269) als einen 'nicht unbedeutenden Gewinn für die Wissenschaft' bezeichnet; und als zweites muß mit Benfey (1869:270), Jespersen (1925:4), Thomsen (1927:40), Pedersen (1962:240), Dinneen (1967:179) und Arens (1969:149) nachdrücklich darauf hingewiesen werden, daß Lorenzo Hervás y Panduro nicht nur die Bedeutung des grammatischen Strukturvergleichs für die Beurteilung der Sprachverwandtschaft anerkannte, sondern auch selbst diesen Strukturvergleich schon durchzuführen suchte.

Aus diesem Grunde war er auch an dieser Stelle zusammen mit den übrigen Vorläufern der vergleichenden Grammatik zu würdigen. Leider aber blieb allen diesen Männern von Ludolf über Kraus, Sajnovics und Gyármathi bis zu Hervás der wissenschaftsgeschichtliche Durchbruch ihrer Ideen versagt, wofür — wie Holger Pedersen (1962:240–1) wohl richtig darlegt — mit ausschlaggebend war, daß sie ihre neue Erkenntnis überwiegend auf nicht-indoeuropäische Sprachen angewendet hatten.

II. *Rasmus Kristian Rask*

Wenn Vilhelm Thomsen noch zu Anfang unseres Jahrhunderts darüber klagen mußte, daß der große dänische Sprachforscher Rasmus Kristian Rask (1787–1832) außerhalb seines Vaterlandes 'leider keineswegs nach Verdienst bekannt oder geschätzt' ist (Zitat nach der dt. Übers. durch Hans Pollack, Thomsen 1927:51), so darf man heute sagen, daß sich diese Situation von Grund auf geändert hat. Denn inzwischen ist die Leistung Rasks nicht nur durch Hjelmslevs hervorragende dänische und deutsche Ausgabe seiner *Ausgewählte(n) Abhandlungen* (1932–1937, 3 Bde.) und die ebenfalls von Hjelmslev edierten *Breve fra og til Rasmus Rask* (1941) einem breiteren Kreis bekannt geworden, vielmehr wurde sie auch in mehreren Aufsätzen und wissenschaftsgeschichtlichen Darstellungen ausführlich gewürdigt. Zu nennen wären hier vor allem die *Einleitung* von Holger Pedersen zu der bereits erwähnten Rask-Ausgabe (dt. Fassung Bd. I, 1932:XIII–LXIII), die Untersuchungen von Louis Hjelmslev (1950–1951), Kemp Malone (1952), Marie Bjerrum (1959) und Paul Diderichsen

(1960) sowie etwa die historiographischen Würdigungen bei Jespersen (1925), Agrell (1955), Porzig (1957), Diderichsen (1966), Dinneen (1967), Mounin (1967), Arens (1969), Lockwood (1969), oder Waterman (1970). Dies mag als Beweis genügen, und so soll als letztes Indiz dafür, daß die besondere Bedeutung Rasks für die Entwicklung der Linguistik heute allgemein bekannt ist, nur noch darauf hingewiesen werden, daß er selbstverständlich auch in den sprachwissenschaftlichen Anthologien wie beispielweise der von Winfred Philipp Lehmann (1967) seinen Platz gefunden hat.

Über die einzelnen Lebensdaten und das umfangreiche Werk dieses äußerst produktiven Mannes informieren wohl immer noch am besten die von Louis Hjelmslev besorgte Ausgabe seiner *Ausgewählte(n) Abhandlungen* (1932–1937) mit den darin enthaltenen Einleitungen und der umfangreichen Bibliographie der Schriften Rasks sowie der biographische Artikel "Rasmus Rask" von Kristian Sandfeld (1940) und die *Breve fra og til Rasmus Rask* (1941) mit dem erst jüngst erschienenen Ergänzungsband von Marie Bjerrum, der u.a. auf den Seiten 515–93 sämtliche Manuskripte Rasks verzeichnet. Daneben sind aber auch die Darstellungen von Rudolf von Raumer (1870:470–86) und Kemp Malone (1952) nicht zu vergessen, die wenigstens die wichtigsten Stationen im Leben Rasks verfolgen. Doch selbst auf alle dort erwähnten Punkte näher einzugehen, würde den Rahmen unseres Berichtes sprengen, und daher seien lediglich derjenigen Schrift einige Bemerkungen gewidmet, die auch Rask selber als sein Hauptwerk ansah.

Wie Johann Gottfried Herders berühmte Abhandlung *Über den Ursprung der Sprache* war diese Schrift ebenfalls als Antwort auf eine Preisfrage entstanden, und zwar hatte die Königlich Dänische Gesellschaft der Wissenschaften die Aufgabe gestellt: 'Mit historischer Kritik zu untersuchen und mit passenden Beispielen zu erläutern, aus welcher Quelle die alte skandinavische Sprache am sichersten hergeleitet werden kann; den Charakter der Sprache und das Verhältnis anzugeben, worin sie seit den älteren Zeiten und während des Mittelalters teils zu nordischen, teils zu germanischen Dialekten gestanden hat; und die Grundsätze genau zu bestimmen, worauf alle Herleitung und Vergleichung in diesen Sprachen aufgebaut werden muß' (Pedersen 1932:XVI–XVII). Seine Lösung mit dem Titel *Undersøgelse om det gamle Nordiske eller Islandske Sprogs Oprindelse* hatte Rask zwar schon im Jahre 1814 der Gesellschaft der Wissenschaften in Kopenhagen zugeschickt, doch konnte dieses Buch, obwohl es den ausgesetzten Preis errang, erst vier Jahre darauf erscheinen. Dieser Verzögerung aber ist es zuzuschreiben, daß Rask zur damaligen Zeit nicht der Ruhm zuteil wurde, der seiner Leistung eigentlich gebührte. Denn bereits im Jahre 1816, also genau zwei Jahre vor der endgültigen Veröffentlichung seiner *Undersøgelse...*, war zu Frankfurt die epochemachende Arbeit *Über das Conjugationssystem der Sanskritsprache in Vergleichung mit jenem der griechischen, lateinischen, persischen und germanischen Sprache. Nebst Episoden des Ramajan und Mahabharat in genauen metrischen Übersetzungen aus dem Originaltexte und einigen Abschnitten aus den Veda's* von Franz Bopp (1791–1867) erschienen. Und da Franz Bopp hier das Problem der Sprachverwandtschaft nicht nur methodisch ähnlich wie

Rask angegangen, sondern über ihn hinaus auch das Sanskrit miteinbezogen hatte, war so manches von Rasks ursprünglich neuen Ideen und Ergebnissen bei seinem Bekanntwerden beinahe schon veraltet (vgl. dazu Pedersen 1932:XV). Zudem hat noch der Umstand, daß Rasks Preisschrift in Dänisch und nicht in einer bekannteren Sprache abgefaßt war, ihrer weiteren Verbreitung sehr geschadet, und da auch die spätere deutsche Übersetzung durch Johann Severin Vater im Jahre 1822 allein den Teil der *Undersøgelse* enthielt, der dem 'Thrakischen' (d.h. dem Lateinischen und Griechischen) gewidmet war, waren die im ersten Teil enthaltenen wichtigen theoretischen Gedanken sogar weithin unbekannt geblieben. Heutzutage wird dieses Werk, mit dessen Inhalt sich etwa v. Raumer (1870:481–5), Jespersen (1925:19–21), Thomsen (1927:45–8), Agrell (1955:37–9; 45–8), Pedersen (1932 sowie 1962:248–54), Diderichsen (1960; 1966) und Jankowsky (1972:62–76) ausführlich auseinandersetzen, jedoch zu Recht als ein wichtiger Grundstein der vergleichenden indoeuropäischen Sprachwissenschaft betrachtet. Denn wenn Rask auch im einzelnen bei seiner Untersuchung zahlreiche Fehler unterlaufen sind, so hat er doch zwei Dinge klar herausgestellt, die für die weitere Entwicklung der Linguistik sehr bedeutsam waren.

Als erstes ist hier, wie es in der neueren Literatur auch allgemein geschieht, auf eine Stelle hinzuweisen, an der Rask sich zur Methode der Sprachvergleichung äußert. In dieser Passage, die in der Einleitung zu seiner Preisschrift steht und die vor manchen Historiographen wie etwa Pedersen (1932:XXXVI; 1962:250–1), Mounin (1967:165), Arens (1969:192) und Jankowsky (1972:68–9) sogar wortgetreu zitiert wird, legt er nämlich ausführlich dar, daß die lexikalische Übereinstimmung als Kriterium der Sprachverwandtschaft höchst unzuverlässig sei und man in erster Linie das grammatische System vergleichen müsse, um zu haltbaren Ergebnissen zu kommen. Denn während einzelne Wörter sehr oft aus einer Sprache in die andere übernommen würden, geschehe dies mit den grammatischen Formen äußerst selten.

Dieser Erkenntnis waren wir zwar auch schon im vergangenen Kapitel bei Ludolf, Kraus, Sajnovics, Gyármathi und Hervás begegnet. Aber noch nirgendwo war sie so systematisch auf die Untersuchung aller damals wissenschaftlich zugänglichen Sprachen angewendet worden wie bei Rask, der hier bei der Suche nach dem Ursprung des Altnordischen auf die besondere Bedeutung der Grammatik — d.h. vor allem: der Flexion — gestoßen war und auf dieser Basis eine für die damalige Zeit hervorragend genaue vergleichende Grammatik des Germanischen, Slavischen, Litauischen, Lateinischen und Griechischen geschrieben hatte.

Das zweite große Verdienst von Rasmus Kristian Rask ist gleichsam als komplementäres Gegenstück zu seiner erstgenannten Einsicht zu verstehen. Nach seinen Ausführungen über die Bedeutung der Flexion weist er nämlich darauf hin, daß es außer der grammatischen Übereinstimmung noch ein anderes Kennzeichen der Sprachverwandtschaft gibt, indem er sagt: 'Eine Sprache, wie gemischt sie auch sein mag, gehört zu demselben Sprachzweig wie eine andere, wenn sie die wesentlichsten, sinnlichsten, unentbehrlichsten und ersten Wörter, das Fundament der Sprache, mit ihr gemeinsam hat.' Und ein wenig später fährt er fort: 'Wenn es in dergleichen Wörtern Übereinstimmungen zwischen zwei Sprachen gibt, und zwar so viele, dass man Regeln für die Buchstabenübergänge von der einen in die andere herausfinden kann, dann gibt es eine Grundverwandtschaft zwischen diesen Sprachen; besonders wenn die Ähnlichkeiten im Bau und System der Sprache dem entsprechen' (dt. Übersetzung nach H. Pedersen 1932:XXXVI–XXXVII). Diese Ausdrucksweise ist zwar nicht ganz modern — zumal in der damals allerdings auch bei Franz Bopp und Jacob Grimm üblichen Verwendung des Wortes BUCHSTABE in der Bedeutung 'Laut' —, doch wird ohne weiteres ersichtlich, daß Rasmus Kristian Rask neben der Ähnlichkeit in der grammatischen Struktur auch die lautgesetzliche Übereinstimmung im zentralen Wortschatz als Beweis für eine Sprachverwandtschaft ansieht.

Welche Entdeckungen im einzelnen hinter dieser Einsicht stecken, ist sehr ausführlich von v. Raumer (1870:507–20), Pedersen (1932:XXXVI–LV; 1962:252–3), Porzig (1957:325–6), Arens (1969:192–3) u.a. gewürdigt worden. Daher brauchen wir an dieser Stelle lediglich darauf hinzuweisen, daß Rask bei seiner Untersuchung im Grunde schon auf das Gesetz der ERSTEN oder auch GERMANISCHEN LAUTVERSCHIEBUNG stieß, nach dem beim Übergang vom Indoeuropäischen zum Germanischen anlautende Tenues zu Spirantes, Mediae aspiratae zu Mediae und Mediae zu Tenues werden (vgl. Iordan 1962:17 und zur Entdeckungsgeschichte der Lautverschiebung besonders die eingehende Darstellung von Jan Agrell, 1955). Allerdings hat er selbst — wie schon v. Raumer (1870:512–4) nachwies und sogar Rasks Landsmann Vilhelm Thomson (1927:59–60) zugesteht — die große historische Bedeutung und Tragweite der Lautverschiebung nicht erkannt. Das sollte Jacob Grimm (1785–1863) vorbehalten bleiben, nach dem denn auch noch heute die germanische Lautverscheibung im angelsächsischen Bereich sehr häufig als GRIMM'S LAW bezeichnet wird.

Da Jacob Grimm jedoch unzweifelhaft auf den Entdeckungen Rasks aufbaut — man vergleiche hier vor allem v. Raumer (1870:507–20), Bjerrum (1959:161–9), Jankowsky (1972:61–73) sowie Elmer H. Antonsens Abhandlung *Rasmus Rask and Jacob Grimm: Their relationship in the investigation of Germanic vocalism* (1962) — war Rask in dem Bereich der Lautverschiebung eine wesentlich größere Wirkung vergönnt als auf dem Gebiete des grammatischen Strukturvergleichs. Dort war er, wie wir ja bereits gesehen haben, von Bopp überrundet worden, der das für die Sprachvergleichung so bedeutsame Sanskrit in seine Untersuchung einbezogen hatte. Aber so nachteilig es sich im einzelnen auch ausgewirkt hat, daß Rasmus Kristian Rask zu der Zeit, da er seine *Undersøgelse* verfaßte, das Sanskrit nicht kannte, so darf doch auf der anderen Seite mit Jespersen (1925:37), Thomsen (1927:48) und Jankowsky (1972:61) in diesem Umstand der endgültige Beweis dafür gesehen werden, daß man auch ohne Kenntnis des Sanskrit die richtige Methode der Sprachvergleichung finden konnte.

Ein Bericht über die wissenschaftsgeschichtliche Einordnung der Leistung Rasks wäre freilich unvollständig, wenn man (abgesehen von seinen Untersuchungen zum

Dänischen (Bjerrum 1959) oder seinen bedeutenden Erkenntnissen über das Zendavesta, die finnisch-ugrischen Sprachen usw.) nicht auch einen Punkt hervorhöbe, dem Hjelmslev (1950–1951) sein besonderes Augenmerk gewidmet hat und den auch Mounin (1967:166–8) jetzt stark betont. Und zwar ist dies die Tatsache, daß Rask — wie sein unter dem Titel *Leçon sur la philosophie de langage* (Ausgewählte Abhandlungen, Bd. II) veröffentlichtes Manuskript recht deutlich zeigt — hinter den nackten sprachlichen Einzelfakten immer das Sprachsystem im Auge hatte und daß ihm wohl als höchstes Ziel seines Bemühens eine Grammaire générale vorschwebte, die jedoch nicht wie bisher auf apriorischer Philosophie beruhen, sondern auf empirisch gewonnenen Daten aufgebaut sein sollte.

III. *Die vergleichende Sprachwissenschaft nach der Entdeckung des Sanskrit*

1. *Erste Sanskritkenntnisse*

Trotz der bewundernswerten Leistung Rasks hat die Epoche der vergleichenden Indogermanistik aber erst mit dem Erscheinen von Franz Bopps *Conjugationssystem* begonnen. Und das liegt weniger an der verspäteten Publikation des Raskschen Werkes als daran, daß Franz Bopp als erster das Sanskrit systematisch für die Sprachvergleichung nutzte, das aufgrund seines hohen Alters natürlich eine ganz andere Bedeutung für die Einsicht in das ursprüngliche indoeuropäische Flexionssystem besaß als die von Rask herangezogenen Sprachen. Doch bevor wir uns genauer mit der Historiographie Franz Bopps befassen, ist — so wie auch Theodor Benfey (1869) oder Vilhelm Thomsen (1927:52–53) ganz zu Recht verfahren — noch kurz auf diejenigen Männer hinzuweisen, die überhaupt die Kenntnis des Sanskrit nach Europa brachten.

Über diese Wegbereiter der Sanskritphilologie informieren recht ausführlich Ernst Windisch in seinem zweiteiligen Buch *Geschichte der Sanskrit-Philologie und indischen Altertumskunde* (1917–1920:1–22) und vor diesem schon Theodor Benfey in dem Kapitel *Beachtung des Sanskrit durch die Europäer bis zur Einführung desselben in die deutsche Wissenschaft* (1869:333–357) sowie Max Müller in seinem bekannten Werk *Science of language* (1891; deutsche Übersetzung durch R. Fick und W. Wischmann: *Die Wissenschaft der Sprache*, 1892-1893).

Max Müller (1892-1893, I:196ff.) hat dabei eine gewisse Kenntnis des Sanskrit bis zu dem spanischen Basken Francisco de Yasu y Xavier (1506–1552) zurückverfolgen können, der im Jahre 1542 als jesuitischer Missionar nach Goa (Ostindien) kam und in der christlichen Welt im allgemeinen als Franciscus Xaverius bekannt ist. Ansonsten wird dann in der Regel (vgl. Benfey 1869:222–223, 333; Windisch 1917–1920:6; Bonfante 1954:686–7; Robins 1967:135; Arens 1969:73; Lockwood 1969:22) auf den Florentiner Kaufmann Filippo Sassetti hingewiesen, der von 1583 bis 1588 in Indien weilte und in seinen — allerdings erst 1855 in Florenz veröffentlichten — *Lettere* darauf aufmerksam machte, daß das Sanskrit manche Wörter mit dem Italienischen gemeinsam habe wie etwa die Zahlwörter für 6, 7, 8 und 9.

Etwas tiefer in die altindische Gelehrtensprache einzudringen ist aber erst über hundert Jahre später einigen Missionaren gelungen, die trotz aller Schwierigkeiten Kontakt zu den Brahmanen, den Pflegern und Erhaltern der alten Literatur, gewonnen hatten. Unter diesen Männern sind nun vor allem vier hervorzuheben:

1. der deutsche Jesuit Johann Ernst Hanxleden (1680–1732), der nicht nur ein malabarisch-sanskrit-portugiesisches Wörterbuch mit dem Titel *Dictionarium Malabaricum Samscridamicum Lusitanum* verfaßte, sondern nach Theodor Benfey (1869: 335) auch der erste Europäer war, der eine Sanskrit-Grammatik schrieb. Beides ist zwar Manuskript geblieben, wurde aber später von dem Karmeliten Philipp Weszdin (1748–1806), der den Ordensnamen Paulinus a Sancto Bartholomaeo trug, verwertet (vgl. dazu Windisch 1917–1920:20–22).

2. der Missionar Benjamin Schultze, der im Jahre 1725 erneut die Zahlwörter des Sanskrit mit lateinischen, griechischen und deutschen Zahlwörtern verglich.

3. der ehemals französische Mönch und spätere Bibliothekar und Antiquar am preußischen Hofe Maturin Veyssiere La Croze (1661–1739), der Theodor Benfey (1869:339) zufolge 'der erste war, der die Verwandtschaft des Altindischen mit dem Persischen andeutete' (so auch Bonfante 1954:696).

Als letzter dieser Reihe wäre dann noch der französische Jesuit G. L. Cœurdoux zu erwähnen, der ebenfalls die Ähnlichkeit zwischen Sanskrit, Griechisch und Latein bemerkte und in einem Briefe aus dem Jahre 1767 eine umfangreiche Liste derartiger Wortgleichungen aufgestellt hat. Nach dem Bericht Theodor Benfeys (1869:341) soll Cœurdoux in diesem Schreiben, das an die Pariser Académie des Inscriptions et Belles-Lettres weitergeleitet werden sollte und dort auch in Jahre 1768 vorgelesen wurde, bereits ausdrücklich darauf hingewiesen haben, daß als Ursache für diese Ähnlichkeit der Sprachen die 'ursprüngliche Verwandtschaft der Inder, Griechen und Lateiner' anzusehen sei. Zufolge dieser These, der übrigens Ernst Windisch (1917–1920:24, Anm. 1) vorbehaltlos zustimmt und die auch Bonfante (1954:696) noch vertritt, wäre in der Tat Cœurdoux — und nicht erst William Jones (1746–1794) — der erste, der den wahren Grund für die große Ähnlichkeit zwischen Sanskrit, Latein, und Griechisch angesprochen hätte. Doch wie Franklin Edgerton in einem Aufsatz aus dem Jahre 1946 nachgewiesen hat und neuerdings auch W. B. Lockwood (1969:22) richtig darlegt, hat Cœurdoux an die Akademie die Anfrage gerichtet, wie die auffällige Ähnlichkeit in Grammatik und Vokabular der betreffenden drei Sprachen zu erklären sei. Und dabei hat er lediglich als eigenen Lösungsvorschlag kundgetan, daß erstens nach der babylonischen Sprachverwirrung auch den neuentstandenen Sprachen einige Wörter gemeinsam blieben und zum zweiten die damaligen Völkerstämme vor ihrer endgültigen Trennung noch eine Zeitlang in Verbindung standen, so daß sich ihre Sprachen außerdem vermischten.

Diese Kombination von mythologischer Deutung und Annahme von Lehnbeziehungen kann wirklich nicht als Hinweis auf einen gemeinsamen Sprachursprung oder eine nähere Verwandtschaft des Griechischen, Lateinischen und Sanskrit angesehen werden, und so sind Benfey, Windisch und Bonfante einem Irrtum unterlegen, wenn sie schon Cœurdoux diese bedeutende Erkenntnis zuerkennen wollen.

Dessen ungeachtet ist Cœurdoux' Brief wegen seiner vielen zutreffenden Wortgleichungen, zu denen sogar schon die Gegenüberstellung des Indikativs und Konjunktivs Praesens von skr. *ásmi* 'ich bin' mit den entsprechenden lateinischen Formen gehörte, äußerst wertvoll. Aber unglücklicherweise wurde dieses Schreiben erst im Jahre 1808 gedruckt, und da hatte das Sanskrit bereits Eingang in die Wissenschaft gefunden.

Daß es dazu kam, ist jedoch weniger den Missionaren zu verdanken, deren Erkenntnisse bei der gelehrten Welt Europas kaum Beachtung fanden, als — wie Theodor Benfey (1869:341) zutreffend sagt — 'dem Handel und ... dem Rechtsgefühl' der Briten. Im Laufe des 18. Jahrhunderts gelang es nämlich der von englischen Kaufleuten gegründeten East India Company, in Indien fester Fuß zu fassen und dieses Land nach und nach in englischen Besitz zu bringen. Dabei war man jedoch bestrebt, für die Inder eine Rechtsprechung zu schaffen, die auf deren eigenen Gesetzen aufgebaut war, und so kam es, daß auf Veranlassung des Generalgouverneurs Warren Hastings (1732–1818) schließlich elf gebildete Brahmanen, sogenannte Pandits also, aus Sanskrittexten ein Werk über das indische Recht zusammenstellten. Da jedoch niemand in England das Sanskrit beherrschte und die Verfasser der Gesetzessammlung sich strikt weigerten, einen Ausländer in ihre heilige Sprache einzuweihen, wurde dieses Buch zunächst ins Persische übertragen und erst dann von Nathaniel Brassey Halhed (1751–1830) ins Englische übersetzt. In dieser Fassung erschien es schließlich im Jahre 1776 in London mit dem Titel *A code of Gentoo laws, or, Ordinations of the pundits, from a Persian translation, made from the original, written in the Shanscrit language*.

Nach dem sicher zutreffenden Urteil von Ernst Windisch (1917–1920:19–20) hat zwar auch dieses Buch noch nicht unmittelbar auf die Entwicklung der Sanskritphilologie gewirkt, doch es hat ihr gleichsam den Weg geebnet. Denn auf der einen Seite hat es, zumal es im Jahre 1778 auch in französischer und deutscher Version erschien und in seiner Einleitung zudem schon einige genauere Angaben über das Sanskrit und dessen Literatur enthalten waren, das Interesse an der altindischen Sprache und Kultur gefördert. Und auf der anderen Seite war es Nathaniel Brassey Halhed kurz nach dem Abschluß seiner Übersetzung doch noch gelungen, einen etwas liberaleren Brahmanen als Sanskritlehrer zu gewinnen, und damit 'scheint' — wie Theodor Benfey (1869:344) formuliert — 'das Eis gebrochen'. Bald nachdem Halhed in Bengalen eine nähere Kenntnis des Sanskrit erworben hatte, wovon u.a. die Vorrede zu seiner 1778 publizierten *A grammar of the Bengal language* zeugt (vgl. dazu Benfey 1869:344, Arens 1969:146, Jankowsky 1972:27), gelang es nämlich auch den Männern, sich mit dem Sanskrit vertraut zu machen, deren Werk den endgültigen Grundstock für die neue Wissenschaft der Sanskritphilologie und indischen Altertumskunde legen sollte. Es sind dies die drei Engländer Charles (später Sir Charles) Wilkins, Sir William Jones und Henry Thomas Colebrooke.

2. *Begründung der Sanskritphilologie durch Sir Charles Wilkins, Sir William Jones, und Henry Thomas Colebrooke*

Sir Charles Wilkins (1750–1833), der als erster der drei Genannten im Dienste der East India Company nach Indien kam, lernte Sanskrit im Zentrum der brahmanischen Gelehrsamkeit, nämlich in der alten, am Ganges gelegenen Tempelstadt Benares, und wurde später von Sir William Jones, Henry Thomas Colebrooke, und vielen anderen (vgl. Windisch 1917–1920:23 mit Anm. 1) als der erste Europäer angesehen, der diese Sprache in der Tat beherrschte. Von seinen bei Theodor Benfey (1869:345) angeführten Werken ist am bekanntesten die Übersetzung der Bhagavadgitā *The Bhăgvăt-Gēētā or dialogues of Krēēshnă and Ărjŏŏn in eighteen lectures, with notes, translated from the original in the Sănskrēēt or ancient language of the Brăhmăns*, die 1785 in London erschien und bereits im selben Jahr in russischer, 1787 in französischer und 1801 in deutscher Sprache auf den Markt kam. Dieses Buch, das nach den Worten August Wilhelm von Schlegels (1767–1845) 'das schönste, ja vielleicht das einzig wahrhafte philosophische Gedicht' enthält, 'das alle uns bekannte Literaturen aufzuweisen haben' (Indische Bibliothek 2, 1827:219), erregte überall sehr großes Interesse und trug so viel zu dem Bekanntwerden der altindischen Schriften in Europa bei. Darüberhinaus werden als besonderes Verdienst von Wilkins aber auch noch ein 1815 publiziertes Verzeichnis von Sanskritwurzeln erwähnt sowie vor allen Dingen die Sanskritgrammatik, die er 1808 in London drucken ließ und die unter anderem die deutschen Sanskritisten Othmar Frank (1770–1830), August Wilhelm von Schlegel und Franz Bopp benutzten.

Wesentlich bedeutsamer für die Kenntnis des Sanskrit und die später einsetzende komparative Linguistik war jedoch die Tätigkeit Sir William Jones' (1746–1794). Dieser Mann, über dessen Werk und Leben nicht nur sein Freund und Biograph Lord Teignmouth (Jones 1807:Bd. I und II), sondern in neuerer Zeit auch etwa Franklin Edgerton (1946) sowie Garland H. Cannon (1952 und 1964) ausführlich berichten, kam im Jahre 1783 als Oberrichter nach Kalkutta. Da er äußerst sprachbegabt war — seinem eigenen bei Lord Teignmouth (Jones 1807:Bd. II, 264) überlieferten Zeugnis zufolge beherrschte er an seinem Lebensende 28 Sprachen — und zudem die Kenntnis der altindische Gelehrtensprache für seinen Beruf als Richter für sehr nützlich hielt, vertiefte er sich einige Zeit nach seiner Ankunft auch in das Sanskrit. Genau genommen begann er damit im Spätsommer des Jahres 1785, und schon knapp ein halbes Jahr darauf hielt er am 2. Februar 1786 vor der von ihm gegründeten "Asiatick Society" (von 1839 an hieß diese Gesellschaft "Asiatic Society of Bengal") seine berühmte Rede *On the Hindus*, die die so häufig zitierte Äußerung enthält:

The Sanscrit language, whatever be its antiquity, is of a wonderful structure; more perfect than the Greek, more copious than the Latin, and more exquisitely refined than either, yet bearing to both of them a stronger affinity, both in the roots of verbs and in the forms of grammar, than could possibly have been produced by accident; so strong indeed, that no philologer could examine them all three, without believing them to have sprung from some common source, which, perhaps, no longer exists: there is a similar reason, though not quite so forcible, for supposing that both the Gothick and the Celtick, though blended with a very different idiom, had the same origin with the Sanscrit; and the old Persian might be added to the same family, if this were the place for discussing any question concerning the antiquities of Persia (1788 b: 422–3).

Nun wendet sich zwar Cannon in dem Aufsatz "Sir William Jones's Persian linguistics" (1958) mit gutem Grund dagegen, daß man in wissenschaftsgeschichtlichen Darstellungen die Leistung Jones' auf seine hervorragenden Übersetzungen, das in der Abhandlung *A dissertation on the orthography of Asiatick words in Roman letters* (1788a) vorgestellte System der Transliteration des Sanskritalphabetes und die eben angeführten Sätze reduziert. Aber da wir hier ausschließlich die Entwicklungslinie der komparativen Linguistik aufzuzeigen suchen, müssen wir uns an dieser Stelle ebenfalls auf die Beobachtungen Jones' bezüglich des Sanskrit beschränken. Zu weiteren Informationen sei daher einerseits verwiesen auf die von Anna Maria Jones besorgte und mit der bereits erwähnten Biographie versehene dreizehnbändige Gesamtausgabe der Werke William Jones' (1807) sowie *The letters of Sir William Jones* von Garland Cannon (1970), und andererseits vor allem auf die Darstellungen von Chatterji (1948) und Cannon (1952; 1958; 1964) und auf das sehr instruktive Kapitel "Sir William Jones and the new philology" von Aarsleff (1967:115–61).

Doch kehren wir zurück zu den zitierten Sätzen aus der Rede *On the Hindus*, die in der wissenschaftsgeschichtlichen Literatur von Benfey (1869:348) über Jespersen (1925:15) und Thomsen (1927:52) bis hin zu Mounin (1967:156–7), Arens (1969:147), Lockwood (1969:22), Waterman (1970:16) und Jankowsky (1972:25–6) immer wieder in Übersetzung oder originalem Wortlaut ausgeschrieben werden. Die ungewöhnlich große Aufmerksamkeit, die man diesem Texte widmet, läßt schon auf seine hervorragende Bedeutung schließen. Und in der Tat wird in ihm erstmals klar und deutlich die für die spätere Indogermanistik grundlegende Erkenntnis ausgesprochen, daß das Sanskrit mit dem Lateinischen und Griechischen, ja, wahrscheinlich auch mit dem Gotischen, Keltischen und Persischen verwandt ist. Jones spricht sogar von einer gemeinsamen Ursprache ('some common source'), die vielleicht schon nicht mehr existiert, auf die aber die genannten Sprachen zurückzuführen seien, und gleichsam im Vorgriff auf Rasmus Kristian Rask nennt er als Kriterien für die Beurteilung der Sprachverwandtschaft die Übereinstimmung in 'the roots of verbs and in the forms of grammar'. Daher ist es nicht zu hoch gegriffen, wenn Hans Aarsleff (1967: 134) die hier umrissenen Gedanken einer historischen, vergleichenden und strukturbezogenen Sprachbetrachtung 'a revolution in the study of language' nennt.

Leider hat Sir William Jones diese Gedanken nicht weiter entwickeln können, doch hat — wie auch schon Alfred Master in dem Aufsatz "The influence of Sir William Jones upon Sanskrit studies" (1946) deutlich machte — Jones' Erkenntnis über das Sanskrit wie überhaupt dessen Begeisterung für die altindische Kultur und Sprache den weiteren Gang der Linguistik nachhaltig beeinflußt.

Unmittelbar nach dem Tode William Jones' veröffentlichte Henry Thomas Colebrooke (1765–1837), der anfangs als Verwaltungsbeamter, dann als Richter und später als 'Professor of the Sanscrit Language' am College von Fort William in Indien tätig war, seinen ersten Essay im vierten Band der von Sir William Jones begründeten *Asiatick Researches* (1799). In dieser Abhandlung, die den Titel "On the duties of a faithful Hindu widow" trug, befaßte er sich mehr mit kulturell-religiösen Dingen wie der Witwenverbrennung, doch wandte er sich auch sehr intensiv der Sprache zu. So erschien im Jahre 1803 im siebten Band derselben Reihe sein Aufsatz "On the Sanscrit and Pracrit languages", in dem er einen Überblick über die grammatische Literatur zum Sanskrit, insbesondere über das System Pāṇinis, gibt und in dem er auch die einheimische Lexikographie behandelt. Als weitere Früchte dieser Arbeit sind dann später *A grammar of the Sanscrit language* (1805) sowie die Herausgabe des lexikographischen Werkes *Amarasiṃha-Cósha, or, dictionary of the Sanscrit language, with an English interpretation and annotations* (1808) und der berühmten Grammatik des Pāṇini (1810) gefolgt, wodurch dann die Sanskritphilologie endlich auf einen sicheren Boden gestellt wurde. Dies war aber auch für die weiteren Forschungen auf dem Gebiet des Sprachvergleichs von nicht gering zu achtender Bedeutung, und daher schien uns dieser kurze Hinweis auf Henry Thomas Colebrooke unumgänglich, obwohl er bei den meisten linguistisch orientierten Historiographen keinerlei Erwähnung findet.

3. *Johann Christoph Adelung*

Johann Christoph Adelung (1732–1806), über dessen Lebenslauf der erste Teil der Dissertation von Karl-Ernst Sickel (1933:7–98) ein anschauliches Bild vermittelt, ist vor allem bekannt geworden durch sein Wirken auf dem Gebiet der deutschen Grammatik und des deutschen Wörterbuches sowie durch seine große Polyglottensammlung *Mithridates oder allgemeine Sprachenkunde mit dem Vater Unser als Sprachprobe in bey nahe fünfhundert Sprachen und Mundarten* (Berlin 1806–1817, 4 Bde.). Da uns im Augenblick jedoch nur seine Leistung innerhalb der komparativen Linguistik interessiert, wollen wir an dieser Stelle lediglich auf den *Mithridates* etwas näher eingehen und Adelungs Wirken im Bereiche der Grammatik und des Wörterbuches dann in Zusammenhang mit Jacob Grimm behandeln.

Ganz allgemein betrachtet gehört der *Mithridates*, von dem Adelung selbst nur noch den ersten Band vollenden konnte und dessen weitere Ausarbeitung in den Händen Johann Severin Vaters (1771–1826) lag, in die Reihe der von Leibniz angeregten und von Peter Simon Pallas sowie Lorenzo Hervás y Panduro verwirklichten Universalglossare. Ebenso wie diese beiden Werke ist er nach geographischen Gesichtspunkten geordnet, und auch in dem Ziel, mit Hilfe der Sprachvergleichung das gegenseitige Verhältnis der Völker, ihre Herkunft und ihre Verwandtschaft zu ergründen, steht er diesen nahe. Aber weniger die Einzelheiten seines Aufbaus oder seine speziellen Vorzüge und Fehler, auf die Theodor Benfey (1869:271–81, 354–6), O. Schrader (1906:3–7), Vilhelm Thomsen (1927:40–2), Hans Arens (1969:150–2) und Kurt R. Jankowsky (1972:34–5) näher eingehen, sollen hier betrachtet werden, als die aus ihm hervorgehende Ansicht Adelungs über die Kriterien des Sprachvergleichs und die Sprachverwandtschaft.

In diesen beiden Fragen nimmt der *Mithridates* jedoch eine eigenartig zwielichtige Stellung ein, denn wie Hans Arens (1969:149) innerhalb seines allgemeinen Urteils über Adelung treffend formuliert, stehen auch dort 'vernünftige Ansichten, richtige Bemerkungen, flüchtige Ahnungen und rückständige Meinungen ... nebeneinander'. So äußert Adelung einerseits in der Vorrede des ersten Bandes (1806:VIII) ernsthafte Bedenken dagegen, daß man einen Sprachvergleich lediglich aufgrund einzelner Wortsammlungen durchführt, während er andrerseits — was denn auch Vilhelm Thomsen (1927:41–2) und Hans Arens (1969:150) zu Recht monieren — in seinem Werke selbst kaum mehr als eine Zusammenstellung einzelner Wörter bietet. Denn wenn er in den meisten Fällen auch den Text des *Vater Unser* als 'Sprachprobe' hinzufügt, so geht er bei der Sprachvergleichung doch in erster Linie von Einzelwörtern und eben nicht von diesem Texte aus.

Desweiteren hat Adelung zwar bereits im Jahre 1781 (also noch vor Christian Jacob Kraus) an einer bei Hans Arens (1969:149–50) und Kurt R. Jankowsky (1972:33) zitierten Stelle seiner Schrift *Über den Ursprung der Sprachen und den Bau der Wörter, besonders der Deutschen. Ein Versuch* auf die Bedeutung der grammatischen Struktur für die Beurteilung der Sprachverwandtschaft hingewiesen, aber dennoch ist in seinem *Mithridates* von dieser Einsicht kaum etwas zu spüren.

Ähnlich widersprüchlich sind auch Adelungs Ansichten über die indogermanische Sprachverwandtschaft bzw. über die Gründe, die zu der großen Ähnlichkeit der indogermanischen Sprachen geführt haben. Hier macht z.B. Schrader (1906:6–7) darauf aufmerksam, daß Adelung in seiner *Älteste(n) Geschichte der Deutschen, ihrer Sprache und Literatur, bis zur Völkerwanderung* (Leipzig 1806:350) die 'deutschen Bestandtheile im Persischen' auf eine Sprachmischung zurückführt, die zur Zeit der Völkerwanderung (der Goten) stattgefunden habe, während er in dem im gleichen Jahr erschienenen *Mithridates* (Bd. I, 279) die wesentlich richtigere Hypothese äußert, die Perser und Germanen hätten vielleicht 'gleichzeitig aus einer und derselben Sprachquelle geschöpft'.

Schrader findet diese Differenz 'sehr merkwürdig', doch ist sie mit Rudolf von Raumer (1870:240) wohl dadurch zu erklären, daß zwischen der Veröffentlichung und der Ausarbeitung der *Älteste(n) Geschichte* ... etwa zehn Jahre lagen und Johann Christoph Adelung in dieser Zeit Bekanntschaft mit dem Sanskrit machte. Adelung selbst hat diese Sprache zwar nicht mehr erlernt, aber aus zweiter Hand stellt er im *Mithridates* (Bd. I, 149ff.) eine ganze Reihe von Sanskritwörtern zusammen, die er mit zahlreichen Wörtern anderer Sprachen verbindet. Und aufgrund dieses Vergleiches kommt er zu dem Ergebnis, daß die Ursache für die Übereinstimmung so vieler Wörter innerhalb dieser Sprachen nur darin liegen kann, daß 'alle diese Völker bei ihrem Entstehen und vor ihrer Absonderung zu einem gemeinschaftlichen Stamme gehöret haben'.

So ist denn Adelung in der Tat durch die Entdeckung des Sanskrit bei seinem eigenen Versuch, die Ähnlichkeit der indoeuropäischen Sprachen zu erklären, ein Stück vorangekommen. Dies müssen wir als unbestreitbares Faktum anerkennen;

doch darf man auf der anderen Seite nicht so weit wie Schrader (1906:7) gehen und behaupten, Adelung habe demnach kurz vor seinem Tode 'zu demselben Resultat' gefunden wie Sir William Jones in seiner denkwürdigen Rede aus dem Jahre 1786. Denn im Gegensatz zu Jones, der ja als Grundlage des Sprachvergleichs 'the roots of verbs and ... forms of grammar' angab und auch nur wirklich verwandte Sprachen mit dem Sanskrit in Verbindung brachte, hat Adelung mangels zuverlässiger Kriterien für die Beurteilung der Sprachverwandtschaft auch Sprachen wie Hebräisch, Syrisch, Türkisch, Ungarisch und Finnisch mit dem Sanskrit verbunden, die ganz außerhalb der indoeuropäischen Sprachfamilie stehen.

Infolgedessen erscheint auch nicht das eben angeführte Urteil Schraders angemessen, sondern eher das von Benfey (1869:355), der die Ansicht Adelungs im Vergleich zu William Jones' Erkenntnis 'einen Rückschritt' nennt.

Schon wenige Jahre später aber sollte ein anderer Deutscher an die Öffentlichkeit treten, der — mit den Werken von Sir William Jones und Sir Charles Wilkins wohlvertraut — nicht nur das Studium des Sanskrit und der altindischen Literatur in hohem Maß gefördert hat, sondern auch die weitere Entwicklung der vergleichenden Grammatik. Sein Name lautet Friedrich von Schlegel.

4. *Die Brüder Schlegel*

Friedrich von Schlegel (1772–1829), der geistreiche, ja geniale Kopf der älteren Romantik, war wie viele seiner Zeitgenossen auf zahlreichen Gebieten tätig. Als die wichtigsten Bereiche seines Schaffens seien an dieser Stelle nur Philosophie, Sprachtheorie, allgemeine Ästhetik sowie die Universal- und Literaturgeschichte angeführt, und wer sich ein genaues Bild von seinem umfangreichen Werk verschaffen möchte, der sei vor allem auf die *Kritische Ausgabe seiner Werke* verwiesen, die Ernst Behler mit großer Sorgfalt vorbereitet hat (vgl. Behler 1957; 1958) und die er seit dem Jahre 1958 unter Mitwirkung von Jean-Jacques Anstett und Hans Eichner herausgibt. Desweiteren geben aber auch die neueren Monographien von Ludwig Wirz (1939), Werner Mettler (1955), Alois Dempf (1958), Heinrich Nüsse (1962) und Eugeniusz Klin (1964; 1971), in denen Friedrich Schlegels philosophische Entwicklung, sein Verhältnis zur klassischen Antike sowie seine Sprach- und Literaturtheorie beschrieben werden und die hier stellvertretend für viele weitere genannt sind, ein eindrucksvolles Zeugnis von dem vielseitigen Denken dieses Mannes. Und da für das bessere Verständnis eines Werkes ebenfalls die Kenntnis der persönlichen Entwicklung und der äußeren Lebensumstände seines Verfassers wichtig ist, wie Thomas A. Sebeok ganz richtig in der Einleitung zu seiner biographischen Anthologie *Portraits of linguists: A biographical source book for the history of western linguistics, 1746–1963* (1966: Bd. I:X) hervorhebt, sei hier auch auf die Darstellungen Rudolf Hayms (1870), C. Enders' (1913) und Heinrich Finkes (1918) hingewiesen sowie besonders auf Ernst Behlers ausgezeichnete Biographie mit dem Titel *Friedrich Schlegel in Selbstzeugnissen und Bilddokumenten* (1966).

Über die Zeit, die uns in unserem Zusammenhang allein interessiert, nämlich die Jahre, in denen Friedrich Schlegel sich mit dem Sanskrit und der Sprachvergleichung auseinandersetzte, gibt neben den älteren Berichten von Theodor Benfey (1869:357–69) und Ernst Windisch (1917–1920:57–8) vor allem das in der Dissertation von Ursula Oppenberg (1965:110–20) enthaltene Kapitel *Die Lebenslage Friedrich Schlegels zur Zeit seiner Sanskritstudien in Selbstzeugnissen, Briefen und zeitgenössischen Dokumenten* Auskunft. Demnach war Friedrich Schlegel Ende Juli 1802 nach Paris gekommen, um dort Interesse für die romantische Literatur und die idealistische Philosophie zu wecken. In der Tat hat er dann auch vor prominentem Kreise Vorlesungen über die neuere deutsche Literatur und Philosophie gehalten, aber schon am 16. September desselben Jahres schrieb er an seinen älteren Bruder August Wilhelm: 'Erlauben meine Verhältnisse mir, so lang hier zu bleiben als es dazu nöthig ist, so denke ich Sanskrit zu lernen, und wenn es dazu nöthig ist, auch Persisch' (vgl. *Friedrich Schlegels Briefe an seinen Bruder August Wilhelm*, hrsg. v. Oskar F. Walzel, Berlin 1890:497).

Wie aus seinen weiteren Briefen deutlich wird, hat er dieses Vorhaben bezüglich des Persischen schon sehr bald durchgeführt, und zwar studierte er diese Sprache bei dem Orientalisten Antoine Léonard de Chézy (1773–1832), der damals noch in der Manuskriptabteilung der Pariser Nationalbibliothek tätig war und später am Collège de France die erste in Frankreich eingerichtete Sanskritprofessur erhielt. Sein Studium der altindischen Gelehrtensprache begann Friedrich Schlegel seinen eigenen Angaben (vgl. *Ueber die Sprache und Weisheit der Indier*, 1808: Vorrede) zufolge dann im Frühjahr bei Alexander Hamilton (1762–1824), einem in Ostindien geborenen Schotten, der durch die napoleonische Kontinentalsperre an seiner Rückkehr nach England gehindert war. Über die besondere Bedeutung, die diesem Mann für die Verbreitung des Sanskrit auf dem europäischen Kontinent und in England zukam, unterrichtet jetzt Rosane Rocher, die in ihrer instruktiven Abhandlung *Alexander Hamilton* (1762–1824): *A chapter in the early history of Sanskrit philology* (1968) das gesamte Leben und Wirken Hamiltons untersucht und dabei eine Reihe verbreiteter Irrtümer berichtigt. Insgesamt gesehen nahm Schlegel nun bei Hamilton etwa ein Jahr lang, und zwar bis zum Ende seines Frankreichaufenthaltes, Unterricht, doch konnte er sich auch in dieser kurzen Zeit keineswegs ununterbrochen und mit ganzer Hingabe dem Sanskrit widmen. Dazu war, wie Ursula (Struc-)Oppenberg (1965:128) und Ernst Behler (1966:94–5) nachdrücklich betonen, seine finanzielle Lage viel zu schlecht. Denn da es ihm trotz seiner vielfältigen Tätigkeiten nicht gelang, in Paris beruflich Fuß zu fassen, war er weiterhin gezwungen, private Vorlesungen abzuhalten. Und diese nahmen ein Großteil seiner Zeit in Anspruch.

Die durch diese mißliche Situation bedingte Kürze seines Sanskritstudiums sowie den Umstand, daß Friedrich von Schlegel der erste Europäer war, der das Sanskrit nicht in dessen Ursprungsland erlernte, muß man aber in Rechnung stellen, wenn man das Werk beurteilt, das Schlegel dann im Jahre 1808 als Frucht seiner Beschäftigung mit dieser Sprache vorgelegt hat.

Der vollständige Titel dieses Buches lautet *Ueber die Sprache und Weisheit der In-*

dier: Ein Beitrag zur Begründung der Alterthumskunde von Friedrich Schlegel. Nebst metrischen Uebersetzungen indischer Gedichte (Heidelberg, 1808). Außer den im Titel erwähnten Übersetzungen aus der Bhagavadgitā, dem Mahābhārata Rāmāyaṇa usw. enthält diese Schrift im einzelnen die drei Teile *Von der Sprache*, *Von der Philosophie* und *Historische Ideen*. Wie aus diesen Überschriften bereits deutlich wird, ist für die Linguistik vor allen Dingen der erste Teil von Interesse, dessen wichtigste Passagen sogar im originären Wortlaut bzw. in englischer Übersetzung in die Textsammlungen von Hans Arens (1969:160–5) und Winfred Philipp Lehmann (1967:23–8) aufgenommen wurden.

Nun würde es zwar zu weit führen, wenn wir auf alle linguistisch bedeutsamen Aspekte dieses Teiles eingehen wollten, doch seien wenigstens diejenigen Gedanken Friedrich Schlegels in knappen Zügen referiert, die nach dem Urteil der heutigen Historiographen auf die weitere Entwicklung der vergleichenden Grammatik großen Einfluß übten.

Als erstes wäre hier die Feststellung der Sprachverwandtschaft zwischen Sanskrit, Griechisch und Lateinisch, Germanisch, Persisch, Keltisch usw. zu erwähnen sowie der Hinweis, daß die Ähnlichkeit der genannten Sprachen nicht bloß auf eine große Zahl von Wortwurzeln beschränkt sei, sondern sich 'bis auf die innerste Struktur und Grammatik' erstrecke. Der zweite fruchtbare Gedanke, der häufig hervorgehoben wird, findet sich dann ein wenig später dort, wo Friedrich Schlegel noch näher auf die Ähnlichkeit der Wurzeln als Kriterium für Sprachverwandtschaft eingeht. Denn an dieser Stelle fordert er zwar einerseits noch ängstlich zum Beweis der Abstammung die 'völlige Gleichheit' des Wortes, doch fährt er fort: 'Freilich wenn sich die Mittelglieder historisch nachweisen lassen, so mag *giorno* von *dies* abgeleitet werden.' Und im folgenden teilt er dann einige 'Buchstaben'-Übergänge vom Lateinischen zum Spanischen bzw. Deutschen mit, worin man ganz zu Recht mit Otto Jespersen (1925:16), Friedrich Kainz (1939:281) und Winfred Philipp Lehmann (1967:22) einen ersten Schritt hin auf die Lautgesetze sehen kann, die einige Zeit danach von Rasmus Kristian Rask und Jacob Grimm gefunden wurden.

Zum dritten aber geht Friedrich von Schlegel, wie Walter Porzig (1957:324) einmal formulierte, noch entschieden 'über die Vergleichung einzelner Wörter und Wortformen hinaus', indem er fordert, daß man zur Feststellung der Sprachverwandtschaft vor allem die grammatische Struktur vergleichen müsse. An der betreffenden, häufig zitierten Stelle heißt es wörtlich: 'Jener entscheidende Punct aber, den hier alles aufhellen wird, ist die innre Structur der Sprachen oder die vergleichende Grammatik, welche uns ganz neue Aufschlüsse über die Genealogie der Sprachen auf ähnliche Weise geben wird, wie die vergleichende Anatomie über die höhere Naturgeschichte Licht verbreidet hat' (1808:28; auch in: Friedrich von Schlegel's sämtliche Werke, Zweite Originalausgabe, VIII., Wien 1846, 291).

Aber nicht nur wegen seiner allgemein gewürdigten Bedeutung für die weitere Entwicklung der komparativen Linguistik haben wir diesen Satz im originalen Wortlaut angeführt, sondern auch, weil die beiden Zentralbegriffe dieses Abschnitts, die

Termini VERGLEICHENDE GRAMMATIK und VERGLEICHENDE ANATOMIE, in der heutigen Literatur recht kontrovers beurteilt werden.

So findet man zum einen — beinahe wie ein Dogma — von Benfey (1869:363) über Jespersen (1925:16), Porzig (1957:324), Nüsse (1962:42), Robins (1967:170), Lehmann (1967:22) und Arens (1969:165) bis hin zu Jankowsky (1972:53) die Ansicht vertreten, der Begriff 'vergleichende Grammatik' sei hier überhaupt zum ersten Mal verwendet worden und somit als eigene Schöpfung Friedrich Schlegels anzusehen. Demgegenüber hat jedoch Hans Aarsleff (1967:157 Anm. 115) darauf hingewiesen, daß dieser Terminus — sogar gesperrt gedruckt — bereits fünf Jahre früher, nämlich im Jahre 1803, in einer Rezension über A. F. Bernhardis *Reine Sprachlehre* erscheint, die Friedrichs älterer Bruder August Wilhelm im 2. Bande der Zeitschrift *Europa* veröffentlicht hatte. Infolgedessen ist die Frage der Priorität wohl eindeutig zu Gunsten August Wilhelms zu entscheiden. Doch wenn man auch die jeweilige Auswirkung bedenkt, d.h. wenn man die Rezeptionsgeschichte des Begriffes mit im Auge hat, dann muß man zugleich zugestehen, daß der Begriff 'vergleichende Grammatik' und die mit ihm verknüpfte Konzeption der Sprachbetrachtung vor allem durch die hier zitierten Ausführungen Friedrich Schlegels weitere Verbreitung fanden und für die Linguistik fruchtbar wurden.

Die zweite Kontroverse betrifft die Interpretation von Schlegels Hinweis auf die Erfolge der vergleichenden Anatomie. Diese Anspielung ist nämlich des öfteren (vgl. etwa Kainz 1939:279, Lehmann 1967:22, Arens 1969:166, Jankowsky 1972:53–5) hervorgehoben und mutatis mutandis so gedeutet worden, als ob Friedrich Schlegel — wie Jankowsky es so plastisch formulierte (1972:54)– hier 'at the dawn of comparative linguistics, had already thought of the necessity for the linguist to follow closely the methods developed and successfully applied by the natural sciences'. Gegen eine derartige Interpretation wendet jedoch Heinrich Nüsse (1962:42) ein, daß sie 'allzusehr' auf dem 'Wissen um Auseinandersetzungen, die erst Mitte des 19. Jahrhunderts einsetzten', basieren, und er fährt wörtlich fort: 'Schlegel wollte die Sprachwissenschaft keinesfalls in die Nähe der Naturwissenschaft rücken .... Der Hinweis auf die Naturwissenschaft muß als das belassen werden, was er ist: ein Vergleich, der um 1808 sich noch unbelastet anbot.'

Im ersten Augenblick scheint dieser Einwurf einzuleuchten; aber ganz zu Recht machen Arens (1969:166) und Jankowsky (1972:54) darauf aufmerksam, daß auch Friedrich Schlegels Zeitgenosse Jacob Grimm die Sprachwissenschaft zu der 'vergleichenden Anatomie' in Parallele setzte (vgl. Grimm 1819:XII bzw. 1890:32), und daher ist in diesem Falle wohl Hans Arens beizupflichten, wenn er — womit er etwa auch die Zustimmung Jankowskys findet — zu Friedrich Schlegels Darlegung erklärt: 'Dies scheint mir mehr als ein zeitgemäßer Vergleich zu sein, nämlich der Ausdruck der Hochachtung für die Leistungen der aufblühenden Naturwissenschaft und des Wunsches, es ihr gleichzutun in dem Fortschreiten zu gesicherten, d.h. aber beweisbaren neuen Erkenntnissen....'

Als letztes sei bei diesem dritten Punkt nicht unerwähnt gelassen, daß Friedrich

Schlegel im weiteren Verlaufe der Erörterung auch noch ein wenig ins Detail geht und anhand von Beispielen beweist, daß der Vergleich der Konjugation wesentlich mehr ergibt als der der Deklination. Zum vierten ist dann Schlegels Forderung nach 'historischer' Betrachtung der Sprache und ihrer Entstehung zu erwähnen, und hier hat Heinrich Nüsse (1962:42–4) das Verdienst, deutlich gezeigt zu haben, daß die Methode des historischen und systematischen Vergleichens im Denken Friedrich Schlegels tief verwurzelt ist und sich z.B. auch in dessen Ansätzen zu einer kritischen Philosophiegeschichte findet.

Als fünfter und letzter Punkt sei schließlich noch Friedrich Schlegels Klassifikationsversuch hervorgehoben, bei dem aufgrund des 'inneren Baus' der Sprachen 'zwei Hauptgattungen' unterschieden werden; nämlich 1. Sprachen, bei denen 'die Nebenbestimmungen der Bedeutungen durch innre Veränderung des Wurzellautes' angezeigt werden, und 2. solche, bei denen dies 'durch ein eignes hinzugefügtes Wort' geschieht. Wenn auch diese Einteilung nach heutigem Ermessen völlig unzureichend ist, so hat sie doch die weiteren Klassifikationsversuche von August Wilhelm von Schlegel, Wilhelm von Humboldt usw. angeregt.

Insgesamt gesehen bietet Friedrich Schlegels Schrift also eine Fülle von Gedanken, die die Entwicklung der historischen und komparativen Linguistik wesentlich gefördert haben. Es ist zwar unbestreitbar, daß ihm im einzelnen zahlreiche Ungereimtheiten und Fehler unterlaufen sind und daß auch seine Sanskritkenntnisse nicht sehr gründlich waren, wie Theodor Benfey (1869:361) schon bemerkte und Ursula (Struc-)-Oppenberg (1965) jetzt in ihrer eingehenden Überprüfung seiner Übersetzungen ganz klar gezeigt hat. Desweiteren ist auch zweifellos Hans Aarsleff (1967:156–7) zuzustimmen, wenn er mit Nachdruck in Erinnerung ruft, daß viele der von Schlegel vorgetragenen Anregungen und Ideen schon bei William Jones zu finden sind. Auf diese Tatsache hat sogar Friedrich Schlegel selbst am Ende seines ersten Teiles *Von der Sprache* hingewiesen, indem er William Jones den ersten nennt, der 'Licht in die Sprachkunde ... gebracht hat.' Trotz allem aber ist der Anstoß zu dem folgenden schwunghaften Aufstieg der neuen Disziplin der Indogermanistik diesem Werk *Ueber die Sprache und Weisheit der Indier* zu verdanken.

In unmittelbarem Zusammenhang mit dem Erscheinen dieses Buches (vgl. dazu etwa Windisch 1917–1920:75 oder Nüsse 1962:42) steht zum Beispiel die Hinwendung von Friedrich Schlegels Bruder August Wilhelm (1767–1845) zum Sanskrit, der dann im Jahre 1818 auf den ersten deutschen Lehrstuhl für dieses Fach in Bonn berufen wurde. Ihm ist es in der Folgezeit gelungen, das Sanskritstudium in Deutschland einzubürgern, und abgesehen von der Herausgabe der Zeitschrift *Indische Bibliothek* und dem bereits erwähnten Klassifikationsversuch hat er sich nach allgemeinem Urteil (vgl. etwa Arens 1969:187, Rocher 1972:52) vor allem durch die Edition zahlreicher Sanskrithandschriften verdient gemacht.

Doch schon einige Jahre vorher hatte Friedrich Schlegels Werk durch die Vermittlung Windischmanns einen anderen Deutschen für den Orient begeistert, dessen Wirken für die Linguistik noch wesentlich fruchtbarer werden sollte, nämlich den im

Jahre 1791 in Mainz geborenen Franz Bopp. Im Zusammenhang mit Rasmus Kristian Rask waren wir ihm schon kurz begegnet, und nun wollen wir sein Werk etwas ausführlicher behandeln.

IV. *Die vergleichende indoeuropäische Grammatik bei Franz Bopp*

Wer sich über das Leben Franz Bopps (1791–1867) näher informieren will, tut immer noch gut daran, die alte Biographie von Salomon Lefmann mit dem Titel *Franz Bopp, sein Leben und seine Wissenschaft* (1891–1897) zu konsultieren. Denn einmal ist bis heute keine neuere, ebenso detaillierte Darstellung erschienen, die die leider oft recht sentimental (vgl. Neumann 1967:7) und überschwenglich klingende Monographie Lefmanns ersetzen könnte, und zum anderen hat dieses Werk auch einen unschätzbaren Wert durch den im *Nachtrag* und *Anhang* veröffentlichten Briefwechsel Franz Bopps mit den berühmtesten Gelehrten seiner Zeit wie etwa Wilhelm von Humboldt, August Wilhelm von Schlegel, Antoine Léonard de Chézy, Jacob Grimm u.v.a. Darüberhinaus sei dann noch auf den Nachruf hingewiesen, den Russell Martineau seinem Lehrer widmete (Martineau 1867), sowie auf die mehr oder minder eingehenden Würdigungen von Theodor Benfey (1869:370–99; 470–515), August Leskien (1876) und Ernst Windisch (1917–1920:67–73). Und last but not least ist hier die kleine, aber instruktive Studie Günter Neumanns (1967:5–20) zu erwähnen, die sich besonders mit der Schulzeit und den ersten Studienjahren Bopps befaßt und außerdem noch weitere biographische Literatur verzeichnet.

Den bedeutendsten Grundstein für sein späteres fruchtbares Wirken innerhalb der Sanskritphilologie und der vergleichenden Grammatik legte Franz Bopp in der Zeit von 1812 bis 1816. Im Herbst des Jahres 1812 ging er nämlich, gerade einundzwanzigjährig, als Stipendiat der Bayerischen Regierung nach Paris, um sich dort dem Studium des Orients zu widmen. Sein Interesse für die Orientalistik und insbesondere die Sanskritliteratur war, wie wir schon angedeutet haben, durch seinen Freund und Lehrer Karl Joseph Hieronymus Windischmann (1775–1839) sowie Friedrich von Schlegels Schrift *Ueber die Sprache und Weisheit der Indier* geweckt worden, und da auf dem europäischen Kontinent lediglich die Pariser Nationalbibliothek über die für das Sanskritstudium unentbehrlichen Handschriften und Hilfsmittel verfügte (vgl. hierzu vor allem Jan Filliozat, 1941), lag nichts näher, als daß Bopp eben dorthin ging, um diesem Interesse nachzukommen. Außerdem lehrte in Paris zu jener Zeit der bekannte Orientalist Antoine Isaac Silvestre de Sacy (1758–1838; vgl. Fück 1955:140–57), bei dem denn auch Franz Bopp nach seiner Ankunft zuerst Arabisch und nachher noch Persisch hörte.

Nach dem Bericht von Russell Martineau (1867) und Georges Mounin (1967:170) studierte er dann später Sanskrit bei Antoine Léonard de Chézy, demjenigen Manne also, bei dem schon Friedrich Schlegel einige Jahre vorher Persisch gelernt hatte und der sich, wie Rocher (1968:59–61) vor kurzem nachwies, — vom Beispiel Hamiltons begeistert — dem Sanskritstudium zugewandt und sich diese Sprache völlig als Autodidakt angeeignet hatte. Doch wie schon Benfey (1869:371–2) und Leskien (1876) betonen, widerspricht dem die in einer Londoner Publikation enthaltene Äußerung Franz Bopps, er habe sich das Sanskrit ohne Hilfe eines Lehrers angeeignet (vgl. *Nalus, carmen sanscritum e Mahábhárato edidit, latine vertit et annotationibus illustravit Fr. Bopp*, London 1819:III), aber vielleicht kann hier in dieser Streitfrage mit Günter Neumann (1967:13, Anm. 9) dahingehend vermittelt werden, daß Bopp bei dem in erster Linie *literarisch* orientierten de Chézy möglicherweise einen Kurs besuchte, jedoch keine Anregung für seine eigenen *sprachlichen* Überlegungen gefunden hat.

So hat sich Bopp, wie er auch selbst sehr anschaulich in einem Brief vom 29. 4. 1814 an Windischmann berichtet (vgl. Lefmann 1891–1897:Anhang 5*–7*), 'ohne alle fremde Hilfe', lediglich auf einige bereits vorhandene Übersetzungen und Grammatiken gestützt, an die Lektüre der Sanskrithandschriften herangewagt und die Kenntnis dieser Sprache in mühevoller Kleinarbeit erworben. Aber dieses schwierige Werk der Entzifferung der oft continuo geschriebenen Manuskripte sollte seinen Blick für die Analyse der grammatischen Formen schärfen und schon bald in seinem Erstlingswerk reiche Früchte tragen, das er im Jahre 1816 in Frankfurt/Main unter dem noch ungelenken Titel publizierte: *Über das Conjugationssystem der Sanskritsprache in Vergleichung mit jenem der griechischen, lateinischen, persischen und germanischen Sprache. Nebst Episoden des Ramajan und Mahabharat in genauen metrischen Übersetzungen aus dem Originaltexte und einigen Abschnitten aus den Veda's. Herausgegeben und mit Vorerinnerungen begleitet von Dr. K. J. Windischmann.* Ähnlich wie die oben zitierte Schrift von Friedrich Schlegel besteht auch dieses Buch aus einem ersten Teil, in dem die für unseren Zusammenhang bedeutsamen sprachlichen Fragen erörtert werden, und einem zweiten Teil, der hauptsächlich Übersetzungsproben bietet und somit an dieser Stelle übergangen werden kann. Zur ersten Information über das Ziel und die Hauptgedanken des linguistisch relevanten Teiles kann wieder auf die Textsammlungen von Winfred Philipp Lehmann (1967:38–45) und Hans Arens (1969:175–9) hingewiesen werden, dann aber auch auf die kritischen Berichte bei Leskien (1876), Benfey (1869:374–9), Delbrück (1908:57ff.), Jespersen (1925:29–34), Porzig (1957:328–34), Pedersen (1962:255–7), Mounin (1967:170–5) und Neumann (1967:13–9).

Im einzelnen sah nun Franz Bopp nach seinen eigenen Worten (1816:8) seine Aufgabe darin,

> zu zeigen, wie in der Conjugation der altindischen Zeitwörter die Verhältnißbestimmungen durch entsprechende Modificationen der Wurzel ausgedrückt werden, wie aber zuweilen das verbum abstractum mit der Stammsylbe zu einem Wort verschmolzen wird, und Stammsylbe und Hilfszeitwort sich in die grammatischen Functionen des verbum theilen; zu zeigen, wie dasselbe in der griechischen Sprache der Fall sey, wie im Lateinischen das System der Verbindung der Wurzel mit einem Hilfszeitworte herrschend geworden, und wie nur dadurch die scheinbare Verschiedenheit der lateinischen Conjugation von der des Sanskrit und des Griechischen entstanden sey; zu beweisen endlich, daß an allen den Sprachen, die von dem Sanskrit, oder mit ihm von einer gemeinschaftlichen Mutter abstammen, keine Verhältnißbestim-

mung durch eine Flexion ausgedrückt werde, die ihnen nicht mit jener Ursprache gemein sey, und scheinbare Eigenheiten nur daraus entstehen, daß entweder die Stammsylben mit Hilfszeitwörtern zu einem Worte verschmolzen werden, oder daß aus Participien, die schon im Sanskrit gebräuchlichen tempora derivata abgeleitet werden, nach Art, wie man im Sanskrit, Griechischen und vielen anderen Sprachen aus Substantiven verba derivata bilden kann.

Kurz gesagt will Bopp also in seiner Studie den grammatischen Bau oder, wie es heutzutage heißt, die Morphologie des Sanskritverbums untersuchen und durch Sprachvergleich beweisen, daß die Verben aller Sprachen, die zur indoeuropäischen Familie gehören, ursprünglich aus denselben Formantien gebaut sind. Und desweiteren möchte er, wie er an späterer Stelle ausführt, mit Hilfe dieses Sprachvergleichs in die geschichtliche Entwicklung des 'Sprachorganismus' Einblick nehmen, um dann sogar den 'Ursprung der grammatischen Formen' zu erkennen (vgl. dazu beispielsweise 1816:12 und 137). Dieses letztgenannte Ziel war freilich unerreichbar, und vor allem wird Bopp heute vorgeworfen (cf. Jespersen 1925:30–2, Pedersen 1962:256, Lehmann 1967:39, Mounin 1967:172–4, Watermann 1970:30–1), daß er bei seinen diesbezüglichen Überlegungen von der Idee beherrscht war, als wesentlichen Bestandteil jeglicher Verbalendung das verbum abstractum oder verbum substantivum 'sein' zu finden, und zwar in Form der beiden Sanskritwurzeln *as* und *bhu*. Aber wenn Bopp mit dieser These auch einem Irrtum unterlegen ist, so war seine sonstige Analyse der Verbalformen doch sehr erfolgreich. Welche Entdeckungen hier im einzelnen besonders wichtig sind, ist in der bisher zitierten Literatur ausführlich dargestellt und kann hier nicht mehr in extenso nachgezeichnet werden. Aber vielleicht sollte man doch noch erwähnen, daß Bopp in seiner Studie unter anderem die Bedeutung des Ablauts — er selbst spricht noch von 'innerer Umbiegung der Stammsylbe' — für die Kennzeichnung der Tempora erkannt und durch seine Erklärung des Flexionssystems auch stillschweigend den im vorigen Kapitel erwähnten Klassifikationsversuch von Friedrich Schlegel korrigiert hat (vgl. besonders Neumann 1967:14–8). Als wissenschaftsgeschichtlich wichtigstes Ergebnis bleibt jedoch festzuhalten, daß Bopp hier die Methode der grammatischen Vergleichung systematisch an den Verbalsystemen mehrerer indoeuropäischer Sprachen erprobt hat und damit nicht nur den endgültigen wissenschaftlichen Beweis für deren Zusammengehörigkeit erbrachte, sondern auch — wie Lockwood kürzlich formulierte — 'the foundations of comparative Indo-European grammar' legte (Lockwood 1969:23; vgl. auch Jankowsky 1972:55–61). Im weiteren Verlaufe seines Lebens hat Franz Bopp, der übrigens im Jahre 1821 auf Vermittlung Wilhelm von Humboldts als Professor für orientalische Literatur und allgemeine Sprachenkunde nach Berlin berufen wurde, die in dieser Erstlingsschrift entwickelten Gedanken stetig weiter ausgebaut. So erweiterte er bereits die englische Fassung des *Conjugationssystems*, die 1820 in den Londoner *Annals of Oriental Litterature* erschien und dort den Titel *Analytical comparison of the Sanscrit*, *Greek*, *Latin and Teutonic languages showing the original identity of their grammatical structure* trug, um die Untersuchung der Deklinationen. Und außerdem formulierte er dort seine Grundideen von der Sprachvergleichung und Wortanalyse, deren geistesgeschichtlichen Hintergrund vor einigen Jahren Verburg (1950; 1951) und Orlandi (1962) aufzuzeigen suchten, noch etwas klarer, so daß z.B. Berthold Delbrück (1908) und Otto Jespersen (1925) in erster Linie diese Ausgabe für ihre Schilderung der Boppschen Ansichten benutzten.

Die wichtigste Erweiterung liegt freilich in Bopps sogenannter *Vergleichende(r) Grammatik* vor. Eigentlich lautet der volle Titel dieses von 1833 an in Berlin erschienenen Werkes *Vergleichende Grammatik des Sanskrit, Zend, Griechischen, Lateinischen, Litauischen, Gothischen und Deutschen,* doch wird wie so häufig auch in diesem Fall meistenteils die Kurzform zitiert. Wie der vollständige Titel schon erkennen läßt, hat Bopp hier seine Untersuchungen auf weitere Sprachen ausgedehnt, und außerdem hat er jetzt alle Teile der Grammatik in seine Betrachtung einbezogen. In der zweiten Abteilung dieses Werkes, dessen Veröffentlichung insgesamt bis 1852 dauerte, kam dann noch das Altslavische hinzu und in der zweiten Auflage, die in der Zeit von 1857 bis 1861 stattfand, sogar noch das Armenische, weshalb denn auch der neue Titel lautet: *Vergleichende Grammatik des Sanskrit, Zend, Armenischen, Griechischen, Lateinischen, Litauischen, Altslavischen, Gothischen und Deutschen.*

Abgesehen von dieser ständigen Erweiterung und der Verfeinerung der Methode unterscheidet sich diese Grammatik, über deren Inhalt beispielsweise Martineau (1867), Benfey (1869:470–509), Jespersen (1925:35–7), Thomsen (1927:55–6), Pedersen (1962:257–8) und Arens (1969:218–27) informieren, von seiner Erstlingsschrift vor allem dadurch, daß hier die genetische Seite der Sprachvergleichung viel stärker in den Vordergrund gerückt ist. Infolgedessen aber hat Bopp sich unter anderem in diesem Werk nicht nur noch intensiver mit der Klassifikation beschäftigt, sondern auch mit den 'Gesetzen', die dem Sprachwandel zugrundeliegen und denen dann in der Nachfolge von Bopp besonders August Friedrich Pott (1802–1887) und August Schleicher (1821–1868) ihre Aufmerksamkeit gewidmet haben.

Schließlich sei nur noch am Rande vermerkt, daß Franz Bopp für die Bezeichnung der von ihm als verwandt erwiesenen Sprachen in der *Vergleichende(n) Grammatik* (vgl. Vorrede zur 2. Aufl., XXIV) den Terminus 'indoeuropäisch' gegenüber dem Begriff 'indogermanisch' vorzog; und diese von Bopp bevorzugte Bezeichnung ist dann auch außerhalb von Deutschland, wo man lieber das von Klaproth vorgeschlagene 'indogermanisch' verwendet, allgemein üblich geworden.

V. *Die historisch-vergleichende Grammatik Jacob Grimms*

Im Anschluß an die Würdigung der großen Leistung Bopps auf dem Gebiete der vergleichenden Grammatik heißt es bei Walter Porzig (1957:336) lapidar: 'Inzwischen aber hatte die Methode der Sprachvergleichung wieder eine neue Stufe erstiegen.' Was Porzig hier mit Understatement eine 'neue Stufe' nennt, ist nichts Geringeres als die Begründung einer neuen Disziplin der Linguistik, nämlich die Einführung der sogenannten *historischen* Grammatik durch den im hessischen Hanau geborenen Jacob Grimm (1785–1863).

Über das wechselvolle Schicksal dieses Mannes und sein umfangreiches Wirken auf so verschiedenen Gebieten wie dem deutschen Recht, der Religion und Mythologie, der Sage, dem Märchen und der Fabel, der Poesie, der Sprache und der Literatur, geben einmal seine eigenen Zeugnisse umfassend Auskunft, von denen jetzt die wichtigsten bequem in Gerstners kommentierter Auswahl *Die Brüder Grimm: Ihr Leben und Werk in Selbstzeugnissen, Briefen und Aufzeichnungen* (1952) greifbar sind. Zum anderen aber sind aus der kaum übersehbaren Literatur (vgl. hierzu etwa die umfangreichen bibliographischen Angaben bei Ludwig Denecke 1971) vor allem die kritischen und in erster Linie sprachwissenschaftlich orientierten Darstellungen von Benfey (1869:427–70), v. Raumer (1870:378–452, 495–539), Scherer (1879), Jespersen (1925: 22–9, 42–4), Stegmann von Pritzwald (1936), Newald (1949:73–120), Dünninger (1957:148–61), Magon (1963), Friedrich Neumann (1971:50–65) und Jankowsky (1972:76–83) zu nennen. Diese allgemeineren Berichte werden zudem vortrefflich ergänzt durch viele Einzeldarstellungen, in denen beispielsweise Grimms Sprachphilosophie (Beneš 1958), seine Ansichten zur Frage des Sprachursprungs (Ulmer 1950–1951; Lun 1960; Hermann 1965; Löther 1965; Schankweiler 1965), sein Wirken im Bereich der Etymologie (Trier 1964), der Märchen- und Sagenforschung (Woeller 1965), der deutschen Literatur (Mettke 1965), der nhd. Schriftsprache (Bondzio 1965) und der Dialektgeographie (Schoof 1963–1964) sowie etwa seine Anregungen auf die Romanistik (Kabilinski 1914), Neogräzistik (Irmscher 1965) und Nordistik (Bergsveinsson 1965) detailliert beschrieben werden. Alle diese Literaturhinweise stellen zwar nur eine geringe Auswahl dar, doch mögen sie zur Aufhellung des Hintergrundes, vor dem die drei im folgenden behandelten sprachwissenschaftlich bedeutsamsten Werke Grimms zu sehen sind, genügen.

Das erste Werk, auf das wir näher eingehen müssen und das auch in allen älteren und neueren Geschichten der Linguistik mehr oder minder ausführlich gewürdigt wird (vgl. z.B. Benfey 1869:431–51; v. Raumer 1870:499–520; Jespersen 1925:24–9; Thomsen 1927:57–62; Agrell 1955:25–9; Porzig 1957:336–41; Pedersen 1962:36–43; 258–62; Dinneen 1967:184–6; Robins 1967:171–3, Arens 1969:195–203; Waterman 1970:20–30; Helbig 1971:11–2 und Jankowsky 1972:82–3), ist Jacob Grimms *Deutsche Grammatik*, deren erster Band im Jahre 1819 zu Göttingen erschien, aber bereits im Jahre 1822 in völlig umgearbeiteter Fassung nochmals herauskam. Der zweite, der dritte und der vierte Band wurden dann in kontinuierlicher Folge etwas später, und zwar 1826, 1831 und 1837 publiziert.

Der Titel dieses Buches ist nach heutigem Sprachgebrauch freilich etwas irreführend, und schon Grimm selbst sah sich zu seiner Zeit zur Verteidigung gezwungen (vgl. v. Raumer 1870:506 mit Anm. 3 sowie Denecke 1971:91), weil er das Wort *deutsch* in der Bedeutung 'germanisch' verwandte und dementsprechend in seiner Grammatik nicht nur eine Darstellung des Deutschen, sondern vieler älterer und jüngerer germanischer Sprachen wie des Gotischen, Altnordischen, Dänischen, Schwedischen, Englischen usw. gab.

Grimms epochemachende Bedeutung liegt aber nicht so sehr darin, daß er — ähnlich wie schon Rasmus Kristian Rask — die grammatischen Systeme der germanischen Sprachfamilie vergleicht, sondern darin, daß er mit dieser Grammatik die *historische* Sprachbetrachtung einführt.

Schon gleich in der Vorrede des ersten Bandes (*Deutsche Grammatik*, Erster Theil, Göttingen 1819; wieder abgedruckt in: *Kleinere Schriften*, VIII., Gütersloh 1890 sowie Grimm 1968:1–17) spricht er davon, er sei 'von dem Gedanken, eine historische Grammatik der deutschen Sprache zu unternehmen, ... lebhaft ergriffen worden' (1968:9), und gegen Ende dieser Prolegomena bezeichnet er als Hauptzweck seines Werkes, er wolle den Beweis erbringen, 'daß und wie alle deutschen Sprachstämme innigst verwandt und die heutigen Formen unverständlich seyen, wo man nicht bis zu den vorigen, alten und ältesten hinaufsteige, daß folglich die gegenwärtige grammatische Structur nur geschichtlich aufgestellt werden dürfe' (1968:16). 'Historische' Sprachbetrachtung bedeutet also einerseits, eine Sprache oder Sprachengruppe aufgrund ihrer geschichtlichen Entwicklung zu verstehen und die gegenwärtige Sprachstruktur aus den vorhergehenden Sprachzuständen abzuleiten. Zum anderen aber hat *historisch*, worauf Telegdi (1966; 1967) mit besonderem Nachdruck hinweist, zu jener Zeit auch die Bedeutung von 'empirisch', und zwar direkt im Gegensatz zu 'logisch-philosophisch'.

Mit diesen beiden Inhaltskomponenten des Begriffs *historische Grammatik* ist zugleich auch schon die Stellung angedeutet, die Jacob Grimm gegenüber allen anderen zeitgenössischen Grammatiken bezieht. So ist es kaum überraschend, daß er die logisch-philosophische Grammatik, wie sie in der berühmten *Grammaire générale et raisonnée* von Port-Royal (1660) oder in Deutschland in der von 1801 bis 1803 in Berlin veröffentlichten *Sprachlehre* August Ferdinand Bernhardis (1769–1820) greifbar ist, aus dem Grunde ablehnt, weil sie 'ohne Rücksicht auf die Wurzeln der Wörter (d.h. ihre Geschichte) die bloß allgemein gedachten Formen und Formeln einer Sprache logisch erörtert'.

Desgleichen steht er selbstverständlich auch den normativen und kritischen Grammatiken in ablehnender Haltung gegenüber, die gleichsam als 'gesetzgebendes System' (Schoof 1957:413) den Sprachgebrauch reglementieren wollen. Mit dieser Auffassung steht Jacob Grimm zu seiner Zeit allerdings keineswegs alleine da. Vielmehr ist an dieser Stelle etwa auf den weithin unbekannt gebliebenen Carl Gustav Jochmann (1789–1830) hinzuweisen, dessen originelles Werk *Über die Sprache* (1828) jetzt in der dankenswerten Neuausgabe von Christian Johannes Wagenknecht (1968) greifbar ist und der in dem Kapitel *Die Sprachreiniger* (1968:49–194) mit scharfen Worten gegen die 'Sprachgesetzgeber' polemisiert.

Grimm selbst hebt sich nun in seinen Ausführungen vor allem von Johann Christoph Adelung ab, der auf Veranlassung des preußischen Ministers für Kirchen- und Schulangelegenheiten Karl Abraham Freiherr von Zedlitz (1731–1793) eine *Deutsche Sprachlehre. Zum Gebrauche der Schulen in den Königl. Preuß. Landen* (Berlin 1781) geschrieben und kurz darauf sogar noch ein *Umständliches Lehrgebäude der Deutschen Sprache, zur Erläuterung der Deutschen Sprachlehre für Schulen* (2 Bde.,

Leipzig 1782) herausgegeben hatte. Doch wenn Grimm sich auch zu Recht von diesen Büchern distanziert, so darf man andrerseits nicht übersehen, daß Adelung hier in gewisser Weise der historischen Grammatik sogar den Weg geebnet hat. Denn wie etwa v. Raumer (1870:224–9), Jellinek (Bd. I, 1913:336–60) und Sickel (1933:96–8) in ihren Würdigungen der Verdienste Adelungs mit gutem Grund betonen, finden sich bei diesem auch Gedanken, die der Ansicht Jacob Grimms sehr nahe kommen. So sagt Adelung in der Vorrede zu seinem *Umständlichen Lehrgebäude* (Bd. I, 1782: V): 'Eine gründliche Sprachlehre ist gewisser Maßen eine pragmatische Geschichte der Sprache', und an anderer Stelle heißt es noch präziser: 'Ohne eine genaue Kenntniß des Stufenganges, welchen eine Nation in dem Baue und der Bildung ihrer Wörter von dem ersten Ursprunge ihrer Sprache an, bis zu ihrer höchsten Verfeinerung beobachtet hat, wird in keiner Sprache eine erträgliche Sprachlehre zu Stande kommen' (vgl. *Kurzer Begriff menschlicher Fertigkeiten und Kenntnisse so fern sie auf Erwerbung des Unterhalts, auf Vergnügen, auf Wissenschaft, und auf Regierung der Gesellschaft abzielen. Für Realschulen und das bürgerliche Leben*, 4 Teile, Leipzig 1778–1781, Bd. III:232 und dazu Sickel 1933:97, 247).

Aber ähnlich wie vorhin bei der Behandlung des *Mithridates* deutlich wurde, hat Adelung auch hier seine eigenen Grundsätze nicht befolgt und statt dessen zwei normative Grammatiken geschrieben, in denen er den Sprachgebrauch der besten und weisesten Schriftsteller als 'gesetzgebende Theile der Sprache' deklariert (vgl. *Umständliches Lehrgebäude*, Bd. I, 1782:107 und dazu Jellinek Bd. I, 1913:371). Infolgedessen blieb es also trotz der Ansätze bei Adelung und auch trotz der ersten Schritte, die Franz Bopp und Rasmus Kristian Rask auf dem Weg zur Sprachgeschichte taten, Grimm vorbehalten, den Gedanken der historischen Grammatik auszuführen und so eine neue Disziplin zu etablieren.

Die zweite bedeutsame Erkenntnis Jacob Grimms ist die Entdeckung der sogenannten LAUTVERSCHIEBUNG. Wie wir in dem Kapitel über Rasmus Kristian Rask schon angedeutet haben, verdankt Grimm diese Einsicht allerdings zum großen Teil dessen *Undersøgelse*, und so ist es auch nicht verwunderlich, daß die diesbezüglichen Kapitel "Von den Buchstaben" erst in der völlig umgearbeiteten zweiten Auflage des ersten Bandes der *Deutschen Grammatik* erscheinen. Aber über Rask hinaus hat Jacob Grimm aufgrund seiner historischen Betrachtungsweise klar erkannt, daß die von Rask entdeckten Lautentsprechungen nicht als einzelne, voneinander unabhängige Phänomene zu betrachten sind, sondern als Teile zweier großer Lautbewegungen, die jeweils bei dem Übergang vom Indoeuropäischen zum Germanischen und vom Germanischen zum Althochdeutschen stattgefunden haben. Und wenn Grimm auch im Detail noch viele Fehler unterlaufen sind, von denen man heute vor allem seine These vom KREISLAUF der Verschiebungen von Tenuis zu Aspirata, Aspirata zu Media und Media zu Tenuis hervorhebt (vgl. Jespersen 1925:27, Porzig 1957:339, Robins 1967: 171–2, Waterman 1970:28–9), so war in seiner Untersuchung doch erstmals sowohl die ERSTE (GERMANISCHE) als auch die ZWEITE oder HOCHDEUTSCHE LAUTVERSCHIEBUNG nachgewiesen. In der Folgezeit wurde Grimms Erkenntnis dann vor allen Dingen von den sogenannten JUNGGRAMMATIKERN ('neo-grammarians') erweitert, die jedoch im Gegensatz zu ihm von LAUTGESETZEN sprachen.

Als letztes sei dann noch erwähnt, daß Jacob Grimm mit diesem Werk auch die Begriffe STARKE und SCHWACHE VERBEN sowie ABLAUT ('vowel gradation') und UMLAUT ('vowel change ascribable to earlier environmental conditions', Robins 1967:171) in die Linguistik eingeführt hat.

Die beiden anderen Werke, auf die wir an dieser Stelle noch kurz eingehen müssen, sind die *Geschichte der deutschen Sprache* (2 Bde., Leipzig 1848) und das deutsche Wörterbuch, das Jacob Grimm zusammen mit seinem Bruder Wilhelm (1786–1859) publizierte. Die erstgenannte Abhandlung wird zwar von den meisten linguistisch orientierten Historiographen übergangen, doch läßt sie, wie schon Theodor Benfey (1869:451–66) und in jüngerer Zeit vor allem Burkhard Löther (1965) zeigten, gut erkennen, wie sehr Jacob Grimm darum bemüht hat, Klarheit über das schwierige dialektische Verhältnis von Sprach- und Volksgeschichte zu erlangen (vgl. hierzu auch die knappe Würdigung bei Friedrich Neumann 1971:62–3). Und da er dabei unter anderem auf die innige Beziehung zwischen Kultur- und Wortgeschichte stieß und aus diesem Grunde die These 'von den Wörtern zu den Sachen' formulierte (vgl. *Geschichte der deutschen Sprache*, Bd. I, 1848:XIII), könnte dieses Werk sogar in mancher Hinsicht als Vorläufer der sogenannten WÖRTER UND SACHEN-Forschung unseres Jahrhunderts angesehen werden.

Das größte Unternehmen Jacob Grimms, sein mit dem Bruder Wilhelm gemeinsam publiziertes *Deutsches Wörterbuch*, ist zu seinen Lebzeiten nur bis Band 4 gediehen und erst im Jahre 1960 vorläufig abgeschlossen worden. Auch dieses heute noch unübertroffene Werk, dessen erste Lieferung 1852 in Leipzig erschien und über dessen wechselvolle Entstehungsgeschichte Ludwig Denecke (1971:119–29) und die dort verzeichnete Literatur eingehend berichten, steht ganz auf dem Boden der historischen Sprachbetrachtung. Denn ebenso wie die *Deutsche Grammatik* und die *Geschichte der deutschen Sprache* sollte dieses Wörterbuch einen Einblick in die deutsche Sprachgeschichte geben, und zwar sollte es die Verwendung jedes wichtigen Wortes von Martin Luther (1483–1546) bis zu Johann Wolfgang Goethe (1749–1832) hin verfolgen. Auch damit sind die Brüder Grimm wieder in direkten Gegensatz zu Adelung getreten, dessen *Versuch eines vollständigen grammatisch-kritischen Wörterbuches der Hochdeutschen Mundart, mit beständiger Vergleichung der übrigen Mundarten, besonders aber der oberdeutschen* (5 Bde., Leipzig 1774–1786) sie mit den Worten kritisieren: 'Das Wörterbuch Adelungs, des unter allen Vorgängern allein nennenswerthen, ist weit hinter der Fülle des Materials zurückgeblieben und ruht auf keiner ausreichenden Grundlage, die, wie sich von selbst versteht, nur eine historische sein kann' (Kasseler Allgemeine Zeitung vom 1. September 1838, Beilage Nr. 27).

Ihr eigenes Werk ist aber bis zu seinem Abschluß in unseren Jahrhundert nicht nur immer wieder entsprechend ihren Grundgedanken fortgeführt (vgl. Schoof 1938a, 1938b, 1961), sondern sogar quellenmäßig noch erweitert worden, so daß es heute für die Wortforschung von 'unschätzbarem Wert' ist und auch in anderen Ländern wie etwa der Schweiz, Schweden, England und den Niederlanden Nachahmung gefunden hat (Denecke 1971:123, 129).

B. DIE BEGRÜNDUNG DER ALLGEMEINEN SPRACHWISSENSCHAFT UND DER MODERNEN SPRACHPHILOSOPHIE

I. *Die Vorläufer: Johann Georg Hamann und Johann Gottfried von Herder*

Wenn man die Entwicklung der Sprachwissenschaft im Zeitalter der Romantik in Deutschland beurteilen will, muß man zwei Männer berücksichtigen, die Wegbereiter wichtiger neuer Ideen waren und die einen großen Einfluß ausgeübt haben. Der für die Sprachphilosophie und Sprachwissenschaft bedeutendste war sicher der aus Ostpreußen stammende evangelische Prediger, Theologe und spätere Generalsuperintendent in Weimar, Johann Gottfried von Herder (1744–1803). Aber Herder ist kaum ausreichend zu verstehen ohne den Einfluß seines älteren Landsmannes und Freundes, des nebenberuflich philosophischen Schriftstellers Johann Georg Hamann (1730–1788). Dieser höchst originelle christlich-protestantische Denker hat in einer oft dunklen, bilderreichen Sprache Ansichten über Sprache und Mensch ausgesprochen, die zwar kaum wissenschaftlich genannt werden können, die aber an die Fundamente der menschlichen Existenz heranführen. Die Bedeutung von Hamann und Herder für das Sprachdenken der Romantik und für die allgemeine Sprachwissenschaft ist in den letzten Jahren in mehreren Spezialuntersuchungen erneut hervorgehoben und präzisiert worden. Hamann ist eine höchst eigenartige Persönlichkeit. Man darf ihn als einen 'gläubigen Weisen' bezeichnen, der wortgewaltig und kompromißlos seine christliche Deutung des Menschen aus dem Geist der Bibel vorträgt. Die Sprache Hamanns ist, wie bereits erwähnt, sehr schwierig, überaus metaphernreich und oft rätselhaft. Ohne ausführliche Erklärungen bleiben ganze Passagen unverständlich. Daher ist mit Nachdruck auf die ausgezeichnete Darstellung von Elfriede Büchsel zu verweisen, in der auch die Wirkungsgeschichte der 'Herderschriften' Hamanns und die wichtigste Sekundärliteratur kritisch behandelt sind (Hamann/Büchsel 1963). Die Hamannschen Originale sind hier abgedruckt und ausführlich erklärt. Aus dem Umstand, daß die Kommentare den Urtext an Umfang stellenweise weit übertreffen, geht deutlich hervor, wie zahlreich die Andeutungen und Anspielungen Hamanns sind, die ohne eingehende Kenntnis seiner Denkweise und seiner Quellen verschlossen bleiben.

Die wichtigste Überzeugung des sogenannten Magus aus dem Norden ist die, daß der Mensch als Geschöpf Gottes nach dessen Ebenbild ein vernunft- und sprachbegabtes Wesen von Anbeginn an ist. Nicht der Mensch hat das Wort gemacht, sondern das Wort den Menschen. Gott hat sich zum Menschen als seinem Geschöpf 'herabgelassen', und dieser 'Herablassung' Gottes hat der Mensch alles zu verdanken. Georg Baudler hat den existentialen Kern des Hamannschen Sprachdenkens, den

Glauben an die gottmenschliche Urkorrespondenz des Daseins, in einer neuen Untersuchung mit dem bezeichnenden Titel *Im Worte sehen* (1970) herausgearbeitet. Diese Arbeit ist besonders für die Beurteilung des religiösen und theologischen Hintergrundes von Hamanns Schaffen wichtig.

Vernunft und Sprache sind für Hamann eines, es gibt keine Sprache ohne Vernunft und keine Vernunft ohne Sprache. Trotz dieser rückhaltlosen Bejahung des göttlichen Ursprungs der Sprache gerät Hamann in eine überraschend modern anmutende sprachkritische Haltung. Sie entspringt aus seiner Skepsis gegenüber den leeren Abstraktionen der ALLGEMEINBEGRIFFE, die den Sprachgebrauch der rationalistischen Philosophen beherrschten. Josef Simon hat darauf in seiner Einleitung zu Hamanns *Schriften zur Sprache* (1967) mit Recht hingewesen. Hamann kämpft gegen den abstrakten Allgemeinbegriff, der den individuellen Gedanken zu ersticken droht. Deshalb ringt er um eine unverwechselbare eigene Ausdrucksform seines Gedankens. Das aber geht nur auf Kosten der Allgemeinverständlichkeit, die ohne Konzessionen an das vorhandene Begriffsgut nicht möglich ist. Wir stehen hier vor dem gleichen Problem, vor das sich große Dichter wie Hugo von Hofmannsthal, Bert Brecht, Gottfried Benn u.a. später wieder gestellt sahen und das auch in der analytischen Sprachphilosophie eine Rolle spielt (Gipper 1967).

Hamann gelangt bei seinen eigenwilligen Formulierungen zu großartigen Aussagen, denen Bruno Liebrucks im ersten Band seines großen Werkes *Sprache und Bewußtsein* (1964) höchstes Lob gespendet hat. Liebrucks beurteilt die Gedanken Hamanns als einen Gipfel der Sprachbetrachtung und würdigt ihn als einen bedeutenden Denker, der gegen jede leichtfertige Kritik in Schutz zu nehmen ist (Liebrucks 1964:286–340).

Durch die hohe Einschätzung der Sprache gerät Hamann in Gegensatz zu seinem großen Lehrer Immanuel Kant, für den die Vernunft primär und entscheidend war und der die fundamentale Bedeutung der Sprache im menschlichen Erkenntnisprozeß nicht erkannt hat. An dieser Stelle wird nun auch Hamanns Einfluß auf Herder deutlich, der ebenfalls Schüler Kants in Königsberg gewesen war. Auch Herder sieht die zentrale Bedeutung der Sprache, auch er wendet sich gegen Kant und greift dabei auf Gedanken Hamanns zurück. Wilhelm Streitberg hat in seinem Aufsatz "Kant und die Sprachwissenschaft" (1909) die Zusammenhänge näher untersucht und besonders darauf hingewiesen, daß es vor allem John Lockes drittes Buch von der Sprache im *Essay concerning human understanding* (1690) war, das die beiden Freunde bei ihrer Auseinandersetzung mit Kant als hilfreich empfanden. Beide, Hamann und Herder, begreifen den Menschen als Sprachwesen, und diese Überzeugung geben sie weiter an Wilhelm von Humboldt, der sie als zentrales Motiv in seine Sprachphilosophie aufnimmt.

Hierzu ist jedoch folgende Erläuterung am Platze:

Da Humboldt in den betreffenden Schriften weder Hamann noch Herder erwähnt, ist dieser Einfluß gelegentlich bezweifelt worden. Dieser Frage ist Friedrich Lauchert in seiner Untersuchung über *Die Anschauungen Herders über den Ursprung der Sprache, ihre Voraussetzungen in der Philosophie seiner Zeit und ihr Fortwirken* (1894) nachgegangen. Er bemerkt, daß H. Steinthal einen Einfluß Herders auf Humboldt entschieden ablehnt (Steinthal 1858:12; [4]1888:10) und daß F. Pott diese Auffassung in seinem Humboldt-Kommentar (Pott 1876) übernimmt. Demgegenüber bejaht Rudolf Haym, der Biograph Herders und Humboldts, die Frage mit Nachdruck (Haym 1880:I, 408; 1856:494). Lauchert weist dann in Humboldts Arbeiten wörtliche Anklänge an Herder nach und betrachtet Herder geradezu als den Vater der von Humboldt entwickelten Sprachphilosophie (766). Edward Sapir, der ebenfalls auf diese Frage eingeht, hält einen direkten Zusammenhang für sehr wahrscheinlich (Sapir 1907/08:33). Und schließlich weist auch Clemens Menze in der neueren Untersuchung *Wilhelm von Humboldts Lehre und Bild vom Menschen* (1965:224) auf nahezu wörtliche Entsprechungen zu Herder bei Humboldt hin. Eine erneute Überprüfung dieser Thesen zeigt nun folgendes Ergebnis: In Humboldts gesammelten Schriften ist Herder mehrfach erwähnt, allerdings nicht in den Aufsätzen, sondern in Briefen und Tagebuchnotizen. Demnach hat Humboldt Herder persönlich gekannt, ihn besucht, und mit ihm korrespondiert. In den Paralipomena (7. Band, 2. Hälfte 1907) ist in den Notizen *Aus Engels philosophischen Vorträgen* sogar Herders Preisschrift ausdrücklich erwähnt (a.a.O.:372). Daß Humboldt Herders Schriften gekannt hat, steht also ganz außer Frage.

Eine zweite ergänzende Bemerkung sei gleich angeschlossen:

Es ist den meisten Kommentatoren entgangen, daß sich verwandte Gedankengänge fast gleichzeitig auch in Frankreich finden, so bei dem sog. Illuminaten Claude de Saint-Martin (1743–1803), dessen Lebensdaten sich fast mit denen Herders decken. Der Romanist Hugo Friedrich hat in seinem Aufsatz "Die Sprachtheorie der französischen Illuminaten des 18. Jahrhunderts, insbesondere Saint-Martins" (1935) auf diesen esoterischen, aber philosophisch und theologisch hochgebildeten Theosophen hingewiesen und gezeigt, daß auch nach dessen Überzeugung Sprachursprung und Ursprung des Geistes, Menschwerdung und Sprachentstehung zusammenfallen. Friedrich hebt die Nähe dieser Auffassung zu Hamann und Herder hervor, ohne eine direkte Verbindung nachzuweisen. Saint-Martin begegnet sich auch mit Herder und mit Humboldt darin, daß er in seiner Sprachtheorie dem Verbum eine zentrale Stellung einräumt. Der Grund hierfür liegt in Saint-Martins Auffassung, daß die schöpferischen Kräfte das schaffende Prinzip, das Wesen der Welt ausmachen. Auf diesen energetischen Grundgedanken gründet er die erste idealistische Sprachtheorie (neben Diderot) in Frankreich, die wie Friedrich betont, den Weg in die Romantik freilegen hilft.

Trotz der oben erwähnten Gemeinsamkeit der Auffassungen blieb das Verhältnis der beiden Freunde Hamann und Herder nicht ungetrübt. Anlaß zu einem schweren Zerwürfnis war Herders berühmte Abhandlung *Über den Ursprung der Sprache*, die er 1771 auf eine Preisfrage der Berliner Akademie der Wissenschaften einreichte und für die er ausgezeichnet wurde. Da die Frage des Sprachursprungs eine zentrale Frage der intellektuellen Welt jener Zeit war (30 Antworten waren auf die Preisfrage der Akademie eingegangen) und da sich hieraus wichtige Einsichten Herders für die

Sprachwissenschaft ergaben, sei näher darauf eingegangen:

Wie schon angedeutet, hatte man im 18. Jahrhundert zahlreiche Sprachursprungstheorien aufgestellt. Das allgemeine Interesse an diesem Problem muß mit dem besonderen Anliegen des Aufklärungsdenkens in Zusammenhang gebracht werden, das die Wurzeln der menschlichen Vernunft freizulegen suchte. Über die verschiedenen Ansätze unterrichten etwa Krüger 1967, Salmon 1968/69, Sapir 1907/08, Sommerfelt 1953/54, Révész 1946, Rosenkranz 1961 und Terray 1958 recht ausführlich.

Wer nun in jener Zeit über den Ursprung des Menschen und seiner Sprache nachdenken wollte, konnte nicht an dem Schöpfungsbericht der Bibel vorbeigehen. Hiernach war der Mensch als Ebenbild Gottes erschaffen und als Ebenbild des Schöpfers auch bereits mit Sprache ausgestattet. Gott selbst schuf die Welt, indem er aussprach, was entstehen sollte, und er nannte die Elemente und kosmischen Erscheinungen als das, was sie waren. Ähnlich stellt das Johannes-Evangelium an den Anfang den Logos, der bei Gott war und der gleich Gott war. Die Übersetzung des griechischen Logos mit 'Wort' ist sicher eine Einengung des Begriffs, aber sie zeigt, wie zentral die Stellung der Sprache gesehen wurde. Nach Mose 1, 2, 19, bringt Gott dann die erschaffenen Tiere zu Adam, 'daß er sähe, wie er sie nennte', denn 'so sollten sie heißen'. Und Adam gab jeglichem Tier seinen 'Namen'. Der erste Mensch spricht also bereits, besitzt also Sprache, und zwar auch schon, bevor er eine Gefährtin bekommt. Das kommunikative und soziale Element ist infolgedessen keine Vorbedingung für den Ursprung der Sprache: Diese ist vielmehr Geschenk aus der Hand des Schöpfers.

Die Schöpfung der Welt lag aber nach kirchlich-orthodoxer Ansicht nur wenige Jahrtausende zurück. Der englische Erzbischof James Ussher hatte sogar den genauen Zeitpunkt errechnet und zwar den 23. Oktober des Jahres 4004 vor Christi Geburt, Sonntagvormittag, 9 Uhr. Usshers Berechnung aus dem Jahre 1650 blieb für die wörtlichen Bibelausleger fast drei Jahrhunderte lang ein fester Markierungspunkt (Beiser 1967:35). Die Erde war demnach nicht einmal 6000 Jahre alt. In diesem uns heute geradezu lächerlich gering erscheinenden Zeitraum wäre für die Annahme einer Evolution von niederen zu höheren Lebewesen einfach kein Platz gewesen.

Sogar noch der große schwedische Biologe Carl von Linné (1707–1778) hält in seinem *Systema naturae* (1735) an der strengen Trennung der Arten fest, obwohl er den Menschen mit den Affen in dieselbe Klasse der Herrentiere, der Primaten, stellt. Wohl wußte man, daß Völker und Kulturen entstehen und vergehen, und es war auch bekannt, daß man z.B. durch Züchtung leistungsfähigere Pflanzen und Tiere hervorbringen konnte. Eine Entwicklung des Menschen war also an sich wohl vorstellbar, aber nur als Entwicklung innerhalb der sich prinzipiell gleichbleibenden Spezies.

Zur Zeit Herders war man nun über diese unhaltbaren Vorstellungen noch nicht weit hinausgelangt, denn die historischen Kenntnisse waren noch recht begrenzt. Als älteste Sprache galt vielen immer noch das Hebräische (vgl. u.a. Agrell 1955:204), und auch Herder hielt es für eine, wenn nicht *die* Ursprache (Sapir 1907/08:4; Jankowsky 1972:37–8). Dem Hebräischen machte dann ein wenig später das wiederentdeckte Sanskrit den Rang streitig. Fabre d'Olivet, der französische Semitist, dessen Buch *La langue hébraïque restituée et le véritable sens des mots hébreux rétabli et prouvé par analyse radicale* (1815) so starken Eindruck auf B. L. Whorf gemacht hat, geht z.B. von der Existenz dreier gleichberechtigter Ursprachen ('langues fondamentales') aus, dem Sanskrit, dem Hebräischen und dem Chinesischen. Über die Bedeutung dieser Anschauungen berichtet Judith E. Schlanger in einem aufschlußreichen Aufsatz *La langue hébraïque, problème de linguistique spéculative* (1967).

Wenn diese Sprachen nach damaliger Ansicht zwei bis drei Jahrtausende alt sein mochten, standen sie dem Ursprung der Menschheit in jedem Falle beträchtlich näher als alle lebenden Sprachen. Ihre Ursprünglichkeit mußte daher zwangsläufig überbewertet werden. Auf diesen Umstand hat kein geringerer als Edward Sapir in seinem ausgezeichneten Aufsatz über "Herder's Ursprung der Sprache" (1907/08) aufmerksam gemacht. Andererseits war jedoch eine historische Entwicklung der schon länger bekannten Sprachen durchaus erkennbar. Man brauchte nur das Latein mit den romanischen Sprachen oder das Deutsche mit den Texten aus alt- und mittelhochdeutscher Zeit zu vergleichen. Daß bei dieser Entwicklung der grammatische Formenreichtum früherer Epochen abgenommen hatte, war unschwer festzustellen. Es stellte sich daher die Frage, ob diese Entwicklung als Verfall oder als Aufwärtsbewegung zu interpretieren war. Nahm man einen göttlichen Ursprung der Sprache an, lag es nahe, den Formenschwund als Niedergang zu deuten. (Damit konnte aber auch leicht eine Minderbewertung der Leistungsfähigkeit des menschlichen Geistes verbunden werden).

Unter solchen Voraussetzungen muß man die Sprachursprungshypothesen, die manche Denker des 17. und 18. Jahrhunderts aufstellten, als kühn bezeichnen. Wenn sie, wie z.B. Condillac, annahmen, daß sich die Sprache aus tierischen Lauten entwickelt haben könnte, wobei Affekt, Instinkt, Imitation, Ausdrucks- und Mitteilungsabsicht eine Rolle gespielt haben mochten, dann verstießen sie nicht nur gegen den Wortlaut der Bibel, über deren Geltung immer noch die Zensur großer Universitäten wachte, sondern sie zogen auch bereits Vergleiche, die heute wie Vorahnungen des Evolutionsgedankens wirken. Charles Robert Darwins (1809–1882) epochemachendes Buch *The origin of species by means of natural selection* erschien aber erst im Jahre 1859, und auf das Problem der Menschwerdung war auch dieser vorsichtige Forscher nur mit dem Satz eingegangen: 'Light will be thrown on the origin of man and his history.' Und es sollte noch Jahrzehnte dauern, bis der Gedanke der Evolution auf die Stufe gesicherter wissenschaftlicher Erkenntnis gehoben werden konnte. Die zweite Hälfte des 18. Jahrhunderts bot also noch Anlaß genug, die Frage des göttlichen Ursprungs der Sprache öffentlich zu diskutieren. Bibel- und Offenbarungsgläubige mußten sich neue Argumente einfallen lassen, um der Skepsis der Rationalisten zu begegnen. Man muß sich diese Lage vor Augen halten, um Herders *Abhandlung über den Ursprung der Sprache* gerecht beurteilen zu können.

Konkreten Anlaß zur Verfassung dieser Schrift boten Ereignisse an der Berliner Akademie der Wissenschaften. Deren Präsident Pierre-Louis Moreau de Maupertuis (1697–1759) hatte sich in zwei Abhandlungen für einen Sprachursprung aus Gesten und Geschrei ausgesprochen (Maupertuis 1756) und damit den Widerspruch eines anderen Akademiemitgliedes, des Theologen und Begründers der Bevölkerungsstatistik Johann Peter Süßmilch (1708–1767) hervorgerufen. Süßmilch antwortet mit einer Schrift *Versuch eines Beweises, daß die erste Sprache ihren Ursprung nicht von Menschen, sondern allein vom Schöpfer erhalten habe.* Sie war bereits 1756 in der Akademie vorgetragen worden, erschien aber erst 1766 im Druck. Um den Streit zu schlichten, stellte die Berliner Akademie der Wissenschaften 1769 die für den Zeitgeist typische Preisfrage: *En supposant les hommes abandonnés a leurs facultés naturelles, sont-ils en état d'inventer le langage? et par quels moyens parviendront-ils d'eux-mêmes à cette invention?*

Es geht also um die Frage, ob die Sprache 'natürlichen', d.h. menschlichen Ursprungs, oder 'übernatürlichen', d.h. göttlichen Ursprungs ist. Herder ergreift diesen Anlaß, gegen Süßmilch zu Felde zu ziehen und eigene Gedanken zu sprachlichen Problemen erneut zusammenzufassen. Er verfaßt seine Schrift in Eile und reicht sie zum letztmöglichen Termin ein. Die Arbeit erhielt den Preis, sie wurde 1772 auf Geheiß der Akademie veröffentlicht.

Edward Sapir hat in dem bereits erwähnten Aufsatz über "Herder's Ursprung der Sprache" (Sapir 1907/08) darauf hingewiesen, daß die Fragestellung der Akademie bereits verrät, welche wissenschaftliche Sicht des Problems man dort gewonnen zu haben glaubte. Die Formulierung zeigt, daß man weit davon entfernt ist, den biblischen Schöpfungsbericht noch für verbindlich zu halten. Es wird hier schlicht vorausgesetzt, daß es Menschen ohne Sprache gegeben hat. Der Spracherwerb wird mit einer Erfindung verglichen, so wie Werkzeuge, Geräte und Maschinen erfunden werden. Zu Erfindungen gehören, wie man aus Erfahrung weiß, bestimmte Fähigkeiten der Intelligenz. Damit spitzt sich die Frage so zu: Reichten die natürlichen intellektuellen Fähigkeiten des noch sprachlosen Menschen zur Erfindung eines so komplizierten Werkzeugs wie der Sprache aus — oder mußte Gott, dessen primäre Schöpfungstat nicht in Frage gestellt war, erneut eingreifen und dem Menschen noch nachträglich das Geschenk der Sprache machen?

Herders Antwort ist klar: Der Mensch hat sich selbst Sprache geschaffen, aber es handelt sich um keine Erfindung, sondern um einen langen Prozeß, dessen Möglichkeit bereits vom Schöpfer in ihn hineingelegt war. Insofern ist es ungenau, wenn immer wieder behauptet wird, Herder habe den menschlichen Ursprung der Sprache beweisen wollen. Aus dem Munde eines Theologen hätte eine solche Behauptung wohl auch befremdlich gewirkt. Vielmehr möchte Herder Gottes Schöpfertat, von der auch er überzeugt ist, in einem noch größeren Lichte zeigen, indem er die von Gott geschenkte menschliche Seele als die Kraft hinstellt, die den Menschen befähigt, sich selbst die Sprache zu schaffen. Es ist daher zutreffender, vom 'menschlich-göttlichen Ursprung der Sprache' bei Herder zu sprechen, wie es Manfred Krüger in seinen *Bemerkungen zu Herders Sprachtheorie* (1967) getan hat.

Folgende Stelle am Ende von Herders Abhandlung macht diesen Zusammenhang ganz deutlich:

Der höhere Ursprung ist, so fromm er scheine, *durchaus ungöttlich.* Bei jedem Schritte verkleinert er Gott durch die niedrigsten, unvollkommensten Anthropomorphien. Der menschliche zeigt Gott im größesten Lichte: *sein Werk, eine menschliche Seele, durch sich selbst eine Sprache schaffend und fortschaffend, weil sie sein Werk, eine menschliche Seele ist.* Sie bauet sich diesen Sinn der Vernunft als eine Schöpferin, als ein Bild seines Wesens. Der Ursprung der Sprache wird also nur auf eine würdige Art göttlich, sofern er menschlich ist. (1966:123)

Diesen theologischen Hintergrund darf man bei Hamann und Herder nie außer Acht lassen. Es mutet daher seltsam an, wenn Hannelore Pallus in ihrem Beitrag "Die Sprachphilosophie Johann Georg Hamanns als eine Quelle für Herders Anschauungen über das Verhältnis von Sprache und Denken" aus marxistischer Sicht mit aller Gewalt versucht, bei beiden Autoren Ansätze für materialistische und 'antifeudale' Anschauungen nachzuweisen. So glaubt sie z.B. in den Stellungnahmen Hamanns gegen einige herrschende kirchliche Formen auch einen 'ersten Ansatz zur Kritik an der Religion über die Kritik an der Kirche' erblicken zu dürfen. Dann folgt der erstaunliche Satz: 'Auch Herder gelang es nicht, bis zur völligen Ablehnung der Religion vorzudringen, wie es die Atheisten, Herders Freunde Einsiedel und Knebel, taten' (367). Das ist denn doch wohl für einen evangelischen Theologen, Generalsuperintendenten und Oberpfarrer an der Stadtkirche zu Weimar, ein wenig zuviel verlangt.

Für die heutige Sprachwissenschaft ist der alte Streit um den göttlichen oder menschlichen Ursprung der Sprache nurmehr von rein historischer Bedeutung. Wir verstehen kaum mehr, wie sich die Gemüter an dieser Frage derart erhitzen konnten. Übrigens war schon dem realistisch denkenden Goethe diese Aufregung unbegreiflich. Ihm schien die Frage, mit der Herder ihn in Straßburg vertraut machte, 'einigermaßen müßig. ... War der Mensch göttlichen Ursprungs, so war es ja auch die Sprache selbst, und war der Mensch, in dem Umkreis der Natur betrachtet, ein natürliches Wesen, so war die Sprache gleichfalls natürlich' (Gedenk-Ausgabe, X: 445–446).

Heute ist die Evolutionstheorie durch Fakten gesichert. Der Prozeß der Menschwerdung darf als eine Tatsache gelten. Es hat ein Tier–Mensch-Übergangsfeld gegeben, das führende Anthropologen ins Erdzeitalter des Pliozän, etwa sechs Millionen Jahre zurückverlegen (Heberer 1968). Ein geradezu phantastisch weiter Zeitraum, verglichen mit den wenigen Jahrtausenden, mit denen Herder rechnen konnte. Trotzdem wissen auch wir — noch — nicht, wie die menschliche Sprache tatsächlich entstanden ist. Aber wir sind sicher, daß sie einen bestimmten Entwicklungsgrad des zentralen Nervensystems und der Sprachorgane voraussetzt, daß sie, wenn auch mit mutativen Sprüngen, aus einfachsten Anfängen heraus entstanden sein muß, an die kein Rekonstruierungsversuch aus historisch belegten Sprachen heranreicht. Wir dürfen weiter vermuten, daß eine systematische Erforschung des Prozesses der kind-lichen Spracherlernung zum besseren Verständnis jener nicht mehr erreichbaren Anfänge beitragen kann, ohne daß wir damit eine Parallele zwischen Phylogenese und Ontogenese behaupten wollen.

Herders Auffassungen verdienen aber noch heute unser Interesse. Sie enthalten geniale Einsichten, die uns manche aus reiner Unkenntnis gefällten Fehlurteile des Autors übersehen lassen. Aus diesem Grunde ist dieser epochemachenden Arbeit hier mehr Platz eingeräumt als Herders anderen Äußerungen zu sprachlichen Problemen.

Bereits der erste Satz der Herderschen Abhandlung rüttelt auf und schockiert: 'Schon als Tier hat der Mensch Sprache'. Man hat diesen Satz als Widerspruch in sich bezeichnet, man hat auch einen evolutiven Gedanken hineingedeutet. Beides ist falsch. Herder will lediglich sagen, daß der Mensch als Lebewesen, das er ja wie das Tier zweifellos ist, bereits ein Sprachwesen ist. Mit dem Tier hat der Mensch manches gemeinsam, so auch die 'Sprache der Empfindungen', die affektiven Laute des Wohlbefindens und des Schmerzes. Aber aus diesen Naturtönen, die beim heutigen Menschen nur noch in Resten lebendig sind, hat sich nie menschliche Sprache entwickeln können. Denn das 'Naturgesetz empfindsamer Maschinen', ihr Geschrei der Empfindungen, ist etwas ganz anderes als Sprache.

Herder weist mit Recht Spekulationen Süßmilchs zurück, die jener zum Beweis des göttlichen Ursprungs der Sprache geltend macht, z.B. den Hinweis darauf, daß alle Sprachen mit einer ganz geringen Anzahl von 'Buchstaben' — richtiger: von Lauten — auskommen. Paul Salmon hat darin in seinem Aufsatz "Herder's Essay on the origin of language, and the place of man in the animal kingdom (1968/69) eine Vorahnung des phonologischen Systems erblicken wollen. (S. 60). Herder lehnt auch Étienne Bonnot de Condillacs (1715–1780) Annahme der Spracherfindung zwischen einsam aufwachsenden Kindern und ähnliche Gedanken Maupertuis' und Rousseaus ab.

Seine eigene Begründung stützt sich auf philosophische, anthropologische, biologische und psychologische Argumente, die nicht selten eigenem Scharfsinn entstammen und sich nicht auf wissenschaftlich gesicherte Fakten stützen. Der Mensch ist im Gegensatz zum Tier arm an Instinkten und schwach in Bezug auf die Qualität seiner Sinne. Er ist körperlich benachteiligt, ein Mängelwesen. (Dieses Moment hat Arnold Gehlen in seiner biologischen Anthropologie aufgegriffen und ausgewertet; Gehlen 1950.) Kompensiert werden die Mängel durch die 'breitere Sphäre', die die geschwächten Sinne dennoch eröffnen, durch das breitere Spektrum möglicher Interessenahme, durch das göttliche Geschenk der Freiheit, die den Menschen befähigt, der Welt ganz anders als das Tier zu begegnen. Der Mensch hat eine unteilbare Seele, geistige Kräfte, die ihn befähigen, sich Sprache zu schaffen. Besonders ist es die BESONNENHEIT, die Fähigkeit zur Reflexion, die es ihm ermöglicht, Distanz zur Flut der Erscheinungen zu gewinnen, die Gegenstände der Erfahrung nicht nur wahrzunehmen, sondern sie auch zu erkennen und wiederzuerkennen. Besonnenheit versetzt den Menschen in die Lage, den Strom der Empfindungen anzuhalten, aus den komplexen Erfahrungsgegenständen einzelne Merkmale herauszugreifen, sie mit lautlichen Merkzeichen festzuhalten und geistig verfügbar zu machen. Das berühmte Beispiel des Schafes, dessen Blök-Laut zum Merkmal, zur 'tönenden Bezeichnung' wird, ist allgemein bekannt. Das erste erkannte 'tönende Merkmal' wird zum 'Wort der Seele'. Damit ist die Sprache gegeben.

Alf Sommerfelt hat den Ansatz beim Blök-Laut des Schafes als Zeichen dafür gedeutet, daß Herder an einen onomatopoetischen Sprachursprung dachte (Sommerfelt 1953/54). Diese Überlegung ist trotz mancher in diese Richtung weisenden Äußerungen Herders nicht zwingend. Denn Herder nennt bemerkenswerterweise den Laut des Schafes an dieser Stelle nicht, er hütet sich auch, etwa das deutsche Wort *Schaf* auf die Lautäußerung des Tieres zurückzuführen, was zu einer völlig falschen Etymologie hätte führen müssen. Sein Satz 'Ha, du bist das Blökende!' enthält gerade keinen onomatopoetischen Ausdruck. Entscheidend ist vielmehr die Merkmalheraushebung als solche, ganz gleich, über welchen Sinn sie gewonnen ist. Dies ist das Bleibende für die Sprachwissenschaft, die Einsicht, daß es sich bei der Merkmalfindung, bei der abstraktiven Hervorhebung von Kennzeichen um ein konstitutives Element sprachlicher Begriffsbildung handelt.

Ein weiterer Einwand gegen Herders Ansatz verdient Erwähnung. Ewald Schankweiler hat in seinem Aufsatz "Zum Wesen und Ursprung der Sprache bei Jacob Grimm und Wilhelm von Humboldt" (1965) behauptet, Herders Deutung sei rein psychologischer Natur, und er wendet gegen Herder ein, dieser habe das entscheidend wichtige soziale Element im Prozesse der Sprachentstehung übersehen. Hier hätten Wilhelm von Humboldt und Jacob Grimm schärfer gesehen. Auch das ist nicht richtig. Das 'zweite Naturgesetz', das Herder im zweiten Teil seiner Abhandlung formuliert, lautet: 'Der Mensch ist in seiner Bestimmung ein Geschöpf der Herde, der Gesellschaft: die Fortbildung einer Sprache wird ihm also natürlich, wesentlich, notwendig.' Herder sieht also durchaus den gesellschaftlichen, den sozialen Charakter der Sprache. Er hebt in diesem Zusammenhang die Wichtigkeit der Familie als Ausgangspunkt der Spracherlernung für das Kind hervor. (Freilich gibt es auch zahlreiche in Gemeinschaften lebende Tiere, die dennoch keine Sprache entwickelt haben. Wohl wissen wir heute, daß sie über Zeichensysteme verfügen, die das Zusammenleben und Überleben sichern.) Die Einsicht in den sozialen Charakter der menschlichen Sprache läßt sich aber auch aus Herders Äußerungen über die wichtige Vermittlungsfunktion des Gehörsinnes herauslesen. Herder glaubt an die Ausdruckskraft des Schalles. An die Tatsache, daß die menschliche Sprache durch die Lauterzeugung eng mit dem Gehörsinn verbunden ist, knüpft er bemerkenswerte Ausführungen über das Gehör, den 'mittleren' Sinn des Menschen. Die besonderen Vorzüge dieses Sinnes für die Sprache begründet er ausführlich, und seine Argumente werden bis zum heutigen Tage bei der Diskussion dieser Zusammenhänge wiederholt.

Freilich fehlt es bei Herder auch nicht an unhaltbaren Spekulationen. Die tönenden Merkmale werden als Zeichen innerer Bewegung gedeutet, und das Bewegung ausdrückende Verbum wird zum Zentrum der Sprachentwicklung. Der Sprachursprung wird zudem eng mit dem Gesang verknüpft. Der Mensch als Geschöpf der Sprache ist auch ein singendes Geschöpf. Romantische Auffassungen strömen hier ein.

Wichtig für die weitere Entwicklung der Sprachwissenschaft wurden Herders Äußerungen über die Sprachverschiedenheit und die 'Nationalsprachen'. Trotz der Annahme eines monogenetischen Sprachursprungs hält Herder die Aufspaltung in viele Einzelsprachen für notwendig und natürlich. Sein 'Drittes Naturgesetz lautet: 'So wie das ganze menschliche Geschlecht unmöglich eine Herde bleiben konnte, so konnte es auch nicht eine Sprache behalten. Es wird also eine Bildung verschiedener Nationalsprachen.' Hier ist ein für das romantische Sprachdenken bedeutsamer Punkt erreicht: die Entdeckung der Nationalsprachen, die an bestimmte Sprachgemeinschaften gebunden sind. Die Sprachen werden als Spiegel des 'Volksgeistes', als Ausdruck der Mentalität ihrer Sprecher gesehen. Herder betont, daß jeder Mensch 'im eigentlichen metaphysischen Verstande' seine eigene Sprache spricht, ein Gedanke, der auch bei Humboldt wieder auftaucht. Jedes Geschlecht wird, der Aussprache nach, eine verschiedene Mundart sprechen, viele Gründe lassen sich für die Ausdifferenzierung der Sprachen auf der Erde nennen, aber ein bestimmter Grad der Gemeinsamkeit muß doch die Verständigung innerhalb einer Sprachgemeinschaft garantieren. Haß kann jedoch zwischen benachbarten kleinen Völkern die Sprachverschiedenheit verschärfen. Hier erwähnt Herder auch den biblischen Bericht von der babylonischen Sprachverwirrung, aber er tut es nicht, um diesem 'Poem' Wahrheitscharakter zuzusprechen, sondern um zu unterstreichen, daß 'die Vielheit der Sprachen keinen Einwand gegen das Natürliche und Menschliche der Fortbildung einer Sprache abgeben könne'.

Wer sich über die verschiedenen Deutungen unterrichten möchte, die *Der Turmbau von Babel* in der Geistesgeschichte gefunden hat, sei auf das monumentale sechsbändige Werk gleichen Titels von Arno Borst hingewiesen (Borst 1957–1963). Hier ist eine Fülle von Material zusammengetragen, das auch für die Sprachwissenschaft von hohem Interesse ist. Besonders hervorzuheben ist hier das einschlägige Kapitel "Revolution und Romantik" (Borst III 2, 1961:1521–1629), in dem über sämtliche Denker der Zeit, die sich zu dieser Frage geäußert haben, ausführlich berichtet ist.

Auf Herders Ausführungen über die Sprachentwicklung einzugehen, lohnt sich in unserem Zusammenhang nicht. Es fehlen ihm ausreichende Kenntnisse, um hier weiterführende neue Einsichten gewinnen zu können. Für die Sprachwissenschaft ist vor allem Herders Hinwendung zu den Sprachen der Völker und zu ihrer Geschichte wegweisend geworden. Hier finden Humboldt und Grimm den Boden vorbereitet, auf dem sie ihre eigenen Auffassungen entwickeln konnten.

Die scharfe ablehnende Reaktion des Freundes Hamann auf die Abhandlung über den menschlichen Ursprung der Sprache hat Herder schwer getroffen. Er bedauert seine zu eilig verfaßte Schrift und distanziert sich von ihr. Er sucht Hamann zu besänftigen: 'Daß Gott durch Menschen die Sprache würke — wer zweifelt?' schreibt er 1772 an seinen erzürnten Freund (Salmon 1968/69:68). Trotzdem läßt er die zweite Auflage seiner Abhandlung 1782 fast unverändert. 1784 erkennt er jedoch in einem

Vorwort zu James Burnett Lord Monboddos (1714–1799) Werk *Of the origin and progress of language* (1773–1792), das ein Jahr nach der eigenen Arbeit zu erscheinen begann, dem Engländer 'die Palme' zu. Monboddo geht ausführlich auf die geistigen und körperlichen Voraussetzungen der Sprache ein, zieht Darstellungen von Indianersprachen mit heran, um die Entwicklung vom unartikulierten Naturlaut zum artikulierten Sprachlaut begreiflich zu machen. Er hebt besonders das wachsende Vermögen zur Abstraktion als entwicklungs förderndes Element hervor. Aber in entscheidenden Punkten weicht er erheblich von Herder ab.

Herders eigene Auffassungen schwankten in seinem wechselvollen Leben. Kritiker sind der Ansicht, daß die späteren Gedanken über die Sprache gegenüber der Jugendarbeit über den Sprachursprung einen Abstieg bedeuten. Am Hofe des Grafen von Schaumburg–Lippe gerät Herder unter den Einfluß mystischer Anschauungen der Gräfin Maria, aber trotz aller Wandlungen seiner Auffassungen, trotz aller romantischen Züge seines Denkens blieb er insofern auch ein Sohn der Aufklärung, als er an die Kraft reiner Verstandesargumente zu glauben nie aufgab.

Fassen wir die Nachwirkungen Herders auf die Sprachphilosophie ins Auge, so ist festzustellen, daß Herders Begriff der Besonnenheit spätere Interpreten immer wieder angezogen hat. Manfred Krüger hat gezeigt (1967), daß dieser zentrale Begriff bei Herder mehr und mehr durch den Begriff der REFLEXION abgelöst und verdrängt wird und zwar in einem ganz bestimmten Sinne. Die Besonnenheit zielt, so meint Krüger, mehr auf das 'Woraus' des Ursprungs, die Reflexion mehr auf das 'Wie' des Entspringens. Über den Ursprung der Besonnenheit selbst denkt Herder nicht weiter nach. Die Besonnenheit ist der genetische Grund der Reflexion. Sie ist noch ungerichtet, Ausdruck der harmonisch zusammenwirkenden Seelenkräfte; aber die Reflexion ist zielgerichtet, sie führt zur Ausrichtung auf Einzelmerkmale und macht begriffliche Erkenntnis möglich (Krüger 1967:5). Da sie zur Heraushebung von Merkmalen aus der Vielfalt der Erscheinungen führt und da diese Merkmalauswahl in den einzelnen Sprachen verschieden erfolgt, löst, so sagt Krüger, die Reflexion zwar nicht das Problem des Sprachursprungs, wohl aber das der Sprachmannigfaltigkeit. Diese besonderen Bedingungen, die Herder an den Begriff der Reflexion knüpft, sollten, so fügen wir hinzu, zugleich vor einer voreiligen Identifikation mit Condillacs in ähnlichem Zusammenhang gebrauchtem Ausdruck *réflexion* warnen. Ganz fernzuhalten ist aber Rousseaus vager Gebrauch des Wortes in seinem *Discours sur l'origine et les fondements de l'inégalité parmi les hommes* (1795), wo er von '*quelque sorte de réflexion ou plutôt une prudence machinale*' (27, 60) spricht, die den Naturmenschen bei der Begegnung mit wiederkehrenden Naturerscheinungen leiteten (vgl. F. Lauchert, 1894:757).

Große Bedeutung mißt auch der deutsche Sprachphilosoph Bruno Liebrucks im ersten Band seines mehrbändigen Werks *Sprache und Bewußtsein* (1964) Herders Besonnenheit für die Deutung des Wesens des Menschen zu. Mit dieser entscheidend wichtigen Einsicht wird, so meint Liebrucks, der verhängnisvolle Versuch, den Menschen als handelndes Wesen zu definieren, überwindbar gemacht. Aus Handeln allein, ohne vorgeschaltete Besonnenheit, ohne Reflexion, ohne distanzierende Überlegung, kann, so meint er, nur Unheil erwachsen. Gerade dadurch, daß der Mensch nicht einfach reflexartig reagiert und handeln muß, sondern die Besonnenheit, also Überlegung, zwischenschalten kann und soll, wird menschliches, d.h. sinnvolles, vernünftiges Handeln möglich. Liebrucks wendet sich damit scharf gegen Arnold Gehlens handlungsbetonende Anthropologie, die bereits weitgehende Zustimmung gefunden hatte (Liebrucks 1964:79–128).

Eine eingehende Würdigung der sprachphilosophischen Schriften Herders hat der österreichische Philosoph Erich Heintel in seiner Einleitung zur Neuausgabe einer Auswahl aus Herders Gesamtwerk 1960 vorgelegt. Wenn Heintel es auch als ein bedauerliches Faktum betrachtet, daß es zu keiner echten Begegnung zwischen der großen Philosophie Kants und Hegels und den Sprachdenkern der Romantik, von Herder bis Humboldt, gekommen sei, so würdigt er doch die sprachphilosophischen Ansätze Herders vollauf. Er weist auf manche Mißverständnisse hin, auf eine folgenschwere Vermischung der Problemebenen, aber er erkennt doch an, 'daß die grundsätzlichen Formulierungen Hamanns, Herders und Humboldts gar nichts anderes besagen als die sprachphilosophische Fassung der transzendentalphilosophischen Fundamentalproblematik' (Herder/Heintel 1960:XX–XXI). Wie dies zu verstehen ist, zeigt Heintel in einer ausführlichen Begründung. Die Lektüre dieser Einleitung setzt allerdings Vertrautheit mit der Philosophie von Leibniz, Kant und Hegel voraus. Genannt seien hier nur die Hauptproblemkreise, die Heintel als entscheidend aus dem Werk Herders heraushebt: 1. Sprache und Philosophie (Logos-Weltschöpfung-Menschsein), 2. Sprache und Biologie (das Tier Mensch und die Sprache), 3. Sprache und Geschichte (Kultur, Tradition, Gemeinschaft) (1960: XLV).

Die Wirkung Herders auf den sog. sprachwissenschaftlichen Neuromantismus in Deutschland ist bedeutend. Leo Weisgerber nennt immer wieder Herder neben Humboldt als den wichtigsten Anreger seiner inhaltlich orientierten energetischen Sprachauffassung.

Das Problem des Sprachursprungs wird in der Epoche der Romantik noch mehrfach aufgegriffen. Auch für Humboldt gilt 'Der Mensch ist nur Mensch durch Sprache; um aber die Sprache zu erfinden, müßte er schon Mensch seyn' (Humboldt: IV 16). Jacob Grimm zeigt sich unzufrieden über Herders Antwort. Als Schelling der Preußischen Akademie der Wissenschaften nochmals die Behandlung der Themas vorschlägt, versucht Grimm in einer eigenen Abhandlung *Über den Ursprung des Sprache*, die er in einer Akademiesitzung am 9. Januar 1851 vorträgt, eine sprachwissenschaftliche Antwort zu geben. Aber wie Karl Ulmer in einem Aufsatz über "Die Wandlung des Sprachbildes von Herder zu Jacob Grimm" (1950/51) gezeigt hat, ist ihm dies nicht gelungen. Denn wenn er auch die sprachphilosophische Problematik durch eine sprachwissenschaftliche Argumentation zu ersetzen trachtet, so kann er gleichwohl auf bestimmte philosophische Voraussetzungen im Sinne Herders nicht verzichten. Zu einer sprachwissenschaftlichen Begründung reichen aber auch Grimms Kenntnisse keineswegs aus. Wenn er unter dem gewaltigen Eindruck der genetisch-sprachvergleichenden Forschung auf dem Gebiete der indogermanischen Sprachen den Gedanken der Ursprache ins Zentrum seiner Überlegungen stellt, so verkennt er, daß erstens der Zugang zu dieser hypothetischen Ursprache noch keineswegs eröffnet war und daß zweitens die gemeinsame Grundsprache des Indogermanischen, selbst wenn es sie wirklich gegeben haben sollte, in gar keiner Weise mit dem menschlichen Sprachursprung gleichgesetzt werden kann.

Trotz mancher wertvoller Passagen bleibt Grimms Abhandlung, wie Ulmer zu recht bemerkt, hinter der Herders zurück. Auch bei ihm stehen richtige Einsichten neben kühnen Hypothesen und bedauernswerten Fehleinschätzungen. Reichlich unkritisch erscheint dem heutigen Betrachter eine Grimmsche Überlegung wie etwa die, daß sich bei Annahme der Entstehung der Menschheit aus einem Elternpaar die Kinder gegenseitig hätten heiraten müssen, um sich zu vermischen, 'wovor die natur ein grauen hat' (S. 36). Und er fährt an dieser Stelle fort: 'Die Bibel geht darüber still hinweg, daß Adams und Evas, wenn sie allein standen, kinder untereinander sich begatten mußten' (S. 36). Auch daß 'mann und weib zusammen, vollwüchsig und zeugungsfähig erschaffen wurden' (S. 35), nimmt Grimm ohne weiteres an. Man ist überrascht, bei einem Forscher vom Range Grimms derartig naive Gedanken zu finden, und es ist eigentlich kaum zu erwarten, daß dieser Mann wesentlich mehr zur Klärung der Frage nach dem Sprachursprung beitragen konnte als der philosophisch, anthropologisch und biologisch umfassender gebildete Herder.

Alle bedeutenden Sprachursprungstheorien der Zeit stellt Heymann Steinthal 1877 zusammen. Auch wenn hier die obere zeitliche Grenze unseres Kapitels bereits überschritten ist, werden diese wichtigen Hinweise erwünscht sein. In der vierten, 'abermals erweiterten' Auflage von 1888 behandelt er neben Hamann, Herder, Grimm und Humboldt auch Friedrich Wilhelm J. von Schelling, Karl Wilhelm Ludwig H. Heyse (1797–1855), Ernest Renan (1823–1892), Lazarus Geiger (1823–1900), Gustav Jäger, Charles Robert Darwin (1908–1882), Caspari, Ludwig Noiré (1828–1889), Wilhelm Wundt. Steinthals Urteil über die Theorien von Herder, Humboldt, Grimm und Heyse gipfelt in der Feststellung, daß die Genannten nur die Lage des menschlichen Bewußtseins zeichnen wollten, 'bei welcher Sprache entstand und entstehen mußte, oder den Weg entdecken, auf welchem sich der Mensch Sprache schuf und schaffen mußte'. Es ging 'um ein Kapitel der Metaphysik. Dabei blieb der Ursprung als historische Tatsache ganz unberührt' (1877:350). Für Steinthal selbst, der Sprache als psychisches Organ betrachtete, 'handelte es sich um die Lage des Bewußtseins und um die dasselbe beherschende (sic) Gesetze bei der Erzeugung der Sprache im Uranfang, wie im Kinde, und wie im jedesmaligen Augenblick der Rede' (351). Es war also eine Frage der empirischen Psychologie.

Steinthal bemühte sich, den Ursprung des Menschen aus dem Tier nachzuweisen, wobei ihm der Übergang von der vorsprachlichen tierischen Wahrnehmung oder Anschauung zur höheren Stufe der Vorstellung oder Sprache besonders wichtig erschien. Er geht dabei behutsam vor, setzt ähnlich wie Herder bei den Sinnesempfindungen ein, betont die Wichtigkeit des aufrechten Ganges und dessen Einfluß auf die

Entwicklung der Sinne und die damit verbundene wachsende Intellektualität. Diese wiederum stellt der Mensch in den Dienst nutzbringender Arbeit. Die Arbeit ihrerseits schafft Bedürfnisse, führt zugleich zur Gesellschaft. Diese wird ein neuer Keim zur Erweiterung des Intellekts und zur Schöpfung der Sprache. Dabei wird das Familienleben wichtig.

Steinthal legt Wert darauf, bei seinen Überlegungen den Boden der Kausalität nicht zu verlassen, und er nimmt für sich in Anspruch, Herders Darstellung entscheidend zu ergänzen. Er greift auch Argumente Darwins, Jägers, und Casparis auf, denen zufolge die physiologische Seite der Sprache für die Ursprungsfrage von untergeordneter Bedeutung sein soll. Der Schwerpunkt liegt auf der geistigen Seite, die Frage ist für ihn daher hauptsächlich eine Frage der Psychologie. Es mag den heutigen Beobachter überraschen, daß der nach positiver Faktizität einer Beweisführung strebende Steinthal die physiologischen Grundlagen der menschlichen Sprachfähigkeit und des menschlichen Sprachbesitzes so gering veranschlagt und daß er übersieht, daß auch die Psyche des Menschen auf physiologischen Voraussetzungen beruht. Aber über das Gehirn wußte man zu seiner Zeit noch so wenig, daß dieser Mangel seiner Argumentation entschuldbar bleiben mag. Überraschend ist auch, daß Steinthal die Deszendenz-Theorie, die er (als Hypothese) durchaus anerkannte, dennoch unbeachtet ließ. Er begründete dies selbst mit der Feststellung, daß ausreichende Grundlagen noch fehlten.

Geradezu unglaublich wirkt jedoch, daß Steinthal es durchaus für möglich hält, daß sich, wie der Wiener Anatom F. Müller annahm, zwölf Menschenrassen noch vor der Sprache entwickelt haben könnten. Hier zeigt sich ein krasser Gegensatz gegenüber Hamann, Herder, Humboldt und Grimm. Steinthal stört die Annahme eines sprachlosen Menschen keineswegs, er spricht sogar die für einen Sprachforscher überraschenden Sätze aus: 'durch Sprechen wird man nicht klug; der Mangel an Sprache macht nicht dumm' (a.a.O.: 356). Eine direkte Notwendigkeit zur Sprachentwicklung liegt für Steinthal nicht vor. Lediglich ein erwachender Trieb zur Vervollkommnung, zur Mitteilung, zur Geselligkeit u.a. werden als Keime des Sprachursprungs genannt, die sich, so nimmt der Autor an, in der Eiszeit entwickelt haben müssen. Ein 'quaternärer' (diluvialer) Mensch scheint ihm unter Berufung auf den Anatomen Robert Hartmann erwiesen, ein tertiärer Mensch bleibt noch hypothetisch. Es ist weiterhin festhaltenswert, daß Steinthal die Seelenkräfte, die zur Sprache, die Triebe, die zur Artikulation lautlicher Zeichen führen, auf Reflexe reduzieren zu können glaubt. Er wendet sich damit besonders gegen Auffassungen Wilhelm Wundts. Selbst der Wille ist für Steinthal eine ganz mechanische Kraft, die nach bestimmten Gesetzen des Bewußtseins funktioniert, als auch eine Art Reflex. Man wird hier an spätere Postulate des Behaviorismus oder der sog. objektiven Psychologie erinnert, die im klassischen Strukturalismus unseres Jahrhunderts eine so große Rolle gespielt haben.

Was die Entwicklung der Sprachen selbst anbetrifft, so spielt auch hier die Reflex-Auffassung Steinthals eine Rolle. Z.B. deutet er auf diese Weise das Wesen der Onomatopöie, die er als ein stets lebendiges konstitutives Prinzip der Sprache bezeichnet, ohne daß es jedoch regulativ wäre. Von Anbeginn ist Sprache für Steinthal jedoch geschichtlich und er stimmt wieder mit Humboldt überein, wenn er den Ursprung der Sprache als Geschichte der menschlichen Rede versteht. Steinthal nimmt dabei Perioden des Werdens an: Die Urgeschichte zeigt, wie das menschliche Bemerken, das Wachstum des objektiven Interesses an den Dingen dabei wirksam wird. Diese Einsicht sieht Steinthal vor allem durch die Arbeiten Geigers und Noirés gefestigt.

Obwohl Steinthal Geselligkeit und Mitteilung als Ursachen des Sprachursprungs anerkennt, legt er doch Wert auf die Feststellung, daß Sprache nicht nur als Mittel der Mitteilung zu sehen ist, vielmehr dient sie zum Selbstverständnis des Redenden und ist in ihrem Wesen vor allem hierin zu begründen. Für die Sprachentwicklung selbst betrachtet Steinthal die Entwicklung der zweigliedrigen Rede, des Satzes aus Subjekt und Prädikat, die Differenzierung von Subjekt und Objekt als entscheidend, denn darin wird der Fortschritt von der Wahrnehmung zur Vorstellung greifbar, dem in seiner Theorie zentrale Bedeutung zukommt.

Im übrigen bleibt Steinthals Ansatz in den genannten Überlegungen stecken. Zu einer vollen Ausarbeitung seiner Anschauungen ist er nicht gekommen.

Damit können wir diesen Abschnitt abschließen und uns einer zentralen Gestalt der Epoche, Wilhelm von Humboldt, zuwenden.

II. *Wilhelm von Humboldt*

Wilhelm von Humboldt (1767–1835), der ältere Bruder des allgemein bekannteren Naturforschers Alexander von Humboldt (1769–1859), hat sich in der Geschichte Preußens als Diplomat und Staatsmann, als Chef des preußischen Unterrichtswesens und Begründer der Berliner Universität einen Namen gemacht. Neben seinen vielen Ämtern und Pflichten hat er sich von Jugend an für das Sprachenstudium interessiert. Er hat zahlreiche Länder Europas bereist, kannte viele tote und lebende indoeuropäische und nichtindoeuropäische Sprachen, lernte noch in hohem Alter Sanskrit und gehörte zu den besten Sprachenkennern seiner Zeit. Er hat sowohl spezielle, empirische Sprachstudien vorgelegt, als auch wichtige sprachphilosophische Schriften verfaßt. In seinem Werk sind die Grenzen zwischen Sprachwissenschaft und Sprachphilosophie fließend.

Die letzten Jahre seines Lebens waren ganz sprachwissenschaftlichen und sprachphilosophischen Studien gewidmet. Die hervorragendste Arbeit ist die Einleitung zum sog. Kawi-Werk, einer geplanten Darstellung der Sprache Javas, die als Mittelglied zwischen den westlichen und östlichen Sprachtypen in Humboldts Sicht besondere Wichtigkeit erlangt hatte. Wenn man Humboldt als Begründer der allgemeinen Sprachwissenschaft bezeichnen kann, so ist das besonders dieser programmatischen Einleitung zuzuschreiben, in der die verschiedensten Seiten des Sprachproblems beleuchtet werden.

Schon der Titel ist kennzeichnend für die Einstellung des Autors: *Ueber die Ver-*

schiedenheiten des menschlichen Sprachbaues und ihren Einfluß auf die geistige Entwicklung des Menschengeschlechts (1830–1835). Das Werk wurde erst nach Humboldts Tode von seinem Bruder Alexander veröffentlicht.

Über sämtliche Äußerungen Humboldts in diesem weiten Bereich unterrichtet das *Bibliographische Handbuch zur Sprachinhaltsforschung* (Gipper/Schwarz 1962ff.) in den Titelnummern 8807–8851 (S. 1175–1209). In zahlreichen Besprechungen sind hier auch alle bedeutsamen Gedankengänge Humboldts hervorgehoben worden. Ein ausführliches Sachregister zu allen sprachlich relevanten Aufsätzen Humboldts von Edeltraud Bülow schließt das Gesamtwerk zum ersten Mal völlig auf und ist eine unentbehrliche Hilfe für die künftige Humboldt–Forschung.

Die Wirkung von Humboldts Ideen war jedoch zunächst nicht sonderlich groß. Zu sehr zog eine andere sprachwissenschaftliche Disziplin in den ersten Jahrzehnten des 19. Jahrhunderts die Aufmerksamkeit der interessierten Fachwelt auf sich: die entstehende historisch-vergleichende Sprachwissenschaft. Diese in wichtigen Punkten von Rasmus Kristian Rask (1787–1832) eingeleitete, aber aus verschiedenen Gründen doch von Franz Bopp (1791–1867) ausgelöste Entwicklung, die zur Ausbildung der Indogermanistik führte und als solche Eingang in die deutschen Universitäten gefunden hat, weist zwar in eine andere Richtung, ist Humboldt aber trotzdem in vieler Hinsicht verpflichtet. So hat Wilhelm von Humboldt, der mit den bedeutendsten Persönlichkeiten seiner Zeit in lebhaftem Gedankenaustausch stand, auch wesentlich zur Entdeckung junger wissenschaftlicher Talente beigetragen. Er war es auch, der die junge historisch-vergleichende Sprachwissenschaft entscheidend gefördert hat, indem er Franz Bopp auf einen Lehrstuhl für orientalische Literatur und allgemeine Sprachkunde, d.h. praktisch auf den ersten Lehrstuhl für allgemeine Sprachwissenschaft, an die Universität Berlin berief. Er hat aber das junge Fach nicht nur durch seinen politischen Einfluß nach Kräften gefördert, sondern an der Forschung selbst aktiven Anteil genommen. Durch regen Briefwechsel mit den führenden Kapazitäten auf dem Gebiete der orientalischen und asiatischen Sprachen, wie z.B. mit August Wilhelm von Schlegel, der seit 1818 als Sanskritist einen Lehrstuhl an der Universität Bonn innehatte, hat er wiederholt in die Diskussion um philologische Einzelfragen eingegriffen und in dem Streit der Lehrmeinungen zu vermitteln gesucht (Briefwechsel Humboldt/A. W. v. Schlegel, 1908).

Humboldt war aber zugleich ein philosophisch und literarisch gebildeter Mann. Die intensive Beschäftigung mit der idealistischen und kritischen Philosophie, vor allem mit Kant, sowie die persönliche Begegnung, ja, Freundschaft mit Schiller und Goethe haben zu einer Weite des Blickes und zu einer Höhe der Anschauung geführt, die einmalig genannt werden kann.

Von der hohen Warte eines erfahrenen Weltmannes, eines 'homme de lettres' und klassisch gebildeten Humanisten aus war es diesem außergewöhnlichen Manne möglich, auch die Sprachforschung auf eine Höhe der Betrachtungsweise zu heben, die vor ihm und nach ihm selten erreicht worden ist. Allerdings gelten seine Schriften als schwer verständlich und unklar. Vilhelm Thomsen wiederholt in seiner *Geschichte der*

Sprachwissenschaft bis zum Ausgang des 19. Jahrhunderts (1927) die alten Einwände und findet in Humboldts Schriften so viel Abstraktes, Unwirkliches, ja Mystisches, so viel, das uns 'wunderlich fern' steht, daß es ihm schwer fällt, Humboldt voll zu würdigen oder gar seinen Einfluß auf die Sprachwissenschaft zu verstehen (S. 63f.). Auch R. H. Robins hat in seiner *Short history of linguistics* (1967) den diffusen Stil Humboldts bedauert. Im Gegensatz zu Thomsen erkennt er aber die große Bedeutung Humboldts an und hält es für wahrscheinlich, daß ihm ein Platz neben F. de Saussure eingeräumt worden wäre, wenn er seine Ideen mehr ausgearbeitet hätte und diese infolgedessen auch mehr verbreitet und gelesen worden wären (1967:174–178).

Derartige Vorurteile haben sicher viele Leser von der Lektüre der Originaltexte abgehalten. In der Tat ist Humboldt nicht leicht zu lesen. Sein Stil setzt gründliche Deutschkenntnisse und vor allem Geduld voraus. Leider fehlen auch immer noch ausreichende Übersetzungen in die übrigen Kultursprachen. Aber die Mühe des Eindringens in die komplizierte Materie lohnt sich.

Vortrefflich hat Heymann Steinthal in seiner Habilitationsschrift *Die Sprachwissenschaft Wilhelm v. Humboldt's und die Hegel'sche Philosophie* (1848) den Kern der Schwierigkeiten erkannt. Da diese Stelle lange Kommentare überflüssig macht, sei sie hier im vollen Wortlaut zitiert:

> Die Dunkelheit, welche in Humboldts Schriften unleugbar sich findet, rührt keineswegs von der Methode her, sondern ganz vorzüglich aus der Neuheit und der Gediegenheit der Ideen, denen sich nicht sogleich die Sprachform anschmiegen will. Für die Tiefe seines Gefühls und seiner Gedanken fanden sich nicht immer die sie ganz in sich begreifenden und wiedergebenden Worte. Aus jedem Satze wehet uns ein unaussprechliches Etwas an, was uns ahnen lässt, es liege in den Worten nicht alles wirklich ausgedrückt, was sie bedeuten sollen; und wir fühlen uns immer von neuem getrieben, dieses über den wörtlichen Ausdruck Ueberschwankende uns klar zu machen. Wir fürchten immer, Humboldts Worte noch nicht vollkommen verstanden zu haben. So verstärkt ihre Dunkelheit nur den Reiz, sie aufzuhellen. Darin liegt das Anregende, welches Humboldts Werke für immer ausüben werden. Sie werden nur bei reger, lebendiger Selbstthätigkeit des Lesers verstanden und wollen weniger nur aufgefasst als nachgeschaffen werden. Humboldt hat keine feststehenden Formeln, die man sich aneignen, mit einer gewissen Geschicklichkeit handhaben könnte, ohne dass man ihren wahren Geist erfasst hat. Wer sich aber mit Fleiss und auch mit Liebe, d.h. mit Vergessung seiner eigenen vorgefassten Gedanken den Ideen Humboldts hingegeben hat, der findet dann auch sicherlich zum Lohne mehr als er gesucht hatte.

Es geht hier um grundlegende Fragen der menschlichen Existenz und der Bedeutsamkeit der Sprache für die Menschheit und ihre geistige Entwicklung, um Themen also, die ebenso schwierig wie vielschichtig sind. Man darf nicht vergessen, daß Humboldt kein Berufswissenschaftler war. Er konnte es sich erlauben, als Liebhaber, als freier Schriftsteller zu schreiben und er brauchte sich an keine bestimmte Leserschaft gebunden zu fühlen. Das gab ihm die Freiheit, sich nicht dem Zwang einer systematischen Darstellung zu beugen. Er verweilte bei Einzelfragen, die ihn interessierten und ging großzügig über Fragen hinweg, die ihn im Augenblick nicht fesselten. Trotzdem sind seine Ausführungen durchaus von sprachwissenschaftlicher Relevanz. Bei der

Beschreibung schwieriger sprachlicher Probleme gelingen ihm bisweilen genaue und treffende Formulierungen, die den Neid der Fachleute zu erregen geeignet sind.

Über Leben und Werk Wilhelm von Humboldts unterrichten zahlreiche Biographien und Einzeldarstellungen. Peter Berglar hat in seiner Monographie *Wilhelm von Humboldt in Selbstzeugnissen und Bilddokumenten* (1970) das Material zusammengestellt. Welche Darstellungen auch Aufschluß über Humboldts Sprachforschung gewähren, hat Wilhelm Lammers in seiner Arbeit *Wilhelm von Humboldts Weg zur Sprachforschung* (1936) gezeigt. Die ausführlichste, immer noch unübertroffene Biographie, die auch das sprachwissenschaftliche Werk eingehend behandelt, stammt von Rudolf Haym (1856). Sie ist jetzt wieder als Neudruck greifbar (1965) und sei hier stellvertretend für alle weiteren Untersuch hervorgehoben.

Was die sprachwissenschaftliche Seite betrifft, so hat Theodor Benfey Humboldt in seiner *Geschichte der Sprachwissenschaft und orientalischen Philologie in Deutschland* (1869) besonders gewürdigt (1869:515–556). Er lobt seine sprachwissenschaftlichen Schriften 'trotz aller ihrer nicht weg zu läugnender Mängel' als 'einen unerschöpflichen Born sprachwissenschaftlicher Weisheit' (1869:555). Auch die marxistische Linguistin Gertrud Pätsch beurteilt Humboldt in ihren *Grundfragen zur Sprachtheorie* (1955) als einen der größten Gelehrten des vorigen Jahrhunderts. Ihre z.T. heftige Kritik richtet sich mehr gegen die Nachfolger, und zwar ist ihre Ablehnung um so schärfer, je mehr diese sich aus ihrer Sicht als Anhänger idealistischer Anschauungen erweisen und somit von der materialistischen Überzeugung der Verfasserin abweichen. Trotz aller ideologisch bedingten Kritik steht auch Gerhard Helbig in seiner *Geschichte der neueren Sprachwissenschaft* (1971:12–13, 119–161) im Grunde positiv zu Humboldt. Er mißt der Sprachphilosophie große Bedeutung zu und seine aus marxistischer Sicht vorgetragenen Einwände stellen einen beachtenswerten Beitrag dar. Ausführlich gewürdigt hat ebenfalls Hans Arens das sprachwissenschaftliche Werk Wilhelm von Humboldts in seinem großen Buch *Sprachwissenschaft: Der Gang ihrer Entwicklung von der Antike bis zur Gegenwart* (^{2}1969). Er verfolgt die einzelnen Etappen der romantischen Geisteswissenschaft und weist ihnen die Arbeiten Humboldts aus den entsprechenden Lebensabschnitten zu. Arens sagt, Humboldt sei 'der erste damals und der einzige seiner Art bis heute, der, soweit ein Mensch das kann, das Idealbild des Sprachforschers verwirklichte' (1969:170). Da bei Arens auch die wichtigsten Passagen der Originaltexte abgedruckt sind, empfielt sich seine Darstellung besonders als ausgezeichneter Überblick über Humboldts Werk.

Erwähnt werden muß hier noch die umfassendste Darstellung Humboldts aus sprachphilosophischer Sicht. Bruno Liebrucks hat in seinem monumentalen mehrbändigen Werk *Sprache und Bewußtsein* (1964ff.) den ganzen zweiten Band Wilhelm von Humboldt gewidmet (1965). Liebrucks geht es besonders darum, Humboldts Weg zur 'dialektischen Sprachbewegung' herauszuarbeiten, d.h. zu einer philosophischen Betrachtungsweise, die der Autor für die dem Gegenstand Sprache einzig wirklich angemessene hält. Zwar bleibt Humboldt, so meint Liebrucks, noch 'im Vorhof der Dialektik' — im Hegelschen Sinne — stehen, aber seine Gedanken werden als wegweisend für alle künftige Sprachphilosophie bezeichnet.

Es ist nicht unsere Aufgabe, eine Gesamtübersicht über Humboldts Ideen zu geben. Wohl aber scheint es uns unerläßlich, die wichtigsten Gedanken herauszuheben und zu zeigen, wie sie in der Sprachwissenschaft fruchtbar geworden sind. Vor allem wird auch auf zahlreiche Arbeiten zu verweisen sein, die sich in neuerer Zeit mit Einzelfragen beschäftigt haben.

Humboldts Interesse an den Sprachen ist anthropologischer, philosophischer, aber auch literarischer und ästhetischer Art. Man kann es auch humanistisch im weitesten Sinne des Begriffs nennen. Es geht ihm um die geistige Entwicklung der ganzen Menschheit, die sich unter entscheidender Mitwirkung der Sprachen innerhalb der Völker und Kulturen vollzieht. Die Gesamtentwicklung zielt, so glaubt er, auf eine wachsende Vollendung des Geistes und des Denkens hin. Die Sprachen stehen mit dem Denken in enger Wechselwirkung. Das Denken vollzieht sich zwar nach allgemeinen Gesetzen, und hier ist deutlich der Einfluß Kants spürbar, aber doch in verschiedener, nämlich sprachbedingter Weise. Humboldts Einsicht, daß sich das Denken der Menschen praktisch in den Bahnen vorgegebener Sprachstrukturen bewegt, liefert ihm den Schlüssel zu wegweisenden Erkenntnissen.

Allerdings interessiert ihn die Frage nach dem Sprachursprung weniger. Für ihn ist die Sprache so eng mit der menschlichen Existenz verbunden, daß er sagen kann: 'Der Mensch ist nur Mensch durch Sprache; um aber die Sprache zu erfinden, mußte er schon Mensch sein.' Hier klingt Herder an, der wie Hamann den Menschen nicht ohne Sprache denken kann. Die Sprache muß, so meint Humboldt, mit einem Male da sein, keine Sprache ist je im ersten Werden ihrer Formen überrascht worden, wir finden sie alle bereits als fertige Organismen vor. Und wir treffen sie an in der Vielfalt historisch gewachsener Erscheinungen. Die große Verschiedenheit der Formen und Strukturen muß die Aufmerksamkeit des Sprachforschers auf sich ziehen.

Humboldts Begriff der Form gewinnt dabei eine zentrale Bedeutung. FORM ist bei Humboldt nicht statisch gegebene Gestalt, sondern formendes Prinzip, man könnte auch sagen: FORMA FORMANS, nicht FORMA FORMATA. Die äußeren Formen der Sprachen, ihre lautlichen und grammatisch-formalen Gestalten sind sehr verschieden. Aber es lassen sich Verwandtschaften, bestimmte Bauprinzipien nachweisen. Eine Klassifikation der verschiedenen Sprachtypen ist möglich. Hatten die Brüder Schlegel bereits einen isolierenden, einen agglutinierenden, und einen flektierenden Typus unterschieden, und hatte August Wilhelm von Schlegel auf den wichtigen Unterschied synthetischer und analytischer Formbildung hingewiesen, so fügt Humboldt aufgrund seiner Kenntnis neuentdeckter Indianersprachen einen einverleibenden, inkorporierenden Typus hinzu. Heymann Steinthal setzt Humboldts Klassifikationsversuche fort, Franz Misteli arbeitet das System erneut um (Misteli 1893), August Schleicher greift mit einem präzisierenden Darstellungsversuch ein (1850), Franz Nikolaus Finck (1909, ⁴1936), Edward Sapir (1921) u.a. leisten eigene Beiträge, und Ernst Lewy (1942) und Johannes Lohmann (1965) suchen neue, zeitgemäße Lösungen des alten Problems, letzterer unter Einbeziehung philosophischer Kategorien von Martin Heidegger. Wir können dieses wichtige Problem der Sprachtypologie hier verlassen, weil es in diesem Band von Anna Morpurgo-Davies in dem Kapitel "Language classification" behandelt wird.

Humboldt als Verehrer des klassischen Altertums ist wie die meisten seiner Zeitgenossen vom hohen Rang einer formenreichen Grammatik, wie sie das Altgriechische zeigt, überzeugt, aber er vermag auch die Vorzüge des formenarmen, isolierenden Chinesisch zu sehen. Kennzeichnend für seinen Weitblick ist die wichtige Einsicht, daß der unleugbare Formenschwund, der sich in der Entwicklung der indogermanischen Sprachen beobachten läßt, keinen Niedergang, keinen Verfall bedeutet, wie es auch der Sicht mancher Romantiker erscheinen mochte, sondern daß es sich um eine geistige Höherentwicklung handelt. Denn was an Formenreichtum aufgegeben wurde, bedeutet, aufs Ganze gesehen, keinen Verlust, sondern ökonomische Einsparung, die Platz schafft für höhere begriffliche Leistungen. Ähnlich positiv äußert sich übrigens später auch Jacob Grimm, der trotz seiner Bewunderung für die frühere Formvollkommenheit und den alten Wohllaut der Sprachen den 'Trieb zum Gedanken' als leistungssteigernde Kraft wirksam sieht (Grimm [1851] 1958: 38–9).

Wichtiger aber als die äußere lautliche Verschiedenheit der Sprachen ist ihre innere semantische Verschiedenheit. Zwei zentrale Begriffe Humboldts tragen diesem Faktum Rechnung: der Begriff der SPRACHLICHEN WELTANSICHT und der Begriff der INNEREN SPRACHFORM. Humboldt ist der Überzeugung, daß die Verschiedenheit der Sprachen nicht nur eine Verschiedenheit der 'Schälle' ist, sondern eine Verschiedenheit der Weltansichten selbst. Dieser Begriff der sprachlichen Weltansicht hat zahlreiche Mißverständnisse ausgelöst. Leo Weisgerber, der konsequenteste Fortführer Humboldts, hat hierfür den Begriff des SPRACHLICHEN WELTBILDES eingeführt, aber auch dieser Begriff, der oft mit dem belasteten Begriff der (ideologischen) Weltanschauung verwechselt wurde, hat Angriffe und Fehldeutungen nicht zu verhindern vermocht. Will man den rationalen Kern dieses Gedankens herausarbeiten, wie es auch Adam Schaff in seinem Buche *Sprache und Erkenntnis* (1964) versucht hat, so muß man betonen, daß die sprachliche Weltansicht bzw. das sprachliche Weltbild sich auf die Art des Gegebenseins der Welt in den Kategorien einer Sprache, in ihrem grammatischen, d.h. morphologischen und syntaktischen sowie in ihrem semantischen Aufbau bezieht. Es geht also, Humboldtisch ausgedrückt, darum, in welcher Weise in einer bestimmten Sprache die Welt in den Gedanken überführt worden ist. Daß hier keine Spekulation vorliegt, sondern Fakten und Tatsachen angesprochen werden, ist mit Nachdruck zu betonen. Ein Blick auf die inhaltliche Gliederung und den Aufbau des Wortschatzes einer Sprache überzeugt schnell davon, daß das erfahrbare und denkbare Seiende in einer bestimmten Weise "auf den Begriff" gebracht worden ist. Dies ist in einem jahrhundertelangen wechselvollen Prozeß geschehen und setzt sich fort, solange eine Sprachgemeinschaft mit dieser Sprache lebt und handelt. Jeder, der in die Gemeinschaft hineinwächst, übernimmt die sprachlichen Schweisen, er beginnt die Welt, bildlich gesprochen, durch die Brille seiner Muttersprache zu sehen.

Zweifellos wird auch sein Denken und Handeln durch die vorgegebenen semantischen Strukturen und Aussagemöglichkeiten gelenkt, aber er wird deshalb kein Sklave seiner Sprache, sondern kann über seine Sprache hinausdenken und gegen sie andenken. Die sprachliche Weltansicht ist insofern apriorischen Charakters, als sie dem individuellen Denken und Erfahren des Einzelnen notwendig vorausliegt. Alle weiteren Weltentwürfe, wissenschaftliche Weltbilder und ideologische, religiöse und politische Weltanschauungen werden erst später, sekundär erworben.

Sie mögen auch unter sprachlicher Wirkung stehen, sind aber nicht mit der vorgegebenen sprachlichen Weltansicht zu verwechseln. Daß der Mensch kein Sklave seiner Sprache ist, geht schon aus der Tatsache hervor, daß er die Eigenart der sprachlichen Weltansicht im Vergleich mit der erfahrbaren Welt und vor allem mit anderen Sprachen zu erkennen vermag und daß er auf sie einwirken, d.h. sie verändern helfen kann. Man braucht also hier nicht der *linguist's fallacy*, d.h. einer Zirkelargumentation, zu verfallen. Allerdings ist vor einer folgenschweren Verwechslung des wertneutralen Begriffs Humboldts mit den konkurrierenden Ausdrücken "(wissenschaftliches) Weltbild" und "(ideologische) Weltanschauung" zu warnen. Da diese Unterscheidungen bei den Übersetzungen aus dem Deutschen meist verwischt werden, entsteht hier ein ständige Quelle der Mißverständnisse. Darauf hat Helmut Gipper in seinem Buch *Gibt es ein sprachliches Relativitätsprinzip? Untersuchungen zur Sapir–Whorf-Hypothese* (1972) mit besonderem Nachdruck hingewiesen.

Leo Weisgerber hat den existentiellen und prozeßartigen, energetischen Charakter des sprachlichen Weltbildes durch eine Definition zu fassen versucht, die ebenfalls manchen Mißverständnissen ausgesetzt war. Er bestimmte eine Sprache, d.h. eine Muttersprache, 'als Prozeß des Wortens der Welt (d.h. des Überführens der Welt in Sprache) durch eine Sprachgemeinschaft' und meinte damit nicht etwa, daß es sich hier um ständige sprachliche Neuschöpfungen handelt, denn selbstverständlich liegt die Zeit der eigentlich schöpferischen Spracherzeugungen weit zurück. Vielmehr möchte er die im Leben einer Menschengruppe ständig sich vollziehende Leistung erfassen, die darin liegt, daß immer wieder die Welt über die verfügbare Sprache in den Gedanken überführt wird. Daß das sprachliche Weltbild keine autonome Größe ist und keine isolierte Existenz besitzt, sondern stets als Vermittlung zwischen Mensch und Mitmensch und zwischen Mensch und Welt verstanden werden muß, sollte kaum betont zu werden brauchen.

Es ist oft darauf hingewiesen worden, daß B. L. Whorf mit seinem Begriff der *view* (*picture*) *of the world* eine ganz verwandte Anschauung vertritt. Auch ist die Sapir–Whorf-Hypothese, die Konzeption eines sprachlichen Relativitätsprinzips, mit der Humboldt–Weisgerberschen Sprachauffassung verglichen worden. Die wahren Verhältnisse sind jedoch komplizierter, als viele Kritiker beider Richtungen angenommen haben. Daß Sapir Herders und Humboldts Schriften gekannt hat, ist sicher. Für Whorf ist dies bisher nicht eindeutig bewiesen worden, obwohl H. H. Christmann in seinen *Beiträgen zur Geschichte der These vom Weltbild der Sprachen* (1967) diese

Ansicht vertritt. Daß Whorf mit "VIEW OF THE WORLD" verschiedenes meint, geht aus der Analyse seiner Aufsätze, besonders der Arbeiten über die Hopi-Indianer und ihre Sprache, hervor. Diesen ganzen Fragenkomplex hat jetzt H. Gipper im bereits erwähnten Buch *Gibt es ein sprachliches Relativitätsprinzip? Untersuchungen zur Sapir-Whorf-Hypothese* (1972) ausführlich untersucht. Er ist auch auf die Kritiken eingegangen, die in der Diskussion vorgebracht worden sind, besonders auf die des polnischen Philosophen Adam Schaff in dessen Buch *Sprache und Erkenntnis* (1964). Vor allem hat er auch Whorfs Thesen über die angeblich andersartige Raum-Zeit-Auffassung der Hopi-Indianer an Ort und Stelle verifiziert und bestimmte Korrekturen an den z.T. übertriebenen und unzureichenden Angaben Whorfs vorgenommen. Es kann daher an dieser Stelle auf eine ausführlichere Diskussion des Weltbildgedankens in der deutschen und amerikanischen Sprachwissenschaft verzichtet werden.

Kehren wir zu Humboldt zurück: die Weltbildverschiedenheit der Sprachen muß sich auch strukturell erfassen lassen. Man hat in diesem Bereich oft sehr vordergründig argumentiert: die Vielfalt konkreter Bezeichnungen für manche Gegenstandsbereiche in einzelnen Sprachen, das Fehlen mancher Begriffe, die Aufspaltung einzelner Begriffe in zwei oder drei Synonyme oder Antonyme usw. wurden immer wieder als Beweise für die inhaltliche Verschiedenheit der Sprachen angeführt. Dabei sind dies im Grunde Selbstverständlichkeiten, Zufälligkeiten oder Belanglosigkeiten.

Wichtiger sind durchgängige strukturelle Verschiedenheiten, auf die im formalen Bereich die sprachtypologische Betrachtungsweise abzielt. Humboldt stellt hier aber einen weiteren Begriff bereit, der unsere Aufmerksamkeit verdient. Er unterscheidet neben der äußeren Sprachform eine INNERE SPRACHFORM. Dieser Begriff ist ebenso bekannt wie umstritten. Humboldt hat ihn nie definiert, er ist mehr Aufgabe als festes Programm geblieben. Aber was gemeint ist, läßt sich durchaus begreifen. Es geht um die Art der Begriffsbildung, der Urteilsbildung, um den semantischen Aufbau von Wörtern und Sätzen in einer Sprache. Hier lassen sich Bauprinzipien nachweisen, die für das gedankliche Verfahren in einer Sprache kennzeichnend sind. Einzelne Untersuchungen in dieser Richtung liegen bereits vor (Bally [4]1965, Gipper 1967, Leisi [4]1970, Malblanc [3]1966, Vinay/Darbelnet 1958).

Ein Blick auf die Diskussion um den Begriff der inneren Sprachform zeigt, wie unterschiedlich er verstanden worden ist. Ein deutscher Kritiker, E. Stolte, bezeichnet in seinem Aufsatz "Wilhelm von Humboldts Begriff der inneren Sprachform" (1948) schon die Begriffsbildung 'innere Sprachform' als einen Widerspruch in sich, als contradictio in adiecto, weil er Form nur als etwas Äußeres zu verstehen vermag.

Die Sprachen haben aber nun einmal eine inhaltliche Seite, die keineswegs immer parallel zur äußeren verläuft. Es handelt sich um die SIGNIFIÉ-Ebene im Sinne F. de Saussures, in die auch komplexe Zeichen, d.h. Sätze und Texte, einzubeziehen sind.

Verschiedene Forscher haben sich um eine Präzisierung des Begriffs der inneren Sprachform bemüht. Heymann Steinthal stellt die Gleichung auf: INNERE SPRACHFORM = BEDEUTUNG = VORSTELLUNG ODER SPRACHLICHER BEGRIFF = WORT (vgl.

Bumann 1965:129). Psychische Vorstellungen, die das Produkt sinnlicher Wahrnehmungen sind, werden in den sprachlichen Begriffen festgehalten und im Sprachgebrauch reproduziert. Auf diese Weise wird aber noch nicht das Typische, das formende Prinzip sichtbar, das die innere Form einer Sprache auszeichnet und von der inneren Form einer anderen Sprache unterscheidet.

Der Philosoph Anton Marty (1847–1914) versteht unter innerer Sprachform etwas, was man eher als die wörtliche Bedeutung eines sprachlichen Ausdrucks bezeichnen kann, und ganz in seinem Sinne behandelt auch der Anglist Otto Funke diesen Fragenkomplex in der Untersuchung *Innere Sprachform: Eine Einführung in A. Martys Sprachphilosophie* (1924). An einem Beispiel läßt sich am besten verdeutlichen, was gemeint ist: Wenn ein bestimmtes Insekt im Englischen als 'butterfly' bezeichnet wird, so ist klar, daß wörtlich von einer 'Butter-Fliege' die Rede ist. Dieser wörtliche Ausdruck wäre aber ganz fehlleitend, sein eigentlicher Sinn führt zu grotesken und belustigenden Auffassungen, wie sie in Lewis Carolls *Alice in Wonderland* (1865) ausgenutzt worden sind. Die Bestandteile 'butter' und 'fly' müssen trotzdem früher einmal als sinnsteuernde Elemente empfunden worden sein, als Metapher etwa, die zur Erfassung des so bezeichneten Tieres hinführen sollte. Das müßte im einzelnen die Wortgeschichte zeigen. Die Ursprungsbedeutung ist heute jedenfalls tot. Kein kompetenter Sprecher des Englischen wird, wenn er 'butterfly' ausspricht oder hört, an 'butter' und 'fly' denken. Marty nennt diese unterliegende Bedeutung die FIGÜRLICHE INNERE FORM und unterscheidet davon eine analoge Erscheinung auf syntaktischem Gebiet, die er als KONSTRUKTIVE INNERE FORM bezeichnet. Sie liegt etwa in der wortwörtlichen Bedeutung der englischen Redewendung vor: 'How do you do?', aber auch in dem entsprechenden deutschen 'Wie geht es Ihnen?' oder französischen 'Comment allez-vous?'. Wörtlich geben diese Sätze kaum einen plausiblen Sinn, aber als feste Redewendungen werden sie verstanden, und zwar als Fragen nach dem Wohlbefinden dessen, an den sie gerichtet sind. Es ist nicht zu bestreiten, daß Marty ein tatsächlich vorhandenes wichtiges Phänomen richtig erkannt hat, aber selbst die große Mühe, die der Marty–Schüler Otto Funke darauf verwandt hat, diese eigenwillige Martysche Interpretation der inneren Sprachform als die einzig richtige zu erweisen, ändert nichts an der Tatsache, daß dies mit Humboldts innerer Sprachform wenig zu tun hat.

Kritik an Martys und Funkes Deutung haben vor allem Walter Porzig und Leo Weisgerber (1929) geübt. Grundsätzlich hat sich Porzig in den beiden Aufsätzen "Der Begriff der inneren Sprachform" (1923) und "Sprachform und Bedeutung: Eine Auseinandersetzung mit A. Marty's Sprachphilosophie" (1928) zu diesem Problem geäußert. Dabei unterscheidet er vier Stellungnahmen zur inneren Sprachform: 1. Die positivistische Auffassung, die die Brauchbarkeit des Begriffes überhaupt leugnet; 2. Die psychologische Interpretation, wonach es sich, wie bei Wilhelm Wundt (1832–1920), vor allem um die psychischen Vorgänge handeln soll, die die äußere Form des Sprechens bestimmen; 3. Die phänomenologische Deutung, wonach es vor allem um die Gesetzlichkeit der Beziehungen zwischen den 'reinen' Bedeutungen geht, also um die Frage, inwieweit es dem Sprecher gelingt, 'ideale' Gedankeninhalte sprachlich adäquat wiederzugeben; hier ist Edmund Husserls (1859–1938) Idee einer reinen Grammatik mit idealen Bedeutungsintentionen gemeint; 4. Die genannte Deutung Martys, bei der es sich um das Prinzip der Auswahl der konkreten Sprachmittel handelt, die zur Wiedergabe eines gemeinten Sinnes tatsächlich herangezogen werden.

Die posivistisch-ablehnende Haltung findet sich z.B. bei dem Junggrammatiker Berthold Delbrück (1842–1922), der nur einzelne Züge einer Sprache zu erkennen vermag, die sich weder addieren noch in ein System bringen lassen.

Die psychologische Deutung führt an die Intentionen des Sprechers, nicht aber an die vorgegebenen sprachlichen Möglichkeiten heran, in denen die innere Sprachform steckt. Der intersubjektive und überindividuelle, d.h. sozial bedingte Charakter der Bedeutungen wird bei dieser individualpsychologischen Sehweise nicht erkennbar.

Anders steht es wieder bei dem phänomenologischen Ansatz Edmund Husserls. Seiner Unterscheidung von sprachlichem Ausdruck, d.h. äußerer Sprachform, Bedeutung und (außersprachlichem) Gegenstand ist zwar zuzustimmen, und auch sein Begriff der Bedeutungsintention, d.h. der Zielgerichtetheit der Bedeutung auf den gemeinten Gegenstand, kann akzeptiert werden. Aber seine Vorstellung einer reinen Grammatik, 'reiner', 'idealer' Bedeutungen führt in eine Richtung, die der Besonderheit der historisch entstandenen semantischen Werte in einer gegebenen Sprache nicht gerecht wird. Hier drohen außersprachlich-logische Gesichtspunkte den Blick auf das Spezifische der inneren Form einer bestimmten Sprache zu verstellen.

Walter Porzig weist demgegenüber darauf hin, daß es sich um ein formgebendes Prinzip handelt, das Verständigung innerhalb der Sprachgemeinschaft ermöglicht, und bestimmt die innere Sprachform infolgedessen als 'die mit der äußeren Sprachform in Wechselwirkung stehenden eigentümlichen Apperzeptionsformen einer Sprachgemeinschaft' (1923:167). Die Schwierigkeit liegt hier im Ausdruck APPERZEPTION, einem Begriff, der philosophisch und psychologisch mehrdeutig ist und den Porzig leider nicht näher erläutert. Gunther Ipsen (geb. 1899), der sich ebenfalls mit Humboldt beschäftigt hat, bestimmt in seiner *Sprachphilosophie der Gegenwart* (1930) die innere Sprachform als 'das Bildungsgesetz des tragenden Bedeutungsgefüges der Sprache, das eine kategorial geformte Wirklichkeit meint' (20). Diese Auffassung findet Leo Weisgerber unzureichend, und er stellt ihr in *Muttersprache und Geistesbildung* (1929) die Definition gegenüber: 'Wir verstehen unter der inneren Sprachform einer Sprache die Gesamtheit der Inhalte dieser Sprache, also alles, was in dem begrifflichen Aufbau des Wortschatzes und dem Inhalt der syntaktischen Formen einer Sprache an gestalteter Erkenntnis niedergelegt ist' (86). Außerdem ist Weisgerber der Ansicht, daß Humboldt mit dem Begriff der inneren Sprachform eine mehr statische Betrachtungsweise, wie sie der 'sprachlichen Weltansicht' noch anhaftet, in eine energetische Betrachtungsweise wandeln wollte. Er begreift diese innere Sprachform in einem späteren Aufsatz als 'Stil der sprachlichen Anverwandlung der Welt durch eine Sprachgemeinschaft' (Weisgerber 1954). Josef Derbolav möchte dem Begriff der inneren Sprachform in einer speziellen Untersuchung aus dem Jahre 1951 einen bestimmten Platz in der modernen Sprachphilosophie zuweisen und zieht dazu den sprachkritischen Positivismus des Wiener Kreises, die alte sprachphilosophische Idee einer Norm- oder Idealsprache, die sprachpsychologischen Ansätze Karl Bühlers und Friedrich Kainz' heran und gelangt zu dem Versuch einer Verbindung von aristotelischer 'Form' und idealistischer 'Innerlichkeit'. Innere Sprachform wird dann bestimmt als die Verklammerung der beiden Grundpostulate der Wirklichkeitsnähe und der logischen Exaktheit, in deren lebendiger Spannung alle Sprache steht (Derbolav 1951:301).

H. Mueller hat in seinem Aufsatz "On re-reading Humboldt" (1966) auf das *dynamic principle* hingewiesen, das der inneren Form Humboldts innewohnt. Er bezieht sich dabei auf Goethes Idee der Urpflanze, die auf einem verwandten gedanklichen Prinzip beruht. H. Gipper hat in zwei Humboldt-Aufsätzen (1956/66, 1968) auf die Nähe des Begriffes der inneren Sprachform zu Goethes Naturauffassung aufmerksam gemacht. So wie für Goethe in der Natur, so kann es für Humboldt in der Sprache keinen ungeformten Stoff geben. Die innere Sprachform ist das Prinzip der Formprinzipien, welche die semantische Seite des 'Organismus' einer Sprache erfassen und ihm ihre eigentümliche Struktur verleihen.

Zu erwähnen bleibt, daß Johannes Lohmann den Begriff der inneren Sprachform ganz auf die grundsätzliche Verschiedenheit der großen Sprachtypen bezogen wissen möchte. Er begreift Humboldts Idee als zentrale Aufgabe der Sprachwissenschaft, 'das systematische Bildungs-Gesetz der Sprache (in allen seinen Einzelheiten) von den vorhandenen Sprachen her aufzuweisen' (Lohmann 1960:453), und er erblickt einen entscheidenden Schritt in dieser Richtung in Steinthals Begriff des TYPUS DES SPRACHBAUES, der später von Franz Nikolaus Finck und Ernst Lewy präzisiert wurde.

Ausführlich hat Peter Hartmann in seinem Buch *Probleme der sprachlichen Form* (1957) im 5. Kapitel über "Die sprachliche Geformtheit in W. v. Humboldts Verschiedenheit des menschlichen Sprachbaues" Humboldts Interpretationen des Phänomens der Form in der Sprache referiert. Hartmann weist auf deutliche Parallelen zu Sapir hin, zeigt aber auch bestimmte Abweichungen auf.

Beachtung verdient an dieser Stelle ferner die lesenswerte Abhandlung des georgischen Sprachforschers Guram Ramischvili "Zum Verständnis des Begriffes der Sprachform bei Wilhelm von Humboldt" (1967), die in der Übersetzung von Gertrud Pätsch vorliegt. Ramischvili arbeitet die Auffassungen Humboldts in enger Anlehnung an die Originaltexte heraus und hebt sie von denen der sprachhistorischen Schule ab. Auch der historische Hintergrund findet in dieser Darstellung Berücksichtigung. Ramischvili betont, daß Humboldt mit Ideen der romantischen Philosophie aufgewachsen ist, die von den späteren Junggrammatikern nicht geteilt wurden. Bemerkenswert ist, daß der georgische Gelehrte trotz seiner Vorbehalte gegen Humboldts idealistische und metaphysische Theorie der historischen Entwicklung die Auffassung vertritt, daß dessen allgemeine Theorie von den sozialen (historischen) Wissenschaften der Semeologie F. de Saussures und den heutigen panchronistischen Bemühungen auf diesem Gebiet nähersteht als etwa die betont historisch ausgerichtete Prinzipienlehre Hermann Pauls. Ramischvili macht auch deutlich, weshalb die Entwicklung der Sprachwissenschaft im 19. Jahrhundert der Weiterführung der Humboldtschen Anschauungen nicht günstig war. Auf die Humboldt-Renaissance im Neuhumboldtianismus geht der Autor jedoch nur mit wenigen Worten ein. Wohl weist er auf die Übereinstimmung zentraler Ansichten Humboldts mit denen F. de Saussures hin. In einer Anmerkung hebt er allerdings auch eine wichtige Verschiedenheit hervor: Humboldt habe den Energeia-Charakter der Sprache, Saussure dagegen mehr den Ergon-Aspekt betont. Diskussionwürdig bleibt Ramischvilis Behauptung, daß Humboldt und de Saussure übereinstimmend die Sprache als "reine Form" aufgefaßt haben. Die Schwierigkeit liegt darin, das Epitheton "rein" zu definieren. Angesichts des medialen Charakters der Sprache, d.h. ihrer Vermittlungsfunktion zwischen Mensch, Mitmensch und Welt, wird es problematisch, die Möglichkeit "reiner" Formen zu vertreten. Unverfänglicher scheint es uns, von einer durchgängigen Wirksamkeit formender Kräfte oder Prinzipien bei jedem sprachlichen Erzeugungsprozeß zu sprechen. Auch sollte man aus dem Begriffspaar Ergon/Energeia keine sich ausschließende Gegensätzlichkeit herauslesen, sondern darin zwei sich wechselseitig bedingende Aspekte des Phänomens Sprache erblicken.

Mit der Betonung des dynamischen Charakters des Humboldtschen Formbegriffs gelangen wir zu einem weiteren Kerngedanken unseres Autors, wonach Sprache nicht WERK (ERGON), sondern TÄTIGKEIT (ENERGEIA) sei. Auch dieser Begriff der Energeia ist oft mißverstanden worden und spielt in der heutigen Diskussion um die Humboldtsche Sprachphilosophie eine wichtige Rolle. So wurde er im Sinne der Saussureschen Unterscheidung von LANGUE und PAROLE als Hinweis auf den Sprechakt, die PAROLE, gedeutet. Doch Leo Weisgerber hat sich entschieden gegen diese Auffassung gewandt und in einem Beitrag "Zum Energeia-Begriff in Humboldts Sprachbetrachtung" (1953/54) betont, daß Humboldt ausdrücklich nicht auf den einzelnen Sprechakt abzielt, sondern 'die sich ewig wiederholende Arbeit des Geistes, den artikulierten Laut zum Ausdruck des Gedankens fähig zu machen', also die "Totalität" alles Sprechens, das ständige Wirken der "Sprachkraft" meint. Sprachkraft ist nach Weisgerber hier aufzufassen als Sprachfähigkeit, als eine Grundkraft im Dasein des Menschen, als eine Wirklichkeit in dem Sinne, daß von ihr ständig Wirkungen auf das Verhalten des Menschen, sein Denken und Handeln ausgehen. Die Existenz des Ergons, der Sprache als gegebenen Systems, braucht deshalb nicht in Frage gestellt zu werden, aber erst Sprache in actu, ob lautlich artikuliert oder nicht, ist die Existenzform, die ihr essentiell zukommt.

Leonhard Jost hat in einer Untersuchung über *Sprache als Werk und wirkende Kraft* einen wichtigen *Beitrag zur Geschichte und Kritik der energetischen Sprachauffassung seit Wilhelm von Humboldt* (1960) geleistet. Hier ist auch die Auffassung der Sprache als Energeia bei Rudolf Haym, dem Biographen Herders und Humboldts, Heymann Steinthal, Hermann Paul (1846–1921), Franz Nikolaus Finck (1867–1910), Wilhelm Wundt, Leo Weisgerber und Martin Heidegger geschildert, und es ist aufschlußreich zu verfolgen, wie verschieden dieser Begriff ausgedeutet werden konnte und wie er in die unterschiedlichen Sehwiesen der einzelnen Forscher hineingezogen wurde.

H. Gipper hat dann in der Einleitung zu den *Bausteinen zur Sprachinhaltsforschung* ([2]1969:26–7) noch auf eine weitere Interpretation durch den Philosophen Erich Heintel hingewiesen, der die Energeia Humboldts als Sinnerzeugung überhaupt versteht und ihr damit im Denken eine gegenstandskonstitutive Funktion zuerkennt, die mit der philosophischen Frage nach der Möglichkeit der Vermittlung (Kants Synthesis im Erkennen) zu verbinden ist. Sinnerzeugung in und mit der Sprache ist aber stets nur als Prozeß, als Geschehen möglich, denn die Sprache kann tönenden Sinn nur im Nacheinander eines simultan Gemeinten artikulieren.

Will man Humboldts Urteil über die Bedeutung der Sprache für den Menschen als Einzelwesen und als Glied einer Sprachgemeinschaft zusammenfassend kennzeichnen, so muß man auf die Kernformulierungen hinweisen, mit denen er die Sprache als wesenhaft mit der Existenz des Menschen verbunden hinstellt: Sprache ist, so drückt sich Humboldt aus, ein 'intellektueller Instinkt der Vernunft', ein 'Organ des inneren Seins'. Das sind biologische Metaphern, aber es handelt sich um keinen Biologismus. Vielmehr weist schon Wilhelm Streitberg in seinem Aufsatz "Kant und die Sprachwissenschaft: Eine historische Skizze" (1910) darauf hin, daß Humboldts Organismusbegriff von einer Definition Kants in der *Kritik der Urteilskraft* mitgeprägt sei, und er führt verschiedene Stellen Humboldts an, die zeigen daß er diese Vergleiche stets bildlich meinte und deren begrenzten Aufschlußwert betonte. Die Sprache gehört eben zur 'Physiologie des intellektuellen Menschen', ist also kein Produkt der Natur schlechthin, sondern der Natur der menschlichen Vernunft. Damit ist weiteres eng verbunden: das Problem von Individualität und Gemeinschaft, von Besonderem und Allgemeinem, von Sprechen, Hören und Verstehen, vom Verstehenshorizont der einzelnen Sprachen und von allgemeingültiger Erkenntnis. In all diesen Fragen hat Humboldt Wesentliches gesagt, wie in den bereits erwähnten Aufsätzen von H. Gipper weiter ausgeführt ist.

Wir haben bisher versucht, die Hauptideen Wilhelm von Humboldts zu skizzieren und zu zeigen, wie man sich um eine Klärung umstrittener Begriffe in neuerer Zeit bemüht hat. Stellenweise wurde auch bereits angemerkt, welche Forscher und Anschauungen auf Humboldt eingewirkt haben. Eine eigentliche Vorgeschichte der tragenden Begriffe ist damit natürlich nicht geleistet, und sie gehört auch nicht in den Rahmen dieser Darstellung hinein. Dennoch sollten einige Bemerkungen zu dieser wichtigen Frage nicht ganz fehlen, zumal auch einige spezielle Untersuchungen zu diesem Punkte zu erwähnen sind. Dabei sei jedoch betont, daß es uns schwierig und oft auch mißlich erscheint, das Werk eines Denkers sozusagen aus verschiedenen Einflüssen 'zusammenzusetzen'. Denn oft ist ein direkter Einfluß eines Vorgängers gar nicht mit Sicherheit nachzuweisen, und meist wird ein Gedanke, falls er wirklich übernommen ist, doch umgedacht und abgewandelt. Ideen- und wissenschaftsgeschichtlich mag daher das Verfolgen der einzelnen Fäden aufschlußreich sein, für die Leistung eines Forschers besagt es indessen nicht sehr viel.

So ist es z.B. möglich, den Humboldtschen Gedanken der 'Form' und der 'inneren Form' zurückzuverfolgen über Shaftesburys INWARD FORM und J. Harris' FORM INTERNAL bis zu Plotins TÓ ÉNDON EÍDOS und Aristoteles' Entelechie-Gedanken. Dies hat Reinhold Schwinger in seiner lesenswerten Dissertation *Innere Form: Ein Beitrag zur Definition des Begriffes auf Grund seiner Geschichte von Shaftesbury bis Wilhelm von Humboldt* (1934) getan. Aber damit ist weder erklärt, was Humboldt meint, noch gezeigt, wo er diesen Begriff tatsächlich aufgenommen hat. Ähnlich läßt sich der Begriff ENERGEIA, der bei Humboldt nur einmal auftaucht, ideengeschichtlich bis zur Antike hin zurückverfolgen, und auch der Gedanke, wonach in jeder Sprache eine bestimmte Weltansicht beschlossen ist, kann bis auf weit entfernte Wurzeln zurückgeführt werden. Zu nennen wären hier Nikolaus von Kues (Cusanus, 1401–1464), Francis Bacon (1561–1626), John Locke (1632–1704) und Giambattisto Vico (1668–1744). Aber es bedarf noch genauer Untersuchungen, um etwaige Einflusse auf Humboldt im einzelnen nachzuweisen.

Bei einer solchen Prüfung kann sich dann sogar herausstellen, daß die Anzahl der vorausliegenden Parallelen noch größer ist, als man bisher wußte. So hat z.B. Karl-Heinz Weimann in seinem wichtigen Aufsatz *Vorstufen der Sprachphilosophie Humboldts bei Bacon und Locke* (1965), gezeigt, wie stark die Ansichten dieser Denker konvergieren. Besonders die Äußerungen Lockes in Richtung auf den sprachlichen Weltbildgedanken erinnern überschend stark an Humboldt, und Weimann weist mitra Recht darauf hin, daß diese Vorläuferposition Lockes bisher nicht genügend beachtet worden ist, weil Locke seine diesbezüglichen Aussagen nicht in einem zusammenhängenden Kapitel des sprachphilosophischen III. Buches seines *Essay concerning human understanding* (1690) dargestellt hat. Infolgedessen wurden sie auch, wie Weimann berichtet, von Locke-Spezialisten wie Karl Fahrion (1913), Richard Ithamar Aaron (^{2}1955) und Arthur Zobel (1928) übersehen. Gerade deshalb ist es aber denkbar, daß Humboldt, obwohl er die Schriften Lockes kannte, dennoch seine Idee nicht diesen Stellen unmittelbar verdankt.

Wenn man nach Einflüssen sucht, findet man natürlich bei einem so umfassend gebildeten und belesenen Manne wie Humboldt Ansatzpunkte genug. Wirkungen zahlreicher Philosophen und Dichter sind sicher, z.B. die von Leibniz, Kant, Fichte und Schelling, Goethe und Schiller. Auf den besonderen Einfluß Kants wird noch zurückzukommen sein. Mit zahlreichen Gelehrten seiner Zeit stand er in Briefwechsel oder kannte ihre Werke. So erwähnt er z.B. lobend August Friedrich Bernhardi (1768–1820), obwohl dieser Grammatiker mit seiner rationalistischen Einstellung und seiner Vorliebe für formalistisch-logische Erörterungen der Denkweise Humboldts kaum entgegenkam. Die Beziehungen zu den Brüdern Schlegel, zu Franz Bopp, August Boeckh, Jacob Grimm, Friedrich August Wolf bzw. zu den Werken dieser Forscher sind ebenfalls von Humboldt selbst bezeugt. Moritz Scheinert erwähnt in seinem Aufsatz "Wilhelm von Humboldts Sprachphilosophie" (1908:175–

185) eine ganze Reihe weiterer Namen und weist nachdrücklich auf August Friedrich Potts Einleitung zu Humboldts Hauptwerk und Berthold Delbrücks *Einleitung in das Studium der indogermanischen Sprachen* (1893) als wichtige Quellen zum Studium derartiger Zusammenhänge hin. Worauf es aber letztlich ankommt, ist das, was Humboldt aus dem Studium fremder Anregungen und Lehrmeinungen gemacht hat. Hier zeigt sich die unvergleichliche Begabung dieses Mannes, selbst alte Probleme aus neuer Sicht zu beleuchten und ihnen neue Aspekte abzugewinnen.

Diese Stellen haben wir herauszustellen versucht und mit den notwendigen Hinweisen auf einige Werke erläutert, in denen der an Detailfragen Interessierte weitere Auskünfte finden kann.

III. *Die Humboldt-Renaissance im 20. Jahrhundert*

Die Sprachphilosophie Wilhelm von Humboldts ist in der Folgezeit mehr und mehr in Vergessenheit geraten. Zwar versuchte Heymann (Hajim) Steinthal (1823–1899), Professor der allgemeinen Sprachwissenschaft an der Universität Berlin, das Werk Humboldts fortzusetzen und zu vollenden, aber die Art, wie dies geschah, war kaum geeignet, dessen Wirkung auf die Sprachwissenschaft zu verstärken. Vor allem glaubte Steinthal, daß nicht die Philosophie, sondern vielmehr die Psychologie die angemessene Wissenschaft zur Erforschung der Sprache sei. Unter dem Einfluß des Pädagogen, Philosophen und Psychologen Johann Friedrich Herbart (1776–1841) hoffte Steinthal, Humboldts Ideen durch eine psychologische Interpretation präzisieren zu können. Damit folgte er einer allgemeinen Tendenz, die auf Ablösung der philosophischen Spekulation durch eine realitätsnähere Psychologie auf naturwissenschaftlicher Basis zielte. Es besteht im übrigen kein Zweifel, daß Steinthal ein hochbegabter Kopf war und daß er sich besonders beim Ausbau der sprachtypologischen Ansätze Humboldts große Verdienste erworben hat. Das Wirken Steinthals gehört aber nicht mehr in den Rahmen unseres Kapitels, und daher sei lediglich verwiesen auf die aufschlußreiche Darstellung von Waltraud Bumann *Die Sprachtheorie Heymann Steinthals dargestellt im Zusammenhang mit seiner Theorie der Geisteswissenschaft* (1965).

Im weiteren Verlaufe des 19. Jahrhunderts gewann die durch Rask und Bopp eingeleitete und durch die Junggrammatiker verstärkte mehr positivistische Art der Sprachbetrachtung an Boden. Sie führte zum Triumph der historisch-vergleichenden indogermanischen bzw. indoeuropäischen Sprachwissenschaft, also der diachronen Sprachbeschreibung. Erst in unserem Jahrhundert erlangte unter dem Einfluß der Sprachtheorien von Ferdinand de Saussure (1857–1913), Leonard Bloomfield (1887–1949) und anderen Forschern die synchrone Betrachtung sprachlicher Systeme wieder Vorrang. De Saussures Systembegriff nähert sich wieder dem Strukturbegriff des Organismus bei Wilhelm von Humboldt. Hierauf hat schon Gunther Ipsen aufmerksam gemacht (Ipsen 1932:63). Eine ausgesprochene Humboldt-Renaissance setzte aber in Deutschland in den dreißiger Jahren dieses Jahrhunderts ein. Sie wurde ausgelöst und weitergeführt durch Gelehrte wie Gunther Ipsen (geb. 1899), Walter Porzig (1895–1961), Jost Trier (1894–1970), und besonders durch Leo Weisgerber (geb. 1899), den man einen HUMBOLDT REDIVIVUS genannt hat (vgl. z.B. Ivić 1971:256). Harald Basilius hat in seinem Aufsatz "Neo-Humboldtian ethnolinguistics" (1952) diese sprachwissenschaftliche Strömung als Neuhumboldtianismus bezeichnet, und unter dieser Kennmarke ist sie in der angloamerikanischen Welt bekannt geworden. Systematische und methodische Anregungen zur Wiederentdeckung Humboldts gingen von Ernst Cassirers (1874–1945) *Philosophie der symbolischen Formen* (1923–1929) aus. Besonders im ersten, der Sprache gewidmeten Band des epochalen Werks wird das Sprachproblem in der Geschichte der Philosophie behandelt und neben Vico, Hamann und Herder vor allem Humboldt gewürdigt. Cassirers Gedanke, die Sprache als Erkenntnisform zu deuten, die die Wirklichkeit des Menschen erschafft, barg allerdings die Gefahr einer einseitig idealistischen Überzeichnung der wirklichen Zusammenhänge in sich, die auch in der neuhumboldtianischen Sprachbetrachtung spürbar blieb. Auf der anderen Seite drohte von Cassirers Auffassungen insofern die Gefahr einer Unterbewertung der Sprache, als diese nur als *eine* Erkenntnisform neben anderen hingestellt wurde. Die symbolischen Formen des Mythos und der Kunst dürften aber ohne die vermittelnde Wirkung der Sprache kaum denkbar sein. Hierauf hat Adam Schaff in seinem Buch *Sprache und Erkenntnis* (1964:37–46) hingewiesen. Auf die neuhumboldtianische Bewegung haben auch die Völkerpsychologie Wilhelm Wundts (1832–1920), die phänomenologische Methode Edmund Husserls (1859–1938) und die idealistisch-ästhetische Sprachauffassung des Romanisten Karl Vossler (1872–1949) eingewirkt. Gunther Ipsen hat diese Zusammenhänge in seinem Buch *Sprachphilosophie der Gegenwart* (1930) dargestellt. Allerdings läßt der zu allgemein gefaßte Titel nicht erkennen, daß er fast ausschließlich auf die Entwicklung in Deutschland eingeht. Antoine Meillet hat dies in einer verärgerten Rezension gerügt. Was jedoch die Wiederentdeckung Humboldts anbelangt, so entspricht Ipsens Darstellung den Tatsachen. In seinem Aufsatz "Der neue Sprachbegriff" (1932) hat Ipsen seine Ausführungen noch ergänzt. Hier wird auch deutlich, weshalb im 19. Jahrhundert das Erbe der romantischen Sprachphilosophie im Sinne der sog. realistischen Wendung an die Psychologie überging und erst um die Jahrhundertwende wiedergewonnen wurde. Eine kritische Stellungnahme zu der neuen Entwicklung hat auch Alfons Müller in seiner Untersuchung *Betrachtungen zur neuen deutschen Sprachphilosophie* (1938) abgegeben. Er geht auch auf Julius Stenzel (1883–1935) und Georg Schmidt-Rohr, den Autor in Deutschland später umstrittenen Buches *Mutter Sprache: Vom Amt der Sprache bei der Volkwerdung* (1933), ein und erblickt in den Auffassungen Weisgerbers und Schmidt-Rohrs insofern eine Einschränkung der menschlichen Freiheit, als hier die Vorrangstellung der Sprache gegenüber dem Denken überbetont werde. Daraus folgert er, ganz im Gegensatz zu den üblichen Kritiken, daß dies als eine Gegenposition zum Idealismus gedeutet werden könne.

Wie dem auch sei, es bleibt unbestreitbar, daß Weisgerbers Sprachauffassung völlig auf den von Herder und Humboldt geschaffenen Voraussetzungen basiert. Sie ist bereits in den Jahren 1924–1925 in den Grundzügen entwickelt und liegt in dem wichtigen Werk *Muttersprache und Geistesbildung* (1929) ausgebildet vor.

Weisgerbers zentrales Thema ist die Darstellung der "Kräfte" der "Muttersprache" die er in allen geistigen Bereichen einer Kultur am Werk sieht. Da er dies vornehmlich an der deutschen Sprache demonstrierte, deren "sprachliches Weltbild" er in immer neuen Ansätzen zu erfassen suchte, war es naheliegend, daß diese Gedanken in den dreißiger Jahren in Berührung mit den nationalsozialistischen Bestrebungen nach Rückführung aller Deutschen ins Reich gerieten. Die verbindende Kraft der deutschen Muttersprache war zwar geistig gemeint, sie konnte aber auch politisch verstanden werden. Hieraus erklärt sich die heftige Kritik, die man nach dem zweiten Weltkrieg gegen Leo Weisgerber erhoben hat. Es wurde dabei außer Acht gelassen, daß der Kritisierte in der nationalsozialistischen Zeit auch wegen seiner Humboldtischen Betonung der sprachlich-geistigen — und nicht der rassischen — Grundlagen der Gemeinschaft eines Volkes heftig angegriffen worden war: Man hatte ihm "volksfeindliche Sprachphilosophie" und "Sprachwissenschaft auf Schleichwegen" vorgeworfen (Banniza von Bazan 1933, Glässer 1939). Dies alles mag zwar heute nur noch von rein historischem Interesse sein, sollte aber nicht ganz unerwähnt bleiben, weil diese politisch ausgerichtete Kritik der neuhumboldtischen Sprachwissenschaft sehr geschadet hat.

In den fünfziger Jahren kam es jedoch zu einer Neubelebung der Weisgerberschen Bestrebungen in dem Arbeitskreis "Sprache und Gemeinschaft", dem neben Leo Weisgerber Gunther Ipsen, Jost Trier, Hennig Brinkmann (geb. 1901), Theodor Frings (1886–1968), Hans Glinz (geb. 1913), Johannes Erben (geb. 1925), Helmut Gipper (geb. 1919), Paul Grebe (geb. 1908), Peter Hartmann (geb. 1923), Karl Kurt Klein (1897–1971), Lutz Mackensen (geb. 1901), Hugo Moser (geb. 1909), Gilbert de Smet (geb. 1921) angehörten. An der Arbeit nahmen auch Hans Eggers, Jean Fourquet, Günther Kandler und Els Oksaar teil. Da es bei diesen Bestrebungen vor allem um die inhaltliche Seite der Sprache ging, wurde es üblich, sie als Sprachinhaltsforschung zu kennzeichnen. Eine Reihe von Publikationen zeigt die Ergebnisse dieser Arbeit. Das große Projekt einer inhaltbezogenen Grammatik des Deutschen, in der die sprachtheoretischen Vorstellungen empirisch erprobt werden sollten, blieb jedoch in den Anfängen stecken. Wohl publizierten einige Mitarbeiter eigene Grammatiken, so Hennig Brinkmann sein großes Werk *Die deutsche Sprache: Gestalt und Leistung* (²1971), Johannes Erben seinen *Abriß der deutschen Grammatik* (¹¹1972), Hans Glinz *Die innere Form des Deutschen* (²1961) — wobei der Titel irreführt, denn es handelt sich hier nicht eigentlich um Humboldts innere Form, sondern um einen eigenständigen Versuch, das, was Glinz die 'grammatischen Inhalte' nennt, mit einem struktural-experimentierenden Verfahren zu erfassen — und Paul Grebe mit seinen Mitarbeitern die neue *Dudengrammatik* (³1973). Helmut Gipper versuchte in seinen *Bausteinen zur Sprachinhaltsforschung* (²1969), die inhaltbezogene Sprachauffassung mit der neueren Philosophie und Grundlagenforschung zu vergleichen und sie weiter auszubauen. In der Einleitung dieses Buches wird die Sprachauffassung selbst nochmals im Überblick dargestellt.

Alle diese Arbeiten sind in diesem Kapitel zu erwähnen, weil sie im weiteren Sinne der romantischen Epoche verpflichtet sind, sei es im direkten Bezug auf Herder und Humboldt, sei es auf dem Wege über Ferdinand de Saussure.

Neben dem Versuch Leo Weisgerbers, Herders und Humboldts Sprachauffassung auszubauen und in der empirischen Sprachforschung zu erproben, bildet die von Jost Trier entwickelte Lehre vom sprachlichen Feld das Kernstück der neuen inhaltlich orientierten Sprachbetrachtung. Hier wird Humboldts zentraler Gliederungsgedanke, die ARTIKULATION der sprachlichen Erscheinungen, im Bereich des Wortschatzes und dann bei Weisgerber auch für die Syntax ausgewertet. Trier empfing zwar seine Anregungen weniger von Humboldt als von Ferdinand de Saussure, aber der Grundgedanke entspricht durchaus Humboldtschen Gedankengängen. Es geht hier um die am konkreten Sprachmaterial gewonnene Einsicht, daß die Bedeutung, besser: der Inhalt eines Wortes, nie völlig isoliert steht, sondern daß sein Stellenwert vom Inhalt benachbarter sinnverwandter Wörter mitbestimmt wird. Solche Gruppen sinnverwandter Wörter stehen in einem gegenseitigen Abhängigkeitsverhältnis, sie bilden Felder, die mit entsprechenden synchronen Beschreibungsverfahren nachgewiesen werden können. Man kann das Gemeinte mit den bekannten Termini de Saussures etwa so beschreiben: die *signifiés* semantisch verwandter Wörter weisen sich wechselseitig einen Stellenwert, eine *valeur* im System zu, die für das genaue Verständnis wichtig ist. Ein Farbwort wie *rot* zielt zwar auf eine außersprachliche sichtbare Erscheinung, aber der Umfang des Begriffes, die Reichweite seiner Anwendungsmöglichkeit, wird durch *orange* mitbestimmt, und *orange* seinerseits wird durch *gelb* begrenzt. Eine Sprache, die den Wert '*orange*' nicht besitzt, aber '*rot*' und '*gelb*' hat, dehnt die Grenzen beider Inhalte gegeneinander aus und schließt so die Lücke, die sonst '*orange*' füllt. Zwar wird dadurch das Unterscheidungsvermögen der Sprecher nicht betroffen, wohl aber der praktisch wirksame Unterscheidungswille.

Zahlreiche Felder sind erforscht worden (Verwandtschaft, Farben, moralische und ethische Werte, usw.). Der gesamte Wortschatz erweist sich als ein kohärentes Netz mehr oder minder dicht besetzter Felder. Deren Struktur hängt ab von den Interessen der Sprachgemeinschaft, die sie im Laufe langer Zeit ausgebildet hat, und von der Struktur des außersprachlichen Gegenstandsbereiches, der erfaßt wird. Der sprachbesitzende Mensch bedient sich unbewußt dieser vorgegebenen Gliederungen, wenn er über bestimmte Tatbestände spricht. Die Schicht der 'signifiés', der sprachlichen Inhalte, schiebt sich dabei unbemerkt zwischen Sprecher und Welt, was Weisgerber dazu veranlaßt, den Begriff der SPRACHLICHEN ZWISCHENWELT zur Kennzeichnung dieses Zusammenhangs einzuführen. Dieser sehr oft mißverstandene Ausdruck entspricht ebenfalls völlig Humboldtschen Gedankengängen.

Über die wechselvolle Geschichte der Feld-Methode, über die Kontroversen die sie hervorgerufen hat, und den heutigen Stand der Forschung unterrichtet u.a.

Rudolf Hoberg, ein Schüler Triers und Weisgerbers, in seiner Arbeit *Die Lehre vom sprachlichen Feld* (1970), in der auch die Anknüpfungspunkte an Humboldt aufgezeigt werden. Eine ausführliche Darstellung der Verfahrensweise der Feldforschung liefert Hans Schwarz in der Einleitung zu H. Gipper/H. Schwarz *Bibliographisches Handbuch zur Sprachinhaltsforschung* (Bd. I 1962–1966: LX–LXVI). Die wichtigsten Aufsätze zur Lehre vom sprachlichen Feld sind jetzt in einem Sammelband mit dem Titel *Wortfeldforschung: Zur Geschichte und Theorie des sprachlichen Feldes* (1973) von Lothar Schmidt herausgegeben worden. Die Feldlehre hat sich inzwischen als ein brauchbares Instrument der Semantik erwiesen. Das beweisen zahlreiche Einzeluntersuchungen, die in den letzten Jahren durchgeführt worden sind. Horst Geckeler hat in seiner Arbeit *Strukturelle Semantik und Wortfeldforschung* (1971) gezeigt, inwiefern die Wortfeldforschung manchen anderen Ansätzen auf dem Gebiet der modernen Semantiktheorie überlegen ist, wenn ein formaleres Deskriptionsverfahren angewandt wird. Er nimmt dabei bestimmte Vorschläge seines Lehrers Eugenio Coseriu auf, der die Feldforschung ebenfalls für eine aussichtreiche Methode hält. Streng genommen handelt es sich hier um das erste semantische Verfahren, das das Prädikat "strukturell" wirklich verdient. Denn hier wird nicht völlig un-strukturell von Einzelwörtern ausgegangen, wie z.B. bei Fodor und Katz, und nach deren Polysemien gefragt (die in Wahrheit häufig Homonymien sind!), sondern die Wortinhalte werden im realen Zusammenhang der strukturierten Wortverbände, d.h. der Felder, aufgesucht und beschrieben, in denen sie erlernt worden sind und gebraucht werden.

Da die Feldlehre in der Tat ein Kernstück der auf Humboldt zurückgehenden Sprachinhaltsforschung darstellt, konnte es kaum ausbleiben, daß sie auch in die Diskussion um die Beziehungen der Humboldtschen Sprachauffassung zu der geistig verwandten Sapir–Whorf-Hypothese einbezogen wurde. Dies zeigt sich z.B. deutlich in der Untersuchung von Robert L. Miller *The linguistic relativity principle and Humboldtian ethnolinguistics* (1968). Da diese Arbeit eine harte Kritik an der Feldlehre enthält, muß darauf eingegangen werden. Millers Arbeit beschäftigt sich nicht nur mit Hamann, Herder und W. von Humboldt, sondern geht auch auf de Saussure, Cassirer und besonders auf Weisgerber ein. Dessen Sprachtheorie, insonderheit die Theorie des sprachlichen Feldes, rückt sogar in den Mittelpunkt der Darstellung. Miller gelangt zu einem durchweg ablehnenden Urteil, wobei zu betonen ist, daß er sich auf frühe Arbeiten zur Feldforschung beruft, die nicht mehr den heutigen Auffassungen ihrer Verfasser entsprechen. Miller sieht auch nicht, daß man zwischen den in einer Sprache vorgegebenen semantischen Gliederungen, dem also, was Weisgerber unter 'sprachlichem Weltbild' versteht, und dem, was ein Sprecher darüber hinaus an eigener Weltauffassung sekundär erwirbt, unterscheiden muß. Er zweifelt ferner — wie viele andere — an der Gemeinsamkeit und Verbindlichkeit des Sprachbesitzes innerhalb einer Sprechergemeinschaft und meint, man könne höchstens sagen, daß jeder Sprecher ein eigenes Feld mit eigenen Werten besitzt (104). Er bestreitet die Brauchbarkeit der von Weisgerber angebotenen Kriterien zur Bestimmung einzelner Felder und betont, daß auch Triers Arbeiten im Bereich des Sinnbezirks des

Verstandes zu sehr auf der ungenügend kontrollierbaren Intuition des Autors beruhen. Auf diese Weise sei aber kaum zu erwarten, daß zwei Forscher in der Beurteilung eines gegebenen Feldes übereinstimmten (106). Außerdem vertritt er unter Berufung auf R. E. Longacre (1956) die Auffassung, daß der Kontext für die Wertigkeit einer bestimmten Wortbedeutung entscheidener sei als die angebliche Feldbestimmtheit (108). Er wirft Weisgerber ferner unter Hinweis auf Josep H. Greenbergs Kritik an der Sapir-Whorf-Hypothese (Greenberg, in Hoijer 1954) vor, er habe die metaphorische Bedeutung einzelner Sprachmittel überwertet (ein Vorwurf, der u.E. mit mehr Berechtigung gegen Whorf erhoben worden ist). Allgemein scheint ihm die Annahme hypostasierter Bedeutungen oder Inhalte auf dem unhaltbaren Glauben an einen Dualismus zwischen Geist und Körper oder zwischen geistigem Bereich und physikalischem Bereich zu beruhen. Als Kronzeugen für die Widerlegung dieser Auffassung nennt er L. Wittgenstein, G. E. M. Anscombe, G. Ryle und J. R. Firth (110). Zutreffender findet er Wittgensteins funktionale Bestimmung der Bedeutung als deren Gebrauch in der Sprache. Er greift dann auch ein Argument Max Blacks auf, daß der Besitz von Begriffen nicht an den Besitz entsprechender Wörter gebunden sei (Black 1959), und folgert daraus, daß das Fehlen bestimmter Wörter, etwa im Sinnbezirk des Verstandes, im Deutschen des 13. Jahrhunderts lediglich zeige, daß die Sprecher gewöhnlich bestimmte Unterscheidungen nicht trafen, die sie aber sehr wohl hätten machen können.

Die Einwände gegen Trier und Weisgerber setzt Miller mit ähnlichen Argumenten auf der Ebene der Wortarten und Redeteile fort und beruft sich dabei auf G. Ryles Ausführungen über "Systematically misleading expressions" (1952), die zugleich als Warnung vor einer sprachtheoretischen Überbewertung normaler Sprachgepflogenheiten gedeutet werden können. Schließlich werden auch Weisgerbers Äußerungen bezüglich der Eigenart deutscher Satzbaupläne, also z.B. die Hinweise auf die gedanklichen Konsequenzen der für den deutschen Satzbau typischen Klammergefüge, mit der Bemerkung zurückgewiesen, im Grunde könne man derartige Aussagen auf die Feststellung reduzieren, daß einer, der Deutsch spricht oder schreibt, eben bestimmte grammatische Regeln befolgen muß (119).

Die Schlußfolgerung Millers ist ziemlich vernichtend: 'The conclusion reached in this study is that the Neo-Humboldtians' position with regard to linguistic relativity cannot withstand serious analysis' (119). Wenn wirklich ein Fortschritt auf diesem Gebiet erreicht werden soll, so fordert Miller, dann muß zunächst einmal die allgemeine These in expliziter Weise mit brauchbaren, sorgfältig definierten Begriffen formuliert werden. Dann müssen Möglichkeiten experimenteller Nachprüfung geboten werden. Wenn bewiesen werden soll, daß Sprecher verschiedener Sprachen verschieden denken, dann ist es letztlich nötig, auf nichtsprachliche Fakten zurückzugreifen: 'it is necessary to appeal ultimately to nonlinguistic facts' (120). Miller schließt mit den Hinweis auf R. W. Browns Vorschlag (Brown 1958:262), daß Sprache so definiert werden sollte, daß sie die Semantik einschließt und daß das Denken ('thought') 'in terms of some nonlinguistic behavior' zu definieren sei. Die Kern these könnte dann — mit Browns Worten — lauten: 'that some nonlinguistic evidence covaries with some linguistic evidence' (120). Ohne einen derartigen Ansatz werde man zu keiner Beantwortung der Fragen der linguistischen Relativität gelangen.

Schon bei unseren Ausführungen über Humboldts Sprachauffassung und ihre wichtigsten Grundbegriffe wurde auf einige Mißverständnisse und Fehldeutungen hingewiesen, die auch bei R. L. Miller wiederkehren. Deshalb darf hier dieser Verweis genügen. Es sei aber nochmals wiederholt, daß H. Gipper in seinem Buch *Gibt es ein sprachliches Relativitätsprinzip?* (1972) diese Fragen ausführlich behandelt hat. Was Millers harte Kritik am Gedanken der Vorgegebenheit semantischer Gliederungen in den einzelnen Sprachen, also das Problem der sprachlichen Felder, anbetrifft, so ist mit Nachdruck zu fordern, daß die Theorie und die Methode der Feldforschung im Sinne J. Triers und L. Weisgerbers nicht nach den Anfängen, sondern nach ihrem heutigen Stande beurteilt werden sollte. Auf die Arbeiten, die hierüber berichten, wurde bereits hingewiesen.

Viele der Argumente, die Miller gegen das Feld vorbringt, sind inzwischen längst widerlegt. Die Möglichkeit einer Verständigung zwischen Angehörigen derselben Sprachgemeinschaft ist wohl kaum zu begründen und zu erklären, wenn man nicht davon ausgeht, daß die Sprecher trotz der verschiedenen individuellen Bedingungen der Spracherlernung über einen hinreichend ähnlichen Sprachbesitz verfügen, der sinnvolle Kommunikation erlaubt. Die semantischen Gliederungen, die in einer Sprache ausgebildet sind und als geltend anerkannt werden müssen, begründen die Kompetenz der Sprecher, die sie erlernt haben, und verleihen ihnen jenes unleugbare "Sprachgefühl" (*intuition of the native speaker*), ohne das niemand seine Sprache zu gebrauchen vermag. Wo aber sprachliche Gliederung ist, die den Sprachbesitz überschaubar und handhabbar macht, da ist Feld, d.h. Stellenwerthaftigkeit oder Strukturbedingtheit der einzelnen Sprachmittel. Sie liegt systematisch jedem Sprachgebrauch und jedem möglichen Kontext voraus. Diese Voraussetzungen müssen klar erkannt sein, wenn man zu einem objektiven Urteil über das Feldprinzip gelangen will. Im übrigen treffen sich einige Forderungen Millers durchaus mit den Intentionen der Feldforschung: Miller wendet sich gegen idealisierende und hypostasierende Tendenzen des Feldgedankens und betont demgegenüber die Wichtigkeit des Sprachgebrauchs, des Kontextes, der außersprachlichen Faktoren. Damit rennt er im Grunde offene Türen ein, denn die genannten Gesichtspunkte sind z.B. in den Arbeiten von H. Gipper auf diesem Gebiet ausdrücklich einbezogen und berücksichtigt worden (Gipper 1959, ²1966).

Zu einer gerechteren Beurteilung des Zusammenhänge zwischen den Anschauungen Humboldts, seiner Nachfolger und der verwandten ethnolinguistischen Bestrebungen in Amerika gelangt Roger L. Brown in seiner Untersuchung *Wilhelm von Humboldt's concept of linguistic relativity* (1967). Seine Arbeit gibt einen guten Überblick über die Intentionen und das Schaffen Humboldts. Der Autor ordnet die sprachphilosophischen Auffassungen des deutschen Forschers in die geistigen Strömungen der Aufklärung und der Romantik ein und zeigt auch die über F. Boas und

E. Sapir laufenden Verbindungen zu den parallelen amerikanischen Ansätzen auf. Die lesenswerte Darstellung versucht den Tatsachen in fairer Weise gerecht zu werden. Brown weist mit Recht darauf hin, daß die Vernachlässigung Humboldts mit dem Fehlen ausreichender Übersetzungen (20) sowie mit der strukturalistischen Abneigung gegen Bedeutungsfragen zusammenhängt (120). Er kann sich bei der letzteren Feststellung auf eine entsprechende Äußerung von D. Hymes berufen (Hymes 1961:26).

Es ist bekannt, daß die Entwicklung der modernen Linguistik nach dem zweiten Weltkrieg in wachsendem Maße vom taxonomischen Strukturalismus und seinen Ausläufern bestimmt wurde. Dessen positivistisch-behavioristische Sprachauffassung war mit einer antimentalistischen Grundeinstellung verknüpft, die die Behandlung von Bedeutungsfragen hintanstellte. Diese Zeit war infolgedessen ungünstig für die Weiterführung sprachwissenschaftlicher Arbeit im Humboldtschen Sinne. Auch die in vieler Hinsicht verwandten Ansätze bei Edward Sapir und Benjamin Lee Whorf in den Vereinigten Staaten fanden im Schatten dieser Entwicklung keine Breitenwirkung. Diese Lage hat sich jedoch seit der Verbreitung von Noam Chomskys generativer Transformationsgrammatik geändert. Man darf von einer Überwindung der vorherrschenden antimentalistischen Einstellung in der Linguistik sprechen. Das hatte zur Folge, daß man sich auch auf breiter Front wieder dem vernachlässigten Bedeutungsproblem zuwandte.

Eine weitere Blickwendung ist kaum weniger folgenschwer gewesen: Chomsky suchte wieder Anschluß an alte Traditionen zu gewinnen. Nicht nur auf die Grammaire de Port-Royal und auf Descartes berief er sich, sondern zur Überraschung vieler auch auf Wilhelm von Humboldt. Wenn es sich auch bei den Bemühungen, Humboldts Energeia-Begriff mit Chomskys generativem Prinzip und die innere Sprachform mit der DEEP STRUCTURE der Transformationsgrammatik zu verbinden, mehr um furchtbare Mißverständnisse handelt, so ist damit doch Humboldt in den Linguistenkreisen, wo man ihn für überholt hielt, sozusagen wieder hoffähig geworden.

Die Vertreter der strukturalen Semantik gehen zwar eigene Wege, aber es kann doch kaum ausbleiben, daß zumindest in neueren Darstellungen und Einführungen in die allgemeine Problematik der Semantik auch die von Humboldt ausgehenden Gedanken wieder Beachtung finden. Die Autoren sehen sich auch veranlaßt, auf Jost Trier und Leo Weisgerber einzugehen. Überall wird der Zusammenhang ihrer Auffassung mit dem Gedankengut Herders und Humboldts betont. Es hängt dann allerdings von der Einstellung des jeweiligen Autors ab, wie diese Bemühungen bewertet werden. In marxistisch orientierten Arbeiten werden in der Regel besonders die als idealistisch eingestuften Züge der inhaltlich orientierten Sprachwissenschaft mehr oder minder radikal zurückgewiesen. So etwa in der *Einführung in die Semasiologie* (1972) von Thea Schippan. Hier ist es besonders der auf Humboldtischen Auffassungen begründete Gedanke der 'sprachlichen Zwischenwelt', gegen den ernste Bedenken vorgetragen werden.

Auch in den *Grundfragen der Linguistik* (1972) von Volker Heeschen geht dessen Bruder Claus Heeschen auf die von Weisgerber weiterentwickelte Sprachphilosophie

Humboldts ein und bemerkt, die 'idealistischen Voraussetzungen der philosophischen Überlegungen' schienen 'teilweise unreflektiert zu bleiben' (1972:56). Eine nähere Begründung dieser unpräzisen Bemerkung unterbleibt allerdings.

Erwähnt werden die Humboldt–Weisgerberschen Bezüge auch in dem Buch *Allgemeine Sprachwissenschaft: Eine Einführung* (1972) von Vermeer. Hier werden u.a. die Stellungnahmen von Gertrud Pätsch und Wilhelm Schmidt angeführt, doch eine eingehende Auseinandersetzung erfolgt leider nicht.

Daß in einer so ausführlichen Darstellung wie den *Principles of Semantics* (^{3}1967) von Stephen Ullmann auch Humboldts und de Saussures Einfluß auf Trier und Weisgerber vermerkt wird, bedarf kaum der Erwähnung. Ullmann betrachtet Humboldt als 'the spiritual ancestor of the field theory' (154). Er berichtet ausführlich über Triers und Weisgerbers Bemühungen, geht auch auf die Kritiken ein und gelangt zu einer positiven Beurteilung. Ähnlich äußert er sich auch in seinem Werk *Semantics: An introduction to the science of meaning* (1962:243f.).

Recht positiv stellt sich Oskar Reichmann in seinem Buch *Deutsche Wortforschung* (1969) zur Sprachinhaltsforschung, deren Zusammenhang mit den Auffassungen Humboldts er ausdrücklich würdigt. Er wertet es als ein bestätigendes Argument, daß von Sapir und Whorf unabhängig ähnliche Anschauungen entwickelt worden sind.

In Milka Ivić's *Wege der Sprachwissenschaft* (1971) ist ein Kapitel der Humboldtschen Sprachauffassung und ihrer Weiterführung in der *Inhaltsbezogenen Sprachwissenschaft* gewidmet. Ivić würdigt diese Bemühungen ausdrücklich, allerdings verschieben sich in ihrer Sicht die Perspektiven ein wenig. So werden z.B. die Arbeiten von Peter Hartmann als Musterbeispiele der inhaltbezogenen Sprachwissenschaft vorgestellt, obwohl sich Hartmann mehrfach von dieser Forschungsrichtung distanziert hat und inzwischen eigene Wege gegangen ist.

Eingehendere Würdigungen haben die sprachphilosophischen Ideen Humboldts in neueren philosophischen Arbeiten gefunden. Georg Jánoska geht in seinem Buch *Die sprachphilosophischen Grundlagen der Philosophie* (1962) im 10. Kapitel, "Sprache und Wirklichkeit", auf die erkenntnistheoretischen Grundlagen des Weltansicht-Gedankens ein. Er bezieht hier auch ausdrücklich die einschlägigen Äußerungen Jost Triers und Leo Weisgerbers ein. Er verweist auf ähnliche Gedanken bei Martin Heidegger und Benjamin Lee Whorf. Jánoska hebt hervor, daß Weisgerber sich selbst gegen den Vorwurf des Idealismus verwahrt habe, indem er betonte, daß er keinerlei Anlaß habe, das Dasein des realen Seins der Dinge anzuzweifeln. Auch bei Whorf findet Jánoska 'realistische Stellen'. Er selbst möchte einen eigenen Beitrag zur Klärung der Rolle der Sprache im Erkenntnisprozeß leisten und hält es für eine wichtige, auch realistisch zu begreifende Einsicht, 'daß der Sprache ein konstruktiver Anteil bei der Begriffsbildung' (83) zukommt. Jánoska begründet dann seinen eigenen Standpunkt, den er als 'konstruktiven Realismus' kennzeichnet, und entwickelt eine sprachphilosophische Betrachtungsweise, für die er den Ausdruck 'ontosemantisch' wählt. Hierbei handelt es sich um einen bemerkenswerten Ansatz, der Humboldtische Gedanken aufnimmt und positiv auswertet.

Ausführlich hat sich Wilhelm Luther in seinem Buch *Sprachphilosophie als Grundwissenschaft* (1970) zu den Bemühungen um eine wissenschaftliche Bescheibung und Darstellung des Problemkomplexes "Sprache und vorgegebenes Weltverständnis" seit Wilhelm von Humboldt geäußert und eigene Vorschläge zu einer seiner Ansicht nach realistischeren Behandlung dieser Fragen gemacht. Trotz kritischer Äußerungen zu manchen Postulaten Humboldts und der Sprachinhaltforschung steht Luther dieser Forschungsrichtung im ganzen positiv gegenüber.

Auf den hermeneutischen Aspekt in Humboldts Sprachphilosophie geht Hans-Georg Gadamer in seinem wichtigen Buch *Wahrheit und Methode: Grundzüge einer philosophischen Hermeneutik* (1960) ein. Er behandelt auch die romantische Hermeneutik Schleiermachers und zeigt, welche Schranken ihr aufgrund ihrer theologischen Prämissen gesteckt bleiben. Am wichtigsten für unseren Zusammenhang ist der dritte Teil des Buches, betitelt *Ontologische Wendung der Hermeneutik am Leitfaden der Sprache*, der unter ein Motto Schleiermachers gestellt ist: 'Alles Vorauszusetzende in der Hermeneutik ist nur Sprache.' Die Sprache versteht Gadamer als Medium der hermeneutischen Erfahrung. Im dritten Abschnitt, "Sprache als Horizont einer hermeneutischen Ontologie", wird unter a) "Sprache als Welterfahrung" Humboldt als Schöpfer der modernen Sprachphilosophie gewürdigt. Seine wichtigsten Gedanken über das Wechselverhältnis von Mensch, Sprache und Welt werden auf ihre Auswertbarkeit für eine philosophische Hermeneutik geprüft. Gadamers besonnene Darstellungsweise macht dieses Kapitel — wie das ganze Buch — auch für den am Problem des Verstehens interessierten Sprachwissenschaftler äußerst lesenswert.

Eine aufschlußreiche Darstellung der Sprachanthropologie Wilhelm von Humboldts findet sich schließlich in der Schrift vom Clemens Menze *Wilhelm von Humboldts Lehre und Bild vom Menschen* (1965), und zwar im zweiten Teil. Besonders wichtig sind die Abschnitte I.,2: "Die Auffassung des Problems der Sprache", II. "Der Neuansatz: Der Mensch als Sprachgeschöpf", mit den Teilen A. "Sprachphilosophische Grundfragen" und B. "Sprachanthropologische Grundfragen". Unter anderem wird das Sprachursprungsproblem von Rousseau über Condillac bis zu Herder und Humboldt verfolgt und beurteilt. Die Probleme "Menschsein und Sprache", "Volk, Nation und Sprache" sowie "Bildung und Sprache" sind ausführlich behandelt.

IV. *Sprachphilosophie und Sprachästhetik: Zu den Darstellungen von Eva Fiesel und Friedrich Kainz*

Die einzige umfassende Monographie über die *Sprachphilosophie der deutschen Romantik* ist die ältere Arbeit von Eva Fiesel aus dem Jahre 1927. Sie verdient daher in unserer Darstellung besondere Beachtung. Zur gerechten Beurteilung dieses Buches ist es nützlich zu wissen, daß die Autorin stark von Fritz Strichs Untersuchung *Deutsche Klassik und Romantik oder Vollendung und Unendlichkeit* (1922, ^{4}1949) beeinflußt ist. Strichs Buch steht methodisch wiederum unter dem Einfluß von Heinrich Wölfflins Buch *Kunstgeschichtliche Grundbegriffe: Das Problem der Stilentwicklung in der neueren Kunst* (1915, [9]1948). Kennzeichnend für die Arbeitsweise von Wölfflin und Strich ist ein vergleichendes Verfahren mit Hilfe leitender Begriffspaare (Vollendung und Unendlichkeit!). Diese Methode kann, besonnen angewandt, den Blick für das Wesentliche schärfen, sie birgt aber zugleich die Gefahr in sich, daß komplexen Phänomenen durch die Einpassung in oppositionelle Begriffsschemata Gewalt angetan wird. Diese Gefahr ist auch bei der Darstellung Eva Fiesels spürbar.

Die Verfasserin unterscheidet eine frühe, transzendentale[1] Romantik, die das letzte Jahrzehnt des 18. Jahrhunderts beherrscht und mit dem Tod ihrer Zentralgestalt, des Dichters Georg Philipp Friedrich Freiherr von Hardenberg, genannt Novalis (1772–1801), zum Abschluß kommt, und eine jüngere, diesseitige Romantik, für die der Dichter Joseph Freiherr von Eichendorff (1788–1857) als eine charakteristische Gestalt gelten darf. Davon abgehoben wird die Nachromantik und die politisch engagierte Bewegung des neuen Deutschlands, der sich Heinrich Heine (1797–1856) trotz seiner romantischen Grundeinstellung verbunden fühlte. Überlagert wird die romantische Epoche von der deutschen Klassik, die keine eigene Sprachphilosophie entwickelt hat. Die Sprachphilosophie der deutschen Romantik betrachtet Eva Fiesel als Ausdruck der romantischen Weltanschauung. Die zentrale Sprachidee dieser Geistesströmung ist verankert in der Religion. Sprachphilosophie wird verstanden als innere Sprachphilosophie, die auf einen göttlichen Mittelpunkt bezogen ist (3). Für die frühen Romantiker war die Sprachphilosophie ein zentrales und universelles Erlebnis. Sprachphilosophie ist Schöpfung und Spiegel des Geistes, der von Gott stammt. Sie gilt als Sinnbild einer verlorenen Einheit von Sinnenwelt, Geist, Poesie, Philosophie und Religion (2). Dies entspricht zugleich einer poetischen Weltanschauung, für die Sprache Poesie und Poesie letztlich Musik ist. Damit verbunden ist die Idee einer ursprünglichen Einheit aller Sprachen. Es handelt sich also um eine metaphysische Sprachidee, deren Form notwendig symbolisch ist (120). Sie findet im Werk der frühen Romantiker, unter denen sich Dichter, Philosophen und andere Denker befinden, ihren Ausdruck, ohne daß dies am Titel der einzelnen Schriften äußerlich erkennbar wäre. Genannt werden in diesem Zusammenhang Friedrich Hölderlin (1770–1843), Georg Philipp Friedrich Freiherr von Hardenberg, genannt Novalis (1772–1801), Wilhelm Heinrich Wackenroder (1773–1798), Ludwig Tieck (1773–1853), Philipp Otto Runge (1777–1810), Otto Heinrich Graf von Loeben (1786–1825), Johann Wilhelm Ritter (1776–1810) und Franz Xaver Baader (1765–1835).

Eva Fiesel weist auf Bezüge dieser frühromantischen Denker zu Platon, Jean-Jacques Rousseau (1712–1778), Louis de Bonald (1754–1840), Claude de Saint-Martin (1743–1803), Herder und dem sog. Sturm und Drang hin, betont aber, daß eine noch engere geistige Verwandtschaft zu den Anschauungen des deutschen Mystikers Jakob

[1] Transzendental ist hier im vorkantischen Sinne ('erfahrungsüberschreitend') zu verstehen, besser wäre, von 'transzendent' zu sprechen.

Böhme (1575–1624), zu dem niederländischen Philosophen Frans Hemsterhuis (1721–1790) und zu Johann Georg Hamann (1730–1788) besteht (7). Die Autorin unterstreicht auch, daß diese Sprachideen nicht am Maßstab einer modernen Sprachwissenschaft gemessen werden dürfen, deren Ziele und Methoden völlig andere sind. Charakteristisch ist, daß die romantischen Ideen nicht von der empirischen Erfahrung ausgehen, sondern vom Begriff. Es sei, so sagt Eva Fiesel, daher nicht verwunderlich, daß sie in der Problemgeschichte der Sprachwissenschaft kaum berücksichtigt worden sind.

Unter diesen generellen Vorbehalt stellt die Verfasserin auch manche Äußerungen Friedrich Schlegels. In seinem Werk vollzieht sich in der Mitte der Romantik eine entscheidende Wandlung, die eine neue Epoche einleitet: Die jüngere, diesseitige deutsche Romantik wendet sich seit dem Beginn des 19. Jh.s von der Idee zur geschichtlichen Wirklichkeit. Die Sprache wird nun in wachsendem Maße als historische Erscheinung gewertet. Damit werden zugleich die Voraussetzungen für die folgende historisch-philologische Erforschung der Sprache geschaffen. Man betrachtet die Sprache vor allem als Ausdruck des Volksgeistes und richtet das Augenmerk auf die Erforschung der nationalen Vorzeit. Dabei gewinnt auch die Mythologie entscheidende Bedeutung. Die Philosophie der Sprache wird mehr und mehr zu einer Philosophie der Mythologie. Schließlich weicht auch die romantische Mythenforschung rationaleren Deutungen und die Sprachbetrachtung entfernt sich allmählich ganz von der Philosophie und endet am Ausgang des Jahrhunderts in reiner Materialforschung. In der nachromantischen Phase wird die Erforschung der Nationalsprachen zur eigentlichen Aufgabe der Sprachwissenschaft. Jacob Grimm begründet die strenge Textkritik und das Quellenstudium. Damit entwickelt sich die Sprachwissenschaft zu einer historisch-vergleichenden Disziplin, die auf empirisch gefundenen Daten aufbaut. In der Nachromantik erlischt, so sagt Eva Fiesel, der "Sprachsinn" vollends, die Sprache hört nun auf, die zentrale Rolle zu spielen.

In diesen ideengeschichtlich begründeten Rahmen ordnet Eva Fiesel die von ihr behandelten Persönlichkeiten ein. Auch die eigentlichen Sprachforscher finden hier ihren Platz. Als Anreger frühromantischer Sprachideen wird Hamann herausgehoben, während Herders realistische Grundeinstellung nach Fiesels Urteil in der späteren Romantik mehr Anklang fand.

Die zentrale Gestalt des deutschen romantischen Sprachdenkens ist nach Ansicht der Autorin Friedrich Schlegel. Als enger Freund des Novalis steht er anfänglich ganz unter dem Einfluß transzendent-metaphysischer Gedanken und bleibt in seiner Sprachauffassung trotz mancher Wandlungen diesen Anfängen verpflichtet. Die Beschäftigung mit den realen Spracherscheinungen lenkt ihn auf die Beachtung der sprachlichen Form und damit auf historisch verfestigte Fakten, die dem entgrenzenden, auf die Idee gerichteten romantischen Denken als unzulänglich erscheinen. Den entscheidenden Übergang von der älteren zur jüngeren Romantik erblickt Eva Fiesel in F. Schlegels *Sprache und Weisheit der Indier* (1808), dem genialen Werk, das den Beginn der neuen Sprachwissenschaft markiert. Hier werden die Aufgaben und

Methoden einer historisch orientierten Sprachwissenschaft formuliert, die den weiteren Gang der Forschung bestimmen. Aber Schlegel selbst geht diesen Weg nicht zu Ende. Vielmehr bleibt er seinen Anfängen im Grunde treu und findet im Alter zu den universellen, in der Religion wurzelnden Ideen zurück (79). Eva Fiesel hebt hervor, daß er sich dadurch seinen andersdenkenden Zeitgenossen entfremdet habe und schließlich völlig vereinsamt gewesen sei (120).

Den älteren Bruder August Wilhelm von Schlegel, der ebenfalls in seinem Werk die verschiedenen Phasen romantischen Sprachdenkens erkennen läßt, stuft Eva Fiesel weit unter dem genialeren Friedrich ein. Die sprachtypologischen Ansätze beider Brüder hält sie für völlig unbefriedigend, ebenso auch die Erweiterungen Wilhelm von Humboldts. Besonders die Evolutionstheorie Friedrich Schlegels sei, so betont die Autorin, ganz in der transzendentalen Romantik begründet und nur aus ihr heraus zu verstehen (153).

Eine Schlüsselstellung weist Eva Fiesel auch dem Sprachforscher August Ferdinand Bernhardi (1769–1820) zu, der die meisten Sprachdenker, so auch Franz Bopp und Wilhelm von Humboldt, beeinflußt hat. Bernhardi zeigt an vielen Stellen seiner Sprachlehre romantische Gedankengänge. Diese Sprachlehre stellt aber vor allem den Versuch dar, die Grundanschauungen der idealistischen Philosophie Fichtes auf die Sprachbetrachtung zu übertragen. Bezeichnend ist, daß Bernhardi die Grammatik ganz auf die Kategorien der Logik zurückführen zu können glaubt. Er glaubt an eine "unbedingte Form der Sprache", auf deren Erfüllung alle Sprachen zustreben. Mit diesen Anschauungen hat Bernhardi auch auf Humboldt gewirkt. Bernhardi entfernt sich aufgrund seiner "Heiligsprechung der Form", wie Eva Fiesel es nennt, von der frühromantischen Auffassung. Mit diesem Bezug der grammatischen Kategorien auf die als absolut aufgefaßten Kategorien der Logik wird aber auch der Boden der geschichtlichen Wirklichkeit verlassen. Trotzdem kommt es, so betont Eva Fiesel, bei Bernhardi immer wieder zu einer Verschmelzung seiner philosophischen Deduktionen mit der tatsächlichen historischen Entwicklung.

Jacob Grimm steht nach Auffassung Eva Fiesels schon ganz diesseits der durch Friedrich Schlegel bezeichneten Grenze, ja die Autorin möchte ihn nur mit Einschränkungen zur jüngeren Romantik rechnen. Obwohl er heute meist als Romantiker betrachtet wird, ist er es von der Romantik selbst aus gesehen schon nicht mehr (129ff.). Denn mit seiner entschiedenen Hinwendung zur Sprachgeschichte und zur nationalen Vorzeit, mit seiner Forderung nach Textkritik und Quellenstudium schwindet das metaphysische Kernelement romantischen Denkens. Grimms poetische Bilder und Gleichnisse nehmen sich, so sagt Eva Fiesel, nur noch wie Requisiten aus. Denn in Wahrheit sei hier bereits die historisch-materialistisch orientierte Wissenschaftshaltung erreicht, die für die Folgezeit kennzeichnend wurde.

Als den bedeutendsten Sprachforscher damaliger Zeit betrachtet Eva Fiesel jedoch Wilhelm von Humboldt. Sie weist darauf hin, daß auch er von romantischen Gedankengut beeinflußt ist, z.B. in der Beurteilung der schöpferischen Sprachkraft des Menschen als einer Emanation des Geistes (153). Aber andererseits sieht sie ihn bereits entscheidend vom Geist der deutschen Klassik geprägt (4; 241). Die großen sprachwissenschaftlichen Probleme haben bei ihm eine geniale Gestaltung erfahren, die sie nach ihrer Überzeugung über die Unzulänglichkeiten des zeitbedingten Wissens hinausheben.

Als einen wichtigen Grund für den Wandel der Auffassungen in der jüngeren Romantik betrachtet Eva Fiesel den Umstand, daß die Lehre des Naturphilosophen Friedrich Wilhelm Schelling diejenige des idealistischen Fichte ablöste. Damit erwacht ein neues Gefühl für das Leben und die Wirklichkeit, das aus überzeitlichen und übergeschichtlichen Fernen frühromantischer Ideen wieder in die Zeit und in die Geschichte hineinführt. Die mit der Hinwendung zur Vergangenheit von Volk und Sprache verbundene neue Mythenforschung ist immer noch aus romantischen Quellen gespeist. Sie strebt zu einer "Urmythologie", in welcher sich die ewige Wahrheit der Religion offenbaren soll. Eva Fiesel nennt in diesem Zusammenhang Forscher wie Joseph von Görres (1776–1848), Arnold Kanne (1773–1824), Lorenz Oken (eigentlich Ockenfuß) (1779–1851), Johann Jakob Wagner (1775–1841) und Gotthilf Heinrich Schubert (1780–1860). Aber gegen diese stellenweise mystische und irrationale Deutung der Mythologie und ihrer Symbole erheben sich alsbald auch gewichtige Gegenstimmen: Gottfried Hermann (1772–1848) wendet sich gegen die romantische Mythenforschung, indem er die Mythologien als geschichtlich und psychologisch bedingte Gebilde erklärt.

Eva Fiesel kommentiert diesen Bereich romantischen Denkens mit der Bemerkung, daß die Werke der romantischen Mythologen ihre Zeit nicht überdauert haben und von der Wissenschaft mit Recht vergessen worden sind (152).

Lesenswert bleibt das Buch über die deutsche Sprachphilosophie der Romantik, dem wir hier bewußt einen breiteren Platz einräumen, auch deshalb, weil sich daraus entnehmen läßt, wie sich die Einstellung zu einzelnen Sprachproblemen im Laufe der Zeit gewandelt hat. So hatten z.B. die Denker des 17. und 18. Jahrhunderts den Optimismus besessen, etwa die Frage des Sprachursprungs mit den Denkmitteln ihrer Zeit lösen zu können. Für die Frühromantiker entzieht sich dahingegen das Geheimnis der Entstehung der Sprachen dem menschlichen Erkenntnisvermögen. Die diesseitige Romantik wiederum hofft durch den Rückgriff auf die Mythen das Problem lösbar zu machen. Teilweise wird die Sprache sogar wie eine reine Naturerscheinung behandelt, dem Geist also keine Sonderstellung eingeräumt. Ähnlich wandelt sich die Einstellung zum Laut und zum Buchstaben, zum Wort und zum Satz, zu den Größen Name, Symbol und Bild, zur Form, zur Etymologie, zur Grammatik, zur Stilistik und zum Übersetzungsproblem. Im Ganzen ist diese Entwicklung gekennzeichnet durch eine allmähliche Zurückdrängung transzendenter, idealistischer und religiöser Grundanschauungen zugunsten einer erneuten Hinwendung zu rationaleren Deutungen der sprachlichen Phänomene, die verbunden ist mit einer stärkeren Beachtung historisch belegbarer Fakten unter naturwissenschaftlichen materialistischen Vorzeichen.

Es ist unverkennbar, daß Eva Fiesels Sympathien der frühen Romantik gehören und daß sie die weitere Entwicklung als eine Verflachung empfindet. Das geht aus ihren Formulierungen deutlich hervor. Der neue wissenschaftliche Rationalismus, der Sprachutilitarismus des jungen Deutschland, das naturwissenschaftlich-materialistische Denken, das sich in der Sprachwissenschaft ausbreitet, wird von der Autorin skeptisch beurteilt. Sie fragt, ob diese neue Art wissenschaftlichen Erkennens schon wahrhafte philosophische Erkenntnis ist (224).

Hier ist in der Tat der Punkt erreicht, an dem sich auch heute die Geister scheiden. Es geht letztlich um die Frage, ob idealistische Sprachauffassungen, die den subjektiven Pol der Erkenntnis betonen, Anspruch auf Wissenschaftlichkeit verdienen oder ob dies vielmehr ausschließlich den materialistischen Sprachauffassungen zukommt, die den objektiven Pol der Erkenntnis hervorheben. Zweifellos können viele romantische Anschauungen heute nicht mehr wissenschaftlich ernst genommen werden. Andere dagegen haben einen durchaus rationalen Kern und werden die Sprachwissenschaft, wenn auch in gewandelter Form, erneut beschäftigen. Ringt man sich zu der Einsicht durch, daß nur in der dialektischen Verknüpfung des subjektiven und des objektiven Pols menschliche Erkenntnis überhaupt möglich ist, werden die alten Konfrontationen von Idealismus versus Materialismus letztlich gegenstandslos und schaffen Raum für übergreifendere, dem Gegenstand angemessenere Sehweisen. Nicht zu leugnen ist, daß gerade die idealistisch ausgerichtete Romantik besonders in künstlerischer Hinsicht auf allen Gebieten Meisterwerke hervorgebracht hat. Auch auf sprachphilosophischem Gebiet hat die Romantik Großes geleistet. Dies herausgearbeitet zu haben, bleibt ein Verdienst der Arbeit Eva Fiesels. Allerdings ist es ein Mangel des Buches, daß die zahlreichen Zitate unzureichend belegt sind, so daß eine Nachprüfung schwierig und zeitraubend ist. Auch fehlen die dringend erwünschten bibliographischen Angaben und ein Literaturverzeichnis.

Eine wichtige kritische Ergänzung der Darstellung Eva Fiesels verdanken wir dem gründlichen Kenner der romantischen Epoche, Friedrich Kainz. In seinem Aufsatz "Die Sprachästhetik der Jüngeren Romantik" (1938) bemängelt er, daß Eva Fiesel überscharfe Trennungslinien zwischen Früh- und Spätromantik gezogen hat. Demgegenüber weist er auf die Gemeinsamkeiten hin, die sich besonders auf dem Gebiet der Sprachästhetik zeigen. Kainz zeigt, daß auch in der Spätromantik trotz der von Fiesel beobachteten Wandlungen frühromantische Auffassungen noch durchaus lebendig sind. Er betont auch, daß einzelne Sprachprobleme von den Zeitgenossen teilweise so verschieden beurteilt wurden, daß es gefährlich ist, von durchgängigen Auffassungen zu sprechen.

Da die Sprachästhetik als ein besonderer Zweig der Sprachphilosophie in den meisten Darstellungen zu kurz kommt, seien die wichtigsten Probleme genannt, auf die Kainz eingeht. Sie verdienen diese Erwähnung um so mehr, als die moderne Textlinguistik wieder Anlaß bietet, die engen Bezüge zwischen Sprach- und Literaturwissenschaft zu unterstreichen. Kainz hebt folgende Problemkreise hervor:

1. *Das Problem der ästhetischen Bedeutsamkeit von Sprachfügungen.* Für die Früh-

romantik stand die Ästhetizität der Sprache außer Frage, die Spätromantik sucht sie in stimmungsvoller Altertümlichkeit und Volkstümlichkeit des sprachlichen Ausdrucks.

2. *Die Frage des Sprachursprungs unter ästhetischem Blickwinkel.* Die Frühromantik hatte sich die Interjektional- und Ausdruckstheorien zu eigen gemacht, die mittlere und die späte Romantik bringen den Gedanken der Nachbildung und Abbildung der gegenständlichen Welt durch die Sprache stärker zur Geltung.

3. *Die Lautästhetik*, verbunden mit den Fragen der Lautsymbolik, der Beziehungen von Laut und Sinn, der Lautcharakteristik (Onomatopoetik, Lautmetaphorik und der Synästhesie). Die Vorliebe mancher romantischer Dichter für lautsymbolische Bezüge geht so weit, daß sie gebräuchliche Wörter ohne weiteres lautlich verändern, wenn dies ihren Intentionen entspricht (so z.B. bei Tieck und Brentano). Für die romantische Auffassung ist der Sprachlaut mehr als willkürliches Zeichen, er steht vielmehr in notwendigem Wesensbezug zu den bezeichneten Sachverhalten. Freilich stehen die Theoretiker — Kainz nennt Hegel und Schleiermacher — dieser Auffassung skeptisch gegenüber.

Unterschiedlich ist auch das Urteil über die Synästhesie, die z.B. bei Tieck und Brentano eine große Rolle spielt. Unter dem Stichwort "Lautästhetik" geht Kainz auch auf 'bestimmte höhere Wirkungsmittel der Klanggestalt' ein, worunter er vor allem Rhythmus und Reim versteht. Hierüber hat sich z.B. ein Theoretiker der jüngeren Romantik, Karl Wilhelm Ferdinand Solger (1780–1819) ausführlich geäußert.

4. *Das Verhältnis von Sprache und Musik* und dessen Wandel von der Früh- zur Spätromantik. In diesem bereits von Eva Fiesel erörterten Zusammenhang weist Kainz auf die romantische Sprachtheorie von Carl Gustav Carus (1789–1869) hin, die dieser in einem Kapitel seiner Psychologie (über den Gehörsinn) entwickelt. Carus nimmt u.a. einen synästhetischen Zusammenhang zwischen Sprachlaut und Buchstabe, also zwischen Sprache und Schrift an. Akustische Erlebnisse vermögen sich nach romantischer Auffassung in Lineamente und graphische Figuren umzusetzen. Kainz bemängelt, daß Carus von Eva Fiesel nicht erwähnt werde. Das trifft jedoch nicht zu.

5. *Das sprachästhetische Problem der dichterischen Bildlichkeit.* Zwar neigen alle Romantiker der Auffassung zu, daß nur eine bildliche Sprache künstlerisch sein kann, aber in der jüngeren Romantik wird das dichterische Bild noch körperlicher und sinnennäher erlebt. Solger beschreibt die sprachlichen Mittel zur Erzeugung dieser Bildlichkeit. Er geht von einer Antithese von Symbol und Allegorie aus und untersucht die symbolhaften Tropen Metapher, Metonymie und Synekdoche. Diese Untersuchungen verdienen noch heute Beachtung. Erwähnenswert ist, daß das Interesse für mythologisch-symbolhafte Zusammenhänge in dieser Zeit bis zu parapsychologischen und tiefenpsychologischen Deutungen der Dichtersprache und der Symbolsprache des Traumes führt, so in dem Buch des Arztes Albert Steinbeck *Der Dichter ein Seher oder über die innige Verbindung der Poesie und der Sprache mit den Hellsehern* (1836).

6. *Das Problem des Verhältnisses von Sprache und Anschauung.* Die im Alltagsgebrauch verdeckte Anschaulichkeit der Sprache soll in der Dichtung wieder hervorgekehrt werden. Dafür tritt besonders der Dichter Jean Paul (Johann Paul Friedrich Richter, 1763–1825) ein, der ansonsten gedanklich am Rande der Romantik steht. Seine *Vorschule der Ästhetik* (1804) enthält zahlreiche noch heute lesenswerte Sprachbetrachtungen.

7. In dem Problemkreis, den Kainz als das *Verhältnis von Sprache und ästhetischem Grundgehalt* kennzeichnet, geht es um spracherzeugte Formen des Witzes, der Ironie, des Humor und des Wortspiels. Kainz spricht von 'glossomorpher Komik' und stellt einen Wandel in den diesbezüglichen romantischen Einstellungen fest: Die Frühromantik bevorzugt Witz und Ironie, die mittlere und späte Romantik Laune und Humor. (Was mit diesen Begriffen genau gemeint ist, wird nur in einer sprachwissenschaftlichen Untersuchung dieses sprachlichen Feldes so explizit gemacht werden können, daß auch die außerdeutsche Sprachwissenschaft diese romantischen Auffassungen für die Beurteilung analoger Probleme in anderen Literaturen nutzen kann.)

8. Die '*Nationalästhetik*', ein Kernproblem der jungromantischen Sprachbetrachtung und -bewertung. Im Laufe des Übergangs von der frühen zur späten Romantik ergibt sich — durch die politischen Ereignisse mitbedingt — ein Wandel in der Wertschätzung der Sprachen. In der jüngeren Romantik bekennt man sich zur Schönheit der Muttersprache und gelangt zu einer ethischen Bewertung des Deutschen, zur Pflege des "Nationalstils" und der volksliedartigen, altertümlichen Dichtung. Hiermit stehen bestimmte sprachwissenschaftliche Diskussionen der Zeit in engem Zusammenhang: so z.B. die Sprachreinigungsbestrebungen, die von einigen Romantikern unterstützt, von anderen jedoch abgelehnt werden.

Die Brüder Schlegel und besonders der Philosoph Fichte in seinen *Reden an die deutsche Nation* (1808) treten für Sprachreinigung ein, Jacob Grimm, Adam Müller u.a. wenden sich gegen "die Jagd auf Fremdworte". Ein Theoretiker wie Loeben hält es sogar für einen wichtigen Zug des deutschen Nationalcharakters, in dem Streben nach Universalität Fremdes aufzunehmen.

9. *Die Kategorie des Archaismus* als ein Zentralproblem der jüngeren Romantik. In diesem Problemkreis wird die Einstellung zur Volkssprache und zu den Mundarten diskutiert. Als ästhetisch bedeutsam gilt eine altertümliche, klang- und formenreiche Sprache mit Bildreichtum und Anschauungsfülle. Sie trifft man in der Volkssprache und den Mundarten an, die sich deshalb, im Gegensatz etwa noch zur Einstellung A. W. v. Schlegels, wachsender Wertschätzung erfreuen. Freilich ist damit auch ein Provinzialismus verbunden, der zur Verengung des geistigen Horizonts führen kann.

10. *Das Problem der ästhetischen Charakteristik einzelner Sprachen* wird in der jüngeren Romantik lebhaft diskutiert. Jean Paul versucht eine Beschreibung der Eigenart verschiedener europäischer Sprachen, die sich durch eine erstaunliche Unvoreingenommenheit auszeichnet.

11. *Das Übersetzungsproblem* gewinnt mit der Hinwendung zur Erforschung der Nationalsprachen erneut an Bedeutung. Während die Frühromantiker die Möglichkeit adäquater Übersetzungen durchaus bejahten, wird man nun skeptischer und gelangt zu einer Verneinung dieser Frage.

Kainz empfiehlt schließlich, einmal eine kritische Bestandsaufnahme der ästhetischen Beschreibungs- und Bewertungsbegriffe der Romantiker vorzunehmen. Diese romantische Metasprache könnte auch für heutige sprachästhetische Untersuchungen nützlich sein.

Mit diesen Hinweisen auf die von F. Kainz herausgestellten sprachästhetischen Probleme der Romantik, die die Darstellung Eva Fiesels in wichtigen Punkten ergänzen, wird eine weitere Lücke in den vorliegenden sprachwissenschaftlichen Darstellungen der Epoche geschlossen. Die romantischen Auffassungen mögen zu einem großen Teil spekulativ und wissenschaftlich fragwürdig sein, sie zeigen jedoch eine erstaunliche gedankliche Vielseitigkeit und manche Einsichten, die bewahrt zu werden verdienen.

V. *Das Verhältnis der systematischen Philosophie zur Sprachphilosophie*

Es ist eine überraschende Tatsache, daß die Sprachphilosophen der romantischen Epoche keine Berufsphilosophen waren und daß die großen Philosophen der Zeit keine eigene Sprachphilosophie entwickelt haben. Erich Heintel, ein gründlicher Kenner der Verhältnisse, hat diesen Umstand sehr bedauert. Er erblickt sogar eine Tragik darin, 'daß Hamann und Herder, die Romantik und selbst Humboldt bei allem Reichtum der Ideen und bei aller Tiefe der treibenden Motive, jenes philosophische Rüstzeug vermissen lassen, daß die systematische Philosophie in mühsamer "Anstrengung des Begriffes" in ihrer Entwicklung von Descartes und Leibniz zu Kant und Hegel geschaffen hat' (Heintel 1957, Bd. I: 589). Diese Äußerung Heintels enthält zwar einen wahren Kern, aber sie bedarf doch eines Kommentars. Was Hamann, Herder und Humboldt anbelangt, so waren sie alle nicht nur gründliche Kant-Kenner, sondern darüber hinaus mit der zeitgenössischen Philosophie durchaus vertraut. Wir haben bereits betont, daß Hamann und Herder sich gerade durch Kants Vernachlässigung der Sprache zu deren Verteidigung herausgefordert fühlten. Wilhelm Streitberg hat bereits 1910 in seinem wichtigen Aufsatz *Kant und die Sprachwissenschaft* darauf hingewiesen, daß Hamann Lockes *Essay concerning human understanding* mit Rücksicht auf Kants *Kritik der reinen Vernunft* durchgearbeitet hat und Herder darüber in einem Brief am 3. Juni 1784 'mit Zufriedenheit' berichtet (Streitberg 1909: 385–6). Locke hat Hamanns Gedanken über die Sprache also beeinflußt und auch auf Herder eingewirkt. Freilich reichen die Gegenargumentationen beider gegen Kant an Begriffsschärfe nicht an den gemeinsamen Lehrer heran. Humboldt stand stark unter dem Einfluß Kants. Ernst Cassirer hat "Die kantischen Elemente in Wilhelm von Humboldts Sprachphilosophie" (1923) herausgearbeitet, und Helmut

Gipper hat in einem Aufsatz über "Wilhelm von Humboldt als Begründer moderner Sprachforschung" (1965/66) darauf hingewiesen, daß Humboldts wichtigste sprachphilosophischen Einsichten geradezu gegen Kant errungen worden sind. Über den Einfluß Kants auf das gesamte Denken Humboldts berichtet Eduard Spranger in seiner Untersuchung "Wilhelm von Humboldt und Kant" (1908). Streitberg betont in dem eben genannten Aufsatz, daß Humboldt besonders den "psychischen Aktualitätsbegriff" von Kant übernommen und in seinem Energeia-Begriff auf die Sprache angewandt habe. Auch die Idee der Sprachentwicklung sei in Kants Geschichtsphilosophie zu suchen (Streitberg 1909:408 ff.). Ohne jeden Zweifel ist Humboldt Kant in vieler Hinsicht verpflichtet. Dies ist schon früh erkannt worden. Schon die ersten Biographen Humboldts haben auf die Spuren kantischer Gedankengänge im Werke Humboldts hingewiesen. So bereits Gustav Schlesier, der die erste Lebensgeschichte schrieb (1843–45), dann Rudolf Haym, der sogar von 'platonisiertem Kantianismus' bei Humboldt spricht, und schließlich Heymann Steinthal, der Humboldts Geisteshaltung als 'kantisierten Spinozismus' bezeichnen zu sollen glaubt. Man wird solchen pointierten Formeln mit berechtigter Skepsis begegnen, aber als Zeugnisse dafür, wie sehr Humboldt unter der Wirkung des großen Philosophen gestanden hat, sind sie wertvoll.

Erstaunlich bleibt, daß für Kant selbst die Sprache nicht thematisch geworden ist. Seine Äußerungen zu sprachlichen Erscheinungen hat A. Bezzenberger zusammengestellt. Sie finden in einem Aufsatz von 16 Seiten Platz. Es mag sein, daß aufgrund des neuen Kant-Index noch weiteres Material zutagekommt, aber viel ist kaum zu erwarten. Dessen ungeachtet bleibt Kants Werk wichtig für die Sprachphilosophie. Was er an präziser Begriffsanalyse geleistet hat, fordert auch den Sprachphilosophen auf seinem Felde zur Nachahmung heraus und was er über die Bedingungen der Möglichkeit des Denkens und Urteilens gesagt hat, ist der Sprachphilosophie als eine zu prüfende Aufgabe gestellt. An Versuchen, Kants Kritik der Vernunft durch eine Kritik der Sprache zu ergänzen, hat es nicht gefehlt. Einen Vorstoß in dieser Richtung unternahm Carl Leonhard Reinhold (1758–1823) mit seinen beiden Werken *Grundlegung einer Synonymik für den allgemeinen Sprachgebrauch* (1812) und *Das menschliche Erkenntnisvermögen aus dem Gesichtspunkte des durch die Wortsprache vermittelten Zusammenhangs zwischen der Sinnlichkeit und dem Denkvermögen* (1816). Reinhold will vor allem durch eine Analyse der Wortsprache, durch eine reine Scheidung der Synonyme und Homonyme, also der sinnverwandten und gleichlautenden Wörter, eine allgemeine Sprachregelung vorbereiten, die, so meint er, die Philosophie zu einer Wissenschaft erheben kann. Aber sein sprachkritischer Ansatz erwies sich doch als ungeeignet, die von ihm angestrebte Trennung von reiner und empirischer Erkenntnis durchzuführen. Streitberg hat sich recht ironisch hierzu geäußert (Streitberg 1909:392), doch muß man gerechterweise sagen, daß manche Absichten Reinholds durchaus legitim waren. Weit weniger bedeutsam ist die Bonner Dissertation aus dem Jahre 1868, in der S. Levy *Kants Kritik der reinen Vernunft in ihrem Verhältnis zur Kritik der Sprache* behandelt. Sein Versuch, Kants Grundgedanken als in Übereinstimmung mit den Ergebnissen der Sprachphilosophie zu erweisen, muß als gescheitert gelten. Wichtiger ist das Buch des Sprachphilosophen Ludwig Noiré, *Die Lehre Kants und der Ursprung der Vernunft* (1882), in dem es sich der Autor zur Aufgabe macht darzustellen, wie die menschliche Vernunft entstanden und gewachsen ist. Streitberg hält zwar im Grunde auch diesen Versuch für verfehlt und meint, Kants Intentionen seien hier völlig verkannt, er gibt aber doch zu, daß es sich um den konsequentesten Versuch handelt, Kants *Kritik der reinen Vernunft* für die Sprachwissenschaft fruchtbar zu machen. Trotz der Kritik Streitbergs ist positiv hervorzuheben, daß Noiré Bemerkenswertes über den Unterschied des tierischen und des menschlichen Zugangs zur Welt, über die spezifisch menschlichen Formen objektiver Erkenntnis und über die Rolle der begriffsspendenden Sprache dabei gesagt hat. Seine Einsicht, daß Wörter nicht bloß Zeichen, sondern die conditio sine qua non die Körper der Begriffe sind, verdient noch heute Beachtung.

Kant hat also, so dürfen wir sagen, in vieler Hinsicht anregend gewirkt, selbst — ja, gerade — dort, wo er zum Widerspruch herausforderte.

Wie aber steht es mit den übrigen wichtigen Philosophen jener Zeit, mit Fichte und Schelling, mit Schopenhauer und vor allem mit Hegel? Auch von ihnen ist keiner Sprachphilosoph, aber sie haben sich alle zu Sprachfragen geäußert und die meisten haben direkt oder indirekt auf die Sprachphilosophie der Zeit gewirkt. Johann Gottlieb Fichte (1762–1814) hat u.a. eine Abhandlung *Von der Sprachfähigkeit und dem Ursprunge der Sprache* (1795) verfaßt, doch sie reicht nicht an Herders ältere Arbeit heran, und seine Äußerungen über die Sprache in der vierten Rede an die deutsche Nation zeigen Verwandtschaft mit Ideen Humboldts, ohne deren gedankliche Tiefe zu erreichen (cf. H. Gipper/H. Schwarz 1962ff.: Nummern 4268, 4269/Hans Schwarz).

Friedrich Wilhelm Schelling (1775–1854), ein Freund Hegels, erwähnt und würdigt die Sprache, wie Eva Fiesel gezeigt hat (1927), des öfteren in seinen Werken, aber auch er macht sie nicht zum eigentlichen Thema seiner Naturphilosophie. Auf das Sprachdenken der Romantik wirkt er vor allem durch seinen Begriff des Organischen, den er auch auf den Ursprung und das Wesen der Sprache bezieht. Nach seiner Überzeugung ist die Sprache bereits als ein organisches Ganzes entstanden. Diesen Gedanken finden wir auch bei Humboldt wieder. Übrigens war es auch Schelling, der die Frage des Sprachursprungs nochmals in der Berliner Akademie zur Diskussion stellte. Allerdings begnügte er sich selbst mit einigen *Vorbemerkungen zu der Frage über den Ursprung der Sprache* (1850), in denen er kritisch zu Herder und Hamann Stellung nahm; dagegen übernahm es Jacob Grimm, im folgenden Jahre seine Abhandlung *Über den Ursprung der Sprache* vorzutragen.

Arthur Schopenhauer (1788–1860), der Autor des von pessimistischem Weltgefühl getragenen Werks *Die Welt als Wille und Vorstellung* (1818), ist nicht mit sprachphilosophischen Untersuchungen hervorgetreten. Wohl enthalten seine Schriften verschiedene Äußerungen über die Sprache von recht unterschiedlicher Qualität. Wie bei einem ebenso eigenwilligen wie kompromißlosen Denker nicht anders zu erwarten, urteilt er stets schroff und rückhaltlos. Dabei gelingen ihm treffliche Formulierungen, aber diese stehen oft unvermittelt neben ganz unhaltbaren Fehlurteilen. Schopenhauer zieht gegen die 'Verhunzung' der deutschen Sprache zu Felde und gebärdet sich als Sprachpurist; er urteilt in eigenwilliger Weise *Ueber Sprache und Worte*, nimmt zu Übersetzungsfragen Stellung, rühmt die klassischen Sprachen und fällt teilweise unglaublich abwertende Urteile über neuere Sprachen. Diese Bemerkungen finden sich besonders im zweiten Band der *Parerga und Paralipomena* (1851). Für die Sprachforschung waren und sind Sie nur zum geringen Teil verwertbar.

Anders wiederum steht es mit Georg Wilhelm Hegel (1770–1831), dem großen Philosophen an der Berliner Universität. Hegel war und ist noch heute eine umstrittene Persönlichkeit, von einigen Kritikern als der größte Denker der Zeit gepriesen, von anderen als gefährlicher Scharlatan beschimpft. Auch er hat die Sprache nicht thematisch behandelt, wohl aber zahlreiche Äußerungen über sie gemacht, die freilich erst in jüngerer Zeit systematisch gesammelt und ausgewertet worden sind. Daß auch Humboldt mit Hegels Philosophie in Berührung kommen mußte, versteht sich von selbst. Aber die Geisteshaltung beider Männer war derart verschieden, daß Humboldt sich von Hegel, der übrigens eine seiner indologischen Abhandlungen ohne ausreichende Sachkenntnis ziemlich grob kritisiert hatte, eher abgestoßen fühlen mußte. Heymann Steinthal hat in seiner Schrift *Die Sprachwissenschaft Wilhelm von Humboldt's und die Hegel'sche Philosophie* (1848) viel Mühe darauf verwandt, die Eigenständigkeit des Humboldtschen Denkens gegenüber dem Versuche von Max Schasler zu verteidigen, der die Ideen Humboldts in 'hegelisch-dialektische Form zwängen' wollte. Steinthal stand selbst der dialektischen Methode kritisch gegenüber. Er sah vor allem eine Gefahr für die Sprachwissenschaft in den leeren Abstraktionen, in die sie hineinführte. Im Gegensatz dazu rühmt Bruno Liebrucks, ein Sprachphilosoph unserer Tage, gerade das dialektische Prinzip Hegels und betrachtet es als grundlegend und unentbehrlich für jede Philosophie von der Sprache, ja, er bedauert es, daß Humboldt, wie er meint, im 'Vorhof der Dialektik' stehengeblieben sei. Man wird jedoch zugeben müssen, daß sich Humboldt im Grunde überall, wo er Wechselwirkungen und wechselseitige Bedingungen zwischen Mensch, Sprache, Denken, Erkenntnis und Welt aufzeigt, durchaus in den Bahnen dialektischen Denkens bewegt. Wir bewerten dies positiv, dürfen aber nicht übersehen, daß sich an der Einstellung zur Dialektik und deren Bedeutung für Sprache und Denken noch heute die Geister scheiden.

Während ein so besonnener Forscher wie Karl R. Popper in der Dialektik eine schwere Gefahr für das wissenschaftliche Denken erblickt (1940), ist sie für Männer wie Theodor W. Adorno, Max Horkheimer, Ernst Bloch und Ludwig Marcuse ein unentbehrliches Element des philosophischen, wissenschaftlichen und politischen Denkens. Jürgen Habermas hat zu diesem Streit in fairer Weise vermittelnd Stellung genommen (1963). Wir sind der Überzeugung, daß Sprachphilosophie und Sprachwissenschaft dem Gegenstand Sprache nicht gerecht zu werden vermögen, wenn nicht das Prinzip der Dialektik im Sinne Hegels beachtet wird. Allerdings hat dies mit der gebührenden Vorsicht und unter Berücksichtigung der tatsächlichen Gegebenheiten zu geschehen. Die sprachlichen Prozesse scheinen tatsächlich ausgesprochen dialektischer Natur zu sein, und daher sind sie auch mit entsprechenden Methoden besser zu erfassen.

Hegels Äußerungen zur Sprache sind vor allem in zwei neueren Untersuchungen ausführlich gewürdigt worden. Josef Simon hat das *Problem der Sprache bei Hegel* (1966) untersucht und gezeigt, daß dort, wo Hegel vom 'Absoluten' spricht, auch wesentliche Züge der 'Sprachlichkeit des Menschen', die dessen Endlichkeit begründen, sichtbar werden.

Theodor Bodammer liefert unter dem Obertitel *Hegels Deutung der Sprache* aufschlußreiche *Interpretationen zu Hegels Äußerungen über die Sprache* (1969). Aus seiner Untersuchung geht hervor, weshalb Hegel keine Sprachphilosophie entwickeln konnte, so wie er eine Rechts-, Geschichts-, Kunst-, und Religionsphilosophie geschrieben hat. Die Sprache ist für Hegel, so führt Bodammer aus, nicht 'neben Recht, Staat und Geschichte, sowie schließlich auch der Kunst, Religion und der Philosophie selbst eine "objektive" Gestalt des Geistes, sondern sie besitzt gewissermaßen nur Hintergrundscharakter. Nicht die Sprache selbst wird "objektiv", sondern in ihr "objektivieren" sich geistige Gehalte und nehmen auf diese Weise eine Gestalt an, in der der Geist sich als Selbstbewußtsein realisiert und anschaut' (238).

Einen weiteren wichtigen Beitrag zum Thema hat Josef Derbolav in seinen Aufsatz "Hegel und die Sprache: Ein Beitrag zur Selbstbestimmung der Sprachphilosophie im Systemdenken des deutschen Idealismus" (1959) beigesteuert. Derbolav hebt besonders den Einfluß Herders auf den jungen Hegel hervor und weist auf die Stellen hin, wo Hegel den Zusammenhang von Muttersprache und Sprachgemeinschaft bemerkt hat und dem Sprachproblem noch zugänglicher war als in späterer Zeit. Leider hat Hegel diese Gedanken nicht systematisch weiter verfolgt. Für Hegel ist Sprache die 'erste Tat der theoretischen Vernunft', 'Werk des Gedankens', also prinzipiell dem Denken nachgeordnet. Das dialektische Verhältnis von Sprache und Denken ist also — erstaunlicherweise — nicht erkannt. In Hegels 'universaler Sinntheorie' ist die Sprache zwar stets einbezogen, aber die eigentliche Fundierungsproblematik ist nicht gesehen.

Auch Alfons Müller hebt in einem Exkurs über Hegel in seinen *Betrachtungen zur neuen deutschen Sprachphilosophie* (1938) hervor, daß die Sprache bei Hegel ganz in das System der Tätigkeit der Vernunft eingeordnet ist. Ihr wird zwar eine hohe Bedeutung zuerkannt, aber weder wird sie über das Denken gestellt noch ihm gleichgesetzt. Interessante Aufschlüsse über die Wirkung Hegelscher Ideen auf einzelne Sprachforscher bietet wiederum Wilhelm Streitberg. So führt er z.B. August Schleichers bekannte Periodentheorie auf den Einfluß von Hegels Geschichtsphilosophie zurück (Streitberg 1909:415ff.). Schleichers Auffassung, wonach mit dem Eintritt der Sprache in die Geschichte auch deren Verfallsphase beginnt, steht übrigens in seltsamem Widerspruch zu der Evolutionstheorie Darwins, die der "Amateur-Botaniker" Schleicher ansonsten lebhaft begrüßte.

Hegel, so dürfen wir zusammenfassen, hat zwar Wichtiges über die Sprache gesagt, aber von einer wirklich nennenswerten Wirkung der verstreuten Äußerungen auf die Sprachwissenschaft des 19. Jahrhunderts kann doch kaum die Rede sein. Erst die genannten neueren Spezialuntersuchungen könnten ein Anlaß werden, daß sich auch die Sprachforscher stärker mit Hegel beschäftigen und für ihre Arbeit fruchtbare neue Anregungen gewinnen. – Zum gesamten Fragenkomplex vergleiche auch Henry Lauener *Die Sprache in der Philosophie Hegels mit besonderer Berücksichtigung der Ästhetik* (1962).

Wir haben hier die nach heutigem Urteil bedeutendsten Philosophen der Zeit hervorgehoben, weil der Leser mit Recht erwarten wird, über deren Einstellung zu sprachlichen Problemen etwas zu erfahren. Wir müssen es uns jedoch versagen, auch auf die heute weniger bekannten Philosophen der romantischen Epoche näher einzugehen. Erwähnt seien aber wenigstens der niederländische Philosoph Frans Hemsterhuis (1721–1790), der deutsch-norwegische Naturphilosoph und Schüler Schellings Henrik Steffens (1773–1845), der Arzt, Maler und Philosoph Carl Gustav Carus (1789–1869) und der Naturforscher und Philosoph Lorenz Oken (eigentlich Ockenfuß) (1779–1851). Diese vier Gelehrten haben mit ihren Ideen auf die romantische Bewegung eingewirkt und auch die Sprache gelegentlich mit in ihre Überlegungen einbezogen, ohne sie ausführlich zu thematisieren. Sprachphilosophen im eigentlichen Sinne waren also auch sie nicht. Über den Gesamtzusammenhang haben wir bereits an Hand von Eva Fiesels *Sprachphilosophie der Romantik* (1927) berichtet. In der Sprachwissenschaft haben die Gedanken der Genannten jedoch kaum Spuren hinterlassen. — Leider können wir im Rahmen dieser begrenzten Darstellung nicht auf die z.T. höchst bedeutsamen Sprachauffassungen und Theorien einzelner Dichter und Schriftsteller der romantischen Epoche eingehen. Es sei aber wenigstens auf *Die Sprachtheorie Fr. v. Hardenbergs* (*Novalis*) verwiesen, die Heinrich Fauteck 1939 in einer Dissertation dargestellt hat, und auf Jean Pauls (eigentlich Johann Paul Friedrich Richter, 1763–1825) *Vorschule der Ästhetik* aus dem Jahre 1804, die ebenfalls wichtige Gedanken über die Sprache enthält.

VI. *Die französischen Ideologen*

In den Darstellungen der Geschichte der Sprachwissenschaft und der Sprachphilosophie im Zeitraum der Romantik ist eine Gruppe französischer Gelehrter vergessen bzw. übersehen worden, die bereits wichtige sprachphilosophische Probleme behandelt haben, welche gelegentlich als Errungenschaften der neueren Sprachphilosophie betrachtet werden. Es handelt sich um die sog. Ideologen, d.h. jene Mitglieder des Pariser *Institut National des Sciences et Arts*, das nach der französischen Revolution im Jahre 1795 neu organisiert wurde und die Tradition der französischen Akademie der Wissenschaften fortsetzen sollte. Die uns interessierenden Hauptvertreter dieser Akademie waren Constantin François Chassebeuf Comte de Volney (1757–1820),

Pierre Jean Georges Cabanis, der Freund und Arzt Mirabeaus (1757–1808), Pierre Prévost (1751–1839), der Condillac-Schüler Antoine Louis Claude Destutt de Tracy (1754–1836), Marie François Pierre Gonthier Maine de Biran (1766–1824) und Joseph Marie Degérando (eigentlich de Gérando) (1772–1842). Diese Männer waren der sog. englischen Schule, John Locke (1632–1704), George Berkeley (1685–1753), Thomas Reid (1704–1757), David Hartley (1710–1796) und David Hume (1711–1776) verpflichtet, vor allem aber ihrem Landsmann Étienne Bonnot de Condillac (1714–1780), der die Lockeschen Ideen in sprachphilosophischer Sicht weiterentwickelt hatte. Über die Ideologen und ihre sprachphilosophischeAnschauungen gibt ein wichtiger Aufsatz von J. B. Acton mit dem Titel *The philosophy of language in revolutionary France* (1959) Auskunft. Er verdient hier eine ausführlichere Würdigung.

Acton geht besonders auf die 2. Klasse des Institut National ein, und zwar diejenige für *Sciences morales et politiques*, in der es eine *Section pour l'analyse des sensations et des idées* gab, welche sprachphilosophisch wichtige Fragen behandelte. Der Deist Volney, der die Zielsetzungen der neuen Institution mitbestimmte, war ein vielseitig begabter Gelehrter, der den vorderen Orient und Amerika aus eigener Anschauung kannte, bemerkenswerte Arbeiten zur Vereinfachung des Studiums der orientalischen Sprachen durch die Verwendung der europäischen Buchstabenschrift vorgelegt hat und außerdem auch sprachphilosophisch interessiert war. Er war überzeugt, daß die Menschen nur dann Übereinstimmung in der Beurteiling ihrer Probleme erreichen könnten, wenn sie die Dinge so erfaßten, wie sie tatsächlich sind. Zwischen der Welt der Phantasie und derjenigen der Realität müsse daher eine Demarkationslinie gezogen werden. Theologische und religiöse Meinungen seien z.B. aus der sozialen Sphäre auszuschließen. Wenn dies geschähe, dann würden alle irrige Religionen durch die einzig haltbare Religion der Evidenz und der Wahrheit ersetzt werden. Diese Gedanken, so dürfen wir hinzufügen, erinnern u.a. an Anschauungen der sog. *General Semantics*, wie sie in neuerer Zeit von A. Korzybski vertreten wurden. Auf Volneys sprachphilosophische Bemühungen geht Acton jedoch überraschenderweise nicht ein.

Georges Cabanis, einer der Mitbegründer des Materialismus des 19. Jahrhunderts, ist dadurch berühmt geworden, daß er sich gegen die Erwähnung Gottes im Institut verwahrte und die geistigen Fähigkeiten des Menschen mit natürlichen körperlichen Ausscheidungen der Organe verglich. Dieser Materialismus hat in der Folge die bekannte zugespitzte Formulierung erfahren: "*Le cerveau secrète la pensée comme le foie secrète la bile.*"

Mit diesen Vorbemerkungen ist bereits das geistige Klima bezeichnet, in dem die Akademiegespräche geführt wurden. Es wird auch deutlich, daß hier von spezifisch romantischem Ideengut kaum die Rede sein kann.

Acton hebt in seinem Aufsatz besonders A. L. C. Destutt de Tracy heraus, den Napoleon als das eigentliche Haupt der Ideologen betrachtete. In einer Untersuchung *Mémoire sur la faculté de pensée* (1795) beruft de Tracy sich auf Condillac, der, Lockes Gedanken weiterführend, die Sprache für das Denken selbst als ebenso notwendig erachtete wie für den Ausdruck dieses Denkens. Destutt de Tracy schlägt für diese von Locke und Condillac entwickelte Forschungsrichtung, die auf der Analyse der Empfindungen (*sensations*) und Vorstellungen (*idées*) gerichtet ist, den Ausdruck *idéologie* vor, der damals also durchaus positiv gemeint war und der ganzen Forschergruppe die Bezeichnung "Ideologen" eintrug. Am Rande sei vermerkt, daß der Ausdruck *idée* einer besonderen Klärung bedarf. Er ist, wie Acton hervorhebt, ursprünglich im Sinne von 'perception by means of sight' zu verstehen, wurde jetzt aber erweitert auf alle Sinnesempfindungen, auf die Erfahrung und auf das Denken schlechthin.

Zum besseren Verständnis der Zusammenhänge verweist Acton auf die wichtigsten Anschauungen von Étienne Bonnot de Condillac (1714–1780). Dieser bedeutende Anreger der französischen Ideologen wird in der Geschichte der Philosophie als ein sensualistischer Philosoph gekennzeichnet, der seinerseits den Anschauungen John Lockes (1632–1704) verpflichtet war. Locke hatte bereits betont, daß die Sprache nicht von der Erkenntnis getrennt werden könne. Condillac interpretiert diesen Zusammenhang in dem Sinne, daß Erkenntnis nur durch Analyse der Sinnesempfindungen erreicht werden könne, diese aber sei ohne den Gebrauch von Zeichen, also ohne Sprache, nicht möglich. Es ist an dieser Stelle nicht erforderlich zu erläutern, wie Condillac sich die Genese des menschlichen Zeichengebrauchs, also den Ursprung der Sprache aus natürlichen Lauten und Gesten vorstellte. Hierauf haben wir im Zusammenhang mit Herder bereits hingewiesen. Wichtig ist jedoch festzuhalten, daß er die besondere Leistung der sprachlichen Zeichen in ihrer Fähigkeit erblickte, die sinnlichen Erfahrungen zu ordnen. Sie erlauben vor allem Abstraktionen und somit Verallgemeinerungen, die wiederum die Formulierung allgemeiner Aussagen gestatten. Mehr noch: Condillac betont, daß sich die durch die Zeichen erzielten Klassifikationen jeweils nach den Bedürfnissen der sie gebrauchenden Menschen richten, also auch von Sprache zu Sprache verschieden sind. Damit ist zugleich eine bereits bei Locke nachweisbare Einsicht in das Wesen der Sprachverschiedenheit gewonnen, die später in der Sprachphilosophie W. von Humboldts zentrale Bedeutung gewann.

Für die Wissenschaft ergeben sich aus diesen Einsichten wichtige Folgerungen: Die Kunst des Denkens wird zu einer Kunst des sprachlichen Ausdrucks des Gedachten, und da die Sprachen selbst als analytische Methoden zur Erkenntnisgewinnung betrachtet wurden, erweisen sich die erfolgreichen Wissenschaften im Grunde als gut gemachte Sprachen. Condillac ist daher auch besonders von der Algebra als der Sprache der Mathematik beeindruckt. Nach deren Vorbild hält er alle philosophischen Probleme für lösbar. (Die Verwandtschaft dieser Gedankengänge mit denen A. Korzybskis ist auch hier deutlich.)

Acton weist darauf hin, daß der Chemiker Antoine–Laurent de Lavoisier (1743–1794) als begeisterter Anhänger Condillacs versucht hat, die chemische Terminologie entsprechend zu verbessern. Die Sektion zur Analyse der Empfindungen und Ideen war also gegründet auf Lockes Empirismus, welcher durch Condillac zu einer

Sprachphilosophie ausgearbeitet worden war.

Die Forschung der Ideologen auf diesem Gebiet sollte durch Preisaufgaben gefördert werden. Im Jahre V der Republik, d.h. im Jahre 1796, lautete die Preisaufgabe:

1. Is it really the case that sensations can only be transformed into ideas by means of signs? Or, what comes to the same thing, do our earliest ideas essentially depend on the help of signs?

2. Would the art of thought be perfect if the art of signs were brought to perfection?

3. In those sciences where there is general agreement as to what is true, is this the result of the perfection of the signs used in them?

4. In those branches of knowledge which are a constant source of disputes, is not this division of views a necessary result of the inexactitude of the signs employed?

5. Is there any means of correcting signs that are badly made, and of rendering all sciences equally susceptible of demonstration? (207) (Wir zitieren nach der englischen Fassung Actons, da der Originaltext nicht erreichbar war).

Den ersten Preis erhielt Joseph Degérando, ein überzeugter Katholik, der zunächst gegen den Konvent gekämpft hatte, zweimal geflohen war, einmal in die Schweiz, dann nach Deutschland, wo er einige führende deutsche Denker kennenlernte (Acton nennt leider keine Namen) und später nach Frankreich zurückkehrte. Seine Antwort, ein Werk in vier Bänden, das 1799 veröffentlicht wurde, trug den Titel *Des signes et de l'art de penser, considérés dans leurs rapports mutuels*. Degérando vertritt darin die Auffassung, daß Condillac über das Ziel hinausgeschossen sei. Nicht die Zeichen, von denen Cabanis sogar behauptet hatte, sie seien unentbehrlich, um die Sinnesempfindungen zu stabilisieren (*fixer*), ermöglichten erst die Tätigkeit des Geistes, sondern umgekehrt sei die geistige Aktivität die Voraussetzung für jeden möglichen Zeichengebrauch. Diese Auffassung berührt sich mit derjenigen Maine de Birans, der zwar keine Antwort auf die Akademiefragen einreichte, wohl aber vorbereitende Notizen hierzu anfertigte. Er spricht von einer *puissance motrice*, die das Wort herbeiruft und die Idee erweckt. Ohne sie gibt es keine Wörter.

Degérando kritisiert zwar den Extremismus von Condillac und Cabanis, aber er hält deshalb doch an der Wichtigkeit der Zeichen fest. Hier unterscheidet er prälinguistische und linguistische Zeichen. Erstere lösen Gedanken und Erinnerungen aus: so erinnert ein Schmerz an seine Verursachung. Die sprachlichen Zeichen aber führen die Aufmerksamkeit von sich selbst weg auf ihre Bedeutungen. Innerhalb der sprachlichen Zeichen unterscheidet Degérando dann Zeichen für wahrnehmbare Dinge wie *Hund* und *Haus* und Zeichen zweiter Ordnung für Ideen wie *Nation* und *Verfassung*. Letztere zeigen nicht die Dinge, sondern sie weisen nur den Weg, den man einschlagen muß, um sie zu entdecken.

Degérando kritisiert auch Condillacs Auffassung, wonach Denken nichts weiteres sei als symbolische oder logische Transformation von Sinnesempfindungen.

An dieser Grundannahme hatte auch de Tracy trotz seiner Kritik an Condillac festgehalten. Degérando legt seine schwerwiegenden Einwände vor in dem Werk *Histoire comparée des systèmes de philosophie relativement aux principes des connais sances humaines* (1804). Wer alle Tätigkeiten des Menschen auf Sinnesempfindungen zurückführe, so sagt er, übersehe wesentliche Unterschiede. (Ähnlich hatten sich auch Pierre Prévost und Maine de Biran geäußert.)

Frage 2 und 3 beantwortet Degérando negativ: Die Vorstellung einer vollkommenen Wissenschaftssprache, die von Leibniz u.a. ins Auge gefaßt worden war, hält Degérando für eine Chimäre, zumal keine Generation zukünftige Beobachtungen und Erfahrungen vorauszusehen vermöge.

Was die Abhängigkeit des Fortschritts der Wissenschaft von der Verbesserung der Terminologie betrifft, so glaubt Degérando, daß alle wissenschaftlichen Fortschritte weniger der Sprache als den Zufällen neuer Entdeckungen zu verdanken seien, die dann allerdings durch die Sprache festgehalten würden. Die Nomenklatur bewahrt das Erreichte, sie erlaubt aber weder Voraussagen noch vermag sie die Zukunft zu erklären.

Wenn Condillacs Theorie in der Chemie teilweise bestätigt schien, so führt Degérando dies auf die relativ geringe Zahl der dort zu benennenden Elemente zurück. In anderen wissenschaftlichen Disziplinen, z.B. in der Anatomie und der Physiologie, sei eine derartige Schematisierung nicht möglich.

Hervorzuheben ist, daß auch Degérando, ähnlich wie Locke und Condillac, auf die Kulturbedingtheit der Sprachverschiedenheit hinweist. Er spricht von verschiedenen Bündeln von Ideen, die je nach den kulturellen Verhältnissen gebildet werden. Maine de Biran hatte in diesem Zusammenhang auch auf die emotionale Kraft der ethischen Ausdrücke hingewiesen, die sogar innerhalb einer Gesellschaft bei den einzelnen Individuen verschiedene Gefühle auslösen. (Er nahm damit den Gedanken Lockes auf, daß selbst der Kaiser Augustus durch kein Gesetz die Bedeutung eines lateinischen Wortes hätte ändern können.) Wenn Maine de Biran darauf hinweist, daß der Begriff des Diebstahls in einem Besitzer andere Gefühle erwecke als in einem Armen, so ist dies ein Gedanke, der, so dürfen wir hinzufügen, auch in moderne soziolinguistische Überlegungen durchaus hineinpaßt.

Die vierte Frage der Akademie, ob ungelöste und umstrittene wissenschaftliche Probleme nur ungenügender Exaktheit ihrer Sprachmittel zuzuschreiben seien, beantwortet Degérando einschränkend. Gewiß sei eine ungenaue Sprache mit schuld, aber es seien auch andere Faktoren zu berücksichtigen, z.B. Temperamentsunterschiede der Forscher, bestimmte Vorurteile, Interessen usw.. Wenn derartige Unterschiede zu konkurrierenden Ansichten führten, so sei dies nicht unbedingt ein Nachteil, sondern könne auch der Wahrheitsfindung dienen.

Im Bereiche der Philosophie seien, so hebt Degérando hervor, manche angeblichen Neuerungen dadurch vorgetäuscht worden, daß einzelne den Sinn der Sprache ihrer Vorgänger einfach verändert hätten. Im Übrigen genügten bereits unterschiedliche Lebensauffassungen, um den Sinn einzelner Begriffe zu verändern. So bedeutet *virtus* bei den Stoikern etwas anderes als bei den Epikuräern.

In Bezug auf die Frage 5, die die Möglichkeit einer Verbesserung aller Wissenschaften durch eine Verbesserung ihrer Sprachen zur Diskussion stellt, hütet sich

Degérando wiederum vor einem einseitigen Urteil. Er weist auf Humes Unterscheidung von 'truth of fact (relation of ideas to things)' und 'abstract truth (relation of ideas to one another)' hin, die von Condillac vernachlässigt worden sei. Die meisten Wissenschaften haben es nach der Überzeugung Degérandos mit 'abstract truth' zu tun. Die Algebra, die auf der Idee der Quantität basiert und sämtliche Operationen auf gleichartige Gegenstände bezieht, stelle eine Ausnahme dar. Die nichtmathematischen Wissenschaften könnten nicht den Gewißheitsgrad des Kalküls erreichen.

Acton hebt in seinem Aufsatz folgende Probleme heraus, die von den Ideologen bereits behandelt, aber erst im 20. Jahrhundert zentral wurden:

1) thinking is essentially talking;
2) language is a calculus;
3) philosophical problems are pseudo-problems, they can be exposed and dispersed by means of linguistic reform (216).

Acton hält es für unzweckmaßig, die von Condillac entlehnte und aus Locke hergeleitete Terminologie der Ideologen in die heutige Terminologie transponieren zu wollen. Sein Kommentar bewegt sich daher bewußt im Rahmen der damaligen Begrifflichkeit. Er hebt nochmals hervor, daß die damaligen sprachphilosophischen Probleme nicht nur auf einer grammatisch-philosophischen Ebene geführt, sondern daß z.B. auch soziale Implikationen erkannt wurden (Maine de Biran). Der linguistische Empirismus Lockes und der Sensualismus Condillacs erfuhren seiner Meinung nach eine wohlbegründete Kritik. Besonders Maine de Biran habe die Originalität des individuellen Geistes betont und die treffende Bemerkung gemacht: Wenn die Sprache ein Kalkül wäre, dann könnte man sie getrost den Maschinen überlassen. Wenn Denken Rechnen wäre, würde es im Grunde überflüssig, und man sollte den Menschen dann davon entbinden.

Die Ideologen lehnen auch, so betont Acton, die Idee einer vollkommenen Universalsprache ab. Schon Locke, den Acton als einen 'extreme linguistic individualist' bezeichnet, hatte hervorgehoben, daß jederman frei sei in der Deutung sprachlicher Zeichen, so daß es also keine sprachliche Tyrannei geben könne. Maine de Biran und de Tracy sind ähnlicher Ansicht, sie begründen sie nur anders. De Tracy hält nur das neuerfundene Wort für unmißverständlich: Je mehr es aber gebraucht wird, desto größer wird die Möglichkeit der Bedeutungsänderung. Sprache ist 'inherently imperfect' weil die Menschen eben unvollkommen sind und nur über eine 'natural incompetence' verfügen. Der Einfluß Lockes auf die französischen Denker steht außer Frage. Acton erkennt aber genau, daß die Franzosen die Gedanken des Engländers in die eigene Denkungsart umsetzen. So ersetzt Condillac in dem Bemühen, Ordnung und Ökonomie in die 'sprawling asymmetry' der Gedanken Lockes zu bringen, unbewußt dessen Methode durch ein System.

Erwähnenswert ist hier Degérandos Kommentar über die Britische Philosophie des Jahrhunderts mit dem Acton seinen wichtigen Beitrag beschließt:

The English School has in general a calm, pacific and reserved character, although from time to time it is too dry and too torpid; above all things it respects the findings of common sense; it has a high regard for practical results, and has an attachment for those of its members who write books on moral philosophy. (219) (Zitat nach Acton, da der Originaltext nicht erreichbar war).

Der Aufsatz von J. B. Acton füllt eine Lücke in der allgemeinen Kenntnis der französischen Sprachphilosophie, eine Lücke, die durch mehrere Umstände mitverschuldet sein kann: Erstens handelt es sich bei den Überlegungen, die von den französischen Ideologen angestellt wurden, um Analysen der Empfindungen, Ideen und des Zeichengebrauchs, deren sprachphilosophischer Charakter nicht eigens herausgestellt wurde. Diese wurden zweitens — und das unterstreicht das Gesagte — in einer Sektion des Institut National diskutiert, der keine Sprachforscher oder Grammatiker im eigentlichen Sinne angehörten. Die Spezialisten auf diesem Gebiet gehörten vielmehr der Sektion der schönen Künste an. Es mag also hiermit zusammenhängen, daß die sprachphilosophischen Ideen der Ideologen unbeachtet blieben. Außerdem war die Wirkungszeit dieser Gelehrten relativ kurz. Andere Strömungen gewannen in der Folgezeit mehr Beachtung, vor allem stellte die beginnende Sprachwissenschaft mit ihren spektakulären Erfolgen die Randerscheinungen mehr und mehr in den Schatten.

Es besteht aber kein Zweifel, daß die damals diskutierten Probleme wichtig sind. Sie tauchen fast sämtlich in der neueren Sprachphilosophie wieder auf, sei es in der neopositivistischen Strömung des Wiener Kreises, in der analytischen Sprachphilosophie oder der sog. *ordinary language philosophy*. Auch soziolinguistische Gesichtspunkte sind zu erkennen. Ferner finden sich Einsichten in wichtige Gründe der Sprachverschiedenheit. Hervorzuheben ist die Ausgewogenheit des Urteils, etwa bei Maine de Biran und bei Degérando.

Auf der Suche nach weiteren Aufschlüssen über die Sprachauffassungen der Ideologen stießen wir noch auf einige Arbeiten, die zwar nicht ganz den Erwartungen entsprachen, aber doch wenigstens erwähnt werden sollten.

Wilhelm Köster hat 1933 eine Untersuchung über *Joseph Marie Degérando als Philosoph* vorgelegt. Darin findet sich auch ein Kapitel über die Sprache. Hier werden Degérandos Auffassungen vom Wesen und vom Zustandekommen der Sprache, von den verschiedenen Arten der Sprachzeichen und von der allgemeinen Bedeutung der Sprache für die Bildung der Ideen sowie für die Ausbildung der geistigen Fähigkeiten dargelegt. Einzubeziehen sind auch Degérandos Auffassungen von den Ideen selbst, die in seiner Philosophie eine zentrale Rolle spielen. Bermerkenswert ist, daß dieser Ideologe die geistige Fähigkeit des Menschen, Ideen untereinander auszutauschen, auf die Fähigkeit der Reflexion gründet. Köster paraphrasiert dies mit den Worten: 'Auf Grund der Reflexion erkennt der Mensch seine Akte, "versteht" sich selbst, und erst auf Grund dieses Verstehens seiner selbst ist ein Verstehen anderer und ein Mitteilen an andere möglich' (44). Natürlich erinnert diese Hervorhebung der Reflexion an Herder, aber wir wissen, daß auch schon bei Rousseau und Condillac von diesem Begriff die Rede war. Wir hatten die Auffassung vertreten, daß Herders 'Besonnenheit' und 'Reflexion' tiefer und konsequenter durchdacht ist als die 'réflexion' der Vorgänger. Es würde sich lohnen, die Geschichte dieser Begriffe in einem genauen Vergleich der Texte aufzuhellen. Was jedoch Degérando anbetrifft, so ist hier mit dem Einfluß Herders zu rechnen, den Degérando kannte und schätzte. In den *Archives Littéraires* hat er ihm sogar im Jahre 1804 einen Nachruf gewidmet. Darin begrüßt er Herders Eintreten gegen die Kantbegeisterung der Zeit in dessen *Metakritik*. Degérando war selbst an der damaligen Auseinandersetzung über die Philosophie Kants rege beteiligt (cf. Köster 1933:63, Anm. 9).

Über *Die Logik des Destutt de Tracy* liegt eine recht schmale Dissertation von Oskar Kohler aus dem Jahre 1931 vor, die einige Hinweise auf die Sprachauffassung de Tracys enthält. Kohler hebt hervor, daß dieser Ideologe seine Logik ganz auf dem Begriffsinhalt aufbaut und infolgedessen dem Zustandekommen dessen, was er 'Idee' nennt, seine Aufmerksamkeit widmet. Ausgangspunkt ist dabei das sensualistische Grundprinzip. Die sog. komplexen und allgemeinen Ideen werden durch Zusammenziehen (*contraire*) von Sinneserfahrungen bzw. '*sensations*' gewonnen. Zwar wird der Begriff der Sprache sehr weit gefaßt (es gibt z.B. auch eine Sprache der Aktionen!), aber de Tracy erkennt doch die entscheidende Bedeutung der Wörter für das menschliche Denken. Im Ganzen vereinigt das Werk Destutt de Tracys sensualistische, psychologische und positivistische Züge. Zugleich ist ein soziales Engagement und eine entsprechende pragmatische Einstellung erkennbar. Hieraus erklärt sich auch de Tracys radikale Ablehnung des Syllogismus und alles rein Formalen in der Logik.

Kohler weist mit Recht darauf hin, daß die Argumentationen des Autors nicht immer widerspruchsfrei sind und daß ein dozierender, apodiktischer Ton vorherrscht, was jedoch durch den Lehrbuchcharakter der Schriften erklärlich wird. Sicher verdienen die Äußerungen Destutt de Tracy über Sprache und Denken eine erneute Prüfung.

Die psychologische Einstellung Destutt de Tracys ist auch der Gegenstand einer ebenfalls sehr kurzen Dissertation von Vera Stepanova aus dem Jahre 1908. Die Autorin beginnt mit einer geschichtlichen Orientierung über die philosophischen Strömungen jenen Zeit und geht dann auf die psychologischen Ansichten von Destutt de Tracy ein. Für die Sprachauffassung der Ideologen gibt die Darstellung nicht viel her. Erwähnt werden könnte höchstens das 4. Kapitel, "Von den Ideen", in dem die Autorin leider nur sehr kurz über Destutts Ablehnung der Annahme angeborener Ideen und über die Zeichen und deren Verknüpfungen spricht. Hier hilft also nur der Rückgriff auf die Originaltexte.

Über die sprachwissenschaftlichen Bemühungen des Ideologen Volney, den Acton nur sehr knapp behandelt hat, bietet Jean Gaulmier in seiner Doktoratsthese *L'idéologue Volney* (1951) einige weitere Informationen. Allerdings begnügt er sich in dieser Biographie mit Hinweisen auf die Beschäftigung Volneys mit den orientalischen

Sprachen und auf sein Interesse an Peter Simon Pallas' *Linguarum totius orbis vocabularia comparativa*... (vgl. dazu S. 231ff.). Es ist hier von Volneys Vereinfachungsversuchen des Hebräischen die Rede und von seinen Bestrebungen, ein universelles Alphabet einzuführen, das auch die Verschriftung der arabischen und hebräischen Sprache mit lateinischen Buchstaben gestattet. Nach dem Vorbild von Pallas' Wörtersammlungen schwebt ihm ein Wörterbuch aller in Frankreich gebräuchlichen Dialektwörter vor, die er mit Hilfe von Fragebögen ermitteln möchte. Er schlägt 309 Wörter vor, die auf diese Weise, und zwar in Beispielsätzen, erfaßt werden sollen. Leider blieb dieser Plan zu einem ersten französischen Sprachatlas im Entwurf stecken.

Auf die sprachphilosophischen Gedanken Volneys geht Gaulmier leider nicht ein.

VII. *Die Begründung der Semantik* (*Bedeutungslehre*) *als sprachwissenschaftliche Disziplin*

Ganz am Rande der spektakulären Entwicklungen auf dem Gebiete der historisch-vergleichenden und der allgemeinen Sprachwissenschaft — und daher in den meisten Darstellungen der Geschichte der Linguistik übergangen — sind in der romantischen Epoche auch die Grundlagen einer sprachwissenschaftlichen Disziplin geschaffen worden, die heute noch lebendig ist, obwohl sie vorübergehend unter dem Einfluß antimentalistischer Strömungen vernachlässigt worden war. Es handelt sich um die Bedeutungslehre, also einen Zweig der Linguistik, der auch unter den Bezeichnungen Semasiologie bzw. Semantik (früher auch als Semologie, Semiologie oder Sematologie), franz. sémantique, engl. semantics bekannt ist.

Wie von den Historiographen vor allem Dornseiff (1959), Kronasser (1968), und Rey (1970) aufzeigen, ist das Bedeutungsproblem selbst natürlich alt und reicht in seiner Vorgeschichte bis in die griechische Philosophie (Heraklit, Platon, Aristoteles, die Stoa, usw.) zurück. Als eine eigenständige sprachwissenschaftliche Disziplin wurde die Bedeutungslehre aber erst jetzt etabliert, und zwar wird schon von Oskar Hey (1896:193; vgl. auch Baldinger 1957:4, Dornseiff 1959:41, Kronasser 1968:29, und Schippan 1972:16) mit Recht der deutsche klassische Philologe Christian Carl Reisig (1792–1829) als ihr Begründer angesehen. Dieser hatte nämlich in seinen erst posthum erschienenen *Vorlesungen über lateinische Sprachwissenschaft* (1839) die "Semasiologie" als einen besonderen Forschungsbereich konstituiert und eine Dreiteilung der Grammatik in Etymologie, Semasiologie und Syntax vorgeschlagen. Ein instruktiver Auszug dieses wichtigen Werkes ist jetzt unter dem Titel *Semasiologie oder Bedeutungslehre* in der von Laszlo Antal herausgegebenen Anthologie *Aspekte der Semantik: Zu ihrer Theorie und Geschichte*, 1662–1969 (1972:19–40) greifbar.

Reisigs Arbeit wurde dann von seinen Schülern Agathon Benary (1807–1860) und Friedrich Gottlieb Haase (1808–1867) fortgesetzt, auf deren Wirken etwa Kronasser in seinem *Handbuch der Semasiologie: Kurze Einführung in die Geschichte, Problema-*

tik und Terminologie der Bedeutungslehre (1968:30–2) ein wenig näher eingeht. So wies Benary das Wort als Ausdruck des Gedankens der Bedeutungslehre zu, und er forderte, daß man die Bedeutungen von Wortstamm und Suffix getrennt behandelt. Ähnlich wie Benary nahm dann auch Friedrich Gottlieb Haase Reisigs Dreiteilung der Grammatik in Etymologie, Semasiologie und Syntax auf, doch zergliederte er die Semasiologie noch weiter und nahm dazu noch sprachphilosophische Aspekte in seine Überlegungen hinein, indem er nach dem Verhältnis von Wort und Bedeutung fragte. Diese hier nur knapp umrissenen Gedanken findet man ausführlich dargelegt in den *Vorlesungen zur lateinischen Grammatik* (1874–1880), die nach Haases Tod von Friedrich August Eckstein und Hermann Peter herausgegeben wurden.

Als nächster bedeutender Gelehrter, der die Entwicklung der Semantik förderte, wird in der Regel Gottfried Ferdinand Heerdegen (geb. 1845) genannt, der in seinen *Untersuchungen zur lateinischen Semasiologie* (1875–1881) im Anschluß an Reisig und Haase, aber auch in kritischer Auseinandersetzung mit diesen, die lateinische Semasiologie weiter auszubauen suchte und dabei vor allem den Fragen des Bedeutungswandels nachging (vgl. z.B. Kronasser 1968:32–3, Schippan 1972:16). Heerdegen bearbeitete auch den semasiologischen zweiten Teil von Reisigs *Vorlesungen über lateinische Sprachwissenschaft* und gab diesen zusammen mit seinen eigenen *Grundzüge(n) der Bedeutungslehre* im Jahre 1890 noch einmal heraus.

Trotz dieser beachtenswerten Ansätze wurde die Bedeutungslehre aber erst allgemein in nachromantischer Zeit bekannt, und zwar durch den *Essai de sémantique: Science des significations*, den der Franzose Michel-Jean-Antoine Bréal (1832–1915) im Jahre 1897 veröffentlicht hatte und der schon drei Jahre später unter dem Titel *Semantics: Studies in the science of meaning* ins Englische übersetzt worden war (vgl. Stephen Ullmann 1972:3). Zu Recht kann daher Stephen Ullmann sagen: 'Wenn Reisig der Moses des gelobten Landes der Semantik war, so war Michel Bréal sein Josua' (1972:34). Aber wenn er dann fortfährt: 'Bréal gab ihr den Namen, der heute noch am geläufigsten ist' (1972:34), so stimmt er in dieser Ansicht zwar mit vielen Gelehrten unsere Jh.s überein (vgl. z.B. Liebich 1905:9, Brekle 1972:12, Mounin 1972:8), doch muß hier der Einwurf Dornseiffs (1959:63 Anm. 28) und auch Kronassers (1968:29 Anm. 9) beachtet werden, die darauf verweisen, daß Gaston Paris bereits im Jahre 1887 von einer Wissenschaft spricht, die "man" allgemein SÉMANTIQUE nenne. Demnach kann Bréal entgegen Ullmanns Meinung nicht als der Schöpfer dieses terminus technicus betrachtet werden, aber dennoch bleibt ihm unbestreitbar das Verdienst, diese neue Wissenschaft und ihre Bezeichnung als Semantik (*sémantique*, *semantics*) bekanntgemacht zu haben.

Im einzelnen beschäftigte man sich nun in der klassischen Semasiologie vornehmlich mit der Bedeutung einzelner Wörter der sogenannten Hauptwortarten (Substantiv, Adjektiv, Verb) und fragte in der Regel, ausgehend von der Lautung eines Wortes, danach, was mit ihr gemeint sei bzw. woran man bei ihrem Gebrauche denke. Diese Blickrichtung barg jedoch nach heutigem Urteil die Gefahr in sich, die Bedeutungen der Wörter als etwas außerhalb der Sprache Liegendes zu betrachten, und sie leistete damit einer sprachtheoretisch bedenklichen Auffassung Vorschub, welcher etwa der Logiker Gottlob Frege (1848–1925) durch die Gleichsetzung von Bedeutung und außersprachlichem Gegenstand beredten Ausdruck gab. Auch der junge Wittgenstein (1889–1951) schloß sich in seinem *Tractatus logico-philosophicus* (1922) dieser Auffassung noch an.

Neben der Gefahr der Herausverlegung der Bedeutung aus der Sprache — sei es in die Welt der Gegenstände oder in die Psyche der Sprecher — wird heute als Hauptmangel der traditionellen Semasiologie bezeichnet, daß sie fast ausschließlich bei der Betrachtung einzelner Wörter und deren "Bedeutungswandel" stehen bleibt und somit die strukturalen Zusammenhänge zwischen benachbarten Bedeutungen nicht in den Blick bekommt (Weisgerber 1927, 1971b; Gipper 1969, 1971; Gipper/Schwarz 1962ff.: Nr. 6928, Bespr. Heerdegen). Wie aber beispielweise die neueren Arbeiten von Wilhelm Schmidt (1963, 1965) und Thea Schippan (1972) zeigen, bemüht sich die moderne, mehr synchron orientierte Semasiologie jedoch, diese Fehler zu vermeiden.

LITERATURVERZEICHNIS*

Aaron, Richard Ithamar. 1955. John Locke. 2. Aufl. Oxford, Clarendon.

Aarsleff, Hans. 1964. Leibniz on Locke on language. American Philosophical Quarterly 1.165–88.

——, 1967. The study of language in England. Princeton, N.J., Princeton University Press. (Cf. IV. "Sir William Jones and the new philology", 115–61.)

——, 1969. The study and use of etymology in Leibniz. Studia Leibnitiana, Suppl. 3.173–89.

Abegg, Emil. 1921. Wilhelm von Humboldt und die Probleme der allgemeinen Sprachwissenschaft. Neue Jahrbücher für das Klassische Altertum, Geschichte und Deutsche Literatur 47 (Jg. 24).62–75.

Acton, H. B. 1959. The philosophy of language in revolutionary France. Proceedings of the British Academy 45.199–219.

Adelung, Johann Christoph. 1781. Über den Ursprung der Sprache und den Bau der Wörter, besonders der Deutschen. Ein Versuch. Leipzig, Reimer.

——, 1806. Älteste Geschichte der Deutschen, ihrer Sprache und Litteratur, bis zur Völkerwanderung. Leipzig, Göschen.

——, 1806–1817. Mithridates oder allgemeine Sprachenkunde mit dem Vater Unser als Sprachprobe in bey nahe fünfhundert Sprachen und Mundarten. 4 Teile: I. 1806, II. 1809, III. 1816, IV. 1817 (Teile II.–IV. von Johann Severin Vater). Berlin, Vossische Buchhandlung.

* Für freundliche Hilfe bei der Verifizierung und Beschaffung einzelner Titel möchten wir an dieser Stelle Herrn Ladislaus Hojsak (Bonn) und Herrn Hartwig Kalverkämper (Münster) danken.

ADLER, GEORG J. 1866. Wilhelm von Humboldt's linguistical studies. New York, Wynkoop & Hallenbeck.

AGRELL, JAN. 1955. Studier i den äldre språkjämförelsens allmänna och svenska historia fram till 1827. Mit einer Zusammenfassung auf Deutsch: Studien zur allgemeinen und schwedischen Geschichte der älteren Sprachvergleichung (bis 1827). Uppsala Universitets Årsskrift, 1955, 13. Uppsala, A.-B. Lundequistska Bokhandeln/Wiesbaden, O. Harrassowitz.

ANDERSON, EUGENE N. 1941. German romanticism as an ideology of cultural crisis. Journal of the History of Ideas 2.301–17.

ANTAL, LASZLO (Hrsg.). 1972. Aspekte der Semantik: Zu ihrer Theorie und Geschichte, 1662–1969. Frankfurt a.M., Athenäum Verlag.

ANTONSEN, ELMER H. 1962. Rasmus Rask and Jacob Grimm: Their relationship in the investigation of German vocalism. Scandinavian Studies 34.183–94.

APEL, KARL OTTO. 1963. Die Idee der Sprache in der Tradition des Humanismus von Dante bis Vico. Archiv für Begriffsgeschichte. Bonn, Bouvier.

ARENS, HANS. 1955 [2. Aufl. 1969]. Sprachwissenschaft: Der Gang ihrer Entwicklung von der Antike bis zur Gegenwart. Freiburg/München, Alber.

ARMSTRONG, ROBERT L. 1965. John Locke's 'Doctrine of Signs': A new metaphysics. Journal of the History of Ideas 26.369–82.

ARNDT, ERNST MORITZ. 1804. Ideen über die höchste historische Ansicht der Sprache, entwickelt in einer Rede, am hohen Geburtsfeste Gustav IV. Adolphs, am 1 November 1804. Greifswald, Eckhardt.

ARNDT, ERWIN. 1965. Diachronie und Synchronie in Jacob Grimms "Deutscher Grammatik": Ausnahme und Regel in neuer Sicht. WZUB 14.479–88.

ARNDT, ERWIN/BONDZIO, WILHELM. 1965. Aus den Anfängen der Germanistik: Betrachtungen zum Werk der Brüder Jacob und Wilhelm Grimm. WZUB 14.443–5.

AST, FRIEDRICH. 1808. Grundlinien der Grammatik, Hermeneutik und Kritik. Landshut, Thomann.

BALDINGER, KURT. 1957. Die Semasiologie: Versuch eines Überblicks. Deutsche Akademie der Wissenschaften zu Berlin. Vorträge und Schriften, 61. Berlin.

BALLY, CHARLES. 1965. Linguistique générale et linguistique française. 4. Aufl. Berne, Francke.

BANNIZA VON BAZAN, HEINRICH. 1933. Grenzen der Sprachgemeinschaft. Mu 8. 420–4.

BASILIUS, HAROLD. 1952. Neo-Humboldtian ethnolinguistics. Word 8.95–105.

BATILLORI, MIGUEL. 1951. El archivo lingüístico de Hervás en Roma y su reflejo en Wilhelm von Humboldt. Archivum Historicum Societatis Iesu 20.59–116. Roma.

BAUDLER, GEORG. 1970. Im Worte sehen: Das Sprachdenken Johann Georg Hamanns. Münchener Philosophische Forschungen, 2. Bonn, Bouvier.

BEHLER, ERNST. 1957. Der Stand der Friedrich-Schlegel-Forschung. Jahrbuch der Deutschen Schillergesellschaft 1.253–89.

——, 1958. Neue Ergebnisse der Friedrich-Schlegel-Forschung. GRM 8.350–65.

——, 1966. Friedrich Schlegel in Selbstzeugnissen und Bilddokumenten. Rowohlts Monographien, 123. Reinbek bei Hamburg, Rowohlt.

——, 1968. Das Indienbild der deutschen Romantik. GRM 18.21–37.

BEISER, ARTHUR. 1967. Die Erde. Life: Wunder der Natur. Niederlande (o.O.), Time–Life International.

BENEŠ, BIRGIT. 1958. Wilhelm v. Humboldt, Jacob Grimm, August Schleicher: Ein Vergleich ihrer Sprachauffassungen. Winterthur, Keller.

BENFEY, THEODOR. 1869. Geschichte der Sprachwissenschaft und orientalischen Philologie in Deutschland seit dem Anfange des 19. Jahrhunderts mit einem Rückblick auf die früheren Zeiten. Geschichte der Wissenschaften in Deutschland. Neuere Zeit, 8. München, Cotta. Nachdruck 1965.

BENSE, GERTRUD. 1957–1958. Die vergleichende Sprachwissenschaft in Halle seit F. A. Pott. WZUH 7.901–5.

BERGLAR, PETER. 1970. Wilhelm von Humboldt in Selbstzeugnissen und Bilddokumenten. Rowohlts Monographien, 161. Reinbek bei Hamburg, Rowohlt.

BERGSVEINSSON, SVEINN. 1965. Die Brüder Grimm und der Norden. WZUB 14. 515–6.

BERLIN, ISAIAH. 1956. The age of enlightenment: The 18th century philosophers. New York, Mentor Books.

BEZZENBERGER, A. (o.J.). Die sprachwissenschaftlichen Äußerungen Kants (o.O.).

BINSWANGER, PAUL. 1937. Wilhelm von Humboldt. Frauenfeld, Huber.

BJERRUM, MARIE. 1959. Rasmus Rasks afhandlinger om det danske sprog: Bidrag til forståelse af Rasks tænkning. København, Dansk Videnskaps Forlag.

BODAMMER, THEODOR. 1969. Hegels Deutung der Sprache: Interpretationen zu Hegels Äußerungen über die Sprache. Hamburg, Meiner.

BOHLEN, ADOLF. 1952. Die Sprachtheorie Wilhelm von Humboldts und der Bildungswert des Englischen. Tübingen, Niemeyer.

BOLLNOW, OTTO FRIEDRICH. 1938. Wilhelm von Humboldts Sprachphilosophie. Zeitschrift für Deutsche Bildung 14.102–12.

BONDZIO, WILHELM. 1965. Jacob Grimm und die neuhochdeutsche Schriftsprache. WZUB 14.471–8.

BONFANTE, GIULIANO. 1954. Ideas of the kinship of the European languages from 1200 to 1800. Cahiers d'Histoire Mondial/Journal of World History/Cuadernos de Historia Mundial 3/1.679–99.

BOPP, FRANZ. 1816. Über das Conjugationssystem der Sanskritsprache in Vergleichung mit jenem der griechischen, lateinischen, persischen und germanischen Sprache. Nebst Episoden des Ramajan und Mahabharat in genauen metrischen Übersetzungen aus dem Originaltexte und einigen Abschnitten aus den Veda's.

Herausgegeben und mit Vorerinnerungen begleitet von Dr. K. J. Windischmann. Frankfurt, Andreäische Buchhandlung.

——, 1819. Nalus, carmen sanscritum e Mahábhárato edidit, latine vertit et annotationibus illustravit Fr. Bopp. London.

——, 1833–1852. Vergleichende Grammatik des Sanskrit, Zend, Griechischen, Lateinischen, Litthauischen, Gothischen und Deutschen. 6 Bde. Berlin.

——, 1971. Kleine Schriften zur vergleichenden Sprachwissenschaft. Gesammelte Berliner Akademieabhandlungen 1824–1854. Opuscula, 5. Leipzig.

BORST, ARNO. 1957–1963. Der Turmbau von Babel: Geschichte der Meinungen über Ursprung und Vielfalt der Sprachen und Völker. 4 Bde. Stuttgart, Hiersemann. (cf. Bd. III., 1961, 1521–1626, Kapitel: "Revolution und Romantik").

BOUMANN, ARI C. 1928. Het probleem van de "inwendige taalvorm". NTg 22. 24–37, 293–99.

BRÄUER, JOACHIM. 1921. August Friedrich Bernhardi, der Sprachphilosoph der älteren Romantik. Diss. Breslau.

BRÉAL, MICHEL-JEAN-ANTOINE. 1897. Essai de sémantique: Science des significations. Paris.

BREKLE, HERBERT. 1972. Semantik: Eine Einführung in die sprachwissenschaftliche Bedeutungslehre. Uni-Taschenbücher, 102. München, Fink.

BRINKMANN, HENNIG. 1971. Die deutsche Sprache: Gestalt und Leistung. 2. Aufl. Düsseldorf, Schwann.

BROENS, OTTO. 1913. Darstellung und Würdigung des sprachphilosophischen Gegensatzes zwischen Paul, Wundt und Marty. Diss. Bonn.

BROWN, ROGER LANGHAM. 1967. Wilhelm von Humboldt's conception of linguistic relativity. Janua Linguarum. Series Minor, 65. The Hague, Mouton.

BUMANN, WALTRAUD. 1965 (1966). Die Sprachtheorie Heymann Steinthals, dargestellt im Zusammenhang mit seiner Theorie der Geisteswissenschaft. Monographien zur philosophischen Forschung, 39. Meisenheim am Glan, Hain.

CANNON, GARLAND H. 1952. Sir William Jones: An annotated bibliography of his works. Honolulu.

——, 1958. Sir William Jones's Persian linguistics. JAOS 78.262–73. [Auch in: Portraits of linguists: A biographical source book for the history of western linguistics, 1746–1963, by Th. A. Sebeok, I. Bloomington/London, Indiana University Press, 1966.35–57.]

——, 1964. Oriental Jones: A biography of the English orientalist Sir William Jones (1746–94). London, Asia Publishing House.

CASSIRER, ERNST. 1923. Die Kantischen Elemente in Wilhelm von Humboldts Sprachphilosophie. Festschrift Paul Hensel, Greiz i.V., 105–27.

——, 1923–1929. Philosophie der symbolischen Formen. 3 Bde.: I. Die Sprache. 1923, II. Das mythische Denken. 1925, III. Phänomenologie der Erkenntnis.1929. Berlin, Cassirer. Nachdruck 1953–1954. Darmstadt, Wissenschaftliche Buchgesellschaft.

CHAMBERS, W. W. 1946. Language and nationality in German preromantic and romantic thought. MLR 41.382–92.

CHATTERJI, SUNITI KUMAR. 1948. Sir William Jones: 1746–1794. Sir William Jones Bicentenary of his birth commemoration volume 1746–1946, 81–96. Calcutta. [Auch in: Portraits of linguists: A biographical source book for the history of western linguistics, 1746–1963, ed. by Th. A. Sebeok, I. Bloomington/London, Indiana University Press, 1966, 18–36.]

CHRISTMANN, HANS HELMUT. 1965. Un aspetto del concetto humboldtiano della lingua e i suoi precursori italiani. Problemi di lingua e letteratura italiana del Settecento. Atti del quarto Congresso dell' Associazione internazionale per gli studi di lingua e letteratura italiana. Magonza e Colonia, 28 aprile–1° maggio 1962. A cura di W. Th. Elwert, 328–33. Wiesbaden, Steiner.

——, 1967. Beiträge zur Geschichte der These vom Weltbild der Sprache. AAWL Mainz. Geistes- und sozialwissenschaftliche Klasse, 1966, Nr. 7, 441–69. Wiesbaden, Verlag der Akademie der Wissenschaften und der Literatur in Mainz.

CLARK, ROBERT T. 1946. Herder, Cesarotti, and Vico. SPh 44.645–71.

——, 1955. Herder: His life and thought. Berkeley/Los Angeles, University of California Press.

COLEBROOKE, HENRY THOMAS. 1799. On the duties of a faithful Hindu widow. Asiatick Researches 4.209–19. Calcutta.

——, 1803. On the Sanscrit and Pracrit languages. Asiatick Researches 7.199–231. Calcutta.

——, 1805. A grammar of the Sanscrit language. Calcutta, Honorable Company's Press.

——, 1808. Amarasiṃha–Cósha, or, dictionary of the Sanscrit language, with an English Interpretation and annotations. Serampoor.

COSERIU, EUGENIO. 1970. Semantik, innere Sprachform und Tiefenstruktur. FoL 4.53–63.

DEHÉRAIN, HENRI. 1938. Silvestre de Sacy, ses contemporaines et ses disciples. Bibliothèque Archéologique et Historique, 27. Paris.

DELBRÜCK, BERTHOLD. 1919. Einleitung in das Studium der indogermanischen Sprachen: Ein Beitrag zur Geschichte und Methodik der vergleichenden Sprachforschung. 6. Aufl. Leipzig, Breitkopf & Härtel.

DEMPF, ALOIS. 1958. Weltordnung und Heilsgeschehen. Horizonte, 4. Einsiedeln, Johannes. (Cf. 79–107: "Der frühe und der späte Friedrich Schlegel".)

DENECKE, LUDWIG. 1971. Jacob Grimm und sein Bruder Wilhelm. Realienbücher für Germanisten, Abt. D: Literaturgeschichte. Sammlung Metzler, 100. Stuttgart, J. B. Metzlersche Verlagsbuchhandlung.

DERBOLAV, JOSEF. 1951. Das Problem der inneren Sprachform. Wissenschaft und Weltbild 4.296–303.

——, 1959. Hegel und die Sprache: Ein Beitrag zur Standortbestimmung der Sprachphilosophie im Systemdenken des Deutschen Idealismus. Sprache —

Schlüssel zur Welt. Festschrift für L. Weisgerber, hrsg. von H. Gipper, 56–86. Düsseldorf, Schwann.

DERRIDA, JACQUES. 1967. La linguistique de Rousseau. Revue Internationale de Philosophie 79/80.444–62.

DEVOTO, GIACOMO. 1962. Origini indoeuropee. Firenze, Sansoni.

DIDERICHSEN, PAUL. 1960. Rasmus Rask og den grammatiske tradition. Det Kong. Danske Videnskabernes Selskab. Hist.-filol. Meddelelser, 38, 2. København.

——, 1966. The foundation of comparative linguistics: Revolution or continuation? (1964). Helhed og struktur. Udvalgte sprogvidenskabelige afhandlinger. Selected linguistic papers with detailed English summaries, 340–63. København, Gads Forlag.

DINNEEN, FRANCIS P. 1967. An introduction to general linguistics. New York, Holt, Rinehart & Winston.

DOBBEK, WILHELM. 1969. J. G. Herders Weltbild: Versuch einer Deutung. Köln/Wien, Böhlau.

DORNSEIFF, FRANZ. 1959. Der deutsche Wortschatz nach Sachgruppen. 5. erg. Aufl. Berlin, de Gruyter.

DOVE, ALFRED. 1881. Humboldt. Allgemeine deutsche Biographie 13.338–58. [Auch in: Portraits of linguists: A biographical source book for the history of western linguistics, 1746–1963, ed. by Th. A. Sebeok, I, 71–101. Bloomington/London, Indiana University Press, 1966.]

DÜNNINGER, JOSEF. 1957. Geschichte der deutschen Philologie: Deutsche Philologie im Aufriß. 2. Aufl., hrsg. von Wolfgang Stammler, I, 83–222. Berlin, Schmidt. Nachdruck 1966.

EDGERTON, FRANKLIN. 1946. Sir William Jones. Journal of the American Oriental Society 66.230–9. [Auch in: Portraits of linguists: A biographical source book for the history of western linguistics, 1746–1963, ed. by Th. A. Sebeok, I, 1–18. Bloomington/London, Indiana University Press, 1966.

EICHNER, H. (Hrsg.). 1972. 'Romantic' and its cognates: The European history of a word. Manchester, University Press.

ENDERS, CARL. 1913. Friedrich Schlegel: Die Quellen seines Wesens und Werdens. Leipzig, H. Haessel.

ERBEN, JOHANNES. 1972. Abriß der deutschen Grammatik. 11. Aufl. Berlin, Akademie Verlag/München, Hueber.

——, 1968. Deutsche Grammatik: Ein Leitfaden. Fischer Handbücher, 904. Frankfurt a.M., Fischer.

ERGANG, R. P. 1931. Herder and the foundation of German "nationalism". New York, Col. Univ. phil. Dissertation.

EVANS, CHARLOTTE BUFF. 1967a. Wilhelm von Humboldts Auffassung vom Ursprung der Sprache. Diss. Ohio State University (Cf. DAb 28, 1967, 1073–A).

——, 1967b. Wilhelm von Humboldts Sprachtheorie: Zum Gedächtnis seines 200. Geburtstages am 22. Juni. GQ 40.509–17.

FABRE D'OLIVET, ANTOINE. 1815. La langue hébraique restituée et le veritable sens des mots hébreux rétabli et prouvé par leur analyse radicale. 2 Teile in 1 Bd. Paris.

FAHRION, KARL. 1913. Die Sprachphilosophie Lockes. Archiv für Geschichte der Philosophie 26 (N.F. 19)56–65.

FAUTECK, HEINRICH. 1939. Die Sprachtheorie Fr. v. Hardenbergs (Novalis). Diss. Göttingen 1939. Berlin, Triltsch & Luther.

FICHTE, JOAHANN GOTTLIEB. 1795. Von der Sprachfähigkeit und dem Ursprunge der Sprache. Philosophical Journal 1.255–73, 287–326 [Auch: Sämtliche Werke VIII.301–41.]

——, 1808. Reden an die deutsche Nation. Berlin, Realschulbuchhandlung.

FIESEL, EVA. 1927. Die Sprachphilosophie der deutschen Romantik. Tübingen, Mohr.

FILLIOZAT, JEAN. 1941. Catalogue du fonds sanscrit, Fasc. I, Nos 1 à 165. Bibliothèque Nationale Département des Manuscrits. Paris, Librairie d'Amérique et d'Orient Adrien–Maisonneuve.

FINCK, FRANZ NIKOLAUS. 1899. Der deutsche Sprachbau als Ausdruck deutscher Weltanschauung. Acht Vorträge. Marburg, Elwert.

——, 1961. Haupttypen des Sprachbaus. Nachdruck der 3. Aufl. 1936. Darmstadt, Wissenschaftliche Buchgesellschaft.

FINKE, HEINRICH. 1918. Über Friedrich Schlegel: Schwierigkeiten seiner Beurteilung. Die Arbeitsgebiete seiner zweiten Lebenshälfte. Freiburg i.A., Guenther.

FISCHER, RUDOLF. 1962. August Schleicher zur Erinnerung. SbSAW, 107, 5. Berlin, Akademie Verlag.

FOWKES, ROBERT A. 1964. The linguistic modernity of Jacob Grimm. Linguistics 8.56–61.

FREYER, HANS. 1928a. Sprache und Kultur. Die Erziehung 3.65–78.

——, 1928b. Theorie des objektiven Geistes: Eine Einleitung in die Kulturphilosophie. 2. Aufl. Berlin/Leipzig, Teubner.

——, 1928c. Sprachbegriff der deutschen Bewegung. Verhandlungen der Versammlung Deutscher Philologen und Schulmänner 56, 135. Leipzig, Teubner.

FRIEDRICH, HUGO. 1935. Die Sprachtheorie der französischen Illuminaten des 18. Jahrhunderts. DVLG 13.293–310.

FÜCK, JOHANN. 1955. Die arabischen Studien in Europa bis in den Anfang des 20. Jahrhunderts. Leipzig, O. Harrassowitz.

FUNKE, OTTO. 1924. Innere Sprachform: Eine Einführung in A. Martys Sprachphilosophie. Reichenberg i.B., Kraus.

——, 1928. Studien zur Geschichte der Sprachphilosophie. Bern, Francke.

——, 1934. Englische Sprachphilosophie im späteren 18. Jahrhundert. Bern, Francke.

——, 1954. Form und 'Bedeutung' in der Sprachstruktur. Festschrift für Albert Debrunner, 141–50. Bern, Francke.

——, 1957. Zur Frühgeschichte des Terminus '(Innere) Sprachform'. Beiträge zur Einheit von Bildung und Sprache im geistigen Sein. Festschrift für Ernst Otto, hrsg. von Gerhard Haselbach und Günter Hartmann. Berlin, de Gruyter.

GABELENTZ, GEORG VON DER. 1891. Die Sprachwissenschaft, ihre Aufgaben, Methoden und bisherigen Ergebnisse. Leipzig, Weigel. [Auch: 1901: Leipzig, Tauchnitz. Nachdruck 1969: Tübingen, Tübinger Beiträge zur Linguistik.]

GADAMER, HANS-GEORG. 1960. Wahrheit und Methode: Grundzüge einer philosophischen Hermeneutik. Tübingen, Mohr.

GAJEK, BERNHARD. 1967. Sprache beim jungen Hamann. Europäische Hochschulschriften, Reihe I, Deutsche Literatur und Germanistik, 3. Diss. Frankfurt 1959. Bern, Lang.

GAUDEFROY–DEMOMBYNES, JEAN. 1931. L'œuvre linguistique de Humboldt. Paris, Maisonneuve.

GAULNIER, JEAN. 1951. L'idéologue Volney 1757–1820: Contribution à l'histoire de l'orientalisme en France. Beyrouth, Institut Français de Damas.

GECKELER, HORST. 1971. Strukturelle Semantik und Wortfeldtheorie. München, Fink.

GEHLEN, ARNOLD. 1950. Der Mensch: Seine Natur und Stellung in der Welt. 4. Aufl. Bonn.

GEORGIEV, VLADIMIR I. 1966. Introduzione alla storia delle lingue indoeuropee. Roma, Edizioni dell' Ateneo.

GERSTNER, HERMANN. 1952. Die Brüder Grimm, ihr Leben und Werk in Selbstzeugnissen, Briefen und Aufzeichnungen. München, Langewiesche–Brandt.

GIPPER, HELMUT. 1959. Sessel oder Stuhl? Ein Beitrag zur Bestimmung von Wortinhalten im Bereich der Sachkultur. Sprache — Schlüssel zur Welt. Festschrift für Leo Weisgerber, 271–292. Düsseldorf, Schwann.

——, 1965–1966. Wilhelm von Humboldt als Begründer moderner Sprachforschung. WW 15.1–19.

——, 1966. Sprachliche und geistige Metamorphosen bei Gedichtübersetzungen: Eine sprachvergleichende Untersuchung zur Erhellung deutsch-französischer Geistesverschiedenheit. Düsseldorf, Schwann.

——, 1967. Der Beitrag der inhaltlich orientierten Sprachwissenschaft zur Kritik der historischen Vernunft. Das Problem der Sprache. Achter deutscher Kongreß für Philosophie, Heidelberg, 1966, 407–25. München, Fink.

——, 1968. Wilhelm von Humboldts Bedeutung für die moderne Sprachwissenschaft. Die Brüder Humboldt heute, hrsg. von H. Kessler/W. Thoms, 41–62. Abhandlungen der Humboldt-Gesellschaft für Wissenschaft, Kunst und Bildung, 2. Mannheim.

——, 1969. Bausteine zur Sprachinhaltsforschung. Neuere Sprachbetrachtung im Austausch mit Geistes- und Naturwissenschaft. 2. Aufl. Düsseldorf, Schwann.

——, 1971. Bedeutung. Bedeutungslehre. Historisches Wörterbuch der Philosophie, hrsg. von J. Ritter, I, 757–61. Basel/Stuttgart, Schwabe.

——, 1972. Gibt es ein sprachliches Relativitätsprinzip? Untersuchungen zur Sapir–Whorf-Hypothese. Conditio Humana. Frankfurt a.M., Fischer.

GIPPER, HELMUT/SCHWARZ, HANS. 1962ff. Bibliographisches Handbuch zur Sprachinhaltsforschung. Schrifttum zur Sprachinhaltsforschung in alphabetischer Folge nach Verfassern mit Besprechungen und Inhaltshinweisen. (Abhandlungen der Rheinisch–Westfälischen Akademie der Wissenschaften, 16a). 2 Teile: Teil I. Bd. I. Buchstabe A–G. 1962–1966; Bd. II. Buchstabe H–K. Unter Mitarbeit von Hartmut Beckers, Edeltraud Bülow, Kristina Franke, Eckhard Franzen, Ladislaus Hojsak, Peter Schmitter und Horst Sprengelmeyer. 1965–1973 (wird fortgesetzt). Köln/Opladen, Westdeutscher Verlag.

GIVNER, D. A. 1962. Scientific preconceptions in Locke's philosophy of language. Journal of the History of Ideas 23.340–54.

GLÄSSER, EDGAR. 1939. Einführung in die rassenkundliche Sprachforschung. Kulturgeschichtliche Bibliothek, I, 53–8. Heidelberg, Winter.

GLINZ, HANS. 1955–1956. Aufgabe und Werdegang der deutschen Grammatik. WW 6.328–35.

——, 1961. Die innere Form des Deutschen. Bibliotheca Germanica. 2. Aufl. Bern, Francke.

——, 1965. Grundbegriffe und Methoden inhaltbezogener Text- und Sprachanalyse. Sprache und Gemeinschaft, Grundlegung, 3. Düsseldorf, Schwann.

——, 1970. Deutsche Syntax. Realienbücher für Germanisten, Abt. C: Deutsche Sprachwissenschaft. Sammlung Metzler, 43. 3. Aufl. Stuttgart, Metzlersche Verlagsbuchhandlung. (Cf. 21–55: "Bekannte Darstellungen der deutschen Syntax 1837–1932".)

GLOSZNER, M. 1905. W. v. Humboldts Sprachwissenschaft und ihr Verhältnis zu dem philosophischen System seiner Zeit. Jahrbuch für Philosophie und speculative Theologie 20.129–60. Paderborn.

GREBE, PAUL (Hrsg.). 1973. Grammatik der deutschen Gegenwartssprache. Der Große Duden, 4. 3. Aufl. Mannheim, Bibliographisches Institut.

GRIMM, JACOB. 1819. Deutsche Grammatik, Erster Theil. Göttingen, Dieterich.

——, 1822–1837. Deutsche Grammatik. 4 Theile: I. Theil. Zweite Ausgabe. 1822; II. Theil. 1826; III. Theil. 1831; IV. Theil. 1837. Göttingen, Dieterich.

——, 1848. Geschichte der deutschen Sprache. 2 Bde. Leipzig, Weidmann. 1853: 2. Aufl., Leipzig, Hirzel; 1868: 3. Aufl.

——, 1864–1890. Kleinere Schriften . 8 Bde.: I.–V. hrsg. von Karl Müllenhoff. 1864–1871; VI.–VIII., hrsg. von Eduard Ippel. 1882–1890. Berlin, Dümmler/ Gütersloh, Bertelsmann.

——, 1958. Über den Ursprung der Sprache. Gelesen in der Preussischen Akademie der Wissenschaften am 9. Januar 1851. Mit einem Nachwort von M. Rassem. Wiesbaden, Insel-Verlag.

——, 1961. Vorreden zum deutschen Wörterbuch, Bd. I. und II (1854 und 1860). Darmstadt, Wissenschaftliche Buchgesellschaft.

——, 1968. Vorreden zur Deutschen Grammatik von 1819 und 1822. Mit einem

Vorwort zum Neudruck von Hugo Steger. Darmstadt, Wissenschaftliche Buchgesellschaft.

GRIMM, JACOB/GRIMM, WILHELM. (Begründer) 1852–1960. Deutsches Wörterbuch. 16 Bde. in 32 Teilen. Leipzig, Hirzel.

GUETTI, BARBARA J. 1969. The double voice of nature: Rousseau's 'Essai sur l'origine des langues'. MLN 84.853–75.

GULYA, J. 1965. Some 18th century antecedents of the 19th century linguistics. ALH 15.163–70.

HAASE, FRIEDRICH GOTTLIEB. 1874–1880. Vorlesungen über lateinische Sprachwissenschaft. 2 Bde.: I. Einleitung und Bedeutungslehre 1. Teil, hrsg. von F. A. Eckstein, 1874; II. Bedeutungslehre 2. Teil, hrsg. von H. Peter, 1880. Leipzig, Simmel.

HABERMAS, JÜRGEN. 1963. Analytische Wissenschaftstheorie und Dialektik. Festschrift für Th. W. Adorno. Frankfurt a.M., Europäische Verlagsanstalt.

HÄNSCH, FELIX. 1902. Darstellung und Kritik der Gedanken Herders über die Muttersprache. Pädagogische Studien, Neue Folge.

HALHED, NATHANIEL BRASSEY. 1776. A code of Gentoo laws, or, ordinations of the Pundits, from a Persian translation, made from the original, written in the Shanscrit language. London.

——, 1778. A grammar of the Bengal language. Hoogly (Bengal).

HAMANN, JOHANN GEORG. 1963. Über den Ursprung der Sprache. Zwo Recensionen nebst einer Beylage betreffend den Ursprung der Sprache. Des Ritters von Rosencreuz letzte Willensmeynung über den göttlichen und menschlichen Ursprung der Sprache. Philologische Einfälle und Zweifel. An Salomon de Prusse. Erklärt von Elfriede Büchsel. Hauptschriften erklärt, 4. Gütersloh, Gütersloher Verlagshaus Mohn.

——, 1967. Schriften zur Sprache. Einleitung und Anmerkungen von Josef Simon. Theorie, 1. Frankfurt a.M., Suhrkamp.

HARNOIS, GUY. 1929. Les théories du langage en France de 1660 à 1821. Paris, Les Belles Lettres.

HARTMANN, PETER. 1957. Probleme der sprachlichen Form. Heidelberg, Winter. (Cf. 275–381: "Die sprachliche Geformtheit in W. v. Humboldts Verschiedenheit des menschlichen Sprachbaues".)

——, 1958. Wesen und Wirkung der Sprache im Spiegel der Theorie Leo Weisgerbers. Heidelberg, Winter. [Rezension: Helmut Gipper, 1960, IF 65.56–65.]

HASELBACH, GERHARD. 1966. Grammatik und Sprachstruktur: Karl Ferdinand Beckers Beitrag zur allgemeinen Sprachwissenschaft in historischer und systematischer Sicht. Berlin, de Gruyter.

HAUSSMANN, J. F. 1906–1907. Der junge Herder und Hamann. JEGP 6.606–48.

HAYM, RUDOLF. 1856. Wilhelm von Humboldt: Lebensbild und Charakteristik. Berlin, Gaertner. [Nachdruck: Osnabrück, Zeller, 1965.]

——, 1870. Die romantische Schule: Ein Beitrag zur Geschichte des deutschen Geistes. Berlin, Gaertner. 4. Aufl. 1920.

——, 1880–1885. Herder nach seinem Leben und seinen Werken dargestellt. 2 Bde.: I. 1880; II. 1885. Berlin, Gaertner.

HEBERER, GERHARD. 1968. Homo — unsere Ab- und Zukunft: Herkunft und Entwicklung des Menschen aus der Sicht der aktuellen Anthropologie. Stuttgart, Deutsche Verlagsanstalt.

HEERDEGEN, EUGEN GOTTFRIED FERDINAND. 1875–1881. Untersuchungen zur lateinischen Semasiologie. 3 Teile. Erlangen, Deichert.

HEESCHEN, VOLKER. 1972. L. Weisgerber. Claus Heeschen. Grundfragen der Linguistik mit einem Beitrag von Volker Heeschen, 54–69. Urban Taschenbücher, 156. Stuttgart/Berlin/Köln/Mainz, W. Kohlhammer.

HEGEL, GEORG WILHELM FRIEDRICH. 1807. System der Wissenschaft. Erster Theil: die Phänomenologie des Geistes. Bamberg/Würzburg, Goebhardt. Nach dem Original herausgegeben von Johannes Hoffmeister. 6. Aufl. 1952. Hamburg, Meiner.

HEINTEL, ERICH. 1957. Sprachphilosophie. Deutsche Philologie im Aufriß, 2. Aufl., hrsg. von W. Stammler, 563–619. Berlin/Bielefeld/München, Schmidt. Nachdruck 1966.

——, 1959. Gegenstandskonstitution und sprachliches Weltbild. Sprache — Schlüssel zur Welt. Festschrift für Leo Weisgerber, hrsg. von H. Gipper, 47–55. Düsseldorf, Schwann.

——, 1967. Herders Sprachphilosophie. Revue Internationale de Philosophie 79/80.464–74.

HELBIG, GERHARD. 1961. Die Sprachauffassung Leo Weisgerbers: Zum Problem der "funktionalen" Grammatik. DU 13/3.91–122.

——, 1971. Geschichte der neueren Sprachwissenschaft: Unter dem besonderen Aspekt der Grammatik-Theorie. München, Hueber.

HERDER, JOHANN GOTTFRIED VON. 1877–1913. Sämtliche Werke. Herausgegeben von Bernhard Suphan. 33 Bde. Berlin, Weidmann.

——, 1959. Über den Ursprung der Sprache. Hrsg. von Claus Träger. Berlin, Akademie Verlag.

——, 1960. Sprachphilosophische Schriften. Aus dem Gesamtwerk ausgewählt, mit einer Einleitung, Anmerkungen und Registern versehen von Erich Heintel. Hamburg, Meiner.

——, 1966. Abhandlung über den Ursprung der Sprache. Herausgegeben von Hans Dietrich Irmscher. Stuttgart, Reclam.

HERMANN, LISELOTTE. 1965. Jacob Grimm und die sprachtheoretischen Konzeptionen der französischen Aufklärung. WZUB 14.447–53.

HERVÁS Y PANDURO, LORENZO. 1778–1787. Idea dell' universo che contiene la storia della vita dell'uomo, elementi cosmografici, viaggio estatico al mondo planetario, e storia della terra e delle lingue. 21 Bde. Cesena, G. Biasini.

——, 1800–1805. Catálogo de las lenguas de las naciones conocidas y numeración, división, y clases de estas según la diversidad de sus idiomas y dialectos. 6 Bde. Madrid, Ranz.

HEY, OSKAR. 1896. Die Semasiologie: Rückblick und Ausblick. Archiv für Lateinische Lexikographie und Grammatik 9.193–230.

HJELMSLEV, LOUIS. 1950–1951. Commentaires sur la vie et l'œuvre de Rasmus Rask. Conférences de l'Institut de Linguistique de l'Université de Paris 10.143-57. [Auch in: Portraits of linguists: A biographical source book for the history of western linguistics, 1746–1963, ed. by Th. A. Sebeok, I, 179–95. Bloomington/London, Indiana University Press, 1966.]

HOBERG, RUDOLF. 1970. Die Lehre vom sprachlichen Feld. Sprache der Gegenwart: Schriften des Instituts für Deutsche Sprache, 11. Düsseldorf, Schwann.

HÖPFNER, GERHARD. 1921. Die indischen Studien Friedrich Schlegels im Zusammenhang seines Denkens. Diss. Breslau (Masch.).

HOWALD, ERNST. 1944. Wilhelm von Humboldt. Erlenbach/Zürich, Rentsch.

HUCH, RICARDA. 1908a. Blütezeit der Romantik. 3. Aufl. Leipzig, Haessel. 12. Aufl. 1922.

——, 1908b. Ausbreitung und Verfall der Romantik. 2. Aufl. Leipzig, Haessel. 10. Aufl. 1922.

HUMBOLDT, WILHELM VON. 1883–1884. Wilhelm von Humboldt: Die sprachphilosophischen Werke. Herausgegeben und erklärt von H. Steinthal. 2 Hälften: I. 1883; II. 1884. Berlin, Dümmler.

——, 1903–1936. Wilhelm von Humboldts Gesammelte Schriften. Herausgegeben von der Königlich-Preußischen Akademie der Wissenschaften. 17 Bde. in 4 Sektionen. Berlin, Behr. Nachdruck 1968, 17 Bde. Berlin, de Gruyter.

——, 1960. Ueber die Verschiedenheit des menschlichen Sprachbaues und ihren Einfluß auf die geistige Entwicklung des Menschengeschlechts (1830–1835). Faksimiledruck nach Dümmlers Originalausgabe. Bonn, Dümmler.

——, 1963. Schriften zur Sprachphilosophie. Herausgegeben von Andreas Flitner und Klaus Giel. Darmstadt, Wissenschaftliche Buchgesellschaft.

——, 1969. Cf. Gipper/Schwarz 1962ff.: Bd. II. (Lfg. 11. 1969). Nr. 8801–8851 mit den von E. Bülow zusammengestellten vollständigen Registern zu den Werken W. v. Humboldts.

——, 1972. Linguistic variability and intellectual development. Translation by George C. Buck and Frithjof A. Raven. Pennsylvania Paperback. University of Pennsylvania Press.

HUSSERL, EDMUND. 1900–1901. Logische Untersuchungen. 2. Aufl. 1913–1921. 3 Bde.: I. Prolegomena zur reinen Logik. 1913; II.1. Untersuchungen zur Phänomenologie und Theorie der Erkenntnis. 1913; II.2. Elemente einer phänomenologischen Aufklärung der Erkenntnis. 1921. Halle a.d.S., Niemeyer.

IORDAN, IORGU. 1932. Introducere în studiul limbilor romanice. Iasi. 1937. An introduction to Romance linguistics, its schools and scholars. Rev., transl. and in parts recast by J. Orr. London. 1970. 2nd ed. rev., with a supplement "Thirty years on" by R. Posner. Berkeley/Los Angeles, University of California Press. 1962. Einführung in die Geschichte und Methoden der romanischen Sprachwissenschaft. Ins Deutsche übertragen, ergänzt und teilweise neubearbeitet von W. Bahner. Berlin, Akademie Verlag.

IPSEN, GUNTHER. 1930. Sprachphilosophie der Gegenwart. Philosophische Forschungsberichte, 6. Berlin, Junker & Dünnhaupt.

——, 1932. Der neue Sprachbegriff. Zeitschrift für Deutschkunde 46.1–18. Leipzig/Berlin.

IRMSCHER, JOHANNES. 1965. Jacob Grimm und die Neogräzistik. WZUB 14.517–22.

IVIĆ, MILKA. 1971. Wege der Sprachwissenschaft. München, Hueber. [Engl. Ausgabe: 1965, Trends in linguistics. The Hague, Mouton.]

JANKOWSKY, KURT R. 1972. The Neogrammarians: A re-evaluation of their place in the development of linguistic science. Janua Linguarum. Series Minor, 116. The Hague, Mouton.

JÁNOSKA, GEORG. 1962. Die sprachlichen Grundlagen der Philosophie. Graz, Akademische Druck- und Verlagsanstalt.

JEAN PAUL [RICHTER, JOHANN PAUL FRIEDRICH]. 1804. Vorschule der Ästhetik. 1963. Werke, V. München.

JELLINEK, MAX HERMANN. 1906. Zur Geschichte einiger grammatischer Theorien und Begriffe. IF 19.272–316.

——, 1913–1914. Geschichte der neuhochdeutschen Grammatik von den Anfängen bis auf Adelung. Germanische Bibliothek, 2. Abt. 2 Halbbände. Heidelberg, Winter.

JESINGHAUS, WALTER. 1913. August Wilhelm von Schlegels Meinungen über die Ursprache mit einem Abdruck aus Schlegels Manuscript zu den Berliner Privatvorlesungen über eine Encyclopädie der Wissenschaften. Diss. Düsseldorf, C. Jesinghaus.

JESPERSEN, OTTO. 1922. Language, its nature, development, and origin. London, 1925. Die Sprache, ihre Natur, Entwicklung und Entstehung. Vom Verfasser durchgesehene Übersetzung aus dem Englischen von Rudolf Hittmair und Karl Waibel. Indogermanische Bibliothek. 4. Abt. Heidelberg, Winter.

JOCHMANN, CARL GUSTAV. 1968. Über die Sprache. Faksimiledruck nach der Originalausgabe von 1828, mit Schlabrendorfs "Bemerkungen über Sprache" und der Jochmann-Biographie von Julius Eckardt herausgegeben von Christian Johannes Wagenknecht. Deutsche Neudrucke, Reihe Texte des 19. Jahrhunderts. Göttingen, Vandenhoeck & Ruprecht.

JOLLES, MATHYS. 1936. Das deutsche Nationalbewußtsein im Zeitalter Napoleons. Frankfurt, Klostermann.

JONES, WILLIAM. 1788a. A dissertation on the orthography of Asiatick words in Roman letters. Asiatick Researches 1.1–56. Calcutta.

——, 1788b. On the Hindus. Asiatick Researches 1.415–31. Calcutta.

——, 1807. The works of Sir William Jones. Edited by Anna Maria Jones, with a discourse on the life and writings of Sir W. Jones, by Lord Teignmouth. 13 Bde. London, Robinson.

——, 1970. The letters of Sir William Jones. Edited by Garland Cannon. 2 Bde. Oxford, Clarendon Press.

JOST, LEONHARD. 1960. Sprache als Werk und wirkende Kraft: Ein Beitrag zur Geschichte und Kritik der energetischen Sprachauffassung seit Wilhelm von Humboldt. Sprache und Dichtung, N.F., 6. Bern, Haupt.

JUNKER, HEINRICH F. J. 1935. Rede auf Wilhelm von Humboldt und die Sprachwissenschaft. BSGW 87/3.13–28. Leipzig.

KABILINSKI, FRITZ. 1914. Jacob Grimm als Romanist. Diss. Greifswald 1914. Gleiwitz, Neumann.

KAINZ, FRIEDRICH. 1938a. Zur Sprachpsychologie der deutschen Romantik. Zeitschrift für Psychologie und Physiologie der Sinnesorgane 143.317–90.

——, 1938b. Bernhardis Beitrag zur deutschen Stilistik. ZDPh 63.1–44.

——, 1938c. Die Sprachästhetik der Jüngeren Romantik. Deutsche Vierteljahrsschrift 16.219–57.

——, 1941a. Deutsche Sprachdeutung. Von deutscher Art in Sprache und Dichtung, hrsg. von G. Fricke, F. Koch und K. Lugowski, I, 97–151. Stuttgart/Berlin, Kohlhammer.

——, 1941b. Friedrich Schlegels Sprachphilosophie. Zeitschrift für Deutsche Geisteswissenschaft 3.263–82.

KANTZENBACH, FRIEDRICH WILHELM. 1970. Johann Gottfried Herder in Selbstzeugnissen und Bilddokumenten. Rowohlts Monographien, 164. Reinbek bei Hamburg, Rowohlt.

KIRCHER, ERWIN. 1906. Die Philosophie der Romantik. Aus dem Nachlaß herausgegeben von M. Susmann und H. Simon. Jena, Diederichs.

KIRCHNER, HANS. 1921. Erkenntnis und Sprache: Individualität und Idealität im Sprachausdruck der Erkenntnis nach Wilhelm von Humboldt. Diss. Breslau 1921. Charlottenburg, Winter.

KISSLING, HELMUT. 1937. Sprache – Volk – Geschichte: Bemerkungen zu Fichtes Sprachauffassung. Zeitschrift für Deutsche Bildung 13.275–83.

KLIN, EUGENIUSZ. 1964. Die frühromantische Literaturtheorie Friedrich Schlegels. Acta Universitatis Wratislaviensis, 26. Wrocław.

——, 1971. Die hermeneutische und kritische Leistung Friedrich Schlegels in den romantischen Krisenjahren. Prace Wrocławskiego Towarzystwa Naukowego, Seria A, 143. Wrocław.

KLUCKHOHN, PAUL. 1961. Das Ideengut der deutschen Romantik. Handbücherei für Deutschkunde, 6. 4. Aufl. Halle a.d.S., Niemeyer.

KNOBLOCH, JOHANN. 1956. Die Geschichte der sprachwissenschaftlichen Forschung und Lehre an der Ernst Moritz Arndt-Universität zu Greifswald. Festschrift Greifswald, II.234–8.

KÖSTER, WILHELM. 1933. Joseph Marie Degérando als Philosoph. Geschichtliche Forschungen zur Philosophie der Neuzeit, 2. Paderborn, Schöning.

KOHLER, OSKAR. 1931. Die Logik des Destutt de Tracy. Diss. Freiburg. Borna–Leipzig, R. Noske.

KONRAD, GUSTAV. 1937. Herders Sprachproblem im Zusammenhang der Geistesgeschichte: Eine Studie zur Entwicklung des sprachlichen Denkens der Goethezeit. Berlin, Ebering. [Nachdruck 1967: Nendeln/Liechtenstein, Kraus.]

KRAUS, CHRISTIAN JAKOB. 1787. Rezension des Allgemeinen vergleichenden Wörterbuchs von Pallas. Allgemeine Literatur-Zeitung, Nr. 235–7.

KRONASSER, HEINZ. 1969. Handbuch der Semasiologie: Kurze Einführung in die Geschichte, Problematik und Terminologie der Bedeutungslehre. 2. Aufl. Heidelberg, Winter.

KRÜGER, MANFRED. 1967. Der menschlich-göttliche Ursprung der Sprache. Bemerkungen zu Herders Sprachtheorie. WW 17.1–11.

KÜHLWEIN, WOLFGANG (Hrsg.). 1971. Linguistics in Great Britain. Vol. I: History of linguistics. Tübingen, Niemeyer.

KUEHNER, PAUL. 1944. Theories in the origin and formation of language in the 18th century in France. Philadelphia, University of Pennsylvania.

LAMMERS, WILHELM. 1936. Wilhelm von Humboldts Weg zur Sprachforschung, 1775–1801. Neue Deutsche Forschungen, 56. Diss. Rostock 1936. Berlin, Junker & Dünnhaupt.

LAUCHERT, FRIEDRICH. 1894. Die Anschauungen Herders über den Ursprung der Sprache, ihre Voraussetzungen in der Philosophie seiner Zeit und ihr Fortwirken. Euphorion 1.747–71.

LAUENER, HENRY. 1962. Die Sprache in der Philosophie Hegels, mit besonderer Berücksichtigung der Ästhetik. Sprache und Dichtung: Forschungen zur Deutschen Sprache, Literatur und Volkskunde, 10. Bern, Haupt.

LEFMANN, SALOMON. 1870. August Schleicher. Leipzig, Teubner.

——, 1891–1897. Franz Bopp: Sein Leben und seine Wissenschaft. Berlin, Reimer.

LEHMANN, WINFRED PHILIPP (Hrsg.). 1967. A reader in nineteenth-century historical Indo-European linguistics. Bloomington/London, Indiana University Press.

LEISI, ERNST. 1971. Der Wortinhalt: Seine Struktur im Deutschen und Englischen. 4. Aufl. Uni-Taschenbücher, 95. Heidelberg, Quelle & Meyer.

LEITZMANN, ALBERT. 1908. Briefwechsel zwischen Wilhelm von Humboldt und August Wilhelm Schlegel. Mit einer Einleitung von B. Delbrück. Halle a.d.S., Niemeyer.

——, 1919. Wilhelm von Humboldt: Charakteristik und Lebensbild. Halle a.d.S., Niemeyer.

LEOPOLD, W. 1929. Inner Form. Lg 5.254–60.

LEROUX, ROBERT. 1932. Guillaume de Humboldt: La formation de sa pensée jusqu'en 1794. Paris, Les Belles Lettres.

——, 1958. L'anthropologie comparée de Guillaume de Humboldt. Paris, Les Belles Lettres.

LEROY, MAURICE. 1963. Les grands courants de la linguistique moderne. Paris/Bruxelles, Presses Universitaires.

LESKIEN, AUGUST. 1876. Bopp. Allgemeine Deutsche Biographie 3.140–49. [Auch in: Portraits of linguists: A biographical source book for the history of western linguistics, 1746–1963, ed. by Th. A. Sebeok, I, 207–21. Bloomington/London, Indiana University Press, 1966.]

LEWY, ERNST. 1951. Die Lehre von den Sprachtypen. SG 4.415–22.

——, 1964. Der Bau der europäischen Sprachen. 2. Aufl. Tübingen, Niemeyer.

LIEBICH, BRUNO. 1905. Die Wortfamilien der lebenden hochdeutschen Sprache als Grundlage für ein System der Bedeutungslehre. I.: Die Wortfamilien in alphabetischer Ordnung, nach Heynes deutschem Wörterbuch bearbeitet. 2. Aufl. Breslau, Preuss & Jünger.

LIEBRUCKS, BRUNO. 1964ff. Sprache und Bewußtsein. 6 Bde.: I. Einleitung. Spannweite des Problems. 1964; II. Sprache. Wilhelm von Humboldt. 1965; III. Wege zum Bewußtsein im Raum von Kant, Hegel und Marx. 1966; (In Vorbereitung: IV. Sprachlichkeit des Bewußtseins als "Phänomenologie des Geistes" (Hegel); V. Der menschliche Begriff (Hegels große Logik); VI. Prolegomenon zu einer Phänomenologie des Bewußtseins (Friedrich Hölderlin)). Frankfurt a.M., Akademische Verlagsanstalt.

LOCKE, JOHN. 1690. Essay concerning human understanding.

LOCKWOOD, W. B. 1969. Indo-European philology: Historical and comparative. London, Hutchinson University Library.

LÖTHER, BURKHARD. 1965. Philolog der Nation: Zum Zusammenhang von Sprachgeschichte und Volksgeschichte bei Jacob Grimm. WZUB 14.463–9.

LOHMANN, JOHANNES. 1960. Die Entwicklung der allgemeinen Sprachwissenschaft an der Friedrich-Wilhelms-Universität zu Berlin bis 1933. Studium Berolinense. Gedenkschrift zur 150. Wiederkehr des Gründungsjahres der Friedrich-Wilhelms-Universität zu Berlin, 449–58. Berlin.

——, 1963. Wilhelm von Humboldt und die Sprache. Die Deutsche Literatur 9.41–8. Osaka.

——, 1965. Philosophie und Sprachwissenschaft. Erfahrung und Denken, 15. Berlin, Duncker & Humblot.

——, 1967. Über das Verhältnis der Sprachtheorien von Humboldt, de Saussure und Trubetzkoy. Phonologie der Gegenwart. Wiener Slavistisches Jahrbuch, Ergänzungsband 6.353–63.

LOMMEL, HERMANN. 1930. Friedrich Schlegels Charakteristik des Sanskrit und die deutsche Sprache. DVLG 8.647–59. Halle a.d.S.

LORENZ, W. 1965. Zu einigen Fragen des Zusammenhangs von Sprache und Gesellschaft: Eine kritische Auseinandersetzung mit Leo Weisgerber. Diss. Leipzig.

LOVEJOY, ARTHUR O. 1924. On the discrimination of romanticism. PMLA 29. 229–53.

——, 1941. The meanings of romanticism for the historian of ideas. Journal of the History of Ideas 2.257–78.

LUN, LUIGI. 1960. Da Herder a Jacob Grimm (Diorama di mezzo secolo di storia della filologia germanica). Roma, De Santis.

——, 1962. Il saggio di Jacob Grimm sull' origine del linguaggio. Roma,Ausonia.

MAGON, LEOPOLD. 1963. Jacob Grimm: Leistung und Vermächtnis. Sitzungsberichte der Deutschen Akademie der Wissenschaften zu Berlin, Klasse für Sprachen, Literatur und Kunst, 1963, 5. Berlin, Akademie Verlag.

MAHER, JOHN P. 1966. More on the history of comparative method: The tradition of Darwinism in August Schleicher's work. AnL 8. Nr. 3,2.1–12.

MALBLANC, ALFRED. 1966. Stylistique comparée du français et de l'allemand: Essai de représentation linguistique comparée et étude de traduction. 3. Aufl. Paris, Didier.

MALONE, KEMP. 1952. Rasmus Rask. WSt 28.1–4. [Auch in: Portraits of linguists: A biographical source book for the history of western linguistics, 1746–1963, ed. by Th. A. Sebeok, I, 195–9. Bloomington/London, Indiana University Press, 1966.]

MARTINEAU, RUSSEL. 1867. Obituary of Franz Bopp. TPhS 12.305–12. [Auch in: Portraits of linguists: A biographical source book for the history of western linguistics, 1746–1963, ed. by Th. A. Sebeok, I, 200–6. Bloomington/London, Indiana University Press, 1966.]

MARTY, ANTON. 1908. Untersuchungen zur Grundlegung der allgemeinen Grammatik und Sprachphilosophie. I. Halle a.d.S., Niemeyer.

MASON, EUDO C. 1959. Deutsche und englische Romantik: Eine Gegenüberstellung. Göttingen, Vandenhoeck & Ruprecht.

MASTER, ALFRED. 1946. The influence of Sir William Jones upon Sanskrit studies. BSAOS 11.798–811.

MAURO, TULLIO DE. 1969. Une introduction à la sémantique. Collection Etudes et Documents Payot. Paris, Payot.

MEILLET, ANTOINE. 1921. Linguistique historique et linguistique générale. Collection Linguistique Publié par la Société de Linguistique de Paris, 8. Paris, Champion.

MENDELSOHN, A. 1928. Die Sprachphilosophie und die Ästhetik Wilhelm von Humboldts als Grundlage für die Theorie und Dichtung. Diss. Hamburg. Kirchhain N.–L., Zahn & Baendel.

MENZE, CLEMENS. 1965. Wilhelm von Humboldts Lehre und Bild vom Menschen. Ratingen bei Düsseldorf, A. Henn.

——, 1966. Wilhelm von Humboldt und Christian Gottlob Heyne. Ratingen bei Düsseldorf, A. Henn.

METTKE, HEINZ. 1965. Zur Erforschung der älteren deutschen Literatur durch Jacob Grimm. WZUB 14.495–505.

METTLER, WERNER. 1955. Der junge Friedrich Schlegel und die griechische Literatur. Diss. Zürich. Auszug. Hergen–Zürich, Frei.

METZKE, ERWIN, 1934. J. G. Hamanns Stellung in der Philosophie des 18. Jahrhunderts (Eine Preisarbeit). Schriften der Königsberger Gelehrten Gesellschaft, Geisteswissenschaftliche Klasse, 10. Jahr, Heft 3. Halle a.d.S., Niemeyer.

MEYER, R. M. 1897. Zur "Innren Form". Euphorion 4.445–6.

MILLER, ROBERT L. 1968. The linguistic relativity principle and Humboldtian ethnolinguistics: A history and appraisal. The Hague, Mouton.

MINOR, J. 1897. Die innere Form. Euphorion 4.205–10.

MISTELI, FRANZ. 1893. Charakteristik der hauptsächlichsten Typen des Sprachbaues. Neubearbeitung des Werkes von H. Steinthal. (1861). Berlin, Dümmler.

MONBODDO, JAMES BURNETT LORD. 1773–1792. Of the origin and progress of language. 6 Bde. Edinburgh.

MOSER, HUGO. 1955. Deutsche Sprachgeschichte. Mit einer Einführung in die Fragen der Sprachbetrachtung. CES-Bücherei, 19. 2. Aufl. Stuttgart, Schwab.

MOUNIN, GEORGES. 1967. Histoire de la linguistique des origines au XXe siècle. Paris, Presses Universitaires de France.

——, 1972. Clefs pour la sémantique. Paris, Seghers.

MÜLLER, ALFONS. 1938. Betrachtungen zur neuen deutschen Sprachphilosophie. Gießener Beiträge zur Deutschen Philologie, 64. Diss. Gießen 1938. Gießen, von Münchowsche Universitäts-Druckerei.

MUELLER, HUGO. 1966. On re-reading von Humboldt. MSLL 19.97–107.

MÜLLER, MAX. 1891. Science of language. London. 1892–1893. Die Wissenschaft der Sprache. Übersetzt von R. Fick und W. Wischmann. 2. Bde. Leipzig.

NETTE, HERBERT. 1946. Wilhelm von Humboldts Sprachphilosophie. Wort und Sinn, von den Elementen der Sprache, 35–47. Fulda, Parzeller.

NEUMANN, ERICH. 1927. Johann Arnold Kanne, ein vergessener Romantiker: Ein Beitrag zur Geschichte der mystischen Sprachphilosophie. Diss. Erlangen.

NEUMANN, FRIEDRICH. 1971. Studien zur Geschichte der deutschen Philologie: Aus der Sicht eines alten Germanisten. Berlin, E. Schmidt-Verlag.

NEUMANN, GÜNTER. 1967. Franz Bopp — 1816. Indogermanische Sprachwissenschaft 1816 und 1966, 7–20. IBK, Sonderheft 24. Innsbruck.

NEWALD, RICHARD. 1949. Einführung in die Wissenschaft der deutschen Sprache und Literatur. 2. Aufl. Lahr, Schauenburg.

NOREEN, ADOLF. 1923. Einführung in die wissenschaftliche Betrachtung der Sprache: Beiträge zur Methode und Terminologie der Grammatik. Übersetzt von H. W. Pollak. Halle a.d.S., Niemeyer.

NÜSSE, HEINRICH. 1962. Die Sprachtheorie Friedrich Schlegels. Germanische Bibliothek, Dritte Reihe, Untersuchungen und Einzeldarstellungen. Heidelberg, Winter.

ÖHMANN, SUZANNE. 1951. Wortinhalt und Weltbild: Vergleichende und methodologische Studien zur Bedeutungslehre und Wortfeldtheorie. Stockholm, Norstedt & Söner.

——, 1953. Theories of the "linguistic field". Word 9.123–34.

OPPENBERG (STRUC–OPPENBERG), URSULA. 1965. Quellenstudium zu Friedrich Schlegels Übersetzungen aus dem Sanskrit. Marburger Beiträge zur Germanistik, 7. Diss. Marburg 1963. Marburg, Elwert.

ORLANDI, TITO. 1962. La metodologia di Franz Bopp e la linguistica precedente. RIL 96.529–49.

OSBORNE, JOHN. 1971. Romantik. Handbuch der Deutschen Literaturgeschichte, 2. Abt.: Bibliographien, 8. Bern/München, Francke.

PÄTSCH, GERTRUD. 1955. Grundfragen der Sprachtheorie. Halle a.d.S., Niemeyer.

——, 1960. Franz Bopp und die historisch-vergleichende Sprachwissenschaft. Forschen und Wirken. Festschrift zur 150-Jahrfeier der Humboldt-Universität zu Berlin, 1810–1960, I, 211–28. Berlin, Akademie-Verlag.

——, 1967. Humboldt und die Sprachwissenschaft. Wilhelm von Humboldt, 1767–1967. Erbe – Gegenwart – Zukunft. Beiträge, herausgegeben von Werner Hartke und Henny Maskolat, 101–25. Halle a.d.S., Niemeyer.

PALLUS, HANNELORE. 1964. Die Sprachphilosophie Johann Georg Hamanns als eine Quelle für Herders Anschauungen über das Verhältnis von Sprache und Denken. WZUG 13,363–74.

PEDERSEN, HOLGER. 1924. Sprogvidenskaben i det Nittende Aarhundrede. Metoder og Resultater. København, Gyldendalske Boghandel. 1931. The discovery of language. Linguistic science in the nineteenth century. Translated by J. W. Spargo. Cambridge. Nachdruck. 1962. Bloomington, Indiana University Press.

——, 1932. Einleitung. Rasmus Rask. Ausgewählte Abhandlungen. Herausgegeben von Louis Hjelmslev. I. Kopenhagen, Levin & Munksgaard.

PENN, JULIA MYRLE. 1966. Linguistic relativity versus innate ideas: The origins of the Sapir–Whorf-Hypothesis in German thought of the eighteenth and nineteenth centuries. Diss. University of Texas. [Cf. DAb 27, 1967, 2516-A.]

PERCIVAL, W. KEITH. 1968. Nineteenth century origins of twentieth century structuralism. Papers from the Fourth Regional Meeting. Chicago Linguistic Society, April 19–20, 1968, edited by Bill J. Darden, Charles-James N. Bailey and Alice Davison, 416–20. Chicago, University of Chicago, Dept. of Linguistics.

PFLEIDERER, WOLFGANG. 1953. Die innere Form des Deutschen. Neuere Arbeiten zur Sprachtheorie. DU 6/2.108–28.

PLEINES, JÜRGEN. 1967. Das Problem der Sprache bei Humboldt. Voraussetzungen und Möglichkeiten einer neuzeitlich-kritischen Sprachphilosophie. Das Problem der Sprache. Achter Deutscher Kongreß für Philosophie, Heidelberg 1966, herausgegeben von Hans-Georg Gadamer, 31–43. München, Fink.

PONGS, HERMANN. 1968. Humboldts innere Sprachform zwischen West und Ost, zwischen Manierismus und Sozialismus. Die Brüder Humboldt heute, herausgegeben von H. Kessler und W. Thoms, 87–129. Mannheim, Verlag der Humboldt-Gesellschaft.

PORZIG, WALTER. 1923. Der Begriff der inneren Sprachform. IF 41.150–69.

——, 1928. Sprachform und Bedeutung: Eine Auseinandersetzung mit A. Marty's Sprachphilosophie. Indogermanisches Jahrbuch 12.1–20.

——, 1957. Das Wunder der Sprache: Probleme, Methoden und Ergebnisse der modernen Sprachwissenschaft. 2. Aufl. München, Francke.

POTT, AUGUST FRIEDRICH. 1833. Etymologische Forschungen auf dem Gebiete der Indo-Germanischen Sprachen. Lemgo, Verlag der Meyerschen Hofbuchhandlung.

——, 1876. Wilhelm von Humboldt und die Sprachwissenschaft. Berlin, Calvary.

PRANG, HELMUT (Hrsg.). 1968. Begriffsbestimmung der Romantik. Darmstadt, Wissenschaftliche Buchgesellschaft.

RAMISCHVILI, GURAM. 1967. Zum Verständnis des Begriffes der Sprachform bei Wilhelm von Humboldt. WZUJ 16/5.555–66.

RASK, RASMUS KRISTIAN. 1818. Undersøgelse om det gamle Nordiske eller Islandske Sprogs Oprindelse. Kjöbenhavn, Gyldendal.

——, 1932–1937. Ausgewählte Abhandlungen. Herausgegeben von Louis Hjelmslev. 3 Bde. Kopenhagen, Levin & Munksgaard.

——, 1941. Breve fra og til Rasmus Rask. Udg. ved Louis Hjelmslev. 2 Bde. København; 1968. Bd. III.: Brevkommentar og haandskriftkatalog ved Marie Bjerrum. København.

RAUMER, RUDOLF VON. 1870. Geschichte der germanischen Philologie vorzugsweise in Deutschland. München, Oldenburg.

RAUTER, HERBERT. 1970. Die Sprachauffassung der englischen Vorromantik in ihrer Bedeutung für die Literaturkritik und Dichtungstheorie der Zeit. Bad Homburg, Verlag Gehlen.

REICHMANN, OSKAR. 1969. Deutsche Wortforschung. Realienbücher für Germanisten, Abt. C: Deutsche Sprachwissenschaft. Sammlung Metzler, 82. Stuttgart, J. B. Metzlersche Verlagsbuchhandlung.

REISIG, CHRISTIAN KARL. 1839. Vorlesungen über lateinische Sprachwissenschaft. Herausgegeben von F. Haase. Leipzig.

——, 1890. Vorlesungen über lateinische Sprachwissenschaft. II. Teil: Semasiologie oder Bedeutungslehre. Bearbeitet von F. Heerdegen. Berlin.

RÉVÉSZ, GÉZA. 1946. Ursprung und Vorgeschichte der Sprache. Bern, Francke.

REY, ALAIN. 1970. La lexicologie: Lectures. Initiation à la Linguistique, Série A: Lectures, 2. Paris, Klincksieck.

RIESE, TEUT ANDREAS. 1968. Über den literaturgeschichtlichen Begriff Romantik. Versdichtung der englischen Romantik. Interpretationen, herausgegeben von T. A. Riese und O. Riesner, 9–24. Berlin, Erich Schmidt Verlag.

ROBINS, R. H. 1967. A short history of linguistics. Longmans' Linguistics Library. London, Longmans.

ROCHER, ROSANE. 1968. Alexander Hamilton (1762–1824): A chapter in the early history of Sanskrit philology. American Oriental Series, 51. New Haven, Connecticut, American Oriental Society.

ROMANTIK, DIE EUROPÄISCHE. 1972. Mit Beiträgen von Ernst Behler, Heinrich Fauteck, Clemens Heselhaus, Wolfram Krömer, Wilhelm Lettenbauer, Hans Sckommodau, Helmut Viebrock, Kurt Wais. Frankfurt a.M., Athenäum.

ROTHACKER, ERICH. 1923. Savigny, Grimm, Ranke: Ein Beitrag zur Frage nach dem Zusammenhang der Historischen Schule. Historische Zeitschrift 128.415–45. München/Berlin.

——, 1950. Philosophie und Politik im französischen Denken des frühen XIX. Jahrhunderts: Ein kultursoziologischer Versuch (1942). Mensch und Geschichte. Studien zur Anthropologie und Wissenschaftsgeschichte, 103–29. Bonn, Athenäum.

ROUSSEAU, JEAN-JACQUES. 1795. Discours sur l'origine et les fondements de l'inégalité parmis les hommes.

RÜSTAU, HILTRUD. 1965. Max Müller und Indien. WZUB 14.359–63.

RUPRECHT, ERICH. 1963. Die Sprache im Denken Wilhelm von Humboldts. Die Wissenschaft von deutscher Sprache und Dichtung. Festschrift für F. Maurer, herausgegeben von S. Gutenbrunner, H. Moser, W. Rehm und H. Rupp, 217–36. Stuttgart, Klett.

RYLE, GILBERT. 1952. Systematically misleading expressions. Logic and language, First series, ed. by A. Flew, 11–36. Oxford, Blackwell.

SALMON, PAUL. 1968–1969. Herder's essay on the origin of language and the place of man in the animal kingdom. GLL 22.59–70.

SALMONY, H.-J. 1949. Die Philosophie des jungen Herder. Zürich, Vineta Verlag.

SANDFELD, KRISTIAN. 1940. Rasmus Rask. Dansk Biografisk Leksikon 19.180–94.

SAPIR, EDWARD. 1907–1908. Herder's Ursprung der Sprache. MPh 5.109–42.

SASSETTI, FILIPPO. 1855. Lettere. Firenze.

SAUSSURE, FERDINAND DE. 1955. Cours de linguistique générale. Publié par Charles Bally et Albert Sechehaye avec la collaboration de Albert Riedlinger. 5. Aufl. Paris, Payot.

SCHAFF, ADAM. 1964a. Język a poznanie. Warszawa, Pánstwowe Wydawnictwo Naukowe.

——, 1964b. Sprache und Erkenntnis. Wien/Frankfurt/Zürich, Europa Verlag.

SCHAFFSTEIN, FRIEDRICH. 1952. Wilhelm von Humboldt: Ein Lebensbild. Frankfurt a.M., Klostermann.

SCHANKWEILER, EWALD. 1965. Zum Wesen und Ursprung der Sprache bei Jacob Grimm und Wilhelm von Humboldt. WZUB 14.455–62.

SCHASLER, MAX. 1847. Die Elemente der philosophischen Sprachwissenschaft Wilhelm von Humboldt's. Aus seinem Werke: Ueber die Verschiedenheit ...

in systematischer Entwicklung dargestellt und kritisch erläutert. Berlin, Trautwein.

SCHEINERT, MORITZ. 1908. Wilhelm von Humboldts Sprachphilosophie. Archiv für die Gesamte Psychologie 13.141–95. Leipzig.

SCHERER, WILHELM. 1879. Grimm. Allgemeine Deutsche Biographie 9.678–88. [Auch in: Portraits of linguists: A biographical source book for the history of western linguistics, 1746–1963, ed. by Th. A. Sebeok, I, 154–69. Bloomington/London, Indiana University Press, 1966.]

SCHIPPAN, THEA. 1972. Einführung in die Semasiologie. Leipzig, VEB Bibliographisches Institut.

SCHIROKAUER, ARNO. 1942. Spätromantik im Grimmschen Wörterbuch. GQ 15.204–13.

——. 1957. Das Grimmsche Wörterbuch als Dokument der Romantik. Romantische Philologie. Philobiblion 1.308–23.

SCHLANGER, JUDITH. 1967. La langue hébraïque, problème de linguistique spéculative. Revue Internationale de Philosophie 82.486–507.

SCHLEGEL, AUGUST WILHELM VON. 1803. Rezension von A. F. Bernhardis Reine Sprachlehre. Europa 2/1.193–204.

——. 1827. Ueber die Bhagavad-Gita. Mit Bezug auf die Beurteilung der Schlegelschen Ausgabe im Pariser Asiatischen Journal. Aus einem Brief von Herrn Staatsminister von Humboldt. Indische Bibliothek 2.218–58. Bonn.

SCHLEGEL, FRIEDRICH VON. 1808. Ueber die Sprache und Weisheit der Indier. Ein Beitrag zur Begründung der Alterthumskunde. Nebst metrischen Uebersetzungen indischer Gedichte. Heidelberg, Mohr & Zimmer.

——. 1958ff. Kritische Ausgabe seiner Werke. Herausgegeben von Ernst Behler, Jean-Jaques Anstett und Hans Eichner. München/Paderborn/Wien, Schöningh. (Cf. Bd. X, 1968: "Philosophie des Lebens – Philosophie der Sprache und des Wortes".)

SCHLEICHER, AUGUST. 1871. Compendium der vergleichenden Grammatik der indogermanischen Sprachen. Kurzer Abriss einer Laut- und Formenlehre der indogermanischen Ursprache, des Altindischen, Altiranischen, Altgriechischen, Altitalischen, Altkeltischen, Altslawischen, Litauischen und Altdeutschen. 3. Aufl. Weimar, Böhlau.

SCHLESIER, GUSTAV. 1843–1845. Erinnerungen an Wilhelm von Humboldt. 2 Teile: I. 1843, II. 1845. Stuttgart, Köhler.

SCHMIDT, LOTHAR (Hrsg.). 1973. Wortfeldforschung: Zur Geschichte und Theorie des sprachlichen Feldes. Wege der Forschung, 250. Darmstadt, Wissenschaftliche Buchgesellschaft.

SCHMIDT, WILHELM. 1963. Lexikalische und aktuelle Bedeutung: Ein Beitrag zur Theorie der Wortbedeutung. Schriften zur Phonetik, Sprachwissenschaft und Kommunikationsforschung, 7. Berlin, Akademie-Verlag.

——. 1964. Deutsche Sprachkunde: Ein Handbuch für Lehrer und Studierende mit einer Einführung in die Probleme des sprachkundlichen Unterrichts. Berlin, Volk und Wissen volkseigener Verlag. 7. bearb. Aufl. 1972.

SCHMIDT-ROHR, GEORG. 1933. Mutter Sprache: Vom Amt der Sprache bei der Volkwerdung. Jena, E. Diederichs.

SCHOOF, WILHELM. 1938a. Kritik um das Grimmsche Wörterbuch. ASNS 174.145–62.

——. 1938b. Zur Entstehungsgeschichte des Grimmschen Wörterbuchs. Wörter und Sachen 19.141–54. Heidelberg.

——. 1957. Jacob Grimms Kleine Grammatik. Mu. 412–9. Lüneburg.

——. 1961. Die letzte Lieferung des Grimmschen Wörterbuchs — der Abschluß hundertjähriger Arbeit. WW 11.82–8.

——. 1963. Jacob Grimms Deutsche Grammatik in zeitgenössischer Beurteilung. ZDPh 92.363–77.

——. 1963–1964. Jacob Grimm und die Anfänge der deutschen Dialektgeographie. ZMaF 30.97–103.

SCHRADER, OTTO. 1906. Zur Geschichte und Methode der linguistisch-historischen Forschung. Jena, Costenoble.

SCHULTHEISS, TASSILO. 1936. Sprachwissenschaft auf Schleichwegen. Berlin-Schöneberg, Verlag Deutsche Kultur Wacht.

SCHWARZ, HANS. 1959. Leitmerkmale sprachlicher Felder: Ein Beitrag zur Verfahrensweise der Gliederungsforschung. Sprache – Schlüssel zur Welt. Festschrift für Leo Weisgerber, 245–55. Herausgegeben von H. Gipper, Düsseldorf, Schwann.

——. 1966. Gegenstand, Grundlagen, Stellung und Verfahrensweise der Sprachinhaltsforschung, erörtert an den Gegebenheiten des Wortschatzes. Gipper/Schwarz 1962ff.: XV–LXVI. Bd. I. 1962–1966.

——. 1972. Sprache als energeia. Historisches Wörterbuch der Philosophie, herausgegeben von J. Ritter, II, 492–4. Basel/Stuttgart, Schwabe.

SCHWINGER, REINHOLD. 1934. Innere Form: Ein Beitrag zur Definition des Begriffes auf Grund seiner Geschichte von Shaftesbury bis W. v. Humboldt. Diss. Leipzig 1933. München, Beck.

SEBEOK, THOMAS A. (Hrsg.). 1966. Portraits of linguists: A biographical source book for the history of western linguistics, 1746–1963. 2 Bde.: I. From Sir William Jones to Karl Brugmann, II. From Eduard Sievers to Benjamin Lee Whorf. Bloomington/London, Indiana University Press.

SEIDLER, HERBERT. 1968. Die Bedeutung von W. v. Humboldts Sprachdenken für die Wissenschaft von der Sprachkunst. ZDPh 86.434–51. [Auch in: Die Brüder Humboldt heute, herausgegeben von H. Kessler und W. Thoms, 63–85. Mannheim, Verlag der Humboldt Gesellschaft 1968.]

SEIFFERT, LESLIE. 1968. Neo-Humboldtian semantics in perspective: 'Sprache und Gemeinschaft'. JL 4.93–108.

SEILS, MARTIN. 1961. Wirklichkeit und Wort bei J. G. Hamann. Arbeiten zur Theologie, 6. Stuttgart, Calwer Verlag.

SICKEL, KARL-ERNST. 1933. Johann Christoph Adelung: Seine Persönlichkeit und seine Geschichtsauffassung. Diss. Leipzig 1933. Leipzig, Gerhardt.

SIMON, JOSEF. 1966. Das Problem der Sprache bei Hegel. Stuttgart/Berlin/Köln/Mainz, Kohlhammer.

——. 1971. Philosophie und linguistische Theorie. Berlin/New York, de Gruyter. [Cf. 108–22: XIV. "Humboldts Alternative zu den transformationsgrammatischen Modellen".]

SMITH, COLIN. 1967. Destutt de Tracy's analysis of the proposition. Revue Internationale de Philosophie 79/80.476–85.

SOMMERFELD, SUSANNE. 1943. Indienschau und Indiendeutung romantischer Philosophen. Diss. Zürich 1933. Zürich, Rascher.

SOMMERFELT, ALF. 1953–1954. The origin of language: Theories and hypotheses. Cahiers d'Histoire Mondiale 1.885–902. Paris.

SPECHT, FRANZ. 1948. Die "indogermanische" Sprachwissenschaft von den Junggrammatikern bis zum 1. Weltkriege. Lexis 1.229–63. Lahr i.B.

SPRANGER, EDUARD. 1908. Wilhelm von Humboldt und Kant. Kant-Studien 13.57–129. Berlin.

SPREU, ARWED. 1965. Eine Anmerkung zum Aufbau der "Deutschen Grammatik". WZUB 14.489–90.

SRBIK, HEINRICH RITTER VON. 1950–1951. Geist und Geschichte vom deutschen Humanismus bis zur Gegenwart. 2 Bde. München, Bruckmann/Salzburg, Müller.

STAM, JAMES HENRY. 1964. The question of the origin of language in German thought, 1756–85. Diss. Brandeis. (Masch.).

STEGMANN VON PRITZWALD, KURT. 1933. Der Weg der Sprachwissenschaft in die Wirklichkeit. Neue Jahrbücher für Wissenschaft und Jugendbildung 9.442–54. Leipzig/Berlin.

——. 1936. Kräfte und Köpfe in der Geschichte der indogermanischen Sprachwissenschaft. Germanen und Indogermanen. Festschrift für H. Hirt, herausgegeben von Helmut Arntz, II, 1–24. Heidelberg, Winter.

STEHR, A. 1957. Die Anfänge der finnisch-ugrischen Sprachvergleichung. Diss. Göttingen. (Masch.).

STEINBECK, A. 1836. Der Dichter ein Seher oder über die innige Verbindung der Poesie und der Sprache mit den Hellsehern.

STEINTHAL, HEYMANN. 1848. Die Sprachwissenschaft Wilhelm von Humboldt's und die Hegel'sche Philosophie. Berlin, Dümmler. [Nachdruck 1971. Hildesheim/New York, Olms.]

——. 1850. Die Classification der Sprachen, dargestellt als die Entwicklung der Sprachidee. Berlin, Dümmler.

——. 1855. Grammatik, Logik und Psychologie: Ihre Prinzipien und ihr Verhältnis zueinander. Berlin, Dümmler.

——. 1858; 4. Aufl. 1888. Der Ursprung der Sprache in Zusammenhang mit den letzten Fragen des Wissens: Eine Darstellung der Ansicht Wilhelm von Humboldts, verglichen mit denen Herders und Hamanns. Berlin, Dümmler.

——. 1860. Charakteristik der hauptsächlichsten Typen des Sprachbaues. Zweite Bearbeitung der Classification der Sprachen. Berlin, Dümmler.

STENZEL, JULIUS. 1921. Die Bedeutung der Sprachphilosophie W. v. Humboldts für die Probleme des Humanismus. Logos 10.261–74.

STEPANOVA, VERA. 1908. Destutt de Tracy: Eine historisch-psychologische Untersuchung. Diss. Zürich 1908. Zürich, Zürcher & Furrer.

STOLPE, HEINZ. 1964. Herder und die Ansätze einer naturgeschichtlichen Entwicklungslehre im 18. Jahrhundert. Neue Beiträge zur Literatur der Aufklärung, 289–316. Neue Beiträge zur Literaturwissenschaft, 21. Berlin, Rütten & Loening.

STOLTE, ERICH. 1948. Wilhelm von Humboldts Begriff der Inneren Sprachform. ZPhon. 2.205–7.

STREITBERG, WILHELM. 1897. Schleichers Auffassung von der Stellung der Sprachwissenschaft. IF 7.360–72.

——. 1910. Kant und die Sprachwissenschaft: Eine historische Skizze. IF 26.382–422.

—— (Hrsg.). 1916–1936. Geschichte der indogermanischen Sprachwissenschaft seit ihrer Begründung durch Franz Bopp. 5 Bde. Straßburg/Berlin/Leipzig, de Gruyter.

STRICH, FRITZ. 1949. Deutsche Klassik und Romantik oder Vollendung und Unendlichkeit: Ein Vergleich. 4. Aufl. Bern, Francke. [Cf. 164–96: "Die Sprache".]

STROH, FRITZ. 1933. Der volkhafte Sprachbegriff. Halle a.d. S., Niemeyer.

STURM, WILHELM. 1917. Herders Sprachphilosophie in ihrem Entwicklungsgang und ihrer historischen Stellung. Diss. Breslau. Breslau, Fleischmann.

SÜSSMILCH, JOHANN PETER. 1766. Versuch eines Beweises, dass die erste Sprache ihren Ursprung nicht von Menschen, sondern allein vom Schöpfer erhalten habe. Berlin, Realschulbuchhandlung.

SVANBERG, N. 1936. W. v. Humboldt und die Sprachforschung unserer Zeit. Uppsala Universitets Årsskrift, 10.

TAGLIAVINI, CARLO. 1968a. Panorama di storia della filologia germanica. Bologna, Pàtron.

——. 1968b. Panorama di storia della linguistica. 2. Aufl. Bologna, Pàtron.

TELEGDI, ZS. 1966. Zur Geschichte der Sprachwissenschaft. ("Historische Grammatik"). ALH 16.225–37.

——. 1967. Struktur und Geschichte: Zur Auffassung ihres Verhältnisses in der Sprachwissenschaft. ALH 17.223–43.

TERRAY, ELEMIR. 1958. Herders Theorie des Sprachursprungs. SFFUK 10.9–20.

THOMSEN, VILHELM. 1902. Sprogvidenskabens historie: En kortfattet fremstilling af dens hovedpunkter. København. 1927. Geschichte der Sprachwissenschaft bis zum Ausgang des 19. Jahrhunderts. Übersetzt von H. Pollak. Halle a.d. S., Niemeyer.]

THYSSEN, JOHANNES. 1952–1953. Die Sprache als "Energeia" und das "Weltbild" der Sprache (eine kritische Betrachtung zu Leo Weisgerbers Sprachphilosophie). Lexis 3.301–7. Lahr i.B.

TRIER, JOST. 1934. Das sprachliche Feld: Eine Auseinandersetzung. Neue Jahrbücher für Wissenschaft und Jugendbildung 10.428–49.

——. 1964. Jacob Grimm als Etymologe. Münster, Aschendorff.

TRNKA, BOHUMIL. 1952. Zur Erinnerung an August Schleicher. ZPhon 6.134–42.

ULLMANN, RICHARD, und HELENE GOTTHARD. 1927. Geschichte des Begriffes "Romantik" in Deutschland. Berlin.

ULLMANN, STEPHEN. 1967. The principles of semantics. 2. Aufl. Nachdruck. Oxford, Blackwell & Mott.

——. 1972. Sprache und Stil: Aufsätze zur Semantik und Stilistik. Deutsche Fassung von S. Koopmann. Konzepte der Sprach- und Literaturwissenschaft, 12. Tübingen, Max Niemeyer Verlag.

ULMER, KARL. 1950–1951. Die Wandlung des Sprachbildes von Herder zu Jacob Grimm. Lexis 2/2.263–86. Lahr i.B.

UNGEHEUER, GEROLD. 1969. Paraphrase und syntaktische Tiefenstruktur. FoL 3.178–227.

UNGER, RUDOLF. 1905. Hamanns Sprachtheorie im Zusammenhange seines Denkens: Grundlegung zu einer Würdigung der geistesgeschichtlichen Stellung des Magus im Norden. München, Becksche Verlagsbuchhandlung.

VALVERDE, JOSE MARIA. 1955. Guillermo de Humboldt y la filosofía del lenguaje. Biblioteca Románica Hispánica. Madrid, Gredos.

VERBURG, PIETER ADRIANUS. 1950. The background to the linguistic conceptions of Franz Bopp. Lingua 2.438–68. [Auch in: Portraits of linguists: A biographical source book for the history of western linguistics, 1746–1963, ed. by Th. A. Sebeok, I, 221–50. Bloomington/London, Indiana University Press, 1966.]

——. 1951. Taal en functionaliteit: Een historisch-critische studie over de opvattingen aangaande de functies der taal vanaf de prae-humanistische philologie van Orléans tot de rationalistische linguistiek van Bopp. Diss. Vrije Univ. Amsterdam. Wageningen, Veenman.

VERMEER, HANS J. 1972. Allgemeine Sprachwissenschaft: Eine Einführung. Mit 10 Abbildungen. Rombach Hochschul Paperback, 48. Freiburg, Verlag Rombach.

VIERTEL, J. 1966. Concepts of language underlying the 18th century controversy about the origin of language. MSLL 19.109–32.

VINAY, J.-P., und J. DARBELNET. 1958. Stylistique comparée du français et de l'anglais: Méthode de traduction. Paris, Didier.

VOLNEY, CONSTANTIN. 1864. Discours sur l'étude philosophique des langues. Œuvres complète de Volney, 103–15. Paris.

WALD, LUCIA. 1962. Aspecte dialectice in teorie limbii a lui Wilhelm von Humboldt. PLG 4.193–201.

WARTBURG, WALTHER VON. 1943. Einführung in die Problematik und Methodik der Sprachwissenschaft. Halle a.d. S., Niemeyer.

WATERMAN, JOHN T. 1970. Perspectives in linguistics. 2. Aufl. Chicago/London, The University of Chicago Press.

WEBER, HANNA. 1939. Herders Sprachphilosophie: Eine Interpretation im Hinblick auf die moderne Sprachphilosophie. Germanische Studien, 214. Berlin, Ebering.

WEIMANN, KARL-HEINZ. 1965. Vorstufen der Sprachphilosophie Humboldts bei Bacon und Locke. ZDPh 84.498–508.

WEIN, HERMANN. 1965. Sprache und Weltbild. Westermanns Pädagogische Beiträge 1.1–12.

WEISGERBER, LEO. 1925. Sprache als gesellschaftliche Erkenntnisform. Habilitationsschrift. Bonn (unveröffentlicht).

——. 1926. Das Problem der inneren Sprachform und seine Bedeutung für die deutsche Sprache. GRM 14.241–56.

——. 1927. Die Bedeutungslehre, ein Irrweg der Sprachwissenschaft? GRM 15. 161–83.

——. 1930. "Neuromantik" in der Sprachwissenschaft. GRM 18.241–59.

——. 1939. Muttersprache und Geistesbildung. 2. Aufl. Göttingen, Vandenhoeck & Ruprecht.

——. 1948. Die Entdeckung der Muttersprache im europäischen Denken. Lüneburg, Heliand-Verlag. [Cf. 106–18: VIII. "Die Hochblüte des Sprachgedankens in der deutschen Bewegung um 1800".]

——. 1950–1962. Von den Kräften der deutschen Sprache. 4 Bde.: I. Grundzüge der inhaltbezogenen Grammatik. 3. Aufl. 1962, II. Die sprachliche Gestaltung der Welt. 3. Aufl. 1962, III. Die Muttersprache im Aufbau unserer Kultur. 2. Aufl. 1957, IV. Die geschichtliche Kraft der deutschen Sprache. 1950. Düsseldorf, Schwann.

——. 1951a. Die Wiedergeburt des vergleichenden Sprachstudiums. Lexis 2.3–22. Lahr i.B.

——. 1951b. Die Sprache als wirkende Kraft. SG 4.127–35.

——. 1953–1954. Zum Energeia-Begriff in Humboldts Sprachbetrachtung. WW 4.374–77.

——. 1954. Innere Sprachform als Stil sprachlicher Anverwandlung der Welt. SG 7.571–79.

——. 1956–1957. Die Erforschung der Sprach"zugriffe". I. Grundlinien einer inhaltbezogenen Grammatik. WW 7.65–73.

——. 1959. Sprache — Schlüssel zur Welt. Festschrift für Leo Weisgerber. Herausgegeben von H. Gipper. Düsseldorf, Schwann.

——. 1961. Zur Entmythologisierung der Sprachforschung. WW Beiheft 3.30–50.

——. 1963. Die vier Stufen in der Erforschung der Sprachen. Sprache und Gemeinschaft, Grundlegung, 2. Düsseldorf, Schwann.

——. 1964. Die Grundlegung der ganzheitlichen Sprachauffassung: Aufsätze 1925–1933. Herausgegeben von H. Gipper. Düsseldorf, Schwann.

——. 1971a. Die geistige Seite der Sprache und ihre Erforschung. Sprache der Gegenwart, 15. Düsseldorf, Schwann. [Cf. 193–205: "Die vergleichende Sprachwissenschaft"].

——. 1971b. Bedeutungswandel. Historisches Wörterbuch der Philosophie, herausgegeben von J. Ritter, I, 761–2. Basel/Stuttgart, Schwabe.

WEISWEILER, JOSEF. 1949. Die indogermanische Sprachwissenschaft: Eine geistesgeschichtliche Studie. Historisches Jahrbuch 62–69.464–90. München.

WELLEK, RENÉ. 1963. Concepts of criticism. New Haven/London, Yale University Press. [Cf. 128–98: "The concept of romanticism in literary history", und 199–221: "Romanticism re-examined"].

——. 1965. German and English romanticism: A confrontation. Studies in romanticism, 33–56. Boston.

WILL, WILFRIED VAN DER. 1969. Name, semeion, energeia: Notes in the permutations of language theories. Essays in German language, culture, and society, ed. by S. S. Prawer, R. H. Thomas, and L. Forster, 211–30. London, University of London, Inst. of German Studies.

WINDISCH, ERNST. 1917–1920. Geschichte der Sanskrit-Philologie und indischen Altertumskunde. Grundriß der Indo-arischen Philologie und Altertumskunde, 1,1. 2 Teile. Straßburg, Trübner.

WIRZ, LUDWIG. 1939. Friedrich Schlegels philosophische Entwicklung. Bonn, Hanstein.

WOELLER, WALTRAUD. 1965. Die Bedeutung der Brüder Grimm für die Märchen- und Sagenforschung. WZUB 14.507–14.

WOLFF, HANS M. 1952. Der junge Herder und die Entwicklungsidee Rousseaus. PMLA 57.753–819.

WUNDT, WILHELM. 1911. Völkerpsychologie: Eine Untersuchung der Entwicklungsgesetze von Sprache, Mythus und Sitte. I: Die Sprache. 3. Aufl. 1. Teil. Leipzig, Engelmann.

ZIEGLER, KLAUS. 1952. Die weltanschaulichen Grundlagen der Wissenschaft Jacob Grimms. Euphorion 46.241–66.

ZOBEL, ARTHUR. 1928. Darstellung und kritische Würdigung der Sprachphilosophie John Lockes. Anglia 40.289–324.

ZSIRAI, MIKLÓS. 1951. Sámuel Gyarmathi: Hungarian pioneer of comparative linguistics. ALH 1.5–16. [Auch in: Portraits of linguists: A biographical source book for the history of western linguistics, 1746–1963, ed. by Th. A. Sebeok, I, 58–70. Bloomington/London, Indiana University Press, 1966.]

Zwirner, Eberhard. 1969. Zum Begriff der allgemeinen Sprachwissenschaft und der allgemeinen Grammatik. Mélanges pour Jean Fourquet, par M. Adamus et al. réunis par P. Valentin et G. Zink, 407–15. München, Hueber/Paris, Klincksieck.

LANGUAGE CLASSIFICATION IN THE NINETEENTH CENTURY

A. MORPURGO DAVIES

1. INTRODUCTION

1.1 Attempts to classify the known languages or dialects go back to a very early period: they aim both at establishing differences and similarities on what we would now call a synchronic or an 'achronic' basis, and at pointing out a genetic relationship from a diachronic angle. The terminology, or part of it, may be new, but neither the concept of language affinity nor that of genetic or genealogical relationship were in any way a discovery of the nineteenth century scholars or of their immediate predecessors. It is true, however, that it was in the nineteenth century that a new wealth of linguistic material became available and that new methodological tools were created which allowed the various types of linguistic affinity to be distinguished with some clarity and to be explored in greater depth than had previously been possible. Thus there is some reason to confine this chapter to the nineteenth century, ignoring not only previous achievements but also more recent research, which, in spite of different methods and different emphasis, still continues to plough some of the same fields.

Though it has often been done, it would be deceptive to make a sharp distinction between the different ways in which the languages were classified in our period. It would be equally deceptive to dissociate the concrete achievements of language classification from the general thinking about language and about the problems connected with it. Some of the earlier monographs and articles concerned with nineteenth century linguistics have been guilty of this particular sin. They reveal an excessive attention to the exploration of effective results (with all the related questions of priority and authorship) but a lack of interest in the method by which these were prompted and the background against which they were reached: a great deal of history of technology, but little history of ideas. The outcome is often a 'technical' history which registers the successes and ignores the mistakes: it may appear either as a triumphant and unimpeded progress towards greater knowledge or as a succession of dull squabbles about trivialities.

1.2 Paradoxically, some of the troubles which beset the historiography of the period depend on the richness of the material available. There is a large amount of what we could call primary sources. Grundrisse, monographs, articles, reviews give us direct access to the thought of the scholars of the time. Letters, memoirs, biographies, autobiographies, documents etc. provide the necessary background knowledge.[1] A probably larger amount of material remains to be discovered in public and private archives and made available to a wider public, but it is still true that what is in fact available is hardly ever made use of. More easily accessible — and consequently more influential — is another type of contemporary evidence which is in the ambiguous position of having the status of primary and secondary source at the same time. More than in any other period, except our own, in the nineteenth century linguistics excelled in writing its own history, while it was making it. Not only were most monographs preceded — as is only right — by a chapter on the 'history of the question', but, more important, entire books were dedicated to the history of the subject for its own sake. F. Max Müller's *Lectures on the science of language*, which appeared in their first edition in 1861, contained what might count as a history of linguistics from classical times to the author's own days. In 1869 Theodor Benfey published his history of linguistics and oriental philology in Germany from the beginning of the nineteenth century; the *Geschichte der germanischen Philologie* by Rudolf von Raumer was published in 1870 and included a discussion of the work done by Raumer's contemporaries. Gustav Gröber's *Grundriss* with his *Geschichte der romanischen Philologie* started appearing in 1886. The highly influential *Einleitung in das Sprachstudium. Ein Beitrag zur Geschichte und Methodik der vergleichenden Sprachforschung* by Berthold Delbrück appeared in the first of its numerous editions in 1880 and was essentially concerned with the work of the three latest generations of scholars. This absence of a time gap between the historian and his subject gives to some earlier historiographical work a curious position in between real historiography and the innumerable obituaries, encomia, laudatory biographies and polemical reviews in which the period is rich. In the first half of the present century most works of historiography have directly descended from the earlier work. However, at the same time as twentieth century historiography has accepted many of the views and perhaps the preconceptions of its predecessors, it has also lost some of the contemporary awareness of the finer distinctions and the clarifying background. In some cases even the semantic value of some key terms has been forgotten (cf., e.g., the very valuable essay by Telegdi [1966] on terms like *historisch*). At present the 'accepted history of linguistics is partly myth and partly serious history' (Hoenigswald 1971: 423); this is certainly true for nineteenth century studies, but the signs are that here — as elsewhere — the situation may be changing.[2]

[1] Malkiel has compiled a tentative typological inventory of the varieties of primary material available to the historian of linguistics (cf. Malkiel and Langdon 1968–69: 541ff.).

[2] For some reflections on the recent interest in the history of linguistics cf. Malkiel (Malkiel and Langdon 1968–9: 530–32) and Koerner (1972a). It is probably true that after the experiences of structuralism and generative grammar we now look at nineteenth-century work through different eyes.

1.3 What follows aims at giving a brief critical survey of recent work about the theories and methods of language classification proposed in the last century, but also tries to point out some problems which are either ignored or unsolved. The starting point is perhaps a precursor, Sir William Jones, and the point of arrival F. N. Finck, but there will be occasional references to earlier and later authors. Incompetence has obliged me to concentrate on western scholars operating mostly on (and in) western Indo-European languages; even the history of Finno-Ugric studies is largely neglected. Other Oriental, African and American languages cannot be dealt with here. Some of the specialized historiography about particular sub-groups like Romance, Slavonic, Germanic, etc., is also neglected except when it is felt that it impinges directly on more general studies.[3]

The historiographical work considered belongs for the most part to the period 1945–70, but occasionally it will be necessary to discuss earlier work.[4] A few articles and books published after 1970 have been quoted, but, in the absence of reliable bibliographical repertories (like the *Bibliographie linguistique*), chance more than anything else has dictated the choice.

The original aim, completeness, has long since been lost sight of, both in the bibliography and in the preceding survey. The latter was meant to be selective from the start, the former soon became so; lack of time, inadequate libraries, and an unclear delimitation of the subject have proved insuperable obstacles.[5]

1.4 The first question concerns periodization. Traditionally, the beginning of 'scientific linguistics' is dated at the turn of the nineteenth century, just after or just before, and is identified with the discovery of the historical and comparative method and with the demonstration of the kinship of the Indo-European languages, that is to say with two achievements which are both relevant to the problem of language classification. Most prewar and postwar histories of linguistics reflect this view

[3] The problem is particularly difficult in the case of works in — and about — Slavonic languages. Scholars like, e.g., Potebnja and Fortunatov do not seem to have had much influence outside Russia, in spite of the originality of their theories. In a short survey perhaps the safest course was to ignore them, just as it has seemed best to ignore scholars such as Renan or Gaston Paris, or earlier authors like Bredsdorff.

[4] The bibliography lists a few works which could count as primary sources, but the choice is entirely dictated by the references made in the text. I have not aimed at completeness.

[5] I have ignored work specifically concerned with problems of the philosophy of language. Those introductions to general linguistics which dedicate a short chapter to the history of the subject have also been left aside. On the other hand I have tried to include in the bibliography all the recent histories of linguistics which I have been able to consult. Some omissions are due to library deficiencies: for a fuller list see the bibliography of Koerner (1972a). I particularly regret not to have been able to see Drăganu (1945), Džahoukjan (1960–62), Gagkaev (1957), Hamel (1945), Loja (1968), Verburg (1951): an asterisk premitted to the title of any work in the bibliography indicates that the quotation is second-hand and that I have not been able to see the actual book or periodical. A number of recent works on the history of linguistics have been translated into most European languages; I have made no attempt to list these translations nor have I listed the modern reprints of earlier works. However, in the cases in which a translation or a reprint was available, while the original text was not, the bibliography mentions them.

(together with the evaluative judgement implied in the adjective 'scientific'): sometimes they even give the impression of a science created ex nihilo.[6] It is against this that a recent reaction has taken place. It is useful not to confuse the two different and often contrasting angles from which the attack has come. On the one side, there have been attempts to revalue the linguistic thought of earlier centuries, its general insights and its profound concern with the theory of language. Chomsky's *Cartesian linguistics* (1966) is neither the first nor the last work on the subject, but in spite of its obvious defects and the polemics that it has aroused (cf. Rosiello 1967; Hall 1969; Aarsleff 1970, etc.), it has helped to bring works and authors of this period into the limelight.[7] An extreme result of its impact could be described in the paradoxical claim that, far from opening 'la voie rationelle' to linguistic thought (Leroy 1971:17), this period marks the end of a truly 'philosophical' approach to the theory of language and the beginning of a time of uninspired drudgery, from which some empirical results, but few new insights were gained. In a sense, then, the gap between nineteenth-century and pre-nineteenth century thought is not reduced, but increased. The only real difference in periodization would then concern the figure of Wilhelm von Humboldt, no more one of the founders of the 'new' linguistics, but the surviving hero of time past.

On the other side some less glittering but perhaps more solid work has tried to show that the gap between the two periods is not as wide as was assumed. Here too we may recognize two different directions. A number of scholars have concentrated on earlier periods and authors (Bacon, Leibniz, Locke, Condillac, Vico, Herder, etc.) and have recognized in them the beginning of an empirical and sometimes historical approach to language. The aim was to demonstrate that in linguistics empiricism and historicism do not arise in the nineteenth century as the result of the anti-Enlightenment bias of Romanticism, but are rather the outcome of a long and gradual process which had started and partly come to fruition one or two centuries before (cf., e.g. Apel 1963, de Mauro 1963, 1970a:52ff., Rosiello 1967 etc.).[8] In this the history of linguistics probably follows a general historiographical trend towards reducing to more sensible proportions the exaggerated claims of novelty made by European Romanticism.[9] An important factor is obviously the interest which modern linguistics takes in investigating theoretical and methodological problems in preference to concrete questions.

Other scholars — so far a minority — have preferred to explore in depth the

[6] Obviously, the position of those histories of linguistic thought which concentrate on philosophy of language is different: cf. for instance the panorama traced in Cassirer's *Philosophie der symbolischen Formen* (1923). Some very thoughtful discussions about theory and methodology can also be found in Pagliaro 1930.

[7] In this paragraph all references are purely indicative of particular trends and do not aim at completeness.

[8] It may be instructive to see the somewhat exacerbated polemics on the subject between Bolelli (1966, 1967) and de Mauro (1967b).

[9] This has often been pointed out: cf., e.g., Christmann 1966 (453ff.), Ginschel 1967 (5ff.), Hermann 1965 (447), Timpanaro 1972a (72).

intellectual background and presuppositions which determined the work of some of the 'new' linguists. The outcome of this work is two-fold: on the one side it has helped to differentiate the theoretical outlooks of the founders of the 'new' linguistics, so that the traditionally monolithic view is now shattered; on the other side it has recognized, in the thought of these authors, survivals — often important — of earlier doctrines. Verburg's (1950) brilliant analysis of Bopp's interests and assumptions (which has brought out the rationalistic element in his formation), Hjelmslev's (1950–51) challenging and somewhat perverse interpretation of Rask's work, M. Bjerrum's (1959) detailed study of his views, Diderichsen's (1960) important and solid reply with his study of Rask's background, L. Hermann's (1965) notes on Jacob Grimm, G. Ginschel's (1967) useful study of his progress towards linguistic history, and some of the more recent works on Wilhelm von Humboldt (e.g. Brown 1967, Christmann 1966, Heintz 1969, Viertel 1966) should be ranged in this category. In this way too the yawning gulf between rationalism and empiricism, Enlightenment and Romanticism, anti-historicism and historicism, in a word, between 'prescientific' and 'scientific' linguistics appears to be bridged.[10]

This new historiographical trend is so recent that there has been little time to judge of its validity.[11] Timpanaro's (1972a:72–5) balanced assessment of it, together with his reminder that the 'technicians' (e.g. Bopp and Rask) often had general views as interesting as those of the 'theoreticians' (e.g. Humboldt and Schlegel), is a first step in this direction. An equally balanced statement of the problem will be found in Koerner's (1972a) review of Arens (1969). He adopts a relatively traditional view (cf. also Koerner 1972c:216–7), but pleads for a suspension of judgement until more evidence is available about the epistemology of the earlier centuries.[12] One point which Koerner makes (1972a:430) but is oddly ignored in some histories of linguistics (though, see Mounin 1967:175) is that Bopp seems to have been the first scholar to 'emphasize the study of language for language's sake'. The claim to priority may need checking, but the point can be stressed by comparing, for instance, Adelung's attempts, in the introduction to his Mithridates (Adelung 1806–17:I iii), to justify the study of linguistics in terms of historical-ethnographical studies about migrations and the origins of peoples, with Bopp's stated purpose to treat languages 'als Gegenstand und nicht als Mittel der Erkenntniss' (Bopp 1833:I xiii-xiv).[13]

[10] Cf. also Teeter 1966 for some strictures upon the standard accounts of the history of linguistics.

[11] Even so, it has already yielded fruit: Jankowsky (1972), for instance, starts his account of the linguistic background of the neogrammarians not with Jones or Schlegel but with Francis Bacon and Leibniz.

[12] Whether Thomas Kuhn's ideas about the development of science (cf. Kuhn 1970) could or should be applied to the history of linguistics is still dubious: for a few observations on this point see Bursill-Hall (1970a:114–15; 1970b:231–2, 239–40).

[13] Even more impressive is Bopp's description, in an early curriculum, of his intellectual progress from a love of Oriental literature to an interest in 'Sprachen an und für sich' (cf. Lefmann 1891–97: II, 116*). Similarly, in a letter of 1815 to Windischmann he declared that he intended to dedicate himself to the study of languages and to endeavour 'das Sprachstudium zu einem philosophischen und historischen Studium zu machen' (*ibid.* 33*). In spite of the apparent clarity of these statements

1.5 This is not the place to discuss the ties between linguistics and Romanticism, a subject dealt with elsewhere in this volume. Nor can we consider the equally important question of the relationship between linguistics and other disciplines, though, e.g. law and classical philology come to mind.[14] But even at the risk of repeating something said elsewhere in this volume, we cannot entirely pass over in silence two other problems which are closely related to each other: that of the influence of the natural sciences on linguistics and that of the organic concept of language.

It has often been noticed — and not only recently — that the language of the early nineteenth century scholars is rich in scientific jargon and scientific metaphors and comparisons: for some observations on the subject, cf. for instance Delbrück (1880: *passim*). More recently, the problem has been tackled again, both in general terms, and (more frequently) with reference to individual authors. However, we still lack a history of linguistics which traces not only the ideal parallelism, but also the effective connections between the study of language and that of the natural sciences.

Observations on the connections between sciences and linguistics (including phonetics) are found in most works by Zwirner (cf. especially Zwirner 1962; Zwirner and Zwirner 1966: 74ff.); see also Maher 1966 and Trim 1959. Attention has often been called to the influence of comparative anatomy on comparative grammar and to the frequent references to it which we find in the early nineteenth century: cf. Aarsleff 1967 (172, 210), Arndt 1965 (482f.), Hoenigswald 1963, Jankowsky 1972 (54ff.), Putschke 1969, Ruprecht 1963, Schwankweiler 1965 (458ff.), etc. Friedrich Schlegel's famous passage about 'vergleichende Grammatik' and 'vergleichende Anatomie' (F. Schlegel 1808:28) has been dismissed as a concession to the spirit of the time by Nüsse (1962:42), who argues that Schlegel was brought to the problem of language classification by his systematic temperament and not through the influence of his scientific studies. Timpanaro (1972a) is more willing to find in Schlegel a reference to Cuvier's work and a sort of programmatic statement aimed at upholding the functions of comparative anatomy as a guide for linguistics.[15]

At first sight it may appear that the frequent use of 'organic' and 'organism' reflects yet another of these scientific metaphors, but this time the problem is far more important, since the whole definition and understanding of language is involved. A useful chapter by R. L. Brown (1967:40–53) collects some evidence about the begin-

they pose a double problem of interpretation. First, are they simply meant to contrast the linguistic study of language with that directed towards 'l'explication des textes', or is there something more in them? Do they foreshadow, for instance, the mid-century discussions about the respective roles of *Philologie* and *Sprachwissenschaft*? Secondly, how should they be understood? Do they represent a new view of linguistic studies, or do they imply a return to a rationalistic 'philosophical' attitude? See below note 32 for Aarsleff's reflections on Jones' views.

14 For the influence of classical philology on linguistics Oertel 1901 is still useful. The more or less violent reactions of the classicists to the first appearance of the new theories about comparison have been discussed in detail by L. Rocher (1957–58); for the later period, cf. also Hoenigswald 1963 and Timpanaro 1963 (5ff., 39ff., 72ff.).

15 Timpanaro (1972a:96) corrects the popular misapprehension that Friedrich Schlegel was the first to speak of 'vergleichende Grammatik', and refers inter alia to earlier works by J. S. Vater.

nings of these organic conceptions. In an impressive but sweeping article Cassirer (1945) has compared the organic view of language with some forms of modern structuralism. Some qualifications, and an interesting study of the development of the concept of organism, can be found in Lepschy (1962), while the contrast and similarities between organism, system and structure are also the subject of an article by Rensch (1967), who does not seem to have made use of Lepschy 1962. Finally, a great deal of information is available in Haselback's (1966) book on Becker.

Numerous problems could be raised, but here it must be sufficient to point out the difficulties which arise when we try to give a closer definition of organic and organism in their application to language. As Cassirer (and Lepschy) have pointed out, the emphasis may be on 'organism' in the sense of structure (which sometimes incorporates the idea of the whole as distinguished from the sum of its parts), or on the equation of 'organism' and living being, i.e. on the ontological meaning of organism. Finally, 'organic' may be taken as quasi-synonymous to individual or individualized. Needless to say, the first view may lead to some form of structuralism, but the second, as Lepschy has shown, is far more likely to lead towards evolutionism or transformationism, or at any rate towards a conception of language as endowed with a life of its own and towards a conception of linguistics as a natural science. The difficulty consists in establishing whether and how any of these developments took place, and — at a more pedestrian level — in deciding which one of these meanings of organic and organism can be attributed to each author. There is an additional risk: it is all too easy to forget the distinction between a technical term used with its full value in any of the meanings indicated above and a stereotype adjective or noun introduced by some particular writer as a concession to the current fashion. Even so, at the very least it is possible to say that the introduction of the concept of organism in linguistics provides a verbal link with the biological sciences, i.e. with those sciences which had been most concerned with classification problems.[16]

1.51 It is likely that it is not the history of the various views of language which is the most profitable field for an enquiry into the influences of the natural sciences on linguistics, but the history of language classification, of its aims, and — up to a point — of its methods. Here historiography lets us down again, because such an enquiry, bearing on language classification, is just what we do not have.[17] This function is not fulfilled by a difficult, controversial, and at times fascinating book by M. Foucault (1966), which among other things discusses the problems of classification in the history of Western thought. Even so, Foucault's book can perhaps provide a starting point which may be accepted because of its brilliant insights or rejected because of its lack of qualifications and distinctions (see Rosiello 1967:168ff.).[18] At a different level

[16] We shall discuss later (see 3.91) the evolutionary theories in linguistics. Here it is sufficient to point out that organic comparisons carry the immediate consequence of continuous reference to life, growth, maturity and decay of language. Yet, even within this context it was possible to conceive of language as undergoing a process of continuous growth or continuous decay (see below note 120).

[17] For Sharadzenidze 1958 see below p. 654.

[18] In spite of some very interesting points it seems to me that the paragraphs which Foucault (1966:

from that explored by Foucault, it becomes clear that the development of scientific classification from Linnaeus through Jussieu to Cuvier (and then to Darwin and Haeckel) had a definite reflection on linguistic thought, even if there may have been a time gap between the two developments. Some examples may prove the point. J. von Farkas (1952:2ff.) has pointed out that already in the eighteenth century August Ludwig Schlözer aimed at introducing Linnaeus's method into ethnology (thus following in the steps of Leibniz) and at using language as the classificatory criterion (cf. also Lauch 1968:278). Later on we find that Rask wanted to replace Linnaeus's division into *classis*, *ordo*, *genus*, *species* and *varietas* by a (genealogical?) classification of languages into *Race* (*Aet*), *Klasse*, *Stamme*, *Gren*, *Sprog*, *Sprogart* (cf. Diderichsen 1960:139, but see also Pott 1856:192ff.);[19] still later Pott, then in the full maturity of his thought, argued that for a linguist the highest task would consist in being a new Linnaeus capable of producing a classification of the languages of the world (Pott 1856:191). This was hardly a new idea, but from the context it becomes clear that Pott was also thinking of a 'physiological' i.e. a typological classification (*ibid.*: 197). A further qualification which Pott added is even more enlightening: the new classification — we are told — must not be 'artificial', like that of the Swedish naturalist, but 'natural' like that of Jussieu (*ibid.*: 196). We may contrast this statement with the words which an English scientist and philologist, T. Young, had written some forty years before in a review of Adelung's Mithridates: 'A perfect NATURAL order of arrangement, in treating of the peculiarities of different languages, ought to be regulated by their descent from each other and their historical relations: a perfect ARTIFICIAL order ought to bring together into the same classes all those genera which have any essential resemblance ...' [my emphasis] (Young 1813–14:252).[20]

Well after Pott and Young the artificial/natural distinction reappears in the writings

292ff.) has dedicated to the beginning of comparative linguistics in the nineteenth century are among the least satisfactory of the book. I am not certain, for instance, that 'tout l'être du langage est maintenant sonore' as Foucault maintains (*ibid.* 298), nor am I certain that, in contrast to the earlier period, in the nineteenth century 'toutes les langues se valent' (*ibid.*). As we shall see, attempts to evaluate the various languages continue all through the century. The main point, however, is that Foucault too is mesmerized by the development of the comparative method and of genealogical classification, and, in spite of his reference to the theories of Bopp and Schlegel, he almost entirely ignores contemporary typological classifications. As I have tried to show above, typological and genealogical classifications appear in the course of the nineteenth century to follow a route which is similar to that reconstructed by Foucault for the earlier history of biological classification; this very fact makes it difficult to accept Foucault's point that similar developments had taken place at the same time in linguistics and in the sciences.

19 For the whole problem of Rask's attitude towards the classification of the natural sciences see Bjerrum (1959:63ff.). It is also worth remembering that Rask's compatriot J. H. Bredsdorff [1790–1841], who is best known to linguists for his very modern views on the causes of language change (cf. Thomsen 1927: 62–3, Jespersen 1922:70–1; I regret that I have not been able to see Bredsdorff 1970), was also the author of an interesting dissertation *De regulis in classificatione rerum naturalium observandis* (1817).

20 According to the O.E.D. this review marks the first occurrence of the word Indo-European in written English. It should also be pointed out that in it Young argued that language had to be identified with a 'species', as Schleicher was to do much later (see below 3.7 and note 99).

of R. de la Grasserie (1889–90) who criticized as artificial all the previous typological classifications and proposed a natural classification based like those of botany and zoology on the principle of 'subordination des caractères'. In a period in which the controversy on evolution was just subsiding he then proceeded to wonder whether a typologically based natural classification, such as the one he had proposed, could also be proved to have a genealogical value.[21]

To sum up: in this field the natural sciences seem to set the task: first a comprehensive classification, secondly a 'natural' classification. The way in which nineteenth-century scholars tackled it is significant for the development of linguistics; even more so is the interplay, which we cannot help noticing, between genealogical and typological classifications as possible ways of solving the problem.

1.6 Neither the traditional nor the more modern historiography appear to have explicitly discussed the problems posed by the relationship between the various types of language classification in the nineteenth century.[22] The 'comparative method' with its spectacular achievements has monopolized attention. However, at the same time in which this was being developed and experimented with, scholars (often the same scholars) were also interested in a so-called morphological classification, i.e. in a typological classification which aimed at grouping languages not according to their origin, but according to their structural similarities. Genetic and morphological classification had an important point of contact. By the turn of the century (and probably long before) it had become clear that a genetic (or genealogical) relationship between languages could not be established only on the basis of lexical agreement; structural similarity appeared to be a more important criterion. In the same period, however, we find that typological classification is also based on grammatical and structural considerations. Is this coincidence entirely accidental?

A posteriori we can see that another point also helped to bring the two classifications together: they both disclaimed any arbitrariness and artificiality and were confident that they rested on some essential characteristics of the languages which they classified. The pressing question — and one that impinges both on the history of comparative method and on that of typology — is whether all leading scholars in the first part of the century made a clear distinction between genetic and typological affinity. It is often not seen that this is in fact a problem, but once it is posed it appears that, in the early period at least, there is little justification for keeping apart the histories of the two types of classification. If we are obliged to do so in this survey, it is because there is so little overlap in the historiographical work concerned with the one field or the other. This conflict between history and history of historiography may perhaps explain some of the uneasiness which no doubt will emerge from the exposi-

[21] For R. de la Grasserie see below 3.10 and note 127.

[22] There have been a few relevant contributions, but they have concerned the interpretation of individual authors; cf., e.g., Hjelmslev 1950–51, Bjerrum 1959, and Diderichsen 1960 for Rask, Timpanaro 1972a for Schlegel.

tion, the frequent references from one section to the other, and the repetitions which we have tried to avoid but have kept creeping in. We shall first discuss the history of the comparative method and then that of typological classification; towards the end we shall try to gather the common threads.

2. GENEALOGICAL CLASSIFICATION

2.1 We have seen that most of the challenges to the traditional periodization have been based on the assumption that technical achievements count but little: what matters is the general outlook on which they are founded, and this is the result of a lengthy and continuous process. However, there is some agreement in pinpointing the comparative method as one of the concrete results which had a more lasting influence. If so, the challenge could also be posed from a different angle: how correct is the claim of absolute novelty made by — or on behalf of — the 'technicians' of the nineteenth century?

Work on this point appears to be either non existent or somewhat disjointed and lacking in continuity. Even so, it is one of the great merits of some recent histories of linguistics that they have made available some information, however elementary and incomplete, about the first studies which impinged on language comparison and genetic classification.

Thus Arens (1969) devotes some space to early attempts at classification (Dante, J. J. Scaliger, Gesner, Leibniz, Ludolf, Ten Kate, etc.) up to Adelung's *Mithridates* (but more space should be dedicated to Hervás than has been done). Robins (1967: 164–9) briefly traces very much the same story and stresses the point that what characterizes early work is not so much lack of insight as lack of that continuity in scholarly production which characterizes the nineteenth century (*ibid.*: 164). Tagliavini (1968a: 32ff.) provides as usual rich factual information and is far better informed than most histories of linguistics about the comparison of non-Indo-European languages. Mounin (1967) makes an interesting effort to give the full picture of the concrete work attempted during the sixteenth, seventeenth and eighteenth centuries with its merits and its absurdities, but lack of space does not allow him to go much into detail.[23] Some of the earlier stages of pre-nineteenth-century comparative work have been discussed by Agrell (1955) in a useful monograph which concentrates on methodology, with particular reference to Germanic languages, and goes back as far as the Renaissance. In the fifties Bonfante (1953) reacted against the traditional assumption that the inter-relationship of the Indo-European languages had been first thought of at the end of the eighteenth century. In a twenty-page article he collected evidence about the various classifications of European languages from the Middle Ages to the

[23] For some information, which partly depends on Arens, see Apel 1963 (280–5). Neither here, nor in the bibliography, have we listed all work about individual authors, though some of them (e.g. Gesner) have come in for a large share of attention.

time of Sir William Jones. As a source of basic material this article still remains unsurpassed; it should be integrated with Bonfante's note on E. Brerewood (Bonfante 1955). More recently — and at a more popularizing level — Otto Zeller (1967) in his history of comparative Indo-European philology has broken with the tradition and started his exposition from Gesner, Megiser and J. J. Scaliger, arguing, somewhat perversely but interestingly, that comparative linguistics in our sense of the word was created by these three scholars. Zeller analyses their classifications and contrasts the alphabetic arrangement (with some genetic subgrouping) of the languages of the world, adopted by Gesner, both with the partly genetic, partly geographical classification of Megiser, and with the sound genetic classification of Scaliger linked with his firm denial of any religious presupposition. The next author discussed, before Friedrich Schlegel, is Leibniz, with his interest in language development, his distinction between language similarities due to common origin and those due to secondary contacts, and his dual subdivision of languages into an Aramaic and a Japhetic group. The information provided is not new, and consists largely of reproduction of primary sources. Even so, this short book has an unusual character of freshness and novelty which is obviously connected with its constant use of first-hand evidence.

2.12 The standard works of reference provide only very scanty information about the early stages of those comparative studies which do not concern Indo-European languages (though, as we have seen, Tagliavini 1968a is an exception).[24] This is understandable, but we must hope that some way (team work?) can be found to fill the gaps. Arens (1969:105–6) has a tantalizing quotation from the Orientalist Ludolf who at the end of the seventeenth century was convinced that in order to prove that two languages are related it is necessary to show that their 'grammaticae ratio' is similar. We should like to be told much more about Ludolf, but Arens himself quotes second-hand from Benfey (1869) (cf. also Jankowsky 1972:23). Elsewhere Arens (1969:148) mentions without any direct quotation the works of Sajnovics and Gyarmathi on Finno-Ugrian and points out the attention given to grammar in the latter's *Affinitas linguae hungaricae cum linguis fennicae originis grammatice demonstrata* (1799). It would have been possible to make use of some recent and less recent articles and monographs about the development of Finno-Ugrian linguistics. Information about the early period of these studies is available, for instance, in a 1957 dissertation by A. Stehr, a pupil of J. von Farkas (but cf. also Farkas 1948 and 1952, Gáldi 1955 and 1956, Hormia 1964–65, Lakó 1970, Mezey 1965, Pražák 1967, etc.). Mention should be made of Stehr's (1957:7–23) study of the *Nachlass* of Martin Fogel [1634–1675], with his very clear distinction between loan words and inherited words and his demonstration, based on structural considerations, of the kinship of Hungarian and Finnish. Similarly the observations of J. E. Fischer [1697–1771] about the phonetic correspondences between Hungarian and the other Finno-Ugrian languages should

[24] I have not found mentioned in the recent histories of linguistics the *Dissertationes miscellaneae* (1706–08) of the Dutch scholar Relandus, who, according to Gabelentz (1891:26), was the first author who established 'Lautvertretungsgesetze' between two related languages (Malay and Malagasy).

be rescued from oblivion (Stehr 1957:51–100, especially 93–4; cf. also Vdovin 1954 and Gulja 1965 with interesting accounts of early work devoted to collecting and organizing linguistic data). Before the diffusion of specialization in the second half of the nineteenth century it was conceivable, and indeed normal, that a scholar working on Indo-European languages should have been influenced by a Semitist or an Ugrologist: Stehr has pointed out that Leibniz went to Hamburg to see Fogel's manuscripts, we know that Rask admired Gyarmathi and was a Finno-Ugrian scholar himself, and we have evidence of Grimm's interest in Finnish language and poetry (cf. Kunze 1957). However, until we have more detailed studies of the methodology involved in these earlier classifications, both when they were successful and when they were not, it seems necessary to suspend judgement about the degree of continuity that can be postulated between them and nineteenth century work.[25]

2.2 We cannot discuss here the historical background against which the development of linguistics must be considered (for some general observations, cf. Pätsch 1960:211ff.). It suffices to repeat the banal observation that the end of the eighteenth century saw an increase in the linguistic material available (missionaries and colonizations contributed to it) and a deeper understanding of — as well as a greater interest in — the earlier phases of national languages, together with a stress placed on descriptive rather than normative grammar.[26] The great compilations by Hervás and Adelung (not to mention Pallas) continue an older tradition of similar collections of material, but the richness of the evidence confirms our point. They would deserve a far closer analysis than they have received in recent years; in particular Hervás's *Catálogo* (cf. Hervás 1784 and 1800–05) and his more theoretical works (e.g. Hervás 1787) are worth remembering both for their historical importance and for their intrinsic methodological interest. Not much has been written about them; at the moment we can only quote a very interesting discussion by Lázaro Carreter (1949:100–12), some factual articles by Batllori (1951 and 1959) and a few paragraphs in Mourelle-Lema (1968: 162f.). For Adelung, whose *Deutsche Sprachlehre* has always attracted some attention, some valuable information is now available in Diderichsen 1960 where his views are often compared with those of Rask (cf. also Jankowsky 1972:33ff. and Spiridonova 1961).

Far more is known, though still not enough, about the first Western contacts with

[25] For Gyarmathi cf. also Zsirai 1951. I have not been able to make use of bibliography in Finnish and Hungarian and I have found it impossible to see some Finnish periodicals.

[26] In the history of linguistics more space should be devoted to earlier studies of individual branches of Indo-European. We have mentioned above Annelies Lauch's article (1968) about Schlözer's contributions to Slavonic studies, but figures like those of Josef Dobrovský [1753–1829], Bartholomäus (Jerney) Kopitar [1780–1844] and Vuk (i.e. Vuk Stefanović Karadzić) [1787–1864] should certainly not be forgotten, not only for the value of their contributions, but also because of the importance attributed to their work by Jacob Grimm. Some general information on Schlözer will be found in Winter 1916 and 1962 as well as in Lauch 1968; cf. also Eichler 1966 and Grau 1966. For information and bibliography on Dobrovský cf. Krbec-Michálková 1959 and Krbec-Laiske 1968 and 1970.

Sanskrit and with some of the Oriental languages. Benfey 1869 and Windisch 1917–20 remain indispensable, but Schwab 1950 is a mine of information (which sometimes needs checking) about anything oriental in Europe (and particularly in France) between the end of the eighteenth century and the beginning of the twentieth century. Willson 1964 is also useful as a German counterpart for the earlier period and makes good reading, but is less rich in information about linguistic matters. More recently a detailed and reliable monograph on Alexander Hamilton (R. Rocher 1968, cf. R. Rocher 1970) has provided us with first-hand evidence about one of the men who had a determining influence in introducing Sanskrit in Europe. Some more information can be obtained from the rich literature on Sir William Jones (see below 2.3). A useful piece of research (Oppenberg 1965) has tested at close quarters the knowledge of Sanskrit which appears in the translations of the first German who learnt this language, Friedrich Schlegel.

Traditionally Sanskrit is seen as the catalyst which accelerated or even determined the success of Indo-European comparative studies. No doubt, the causes are many and need not all be of a linguistic nature; however, it has frequently been suggested that the structural clarity or the transparency of the language is one of them.[27] Recently, Emeneau (1955 and 1971) has stressed the vagueness and possible irrelevance of this notion, and has pointed out that what mattered more was the contact with a different grammatical tradition and a type of grammatical analysis clearly distinguished from that of the Western tradition.[28]

Whatever the cause, it seems likely that the contact with Sanskrit pushed further a preexisting tendency towards grammatical analysis and segmentation: this may possibly help to account for the persistent morphological interests of scholars like Bopp who had come to comparative grammar from Sanskrit. Another question, which has not been asked but is important, is whether Sanskrit had a determining influence only on the progress of the comparative method. Or did it have a part to play also in the beginning of 'morphological' classification?

[27] Georg von Gabelentz (1891:26) is more explicit; language comparison — he argues — requires etymological analysis and this is a difficult task in languages like the Western ones in which forms cannot be easily segmented; Sanskrit offers more promising material. But this is the moot point: Emeneau (1955:149) has maintained that he does not find Sanskrit more transparent than Greek. Perhaps another factor should be considered. Any teacher of Indo-European comparative grammar knows that it is difficult to induce a student steeped from youth in the classical languages to analyze those forms which he has learnt as indivisible wholes. The same student, however, when faced with a set of Sanskrit forms, and with an explanation of their meaning, will automatically proceed to segment them, if only to provide himself with a mnemonic aid. It is then likely that the similarity between some Sanskrit and some Greek or Latin morphs will lead him back to the more familiar forms and will induce him to look at them with different eyes. Conceivably this or a similar phenomenon contributed to the generally held assumption that Sanskrit was more transparent than the other European languages.

[28] The importance of the contact with Sanskrit grammarians had been mentioned before: cf., e.g., Gabelentz (1891:26), Pedersen (1962:21–2). In the 1950s the question has been the object of a short controversy between Emeneau (1955) and Master (1956). Emeneau argued that Sir William Jones's analyses were helped by Indian grammatical teaching in the Pāṇini tradition; Master has denied any influence of Pāṇini on Jones and indeed any originality in Jones's views on Indo-European, which he assumed were in part taken from Wilkins. A convincing answer has come from Emeneau (1971).

2.3 Even within the narrower limits imposed by dating the start of the comparative method at the end of the eighteenth century questions of evaluation and priority have arisen. Traditionally Bopp is hailed as the founder of comparative linguistics, but Arens (1969:165ff.) follows the line first developed by Benfey (1869:357ff.) and gives priority to Friedrich Schlegel. However, in his important book on the study of language in England from 1780 to 1860, Aarsleff (1967:124; cf. also 156 and note 112) points out that the credit normally given to Friedrich Schlegel as instigator of the new linguistic trend really belongs to Sir William Jones. Interestingly enough Aarsleff's challenge against the Schlegel 'orthodoxy' seems to proceed in parallel with the opposite challenge against the Bopp 'orthodoxy'. According to de Mauro (1970a: 84ff.) it is one of the great merits of Arens that he has modified decisively the traditional view which saw in the factual Bopp the founder of the new discipline. Wise words on the subject have been said by Timpanaro (1972a), who has put the question in its historical perspective. We might be somewhat amused by the parallelism of the two disputes but in fact there is a considerable difference between them. De Mauro's championing of Schlegel (and Humboldt) is in line with his wish to assert the continuity of linguistic thought from Leibniz to the nineteenth century; Aarsleff's interest in Sir William Jones vis-à-vis Schlegel is partly due to reaction against some of the 'mystical' attitudes of Schlegel, and partly to the observation that the fight against arbitrary etymologies, the emphasis on structural analysis of words, and the insistence on historical and comparative study of languages (Aarsleff 1967:156) had already found an expression in Jones's *Anniversary discourses*.[29]

It is doubtful whether those scholars who, like Hockett (1965:185), date the first break-through in linguistics to 1786 (the year in which Sir William Jones gave the third anniversary speech to the Asiatic Society at Calcutta and prounounced the famous statement about the relationship of Sanskrit with the other European languages) are doing this for the same historical reasons as Aarsleff. However, the contrast is there. For people like Lehmann (1967:7ff.), Lounsbury (1968:174) and up to a point Waterman (1963:15ff., where Schlegel is ignored) Jones has a prominent position; for others (Bonfante 1953:696–7; Hoenigswald 1963:2–3, Ivić 1970:33, Kukenheim 1966:41, Tagliavini 1968:50; etc.; Zeller 1967 ignores Jones altogether) Jones is a remote precursor and Schlegel and Bopp (or Rask) the founding fathers. Aarsleff's intervention has put the discussion on a somewhat different level, but it may be useful to remember that in this type of argument it is all too easy to confuse a number of problems.

The first task is that of extracting from the sources enough evidence to allow an evaluation of the scholar or scholars under consideration. In this case Aarsleff rightly complains that, with the exception of the all too famous 'philologer' passage, Jones is more quoted than read. Recently, Jones's life and work have been the object of numerous articles and monographs (cf. Arberry 1943–46, 1944, 1946, 1960, Cannon

[29] Aarsleff's line is entirely adopted by Salus (1969:15-6), but not, for example, by Koerner (1972a: 434, 1972c: 216).

1952, 1953, 1958, 1963, 1964, 1968, 1970, Chatterji 1948, Edgerton 1946, Emeneau 1955, 1971, Fan 1946, Kirketerp-Møller 1962, Lohuizen-de Leeuw 1948, Master 1946, 1956, Mukherjee 1968, Waley 1943–46, 1952), but most of them have concentrated on the Orientalist rather than on the Comparativist.[30] Aarsleff's (1967) analysis is far more detailed.

Secondly, there is a real question of priority, both in the use of particular techniques (grammatical comparison etc.) and in the formulation of a general outlook. As far as the techniques used in comparison are concerned, it is dubious whether priority belongs to the students of Indo-European languages (see above para. 2.12). In particular, interest in grammatical similarity seemed to be in the air in the second half of the eighteenth century. Both Arens (1969:136–46) and Timpanaro (1972a:78) have called attention in this respect to Kraus's review of Adelung's Mithridates published in 1787. Timpanaro has also recalled the importance attributed by Hervás to the 'artifizio delle lingue', i.e. to their grammar. It is worth stressing that in Hervás this is not an isolated dictum but is part of an interesting and well worked out theory about language plurality.[31] Even so, priority does not certainly belong to Hervás: Lázaro Carreter (1949:105–9) has identified some of the Spanish antecedents of his ideas. Heinz Pohrt (1964:328) has underlined the importance given to grammatical structure in the somewhat fantastic monogenetic views of K. G. von Anton [1751–1818]; Diderichsen (1960:106) has referred in this connection to Gatterer's *Einleitung in die synchronistische Universalhistorie* (1771), and A. L. von Schlözer's [1735–1809] views have also been mentioned (e.g. by Lauch 1968:279). Some of the studies on Finno-Ugrian have already been quoted (cf. above para. 2.12); for the earlier period Lakó (1970) has referred to Mikael Wexionius-Gyldenstolpe and to his 1650 work on the grammatical structure of Finnish and Estonian. This list could continue, but the point is abundantly proved already. Obviously, general outlook is more important, but less easily definable. It would be useful, for instance, to know how to interpret the fact that linguistic considerations were never primary in Jones's work in the way in which they were, e.g. in Bopp.[32]

Thirdly, a problem of influence and continuity arises. All too often, the real founder of a school is not the man who first formulated its tenets, but the man who managed to do so most effectively and who was then generally recognized as master. In the development of comparative linguistics, which according to Benfey (1869:15; cf.

[30] I have ignored those articles on Jones which do not give primary attention to his linguistic work. The biografies and the edition of his letters are quoted as sources of first-hand material and for further bibliography.

[31] In his *Saggio pratico delle lingue* (1787:17) Hervás argued: 'Gli idiomi per la loro sintassi differiscono più che non per le parole' and, later on (*ibid.* 53): 'consistendo la vera diversità degl'idiomi nella loro differente sintassi, a metter questa in chiaro lume sono necessarj i loro elementi grammaticali'. The interesting point, however, is that Hervás's theory about language relationship is coupled with a theory about language change (see below 3.91).

[32] Cf. above 1.4 and note 13. According to Aarsleff (1967:124) Jones's attitude to linguistics (which he considered a means rather than an end in itself) is a healthy sign of his rejection of the philosophical dreams of his predecessors and of a more empirical approach.

Robins 1967:170) is entirely German, what part is played by Jones the comparativist (as contrasted with Jones the Indologist, who was largely responsible for the wild enthusiasm with which Sanskrit literature was greeted in Europe)? We have evidence enough to prove unquestionably that the Anniversary Discourses were widely read, first of all by Schlegel (cf. Aarsleff 1967:156–7), but on the one side the extensive quotation of examples which Schlegel introduced into his 1808 book, and which Jones would have found impossible to introduce into the Discourses, was likely to be more impressive for potential followers, like the young Bopp; on the other side, in spite — or perhaps because — of some vagueness and nebulosity, Schlegel's philosophical background and what Aarsleff (1967:157) calls his 'nearly mystical idealism' helped to give the impression that the historical method and the comparison of languages could reveal endless new horizons (not only of an ethnological nature). This last point is perhaps more important than the rest, especially now that it is becoming more and more clear that not only the principle of grammatical comparison, but also the actual detailed comparison of forms in Sanskrit, Greek, Latin, German, etc. were not peculiar to Schlegel, let alone Bopp.[33] Some ten years ago Ludo Rocher (1961) published an interesting analysis of the comparative writings of Paulinus a Sancto Bartholomaeo, whose work appeared between 1790 and 1802; more recently Rosane Rocher (1968; cf. also R. Rocher 1970) has called attention to the man who taught Sanskrit to Schlegel, Alexander Hamilton. In an earlier article Chambers and Norman (1929) had reached the conclusion (to which R. Rocher subscribes) that the surprising coincidences between the observations made in Hamilton's review of Wilkins's Sanskrit Grammar (Hamilton 1809) and those of Schlegel's 1808 book (which Hamilton could not have read at the time) are due to the earlier influence of Hamilton on Schlegel. This is possible, and could perhaps serve as a further link between Jones and Schlegel. Even if it were mistaken, the coincidences would confirm that around the same time a number of scholars had reached — or was acquainted with — the same conclusions. What is not certain, however, is that the conclusions were in themselves shattering. They needed to be put in a more general framework, and this — with all its limitations — is what Schlegel could and did provide.[34]

[33] A recurrent priority question concerns the supposed discovery of the common origin of Sanskrit, Greek and Latin by the French Jesuit G. L. Coeurdoux, who would have preceded Jones by almost twenty years, though the letter in which he discussed his theories was not published until 1808. Edgerton (1946:236, note 44) pointed out that Coeurdoux's words cannot be interpreted in this sense, but this did not stop J. Godfrey (1967), who does not seem to have known Edgerton's article, from pressing Coeurdoux's claim again (nor A. Arlotto [1969] from refuting him).

[34] In order to emphasize the importance of Fr. Schlegel's work in the history of comparative linguistics, I cannot refrain from quoting an inedited letter by Rask, which I hope to publish soon. On 27 April 1824, Rask wrote to Joseph Bosworth, the Anglo-Saxon specialist, discussing some problems in the classification of the Germanic languages. In the course of the argument he reiterated his belief that 'the European languages of the Gothic stock are related to those of India and Persia' and concluded advising Bosworth to read Schlegel's 1808 book. This is significant, if we consider that by 1824 the subject had advanced far beyond the stage of *Ueber die Sprache und Weisheit der Indier*.

2.4 The names of Humboldt, Rask, Bopp and Grimm are regularly mentioned in any history of linguistic concerned with the development of the comparative method. We shall refer to the literature on Humboldt further on (see below para. 3.5). Some works about Rask have already been quoted (cf. p. 611): one of the encouraging tendencies in modern historiography is the concentration on a correct interpretation of Rask and Grimm rather than on the older questions of priority; even when the latter are raised the emphasis is different (cf., e.g., Antonsen 1962, Ginschel 1967: 357ff.). There has been a number of shorter contributions discussing particular aspects of Rask's life and work (Bjerrum 1956, 1957; Djupedal 1956a, 1956b, 1958, Clavería 1946; Henning 1963; Meisner 1972; Nordstrand 1955, 1961; Skårup 1960, 1964; Sletsjøe 1957; de Tollenaere 1948, 1951, 1953, 1954),[35] but undoubtedly the most important question was raised by Hjelmslev (1950–51): was Rask a typologist or an historical linguist. Hjelmslev favours the first hypothesis and argues that historical-comparative linguistics, in our sense of the word, really begins with Jacob Grimm; M. Bjerrum's monograph (1959), which is also rich in detailed analyses, seems to follow in this line, but with a number of qualifications. Independently of Hjelmslev's article and before Diderichsen's monograph an interesting contribution by F. de Tollenaere (1951) had adopted a mid-way position and shown some of the oscillations in Rask's thought, while firmly upholding his genealogical interests. Diderichsen's work (1960) has provided a clear analysis of Rask's background and interests, of his compromise between Romanticism and Rationalism, of the contrast between his and Grimm's approach to language, and also of his striving towards a genealogical classification. Undoubtedly it is, and will remain for some time, the standard work on Rask. More recently, Percival 1970 has discussed Rask's views on language change, as attested in his review of Grimm's *Deutsche Grammatik*.

2.41 Understandably Bopp's work has called for less attention; there was no need to vindicate someone who since 1833 at least had been hailed as the founder of the new linguistics (cf. Pätsch 1960:211, Orlandi 1962:528ff.). On the contrary, as we saw before, there have been attempts to remove Bopp from this enviable position in order to allow some of the aura which surrounds him to pass to Schlegel or to some earlier scholar (cf. above para. 2.3). However, in 1969 the 150th anniversary of Bopp's birth was celebrated by the Humboldt University in Berlin with a collection of shorter contributions on Bopp, some of which dealt rather interestingly with Bopp's solution of specific comparative problems (cf. Barschel 1969, Desnickaja 1969, Fiedler1969, Seidel 1969, Seidel-Slotty 1969, Sternemann 1969, Uhlish 1969; Valderrama 1969 does not belong to this series and does not really concern Bopp).

Other articles or sections of books have concentrated on Bopp's methodology and intellectual background (cf. Lohmann 1941, Neumann 1967, Orlandi 1962, Pätsch 1960, Rosiello 1967:173ff., Terracini 1949:61–72, Verburg 1949–50, as well as the

[35] Unfortunately I have not been able to see two recent works on Rask: one is the commentary (Bjerrum 1968) which has followed the earlier publication of his letters (cf. Hjelmslev 1941), the second is a 1971 monograph by G. A. Piebenga about Rask's Frisian grammar.

histories of linguistics quoted in the bibliography). In contrast to the traditional image of Bopp as an exponent of Romanticism, deeply influenced by Humboldt's ideas (cf. Terracini 1949), Verburg (1949–50) has effectively underlined the rationalistic slant of his interests, his connection with a tradition of linguistic thought started by Leibniz, and the static aspect of his view of language comparison if contrasted, e.g. with that of Grimm. Orlandi (1962) has brought the argument even further in his attempt to show that an understanding of Bopp can only come from a study of his concrete work as contrasted with his theoretical statements. According to him Bopp's only aim was that of using Sanskrit as a parameter or a lens to systematize the empirical data provided by the various languages (cf. also Lohmann 1941): his interests were not historical but methodological. This thesis, to which Rosiello (1967) seems to subscribe, may be too extreme; we should not forget that Bopp is really looking for a historical explanation of the forms in which he is interested. Terracini (1949) is probably right when he maintains that Bopp uses comparison and history to solve a problem of general linguistics. Neumann's (1967:16) point that Bopp applies to linguistics that principle of 'genetische Erklärung' to which Herder had given a theoretical expression is relevant. If Bopp believed (with a number of his contemporaries) that a correct explanation of any phenomenon could only be obtained by going back to its origin, then he must also have realized that his systematic interests were better served by a historical approach. A balanced view is perhaps that of Pätsch (1960), who recognizes in Bopp both a number of Romantic ideas and a strong rationalistic streak, but we still need a new synthesis to take into account Verburg's findings and to replace the well-informed but quasi-hagiographic biography by Lefmann (1891–97). Possibly this will refute or clarify the often quoted dictum by Meillet (1937:458) that 'Bopp a trouvé la grammaire comparée en cherchant à expliquer l'indo-européen, comme Christophe Colomb a découvert l'Amérique en cherchant la route des Indes' (cf. Mounin 1967:174, Leroy 1971:21). If Columbus really meant to reach the Indies, America could only be an obstacle in his way, but — in 1816 at least — for Bopp the 'discovery', or rather the exploitation, of the comparative method was a necessary factor in the demonstration of the point which he had set out to prove: the agglutinative origin of the inflectional forms.[36]

2.42 It is hopeless to try to give in a few lines a survey of the recent work on Jacob Grimm. A number of contributions which are primarily concerned with the man, the collector of folk tales, the patriot, the German philologist, the comparative mythologist, etc., also provide some accidental information about the linguist. Denecke 1971 may serve as an introduction to this multifarious literature. Our bibliography only mentions articles and monographs of prevailing linguistic interest and

[36] It is well known that Bopp argued — against Fr. Schlegel — that a number of Indo-European inflections arose from the agglutination of monosyllabic roots with pronominal elements or with forms of the verb 'to be'. For the further history of this view it is still worthwhile to consult Pagliaro (1930:64ff.). We still lack a history of agglutinative theories, but Timpanaro (1972a:83 note 35) has announced that he will discuss the earlier origins of the doctrine and its diffusion in the eighteenth century in a forthcoming paper. Cf. also *infra* note 121.

ignores both the general biographies and the editions of primary sources, like documents, letters, etc. While in the case of Rask and Bopp it is possible to recognize some definite historiographical tendencies at work, the same is difficult to establish for Grimm. Some recent articles are concerned with background information and with specific Germanic problems (cf. Antonsen 1962, Bergsveinsson 1965, Bondzio 1965, Henning 1963, Hiehle 1949, Kunze 1957, Löther 1965, Mojasevic 1963, Peukert 1964, 1966, Pfeifer 1963, Schoof 1941, 1963a, 1963b, 1963–64, 1967, Trier 1964, Wanner 1963) or with questions of terminology (Ginschel 1955; cf. also Telegdi 1966, 1967a). A substantial contribution is G. Ginschel's attempt (1967) to trace Grimm's intellectual biography and to emphasize his originality both in the ideas which he shared with Savigny and the *Historische Schule* and in his approach to historical linguistics. A few other articles aim at a general assessment, and here too we sometimes recognize a reaction against the traditional view of Grimm: the stress is often put on the a-priori, non-historical and non-empirical elements of his thought (cf. Hermann 1965, Spreu 1965, and the very interesting discussion in Heinimann 1967 of the outlook of Grimm, Diez, and Meyer-Lübke). However, it is difficult to deny that, even when allowance has been made for these elements, there is in Grimm an overwhelming interest in historical development and in national language; this has often been reasserted (cf. Ginschel 1967, Hammerich 1963, Löther 1965, Ulmer 1951, and especially Arndt 1965). An interesting contrast is provided by two works both of which set out to compare Humboldt's and Grimm's 'Sprachauffassungen': Beneš (1958) and Schwankweiler (1965). Schwankweiler is eager to point out the common ground on which Humboldt and Grimm move (social character of language, historical conception, organicistic views etc.), while Beneš aims at stressing the differences both in their conceptions of language and in the largely historical approach of Grimm as against the descriptive and systematic interests of Humboldt. Finally, the 'modernity' of Jacob Grimm has been underlined by R. A. Fowkes (1964) in a rather schematic list of the seven chief services which he has contributed to linguistics (cf. also Arndt 1965, Waterman 1963:20–30, and the very interesting observations of Telegdi 1967b).

2.5 What were the arguments used to demonstrate genetic relationship? Historians of linguistics seem to agree that by the beginning of the nineteenth century the emphasis was on structural similarity rather than on lexical equivalences. Regularity of sound correspondences was sometimes mentioned, but certainly not by all linguists.

It is easy to give the wrong impression: even in the golden period of structural similarity, lexical correspondences were by no means neglected. In fact, the history of the way in which they were used both before and during the nineteenth century would deserve a separate study, similar to that which Mary Haas has dedicated to Amerindian linguistics in her paper on *Grammar or lexicon*? (Haas 1969). At present it is not easy — if indeed possible — to find out from the relevant histories of linguistics how well defined at any one time were notions which subsequently became banal, such as those of loan-word, of fundamental vocabulary (which is less subject to change), of lexical similarities due to onomatopoeia, etc. Certainly we find them all in Hervás, but they did not start with him. In Adelung's *Mithridates* (1806–17:I xiii) we also find the observation (which need not be original) that the relationship of languages can only be shown through the comparison of root syllables, and the warning that comparison must be preceded by a correct identification of the root, in order to avoid equating e.g. Gr. *anainomai* with any word including just *an*, *na* or *in*.[37]

Equally important — and perhaps more so — would be to trace the development of the criterion of structural similarity; at the moment we only have odd observations about the use made of it by individual authors (for the earlier period see above para. 2.3). Timpanaro (1972a:80ff.) points out that in Friedrich Schlegel it assumed an almost mystical, *a priori* value and became the absolute criterion for the classification of languages. This attitude is contrasted with that of e.g. Gyarmathi and Rask who reached the criterion inductively through their own experience of work on language. It would be possible to challenge this last point for Rask, whose methodology, though different from that of Schlegel, is not always determined by empirical considerations, as Diderichsen (1960) has shown (but cf. also Bjerrum 1959 *passim*). In the case of Gyarmathi we should like to know much more about the influences which he underwent in his Göttingen days.

So far it does not seem that we have sufficient evidence to allow the emphasis on structural similarity to be traced back to its origins. It is tempting to recognize in it (with Lázaro-Carreter 1949:108–10) a much older influence: that of the Aristotelian-Tomistic distinction between *forma* and *materia* and that of the identification of *forma* with the *nexus partium grammaticalium*. The 'formal' criterion would first become a mark of distinction between different languages and then a criterion for genetic affinity. However, it is possible that even in this case the end of the eighteenth and the beginning of the nineteenth century signal the merging of two different traditions: a 'philosophical', theory-oriented, one and a data-oriented one which arises from the practical experience of comparative work.

Two main problems concern (a) the exact definition of the structural similarity criterion and (b) the purposes for which it is used.

The first question arises because of ambiguities in formulation. Given the morphological-syntactical slant which the criterion acquires, it could conceivably refer to similarity in grammatical categories independently of the form in which they are expressed (as in the case of e.g. Ancient Greek and Ostjak which show a similar contrast of singular/dual/plural in noun inflection). Alternatively it could refer to a functional and formal similarity of morphemes (as in the case of e.g. the Sanskrit verbal endings *-mi*, *-si*, *-ti* compared with the Greek *-mi*, *-(s)i*, *-ti*, three morphs which fulfill the same functions as the Sanskrit ones).

[37] For Adelung's definition of language relationship see also Jankowsky (1972:33ff.). For some reflections on the use of lexical comparison, cf. Gatterer quoted by Diderichsen (1960:106). Kylstra (1961:3ff.) offers a useful study of the work done from the seventeenth century onwards on Finnish vocabulary and its connections with that of Germanic.

We may want to ask how real these alternatives are and whether the criterion of structural similarity was in fact used in both these interpretations, but for the moment it may be convenient to leave these questions aside and to turn to the second of the problems mentioned above, *viz.* the purpose for which the criterion was used. It should be clear, by now, what this means. If structural similarity is taken in the first of the two meanings indicated, a comparison based on it may (though need not) lead to a typological and not to a genetic classification. If genetic (or genealogical) classification is what is aimed at, the second meaning should apply. Was this always clear? We are once again back to the problem mentioned in 1.6: did all nineteenth century scholars make a clear distinction between the two types of classification?

None of these questions is answered in the standard histories of linguistics, though we find occasional hints. Here we cannot deal with them at length, but it may be worthwhile to give some references to relevant authors, if only to show that the problems do in fact exist.

In the introduction to his *Mithridates* Adelung (1806–1817:I xii) argued that it was useless to give a list of grammatical 'Erscheinungen' in order to prove language kinship, since many languages may share them without being related. This (a) confirms that the structural criterion was already in operation before Adelung (as we knew) and (b) shows that Adelung understood it in the first of the two ways mentioned.[38] Shortly after, we find that the primary importance given by Friedrich Schlegel to the criterion leads indeed to some confusion: in his 1808 book we are told that all inflectional languages are organic and that all organic languages are related (cf. Timpanaro 1972a). The distinction between the two types of classification is there, but only in nuce; not for nothing has Schlegel been acclaimed as the founder of both comparative linguistics and typological classification (see below 3.4). At a much later stage, when the 'morphological' classification was well established, Max Müller could still claim on structural grounds that all Turanian (i.e. agglutinative) languages were related (F. Max Müller 1854). Pott's fierce rebuke (1855) is worth reading.[39]

So much for the ambiguity; now for the clarification. Humboldt and Pott may well serve as protagonists.

In an Essay which was read to the Asiatic Society in 1828 (but published in 1830), and is an outstanding explanation of the aims and methods of comparative linguistics, Humboldt (1903–36:VI 76–84) argued that even the fundamental vocabulary cannot be guaranteed against the intrusion of foreign elements, warned against any comparison based exclusively on lexicon, and finally maintained that 'if two languages ... exhibit grammatical forms which are identical in arrangement, and have a close analogy in their sounds, we have an incontestable proof that these two languages

[38] Aarsleff (1967:132) refers to Jones's statement that Arabic could not be related to Sanskrit because 'Arabick ... and all its sister dialects, abhor the composition of words ...'. This is a typical example of an observation for which it is impossible to indentify the underlying concept of grammatical similarity.

[39] Also interesting is Whitney's attempt (1867:291ff.) to argue that structural similarity (in Max Müller's sense) is not a sufficient, but an additional criterion for demonstrating language kinship.

belong to the same family'.[40] He then explained at length, with a number of examples and counterexamples, what was meant by 'close analogy in their sounds', and why this qualification was fundamental.[41] The tone is that of someone fully aware that he was introducing a concept which needed clarification. Further on he proceeded to distinguish 'between the real affinity of languages, which presumes a filiation as it were among the nations who speak them, and that degree of relation which is purely historical, and only indicates temporary and accidental connexions among nations'.[42]

It was Pott who made the distinction between 'physiological' and 'genealogical' classification into one of the leit-motivs of his life work.[43] Physiological classification — we are told — is determined according to 'den Besonderheiten der Structur und dem durch sie bedingten Sprachcharakter, welche sich auch bei genealogisch-verschiedenen Sprachen gleichartig zeigen können' (Pott 1833–36: I xxvi). The same points were often repeated and amplified, since Pott did not hesitate to describe in detail the task of the comparativist. That his arguments were not without influence is shown inter alia by the remarkable introduction which Böhtlingk added to his *Ueber die Sprache der Jakuten* (1851) where terminology and concepts first found in Pott are recognizable, though here they are sharpened to an even higher level of critical awareness.

2.51 In addition to lexical and structural similarity, a third criterion, that of regular 'letter permutations', i.e. sound correspondences, is also mentioned. Rask

[40] By way of contrast we can refer to A. W. Schlegel's 1833 essay *De l'origine des Hindous* (cf. A. W. Schlegel 1846: III, 24–93, especially 64 and 82), where it is repeatedly stated that comparison must start with grammar, but the concept of grammatical comparison is never closely defined and the ambiguity persists. Ten years before the date of Schlegel's essay, Julius von Klaproth (1823: ix–x) had argued that *Stammverwandtschaft* (which he distinguished from *allgemeine Sprachverwandtschaft* which joined all languages) was mainly founded on word-similarity. The comparison of grammatical structures — he maintained — was not useless, since it helped to illuminate the development and progress of human *Geist*, but came into its own only when it served to establish the similarities or differences of dialects (as contrasted with languages). Once more the concept of *grammatischer Bau* is not closely defined.

[41] Most of the same points were made by Humboldt — with more detailed explanations — in his 1827–29 work *Ueber die Verschiedenheiten des menschlichen Sprachbaues* (cf. Humboldt 1903–36: VI, 248f. and especially 250): 'Die Gleichheit der grammatischen Form in dem hier angedeuteten Sinne genommen, ist daher allein das die Einerleiheit der Sprache bedingende. Allein und für sich würde sie indess nicht hinreichen, dieselbe in zwei Sprachen zu beurkunden, wenn dabei das Lautsystem unbeachtet bliebe.' Further on he expressed much the same idea, spoke of the correspondences of 'concrete' grammatical forms, and then concluded (*ibid.* 254): 'Entkleidet man die Sprachform von ihren Lauten und lässt man bloss den Begriff, die Behandlungsart ihrer Wörter in der verbundenen Rede, in ihr zurück, so berechtigt sie durchaus zu keinem Schluss auf geschichtlichen Zusammenhang.'

[42] It is perhaps worth mentioning that as late as 1885 K. Abel found it worthwhile to give extensive quotations of — and in practice to reprint — Humboldt's 1828 essay in his own article *Zur Frage nach den Kennzeichen der Sprachverwandtschaft* (1885).

[43] I am indebted to Mrs. Joan Leopold for parts of what is said here and elsewhere (cf. especially 2.61) about Pott. – As G. Pätsch (1967: 107ff.) has shown, Humboldt too had earlier made a distinction similar to that of Pott. Structural similarity — he argued — could prove membership of a linguistic class, but could not prove genetic relationship; cf. e.g. Humboldt (1903–36: VI, 254): 'Die Semitischen Sprachen stehen den Sanskritischen ... sehr viel näher, als beiden die Koptische und andre in die gleiche Kategorie gehörende, allein die Aehnlichkeit scheint doch nur eine Classenverwandtschaft, auf keine Weise eine zu Voraussetzung geschichtlichen Zusammenhanges berechtigende.'

and Grimm are normally quoted in this connection (cf., e.g., Leroy 1971:19, Mounin 1967:165, Waterman 1963:21, etc.) and in most histories of linguistics the history of the criterion appears to be inextricably linked with that of the discovery of the Germanic Lautverschiebung. In his brief sketch of earlier phonetic work, Timpanaro (1972a:78) has pointed out the arbitrariness of the method by which before the nineteenth century phonetic alternations were established for one language and then invested with general validity. Even so, he admits that some more serious work had been done, though not in the Indo-European field, and quotes with respect Turgot's statement (in his article on etymology for the *Encyclopédie*) that phonetic phenomena require historical study and that some changes are limited to individual languages. However, Sajnovics (quoted by Timpanaro) and Turgot are perhaps less isolated and less original than they seem. The contributions of J. E. Fischer have been mentioned in 2.12. In the Indo-European field we may choose to ignore the long list of scholars who anticipated parts at least of Grimm's law (cf. Arens 1969:192f., Jankowsky 1972:72, and especially Agrell 1955), but Sommerfelt (1952) has called attention to some impressive contributions by Edward Lhuyd [1660–1709]. Not only do we find in his works a long list of sound correspondences between some Indo-European languages, but it is also said that it is necessary to distinguish between letters and their 'potestates' and between 'idiomatal' and 'accidental' alternations, i.e. between alternations which can be established for one particular language and alternations which recur in an accidental way. The regularity of sound correspondences is considered to be a proof of common origin. The list of precursors could be lengthened, but perhaps the most important contribution in recent years has been Diderichsen's analysis (1960:66ff.) of the direct link which joins Rask and one of them. As early as 1737 G. J. Wachter distinguished between sound alternations due to articulatory similarity and sound alternations peculiar to one given language. Rask took up and developed this principle, which is not new in him. His own thought, on the other hand, includes a number of layers, some of which are far from 'modern'. In the *Undersøgelse* published in 1818 (cf. Rask 1932–35: vol. I) three arguments which are considered equally important are advanced to prove the kinship between Greek and Icelandic: (a) the two languages (if correctly interpreted) have the same sounds; (b) they show the same rules of 'euphony'; (c) they show regular sound alternations (here the Lautverschiebung is explained). In other words, at this stage Rask does not yet distinguish between a typological statement (two languages have the same or a similar phonemic inventory and similar morphophonemic rules) and a historical statement intended to prove genealogical relationship. Yet Diderichsen (1960) has abundantly demonstrated in the course of his argument with Hjelmslev (1950–51) that genealogical relationship was what Rask was aiming at.

We may leave aside the rather tiresome question whether Grimm did or did not improve on Rask's formulation of the Germanic Lauverschiebung (cf. the opposite views of e.g. Jespersen 1922: 41ff. and Waterman 1963:20f.), but it is worth observing that Grimm, who certainly aimed at demonstrating the kinship of the Indo-European languages, concluded his discussion of the Lautverschiebung with the statement that 'Aus dem verhältnis der consonanten geht also genügender beweis einer urverwandtschaft der verglichenen sprachen hervor' (Grimm 1822:592). The next question discussed is whether the same type of correspondence applies to the vowels.

In the history of linguistics Rask and Grimm, and after them R. von Raumer, Pott and Schleicher count as 'phonetically-minded', i.e. as interested in sound correspondences. What was the position of their contemporaries? This has not been closely discussed, or, at least, not recently. Pätsch (1960:218) rightly reproaches Delbrück for his unduly severe attitude towards Bopp's lack of rigour in his treatment of sound laws.[44] The point is that any history of neogrammarian inspiration is likely to notice the cavalier behaviour towards phonetic correspondences and not to make any further distinctions. What we should like to know for Bopp — and are not told — is how much importance he assigns to a certain type of sound correspondences as a convincing argument for genetic relationship. It is sufficient, however, to read the introduction to Bopp's 1833 *Vergleichende Grammatik* to see how all-important grammar is for him and how much sound correspondences were to take a second place, if they had a place at all. If Delbrück (1880:23f.) is unjust towards Bopp, Jespersen (1922:34) is no less unfair towards Schlegel, on whom he pours scorn for his self-imposed rule to compare only phonetically similar or identical words (cf. also Jankowsky 1972:53). Humboldt's position has been partly discussed by Pätsch (1967:107), who in spite of her close acquaintance with the sources, does not seem to make use of the 1828 paper quoted above (in 2.5). There Humboldt argued that in order to establish the common origin of two or more languages the systems of sounds and 'regular transformations of sounds' should be considered, but grammar is the decisive factor — in fact a position not very different from that of Rask. But in the almost contemporaneous *Ueber die Verschiedenheiten des menschlichen Sprachbaues* Humboldt (1903–36:VI 250) distinguished between 'dem Lautsystem in Allgemeinen, und concreten Lauten in Wörtern und grammatischen Formen' and argued that the comparison of the former did not lead very far; the real proof of kinship was given by the comparison of grammatical forms. In related languages these either appeared unaltered or almost unaltered, or could be traced back to each other 'nach aufzufinden Gesetzen' (*ibid.*: 267). In other words, as appears elsewhere, and as Pätsch has argued, Humboldt has formulated the concept of a sound law (though not, obviously, in the neogrammarians' sense), but still for him grammar remains the most important factor in proving kinship (cf. also Kovács 1971:223ff.). Why this is so, is again something which should be discussed, but the answer is probably to be found in Humboldt's concept of *Sprachform* as residing in grammatical structure (cf. Humboldt 1907–36:

[44] The reference is to Delbrück (1880:23f.) who pours scorn on Bopp's attempt at demonstrating the relationship of the Malay-Polynesian languages with Indo-European. In fact the monograph which Bopp (1841) dedicated to the subject is worth reading. Among other things it demonstrates that Bopp believed that the grammatical structure of a language could change to the point of becoming unrecognizable, and that other criteria had then to be used in order to prove genetic relationship.

VI 248), i.e. not in an empirical heuristic reason dictated by experience of comparison (though this probably played a part) but in a particular view of language and of language change.

2.6 What are the developments of the comparative method after Bopp? And how are they described by modern historiography? The second question is not easy to answer; if hitherto we could complain of a lack of attention to some specific problems, but also of an embarras de richesse from the bibliographical point of view, now the situation is reversed. If we exclude the general histories of linguistics, for the second part of the century we can list only some work on Ascoli and Schleicher (largely of a biographical nature), and some very recent work on the neogrammarians and the precursors of de Saussure. Steinthal, whom we shall discuss elsewhere, has recently received some attention (see below 3.71). The standard view, as represented in most histories of linguistics, has not varied greatly over the years: it sees the period between the later 1830s and the '70s as a period of increased philological knowledge of the various languages, of greater interest in phonetics, of more solid etymologizing and of slow progress towards the concept of a sound law in the stricter sense.[45] It also posits a contrast, greater or lesser, according to the historian's tendency, between the time at which the neogrammarians' influence made itself felt and the earlier part of the century. This is the period of Pott's *Etymologische Forschungen* (1st ed. 1833–36, 2nd ed. 1859–76), of von Raumer's etymological work, of Schleicher's *Compendium* (1861–62), and in more limited domains of Miklosich's *Vergleichende Grammatik der slavischen Sprachen* (1852-74), of Diez's *Grammatik der romanischen Sprachen* (1836–44), and of Zeuss's *Grammatica celtica* (1853). Mounin (1967:176) partly follows this tradition when he discusses the various historiographical attempts to distinguish a period in which comparative work was the main interest from a period geared towards historical research, and wonders where to draw the line: after the thirties, with Kukenheim, or between the sixties and the seventies, with Meillet.[46] But, as Mounin is the first to point out, definitions of comparative and historical grammar vary and in most cases it is difficult, if not impossible, to distinguish between work prompted by the one or the other interest. Two other factors complicate the question. First, this is the time of the merging of two traditions which in some cases had remained separated, that of philological work based on the examination of the texts (be they classical or Germanic or Romance) and that of comparative study. Secondly, it is also the time in which national contrasts become clearer. We may recall, for instance, Aarsleff's study (1967) and its conclusion that a new approach to philology was introduced to England

[45] The history of phonetics is dealt with elsewhere in this volume. It would be interesting to follow from the middle of the century onwards the beginning of a functional theory of phonetic distinctions: cf., e.g., Imart (1968) on Uslar, and Lepschy (1962:190, note 123) about some observations by Max Müller.

[46] In any case some work on language change as such seems to have been produced at all periods: for Bredsdorff's views see above, note 19.

by two scholars who had been in direct contact with Rask and Grimm. The German situation was very different, as we know, and the position of France, where comparative studies were introduced at a relatively late date, diverse again. In Italy too the problems discussed and the prevailing trends had their own distinctive character (cf. Timpanaro 1969).

2.61 Arens (1969:228ff.) groups Pott, von Raumer, Steinthal (or at least that part of his work which concerns classification), Curtius and Schleicher under the heading 'Der Weg zur Naturwissenschaft'. No doubt these scholars, with the possible exception of Steinthal, share a greater interest in phonology than e.g. Bopp, but here too it would probably be worthwhile to stress the differences rather than the similarities.[47]

Pott may be mentioned as a test case. All too often he is remembered only because of Meillet's praise for his statement that the discovery of the Germanic Lautverschiebung was more important a result than many a philosophy of language (cf. Leroy 1971:20, de Mauro 1963:145, 1970a:89 [and 88]). Together with his etymological work (for which see Thieme 1952–53) this may have given the impression that he marks the beginning of that narrower and more specialized approach for which the linguists of the second half of the century have been so often reproached (or praised). The contrary is true, and what is so interesting in Pott is just his combination of a wide spectrum of anthropological, philosophical and linguistic concerns with a willingness to explore the methodology of his subject and its limitations. His distinction between genealogical and physiological enquiry (cf. above p. 628) and his polemics against any superficial exploitation of half-baked doctrines (cf., e.g., his attack against Max Müller) fit within this picture — as also does his determined fight against the confusion of language and race (cf., e.g., Pott 1852:508 and Pott 1856). At a time when language comparison was reaching its peak of success, he was no less aware of the limitations of genealogical classification: a comparison of syntax and style in different languages — he wrote in 1833 — may be less profitable for an enquiry into 'Völkergenealogieen, desto fruchtbarere aber für Geistes-, Menschen- und Völkercharakteristik' (Pott 1833–36:I xx).

Jankowsky (1972:83-8), who is among the few modern scholars who remember

[47] Arens (1969) ignores J. N. Madvig [1804–1886] in spite of the theoretical interest of his monographs and articles on linguistics, but this lack of interest for the Danish philologist is shared by most histories of linguistics. Earlier exceptions are Thomsen (1927:64ff.) and Jespersen (1922:84f.). More recently, Devoto (1958) has called attention to a number of motifs in Madvig's work which anticipate much later research: his interest in language change rather than in language comparison, the emphasis he put on the social character of language, the distinction he made between study of etymology and study of word-meanings, etc. De Mauro (1970a) has frequently quoted Bréal and Madvig as upholders of those syntactical and semantic interests which were shunned by most linguists 'who went the way of Pott' (but see below). Coseriu (1967b) has mentioned Madvig and Whitney in his history of 'l'arbitraire du signe', and Jensen (1958) has assessed his importance in the history of Danish philology. However, from the point of view of the history of linguistics, the most important contribution has been K.F. Johansen's lengthy introduction to his edition of Madvig's *Sprachtheoretische Abhandlungen* (cf. Madvig 1971:1–46; for Madvig see also below, note 57 and 3.10).

Pott at all, seems to agree with Arens in seeing in him an immediate precursor of Schleicher and an upholder of 'the inherent similarity between language study and the natural sciences'. But this, like Arens' heading, remains vague; if taken in a very precise sense, it is likely to be wrong. Pott, an Humboldtian, was fully conscious of the difference in methodologies required for his subject and for any scientific discipline — and he was at pains to make this explicit. In his discussion of the contrast between genealogical and physiological classification he emphasized that it was the latter which came nearer to scientific classification and at the same time he specified where the similarity lay (Pott 1856:197). Elsewhere he seemed to imply that there was no reason why languages should not move in opposite ways: e.g. not only from synthetic to analytic, but also from analytic to synthetic (1852:514, cf. also 1856:214f.). This would presumably clash with a theory of language as an organism which develops according to fixed rules: that Pott was no Schleicherian is no mystery (cf. Pott 1856: 213f. about the non-independent existence of languages).

2.7 According to most histories of linguistics a rather curious combination of approaches and results marks Schleicher's contributions to the study of language. His system seems to embrace a Hegelian belief in a process of prehistoric growth followed by historical decay, a Darwinian theory of evolution, a greater rigour in the application of sound laws, the *Stammbaumtheorie*, and finally an interest in the reconstruction of *Ursprachen*. Together with this goes his claim that linguistics, or *Glottik*, is a natural science and not a form of historical knowledge (a task reserved for philology) and that all languages may be classified into three classes (isolating, agglutinative and inflectional).

The specific work about him emphasizes one or the other of these points. If we leave aside a few biographical and documentary articles (Dietze 1960, 1964, 1965a, 1965b, 1969, Fischer 1953–54, 1961a, 1961b, 1962, 1963) we are left with the 1958 dissertation by Beneš who sees Schleicher's comparative work as a continuation and systematization of Bopp's achievements and at the same time as the precursor of all subsequent further contributions in the field of Indo-European studies. In his general work she is eager to stress Humboldt's influence. In a more detailed monograph Dietze (1966) deals with Schleicher's life and work and then concentrates on his achievements in the Slavonic field. Trnka's appreciation (1952) is largely biographical and offers only a few general (but interesting) comments. Maher (1966) has rightly argued against the common belief in Darwin's influence on Schleicher and has shown that the chronological data, Schleicher's own statements about his intellectual development, and, above all, his non-Darwinian approach to the theory of evolution, conflict with this assumption. For his part Cassirer (1945:109ff.) has emphasized that Schleicher's system is built on an ontological interpretation of that organic theory of language which is at least as old as Herder (cf. above 1.5). Thus both Cassirer and Maher (cf. also Putschke 1969) appear to see in Schleicher a scholar tied in outlook and interests to the first part of the century. On the other side Percival (1969) has stressed the continuity between some of Schleicher's general views (e.g. about language difference and general grammar) and those of scholars like Bloomfield.[48] This contrast may provide a means of assessing some of his achievements: do they point to a systematizer or to an innovator?

Pulgram (1953) has argued that the family tree model of language genealogy (i.e. the so-called *Stammbaumtheorie*) is only a schematization of the views generally held in Schleicher's time or before (cf. also Jankowsky 1972:106). Hoenigswald (1963:6f.) has assumed that both the family tree model and the techniques which Schleicher used in reconstruction show a strong influence of the techniques of textual criticism which Schleicher must have learnt during his classical training. Timpanaro (1963:73ff.), who has covered much the same ground, though in more general terms, is more doubtful, but points out that the comparison between textual criticism and linguistic reconstruction was explicitly made by Georg Curtius, Schleicher's friend and colleague. So far we have been looking backward, but other points may reverse the situation. Pisani (1949) does not hesitate to stress the inherent contradictions in Schleicher's theory, but also emphasizes his influence. Pulgram (1953), preceded by Leskien (cf. Jankowsky *loc. cit.*), points out that the *Stammbaumtheorie* still has modern validity. Timpanaro (*loc. cit.*) seems to argue that Schleicher marks a dividing line after which the development of textual criticism and that of the comparative method proceed in the parallel. More important, even the sound law question and the *Ursprache* reconstruction can appear under two different aspects. The polemics of the neogrammarians against Schleicher are well known, and equally well known is Johannes Schmidt's reply (1886) stressing how important the *Lautgesetze* were for Schleicher. These two viewpoints have their reflection in modern historiography. For Kovács (1971:235), who, admittedly, is an extreme case, Schleicher 'and his followers (Osthoff and especially Brugman) fought doggedly to make the principle of 'iron consistency' and 'exceptionless' accepted'. But for Robins (1967:183), Schleicher was not 'troubled by apparent exceptions to the general run of sound changes in the language'. Similarly, Schleicher's reconstructions have appeared as the culmination of the early nineteenth-century interest in primitive language (cf. Leroy 1971:23), but also as a preliminary to Saussure's Indo-European work (Pisani 1949).[49]

[48] Unfortunately I have not been able to see Häusler's article on *Jan Baudouin de Courtenays Kritik an der Sprachtheorie August Schleichers*, quoted by Koerner (1972:65, note 8); the reference to GZH (*sic*, but GHZ?) 10 (1967) seems to be wrong. However, for the contrast between Schleicher and Baudouin see Häusler 1968 (27–33). Similarly, I have not been able to find A. Sabaliauskas 1969; Desnickaja 1971 came to my notice too late to be used here. Among the older contributions two articles by Streitberg (1897, 1909–10) are still very important.

[49] Jankowsky (1972:102ff.) has put up a spirited defence of Schleicher's reconstructions, but long before him Delbrück (1880:49), and especially Kretschmer (1896:8) had argued that it was far from certain that Schleicher did in fact attribute an historical value to his starred forms. The whole question of what is assumed to be the purpose and value of reconstruction at different moments of the history of linguistics would merit a discussion of its own. It is all too easy to give the impression that because Schleicher was the first to make constant use of starred forms he was also the first who thought of reconstruction at all, but we should not forget, inter alia, the intense work on Indo-European *Alter-*

The banal truth is probably that Schleicher succeeded better than anyone else in extracting the implications of a number of ideas which had been floating round for some time and to organize them into a system. The result is the impression of striking clarity which is left from the reading of any of his works, even when they are marred by contradictions and inconsistencies. Schleicher's courage and his determined attempts to carry any argument to its logical conclusion had the result that his successors could take sides for or against him in full awareness of what the points at issue were and what the consequencies were of accepting or rejecting them.[50]

2.71 It is regrettable that no attempt has been made to analyze the full import of Schleicher's ideas about language classification. As we have seen, his *Stammbaumtheorie* and his concepts of *Ursprache* and typological classification are often mentioned; yet it is rarely said — if at all — that Schleicher is one of the first scholars who, while being fully aware of the distinction between 'morphological' and genealogical classification, made an honest effort to propose an integrated theory which took account of them both. The starting point is Schleicher's assumption that genealogical relationship is not proved by structural similarity but by sound correspondences. This is not new: we have seen the beginning of the theory in Rask and Grimm and noted Humboldt's and Pott's contributions (cf. above 2.5 and 2.51). Practically the same statement was made by Böhtlingk (1851:xxvf.). What is new is the clarity with which Schleicher proceeds to ask some other questions: if there were two languages which belonged to two different morphological classes but were genealogically related, should we be able to recognize such a case of genealogical relationship? And are there two languages in this position? According to Schleicher, the answer to the first question can be positive (since the proof or relationship is no more based on grammatical structure but on sound correspondences). The answer to the second question is negative; that is to say — Schleicher argued — since we have no examples of the phenomenon, there is no reason to suppose that it ever occurred. Schleicher's final conclusion is that genealogical relationship implies membership of the same morphological class (though the converse is not true) and that consequently the first subdivisions of each morphological class can be the *Sprachstämme*. The next step is then that of looking for further subdivisions of each *Sprachstamm* and these are to be found in the *Sprachfamilien*, which in their turn are subdivided into *Sprachen* or *Mundarten*.[51] Given the framework in which it is inserted, it would then

---

tumskunde which started in the first part of the nineteenth century (the names of Adalbert Kuhn and Adolphe Pictet come to mind in this connection) and which by its own nature was based on some form of reconstruction (for some recent discussion of it see Pisani 1966, and for a more detailed account Schrader 1890:1–148).

[50] Koerner (1972c:216–17) has tried to make explicit the reasons which justify a distinction in the history of linguistics between a pre- and a post- 1865–70 period; among his points is the fact that Schleicher's *Compendium* (1861–2) represented 'the synthesis of the Indo-European linguistics of the first two thirds of the 19th century' (cf. also Putschke 1969).

[51] Most of this paragraph is based on the first chapter of the introduction to *Die deutsche Sprache* (Schleicher 1869); some other points will be discussed later (cf. 3.7).

appear that the family tree model has both a genealogical and a typological value. In other words, the members of a language family are joined by a common historical origin and by a number of typological features which they share. This is worth pointing out, because it is probably at the origin of a number of methodological hesitations which accompanied the attempts at sub-grouping the Indo-European languages.

However, even when the typological implications were ignored, the family tree model served to give a graphic representation of a series of problems which were being discussed at the time. The question was no longer: how do we prove genetic or genealogical relationship? It had become: in a group of related languages, how do we conceive of the relationship of one language to the others? The same problem could be put in dynamic terms: how does it happen that any *Ursprache* or any language splits into more than one language or dialect?[52] As became clear later, the *Stammbaumtheorie* could serve as a model for language classification and also as a model for the process of language change and differentiation. In some of Schleicher's formulations it also provided a concrete representation of the development and prehistory of the Indo-European languages. It could be tested (and attacked) from at least three different angles, and the following developments showed that the opportunity was not missed.[53]

2.8 If we try to follow the history — and the historiography — of the comparative method and of genealogical classification after Schleicher, we soon realize that there are far too many independent (but related) strands. They can be pursued along a number of different lines.

First, the very existence from the early 1860s onwards of such works as Max Müller's *Lectures on the science of language* (1861 and 1864), Whitney's *Language and the study of language* (1867), *Life and growth of language* (1875), Paul's *Principien der Sprachgeschichte* (1880), and Gabelentz's *Sprachwissenschaft* (1891) — to quote only a

[52] Pisani (1959:14) has pointed out that the theory involves a basic ambiguity. It was based on the concept of language as an organism which develops according to inherent laws, but this could hardly explain the differentiation of languages. To account for it Schleicher was obliged to appeal to geographical differences, but that meant that he had to reintroduce those historical considerations which he wanted to avoid. The contradiction is even stronger than it appears. Schleicher could not allow historical factors to play a part in language change because, if he had done so, he would have destroyed that absolute overlapping of typological and genealogical classification which he had proposed. As long as language change was gradual and 'organic' (as Schleicher wanted it to be), two dialects which arose as the result of a language split were bound to be typologically near to each other. However, if historical factors were allowed to have a determining influence on language development, then it became conceivable that in particular circumstances one of these dialects could alter up to a point at which it was typologically closer to another dialect with different origins.

[53] Maher (1966) has argued that the actual image of a family tree with its branches is too banal to require any particular explanation, and that there is no reason to suppose that Schleicher borrowed it from Darwin or Häckel. The last point is certainly correct. As for the first point, the question of possible influences from textual criticism has been mentioned before, but here it may be opportune to remember that, whatever the origin of the procedure of mapping languages on genealogical trees, it was already established by the first part of the century: cf. for instance the table of languages presented in Klaproth's *Asia polyglotta* (1823: near p. 217).

small number of works which came from different and often contrasting backgrounds — shows an interest in linguistic theory and in the systematization of current methodology.[54] The psychological view of language, which was explicitly advocated by Steinthal and then received far more general acceptance in the last quarter of the century, comes under this heading, as also does the continuing interest in Humboldt, exemplified by the works and editions of Steinthal and Pott.

At the same time a number of contributions of more specific theoretical interest start appearing: for the last part of the century the names of Bréal, Schuchardt, Kruszewski and Baudouin de Courtenay come to mind, but any choice is invidious. It would be useful to distinguish the work of those more theoretically minded scholars who proposed new ways of looking at language and pointed out new paths to explore from the work of those who were more interested in methodological clarification and in an exact definition of discovery procedures. The distinction is not easy to draw, and it is possible that this difficulty accounts for the different judgement passed on some linguistic trends. For some the end of the century is a time of retrenchment and disarray, for others it is a period of excessive confidence in the historical side of linguistic work. At any rate it is certainly true that in various ways and at various times we can recognize the first signs of a movement which will lead to the main currents of study of general linguistics: Saussure and the beginnings of structuralism on the one side, individualism and idealism on the other side.

It may well appear that these trends have little or nothing to do with the history of genealogical classification; that it is not so can be shown by referring to the work of some of the relevant scholars. First, a less well known writer: in 1881, the French scholar, Lucien Adam (1881a) started an article on *Les classifications de la linguistique* by saying that in rereading Whitney and Max Müller he had come to the conclusion 'qu'il est dévenu necessaire de soumettre dans notre Revue à l'épreuve de la discussion les points fondamentaux de la science du langage.' Secondly, Schuchardt, who is regarded as one of the founders of individualism in linguistics, is also the man who started the harshest attack against the comparative method and argued that no real classification of languages was possible, since by nature languages were non classifiable entities. Much later on Trubeckoj, with whom we are well within the domain of structuralism, tried to vindicate typology as a classificatory criterion and to introduce it into the traditional domain of genealogical classification, as the only adequate means of defining the Indo-European languages (Trubeckoj 1939). At this point — which unfortunately goes beyond the limits of this survey — it may well be said that the history of classification has come full circle since Friedrich Schlegel.[55]

[54] Perhaps we should add to our list at least Sayce's *Principles of comparative philology* (1874) and Hovelacque's *La linguistique* (1876). The latter book had some importance in popularizing Schleicher's ideas about linguistic classification.

[55] Most of the points made by Trubeckoj were anticipated by Baudouin de Courtenay in a series of works which started in the last quarter of the nineteenth century and continued through the first decades of the twentieth century: cf., e.g., Baudouin de Courtenay 1972:312ff. [1884], 219ff. [1901], 296ff. [1930].

Closely related to these general studies — and at the same time to the problems of classification and dialectology which we shall mention below — is the scrutiny to which the very concept of language was subjected. Schleicher's work had brought the organic view of language (in the ontological sense) to the point where compromise was no longer possible. Above all it had shown what the consequences were of endowing language with a life of its own. A few scholars accepted his conclusions, but a number reacted against them. In various ways this reaction diverted attention from language as such towards the speaker. In this respect even the sociologically minded like Whitney, the 'mentalists' like Paul, or the individualists like Schuchardt could come to some measure of agreement. A formula which very few would have disclaimed is probably that of Paul (1880:232 [=1920:37]): 'wir müssen eigentlich so viele sprachen unterscheiden als es individuen gibt'.

A second line of investigation could follow the increasing interest in dialect studies through to the creation of an almost independent discipline, which reached its acme in the dialect geography of the twentieth century. Even at an earlier stage its impact cannot be underestimated. The interest in the study of some more modern linguistic phases is often quoted as one of its results, but there is more. Once again, a different definition, or perhaps a special definition of language, became necessary. How was it possible to distinguish one dialect from another? Or, for that matter, a dialect from a language? What indicated the boundaries? And what did it mean to say that a language split into dialects? Here too attention was drawn to the problems of classification and to the how and why of language change.

Thirdly, there was a new widely spread interest in experimental and descriptive phonetics. We may leave this point aside, since the history of phonetics is discussed elsewhere in this volume, but we must remember that most of the theoretical discussions which went on during the last quarter of the century would have been unthinkable without this particular background.

Fourthly, we should perhaps isolate (though it would be a somewhat artificial separation) that particular set of problems and discussions which went together with the so-called *Junggrammatische Richtung*. It was certainly not divorced from contemporary currents of theoretical thought (from which it absorbed a great deal and to which it contributed substantially), but it merits a place of its own because of the immediate and powerful impact that it had on the theory and practice of linguistic theory and comparison.

Fifthly and sixthly, there are special problems which concern genetic classification in particular. The need for a classification of the languages of the world was still there — and was more and more pressing. The material available increased daily, and anthropologists and ethnologists looked to linguists for a reliable and useful classification. This very fact encouraged a genealogical rather than a typological classification, but the emphasis was also determined by other reasons. On the one side the natural development of the subject was suggesting new attempts to demonstrate a genetic relationship between some of the linguistic families previously established.

The work of R. von Raumer, Ascoli, and, later on, Hermann Möller on Semitic and Indo-European is well known. For much of the last century it was still possible to hope that more sophisticated comparative work could drastically reduce the total number of families and eventually even create a gigantic family tree demonstrating the original kinship of all languages and affording a satisfactory and complete classification.[56] On the other side, some of the more theoretically minded scholars (Whitney and Pott could serve as examples) seemed to be moving more and more towards genetic rather than typological classification, although they certainly did not believe in linguistic monogenesis. The reasons for this would need a much deeper exploration than can be offered here (but *à propos* of Whitney see Terracini 1949:88f. and 94f.). An additional point which would be worth considering is the extent to which the views of linguists (even when they were not followers of Schleicher) were influenced by Darwin's criticism of the classifications used in the natural sciences and by his argument that it made little sense to speak of a natural classification which was not genealogical (Darwin 1859: chapter 14).

At a different level the attention of Indo-European scholars shifted towards a problem which had come to concern them directly. The kinship of the Indo-European languages did not call for further demonstration, but their internal classification needed more extensive discussion at both a theoretical and a concrete level. The question concerned, in equal measure, the classification of the Indo-European languages, of the Romance languages, of the Germanic languages, etc. and that of any smaller group of dialects. Yet, any study on the problems of sub-grouping was bound to have major repercussions on most problems about language relationship. We thus return to Schuchardt's criticism of the concept of *Sprachverwandtschaft*.

2.9 What is the position of recent historiography? In this survey we can only refer briefly to some of the lines of enquiry mentioned above. The first two in particular will receive only very summary treatment, and the third will be ignored.

Few of the general works have been studied for their own sake (for Becker see above p. 613). Likewise, the initial links between psychology and linguistics (Steinthal, Lazarus, Geiger) and the varying attitudes of scholars like Scherer, the neogrammarians' group (including Paul) and then Wundt (including the polemics between Delbrück and Wundt), have also been largely ignored by historians of linguistics (but for Steinthal, see below 3.71): two recent books by psychologists (Esper 1968 and Blumenthal 1970; cf. also Alkon 1959) are mostly concerned with the later period and with the links between this earlier tradition and the psychologism of the young Bloomfield, though Esper makes a number of very interesting excursions into the second half of the nineteenth century.

Even the recent anthology of Whitney's writings (Whitney 1971) does not offer a complete analysis of his thought, in spite of a brilliant essay by Roman Jakobson on

[56] The attempt was, of course, made; here it should be enough to refer to Trombetti's work (cf. Assirelli 1962).

other scholars' reactions to Whitney (*ibid.*: xxv-lxv) and of a very interesting introduction by Silverstein (*ibid.*: x–xxiii), whose main defect to my mind is that it does not sufficiently stress the influence of earlier scholars on Whitney and the effective points of contact which he had with his adversary Max Müller. Terracini's chapter on Whitney (1949:73–121) is still the most complete treatment and the only one which underlines both the new and the old features of Whitney's thought. For the connections with Saussure, cf. also de Mauro (1970b:299ff. and 327ff.).[57] Paul — to quote another great name — is mentioned in all works on the neogrammarians (cf., e.g., Jankowsky 1972 *passim*), but we have no complete analysis of the *Prinzipien*. Two very different (and very recent) contributions should be mentioned. In a paper which is mainly concerned with the theory of language change and not with the history of linguistics, Weinreich, Labov, and Herzog (1968) have offered a very closely documented discussion of Paul's theories about linguistic change; it is a brilliant piece of work in spite of some disputable points. Even more recently, Koerner (1972d) has tried to show once more that there is a direct link between Paul and Saussure (while denying the often postulated influence of Gabelentz on Saussure) and has offered an interesting examination of Paul's views with special reference to his attitude towards historical and descriptive linguistics (cf. also Kandler 1954:15 and Lieb 1967:22f.).

Georg von Gabelentz has both gained and suffered from the attempts to connect him with Saussure. They have rescued him from the almost complete obscurity into which he had fallen, but at the same time they have called attention to some particular parts of his work rather than to others which are equally deserving.[58] For the most detailed comparisons of the views of Saussure and Gabelentz we can refer to Rensch (1966) and Coseriu (1967c): for some reactions see de Mauro (1970b:xxii–xxiv) and Koerner (1972d). Christmann (1972) has tried to establish a link between Humboldt and Gabelentz and Gabelentz and Saussure, while in a paper which is more a programmatic declaration than a piece of historiography Lohmann (1967) has aimed at stressing the differences between Humboldt and Saussure.

A number of contributions, among which are some of those just quoted, arise from recent exploration of the sources of Saussure's thought and of his possible precursors: for a general account see de Mauro (1970b:347ff.) and for a complete bibliography Koerner (1972c). Principles such as that of the arbitrarity of the sign (cf. Coseriu 1967b, de Mauro 1970b:348ff., Koerner 1972c:128ff.), or dichotomies like those between synchrony and diachrony (cf. de Mauro 1970b:350, Koerner 1972c:97ff., Christmann 1971, 1972, Koerner 1972d, Lieb 1967, Scheller 1968 etc.),[59] between

[57] The similarities between Whitney's views and Madvig's would deserve a separate treatment; for some hints cf. Johansen's discussion (Madvig 1971:37, 468ff,).

[58] His thoughts on linguistic typology come to mind; cf. Gabelentz (1894) and see below, notes 124 and 129.

[59] As de Mauro and Koerner make clear, a number of scholars have been quoted as precursors of this distinction: Humboldt, Grimm, Comte, Ascoli, Kruszewski, Baudouin de Courtenay, G. von Gabelentz, Masaryk, Paul, Marty, Liebich, Schuchardt, etc. For the sake of completeness — and not because we have much faith in what has become a popular pastime — we could add here the names of

langue and parole (cf. de Mauro 1970b:350, Koerner 1972c:112ff.),[60] and between sound and phoneme (cf. de Mauro 1970b:352ff. and 401f.) have all been explored with regard to their origin. In this way we have indirectly gained a general view of the pre-Saussurean theories. It has also been shown that the all-important distinction between synchrony and diachrony had in fact been formulated in various ways (admittedly not always as impressive as that of Saussure) well before the publication of the *Cours*. This fact, which obviously does not detract from the importance of Saussure, is important for a correct understanding of the work done in the three last decades of the nineteenth century. It is all too easy to give the impression that the emphasis was on historical linguistics simply because no other type of work was conceived of; this is as wrong as the often repeated statement that all the work of the nineteenth century is atomistic in nature because of a lack of interest in synchronic studies and of the absence of the concept of system (against the opposite exaggeration see Buyssens 1961).

Here it would be useless to refer to all the theoretical contributions of scholars like Marty, Noreen, etc. who have been quoted in connection with particular trends of twentieth century linguistics. More to the point, however, is a mention of recent historiographical interest in the so called Kazan school and in its exponents, Kruszewski and Baudouin de Courtenay. Most Western histories of linguistics barely pay lip service to them, but Graur-Wald (1961:54ff.), Ivić (1970:97ff.) and especially Zvegincev (1960:I 197ff.) give a more complete account. A far more detailed treatment is in Berezin (1968:100ff.); for a general introduction see Jakobson (1971b). The connections between Baudouin de Courtenay and Saussure have often been discussed (cf., e.g., Benveniste 1964:129–30, Leont'ev 1966, Slusareva 1963, and the general account of de Mauro 1970b:306–8). Yet, we cannot forget that both Kruszewski and Baudouin started as Indo-Europeanists and that part at least of Kruszewski's work had a definite influence on Paul's *Prinzipien* (to give a single example).

Indications about recent work on Kruszewski can be found in Berezin (1968) and in Koerner (1972d:294ff.); for an appreciation of his work see Jakobson (1965) and for an edition of his writings Kruszewski (1967) with Kurylowicz's introduction (*ibid.*: iii–ix), and the edition announced by Koerner (cf. Koerner 1972c:278 no. 1746). The Russian, Polish, etc. literature on Baudouin has by now reached unmanageable proportions; it would be useless to give the details here or in the bibliography, since most of it can be easily traced through the 1960 Russian collection of essays about him (Baudouin de Courtenay 1960), the Russian anthology of his works (Baudouin de Courtenay 1963), and the very recent anthology translated into English and edited

Thurot (see Coseriu 1967a) and Savigny (cf. Ginschel 1967:15). It is odd to see that Henry Sweet is not often mentioned in this connection (but cf. Trim 1959 and for Sweet see Jakobson 1966 and Wrenn 1946). An interesting essay is that of Christmann (1971) on the attitude taken by the *Grammaire des grammaires* to historical and descriptive linguistics.

[60] To the references given in de Mauro and Koerner, add Coseriu (1976a), who refers to Hegel for a similar distinction, and Bumann (1965:42f.), where the similarities between Steinthal and Gabelentz and Gabelentz and Saussure are again emphasized (see also Belke 1971:cx).

with a long and important introduction by E. Stankiewicz (Baudouin de Courtenay 1972).[61] Further information can be obtained from Häusler's excellent monograph on phonetics and phonology in Baudouin (Häusler 1968, cf. also Koerner 1972b), and from Berezin's study of the history of linguistics in Russia (1968:100–50).[62]

2.91 Linguistic geography may be left aside since it belongs to a later period than that in which we are interested, but dialect studies started well before the twentieth century and played an important part in the development of linguistic thought. General information is provided by most histories of linguistics: cf., e.g., Arens (1969:329–37 and 765f., 793f.). Particularly rich in detailed accounts are the histories of Romance philology (cf., e.g., Iordan-Orr-Posner 1970:144–278, 465–72). Other useful sources of evidence are provided by the general books on linguistic geography and dialectology (see especially Pop 1950–51). An up-to-date survey can also be found in the collective volume on *Sprachatlanten* which was published a few years ago (*Sprachatlanten* 1969).

A shorter account of the earlier collections of dialect material (especially in Germanic territory) and of the beginning and development of dialectology from the end of the eighteenth century onwards is given in Freudenberg (1965; cf. also Gerhardt 1947).[63] Some interesting factual articles have concentrated on the first Idiotika and the dialectological interests of the brothers Grimm: cf., e.g., Niemeyer (1962; on G. Landau), Schoof (1941, 1963/4 and 1967; on Grimm), Sonderegger (1967; on Heusler), Studer (1954; on F.J. Stalder), Wanner (1963; on Grimm). Malkiel (1967–68) has drawn attention to an earlier Romance dialectologist, August Fuchs; for the later work in the field cf. Kuhn (1947–48).

A detailed discussion of this and other work would be impossible, but some historiographical trends must be mentioned. In Italy there has been a great deal of research on Graziadio Isaia Ascoli and the many aspects of his activity; his general views on language, his substratum theory,[64] his work on dialects and his position in the neogrammarians controversy. A number of new documents offer an inside view of the problems of the time (cf. de Felice 1954 for Ascoli's terminology, Bolelli 1963, Conti Peca 1965, Cronia 1962, Faré 1964, Gadzaru 1967, Prosdocimi 1969, Timpanaro 1959, etc. for letters and other evidence). In addition to some interesting

[61] This is the most recent publication on Baudouin de Courtenay but the bibliography is not meant to be complete and some omissions (like that of Häusler 1968) are odd. It is also a pity that Stankiewicz has missed the chance of giving a complete list of the recent publications of documents, letters, etc. by and about Baudouin. For Häusler's article on Schleicher and Baudouin see above, note 48.

[62] I have not mentioned here F. F. Fortunatov and the so-called 'Moscow school' because in the nineteenth century its influence outside Russia seems to have been very limited. For some basic information cf. the Russian anthology of Fortunatov's writings (Fortunatov 1956–57) with Peterson's introduction (*ibid.* I, 5–16), Zvegincev (1960: I, 197ff.) and Berezin (1968:28–99). There are a number of articles on Fortunatov, mostly in Russian publications (but see Vascenco 1960): cf., e.g., Kacnel'son 1954, Kert 1965, Tolkačev 1964, Ščerba 1963, Žirmunskij 1953.

[63] For a general bibliography on Swiss dialectology cf. Sonderegger 1962, which also includes some historiographical information.

[64] Most histories of linguistics give some information about the further development of the substratum theory; cf. also Jarčeva 1956, Nemirovskij 1956.

work by Terracini, which stretches almost over half a century (most recently see Terracini 1949:123–47, 1956, 1966 and 1967), and some chapters included in more general books (e.g. Vitale 1955:118–24 and Várvaro 1968:104–16) the most penetrating contributions have come from Timpanaro's studies (cf. especially Timpanaro 1969:229–357, 419–24, and 1972b).[65] The picture which emerges is that of a scholar who is much nearer to Schleicher and the neogrammarians than has been claimed by his later idealistic followers.[66] What we still do not know is how great Ascoli's influence was outside Italy (but see Gadzaru 1967), if we except the general favour with which some of his concrete results in the field of Indo-European reconstruction were received. However, the reasons why Ascoli is mentioned in this section rather than elsewhere are provided by his later studies of Romance dialects, and by his persistent faith in a linguistic (rather than ethnic or political) definition of dialects and in the possibility of their classification on linguistic grounds. This view, which offers an interesting contrast with the scepticism of Schuchardt, provoked the attacks of Paul Meyer and Gaston Paris (cf. Várvaro *loc. cit.*), thus starting the discussion about the definition and classification of dialects which was to continue for a long time after the 1870s and which can be regarded both as the origin and the result of a greater interest in descriptive techniques and in the study of language change.[67]

A further enquiry into dialect studies would bring us to discuss, on the one hand, Schuchardt (for whom see below) and Gilliéron (for whom see the collective volume Pop and Pop 1959 and the sobering remarks of Malkiel 1967a and 1957:10 = 1968: 213f.), and on the other hand Rousselot and the new data of experimental phonetics. We should also mention the beginning of field work and the first linguistic atlases which start appearing towards the end of the nineteenth century. All this must be left aside, if the limits of this survey are not to expand to impossible proportions. It may be useful, however, to conclude this paragraph with a note of warning. All too frequently general histories of linguistics give the impression that nineteenth century dialect study inevitably led to a drastic revision of the tenets of genealogical comparison

65 I have ignored here the part played by Ascoli in the Italian 'questione della lingua'; for a general bibliography on the subject cf. Ascoli 1968, where Grassi reprints some of the relevant texts, and Timpanaro 1969 (xxivff.).

66 This is essentially Timpanaro's view: some comments about the differences between Ascoli and the neolinguist Bartoli had been previously made by W. von Raffler (1953).

67 In spite of the large number of monographs and articles about him, I have hesitated to devote even a page to Ascoli in a survey which is obliged to ignore works like those of Raynouard, Diez and Meyer-Lübke, and does not mention any of the earlier Italian scholars (Cattaneo, Biondelli, etc.). Some points may justify my decision. First, as Timpanaro has shown, so many linguistic trends merge in Ascoli that a study of his intellectual biography is almost paradigmatic for the period. *Inter alia* Ascoli shares with Johannes Schmidt the honour of being claimed as precursor by two very different schools; in the case of Ascoli the reference is to the Italian neogrammarians and the Italian 'neolinguisti'. Secondly, Ascoli's work is a good example of that phenomenon which we mentioned before: the different coloring taken by linguistics in various countries. Thanks to Aarsleff (1967) and to Timpanaro (1969) we are now quite well informed about Britain and Italy, i.e. two countries which were not in the forefront of linguistic developments (for France see Kukenheim 1966, for Russia Berezin 1968, Vinogradov 1958, for Spain Lázaro Carreter 1949, Mourelle-Lema 1968).

and therefore stood in strong contrast to it. As we have seen this can scarcely apply to scholars like Ascoli who, as Malkiel put it (1957:9 = 1968:213), elevated dialect studies to 'the rank of a respectable scholarly endeavour'. It applied even less to those who are considered the traditional enemies of dialect geography, the neogrammarians. Some of the first detailed enquiries into living dialects (e.g. Winteler 1876) were quoted by them in support of their thesis, and we must not forget that some of the most thoughtful phoneticians (Sweet, Sievers), who were directly involved in the study of living languages, were more for them than against them.

2.92 These observations bring us to our fourth line of enquiry: the neogrammarian school. The relevance to our main theme is clear; there was a time at which comparison and neogrammarians' work were almost synonymous. In spite of this — or perhaps because of it — few other nineteenth century movements have had a more curious historiographical reception. The neogrammarians have not been forgotten, but historians of linguistics either have treated them with undisguised and uncritical admiration (for a part of the American tradition cf., e.g., Hockett 1965:186ff.), or have underlined the concrete results (Verner's law, the nasal sonants, etc.) and forgotten the theory, or have branded the whole school with total disapproval (cf., e.g., Iordan in Iordan-Orr-Posner 1970:18). In spite of some attempts at conciliation, until very recently it has been difficult to speak about the neogrammarians without implying a quasi-moral judgement; in some academic circles the very word 'neogrammarian' has assumed particular connotations. The result has been in most cases a remarkably one-sided view. What historiography most needs now is a series of attempts to investigate both the neogrammarians' concrete achievements (about which much is known) and their theoretical presuppositions in their entirety (about which we are far less clear), to compare the two, and to set them in some sort of historical perspective.

Some very recent work has moved in this direction: cf. for instance the article by Putschke (1969) and the monograph by Jankowsky (1972).[68] In order to account for the basic ideas of the movement Putschke has felt the need to go back to the beginning of the century; Jankowsky has taken the enquiry back to Francis Bacon, but has perhaps lost in depth what he has acquired in the temporal dimension. Putschke firmly denies that the neogrammarians brought about a breakthrough in linguistic science (cf. for this view Hockett 1965, Robins 1967:186) and is ready to underline the motifs and principles which they inherited from their predecessors. According to him the school marks the confluence of the psychological and physiological approaches which linguistics had been developing from the beginning of the nineteenth century. The immediate influences were those of Scherer, with his concept of analogy, and of Schleicher, with his concept of sound law. Jankowsky is equally eager to stress the importance of Scherer and Schleicher, but also wishes to emphasize the difference between them and the neogrammarians. Both authors — to my mind — do not sufficiently explore the psychologism of the second half of the century, and in particu-

[68] About the neogrammarians cf. also Meriggi 1966, Pulgram 1955, and Raven 1954.

lar do not concentrate enough on Steinthal. Perhaps as a result of the anti-mentalistic attitudes of parts of twentieth century linguistics, they do not seem too eager to enquire how important psychology was in the neogrammarians' system.[69]

Both works have obvious theses to defend. Putschke argues that the neogrammarians were slowly moving in the direction of a diachronic structuralism and that this attitude descended directly from their methodology, i.e. from their theory of analogy and their theory of sound change. The thesis may appear paradoxical, in view of the constant allegations of atomism, but has much to be said for it, as Putschke has shown. Jankowsky is far more eager to demolish some of the criticism of the neogrammarians and to give them credit for their achievements: the refinement of comparative and historical methodology, the interest in formal analysis, and the collection of an enormous amount of data.

A historiographical problem, which is not often discussed, concerns the subsequent fortunes of the neogrammarians: why did they pass into history almost exclusively as supporters of the principle of regularity of sound change, while no mention is normally made of their other theories? Yet some other points at least should be mentioned: their fight against Schleicher's concept of organism with their determined attempt to bring language back into the domain of history rather than in that of the natural sciences; their self-avowed mentalism; their uniformitarian principle, according to which language develops at all times according to similar rules, and there is no question of a period of growth followed by a period of decay; and their interest in modern phases of languages as the best source of information about what we could call diachronic universals.[70] That none of these tenets is entirely original hardly

[69] Esper (1968) gives a detailed analysis of the controversy which took place between Delbrück and Wundt at the beginning of this century, but also offers important information about the psychological views of Paul. For the earlier period, rather than refer to the famous preface to the *Morphologische Untersuchungen*, written by Brugmann when he was not yet thirty, it is better to emphasize the importance of Brugmann's inaugural lecture in Freiburg (cf. Brugmann 1885:33ff.) with its clear analysis of the tenets which the neogrammarians accepted from their predecessors (above all Steinthal). Gadzaru (1967:58) has published a letter which Brugmann wrote to Ascoli in 1887 and in which it is stated that the great controversy which followed the neogrammarians' declarations did not centre so much 'um solche Fragen ... welche die Verbindung der Sprachforschung mit der Sprachphysiologie betreffen, als um solche, welche sich auf das Verhältniss der Einzelforschung zur Psychologie beziehen'.

[70] A problem which calls for some attention concerns the position of the young Saussure; how close was he to the neogrammarians' views? His first book has been analyzed in detail by Vallini (1969) who has tried to look at it from the point of view of the *Cours*. De Mauro (1970b:292ff.) appears inclined to stress the differences between Saussure and the neogrammarians, both from the point of view of the concrete results (e.g. in the theory of Ablaut) and from that of Saussure's interests and theories. To my mind, some of these points have been carried too far; an interest in syntax is not altogether unknown in the school to which Delbrück belonged, so that Saussure's dissertation on the genitive absolute in Sanskrit is not altogether isolated, the influence of Whitney (which according to de Mauro is very recognizable in Saussure) is officially acknowledged by Brugmann in more than one occasion, and as for the journey to Lithuania, which according to de Mauro is a proof of Saussure's interest in living languages and in descriptive linguistics, this must have been almost de rigueur for a budding comparativist at some stage (cf. the parallel enterprises first of Schleicher and then of Brugmann and Leskien). In any case the neogrammarians had vociferously claimed that the study of

matters: perhaps the greatest single achievement of the neogrammarians is to have shown that even a data-oriented movement needs a coherent methodology and that such a methodology is only possible within an explicit theoretical framework. It is not worth while to discuss here the ambiguities which existed in the theory (Putschke 1969 has mentioned some of them); they do not detract from the importance of the attempt.

We shall return later to the neogrammarians and to their views about sub-grouping (cf. 2.941). Here we must still examine their attitude towards the problems of language classification. Once again, this has not been formally explored, but some facts at least are obvious. Schleicher's elaborate construction could not be accepted by the supporters of the uniformitarian principle. The neogrammarians were bound to reject in toto any theory which combined morphological and genealogical classification at the cost of postulating a prehistoric period of linguistic growth followed by a period of historical decay. More important, their whole attitude to the problems of classification was different. On the one side, these were bound to appear less urgent, since linguistics was no longer to be treated as one of the natural sciences, nor language as an independent organism. On the other side, the primary task for the neogrammarians had become the exploration of language change. This called for an intensive analysis of the history of individual languages or language families, but the aim was that of tracing a historical process, not of arriving at a classification.[71] From this angle, too, typological classification receded into second place; the interest in comparison and in the comparative method remained — all the more so since it seemed that for the first time it was put on firm methodological basis — but of course the bias was different. The result, however, was that the new rigour employed in the study of language change was reflected in the practical work of language comparison and reconstruction. The data speak for themselves: in the course of a few years the neogrammarians and their contemporaries almost completely altered the view of Indo-European that they had inherited. At the same time a clearer understanding of the methodology used meant also a clearer understanding of its limitations: it is noticeable that Brugmann's

---

living languages was as important as that of the ancient Indo-European languages, if not more so. It is possible to wonder whether at the time in which Saussure was in Leipzig the disagreements — or rather the lack of sympathy — between him and his German contemporaries really depended on profound theoretical divergences rather than on differences in temperament and inclinations. Another problem which should be discussed in the context of any work on the neogrammarians concerns the numerous coincidences between their views and those of the young Baudouin de Courtenay (and perhaps of Kruszewski).

71 In the paper which they wrote to celebrate the 100th birthday of Bopp, and which was published in the first number of the *Indogermanische Forschungen*, Brugmann and Streitberg (1891: vii) stated: 'Die wahre Aufgabe der indogermanischen Sprachwissenschaft — daran lässt sich nicht zweifeln — besteht viel mehr darin den gesamten Entwickelungsgang der indogermanischen Sprachen von den dunkelsten Zeiten ferner Vergangenheit bis zum hellen Tage lebendiger Gegenwart zu durchforschen und die Gesetze aufzudecken die seine Richtung bestimmt haben.'

reconstructions of Indo-European forms are far less daring than those of Bopp or Schleicher.[72]

2.93 Concrete work about genealogical classification has attracted little attention. The motives which determined very different scholars (e.g. Rudolf von Raumer, Ascoli, Möller, Trombetti, etc.) to explore the possibilities of linking the Indo-European languages with other language families still need exploring; at present we know little about them, and even less about the methodology used in each case. Similarly, there has not been much discussion of the attempts to provide a genealogical classification of all languages of the world. The books of Fr. Müller and F.N. Finck (published in 1876–88 and 1909 respectively) where all language families are listed and then grouped according to racial criteria, are sometimes mentioned (cf., e.g., Tagliavini 1963:415ff.), but almost exclusively in order to deplore this connection of language and race. Here too a number of distinctions should be drawn. The spirit in which the anthropologist and ethnologist Fr. Müller undertook his classification was certainly different from that of the linguist Finck, who was more interested in typology (see below 3.81) and for whom a genealogical classification (presented with all possible hesitations and qualifications) was very much a preliminary step to some more important work. Other works which are on the borderline between linguistics and anthropology (cf., e.g., Maury 1857 and perhaps Pott 1884–90 with Pott 1887) have not even been mentioned in the relevant literature (but for a list of these works cf., e.g., Meillet-Cohen 1952 and Veith 1969).

2.94 The problems of sub-grouping have aroused more interest. In the 'Geschichte der Forschung' section of his book on *Die Gliederung des indogermanischen Sprachgebiets*, W. Porzig (1954:17–52) has given a detailed history of the controversies over the internal classification of the Indo-European languages and the related questions of Indo-European reconstruction and *Altertumskunde*.[73] The facts are all there, but because of the purpose of the book, no attempt is made at any general historiographical statement. Even so, Porzig's analysis is a healthy reminder of the weight that concrete problems may have in the evaluation of theoretical positions. Any scholar who wanted to give an account of the differentiation of the Indo-European languages from the Ursprache to modern times and to use for this the family tree model had to answer questions such as: to what branch do the Slavonic languages belong? Are they closer to Indo-Iranian or to Germanic? If these and similar problems could not be solved in spite of what appeared to be a wealth of material, attention was redirected towards the model, and its very validitity could be challenged. It is probably within this framework that we should consider Johannes Schmidt's criticism of the *Stammbaumtheorie* and his own alternative proposal for a model (the so called *Wellentheorie*) which laid the stress on the horizontal rather than on the vertical

[72] It is just this paradox — of apparent retrenchment in some fields, balanced by advance in comparative and historical method — which may account for the ambivalence of attitude (still discernible) towards the achievements of the neogrammarians.

[73] A useful analysis of the early discussions about classification of the Indo-European languages from Schleicher onwards is to be found in Schrader (1890:68–110).

spread of linguistic features and on geographical continuity rather than on genealogical transmission (cf. also Terracini 1949:218). Schmidt's pamphlet on *Die Verwandtschaftverhältnisse der indogermanischen Sprachen* (1872) is constantly mentioned, but especially among Romance philologists, priority for the *Wellentheorie* is often given to Schuchardt rather than to Schmidt (cf. Iordan in Iordan-Orr-Posner 1970:52 note for an account of the question, and see Höfler 1955:30, Gadzaru 1967:144–64, Malkiel 1955–56, 1968:18). However, we miss in general historiography a discussion of some different, though interlocking, problems.

First, it is often not realized that in their simplest form the questions of sub-grouping are as old as the beginning of genealogical comparison. The decision taken by some of the earliest comparativists that Sanskrit was one of the Indo-European languages and not the mother tongue of all of them comes under this heading. Similarly A.W. Schlegel's 1818 attack on Raynouard's thesis that all Romance languages derived from Old Provençal revolves round a problem of sub-grouping. As early as 1833 Pott felt the need to stress the difficulties inherent in this field (cf., e.g., Pott 1833–36:I xxviiiff.). Later on he argued that within a group of genealogically related languages further distinctions could only be based on the different grades of relationship, but gave a warning against confusing human and linguistic kinship. The worst complications — he maintained — were likely to arise in the attempt to distinguish between ascendents and collaterals and to give a correct definition of daughter languages. Somewhat earlier, similar problems had been discussed by Steinthal (1849), to whom Pott referred (cf. Pott 1856:213ff.).[74]

Secondly, even the earlier controversies about the family tree model or similar models are hardly ever mentioned. Yet, as Porzig has pointed out, Schmidt was not the first to imply that those Indo-European languages which were geographically contiguous were also linguistically nearest, even when the traditional classification attached them to different branches of the family tree. In the late fifties and early sixties he had been preceded by Pictet and Ebel, who had compared the connections among the Indo-European languages to those between the links of a chain. In more general terms, Pott had pointed out that language and dialect boundaries keep crossing, and that languages influenced each other in a way which cannot even be compared to grafting because reciprocal influences were not limited to languages of the same type (cf. Pott 1856: *passim* and especially 203 and 213–20).

Arens (1969:304) argues that an important feature of Schmidt's theory is that he shattered the belief in the unity of the Indo-European *Ursprache* and put in its place a multiplicity of dialects. However, this point too should be considered within the framework of a discussion which had been going on for some time. Brugmann in 1884

[74] Steinthal's review (1849) is very much worth reading. The beginning shows a profound dissatisfaction with the vagueness of the current terminology and current theories: 'Noch ist die Sprachclassification nicht so weit gediehen, dass man auch nur über die ersten Grundbestimmungen derselben im Klaren wäre. Man versteht sich wohl so ungefähr, wenn von Sprachstämmen, -familien, -geschlechtern die Rede ist; aber noch ist man in Verlegenheit, wenn man genau und scharf anzugeben hat, WAS, d.h. welcher bestimmte Grad von Verwandtschaft oder Aehnlichkeit damit ausgesagt ist.

(239f.) could still refer to Max Müller as the author of similar observations (cf., e.g., Max Müller 1861:177ff., but see also the earlier references given in Schrader 1890: 72ff.). This is worth remembering since in more than one respect Max Müller can count as a Schleicherian. More important, however, is the polemical attack of Whitney (1867:177) on those writers who 'have committed the very serious error of inverting the mutual relations of dialectic variety and uniformity of speech, thus turning topsy-turvy the whole history of linguistic development'. They 'affirm that the natural tendency of language is from diversity to uniformity; that dialects are, in the regular order of things, antecedent to language; that human speech began its existence in a state of infinite dialectic division, which has been, from the first, undergoing coalescence and reduction'. (*ibid.*; cf. also Whitney 1875:177). The reference is to Max Müller, but especially to Renan and to his highly influential *Histoire générale et système comparé des langues sémitiques* (1858b:98ff.) and his *De l'origine du langage* (1858a:183ff.).[75] It is unlikely that if Schmidt had been obliged to take part in this controversy he would have sided with Renan and Max Müller: his point seems rather to be that we are incapable of reconstructing a unitary *Ursprache* and that we should suspend judgement when we are confronted with what appear to be dialect variations (Schmidt 1872:29). One of his concluding sentences could hardly have been acceptable to Renan: 'Dass eine einheitliche indogermanische ursprache einmal vorhanden gewesen sei, ist höchst warscheinlich, ja ganz sicher, wenn sich erweisen lässt, dass das menschengeschlecht von einigen wenigen individuen seinen anfang genommen hat.' (*ibid.*: 29–30).[76]

2.941 This last reference brings us back to our original problem and to a question which deserves more attention than it has received: what were the reactions to the *Wellentheorie*? But there is a preliminary point which cannot be ignored. We have seen that the paternity of the *Wellentheorie* has often been attributed both to Schmidt and to Schuchardt. Yet no attempt has been made to contrast the positions of these two scholars. In recent times there has been practically no historiographical work on Johannes Schmidt per se, and even the recent work which concentrates on Schuchardt, either in order to extol his contributions (cf., e.g., Vitale 1955:125–33, Vàrvaro 1968:91ff.) or to criticize him (cf. Hall 1963:10–17), fails to consider this very problem (though Terracini 1949:205–33 and Vitale *loc. cit.* come near to it). It is perhaps worth noticing that, while no compromise was suggested between the views of Schuchardt (in their later version) and those of the more traditional comparativists, a

[75] Yet another attack against Renan was made by Whitney in that passage of his 1867 book where he challenged the definition of roots as pure abstractions (1867:284). Whitney's whole theory of original monosyllabic roots contrasts strikingly with Renan's (and not only Renan's) fight against 'ce besoin de l'esprit qui nous porte à expliquer la complexité actuelle par la simplicité primitive' (Renan 1858b:98; cf. 1858a: 107ff.).

[76] For some views of the Italian Cattaneo which anticipate the criticisms of Schmidt and Schuchardt cf. Timpanaro 1969: 273ff. It is also worth noticing that in his 1877–78 programme of lectures Baudouin de Courtenay (1972:118) proposed to discuss precisely the problems raised by Max Müller and Renan.

compromise between the *Stammbaumtheorie* and Schmidt's *Wellentheorie* was often proposed. Arens (1969:311ff.) quotes Leskien's 1876 discussion, where it is argued that the two models are complementary, and the same point is often repeated (cf. Jankowsky 1972:106ff. with his reference to Pulgram 1953 and see also Graur 1967). The neogrammarians, as often, took their clue from Leskien, at least if we are to judge from Brugmann's discussion in his paper about the classification of the Indo-European languages (Brugmann 1884).

The contrast between the paper by Brugmann just mentioned and other reactions to Schmidt's pamphlet is also enlightening. In his 1873 book Fick objected to Schmidt's suggestion that Balto-Slavonic was particularly close to Indo-Iranian, since this went against his dichotomy between Asian and European languages (made in a strict 'family tree' spirit); in order to do so he plunged straight into a discussion of the detailed connections between the two groups. Brugmann's attitude was different: he realized that the whole question really concerned a particular model of sub-grouping and revolved round the criteria which could prove or disprove the connection of two languages or dialects within a certain group. After having stressed the point that any argument adduced was equally relevant to all language families and all genealogical classifications, he proceeded to take the discussion a step further. Schmidt had shown the importance of innovations as a criterion for sub-grouping, but had ignored the possibility of parallel innovations which could occur independently in similar circumstances. The introduction of this new factor showed that even Schmidt's model was unrealistic and that the problem was even more complicated than he had imagined. Brugmann's conclusion was that no single criterion could ever be sufficient to demonstrate the closer relationship of two languages or dialects: a very large number of agreements in phonetic, inflectional, syntactical and lexical innovations was necessary.[77]

The next point concerned the possibility of reconstruction. Brugmann agreed with Schmidt that, while a family tree model allowed an almost mechanical process of reconstruction, things had become more difficult now that the model had been challenged. Reconstruction had to be based on a clear understanding of the how and why of language change. This involved (if we can put some more modern terminology in Brugmann's mouth) a series of generalizations about diachronic events (i.e. an interest in diachronic typology and diachronic universals), conjoined with a study of the particular linguistic systems concerned, in order to understand whether some phenomena could have arisen in them as innovations or were bound to be archaisms.

There is a sense, then, in which Brugmann is in a direct line of descent from Schmidt. To argue, as it is sometimes done, that the neogrammarians were strict upholders of the family tree theory seems to be impossible. On the contrary, it would be

[77] Jakobson (1938:49–50) gives Meillet the credit for having established that 'les concordances entre deux ou plusieurs langues ... proviennent, beaucoup plus qu'on ne l'imagine au premier abord, de développements parallèles'. It is proper to recognize that Brugmann too had emphasized the same principle. Cf. also note 78.

possible to stress some points of agreement with the contemporary views of Baudouin de Courtenay, who was also ready to criticize both models. But Baudouin's arguments were different: even the *Wellentheorie*, he maintained, was too abstract and treated language as if it were something separate from the speakers (cf. Baudouin de Courtenay 1910 and for references to earlier work Baudouin de Courtenay 1972:113, 311f.; see below 3.8).

However, if Brugmann was not too far from Schmidt, he was certainly not near to Schuchardt. The Romance philologist was far more drastic than Schmidt in his attitude. Admittedly, like Schmidt, he had spoken of linguistic waves, but he had then proceeded to argue, as we have seen, that by their nature language and dialects were not classifiable (cf. Schuchardt 1928:187 [published 1900]). He had also quoted Darwin's dictum, that every real classification is genealogical, but merely in order to point out that any genealogical classification could only be an external one (*ibid.*: 166). On the one side he felt obliged to extend his misgivings about the possibility of the genealogical sub-grouping of dialects to the whole concept of genealogical classification, on the other side he found that the distinction between similarities due to common origin, similarities due to early influences, and similarities due to what he called *Elementarverwandtschaft*, was far from clear (1928:248ff. [first published 1912]) and he came to argue that any attempt to establish a genealogical classification broke down when it was not supported by ethnological, historical, and anthropological evidence.[78]

2.10 Practically anything that we can say — or have said — about Schuchardt is an oversimplification, but we have now reached a stage where — in the context of an enquiry into the history of language classification — we are entitled to ask whether he should be listed among the comparativists or among the typologists (or among neither of them). The dilemma is typical of this period: the end of the century seems to be marked by a polarization of interests and opinions. The neogrammarians had brought into the open their criticism of earlier methods of comparison and had pleaded for a more historically minded approach and for a greater methodological rigour. In their case, the result was a new fervour of historical and comparative work. Classification,

[78] At this stage virtually every word needs qualification. What is the theoretical difference between Brugmann's point that identical innovations may occur independently and the explanation in terms of *Elementarverwandtschaft* which Schuchardt gives of some linguistic changes (e.g. 1928:252)? Sometimes we have the impression that the theories differ less than at first appears, but that the practical conclusions diverge: Schuchardt would never have written Brugmann's *Grundriss*. The opposite may of course be true. On the other hand when we speak of Schuchardt as a typologist further qualifications are necessary: he is interested in historical events in a way in which the earlier typologists were not, and consequently he is far less interested in generalizing statements. Since it is normal to speak of the neogrammarians as data oriented, we may wonder whether the same adjective might not apply to Schuchardt too. In a somewhat paradoxical vein we may also ask whether the real difference between Schuchardt and the neogrammarians does not consist in the fact that the latter are structuralists before their time (see above for Putschke's views), while Schuchardt is much nearer to individualism and idealism.

as we have seen, was not their main concern, but when in the early 1920s Meillet affirmed that the only way in which languages could be usefully classified was genealogically, he was in fact well within the tradition which they had started.[79] In other circles the criticism had gone further, and the very bases of the comparative method were called in doubt: we have mentioned the position of Schuchardt, but it would be equally and, perhaps, more interesting to discuss the views of Baudouin de Courtenay. The obvious consequence, this time, was a shift of interests: hence the numerous studies of word histories, *Wörter und Sachen*, history of culture and history of language, etc. In the rare cases in which attention did concentrate on language classification, this rejection or criticism of the comparative method was bound to stimulate interest in areal classification and in a typological characterization of languages. Along this line it would be possible to follow one of the trends of thought which, in the twentieth century, led for instance to Trubeckoj's definition of the notion of *Sprachbund*. However, this lies outside our chronological limits, and the moment has now come to abandon the history of the comparative method and pass to the second part of our survey.

3. TYPOLOGICAL CLASSIFICATION

3.1 The typological views of the nineteenth century have not found a generous reception in standard histories of linguistics: all mentions of them are accidental and almost apologetic in nature. Historically this is understandable. As we shall see, the traditional form of 'morphological' classification was discredited by the end of the nineteenth century, and modern historiography has reflected this attitude. Moreover, the tendency has been to concentrate on what, for most scholars, marked the real dividing line between the nineteenth century approach and the 'philosophical' outlook of the century which preceded it (see above 1.4): the genealogical method of comparison, with its historical aims, seemed to fulfil this function, while linguistic typology, with its inevitable element of arbitrariness and its synchronic or perhaps achronic methodology, did not. This may account for instance for the views of Pedersen (1962: 99) who dismisses in less than a page the fact that 'in the course of the nineteenth century certain attempts were made to devise a short-cut by establishing a number of types under which all languages could be classified'. A similar attitude had been taken long before by Berthold Delbrück (1901:47): 'Wie bekannt, hatten sich die Sprachforscher einmal dahin geeinigt, die Sprachen nach ihrem Bau in isolierende, einverleibende, agglutinierende und flektierende einzuteilen. Aber diese Klassifikation ist uns allmählich unter den Händen zerronnen'. Delbrück was not the first with his criticism: similar doubts had been expressed in an equally influential work, Fr.

[79] See below 3.1.

Müller's *Grundriss der Sprachwissenschaft* (1876–88:I,1, 81ff.).[80] As we have seen before (2.10) a classic sentence by Meillet (1924:1) gave the accolade to a similar position: 'La seule classification linguistique qui ait une valeur et une utilité est la classification généalogique, fondée sur l'histoire des langues.'

3.11 In a recent article Greenberg (1970) has underlined the dramatic features of the history of typology. At the beginning of the nineteenth century it shared the stage with the new comparative linguistics; towards the end of the century it fell into neglect and disrepute. Sapir appears to have saved it from complete extinction. During the last two decades it has revived, thus showing the intrinsic vitality of the subject, its tenacity and its adaptability.

Parts of this picture could be challenged. We may choose to ignore the link between the work of Finck and that of his pupil Ernst Lewy (cf. Lewy 1951 and 1952), but we should not forget Schuchardt's interest in an *Elementarverwandtschaft* with no historical connotations (see above p. 651), or, later on, Trubeckoj's paper on the typology of Indo-European (1939, see p. 637) or Jakobson's contributions to the subject. Particularly important is the prominence given to typology in Hjelmslev's linguistic theory (cf. Bès 1967, and especially Lepschy 1970:xii), not least because with its undeniable influence on, e.g., the work of Uspenskij and Birnbaum, it seems to guarantee some continuity between the recent revival and earlier doctrines (cf. Birnbaum 1970: *passim* and especially 80). Even Marr's typological-genealogical theories, which are outside the chronological limits of this survey, should not be entirely forgotten. However, if by typology we refer to the 'morphological' classification in its standard form, Greenberg's statements are essentially correct for the nineteenth century.

3.2 For the reasons given in 3.1 an account of the basic facts concerning the typological classifications of the nineteenth century is not easy to find. As a list of primary material to turn to in the first instance, the long bibliographical introduction to the second edition of *Les langues du monde* (Meillet and Cohen 1952:I) remains unrivalled. It offers an almost complete list of works dedicated to language comparison and typology from the beginning until recently; nineteenth-century titles form the greatest part of the list. A short survey of the most important books is also offered by Veith (1969) who gives a brief summary of their content and offers some comments on their importance (cf. especially Veith 1969:11–18). Yet another brief account of various types of classification (geographical, genealogical, typological) from Dante until the present day will be found in Leroy (1960); parts of the text are repeated in Leroy (1971: *passim*).

In his *Introduzione alla glottologia* Tagliavini (1963:381ff.) offers a clear account (which relies in part on earlier work of his) of the various classifications proposed from Schlegel onwards till the present day. The starting point is the usual distinction

[80] Baudouin de Courtenay could also be quoted: cf., e.g., Stankiewicz's discussion (Baudouin de Courtenay 1972: 39) with his reference to Baudouin's programme of lectures for 1877–78 (*ibid.* 119).

between typological and genealogical classification, but Tagliavini postulates a further subdivision between morphological and psychological classifications. According to him Schlegel, Bopp, Pott and Schleicher based their theories on a structural comparison of languages, while Humboldt, Steinthal, Misteli and Finck arranged their evidence according to psychological criteria. The distinction goes back to Fr. Müller's *Grundriss* (1876–88:I,1,63–4).

Linguistically inaccessible to me is T.S. Sharadzenidze's book in Georgian on the classification of languages and their principles, which I know only through the brief Russian summary at the end (Sharadzenidze 1958:503ff.). Sharadzenidze distinguishes seven types of classification: genealogical, morphological (Schlegel, Humboldt, Schleicher), psychological (Steinthal, Misteli), conceptual (Sapir), 'in Sprachkreise' (W. Schmidt), in stages (Marr, Meščaninov), in *Sprachbünde* (Trubeckoj). The distinction between morphological and psychological classifications is similar to that of Müller and Tagliavini, but Humboldt is assigned to the former and not to the latter group.[81]

In the last two decades the renewed interest in the problems of language classification has produced two monographs which aim at providing the reader with a simple history (chronologically arranged) of the studies of typological classification. Kuznecov (1960) offers a brief resumé of the theories of the most obvious authors (from Schlegel to Sapir and then to Marr). Horne (1966) starts with a theoretical chapter which relies heavily on Greenberg's work and discusses the various ways of approaching language classification. He then follows very much the same pattern as Kuznecov, though the emphasis varies slightly, especially for the more modern authors. Kuznecov emphasizes the importance of Marr in the USSR, while Horne dedicates more space to Sapir and introduces two more modern theorists: Greenberg and Martinet. For the earlier period Horne and Kuznecov do not differ much: both authors consider the contributions of the two Schlegels, Humboldt, Bopp, Schleicher, Steinthal, Misteli, and Finck, and are practically alone in mentioning Fortunatov.

Lounsbury's brief survey of the history of classification (1968) is less propaedeutic and more argumentative; it adopts a line which is very similar, at least in its first part, to that of Jespersen's article on language classification (Jespersen 1962:693–704 [first published 1920]). It starts with the observation that the concern with differences among languages was linked in the nineteenth century with the attempt to discern their mental and cultural significance. Linguistic typology was comparative, in a non-historical sense of the word, but it also came to have a time dimension thanks to its evolutionary tendencies. Humboldt was the first to postulate a development from one linguistic type to another, and this assumption was accepted by some of his successors

81 I am grateful to Mrs. Joan Leopold for bringing this book and Lounsbury's article to my attention. The main purpose of Sharadzenidze's book does not seem to be historical, and it is no oddity that it appears to have been written outside the main Western tradition of the history of linguistics. Even so, the book seems to be solidly based on a good acquaintance with the primary sources, and this increases the regret that it cannot be accessible to a wider public.

until Max Müller connected the evolution of language with the evolution of society and assumed that each of the three major language types (isolating, agglutinative, inflectional) corresponded to one stage of the development of community life (family stage, nomadic stage, political or state stage). The attention then shifts to the typological views of the American school: Whitney and then Boas, and Sapir.

3.3 From most of the literature just quoted the development of typological research appears as relatively unproblematic. The aim was to find some criterion which could be meaningfully used to classify all languages of the world. After Fr. Schlegel's distinction between affixing and inflectional (or organic) languages, which in practice contrasts Indo-European with all other language types, we have a series of further refinements, due to A.W. Schlegel, Humboldt, Schleicher, etc. A common feature is the attention given to word structure which allows the famous tripartite division into isolating (or monosyllabic), agglutinative (or affixing), and inflectional languages. Other distinctions may be introduced, such as a fourth class of incorporating languages, intended to accommodate, inter alia, most of the Amerindian types (which Schleicher prefers to consider agglutinative). A further subdivision which gained popularity was that proposed by A.W. Schlegel, between synthetic and analytic languages, which was meant to take care of the contrast between two inflectional languages such as Latin and English. Steinthal's analysis followed different lines, but it is this 'morphological' classification which gained prevalence until its partial rejection towards the end of the century and its reformulation and reintegration in Sapir's theory.

3.31 Yet, for all its apparent simplicity, even this view of the history of typological classification may be challenged. We are given a list of scholars, which, needless to say, is not exhaustive, but we are left in doubt about the criteria which determined the selection. Other names come to mind. Steinthal (1860:13) quotes with some respect the theories of the psychologist-anthropologist Th. Waitz, who now appears to be forgotten.[82] Should we yield to the urgent plea of Ernst Lewy (1961b [first published 1944]) and mention James Byrne with his psychological classification?[83] What is the position of Georg von Gabelentz, whose theoretical contributions have recently been revalued (cf. above 2.9), and to whom we owe, inter alia, a very interesting article on typology (Gabelentz 1894)? Most authors ignore R. de La Grasserie: is this a wise

[82] The first volume of the *Anthropologie der Naturvölker* appeared in Leipzig in 1859 and was translated into English 'with numerous additions by the Author' by J. F. Collingwood in 1863. The book appeared as the first of a series of translations published by the Anthropological Society of London (founded in that year). The chapter on language classification which is part of section 5 [part 1] ('On the classification of Mankind'), though not new in its approach, is an interesting reminder for the linguist of the importance that typological classification had for the anthropologists of the first three quarters of the nineteenth century. It also shows some vagueness in the distinction between genealogical and typological classification.

[83] Byrne was more influential than is normally supposed. Lewy has repeatedly stressed the connection between him and Finck, but we may also remember the high praise bestowed upon him by G. von Gabelentz (1894:1).

decision? And what about the views of Baudouin de Courtenay? Other problems arise from the divergent interpretations of some authors. Should we count Rask among the typologists, as suggested by Hjelmslev (cf. above 2.4)? The starting point of the list requires some comment too. Why should we start the canon with Friedrich Schlegel rather than with J.C. Adelung or even D. Jenisch (for the latter see Jespersen 1922:29–31 and Timpanaro 1972a:97–8)?[84] To Adelung we owe a clear-cut distinction between monosyllabic and polysyllabic languages, which, for all its evolutionary overtones, is not too remote from that between isolating and agglutinative languages. The name of Adam Smith is not normally associated with linguistic typology, but Coseriu (1968) has suggested that he is the source of A.W. Schlegel's distinction between analytic and synthetic languages. In an independent essay Scott Elledge (1967) has tried to show that Adam Smith's views were influenced by Bacon. But even if we do not go so far back as Bacon, we should not forget the typological distinction between 'langues transpositives' (like Latin), 'analogues' (like French) and 'mixtes' (like German) made by the abbé Girard as early as 1747 (cf. Diderichsen 1960:127, Rosiello 1967:146). If so the history of typology seems to stretch far back through the centuries.

All these are open problems and in view of their existence the agreement about the name of F. Schlegel as the first author of a typological classification may be puzzling. Here too, the usual explanation is forthcoming. Modern historiography has accepted the views of the past century. This is probably a right decision; there is little doubt that there is a strong sense of continuity between Schlegel and the later typologists, while Adelung, Jenisch, Adam Smith and l'abbé Girard, not to mention Bacon, remain at a distance. Even so, the choice is derivative and few attempts have been made to give it an explicit justification (for an exception see Timpanaro 1972a:97–101, who offers an interesting sketch of the early non-genealogical comparisons, and see also Diderichsen 1960:125ff., for the contrast between the nineteenth century and the earlier period).

Other questions arise; they concern first and foremost the correct interpretation of the authors mentioned, but also some more general problems. We have spoken already of the difficulties which we find in distinguishing between the early typological and genealogical classifications (cf. 1.6) and between the criteria used in each type of enquiry. This is not the only trouble. What justifies the fervour of typological research which we find in the first three quarters of the century? Should it be taken as a con-

[84] Jenisch is scarcely ever mentioned, but Jespersen's own interests induced him to give some attention to Jenisch's attempt to characterize each language in order to find out which one came nearest to the 'Ideal einer vollkomnen Sprache'. Timpanaro (1972a:97) points out that in spite of Jenisch's rare impartiality the book reveals the basic subjectivity and infertility of this type of comparison. In fact what is interesting in Jenisch (1796) is not so much his evaluation of the various languages as the attention which he gives to language as a whole, including grammar, which is also considered as a means of establishing language kinship (cf., e.g., his statement about English, *ibid.* 57, note). Jenisch was well aware of the possibilities of historical research and knew the correct methodology for it (cf., e.g., *ibid.* 41); at the same time as he stated that similarities due to common origin go deeper than any other form of similarity, he seemed to exclude any form of evolution which would drastically alter a language type.

tinuation of eighteenth-century classificatory interests? Or is it due to the influence of the natural sciences (cf. above 1.51)? Or does it simply correspond to the practical need to arrange in some way the new wealth of linguistic material available? And finally, what can explain the disenchantment with morphological typology which prevailed in some circles by the end of the century? None of these questions can be answered here, but they may be kept in mind and used as a framework for our survey of recent work on the subject.

3.4 The first problematic figure is F. Schlegel. The enormous influence which his equation of organic and inflectional exerted on the history of nineteenth-century linguistics in general, is well known.[85] An analysis of F. Schlegel's thinking about language differences can be found in Nüsse (1962:37–49), who argues that his typology arises from the merging of his systematic interests with his concept of organism. However, Timpanaro (1972a) is certainly right when he emphasizes that in Schlegel's statements there is still something of the old classifications of the eighteenth century which were concerned with the genius of languages. While his 'vergleichende Grammatik', in contrast with that of his predecessors,[86] appears to aim at a genealogical classification, his typological classification is essentially static and has evaluative overtones: the contrast between the two language types becomes in his mind a contrast of divine and ferine languages (Timpanaro 1972a:101). Yet, to my mind, not even Timpanaro stresses sufficiently that nowhere in *Ueber die Sprache und Weisheit der Indier* (Schlegel 1808) is there a clear statement of the distinction between linguistic comparison which aims at genealogical results and linguistic comparison which aims at typological statements or classification. The purpose of genealogical comparison is stated once at the beginning: it elucidates the historical origins and progress of nations and their early migrations and wanderings. Later on, the chapter on typological classification states clearly that all organic languages share the same structure and are genetically related. It then appears that the organic/non-organic distinction is meant to provide further evidence about the kinship of the organic languages, while at the same time stressing their superiority. If so, typological classification may seem to play a subordinate role vis-à-vis genealogical classification. And indeed Sharadzenidze (1958: Russian resumé 513–4) argues just this: Schlegel is only interested in genealogical relationship; he knows that Semitic is not related to Indo-European and consequently he is compelled to make the somewhat surprising statement that Semitic, differently from Indo-European, is a non-inflectional, non-organic language. However, this view too is probably too drastic. Apropos of the non-organic languages Schlegel denies the possibility of tracing them back to a common source, so that it

[85] Cf. above 2.3. It is certainly wrong to argue that by inflection Schlegel means only the modification of the root vowels (as in Latin *foedus* vs. *fides*), yet this has been frequently maintained (most recently by Horne 1966:11f.). For a correct interpretation (scil. inflection refers both to ablaut, umlaut and the like, and to a particular type of suffixes and prefixes) cf. Timpanaro 1972a (82f.). For La Grasserie's point that the concept of inflection had never been properly defined see below note 127.

[86] For the earlier history of this phrase see above, note 15.

would seem that the organic/non-organic classification had a wider scope than the genealogical one.

The problem which has not been tackled a propos of F. Schlegel is why his somewhat rough classification, with all its ambiguity, was regarded with respect, even when attacked, for most of the nineteenth century. The beginnings of a solution could perhaps be found in the observation that all through the work of Humboldt, Schleicher, Steinthal, etc. — in spite of the difference of presuppositions and backgrounds — we can recognize a continual search for a non-arbitrary principle on which linguistic classification could be based. Non-arbitrary in this context can only mean essential to language, i.e. based on the study of the nature of language. From this point of view the aesthetic classifications of the previous centuries were bound to appear unacceptable, but F. Schlegel's classification, even when bitterly opposed — as it often was —, seemed to be on a different level.[87] In the first part of the century there could be debate about the way in which the idea of 'organic' should be applied to language, but no one would have denied its essential and non-arbitrary nature.[88]

3.41 Timpanaro (1972a) is eager to underline, against Nüsse (1962), the development in F. Schlegel's ideas. In his earlier work the distinction between inflectional or organic and non-inflectional or non-organic languages impelled him to deny any genetic connection between the two types; later on, religious scruples induced him — a new convert — to accept the traditional monogenetic view and to postulate a sort of degenerative process which was supposed to bring the organic languages to a non-organic or mechanical stage. As Timpanaro (1972a) points out, this phase of Schlegel's thought, however interesting biographically, remains outside the main stream of the history of linguistics. This was influenced, and in a sense directed, by Friedrich Schlegel only through his 1808 book and through the modified version of his theory proposed by his brother A. W. Schlegel.

It is to A. W. Schlegel in fact that we owe the traditional distinction between languages without grammatical structure, languages with affixes and languages with inflection, and it was he who canonized the division of inflectional languages into analytic and synthetic and the theory that synthetic languages had to become analytic in the process of time.[89] Nüsse (1962:48) points out that in fact the three-fold dis-

[87] Steinthal (1860:4f.) sharply criticized Schlegel's classification but gave him credit for having introduced the concept of organism into linguistics (though, see *ibid.* 21, where he gives priority to Humboldt). Further on, he argued that Schlegel's classification should be grouped with other classifications of languages into masculine and feminine, or crystal-like, plant-like and animal-like (an obvious dig at Schleicher); they all contained part of the truth, but only touched the surface of the language phenomenon (*ibid.* 7).

[88] Needless to say, other reasons, which were more concerned with the history of linguistics in general than with that of typological classification in particular, helped to give the views of Fr. Schlegel's an authority which those of his predecessors lacked.

[89] The history of this distinction, which still enjoys some popularity, deserves a separate study. I have given above some hints about its earlier history (cf. 3.31). From the point of view of the terminology employed it could be added here that, well before A. W. Schlegel, S. de Sacy (1808:255f.) spoke of a 'système de synthèse' for the grammar of Coptic (cf. also Humboldt 1903–36:IV, 312),

tinction destroyed the whole point of F. Schlegel's organic/inorganic contrast, while at the same time showing some progress in the application of the comparative method. This is worth stressing; another point, however, which is often ignored is that A.W. Schlegel, in contrast to his brother, refused to prejudge the possibility of an evolution from the first of his language classes to the second or the third. His statements on the subject (A.W. Schlegel 1846:214 note 7 [first published 1818]) implied that the problem of the evolutionary interpretation of his scheme could only be solved by empirical evidence and that this was not available at the time. The very existence of this sceptical position at the beginning of the century is important. We shall have to return to the question later, when talking about evolution (see 3.91); for the moment it is sufficient to point out how much more aware A.W. Schlegel appears than his brother of the importance of the historical method. It is to be hoped that the promised work of S. Timpanaro on his thought (cf. Timpanaro 1972a:93 note 63) will shed some more light on this and other points.

3.5 We mentioned above (in 2.5) Wilhelm von Humboldt's definition of the criteria which prove genealogical relationship. Here we must concentrate on other parts of his work. In the last twenty years or so, he has attracted great attention from numerous angles, not all of which need concern us here. However, even if we limit ourselves to strictly linguistic work, we have to register a number of contributions of very unequal value, often written in ignorance one of the other. A book has attempted a summary of Humboldt's linguistic thought accompanied by a resumé of his posthumous book (Valverde 1955). A lengthy monograph (Liebrucks 1964–70:II, cf. also I) has examined Humboldtian problems more from a philosophical than from a historiographical point of view. No less than three monographs and a number of articles have concentrated on Humboldt's role as founder or upholder or precursor of the so-called Sapir-Whorf hypothesis (Brown 1967, Miller 1968, Penn 1972, Apel 1959, Christmann 1965, 1966, Mattoso Camara 1970, Politzer 1963a, 1963b; cf. also Hansen-Løve 1972). His thought has been discussed in general (Evans 1967, Gipper 1965, H.J. Mueller 1966, Seidel 1968, Teeter 1966, Wald 1962, etc.) or with reference to particular concepts (Beneš 1958, Pleines 1967, Rensch 1967, Stolte 1948, Schwankweiler 1965,

though he was only concerned with the way in which languages pass from a monosyllabic isolating stage to a plurisyllabic agglutinative form. The popularity of A. W. Schlegel's distinction must have been partly due to the fact that it fulfilled the (more or less explicit) need to believe that all languages belonging to the same family also belonged to the same linguistic class (cf. 3.93). Since some Indo-European languages had been taken as a model for the inflectional type, it did not seem possible to give a different label to the younger offshoots of the family, even if by rights they appeared to be nearer to the agglutinative or the isolating type. However, this sub-classification was not universally accepted. Soon after its formulation, Humboldt rejected it because it was too vague and because linguistic history showed that the so-called analytic languages often created synthetic forms as secondary developments not inherited from the parent language (cf. Humboldt 1903–36: VI, 260f.). At a much later stage (see below 3.93) Baudouin de Courtenay argued that English was really an isolating language on a par with Chinese, which implied a de facto rejection of the analytic/synthetic distinction as a sub-classification of the inflectional class.

Weisgerber 1953–54).[90] The connections between Humboldt and modern linguistics have often been explored, though sometimes in a desultory and uncoordinated manner (but cf. Christmann 1972, Lohmann 1967, Pätsch 1968), and attempts have been made to put Humboldt in his setting and to trace the influences which helped to form his setting and theoretical outlook (Apel 1963:372ff., Christmann 1965, Funke 1957, Heintz 1969, Viertel 1966, Weimann 1965, cf. also above 1.4). Modern anthologies and translations[91] document a lively interest in this author even from outside the traditional territory of the German Neohumboldtians.

Few works, however, have been concerned directly with Humboldt's classification. This may perhaps explain a puzzling phenomenon: the general books and monographs mentioned above in 3.2 present different accounts of his classificatory schemas. Kuznecov (1960:10) and Horne (1966:13–15) attribute to him a four-tier classification of languages into isolating, agglutinative, inflectional and incorporating classes, while recognizing that this is basically A.W. Schlegel's classification schema with a fourth class added. Lounsbury (1968:191ff.) follows very much the same line, with some qualifications. Other scholars go further and mistakenly seem to attribute to Humboldt rather than to A.W. Schlegel the paternity of the whole schema (cf., e.g., Robins 1967:176). Tagliavini (1963:I, 393) attributes these views to an error of Schleicher,[92] while he accepts another schema (obviously taken from Steinthal 1850 and 1860) according to which all languages are to be categorized as being more or less 'complete'. The former may be either isolating or inflectional, the latter may be either particle languages (in which the verb has no special expression) or pronominal languages (in which the verb is characterized by the juxtaposition of pronominal elements).

In a thoughtful article, in which she is practically unique in considering both the concrete and the theoretical work of Humboldt, G. Pätsch (1967) has pointed out that, although Humboldt is always quoted for one or the other version of linguistic classification, in fact he never reached any firm conclusion on the subject. He simply distinguished the two extremes (the inflectional languages versus the languages like e.g. classical Chinese) and assumed that the affixing languages represented an intermediate point. Warnings about the misunderstandings which have arisen in the interpretation of Humboldt's theories are also to be found in Gipper (1965:9ff.). Hansen-Løve (1972:37f.) goes a step further and denies that Humboldt ever admitted the possibility of any language classification.

In fact, most of the various schemas attributed to Humboldt are in some way

[90] Some books or articles which I have not been able to see are not quoted here or in the bibliography. I particularly regret that I have not found the series of essays *Die Brüder Humboldt heute* (Abhandlungen der Humboldt Gesellschaft, 2), Mannheim 1968, mentioned in BL 1969: 20 no. 46.

[91] Anthologies and translations are not quoted here or in the bibliography with the exception of Cowan 1963, which is frequently referred to in American publications, but which I have not been able to see.

[92] The reference is to Schleicher 1848:6, note; the error had already been pointed out by Steinthal (1970:132 [first published, 1850]).

grounded in his own work. A distinction between isolating, agglutinative, and inflectional types occurs frequently (with this terminology) in the posthumous (1836) *Ueber die Verschiedenheit des menschlichen Sprachbaues und ihren Einfluss auf die geistige Entwicklung des Menschengeschlechts* (Humboldt 1903–36:VII, 1ff.) and is also implied in the earlier work (1822) *Ueber das Entstehen der grammatischen Formen, und ihren Einfluss auf die Ideenentwicklung* (*ibid.*:IV, 285ff.). However, a contrast between agglutinative and inflectional types is explicitly denied in VII,117, where only two types seem to be envisaged; elsewhere (VII,117, cf. also VI,275ff.) it is stated that these must be interpreted as abstract forms and all languages are mixtures of two or more types.[93] The last chapters of the 1836 book (on which Steinthal's schema is based) seem to express strong doubts about the possibility of an exhaustive classification of all languages, but it is reiterated that this is feasible with a particular aim in mind and using a particular phenomenon as a criterion (cf. VII,254ff., and especially VII,278–9). Then a sort of classification is suggested which corresponds, though not exactly, to that given by Steinthal. The main defect of the histories of typology mentioned before is not so much that they give a wrong interpretation of Humboldt's theories as that they do not add the necessary qualification to their statements. An easy reminder of the difficulties encountered in understanding Humboldt's views on the subject could have come from a first-hand acquaintance with the polemical (but friendly) exchange about this problem which took place in the 1850s and later between Steinthal and Pott (cf., e.g., Pott 1852a, 1852b, Steinthal 1970: 139–64 [first published 1852], Pott 1859–76:II,4,ii).

3.51 Telegdi (1970) has competently discussed the part which typology plays in the linguistic work of Humboldt: it is interesting to see that some of his conclusions come near to those of Steinthal, but it is a pity that he does not discuss the earlier work on the subject (e.g. Pätsch 1967, Gipper 1965, parts of Liebrucks 1964–70:II). According to Telegdi, Humboldt's typological studies are a direct consequence of his linguistic theory; they represent an essential part of his search for universals and they indicate the extent of his reactions against the universal or philosophical grammar of his predecessors. Moreover, Humboldt's conception of language as an organism with a unity and a reality of its own accounts for the attention which the problem of language plurality receives in his system. It is at this stage that the problem of Humboldt's views about linguistic relativity should be considered (cf. the literature quoted above in 3.5). One of Brown's key points is that it was his organicistic view of language which allowed Humboldt to set up language as the independent variable required for a strong version of a linguistic relativity theory (Brown 1967: *passim* and especially 53).

It may be added here that the primary importance given to typology, as the main source of information about the language faculty and its expression, may well explain Humboldt's hesitations and the reluctance with which he proposed — or perhaps did

[93] Steinthal (1970:145 [first published, 1852]) pointed out that this implied that according to Humboldt the division into isolating, agglutinative, and inflectional types could not be sufficient by itself to provide a classification of languages.

not propose — a classification schema: too much depended on it. However, we should not forget Steinthal's detailed analysis of this very question (1860). According to him, Humboldt was clear in his mind that any classification had to depend on a correct identification of the *Sprachform* of each language, but he did not succeed in defining this key concept clearly and oscillated between two opposite views; on the one side he identified the *innere Sprachform* with the general form of thought and on the other side he treated it as the organic principle which introduced an essential — i.e. non-superficial — difference between the various languages.[94]

We have to refrain here from any discussion of the Humboldtian concept of *innere Sprachform*, which would take us too far, and which is indeed examined in practically all works quoted above (for a short introduction see Funke 1957), but we may add by way of postilla to what precedes that it is regrettable that, in spite of a few exceptions (e.g. Liebrucks 1964–70:II), most linguists have not given attention to the anthropological essays which Humboldt wrote in the last decade of the eighteenth century and which have been recently discussed again by Leroux (1958; cf. also Brown 1967:106). His conclusion: 'c'est donc en anthropologue et afin de promouvoir la connaissance des mentalités et des caractères des peuples que Humboldt aborda l'étude des langues' (*ibid.*:69, note 2) is important, and some of the endless discussion about Humboldt's key concepts (like that just mentioned of *innere Sprachform*) could receive some light from a comparison with his early psychological-anthropological work.

Another important point to consider concerns the relationship between Humboldt's views and those of Friedrich Schlegel. In his view of 'organic' inflection Humboldt is obviously on the side of Bopp, and assumes that inflection may arise from agglutination, something which Schlegel hotly denied. Nüsse (1962:46) has pointed out that Humboldt managed to overcome Schlegel's dualism. All languages (including the isolating ones) are characterized by an organic principle (the *innere Sprachform* again!) so that the organic/non-organic contrast loses its value as a classificatory criterion. Even so, Humboldt, like Schlegel, has no hesitation in arranging the different languages on a priority scale. Gertrud Pätsch (1967:114ff.) has tried to establish what it was that impelled Humboldt to take this evaluative position, and attributes it to three causes. First, for him language is simply a *Vehikel* used in order to penetrate the secrets of the 'geistige Welt', i.e. Humboldt looks at language from an extralinguistic point of view. Secondly, his philosophical presuppositions induce him (like Bernhardi) to look for an ideal language as an 'unbedingte Form'. Thirdly, like all his contemporaries he is conditioned by his interest in Indo-European languages. There is little to add to this analysis, but the first point needs some clarification. This comes — in my opinion — from Humboldt's relativity theory. Since language can influence

[94] It is possible to give weight to this interpretation without necessarily following Steinthal all the way or seeing the real cause of Humboldt's hesitations in a conflict between *Theorie* and *Empirie* which would have blighted the whole life of this 'wahrhaft tragischer Held' (Steinthal 1970:139 [first published, 1852]).

thought, it can also hinder it. It follows that the nearer a language comes to a formal expression of logical relationship the more it fulfils this aim of favouring rational thought. As Humboldt argued in his 1822 paper (1903–36:IV,285ff.) this does not exclude, of course, that anything can be expressed in any language, provided that some external cause (such as contact with other cultures) has created the need for it in the mind of the speaker; it simply means that some languages make a particular type of thought easier than some others.

3.6 Two other scholars are referred to in the histories of typology: Franz Bopp (cf. above 2.41) and August Friedrich Pott (cf. 2.61). Bopp's attempt to classify languages according to the form of their roots and their capacity for composition and internal alteration is often mentioned (cf. Tagliavini 1963:I,384f., Horne 1966:15), but this classification is meaningful only if considered in connection with Bopp's theory of the root and of Ablaut (cf. 2.61 and see Verburg 1950) and only if one understands Bopp's early fight against Friedrich Schlegel's concept of the organic development of the root (for some hints about this see Lounsbury 1968). In fact the whole question is more interesting for an understanding of Bopp than for the history of typology, to which Bopp contributed but little. Yet, Bopp's views about the superiority of the Indo-European languages over the others (cf. Bopp 1833:113) would deserve some mention, if only because, based as they were on a somewhat vague notion of richness and harmony, they emphasize by contrast the greater impact of Humboldt's and F. Schlegel's evaluative criteria.[95]

Tagliavini (1963:I,385), Horne (1966:15f.), who follows Steinthal (1860) and Jespersen (1962:693–704 [first published 1920]), Lounsbury (1968), who follows Steinthal (1850) and Jespersen (*loc. cit.*), all agree in attributing a particular classification schema to Pott. The same statement is found in Steinthal, as we have seen, and in Fr. Müller (1876–88:I,67). Directly or indirectly reference is made to an article by Pott in an obscure periodical, the *Jahrbücher der freien deutschen Akademie* (Frankfurt a.M.) for 1849. Pott himself has tried to correct this mistaken attribution (cf., e.g., Pott 1852a, and 1859–76:II,4, iff,); he repeatedly argued that he had always felt incompetent to produce any classification and that what passed for his own effort was in fact the way in which, after due warning, he had set out in a short and popularizing article his interpretation of Humboldt's views on the subject.[96] The misunderstanding has lasted too long. Pott's reflections about the whole problem of classification have

[95] Obviously I do not mean to select here for praise, still less acceptance, the criteria and conclusions of Humboldt and Schlegel, but it is important to point out that at least in the case of Humboldt these were far more thoughtful and theoretically well grounded than the traditional aesthetic judgments about the relative value of languages. Bopp's attitude meant a regression to earlier views (while at the same time his version of the morphological classification was perhaps naive but far better defined).

[96] As far as one can see, the periodical was almost always quoted at second hand. Already in 1851 Böhtlingk (1851:i) mentioned that he had found it impossible to get hold of Pott's article, and a similar declaration was made in the late 1850s by Madvig (cf. Madvig 1971:168 note 1). Steinthal withdrew part of his statements in 1852 and again in 1860 (cf. Steinthal 1970:139ff., 1860:10).

been quoted above (cf. 1.51 and 2.61) and certainly earn him a place in the history of typology and in that of genealogical studies, but he should not be attributed views which he himself maintained that he had never held.

3.7 In the main stream of typological work are two contrasting and often antagonistic figures, A. Schleicher and H. Steinthal. We shall discuss them in turn.[97]

All the works mentioned above point out that Schleicher's version of typological classification (with its evolutionary or transformationistic statements and its division of languages into isolating, or monosyllabic, agglutinative, and inflectional) became widely known and still holds the field at a lower level of vulgarization. They also illustrate Schleicher's formulae for indentifying languages according to the different ways in which they express lexical meaning and relations (*Beziehungen*). Most accounts give the impression that we are dealing with a somewhat modernized version of Humboldt's and A. W. Schlegel's classifications. Humboldt's influence on Schleicher must indeed have been great, and is often recognizable even in minor details, but it is all too easy to forget that the general approach and the thought behind the schema differ considerably. We have seen that for Humboldt the plurality of languages was strictly tied to the spiritual differences of nations (as it was in Herder): his 'vergleichendes Sprachstudium' was the outcome, and, in a sense, the precondition of his 'vergleichende Anthropologie'. For Schleicher any attempt at analyzing the spiritual life of peoples came under the purview of philology and not of linguistics or *Glottick*. Since language was an organism which obeyed natural laws, the normal methodology of the natural sciences was relevant, and called in all cases for a comparative, classificatory study. Dietze (1966:68–9) has mentioned some of these points (cf. also the observations by Esper 1968:95ff.), but Schleicher's classification theory needs further exploration. How does he, for instance, justify the choice of his linguistic parameter, the relationship of meaning and *Beziehungen*? He himself tells us (1850:6–7) that this contrast is basic to human thought. But if language is envisaged as being closely connected with thought, how can it be an independent, 'natural' organism?[98] We may well ask whether there is here one of those inconsistencies in Schleicher's theoretical position which have been underlined by Trnka (1952:140).

Yet another problem arises when we consider the details of Schleicher's classification theory. We have mentioned above (in 2.71) the way in which he tried to combine genealogical and morphological classifications. This is not all: most text books also refer to his evolutionary theories to the effect that in prehistoric times every inflectional language passed through a monosyllabic and an agglutinative stage. It would be easy to make use of this belief in evolution in order to argue that Schleicher extended the genealogical principle to all classification, as Darwin wanted to do, but this conflicts with all that we know about his thought. For Schleicher, who did not believe in

[97] For the bibliography on Schleicher, cf. above 2.7.
[98] Cf. Schleicher 1869:5: 'Die Sprache ist also lautlicher Ausdruck des Denkens, lautes Denken ... (cf. also Dietze 1966:65).

monogenesis, two *Ursprachen*, which belonged to the same morphological class, did not need to be genealogically related — and in fact could not, if the distinction between evolution period and decay period had to be taken seriously. Let us combine this conclusion with the point mentioned by Schleicher (e.g. in 1850:23) that the concepts of species and genus are relative: the *Sprachstämme* are to the morphological classes as species to genus, but to the *Sprachfamilien* as genus to species. In this way we find another ambiguity in the schema (in addition to those pointed out by Lepschy 1962: 189).[99] The criterion used for identifying e.g. the species Germanic versus the genus Indo-European (or European) is a genealogical one and is very different from the typological criterion used for identifying the species Indo-European versus the genus 'inflectional'.

That for Schleicher typological classification was not simply a side interest is shown, inter alia, by some work which has often been neglected. His first large scale book, *Zur vergleichenden Sprachgeschichte* (1848), as well as one of his last essays (1865b), are attempts at typological analyses, in the first case of a phonetic phenomenon which is studied diachronically, in the second case of the distinction between noun and verb (cf. for this Percival 1969). It is in this latter paper that Schleicher argued more clearly than most of his contemporaries had done that a study of language plurality had to rest on a description of the linguistic categories of the individual languages, and that this task was only possible if we had a criterion which allowed us to define the categories. According to him the real problem was: are there linguistic functions which have no formal definition? Or alternatively: do we start in our description of languages from the function or from the form? Is there an 'inner form' which is independent of the external form? More concretely: can we say that a language has a noun/verb distinction when there is no formal sign of this distinction? Schleicher's answer was that we should not attribute to any language a category which is not formally identifiable in it. From our point of view what matters here is not so much that — admittedly with a more sophisticated meaning of 'form' — these views have been claimed as a conquest of the first half of the twentieth century (cf. Percival 1969), but that here the view is implied that typology depends on synchronic description and that a correct description depends on the solution of some theoretical problems.[100] Obviously some of the same thoughts were in Humboldt's mind too (cf., e.g., Humboldt 1903–36:IV,289), but it is more interesting to find them in a man who passed to fame as a comparativist rather than as a theoretical thinker.

[99] Lepschy (1962:187ff.) offers a very interesting discussion of some points concerning the interpretation of Schleicher's theories; among other things he mentions Schleicher's identification of language with species and the difficulties which this creates within the context of his organicistic views (for language as species see above note 20 and cf. 3.91). Interestingly Lepschy also stresses the survival of Schleicher's theories in both the contendants of the later generation, Whitney and Max Müller (*ibid.* 190).

[100] Even so, Schleicher does not tackle the basic problem and does not ask how can it be that while he is willing to identify his categories on a formal basis, he still feels able to to use the same labels for categories of different languages.

3.71 The impact of H. Steinthal on the history of linguistics is difficult to assess. Part of the twentieth century seems to have surrounded him with a curtain of silence: Jespersen (1922 and 1962), Pedersen (1962), Mounin (1967), Robins (1967), Waterman (1971), Leroy (1971) either ignore him or barely mention him. Graur-Wald (1961: 42ff.) and Ivić (1970:52ff.) are almost exceptional in devoting some space to him as a prelude to their discussions of Potebnja and (in the case of Ivić) of Marty, Gabelentz, and Wundt. Arens (1969:242–5, 277–85) and Zvegincev (1960:I,105–50) are far more interested, but they are isolated. The scarcity of twentieth century work about Steinthal emerges clearly from Bumann's bibliography (1965:149–53). The short dissertation by Beneš (1958) discusses some of Steinthal's views, but with a lack of sympathy which at times comes near contempt and prevents understanding. The constant reproach, that of obscurity, woolliness, and metaphysical inclinations, levelled at him by some of his contemporaries (e.g. Max Müller and Whitney) has stuck. Even works such as de Mauro (1970a) which aim at tracing within the nineteenth century the theoretical interests of the previous century only quote Steinthal in order to reproach him for his too simple dismissal of Aristotle's theories or to put him together with Pott, Rudolf von Raumer and Brücke (de Mauro 1970a:82, 89). In the last ten or fifteen years, Lohmann's attempt (1960) to put Steinthal in his setting, the teaching of *allgemeine Sprachwissenschaft* in Berlin, Jost's study of the concept of language as energeia with his chapter on Steinthal (Jost 1960:83–92), Haselback's references to him in his monograph on Becker (1966), and Bumann's excellent monograph (1965) together with his edition of some of Steinthal's minor essays (Steinthal 1970) have slightly altered the balance (cf. also Esper 1968 *passim* and Jankowsky 1972 *passim*). Even more recently, in the lengthy introduction to her publication of the Lazarus-Steinthal correspondence, Ingrid Belke (1971) has dedicated some space to Steinthal's linguistic thought (including his theories about classification and about the origin of language) and to the differences between him, Paul, and Wundt (Belke 1971: ciii-cxii).[101] In spite of this recent work, it is no wonder that Horne, Kuznecov and Tagliavini simply summarize Steinthal's classification of languages without any close attempt at setting it against its theoretical background. Tagliavini (1963:393f.) sees in Steinthal a continuator of Humboldt's psychological classification, while Horne (1966:17f.) is eager to stress that his classification is based on a syntactical concept of 'form'.[102]

Bumann's explanation of Steinthal's views on language classification follows closely that of Steinthal's own books: the earlier *Die Classification der Sprachen, dargestellt als die Entwickelung der Sprachidee* (1850), and the later *Charakteristik der hauptsächlichsten Typen des Sprachbaues* (1860). Here, as elsewhere, Steinthal finds

[101] *Inter alia*, Belke (1971:cxiii) points out that some of Steinthal's theories changed considerably after he had read Darwin's *Descent of man* (1871).

[102] More surprising is Jespersen's statement (1962:703): 'Steinthal ... in various works tried to classify languages partly from geographical, partly from structural points of view, without however arriving at any definite and consistent system.'

his starting point in an appraisal and criticism of Humboldt's views. We have mentioned before (in 3.51) some of the points he makes. Humboldt's definition of *innere Sprachform* — we are told — is inadequate; he tended to identify it with the general form of thought without realizing that this effectively prevented him from giving any serious consideration to the problems of language plurality. Moreover he seemed to share the common assumption of philosophical and historical [i.e. empirical?] grammar that there is a set of categories common to all languages. This is just the point that Steinthal is eager to deny: it is absurd, he argued, to want to find logical categories in grammar, since language is not an expression of logical thought. There was no such thing as an *allgemeine Grammatik* and indeed there were no language categories outside the language to which they belonged. According to Steinthal the sort of typological work which looks for the different expressions of some linguistic category in different languages is misguided and is incompatible with any theory which takes seriously its definition of language as an organism. Categories must be extracted from each language, not imposed onto it a priori.[103] Thus, starting from his own psychological or socio-psychological presuppositions, Steinthal seems to have reached some conclusions which could well belong to the thirties or the forties of this century.[104]

Equally important, from our point of view, is that Steinthal explicitly mentions the function which he assigns to language classification: it was to replace the old *allgemeine Grammatik* as the supreme task of linguistics. Its aim was to show how each individual language in its organic unity was an implementation of the concept of language (*Sprachidee*) and how all languages in their turn could be considered as organic elements of a system in which they participated in various ways according to their relationship and the value of their inner organization (cf. Bumann 1965:110f.).

Bumann's otherwise excellent exposition does not sufficiently emphasize, to my mind, how it was just this explicit need to compare and classify linguistic organisms (i.e. organized wholes) rather than single linguistic elements and categories which induced Steinthal to reject any classification based on individual *Merkmäle* and to break new ground, using simultaneously a multiplicity of syntactical, morphological, etc. criteria in order to characterize the various languages and to assign them to classes.[105] Yet, the point is important in the history of language classification, and perhaps of classification in general. 'La classification, comme problème fondamental et constitutif de l'histoire naturelle, s'est logée historiquement, et d'une façon nécessaire, entre une théorie de la *marque* et une théorie de l'*organisme*.' (Foucault 1966:

[103] This emerges very clearly from the short explanation given in Steinthal's book on *Grammatik, Logik, und Psychologie* (1855:386–7). Steinthal 1850, which is closely followed by Bumann, is more long winded and less perspicuous.

[104] For some very structuralistic views about the meaning of words and the function of grammatical categories see Steinthal 1855:387. Some of Steinthal's assumptions in this field may have been inherited from his teacher Heyse, whose work he edited. For Heyse's theories about structural semantics, cf. Coseriu 1967d.

[105] Cf. especially Steinthal 1970:156f. [first published 1852].

158). What Steinthal had to offer was obviously a 'théorie de l'organisme'. But there is more. While breaking away from the idea of a single *Merkmal* as principle of classification, Steinthal foreshadowed more modern developments, which, though starting from different presuppositions, came to similar conclusions: Sapir's classification comes to mind, but we could also refer to some tendencies of statistical typology.

However, the development of Steinthal's thought is not altogether clear (and has hardly been explored). Between the classificatory schema proposed in *Classification* (1850) and that of *Charakteristik* (1860) there is a sharper distinction than is often realized. Bumann (1965:113) points out, rightly, that in the latter work a greater simplicity was obtained by limiting the classification to some linguistic types — a concept and method which, as Lewy (1951) and Lohmann (1960) have shown, was first introduced by Steinthal.[106] In an interesting article on the notion of linguistic type, Petr Sgall (1971:77) argues that in his earlier work Steinthal looked for substantial distinctions (while Humboldt aimed at distinctions of degrees) but later on he preferred to concentrate on the detailed analysis of a variety of a linguistic features and their combinations, without aiming at a rigid classification. Yet, the 1860 schema also introduced a straightforward distinction between *Form-Sprachen* and *formlose Sprachen*, which almost implied a return to the dualism of the younger Schlegel and to a more metaphysical interpretation of Humboldt's concept of form.[107] On the other hand there were, in the more recent book, some other new features in addition to the notion of linguistic type which we mentioned earlier: first, the explicit affirmation that form may be expressed in a number of ways, and secondly the practical consequence drawn from it, that Classical Chinese was listed among the *Form-Sprachen* because of its fixed word order. The necessary background for this last conclusion was a less naive view of grammar than that which stated without qualms that Classical Chinese had no grammar at all. Here, as elsewhere, Steinthal's thought is marked by a mixture of new insights, some of which had a considerable part to play in the further development of linguistics, and of unprovable assumptions. Whitney's criticism was justified, but one-sided.

3.8 Three other scholars are regularly mentioned in the works quoted above (3.2): Max Müller, Misteli and Finck. The latter is perhaps outside our chronological

[106] This is probably correct, but we should not forget the admirable preface which Böhtlingk wrote for his *Sprache der Jakuten* (1851). There he argued that any grammar should include a characterization of the language which it describes, so that this could be used for typological purposes, and advocated a study of both 'external' and 'internal' *Merkmäle* for the purpose of 'physiological' (i.e. structural) classification. In his characterization of the language he was describing he listed phonological and morphophonemic phenomena (number of vowels, consonants, etc., existence of vocalic harmony) as well as a number of morphological and syntactical features.

[107] But Gabelentz (1891:405) pointed out that the terminology represented an advance on Humboldt's distinction between *vollkommene* and *minder vollkommene Sprachen*, in which it was still possible to recognize the survival of earlier contrasts between Hellenes and Barbarians, 'Culturmenschen und Wilde'.

limits, but the ties which join him to his predecessors, Steinthal and Byrne on the one side, and Fr. Müller on the other, are so close that he cannot be ignored here. None of these authors has been very fortunate with modern scholarship: Misteli has been almost entirely ignored in spite of Koerner's recent interest in his review of Paul's *Prinzipien* (cf. Koerner 1972d). Max Müller has received some attention, mostly due to his political activity (Voigt 1967, Rüstau 1965), but his linguistic work — in spite of its earlier popularity — had partly fallen into discredit by the time of his death (1900), and has never been the object of thorough analysis.[108] Some basic information can be found in the pages dedicated by Terracini to Whitney (1949:73–121), in a short chapter by Jankowsky (1972:177–181), and in Graur-Wald (1961:40f.), Ivić (1970:46). As far as his typological classification is concerned, Lounsbury (1968: 194f.) follows Jespersen in mentioning Max Müller's tripartite classification of the languages of the world, his evolutionary views, and his attempt to connect the language classes with different stages of the culture of society (family stage ~ isolating languages; nomadic stage ~ agglutinative or Turanian languages; 'political' stage ~ inflectional languages).[109] Horne (1966) does not mention this attempt at historical interpretation. It is probably worth stating here that, though Max Müller made much of it in his superficial and often contradictory essay published together with Bunsen's magnum opus (cf. Max Müller 1854), the whole suggestion was toned down in the successive editions of his *Lectures on the science of language* and did not appear at all in his 1868 Rede lecture *On the stratification of language*.

3.81 Horne (1966:25–7) starts his chapter on twentieth century views of classification with a paragraph on F.N. Finck, but the sub-heading 'Continuation of older views' is significant for his assessment. Tagliavini (1963:394–95) mentions Finck as a follower of Steinthal and Misteli and as an exponent of psychological classification, but points out that in his last work he implicitly rejected his earlier classification based on different grades of 'excitability' of the speakers. Elsewhere Tagliavini (*ibid.*:418ff.) criticizes the anthropological and racial presuppositions of the genealogical classifications proposed by Finck (see above 2.93, but cf. also Koerner 1970a: 93).

If we ignore the close ties which joined Finck to Ernst Lewy (cf. Lewy 1952), and the intellectual bonds which still exist between him and the group of German scholars which in the forties and the fifties of this century congregated round the periodical *Lexis* (cf., e.g., Lohmann 1960:454–6), his figure is almost forgotten. There are some exceptions: Leroy (1971:166–7) is critical but interested; Arens (1969:405–15) stresses the importance of Finck's views in a period which foreshadowed a renewal of linguistic thought. Some valuable information can also be obtained from the criticism which Jost levels at Finck's interpretation of a Humboldtian principle (Jost

108 But it is certainly exaggerated to say with Dussaud (1951:10) that together with Renan and Mommsen 'Max Müller est un des trois philologues qui ont dominé leur époque'.

109 For Max Müller's theories about the Turanian languages cf. *supra* 2.5; for his evolutionary views see 3.92 and note 121.

1960:100–02), and from the more violent attack of G. Pätsch (1955:8–13); cf. also Gipper (1963 *passim*) and Lehmann 1965. More recently a short article by Koerner (1970a) gives a summary of Finck's views and of his biography.[110]

In a history of language classification Finck should certainly not be neglected, but it is permissible to doubt whether a list of the schema or schemata for classification which he proposed is particularly significant. Once again, what matters more is the theoretical framework which led him to the problems of classification, and which Tagliavini and Horne ignore. Basic is his denial of the existence of language as a supra-individual phenomenon: 'gibt es doch in Wirklichkeit NUR ein ganz INDIVIDUELLES Sprechen' (Finck 1910:3). It follows that any study of language which is not limited to a single speech-act implies a classification, i.e. the establishing of particular groups or types and that classification is indeed at the centre of linguistics (*ibid.*). There is more: not only did Finck challenge the concept of language with which most of the previous century's work had operated (as we saw, he was not unique in this: cf. 2.8 etc.), but he also drew from this the consequence that the primacy given by his predecessors to historical linguistics was to be rejected. Historical grammar was in no position to explain linguistic facts: all that it did was to contrast two different *Sprachwesen*, one of which had served as a model for the other, though it had in no way originated it (cf. Finck 1905:16 and see also 1909:5 and 45ff.).[111] Any causal explanation that it claimed to provide was — according to Finck — out of place since language transmission was simply a process through which an individual in all freedom created language using a model (or more than one model) in different ways. Hence genealogical classification could be used as a *Vorarbeit*, but it could not be the aim of linguistics and had no theoretical validity by itself. The real explanation of the linguistic facts arose from the individual characters of the *Geist*. There is a wealth here of old and new motifs, often inextricably connected, which would deserve a thorough exploration. It is perhaps too easy to label Finck as an individualist; even if we were to do so we would be obliged to explain how his position differed from, for example, that of Schuchardt.

The historian of linguistics will no doubt recognize in his thought one of the numerous attempts at a new start in linguistic theory which characterize this part of the century. The historian of classification will at least want to bring out two points: one is the importance which Finck gave to his notion of linguistic type (cf. Lohmann 1960 and see above 3.8). Sgall (1971) has pointed out that Finck's later writings belong 'to the foundations of a more modern approach to typology' and that he was clear

[110] Short resumés of two of his works can also be found in Gipper-Schwarz (1961ff.: I, nos. 4304, 4305). Also useful is Lewy (1961c).

[111] In Finck (1909:1ff.) the attack is obviously turned against Schleicher's *Stammbaum* model, and the criticism of genealogical classification is toned down but not abandoned. Here too the aim of linguistics consists in explaining the more or less unitary *Redearten* of each people from their 'geistigen' peculiarities. This calls for a work of description of languages (*Sprachkunde*) and of combination of of the various idioms into *Sprachgruppen*. Some of the similarities may then be explained as derived from a common model: hence the preliminary usefulness of genealogical and historical work.

about the distinction between linguistic type and linguistic class and about the fact that a given language can show a combination of the properties of different types. In other words, Finck's methodology was not too far from that of Sapir.[112] The second point concerns Finck's earlier psychological classification, on which it is all too easy to pour scorn. In fact this is a logical (though naive) corollary of Finck's general theory. Those scholars who had claimed that the explanation of a linguistic fact could only be given in terms of its history obviously favoured a genealogical classification, or at least a historical classification of some type; but if the principle of *genetische* (i.e. historical) *Erklärung* was to be given up it was all too natural to turn to other explanations: psychology offered one. The historical antecedents of this line of thought are clear: Humboldt's concept of language as *energeia* on the one side, Steinthal's psychological interpretation of Humboldt's theories on the other.

We may support both our points with a quotation from a very different scholar: Baudouin de Courtenay. In his 1910 paper on language classification he claimed that all previous attempts at morphological classification had been failures; the correct aim was not a classification of languages but a *vergleichende Charakteristik*. He then proceeded to argue that the 'reelle Grösse' was not language, abstracted from the speaker, 'sondern DER MENSCH, ALS TRÄGER DES SPRACHLICHEN DENKENS'. And he continued 'Wir sollen nicht Sprachen klassifizieren, respektive vergleichende charakterisieren, sondern eine VERGLEICHENDE CHARAKTERISTIK DER MENSCHEN nach dem ihnen eigenen sprachlichen Denken geben' (Baudouin de Courtenay 1910:55).[113] There is considerable difference between Baudouin's suggestions and the 'excitability' of which Finck spoke in his early works, but we should recognize that the two scholars shared a number of presuppositions and that these did indeed diverge from those of, for example, Schleicher.

3.9 Before we turn to a general overview of the typological classifications of the nineteenth century we must consider some other features which we have occasionally mentioned without an explicit discussion. Two problems call for attention. First, most classifications are accompanied by an evaluation of the language types or language classes in terms of some particular criterion. In other words, each type or class is assigned a certain rank according to a definite scale of values. Secondly, a classifica-

[112] Cf. below 3.10 for Sgall's appreciation of Finck. So far there has been no attempt to investigate how much Finck's thought was influenced by Gabelentz, but cf. Coseriu 1967c:75 and for Gabelentz's definition of language type *ibid.* 95.

[113] Baudouin's formulation in an earlier programme of lectures (1877–78; cf. Baudouin de Courtenay 1972:119) is nearer to Finck's early views: 'Internal form simultaneous with phonetic form. However, one should define first the psychological character of language and then its external form as a reflection of internal (psychological) activity'. Baudouin's views on the subject changed in the course of time, but he never abandoned his psychological interests. In a 1930 article (cf. Baudouin de Courtenay 1972:296ff.) he distinguished between historical affinity (mostly based on genetic transmission), affinity based on geographical continuity, and similarities common to all mankind, and concluded by arguing that in all three types of affinity the explanation of facts required 'simultaneous reference to history and geography, physiology and psychology, and even to physics and mechanics'.

tion may be static or dynamic, that is to say it is assumed either that the linguistic types or classes are unchangeable or that they are derived from each other through a continuous process of alteration.

It has often been pointed out that, whatever the criterion, the Indo-European languages always seemed to appear at the top of the scale. The chauvinism which prompted this conclusion has been repeatedly attacked and rejected (though occasionally keeps cropping up). Yet, in the enthusiasm for the truth, the duties of the historian have been forgotten. The problem is no so much that of destroying an obsolete belief as that of understanding it. If so, a double question arises. Why did contemporary scholars feel this almost compulsive need to arrange all linguistic types on a given scale? And what justified one particular arrangement in preference to another? To my knowledge little or nothing has been done to provide an answer to the first part of the question — and indeed it is likely that more than one answer is necessary. From a linguistic point of view the influence of the aesthetic classifications of the previous centuries and the belief in an absolute idea of language, variously realized in different languages, both come to mind as possible causes. Others could be added, but would still not be sufficient. It is possible that here too a substantial part of the explanation would have to depend on a comparison with the classifications of the natural sciences. A sentence of Pott (1856:197) may clarify this point: 'Auch kann zwar in der ersteren Rücksicht, in physiologischer, aber nicht eigentlich in genealogischer nach einer stufenmässigen Rangordnung und Werth-Abschätzung der Sprachen vom Niederen zum Höheren und edler Gebildeten hinauf, wie etwa im Thierreich — höchstens nach mehr oder minder edler Abkunft — gefragt werden.' At the same time we find that the comparisons of the isolating languages with the zoophytes of the animal kingdom keep appearing again and again.

As we have seen (3.51), Gertrud Pätsch has tried to give a solution to the second part of our question in the case of Wilhelm von Humboldt; it is likely that *mutatis mutandis* most of her conclusions can be applied to the views of other scholars (but for Bopp, see above 3.6).[114] It may be worthwhile to remember here that, according to G. Pätsch, Humboldt was impelled towards his evaluation by extralinguistic reasons. We have discussed this point before (3.51); here it may be useful to show how at the beginning of the twentieth century scholars had reached a very different position. At the end of his booklet on the tasks and division of linguistics F. N. Finck (1905:54–5) mentioned the question of the respective values of human languages and concluded that the problem was legitimate, but did not belong to linguistics any more than the question of the relative usefulness of domestic animals belonged to zoology; if anything, it had to be discussed under the heading of *Völkerkunde*, since this discipline was concerned inter alia with the influence of language on the nature of peoples. There is a general lesson to be extracted from this: when linguistics moves towards a

[114] For a discussion of Steinthal's evaluative criteria see Bumann 1965:114f. and Belke 1971:cxiif.

clearer conception of its own autonomy the problem of language evaluation assumes secondary importance.[115]

3.91 A satisfactory history of the evolutionary or anti-evolutionary views which accompanied typological classification has yet to be written. In the history of scholarship the question is closely related to that of monogenesis versus polygenesis and in the last resort to all religious implications which accompany the biblical history of the Tower of Babel.[116] Yet, in the course of the nineteenth century it became more and more possible, both in theory and in practice, to preserve an agnostic attitude towards monogenesis and its religious implications, while taking a definite stand on the problems of evolution.

In two interesting essays on *Language and evolutionary theory* and *Language and evolution* Greenberg (1971:78–92, 106–25) has pointed out that in the history of linguistics, even more than in that of the natural sciences, it is necessary to distinguish between 'transformationism', which is contrasted with 'creationism' and assumes that 'species develop from other species' (*ibid.*: 106), and the natural selection theory (or theories) which asserts that 'natural selection has played a major role in producing this result'. Associated with the latter view, according to Greenberg, is often a concept of advance or progress which need not accompany simple transformationism. No doubt Greenberg is right in stressing that linguistic transformationism arose well before Darwinism, but I find it difficult to accept his statements that in linguistics 'the triumph of transformationism over creationism' was most clearly marked by the discovery of the interrelationship of the Indo-European languages, and previously by that of the Semitic and Finno-Ugric languages' (*ibid.*:111). In view of Greenberg's own definition of transformationism, the statement is only valid if individual languages are equated with species — but this is just one of the problems which linguistic classification had to solve.[117] Languages may also be compared to individuals; if so, the differences between, e.g., Latin and French, or Indo-European and Latin, could be compared to the normal differences which obtain between father and son (or mother and daughter) and the problem of the development of a species into another species does not arise. In the history of linguistics this particular position could be represented by Hervás, who recognized the existence of a number of language families, but was a creationist and denied that the members of the same family could show any structural difference.[118]

[115] Obviously this conclusion does not apply to that type of evaluation which is based on particular views of historical development, but for it see below, note 120.

[116] A complete account of the theories about the subject from the beginning until modern times can be found in Borst 1957–63 (especially III,2 for our period), which is a mine of information on a number of problems. However, Borst is not exclusively concerned with the development of linguistic thought as such, but extends his enquiries to literature, poetry, etc.

[117] For the identification of language and species see above, notes 20 and 99.

[118] Cf., e.g., Hervás (1787:15f.): 'Bisogna dunque dire, che la perfezione, o rozzezza dell'artificio degli idiomi non ha nessuna relazione alla civiltà, o rusticità delle nazioni: hanno questa relazione le scienze, e le manifatture; ma non gli idiomi, che troviamo sostanzialmente invariabili. Osserviamo in nazioni barbare, e civili, i dialetti provenienti d'una stessa lingua madre, e sempre vi ritroveremo l'ossatura del corpo onde furono formati.'

Greenberg is obviously right in calling for some clarification, but he does not go far enough. Even if we retain his distinction between natural selection theories and transformationism, there are some other distinctions to make. First, we must acknowledge that there is an element of transformationism in any theory which at all recognizes the existence of language change.[119] From this point of view, if interest in — and indeed emphasis on — linguistic change is synonymous with transformationism, the whole of the nineteenth century is transformationist.[120]

Secondly, there is a different version of transformationism which assumes, in a somewhat ill-defined way, that some types or classes of languages (without necessarily establishing a distinction between the two) can arise from each other. Diderichsen (1960:125) mentions the 'genetic' theories of the eighteenth century, which postulated that languages developed from a simpler to a more complex stage, but which made no attempt to establish a genealogical link between any exponent of the various types.

Thirdly, some transformationist theories are far more explicit (in spite of some remaining ambiguities). These could only arise (and survive) in a period in which linguists were convinced, a) that it was possible to give a non-arbitrary definition of the notions of language type and typological class, and to base a typological classifica-

[119] We may notice here that this recognition is not as immediate as it may appear. The layman is aware only of very minor and unimportant variations, and does not realize the magnitude of the changes except when he is shown documentary evidence provided by written tradition. Interestingly enough as late as 1863 Sir Charles Lyell found it useful to dedicate some pages of his book on 'The geological evidences of the antiquity of man' (1863:457ff.) to wondering how difficult it would have been for a philologist to convince a lay audience that languages did indeed change. However, at a certain level of learning, evidence proving the basic facts of change had been known in the West for a very long time. Even if we forget the classical theory that Latin derived from Aeolic, we may remember that the derivation of the Romance languages from Latin (with the possible, but doubtful, exception of Rumanian) was never doubted.

[120] Of course some distinctions are necessary here too. Even within this mild form of transformationism, which is perfectly compatible either with an interest in genealogical classification and an agnostic or negative position towards typological classification, or even with a study of change within the same typological class, it is permissible to ask what direction the change is likely to take. In the first part of the nineteenth century it was customary to speak of language growth, maturity and decay, in terms which were obviously inspired by the identification of language with an organism or a living being, but which often remained ill defined. Alternatively, change could be conceived of as a linear process, often with an associated idea of progress. In both cases, then, an evaluative conception seemed to be associated with linguistic development. However, if we try to understand what was in effect meant by 'growth' or progress in both types of analysis, we often find that the concept is tied to a historical view of the root-development and of its composition processes. For Bopp, for instance, (who distinguished typologically between languages whose roots were monosyllabic and did not admit of composition and languages which also had monosyllabic roots but did admit of composition and agglutination), it made perfect good sense to speak of growth with reference to his second class. His thesis was that linguistic change caused a shift from an earlier stage in which a small amount of agglutination occurred to a later stage in which inflection prevailed. Whitney's position was in some respects similar: cf. Silverstein (Whitney 1971:xviif.), who rightly observes that 'in such a unilinear evolutionary schema [as that of Whitney] it is fitting and proper to speak of Indo-European languages as the "highest" or most developed, since no other languages investigated by his day were inflective in the same manner, and also because the farther back we trace the history of forms in, say, Indo-European, the closer we get to a completely syntactic — formless — tongue, the root or radical stage of language'.

tion of languages on it, and b) that it was possible to demonstrate that two languages were genetically related. It is only at this stage that the contrast between transformationists and non-transformationists can be clearly stated. The former argued that there was nothing to prevent a language from going through different typological stages while remaining in a meaningful sense of the word the 'same' language. They also assumed that the different linguistic types had in fact arisen through a slow process of development from the lower to the higher type and that the representatives of the higher types still preserved traces of the earlier stages. Yet, at this stage an element of ambiguity crept into the theory. In spite of their general views a number of transformationists were unwilling to admit the possibility that two existing languages could be genealogically related, while belonging to two different language classes.

A number of points in these theories were of direct concern not only to the typologists but also to the historical linguists. The extent of variation caused by linguistic change, and the effect that this could have on linguistic structure, was their problem too. Similarly, it was their evidence that was required in order to elicit the traces of earlier types in the attested phases of languages. The attempt to substantiate the claim that even the 'organic' Indo-European languages showed an agglutinative stratum had first come from Bopp. Once more we return to the observation that the histories of typological and genealogical classifications cannot be kept entirely apart.

3.92 Transformationist and evolutionary theories have often been discussed in recent literature (cf. also Jakobson 1958:18f.), but there is not always agreement about the plain statement of the facts. Lounsbury (1968:191), who follows Jespersen (1962), states that Humboldt was the first scholar to introduce 'an explicit theory of linguistic development to go along with the concepts on which Schlegel [*sic*] typology was based'. Kuznecov (1960:39) appears to share this view, but Sharadzenidze (1958:514 [Russian summary]) argues that the whole idea of development was foreign to Humboldt's conception of the morphological classification of languages. In a pamphlet dedicated to the concept of evolution in linguistics, Leroy (1950:17) states that the tripartite classification, which was originally static, first became dynamic with Schleicher. To sum up, it seems that Schleicher and Max Müller are the two authors whose transformationist views have never been doubted. Modern scholars are eager to stress Schleicher's belief in a prehistoric period during which all languages progressed towards their more developed expression and which was followed by a historical period of decay. As we have seen (2.7), Maher (1966) has pointed out that this form of evolutionism or transformationism preceded that of Darwin and that Schleicher's views are nearer to those prevailing at the beginning of the century that to those inspired by Darwin himself.[121]

[121] Max Müller repeatedly argued in his Rede Lecture (1868) that there was no clear dividing line between the three basic linguistic types (isolating, agglutinative, and inflectional), and that this fact could be used as a proof of his transformationist views. However, agreement among the various followers of Schleicher was far from complete. In the second part which Max Müller added to the reprint of his lecutre (1875), he took issue with Georg Curtius's somewhat too rigid conception of seven different periods of growth in the prehistory of Indo-European (cf. G. Curtius 1867). Max

It seems then that the real historiographical problems concern the earlier period. We have mentioned Hervás's views above (3.91), but here we should not forget the transformationism of Adelung, who argued that all languages were on a developmental scale (cf. supra, the second type of transformationism); in this he was preceded by Rüdiger, as Steinthal (1860:4) was at pains to point out. We have also seen (3.4) how F. Schlegel made a sharp distinction between organic and non-organic languages and at first denied the possibility of a development from one type to the other. In view of this background the agnosticism of A.W. Schlegel appears all the more remarkable (cf. above 3.41). But we are now led back to Humboldt and to the contrasting interpretations of his views. Gertrud Pätsch (1967:113f.) has argued that part of the difficulties arise from oscillations in Humboldt's own thought which are reflected in his writings. But there is another source of confusion. As early as 1855, Pott (1855:412) argued that we must distinguish between two different concepts, that of typological 'Stufengang' or 'stufenweise' progress, and that of genetic-historical development. Neither of the two concepts, according to Pott, is logically dependent on the other, and Humboldt, who recognized different degrees of 'completeness' in the different language types, remained agnostic about the possibility of a historical development from one class to the next (see e.g. Humboldt 1903–36: VII, 344, but cf. also the more ambiguous observations of VI, 275). It seems to follow that, though the terminology is at times confusing, we should probably accept Humboldt's statement at their face value and refuse to commit him to any evolutionary or transformationalist theory (cf. also Ruprecht 1963:231f.).[122]

The position of Steinthal was not very different. Here too, however, it is difficult to reach a clear interpretation. At times he seemed to imply that a shift from e.g. agglutinative to inflectional languages was possible (cf. Bumann 1965:112), but we must remember that for Steinthal agglutination and inflection were not in themselves marks of different linguistic types; on other occasions he was obviously concerned with an ideal ordering of the linguistic types. A sentence by Finck may perhaps show that even at a much later stage the problem of distinguishing between these two forms of development (ideal and historical) was still very much alive. At the beginning of his

---

Müller's point was that 'the growth of language does not lend itself to a chronological division in the strict sense of the word ... Inflection does not put a sudden end to combination, nor combination to juxtaposition' (1875:144). He even went so far as to state that 'combination', the main power which operated in the prehistory of languages, 'is not extinct even in our own time' (*ibid.*). The inconsistency is obvious; if Max Müller had seen the implications of this point, he should have concluded (like Gabelentz: cf. note 124) that language development moved in a sort of never ending spiral and should have refused to acknowledge any distinction between a prehistoric period of growth and a historical period of decay. Curtius was more rigid and his picture was less plausible but more consistent.

[122] If this is so, there is an interesting side result. Humboldt, as we know, accepted Bopp's agglutinative theory. Now, if he had also accepted a division into typological classes based on the contrast between agglutination and inflection, this would have implied that he was as much of a transformationist as Schleicher, which is just what we have been arguing against. It should follow that Steinthal's criticism of the traditional interpretation of Humboldt is right (cf. above 3.5) and that Humboldt did not classify languages into isolating, agglutinative and inflectional.

booklet on *Die Haupttypen des Sprachbaus* he felt the need to point out that the ordering of the linguistic types 'entspricht nicht etwa einer historischen Entwickelung, auch nicht einer ideellen in dem Sinne, dass ein Aufsteigen von Einfachsten zum Kunstvollsten oder vom Urzustande zur vollendeten Geistesbildung veranschaulicht werden sollte' (Finck 1910:6).

The conclusion seems to be that, while there is ample evidence in the history of linguistics for our first and second versions of transformationism, far fewer scholars were committed to the third — and more powerful — version. Schleicher was among these few, but even he denied the possibility that two genealogically related languages belonged to two different typological classes and relegated that form of development which involved typological change to the prehistoric period. In the historical period only 'decay' could occur, and apparently 'decay' did not allow for a shift from one typological class to the other (cf. *supra* 2.7).

3.93 We are then left with yet another problem. What justifies this reluctance to assume that within the limits of our experience linguistic change may involve a change of typological class?[123] Clearly, there is no single answer to this question, and here we can only suggest some possible causes. As we have seen, the typological classification of the nineteenth century was based on grammar; it is likely that in the early period at least this reluctance was justified by the importance given to grammatical similarity (in the ambiguous sense which we discussed in 2.5) as the main, and perhaps the only, criterion used to prove genetic relationship. Another factor which may have been relevant was the lack of an explicit distinction between synchrony and diachrony. Any distinction between linguistic types or classes was bound to be descriptively based, but at a period in which the emphasis was on history, and in which history seemed to offer the only acceptable explanation of any synchronic phenomenon, a distinction which had no diachronic validity was likely to be challenged as arbitrary. Hence for any typologist the temptation must have been either to reject the third version of transformationism, thus guaranteeing the 'non-arbitrary' character of the whole classification, or to project it back into mythical times, as Schleicher did. This last solution was soon exploded; the neogrammarians' vociferous propaganda for the so-called uniformitarian hypothesis, i.e. for the theory that the development of

[123] Meillet (1938:169f.) was well aware of the beliefs generally held round the middle of the century. A propos of Renan he wrote: '... au temps, où Renan a fixé ses idées, on croyait couramment à la perennité des espèces. Et l' on admettait volontiers pour chaque groupe de langues un type idéal — situé assez loin dans le passé — dont les langues attestées même à date ancienne seraient des déformations plus ou moins prononcées. On était loin de la conception moderne suivant laquelle tout état linguistique est simplement un moment de transition entre un état antérieur et un état suivant, et où l'on constate des changements radicaux du type linguistique d'une période à l'autre d'une même langue. Comme tous les savants de son temps, Renan croyait donc à la fixité des types linguistiques. A cet égard, il va très loin, allant jusqu' à écrire que 'les caractères de famille sont immuables'.' If Renan was certain of his ground, Pott, who is perhaps more representative, was considerably worried by the problem and discussed it repeatedly, but he too ended taking refuge in the old saying 'Art lässt nicht von Art' and came down against the possibility that a language could change type (cf., e.g., Pott 1856:204ff.).

language had always occurred in similar ways and similar conditions, was bound to kill it at the roots.[124]

Here we cannot go into details, but that our suggestions are not entirely wrong can perhaps be shown by a reference to two linguists, Saussure and Baudouin de Courtenay, both of whom have received credit for the clarity with which they distinguished between synchronic and diachronic study. Well within the limits of the twentieth century they still felt that the subject called for some strong pronouncements. In the notes on which Saussure's *Cours* is based we read: 'poser une question de caractères dans une famille de langues, c'est s'attendre à une réponse non absolue, parce que le temps peut amener changement total' (Saussure 1967–68: I, 510) or 'On ne peut pas attacher une famille non plus à un type, à une classe préétablie, comme par example le type flexionnel et le type agglutinant; aucune guarantie qu'une langue, qu'une famille guarde ces caractères' (*ibid.* 511); and elsewhere 'En reconnaissant que la pretention de Schleicher de faire de la langue une chose organique (indépendente de l'esprit humain) était une absurdité, nous continuons, sans nous en douter, à vouloir faire d'elle une chose organique dans un autre sens en supposant que le génie indo-européen ou le génie sémitique ⟨veille⟩ sans cesse ⟨à⟩ ramener la langue dans les mêmes voies fatales' (*ibid.*: 514). In 1910 Baudouin was even more explicit: '... Die landläufige sprachwissenschaftliche Theorie von der Stufenmässigkeit in der Entwicklung der sprachlichen Formen erblickt darin aber einzig und allein eine Vervollkomnung d.h. einen Übergang von einer noch ganz unvollendeten 'Isolation' durch eine mehr vollendete 'Agglutination', zu der vollendetsten 'Flexion'. ... Die Erfinder ähnlicher 'morphologischer Klassificationen' schliessen ihre Augen vor evidenten geschichtlichen Tatsachen. Es ist ja, so recht eigentlich die englische Sprache eine 'einsylbige', nebensetzende, 'isolierende' Sprache, wie die chinesische. Und doch gehört die englische Sprache zu den 'indogermanischen' (arioeuropäischen) Sprachen. ... Aus dem Vorhergesagte erhellt, dass unsere vermeintlichen Evolutionisten die Evolution gerade dann vergessen, wenn dieser Begriff sich sozusagen selbst zur Anwendung anbietet. ... Wir sehen also dass die LANDLÄUFIGEN SYSTEME MORPHOLOGISCHER KLASSIFICATIONEN der Sprachen GEGEN DEN richtigen BEGRIFF DER EVOLUTION VERSTOSSEN' (Baudouin de Courtenay 1910: 53). We have seen above the conclusion of this paper: 'morphological' classification was antiquated and had to go. The real aim was that of a comparative characterization of languages (*ibid.*: 54).

3.10 As we have seen, few attempts have been made to give an overall view of the development of typological classification. It is frequently said that there was an early

[124] The position of Georg von der Gabelentz was different. He was ready to point out (1894: 5) that there were both isolating and agglutinative languages which belonged to the same family, and he assumed that all languages moved repeatedly from agglutination through inflection to isolation and back again, this movement being a spiral-like development determined by two main forces which direct language change: *Bequemlichkeitstrieb* and *Deutlichkeitstrieb* (cf. Gabelentz 1891: 250ff., and see also Sgall 1971: 77).

period in which typological and genealogical classifications flourished side by side and that at a later stage the former fell into discredit. We have tried to show that any such statement is only a partial account of the evidence, if it does not emphasize the hesitations which accompanied the beginning of a distinction between the two types of classification. Moreover, all too often it is implied that the only typological classification envisaged was that which proposed a partition of languages into isolating, agglutinative and inflectional, i.e. the traditional morphological classification. Yet it is clear from what precedes that there were also suggestions for other schemas, intended to classify languages from a non-genealogical point of view.[125] In fact, if we ignore its great vogue at a lower level of popularization, it is difficult to pinpoint any one time at which the traditional form of morphological classification was generally accepted. A.W. Schlegel proposed it, but did not dwell on it; Humboldt was too cautious to commit himself (even if some of his contemporaries believed otherwise), Bopp's views were somewhat different, and Pott tended to be sceptical or at least agnostic. This is not all: criticism was not late to come. We have already mentioned some of the reasons which justified the rejection of morphological classification in the second part of the century, but it should be added here that the tripartition could also be found wanting in two basic senses. First, it was possible to prove that real languages could show both agglutination and inflection, or isolation and agglutination, or any other combination of these features. In other words, if what was required was a mathematical partition of the set of all languages, properties like agglutination, inflection, etc. were not sufficient to establish it. Moreover, as it was pointed out before, since it was not clear whether a synchronic or a panchronic classification was being aimed at, those scholars who were not willing to commit themselves to a strong version of transformationism found that the current belief that inflection derived from agglutination was a stumbling block which prevented them from accepting the whole schema. For some this was no impediment, and indeed it was the transformationists like Max Müller and Schleicher who gave the tripartition a new lease of life.[126] However, as soon as the classification appeared to be necessarily tied to an idea of historical development, it was possible to attack it on empirical grounds. Could the development be proved by means of the normal techniques of reconstruction?

The second criticism came at different times and in different ways from a number of scholars. Nineteenth-century linguists prided themselves on having moved a step further than their predecessors. They were interested in a non-arbitrary non-artificial classification, which touched the real nature of language; but were agglutination, inflection etc. properties which could justify this claim? The contrast of *Beziehungen* and meaning (to use Schleicher's formula) was often identified with that of form and content: Schleicher had argued that since this contrast was essential to human thought

[125] I feel reluctant to accept Fr. Müller's distinction between psychological and morphological classification (see above 3.2), since the classifications of Steinthal and Misteli were as much based on linguistic data as was the standard tripartition into isolating, agglutinative and inflectional languages.
[126] Cf. above, note 121.

it could provide a non-arbitrary non-artificial criterion for classification. But in the 1850s Madvig pointed out that it was a gross mistake to argue that the relation of ending and stem in inflectional languages was one of form and content; inflectional endings could be as relevant to the content as the stems: 'Das, was durch die Biegung bezeichnet wird, ist entweder eine besondere Modifikation des Inhalts der Vorstellung, wie dieser durch das Wort selbst gegeben ist (z.B. die Mehrzahl, die Passivauffassung), oder eine Relation ausserhalb des Inhalts' (Madvig 1971:171 [first published 1856]). Steinthal had shown similar signs of disquiet.[127] In other words we do not need to wait until the last quarter of the century to see the first attacks on morphological classification: the discussion continued all through the century.

The conclusion seems to be that the standard historiographical account is somewhat too simple. First, it is mistaken to have a monolithic view of morphological classification itself, for there were sufficient differences among its upholders to justify individual treatments of their theories and of the motives which determined them; secondly it is equally mistaken to identify all non-genealogical classification of the century with morphological classification.

In a recent article Petr Sgall (1971) has given a more articulated and altogether more faithful picture of the development of typological classification. His view is that with Humboldt, and before him with Fr. Schlegel, linguistic thought became interested in a notion of language type which was not yet distinguished from that of of language class. While Humboldt saw only a distinction of degrees between the various linguistic types, Fr. Schlegel aimed at an effective partition in terms of types, and so did Steinthal in his early work. At a later stage, however, Steinthal, like Humboldt, renounced his rigid classification and preferred to concentrate on a more detailed analysis 'of the variety of typological properties and of their combinations in individual languages' (*ibid.*:77).[128] Much later Finck established a clear distinction between language type and language class, and acknowledged that the individual languages could combine properties belonging to different types. Sgall's conclusion is that at this stage typological classification has ceased to aim at a partition of the set of all languages into subsets corresponding to their types, but aimed rather at a more complex analysis. However, according to Sgall, it was only Sapir who 'came to the conclusion that it was necessary to classify languages in various manners, corresponding to various groups of typological properties' (*ibid.*). The result was a final classification which could be stated

[127] Yet other criticisms were put forward by R. de la Grasserie (1889–90: II, 296–7): 'D'ailleurs elle [*scil.* 'morphological classification'] ne péchait pas seulement parce qu'elle ne prenait pour terme de compairison que le mot vide auxiliaire, en excluant tout le reste, mais encore en ce que l'école qui l'avait adoptée n'a jamais pu définir ce que c'est que la flexion et dire si celle-ci consistait dans la modification vocalique de la racine, ou dans celle de la syllabe thématique, ou dans celle de la désinence, ou dans la soudure de ces trois parties ou des désinences entre elles; enfin l'écart qui existe entre l'isolement et l'agglutination est immensement plus grand que celui qui sépare l'agglutination sans flexion de l'agglutination avec flexion, de telle sorte que la division tripartite aurait dû céder en tout cas la place à une division binaire suivie dans un de ces termes d'une subdivision ....'

[128] This would require further study, but see above, 3.71.

'in terms of a Cartesian product of those partitions of the set of languages that correspond to the groups of typological properties' (*ibid.*).

Here too there are some observations to make. In a sense Sgall is on the same wavelength as Baudouin, who argued that the efforts towards language classification had to make way for attempts at language characterization. Presumably Sgall would be willing to accept that this is the direction in which typological studies (or rather that part of them which was interested in classification) moved during the nineteenth century. But once more it should be pointed out that the development was not linear. As we said before, the problem was complicated at first by an insufficient distinction between typological and genealogical work, and later on by the wish to believe that a family of interrelated languages could only count as a subset of the set of those languages which showed the same typological property or properties. At this point development could occur in different directions, not necessarily correlated. The possibility of defining or redefining the typological properties involved could be considered; Steinthal's attempt to get away from the standard morphological classification and to introduce a number of additional criteria is a step in this direction. Transformationist views could be introduced in an attempt to solve the ambiguity between genealogical and typological classification. Alternatively, genealogical problems could be left aside and research could turn towards a language characterization which would either be sufficient in itself or would count as a first step in the direction of classification (well before Baudouin, Böhtlingk seemed to have reached this stage). Finally, extra-linguistic criteria could be appealed to within particular theoretical frameworks.

As a corollary to the first of these possibilities, we should perhaps mention R. de la Grasserie's attempt to provide a number of provisional and subjective classifications in terms of individual features (phonological, morphological, syntactical, etc.) and to argue that this preliminary work could be used as the foundation for a 'classification totale, naturelle et objective' of all languages (la Grasserie 1889–90: II, 335). The principle to be used for it was that of the 'subordination des caractères' (cf. Cuvier's principle of 'corrélation des formes') and the model that of the biological sciences. In other words, la Grasserie suggested that typological features occur in clusters: e.g. some languages which show vocalic harmony turn out to be also agglutinative and 'enveloppant', as if there were a sort of necessary correlation between these properties. Why this was so — la Grasserie continued — was doubtful; it was possible that, as the evolutionists argued for biology, so too in the case of language the answer was to be found in genealogical relationship. However that might be, nonetheless, if the principle was valid, it could provide an obvious criterion on which to base a classification. It is apparent how much — in 1890 — the discussion was still being conducted within the tradition of nineteenth century typological speculation, but another aspect is also noticeable. There is a sense in which R. de la Grasserie's findings anticipate the current interest in implicational universals (cf., e.g., Jakobson 1958:20ff.; Greenberg, Osgood, Jenkins in Greenberg 1966:xix–xx, xxiv–xxvi).

In this respect too the work of la Grasserie, though not prominent perhaps for depth or novelty of enquiry, was symptomatic of the typological classification of the whole period.[129] In spite of its numerous hesitations, contradictions and false starts, this type of work fulfilled an important function in the history of linguistics. One of its achievements was that it obliged scholars not to forget the existence of theoretical and descriptive problems. If we ignore its existence we do so at our own risk; it means that we effectively prevent ourselves from understanding much of the background of this century's views on general linguistics.

4. CONCLUSION

4.1 We may be brief. Most of the conclusions that we want to draw at the end of this survey are, or should be, implicit in what precedes. Since we still lack a monograph which traces the history of language classification from the Renaissance or even from the beginning of the nineteenth century until modern times, we have been obliged to concentrate on work bearing on the general history of linguistics in the nineteenth century. We have inherited from the last century and from the first half of this century a number of works concerned with the concrete results of linguistics. In practice this means that we are relatively well acquainted with the technical progress of one particular branch of comparative studies, that which concerned Indo-European languages. Yet, even in this well trodden field we remain ignorant about methodology and theory. The last few years, with their renewed emphasis on history of linguistics, have produced a steady flow of books and articles which have gone some

[129] Some of the points made by la Grasserie were criticized, and some others explored in greater depth, by Georg von der Gabelentz (1894) in a remarkable article which appeared posthumously — and in which la Grasserie was not mentioned. Gabelentz was sceptical about the possibility of applying Cuvier's method to linguistics: 'Es leuchtet auch ein, dass gewisse Züge in der Physiognomie der Sprachen, zumal lexikalische, stilistische und syntaktische, besonders charakteristisch sind. Geht man aber weiter, will man es der Zigeunerin nachmachen, die aus den Zügen der Handfläche den ganzen Menschen deutet, oder einem Cuvier, dessen Geist aus dem einzelnen Knochen das ganze Tier aufbaute, — misst man die Theorie an der Thatsachen: so scheint es bald, als hätte man nur die traurige Wahl, sich sofort für insolvent zu erklären oder mit Kunstmitteln Wechselreiterei zu treiben bis der Bankerott von selbst ausbricht' (*ibid.* 4). However, in the same paper Gabelentz (*ibid.* 5) observed that the frequent cases in which two or more non related and geographically remote languages showed identical or similar clusterings of linguistic features could hardly be due to chance. He explained that we should aim at a series of statements like: 'die Erscheinung A trifft mit so und so grosser Wahrscheinlichkeit mit B, C, D, usw. zusammen, selten mit E, nie mit F' (*ibid.* 5–6). And he continued (*ibid.* 6): 'Und dies ist die Statistik, die ich zunächst verlange. Es fragt sich: Ist sie schon jetzt erreichbar? und was würde mit ihr erreicht?'. The immediate aim for Gabelentz was to establish a programme of future work; its first task was to be a purely descriptive one, that of formulating a sort of questionnaire 'der kategorienweise alle grammatischen Möglichkeiten erschöpft'. The gist of the whole article is clear; the study of these linguistic features with their universal or statistical implications cannot lead us to a classification, but is a basic prerequisite for a greater knowledge of language differences and similarities. Like Baudouin, Gabelentz is obviously more concerned with language characterization than with language classification in the strict sense of the word.

way towards closing the gap. A great deal still remains to be done. In particular it is easy to predict that in this field too it will soon become necessary to return from theory to practice and to see how the two overlap or disagree. At the moment this remains unknown territory. Humboldt's views, to give just an example, have been repeatedly discussed and analyzed, but little has been written about the way in which he tackled his descriptive and comparative problems. Similarly, though we know something about the theoretical views of the neogrammarians, and though we know a great deal about their concrete results, we are still in ignorance, for instance, of how, if at all, they applied their psychological theories to the reconstruction of linguistic history.[130]

Yet, at the moment the worst gap in our historiography concerns non-genealogical work. Morphological classification is often mentioned in 'Introductions to linguistics', but only to be immediately rejected. The result is that we still lack the basic preconditions of any historiographical work: a knowledge of the data and an understanding of the background. The strictures bestowed by Léon Wagner (1950–51:123) upon the historians of Romance philology are applicable here too — not to any particular individual but to the situation in general: 'Chez tous les critiques perce ou du dédain ou une moquerie à l'égard des 'irréguliers', des 'rêveurs', des 'fous'. J'ai tenté de dire que l'on ferait mieux d'essayer de comprendre ces bizarries.' In this survey we have tried to show the number and the magnitude of the problems which still remain open; we have also made an attempt to recognize a line of development or to endorse views put forward by others. Perhaps all this is premature: what we need at the moment is a series of detailed analyses and a correct assessment of the data available. One point, however, is worth making; if we do not make a serious attempt to explore the problems and the discussions which centered round typological classification we shall lose any chance we might otherwise have of fully understanding the development of genealogical classification and later on that of areal linguistics and modern typology.

REFERENCES

AARSLEFF, HANS. 1967. The study of language in England, 1780–1860. Princeton, Princeton University Press.

——. 1970. The history of linguistics and Professor Chomsky. Lg 46.570–85.

ABEL, KARL. 1885. Zur Frage nach den Kennzeichen der Sprachverwandtschaft. Internationale Zeitschrift für allgemeine Sprachwissenschaft 2.43–53.

ADAM, LUCIEN. 1881a. Les classifications de la linguistique. Revue de linguistique et de philologie comparée 14.217–68.

——. 1881b. La linguistique est-elle une science naturelle ou une science historique? Revue de linguistique et de philologie comparée. 14.373–95.

ADELUNG, JOHANN CHRISTOPH. 1806–17. Mithridates oder allgemeine Sprachen-

[130] From this point of view Brugmann's later syntactical work would repay a full study.

kunde mit dem Vater Unser als Sprachprobe in bey nahe fünfhundert Sprachen und Mundarten (fortgesetzt und bearbeitet von Dr. Johann Severin Vater). 4 vols. Berlin, Vossische Buchhandlung.

AGRELL, JAN. 1955. Studier i den äldre språkjämförelsens allmänna och Svenska historia fram till 1827. Uppsala Universitets Årsskrift 1955.13. Uppsala/Lundequist/Wiesbaden, Harrassowitz.

ALKON, PAUL K. 1959. Behaviourism and linguistics: An historical note. LS 2.37–51.

ANTONSEN, ELMER H. 1962. Rasmus Rask and Jacob Grimm: Their relationship in the investigation of Germanic vocalism. ScS 34.183–94.

APEL, KARL OTTO. 1959. Der philosophische Wahrheitsbegriff als Voraussetzung einer inhaltlich orientierten Sprachwissenschaft. Sprache: Schlüssel zur Welt. Festschrift für Leo Weisgerber, hssg. von Helmut Gipper, 11–38. Düsseldorf, Pädagogischer Verlag Schwann.

——. 1963. Die Idee der Sprache in der Tradition des Humanismus von Dante bis Vico. Archiv für Begriffsgeschichte, 8. Bonn, Bouvier & Co.

ARBERRY, A.J. 1943–46. New light on Sir William Jones. BSOAS 11.673–85.

——. 1944. Persian Jones. Asiatic Review 40.186–96.

——. 1946. Asiatic Jones. The life and influence of Sir William Jones (1746–1794) pioneer of Indian studies. London/New York/Toronto, Longmans, Green & Co.

——. 1960. The founder. William Jones. Oriental Essays. Portraits of seven scholars, 48–86. London, Allen & Unwin.

ARENS, HANS. 1969². Sprachwissenschaft. Der Gang ihrer Entwicklung von der Antike bis zur Gegenwart. Orbis Academicus. Freiburg/München, Karl Alber [1st ed. 1955.]

ARLOTTO, ANTHONY A. 1969. Jones and Coeurdoux: Correction to a footnote. JAOS 89.416–17.

ARNDT, ERWIN. 1965. Diachronie und Synchronie in Jacob Grimms 'Deutscher Grammatik'. Ausnahme und Regel in neuer Sicht. WZUB 14.479–88.

ASCOLI, GRAZIADIO ISAIA. 1968². Scritti sulla questione della lingua, a cura e con introduzione e nota bibliografica di Corrado Grassi. Torino, Edizioni Giappichelli. [1st. ed. 1967.]

ASSIRELLI, ODDONE. 1962. La dottrina monogenistica di A. Trombetti. Faenza, Tipografia Fratelli Lega.

BARSCHEL, BERND. 1969. Das Sprachbundproblem und die Divergenzen in der indoeuropäischen o-Deklination. WZUB 18.301–04.

BATLLORI, MIGUEL., S.J. 1951. El archivo lingüístico de Hervás en Roma y su reflejo en Wilhelm von Humboldt. Archivum Historicum Societatis Jesu 20.59–116.

——. 1959. Provençal i català en els escrits lingüístics d'Hervás. Studi in onore di Angelo Monteverdi 1.76–81. Modena, Società tipografica modenese.

BAUDOUIN DE COURTENAY, JAN. 1910. Klassification der Sprachen. Bericht über die

Grazer 50. Versammlung deutscher Philologen und Schulmänner. IF 26 Anzeiger. 51–8.

——. 1960. I. A. Boduèn de Kurtenè (k 30-letiju so dnja smerti). Moscow, Idz. Akademii Nauk SSSR.

——. 1963. I. A. Boduèn de Kurtenè. Izbrannye trudy po obščemu jazykoznaniju. 2 vols. Moscow, Izd. Akademii Nauk SSSR.

——. 1972. A Baudouin de Courtenay Anthology. The beginnings of structural linguistics, trans. and ed. with an introduction by Edward Stankiewicz. Indiana University Series in the History and Theory of Linguistics. Bloomington/London, Indiana University Press.

Beiträge zur Geschichte der Slawistik. 1964. Deutsche Akademie der Wissenschaften zu Berlin. Veröffentlichungen des Instituts für Slawistik, ed. by H. H. Bielfeldt, Nr. 30. Berlin, Akademie Verlag.

BELKE, INGRID, ed. 1971. Moritz Lazarus und Heymann Steinthal. Die Begründer der Völkerpsychologie in ihren Briefen. Mit einer Einleitung hssg. von Ingrid Belke. Schriftenreihe wissenschaftlicher Abhandlungen des Leo Baeck Instituts, 21. Tübingen, J. C. B. Mohr (Paul Siebeck).

BENEŠ, BRIGIT. 1958. Wilhelm von Humboldt, Jacob Grimm, August Schleicher. Ein Vergleich ihrer Sprachauffassungen. Diss. Bonn. Winterthur, P. G. Keller.

BENFEY, THEODOR. 1869. Geschichte der Sprachwissenschaft und orientalischen Philologie in Deutschland seit dem Anfange des 19. Jahrhunderts mit einem Rückblick auf die früheren Zeiten. Geschichte der Wissenschaften in Deutschland. Neuere Zeit, 8. München, Cotta.

BENSE, GERTRUD. 1957–58. Die vergleichende Sprachwissenschaft in Halle seit F. A. Pott. WZUH 7.901–6.

BENVENISTE, EMILE. 1964. Lettres de Ferdinand de Saussure à Antoine Meillet. CFS 21.89–130.

BEREZIN, FEDOR MIXAJLOVIČ. 1968. Očerki po istorii jazykoznanija v Rossii (konec XIX- nacalo XX v.). Moscow, Izd. 'Nauka'.

BERGSVEINSSON, SVEINN. 1965. Die Brüder Grimm und der Norden. WZUB 14. 515–16.

BERNHAGEN, WOLFGANG. 1964. J. S. Vater, ein vergessener Slavist des 19. Jahrhunderts. Beiträge... 1964, 162–70.

BÈS, GABRIEL G. 1967. Parenté génétique et parenté typologique. Linguistique 2. 139–50.

BIELFELDT, HANS HOLM. 1964. Die Geschichte des Lehrstuhls für Slawistik an der Berliner Universität. Beiträge... 1964. 267–80.

BIRNBAUM, HENRIK. 1970. Problems of typological and genetic linguistics viewed in a generative framework. Janua Linguarum. Series minor, 106. The Hague/Paris, Mouton.

BJERRUM, MARIE. 1956. Hvorfor kom Rask ikke til Sverige i 1810. Festskrift til Peter Skautrup 21. Januar 1956. Aarhus, Universitetsforlaget.

——. 1957. Hvorfor rejste Rask til Kaukasus og Indien? DS 1957. 80–100.

——. 1959. Rasmus Rask afhandlinger om det danske sprog. Bidrag til forståelse af Rasks taenkning. Copenhagen, Dansk Videnskabs Forlag.

*——. 1968. Breve fra og til Rasmus Rask. III. Brevkommentar og håndskrifts-katalog. Udg. for Det danske Sprog- og Litteraturselskab af Marie Bjerrum. Copenhagen, Munksgaard. [Cf. BL 1969. 24, no. 577.]

BLUMENTHAL, ARTHUR L. 1970. Language and psychology. Historical aspects of psycholinguistics. New York/London/Sidney/Toronto, John Wiley & Sons.

BÖHTLINGK, OTTO. 1851. Ueber die Sprache der Jakuten. Grammatik, Text und Wörterbuch. St. Petersburg, Buchdruckerei der kaiserlichen Akademie der Wissenschaften.

*BOLELLI, TRISTANO. 1949. Tra storia e linguaggio. Arona, Paideia.

——. 1963. Ascoli e la Grammatica di Bopp. SSL 3.87.

——. 1965. Per una storia della ricerca linguistica. Testi e note introduttive. Collana di storia, 4. Napoli, Morano.

——. 1966. Review of Introduzione alla semantica, by T. de Mauro. SSL 6.206–11.

——. 1967. Chiose ad una replica di T. De Mauro. SSL 7. 189–206.

BONDZIO, WILHELM. 1965. Jacob Grimm und die neuhochdeutsche Schriftsprache. WZUB 14.471–8.

BONFANTE, GIULIANO. 1953. Ideas on the kinship of the European languages from 1200 to 1800. Cahiers d'histoire mondiale 1.679–99.

——. 1955. Una descrizione linguistica d'Europa del 1614. Paideia 10.224–7.

BOPP, FRANZ. 1833. Vergleichende Grammatik des Sanskrit, Zend, Griechischen, Lateinischen, Litthauischen, Gothischen und Deutschen, vol. 1. Berlin, Dümmler.

——. 1836. Vocalismus oder Sprachvergleichende Kritiken über J. Grimm's deutsche Grammatik und Graff's althochdeutschen Sprachschatz mit Begründung einer neuen Theorie des Ablauts. Berlin, Nicolaische Buchhandlung.

——. 1841. Ueber die Verwandtschaft der malayisch-polynesischen Sprachen mit den indisch-europäischen. Berlin, Dümmler.

BORST, ARNO. 1957–63. Der Turmbau von Babel: Geschichte der Meinungen über Ursprung und Vielfalt der Sprachen und Völker. 4 parts, 6 vols. Stuttgart, Hierschmann.

——. 1960. Die Geschichte der Sprachen im abendländischen Denken. WW 10. 129–43.

BOTTIGLIONI, GINO. Un ignorato precursore delle teorie etnico-linguistiche di G.I. Ascoli. Annali della facoltà di Lettere, Filosofia e Magistero della Università di Cagliari 18.1–11.

BREDSDORFF, JACOB HORNEMANN. 1817. De regulis in classificatione rerum naturalium observandis commentatio. Diss. inauguralis. Hauniae [Copenhagen], Typis Andreae Seidelini.

——. 1886. Om Aarsagerne til Sprogenes Forandringer. Paa ny udgivet af Vilh. Thomsen. Copenhagen, Gyldendal. [1st ed. 1821.]

*——. 1970. Ueber die Ursachen der Sprachveränderungen, übersetzen und hsg. von Uwe Petersen. Tübingen, Tübinger Beiträge zur Linguistik.

BROSS, DIETER. 1968. Epistolario de Rufino José Cuervo y Hugo Schuchardt. Edición, introducción y notas de Dieter Bross. Publicaciones del Instituto Caro y Cuervo. Archivo epistolar Colombiano, 2. Bogotá, Imprenta Patriótica del Instituto Caro y Cuervo.

BROWN, ROGER LANGHAM. 1967. Wilhelm von Humboldt's conception of linguistic relativity. Janua Linguarum. Series minor, 65. The Hague/Paris, Mouton.

*BRÜDER HUMBOLDT. 1968. Die Brüder Humboldt heute. Abhandlungen der Humboldt- Gesellschaft, 2. Mannheim, Verlag der Humboldt-Gesellschaft. [BL 1969. 20, no. 416.]

BRUGMANN, KARL. 1884. Zur Frage nach den Verwandtschaftverhältnissen der indogermanischen Sprachen. Internationale Zeitschrift für allgemeine Sprachwissenschaft 1.226–56.

——. 1885. Zum heutigen Stand der Sprachwissenschaft. Strassburg, Trübner.

——, and WILHELM STREITBERG. 1891. Zu Franz Bopps hundertjährigem Geburtstage. IF 1. v–x.

BUMANN, WALTRAUD. 1965. Die Sprachtheorie Heymann Steinthals: Dargestellt im Zusammenhang mit seiner Theorie der Geisteswissenschaft. Monographien zur philosophischen Forschung, 39. Meisenheim am Glan, Verlag Anton Hain.

BURSILL-HALL, G.L. 1970a. Review of On language by Peter H. Salus. Glossa 4.111–15.

——. 1970b. Review of A short history of linguistics by R.H. Robins, Trends in linguistics by M. Ivić, Les grands courants de la linguistique moderne by M. Leroy. Glossa 4.229–44.

BUSSENIUS, ARNO. 1952. Vom sprachlichen Bedeutung. Eine wissenschaftsgeschichtliche Studie. ZPhon 6.315–27.

BUYSSENS, ERIC. 1961. Origine de la linguistique synchronique de Saussure. CFS 18. 17–33.

BYRNE, JAMES. 1892². General principles of the structure of language. 2 vols. London, K. Paul, Trench, Trübner & Co. [1st. ed. 1885.]

CANNON, GARLAND H. 1952. Sir William Jones, Orientalist. An annotated bibliography of his works. Honolulu, University of Hawaii Press.

——. 1953. Sir William Jones and the *Sakuntala*. JAOS 73.198–202.

——. 1958. Sir William Jones's Persian linguistics. JAOS 78.262–73. [Reprinted in Sebeok 1966: I. 36–57.]

——. 1963. Sir William Jones's Summary of *Sakuntala*. JAOS 83.241–3.

——. 1964. Oriental Jones. A Biography of Sir William Jones (1746–1794). London, Indian Council for Cultural Relations. Asia Publishing House.

——. 1968. The correspondence between Lord Monboddo and Sir William Jones. AmA 70.559–62.

——. 1970. The letters of Sir William Jones, edited by Garland Cannon. 2 vols. Oxford, Clarendon Press.

CASSIRER, ERNST. A. 1923. Philosophie der symbolischen Formen: Die Sprache. Vol. 1. Berlin, Bruno Cassirer. [English translation, 1953. New Haven and London, Yale University Press.]

——. 1945. Structuralism in Modern Linguistics. Word 1.99–120.

CHAMBERS, R. W., and F. NORMAN. 1929. Alexander Hamilton and the beginning of comparative philology. Studies in English philology. A miscellany in honor of Frederick Klaeber edited by Kemp Malone and Martin B. Ruud, 457–66. Minneapolis, The University of Minnesota Press.

CHATTERJI, SUNITI KUMAR. 1948. Sir William Jones (1746–1794). Sir William Jones: Bicentenary of his birth commemoration volume 1746–1946, 81–96. Calcutta, Royal Asiatic Society. [Reprinted in Sebeok 1966: I, 18–36.]

CHOMSKY, NOAM. 1966. Cartesian linguistics: A chapter in the history of rationalist thought. New York/London, Harper and Row.

CHRISTMANN, HANS HELMUT. 1965. Un aspetto del concetto humboldtiano della lingua e i suoi precursori italiani. Problemi di lingua e letteratura italiana del Settecento. Atti del Quarto Congresso dell'Associazione Internazionale per gli Studi di lingua e letteratura italiana, Magonza e Colonia, 28 Aprile–1° Maggio 1962, 328–33. Wiesbaden, F. Steiner.

——. 1966. Beiträge zur Geschichte der These vom Weltbild der Sprache. AAWL 7.441–69.

——. 1971. Die Begegnung von descriptiver und historischer Sprachbetrachtung in der Grammaire des Grammaires. RF 83.173–81.

——. 1972. Saussure und die Tradition der Sprachwissenschaft. ASNS 208.241–55.

CLAVERÍA, CARLOS. 1946. La 'Gramática Española' de Rasmus Rask. RFE 30.1–22.

COLLINDER, BJÖRN. 1968. Kritische Bemerkungen zum Saussure'schen Cours de linguistique générale. ASLU 1(5).181–210.

CONTI PECA, RITA. 1965. Quattro lettere dal carteggio inedito Ascoli–Teza. SSL 5. 161–71.

COSERIU, EUGENIO. 1967a. François Thurot. ZFSL 77.30–4.

——. 1967b. L'arbitraire du signe. Zur Spätgeschichte einer aristotelischen Begriffes. ASNS. 204.81–112.

——. 1967c. Georg von der Gabelentz et la linguistique synchronique. Word 23.74–100. [Reprinted in Gabelentz 1891; reprint 1969.]

——. 1967d. Zur Vorgeschichte der strukturellen Semantik: Heyses Analyse des Wortfeldes 'Schall'. To honor Roman Jakobson. Essays on the occasion of his seventieth birthday 11 October 1966, vol. 1, 489–98. Janua Linguarum, Series maior, 33. The Hague/Paris, Mouton.

——. 1968. Adam Smith und die Anfänge der Sprachtypologie. Wortbildung, Syntax und Morphologie. Festschrift zum 60. Geburtstag von Hans Marchand, hssg. von Herbert E. Brekle und Leonhard Lipka, 46–54. The Hague/Paris, Mouton.

*COWAN, M. 1963. Humanist without portfolio. An anthology of the writings of Wilhelm von Humboldt. Detroit, Wayne State University Press.

CRONIA, ARTURO. 1962. Lettere di Graziadio Ascoli a Franz Miklosich. Studi in onore di Ettore Lo Gatto e Giovanni Maver. Collana di Ricerche Slavistiche, 1, 153-58. Firenze, Sansoni.

CURTIUS, ERNST ROBERT. 1947. Bonner Gedenkworte auf Friedrich Diez (zum 15. März 1944). RF 60.389–410 [Reprinted in Curtius 1960: 412–27.]

——. 1951. Gustav Gröber und die romanische Philologie. ZRPh 67.257–88. [Reprinted in Curtius 1960: 428–55.]

——. 1960. Gesammelte Aufsätze zur romanischen Philologie. Bern/München, Francke Verlag.

CURTIUS, GEORG. 1867. Zur Chronologie der indogermanischen Sprachforschung. Abhandlungen der philologisch-historischen Classe der Königlichen Sächsischen Gesellschaft der Wissenschaften Nr. 3, 185–261. Leipzig, S. Hirzel.

ČEMODANOV, N.S. 1958. Iz istorii sravitel'no-istoričeskogo metoda v russkom jazykovedenii. Sbornik statej po jazykoznaniju: Professory Moskovskogo Universiteta akademiku V. V. Vinogradovu, 312–29. Moscow, Izd. Moskovskogo Universiteta.

DARWIN, CHARLES. 1859. On the origin of species by means of natural selection or the preservation of favoured races in the struggle for life. London, John Murray.

——. 1871. The descent of man, and selection in relation to sex. 2 vols. London, John Murray.

DE FELICE, EMIDIO. 1954. La terminologia linguistica di G. I. Ascoli e della sua scuola. Comité International permanent des linguistes. Publication de la commission de terminologie. Utrecht/Anvers, Editions Spectrum.

DELBRÜCK, BERTHOLD. 1880. Einleitung in das Sprachstudium. Ein Beitrag zur Methodik der vergleichenden Sprachforschung. Bibliothek indogermanischer Grammatiken, 4. Leipzig, Breitkopf und Härtel. [6th ed. 1919.]

——. 1901. Grundfragen der Sprachforschung mit Rücksicht auf W. Wundts Sprachpsychologie erörtert. Strassburg, Trübner.

DE MAURO, TULLIO. 1963. A proposito di J.J. Becher. Bilancio della nuova linguistica. De Homine 7–8.134–46.

——. 1967a. Ludwig Wittgenstein. His place in the development of semantics. FL Supplementary Series, vol. 3. Dordrecht, D. Reidel Publishing Co.

——. 1967b. Il prof. Bolelli e il metodo della linguistica. La Cultura 5.267–76.

——. 1970a³. Introduzione alla Semantica. Universale Laterza, 146. Bari, Laterza. [1st. ed. 1965.]

——. 1970b. Ferdinand de Saussure, Corso di linguistica generale. Introduzione, traduzione e commento. Universale Laterza, 151. 3rd (?) ed. Bari, Laterza. [1st ed. 1967].

DENECKE, LUDWIG. 1971. Jacob Grimm und sein Bruder Wilhelm. Stuttgart, J. B. Metzlersche Verlagsbuchhandlung.

——, and INA-MARIA GREVERUS, eds. 1963. Brüder–Grimm–Gedenken. Gedenkschrift zur hundertsten Wiederkehr des Todestages von Jacob Grimm. HBVk 54.1–610. Marburg, N. G. Elwert.

DESNICKAJA, AGNIA V. 1969. Franz Bopp und die moderne Sprachwissenschaft. WZUB 18.305–7.

——. 1971. O lingvističeskoj teorii Avgusta Šlejxera. (k 150-letiju so dnja roždenija). VJa (6).3–15.

DEVOTO, GIACOMO. 1958. Madvig grammairien et linguiste. Acta Congressus Madvigiani, vol. 1 (Proceedings of the second International Congress of Classical Studies), 57–63. Copenhagen, Munksgaard. [Reprinted in Scritti Minori, vol. 1, 379–85. Firenze, Le Monnier. 1958.]

DICKENHAMM, ERNST. 1954. Franz Miklosich (1813–1891). Onoma 5.21–44.

DIDERICHSEN, PAUL. 1960. Rasmus Raks og den grammatiske tradition. Studier over vendepunktet i sprogvidenskabens historie. Historisk-filosofiske Meddelelser udgivet af Det Kongelige Danske Videnskabernes Selskab, Bind 38, nr. 2. Copenhagen, Munksgaard. [German translation announced, Internationale Bibliothek für allgemeine Linguistik, 33. München, Wilhelm Fink Verlag.]

DIETZE, JOACHIM. 1960. Briefe August Schleichers an Reinhold Köhler. ZSl 5.267–80.

——. 1964. Das Bild Leskiens in den Briefen August Schleichers. Beiträge... 1964. 353–86.

——. 1965a. Leben und Leistung August Schleichers im Spiegel seiner Briefe an Miklosich. ZSl 10. 533–63.

——. 1965b. Salomon Lefmann — der Biograph August Schleichers. FF 39.19–20.

——. 1966. August Schleicher als Slawist. Sein Leben und sein Werk in der Licht der Indogermanistik. Berlin, Akademie Verlag.

——. 1969. August Schleicher und die frühe Baltistik, ZSe 14.591–7.

DIEZ, FRIEDRICH CHRISTIAN. 1836–44. Grammatik der romanischen Sprachen. 2 vols. Bonn, E. Weber.

DINNEEN, FRANCIS P., S.J. 1967. An introduction to general linguistics. New York/Chicago/San Francisco/Toronto/London, Holt, Rinehart & Winston.

DJUPEDAL, REIDAR. 1956a. Rasmus Rask og 'Videnskabernes Selskabs Danske Ordbog'. Festskrift til Peter Skautrup 21. Januar 1956, 383–96. Aarhus, Universitetsforlaget.

——. 1956b. Eit brev frå Rasmus Rask om dansk rettskriving. DS 1956. 107–10.

——. 1958. In brief fan Rasmus Rask út 1825 oer 'Die Sprache der Nord-friesen' fan Bende Bendsen. Us Wurk 7.83–86.

DOBROVSKÝ, JOSEF. 1953. Josef Dobrovský 1753–1953. Sborník studií k dvoustému výročí narození. Prague, Nakladatelství Československé Akademie Věd.

*DRĂGANU, NICOLAE. 1945. Istoria sintaxei. Societatea Română de Linguistică I, 5. Bucharest, Institutul de Linguistică Română. [Cf. BL 1948. 117.]

*——. 1970. Storia della sintassi generale, trans. by P. Bardelli Plomteux. Bologna, Pàtron.

DÜNNINGER, JOSEF. 1957. Geschichte der deutschen Philologie. Deutsche Philologie im Aufriss, ed. by Wolfgang Stammler, vol. 1, 83–222. Berlin, Eric Schmidt. [1st ed. 1951.]

DUSSAUD, RENÉ. 1951. L'œuvre scientifique d'Ernest Renan. Paris, Paul Geuthner.

*DŽAHOUKJAN, G.B. 1960–62. Lezwabanouthjan patmouthjoun. [Džaukjan, G. Istorija Jazykoznanija]. 2 vols. Erevan, Izd. Erevanskogo univ. [Cf. BL 1963.37, no. 840.]

EDGERTON, FRANKLIN. 1946. Sir William Jones (1746–1794). JAOS. 66.230–39. [Reprinted in Sebeok 1966: I, 1–18).

ELLEDGE, SCOTT. 1967. The naked science of language, 1747–86. Studies in criticism and aesthetics, 1660–1800. Essays in honor of Samuel Holt Monk, ed. by Howard Anderson and John S. Shea, 266–95. Minneapolis, University of Minnesota Press.

EMENEAU, M.B. 1955. India and linguistics. JAOS 75.245–53.

——. 1971. Review of The letters of Sir William Jones, edited by Garland Cannon. Lg 47.959–64.

ESPER, ERWIN A. 1968. Mentalism and Objectivism in linguistics. The sources of Leonard Bloomfield's Psychology of language. Foundations of Linguistics, 1. New York, American Elsevier Publishing Company.

EVANS, CHARLOTTE B. 1967. Wilhelm von Humboldt's Sprachtheorie. Zum Gedächtnis seines 200. Geburtstages am 22. Juni. GQ 40.509–17.

FAN, T.C. 1946. Sir William Jones's Chinese Studies. RES 22.304–14.

FARÉ, PAOLO A. 1964. I carteggi Ascoli-Salvioni, Ascoli-Guarnerio. Memorie dell'-Istituto Lombardo — Accademia di Scienze e Lettere. Classe di Lettere — Scienze morali e storiche, vol. 28, fasc. 1. Milano, Istituto Lombardo di Scienze e Lettere.

FARKAS, JULIUS VON. 1948. Samuel Gyarmathi und die finnisch-ugrische Sprachvergleichung. NAWG 1948 Nr. 3.109–36.

——. 1952. August Ludwig Schlözer und die finnisch-ugrische Geschichts-, Sprach- und Volkskunde. UAJb 24.1–22.

FICK, AUGUST. 1873. Die ehemalige Spracheinheit der Indogermanen Europas. Eine sprachgeschichtliche Untersuchung. Göttingen, Vandenhoeck und Ruprecht.

FIEDLER, WILFRIED. 1969. Franz Bopps Verdienste um die Erforschung der Albanischen Morphologie. WZUB 18.313–4.

FINCK, FRANZ NIKOLAUS. 1899. Der deutsche Sprachbau als Ausdruck deutscher Weltanschauung. Acht Vorträge. Marburg, N.G. Elwert.

——. 1901. Die Klassification der Sprachen. Marburg, N.G. Elwert.

——. 1905. Die Aufgabe und Gliederung der Sprachwissenschaft. Halle (Saale), Rudolf Haupt.

——. 1909. Die Sprachstämme des Erdkreises. Leipzig, B.G. Teubner.

——. 1910. Die Haupttypen des Sprachbaus. Leipzig, B.G. Teubner.

FIRTH, JOHN R. 1949. Atlantic linguistics. ArchL1.95–116. [Reprinted in Firth, J.R. Papers in Linguistics 1934–1951, 156–72. London/New York/Toronto, Oxford University Press.]

FISCHER, RUDOLF. 1953–54. Jena und Leipzig in der Slawistik. WZUL 3.153–6.

——. 1961a. Zum Leben und Schicksal August Schleichers. ZSl 6.449–51.

——. 1961b. Zum Charakterbilde August Schleichers. Ein Sprachgelehrter als Kritiker seiner Wirklichkeit. FF 35.115–18.

——. 1962. August Schleicher zur Erinnerung. SbSAW 107 Heft 5.

——. 1963. Zur Erforschung der Sprache der Elbslawen. Ein bisher unveröffentlichter Brief Schleichers an einen tschechischen Freund. FF 37.187–9.

FORTUNATOV, FILIPP FEODOROVIČ. 1956–57. Izbrannye Trudy. 2 vols. Moscow, Gosudarstvennoe učebno-pedagogičeskoe izd. Ministerstva prosveščenija RSFSR.

FOUCAULT, MICHEL. 1966. Les mots et les choses. Une archéologie des sciences humaines. Paris, Gallimard.

FOWKES, ROBERT A. 1955. Friedrich Hebbel and comparative linguistics. GR 30. 294–300.

——. 1964. The linguistic modernity of Jakob Grimm. Linguistics 8.56–61.

FRAENGER, WILHELM, and WOLFGANG STEINITZ, eds. 1963. Jacob Grimm. Zur 100. Wiederkehr seines Todestages. Festschrift des Instituts für deutsche Volkskunde. DJbVk 9.1–290. Berlin, Akademie Verlag.

FRANCIS, E.D. 1969–70. History of linguistics: Some early uses of the term 'stratification'. RomPh 23.64.

FREUDENBERG, RUDOLF. 1965. Zur Entwicklungsgeschichte der dialekt geographischen Methode. ZMaF 32.170–82.

FUNKE, OTTO. 1957. Zur Frühgeschichte des Terminus '(Innere) Sprachform'. Beiträge zur Einheit von Bildung und Sprache im geistigen Sein. Festschrift zum 80. Geburtstag von Ernst Otto, hssg. von Gerhard Haselbach and Günter Hartmann, 289–94. Berlin, Walter de Gruyter & Co.

GABELENTZ, GEORG VON DER. 1891. Die Sprachwissenschaft. Ihre Aufgaben, Methoden und bisherigen Ergebnisse. Leipzig, T.O. Weigel Nachfolger. [2nd. ed. 1901; reprinted by *Gunter Narr and Uwe Petersen, 1969, Tübingen, Tübinger Beiträge zur Linguistik.]

——. 1894. Hypologie (sic) der Sprache, eine neue Aufgabe der Linguistik. IF 4.1–7.

GADZARU, DEMETRIO. 1967. Controversias y documentos lingüísticos. Buenos Aires, Instituto de Filología. Facultad de Humanidades y Ciencias de la Educación. Universidad Nacional de la Plata.

*GAGKAEV, KAZAN EGOROVIČ. 1957. Kurs lekcij po istorii jazykoznanija. Odessa, Odesskij gosud. univ. [Cf. BL 1957.26.]

GÁLDI, L. 1955. Sur quelques pionniers des rapprochements étymologiques slavo-hongrois. SSlav 1.5–28.

——. 1956. De Gyarmathi à Miklosich. Un chapitre de l'histoire des recherches étymologiques slavo-hongroises. SSlav 2. 289–329.

GERHARDT, DIETRICH. 1947. Zu den Epochen der deutschen Mundartenforschung. ZPhon 1.5–18, 130–47. [Partly reprinted in Phonetica (1960)5. 4–8.]

GERMANN, DIETRICH. 1955–56a. Die Berufung von Eduard Sievers als ausserordentlicher Professor der deutschen Philologie nach Jena 1871. WZUJ 5.699–701.

——. 1955–56b. Die Gründung des Ordinariats für deutsche Philologie an der Universität Jena 1876. WZUJ 5.703–7.

——. 1957a. E. Sievers' Bericht von seinen Handschriftenfunden in der Bodleiana und dem Britischen Museum im Frühjahr 1871. PBB (H) 79 (3).321–35.

——. 1957b. E. Sievers und die Gründung des Ordinariats für deutsche Philologie an der Universität Jena 1876. Wissenschaftliche Annalen Berlin, Akademie Verlag. 6. 485–93.

——. 1968. Aus Eduard Sievers' Jenaer Zeit (1871–1883). Briefe und Aktenstücke über Berufungen aus den Archiven deutscher Universitäten und dem Archiv der Harvard-Universität. PBB (T) 90 (2–3).303–14.

GINSCHEL, GUNHILD. 1955. Jacob Grimm. Aufgaben und Probleme der Exzerption. SbDAW 1955, no. 3.47–110.

——. 1967. Der junge Jacob Grimm (1805–1819). Berlin, Akademie Verlag.

GIPPER, HELMUT. 1963. Bausteine zur Sprachinhaltsforschung. Neuere Sprachbetrachtung im Austausch mit Geistes- und Naturwissenschaft. Düsseldorf, Pädagogischer Verlag Schwann.

——. 1965. Wilhelm von Humboldt als Begründer moderner Sprachforschung. WW 15.1–19.

——, and HANS SCHWARZ. 1961ff. Bibliographisches Handbuch zur Sprachinhaltsforschung. Schrifttum zur Sprachinhaltsforschung in alphabetischer Folge nach Verfassern mit Besprechungen und Inhaltshinweisen. Wissenschaftliche Abhandlungen der Arbeitsgemeinschaft für Forschung des Landes Nordrhein Westfalen, 16 a. Köln und Opladen, Westdeutscher Verlag.

GODFREY, JOHN J. 1967. Sir William Jones and Père Cœurdoux: A philological footnote. JAOS 87.57–9.

GRAU, C. 1966. Zwei unbekannte Briefen A.L. Schlözers über seine Anfänge in Russland. Ost und West in der Geschichte des Denkens und der kulturellen Beziehungen. Festschrift für Eduard Winter zum 70. Geburtstag, 321–31. Berlin, Akademie Verlag.

GRAUR, ALEXANDRU. 1967. 'Wellentheorien'. PLG 5.69–75.

——, and LUCIA WALD. 1965. Scurtă istorie a linguisticii. Bucharest, Ed. ştiinţifica.

GREENBERG, JOSEPH H. 1957. Essays in linguistics. Chicago, University of Chicago Press.

——. 1966². Universals of language. Cambridge Mass./London: The M.I.T. Press. [1st ed. 1963.]

——. 1970. The role of typology in the development of a scientific linguistics. Theoretical problems of typology and the Northern Eurasian languages, ed. by

L. Dezsö and P. Hajdú, 11–24. Amsterdam, B.R. Grüner; Budapest, Akadémia Kiadó.

——. 1971. Language, culture, and communication. Essays by Joseph H. Greenberg. Selected and introduced by Anwar S. Dil. Stanford, Stanford University Press.

GRIMM, JACOB. 1822². Deutsche Grammatik. vol. 1. Göttingen, Dieterische Buchhandlung. [1st. ed. 1819.]

GRÖBER, GUSTAV. 1886–88. Grundriss der Romanischen Philologie. 1. Band: Geschichte und Aufgaben der romanischen Philologie — Quellen der romanischen Philologie und deren Behandlung — Romanische Sprachwissenschaft — Register. Strassburg, Trübner.

GUCHMAN [GUXMAN], M.M. 1966. Grammatische Kategorie und typologische Forschung. Zeichen und Systeme der Sprache. Veröffentlichung des 2. Int. Symposium 'Zeichen und Systeme der Sprache' von 8.9. bis 15.9. 1964 in Magdeburg. Vol. 3, 262–73. Berlin, Akademie Verlag.

GULYA, J. 1965. Some eighteenth century antecedents of the nineteenth century linguistics. ALH 15.163–70.

HAAS, MARY R. 1969. Grammar or lexicon? The American Indian side of the question from Duponceau to Powell. IJAL 35.239–55.

HÄUSLER, FRANK. 1968. Das Problem Phonetik und Phonologie bei Baudouin de Courtenay und in seiner Nachfolge. Halle (Saale), VEB Max Niemeyer Verlag.

HAFNER, STANISLAUS. 1963. Franz Miklosichs Stellung und Leistung in der europäischen Wissenschaft. Zu Franz Miklosichs 150. Geburtstag. WSlav 8.299–319.

HALL, ROBERT A. Jr. 1963. Idealism in Romance linguistics. Ithaca, New York, Cornell University Press.

——. 1969. Some recent studies on Port-Royal and Vaugelas. AL 12.207–33.

HALTSONEN, SULO. 1962. Ein Brief von M.A. Castrén. Commentationes Fenno-Ugricae in honorem Paavo Ravila. MSFOu 125.65–8. Helsinki, Suomalais-ugrilainenseura.

*HAMEL, A.G. VAN. 1945. Geschiedenis der taalwetenschap. Den Haag, Servire. [Cf. BL. 1939–47.5.]

[HAMILTON, ALEXANDER]. 1809. Review of A grammar of the Sanskrit language, by Ch. Wilkins. Edinburgh Review 13.366–81.

HAMMERICH, LOUIS L. 1963. Jacob Grimm und sein Werk. Brüder-Grimm-Gedenken, ed. by L. Denecke and I.M. Greverus, 1–21. Marburg, N.G. Elwert.

HANSEN-LØVE, OLE. 1972. La révolution copernicienne du langage dans l'œuvre de Wilhelm von Humboldt. Paris, J. Vrin.

HARTKE, WERNER. and HENNY MASKOLAT, eds. 1967. Wilhelm von Humboldt: 1767-1967. Erbe — Gegenwart — Zukunft. Beiträge vorgelegt von der Humboldt Universität zu Berlin anlässlich der Feier des zweihundertsten Geburtstages ihres Gründers. Halle (Saale), VEB Max Niemeyer Verlag.

HASELBACH, GERHARD. 1966. Grammatik und Sprachstruktur. Karl Ferdinand

Beckers Beitrag zur Allgemeinen Sprachwissenschaft in historischer und systematischer Sicht. Berlin, Walter de Gruyter & Co.

HEINIMANN, SIEGFRIED. 1967. Zur Auffassung des Geschichtlichen in der historischen Grammatik des 19. Jahrhunderts. Festgabe Hans von Greyerz zum sechzigsten Geburtstag, 783–807. Bern, Herbert Lang.

HEINTZ, G. 1969. Point de vue. Leibniz und die These vom Weltbild der Sprache. ZDAlt 98.216–40.

HELBIG, GERHARD. 1970. Geschichte der neueren Sprachwissenschaft. Leipzig, VEB Bibliographisches Institut.

HENNING, HELMUT. 1963. Die Wechselbeziehungen zwischen den Brüdern Grimm und dem Norden. Brüder-Grimm-Gedenken, ed. by L. Denecke and I.M. Greverus, 451–67. Marburg, N.G. Elwert.

HERMANN, LISELOTTE. 1965. Jacob Grimm und die sprachtheoretischen Konzeptionen der französischen Aufklärung. WZUB 14.447–53.

HERVÁS, LORENZO. 1784. Catalogo delle lingue conosciute e notizia delle loro affinità, e diversità. Cesena, Gregorio Biasini all'insegna di Pallade.

——. 1787. Saggio pratico delle lingue. Idea dell' Universo che contiene Storia della vita dell'Uomo, viaggio estatico al mondo planetario, e storia della terra, e delle lingue, 21. Cesena, Gregorio Biasini all'insegna di Pallade.

——. 1800–05. Catálogo de las lenguas de las naciones conocidas, y numeración, división, y clases de estas según la diversidad de sus idiomas y dialectos. 6 vols. Madrid, Librería de Ranz.

HIEHLE, KURT. 1949. Jacob Grimm als Wegbereiter einer lautrichtigen Rechtschreibung. ZPhon 5.303–16.

HJELMSLEV, LOUIS, ed. 1941. Breve fra og til Rasmus Rask. 2 vols. Copenhagen, Munksgaard.

——. 1950–51. Commentaires sur la vie et l'œuvre de Rasmus Rask. Conférences de l'Institut de linguistique de l'Université de Paris 10.143–57. [Reprinted in Sebeok 1966: I, 179–99.]

HOCKETT, CHARLES F. 1965. Sound change. Lg 41.185–204.

HÖFLER, OTTO. 1955. Stammbaumtheorie, Wellentheorie, Entfaltungstheorie. PBB (T) 77.30–46 [continued ibid. 78.1–44].

HOENIGSWALD, HENRY M. 1963. On the history of the comparative method. AnL 5(1).1–11.

——. 1971. Review of A reader in nineteenth-century historical Indo-European linguistics, by W. P. Lehmann. Lingua 26.423–7.

HORMIA, OSMO. 1964–65. Ueber die fennougristischen Interessen von Olaus Rudbeck d. Ä. FUF 34.1–43.

HORNE, KIBBEY M. 1966. Language typology: 19th and 20th century views. Washington D.C., Georgetown University Press.

HOVELACQUE, ABEL. 1877². La linguistique. Histoire naturelle du langage. Bibliothèque des sciences contemporaines, 2. Paris, Reinwald. [1st. ed. 1876.]

HUMBOLDT, WILHELM VON. 1903–36. Gesammelte Schriften, herausgegeben von der königlichen Preussischen Akademie der Wissenschaften. 17 vols. Berlin/Leipzig, B. Behrs Verlag, Friedrich Feddersen.

——. 1969[3]. Schriften zur Sprachphilosophie, herausgegeben von Andreas Flitner und Klaus Giel. Werke in fünf Banden, 3. Darmstadt, Wissenschaftliche Buchgesellschaft.

HYMES, DELL H. 1963. Notes towards a history of linguistic anthropology. AnL 5(1).59–103.

IMART, G. 1968. Uslar et la phonologie. Linguistique 1.31–42.

*IORDAN, IORGU. 1932. Introducere în studiul limbilor romanice. Evoluţia si starea actuală a linguisticii romanice. Jassy.

——. 1962. Linguistica romanică: Evolutie, curente, metode. Bucharest, Ed. Acad. Republicii Populare Romine.

——, and MANUEL ALVAR. 1967. Lingüística románica: Evolución — Corrientes — Méthodos. Reelaboración parcial y notas de M. Alvar. Madrid, Alcalá.

——, and WERNER BAHNER. 1962. Einführung in die Geschichte und Methoden der romanischen Sprachwissenschaft. Ins Deutsche übertragen, ergänzt und teilweise neubearbeitet von Werner Bahner. Berlin, Akademie Verlag.

——, and JOHN ORR. 1970. An introduction to Romance linguistics, its schools and scholars. Revised with a supplement 'Thirty years on' by R. Posner. Language and Style series, 8. Oxford, Basil Blackwell.

IVANOV, V.V. 1954. Genealogičeskaja klassificacija jazykov i ponjatie jazykovogo rosstva. Materjaly k kursam jazykoznanija. Pod obščej redakciej V.A. Bvegínceva. Moscow, Izd. Moskovskogo Universiteta.

*——. 1956. Die genealogische Klassification der Sprachen und der Begriff der Sprachverwandtschaft German transl. by K.A. Paffen. Halle (Saale), Niemeyer. [Cf. BL 1956. 29.]

*IVIĆ, MILKA. 1963. Pravci u lingvistici. Ljubljana, Državna založba Slovenije.

——. 1970. Trends in linguistics. Trans. by Muriel Heppell. Janua Linguarum. Series minor, 42. 2nd printing. The Hague/Paris, Mouton.

JACOB, ANDRÉ. 1969. 100 Points de vue sur le langage: 270 textes choisis et presentés avec introduction et bibliographie. Paris, Klincksieck.

JACOBSON, RODOLFO. 1968. Wilhelm von Humboldt, the linguist. Linguistics 44.69–74.

JAGIĆ, I.V. 1910. Istorija Slavjanskoj Filologii. St. Petersburg, Tipografija Imperatorskoj Akademii Nauk.

JAGODITSCH, RUDOLF. 1950. Die Lehrkanzel für slavische Philologie an der Universität Wien 1849–1949. WSlJb 1.1–52.

JAKOBSON, ROMAN. 1938. Sur la théorie des affinités phonologiques entre les langues. Actes du quatrième Congrès International de linguistes tenu à Copenhague du 27 août au 1er septembre 1936, 48–58. Copenhagen, Munksgaard. [Reprinted in Jakobson 1971a: I, 234–46.]

——. 1942–43. Polish-Russian cooperation in the science of language. Bulletin of the Polish Institute of Arts and Sciences in America 1.970–74. [Reprinted in Jakobson 1971a: II, 451–5.]

——. 1958. Typological studies and their contribution to historical comparative linguistics. Proceedings of the eighth International Congress of Linguists, 17–25. Oslo, Oslo University Press. [Reprinted in Jakobson 1971a: I, 523–31.]

——. 1965. L'importanza di Kruszewski per lo sviluppo della linguistica generale. RSlav 13.3–23. [Polish version printed in Kruszewski 1967: x–xxv; Russian version printed in Jakobson 1971a: II, 429–50.]

——. 1966. Henry Sweet's path towards phonemics. In memory of J.R. Firth, 242–54. London, Longmans, Green & Co. [Reprinted in Jakobson 1971a: II, 456–67.]

——. 1971a². Selected writings. Vols. I and II. The Hague/Paris, Mouton.

——. 1971b. The Kazan School of Polish linguistics and its place in the international development of phonology. Selected writings (1971a), II 394–428. [First appeared in Polish, *BPTJ 19 (1960). 3–34.]

Jankowsky, Kurt R. 1972. The Neogrammarians. Janua Linguarum. Series minor, 116. The Hague/Paris, Mouton.

Jarčeva, V.N. 1956. Teorija substrata v istorii jazykoznanija. DSlJa 9.8–32.

Jarosch, Günther. 1968. Karl Gottlob von Antons 'Erste Linien eines Versuches über der alten Slawen Ursprung, Sitten, Gebräuche, Meinungen und Kenntnisse' — ein früher deutscher Beitrag zur Geschichte und Volkskunde der slawischen Völker. WZUB 17.283–8.

Jenisch, D. 1796. Philosophisch-kritische Vergleichung und Würdigung von vierzehn ältern und neuern Sprachen Europens, namentlich: der Griechischen, Lateinischen; Italienischen, Spanischen, Portugiesischen, Französischen; Englischen, Deutschen, Holländischen, Dänischen, Schwedischen; Polnischen, Russischen, Litthauischen. Berlin, Friedrich Maurer.

Jensen, Povl Johannes. 1958. Madvig's Place in Danish Philology. Acta Congressus Madvigiani, 1 (=Proceedings of the second International Congress of Classical Studies), 65–7. Copenhagen, Munksgaard.

Jespersen, Otto. 1922. Language. Its nature, development and origin. London, Allen & Unwin, Ltd.

——. 1962. The classification of languages. A contribution to the history of linguistic science. Selected writings of Otto Jespersen, 693–704. London, Allen & Unwin. Tokyo, Senjo Publishing Co. Ltd. [First printed in *Scientia 28 (1920).]

Jones, Sir William. 1948. Sir William Jones. Bicentenary of his birth. Commemoration volume 1746–1946. Calcutta, Royal Asiatic Society of Bengal.

Jost, Leonhard. 1960. Sprache als Werk und wirkende Kraft. Ein Beitrag zur Geschichte und Kritik der energetischen Sprachauffassung seit Wilhelm von Humboldt. Sprache und Dichtung, Neue Folge, 6. Bern, Paul Haupt.

Kacnel'son, S.D. 1954. Teorija sonantov F.F. Fortunatova i ee značenie v svete sovremnyx dannyx. VJa 1954 (6). 47–61.

KANDLER, GÜNTHER. 1954. Das Geschichtliche in der Sprachwissenschaft und seine Ergänzungen. Lexis 4.5–20.

KERT, G.M. 1965. F.F. Fortunatov i finno-ugrovedenie. SovFU 1.225–8.

KIRKETERP-MØLLER, HERTHA. 1962. Nadir Shah, Christian VII og William Jones. William Jones' oversaettelse af et persisk Håndskrift. Fund og Forskning i det kongelige Biblioteks Samliger 9.114–27.

KLAPROTH, [HEINRICH] JULIUS [VON]. 1823. Asia Polyglotta. Paris, J.M. Eberhardt.

KNOBLOCH, Johann. 1953. Wege und Ziele der indogermanischen Sprachwissenschaft. Lexis 3.286–99.

KOERNER, E.F.K. 1970a. Franz Nikolaus Finck (1867–1910). Zur 60. Wiederkehr des Todestages eines grossen Sprachwissenschaftlers aus dem Niederrhein. Der Niederrhein 37.91–4.

——. 1970b. Review of On language. Plato to von Humboldt, by P.H. Salus. Lingua 25.419–31.

——. 1972a. Review of Sprachwissenschaft, by H. Arens. Lg 48.428–45.

——. 1972b. Review of Das Problem Phonetik und Phonologie bei Baudouin de Courtenay und in seiner Nachfolge, by F. Häusler. Linguistics 77.63–76.

——. 1972c. Bibliographia Saussureana 1870–1970. An annotated, classified bibliography on the background, development and actual relevance of Ferdinand de Saussure's general theory of language. Methuchen, N.J., The Scarecrow Press, Inc.

——. 1972d. Hermann Paul and synchronic linguistics. Lingua 29.274–307.

KOVÁCS, FERENC. 1971. Linguistic structures and linguistic laws. Trans. from Hungarian by Sándor Simon. Amsterdam, B.R. Grüner; Budapest; Akadémiai Kiadó.

KRBEC, MILOSLAV, and MIROSLAV LAISKE. 1968. Josef Dobrovský II. Příspěvek k soupisu hlavní literatury o jeho díle a životě (Beitrag zur bibliographischen Übersicht der wichtigsten Literatur über dessen Werk und Leben). Sborník prací pedagogické fakulty Palackého university v Olomouci, Jazyk a literatur 1968. 115–54.

——, and MIROSLAV LAISKE. 1970. Josef Dobrovský I. Bibliographie der Veröffentlichungen von Josef Dobrovský. Facultas Philosophica et Paedagogica Universitatis Palackianae Olomucensis. Series Slavica, 1. Prague, Státní Pedagogické Nakladatelství.

——, and VĚRA MICHÁLKOVÁ. 1959. Der Briefwechsel zwischen Josef Dobrovský und Karl Gottlob von Anton. Deutsche Akademie der Wissenschaften zu Berlin. Veröffentlichungen des Instituts für Slawistik, hssg. von H.H. Bielfeldt, 21. Berlin, Akademie Verlag.

KRUSZEWSKI, MIKOŁAJ. 1967. Wybór pism. Z przedmowami Jerzego Kuryłowicza i Romana Jakobsona. Breslau/Warsaw/Cracow, Zakład Narodowy imienia ossolińskich wydawnictwo Polskiej Akademii Nauk.

KUHN, A. 1947–48. Sechzig Jahre Sprachgeographie in der Romania. RJb 1.25–63.

KUHN, THOMAS S. 1970². The structure of scientific revolutions. Chicago, University of Chicago Press. [1st ed. 1962.]

KUKENHEIM, LOUIS. 1966.² Esquisse historique de la linguistique française et de ses rapports avec la linguistique générale. Publications romanes de l'Université de Leyde, 8. Leiden, Universitaire Pers. [1st ed. 1962.]

KUNZE, ERICH. 1957. Jacob Grimm und Finnland. Communications edited for the Folklore Fellows. 65(2). No. 165. Helsinki, Suomalainen Tiedaekatemia, Akateeminen kirjakauppa. Wiesbaden, Harrassowitz.

——. 1962. Aus der Gründerzeit der Finno-Ugristik. (Unbekannt gebliebene Briefe von M.A. Castrén, Ahlqvist und Wiedemann). Commentationes Fenno-Ugricae in honorem Paavo Ravila (MSFOu, 125), 253–62. Helsinki, Suomalaisugrilainen seura.

*KUZNECOV, P.S. 1954. Morfologičeskaja klassifikacija jazykov. Materialy k kursam jazykoznanija. Moscow, Izd. Moskovskogo Universiteta.

——. 1960². Die morphologische Klassification der Sprachen. German trans. by K.A. Paffen. Halle (Saale), Niemeyer. [1st ed. 1956.]

KYLSTRA, A.D. 1961. Geschichte der germanisch-finnischen Lehnwortsforschung. Studia Germanica, 4. Assen, Van Gorkum & Comp. N.V. — Dr. H.J. Prakke & H.M.G. Prakke.

LA GRASSERIE, R. DE. 1889–1890. De la classification des langues. Internationale Zeitschrift für allgemeine Sprachwissenschaft 4.374–87; 5.297–338.

LAKÓ, GYÖRGY. 1970. Janos Sajnovics und die finnisch-ugrische Sprachvergleichung. SovFU 6.239–47.

LAUCH, ANNELIES. 1968. August Ludwig von Schlözer — ein Wegbereiter der Slawistik von Josef Dobrovský. WZUB 17.275–82.

LÁZARO CARRETER, FERNANDO. 1949. Las ideas lingüísticas en España durante el siglo XVIII. RFE 48.

LEFMANN, SALOMON. 1891–97. Franz Bopp, sein Leben und seine Wissenschaft. 2 vols. + Nachtrag. Berlin, Georg Reiner.

LEHMANN, WINFRED P. 1965. Die Kontinuität der Sprachwissenschaft. DVLG 39.16–33.

——. 1967. A reader in nineteenth-century historical Indo-European linguistics. Indiana University Studies in the History and Theory of Linguistics. Bloomington /London, Indiana University Press.

LEONT'EV, A.A. 1966. Boduèn i francuzskaja lingvistika. IzvAN 25.329–32.

LEPSCHY, GIULIO C. 1962. Osservazioni sul termine struttura. A proposito di Sens et usage du terme structure dans les sciences humaines et sociales, edité par R. Bastide. ASNP 31.173–97.

——. 1970. Introduzione alla traduzione italiana. Il linguaggio [by L. Hjelmslev], a cura di Giulio Lepschy. Italian trans. by Anna Debenedetti Wolf, viii-xviii. Piccola Biblioteca Einaudi, 146. Torino, Einaudi.

LEROUX, ROBERT. 1958. L'anthropologie comparée de Guillaume de Humboldt. Publications de la faculté des lettres de l'Université de Strasbourg, 135. Paris, Les Belles Lettres.

LEROY, MAURICE. 1950. Sur le concept d'évolution en linguistique. Bruxelles, Office de publicité. [First printed in *Revue de l'Institut de Sociologie, Université Libre de Bruxelles 1949. 337–75.]

——. 1960. Les langues du monde et la typologie linguistique. Mémoires et publications de la société des Sciences, des Arts et des Lettres du Hainaut 74.169–204.

——. 1963. La classification en linguistique. La Classification dans les sciences, 134-56. Centre national Belge de recherches de logique. Société Belge de logique et de philosophie des sciences. Gembloux, Editions J. Duculout.

——. 1971². Les grands courants de la linguistique moderne. Bruxelles, Editions de l'Université de Bruxelles. [1st ed. 1963. English trans. by Glanville Price, 1967.]

LEWY, ERNST. 1938. Apriorische Konstruktion der Sprachtypen. IF 56.29–31. [Reprinted in Lewy 1961a: 21-3.]

——. 1951. Die Lehre von den Sprachtypen. SG 4.415–22. [Reprinted in Lewy 1961a: 9–21.]

——. 1952. Nachruf auf Franz Nikolaus Finck. Lexis 3.158–62. [Reprinted in Lewy 1961a: 689–94.]

——. 1961a. Kleine Schriften. Deutsche Akademie der Wissenschaften. Veröffentlichungen der Sprachwissenschaftlichen Kommission, 1. Berlin, Akademie Verlag.

——. 1961b. James Byrne. Kleine Schriften (see Lewy 1961 a), 687–9. [First printed in *A Dictionary of Irish Writers, Dublin, 1944.]

——. 1961c. Finck Franz Nikolaus. Neue Deutsche Biographie 5.148–9. Berlin, Duncker & Humblot.

LIEB, HANS-HEINRICH. 1967. 'Synchronic' versus 'diachronic' linguistics; a historical note. Linguistics 36.18–28.

LIEBRUCKS, BRUNO. 1964–70. Sprache und Bewusstsein. 5 vols. Vol. 2: Sprache — 'Wilhelm von Humboldt'. Frankfurt a.M., Akademische Verlagsgesellschaft.

LÖTHER, BURKHARD. 1965. Philolog der Nation. Zum Zusammenhang von Sprachgeschichte und Volksgeschichte bei Jacob Grimm. WZUB 14.463–9.

LOHMANN, JOHANNES. 1941. Franz Bopp geboren am 14. September 1791. AfVPhon 5.93–6.

——. 1960. Die Entwicklung der allgemeinen Sprachwissenschaft an der Friedrich-Wilhelms-Universität zu Berlin bis 1933. Gedenkschrift der Westdeutschen Rektorenkonferenz und der freien Universität Berlin: zur 150. Wiederkehr des Gründungsjahres der Friedrich-Wilhelms- Universität zu Berlin. Vol. 2. Studium Berolinense. Aufsätze und Beiträge zu Problemen der Wissenschaft und zur Geschichte der Friedrich-Wilhelms Universität zu Berlin, hssg. von Hans Leunink,

Eduard Neumann and Georg Kotowski, 449–58. Berlin, Walter De Gruyter & Co.

——. 1967. Ueber das Verhältnis der Sprachtheorien von Humboldt, de Saussure und Trubetzkoy. Phonologie der Gegenwart. WSlJb Ergänzungsband 6.353–63. Graz/Wien/Köln, Hermann Böhlaus Nachf.

LOHUIZEN-DE LEEUW, J.E. VAN. 1948. Sir William Jones, 1746–1794. Orientalia Neerlandica. A volume of Oriental Studies published under the auspices of the Netherlands' Oriental Society, 288–97. Leiden, A.W. Sijthoff.

*LOJA, JĀNIS VILJUMOVIČ. 1968. Istorija lingvističeskix učenij. Materialy k kursu lekcij. Moscow, Izd. 'Vysšaja Škola'. [Cf. BL 1969. 52, no. 1303].

LOUNSBURY, FLOYD G. 1968. One hundred years of anthropological linguistics. One hundred years of anthropology, ed. with an introduction by J.O. Brew, 150–225, 256–64. Cambridge Mass., Harvard University Press.

LUN, L. 1962. Il saggio di Jacob Grimm sull'origine del linguaggio. Roma, Ausonia editrice.

LYELL, CHARLES. 1863. The geological evidences of the antiquity of man, with remarks on theories of the origin of species by variation. London, John Murray.

MACREA, D. 1959. Linguişti şi filologi romîni. Bucharest, Editura Ştiintifica.

MADVIG, J.N. 1955. Johann Nicolai Madvig, et Mindeskrift. Udgivet af det Kgl. Danske Videnskabernes Selskab og Carlsbergfondet, I. Copenhagen, Munksgaard.

——. 1971. Sprachtheoretische Abhandlungen, im Auftrage der Gesellschaft für Dänische Sprache und Literatur hssg. von Karsten Friis Johansen. Copenhagen, Munksgaard.

MAHER, JOHN P. 1966. More on the history of the comparative method: The tradition of Darwinism in August Schleicher's work. AnL 8(3).1–12.

MALKIEL, YAKOV. 1955–56. An early formulation of the linguistic wave theory. RomPh 9.31.

——. 1957. A tentative typology of etymological studies. IJAL 23.1–17. [Reprinted in Malkiel 1968:199–227.]

——. 1963–64. Bibliographic notes: History of linguistics. RomPh 17.823–8.

——. 1967a. Each work has a history of its own ... Glossa 1.137–49.

——. 1967b. Linguistics as a genetic science. Lg 43.223–45.

——. 1967–68. August Fuchs (1818–1847), the founder of comparative Romance dialectology. RomPh 21.285.

——. 1968. Essays on linguistic themes. Oxford, Basil Blackwell.

——, and MARGARET LANGDON. 1968–69. History and histories of linguistics. RomPh 22.530–74.

MALMBERG, BERTIL. 1964. New Trends in linguistics: An orientation. Trans. by Edward Carney. Bibliotheca linguistica, 1. Stockolm/Lund, Naturmetodens Språkinstitut.

*——. 1966³. Nya vägar inom Språksforskningen: En orientering i modern lingvistik. Stockholm, Svenska Bokförlaget. Copenhagen, Munksgaard. [1st ed. 1959.]

MASTER, ALFRED. 1943–46. The influence of Sir William Jones upon Sanskrit studies. BSOAS 11.798–806.

——. 1956. Jones and Pāṇini. JAOS 76.186–7.

MATTOSO-CAMARA, J., JR. 1970. Wilhelm von Humboldt et Edward Sapir. Actes du Dixième Congrès International des linguistes (Bucarest 28 Août- 2 Septembre 1967) 2.327–32. Bucharest, Editions de l'Académie de la République Socialiste de Roumanie.

MAURY, [L.] ALFRED. 1857. On the distribution and classification of tongues, — their relation to the geographical distribution of Races; and on the inductions which may be drawn from these relations. Indigenous races of the earth, or new chapters of ethnological inquiry, ed. by J.C. Nott and Geo. R. Gliddon, 25–86. London, Trübner & Co. Philadelphia, J.B. Lippincott & Co.

MEHLIG, JOHANNES. 1957–58. Die Pflege und Tradition der Indologie in Halle. WZUH 7.891–9.

MEILLET, ANTOINE. 1924. Introduction. Les langues du monde par un groupe de linguistes sous la direction de A. Meillet et M. Cohen, 1–18. Paris, Champion. [Reprinted as Introduction à la classification des langues in Meillet 1938:53–69.]

——. 1937[8]. Aperçu du développement de la grammaire comparée. Introduction à l'étude des langues indo-européennes, 453–83. Paris, Hachette. [1st ed. 1903.]

——. 1938. Linguistique historique et linguistique générale. Vol. 2. Paris, Klincksieck.

——, and MARCEL COHEN. 1952[2]. Les langues du monde par un groupe de linguistes sous la direction de A. Meillet et M. Cohen. 2 vols. Paris, Centre nationale de la recherche scientifique. H. Champion dépositaire. [1st. ed. 1924.]

MEISNER, POVL. 1972. Anquetil du Perron. Avestastudiets pionér og hans danske efterfølgere. Fund og Forskning i det kongelige Biblioteks Samliger 19.33–46.

MERIGGI, PIERO. 1966. Die Junggrammatiker und die heutige Sprachwissenschaft. Sprache 12.1–15.

MEZEY, ISTVÁN. 1965. Schwedische Einwirkungen auf die Entwicklung der älteren ungarischen Sprachwissenschaft. SprB 5 (21).109–36.

MIHĂILĂ, G. 1962. Locul lui Franz Miklosich în studierea elementelor slave din limba romînă (O sută de ani de la aparaţia lucrării 'Die slawischen Elemente im Rumänischen', Viena, 1861). Romanoslavica 6.209–20.

MIKLOSICH, FRANZ. 1852–74. Vergleichende Grammatik der slawischen Sprachen. 4 vols. Vienna, W. Braumüller.

MILLER, ROBERT L. 1968. The linguistic relativity principle and Humboldtian Ethnolinguistics. A history and appraisal. Janua Linguarum. Series minor, 67. The Hague/Paris, Mouton.

MOJASEVIC, MILJAN. 1963. Jacob Grimm und die Jugoslawen. Skizze und Stoff zu einer Studie. Brüder- Grimm- Gedenken, 336–65. [Cf. Denecke and Greverus 1963.] 336–65.

MOUNIN, GEORGES. 1966. La notion de système chez Antoine Meillet. Linguistique 1966, (1), 17–29.

——. 1967. Histoire de la linguistique: des origines au XXe siècle. Le linguiste, 4. Paris, Presses Universitaires de France.

MOURELLE-LEMA, MANUEL. 1968. La teoría lingüística en la España del siglo XIX. Madrid, Editorial Prensa Española.

MÜLLER, FRIEDRICH. 1876–88. Grundriss der Sprachwissenschaft. 4 parts, 6 vols. Vienna, A. Hölder.

MÜLLER, F. MAX. 1854. Letter of Professor Max Müller to Chevalier Bunsen; Oxford, August, 1853; on the classification of the Turanian languages. Christianity and Mankind, their beginnings and prospects, by C.C.J. Bunsen. 3rd part. Outlines of the philosophy of universal history, applied to language and religion 1.263–521. London, Longman, Brown, Green and Longmans.

——. 1861. Lectures on the science of language delivered at the Royal Institution of Great Britain in April, May & June, 1861. London, Longman, Green, Longman and Roberts.

——. 1864. Lectures on the science of language delivered at the Royal Institution of Great Britain in February, March, April & May, 1863. Second Series. London, Longman, Green, Longman, Roberts & Green.

——. 1868. On the stratification of language. Sir Robert Rede's Lecture delivered in the Senate House before the University of Cambridge on Friday May 29, 1868. London, Longmans, Green, Reader & Dyer. [Reprinted in Chips from a German Workshop, vol. 4, 65–116. London, Longmans, Green & Co. 1875.]

——. 1875. Rede Lecture: Part 2. On Curtius' Chronology of the Indo-Germanic languages. Chips from a German Workshop, vol. 4,117–44. London, Longmans, Green & Co.

MUELLER, H.J. 1966. On re-reading von Humboldt. MSLL 19.97–107.

MUKHERJEE, S.N. 1968. Sir William Jones: A study in eighteenth-century British attitudes to India. Cambridge, Cambridge University Press.

NEMIROVSKIJ, M.JA. 1956. Iz istorii razvitija teorii substrata. DSIJa 9.174–9.

NETTE, HERBERT. 1948. Die Sprachphilosophie Wilhelm von Humboldts. Wort und Sinn. Von den Elementen der Sprache, 35–48. Fulda, Parzeller & Co.

NEUMANN, GÜNTER. 1967. Franz Bopp — 1816. Indogermanische Sprachwissenschaft 1816 und 1966, 5–20. Innsbrucker Beiträge zur Kulturwissenschaft. Sonderheft 24. Innsbruck, Sprachwissenschaftliches Institut der Leopold-Franzens Universität.

NIEMEYER, WILHELM. 1962. Georg Landau und die Anfänge deutscher Mundartforschung. ZMaF 29.56–62.

NORDSTRAND, OVE K. 1959. Med Rasmus Rask på Ceylon nov. 1821–aug. 1822. DS 1959.91–106.

——. 1961. Rasmus Rasks Ceylonophold. Fund og Forskning i det kongelige Biblioteks Samliger 8.53–78.

NÜSSE, HEINRICH. 1962. Die Sprachtheorie Friedrich Schlegels. Heidelberg, Carl Winter Universitätsverlag.

OERTEL, HANNS. 1901. Lectures on the study of language. Yale Bicentennial Publications. New York, Charles Scribner's Sons; London, Edward Arnold.

OPPENBERG, URSULA. 1965. Quellenstudien zu Friedrich Schlegels Uebersetzungen aus dem Sanskrit. Marburger Beiträge zur Germanistik, 7. Marburg, N.G. Elwert.

ORLANDI, TITO. 1962. La metodologia di Franz Bopp e la linguistica precedente. RIL 96.528–49.

PÄTSCH, GERTRUD. 1955. Grundfragen der Sprachtheorie. Halle (Saale), VEB Max Niemeyer Verlag.

——. 1960. Franz Bopp und die historisch-vergleichende Sprachwissenschaft. Forschen und Wirken. Festschrift zur 150. Jahr-Feyer der Humboldt-Universität zu Berlin 1810–1960 (Im Auftrag von Rektor und Senat hssg. von Willi Gröber und Friedrich Herneck), vol. 1,211–28. Berlin, VEB deutscher Verlag der Wissenschaften.

——. 1967. Humboldt und die Sprachwissenschaft. Wilhelm von Humboldt.1767 1967. [Cf. Hartke and Maskolat, 1967:101–25.]

——. 1968. Humboldts Beitrag zur modernen Sprachwissenschaft. WZUB 17.353–6.

PAGLIARO, ANTONINO. 1930. Sommario di linguistica ario-europea. Fascicolo 1. Cenni storici e questioni teoriche. Pubblicazioni della scuola di filologia classica presso la R. Università di Roma, II, 2, 1. Roma, 'L'Universale' Tipografia Poliglotta.

PAUL, HERMANN. 1880. Principien der Sprachgeschichte. Halle (Saale), Max Niemeyer. [5th ed. 1920.]

*PEDERSEN, HOLGER. 1924. Sprogvidenskaben i det nittende Aarhundrede: Metoder og Resultater. Det Nittende Aarhundrede, 15. Copenhagen, Gyldendalske Boghandel.

——. 1962². The discovery of language. Linguistic science in the nineteenth century. Trans. by John Webster Spargo. Bloomington, Indiana University Press. [1st ed. 1931, Cambridge Mass., Harvard University Press.]

PENN, JULIA M. 1972. Linguistic relativity versus innate ideas. The origins of the Sapir-Whorf hypothesis in German thought. Janua Linguarum. Series minor, 120. The Hague/Paris, Mouton.

PERCIVAL, WALTER KEITH. 1969. Nineteenth century origins of twentieth century structuralism. PCLS 5.416–20.

——. 1970. Rasmus Rask and the criteria for genetic relationship. Actes du Dixième Congrès International des Linguistes (Bucarest 28 Août–2 Septembre 1967), vol. 2, 261–6. Bucharest, Editions de l'Académie de la République Socialiste de Roumanie.

PERELMAN, CH. 1963. Reflexions philosophiques sur la classification. La Classification dans les sciences, 231–6. Centre national Belge de recherches de Logique.

Société Belge de logique et de philosophie des sciences. Gembloux, Editions J. Duculout.

PETERSON, M.N. 1956–57. Akademik F.F. Fortunatov. Izbrannye Trudy, by F.F. Fortunatov (q.v.), vol. 1,5–16.

PEUKERT, HERBERT. 1964. Jacob Grimm und die Slawen. WZUJ 13.211–20.

——. 1966. Deutsche Südslawen- Klassifikationen. Ost und West in der Geschichte des Denkens und der kulturellen Beziehungen. Festschrift Eduard Winter, 341–55. Berlin, Akademie Verlag.

PFEIFER, WOLFGANG. 1963. Das Deutsche Wörterbuch. Jacob Grimm. Zur 100. Wiederkehr seines Todestages (cf. Fraenger and Steinitz 1963), 190–213.

*PIEBENGA, G.A. 1971. Een Studie over het werk van Rasmus Rask, in het bijzonder over zijn Frisisk Sproglaere. Groningen, Rijkuniversiteit te Groningen.

PISANI, VITTORE. 1949. Augusto Schleicher e alcuni orientamenti della moderna linguistica. Paideia 4.297–319. [Reprinted in Saggi di linguistica storica, 1959, 1–28. Torino, Rosenberg & Sellier, Trans. into German 1954–55. Lingua 4. 337–68.]

——. 1966. Antichità indoeuropee. Nel centocinquantanario del Conjugationssystem. Paideia 21.277–96.

PLEINES, JÜRGEN. 1967. Das Problem der Sprache bei Humboldt. Voraussetzungen und Möglichkeiten einer neuzeitlich-kritischen Sprachphilosophie. Achter deutscher Kongress für Philosophie: Heidelberg 1966. Das Problem der Sprache, hssg. von H.G. Gadamer, 31–43. München, W. Fink.

POHRT, HEINZ. 1964. Karl Gottlob von Anton und seine slawistischen Interessen. Beiträge ... 1964.325–46.

——. 1968. Die deutsche Slawistik im 19. Jahrhundert. Gedenken zu einer Darstellung ihrer Geschichte. WZUB 17.217–21.

POLITZER, ROBERT L. 1963a. On some eighteenth century sources of American and German 'linguistic relativism'. Weltoffene Romanistik. Festschrift Alwin Kuhn, hssg. von Guntiam Plangg und Eberhard Tiefenthaler, 25–33. Innsbrucker Beiträge zur Kulturwissenschaft, 9/10. Innsbruck, Sprachwissenschaftliches Institut der Leopold-Franzens- Universität.

——. 1963b. On the linguistic philosophy of Maupertuis and its relation to the history of linguistic relativism. Symposium 17.5–16.

POP, SEVER. 1950–51(?). La dialectologie. Aperçu historique et méthodes d'enquêtes linguistiques. 2 vols. (n.d.). Louvain, chez l'auteur. Gembloux, Imprimerie J. Duculot.

——, and RODICA DOINA POP. 1959. Jules Gilliéron: vie, enseignement, élèves, œuvres, souvenirs. Préface par Pierre Chantraine. Travaux publiés par le Centre International de Dialectologie générale près l'Université catholique de Louvain, 4. Louvain, Centre International de dialectologie générale.

PORZIG, WALTER. 1954. Die Gliederung des indogermanischen Sprachgebiets. Heidelberg, Carl Winter.

——. 1957². Das Wunder der Sprache. Probleme, Methoden und Ergebnisse der modernen Sprachwissenschaft. Bern, Francke Verlag. [1st ed. 1950. 4th ed. 1967.]

Pott, A.F. 1833–36. Etymologische Forschungen auf dem Gebiete der Indo-Germanischen Sprachen mit besonderen Bezug auf die Lautumwandlung im Sanskrit, Griechischen, Lateinischen, Littauischen und Gothischen. 2 vols. Lemgo, Meyer. [2nd ed. cf. Pott 1859–76.]

——. 1849. Ueber die Eintheilung der Sprachwissenschaft. Jahrbücher der freien deutschen Akademie, hssg. von Nauwerk und Noack, 1, 185–90.

——. 1852a. Die neuere Sprachwissenschaft. Blätter für literarische Unterhaltung 1852 (29 Mai, nr. 22). 505–17.

——. 1852b. Zur Frage über die Classification der Sprachen, mit besonderer Rücksicht auf die Schrift Die Classification der Sprachen, dargestellt als die Entwickelung der Sprachidee von Dr. H. Steinthal. ZDMG 6.287–93.

——. 1855. Max Müller und die Kennzeichen der Sprachverwandtschaft. ZDMG 9.405–64.

——. 1856. Die Ungleichheit menschlicher Rassen, hauptsächlich vom sprachwissenschaftlichen Standpunkte unter besonderer Berücksichtigung von der Grafen von Gobineau gleichnamigem Werke — mit einem Ueberblicke über die Sprachverhältnisse der Völker. Ein ethnologischer Versuch. Lemgo & Detmold, Meyer.

——. 1859–76². Etymologische Forschungen auf dem Gebiete der Indo-Germanischen Sprachen, unter Berücksichtigung ihrer Hauptformen, Sanskrit; Zend-Persisch; Griechisch-Lateinisch; Littauisch-Slawisch; Germanisch und Keltisch. 10 vols. Lemgo & Detmold, Meyer.

——. 1884–1890. Einleitung in die allgemeine Sprachwissenschaft. Internationale Zeitschrift für allgemeine Sprachwissenschaft 1.1–68, 329–54; 2.54–115, 209–51; 3.110–26, 249–75; 4.67–96; 5.3–18. [Cf. Pott 1887.]

——. 1887. Zur Litteratur der Sprachenkunde Europas. Internationale Zeitschrift für allgemeine Sprachwissenschaft, Supplement 1. Leipzig, J.A. Barth. [Continuation of Pott 1884–90.]

Pražák, Richard. 1967. Josef Dobrovský als Hungarist und Finno-Ugrist. Opera Universitatis Purkynianae Brunensis, Facultas Philosophica, 122. Brno, Universita J.E. Purkyní.

Prosdocimi, A.L. 1969. Carteggio di G.I. Ascoli ad A. Mussafia. AGI 54.1–48.

Pulgram, Ernst. 1953. Family tree, wave theory, and dialectology. Orbis 2.67–72.

——. 1955. Neogrammarians and soundlaws. Orbis 4.61–5.

Putschke, Wolfgang. 1969. Zur forschunggeschichtlichen Stellung der Junggrammatischen Schule. ZDL 36.19–48.

Raffler, Walburga von. 1953. Ascoli, forerunner of Matteo Bartoli. Word 9.54–5.

Rask, Rasmus. 1932–35. Udvalgte Afhandlinger (ed. by Louis Hjelmslev). 3 vols. Copenhagen, Levin & Munksgaard.

Raumer, Rudolf von. 1870. Geschichte der germanischen Philologie vorzugsweise in Deutschland. Geschichte der Wissenschaften in Deutschland. Neuere Zeit, 9. München, R. Oldenbourg.

RAVEN, FRITJOF A. 1954. An evaluation of the position of the neogrammarians. Monatshefte für deutschen Unterricht 46.95–101.

RENAN, ERNEST. 1858a². De l'origine du langage. Paris, M. Lévy frères.

——. 1858b². Histoire générale et système comparé des langues sémitiques. Paris, M. Lévy frères.

RENSCH, KARL HEINZ. 1966. Ferdinand de Saussure und Georg von der Gabelentz. Uebereinstimmungen und Gemeinsamkeiten dargestellt an der langue-parole Dichotomie sowie der diachronischen und synchronischen Sprachbetrachtung. Phonetica 15.32–41.

——. 1967. Organismus — System — Struktur in der Sprachwissenschaft. Phonetica 16.71–84.

ROBINS, ROBERT H. 1967. A short history of linguistics. London, Longmans, Green & Co; Bloomington, Indiana University Press.

ROCA FRANQUESA, JOSÉ MARIA. 1953. Las corrientes gramaticales en la primera mitad del siglo XIX: Vicente Salvá y su influencia en Andrés Bello. Archivum 3.181–213.

ROCHER, LUDO. 1957–58. Les philologues classiques et les debuts de la grammaire comparée. RUB 10.251–86.

——. 1961. Paulinus a Sancto Bartholomaeo on the kinship of the languages of India and Europe. ALB 25.321–52.

ROCHER, ROSANE. 1968. Alexander Hamilton (1762–1824). A chapter in the early history of Sanskrit philology. American Oriental Series, 51. New Haven, American Oriental Society.

——. 1970. New data for the biography of the Orientalist Alexander Hamilton. JAOS 90.426–48.

ROSIELLO, LUIGI. 1965. Analisi semantica dell'espressione Genio della lingua nelle discussioni semantiche del settecento italiano. Problemi di lingua e letteratura italiana del Settecento. Atti del quarto congresso dell'Associazione Internazionale per gli Studi di lingua e letteratura italiana, Magonza e Colonia, 28 aprile–1° maggio 1962, 373–85. Wiesbaden, F. Steiner.

——. 1967. Linguistica Illuminista. Saggi, 62. Bologna, Il Mulino.

RUGGERI, RUGGERO M. 1969. La filologia romanza in Italia. Milano, Marzorati.

RUPRECHT, ERICH. 1963. Die Sprache im Denken Wilhelm von Humboldts. Die Wissenschaft von deutscher Sprache und Dichtung. Methoden, Probleme, Aufgaben. Festschrift für Friedrich Maurer zum 65. Geburtstag am 5. Januar 1963. 217–36. Stuttgart, Ernst Klett Verlag.

RÜSTAU, HILTRUD. 1965. Max Müller und Indien. WZUB 14.359–63.

*SABALIAUSKAS, A. 1969. Augustąs Šleicheris. LKK 11.257–69. [Cf. BL 1969, 25, no. 592.]

S[ACY], S[YLVESTRE DE]. 1808. Review of Recherches critiques et historiques sur la langue et la littérature de l'Aegypte, par Et. Quatremère. Magasin encyclopédique, ou journal des sciences, des lettres et des arts, ed. by A. L. Millin, 1808, tome 4.241–82.

SALUS, PETER H. 1969. On language. Plato to von Humboldt. New York/Chicago/San Francisco/Montreal/London/Sidney, Holt, Rinehart & Winston.

SANDERS, WILLY. 1967. Grundzüge und Wandlungen der Etymologie. WW 17. 361–84.

SAUSSURE, FERDINAND DE. 1879. Mémoire sur le système primitif des voyelles dans les langues indo-européennes. Leipzig, B. G. Teubner.

——. 1967–68. Cours de linguistique générale. Edition critique par Rudolf Engler, 1. Wiesbaden, Otto Harrassowitz.

SAYCE, A.H. 1874. The principles of comparative philology. London, Trübner & Co.

SCHELLER, MEINARD. 1968. 'Linguistique synchronique' und 'linguistique diachronique' avant la lettre. Zur Geschichte der neueren Sprachwissenschaft. KZ 82.221–6.

SCHIROKAUER, ARNO. 1942. Spätromantik im Grimmschen Wörterbuch. GQ 15. 204–13.

——. 1957. Das Grimmsche Wörterbuch als Dokument der Romantik. Philobiblon 1.308–23.

SCHLEGEL, AUGUST WILHELM (VON). 1846. Oeuvres écrites en français et publiées par Edouard Böcking. 2 vols. Leipzig, Weidmann.

SCHLEGEL, Friedrich (VON). 1808. Ueber die Sprache und Weisheit der Indier. Ein Beitrag zur Begründung der Altertumskunde, nebst metrischen Uebersetzungen indischer Gedichte. Heidelberg, Mohr und Zimmer.

SCHLEICHER, AUGUST. 1848. Sprachvergleichende Untersuchungen. I. Zur vergleichende Sprachgeschichte. Bonn, H.B. König.

——. 1850. Die Sprachen Europas in systematischer Uebersicht. Bonn, H.B. König.

——. 1861–62. Compendium der vergleichenden Grammatik der indogermanischen Sprachen. Weimann, H. Böhlau.

——. 1863. Die Darwin'sche Theorie und die Sprachwissenschaft. Offenes Sendschreiben an Herrn Dr. Häckel. Weimar, H. Böhlau.

——. 1865a. Ueber die Bedeutung der Sprache für die Naturgeschichte des Menschen. Weimar, H. Böhlau.

——. 1865b. Die Unterscheidung von Nomen und Verbum in der lautlichen Form. ASAW 4 (5).497–587. ...

——. 1869². Die deutsche Sprache. Stuttgart, J.G. Cotta. [1st. ed. 1860.]

SCHLIMPERT, GERHARD. 1964. August Leskien und die Gründung des Lehrstuhls für slawische Sprachen an der Universität Leipzig. Beiträge ... 1964.226–38.

SCHMIDT, JOHANNES. 1872. Die Verwandtschaftverhältnisse der indogermanischen Sprachen. Weimar, H. Böhlau.

——. 1886. Schleichers auffassung der lautgesetze. KZ 28.303–13.

SCHMIDT, K. H. 1966. Historische Sprachvergleichung und ihre typologische Ergänzung. ZDMG 116.8–22.

SCHOGT, HENRY G. 1966. Baudouin de Courtenay and phonological analysis. Linguistique 2.15–29.

SCHOOF, WILHELM. 1941. Jacob Grimm und J.G. Radlof. Ein Beitrag zu deutschen Sprachgeschichte. Archiv für vergleichende Phonetik 5.49–76.

——. 1963a. Jacob Grimm als Vorläufer der heutigen Flurnamenforschung. Zum Gedächtnis seines 100. Todestages am 20. September 1963. BNF 14.148–62, 252–73.

——. 1963b. Jakob (sic) Grimms deutsche Grammatik in Zeitgenössischer Beurteilung. Zum 100. Todestag. ZDPh 82.363–77.

——. 1963–64. Jakob (sic) Grimm und die Anfänge der deutschen Dialektgeographie. Ein Gedenkwort zu seinem 100. Todestag am 20. September 1963. ZMaF 30.97–103.

——. 1967. Karl Bernhardi und die Brüder Grimm. Ein Schwälmer bekam die Stelle von Jacob Grimm. LB 56.120–25.

SCHRADER, OTTO. 1890². Sprachvergleichung und Urgeschichte: Linguistisch-historische Beiträge zur Erforschung des indogermanischen Altertums. Jena, H. Costenoble. [1st ed. 1883.]

SCHUCHARDT, HUGO. 1928². Hugo-Schuchardt-Brevier. Ein Vademecum der allgemeinen Sprachwissenschaft. Zusammengestellt und eingeleitet von Leo Spitzer. Halle (Saale), Max Niemeyer. [1st ed. 1922.]

SCHWAB, RAYMOND. 1950. La renaissance orientale. Paris, Payot. [Preface by Louis Renou.]

SCHWANKWEILER, EWALD. 1959–60. Wilhelm von Humboldts historische Sprachkonzeption. Diss. Berlin 1959, summarized: WZUB 9.512–4.

——. 1965. Zum Wesen und Ursprung der Sprache bei Jacob Grimm und Wilhelm von Humboldt. WZUB 14.455–62.

SEBEOK, THOMAS A., ed. 1966. Portraits of linguists. A Bibliographic source book for the history of Western linguistics, 1746–1963. Indiana University Studies in the History and Theory of Linguistics. 2 vols. Bloomington/London, Indiana University Press.

SEIDEL, EUGEN. 1968. Humboldt und die vergleichende Sprachwissenschaft. WZUB 17.357–8.

——. 1969. Begrüssung und Eröffnung. Zum 150. Geburtstag von Franz Bopp Begründer der Sprachwissenschaft. WZUB 18.296–9.

SEIDEL-SLOTTY, INGEBORG. 1969. Zum Problem des 'Gewichtausgleiches'. WZUB 18.323–4.

SEIDLER, HERBERT. 1967. Die Bedeutung von Wilhelm von Humboldts Sprachdenken für die Wissenschaft von der Sprachkunst. ZDPh 86.434–51.

SGALL, PETR. 1971. On the notion 'type of language'. TLP 4.75–87.

SHARADZENIDZE, T. S. [ŠARADZENIDZE]. 1958. Enat'a klasip'ikatsiis printsipebi. [Klassifikacii jazykov i ix principy.] Tbilisi, Izd. Akademii Nauk Gruzinskoj SSR.

SKÅRUP, POVL. 1960. Anledningen til Rasmus Rasks forelaesning over sprogets filosofi. DS 1960. 103–6.

——. 1964. Rasmus Rask og Faerøsk. Faeroensia, 6. Copenhagen, Munksgaard.

SLEITSJØE, LEIF. 1957. Rasmus Rask romaniste. SNPh 29.39–53.

SLUSAREVA, N. 1963. Quelques considérations des linguistes soviétiques à propos des idées de F. de Saussure. CFS 20.23–46.

SOMMERFELT, ALF. 1952. Edward Lhuyd and the comparative method in linguistics. NTS 16.370–74.

SONDEREGGER, STEFAN. 1962. Die Schweizerdeutsche Mundartforschung 1800–1959. Bibliographisches Handbuch mit Inhaltsangaben. Beiträge zur schweizerdeutschen Mundartforschung, 12. Frauenfeld, Huber & Co.

——. 1967. Andreas Heusler und die Sprache. Studies zur Geschichte der Wissenschaften in Basel, hssg. von der Universität Basel. Basel, Helbing & Lichtenhahn.

SPECHT, FRANZ. 1968. Die 'indogermanische' Sprachwissenschaft von der Junggrammatikern bis zum ersten Weltkriege. Lexis 1. 228–63.

SPIRIDONOVA, L. F. 1961. I. Ch. Adelung i izučenie nemeckogo jazyka v Rossii. (Iz istorii kul'turnyx svjazej Rossii i Germanii). VMU 2.60–68.

SPRACHATLANTEN. 1969. Sprachatlanten. Berichte über sprachgeographische Forschungen, 1, von Martin Durrell, Mieczysław Karás, Bernd Kratz, Werner H. Veith. ZDL, Beiheft NF 8. Wiesbaden, Franz Steiner Verlag GMBH.

SPREU, ARWED. 1965. Eine Anmerkung zum Aufbau der 'Deutschen Grammatik'. WZUB 14.489–90.

STARIKOV, D. V. 1960. Sintaksičeskie vozzrenija F. F. Fortunatova i ego školy. NDVS-F 3.144–54.

STEHR, ALFRED. 1957. Die Anfänge der Finnisch-Ugrischen Sprachvergleichung, 1669–1771. Diss. Göttingen.

STEINTHAL, H. 1849. Review of Ueber das Altai'sche oder Finnisch-Tatarische Sprachengeschlecht, by W. Schott. Allgemeine Literaturzeitung (Halle-Leipzig) 174.233–9; 175.247–8.

——. 1850. Die Classification der Sprachen dargestellt als die Entwickelung der Sprachidee. Berlin, F. Dümmler.

——. 1855. Grammatik, Logic und Psychologie. Ihre Principien und ihr Verhältniss zu einander. Berlin, F. Dümmler.

——. 1860. Charakteristik der hauptsächlichsten Typen des Sprachbaues. Berlin, F. Dümmler.

——. 1970. Kleine sprachtheoretische Schriften neu zusammengestellt und mit einer Einleitung versehen von Waltraud Bumann. Collectanea, 12. Hildesheim/New York, G. Olms.

STERNEMANN, REINHARD. 1969. Das indoeuropäische Verbum in der Darstellung historisch-vergleichender Grammatik seit Franz Bopp. WZUB 18.325–8.

STOLTE, ERICH. 1948. Wilhelm von Humboldts Begriff der inneren Sprachform. ZPhon 2.205–7.

STOLZ, KARL. 1959. Jakob Grimm und Johann Haering, ZDPh 78.94–7.

STREITBERG, WILHELM. 1897. Schleichers Auffassung von der Stellung der Sprachwissenschaft. IF 7.360–72.

——. 1909–10. Kant und die Sprachwissenschaft. Eine historische Skizze. IF 26. 382–422.

STROH, FRIEDRICH. 1952. Geschichte der germanischen Philologie. Handbuch der germanischen Philologie, 38–165. Berlin, De Gruyter.

STRUNK, KLAUS. 1965. Probleme der indogermanischen Sprachwissenschaft nach Brugmann. Glotta 43.199–217.

STUDER, EDUARD. 1954. Franz Josef Stalder. Zur Frühgeschichte volkskundlicher und dialektvergleichender Interessen. Schweizerisches Archiv für Volkskunde 50. 125–277.

STUSSI, ALFREDO. 1963. Ascoli — Tommaseo — Cantù. Lettere inedite. ASNP 32.39–49.

SZÉPE, G. 1963. Review of Perspectives in linguistics, by J. T. Waterman. ALH 16.167–71.

ŠARADZENIDZE, T. S. 1958. See SHARADZENIDZE.

ŠČERBA, L. V. 1963. F. F. Fortunatov v istorii nauki o jazyke. VJa 5.89–93.

TAGLIAVINI, CARLO. 1963[5]. Introduzione alla glottologia. 1. Lingua e linguaggio. Storia e evoluzione della linguistica. Le lingue e i problemi della loro classificazione. Premesse psicologiche. Bologna, R. Pàtron.

——. 1968a[2]. Panorama di storia della linguistica. Bologna, R. Pàtron.

——. 1968b. Panorama di storia della filologia germanica. Bologna, Pàtron.

TEETER, KARL V. 1966. The history of linguistics: New lamps for old. MSLL19. 83–95.

TELEGDI, ZSIGMOND. 1966. Geschichte der Sprachwissenschaft ('Historische Grammatik'). ALH 16.225–37.

——. 1967a. Struktur und Geschichte: zur Auffassung ihres Verhaltnisses in der Sprachwissenschaft. ALH 17.223–43.

——. 1967b. Begründungen der historischen Grammatik; Zur Geschichte der Sprachwissenschaft. To honor Roman Jakobson. Essays on the occasion of his seventieth Birthday 11 October 1966, vol. 3, 1996–2005. Janua Linguarum. Series maior, 33. The Hague/Paris, Mouton.

——. 1970. Humboldt als Begründer der Sprachtypologie. Theoretical problems of typology and the Northern Eurasian languages, ed. by L. Dezsö and P. Hajdu, 25–34. Amsterdam, B.R. Grüner; Budapest, Akadémiai Kiadó.

TERRACINI, BENVENUTO. 1949. Guida allo studio della linguistica storica. 1. Profilo storico-critico. Studi e guide di filologia e linguistica, 1. Roma, Edizioni dell'-Ateneo.

——. 1956. Una lettera poco nota di G.I. Ascoli. AGI 41.139–50.

——. 1966. Review of Classicismo e Illuminismo nell'Ottocento italiano, by S. Timpanaro. AGI 51.86–93.

——. 1967. G. I. Ascoli, direttore dell' 'Archivio' (dal carteggio Ascoli- Salvioni). AGI 52.1–54.

THIEME, PAUL. 1952–53. August Friedrich Pott. Festschrift zur 450- Jahr-Feier der Martin-Luther-Universität, Halle Wittenberg, vol. 2,309–13. Halle Wittenberg, Selbstverlag der Martin-Luther-Universität.

*THOMSEN, VILHELM. 1902. Sprogvidenskabens historie; en kortfattet fremstilling af dens hovedpunkter. Copenhagen, G. E. C. Gadd.

——. 1927. Geschichte der Sprachwissenschaft bis zum Ausgang des 19. Jahrhunderts. Kurzgefasste Darstellung der Hauptpunkte. Trans. by H. Pollak. Halle (Saale), Max Niemeyer.

TIMPANARO, SEBASTIANO. 1959. Graziadio Isaia Ascoli. Note letterario-artistiche minori durante il viaggio nella Venezia, nella Lombardia, nel Piemonte, nella Liguria, nel Parmigiano, Modenese e Pontificio. Maggio-Giugno 1852. ASNP 28.151–91.

——. 1963a. La genesi del metodo del Lachmann. Bibliotechina del Saggiatore, 18. Firenze, Le Monnier.

——. 1963b. A proposito del parallelismo tra lingua e diritto. Belfagor 18.1–14.

——. 1969². Classicismo e Illuminismo nell'Ottocento italiano. Saggi di varia umanità, 2. Pisa, Nistri-Lischi. [1st. ed. 1965.]

——. 1972a. Friedrich Schlegel e gli inizi della linguistica indeuropea in Germania. Critica Storica 9.72–105.

——. 1972b. Graziadio Ascoli. Belfagor 27.149–76.

TOLKAČEV, A. I. 1964. F. F. Fortunatov (1848–1914). IzvAN 23.402–10.

TOLLENAERE, F. DE. 1948. De Briefwisseling R. Rask — R. Posthumus. Miscellanea J. Gessler. vol. 2, 1197–1203. Deurne-Anvers, C. Govaerts.

——. 1951. Indogermaans en Keltisch bij Rasmus Rask. Nph 35.37–46.

——. 1953. Willem de Clercq (15 Januari 1795–4 Februari 1844) en Rasmus Rask (22 November 1787–14 November 1832). TsNTL 71.213–34.

——. 1954. Rasmus Rask en de studie van het Oudfries in Nederland. It Beaken 16.1–9.

TOVAR, ANTONIO. 1968. Review of Language typology, by K. M. Horne. Lg 44.331–4.

TRIER, JOST. 1964. Jacob Grimm als Etymologe. Abhandlungen der Gesellschaft zur Förderung der Westfalischen Wilhelms-Universität, Heft 5. Münster (Westfalen), Aschendorffsche Verlagsbuchhandlung.

TRIM, J. L. M. 1959. Historical, descriptive and dynamic linguistics. L & S 2.9–25.

TRITTON, A. S. 1943–46. The student of Arabic [scil. W. Jones]. BSOAS 11.695–8.

TRNKA, B. 1952. Zur Erinnerung an August Schleicher. ZPhon 6.134–42.

TRUBECKOJ, N. S. 1939. Gedanken über das Indogermanenproblem. AL 1.81–9. [Reprinted in Die Urheimat der Indogermanen, hssg. von Anton Scherer, 214–23. Wege der Forschung, 166. Darmstadt, Wissenschaftliche Buchgesellschaft, 1968].

UHLISCH, GERDA. 1969. Franz Bopp und die historische Lautlehre des Albanischen· WZUB 18.329–31.

ULMER, KARL. 1951. Die Wandlung des Sprachbildes von Herder zu Jacob Grimm. Lexis 2.263–86.

USPENSKIJ, B.A. 1965. Strukturnaja Tipologija Jazykov. Moscow, Izd. 'Nauka'.

——. 1968. Principles of structural typology. Janua Linguarum. Series minor, 62. The Hague/Paris, Mouton.

VALDERRAMA ANDRADE, CARLOS. 1969. Franz Bopp y Miguel Antonio Caro. Ibero-Romania 1.157–8.

VALLINI, CRISTINA. 1969. Problemi di metodo in Ferdinand de Saussure indoeuropeista. SSL 9.1–85.

VALVERDE, JOSÉ MARIA. 1955. Guillermo de Humboldt y la filosofía del lenguaje. Biblioteca románica hispánica. II. Estudios y ensayos. Madrid, Editorial Gredos.

VÁRVARO, ALBERTO. 1968². Storia, problemi e metodi della linguistica romanza. Naples, Liguori. [1st ed. 1966.]

VASCENCO, VICTOR. 1960. F. Fortunatov şi lucrarea sa 'Linguistica comparată'. LbR 9 (6).30–39.

VASMER, MAX. 1947. J. Baudouin de Courtenay. Zur 100. Wiederkehr seines Geburtstages. ZPhon 1.71–7.

VDOVIN, I.S. 1954. Istorija izučenija paleoaziatskix jazykov. Moscow, Izd. Akademii Nauk SSSR.

VEITH, WERNER H. 1969. Die Themakartierung der Sprachen der Welt. Ueberschau und Folgerung. Sprachatlanten 1969.1–26.

VENDRYES, J. 1955. La société de linguistique de Paris (1865–1955). Orbis 4.7–21.

VERBURG, PIETER A. 1950. The background to the linguistic conceptions of Franz Bopp. Lingua 2.438–68. [Reprinted in Sebeok 1966: I, 221–50.]

*——. 1951. Taal en functionaliteit. Een historisch-critische studie over de opvattingen aangaande de functies der taal vanaf de praehumanistische philologie van Orleans tot de rationalistische linguistiek van Bopp. Diss. Vrije Univ. Amsterdam, Wageningen, Veenman & Zonen.

VIERTEL, JOHN. 1966. Concepts of language underlying the 18th century controversy about the origin of language. MSLL 19.109–32.

VINOGRADOV, VIKTOR VLADIMIROVIČ. 1958. Iz istorii izučenija russkogo sintaksisa (ot Lomonosova do Potebni i Fortunatova). Moscow, Izd. Moskovskogo Universiteta.

VITALE, MAURIZIO. 1955. Sommario elementare di una storia degli studi linguistici romanzi. Preistoria e storia degli studi romanzi, ed. by A. Viscardi, C. Cremonesi, E. Mozzati, M. Vitale, 5–169. Milano/Varese, Istituto Editoriale Cisalpino.

VOIGT, JOHANNES H. 1967. Max Mueller. The man and his ideas. Calcutta, Firma K.L. Mukhopadhyay.

WAGNER, LÉON. 1950–51. Contribution à la prehistoire du romanisme. Conférences de l'Institut de linguistique de l'Université de Paris 10.101–24.

WAITZ, THEODOR. 1859–72. Anthropologie der Naturvölker. 6 vols. Leipzig, Friedrich Fleischer.

——. 1863. Introduction to anthropology, ed. with numerous additions by the Author from the first volume of 'Anthropologie der Naturvölker' by J. Frederick Collingwood. Publications of the Anthropological Society of London, 1. London, Longman, Green, Longman, and Roberts.

WALD, LUCIA. 1962. Aspecte dialectice în teoria limbii a lui Wilhelm von Humboldt. PLG 4.193–202.

——. 1962. La notion d'économie dans la théorie linguistique de Baudouin de Courtenay. Actes du dixième Congrès International des Linguistes (Bucarest 28 Aôut–2 Septembre 1967), vol. 2, 321–4. Bucharest, Editions de l'Académie de la République Socialiste de Roumanie.

WALEY, ARTHUR D. 1943–46. Sir William Jones as Sinologue. BSOAS 11.842.

——. 1952. Anquetil Duperron and Sir William Jones. History Today 2.23–33.

WANNER, HANS. 1963. Die Beziehungen zwischen den Brüdern Grimm, ihrem Wörterbuch und der schweizerdeutschen Dialektlexikographie. Brüder-Grimm-Gedenken (cf. Denecke and Greverus), 435–50.

WATERMAN, JOHN T. 1963. Perspectives in linguistics. Chicago/London, University of Chicago Press. [2nd ed. 1970.]

WEIMANN, KARL HEINZ. 1965. Vorstufen der Sprachphilosophie Humboldts bei Bacon und Locke. ZDPh 84.498–508.

WEINREICH, URIEL, WILLIAM LABOV, and MARVIN I. HERZOG. 1968. Empirical foundations for a theory of language change. Directions for historical linguistics: A symposium, ed. by W.P. Lehmann and Y. Malkiel, 98–195. Austin/London, University of Texas Press.

WEISGERBER, LEO. 1953–54. Zum Energeia-Begriff in Humboldts Sprachbetrachtung. WW 4.374–7.

WEISWEILER, JOSEF. 1949. Die indogermanische Sprachwissenschaft. Eine geistesgeschichtliche Studie. Historisches Jahrbuch 62–9.464–90.

WEÖRES, GYULA. 1966. La langue finnoise dans la littérature française au siècle des lumières. NphM 67.257–65.

——. 1966–67. H.G. Porthan und die ungarische Sprache. FUF 36.335–54.

WHITNEY, WILLIAM DWIGHT. 1867. Language and the study of language. Twelve lectures on the principles of linguistic science. New York, Charles Scribner's Sons. London, Trübner & Co.

——. 1875. The life and growth of language. New York, D. Appleton & Co. London, H.S. King.

——. 1971. Whitney on language. Selected writings of William Dwight Whitney ed. by Michael Silverstein. Introductory essay by Roman Jakobson. Cambridge, Mass./ London, M.I.T. Press.

WILEY, R.A. 1971. John Mitchell Kemble and Jacob Grimm. A correspondence 1832–1852, collected, ed. and trans. by R.A. Wiley. Leiden, Brill.

WILLSON, AMOS LESLIE. 1964. A mythical image. The Ideal of India in German Romanticism. Durham, N.C., Duke University Press.

WINDISCH, ERNST. 1917–20. Geschichte der Sanskrit Philologie und indischen Altertumskunde. Grundriss der Indo-Arischen Philologie und Altertumskunde, 1. 2 parts. Strassburg, Karl J. Trübner. Berlin/Leipzig, Vereinigung wissenschaftlicher Verleger, Walter de Gruyter & Co.

WINTELER, JOST. 1876. Die Kerenzer Mundart des Kantons Glarus in ihren Grundzügen dargestellt. Leipzig/Heidelberg, C. F. Winter.

WINTER, EDUARD. 1961. August Ludwig von Schlözer und Russland. Deutsche Akademie der Wissenschaften zu Berlin. Quellen und Studien zur Geschichte Osteuropas, hssg. von E. Winter, 9. Berlin, Akademie Verlag.

——, ed. 1962. Lomonosov — Schlözer — Pallas. Deutsch-russische Wissenschaftsbeziehungen im 18. Jahrhundert, hssg. von E. Winter. Deutsche Akademie der Wissenschaften zu Berlin. Quellen und Studien zur Geschichte Osteuropas, hssg. von E. Winter, 12. Berlin, Akademie Verlag.

WRENN, C. L. 1946. Henry Sweet. TPhS 1946.177–201.

[YOUNG, T.]. 1813–14. Review of Mithridates, by J. C. Adelung. Quarterly Review 10 (October 1813). 250–92.

ZELLER, OTTO. 1967. Problemgeschichte der vergleichenden (indogermanischen) Sprachwissenschaft. Osnabrück, Biblio Verlag.

ZEUSS, J. C. [K.]. 1853. Grammatica Celtica e monumentis vetustis tam hibernicae linguae quam britannicae dialecti cornicae armoricae nec non e gallicae priscae reliquiis construxit J. C. Zeuss. 2 vols. Leipzig, Weidmann.

ZSIRAI, MIKLÓS. 1951. Samuel Gyarmathi, Hungarian pioneer of Comparative Linguistics. ALH 1.5–17. [Reprinted in Sebeok 1966: I, 58–70 and in Gyarmathi, Samuel. 1968. Affinitas linguae hungaricae cum linguis fennicae originis grammatice demonstrata, v–xvii. Bloomington/The Hague, Indiana University and Mouton.]

*——. 1952. A modern nyelvtudomány magyar úttöroi. I. Sajnovics és Gyarmathi. Budapest, Akadémiai Kiadó.

ZVEGINCEV, VLADIMIR ANDREEVIČ. 1960². Istorija jazykoznanija XIX i XX vekov v očerkax i izvlečenijax. 2 vols. Moscow, Gosudarstvennoe učebno-pedagogičeskoe izd. Ministerstva prosveščenija RSFSR. [1st. ed. 1956. *3rd ed. 1964–65.]

ZWIRNER, EBERHARD. 1962. Lebende Sprachen. Beitrag zur Theorie und zur Methodik ihrer Erforschung. SG 15.14–22.

——. 1963. System der Sprachen und System der Wissenschaften. Zum Begriff der 'allgemeinen Sprachwissenschaft' und 'allgemeinen Phonetik'. IF 68.133–48.

——. 1965. Die Bedeutung der Sprachstruktur für die Analyse des Sprechens. Problemgeschichtliche Erörterung. Proceedings of the Fifth International Congress of Phonetic Sciences (held at the University of Münster, 16–22 August 1964) ed. by E. Zwirner and Wolfgang Bethge, 1–24. Basel/New York, S. Karger.

——. 1967. Sprachen und Sprache: ein Beitrag zur Theorie der Linguistik. To honor

Roman Jakobson. Essays on the occasion of his seventieth Birthday 11 October 1966, vol. 3, 2442–64. Janua Linguarum, Series maior, 33. The Hague/Paris, Mouton.

——. 1969a. Zum Begriff der allgemeinen Sprachwissenschaft und der allgemeinen Grammatik. Mélanges pour Jean Fourquet, 407–15. München, Hueber. Paris, Klincksieck.

——. 1969b. Zur Herkunft und Funktion des Begriffpaares Synchronie — Diachronie. Sprache, Gegenwart und Geschichte. Probleme der Synchronie und Diachronie, 30–51. Sprache der Gegenwart: Schriften des Instituts für deutsche Sprache, 5. Düsseldorf, Schwann.

——, and KURT ZWIRNER. 1966². Grundfragen der Phonometrie. (Phonometrie. Erster Teil). Bibliotheca phonetica, fasc. 3. Basel/New York, S. Karger.

ŽIRMUNSKIJ, V. M. 1953. Neizdannaja kniga akad. F. F. Fortunatova. VJa (1).157–8.

UNIVERSITY LIBRARY NOTTINGHAM